The London Gazette

Published by Authority

Registered as a newspaper

The Naval & Military Press Ltd

Published by
The Naval & Military Press Ltd
5 Riverside, Brambleside, Bellbrook
Industrial Estate, Uckfield, East Sussex,
TN22 1QQ England

Tel: +44 (0) 1825 749494
Fax: +44 (0) 1825 765701

www.naval-military-press.com
www.nmarchive.com

In reprinting in facsimile from the original, any imperfections are inevitably reproduced and the quality may fall short of modern type and cartographic standards.

INDEX.

1946	37719	The Battle of Britain. Despatch by Air Chief Marshal Sir Hugh C.T. Dowding, G.C.B., G.C.V.O., C.M.G., A.D.C.
1946	37729	Air Operations in the Middle East from January 1st, 1941, to May 3rd, 1941. Despatch by Air Chief Marshal Sir Arthur Longmore, GCB., DSO.
1946	---	Final Revise.
1946	37838	Air Operations by the Allied Expeditionary Air Force in N.W. Europe from November 15th, 1943 to September 30th, 1944. Despatch by Air Chief Marshal Sir Trafford Leigh-Mallory, K.C.B., D.S.O.
1947	37846	Air Operations in Greece, 1940-1941. Despatch by Air Vice-Marshal J.H. D'Albiac, D.S.O.
1947	38111	Liberation of Europe (Operation "Overlord") Operations of Coastal Command, Royal Air Force, from May to August, 1944 Despatch by Air Chief Marshal Sir Sholto Douglas, K.C.B., M.C., D.F.C.
1948	38183	Operations in the Far East, from 17th October, 1940 to 27th December 1941. Despatch by Air Chief Marshal Sir Robert Brooke-Popham, G.C.V.O., K.C.B., C.M.G., D.S.O., A.F.C.
1948	38216	Report on the Air Operations During the Campaigns in Malaya and Netherland East Indies from 8th December, 1941 to 12th March, 1942. Despatch from Air Vice-Marshal Sir Paul Maltby, K.B.E., C.B., D.S.O., A.F.C.
1948	38229	Air Operations in Burma and Bay of Bengal, January 1st to May 22nd, 1942. Despatch by Air Vice-Marshal D.F. Stevenson, CBE., DSO., MC.
1948	38404	Air Operations by Fighter Command from 25th November 1940 to 31st December 1941. Despatch by Marshal of the Royal Air Force Sir Sholto Douglas, G.C.B., M.C., D.F.C.
1948	38437	Air Operations by Air Defence of Great Britain and Fighter Command in Connection with the German Flying Bomb and Rocket Offensives, 1944-1945. Despatch by Air Chief Marshal Sir Roderic Hill, K.C.B., M.C., A.F.C.
1951	39173	Air Operations in South East Asia 16th November, 1943 to 31st May, 1944. Despatch by Air Chief Marshal Sir R.E.C. Peirse, K.C.B., D.S.O., A.F.C.
1951	39196	Air Operations in South East Asia from 1st June, 1944, to the Occupation of Rangoon, 2nd May, 1945. Despatch by Air Chief Marshal Sir Keith Park, K.C.B., K.B.E., M.C., D.F.C.
1951	39202	Air Operations in South East Asia 3rd May, 1945 to 12th September, 1945. Despatch by Air Chief Marshal Sir Keith Park, G.C.B., K.B.E., M.C., D.F.C.
1951	39367	The Part Played by the Allied Air Forces in the Final Defeat of the Enemy in the Mediterranean Theatre, March to May, 1945. Despatch by Air Chief Marshal Sir Guy Garrod, K.C.B., O.B.E., M.C., D.F.C.
1951	39172	Burma Campaign Maps (in case).

Numb. 37719　　　　4543

SUPPLEMENT
TO
The London Gazette
Of Tuesday, the 10th of September, 1946

Published by Authority

Registered as a newspaper

WEDNESDAY, 11 SEPTEMBER, 1946

The Air Ministry,
September, 1946.

THE BATTLE OF BRITAIN.

The following despatch was submitted to the Secretary of State for Air on August 20th, 1941, by Air Chief Marshal Sir Hugh C. T. Dowding, G.C.B., G.C.V.O., C.M.G., A.D.C., Air Officer Commanding-in-Chief, Fighter Command, Royal Air Force.

PREAMBLE.

1. I have been instructed by the Air Council to write a Despatch on the Air Fighting of last Autumn, which has become known as the " Battle of Britain." The conditions are a little unusual because, firstly, the Battle ended many months ago, secondly, a popular account of the fighting has already been written and published, and, thirdly, recommendations for Mention in Despatches have already been submitted.

2. I have endeavoured, therefore, to write a report which will, I hope, be of Historical interest, and which will, in any case, contain the results of more than four years' experience of the Fighter Command in peace and war.

August 20, 1941.

THE BATTLE OF BRITAIN.
PART I.—PRELIMINARY.

3. In giving an account of the Battle of Britain it is perhaps advisable to begin by a definition of my conception of the meaning of the phrase. The Battle may be said to have started when the Germans had disposed of the French resistance in the Summer of 1940, and turned their attention to this country.

4. The essence of their Strategy was so to weaken our Fighter Defences that their Air Arm should be able to give adequate support to an attempted invasion of the British Isles. Experiences in Holland and Belgium had shown what they could do with armoured forces operating in conjunction with an Air Arm which had substantially achieved the command of the Air.

5. This air supremacy was doubly necessary to them in attacking England because the bulk of their troops and war material must necessarily be conveyed by sea, and, in order to achieve success, they must be capable of giving air protection to the passage and the landing of troops and material.

6. The destruction or paralysis of the Fighter Command was therefore an essential pre-requisite to the invasion of these Islands.

7. Their immediate objectives might be Convoys, Radio-Location Stations, Fighter Aerodromes, Seaports, Aircraft Factories, or London itself. Always the underlying object was to bring the Fighter Command continuously to battle, and to weaken its material resources and Intelligence facilities.

8. Long after the policy of " crashing through " with heavy bomber formations had been abandoned owing to the shattering losses incurred, the battle went on. Large fighter formations were sent over, a proportion of the fighters being adapted to carry bombs, in order that the attacks might not be ignorable.

9. This last phase was perhaps the most difficult to deal with tactically. It will be discussed in greater detail later on.

10. Night attacks by Heavy Bombers were continuous throughout the operations, and, although they persisted and increased in intensity as Day Bombing became more and more expensive, they had an essentially different purpose, and the " Battle of Britain " may be said to have ended when the Fighter and Fighter-Bomber raids died down.

11. It is difficult to fix the exact date on which the "Battle of Britain" can be said to have begun. Operations of various kinds merged into one another almost insensibly, and there are grounds for choosing the date of the 8th August, on which was made the first attack in force against laid objectives in this country, as the beginning of the Battle.

12. On the other hand, the heavy attacks made against our Channel convoys probably constituted, in fact, the beginning of the German offensive; because the weight and scale of the attack indicates that the primary object was rather to bring our Fighters to battle than to destroy the hulls and cargoes of the small ships engaged in the coastal trade. While we were fighting in Belgium and France, we suffered the disadvantage that even the temporary stoppage of an engine involved the loss of pilot and aircraft, whereas, in similar circumstances, the German pilot might be fighting again the same day, and his aircraft be airborne again in a matter of hours.

13. In fighting over England these considerations were reversed, and the moral and material disadvantages of fighting over enemy country may well have determined the Germans to open the attack with a phase of fighting in which the advantages were more evenly balanced. I have therefore, somewhat arbitrarily, chosen the events of the 10th July as the opening of the Battle. Although many attacks had previously been made on convoys, and even on land objectives such as Portland, the 10th July saw the employment by the Germans of the first really big formation (70 aircraft) intended primarily to bring our Fighter Defence to battle on a large scale.

14. I had 59 squadrons in various stages of efficiency. A list of these units, with supplementary information, is given in Appendix A. Many of them were still suffering from the effects of the fighting in Holland and Flanders, at Dunkerque, and during the subsequent operations in France. Others were in process of formation and training. But, if the lessons of the Battle are to be correctly appreciated, due consideration must be given to the factors leading up to the situation existing when it began. Leaving out of account peace-time preparations and training, the Battle of Britain began for me in the Autumn of 1939.

15. The first major problem arose during the discussion of the question of sending Fighter Squadrons to France. The decisive factor was that of Supply. Our output at the beginning of the war was about 2 Hurricanes and 2 Spitfires per diem; and, although there were hopes of increasing Hurricane production, there was then no hope that Spitfire production would be materially increased for about a year. It is true that certain optimistic estimates had been made, but there were reasons to believe that these could not be implemented. At that time, we in England were out of range of German Fighters, and I had good hopes that unescorted bomb raids on this country could be met and defeated with a very small loss in Fighters; but there could be no illusions concerning the wastage which would occur if we came up against the German Fighters in France.

16. I therefore regarded with some apprehension the general policy of sending Home Defence Fighter Units to France; but, as it was clear that such an attitude was politically untenable, I wrote on the 16th September, 1939, a letter to the Air Ministry. In this letter I pointed out that the Air Staff Estimate of the number of Fighter Squadrons necessary for the defence of this country was 52, and that on the outbreak of war I had the equivalent of 34 (allowing for the fact that some Auxiliary Squadrons were only partially trained and equipped).

17. I wanted 12 new squadrons, but asked that 8 should be raised immediately, and made proposals for their location and employment. In a letter dated the 21st September the Air Ministry regretted that the most they could do towards meeting my requirements was to form 2 new squadrons and 2 operational training units. I was invited to a meeting of the Air Council on the 26th September,

18. On the 25th September I wrote expressing my disappointment and asking for a reconsideration. As a result of this letter, the Air Council Meeting, and a further meeting under the Chairmanship of the Deputy Chief of Air Staff, the Air Ministry wrote on the 9th October sanctioning the immediate formation of 8 new squadrons, though 6 of these could be formed initially only as half-squadrons owing to shortage of resources. This correspondence is too lengthy to reproduce here, but it deals also with my apprehensions concerning Hurricane wastage in France, which were realised in the Spring of 1940. It also dealt with an estimate worked out by the Air Ministry Organisation Staff that after 3 months of fighting we might expect the Fighter strength to have been reduced to 26 squadrons.

19. In October, 1939, the Air Ministry further reconsidered their policy, and ordered the formation of 10 additional Fighter Squadrons, 4 of which were destined for the Coastal Command.

20. In January, 1940, the Northern flank of our continuous Defence organisation was on the Forth, and the South-Western flank was at Tangmere in Sussex (with the exception of an isolated station at Filton for the local defence of Bristol and the mouth of the Severn). On the 2nd and 4th February I wrote two letters pointing out these limitations, and asking for an extension of Aerodrome facilities, Intelligence cover and communications.

21. On the 9th February I was told that a paper was in preparation, and that I would be given an opportunity to remark on the proposals at a later stage.

22. On the 16th March I received the paper referred to and forwarded my comments on the 23rd March.

23. On the 8th May I received a letter saying that a reply had been delayed. The proposals were now approved, and decisions would shortly be taken.

24. This delay was presumably unavoidable, but the result was that the organisation and development of the defences of the South and West of England were very incomplete when they were called upon to withstand the attacks which the German occupation of French aerodromes made possible.

25. The fighting in Norway has only an indirect bearing on this paper. Certain useful tactical lessons were gained, particularly with regard to deflection shooting, and I trust

that the story of the epic fight of No. 263 Squadron under Squadron-Leader J. W. Donaldson, D.S.O., near Andalsnes, may not be lost to History.

26. The outcome, as it affects this account, was the virtual loss of 2 squadrons in the sinking of the Aircraft Carrier *Glorious* after the evacuation of Narvik.

27. Next came the invasion of Holland, and the call to send Fighters to the assistance of the Dutch. The distance to Rotterdam was about the extreme range of the single-seater Fighter, which therefore operated under the disadvantage of having a very brief potential combat-time, followed by the necessity of a long sea crossing on the homeward way. The Blenheims, of course, had the necessary endurance, but they had not been designed as fighters, and their use against day fighters proved costly in comparison with the limited success which they attained.

28. The Defiants were used here for the first time, and, although they proved very effective against unescorted bombers, they, too, suffered heavy casualties when they encountered fighters in strength. As the result of this experience I formed the opinion that the Blenheims should be kept exclusively for night fighting, if possible, while I retained an open mind about the Defiants pending some experience of short-range fighting.

29. Then began the fighting in Belgium and Northern France, and at once my fears about the incidence of wastage in this type of fighting began to be realised.

30. At the beginning of April, 1940, there were 6 Fighter Squadrons in France.

31. Then 4 more complete squadrons were sent when the fighting began.

32. Then on the 13th May 32 pilots and aircraft were sent—say the equivalent of 2 squadrons.

33. Almost immediately afterwards 8 Half-Squadrons were sent. This was done under the impression that the loss of 8 Half-Squadrons would affect me less than that of 4 entire Squadrons, because it was supposed that I should be able to rebuild on the nuclei left behind. But this assumption was incorrect because I had neither the time nor the personnel available for purposes of reconstruction, and the remaining half-squadrons had to be amalgamated into Composite Units with a resulting disorganisation and loss of efficiency. At this time, too, I was ordered to withdraw trained pilots from squadrons and to send them overseas as reinforcements.

34. I had now lost the equivalent of 16 Squadrons, and in addition 4 Squadrons were sent to fight in France during the day and to return to English bases in the evening.

35. Other pilots were withdrawn from the Command through the system by which the Air Ministry dealt direct with Groups on questions of Personnel.

36. It must be remembered that during this period the Home Defence Squadrons were not idle, but that Hurricane Squadrons were participating in the fighting to a considerable extent, 4 Squadrons daily left S.E. England with orders to carry out an offensive patrol, to land and refuel in France or Belgium, and to carry out a second sortie before returning to England.

37. Hitherto I had succeeded generally in keeping the Spitfire Squadrons out of the Continental fighting. The reason for this, as stated above, was that the supply situation was so bad that they could not have maintained their existence in face of the Aircraft Casualty Rate experienced in France: between the 8th May and the 18th May 250 Hurricanes were lost.

38. When the Dunkerque fighting began, however, I could no longer maintain this policy, and the Spitfires had to take their share in the fighting.

39. When the Dunkerque evacuation was complete I had only 3 Day-Fighting Squadrons which had not been engaged in Continental fighting, and 12 Squadrons were in the line for the second time after having been withdrawn to rest and re-form.

40. All this time, it must be remembered, the attack on this Country had not begun; with a few accidental exceptions no bomb had been dropped on our soil. I was responsible for the Air Defence of Great Britain, and I saw my resources slipping away like sand in an hour-glass. The pressure for more and more assistance to France was relentless and inexorable. In the latter part of May, 1940, I sought and obtained permission to appear in person before the War Cabinet and to state my case. I was accorded a courteous and sympathetic hearing, and to my inexpressible relief my arguments prevailed and it was decided to send no more Fighter Reinforcements to France except to cover the final evacuation.

41. I know what it must have cost the Cabinet to reach this decision, but I am profoundly convinced that this was one of the great turning points of the war.

42. Another decision, of perhaps equal importance, was taken at about this time. I refer to the appointment of Lord Beaverbrook to the post of Minister of Aircraft Production. The effect of this appointment can only be described as magical, and thereafter the Supply situation improved to such a degree that the heavy aircraft wastage which was later incurred during the "Battle of Britain" ceased to be the primary danger, its place being taken by the difficulty of producing trained fighter pilots in adequate numbers.

43. After the Evacuation from Dunkerque the pressure on the Fighter Command became less intense, but it by no means disappeared. Hard fighting took place along the coast from Calais to Le Havre to cover the successive evacuations from that coast. Then the centre of gravity shifted to Cherbourg and its neighbourhood, and the "Battle of Britain" followed on without any appreciable opportunity to rest and re-form the units which had borne the brunt of the fighting.

44. The above considerations should be kept in mind when Appendix A (Order of Battle on the 8th July, 1940) is being studied.

45. The Guns and Searchlights available for the Air Defence of Great Britain were arranged as shown on the map which constitutes Appendix B.

46. The fall of Belgium and France had increased the danger to the South and West of England, and had necessitated a considerable modification of the original arrangements when bombing attacks could start only from German soil.

47. The distribution of Army Units was, as a matter of fact, in a condition of perpetual change to meet new situations as they arose, and I must pay a very sincere tribute to the flexibility of the Army organisation, and to the tact, patience and loyalty of the Commander-in-Chief of the Anti-Aircraft Command, Lt.-Gen. Sir Frederick A. Pile, Bart., K.C.B., D.S.O., M.C., which enabled these constant changes to be made without disorganisation.

48. In theory the Commander-in-Chief, Fighter Command, was the authority responsible for settling the dispositions of all guns allotted to the Air Defence of Great Britain; but this was little more than a convenient fiction. The number of guns available was so inadequate for the defence of all the vulnerable targets in the country, and the interests concerned were so diverse and powerful, that it was not to be supposed that an individual member of any one Service would be left to exercise such a prerogative uninterruptedly. A disproportionate amount of my time was taken up in discussions on gun distribution, and each decision was at once greeted with a fresh agitation, until finally I had to ask that all proposals should be discussed by a small Committee on which all interests were represented, and I normally accepted the recommendations of this Committee during quiet periods. During active operations I consulted General Pile, and we acted according to our judgment.

One rather important lesson emerged from our experience, viz., that the general fire-control of all guns in the Air Defence System should be vested in the Air Defence authorities. I do not, of course, mean that, if an invasion had taken place, the guns co-operating with the troops in the Field should have been subordinated to any A.A. Defence Commander, but the existence of "free-lance" guns*), the positions and even the existence of which were unknown to me, was an appreciable handicap, especially at night. It was impossible to acquaint them with the approach of enemy raiders, or of the fact that our own aircraft were working in the vicinity.

49. When the night attacks on London began to be really serious, General Pile, in consultation with myself, decided to send heavy reinforcements. Within 24 hours the defences to the South and South-East of London were approximately doubled, and the great increase in the volume of fire was immediately noticed and had a very good effect on public morale. The physical effect in the shape of raiders destroyed was by no means negligible, but the main effect was never generally known. The track of every raid was, of course, shown on various operations tables, and on some nights as many as 60 per cent. of the raiders approaching London from the South turned back after dropping their bombs in the open country or on the fringe of the Barrage.

50. The A.A. Guns at Dover enjoyed unusual opportunities for practice, with the result that their crews became acknowledged experts in the art of Anti-Aircraft Gunnery. Their skill, however, was attained through the circumstance that they and the Dover Balloon Barrage were continuously the objectives of German attack; they manned their guns continuously night and day, and I must pay a high tribute to their morale, enthusiasm and efficiency.

A report from the 6th A.A. Division, which was busily and typically employed, is included at Appendices C, C.A, C.B. and C.C.

51. A short Appendix (C.D) is added showing the number of rounds fired per aircraft destroyed, for the whole Anti-Aircraft Command.

52. On the map which constitutes Appendix A.A. are shown the boundaries of Groups and Sectors, and also the positions of the Balloon Barrages, together with an indication of the front covered by Radio Location Stations and the area covered by the Observer Corps.

53. The Balloon Barrages had, at this stage, had little opportunity of justifying their existence, except perhaps at Rosyth and Scapa Flow, since bombing attacks against land objectives in Britain had not yet begun. It was thought, however, (and later experience confirmed this opinion), that the heavy cost of their installation and maintenance, and their drain on man-power, were on the whole justified. It is true that their material results, in terms of enemy aircraft destroyed, were not impressive, they suffered staggering casualties in electric storms, and had brought down a number of our own aircraft; on the other hand, they exercise a very salutary moral effect upon the Germans and to a great extent protected the vital objectives, which they surrounded, against low-altitude attacks and dive-bombing.

54. This is not the place to give an account of the romantic discovery and development of Radio Location. It may be explained, however, that the backbone of the system consisted of a series of large "chain" stations at intervals averaging about 30 miles. These gave warning, by means of reflected electrical echoes, of the presence of aircraft within the radius of their effective action, which attained to nearly 200 miles in the most favourable circumstances. The average effective radius was about 80 miles, but they had the serious limitation that they failed altogether to give indications of aircraft flying below 1,000 feet.

55. To overcome this disability, which was particularly hampering to operations against low-flying minelayers, smaller units called "C.H.L. Stations" were included in the protective line.

56. These had a restricted range (about 30 miles), and were incapable of giving heights with any degree of accuracy; they were, however, extremely accurate in azimuth, and constituted an essential feature of the Defensive and Warning Systems.

57. The Radio Location system was growing so fast and had to meet so many calls from overseas that the training of the technical personnel and the maintenance of the elaborate scientific apparatus presented great difficulties. In spite of these handicaps, however, the system operated effectively, and it is not too much to say that the warnings which it gave could have been obtained by no other means and constituted a vital factor in the Air Defence of Great Britain.

---

* These guns belonged to Field Force Units. As such units were, of necessity, highly mobile, their exact location was not always known to Fighter Command. Nor, after a recent move, were they always included in the telephone system.

58. The functions of the Observer Corps (since granted the "Royal" prefix) are too well known to require description here. Suffice it to say that this loyal and public-spirited body of men had maintained their watch with admirable efficiency since the beginning of the war and throughout a winter of exceptional severity. It is important to note that, at this time, they constituted the sole means of tracking enemy raids once they had crossed the coast line. Later experience was to show that "sound plots," which were all that could be given for night raiders, and aircraft flying above clouds or at extreme altitudes, were not adequate for purposes of accurate interception; but their work throughout was quite invaluable. Without it the Air Raid Warning systems could not have been operated, and Inland Interceptions would rarely have been made.

59. The credit for building up and developing the Observer Corps in recent years is due largely to its Commandant, Air Commodore A. D. Warrington Morris, C.M.G., O.B.E.

60. The Air Raid Warning System was operated centrally from Fighter Command Headquarters (with a small exception in the Orkneys and Shetlands).

61. The country was divided into about 130 "Warning Districts," the boundaries of which were determined by the lay-out of the public telephone system. These districts were shown on a map in my Operations Room, and the tracks of all enemy raids, whether over the land or sea, were plotted by means of counters deposited and removed as necessary by a number of "Plotters."

62. The counters were of three colours, according to the 5-minute period in which they were placed on the table. This was necessary to facilitate their removal at the end of 15 minutes, and so to obviate the confusion caused by "stale plots."

63. Three telephone operators were in continuous communication with the Trunk Exchanges in London, Liverpool and Glasgow, and when a raid was within 20 minutes' flying distance of a warning district the Air Raid Warning officer would send a message, as, for instance: "10. Norwich. Yellow." The London operator would transmit this to the London Trunk Exchange, and the London operator would immediately retransmit it to Norwich, where other operators would pass it on to approved recipients in the Warning District. This was a preliminary caution for the information of Police, Fire Stations, &c., and involved no public warning.

64. About 5 minutes later, if the said District were still threatened, a "Red Warning" would be given. This was the signal for the Sirens to sound. A "Green" signal indicated "Raiders Passed," and the Sirens sounded the "All Clear."

65. At night, when it became essential to maintain exposed lights in Dockyards, Railway Sidings and Factories up to the last minute, so as to obviate unnecessary loss of working time, a "Purple" warning was introduced. This was a signal for the extinction of exposed lights, but it did not connote a public warning.

66. There were also subsidiary warnings, transmitted by a fourth operator, to close down Radio Stations which might assist the enemy's navigation by enabling him to use wireless Direction Finding.

67. The credit for working out this system in conjunction with the Home Office is due largely to Air Vice-Marshal A. D. Cunningham, C.B.E.

68. The Fighter Command was divided into Groups and Sectors in accordance with the arrangement shown in Appendix A A. Only Nos. 11, 12 and 13 Groups were fully organised at the beginning of the Battle. Each Group and Sector Headquarters had an Operations Table generally similar to that already described at Command Headquarters, but covering an appropriately smaller area. The British Isles and neighbouring seas were covered by an imaginary "grid" which was used by all concerned for plotting purposes. An expression consisting of one letter and four digits gave the position of a point with an accuracy of 1 square kilometre.

69. Plots from which tracks could be built up were received first from the Radio Location Station, and later from the Observer Corps (and to a small extent from Searchlight Detachments) after a raid had crossed the coast.

70. All Radio Location plots came to a "Filter Room" table at Command Headquarters (next door to the room in which the Operations Table was situated), and, after surplus information had been eliminated, tracks were passed by direct telephone line simultaneously to my Operations Table and to those of Groups and Sectors concerned.

71. Observer Corps plots, on the other hand, went first to Observer Group Centres (where plotting tables were also installed) and thence to Sector and Fighter Group Operations tables. The tracks were then "told" to my Operations Room from the Group Tables.

72. In order to avoid waste of flying effort and false Air Raid Warnings it was obviously very necessary to differentiate between friendly and enemy formations, and this was the most difficult as well as the most important task of my Filter Room. Liaison Officers from Bomber and Coastal Commands were permanently on duty, and they were in possession of all available information concerning the operations of our own Bombers and Coastal patrols. During 1940 an electrical device became generally available which modified the echo received by the Radio Location System from our own aircraft in a characteristic manner. This was of the greatest value.

73. The credit for working out the complicated details of the Filter Room belongs largely to Wing Commander (now Group Captain) R. G. Hart, C.B.E.

74. It appeared to me quite impossible to centralise Tactical control at Command Headquarters, and even Group Commanders would be too busy during heavy fighting to concern themselves with details of Interception.

75. The system was that the Command should be responsible for the identification of approaching formations and for the allotment of enemy raids to Groups where any doubt existed. Group Commanders decided which Sector should meet any specified raid and the

strength of the Fighter force which should be employed. Sector Commanders detailed the Fighter Units to be employed, and operated the machinery of Interception.

76. Various states of preparedness were laid down, *e.g.*, Released, Available (20 minutes), Readiness (5 minutes), and stand-by (2 minutes), and Sectors reported all changes to Group Headquarters, where an up-to-date picture of the state of affairs was recorded by lights on the walls of the Operations Room. Various liaison officers from the Observer Corps, guns and searchlights were maintained in Group and Sector Operations Rooms.

77. It will be seen that the Sector Commander had on his table the best available information as to the position and track of an enemy formation; but, in order to effect an accurate interception, it was necessary that he should also know the position and track of his own Fighters.

78. This was recorded by means of R/T D/F (Radio Telephony Direction Finding). R/T signals were transmitted automatically for 15 seconds out of each minute by selected Fighter aircraft and were picked up by two or three D/F stations installed in Sectors for the purpose. The readings were passed by direct telephone lines to Sector Headquarters, and a mechanical plotting device gave an almost instantaneous plot of the Fighter's position.

79. In the more recently organised Sectors these D/F stations had not been installed, and it was necessary to keep track of the Fighters by giving them precise orders as to speed and direction, and plotting their tracks by Dead Reckoning. This method was adequate only if the force and direction of the wind at various altitudes could be correctly estimated.

80. The Sector Commander could thus see on his operations tables the positions and courses of enemy formations and of his own Fighters, and was enabled so to direct the latter as to make interceptions with the former in a good percentage of occasions by day. Interception depended, of course, on the Fighters being able to see the enemy, and, although the system worked adequately against enemy formations in daylight, the degree of accuracy obtainable was insufficient to effect interception against night raiders not illuminated by Searchlights, or against individual aircraft using cloud cover by day.

81. Orders were given to pilots in their aircraft by means of a very simple code which could be easily memorised. For instance "Scramble" meant Take off. "Orbit" meant Circle. "Vector 230" meant Fly on a course of 230 Degrees.

82. I realised that the enemy might pick up the signals and interpret them, but any elaborate code was out of the question if it included reference to some written list in the air.

83. As a matter of fact the enemy did pick up and interpret the signals in some cases, but not much harm was done, except when they were able to discover the height at which a formation was ordered to operate, and the time when it was ordered to leave its patrol line and land.

84. "Pancake" was the signal for the latter operation, and I therefore introduced several synonyms, the significance of which was not obvious to the enemy.

85. The code word for height was "Angels," followed by the number of thousands of feet; when it appeared probable that the enemy were taking advantage of this information I introduced a false quantity into the code signal. Thus "Angels 18" really meant Fly at 21,000 and not 18,000. On more than one occasion German Fighter formations arriving to dive on one of our patrols were themselves attacked from above.

86. The system as a whole had been built up by successive steps over a period of about four years, and I was not dissatisfied with the way in which it stood the test of war.

87. The steps taken to devise a system of night Interception are described later in this Despatch.

88. I must now give a brief account of the characteristics of the aircraft commonly employed on both sides. As regards the Fighter types available in the Command, the bulk of the force consisted of Hurricanes and Spitfires; the former were beginning to be outmoded by their German counterparts. They were comparatively slow and their performance and manoeuvrability were somewhat inadequate at altitudes above 20,000 ft. The Spitfires were equal or superior to anything which the Germans possessed at the beginning of the Battle.

89. The Hurricanes and Spitfires had bullet-proof windscreens and front armour between the top of the engine and the windscreen. They also had rear armour directly behind the pilot, which was previously prepared and fitted as soon as we began to meet the German Fighters. The early adoption of armour gave us an initial advantage over the Germans, but they were quick to imitate our methods. While German aircraft remained unarmoured, I think it is now generally agreed that the single-seater multi-gun fighter with fixed guns was the most efficient type which could have been produced for day fighting. With the advent of armour some change in armament and/or tactics became necessary, and the subject is discussed in more detail in Appendix F.

90. The Defiant, after some striking initial successes, proved to be too expensive in use against Fighters and was relegated to night work and to the attack of unescorted Bombers.

91. The Blenheim was also unsuitable for day-time combat with Fighters, owing to its low speed and lack of manoeuvrability. It had been relegated to night duties for these reasons, and because adequate space was available in its fuselage for an extra operator and the scientific apparatus which was necessary for the development of a new night-interception technique. The cockpit had not been designed for night flying and the night view was extremely bad. Its already low performance had been further reduced by certain external fittings which were essential for the operation of the Radio Detecting apparatus.

92. The Beaufighter was looked on as a Blenheim replacement in which most of the above disadvantages would be overcome. Its speed promised to be adequate and its armament consisted of 4 20-mm. Cannons instead

of the 5 .303-inch Brownings of the Blenheim. There was thus hope that decisive fire could be brought to bear in the short period during which visual contact could be expected to be maintained at night.

93. Like the Blenheim, it had not been designed as a Night Fighter (it was an adaptation of the Beaufort Torpedo Bomber), and the night view from the cockpit was bad; but Air Vice-Marshal Sir Q. Brand, K.B.E., D.S.O., M.C., D.F.C., a veteran night fighter of the previous war, had designed a new cockpit lay-out, which did not, unfortunately, materialise during my tenure of the Fighter Command. The output of Beaufighters was also very low.

94. Another type which was pressed into service as a Night Fighter was the Douglas D.B.7 (now the Havoc). It had low fire power and comparatively poor performance with its original engines. Its chief advantage lay in its tricycle undercarriage, which proved very popular for landings in bad visibility. Only one Squadron of these was in being when I left the Command.

95. One Squadron of Gladiators was still in use in the Command. As explained above, the organisation of No. 10 Group was not complete, and there was no large aerodrome close enough to Plymouth to allow of direct protection being given to that town and to the Dockyard at Devonport. A squadron of Gladiators was therefore located at a small aerodrome called Roborough in the immediate vicinity. The Gladiators, though slow by modern standards, were very manœuvrable, and had given good results in Norway by deflection shooting in the defence of fixed objectives, where the Bombers could not avoid the Gladiators if they were to reach their targets.

96. Some American single-seater aircraft were in Great Britain, but the types then available were deficient in performance and fire power and were not employed to any material extent.

97. The Whirlwind raised high hopes in some quarters. It claimed a very high top speed and carried 4 Cannon Guns. It had, however, a totally inadequate service ceiling (about 25,000 ft.) and a poor performance at that altitude. It also suffered from a continuous series of teething troubles, and the single Squadron equipped with this type was never fit for operations in my time.

98. It is very difficult to give any kind of concise description of the types of Enemy Aircraft used during the Battle. The Germans, while adhering to broad standard types, were continually modifying and improving them by fitting more powerful engines and altering the armament. The original Messerschmitt 109, for instance, had a performance comparable with that of the Hurricane, but the latest type could compete with the Spitfire, and had a better ceiling. Some of them had 4 machine guns and others had 2 machine guns and 2 cannons. Some of them were fitted to carry bombs and some were not.

99. The Messerschmitt 110 was a twin-engined fighter designed primarily for escorting Bombers and used also as a Fighter-Bomber. It was somewhat faster than the Hurricane, but naturally much less manœuvrable than the single-engined types. Its usual armament was 2 fixed cannons and 4 machine guns firing forward, and one free machine gun firing to the rear. Our pilots regarded it as a less formidable opponent than the later types of M.E. 109.

100. The Heinkel 113 Fighter made its appearance in limited numbers during the Battle. It was a single seater, generally resembling the M.E. 109. Its main attributes were high performance and ceiling, so that it was generally used in the highest of the several layers in which attacking formations were usually built up.

100. The Heinkel 113 Fighter made its Dive-Bomber. It had a low performance (top speed well under 250 m.p.h.). It had 2 fixed machine guns firing forward and one free gun firing to the rear. When it was able to operate undisturbed by Fighters it was the Germans' most efficient Bomber against land or sea targets owing to the great accuracy with which it dropped its bombs; but when it was caught by fighters it was nothing short of a death-trap, and formations of J.U. 87's were practically annihilated on several occasions.

102. The Heinkel 111 and the various types of Dornier (17, 17Z and 215) constituted the main element of the German striking force. They were twin-engined aircraft and were generally similar, although the former was slightly the larger. Their speed was something over 250 m.p.h., and their armament consisted normally (but not always) of 4 free machine guns firing backwards and one firing forwards. Their radius of action varied with tankage and bomb load, but, if necessary, all objectives in England and Northern Ireland could be reached from aerodromes in France.

103. The Junkers 88 was the most modern of the German Bombers. It also was a twin-engined type with a performance of about 290 m.p.h. Its armament was generally similar to that of the H.E. 111 and the Dorniers and it had a slightly longer range. It could be used on occasions as a Dive-Bomber and, though probably somewhat less accurate than the J.U. 87, was much less vulnerable owing to its superior performance and armament.

104. Before beginning an account of the Battle, I must refer briefly to the publication entitled *The Battle of Britain*, issued by the Air Ministry. This, if I may say so, is an admirable account of the Battle for public consumption, and I am indebted to it, as well as to the book *Fighter Command*, by Wing Commander A. B. Austin, for help in the compilation of this Despatch. There is very little which I should have wished to alter, even if circumstances had permitted my seeing it before publication (I was absent in America at the time), but there are two points to which I should like to draw attention:—

105. In the diagram on page 7 the speed of the Hurricane is seriously over-rated at 335 m.p.h. I carried out a series of trials to obtain the absolute and comparative speeds of Hurricanes and Spitfires at optimum heights. Naturally the speeds of individual aircraft varied slightly, but the average speed of six Hurricanes came out at about 305 m.p.h.

106. The second point is of greater importance. I quote from page 33: " What the Luftwaffe failed to do was to destroy the Fighter Squadrons of the Royal Air Force,

which were, indeed, stronger at the end of the battle than at the beginning." (The italics are mine.)

107. This statement, even if intended only for popular consumption, tends to lead to an attitude of complacency which may be very dangerous in the future. Whatever the study of paper returns may have shown, the fact is that the situation was critical in the extreme. Pilots had to be withdrawn from the Bomber and Coastal Commands and from the Fleet Air Arm and flung into the Battle after hasty preparation. The majority of the squadrons had been reduced to the status of training units, and were fit only for operations against un-escorted bombers. The remainder were battling daily against heavy odds.

108. The indomitable courage of the Fighter Pilots and the skill of their Leaders brought us through the crises, and the morale of the Germans eventually cracked because of the stupendous losses which they sustained.

109. Any attempt to describe the events of the Battle day by day would make this Despatch unduly long and would prevent the reader from obtaining a comprehensive picture of the events. I have therefore decided to show the main features of each day's fighting in an Appendix on which our own and the Germans' aircraft casualties will be shown graphically. I shall then be able to deal with the progress of the Battle by phases, thus avoiding the tedious and confusing method of day-to-day description. The information is given in Appendix D.

110. As regards our casualties, we generally issued statements to the effect that we lost " x " aircraft from which " y " pilots were saved. This did not of course mean that " y " pilots were ready immediately to continue the Battle. Many of them were suffering from wounds, burns or other injuries which precluded their return to active flying temporarily or permanently.

111. It might also be assumed that all German crews who were in aircraft brought down during the Battle, were permanently lost to the Luftwaffe because the fighting took place on our side of the Channel. Such an assumption would not be literally true, because the Germans succeeded in rescuing a proportion of their crews from the sea by means of rescue boats, floats and aircraft which will be later described.

112. The decisive features of the Battle were the Ratio of Casualties incurred by ourselves and the Germans, and the Ratio of Casualties to the numbers actively employed on both sides. Appendix D has been drawn up with these points in mind.

113. I must disclaim any exact accuracy in the estimates of Enemy losses. All that I can say is that the utmost care was taken to arrive at the closest possible approximation. Special intelligence officers examined pilots individually after their combats, and the figures claimed are only those recorded as " Certain." If we allow for a percentage of over-statement, and the fact that two or more Fighters were sometimes firing at the same enemy aircraft without being aware of the fact, this can fairly be balanced by the certainty that a proportion of aircraft reported as " Probably Destroyed " or " Damaged " failed to return to their bases. The figures, then, are put forward as an honest approximation. Judging by results, they are perhaps not far out.

114. The German claims were, of course, ludicrous; they may have been deceived about our casualties, but they know they were lying about their own.

115. I remember being cross-examined in August by the Secretary of State for Air about the discrepancy. He was anxious about the effect on the American people of the wide divergence between the claims of the two sides. I replied that the Americans would soon find out the truth; if the Germans' figures were accurate they would be in London in a week, otherwise they would not.

116. Our estimate of German casualties, then, may be taken as reasonably accurate for practical purposes; but our estimates of the strength in which attacks were made is based on much less reliable evidence. The Radio-Location system could give only a very approximate estimate of numbers and was sometimes in error by three or four hundred per cent. This is no reflection on the System, which was not designed or intended to be accurate in the estimation of considerable numbers; moreover, several stations were suffering from the effects of severe bombing attacks. As the average height of operations increased, the Observer Corps became less and less able to make accurate estimates of numbers, and, in fact, formations were often quite invisible from the ground.

117. Even the numerical estimates made by pilots who encountered large formations in the air are likely to be guesswork in many instances. Opportunities for deliberate counting of enemy aircraft were the exception rather than the rule.

118. Although Secret Intelligence sources supplemented the information available, it is possible that on days of heavy fighting complete formations may have escaped recorded observation altogether.

119. This is unfortunate, because it is obviously of the greatest importance to determine the relative strengths of the Attack and the Defence, and to know the ratio of losses to aircraft employed which may be expected to bring an attack to a standstill in a given time. History will doubtless elucidate the uncertainty, but perhaps not in time for the information to be of use in the present war.

120. My personal opinion is that, on days of slight activity, our estimates are reasonably accurate, but that they probably err on the low side on days of heavy fighting when many and large formations were employed.

121. As has been explained above, few squadrons were fresh and intact when the Battle began. No sufficient respite has been granted since the conclusion of the Dunkerque fighting to rest the Squadrons which had not left the Fighter Command, and to rebuild those which had undergone the ordeal of fighting from aerodromes in Northern France. These last had been driven from aerodrome to aerodrome, able only to aim at self-preservation from almost continuous attack by Bombers and Fighters; they were desperately weary and had lost the greater part of their equipment, since aircraft which were unserviceable only from slight defects had to be abandoned.

PART II.—THE BATTLE.

122. The Battle may be said to have divided itself broadly into 4 Phases: First, the attack on convoys and Coastal objectives, such as Ports, Coastal Aerodromes and Radio Location Stations. Second, the attack of Inland Fighter Aerodromes. Third, the attack on London. And fourth, the Fighter-Bomber stage, where the target was of importance quite subsidiary to the main object of drawing our Fighters into the air and engaging them in circumstances as disadvantageous to us as possible. These phases indicated only general tendencies; they overlapped and were not mutually exclusive.

123. It has been estimated that the Germans sent over, on an average throughout the Battle, four Fighters to each Bomber or Fighter-Bomber, but any such estimate must be very rough.

124. I must emphasise, throughout, the extreme versatility of the German methods both in the timing and direction of their attacks, and in the tactical formations and methods employed.

125. They enjoyed the great advantage of having a wide front from which attacks could be delivered. First a blow would be delivered from Calais, perhaps against London; then after a carefully-timed interval, when 11 Group Fighters might be expected to be at the end of their petrol endurance, a heavy attack would be made on Southampton and Portland. Other attacks, after being built up to formidable dimensions, would prove to be only feints, and the Bombers would turn away before reaching coast of England, only to return again in half an hour, when the Fighters, sent up to intercept them, were landing.

126. Time-honoured methods of escort were at first employed. A strong Fighter formation would fly a mile or so behind and above the Bombers. When the Germans found that our Fighters could deliver a well-timed attack on the Bombers before the Fighters could intervene, or when our Fighters attacked from ahead or below, each move was met by a counter-move on the part of the Germans, so that, in September, Fighter escorts were flying inside the Bomber formation, others were below, and a series of Fighters stretched upwards to 30,000 feet or more.

127. One Squadron Leader described his impressions of the appearance of one of these raids; he said it was like looking up the escalator at Piccadilly Circus.

128. I must pay a very sincere tribute to the Air Officer Commanding No. 11 Group, Air Vice-Marshal K. R. Park, C.B., M.C., D.F.C., for the way in which he adjusted his tactics and interception methods to meet each new development as it occurred.

129. Tactical control was, as has already been stated, devolved to the Groups; but tactical methods were normally laid down by Command Headquarters. During periods of intense fighting, however, there was no time for consultation, and Air Vice-Marshal Park acted from day to day on his own initiative. We discussed matters as opportunity offered.

130. He has reported on the tactical aspects of the Battle in two very interesting documents, which are, however, too long to reproduce here.

131. A close liaison was kept between Nos. 10 and 11 and 12 Groups. It sometimes happened that, in the heaviest attacks, practically all 11 Group Fighters would be in the air. 11 Group would then ask 12 Group to send a formation from Duxford to patrol over the aerodromes immediately East of London so that these might not be attacked when defenceless.

132. Mutual help was also arranged between Nos. 10 and 11 Groups. When Portsmouth was attacked, for instance, No. 10 would help No. 11 Group, and *vice versa* when the attack was on Portland or some Convoy to the West of the Isle of Wight.

133. The amount of physical damage done to Convoys during the first phase was not excessive. About five ships (I think) were actually sunk by bombing, others were damaged, and Convoys were scattered on occasion. It was, of course, much easier to protect the Convoys if they kept as close as possible to the English Coast, but one Convoy at least was routed so as to pass close to Cherbourg, and suffered accordingly. Later, it was arranged that Convoys should traverse the most dangerous and exposed stretches by night, and Convoys steaming in daylight either had direct protection by Fighter escorts, or else had escorts at "Readiness" prepared to leave the ground directly danger threatened.

134. Three of the Radio Location Stations in the South of England suffered rather severe damage and casualties. No Station was permanently put out of action, and the worst damage was repaired in about a month, though the Station was working at reduced efficiency in about half that time. The operating personnel, and particularly the women, behaved with great courage under threat of attack and actual bombardment.

135. As regards aerodromes, Manston was the worst sufferer at this stage. It, Hawkinge and Lympne were the three advanced grounds on which we relied for filling up tanks when a maximum range was required for operations over France. They were so heavily attacked with bombs and machine guns that they were temporarily abandoned. This is not to say that they could not have been used if the need had been urgent, but, for interception at or about our own coastline, aerodromes and satellites farther inland were quite effective.

136. Heavy damage was done to buildings, but these were mostly non-essential, because aircraft were kept dispersed in the open, and the number of men and women employed was not large in comparison with the number at a Station which was the Headquarters of a Sector.

137. Works personnel, permanent and temporary, and detachments of Royal Engineers were employed in filling up the craters on the aerodromes. Experience at this stage showed that neither the personnel nor the material provided were adequate to effect repairs with the necessary speed, and the strength and mobility of the repair parties was increased. Stocks of "hard-core" rubble had been collected at Fighter aerodromes before the war.

138. It may be convenient here to continue the subject of damage to Fighter Stations other than those attacked in the first Phase.

139. Casualties to personnel were slight, except in cases where a direct hit was made on

a shelter trench. The trenches commonly in use were lined with concrete and were roofed and covered with earth; but they gave no protection against a direct hit, and, in the nature of things, they had to be within a short distance of the hangars and offices.

140. Only non-essential personnel took cover; aircraft crews and the staff of the Operations Room remained at their posts. The morale of the men and women of ground crews and staffs was high and remained so throughout.

141. At Kenley and at Biggin Hill direct hits were sustained on shelter trenches, at the latter place by a bomb of 500 kilog. or more. The trench and its 40 occupants were annihilated.

142. Wooden hangars were generally set on fire by a bombing attack, and everything in them destroyed.

143. Steel, brick and concrete hangars, on the other hand, stood up well against attack, though, of course, acres of glass were broken. Hangars were generally empty or nearly so, and those aircraft which were destroyed in hangars were generally under repair or major inspection which made it necessary to work under cover.

144. It must, nevertheless, be definitely recorded that the damage done to Fighter aerodromes, and to their communications and ground organisation, was serious, and has been generally under-estimated. Luckily, the Germans did not realise the success of their efforts, and shifted their objectives before the cumulative effect of the damage had become apparent to them.

145. Damage to aerodrome surface was not a major difficulty. It was possible for the Germans to put one or two aerodromes like Manston and Hawkinge out of action for a time, but we had so many satellite aerodromes and landing grounds available that it was quite impossible for the Germans to damage seriously a number of aerodromes sufficient to cause more than temporary inconvenience.

146. This is an important point, because, in mobile warfare, Fighter aerodromes cannot be hastily improvised in broken country, and the number of aerodromes actually or potentially available is a primary factor in the " Appreciation of a Situation."

147. Sector Operations Rooms were protected by high earth embankments, so that they were immune from everything except a direct hit, and, as a matter of fact, no direct hit by a heavy bomb was obtained on any Operations Room. Communications were, however, considerably interrupted, and I must here pay a tribute to the foresight of Air Vice-Marshal E. L. Gossage, C.B., C.V.O., D.S.O., M.C., who commanded No. 11 Group during the first eight months of the war. At his suggestion " Stand-by " Operations Rooms were constructed at a distance of two or three miles from Sector Headquarters, and a move was made to these when serious attacks on Fighter Aerodromes began. They were somewhat inconvenient make-shifts, and some loss of efficiency in Interception resulted from their use. Work was put in hand immediately on more permanent and fully-equipped Operations Rooms conveniently remote from Sector Headquarters; these though in no way bomb-proof, were outside the radius of anything aimed at the Sector Aerodrome, and owed their immunity to inconspicuousness. Most of these were finished by October 1940.

148. Aerodrome Defence against parachute troops, or threat of more serious ground attack, was an important and a difficult problem, because Home Defence troops were few and were needed on the Beaches, and the majority of troops rescued from Dunkerque were disorganised and unarmed. The Commander-in-Chief, Home Forces, did, however, make troops available in small numbers for the more important aerodromes and armoured vehicles were extemporised. The difficulty was enhanced by a comparatively recent decision of the Air Ministry to disarm the rank and file of the Royal Air Force. The decision was reversed, but it was some time before rifles could be provided and men trained in their use.

149. The slender resources of the Anti-Aircraft Command were strained to provide guns for the defence of the most important Fighter and Bomber Aerodromes. High Altitude and Bofors guns were provided up to the limit considered practicable, and the effort was reinforced by the use of Royal Air Force detachments with Lewis guns and some hundreds of 20-mm. Cannon which were not immediately required for use in Aircraft

150. A type of small Rocket was also installed at many aerodromes. These were arranged in lines along the perimeter, and could be fired up to a height of something under 1,000 feet in the face of low-flying attack. They carried a small bomb on the end of a wire. Some limited success was claimed during a low-flying attack at Kenley, and they probably had some moral effect when their existence became known to the Enemy. They were, of course, capable of physical effect only against very low horizontal attacks.

151. The main safeguard for Aircraft against air attack was Dispersal. Some experiments on Salisbury Plain in the Summer of 1938 had shown that dispersal alone, without any form of splinter-proof protection, afforded a reasonable safeguard against the forms of attack practised by our own Bomber Command at the time. Thirty unserviceable Fighters were disposed in a rough ring of about 1,000 yards diameter, and the Bomber Command attacked them for the inside of a week with every missile between a 500-pound bomb and an incendiary bullet, and without any kind of opposition. The result was substantially:—3 destroyed, 1 damaged beyond repair, 11 seriously damaged but repairable, and the rest slightly damaged or untouched.

152. I therefore asked that small splinter-proof pens for single aircraft should be provided at all Fighter Aerodromes. This was not approved, but I was offered pens for groups of three. I had to agree to this, because it was linked up with the provision of all-weather runways which I had been insistently demanding for two years, and it was imperatively necessary that work on the runways should not be held up by further discussion about pens. I think that the 3-aircraft pens were too big. They had a large open face to the front and a concrete area, of the size of two tennis courts, which made an ideal surface for the bursting of direct-action bombs. Eventually, splinter-proof partitions were made inside the

pens, and till then some aircraft were parked in the open. Losses at dispersal points were not serious; the worst in my recollection was 5 aircraft destroyed or seriously damaged in one attack. Small portable tents were provided which could be erected over the centre portion of an aeroplane, leaving the tail and wing-tips exposed. These protected the most important parts and enabled ground crews to work in bad weather.

153. About this time an improvised Repair System was organised and worked well. With the hearty co-operation of the Ministry of Aircraft Production it was decided that Units should be relieved of all extensive repairs and overhauls, both because of their preoccupation in the Battle and because of the danger of further damage being done by enemy action to aircraft under repair. Broadly speaking, any aircraft capable of returning to its base was capable of another 15 minutes' straight flight to a Repair Depot: aircraft incapable of flight were sent by road. Small repairs, such as the patching of bullet holes, were done by the Unit. Two such Repair Depots were improvised about 30 miles to the west of London, and this undoubtedly prevented an accumulation of unserviceable aircraft at Fighter Stations.

154. It was also about this time that the final decision was made to relegate the Defiant to night operations. It had two serious disabilities; firstly, the brain flying the aeroplane was not the brain firing the guns: the guns could not fire within 16 Degrees of the line of flight of the aeroplane and the gunner was distracted from his task by having to direct the pilot through the Communication Set. Secondly, the guns could not be fired below the horizontal, and it was therefore necessary to keep below the enemy. When beset by superior numbers of Fighters the best course to pursue was to form a descending spiral, so that one or more Defiants should always be in a position to bring effective fire to bear. Such tactics were, however, essentially defensive, and the formation sometimes got broken up before they could be adopted. In practice, the Defiants suffered such heavy losses that it was necessary to relegate them to night fighting, or to the attack of unescorted Bombers.

155. The above remarks have carried me beyond the first phase of the Battle and into the second; but I find it impossible to adhere to a description of the fighting phase by phase. The Enemy's Strategical, as well as his Tactical moves had to be met from day to day as they occurred, and I give an account of my problems and the lessons to be derived from them roughly in the order of their incidence. The detailed sequence of events is sufficiently indicated in the Diagram at Appendix "D."

156. Throughout the Battle, of course, fighting continually occurred over the sea, and German aircraft, damaged over England, had to return across the Straits of Dover or the English Channel. Far more German than British crews fell into the sea. The Germans therefore developed an elaborate system of sea-rescue. Their Bombers had inflatable rubber dinghies, and various other rescue devices were adopted. Crews were provided with bags of a chemical known as fluorescine, a small quantity of which stained a large area of water a vivid green. Floating refuges with provisions and wireless sets were anchored off the French coast. "E Boats" and rescue launches were extensively employed, and white-painted float-planes, marked with the Red Cross, were used even in the midst of battle. We had to make it known to the Germans that we could not countenance the use of the Red Cross in this manner. They were engaged in rescuing combatants and taking them back to fight again, and they were also in a position, if granted immunity, to make valuable reconnaisance reports. In spite of this, surviving crews of these aircraft appeared to be surprised and aggrieved at being shot down.

157. Our own arrangements were less elaborate. Life-saving jackets were painted a conspicuous yellow, and later the fluorescine device was copied. Patrol aircraft (not under the Red Cross) looked out for immersed crews, and a chain of rescue launches with special communications was installed round the coast. Our own shipping, too, was often on the spot, and many pilots were rescued by Naval or Merchant vessels.

158. This is perhaps a convenient opportunity to say a word about the ethics of shooting at aircraft crews who have "baled out" in parachutes.

159. Germans descending over England are prospective Prisoners of War, and, as such, should be immune. On the other hand, British pilots descending over England are still potential Combatants.

160. Much indignation was caused by the fact that German pilots sometimes fired on our descending airmen (although, in my opinion, they were perfectly entitled to do so), but I am glad to say that in many cases they refrained and sometimes greeted a helpless adversary with a cheerful wave of the hand.

161. Many of the targets attacked during the first two phases of the Battle were of little military importance, and had but slight effect on our War Effort. Exceptions to this were day-attacks carried out on the Spitfire works at Southampton and the sheds at Brooklands where some of our Hurricanes were assembled and tested. Both these attacks had some effect on output, which would have been serious but for the anticipatory measures taken by Lord Beaverbrook.

162. About this time one Canadian, two Polish and one Czech squadrons became fit for Operations.

163. A squadron of Canadian pilots of the Royal Air Force (No. 242) had been in existence for some months, and was one of the squadrons which went to France in June to cover the evacuation from the West Coast. On its return it became one of the foremost fighting Squadrons in the Command, under the leadership of the very gallant Squadron Leader (now Wing Commander) D. R. S. Bader, D.S.O., D.F.C., No. 1 (Canadian) Squadron, now also came into the line and acquitted itself with great distinction.

164. I must confess that I had been a little doubtful of the effect which their experience in their own countries and in France might have had upon the Polish and Czech pilots, but my doubts were soon laid to rest, because all three Squadrons swung in the fight with a dash and enthusiasm which is beyond praise. They were inspired by a burning hatred for the

Germans which made them very deadly opponents. The first Polish Squadron (No. 303) in No. 11 Group, during the course of a month, shot down more Germans than any British unit in the same period. Other Poles and Czechs were used in small numbers in British Squadrons, and fought very gallantly, but the language was a difficulty, and they were probably most efficiently employed in their own National units. Other foreign pilots were employed in British Squadrons, but not in appreciable numbers. The American "Eagle" Squadron was in process of formation during the Battle.

165. The Auxiliary Squadrons were by this time practically indistinguishable from Regulars. It will be remembered that the Scottish Auxiliaries were responsible for the first Air success of the War in the Firth of Forth. To set off against the discontinuity of their training in peace time they had the great advantage of permanency of personnel, and the Flight Commanders at the outbreak of the War were senior and experienced. At the same time, this very permanence led to the average age of the pilots being rather high for intensive fighting, which exercises a strain which the average man of 30 cannot support indefinitely. This point has now ceased to be of importance because of fresh postings. It is mentioned only because it is a factor to be kept in mind in peace time. No praise can be too high for the Auxiliaries, both as regards their keenness and efficiency in peace time and their fighting record in war.

166. I may perhaps mention the question of the Long Range Guns which were mounted along the coast of France near Cap Grisnez. They were within range of our coastal aerodromes, which they occasionally subjected to a desultory shelling. Their main targets, however, were Dover and the Convoys passing through the Straits. So far as I am aware, neither they nor the guns which we installed as counter measures, had any great influence on the air fighting, but they did of course make it impossible for any of our warships to approach the French coast in clear weather, and might have had an important effect if it had been possible for the Germans to launch an invading army.

167. About the end of the second phase, the problems of keeping units up to strength and of relieving them when exhausted began to assume formidable proportions. It was no new experience, because the drain of units and pilots to France, coupled with the Dunkerque fighting, had created similar problems in the Spring.

168. The comparative relaxation in the intensity of the fighting in June and July had afforded a little respite, but units had only partially recovered and were neither fresh nor up to strength when the fighting again became intense.

169. When Squadrons became exhausted, obviously the most satisfactory way of reinforcement was by means of moving complete units, and this was done when time allowed. Serviceable aircraft were transferred by air, and Operational Aircraft Crews (about 35 men per Squadron) were transferred by Civil Aircraft put at my disposal for the moves. The remainder of the personnel travelled by train or motor transport according to circumstances. Some of the distances involved were considerable, as for instance when a Squadron from Wick had to be brought down in the London Area.

170. The First-line strength of a Squadron was 16 aircraft, of which not more than 12 were intended to be operationally available at any one time. The other 4 would normally be undergoing Inspection or Overhaul. In addition to this there was a small reserve of three to five aircraft per Squadron available on the station.

171. There was a limit to the number of trained pilots which could be kept on the strength of a Squadron even in times of operational passivity, because not more than about 25 could be kept in full practice in Flying Duties.

172. A fresh squadron coming into an active Sector would generally bring with them 16 aircraft and about 20 trained pilots. They would normally fight until they were no longer capable of putting more than 9 aircraft into the air, and then they had to be relieved. This process occupied different periods according to the luck and skill of the unit. The normal period was a month to six weeks, but some units had to be replaced after a week or 10 days.

173. Air Vice Marshal Park found that the heaviest casualties were often incurred by newly-arrived Squadrons owing to their non-familiarity with the latest developments of air fighting.

174. It soon became impossible to maintain the to-and-fro progress of complete unit personnel from end to end of the country, and the first limitation to efficiency which had to be accepted was the retention of the majority of personnel at Sector Stations and the transfer only of flying personnel and aircraft crews. This limitation was regrettable because it meant that officers and men were strange to one another, but worse was to come.

175. By the beginning of September the incidence of casualties became so serious that a fresh squadron would become depleted and exhausted before any of the resting and reforming squadrons was ready to take its place. Fighter pilots were no longer being produced in numbers sufficient to fill the gaps in the fighting ranks. Transfers were made from the Fleet Air Arm and from the Bomber and Coastal Commands, but these pilots naturally required a short flying course on Hurricanes or Spitfires and some instruction in Formation Flying, Fighter Tactics and Interception procedure.

176. I considered, but discarded, the advisability of combining pairs of weak units into single Squadrons at full strength, for several reasons, one of which was the difficulty of recovery when a lull should come. Another was that ground personnel would be wasted, and a third was that the rate at which the strength of the Command was decreasing would be obvious.

177. I decided to form 3 Categories of Squadron:—

(a) The units of 11 Group and on its immediate flanks, which were bearing the brunt of the fighting.

(b) A few outside units to be maintained at operational strength and to be available as Unit Reliefs in cases where this was unavoidable.

(c) The remaining Squadrons of the Command, which would be stripped of their operational pilots, for the benefit of the A Squadrons, down to a level of 5 or 6. These C Squadrons could devote their main energies to the training of new pilots, and, although they would not be fit to meet German Fighters, they would be quite capable of defending their Sectors against unescorted Bombers, which would be all that they would be likely to encounter.

178. The necessity for resorting to such measures as this indicates the strain which had been put on the Fighter Command and the Pilot Training organisations by the casualties which the Command had suffered in this decisive Battle.

179. In the early stages of the fight Mr. Winston Churchill spoke with affectionate raillery of me and my "Chicks." He could have said nothing to make me more proud; every Chick was needed before the end.

180. I trust that I may be permitted to record my appreciation of the help given me by the support and confidence of the Prime Minister at a difficult and critical time.

181. In the early days of the War the question of the provision of Operational Training Units (or Group Pools, as they were called at that time) was under discussion. It was referred to in the correspondence which I have mentioned in paragraph 17 of this Despatch. At that time I was so gravely in need of additional Fighter Squadrons that I was willing to do without Group Pools altogether while we were still at long range from the German Fighters.

182. The functions of these Group Pools, or O.T.Us., was to accept pilots direct from Flying Training Schools or non-fighter units of the Royal Air Force and train them in the handling of Fighter types, formation flying, fighting tactics, and R/T control and interception methods. I realised that the Fighters in France could not undertake this work and must have a Group Pool allotted primarily to meet their requirements, but I felt that, so long as we at Home were out of touch with German Fighters, I would prefer to put all available resources into new Squadrons and to undertake in Service Squadrons the final training of pilots coming from Flying Training Schools, provided that they had done some formation flying and night flying, and had fired their guns in the air.

183. Of course, when intensive fighting began, final training of pilots in Squadrons could no longer be given efficiently, and at the time of the Battle three O.T.Us. were in existence. It was found that three weeks was about the mimimum period which was of practical value, but that a longer course, up to six weeks, was desirable when circumstances permitted.

184. During the Battle the output from the O.T.Us. was quite inadequate to meet the casualty rate, and it was not even possible to supply from the Flying Training Schools the necessary intake to the O.T.Us.

185. The lack of flexibility of the Training system, therefore, proved to be the "bottleneck" and was the cause of the progressively deteriorating situation of the Fighter Command up till the end of September This statement is in no sense a criticism of the Flying Training Command. The problem, as I state it here, can have no ideal solution and some compromise must be adopted.

186. Assuming that in periods of maximum quiescence the Fighter Squadrons of the Royal Air Force require an intake of x pilots per week, in periods of intense activity they require about ten times the number.

187. It is necessary to start the flying training of a pilot about a year before he is ready to engage Enemy Fighters, and therefore the training authorities should be warned, a year ahead, of the incidence of active periods. This is obviously impossible. If they try to be ready for all eventualities by catering for a continuous output to meet a high casualty rate, the result is that, during quiet periods, pilots are turned out at such a rate that they cannot be absorbed, or even given enough flying to prevent their forgetting what they have been taught. If, on the other hand, they cater for the normal wastage rate, Fighter Squadrons are starved of reinforcements when they are most vitally needed.

188. The fundamental principle which must be realised is that Fighter needs, when they arise, are not comparative with those of other Commands, but absolute. An adequate and efficient Fighter force ensures the Security of the Base, without which continuous operations are impossible.

189. If the Fighter defence had failed in the Autumn of 1940, England would have been invaded. The paralysis of their fighters in the Spring was an important factor in the collapse of the French resistance. Later, the unavoidable withdrawal of the Fighters from Crete rendered continued resistance impossible.

190. Day Bomber and Army Co-operation aircraft can operate when their own Fighters are predominant, but are driven out of the sky when the Enemy Fighters have a free hand.

191. I submit some suggestions by which the apparently insuperable difficulties of the problem may be reduced.

(a) Start by aiming at a Fighter output well above that needed in quiescent periods.

(b) Ensure that at Flying Training Schools, pupils earmarked for other duties may be rapidly switched over to Fighter training.

(c) Organise the O.T.Us. with a "Normal" and an "Emergency" Syllabus, the latter lasting for three weeks and the former twice as long.

(d) Fill up the Service Fighter Squadrons to a strength of 25 pilots, or whatever the C.-in-C. considers to be the maximum which can be kept in flying and operational practice.

(e) Form Reservoirs, either at O.T.Us. or in special units where surplus pilots may maintain the flying and operational standard which they have reached.

(f) When the initiative lies in our hands (as, for instance, when we are planning to deliver an offensive some time ahead), the intake of Flying Training Schools should be adjusted to cater for the additional stress which can be foreseen.

(g) (And this applies principally to overseas theatres of war where rapid reinforcement is impossible.) Let the Day Bomber and Army Co-operation Squadrons have a number of Fighters on which they can fly and train as opportunity offers. This is a revolutionary suggestion, but it is made in all seriousness. If their Fighters are overwhelmed the Day Bomber and Army Co-operation units will not be able to operate at all. No very high standard of training should be attempted, especially in Radio-controlled Interception methods: but the intervention of these units as Fighters, working in pairs or small formations, might well prove to be the decisive factor in a critical situation.

192. It will be observed that, at the end of the second Phase of the Battle, the power of reinforcing by complete units had substantially disappeared. We still possessed an effective reserve of trained pilots, but they could be made available only by stripping the Squadrons which were not engaged in the South and South-East of England.

193. The effective strength of the Command was running down, though the fact was not known to the public, nor, I hoped, to the Germans. They for their part must certainly be feeling the effect of their heavy losses, but there was very little indication of any loss of morale, so far as could be seen from a daily scrutiny of the examinations of Prisoners of War. Our own pilots were fighting with unabated gallantry and determination.

194. The confidence of the German High Command probably received something of a shock about this time. The sustained resistance which they were meeting in South-East England probably led them to believe that Fighter Squadrons had been withdrawn, wholly or in part, from the North in order to meet the attack. On the 15th August, therefore, two large raids were sent, one to Yorkshire and one to Newcastle. They were escorted by Fighters. The distance was too great for Me. 109s, but not for Me. 110s.

195. If the assumption was that our Fighters had been withdrawn from the North, the contrary was soon apparent, and the bombers received such a drubbing that the experiment was not repeated. I think that this incident probably had a very depressing influence on the outlook of the German High Command.

196. As I have said, our own pilots were fighting with the utmost gallantry and determination, but the mass raids on London, which were the main feature of the third phase of the Battle, involved a tremendous strain on units which could no longer be relieved as such. Some Squadrons were flying 50 and 60 hours per diem.

197. Many of the pilots were getting very tired. An order was in existence that all pilots should have 24 hours' leave every week, during which they should be encouraged to leave their station and get some exercise and change of atmosphere: this was issued as an order so that the pilots should be compelled to avail themselves of the opportunity to get the necessary rest and relaxation. I think it was generally obeyed, but I fear that the instinct of duty sometimes over-rode the sense of discipline. Other measures were also taken to provide rest and relaxation at Stations, and sometimes to find billets for pilots where they could sleep away from their Aerodromes.

198. During this third phase the problem arose, in an acute form, of the strength of Fighter formations which we should employ. When time was the essence of the problem, two squadrons were generally used by A.V.M. Park in No. 11 Group. He had the responsibility of meeting attacks as far to the Eastward as possible, and the building up of a four-squadron formation involved the use of a rendezvous for aircraft from two or more aerodromes. This led to delay and lack of flexibility in leadership.

199. On the other hand, when No. 12 Group was asked to send down protective formations to guard the aerodromes on the Eastern fringe of London, it was often possible to build up big formations, and these had great success on some occasions, though by no means always.

200. Because a similar situation may well arise in future, I think that it is desirable to enter into some detail in this connection.

201. I may preface my remarks by stating that I am personally in favour of using Fighter formations in the greatest strength of which circumstances will permit, and, in the Dunkerque fighting, where we could choose our time and build up our formations on the outward journey, I habitually employed four-Squadron formations as a preferable alternative to using two-Squadron formations at more frequent intervals; but, during the attacks on London, the available strength of Fighters did not admit of this policy, nor was time available.

202. I quote from Air Vice-Marshal Park's report:—

"The general plan adopted was to engage the enemy high-fighter screen with pairs of Spitfire Squadrons from Hornchurch and Biggin Hill half-way between London and the coast, and so enable Hurricane Squadrons from London Sectors to attack bomber formations and their close escort before they reached the line of fighter aerodromes East and South of London. The remaining Squadrons from London Sectors that could not be despatched in time to intercept the first wave of the attack by climbing in pairs formed a third and inner screen by patrolling along the lines of aerodromes East and South of London. The fighter Squadrons from Debden, Tangmere, and sometimes Northolt, were employed in wings of three or in pairs to form a screen South-East of London to intercept the third wave of the attack coming inland, also to mop up retreating formations of the earlier waves. The Spitfire Squadrons were redisposed so as to concentrate three Squadrons at each of Hornchurch and Biggin Hill. The primary rôle of these Squadrons was to engage and drive back the enemy high-fighter screen, and so protect the Hurricane Squadrons, whose task was to attack close escorts and then the bomber formations, all of which flew at much lower altitude."

203. I think that, if the policy of big formations had been attempted at this time in No. 11

Group, many more Bombers would have reached their objectives without opposition.

204. Air Vice-Marshal Park also quotes the results of the ten large formations ordered from Duxford into No. 11 Group in the last half of October, when the Germans were employing Fighter-types only. Nine of these sorties made no interception, and the tenth destroyed one Me. 109.

205. The most critical stage of the Battle occurred in the third phase. On the 15th September the Germans delivered their maximum effort, when our Guns and Fighters together accounted for 185 aircraft. Heavy pressure was kept up till the 27th September, but, by the end of the month, it became apparent that the Germans could no longer face the Bomber wastage which they had sustained, and the operations entered upon their fourth phase, in which a proportion of enemy Fighters themselves acted as Bombers.

206. This plan, although the actual damage caused by bombs was comparatively trivial, was aimed primarily at a further whittling down of our Fighter strength, and, of all the methods adopted by the Germans, it was the most difficult to counter. Apart from the previous difficulty of determining which formations meant business, and which were feints, we had to discover which formations carried bombs and which did not.

207. To meet this difficulty, Air Vice-Marshal Park devised the plan of using single Spitfires, flying at maximum height, to act as Reconnaissance aircraft and to report their observations immediately by R/T.

208. A special Flight was organised for this purpose, and it was later recommended that the Spitfires should be employed in pairs, for reasons of security, and that the Flight should become a Squadron. A special R/T receiving set was erected at Group Headquarters so that reports might be obtained without any delay in transmission from the Sector receiving station. There is reason to believe that the Germans also adopted a system of using high-flying H.E. 113s as Scouts. Their information concerning our movements was transmitted to the ground and relayed to their Bombers in the air.

209. In the fourth phase, the apparent ratio of losses in our favour dropped appreciably. I say "apparent" because, in fighting at extreme altitudes, fighters often could not see their victims crash, and the percentage reported as Certainly Destroyed was unfairly depressed. Our own casualties, nevertheless, were such that the C. Category squadrons, which I was hoping to build up to operational strength again, remained in their condition of semi-effectiveness.

210. Serious as were our difficulties, however, those of the enemy were worse, and by the end of October the Germans abandoned their attempts to wear down the Fighter Command, and the country was delivered from the threat of immediate invasion.

211. The Order of Battle at the beginning of November is shown at Appendix E. Categories of Squadrons (A, B, or C, *vide* paragraph 177) are indicated.

212. Increasingly throughout the Battle had the importance of a high "ceiling" been manifested. It is by no means necessary that every Fighter shall have its best performance at stratospheric heights; any such policy would result in a loss of performance at lower altitude, and we must never lose sight of the basic principle that the Fighter exists for the purpose of shooting down Bombers, and that its encounters with other Fighters are incidental to this process.

213. There are, nevertheless, arguments for giving to a percentage of Fighters a ceiling (determinable by specific physiological tests) above which no enemy can climb without the use of Pressure Cabins. Just as the "Weather Gauge" was often the determining factor in the tactics of sailing ships, so the "Height Gauge" was often crucial in air combat. Exhaust-driver turbo-superchargers have certain advantages over gear-driven blowers at great height, and should be considered for adoption in spite of their disadvantages.

214. It must be remembered also that the initiative always rests with the Bomber, who can select at will the height at which he will make his attack. We must be prepared, therefore, for the appearance of the pressure-cabin Bomber, flying at a height unattainable by any non-pressurised Fighter. (I should perhaps explain that there is a height, about 43,000 feet, above which the administration of any quantity of oxygen at atmospheric pressure becomes ineffective because it cannot be inhaled and a pressure cabin or a pressure suit becomes essential.) Of course, a pressure-cabin Bomber is inefficient and vulnerable, because it is difficult to operate free guns from a pressure cabin, and pressure leakage from holes made in the walls of the cabin will prostrate the crew. The threat from pressurised Bombers is therefore serious only if we have no Fighters to meet them, and for this reason we should always possess a limited number of pressurised Fighters.

215. Various other lessons were learned from the experience of fighting at extreme altitudes. One very tiresome feature was that a considerable proportion of ultra-high-flying raids was missed by the Intelligence systems, or reported so late that time was not available to climb and intercept. This made it necessary to employ standing patrols just below oxygen height (about 16,000 feet). These patrols climbed to intercept at extreme height when ordered to do so. This cut at the roots of the Fighter Command system, which was designed to ensure economy of effort by keeping aircraft on the ground except when required to make an interception.

216. Another lesson was that the system of using an "Above Guard" should be retained even when an attack was initiated from extreme altitude

217. Flying and fighting-fatigue increases with altitude, and the comfort of the pilot requires unremitting attention. Cockpit heating and the meticulous pursuit and elimination of air leaks are of great importance. Attention should also be paid to the elimination of icing on cockpit hoods (which are apt to freeze immovably) and on the inside and outside of windscreens.

218. A serious handicap, which I have not hitherto mentioned, was the fact that the change over from "High Frequency" to "Very High

Frequency" Radio Telephony was still in progress. The V.H.F. was an immense improvement on the H.F., both in range and clarity of speech; but the change over, which had started nearly a year before, was held up by the slow output of equipment. This meant that much work had to be done on aircraft Radio equipment during the Battle, and Squadrons equipped with V.H.F. could not communicate with H.F. Ground Stations, and *vice versa*.

219. Some of our worst losses occurred through defective leadership on the part of a unit commander, who might lead his pilots into a trap or be caught while climbing by an enemy formation approaching " out of the sun." During periods of intense activity promotions to the command of Fighter squadrons should be made on the recommendation of Group Commanders from amongst Flight Commanders experienced in the methods of the moment. If and when it is necessary to post a Squadron Leader (however gallant and experienced) from outside the Command, he should humbly start as an ordinary member of the formation until he has gained experience. Only exceptionally should officers over 26 years of age be posted to command Fighter Squadrons.

220. The experience of the Battle made me a little doubtful if the organisation of a squadron into 2 Flights, each of 2 Sections of 3 aircraft, was ideal. It was, of course, undesirable to make any sweeping change during the Battle, and I relinquished my Command shortly after its termination; but the weakness lay in the Section of 3 when it became necessary to break up a formation in a " Dog Fight." The organisation should allow for a break up into pairs, in which one pilot looks after the tail of his companion. A Squadron might be divided into 3 Flights of 4 (which would limit the employment of half-Squadrons), or it might consist of 2 Flights of 8, each comprising 2 Sections of 4. This latter suggestion would upset standard arrangements for accommodation.

221. The matter is not one which can be settled without consultation with various authorities and Branches of the Air Ministry. I therefore merely raise the point without making any definite recommendation.

222. A great deal of discussion took place before and in the early stages of the war as to the best method of " harmonisation " of the guns of an 8-gun Fighter: that is to say the direction, in relation to the longitudinal axis of the aircraft, in which each gun should be pointed in order to get the best results.

223. There were three schools of thought:—

One maintained that the lines of fire should be dispersed so that the largest possible " beaten zone " might be formed and one gun (but not more than one) would always be on the target.

The second held that the guns should be left parallel and so would always cover an elongated zone corresponding with the vulnerable parts of a Bomber (Engines, Tanks and Fuselage).

The third demanded concentration of the fire of all guns at a point.

224. Arguments were produced in favour of all three methods of harmonisation, but in practice it was found that concentration of fire gave the best results. Guns were harmonised so that their lines of fire converged on a point 250 yards distant: fire was therefore effective up to about 500 yards, where the lines of fire had opened out again to their original intervals after crossing at the point of concentration.

225. It was very desirable to get data as to the actual ranges at which fire effect had been obtained. The Reflector Sight contained a rough range-finder which the range of an aircraft of known span could be determined if it was approached from astern, but, in spite of this, pilots, in the heat of action, generally underestimated the ranges at which they fired.

226. Cinema guns, invaluable for training purposes, were used in combat also; and many striking pictures were obtained, from which valuable lessons were learned.

227. The types of ammunition used in the guns varied during the course of the Battle. It was necessary to include some incendiary ammunition, but the type originally available gave a distinct smoke-tracer effect. Now tracer ammunition in fixed guns at any but very short range gives very misleading indications, and I wished pilots to use their sights properly and not to rely on tracer indications. (The above remarks do not apply at night, nor to free guns, where tracer is essential for one of the methods taught for aiming.)

228. During the Battle " de Wilde " ammunition became available in increasing quantities. This was an incendiary ammunition without any flame or smoke trace, and it was extremely popular with pilots, who attributed to it almost magical properties. 8-gun Fighters, of course, were always liable to be sent up at night, and it was therefore desirable to retain some of the older types of incendiary bullets. These were preferred to the " tracer " proper, which gave too bright a flame at night.

229. A typical arrangement, therefore, was:—

Old-type incendiary in the 2 outer guns,
de Wilde in one gun while supplies were limited,
Armour piercing in 2 guns, and ball in the other 3.

230. A discussion on the offensive and defensive equipment of aircraft will be found in Appendix F. It will be of interest to all concerned with the Design of Technical Equipment of Aircraft.

PART III.—NIGHT INTERCEPTION.

231. No story of the Battle would be complete without some account of the Night operations. It is true that they constituted only a subsidiary activity in comparison with the main German objective of fighting us to a standstill by day so that Air Superiority might be attained as a preliminary to Invasion. The night attacks did little directly to affect the efficiency of the Day Fighting Squadrons, though they had certain indirect effects. Although actual casualties were insignificant, disturbance and loss of sleep were caused; damage was done to factories where aircraft engines and accessories were produced; and the stress of continuous operations, day and night, imposed a very heavy strain on Formation Commanders and Staff officers, and upon the personnel of all Operations Rooms.

232. I had long been apprehensive of the effect of Night attacks, when they should begin, and of the efficacy of our defensive measures.

233. We relied on daytime interception methods, and on the Searchlights to illuminate and hold the Bombers. If they were capable of doing this, all would be well, since the distance at which an illuminated Bomber can be seen by night is comparable with the range of visibility by daylight.

234. The first night attack worthy of the name was made early in June and the results were encouraging. Aircraft were well picked up and held by the Searchlights and 6 were shot down. The attack was, however, made at comparatively low altitudes (8,000-12,000 ft.) and the Germans, profiting by this lesson, resorted thereafter to greater heights at which the Searchlights were practically ineffective. In close consultation with myself, General Pile tried every conceivable method of operation, but without material success.

235. About this time Radio Location instruments were fitted in Blenheims and it became necessary to develop at high pressure a system of operation which should enable Night Fighters to make interceptions even against unilluminated targets.

236. The difficulty of this task will be realised when it is considered that it became necessary to put the Fighter within one or two hundred yards of the Enemy, and on the same course, instead of the four or five miles which were adequate against an illuminated target.

237. It may be asked why the Searchlights were so comparatively impotent when they had afforded an accessory to successful defence at the end of the last war. The answer lies partly in the height factor already discussed, and partly in the greatly increased speed of the Bomber, which was about three times that obtaining in 1914. The sound locator, on which Searchlights mainly relied at this time, naturally registered the apparent position of the source of sound and lagged behind the target to the extent of the time taken by sound to travel from the target to the Sound Locator. When the speed of the target is low it is comparatively easy to allow for this lag, but at the speeds of modern bombers the angular distance which must be allowed for in searching is so great that the Searchlights were generally defeated.

238. The first thing which appeared obvious to me was that a "sound Plot" track transmitted from the Observer Corps with a variable and unpredictable "lag" was good enough only for Air Raid Warning purposes and was much too inaccurate to be of use for controlled interception at night: height indications also were little better than guesswork. The Radio Location apparatus (known as A.I.) fitted in twin-engined fighters had a maximum range of 2 or 3 miles, but it was limited by the height at which the Fighter was flying. If, for instance, the Fighter was flying at 10,000 feet, ground echoes were reflected from all ranges greater than this, and an aircraft echo from 10,500 feet would be indistinguishable among the ground echoes.

239. The minimum range of the A.I. was also restricted at this time to about 1,000 feet. Below this distance the aircraft echo was swamped by instrumental disturbance. Continuous and intensive development work was in progress to minimise these limitations.

240. No Radio Location apparatus was available at this time for inland tracking, and I turned for help to the Army, which had developed for use with guns a Radio Location apparatus known as the G.L. Set. Within a limited range (about 40,000 feet) this set could give very accurate position plots, and, moreover, could read height to within plus or minus 1,000 feet at average ranges.

241. Although these sets were few in number and were urgently required for their original purpose of gun control, General Pile realised the urgency of our need and made available about 10 sets for an experiment in the Kenley Sector on the usual line of approach of London Raiders, which commonly made their landfall near Beachy Head.

242. The G.L. sets were installed at Searchlight Posts, and direct telephone communication was arranged with the Kenley Sector Operations Room. Here a large blackboard was installed, and the G.L. plots were shown at intervals of about 30 seconds and with a greater accuracy in height than had before been possible by any means.

243. The track of the pursuing fighter was determined by means of the R/T Direction Finding Stations.

244. Major A. B. Russell, O.B.E., T.A.R.O., co-operated in the development of this system in the Kenley Sector. His practical knowledge and tireless enthusiasm were of the greatest value.

245. Promising results were obtained almost from the first and numerous instances occurred where echoes were obtained on the A.I. sets in the aircraft. Practical results were, however, disappointing, partly because the A.I. apparatus proved to be unexpectedly capricious in azimuth, and partly because the Blenheim was slower than many of the German Bombers and was deficient in fire-power. Many Germans escaped after an initial A.I. "pick-up" and even after visual contact had been effected.

246. The A.I. apparatus was then fitted into the Beaufighters, which were just beginning to appear in Service. The machines and their engines suffered from "teething trouble" to an unusual degree, and the adaption of A.I. to a new type was accompanied by certain difficulties. In addition, they were operating from a wet aerodrome at Redhill, and the development of delicate electrical apparatus, combined with a new type of aircraft and engine, with rudimentary maintenance facilities, was a matter of the greatest difficulty. In nine cases out of ten something would go wrong with the aeroplane or with the A.I. set or with the R/T Direction Finding apparatus or with the Communication system before an interception could be made. No. 219 Squadron, under Squadron Leader J. H. Little, were engaged in this work and operated with great energy and enthusiasm under extremely adverse and difficult conditions.

247. It would, of course, have been desirable to carry out all this development work by day when faults would have been much more easily detected and remedied, but the low rate of Aircraft Serviceability precluded Day-and-Night work, and London was being bombed almost every night, so that I could not afford to neglect the chance of getting practical results.

These, though disappointing, were not entirely negligible; several Bombers were shot down in this area during the experimental period, and many discovered that they were pursued and turned back before reaching their objectives. Night Fighting Development work was also going on at the same time at the Fighter Interception Unit at Tangmere in Sussex.

248. A supplementary use was found for the A.I. by the installation of A.I. "Beacons" in the vicinity of Night Flying Aerodromes. These afforded a valuable Navigational aid for "Homing" in cases where any defect occurred in the R/T D/F system.

249. Shortly before I left the Command a new piece of Radio-Location apparatus became available in the shape of the "G.C.I." set with the Plan Position Indicator. This was an Inland-Reading Set which showed the position of all aircraft within its range on a fluorescent screen as the aerial was rotated.

250. The main advantages of this set were that it had a longer range than the G.L. set and it was possible to track the Bomber and the Fighter by the same apparatus instead of following one with the G.L. and the other by R/T D/F. Moreover it was found that in some circumstances the accuracy of the R/T D/F method was inadequate for night interceptions.

251. On the other hand, the accuracy of height readings by the G.C.I. apparatus was less than that obtainable with the G.L. I understand that this has now been improved.

252. Whatever the exact technical method of plotting positions and tracks of aircraft, the object was to place the Fighter behind the Bomber, and in such a position that the echo of the latter would show in the Fighter's A.I. set. The Fighter then tried to overtake the Bomber until it became visible to the naked eye.

253. At that time only multi-seaters could be fitted with A.I., and therefore, concurrently with the Night Interception experiments, methods were tried of using the Searchlights as pointers for Night Fighters, even if the target were out of range of the Searchlight Beam. Experiments were made with the Searchlights in "clumps" to increase their illuminating power and the visibility of their beams to Fighters at a distance.

254. A small Radio-Location set was designed to fit to the Searchlight itself, so as to get over the time-lag which was such an insuperable obstacle to the use of Sound Locators. It is probable that if Searchlights can substitute the speed of light for that of sound they may take on a new lease of useful life.

255. The disadvantage of relying entirely on Radio-controlled methods of Night Interception is that "saturation point" is quickly reached, and when mass raids are in progress only a limited number of fighters can be operated. Results obtained in the Spring of 1941 show that Day Fighters can obtain important results in conditions of good visibility, especially if attention is paid to all methods of improving the night vision of pilots.

256. During the Battle the "Intruder" system was initiated on a small scale. Night fighters without A.I. were sent across to France in an attempt to catch Bombers while taking off from, or landing at, their aerodromes; or to intercept them at points where they habitually crossed the French Coast.

257. I had to leave the Development of Night Interception at a very interesting stage; but it is perhaps not too much to say that, although much remained to be done, the back of the problem had been broken. The experiments had, of course, been carried out in a small area, and raiders which avoided the area could be intercepted only by previously existing methods; but the possibilities had been demonstrated and could be applied on a larger scale as soon as the necessary apparatus was provided.

258. The method is, of course, also applicable to the day interception of raiders making use of cloud cover, which have hitherto proved extremely elusive; and it is not too much to hope that the eventual development of very high-frequency A.I. may enable accurate fire to be opened against unseen targets, so that not even the darkest night nor the densest cloud will serve as a protection to the Raider.

259. The day may come when every Single-Seater Fighter is fitted with A.I., but this is not yet feasible. What can be done is to fit all Searchlights with Radio-Location apparatus so that every Searchlight Beam is a reliable pointer towards an enemy, even if the range is too great for direct illumination.* If then the Fighter can be informed in addition of the height of the Raider, Day Fighters will be able to join usefully and economically in night operations on dark nights.

---

* As a result of the experience gained during this period, all searchlight equipments have since been fitted with Radar control. This, combined with intensified training, has made them, since 1941, extremely accurate.

APPENDIX "A."

FIGHTER COMMAND.

Order of Battle, 8th July, 1940.

No. 10 GROUP.

Squadron.	War Station.	Type of Aircraft.
87	Exeter	Hurricane.
213	Exeter	Hurricane.
92	Pembrey	Spitfire.
234	St. Eval	Spitfire.

APPENDIX "A."—cont.

No. 11 Group.

43	Tangmere	Hurricane.
145	Tangmere	Hurricane.
601	Tangmere	Hurricane.
FIU Unit	Tangmere	Blenheim.
64	Kenley	Spitfire.
615	Kenley	Hurricane.
245	Hawkinge	Hurricane.
111	Croydon	Hurricane.
501	Croydon	Hurricane.
600	Manston	Blenheim.
79	Biggin Hill	Hurricane.
610	Gravesend	Spitfire.
32	Biggin Hill	Hurricane.
54	Rochford	Spitfire.
65	Hornchurch	Spitfire.
74	Hornchurch	Spitfire.
56	North Weald	Hurricane.
25	Martlesham	Blenheim.
151	North Weald	Hurricane.
1	Northolt	Hurricane.
604	Northolt	Blenheim.
609	Northolt	Spitfire.
236	Middle Wallop	Blenheim.

No. 12 Group.

19	Duxford	Spitfire.
264	Duxford	Defiant.
85	Debden	Hurricane.
17	Debden	Hurricane.
29	Digby	Blenheim.
611	Digby	Spitfire.
46	Digby	Hurricane.
23	Wittering	Blenheim.
266	Wittering	Spitfire.
229	Wittering	Hurricane.
66	Coltishall	Spitfire.
253	Kirton-in-Lindsey	Hurricane.
222	Kirton-in-Lindsey	Spitfire.

No. 13 Group.

Squadron.	War Station.	Type of Aircraft.
41	Catterick	Spitfire.
219	Catterick	Blenheim.
152	Acklington	Spitfire.
72	Acklington	Spitfire.
249	Leconfield	Hurricane.
616	Leconfield	Spitfire.
603 "A"	Turnhouse	Spitfire.
141	Turnhouse	Defiant.
602	Drem	Spitfire.
603 "B"	Montrose	Spitfire.
3	Wick	Hurricane.
504	Wick	Hurricane.

Non-Operational Squadrons.
(Forming or reforming.)

Group.	Squadron.	Aerodrome.	Type of Aircraft.
10 Group	238	Middle Wallop	Hurricane.
	1 (Canadian)	Middle Wallop	Hurricane.
11 Group	257	Hendon	Hurricane.
12 Group	242	Coltishall	Hurricane.
13 Group	73	Church Fenton	Hurricane.
	605	Drem	Hurricane.
	607	Usworth	Hurricane.
	263	Grangemouth	Hurricane.

C

APPENDIX "C."

6TH A.A. DIVISION, JULY-OCTOBER 1940.

(*Note.*—This report relates only to 6th A.A. Division. It does not cover the operations of A.A. Command as a whole.)

Glossary of Abbreviations.

H.A.A.	Heavy Anti-Aircraft.
L.A.A.	Light Anti-Aircraft.
G.O.R.	Gun Operations Room.
A.A.L.M.G.	Anti-Aircraft Light Machine-Gun.
V.I.E.	Visual Indicator Equipment.
G.P.O.	Gun Position Officer.
G.L.	Radio Location Set for Gun Laying.
V.P.	Vulnerable Point.
F.A.S.	Forward Area Sight.
S.O.R.	Sector Operator's Room.
G.D.A.	Gun Defended Area.

1. Layout of A.A. Defences.

(a) The area covered by 6th A.A. Division coincided with the R.A.F. sectors Debden, North Weald, Hornchurch, Biggin Hill and Kenley (*i.e.*, the major part of No. 11 Fighter Group, R.A.F.). Thus the coastal boundary extended from Lowestoft (exclusive) in the North to Worthing (exclusive) in the South; the internal boundary marching with that of the Metropolitan area.

(b) Distribution of A.A. defences was briefly as follows:—

(i) H.A.A. Guns.

The Divisional area contained four main "gun defended areas" at Harwich, Thames and Medway North (guns emplaced along the North bank of the Thames Estuary), Thames and Medway South (guns emplaced along the South bank of the Thames Estuary and defending Chatham and Rochester) and Dover (including Folkestone). In addition, H.A.A. guns were deployed for the defence of certain aerodromes.

Each "gun defended area" was based on a Gun Operations Room: at Felixstowe, Vange, Chatham and Dover respectively. This G.O.R. was connected directly to 11 Fighter Group Operations Room at Uxbridge, from which it received plots of enemy raids, which were in turn passed down to all gun sites.

The armament of each H.A.A. site consisted of the following: 4 (sometimes 2) 4.5, 3.7 or 3-inch guns with predictor. Appendix "A" shows the H.A.A. defences as at the beginning of August 1940 and the end of October 1940.

(ii) L.A.A. Guns.

45 Vulnerable Points in the Divisional area were defended by L.A.A. guns. These V.Ps. consisted of Air Ministry Experimental Stations, Fighter Aerodromes, Dockyards, Oil Depots, Magazines, Industrial Undertakings and Factories.

Armament consisted of the following guns: 40-mm. Bofors (with Predictor No. 3 and Forward Area Sights), 3-inch, 20 cwt. (Case I), A.A.L.M.G. and 20-mm. Hispano. Appendix "B" shows the V.Ps. with their armament as in August and October 1940.

(iii) Searchlights.

Searchlights were deployed in single light stations at approximately 6,000 yards spacing throughout the area, but with a closer spacing in certain instances along the coast and in "gun defended areas" where the distance between lights was approximately 3,500 yards.

These lights were deployed on a brigade basis following R.A.F. sectors, and each light was connected by direct telephone line and/or R.T. set No. 17 to Battery Headquarters via troop H.Q. and thence to an army telephone board at the R.A.F. Sector Operations Room.

The equipment of a Searchlight site consisted of the following:—

90-cm. Projector with, in most cases, Sound Locator Mk. III. In some instances sites were equipped with Sound Locators Mk. VIII or Mk. IX. During the late Summer and Autumn the number of Mk. VIII and Mk. IX Sound Locators gradually increased, and V.I.E. equipment and 150-cm. Projectors were introduced. Each Searchlight site was equipped with one A.A.L.M.G. for use against low-flying aircraft and for ground defence.

2. Enemy Tactics.

(a) *High Level Bombing Attacks.*

These took place *generally* between heights of 16,000/20,000 feet. Bombers approached their targets in close protective formations until running up to the line of bomb release, when formation was changed to Line Astern (if there was a definite objective to the attack). Attacks frequently occurred in waves, each wave flying at approximately the same height and on the same course. On engagement by H.A.A. guns, avoiding action was taken in three stages:—

Stage 1.—The bombers gained height steadily and maintained course and formation.

Stage 2.—Formations opened out widely and maintained course.

Stage 3.—Under heavy fire, formations split and bombers scattered widely on different courses. It was after this stage had been reached that the best opportunity was provided for fighters to engage.

(b) *Low Level and Dive Bombing Attacks.*

In the latter stages of the enemy air offensive numerous instances of low level and dive bombing attacks occurred, in particular against fighter aerodromes (Manston, Hawkinge, Lympne, Kenley).

L.A.A. and H.A.A. employed in dealing with these forms of attack met with varying success, but in cases where no planes were brought down the effect of fire from the A.A. defence almost invariably disconcerted the dive bomber so that few bombs were dropped with accuracy.

Considerable efforts were made by Me. 109's and Ju. 87's to destroy the balloon barrage at Dover, and, though at times they partially succeeded, excellent targets were provided for the Dover H.A.A. and L.A.A. guns.

3. Part played by H.A.A. Guns.

Targets of all types presented themselves to H.A.A. sites, ranging from solid bomber formation to single cloud hopping or dive bombers, balloon strafers or hedge hoppers, all of which were successfully engaged by appropriate method of fire.

The action of the defence achieved success in the following ways:—

(a) The actual destruction or disablement of enemy aircraft (see Appendix "C").

(b) The breaking up of formations, thus enabling the R.A.F. to press home attacks on smaller groups of bombers.

(c) Destroying the accuracy of their bombing by forcing the enemy aircraft to take avoiding action.

(d) By pointing out to patrolling fighters the whereabouts of enemy formations by means of shell bursts.

The following methods of fire were in operation at this period:—

(a) *Seen Targets.*

(i) Each gun site was allotted a zone of priority and responsibility for opening fire on a target rested with the G.P.O.

(ii) Targets could be engaged by day if identified as hostile beyond reasonable doubt or if a hostile act was committed. By night, failure to give recognition signals was an additional proviso.

(iii) It was the responsibility of the G.P.O. to cease fire when fighters closed to the attack.

(b) *Unseen Targets.*

Unseen firing at this time was in its infancy and considerable initiative was displayed in evolving methods for engaging targets unseen by day or by night.

The following methods were employed:—

(i) *Geographic Barrages.*

Many forms of barrage were used by different G.D.As. but all were based on obtaining concentrations at a point, on a line, or over an area, through which the enemy aircraft must fly.

Suitable barrages for lines of approach and heights were worked out beforehand. Approach of enemy aircraft was observed by G.L. and, by co-ordination at G.O.Rs., the fire from each site could be controlled to bring a maximum concentration of shell bursts at the required point.

(ii) *Precision Engagements.*

Method A.—Due to poor visibility or wrong speed settings searchlight intersections were often made without actual illumination of the aircraft. By obtaining slant range from G.L. and following the intersection on the Predictor, sufficient data were available to enable shells to burst at or near the intersection.

Method B.—This provided for engagement without searchlight intersections. Continuous bearings and slant ranges from the G.L. were fed into the Predictor and engagement of target undertaken on the data thus provided. For sites which were not equipped with G.L. the appropriate information was passed down from G.O.R.

It will be appreciated that procedure varied with different Gun Zones, according to circumstances and the equipment available. It should be remembered that all engagements of unseen targets were subject to the express permission of the Group Controller at Uxbridge, so that danger of engaging friendly aircraft was obviated.

(c) *Anti-Dive-Bombing Barrage.*

Special barrages against dive bombers were organised round the following V.Ps.: Harwich Harbour, Thameshaven Oil Installations, Tilbury Docks, Chatham Dockyard, Sheerness Dockyard, Dover Harbour, Purfleet Oil and Ammunition Depots.

This barrage could be employed at any time at the discretion of the G.P.O. when he considered that other and more accurate methods were unlikely to be effective. The barrage was designed for a height of 3,000 feet and assumed a dive angle of 60°. It was based on a barrage circle round each gun site which was divided into 4 quadrants in which the barrages were placed.

The maximum effort from H.A.A. guns was required from the 19th August to the 5th October, during which time the crews had little rest, continuous 24 hours manning being required at Dover, a "duty gun station" system being worked in all areas.

Evidence is available to show how time and time again enemy bombers would not face up to the heavy and accurate fire put up by gun stations. Particularly worthy of mention are two attacks on Hornchurch aerodrome when on both occasions fighters were on the ground for refuelling. A.A. fire broke up the formation and prevented *any damage to the station* buildings and aircraft on the ground.

4. *Part played by L.A.A. Guns.*

The targets which offered themselves to L.A.A. guns were in the main small numbers engaged in dive bombing or low level attacks on V.Ps. Opportunity usually only offered fleeting targets, and quickness of thought and action was essential to make fullest use of the targets which presented themselves.

Success against targets by L.A.A. guns was achieved in the following ways:—

(a) The destruction or disablement of enemy aircraft (See Appendix "C").

(b) The prevention of accurate bombing causing the bombers to pull out of their dive earlier than they intended.

Methods of firing employed by L.A.A. guns as follows:—

(i) *Bofors.*

Fire was directed either by No. 3 Predictor or by Forward area Sights; some Bofors were not equipped with the Predictor when the latter method only could be used.

The Predictor equipped guns require a 130 Volt A.C. electric supply which was provided either from engine-driven generators or from the mains. Shooting with the Predictor achieved very great accuracy and the results and destruction of aircraft and the average ammunition expenditure proved the efficiency of this equipment (see Appendix "C"). The F.A.S. method permitted quick engagements of targets although without the accuracy afforded by the Predictor.

(ii) *3-inch 20-cwt. Guns (Case* I).

Some V.Ps. were equipped with the 3-inch 20-cwt. gun without Predictor which was fired from deflection sights; shrapnel was normally used. H.E., however, was used for targets at greater height.

(iii) *A.A.L.M.G.*

Lewis Guns on A.A. mountings proved extremely effective in attacking low-flying enemy aircraft. These guns were mounted in single, double or quadruple mountings and were fired by the Hosepipe method using tracer ammunition.

(iv) *Hispano 20-mm. Equipment.*

A few of these weapons only were deployed and, owing to shortage of ammunition and lack of tracer, were not found very effective.

5. Part Played by Searchlights.

(a) *Day.*

Owing to the close spacing of Searchlight sites they formed a valuable source of intelligence and rapid reports were able to be made upwards of casualties to friendly and enemy aircraft, pilots descending by parachute and other incidents of importance. In addition, they have been able to provide valuable reports of isolated enemy aircraft, trace of which had been lost by the Observer Corps.

The value of the A.A.L.M.G. with which each site was equipped cannot be too highly stressed, and during the 4 months under review no less than 23 enemy aircraft were destroyed, confirmed, by A.A.L.M.G. at Searchlight sites (this includes a few in which A.A.L.M.G. at H.A.A. sites also shared). Prisoner of War reports showed that it was not generally known by the German Air Force pilots that Searchlight sites were equipped with A.A. defence.

(b) *Night.*

Tactical employment of Searchlights at night was by either—

(i) 3-beam rule, in which 3 sites only engaged the target; or

(ii) by the Master-beam system, in which one Master beam per three sites exposed and was followed by the remaining two beams acting under the orders of the Master beam.

The decision to engage was the responsibility of the Detachment Commander, and no direct tactical control was exercised from Battery Headquarters.

In the early stages of the Battle of Britain night activity was on a small scale and Searchlights had few raids to engage. Some illuminations were effected, but throughout it was difficult, by ground observations, to assess the actual numbers. Frequently illuminations were reported by sites not engaging the targets. The difficulty of illumination was increased as the number of night raids increased, owing to the difficulty of sites selecting the same target.

There is evidence to show that Searchlight activity, whilst being difficult to measure, forced enemy aircraft to fly at a greater height than they would otherwise have done. Bombs were frequently dropped when enemy aircraft were illuminated, which were possibly intended to discourage Searchlights from exposing. Evasive tactics by the enemy consisted of changing height and speed continuously to avoid being illuminated rather than a violent evasive action upon illumination.

6. G.L. Equipment.

At the beginning of August experiments had just been completed to determine whether G.L. equipment could satisfactorily be used as a Ships detector. Apart from the results of this experiment three other facts emerged:—

(a) The G.L. principle was of considerable value when used in conjunction with Searchlights.

(b) That G.L. sets sited in an anti-ship rôle, i.e., on the top of a cliff, were of considerable value in detecting low-flying aircraft.

(c) It showed the value of small R.D.F. detectors within the main R.A.F. chain, in plotting enemy aircraft direct to sectors.

At the beginning of the Battle of Britain, 21 G.L. sets were in use by 6th A.A. Division, and by October this number had been increased by another 14.

(i) *G.L. at Gun Stations.*

The main function of these equipments was to provide data for Unseen target engagements as described above. One other function of these sets is worth special mention.

Two sets were specially sited on the cliffs at Dover to pick up targets at low level. These sets were able to register aircraft taking off from the aerodromes immediately behind Calais, thereby obtaining information considerably earlier than could be provided by the main R.D.F. station on the coast. This information was reported back to Uxbridge Operations Room by a priority code message which indicated the approximate number of aircraft which had taken off and their position. This report was received some 5/6 minutes before it could be received through the usual R.D.F. channels, and therefore enabled the Controller to order his Fighters off the ground correspondingly earlier than would otherwise have been the case.

This system, which was also adopted somewhat further along the coast in the neighbourhood of Beachy Head, was of all the more value as the enemy were heavily bombing the R.D.F. stations, which were consequently sometimes out of action.

(ii) *G.L. Stations with Searchlights.*

During the latter stages of the offensive, when the night raids on London commenced, it was realised that the G.L. would be of considerable assistance to Night Fighters. An " elevation " attachment to the equipment was produced and this enabled height to be obtained, which in conjunction with a plotting scheme at S.O.R., enabled Searchlight beams to be directed more accurately on a target to assist night fighters. The results obtained from this were not completely satisfactory, but they showed the way to the development of the present system.

(iii) *Mine-Laying Aircraft.*

It was found that the experiments conducted in the ship-detector rôle could be very satisfactorily applied to detecting mine-laying aircraft which flew in at a height too low to be picked up by the C.H. Stations. It enabled accurate tracks of these aircraft to be kept which were afterwards passed to the Naval Authorities, who were then able to sweep up the mines which had been laid by these aircraft.

7. Statistics.

Careful records have been kept of ammunition expenditure and enemy aircraft shot down, and details are shown in Appendix " C."

The following points are worthy of note:—

(a) The total enemy aircraft Destroyed, Confirmed Category I by 6th A.A. Division during the months July-October 1940, inclusive, was

221; of this total 104 were destroyed on seven days, thus:—

15 August, 1940	...	15
18 ,, ,,	...	22
24 ,, ,,	...	10
31 ,, ,,	...	20
2 September, 1940	...	13
7 ,, ,,	...	14
15 ,, ,,	...	10
		104

(b) A considerable number of enemy aircraft were claimed as Probably Destroyed and Damaged.

(c) The total amount of H.A.A. expended was 75,000 rounds.

(d) The total amount of Bofors ammunition expended was 9,417 rounds.

8. Ground Defence

Preparations were made by all A.A. defences to assume a secondary ground defence rôle; Bofors were provided with A/T ammunition, and sited to cover approaches to aerodromes, V.Ps., &c. Certain 3.7 inch guns suitably sited were given an anti-ship rôle, and preparations were made for barrages to be put on certain beaches. Under the immediate threat of invasion in May 1940, mobile columns of A.A. troops were formed, but these troops reverted to their A.A. rôle before the Battle of Britain began.

9. Lessons Learnt.

(a) The outstanding lesson learnt from this intensive air attack was undoubtedly the soundness and suitability of the organisation and arrangements of the control and direction of the anti-aircraft defences. These measures devised in peace time and perfected during the earlier and quieter period of hostilities, stood the severe test with amazing resilience and adaptability. No major alterations in the system were indicated or, indeed, were made subsequent to these operations.* The way in which the activities of the anti-aircraft linked in and were capable of co-ordination with the major partners in the venture—R.A.F. Fighter Command, No. 11 Fighter Group, and sector commands—is perhaps worthy of special note.

* This statement applies only to the higher organisation, and must not be taken to mean that no improvements were made in the control and direction of A.A. gunnery.

(b) Other lessons learnt are by comparison of minor import. Chief among them was the great vulnerability of aircraft if caught by accurate H.A.A. fire when in close formation. A good instance of this occurred in an action on the 8th September, when a geschwader of 15 Do. 17s, flying in formation at 15,000 feet, approached a gun site South of River Thames. The opening salvo from the four 3.7-inch guns brought down the three leading aircraft, the remaining machines turning back in disorder, scattering their bombs on the countryside in their flight to the coast.

The value of H.A.A. fire as a means of breaking up bomber squadrons to enable them to be more easily dealt with by our fighters was demonstrated on numerous occasions in the Thames Estuary.

The importance of A.A. shell bursts as a "pointer" to fighters, even though the guns cannot themselves effectively engage the enemy, was also frequently demonstrated.

(c) A somewhat negative lesson was the inability of A.A. guns, however well served, to completely deny an area to penetration by determined air attack. Evidence, however, was overwhelming that accurate fire, apart from causing casualties, did impair the enemy's aim, and thus avoid, or at least mitigate, the damage to precise targets.

(d) A rather unexpected result was the high proportion (about 10 per cent.) of planes brought down by A.A.L.M.G. fire. It is doubtful, however, whether with the increased armour now carried by enemy aircraft this lesson still obtains.

(e) The value of training in recognition was repeatedly emphasised throughout these operations. Fortunately, very few instances of friendly aircraft being engaged occurred. Apart from the accuracy of the information as to movement of aircraft furnished to gun sites, this was no doubt due to a reasonable standard in recognition having been attained.

It was, and still is, continually brought home to the A.A. gunner that, before all else, he must not engage a friendly aircraft. With this thought firmly impressed on the G.P.O., some instances of late engagement or failure to engage perforce occurred. In some cases, had the standard of training been higher, to enable the earlier recognition of a machine as "hostile beyond reasonable doubt," the number of machines destroyed would have been increased.

Chelmsford, August 2, 1941.

APPENDIX "C.A."

H.A.A. Gun Defended Areas and Armament.

G.D.A.	August 1940.			October 1940.		
	4·5-in.	3·7-in.	3-in.	4·5-in.	3·7-in.	3-in.
Harwich	—	15	8	—	8	7
T. and M. North	32	8	12	24	4	12
T. and M. South	32	32	14	28	20	10
Dover and Manston	—	12	16	—	12	16
Wattisham	—	—	4	—	—	4
Biggin Hill	—	—	4	—	—	4
Kenley	—	—	—	—	—	2
North Weald	—	+ 4	4 + 2	—	—	4

APPENDIX "C.B."

L.A.A., V.P.'s AND ARMAMENT.

V.P.	August 1940.					October 1940.				
	40-mm.	A.A.L.M.G. (No. of Barrels).	Hispano.	3-in., Case I.	Misc.	40-mm.	A.A.L.M.G.	Hispano.	3-in., Case I.	Misc.
Aerodromes.										
Debden	4	3	—	—	—	4	17	—	—	—
Wattisham	—	12	—	—	—	4	8	—	—	—
Biggin Hill	3	2	—	—	—	6	3	—	—	—
Manston	4	4	—	—	—	4	—	—	—	—
West Malling	2	10	—	—	—	4	10	—	—	—
Croydon	—	12	—	—	—	4	8	—	—	—
Kenley	4	8	—	2	—	4	10	—	3	—
Redhill	—	—	—	—	—	3	—	—	—	—
Gravesend	4	4	—	—	—	4	—	—	—	—
Shorts (Rochester)	—	—	—	—	—	4	8	3	—	—
Detling	—	—	—	—	—	2	12	2	—	—
Eastchurch	—	—	—	—	—	2	10	—	—	—
Hawkinge	4	4	—	—	—	4	4	—	—	—
Lympne	—	—	—	—	—	—	2	—	—	—
North Weald	3	12	—	—	—	5	8	—	—	—
Martlesham	4	10	—	—	—	4	11	—	—	—
Rochford	2	8	—	—	—	4	12	—	—	—
Hornchurch	3	7	—	—	—	5	7	—	—	—
Stapleford Abbotts	—	—	—	—	—	2	—	—	—	—
A.M.E. Stations.										
Darsham	2	7	—	—	—	2	8	—	—	—
Dunkirk	3	6	—	—	—	3	7	—	—	—
Rye	3	6	—	—	—	3	11	—	—	—
Pevensey	3	6	—	—	—	3	21	—	—	—
Bawdsey	—	—	—	—	—	3	3	—	—	—
Great Bromley	—	—	—	—	—	3	11	—	—	—
Canewdon	3	4	—	—	—	3	12	—	—	—
Industrial and Oil.										
Crayford	—	8	—	—	—	3	30	3	1	—
Dartford	—	—	—	—	—	1	20	4	—	—
Northfleet	—	—	—	—	—	—	16	—	—	—
Grain (Barges)	2	4	—	—	—	2	34	2	1	—
Chelmsford	—	8	—	—	—	2	21	—	—	—
Murex (Rainham)	—	20	—	—	—	—	20	—	—	—
Purfleet	—	14	—	2	—	—	16	—	2	—
Canvey	—	12	—	2	—	—	12	—	1	—
Thameshaven	—	4	—	4	—	—	—	—	3	—
Shellhaven	—	8	—	3	—	—	8	—	1	—
Naval.										
Chatham	—	—	—	—	—	—	24	4	3	—
Chattenden	—	—	—	—	—	—	28	—	—	—
Sheerness	—	—	—	—	—	—	22	5	—	—
Landguard	—	—	—	—	—	4	15	—	1	—
Wrabness	—	—	—	—	—	—	23	—	—	—
Parkeston Quay	—	—	—	—	—	—	10	—	—	—
Dover	5	9	—	4	—	9	16	4	—	4 A/T
Tilbury	—	14	—	—	—	—	18	—	—	—
Southend Pier	—	—	—	—	1—2-pdr.	—	—	—	—	1—2-pdr.

APPENDIX "C.C."

I.—AMMUNITION EXPENDITURE AND CLAIMS, CATEGORY I.

	Total Ammunition Expended.	Enemy Aircraft Destroyed.	Average Rounds per E/A.
H.A.A. (seen targets)	48,155	161	298
H.A.A. (barrage and unseen fire)	26,869	11	2,444
L.A.A. Bofors only	9,417	47	200
A.A.L.M.G. (at S.L. and H.A.F. sites)	Not recorded	23	—

NOTES:—
(i) The above table gives records from September 3, 1939 to November 3, 1940.
(ii) The total enemy aircraft destroyed during the months inclusive July–October was 221.
(iii) The following ammunition was expended from September 3, 1939 to June 30, 1940—
    H.A.A. ... 2,995
    L.A.A. (Bofors) ... 1,919
(iv) All the enemy aircraft destroyed by L.A.A. (47) have been credited to Bofors for the purpose of the average; in practice, Lewis guns had a considerable share in several of these as well as in two cases Hispano (2,941 rounds) and 3-in. Case I (194 rounds).
(v) Bofors average may be still further sub-divided thus:—
    With Predictor ... 179 (3,187 rounds)
    With F.A.S. ... 232 (6,230 rounds)

APPENDIX "C.C."—cont.

II.—Table showing Types of Aircraft destroyed July–October 1940.

Type.	No.
HE. III	30
Do. 17	39
Do. 215	14
Ju. 87	15
Ju. 88	19
Me. 109	80
ME. 110	15
Unidentified	9
	221

III.

Destroyed by day	203
Destroyed by night	18
	221

APPENDIX "C.D."

Ammunition Expenditure and Enemy Aircraft destroyed throughout Anti-Aircraft Command for July, August and September 1940.

July 1940—
  Day* ... } 344 rds. per aircraft.
  Night ... } (26 a/c = 8,935 rds.)

August 1940—
  Day* ... } 232 rds. per aircraft.
  Night ... } (167 a/c = 38,764 rds.)

September 1940—
  Day† ... } 1,798 rds. per aircraft.
  Night ... } (144 a/c = 258,808 rds.)

---

* Mainly by day, little night activity.
† Including considerable night activity and large expenditure of ammunition by night.

APPENDIX "E."

Fighter Command.

Order of Battle, November 3, 1940.

No. 9 Group.

Squadron.	War Station.	Type of Aircraft.	Category.
312 (Czech)	Speke	Hurricane	C
611	Ternhill	Spitfire	C
29 (½)	Ternhill	Blenheim	Night-Flying

No. 10 Group.

Squadron.	War Station.	Type of Aircraft.	Category.
79	Pembrey	Hurricane	C
87 (½)	Bibury	Hurricane	B
504	Filton	Hurricane	C
609	Middle Wallop	Spitfire	A
604	Middle Wallop	Blenheim	Night-Flying
238	Middle Wallop	Hurricane	A
56	Boscombe Down	Hurricane	A
152	Warmwell	Spitfire	A
601	Exeter	Hurricane	C
87 (½)	Exeter	Hurricane	B
234	St. Eval	Spitfire	C
247 (½)	Roborough	Gladiator	C

APPENDIX "E."—cont

No. 11 Group.

Squadron.	War Station.	Type of Aircraft.	Category.
25	Debden	Blenheim and Beaufighter	Night-Flying
73	Castle Camp	Hurricane	Night-Flying
17	Martlesham	Hurricane	A
229	Northolt	Hurricane	A
615	Northolt	Hurricane	A
302 (Polish)	Northolt	Hurricane	A
257	North Weald	Hurricane	A
249	North Weald	Hurricane	A
46	Stapleford	Hurricane	A
264	Hornchurch	Defiant	Night-Flying
41	Hornchurch	Spitfire	A
603	Hornchurch	Spitfire	A
222	Rochford	Spitfire	A
141	Gravesend	Defiant	Night-Flying
74	Biggin Hill	Spitfire	A
92	Biggin Hill	Spitfire	A
66	West Malling	Spitfire	A
421 (½)	West Malling	Hurricane	Reconnaissance
605	Croydon	Hurricane	A
253	Kenley	Hurricane	A
501	Kenley	Hurricane	A
219	Redhill	Blenheim and Beaufighter	Night-Flying
145	Tangmere	Hurricane	A
213	Tangmere	Hurricane	Night-Flying
422 (½)	Tangmere	Hurricane	Night-Flying
602	West Hampnett	Spitfire	A
23	Ford	Blenheim	Night-Flying

No. 12 Group.

Squadron.	War Station.	Type of Aircraft.	Category.
303 (Polish)	Leconfield	Hurricane	C
616	Kirton-in-Lindsey	Spitfire	C
85	Kirton-in-Lindsey	Hurricane	C
151	Digby	Hurricane	C
1	Wittering	Hurricane	C
266	Wittering	Spitfire	C
29 (½)	Wittering	Blenheim	Night-Flying
72	Coltishall	Spitfire	C
64	Coltishall	Spitfire	C
242	Duxford	Hurricane	A
310 (Czech)	Duxford	Hurricane	A
19	Duxford	Spitfire	A

No. 13 Group.

Squadron.	War Station.	Type of Aircraft.	Category.
607	Turnhouse	Hurricane	C
65	Turnhouse	Spitfire	B
232 (½)	Drem	Hurricane	C
263 (½)	Drem	Hurricane	C
1 (Canadian)	Prestwick	Hurricane	C
32	Acklington	Hurricane	C
610	Acklington	Spitfire	C
600 (½)	Acklington	Blenheim	Night-Flying
43	Usworth	Hurricane	C
54	Catterick	Spitfire	C
600 (½)	Catterick	Blenheim	Night-Flying
245	Aldergrove	Hurricane	C

No. 14 Group.

Squadron.	War Station.	Type of Aircraft.	Category.
3	Castletown	Hurricane	C
111 (½)	Dyce	Hurricane	C
111 (½)	Montrose	Hurricane	C

APPENDIX "E."—cont.

NON-OPERATIONAL SQUADRONS.

Group.	Squadron.	Station.	Type of Aircraft.
9 Group	308 (Polish)	Baginton	Hurricane
12 Group	306 (Polish)	Church Fenton	Hurricane
	307 (Polish)	Kirton-in-Lindsey	Defiant
	71 (Eagle)	Church Fenton	Buffalo
13 Group	263 (½)	Drem	Whirlwind

NOTE.—Two " B " Squadrons, Nos. 74 and 145, had already been thrown into the battle, leaving only two available at the end.

APPENDIX "F."

NOTE ON THE OFFENSIVE AND DEFENSIVE EQUIPMENT OF AIRCRAFT.

1. The general principle of developing the maximum possible fire power, which is accepted in all Armies and Navies, must presumably be applicable to Fighter Aircraft, provided that this can be done without unduly sacrificing Performance and Endurance.

2. The 8-gun fighter may be said to exemplify this principle, and at the beginning of the war its results were decisive against German Bombers, which were unarmoured at that time.

3. Our Fighter pilots were protected against the return fire of Bombers by their engines, and by bullet-proof glass and armour, for their heads and chests respectively.

4. Furthermore, at this time the return fire from German Bombers was negligible. They had concentrated on Performance as the principle means of evasion (a false lesson drawn from the low speed of the Fighters used in the Spanish War) and the few guns which they carried were manually controlled, and so badly mounted that they were practically useless. These facts, in combination with the fire power and armour protection of our own Fighters, made the latter virtually immune to the fire of unescorted Bombers, and their casualties in Home Defence fighting up to the Spring of 1940 were quite negligible.

5. The German Bombers had good self-sealing tanks, and this was perhaps the only important particular in which they were ahead of us. In our development work we had demanded that tanks should be "Crash Proof" as well as self-sealing, and the drastic conditions, which our experimental tanks had to meet had made them unduly heavy and cumbrous.

6. So far as our Fighters were concerned, the wing tanks in the Hurricane were removed and covered with a fabric known as "Linatex" which had fairly good self-sealing characteristics. The reserve tank in the fuselage was left uncovered, as it was difficult of access and it was thought that it would be substantially protected by the armour which had been fitted. During the Battle, however, a great number of Hurricanes were set on fire by incendiary bullets or cannon shells, and their pilots were badly burned by a sheet of flame which filled the cockpit before they could escape by parachute.

7. The reserve tanks were therefore covered with Linatex as a matter of the highest priority, and a metal bulkhead was fitted in front of the pilot to exclude the rush of flame from the cockpit.

8. The Germans soon began to fit fuselage armour to protect their pilots and crews, but for some unexplained reason neither side had fitted armour behind the engines of their Bombers. The back of the engine is much more vulnerable to rifle-calibre bullets than the front, owing to the mass of ancillary equipment which is there installed. While the back of the engine lies open to attack, the rifle-calibre machine gun remains a useful weapon, and the fact is a fortunate one for us.

9. The application of armour to Bombers did not, of course, come as a surprise to us, and its implications had long been discussed.

10. Excluding devices such as hanging wires, exploding pilotless aircraft, etc., I have always thought that the courses open to the Fighter, when rifle-calibre machine-gun fire from astern becomes ineffective, may be summarised as follows:—

(A) Deliver fire from ahead or from a flank.
(B) Pierce the armour.
(C) Attack the fuel tanks with incendiary ammunition.
(D) Destroy the structure of the aircraft by means of direct hits from explosive shells.
(E) Use large shells with Time and Percussion fuzes.

Discussing these in order:—

11.—(A) Fire from ahead or from a flank is effective but difficult to deliver accurately at modern speeds. Fire from ahead proved very effective on occasions during the Battle, but relative speeds are so high that the time available for shooting is very short, and Fighters generally find themselves in a position to deliver such an attack more by accident than by design.

12. Beam attack is very difficult to deliver accurately, owing to the amount of deflection which had to be allowed. The deflection ring on a Fighter's sight allows for an enemy speed of 100 m.p.h., and therefore a full diameter outside the ring must sometimes be allowed.

13. The method is effective against formations, when the aircraft hit is not always the one aimed at, and certainly the Gladiators in Norway developed this technique with great success. On the whole, however, Fighters which were constrained to this method of attack would have a very limited usefulness.

14.—(B) The simplest reaction for the Fighter is to pierce the armour, but it entails the use of bigger calibres. It must be remembered also that it is not sufficient merely to pierce the armour, but the bullet must have sufficient remaining velocity to do lethal damage thereafter. High velocities, in addition to bigger calibres, are therefore necessary.

15. The .5-inch gun appeared, at first sight, to be the natural successor to the .303 inch, but experiments showed that the type available to us in the Autumn of 1940 was practically defeated by the 8-mm. armour carried in the M.E. 109. It was true that the bullet would pierce 20-mm. or more of armour in the open, but it was found that the minute deceleration and deflection of the axis of the bullet, caused by its passage through the structure of the fuselage, exercised a very important diminution on its subsequent penetrative powers.

16. Experiments carried out with .5-inch guns of higher velocity in America have given encouraging results, and it is not at present possible to dogmatise on the subject. It would, however, be foolish to adopt a gun which could be defeated by a slight thickening of the armour carried by the Bomber and the aim should be to defeat the thickest armour which it is practically possible for the enemy to carry.

17. We have at present no gun of a calibre between .5-inch and 20-mm. (.8 inch). The latter was originally adopted by the French because it was of about the right size to fire an explosive shell through an airscrew of a Hispano Suiza engine, and was adopted by us from them. If, therefore, it proves to be of the best weight and calibre for an armour piercing, that is due to accident rather than design.

18. A study of available data might lead one to suppose that a calibre of about 15-mm. would be the ideal, and I understand that this size has recently been adopted by the Germans; but we cannot now start designing a new gun for this war, and we must choose between the .5-inch and the 20-mm. We shall soon get reliable data from American Fighter types in action. They have faith in the .5-inch gun.

19. The Armament of the Royal Air Force is not its strongest point, and in my opinion we should do our own Design and Experimental work, and satisfy our requirements without being dependent on Woolwich and Shoeburyness.

20.—(C) Incendiary ammunition may be fired from guns of any calibre and Bomber tanks have been set on fire by .303 inch ammunition. The bigger the bullet, however, the bigger the hole, and a small bullet stands a good chance of being quenched before it can take effect. In any case, the fuel tanks of a Bomber constitute so small a proportion of the whole target that they cannot be made the sole objective of attack; and it seems that the adoption of a large-calibre gun and the use of a proportion of incendiary ammunition therein will afford a satisfactory compromise.

21.—(D) It was assumed by the French that the 20-mm. shell would be effective against the structure of modern aircraft. I do not know what trials they carried out, but the tests done by us at Shoeburyness and Orfordness indicate that the effect of a 20-mm. shell exploding instantaneously on the surface of an aircraft is almost negligible, except in a small percentage of lucky strikes. The normal effect is that a hole of about 6-inch diameter is blown in the surface, and that the effect at any distance is nil, since the shell is blown almost into dust. Occasionally the fuze penetrates and does some damage, but this is slight in comparison with the total weight of the shell. Even the big 37-mm. shell, though it may be spectacular damage, will not often bring a Bomber down with a single hit. Greater damage is done if the fuze is given a slight delay action, so that it bursts inside the covering of the aircraft, but small delay action fuzes are unreliable in operation and difficult to manufacture, and, on the whole, it seems doubtful if explosive shells are as efficient as armour-piercing and incendiary projectiles, especially as they will not penetrate armour. Another point must be remembered, viz., that a drum of explosive shells is a very dangerous item of cargo: if one is struck and detonated by a bullet it is not unlikely that they will all go off and blow the aeroplane to pieces.

22.—(E) The use of large shells (comparable to Anti-Aircraft types) from Fighter aircraft is practically prohibited by considerations of weight if a gun is used. The gun itself must be heavy and the structure must be strengthened to withstand the shock of recoil. The walls and base of the shell also have to be made uneconomically heavy to withstand the discharge. All these difficulties, however, can be overcome if the Rocket principle is used. It is true that a Rocket can be discharged only in the direct line of flight, but that is no particular handicap to a Fighter. It can have a light firing tube, there is no recoil, and the shell can be designed for optimum fragmentation effect. (I have been told that a 3-inch Rocket shell develops the same explosive and fragmentation effect as a 4.5-inch Anti-Aircraft gun shell). It also starts with an advantage over the terrestrial rocket in that it has an initial velocity of about 300 m.p.h. through the air, which gives it enhanced accuracy. For this weapon a "Proximity Fuze" would be ideal, but, pending the development of this, there is no reason why the Rocket should not be used with a Time and Percussion Fuze used in conjunction with a range-finder in the Aircraft.

23. This item was put on the programme about 7 years ago, and I think it a great pity that it was allowed to drop. True, unexpected difficulties may be encountered, and nothing may come of the project, but it is an important experiment, and our knowledge of what is and is not possible will not be complete until it has been tried.

24. I think that our decision to adopt the 20-mm. gun is probably the wisest which we could have taken, but to carry increased load efficiently something bigger than the Hurricane or Spitfire is needed. The Typhoon with 2,000 h.p. should be ideal when it has been given an adequate ceiling.

25. In the meantime the Hurricane must be somewhat overloaded with 4 Cannons, and mixed armament (2 Cannons and 4 Brownings) in the Spitfire is merely a compromise necessitated by loading conditions. Might not the high-velocity American .5-inch gun prove a suitable armament for the small fighter?

26. As regards ammunition for the 20-mm. gun, the so-called "solid" bullet was merely a cheap steel bullet produced by the French for practice purposes. Its mass and velocity have enabled it hitherto to smash through armour to which it has been opposed, but an improved design will probably be needed before long; doubtless the matter is receiving attention. I understand that the incendiary bullet—the equivalent of the de Wilde .303-inch—has been giving good results.

27. One other attribute of a naked steel bullet must not be overlooked, viz., its incendiary effect when it strikes a ferrous structure. During ground trials a Blenheim was set on fire by the second hit from a " solid " bullet. Unfortunately, German aircraft do not normally contain much iron or steel.

28. If we look into the not too distant future, I think we shall find that an additional and quite different reason may arise for the adoption of the high-velocity gun with a comparatively heavy projectile. I refer to the increasing intensity and effect of return fire from Bombers.

29. Our Fighters are protected to a very large degree from the return fire of Bombers which they attack from astern, so long as they have to sustain the impact only of rifle-calibre bullets.

30. The situation will be quite different, however, if turrets with .5-inch guns are commonly used in Bombers. The Bomber has the comparative advantage over the pursuing Fighter of firing " down-wind " (one may get a clear idea of the situation by imagining both aircraft to be anchored in space, with a 300-m.p.h. wind blowing from the Bomber to the Fighter). The result is likely to be that effective armouring of Fighters against return fire will be impossible, and fighting ranges in good visibility may be considerably lengthened. In such circumstances high velocity, flat trajectory and a heavy projectile will attain increasing importance; attention will also have to be paid to accurate methods of sighting, and allowance for gravity drop.

APPENDIX "AA"

FIGHTER COMMAND LAYOUT JULY 1940

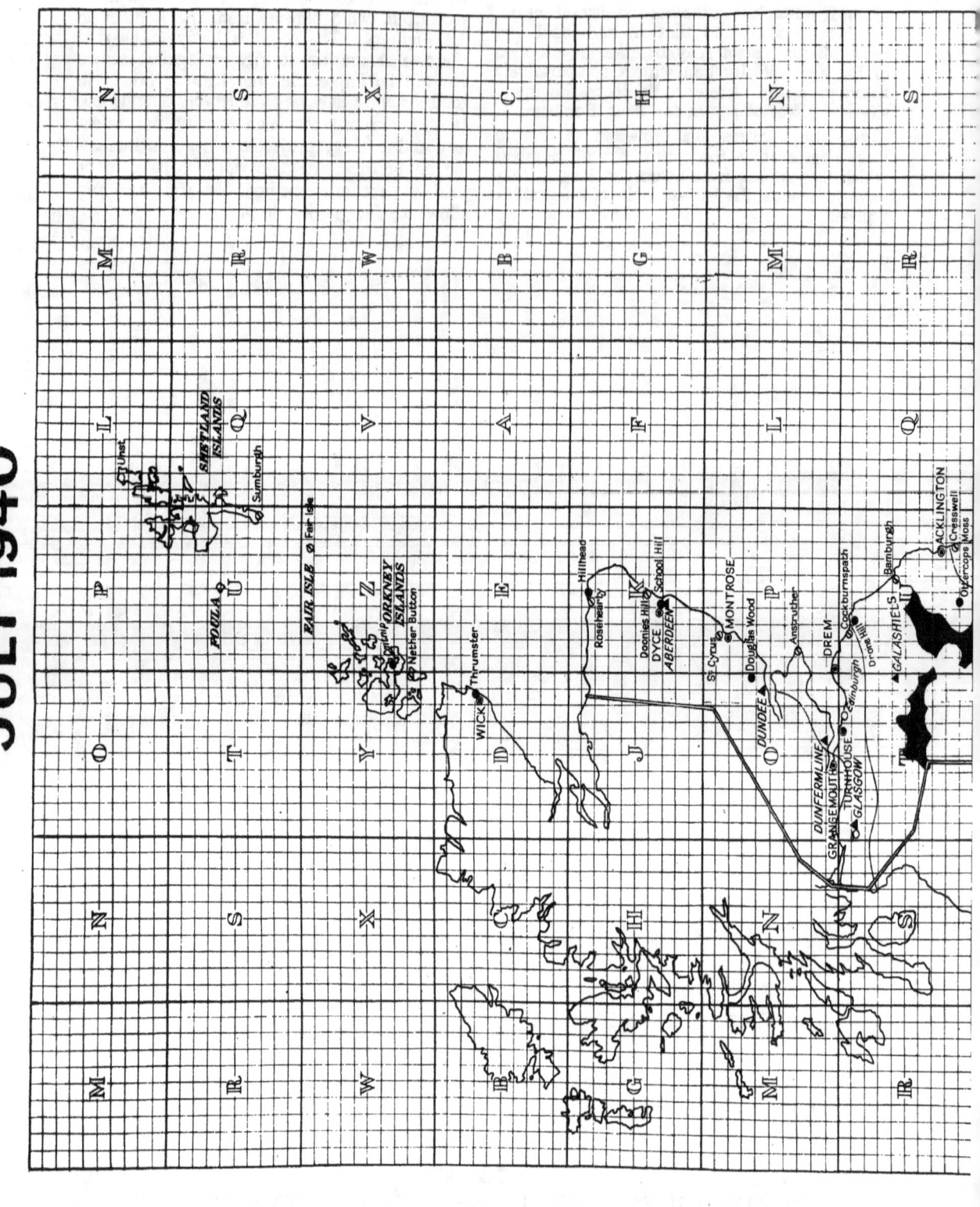

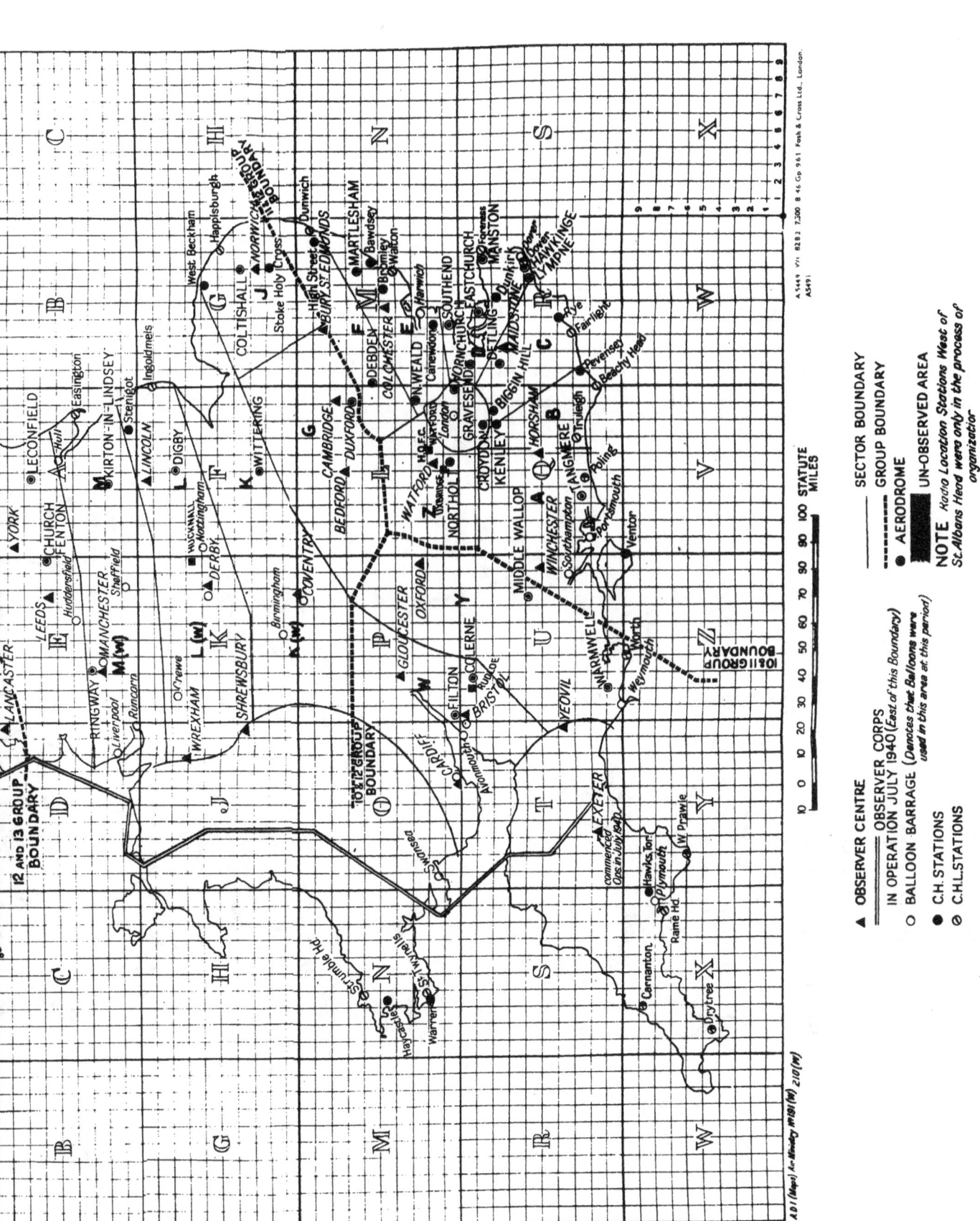

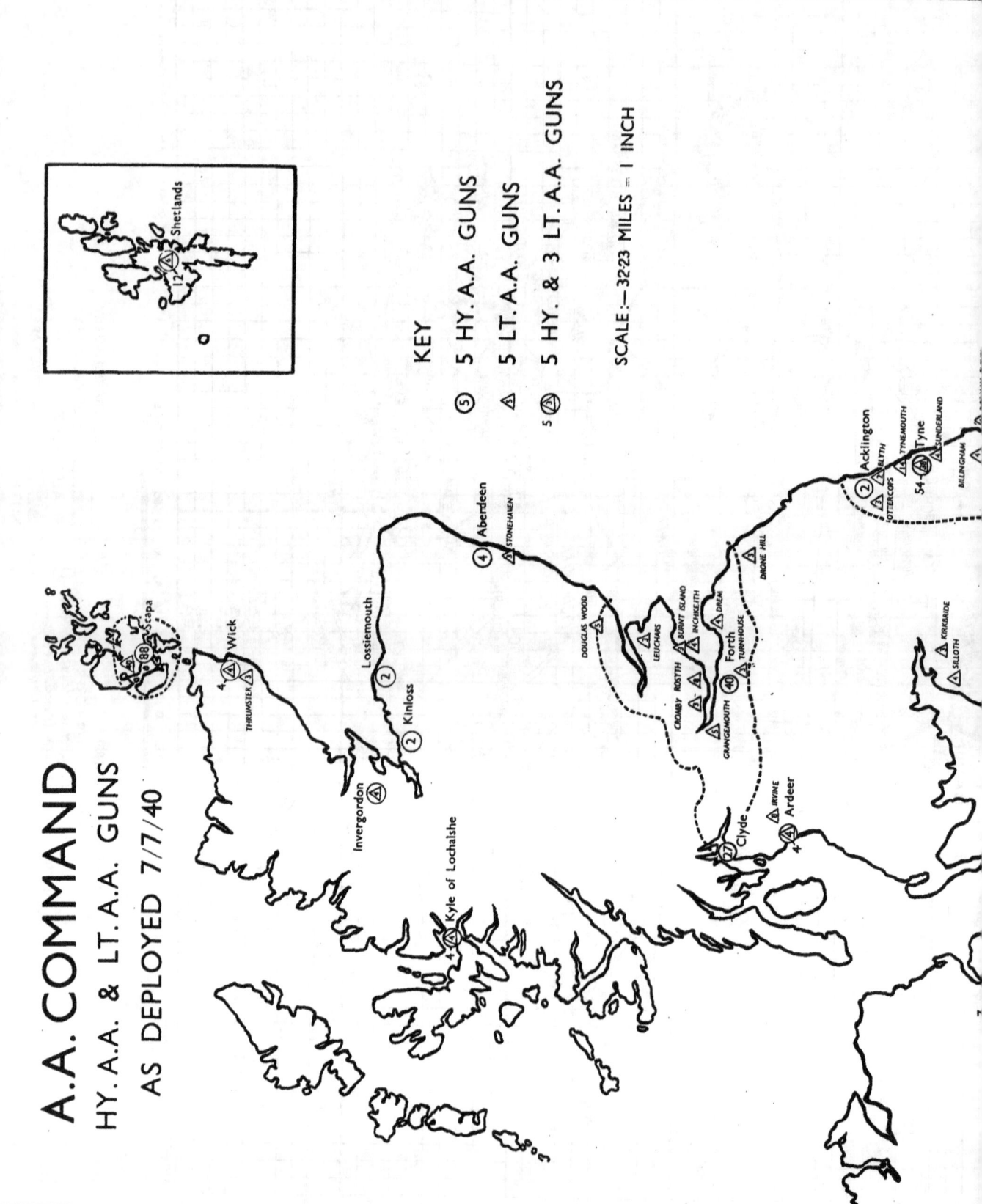

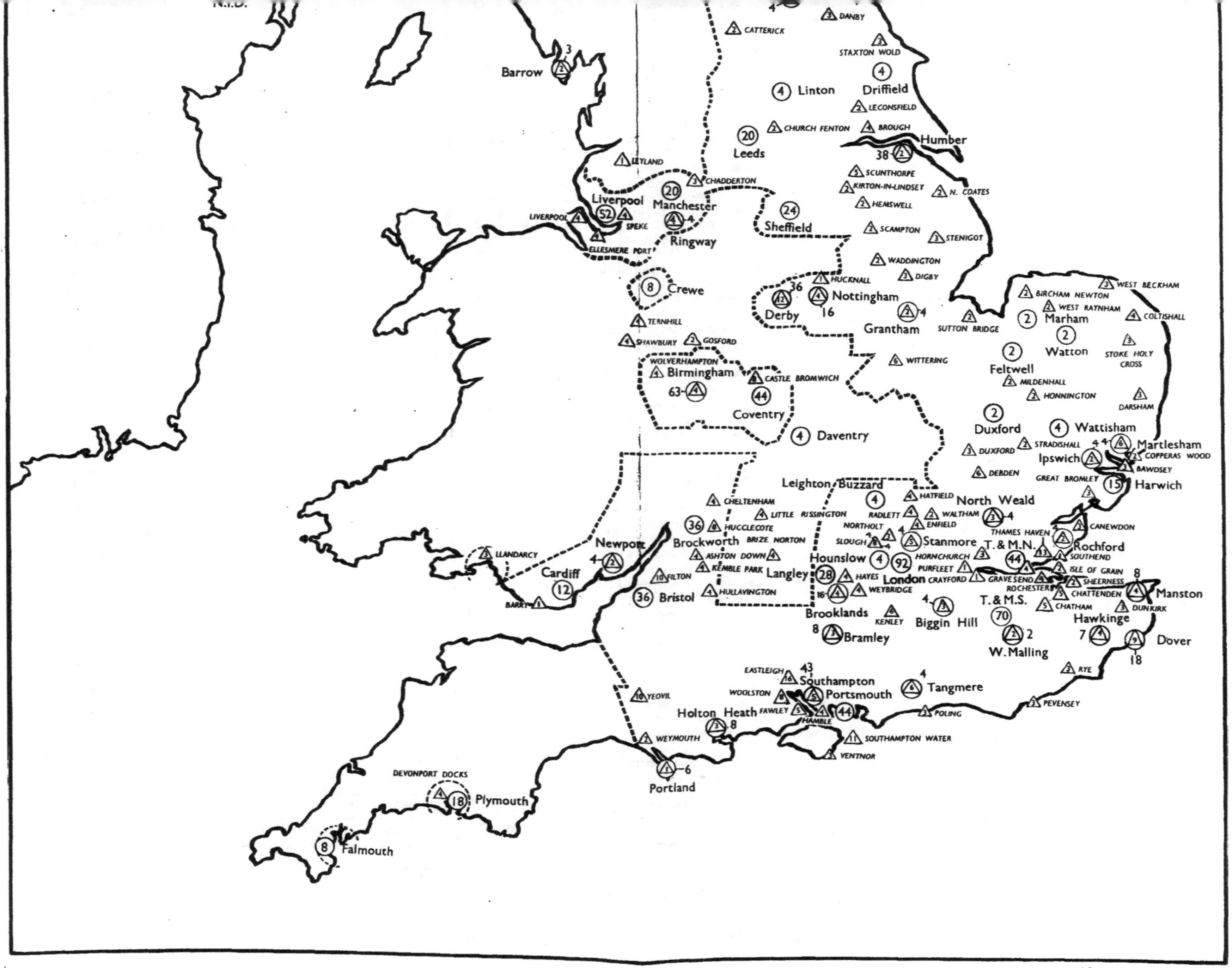

A5449 Fosh & Cross Ltd., London.

AIRCRAFT LOSSES

APPENDIX "D"

COMPARISON of R.A.F. FIGHTER LOSSES WITH CORRESPONDING GERMAN AIRCRAFT LOSSES BY DAY
(BY FIGHTER AIRCRAFT ACTION ONLY)

R.A.F. AIRCRAFT LOSSES ▬▬▬
G.A.F. AIRCRAFT LOSSES -----

Date	R.A.F. Fighters (Sorties)	G.A.F. Aircraft (Sorties)	Main Target	Other Targets
JULY 10	609		S. WALES AREA – DOCKS	SHIPPING
11	432		PORTLAND	SHIPPING: PORTSMOUTH.
12	670		SHIPPING	
13	449		SHIPPING: PORTLAND & DOVER	EAST COAST CONVOYS.
14	593		SHIPPING: DOVER.	SHIPPING: SWANAGE.
15	470		PORTS & CONVOYS	
16	313		SHIPPING	
17	253	FIGS. NOT AVAILABLE BEFORE AUGUST 1ST	SHIPPING	SURREY, KENT, PORTLAND
18	549		SHIPPING	
19	701		SHIPPING: DOVER.	GLASGOW
20	611		DOVER HARBOUR	CONVOYS & SHIPPING.
21	571		SHIPPING: CHANNEL	
22	611		CONVOYS & SHIPPING	
23	470		SHIPPING: NORTH SEA	
24	561		SHIPPING: CHANNEL	
25	641		SHIPPING: CHANNEL	FIRST MENTION OF LARGE FIGHTER ESCORTS
26	581		SHIPPING	
27	496		SHIPPING: DOVER	DOVER HARBOUR
28	794		SHIPPING: STRAITS	
29	758		DOVER	SHIPPING: PORTSMOUTH & HARWICH
30	688		CONVOYS: HARWICH	
31	395		AERODROMES	NAVAL & MILITARY TARGETS, CHATHAM.
AUGUST 1	659	90	SHIPPING	
2	477	60	SHIPPING: CHANNEL	
3	415	50	SHIPPING: S.E. & E. COASTS	RECONN. IN S.W.
4	261	80	SHIPPING	
5	402	110	SHIPPING: STRAITS	
6	416	60	RECONN. DOVER AREA	
7	393	70	RECONN.	
8	655	280	CONVOYS: CHANNEL	CONVOYS: NORFOLK
9	409	110	RECONN. N.E. COAST	CHANNEL SHIPPING
10	336	80	CHANNEL SHIPPING	EAST ANGLIA.
11	729	370	DOVER & SHIPPING	PORTLAND
12	758	440	R.D.F. STATIONS, DOVER & AERODROMES	CONVOYS: ESTUARY
13	861	450	HARBOURS & AERODROMES. S.E. & S. COAST.	SHIPPING: ESTUARY
14	494	400	S. COAST TOWNS & AERODROMES	
15	1254	650	DOVER & E. KENT AERODROMES	NEWCASTLE, SUNDERLAND, HULL, SCARBOROUGH. ESSEX A/DROME
16	850	550	AERODROMES	
17	288	220	MAINLY RECONN.	
18	868	560	AERODROMES	
19	383	290	SHIPPING	AERODROMES
20	453	200	DOVER & AERODROMES.	PEMBROKE DOCK. SHIPPING: YARMOUTH
21	589	170	E. & S.E. COAST AERODROMES.	DOCKS
22	509	220	SHIPPING: CHANNEL	
23	482	200	MAINLY RECONN.	
24	936	550	PORTSMOUTH	KENT (MAINLY MISC. LAND TARGETS)
25	481	325	MAINLY RECONN.	
26	787	440	AERODROMES	PORTSMOUTH.
27	288	115	MAINLY RECONN.	
28	739	400	KENT AERODROMES	
29	498	390	AERODROMES	SHIPPING
30	1054	590	AERODROMES & PETROL STORES	SHIPPING
31	978	700	A/DROMES & FACTORIES	

Date	Sorties (ours)	Sorties (German)	Target Area (Ours)	Target Area (German)	Phase
September 1	661	490	AERODROMES	NAVAL & MILITARY TARGETS — CHATHAM AREA	FIRST PHASE
2	751	750	AERODROMES	THAMES ESTUARY	
3	711	550	AERODROMES	THAMES ESTUARY	
4	678	550	AERODROMES	THAMES ESTUARY	
5	662	460	AERODROMES	OIL STORAGE TANKS, THAMES ESTUARY	
6	987	730	AERODROMES		
7	817	700	AERODROMES	OIL STORAGE TANKS, THAMES ESTUARY	
8	305	200	AERODROMES	DOVER HARBOUR	
9	446	430	AERODROMES	INDUSTRIAL TARGETS IN OR NEAR LONDON	SECOND PHASE
10	224	50	MAINLY RECONN.		
11	678	500	LONDON	PORTSMOUTH	
12	247	80	MAINLY RECONN.		
13	209	150	LONDON		
14	860	400	LONDON	AERODROMES	
15	705	600	LONDON	PORTLAND	
16	428	410	LONDON	KENT AREA	
17	544	350	FIGHTER SWEEPS over KENT		
18	1165	800	THAMES ESTUARY	LONDON	
19	237	75	MISC. TARGETS: LONDON, KENT AND SUSSEX		
20	540	150	FIGHTER SWEEP over KENT. S.E. COAST		
21	503	260	LONDON		
22	158	140	FIGHTER SWEEPS over S.E. COAST		THIRD PHASE
23	710	300	INDUSTRIAL TARGETS IN KENT	SOUTHAMPTON	
24	880	500	FILTON	LONDON	
25	668	290	SOUTHAMPTON	LONDON	
26	417	220	MISC. TARGETS IN KENT & S.E. LONDON		
27	939	850	LONDON	PORTSMOUTH	
28	770	300	S.E. COAST		
29	441	180	INDUSTRIAL ROUND LONDON	AERODROMES	
30	1173	650	LONDON & S.E. KENT	SOUTHAMPTON	
October 1	673	450	S.E. LONDON		
2	807	300	SMALL BUT WIDESPREAD		
3	138	90	LONDON		
4	171	100	LONDON		
5	1074	540	FIGHTER SWEEPS over S.E. COAST	POOLE & PORTSMOUTH	
6	181	130	LONDON	AERODROMES	
7	822	500	LONDON	YEOVIL	
8	561	250	FIGHTER SWEEPS over KENT		
9	456	290	FIGHTER SWEEPS over ESTUARY & KENT	LONDON	
10	712	275	FIGHTER SWEEPS over S.E. COAST	WEYMOUTH	
11	900	480	FIGHTER SWEEPS over S.E. COAST		
12	756	340	FIGHTER SWEEPS over S.E. COAST		FOURTH PHASE
13	552	180	LONDON (MAINLY FIGHTERS)		
14	253	90	MAINLY RECONN.		
15	598	550	LONDON (MAINLY FIGHTERS)	SOUTHAMPTON	
16	234	70	NEGLIGIBLE		
17	563	330	LONDON & S.E. COUNTIES		
18	135	40	MAINLY RECONN.		
19	295	160	LONDON		
20	457	300	LONDON		
21	262	110	LONDON	LIVERPOOL & BLACKBURN	
22	360	80	SWEEPS over KENT		
23	79	40	MAINLY RECONN.		
24	463	30	MAINLY SHIPPING RECONN.		
25	776	440	LONDON & S.E. COUNTIES		
26	678	220	SWEEPS over KENT		
27	967	500	SWEEPS over KENT & ESSEX		
28	606	250	SWEEPS over KENT		
29	649	470	LONDON & S.E. COUNTIES		
30	533	300	LONDON & S.E. COUNTIES		
31	145	70	MAINLY RECONN.		

NOTE. IN MAKING COMPARISONS BETWEEN NUMBERS OF GERMAN SORTIES AND OUR OWN, IT MUST BE REMEMBERED THAT GERMAN SORTIES ARE GENERALLY UNDERSTATED, AND THAT OUR OWN SORTIES INCLUDE NUMEROUS SHIPPING-PROTECTION FLIGHTS ALL ROUND THE COASTS OF GREAT BRITAIN.

SECOND SUPPLEMENT
TO
The London Gazette
Of TUESDAY, the 17th of SEPTEMBER, 1946

Published by Authority

Registered as a newspaper

THURSDAY, 19 SEPTEMBER, 1946

The Air Ministry,
September, 1946

AIR OPERATIONS IN THE MIDDLE EAST FROM JANUARY 1ST, 1941, TO MAY 3RD, 1941.

The following despatch was submitted to the Secretary of State for Air on November 24th, 1941, by Air Chief Marshal SIR ARTHUR LONGMORE, G.C.B., D.S.O., Air Officer Commanding-in-Chief, Royal Air Force, Middle East.

1. This Despatch covers the period from 1st January, 1941, to 3rd May, 1941. On this latter date I was recalled to England and did not return to resume command of the R.A.F., Middle East.

The main features to be recorded during these four months can be summarised as follows:—

(a) The complete defeat of the Italian Air Force in Libya; the successful and rapid advance to Benghazi (6th February) and the subsequent temporary stabilisation in Cyrenaica as far West as El Ageila.

(b) The reduction of British Forces in Cyrenaica, both Army and Air, in order to meet fresh Greek Commitments due to development of the threat to Greece from German Forces which had crossed from Roumania into Bulgaria. The decision being made on the 22nd February to send British Land Forces to Greece.

(c) The subsequent German-Italian offensive in North Africa leading to the withdrawal of British Forces in Cyrenaica to the Frontier and to the isolation of Tobruk.

(d) The German invasion of Yugo-Slavia and Greece on 5th April, resulting in the capitulation of the Armies of both countries and the evacuation of British Forces to Crete and Egypt.

(e) Intensified attacks on Malta and Naval communications in that area by German aircraft based in Sicily.

(f) The successful offensives against Italian East Africa from Kenya and Sudan, including the re-occupation of Berbera.

Note: A separate report has been rendered on the R.A.F. operations in Crete from the 17th April to the 31st May, the control of which ceased to be my responsibility from the 3rd May. On that date the German Air Invasion of the Island had not yet developed.

The full report on Air Operations in East Africa from 10th February to 5th April, 1941, has been forwarded to Air Ministry, but a Summary of these operations is included in this Despatch.

2. The location of units in the Middle East Command on 1st January, 1941, is the same as that given in Despatch No. 1 for the 31st December, 1941, and is repeated at Appendix " A ".* Appendix " B " gives the location of units as at 30th April, 1941.

Libya.

3. In my previous Despatch I recorded in para. 28 that by 31st December, 1940, the whole territory East of the Italian-Egyptian frontier was in our hands. The Army had already advanced to positions surrounding Bardia and forward patrols had already penetrated towards Tobruk.

4. Air operations were continued in direct support of the Army, all types of aircraft contributing to this end during the advance, the role of squadrons being as follows:—

Heavy bombers attacked military objectives by night, such as Bardia and Tobruk, prior to the assault by our troops. At other times their objectives included Benghazi Port and aerodromes.

---

* Appendices not reproduced.

Medium bombers, immediately prior to attacks on Bardia, Tobruk and Derna, were employed in a similar role to the heavy bombers both by day and night and at other times attacked enemy aerodromes. No. 113 Squadron, and later No. 55 Squadron, continued to provide strategical reconnaissance.

The activities of our fighters were varied. They provided reconnaissance, made low flying attacks on mechanical transport on the enemy's lines of communication, in addition to providing air protection to our own troops against enemy air action.

Army Co-operation aircraft were employed mainly on tactical reconnaissance with Hurricanes or Gladiators. Lysanders were used to a limited extent for spotting artillery bombardments.

Early in January the Italian Air Force was still very active despite the heavy losses already inflicted on it.

5. As a prelude to the Army's assault, Bardia was subjected to a heavy Naval and Air bombardment. Thus, during the night 1st/2nd January, following many previous attacks, Wellingtons and Bombays, together with Fleet Air Arm Swordfish, dropped over 20,000 lbs. of bombs on enemy defences and troop positions. Blenheims continued to attack during the day on 2nd January making 44 bombing sorties, followed during the night of 2nd/3rd January by further efforts of Wellingtons and Bombays which dropped another 30,000 lbs. of bombs. The total load of bombs dropped during this series of attacks amounted to over 40 tons.

At the same time Blenheims bombed enemy aerodromes concentrating on Gazala, Derna and Tmimi. Hurricanes of Nos. 33, 73 and 274 Squadrons maintained offensive patrols over Bardia during the attack.

6. The Army attacked Bardia at dawn on 3rd January, the assault being made by armoured forces in co-operation with Australian infantry. During the battle, Blenheims effectively bombed troop concentrations while aircraft of No. 208 (A.C.) Squadron co-operated with artillery. Gladiators of No. 3 R.A.A.F. (Australian) Squadron maintained low flying offensive patrols to cover our troops as they advanced.

As soon as the attack had been launched a large proportion of our bombing effort was turned on to aerodromes in Cyrenaica, with the intention of pinning down and destroying the enemy air force.

Fighting at Bardia continued until 1330 hours on 5th January, when the enemy ceased to offer any further resistance.

7. By the 6th January our Armoured Forces, advancing under cover of offensive fighting patrols, had reached the outer perimeter defences of Tobruk. They also occupied El Adem aerodrome on that date, capturing 40 unserviceable aircraft which had been abandoned by the Italians on the landing ground there. A further 35 burnt out aircraft were found by armoured patrols at Gazala a few days later.

8. On 10th January, Headquarters No. 202 Group, together with the Western Desert Squadrons, started to move forward. By the middle of January, Headquarters, No. 202 Group was established at Sollum, and bomber and fighter squadrons had moved forward to landing grounds in the Sollum-Bardia area, with No. 208 Squadron and No. 3 R.A.A.F. Squadron further forward at Gambut.

9. Operations now passed through a stage of preparation and consolidation before the attack on Tobruk. During this period heavy bombing attacks were continued against Tobruk to wear down the enemy and destroy his defences. Enemy aerodromes were consistently and effectively bombed, particular targets at this time being Berka and Benina, near Benghazi, to which the enemy had been compelled to withdraw his bomber forces as a result of our continued attacks on his more forward aerodromes. Port facilities and shipping at Benghazi and military objectives at Derna were also attacked. It now became evident that the aircraft losses inflicted on the enemy, both on the ground and in the air, were resulting in reduced activity of his air force, and from that time onwards our own aircraft operated with comparative immunity.

10. As in the case of Bardia, the assault on Tobruk was preceded by a Naval bombardment and heavy bombing attacks from the air. On the night of 19th/20th and 20th/21st January, Wellingtons and Blenheims dropped 20 tons of bombs, inflicting heavy damage on the defences and other military objectives at Tobruk, including the A.A. guardship, " San Georgio ". The assault on Tobruk was launched at dawn on 21st January and, simultaneously, Blenheims of Nos. 45, 55 and 113 Squadrons, operating in direct support of our troops, attacked enemy positions within the Tobruk defences, maintaining their attacks throughout the day, and making a total of 87 sorties. The Gladiators of No. 3 R.A.A.F. Squadron, and Hurricanes of Nos. 73 and 274 Squadrons maintained offensive patrols Westwards of Tobruk to cover ground operations, but very few enemy aircraft appeared and only one engagement took place.

Operations continued on 22nd January. Aircraft of No. 208 (A.C.) Squadron provided close support for our troops. Early in the morning the Australians entered the town, while the Free French companies penetrated the perimeter near the sea to the West. All organised resistance was at an end by the evening.

Between the fall of Tobruk and 1st February the following moves were made. Headquarters, No. 202 Group moved forward to Sidi Mahmoud; Nos. 73 (F) and 274 (F) Squadrons to Gazala and No. 3 R.A.A.F. (A.C.) Squadron and No. 208 (A.C.) Squadron to El Tmimi.

11. The main body of our forces now pushed on Northwards to Derna and our armoured formations Westwards to Mechili. Enemy air activity was on a small scale, but as the advance approached Italian base aerodromes a certain number of fighters continued to attack our forward troops. They were, however, successfully dealt with by our own fighter patrols which prevented the enemy from inflicting any serious casualties or from materially influencing the rapid progress of the advance. The intensity of our own air operations at this stage was also somewhat reduced, due partly to unserviceability through long flying hours under desert conditions, but also through our inability to establish forward landing grounds sufficiently rapidly to keep pace with the advance. The over ponderous standard squadron organisation did not lend itself to such conditions, and,

moreover, very few transport aircraft were available. However, the Blenheims and Wellingtons, not being so dependent on advanced landing grounds, were able to continue bombing enemy aerodromes.

12. Our armoured forces entered Mechili on 27th January, and on 30th January Derna fell to the forces which had advanced to the North. Like Bardia and Tobruk, Derna had already been regularly and heavily bombed for a considerable period and was not, therefore, subjected to concentrated bombing attacks immediately prior to the assault. Fighter patrols, however, provided constant cover for the troops and continued to harass the enemy on his lines of communication throughout the operations.

The advance continued and Cyrene was occupied on 3rd February. A rapid withdrawal of enemy forces now took place; M.T. and troop convoys retreating Westwards from Barce were repeatedly attacked by Blenheims and harassed by fighters.

13. The Australians now advanced on Benghazi from the North, while on 4th February our armoured forces started their remarkable dash across the desert from Mechili to the coastal road South of Benghazi. The interception, which completely surprised the enemy, took place at Beda Fomm, approximately 30 miles South of Solluch on 5th February. The enemy, supported by strong armoured car formations, tried to break through, but were repulsed with heavy losses and the greater part of their forces were captured or destroyed.

Meanwhile, as the Australians advanced on Benghazi, our medium and heavy bombers maintained their attacks on Berka and Benina aerodromes and on the railway at Barce which was being used by the enemy for the withdrawal of his forces from that area.

14. Our troops occupied Benghazi on 6th February, meeting little resistance in the final stages. The R.A.F. occupied Benina aerodrome on 10th February and found 87 unserviceable and damaged enemy aircraft there, which, together with those found at other aerodromes, notably El Adem and Gazala, were an indication of the effectiveness of the numerous bombing attacks made on enemy air force objectives and accounted very largely for the virtual collapse of the Italian Air Force during the latter stage of the advance.

15. Following the British occupation of Benghazi, the remnants of the enemy forces retreated Westwards into Tripolitania, while the Italian Air Force had been so depleted as to be incapable of offering any serious threat for the time being. Thus it appeared improbable at that time that the enemy would be able to stage an early counter-offensive in Libya. Meanwhile, the increasing gravity of the situation in Greece called for the early despatch of further air reinforcements to that theatre and the consequent reduction of the Royal Air Force in Cyrenaica.

16. The next phase, therefore, consisted of the reorganisation and redistribution of forces. H.Q. No. 202 Group, Nos. 45 and 113 (B) Squadrons, and No. 274 (F) Squadron were withdrawn to the Delta area in the middle of February. No. 208 (A.C.) Squadron was withdrawn at the end of February, but was replaced by No. 6 (A.C.) Squadron of which two flights were at that time already in Cyrenaica, the remainder of the Squadron being transferred to Aqir (Palestine).

H.Q., R.A.F., Cyrenaica was formed at Barce on 25th February, 1941, under the command of Group Captain L. O. Brown, D.S.C., A.F.C.

The Squadrons remaining in Cyrenaica in March, 1941, were disposed as follows:—

No. 3 Squadron R.A.A.F., which by that time was completely re-armed with Hurricanes, was located at Benina to provide the air defence of Benghazi.

No. 73 (F) Squadron, at first located at Gazala, was moved to Bu Amed on 14th March to defend the Tobruk area.

The Headquarters and one flight of No. 6 (A.C.) Squadron (Hurricanes and Lysanders) was at Barce, with a flight at Agedabia and sections at other landing grounds in Western Cyrenaica.

No. 55 (B) Squadron was at Bu Amed until 10th March, when it moved to Maraua.

17. Enemy air activity increased shortly after our occupation of Benghazi. It was at this time that *German* aircraft, operating from landing grounds near Tripoli began to attack our forces in Cyrenaica, at first using J.U.87's and Ju.88's. German fighters started to operate at a slightly later date from advanced landing grounds, Me.110's making their first appearance, followed shortly afterwards by Me.109's. Before the end of February the Germans had assumed a leading role in the enemy air effort.

The enemy's main bombing objective at first was Benghazi, which was attacked regularly and with some intensity between 14th and 20th February. Subsequent attacks, however, covered a wider range of objectives including Tobruk, our aerodromes in Cyrenaica and troops in the forward area at Agheila and Agedabia. It was in fact due to this somewhat unexpected increase of enemy air activity, coupled with the presence of German fighters, that No. 73 (F) Squadron was retained in Cyrenaica when it had previously been intended to withdraw it from that front to provide further reinforcement for Greece.

18. Reconnaissance of Tripoli harbour from the middle of February onwards revealed considerable quantities of shipping using the port, and it soon became evident that the enemy was being rapidly reinforced. In addition to sea borne reinforcements, the enemy carried considerable numbers of troops to Tripoli by air in Ju.52's. German troops were included in the reinforcements and early in March it was estimated that the greater part of a German division had already arrived in Tripolitania.

It was essential therefore to maintain attacks on shipping and harbour facilities at Tripoli to impede the flow of enemy reinforcements and supplies to Libya. Wellingtons of Nos. 38 and 70 (B) Squadrons, operating from landing grounds in Cyrenaica, accordingly bombed these objectives, making a total of forty sorties against Tripoli during February and March. Further attacks on Tripoli were made by F.A.A. Swordfish as well as Wellingtons operating from Malta. Considerable damage was inflicted during these operations but the total effort which could be made available was insufficient to cause any serious obstruction to the arrival of enemy reinforcements. Other

Wellington operations included attacks on aerodromes in Tripolitania and on shipping at Sirte which the Germans were developing as a forward base.

19. A brief appreciation of the air situation, dated the 6th March, was prepared for the information of the Foreign Secretary, Mr. Eden, who had arrived in Cairo in company with the C.I.G.S. on 19th February. A copy is attached—Appendix " D " (not reproduced).

It was at this time, particularly, that the weakness in number of modern aircraft at my disposal, chiefly Hurricanes and Blenheims, caused me the gravest concern. It had been anticipated that with the defeat of the Italian Air Force in Cyrenaica a quiet period on that front would justify considerable reduction in air strength. This proved to be far from the case, and it became apparent that air reinforcements would have to be sent to Cyrenaica immediately to prevent the enemy thrust from developing into a serious threat to Egypt.

We were already heavily committed in Greece and more help had been promised. Squadrons were awaiting new aircraft in replacement of wastage, yet the promised arrival in Egypt of large air reinforcements from home both via Malta and Takoradi, in spite of periodical emergency ferrying operations by Aircraft Carriers, did not materialise and it was not until the latter end of April that the situation in this respect began to improve. Moreover, though ships were arriving via the Red Sea at Suez quite regularly, there was no steady supply of cased aircraft by this route during the whole of January, February and March.

American Tomahawk fighters, which were beginning to come over from Takoradi, were at this time suffering from various " teething troubles " and were not yet ready for effective operation.

Not only was the Air Force at my disposal insufficient for the commitments which had arisen, but the rate of replacement, either actual or within reach, was not sufficient to keep pace with wastage. Whereas the losses from all causes from the 1st January, 1941 to 31st March, 1941 were 184, during the same period the actual arrivals in Egypt via Takoradi and Malta were 147 and 19 respectively, or a total of 166.

As will be seen later in this Despatch, during the whole of March and April this factor of waning resources had to be taken into account in deciding how to employ the Air Force at my disposal economically and to the best advantage.

20. Early in March, increasing numbers of enemy M.T. were observed by air reconnaissances to be moving eastwards along the coastal roads, and by the 10th March large enemy concentrations were located in the area immediately West of Agheila. Simultaneously the enemy established forward landing grounds at Tamet, Syrte and El Makina.

By the middle of March it was estimated that the German forces in Libya had been built up to two divisions, one of which was armoured. With this increase of strength in personnel and equipment, the enemy forces gradually assumed an offensive role. At the same time enemy aircraft reconnoitred our forward positions apparently with the object of ascertaining the strength of our forces.

On 19th March an enemy patrol occupied the landing ground at Marada, about 80 miles South of Agheila. This move was a forerunner of increased activity by strong enemy patrols which necessitated the withdrawal of our outposts from Agheila, the enemy occupying the fort there on 24th March. Italian infantry, supported by German armoured forces and dive-bombers, moved East of Agheila on 30th March, and on 31st March our forward troops were compelled to fall back on Agedabia. Blenheims of No. 55 Squadron bombed and machine-gunned enemy M.T. concentrations, while the landing ground at Misurata, from which enemy aircraft were operating in support of their advance, was successfully attacked by Wellingtons and Blenheims. The superior weight of the enemy enabled him to continue his advance, however, despite the opposition of our troops and aircraft.

21. On 2nd April, the enemy continued to advance in Cyrenaica, compelling our forward troops to withdraw from Agedabia. The situation in Benghazi thus became precarious, and orders for demolitions were issued. Preparations were made for the withdrawal of all R.A.F. Units from that area, and Benina was evacuated during the early evening of 2nd April, all demolitions having been completed.

Although handicapped by the frequent moves of the ground echelon necessitated by rapid withdrawal, squadrons continued to operate in direct support of the Army. Blenheims of No. 55 (B) Squadron, reinforced by No. 45 Squadron, provided reconnaissances, attacked concentrations of enemy M.T. and A.F.V's., and bombed forward enemy aerodromes. Hurricanes of No. 3 Australian Squadron and No. 73 (F) Squadron maintained constant patrols, covering our troops as they withdrew to new positions and making many effective attacks on enemy M.T. concentrations. Wellingtons also made night attacks on enemy M.T. in addition to maintaining their offensive against Tripoli whilst they were still within striking range of that objective. No. 6 (A.C.) Squadron continued to operate directly under the control of the Army and provided such tactical reconnaissances as were possible with their limited capacity and under conditions in which their ground echelons, like those of the other squadrons, were constantly on the move.

22. For the next few days complete details of the movement of our own and enemy troops remained somewhat obscure. At times it was difficult for Army Co-operation aircraft to keep track of the movements of the particular force with which they were working. For instance, on April 2nd, both the Flight of No. 6 (A.C.) Squadron and the H.Q. of No. 2 Armoured Division with which they were operating spent the night at Antelat, but on the morning of the 3rd April the Flight discovered that Div. H.Q. had left and no information was forthcoming as to their movements. The Flight subsequently moved to the landing ground at Msus where Free French troops were unable to give any information concerning our troops in the area, nor did they know where Div. H.Q. was situated. It was not until noon that a message was received from Second Div. H.Q. which gave their position at that time as 30 miles West of Msus. A tactical reconnaissance about this time, taken by an aircraft of this Flight from Msus, reported

enemy A.F.V's. and M.T. moving towards Msus. Whether this column was, in fact, an enemy one still remains uncertain, but according to the pilot the lorries were Italian and the personnel inside them opened fire on his aircraft.

23. On the 4th April, enemy armoured forces threatened to outflank the Australian Division holding the Benina-Tocra position, necessitating their withdrawal to new positions on the Barce escarpment.

In the meantime, as the Army withdrew to new positions, our Squadrons moved to landing grounds further East. On the 4th April, No. 3 Australian Squadron, No. 6 (A.C.) Squadron and Advanced H.Q., Cyrenaica, moved to Maraua, No. 55 Squadron to Derna and H.Q., Cyrenaica to Tobruk. On the same day 8 Blenheims of No. 45 Squadron reinforced No. 55 Squadron.

The Australian Division withdrew to the Barce escarpment on the 5th April, covered by Hurricane patrols of Nos. 3 and 73 Squadrons. The Hurricane patrols were also extended to cover elements of our troops retiring towards Mechili. In these operations, on 5th April our fighters destroyed 14 enemy aircraft for a loss of 2 Hurricanes.

By the 7th April the Australian Division and support group had withdrawn, first to Derna and then to Gazala area. Meanwhile, our armoured forces, which had already suffered heavy losses, had fallen back on Mechili and joined up with the Indian Motor Brigade. At this stage R.A.F. Squadrons had withdrawn to aerodromes in the Tobruk area, and further movements were necessary on the 8th April when the Blenheim Squadrons and No. 3 R.A.A.F. Squadron withdrew to landing grounds East of the Cyrenaica-Egyptian frontier, and the Wellingtons to their bases in the Fuka area. No. 6 (A.C.) and 73 (F) Squadrons continued to operate from landing grounds within the Tobruk perimeter.

The Australian Division withdrew to the outer perimeter of Tobruk on the 10th April. The following day enemy A.F.V's. cut the road between Tobruk and El Adem and our support group retired towards Sollum. From Mechili the enemy's forward troops continued their advance, and by the 13th April they had occupied Bardia and the Sollum escarpment where their advance was temporarily halted.

24. The situation by 13th April had become more stabilised and was as follows:—

The enemy's thrust in the forward area at Sollum had lost momentum and there were indications that his troops there were experiencing administrative difficulties as a result of their rapid advance.

Tobruk was held by a strong force of our troops and was invested by the enemy whose troops were concentrated West and South of the perimeter, with armoured forces astride the El Adem road.

H.Q. No. 204 Group, which formed at Maaten Bagush on the 12th April under the command of Air Commodore R. Collishaw, C.B., D.S.O., O.B.E., D.S.C., D.F.C., had taken over the control of the Squadrons in the Western Desert from H.Q. Cyrenaica.

The tasks of the R.A.F. at this stage were:—

(a) To continue to attack lines of communication to aggravate the enemy's existing M.T. difficulties.

(b) To provide close support for the Army by attacking enemy A.F.V's., M.T. concentrations and troops both in the forward areas and at Tobruk.

(c) To attack enemy aerodromes, primarily with the intention of destroying his transport aircraft which he was using to supply his forward troops.

(d) To bomb harbour facilities and shipping at Benghazi in order to interrupt the use of the port by the enemy and thereby prevent him from shortening his long lines of communication from Tripolitania.

(e) To provide the fighter defence of Tobruk.

25. Soon after the investment of Tobruk it became evident that it would no longer be possible to maintain No. 6 (A.C.) and No. 73 (F) Squadrons on the aerodrome within the perimeter. In addition to frequent dive bombing attacks, which were liable to destroy or damage the aircraft beyond repair capacity available, the landing ground was within range of enemy artillery fire. These Squadrons were accordingly withdrawn to aerodromes in the vicinity of Maaten Bagush, with advanced landing ground near Sidi Barrani for re-fuelling.

Owing to the distance of Tobruk from these aerodromes and even from the advanced landing ground at Sidi Barrani (120 miles from Tobruk), the task of maintaining fighter defence over Tobruk Harbour at such long range became extremely difficult. In addition, the depth of enemy penetration to the East put Tripoli out of range of our Wellingtons operating from the Western Desert, and made it most difficult to provide fighter escorts to our ships supplying the Tobruk garrison. On the other hand, it enabled the enemy to develop repeated bombing attacks on Tobruk without regular fighter interference, and it reduced the distance for his bombers operating against Alexandria or ships in the Eastern Mediterranean.

26. After a German-Italian attack on Tobruk on April 14th, during which No. 73 (F) Squadron shot down 9 E/A for loss of 2, there followed a period of comparative inactivity from a military standpoint. In the Sollum area, patrols of our mobile forces made raids well behind the enemy's forward troops. The enemy, however, continued to supply his forward areas by means of M.T. and transport aircraft, although harassed by the activity of our mobile patrols and the continued attacks of our aircraft on his lines of communication and forward aerodromes.

Enemy air activity at this stage was concentrated largely on Tobruk, apparently with the primary intention of denying the port to us. Hurricanes of No. 73 Squadron, providing the fighter defence of Tobruk, on several occasions engaged greatly superior numbers of the enemy with success, although not without loss to themselves. As an example, in a series of raids on Tobruk during 22nd and

23rd April in which the enemy employed a total of 100 bombers and about 150 fighters, Hurricanes destroyed 12 enemy aircraft and probably destroyed a further 2 with a loss to themselves of 3 Hurricanes.

The scale of our attack against enemy aerodromes was somewhat increased from about 20th April to the end of the period under review. More than 60 sorties by Wellingtons and Blenheims were made during this particular period, the main weight of this effort being directed against the enemy's forward aerodromes at Derna and Gazala, and the base aerodrome at Benina.

By this time our squadrons in the Western Desert had been further reinforced by detachments of No. 274 (F) Squadron—Hurricanes and No. 39 (B) Squadron—Marylands, the latter being employed mainly for strategical reconnaissances. No. 3 Squadron R.A.A.F. was withdrawn from the Western Desert on 21st April and moved to Aboukir for rest after continuous fighting since 7th November, 1940.

27. Towards the end of the period under review, military activity increased, both in the frontier area and at Tobruk. The enemy's forward troops on the Sollum escarpment after being heavily reinforced with A.F.V's. advanced Eastwards on the 27th April and occupied Halfaya Pass. This appeared to be his main objective for, after establishing a forward line beween Halfaya and Sidi Omar he made no attempt to continue his advance.

At Tobruk the enemy made a further determined attack on 1st May, employing 60 tanks supported by infantry and accompanied by heavy air attacks on our troops and defences. The enemy succeeded in breaking the outer defences of the perimeter but failed to pierce our main defences. Fighting continued for two days and on the 1st May, Hurricanes of Nos. 73 and 274 Squadrons maintained fighter patrols to protect our troops and artillery against enemy fighter and bomber action. The Hurricanes encountered enemy fighters, in greatly superior numbers but shot down 4 Me.109's in flames, with the loss of 1 Hurricane. Our troops successfully counter-attacked, destroying 11 enemy tanks and inflicting other heavy losses. The enemy however, retained a hold on 5,000 yards of the outer perimeter and our line was adjusted accordingly. A further attack by the enemy on the 2nd May was repulsed, after which the enemy effort there appeared to be temporarily spent.

28. A feature of the operations of this period was the high scale of effort maintained by a comparatively small air force working under the difficult conditions imposed by the enemy's rapid advance. From 1st April to 3rd May more than 400 bomber and fighter sorties were made against enemy M.T. convoys and concentrations, A.F.V's. and troops. Over 70 Wellington and 80 Blenheim sorties were made against enemy aerodromes and 64 Wellington and 12 Blenheim sorties were made against Benghazi. In addition, Hurricanes on several occasions machine-gunned aerodromes and in the course of numerous patrols destroyed 73 enemy aircraft in combat and probably destroyed a further 16, with a total loss of 22 Hurricanes.

It would be true to say that the German-Italian success in regaining Cyrenaica was due more to the number, efficiency and mobility of their ground forces than to their numerical air superiority. At no time did the German-Italian Air Forces completely dominate the situation on this front.

29. From January to Mid-February Air Commodore R. Collishaw, C.B., D.S.O., O.B.E., D.S.C., D.F.C., continued in command of No. 202 Group, R.A.F. in these successful operations which culminated in the occupation of Cyrenaica. He maintained the high standard of resource and initative which I had grown accustomed to expect from him, and he was an inspiration to all those under his command. At Appendix "H" will be seen a tribute to the work of his Group by Lieutenant-General O'Connor, Commander of the XIII Corps (not reproduced).

Group Captain L. O. Brown, D.S.C., A.F.C., continued to render most valuable service on the Staff of the G.O.C. in arranging the tasks of the reconnaissance Squadrons under the operational control of the Army. On February 25th he assumed command of the reduced Air Force in Cyrenaica and remained in command during the subsequent withdrawal, during which time he contrived to operate his small Force to the best advantage under most difficult conditions.

The work of No. 3 Royal Australian Air Force, under the command of Squadron Leader I. D. Maclachan, D.F.C., was outstanding. They were continuously in the Western Desert or Cyrenaica for six months, first with a mixture of Gladiators, Gauntlets and Lysanders and later with Hurricanes. Their high morale and adaptability to Desert conditions were remarkable.

Other Squadrons which particularly distinguished themselves on this front were No. 73 —Hurricane—Fighter Squadron and No. 55—Blenheim—Bomber Squadron, which did most of the long distance strategical reconnaissance.

Mention must also be made of No. 2 R.A.F. Armoured Car Company which remained working with the Armoured Division throughout the successful phase of the operations, attached to the XI Hussars.

Greece.

30. The Greek advance had lost its impetus by the beginning of the year as the result of increased enemy resistance, lengthened lines of communication and severe winter conditions. The Greeks still retained the initiative, however, and after operations had apparently become static, they made a further advance, capturing Kelcyre on the 8th January, 1941, and thereafter making slow progress along the Northern side of the Kelcyre-Tepelene gorge. There was little activity in other sectors.

The R.A.F. Squadrons based in Greece, under the command of Air Vice-Marshal J. H. D'Albiac, D.S.O., on the 1st January, 1941, were:—

   No. 30 (F) Squadron (Blenheim Fighters).
   No. 80 (F) Squadron (Gladiators).
   No. 84 (B) Squadron (Blenheims)
   No. 211 (B) Squadron (Blenheims).

In addition, detachments of Wellingtons of Nos. 37 and 70 (B) Squadrons based in Egypt operated during moon periods from aerodromes in Greece.

The continued arrival of Italian reinforcements in Albania presaged an offensive, to counter which the Greeks would require the maximum air support that could be made available. Thus No. 112 (F) Squadron (Gladiators) was withdrawn from the Western Desert early in January, and No. 11 (B) Squadron (Blenheims) and No. 33 (F) Squadron (Hurricanes) were also withdrawn after the capture of Bardia and despatched to Greece, as follows:—

No. 11 (B) Squadron—24th January.
No. 112 (F) Squadron—10th February.
No. 33 (F) Squadron—19th February.

A situation calling for further reinforcements for Greece was created by the threatened German invasion through the Balkans. Accordingly, by the 31st March, No. 113 (B) Squadron (Blenheims) had also been despatched from Egypt to Greece and No. 208 (A.C.) Squadron (Hurricanes and Lysanders) was re-equipping and preparing to move at an early date.

31. Although the Greek Air Force operated with success in the early days of the war its activities were much latterly by the inability of the Greeks to make good their aircraft casualties. Thus, practically the whole of the air effort in this theatre devolved upon the R.A.F. which was consequently called upon to attack strategical objectives, to operate in direct support of the Greek Army, necessary in order to maintain their high morale, and to provide the fighter defence of the Athens area. To meet these requirements Squadrons were employed in the following roles:—

Wellingtons operating by night attacked ports in Albania and to a less extent in S. Italy to interrupt the flow of enemy supplies and reinforcements to Albania.

The primary role of the Blenheims was to provide direct support for the Greek Army by attacking:—

(a) enemy lines of communication and important centres behind the forward area to prevent the distribution of supplies and reinforcements, and

(b) enemy positions in the forward area.

Blenheims also attacked ports in Albania by night and day and provided strategical reconnaissance of ports in Southern Italy and Albania.

Hurricanes and Gladiators were employed in escorting Blenheims during many of their daylight bombing attacks, in maintaining offensive patrols and in protecting the Greek troops against enemy air action.

Blenheim fighters continued to provide the air defence of the Port and Air Bases in the Athens area.

In addition to the commitments already referred to, Wellingtons and Blenheims operating from Greece were called upon to attack enemy aerodromes in the Dodecanese from which enemy aircraft were carrying out mine-laying operations in the Suez Canal, as well as air attacks on our convoys proceeding to Greece.

32. For the first two months of the year extremely unfavourable weather conditions persisted, preventing our aircraft from operating with any degree of intensity. Although both sides were similarly handicapped, it was more to our disadvantage in that, inter alia, it prevented our own aircraft from attacking ports in Albania and Southern Italy with sufficient intensity to do more than embarrass their use by the enemy. Thus, despite the damage inflicted and the nuisance value of our attacks, the Italians still continued to land reinforcements and supplies in Albania.

The bad weather prevailing at the time of the Greeks' capture of Kelcyre on the 8th January prevented our aircraft from operating in close support of their troops during their advance; in fact, until the middle of February operations were of necessity of a sporadic nature, the weather and state of aerodromes on occasions preventing our aircraft from operating for several days at a time. Subsequently, on the 10th January, as the Greeks continued to make slow progress towards Tepelene, Blenheims attacked enemy troops retiring from Kelcyre towards Berat. Otherwise support to the Greek forces at this time was confined to Blenheim attacks on the bases at Berat, West of the Central Sector and Elbasan, beyond the Northern Sector.

Towards the end of January the fighting round Tepelene increased in intensity as reinforcements reached the Italians, enabling them to stiffen their resistance against the Greek thrusts. During this period and up to the middle of February periodical attacks continued against Elbasan in the North, and Berat, Boulsar and Dukaj in the Tepelene area where military buildings and troop concentrations were bombed.

33. By the middle of February there were indications that the threatened Italian counter offensive would not be long delayed. With the Greeks retaining the initiative the ground operations had developed into a series of attacks by the Greeks followed by fierce Italian counter attacks, this activity being concentrated in the Tepelene area. A brief spell of improved weather conditions at this time enabled our aircraft to operate with greater freedom, 108 sorties being made between 11th and 18th February in support of the Greek forces which were making a strong effort at that time to capture Tepelene. In these operations, stores, M.T. convoys and enemy troop and gun positions in the Tepelene area were persistently and effectively attacked by bomber and fighter Blenheims.

Air activity reached a peak on 13th-14th February when, following a series of ineffective Italian counter-attacks, the Greeks launched a new offensive against enemy positions around Tepelene. Our aircraft made 50 sorties in direct and close support of the Greek troops as they advanced and captured important positions in the mountains to the North and South of Tepelene.

Following this short favourable spell, weather conditions again deteriorated after the middle of February, but although this curtailed operations to some extent our aircraft continued to provide support for the Greek Army which maintained its pressure on the enemy. Between 19th February and 4th March approximately 90 Blenheim sorties were made against enemy troop concentrations, gun emplacements and M.T. convoys in the Southern and Central Sectors in an endeavour to wear down the enemy resistance.

34. Owing to enemy fighter activity Blenheims taking part in these operations were on most occasions escorted by Gladiators or Hurricanes. Several combats with large enemy fighter formations took place, to the marked advantage of our own fighters. As an example, during a particular week of activity ending 3rd March, 33 Italian fighters were destroyed and a further 8 probably destroyed, against which our own fighter losses were only 1 Gladiator destroyed, the pilot being safe, and 2 other fighters damaged. Such successes were by no means limited to this period and further reference is made later to the activities of our fighters.

By the beginning of March the continued arrival of enemy reinforcements by sea and air had built up the strength of Italian forces in Albania to an estimated total of 29 divisions. The Greeks, however, retained the initiative, repeatedly repulsing counter-attacks and inflicting heavy losses on the enemy. On the 7th March, the Greeks, taking advantage of improving weather conditions, resumed their offensive against Tepelene, again assisted by our bombers which with fighter escorts continued their attacks against enemy troop positions and lines of communication. The Greeks made local progress.

35. The Italians launched their counter-offensive on the 9th March on a front of about 20 miles, extending from Tepelene in the Southern Sector to the Greek lines West of Corovode in the Central Sector. The enemy forces, which were estimated at about 10 divisions, supported by large numbers of bomber and fighter aircraft, made continuous attacks until the 14th March, but the Greeks, defending resolutely, repulsed all attacks and inflicted very heavy losses on the enemy. The Italians were unable to gain any ground and on the 14th March the Greeks made a successful counter-attack, taking some prisoners.

Throughout these operations, which continued at maximum intensity between the 9th and 14th March, Blenheims escorted by fighters made 43 sorties against enemy troops, gun positions and M.T. columns, concentrating largely on objectives in the Buzi-Gilave area. At the same time Hurricanes and Gladiators engaged on escort duties and offensive patrols made 15 and 122 sorties respectively. They fought several successful combats with enemy fighters during which they destroyed 35 enemy aircraft and probably another 9, with a total loss of 2 Gladiators and 1 Hurricane, the pilots of which escaped.

By the 15th March the Italian offensive was reduced in intensity, although the enemy continued to make local attacks without success until the 27th March. Air operations continued against enemy positions and lines of communication in all sectors although on a somewhat reduced scale as the result of a further deterioration of weather conditions.

36. During the period under review, Wellingtons made 4 sorties and Blenheims 30 sorties against shipping and port facilities at Valona. Against Durazzo Wellingtons made 11 sorties. This effort was augmented by F.A.A. Swordfish operating from Paramythia which made bomb and torpedo attacks against shipping at these objectives, comprising 7 sorties against Durazzo and 12 against Valona. A feature of these operations was the effectiveness of the F.A.A. Swordfish torpedo attacks in which five direct and two probable hits were claimed on shipping. Much damage was inflicted on port facilities, warehouses, military buildings and barracks by the Wellingtons and Blenheims. In Southern Italy, Brindisi was twice attacked by Wellingtons, the railway station being the objective on the first occasion and the aerodrome on the second. A further attack in the Brindisi area was made when fighter Blenheims successfully machine-gunned grounded aircraft at the aerodrome at Lecce (S. Italy).

37. One of the most outstanding features of the campaign in Albania was the marked superiority which our fighters gained over those of the Italians. In a series of combats during the first three months of the year (1941) our fighters destroyed 93 enemy aircraft and probably destroyed another 26, the greater proportion of the total being fighters. Against this our own fighter losses in combat amounted to 4 Hurricanes and 4 Gladiators destroyed, from which 6 of the pilots escaped by parachute.

Enemy aircraft operating from aerodromes in the Dodecanese periodically mined the Suez Canal and also attacked our sea convoys sailing to Greece. It became necessary, therefore, to divert a portion of the available bomber forces in Greece to attack aerodromes in the Dodecanese, with harbours and shipping as an alternative.

The main objectives were the aerodromes at Rhodes, viz. Maritza, Cattavia and Calato, against which 20 Wellington sorties and 25 by Blenheims were made from Greece. Blenheims also made a further 9 sorties against the aerodrome at Scarpanto and shipping at Stampalia. Many fires were started at the aerodromes, and damage was caused to aerodrome buildings and dispersed aircraft. Direct hits were also obtained on one ship at Stampalia.

Other attacks on the Dodecanese were made by Wellingtons operating from Egypt, the total effort from Greece and Egypt combined during the period under review amounting to 70 Wellington sorties and 34 Blenheim sorties.

38. A further operation of note was the combined Naval and R.A.F. action against enemy Naval forces at the Battle of Matapan on 28th March.

Acting on Sunderland reconnaissance reports, Blenheims operating from Greece made five attacks comprising 24 sorties against enemy warships, reporting direct hits with S.A.P. bombs on two cruisers and one destroyer. One cruiser which was hit with a 500 lb. S.A.P. bomb was apparently seriously damaged. At Appendix "J" is a copy of a Signal conveying appreciation by the Board of Admiralty on the part played by the R.A.F. in this action (not reproduced).

39. Towards the middle of February it had become clear that the German infiltration into Roumania was likely to develop into a "drive" through Bulgaria, with Salonika as the preliminary objective. The Greek Government recognised this as a very real threat, but they were anxious to avoid any action originating from their territory which might precipitate events. Though they were continually calling for more air support, they did not accept the offer of British Troops until 22nd February when at a Conference held at Tatoi, attended by the King of Greece, Prime Minister Korysis (who had succeeded the late General Metaxas),

Mr. Eden (Foreign Secretary), General Sir John Dill (C.I.G.S.), General Sir Archibald Wavell (C.-in-C. M.E.), Captain Dick, R.N. (representing C.-in-C. Mediterranean) and myself, the decision was taken to despatch British Troops at the earliest opportunity to form on the Aliakmon line to the West of Salonika.

It followed, of course, that an increased air commitment would be involved both in support of the British Army on this new front and also for air protection of the ships transporting men to Greece. Nevertheless, since the Greeks had decided to oppose a German invasion of Macedonia there was clearly no alternative to giving them the maximum assistance possible. Moreover, though German air and land forces had arrived in Tripoli these might well have been to prevent our further advance, and there was no reason on that particular date to suspect the imminent preparation of a counter-offensive in Libya. It is true, however, that such a threat developed almost immediately after the Greek commitment had been accepted.

40. The landing of British Troops in the Athens area during March proceeded with little or no interference from the air; German infiltration into Bulgaria continued but their air activity was limited to occasional reconnaissances over Macedonia. By the 1st April it was evident that the German invasion of Greece through the Balkans was imminent. Consequently, with the prospect of fighting the war on two fronts, two air formations were created, viz. Eastern Wing and Western Wing. H.Q. Eastern Wing was at Tsaritsani, in close touch with G.H.Q. British Forces and controlled Nos. 11 and 113 (B) Squadrons (Blenheims), No. 33 (F) Squadron (Hurricanes) and No. 208 (A.C.) Squadron (Hurricanes and Lysanders). The role of this force was to provide direct support for the British and Greek Armies against the prospective German attack from the North. H.Q. Western Wing was at Yannina and controlled No. 112 (F) Squadron (Gladiators) and No. 211 (B) Squadron (Blenheims), the role of this formation being to support the Greeks on the Albanian Front. The remainder of the squadrons in Greece, viz. No. 30 (F/B) Squadron (Blenheim Fighters), No. 80 (F) Squadron (Hurricanes and Gladiators) and No. 84 (B) Squadron (Blenheims), together with detachments of Nos. 37 and 38 (B) Squadrons (Wellingtons), were at aerodromes in the Athens area directly under the control of H.Q., B.A.F., Greece. No. 815 Squadron Fleet Air Arm was based on Paramythia and No. 805 Squadron Fleet Air Arm on Maleme (Crete).

41. Germany declared war on Greece and Yugo-Slavia on the 5th April, 1941, and launched her attack at dawn the following day, crossing the Greek frontier into Macedonia by four routes, with the main thrust along the Struma Valley. Simultaneously they advanced Westwards into Yugo-Slavia along the Strumica Valley in the South, from Dragoman to Nis in the North, and by other intermediate routes. The Greeks resisted strongly at Rupel, temporarily checking the German advance through the Struma Valley, but despite this opposition the Germans succeeded in penetrating Thrace and Macedonia and occupied Salonika on the 8th April.

Throughout the German advance the primary task of our Squadrons was to attack his A.F.V.'s, M.T. columns, troops and lines of communication on the Macedonian and Yugo-Slavian Frontiers. Practically the whole of our air effort was directed to this end, Wellingtons making night attacks, Blenheims operating both by night and day, with fighters constantly in support maintaining offensive patrols, making low flying machine-gun attacks on the enemy, and escorting our bombers by day. The first encounter with the German air force on this front took place on 6th April. A patrol of 12 of No. 33 Squadron Hurricanes engaged 30 Me.109's and shot down 5 of them without loss to themselves. During the night of 6th/7th April, 6 Wellingtons of No. 37 Squadron successfully bombed the railway station and marshalling yards at Sofia. From 7th to 9th April, as the Germans advanced in strength, Blenheims of Nos. 11, 84 and 113 Squadrons made heavy and effective attacks on large columns of their M.T., A.F.V.'s and troops near Petrich in Bulgaria, on the Strumica-Lake Doiran Road in Yugo-Slavia and at Axiopolis and Polykastron in Macedonia.

42. By this time the German armoured forces, supported by dive-bombers, advancing Westwards from Bitolj, had overwhelmed the Yugo-Slav Army and had succeeded in joining up with the Italians in Albania. They then advanced Southward from Bitolj to Florina, threatening to isolate the Greeks in Albania from our own forces further East. The Greeks were thus compelled to withdraw from the Northern front of Albania, while our Armoured Brigade and an Australian Infantry Brigade were moved Westwards to close the Florina Gap, where they were joined by a Greek cavalry division from the Koritza area. On 10th April, as the enemy continued his Westward thrust into Yugo-Slavia, Blenheims attacked enemy M.T. columns and A.F.V.'s on the Prilep-Bitolj road inflicting heavy damage on them. During the night of 11th/12th April, Wellingtons followed up this effort with further attacks on the enemy at Prilep and Kilkis.

Meanwhile, our forces holding the Florina Gap had been hotly attacked by the Germans on 9th April and compelled, after a strong resistance, to withdraw on 11th April. By the evening of 12th April, our front had been formed roughly on a line extending from the coast near Mount Olympus, along the Aliakmon River to Servia, thence N.W. towards the Albanian lakes. Continued bombing and machine-gun attacks by Blenheims and Hurricanes contributed to the delay of the enemy's advance during the critical periods in which our troops were falling back on new positions. These operations were inevitably accompanied by considerable losses and in one raid on the 13th April, for example, a complete formation of 6 Blenheims of No. 211 Squadron was destroyed by Me.109's. Wellingtons continued to attack more distant objectives. On the night of 13th/14th April a force of 10 Wellingtons from Nos. 37 and 38 Squadrons made a further effective attack on the railway goods yard at Sofia, destroying a large number of trucks containing explosives. At the same time other Wellingtons bombed and machine-gunned M.T. convoys at Yannitsa and Gorna Djumaya. In operations on the following night Wellingtons destroyed the bridge over the Vardar River at Veles and Blenheims dropped bombs on enemy columns on the road from Ptolomais to Kozani. Our aircraft continued to attack similar objectives during the night of 15th-16th April and throughout the following day, to impede the enemy's advance on Katerini and Kozani.

43. Meanwhile the Army had stubbornly held the Mount Olympus-Aliakmon Line until 14th April when it was turned by the Germans forcing the Kleisoura Pass. Our forces started to fall back on the Thermopylae Position on 15th April, completing the withdrawal by the 20th April. This new situation necessitated the withdrawal of all R.A.F. Squadrons to the Athens Area on 16th April and from that date onwards they were controlled directly by H.Q., B.A.F., Greece. Eastern and Western Wings were consequently disbanded.

Continuous enemy attacks on our aerodromes, coupled with losses from enemy fighter action, had by this time considerably reduced the effective striking power of our Squadrons. In a series of attacks on one day alone, the enemy destroyed 10 Blenheims on the ground at Niamata and damaged several other aircraft which had to be subsequently destroyed and abandoned. Several such attacks were made, during which many aircraft were destroyed or rendered unserviceable, but owing to the loss in several instances of unit records during the ultimate evacuation, full details of enemy raids are not available. Towards the end the repeated enemy attacks on our aerodromes in the Athens Area caused further heavy losses, and as a final blow a force of Hurricanes retained at Argos to cover the evacuation was almost wiped out when 13 of them were destroyed on the ground during intensive enemy air attacks on 23rd April.

In turn our aircraft attacked the German occupied aerodromes on the Salonika and Larissa Plains in an endeavour to reduce the scale of the enemy's air effort. Thus between 15th and 22nd April Blenheims made effective night attacks on the aerodromes at Sedes, Katerina, Kozani and Larissa, starting several large fires. The effort could not, however, be maintained on a sufficiently heavy scale to cause any material reduction of the enemy's air effort, bearing in mind the comparatively large numbers of aircraft and reserves available to him.

Nevertheless, our Squadrons continued to operate until, in the end, the use of aerodromes was virtually denied to them by constant enemy air attacks. In the concluding stages Blenheims attacked enemy columns advancing on the Larissa Plain, concentrating on road bridges between Kozani, Grevena and Kalabaka to impede the enemy's progress. One particularly successful attack was made when Blenheims bombed a large M.T. convoy concentrated in front of a broken bridge across the Aliakmon River a few miles from Kalabaka. Similarly our fighters continued to engage formidable enemy formations with success. Throughout the campaign they had gained many victories against the numerically superior enemy, but at no time was their skill and high morale more in evidence than in the concluding stages. In a number of combats during the period of intensive enemy air activity on 19th and 20th April, Hurricanes of Nos. 33 and 80 Squadrons destroyed a total of 29 German aircraft and probably destroyed another 15. In addition, Fighter Blenheims of No. 30 Squadron probably destroyed 2 Italian bombers. These successes were achieved with a loss of 7 Hurricanes brought down and 2 damaged, a truly remarkable record in view of the increasing disparity of strength between the R.A.F. and the German Air Force.

44. At the beginning of these operations the combined strength of the German and Italian Air Forces amounted to approximately 1,100 aircraft, of which over 40 per cent. were fighters, a little less than 40 per cent. bombers and dive-bombers, and the remainder reconnaissance aircraft. The total strength of the R.A.F. in Greece with reserves was approximately 200 aircraft, of which about half were bombers. Although outnumbered, our Squadrons operated with success in the initial stages of the German advance. It is probable that unfavourable weather and the lack of forward all-weather aerodromes at that stage prevented the enemy from making the best use of his superior numbers. As the enemy advanced, however, he was able to establish forward aerodromes, at first in the Salonika Area and subsequently on the Larissa Plain, from which he was able to exploit his numerical superiority to the fullest advantage. He was thus able to concentrate an overwhelming force which took an increasing toll of our aircraft both on the ground and in the air. These casualties could not be replaced at that time from the slender reserves available in the Middle East, particularly in view of the dangerous situation which had arisen in the Western Desert. The odds which our Squadrons had to face, therefore, increased disproportionately until the Germans had gained virtual air superiority. With that achieved they were able to concentrate the main weight of their attack against our troops, lines of communication, and ports. By 20th April our much-depleted Squadrons were concentrated at the few remaining aerodromes in the Athens Area, where, as already described, they were exposed to continuous air attack. With the complete collapse of the Greek resistance it became evident that even the shortened Thermopylae front could not be held against the superior weight of the enemy and the decision was made to withdraw all British Forces to the coast and embark them for Crete or Egypt.

45. The scheme for the evacuation of R.A.F. personnel aimed at the removal of air crews and certain key personnel by air in Squadron and transport aircraft and flying boats. The remainder were to be evacuated by sea with other British and Imperial Forces. Wellingtons of Nos. 37 and 38 Squadrons had already flown to Egypt on the 17th and 18th April, the personnel and equipment following by sea on 23rd April. In addition, 14 Blenheim Fighters of No. 30 Squadron flew to Crete on 18th April to provide convoy protection during the projected sea evacuation. The remaining aircraft of Nos. 11, 84, 113 and 211 (B) Squadrons and 208 (A.C.) Squadron, amounting to 24 Blenheims and 4 Lysanders, flew to Egypt on 22nd and 23rd April, the Blenheims having previously made several journeys between Greece and Crete evacuating air crews.

The enemy air attack on Argos on 23rd April, already referred to, had reduced the remaining strength of Nos. 33 and 80 Squadron

Hurricanes to 6. These and 14 Gladiators of Nos. 80 and 112 Squadrons were flown to Crete on 23rd April to defend Suda Bay against enemy air attack and to take part with No. 30 Squadron in providing cover for sea convoys engaged in the evacuation. Sunderlands started to evacuate R.A.F. personnel on 19th April, when they flew a 30 Squadron party to Crete. The previous day they had also carried King Peter of Yugoslavia and other important political personages to Egypt, having taken them off from Kotor (Yugoslavia) on 17th April. Sunderlands continued the evacuation of essential personnel in stages from Greece to Crete, thence to Egypt. The King of Greece and members of the Greek Royal Family were included among other important passengers flown to Crete in Sunderlands on 22nd and 23rd April.

46. On 23rd April the Sunderlands were reinforced by two B.O.A.C. Flying Boats which operated between Crete and Egypt and rendered valuable service. These efforts were further augmented on the same day by Bombays of No. 216 Squadron which took two parties from Eleusis to Bagush, and the following day by Lodestars of No. 267 Squadron which carried three parties from Argos to Bagush. Enemy air attacks rendered Eleusis and Menidi aerodromes unusable after 23rd April, and Argos was similarly out of action from 24th April. The Bombays and Lodestars thereafter continued to carry personnel from Crete to Egypt. The last Sunderland loads to leave Scaramanga were taken off on 24th April and included Lieutenant-General Sir T. Blamey, C.B., C.M.G., D.S.O., and Air Vice-Marshal J. H. D'Albiac, D.S.O., and their respective staffs.

On 24th April 1,700 R.A.F. personnel were at Argos awaiting evacuation by sea but by the next day the majority of these had moved to Kalamata and Gytheon, three Sunderland loads being taken off from the former, and one from the latter and flown to Crete. Subsequently all personnel remaining there were evacuated by sea, many of them crossing in small boats to Kythera whence they were later taken off in destroyers. Further Sunderland evacuations from Greece, were made from Nauplia (Morea), transporting Prince Paul of Greece, the Greek Prime Minister and other important passengers including General Sir Maitland Wilson and Generals Mackay and Rankin.

Meanwhile flying boats of Nos. 228 and 230 Squadrons and landplanes continued the evacuation from Crete to Egypt, the last flight being made by a Sunderland on 2nd May. The total number of personnel evacuated by air from Greece to Crete was over 600, and from Crete and Greece to Egypt 870. Two Sunderlands were lost in these operations, one of which crashed while alighting by night at Kalamata, and the other was destroyed by enemy air action at Scaramanga.

47. The main evacuation from Greece of British and Imperial Forces was effected between 24th and 30th April in convoys of H.M. Ships and other vessels. All available aircraft operated in support to protect the convoys against the heavy enemy air attacks to which they were constantly subjected, and which were causing heavy losses. The forces available in Crete were 14 fighter Blenheims of No. 30 Squadron, 9 fighter Blenheims of No. 203 Squadron (recently sent to Crete from Egypt to take part in this operation) and the remaining 6 Hurricanes and 14 Gladiators of Nos. 33, 80 and 112 Squadrons. At this stage, however, only 6 of the 14 Gladiators were serviceable.

Blenheims usually operating in patrols of six aircraft provided such cover for convoys as was possible in the vicinity of the mainland of Greece, while Hurricanes and Gladiators provided patrols over convoys approaching Crete and during their disembarkation at Suda Bay. At the same time, Sunderlands provided Ionian and Mediterranean reconnaissances to guard against possible raids on our convoys by units of the Italian Navy.

During the six months' campaign in Greece our Squadrons contended throughout with numerically superior enemy air forces, emerging in the end with much credit although sadly depleted in strength. Our total aircraft losses amounted to 209, of which 82 had to be destroyed and abandoned by our own forces during the withdrawal and subsequent evacuation. Many of the latter had been damaged during enemy attacks on our aerodromes and in normal circumstances might have been repaired. Our total losses of aircraft, missing and in combat with the enemy were 72.

As a comparison, the losses inflicted on the enemy totalled 259 aircraft destroyed and 99 probably destroyed, with several others damaged. Of these, 231 were destroyed and 94 probably destroyed in combat with our aircraft.

Our personnel losses in Greece amounted to 148 killed and missing and 15 taken prisoner. Of the total, 130 were aircrews. Such losses cannot be considered unduly heavy, bearing in mind the difficulties of the campaign and the hazards of the subsequent evacuation.

48. I cannot speak too highly of the work of Air Vice-Marshal J. H. D'Albiac, D.S.O., who commanded the British Air Force in Greece during the whole six months' campaign. His initiative, his personality and tact in dealings with the Greek High Command, enabled him, right up to the end, to obtain the maximum results in support of the Greeks from the small force at his disposal.

Of those under his Command, the most outstanding for their valuable services were:—

Group Captain A. H. Willets, Senior Air Staff Officer during the whole period.

Wing Commander P. B. Coote, who commanded the Western Wing (The Albanian Front) and himself took part in many of the fighter patrols and bombing raids of his Squadrons, from the last of which he is missing.

Wing Commander J. R. Gordon-Finlayson, D.S.O., D.F.C., commanding No. 211 Squadron, and later the Eastern Wing. A fine leader and an inspiration to his Squadron, with which he had completed over one hundred raids.

Squadron Leader E. G. Jones, D.F.C., commanding No. 80 (F) Squadron; his leadership maintained the high morale and efficiency of this Squadron whose six months' record in Greece, mostly in Gladiators, was quite remarkable.

Wing Commander Lord Forbes, Intelligence Officer on the Staff, who carried out many special missions in his Q.6 aeroplane, some of which were of an unusual and hazardous nature.

Italian East African Campaign.

49. The successful land operations against I.E.A., which resulted in the complete collapse of Italian resistance in that area except for a small " pocket " in the region of Gondar, were supported by Air forces from Sudan, Aden and Kenya. In deciding on the actual strength of the Air force required to give full support to the Land forces operating from the North and South, it was necessary to take into account the fact that:—

(i) It was still possible for the Italians, and Germans if they so decided, to send reinforcements of aircraft direct by air from Tripoli to I.E.A.

(ii) To meet the commitments in Libya and Greece the release of Air and Mechanised forces from this front was important. There was, therefore, need for speed if the campaign was to be completely successful before the rains started in April.

(iii) The majority of our aircraft were of obsolete or obsolescent type which needed the cover of a few modern fighters to enable them to operate by day in face of the Italian C.R.42 fighters which were still active until towards the close of the campaign.

(iv) Patriot activities required constant air support to maintain enthusiasm and morale.

(v) The Red Sea shipping route still remained potentially a very vulnerable line of communication. Its security was the more important since traffic through the Mediterranean had virtually ceased.

50. In the Sudan, at the beginning of the year the R.A.F. under Air Commodore L. H. Slatter, O.B.E., D.S.C., D.F.C., consisted of five Squadrons and one Flight. No. 1 South African Air Force (F) Squadron—Hurricanes and Gladiators, No. 237 Rhodesian (A.C.) Squadron—Hardys, No. 47 (B) Squadron—Wellesleys, No. 223 (B) Squadron—Wellesleys, and No. 14 (B) Squadron—Blenheim IV's. In addition, " K " Flight's (Gladiators) move to Egypt was cancelled pro tem. and they were retained in the Sudan. These Squadrons were mainly used during the whole period to defeat the Italian Air Force and to support the advance of the Army into Eritrea. Other commitments which were met included the Air defence of Port Sudan, occasional special convoy escort work in the Red Sea, attacks on the harbour of Massawa and support of the increasing activities of the Abyssinian Patriots further South, Haile Selassie having entered Abyssinia on the 20th January, 1941.

51. Pressure by General Platt's force on the Kassala area resulted in the fall of the town on January 19th and the retreat of the Italian Forces into Eritrea. Steady progress by two parallel columns continued, Agordat and Barentu falling on the 1st and 2nd February. Early in March the advance was halted in front of the formidable defences on the Keren heights. Here the Italians made a determined stand until March 27, when they were forced to withdraw Southward.

In these operations at Keren the R.A.F. played a prominent part in the close support of the Army. Wellesleys, Vincents, Lysanders, Gauntlets and Hardys were employed for continuous bombing of targets both in and behind the enemy's battle positions. Without doubt this heavy and continuous bombing, combined with the effect of artillery fire, seriously weakened Italian morale and contributed very largely to the capture of this formidable position.

Meanwhile, the offensive against enemy aerodromes, lines of communication and aircraft in the air was continued by Blenheims, Hurricanes and Gladiators. Enemy fighters, whose appearance became less frequent as time went on, continued to " shoot up " our aircraft on the ground, occasionally with success, but their air effort gradually dwindled until by the time Asmara was occupied on March 31st it had virtually ceased.

The Hurricanes of No. 1 South African Squadron were especially prominent in these operations. In two attacks on enemy aerodromes they destroyed 6 C.A.133's, 4 C.R.42's and 6 S.79's, besides damaging a further 3 S.79's.

During the attack on Keren a particularly successful bombing attack on lines of communication resulted in the destruction of an ammunition train reported to be carrying over 20,000 shells.

52. Further South bombing attacks were made in support of the Patriots to help in sustaining their morale; Gubba, Gondar, Asosa, Burye and Debra Marcos being among the places attacked. Blenheims of the Free French Flight took part in these operations. Pilot Officer R. A. Collis, D.F.C., of No. 47 (B) Squadron (Wellesleys), made a series of 19 flights up to a distance of 200 miles into Abyssinia, carrying at various times ammunition, money and supplies for the Patriot forces, and on other occasions representatives of the Emperor and Army Officers.

North of Lake Tana the Italians contrived to maintain themselves in the Gondar area, but South of the Lake the Patriots succeeded in capturing Burye and Debra Marcos and in reaching the Blue Nile.

53. After the occupation of Asmara on the 1st April, the advance continued on Massawa. As our threat to that objective developed, five Italian destroyers based at Massawa left harbour in a Northerly direction on 2nd April. This force was located and attacked on 3rd April by Swordfish of the F.A.A. (H.M.S. Eagle) by No. 14 Squadron (Blenheims) and No. 223 Squadron (Wellesleys). The Swordfish torpedoed two of the destroyers, sinking one of them and leaving the second in a sinking condition, the latter being subsequently bombed and sunk by a Blenheim. A further two destroyers were driven aground on the Hedjaz Coast twelve miles South of Jedda, where they were bombed and destroyed by Blenheims and Wellesleys operating in conjunction with H.M.S. Kingston. The surviving destroyer escaped and returned to Massawa, where she scuttled herself.

Our troops occupied Massawa on 8th April. The capture of this Port, combined with the destruction of the enemy naval forces, greatly reduced the potential threat to our Red Sea communications.

The successful progress of the campaign, coupled with the almost complete destruction of the enemy air force on all fronts of Italian East Africa, now enabled the greater part of the Squadrons previously contained in the Sudan to be released to other theatres. Thus, during the early part of April the remaining forces operating there were reduced to No. 47 (B) Squadron (Wellesleys), No. 237 (B) Squadron (Hardys, Lysanders and Gladiators) and the Free French Flight (Blenheims). Other units, consisting of No. 1 Squadron, S.A.A.F., No. 14 Squadron, No. 223 Squadron, "K" Flight and No. 1430 Flight were moved with what aircraft remained to them to Egypt where they arrived about the middle of April. Nos. 14 and 223 Squadrons took part in the action against enemy naval forces described below before their departure.

54. In the subsequent advance from Asmara towards Dessie the greater part of the offensive effort against objectives in the Dessie area was made by aircraft from Aden and East Africa. These operations are referred to later. Wellesleys of No. 47 Squadron and Gladiators, Lysanders and Hardys of No. 237 Squadron nevertheless made attacks on a light scale on objectives in the vicinity of Amba Alagi where our advance from the North was held up. Bombing and machine-gun attacks were made on enemy troops and M.T. at Mai Ceu, Alomata and Amba Alagi and on the aerodromes at Alomata, Cercer and Sifani. The scale of attack in this area was considerably increased after 27th April when our column from the South captured Dessie, Nos. 47 and 237 Squadrons making over 80 bomber and fighter sorties on enemy positions around Amba Alagi between 28th April and 3rd May to break down the remaining resistance. The enemy was still holding out, however, at the end of the period under review, although the forces there, under the Duke D'Aosta, subsequently capitulated on 16th May.

Operations at Gondar and in the Lake Tana area were continued throughout this period, 27 medium bomber sorties being made by Free French Flight Blenheims and Wellesleys of No. 47 Squadron, the former providing more than half the total effort. The main weight of this attack was against enemy positions and M.T. at Gondar, while other attacks were made on similar objectives at Bahr Dar South of Lake Tana, at Chelga, Gorgora and on the Gondar-Adowa Road.

It appeared likely at the end of this period that, with our troops held up in the Volchit Pass, Gondar would be the last serious military objective in Italian East Africa.

55. Great credit is due to the A.O.C., Air Commodore L. H. Slatter, O.B.E., D.S.C., D.F.C., for his most efficient handling of the R.A.F. and for his excellent team-work with the Army. No praise can be too high for the pilots and aircrews for their accomplishments. Many were flying in obsolescent single engine aircraft. The country was difficult, and much of the flying had to be done at low heights over hostile positions. Great devotion to duty and a high standard of skill were needed to achieve success under these exacting conditions.

56. In Kenya, under the command of Air Commodore W. Sowrey, D.F.C., A.F.C., the Air Force consisted of six South African Squadrons and one Flight of Glenn Martins, No. 2 (F) Squadron—Furies and Gauntlets, No. 3 (F) Squadron—Hurricanes, No. 11 (B) Squadron—Battles, No. 12 (B) Squadron—J.U.86's, Nos. 40 and 41 (A.C.) Squadron—Hartebeestes; a total of 94 aircraft all told.

During January the establishment of advanced landing grounds was completed as far forward as possible on the fronts facing Abyssinia and Italian Somaliland. The advance of General Cunningham's Force started on 10th February and met with some opposition from Italian aircraft operating from Afmadu and Gobwen, but the destruction of 7 C.A.133's and 3 C.R.42's in the first two days went a long way towards establishing the complete air superiority eventually achieved, and which, without doubt, affected the whole course of future operations.

57. On the 11th February, Afmadu was captured and after a further rapid advance Kismayu was occupied on 14th February.

After the fall of Kismayu our aircraft assisted the turning operations which resulted in the forcing of the River Juba and the dash on Mogadiscio. Gobwen, Afmadu, Jelib, Bardera and Dolo were among the targets attacked, also Ischia, Baidoa and Bur Agaba further North.

By the middle of March the forces had reached Gabredarre, having advanced 755 miles in 39 days.

During the remaining operations in March against Harar and Diredawa intense air attacks were made on these places, on military targets in the Jijigga area and on the railway and stations of the Addis Ababa-Djibuti line. Direct hits by bombs were scored on several trains as well as on M.T. on the roads, and traffic was largely immobilised.

Hurricanes of No. 3 S.A.A.F. Squadron "ground-strafed" Diredawa aerodrome on 15th March, damaging 2 S.79's and 5 G.R.32's. Other enemy fighters were shot down in the air over Diredawa.

At this time enemy bombers made a number of attacks on our forward troops at Marda Pass near Jijigga, but did no damage.

On 28th and 30th March enemy fighters machine-gunned Jijigga aerodrome, damaging four of our aircraft on each occasion. Two of the raiders were shot down.

Glenn Martins of the S.A.A.F. did regular long distance reconnaissances in the Addis Ababa direction. Further South in the Boran Area the rains set in early in March, hampering operations. Our bomber aircraft attacked enemy positions at Yavello, Neghelli, Moyale and Mega in support of the Army, and Neghelli was occupied in March. Thus, by the end of March, our forces were firmly established within the Southern boundaries of Abyssinia and further North were already threatening Addis Ababa along the railway.

On this front alone did the enemy show any activity in the air, but it was only spasmodic, and in no way hindered the advance of the Army.

58. After occupying Diredawa on 29th March our forces resumed their advance and after a brief check at Awah moved on to Addis Ababa which surrendered on 6th April. From

Addis Ababa our forces advanced in three directions. One column moved North East towards Dessie, a second column advanced North West towards Debra Marcos to join forces with the Patriots, while a third column moved South West on Gimma to engage the considerable enemy forces in the Galla Sidamo. In the Gojjam the Patriots achieved much success, capturing Debra Marcos, the principal town, on 7th April. By the end of this period the Gojjam was practically cleared of the enemy.

Squadrons of the S.A.A.F. continued to operate in support of our troops, their activities consisting largely of offensive reconnaissances during which bombing and machine-gun attacks, the latter chiefly by fighters, were made on various enemy objectives.

During the advance of our forces on Addis Ababa effective attacks were made on enemy positions and M.T. in the Awash area, and on the aerodrome at Addis Ababa where some of the few aircraft remaining to the enemy were concentrated.

With the advance of the three columns from Addis Ababa in diverging directions, air operations in support of our troops were continued over widely separated areas. The main military objective at this time was Dessie which our troops were approaching from the North and South. The main effort of the S.A.A.F. at this stage was, therefore, against objectives in that area, bombing and machine-gun attacks being made by S.A.A.F. Battles, J.U.86's and Hurricanes on enemy troops and M.T., and against Combolcia (Dessie) aerodrome. Our forces advancing from the South captured Dessie on the 26th April but the enemy still retained his positions at Amba Alagi, holding up our advance on Dessie from the North.

Operations by Nos. 40 and 41 Squadrons, S.A.A.F. (Hartebeestes) and No. 11 Squadron S.A.A.F. (Battles), were carried out against widely scattered groups of the enemy in the Gojjam and the Lakes area and North East of Yavello.

In the Galla Sidamo, operations were concentrated largely against the Gimma area where No. 41 Squadron (Hartebeestes) and No. 3 Squadron (Hurricanes) attacked the aerodrome, enemy troops and M.T. Engagements with the enemy fighters were few at this time, but on the 10th April a formation of No. 3 Squadron Hurricanes attacking Gimma aerodrome encountered two of the remaining enemy fighters and shot them down over their own aerodrome.

59. As was the case in the Sudan, the general success of the campaign in Italian East Africa enabled two Squadrons to be released from the East African Command. No. 2 Squadron, S.A.A.F., and No. 14 Squadron, S.A.A.F., the latter subsequently re-numbered No. 24 Squadron, were therefore transferred to Egypt during the latter part of April, where they awaited re-equipment.

The South African Air Force are to be congratulated on the important and successful part they played in this campaign. They were operating over difficult country and under conditions which tested their initiative, stamina and technical efficiency to the utmost. They contributed largely to the complete defeat of the Italian Air Force in I.E.A. and to the destruction of 300 aircraft, which is the estimated total of enemy aircraft destroyed on the ground or in the air in that theatre of war.

60. At Aden, under the command of Air Vice-Marshal G. R. M. Reid, C.B., D.S.O., M.C., there remained the following Squadrons at the beginning of the year:—

No. 8 (B) Squadron—Blenheims and Vincents, No. 203 (GR/L) Squadron—Blenheim IV's, and No. 94 (F) Squadron—Gladiators (not complete).

Though the Italian Air Force was within easy striking distance of convoys passing up and down the Red Sea they made no attempt to interfere with this line of communication, which was of vital importance to our Forces in Egypt. Whilst they were still capable of such attacks it was necessary to provide Red Sea reconnaissance, and a certain degree of air protection both to convoys and to Aden. The principal effort, however, of these Aden Squadrons during the period under review was in support of the campaigns from North and South into Abyssinia.

Repeated raids were made on Assab, Dessie, Diredawa, Addis Ababa, Alomata and Makalle. Besides damage to buildings, depots and repair shops, numbers of aircraft were destroyed on the ground in the course of these raids, 8 S.A.133s being set on fire at Alomata in one raid by two Blenheims.

In support of the operations, which resulted in the recapture of Berbera by landings from the sea on 16th March, 21 sorties were made against Diredawa aerodrome, 10 enemy aircraft being destroyed on the ground and 8 others damaged. Offensive reconnaissances were also carried out to neutralise possible enemy air action.

61. In April, operations in support of the Army in Italian East Africa were carried out almost entirely in the Dessie area and on the Assab-Dessie Road. Blenheims made a number of successful attacks on M.T. concentrations and troops in these areas and, in addition, attacked the aerodromes at Combolcia (Dessie) and Macaaca (Assab). The scale of effort at this stage was not heavy, only 31 offensive sorties being made during the period, including a number of machine-gun attacks by No. 203 Squadron (Blenheims) engaged on offensive reconnaissances.

Prior to the action on the 3rd April, already described, when four Italian destroyers were sunk or disabled, the considerable force of destroyers and other Italian Naval units at Massawa was a constant threat to our Red Sea communications. Regular reconnaissances of Massawa, Dahlak Island and Assab and the Eritrean Coast were therefore maintained, and a constant check kept on the movements of Italian ships and Naval units. After the occupation of Massawa on the 8th April this threat was greatly reduced, since Assab was the only port then remaining to the enemy. Thereafter operations in the Red Sea were largely confined to reconnaissances of the port.

The reduction of Red Sea reconnaissances, combined with the general success of the campaign in Italian East Africa, enabled No. 203 Squadron to be transferred to Egypt on the 16th April, 1941.

Malta.

62. Early in January, the arrival of the German Air Force in Sicily and Southern Italy changed the situation at Malta very considerably. Whereas the Italian air effort against Malta had been half-hearted, the Germans made determined and persistent attacks on the Grand Harbour, aerodromes and flying boat anchorages.

As these attacks by day, and later more frequently by night, became more numerous and intense, the defence of the Island and of the aircraft base there became more difficult. Some of our aircraft were damaged on the ground, as also were hangars and buildings, although casualties to R.A.F. personnel were fortunately light.

At the beginning of January there were operating from Malta:—

No. 261 (F) Squadron—Hurricanes, No. 228 (F/B) Squadron—Sunderlands, No. 431 G.R. Flight—Glenn Martins and No. 148 (B) Squadron—Wellingtons.

The aircraft strength of these units varied, but seldom, if at any time, were they up to establishment. Moreover, repair and maintenance under conditions of constant bombing became extremely difficult. Flying boats at their moorings were particularly vulnerable. Also, a certain amount of congestion resulted at times on the aerodromes when reinforcing flights which used Malta as a " stage post " arrived from England en route to Egypt. It was necessary to pass them on without delay in spite of enemy interference.

63. Under these circumstances I considered it advisable, after discussion with A.O.C. Malta, temporarily to reduce the number of aircraft based on the Island. In deciding which units to retain, the needs of the Navy had to be considered as well as the requirements of local Fighter Defence. The spirit of the garrison and the morale of the Maltese reacted remarkably to the Hurricanes' successes in air combats over Malta. This was a most important consideration, and it was obvious that as many fighters as possible should operate whilst the " game " remained plentiful and enterprising.

Next in importance came the reconnaissance of enemy ports, their approaches, and of the Eastern Mediterranean itself. The former was done by the Glenn Martins at Malta, within their limited capacity—there were seldom more than three serviceable. A P.R.U. (Photographic Reconnaissance Unit) Spitfire, which was at Malta for special photographic work, proved invaluable for this port reconnaissance, but after its loss, through a forced landing in Italy, no replacement was made available from home. The Sunderlands of Nos. 228 and 230 (F/B) Squadrons on their Ionian Sea and Eastern Mediterranean reconnaissances could still carry on from Alexandria and Suda Bay, and the work of the Wellington Squadron operating against objectives in Italy, Sicily and North Africa could still be done, though on a reduced scale by Wellingtons " on passage ". Thus, No. 228 (F/B) Squadron returned to Alexandria and the Wellingtons of No. 148 (B) Squadron moved to Egypt, detachments being left behind to maintain such Sunderlands as occasionally used Malta, and the Wellingtons on passage to Egypt.

64. In spite of these reductions it was still found possible to operate " passage " Wellingtons occasionally from Malta. An especially successful attack was made on Catania aerodrome on the night of 15/16th January, when 35 German aircraft which had recently arrived were reported to have been destroyed on the ground by 9 Wellingtons.

The Glenn Martins of No. 431 G.R. Flight reconnoitred and photographed Sicilian and Italian Harbours and aerodromes as far North as Naples and Brindisi. They also searched the sea for enemy shipping between Malta, Tunis and Tripoli as well as the West Ionian Sea, supplementing the wider strategical reconnaissance of No. 228 Squadron.

During the period of our occupation of Cyrenaica, Tripoli had remained within range of Wellingtons and Blenheims operating from Benghazi area which reduced the calls on Malta in that direction. However, after the Italian-German counter-offensive in Cyrenaica, which led to our withdrawal to bases outside the range of Tripoli, it became essential to resume operations against that objective from Malta. A detachment of No. 148 Squadron (Wellingtons) was accordingly sent back to Malta during early April, and aircraft of this detachment made 34 night sorties against Tripoli between 13/14th and 24/25th April, dropping upwards of 50 tons of H.E. and incendiary bombs on harbour facilities and shipping with successful results. Fleet Air Arm Swordfish also made torpedo and bombing attacks on convoys off the Tunisian Coast and against shipping at Tripoli.

Towards the end of April Malta was reinforced from home by Blenheims of No. 21 (B) Squadron which made two very effective attacks on enemy shipping. On 1st May, 6 Blenheims of this Squadron bombed and obtained several direct hits on a destroyer and a merchant ship of 3,000 tons near the Kerkenna Islands off the Tunisian Coast. On the following day four Blenheims made another effective bombing attack on a convoy of Italian Naval and merchant ships South-west of Malta, obtaining direct hits on a destroyer and three merchant ships.

65. During the whole period under review the enemy continued to make persistent and heavy scale air attacks at frequent intervals on the Island. The enemy's main objectives appeared to be the Grand Harbour and naval dockyards, as well as the three aerodromes and flying boat anchorage. Especially severe fighting took place over the Island during the repeated dive-bombing attacks on the Grand Harbour and aerodromes on the 16th, 18th and 19th January, and on the Aircraft Carrier H.M.S. " Illustrious " and convoy ships which had arrived in the Harbour on 10th January. The first attacks were recklessly pressed home, and the enemy suffered heavy losses from our fighters and A.A. Batteries. It is reckoned that between the 10th and 19th January, 196

enemy aircraft were destroyed or damaged, including 44 destroyed in two raids by Wellingtons on the Catania aerodrome.

Another heavy attack, this time mostly by night, took place over a period between 28th April and 1st May when 9 enemy aircraft were destroyed and a " probable " 6, for a loss of 6 Hurricanes.

It is noteworthy that once the German Air Force was established in Sicily, Italian bombers scarcely again appeared over Malta. C.R.42's continued to act as escorts and to make a few low machine-gun attacks, but the Germans clearly preferred escorts of their own Me.109's or 110's for their dive-bombers.

To deal with these attacks the number of Hurricanes of No. 261 Squadron was gradually increased to 34 aircraft, partly by reinforcement from the Middle East and partly as a result of operations by Aircraft Carriers from the Western Mediterranean, in which Hurricanes were " flown off " to Malta. In addition, pilots were double-banked to cope with the increased raids and larger number of enemy aircraft taking part in them. This Squadron was in action almost every day and on many nights. Though losses of our own aircraft were serious, a fair proportion of pilots were saved.

66. At the end of the period under review, despite the enemy's persistent air effort, Malta could still be regarded as an effective air base for fighters for a limited offensive against enemy communications in the Mediterranean and as a " stage post " for the reinforcing aircraft en route for Egypt. The damage done to buildings and hangars made conditions of life and work uncomfortable and repair work was difficult.

In spite of these drawbacks, the fact that operations had been carried on throughout this testing period is a great tribute to the spirit and determination of the pilots, aircrews and ground personnel under the very able direction of Air Vice-Marshal F. H. M. Maynard, A.F.C. Amongst those under his Command who rendered valuable service during this period may be mentioned the Senior Air Staff Officer, Group Captain A. C. Sanderson, D.F.C.; Group Captain R. G. Gardner, D.S.C.; Wing Commander A. D. Messenger, the Senior Signals Officer; Squadron Leader P. S. Foss, No. 148 Squadron, and Flying Officer A. Warburton, D.F.C., of the Glenn Martin Reconnaissance Unit.

Palestine and Trans Jordan.

67. During the period covered by this Despatch there is little to record of the activities in this area. No further enemy raids took place on Haifa, or elsewhere. Aqir aerodrome was completed and opened early in the year. Gaza was developed and Lydda taken over as an R.A.F. Station. These aerodromes were prepared for and subsequently occupied by the Squadron personnel evacuated from Greece, for the purpose of re-forming and re-arming them.

Iraq.

68. The political situation described in my previous Despatch continued to deteriorate, particularly after the coup d'état by Raschid Ali and the subsequent removal of the Regent Emir Abdulla Ali. We were at this period more than fully occupied in Greece and the Western Desert, and the only aircraft available in Iraq were those of No. 4 F.T.S. at Habbaniya and the Vincents of No. 244 Squadron at Shaibah. Towards the middle of April it became obvious that air reinforcements would be necessary. The training aircraft of No. 4 F.T.S. had as far as possible been placed on an operational footing, but it was not until the 28th April that it was possible to spare some Wellingtons for Iraq. On that date 10 Wellingtons of No. 37 Squadron flew to Habbaniya and 10 Wellingtons of No. 70 Squadron to Shaibah, followed on the 1st May by a detachment of No. 203 Squadron (Blenheims).

By this time a landing of British troops at Basra had been effected and ships with additional troops were nearing Basra. It was at this moment, on the 30th April, that the Iraqis disclosed the result of their Axis intrigue by surrounding Habbaniya with a strong Iraqi force, including artillery.

Egypt.

69. At the beginning of January the Fighter defence of Egypt consisted of No. 252 Fighter Wing under Group Captain C. B. S. Spackman, D.F.C., who had most ably improvised an organisation which operated one Squadron at Amriya and a Sector Headquarters at Helwan, controlling the defensive patrols of the 2 R.E.A.F. Fighter Squadrons at Almaza and Suez respectively. Information was provided by No. 256 A.M.E.S. Wing.

During January, as a result of minelaying attacks on the Suez Canal, it was decided to build up an organisation, on the lines that had proved so successful in the U.K. Nos. 252 and 256 Wings were amalgamated as the controlling authority, the Sectors being at Amriya, Heliopolis, Fayid and Port Said. As an interim measure, a temporary Sector was formed at Ismailia to deal with the Suez Canal Zone.

In March I decided to re-form No. 202 Group, under Air Commodore T. W. Elmhirst, A.F.C., to co-ordinate all operational problems concerning the air defence of Egypt, and to co-operate with H.Q., B.T.E., on problems concerning A.A. artillery and searchlights.

Experience showed that communications in Egypt were so poor that it proved impossible to operate even 3 Sectors efficiently from one controlling authority, and accordingly the decision was taken to divide the Delta into two by a line from Baltim through Mansura, thence approximately South Eastwards to the Gulf of Suez, and to form two separate Wings each with its own filter room. No. 250 Wing formed at Ismailia to control the Sectors at Port Said and Fayid and be responsible for the defence of the Suez Canal Zone and Eastern portion of the Delta Area. No. 252 Wing was then made responsible for the control of the Sectors at Amriya and Heliopolis, and the defence of Alexandria, Cairo and the Western portion of the Delta.

70. During the actual period of this report the enemy's effort against Alexandria, Suez, Port Said and the Canal, was small in comparison to his activities elsewhere considering the many important and tempting targets open to him. There were, however, two or three effective raids on the Suez Canal which resulted in its being closed for periods up to a week or ten days on account of mines. Only one attack

was made on the Fleet Base at Alexandria, and it was not until later that attacks increased in intensity.

A Balloon Barrage was established at Alexandria under the very able control of Squadron Leader G. M. Trundle, who commanded No. 971 Squadron.

71. Mention must be made of the work of No. 267 Communication Squadron, ably commanded by Wing Commander S. F. Wynne-Eyton, D.S.O., and of No. 216 Bomber Transport Squadron. Their respective functions involved long and frequent flights to all parts of Middle East Command, stretching from Libya to Kenya and from Greece to Takoradi. Frequent use was also made of the services of the British Overseas Airways Corporation on their regular air routes. Their efficiency and reliability was of great assistance in meeting the very heavy demands for air transport.

Health and Morale.

72. The general health of the Command as a whole remained good during the period under review. This was especially noticeable during the advance in Libya and during the operations in Greece where climatic conditions were extremely hard. The morale of all ranks, especially flying crews, remained high throughout.

As recorded in my previous Despatch, credit is due to Air Commodore A. E. Panter, the Principal Medical Officer, and to his Deputy, Group Captain F. J. Murphy. Squadron Leader, The Rev. F. D. Morley, continued his active interest in the welfare of the airmen.

Administration.

73. The work of endeavouring to maintain the Squadrons throughout the Command with replacement aircraft, spare engines and equipment of all kinds, proved most difficult in the absence of regular supplies from home. Re-equipment with new aircraft of those Squadrons using obsolescent types was in most cases seriously delayed. In spite of these handicaps, everything possible was done by the Air Officer in charge of Administration, Air Vice-Marshal A. C. Maund, C.B.E., D.S.O., within the means at his disposal.

Air Commodore F. L. Fay, M.C., the Chief Engineer, continued most successfully to press on with the construction of the new aerodromes and landing grounds.

The ever-increasing financial problems were most ably handled by the Command Accountant, Group Captain T. H. Evans, O.B.E., and in connection with which Mr. C. W. Evans, my Financial Adviser, was of considerable assistance.

74. No praise can be too high for the work of the ground personnel, Officers and men alike, who, in their various capacities, maintained the aircraft, usually under the most trying conditions; whether in the winter snow or slush on the Greek-Albanian Front, or the sand and heat of Aden, Egypt and the Sudan, their devotion to duty, cheerfulness and faithful service remained the same. All maintenance units, repair and salvage organisations, worked to their utmost capacity to keep the Squadrons supplied.

Air Staff.

75. Air Marshal A. W. Tedder, C.B., whose arrival on the 9th December, 1940, I recorded in my previous Despatch, gave me most valuable support at all times as Deputy Air Officer Commanding-in-Chief.

Amongst others who continued to function most efficiently under extremely high pressure conditions were Air Vice-Marshal R. M. Drummond, D.S.O., O.B.E., M.C., the Senior Air Staff Officer; Air Commodore H. E. P. Wigglesworth, D.S.C., Plans; Group Captain N. S. Paynter, Senior Intelligence Officer; Wing Commander C. Bray, Senior R.A.F. Press Officer; Wing Commander T. A. B. Parselle, Air Communications; Squadron Leader Sir Arthur Curtis, K.C.V.O., C.M.G., M.C., my personal Staff Officer. Great credit is also due to Group Captain W. E. G. Mann, D.F.C., the Senior Signals Officer, and all his Staff, for the efficient signal organisation which met each new increase with complete efficiency.

76. In reviewing the part played by the R.A.F. in the Middle East during the period of my Command (May, 1940-May, 1941), the following is a summary of some interesting and prominent features worthy of being placed on record:—

(a) The unexpected survival of Malta as an operational air base. It started without fighters: after one year of war it had 50. It has continued to function as a link on the air reinforcing route to Egypt and as a base for bomber and reconnaissance Squadrons.

(b) The security of the Red Sea shipping route and its comparative immunity from Italian bombers or submarines; a tribute to the Aden and Port Sudan Squadrons and no compliment to the Regia Aeronautica.

(c) The part which the occupation of territory plays on the Mediterranean Littoral, as elsewhere, in adding to or reducing the potential scale of air attack on ships at sea and on our Naval, Army and Air Bases. Instance the Dodecanese (later of course, Greece and Crete), and particularly the North African Coast.

(d) In this respect, the advantage to the enemy of regaining Cyrenaica and the coastal strip of the territory between Tobruk and Sollum. In contrast, our difficulty in providing fighter defence to isolated Tobruk, and the disadvantage to our bombers and reconnaissance aircraft of the increased distance to enemy bases.

(e) The speed of advance by motorised or armoured forces after breaking resistance in breadth, and the importance of mobility of those R.A.F. Squadrons with short range aircraft which must operate at once from rapidly established forward landing grounds if they are to keep pace with, and continue, effective support of the advanced ground forces. Instance the advance into Cyrenaica, December to February, and also General Cunningham's rapid drive into Abyssinia through Italian Somaliland.

(f) The losses in grounded aircraft sustained during a rapid withdrawal through aerodromes being overrun; also the difficulty experienced by Squadrons in offering effective air resistance whilst the ground personnel are constantly on the move to the rear.

Instance the Italian withdrawal in Cyrenaica, and later our own experience in Greece. It was, however, less marked in the case of our withdrawal from Cyrenaica in April.

(g) Finally, the importance of taking into account the " time lag factor " when accepting Air commitments beyond the immediate capacity of the existing force. The interval, which must inevitably elapse with long lines of communication between the date when a decision is taken at home to despatch aircraft from the U.K., until the time they become operationally ready in the Middle East. Though this was considerably shortened by air deliveries in the case of long range aircraft, and also by Aircraft Carrier reinforcing operations, the spares and ground equipment to maintain these aircraft must still come by sea. The figures given at Appendix " C "* of this report show the state of weakness to which my force had been reduced after the campaigns in Greece, Libya, Eritrea and Italian Somaliland.

77. In concluding this Report, I must again pay tribute to the ready co-operation and support of the Naval C-in-C., Admiral Sir Andrew Cunningham, G.C.B., D.S.O., and of General Sir Archibald Wavell, G.C.B., C.M.G., M.C., with whom it was my privilege at all times to work in the closest accord.

To His Excellency the Ambassador, Sir Miles Lampson, G.C.M.G., C.B., M.V.O., once again my thanks and gratitude for his unfailing help and support in dealings with the Egyptian Government.

ARTHUR M. LONGMORE,
Air Chief Marshal.

1st November, 1941.

* Appendices not reproduced.

LONDON
PRINTED AND PUBLISHED BY HIS MAJESTY'S STATIONERY OFFICE
To be purchased directly from H.M. STATIONERY OFFICE at the following addresses:
York House, Kingsway, London, W.C.2; 13a Castle Street, Edinburgh 2;
39-41 King Street, Manchester 2; 1 St. Andrew's Crescent, Cardiff;
80 Chichester Street, Belfast;
or through any bookseller

1946

Price Sixpence net

S.O. Code No. 65-37729

Numb.

FINAL REVISE.

SECOND SUPPLEMENT
TO
The London Gazette
Of TUESDAY, the 17th of SEPTEMBER, 1946
Published by Authority

Registered as a newspaper

THURSDAY, 19 SEPTEMBER, 1946

The Air Ministry,
September, 1946

AIR OPERATIONS IN THE MIDDLE EAST FROM JANUARY 1ST, 1941, TO MAY 3RD, 1941.

The following despatch was submitted to the Secretary of State for Air on November 24th, 1941, by Air Chief Marshal SIR ARTHUR LONGMORE, G.C.B., D.S.O., Air Officer Commanding-in-Chief, Royal Air Force, Middle East.

1. This Despatch covers the period from 1st January, 1941, to 3rd May, 1941. On this latter date I was recalled to England and did not return to resume command of the R.A.F., Middle East.

The main features to be recorded during these four months can be summarised as follows:—

(a) The complete defeat of the Italian Air Force in Libya; the successful and rapid advance to Benghazi (6th February) and the subsequent temporary stabilisation in Cyrenaica as far West as El Ageila.

(b) The reduction of British Forces in Cyrenaica, both Army and Air, in order to meet fresh Greek Commitments due to development of the threat to Greece from German Forces which had crossed from Roumania into Bulgaria. The decision being made on the 22nd February to send British Land Forces to Greece.

(c) The subsequent German-Italian offensive in North Africa leading to the withdrawal of British Forces in Cyrenaica to the Frontier and to the isolation of Tobruk.

(d) The German invasion of Yugo-Slavia and Greece on 5th April, resulting in the capitulation of the Armies of both countries and the evacuation of British Forces to Crete and Egypt.

(e) Intensified attacks on Malta and Naval communications in that area by German aircraft based in Sicily.

(f) The successful offensives against Italian East Africa from Kenya and Sudan, including the re-occupation of Berbera.

Note: A separate report has been rendered on the R.A.F. operations in Crete from the 17th April to the 31st May, the control of which ceased to be my responsibility from the 3rd May. On that date the German Air Invasion of the Island had not yet developed.

The full report on Air Operations in East Africa from 10th February to 5th April, 1941, has been forwarded to Air Ministry, but a Summary of these operations is included in this Despatch.

2. The location of units in the Middle East Command on 1st January, 1941, is the same as that given in Despatch No. 1 for the 31st December, 1941, and is repeated at Appendix " A ".* Appendix " B " gives the location of units as at 30th April, 1941.

Libya.

3. In my previous Despatch I recorded in para. 28 that by 31st December, 1940, the whole territory East of the Italian-Egyptian frontier was in our hands. The Army had already advanced to positions surrounding Bardia and forward patrols had already penetrated towards Tobruk.

4. Air operations were continued in direct support of the Army, all types of aircraft contributing to this end during the advance, the role of squadrons being as follows:—

Heavy bombers attacked military objectives by night, such as Bardia and Tobruk, prior to the assault by our troops. At other times their objectives included Benghazi Port and aerodromes.

---
* Appendices not reproduced.

Medium bombers, immediately prior to attacks on Bardia, Tobruk and Derna, were employed in a similar role to the heavy bombers both by day and night and at other times attacked enemy aerodromes. No. 113 Squadron, and later No. 55 Squadron, continued to provide strategical reconnaissance.

The activities of our fighters were varied. They provided reconnaissance, made low flying attacks on mechanical transport on the enemy's lines of communication, in addition to providing air protection to our own troops against enemy air action.

Army Co-operation aircraft were employed mainly on tactical reconnaissance with Hurricanes or Gladiators. Lysanders were used to a limited extent for spotting artillery bombardments.

Early in January the Italian Air Force was still very active despite the heavy losses already inflicted on it.

5. As a prelude to the Army's assault, Bardia was subjected to a heavy Naval and Air bombardment. Thus, during the night 1st/2nd January, following many previous attacks, Wellingtons and Bombays, together with Fleet Air Arm Swordfish, dropped over 20,000 lbs. of bombs on enemy defences and troop positions. Blenheims continued to attack during the day on 2nd January making 44 bombing sorties, followed during the night of 2nd/3rd January by further efforts of Wellingtons and Bombays which dropped another 30,000 lbs. of bombs. The total load of bombs dropped during this series of attacks amounted to over 40 tons.

At the same time Blenheims bombed enemy aerodromes concentrating on Gazala, Derna and Tmimi. Hurricanes of Nos. 33, 73 and 274 Squadrons maintained offensive patrols over Bardia during the attack.

6. The Army attacked Bardia at dawn on 3rd January, the assault being made by armoured forces in co-operation with Australian infantry. During the battle, Blenheims effectively bombed troop concentrations while aircraft of No. 208 (A.C.) Squadron co-operated with artillery. Gladiators of No. 3 R.A.A.F. (Australian) Squadron maintained low flying offensive patrols to cover our troops as they advanced.

As soon as the attack had been launched a large proportion of our bombing effort was turned on to aerodromes in Cyrenaica, with the intention of pinning down and destroying the enemy air force.

Fighting at Bardia continued until 1330 hours on 5th January, when the enemy ceased to offer any further resistance.

7. By the 6th January our Armoured Forces, advancing under cover of offensive fighting patrols, had reached the outer perimeter defences of Tobruk. They also occupied El Adem aerodrome on that date, capturing 40 unserviceable aircraft which had been abandoned by the Italians on the landing ground there. A further 35 burnt out aircraft were found by armoured patrols at Gazala a few days later.

8. On 10th January, Headquarters No. 202 Group, together with the Western Desert Squadrons, started to move forward. By the middle of January, Headquarters, No. 202 Group was established at Sollum, and bomber and fighter squadrons had moved forward to landing grounds in the Sollum-Bardia area, with No. 208 Squadron and No. 3 R.A.A.F. Squadron further forward at Gambut.

9. Operations now passed through a stage of preparation and consolidation before the attack on Tobruk. During this period heavy bombing attacks were continued against Tobruk to wear down the enemy and destroy his defences. Enemy aerodromes were consistently and effectively bombed, particular targets at this time being Berka and Benina, near Benghazi, to which the enemy had been compelled to withdraw his bomber forces as a result of our continued attacks on his more forward aerodromes. Port facilities and shipping at Benghazi and military objectives at Derna were also attacked. It now became evident that the aircraft losses inflicted on the enemy, both on the ground and in the air, were resulting in reduced activity of his air force, and from that time onwards our own aircraft operated with comparative immunity.

10. As in the case of Bardia, the assault on Tobruk was preceded by a Naval bombardment and heavy bombing attacks from the air. On the night of 19th/20th and 20th/21st January, Wellingtons and Blenheims dropped 20 tons of bombs, inflicting heavy damage on the defences and other military objectives at Tobruk, including the A.A. guardship, "San Georgio". The assault on Tobruk was launched at dawn on 21st January and, simultaneously, Blenheims of Nos. 45, 55 and 113 Squadrons, operating in direct support of our troops, attacked enemy positions within the Tobruk defences, maintaining their attacks throughout the day, and making a total of 87 sorties. The Gladiators of No. 3 R.A.A.F. Squadron, and Hurricanes of Nos. 73 and 274 Squadrons maintained offensive patrols Westwards of Tobruk to cover ground operations, but very few enemy aircraft appeared and only one engagement took place.

Operations continued on 22nd January. Aircraft of No. 208 (A.C.) Squadron provided close support for our troops. Early in the morning the Australians entered the town, while the Free French companies penetrated the perimeter near the sea to the West. All organised resistance was at an end by the evening.

Between the fall of Tobruk and 1st February the following moves were made. Headquarters, No. 202 Group moved forward to Sidi Mahmoud; Nos. 73 (F) and 274 (F) Squadrons to Gazala and No. 3 R.A.A.F. (A.C.) Squadron and No. 208 (A.C.) Squadron to El Tmimi.

11. The main body of our forces now pushed on Northwards to Derna and our armoured formations Westwards to Mechili. Enemy air activity was on a small scale, but as the advance approached Italian base aerodromes a certain number of fighters continued to attack our forward troops. They were, however, successfully dealt with by our own fighter patrols which prevented the enemy from inflicting any serious casualties or from materially influencing the rapid progress of the advance. The intensity of our own air operations at this stage was also somewhat reduced, due partly to unserviceability through long flying hours under desert conditions, but also through our inability to establish forward landing grounds sufficiently rapidly to keep pace with the advance. The over ponderous standard squadron organisation did not lend itself to such conditions, and,

moreover, very few transport aircraft were available. However, the Blenheims and Wellingtons, not being so dependent on advanced landing grounds, were able to continue bombing enemy aerodromes.

12. Our armoured forces entered Mechili on 27th January, and on 30th January Derna fell to the forces which had advanced to the North. Like Bardia and Tobruk, Derna had already been regularly and heavily bombed for a considerable period and was not, therefore, subjected to concentrated bombing attacks immediately prior to the assault. Fighter patrols, however, provided constant cover for the troops and continued to harass the enemy on his lines of communication throughout the operations.

The advance continued and Cyrene was occupied on 3rd February. A rapid withdrawal of enemy forces now took place; M.T. and troop convoys retreating Westwards from Barce were repeatedly attacked by Blenheims and harassed by fighters.

13. The Australians now advanced on Benghazi from the North, while on 4th February our armoured forces started their remarkable dash across the desert from Mechili to the coastal road South of Benghazi. The interception, which completely surprised the enemy, took place at Beda Fomm, approximately 30 miles South of Solluch on 5th February. The enemy, supported by strong armoured car formations, tried to break through, but were repulsed with heavy losses and the greater part of their forces were captured or destroyed.

Meanwhile, as the Australians advanced on Benghazi, our medium and heavy bombers maintained their attacks on Berka and Benina aerodromes and on the railway at Barce which was being used by the enemy for the withdrawal of his forces from that area.

14. Our troops occupied Benghazi on 6th February, meeting little resistance in the final stages. The R.A.F. occupied Benina aerodrome on 10th February and found 87 unserviceable and damaged enemy aircraft there, which, together with those found at other aerodromes, notably El Adem and Gazala, were an indication of the effectiveness of the numerous bombing attacks made on enemy air force objectives and accounted very largely for the virtual collapse of the Italian Air Force during the latter stage of the advance.

15. Following the British occupation of Benghazi, the remnants of the enemy forces retreated Westwards into Tripolitania, while the Italian Air Force had been so depleted as to be incapable of offering any serious threat for the time being. Thus it appeared improbable at that time that the enemy would be able to stage an early counter-offensive in Libya. Meanwhile, the increasing gravity of the situation in Greece called for the early despatch of further air reinforcements to that theatre and the consequent reduction of the Royal Air Force in Cyrenaica.

16. The next phase, therefore, consisted of the reorganisation and redistribution of forces. H.Q. No. 202 Group, Nos. 45 and 113 (B) Squadrons, and No. 274 (F) Squadron were withdrawn to the Delta area in the middle of February. No. 208 (A.C.) Squadron was withdrawn at the end of February, but was replaced by No. 6 (A.C.) Squadron of which two flights were at that time already in Cyrenaica, the remainder of the Squadron being transferred to Aqir (Palestine).

H.Q., R.A.F., Cyrenaica was formed at Barce on 25th February, 1941, under the command of Group Captain L. O. Brown, D.S.C., A.F.C.

The Squadrons remaining in Cyrenaica in March, 1941, were disposed as follows:—

No. 3 Squadron R.A.A.F., which by that time was completely re-armed with Hurricanes, was located at Benina to provide the air defence of Benghazi.

No. 73 (F) Squadron, at first located at Gazala, was moved to Bu Amed on 14th March to defend the Tobruk area.

The Headquarters and one flight of No. 6 (A.C.) Squadron (Hurricanes and Lysanders) was at Barce, with a flight at Agedabia and sections at other landing grounds in Western Cyrenaica.

No. 55 (B) Squadron was at Bu Amed until 10th March, when it moved to Maraua.

17. Enemy air activity increased shortly after our occupation of Benghazi. It was at this time that *German* aircraft, operating from landing grounds near Tripoli began to attack our forces in Cyrenaica, at first using J.U.87's and Ju.88's. German fighters started to operate at a slightly later date from advanced landing grounds, Me.110's making their first appearance, followed shortly afterwards by Me.109's. Before the end of February the Germans had assumed a leading role in the enemy air effort.

The enemy's main bombing objective at first was Benghazi, which was attacked regularly and with some intensity between 14th and 20th February. Subsequent attacks, however, covered a wider range of objectives including Tobruk, our aerodromes in Cyrenaica and troops in the forward area at Agheila and Agedabia. It was in fact due to this somewhat unexpected increase of enemy air activity, coupled with the presence of German fighters, that No. 73 (F) Squadron was retained in Cyrenaica when it had previously been intended to withdraw it from that front to provide further reinforcement for Greece.

18. Reconnaissance of Tripoli harbour from the middle of February onwards revealed considerable quantities of shipping using the port, and it soon became evident that the enemy was being rapidly reinforced. In addition to sea borne reinforcements, the enemy carried considerable numbers of troops to Tripoli by air in Ju.52's. German troops were included in the reinforcements and early in March it was estimated that the greater part of a German division had already arrived in Tripolitania.

It was essential therefore to maintain attacks on shipping and harbour facilities at Tripoli to impede the flow of enemy reinforcements and supplies to Libya. Wellingtons of Nos. 38 and 70 (B) Squadrons, operating from landing grounds in Cyrenaica, accordingly bombed these objectives, making a total of forty sorties against Tripoli during February and March. Further attacks on Tripoli were made by F.A.A. Swordfish as well as Wellingtons operating from Malta. Considerable damage was inflicted during these operations but the total effort which could be made available was insufficient to cause any serious obstruction to the arrival of enemy reinforcements. Other

Wellington operations included attacks on aerodromes in Tripolitania and on shipping at Sirte which the Germans were developing as a forward base.

19. A brief appreciation of the air situation, dated the 6th March, was prepared for the information of the Foreign Secretary, Mr. Eden, who had arrived in Cairo in company with the C.I.G.S. on 19th February. A copy is attached—Appendix " D " (not reproduced).

It was at this time, particularly, that the weakness in number of modern aircraft at my disposal, chiefly Hurricanes and Blenheims, caused me the gravest concern. It had been anticipated that with the defeat of the Italian Air Force in Cyrenaica a quiet period on that front would justify considerable reduction in air strength. This proved to be far from the case, and it became apparent that air reinforcements would have to be sent to Cyrenaica immediately to prevent the enemy thrust from developing into a serious threat to Egypt.

We were already heavily committed in Greece and more help had been promised. Squadrons were awaiting new aircraft in replacement of wastage, yet the promised arrival in Egypt of large air reinforcements from home both via Malta and Takoradi, in spite of periodical emergency ferrying operations by Aircraft Carriers, did not materialise and it was not until the latter end of April that the situation in this respect began to improve. Moreover, though ships were arriving via the Red Sea at Suez quite regularly, there was no steady supply of cased aircraft by this route during the whole of January, February and March.

American Tomahawk fighters, which were beginning to come over from Takoradi, were at this time suffering from various " teething troubles " and were not yet ready for effective operation.

Not only was the Air Force at my disposal insufficient for the commitments which had arisen, but the rate of replacement, either actual or within reach, was not sufficient to keep pace with wastage. Whereas the losses from all causes from the 1st January, 1941 to 31st March, 1941 were 184, during the same period the actual arrivals in Egypt via Takoradi and Malta were 147 and 19 respectively, or a total of 166.

As will be seen later in this Despatch, during the whole of March and April this factor of waning resources had to be taken into account in deciding how to employ the Air Force at my disposal economically and to the best advantage.

20. Early in March, increasing numbers of enemy M.T. were observed by air reconnaissances to be moving eastwards along the coastal roads, and by the 10th March large enemy concentrations were located in the area immediately West of Agheila. Simultaneously the enemy established forward landing grounds at Tamet, Syrte and El Makina.

By the middle of March it was estimated that the German forces in Libya had been built up to two divisions, one of which was armoured. With this increase of strength in personnel and equipment, the enemy forces gradually assumed an offensive role. At the same time enemy aircraft reconnoitred our forward positions apparently with the object of ascertaining the strength of our forces.

On 19th March an enemy patrol occupied the landing ground at Marada, about 80 miles South of Agheila. This move was a forerunner of increased activity by strong enemy patrols which necessitated the withdrawal of our outposts from Agheila, the enemy occupying the fort there on 24th March. Italian infantry, supported by German armoured forces and dive-bombers, moved East of Agheila on 30th March, and on 31st March our forward troops were compelled to fall back on Agedabia. Blenheims of No. 55 Squadron bombed and machine-gunned enemy M.T. concentrations, while the landing ground at Misurata, from which enemy aircraft were operating in support of their advance, was successfully attacked by Wellingtons and Blenheims. The superior weight of the enemy enabled him to continue his advance, however, despite the opposition of our troops and aircraft.

21. On 2nd April, the enemy continued to advance in Cyrenaica, compelling our forward troops to withdraw from Agedabia. The situation in Benghazi thus became precarious, and orders for demolitions were issued. Preparations were made for the withdrawal of all R.A.F. Units from that area, and Benina was evacuated during the early evening of 2nd April, all demolitions having been completed.

Although handicapped by the frequent moves of the ground echelon necessitated by rapid withdrawal, squadrons continued to operate in direct support of the Army. Blenheims of No. 55 (B) Squadron, reinforced by No. 45 Squadron, provided reconnaissances, attacked concentrations of enemy M.T. and A.F.V's., and bombed forward enemy aerodromes. Hurricanes of No. 3 Australian Squadron and No. 73 (F) Squadron maintained constant patrols, covering our troops as they withdrew to new positions and making many effective attacks on enemy M.T. concentrations. Wellingtons also made night attacks on enemy M.T. in addition to maintaining their offensive against Tripoli whilst they were still within striking range of that objective. No. 6 (A.C.) Squadron continued to operate directly under the control of the Army and provided such tactical reconnaissances as were possible with their limited capacity and under conditions in which their ground echelons, like those of the other squadrons, were constantly on the move.

22. For the next few days complete details of the movement of our own and enemy troops remained somewhat obscure. At times it was difficult for Army Co-operation aircraft to keep track of the movements of the particular force with which they were working. For instance, on April 2nd, both the Flight of No. 6 (A.C.) Squadron and the H.Q. of No. 2 Armoured Division with which they were operating spent the night at Antelat, but on the morning of the 3rd April the Flight discovered that Div. H.Q. had left and no information was forthcoming as to their movements. The Flight subsequently moved to the landing ground at Msus where Free French troops were unable to give any information concerning our troops in the area, nor did they know where Div. H.Q. was situated. It was not until noon that a message was received from Second Div. H.Q. which gave their position at that time as 30 miles West of Msus. A tactical reconnaissance about this time, taken by an aircraft of this Flight from Msus, reported

enemy A.F.V's. and M.T. moving towards Msus. Whether this column was, in fact, an enemy one still remains uncertain, but according to the pilot the lorries were Italian and the personnel inside them opened fire on his aircraft.

23. On the 4th April, enemy armoured forces threatened to outflank the Australian Division holding the Benina-Tocra position, necessitating their withdrawal to new positions on the Barce escarpment.

In the meantime, as the Army withdrew to new positions, our Squadrons moved to landing grounds further East. On the 4th April, No. 3 Australian Squadron, No. 6 (A.C.) Squadron and Advanced H.Q., Cyrenaica, moved to Maraua, No. 55 Squadron to Derna and H.Q., Cyrenaica to Tobruk. On the same day 8 Blenheims of No. 45 Squadron reinforced No. 55 Squadron.

The Australian Division withdrew to the Barce escarpment on the 5th April, covered by Hurricane patrols of Nos. 3 and 73 Squadrons. The Hurricane patrols were also extended to cover elements of our troops retiring towards Mechili. In these operations, on 5th April our fighters destroyed 14 enemy aircraft for a loss of 2 Hurricanes.

By the 7th April the Australian Division and support group had withdrawn, first to Derna and then to Gazala area. Meanwhile, our armoured forces, which had already suffered heavy losses, had fallen back on Mechili and joined up with the Indian Motor Brigade. At this stage R.A.F. Squadrons had withdrawn to aerodromes in the Tobruk area, and further movements were necessary on the 8th April when the Blenheim Squadrons and No. 3 R.A.A.F. Squadron withdrew to landing grounds East of the Cyrenaica-Egyptian frontier, and the Wellingtons to their bases in the Fuka area. No. 6 (A.C.) and 73 (F) Squadrons continued to operate from landing grounds within the Tobruk perimeter.

The Australian Division withdrew to the outer perimeter of Tobruk on the 10th April. The following day enemy A.F.V's. cut the road between Tobruk and El Adem and our support group retired towards Sollum. From Mechili the enemy's forward troops continued their advance, and by the 13th April they had occupied Bardia and the Sollum escarpment where their advance was temporarily halted.

24. The situation by 13th April had become more stabilised and was as follows:—

The enemy's thrust in the forward area at Sollum had lost momentum and there were indications that his troops there were experiencing administrative difficulties as a result of their rapid advance.

Tobruk was held by a strong force of our troops and was invested by the enemy whose troops were concentrated West and South of the perimeter, with armoured forces astride the El Adem road.

H.Q. No. 204 Group, which formed at Maaten Bagush on the 12th April under the command of Air Commodore R. Collishaw, C.B., D.S.O., O.B.E., D.S.C., D.F.C., had taken over the control of the Squadrons in the Western Desert from H.Q. Cyrenaica.

The tasks of the R.A.F. at this stage were:—

(a) To continue to attack lines of communication to aggravate the enemy's existing M.T. difficulties.

(b) To provide close support for the Army by attacking enemy A.F.V's., M.T. concentrations and troops both in the forward areas and at Tobruk.

(c) To attack enemy aerodromes, primarily with the intention of destroying his transport aircraft which he was using to supply his forward troops.

(d) To bomb harbour facilities and shipping at Benghazi in order to interrupt the use of the port by the enemy and thereby prevent him from shortening his long lines of communication from Tripolitania.

(e) To provide the fighter defence of Tobruk.

25. Soon after the investment of Tobruk it became evident that it would no longer be possible to maintain No. 6 (A.C.) and No. 73 (F) Squadrons on the aerodrome within the perimeter. In addition to frequent dive bombing attacks, which were liable to destroy or damage the aircraft beyond repair capacity available, the landing ground was within range of enemy artillery fire. These Squadrons were accordingly withdrawn to aerodromes in the vicinity of Maaten Bagush, with advanced landing ground near Sidi Barrani for re-fuelling.

Owing to the distance of Tobruk from these aerodromes and even from the advanced landing ground at Sidi Barrani (120 miles from Tobruk), the task of maintaining fighter defence over Tobruk Harbour at such long range became extremely difficult. In addition, the depth of enemy penetration to the East put Tripoli out of range of our Wellingtons operating from the Western Desert, and made it most difficult to provide fighter escorts to our ships supplying the Tobruk garrison. On the other hand, it enabled the enemy to develop repeated bombing attacks on Tobruk without regular fighter interference, and it reduced the distance for his bombers operating against Alexandria or ships in the Eastern Mediterranean.

26. After a German-Italian attack on Tobruk on April 14th, during which No. 73 (F) Squadron shot down 9 E/A for loss of 2, there followed a period of comparative inactivity from a military standpoint. In the Sollum area, patrols of our mobile forces made raids well behind the enemy's forward troops. The enemy, however, continued to supply his forward areas by means of M.T. and transport aircraft, although harassed by the activity of our mobile patrols and the continued attacks of our aircraft on his lines of communication and forward aerodromes.

Enemy air activity at this stage was concentrated largely on Tobruk, apparently with the primary intention of denying the port to us. Hurricanes of No. 73 Squadron, providing the fighter defence of Tobruk, on several occasions engaged greatly superior numbers of the enemy with success, although not without loss to themselves. As an example, in a series of raids on Tobruk during 22nd and

23rd April in which the enemy employed a total of 100 bombers and about 150 fighters, Hurricanes destroyed 12 enemy aircraft and probably destroyed a further 2 with a loss to themselves of 3 Hurricanes.

The scale of our attack against enemy aerodromes was somewhat increased from about 20th April to the end of the period under review. More than 60 sorties by Wellingtons and Blenheims were made during this particular period, the main weight of this effort being directed against the enemy's forward aerodromes at Derna and Gazala, and the base aerodrome at Benina.

By this time our squadrons in the Western Desert had been further reinforced by detachments of No. 274 (F) Squadron—Hurricanes and No. 39 (B) Squadron—Marylands, the latter being employed mainly for strategical reconnaissances. No. 3 Squadron R.A.A.F. was withdrawn from the Western Desert on 21st April and moved to Aboukir for rest after continuous fighting since 7th November, 1940.

27. Towards the end of the period under review, military activity increased, both in the frontier area and at Tobruk. The enemy's forward troops on the Sollum escarpment after being heavily reinforced with A.F.V's. advanced Eastwards on the 27th April and occupied Halfaya Pass. This appeared to be his main objective for, after establishing a forward line beween Halfaya and Sidi Omar he made no attempt to continue his advance.

At Tobruk the enemy made a further determined attack on 1st May, employing 60 tanks supported by infantry and accompanied by heavy air attacks on our troops and defences. The enemy succeeded in breaking the outer defences of the perimeter but failed to pierce our main defences. Fighting continued for two days and on the 1st May, Hurricanes of Nos. 73 and 274 Squadrons maintained fighter patrols to protect our troops and artillery against enemy fighter and bomber action. The Hurricanes encountered enemy fighters, in greatly superior numbers but shot down 4 Me.109's in flames, with the loss of 1 Hurricane. Our troops successfully counter-attacked, destroying 11 enemy tanks and inflicting other heavy losses. The enemy however, retained a hold on 5,000 yards of the outer perimeter and our line was adjusted accordingly. A further attack by the enemy on the 2nd May was repulsed, after which the enemy effort there appeared to be temporarily spent.

28. A feature of the operations of this period was the high scale of effort maintained by a comparatively small air force working under the difficult conditions imposed by the enemy's rapid advance. From 1st April to 3rd May more than 400 bomber and fighter sorties were made against enemy M.T. convoys and concentrations, A.F.V's. and troops. Over 70 Wellington and 80 Blenheim sorties were made against enemy aerodromes and 64 Wellington and 12 Blenheim sorties were made against Benghazi. In addition, Hurricanes on several occasions machine-gunned aerodromes and in the course of numerous patrols destroyed 73 enemy aircraft in combat and probably destroyed a further 16, with a total loss of 22 Hurricanes.

It would be true to say that the German-Italian success in regaining Cyrenaica was due more to the number, efficiency and mobility of their ground forces than to their numerical air superiority. At no time did the German-Italian Air Forces completely dominate the situation on this front.

29. From January to Mid-February Air Commodore R. Collishaw, C.B., D.S.O., O.B.E., D.S.C., D.F.C., continued in command of No. 202 Group, R.A.F. in these successful operations which culminated in the occupation of Cyrenaica. He maintained the high standard of resource and initative which I had grown accustomed to expect from him, and he was an inspiration to all those under his command. At Appendix "H" will be seen a tribute to the work of his Group by Lieutenant-General O'Connor, Commander of the XIII Corps (not reproduced).

Group Captain L. O. Brown, D.S.C., A.F.C., continued to render most valuable service on the Staff of the G.O.C. in arranging the tasks of the reconnaissance Squadrons under the operational control of the Army. On February 25th he assumed command of the reduced Air Force in Cyrenaica and remained in command during the subsequent withdrawal, during which time he contrived to operate his small Force to the best advantage under most difficult conditions.

The work of No. 3 Royal Australian Air Force, under the command of Squadron Leader I. D. Maclachan, D.F.C., was outstanding. They were continuously in the Western Desert or Cyrenaica for six months, first with a mixture of Gladiators, Gauntlets and Lysanders and later with Hurricanes. Their high morale and adaptability to Desert conditions were remarkable.

Other Squadrons which particularly distinguished themselves on this front were No. 73—Hurricane—Fighter Squadron and No. 55—Blenheim—Bomber Squadron, which did most of the long distance strategical reconnaissance.

Mention must also be made of No. 2 R.A.F. Armoured Car Company which remained working with the Armoured Division throughout the successful phase of the operations, attached to the XI Hussars.

Greece.

30. The Greek advance had lost its impetus by the beginning of the year as the result of increased enemy resistance, lengthened lines of communication and severe winter conditions. The Greeks still retained the initiative, however, and after operations had apparently become static, they made a further advance, capturing Kelcyre on the 8th January, 1941, and thereafter making slow progress along the Northern side of the Kelcyre-Tepelene gorge. There was little activity in other sectors.

The R.A.F. Squadrons based in Greece, under the command of Air Vice-Marshal J. H. D'Albiac, D.S.O., on the 1st January, 1941, were:—

No. 30 (F) Squadron (Blenheim Fighters).
No. 80 (F) Squadron (Gladiators).
No. 84 (B) Squadron (Blenheims)
No. 211 (B) Squadron (Blenheims).

In addition, detachments of Wellingtons of Nos. 37 and 70 (B) Squadrons based in Egypt operated during moon periods from aerodromes in Greece.

The continued arrival of Italian reinforcements in Albania presaged an offensive, to counter which the Greeks would require the maximum air support that could be made available. Thus No. 112 (F) Squadron (Gladiators) was withdrawn from the Western Desert early in January, and No. 11 (B) Squadron (Blenheims) and No. 33 (F) Squadron (Hurricanes) were also withdrawn after the capture of Bardia and despatched to Greece, as follows:—

No. 11 (B) Squadron—24th January.
No. 112 (F) Squadron—10th February.
No. 33 (F) Squadron—19th February.

A situation calling for further reinforcements for Greece was created by the threatened German invasion through the Balkans. Accordingly, by the 31st March, No. 113 (B) Squadron (Blenheims) had also been despatched from Egypt to Greece and No. 208 (A.C.) Squadron (Hurricanes and Lysanders) was re-equipping and preparing to move at an early date.

31. Although the Greek Air Force operated with success in the early days of the war its activities were much reduced latterly by the inability of the Greeks to make good their aircraft casualties. Thus, practically the whole of the air effort in this theatre devolved upon the R.A.F. which was consequently called upon to attack strategical objectives, to operate in direct support of the Greek Army, necessary in order to maintain their high morale, and to provide the fighter defence of the Athens area. To meet these requirements Squadrons were employed in the following roles:—

Wellingtons operating by night attacked ports in Albania and to a less extent in S. Italy to interrupt the flow of enemy supplies and reinforcements to Albania.

The primary role of the Blenheims was to provide direct support for the Greek Army by attacking:—

(a) enemy lines of communication and important centres behind the forward area to prevent the distribution of supplies and reinforcements, and

(b) enemy positions in the forward area.

Blenheims also attacked ports in Albania by night and day and provided strategical reconnaissance of ports in Southern Italy and Albania.

Hurricanes and Gladiators were employed in escorting Blenheims during many of their daylight bombing attacks, in maintaining offensive patrols and in protecting the Greek troops against enemy air action.

Blenheim fighters continued to provide the air defence of the Port and Air Bases in the Athens area.

In addition to the commitments already referred to, Wellingtons and Blenheims operating from Greece were called upon to attack enemy aerodromes in the Dodecanese from which enemy aircraft were carrying out mine-laying operations in the Suez Canal, as well as air attacks on our convoys proceeding to Greece.

32. For the first two months of the year extremely unfavourable weather conditions persisted, preventing our aircraft from operating with any degree of intensity. Although both sides were similarly handicapped, it was more to our disadvantage in that, inter alia, it prevented our own aircraft from attacking ports in Albania and Southern Italy with sufficient intensity to do more than embarrass their use by the enemy. Thus, despite the damage inflicted and the nuisance value of our attacks, the Italians still continued to land reinforcements and supplies in Albania.

The bad weather prevailing at the time of the Greeks' capture of Kelcyre on the 8th January prevented our aircraft from operating in close support of their troops during their advance; in fact, until the middle of February operations were of necessity of a sporadic nature, the weather and state of aerodromes on occasions preventing our aircraft from operating for several days at a time. Subsequently, on the 10th January, as the Greeks continued to make slow progress towards Tepelene, Blenheims attacked enemy troops retiring from Kelcyre towards Berat. Otherwise support to the Greek forces at this time was confined to Blenheim attacks on the bases at Berat, West of the Central Sector and Elbasan, beyond the Northern Sector.

Towards the end of January the fighting round Tepelene increased in intensity as reinforcements reached the Italians, enabling them to stiffen their resistance against the Greek thrusts. During this period and up to the middle of February periodical attacks continued against Elbasan in the North, and Berat, Boulsar and Dukaj in the Tepelene area where military buildings and troop concentrations were bombed.

33. By the middle of February there were indications that the threatened Italian counter offensive would not be long delayed. With the Greeks retaining the initiative the ground operations had developed into a series of attacks by the Greeks followed by fierce Italian counter attacks, this activity being concentrated in the Tepelene area. A brief spell of improved weather conditions at this time enabled our aircraft to operate with greater freedom, 108 sorties being made between 11th and 18th February in support of the Greek forces which were making a strong effort at that time to capture Tepelene. In these operations, stores, M.T. convoys and enemy troop and gun positions in the Tepelene area were persistently and effectively attacked by bomber and fighter Blenheims.

Air activity reached a peak on 13th-14th February when, following a series of ineffective Italian counter-attacks, the Greeks launched a new offensive against enemy positions around Tepelene. Our aircraft made 50 sorties in direct and close support of the Greek troops as they advanced and captured important positions in the mountains to the North and South of Tepelene.

Following this short favourable spell, weather conditions again deteriorated after the middle of February, but although this curtailed operations to some extent our aircraft continued to provide support for the Greek Army which maintained its pressure on the enemy. Between 19th February and 4th March approximately 90 Blenheim sorties were made against enemy troop concentrations, gun emplacements and M.T. convoys in the Southern and Central Sectors in an endeavour to wear down the enemy resistance.

34. Owing to enemy fighter activity Blenheims taking part in these operations were on most occasions escorted by Gladiators or Hurricanes. Several combats with large enemy fighter formations took place, to the marked advantage of our own fighters. As an example, during a particular week of activity ending 3rd March, 33 Italian fighters were destroyed and a further 8 probably destroyed, against which our own fighter losses were only 1 Gladiator destroyed, the pilot being safe, and 2 other fighters damaged. Such successes were by no means limited to this period and further reference is made later to the activities of our fighters.

By the beginning of March the continued arrival of enemy reinforcements by sea and air had built up the strength of Italian forces in Albania to an estimated total of 29 divisions. The Greeks, however, retained the initiative, repeatedly repulsing counter-attacks and inflicting heavy losses on the enemy. On the 7th March, the Greeks, taking advantage of improving weather conditions, resumed their offensive against Tepelene, again assisted by our bombers which with fighter escorts continued their attacks against enemy troop positions and lines of communication. The Greeks made local progress.

35. The Italians launched their counter-offensive on the 9th March on a front of about 20 miles, extending from Tepelene in the Southern Sector to the Greek lines West of Corovode in the Central Sector. The enemy forces, which were estimated at about 10 divisions, supported by large numbers of bomber and fighter aircraft, made continuous attacks until the 14th March, but the Greeks, defending resolutely, repulsed all attacks and inflicted very heavy losses on the enemy. The Italians were unable to gain any ground and on the 14th March the Greeks made a successful counter-attack, taking some prisoners.

Throughout these operations, which continued at maximum intensity between the 9th and 14th March, Blenheims escorted by fighters made 43 sorties against enemy troops, gun positions and M.T. columns, concentrating largely on objectives in the Buzi-Gilave area. At the same time Hurricanes and Gladiators engaged on escort duties and offensive patrols made 15 and 122 sorties respectively. They fought several successful combats with enemy fighters during which they destroyed 35 enemy aircraft and probably another 9, with a total loss of 2 Gladiators and 1 Hurricane, the pilots of which escaped.

By the 15th March the Italian offensive was reduced in intensity, although the enemy continued to make local attacks without success until the 27th March. Air operations continued against enemy positions and lines of communication in all sectors although on a somewhat reduced scale as the result of a further deterioration of weather conditions.

36. During the period under review, Wellingtons made 4 sorties and Blenheims 30 sorties against shipping and port facilities at Valona. Against Durazzo Wellingtons made 11 sorties. This effort was augmented by F.A.A. Swordfish operating from Paramythia which made bomb and torpedo attacks against shipping at these objectives, comprising 7 sorties against Durazzo and 12 against Valona. A feature of these operations was the effectiveness of the F.A.A. Swordfish torpedo attacks in which five direct and two probable hits were claimed on shipping. Much damage was inflicted on port facilities, warehouses, military buildings and barracks by the Wellingtons and Blenheims. In Southern Italy, Brindisi was twice attacked by Wellingtons, the railway station being the objective on the first occasion and the aerodrome on the second. A further attack in the Brindisi area was made when fighter Blenheims successfully machine-gunned grounded aircraft at the aerodrome at Lecce (S. Italy).

37. One of the most outstanding features of the campaign in Albania was the marked superiority which our fighters gained over those of the Italians. In a series of combats during the first three months of the year (1941) our fighters destroyed 93 enemy aircraft and probably destroyed another 26, the greater proportion of the total being fighters. Against this our own fighter losses in combat amounted to 4 Hurricanes and 4 Gladiators destroyed, from which 6 of the pilots escaped by parachute.

Enemy aircraft operating from aerodromes in the Dodecanese periodically mined the Suez Canal and also attacked our sea convoys sailing to Greece. It became necessary, therefore, to divert a portion of the available bomber forces in Greece to attack aerodromes in the Dodecanese, with harbours and shipping as an alternative.

The main objectives were the aerodromes at Rhodes, viz. Maritza, Cattavia and Calato, against which 20 Wellington sorties and 25 by Blenheims were made from Greece. Blenheims also made a further 9 sorties against the aerodrome at Scarpanto and shipping at Stampalia. Many fires were started at the aerodromes, and damage was caused to aerodrome buildings and dispersed aircraft. Direct hits were also obtained on one ship at Stampalia.

Other attacks on the Dodecanese were made by Wellingtons operating from Egypt, the total effort from Greece and Egypt combined during the period under review amounting to 70 Wellington sorties and 34 Blenheim sorties.

38. A further operation of note was the combined Naval and R.A.F. action against enemy Naval forces at the Battle of Matapan on 28th March.

Acting on Sunderland reconnaissance reports, Blenheims operating from Greece made five attacks comprising 24 sorties against enemy warships, reporting direct hits with S.A.P. bombs on two cruisers and one destroyer. One cruiser which was hit with a 500 lb. S.A.P. bomb was apparently seriously damaged. At Appendix "J" is a copy of a Signal conveying appreciation by the Board of Admiralty on the part played by the R.A.F. in this action (not reproduced).

39. Towards the middle of February it had become clear that the German infiltration into Roumania was likely to develop into a "drive" through Bulgaria, with Salonika as the preliminary objective. The Greek Government recognised this as a very real threat, but they were anxious to avoid any action originating from their territory which might precipitate events. Though they were continually calling for more air support, they did not accept the offer of British Troops until 22nd February when at a Conference held at Tatoi, attended by the King of Greece, Prime Minister Korysis (who had succeeded the late General Metaxas),

Mr. Eden (Foreign Secretary), General Sir John Dill (C.I.G.S.), General Sir Archibald Wavell (C.-in-C. M.E.), Captain Dick, R.N. (representing C.-in-C. Mediterranean) and myself, the decision was taken to despatch British Troops at the earliest opportunity to form on the Aliakmon line to the West of Salonika.

It followed, of course, that an increased air commitment would be involved both in support of the British Army on this new front and also for air protection of the ships transporting men to Greece. Nevertheless, since the Greeks had decided to oppose a German invasion of Macedonia there was clearly no alternative to giving them the maximum assistance possible. Moreover, though German air and land forces had arrived in Tripoli these might well have been to prevent our further advance, and there was no reason on that particular date to suspect the imminent preparation of a counter-offensive in Libya. It is true, however, that such a threat developed almost immediately after the Greek commitment had been accepted.

40. The landing of British Troops in the Athens area during March proceeded with little or no interference from the air; German infiltration into Bulgaria continued but their air activity was limited to occasional reconnaissances over Macedonia. By the 1st April it was evident that the German invasion of Greece through the Balkans was imminent. Consequently, with the prospect of fighting the war on two fronts, two air formations were created, viz. Eastern Wing and Western Wing. H.Q. Eastern Wing was at Tsaritsani, in close touch with G.H.Q. British Forces and controlled Nos. 11 and 113 (B) Squadrons (Blenheims), No. 33 (F) Squadron (Hurricanes) and No. 208 (A.C.) Squadron (Hurricanes and Lysanders). The role of this force was to provide direct support for the British and Greek Armies against the prospective German attack from the North. H.Q. Western Wing was at Yannina and controlled No. 112 (F) Squadron (Gladiators) and No. 211 (B) Squadron (Blenheims), the role of this formation being to support the Greeks on the Albanian Front. The remainder of the squadrons in Greece, viz. No. 30 (F/B) Squadron (Blenheim Fighters), No. 80 (F) Squadron (Hurricanes and Gladiators) and No. 84 (B) Squadron (Blenheims), together with detachments of Nos. 37 and 38 (B) Squadrons (Wellingtons), were at aerodromes in the Athens area directly under the control of H.Q., B.A.F., Greece. No. 815 Squadron Fleet Air Arm was based on Paramythia and No. 805 Squadron Fleet Air Arm on Maleme (Crete).

41. Germany declared war on Greece and Yugo-Slavia on the 5th April, 1941, and launched her attack at dawn the following day, crossing the Greek frontier into Macedonia by four routes, with the main thrust along the Struma Valley. Simultaneously they advanced Westwards into Yugo-Slavia along the Strumica Valley in the South, from Dragoman to Nis in the North, and by other intermediate routes. The Greeks resisted strongly at Rupel, temporarily checking the German advance through the Struma Valley, but despite this opposition the Germans succeeded in penetrating Thrace and Macedonia and occupied Salonika on the 8th April.

Throughout the German advance the primary task of our Squadrons was to attack his A.F.V.'s, M.T. columns, troops and lines of communication on the Macedonian and Yugo-Slavian Frontiers. Practically the whole of our air effort was directed to this end, Wellingtons making night attacks, Blenheims operating both by night and day, with fighters constantly in support maintaining offensive patrols, making low flying machine-gun attacks on the enemy, and escorting our bombers by day. The first encounter with the German air force on this front took place on 6th April. A patrol of 12 of No. 33 Squadron Hurricanes engaged 30 Me.109's and shot down 5 of them without loss to themselves. During the night of 6th/7th April, 6 Wellingtons of No. 37 Squadron successfully bombed the railway station and marshalling yards at Sofia. From 7th to 9th April, as the Germans advanced in strength, Blenheims of Nos. 11, 84 and 113 Squadrons made heavy and effective attacks on large columns of their M.T., A.F.V's. and troops near Petrich in Bulgaria, on the Strumica-Lake Doiran Road in Yugo-Slavia and at Axiopolis and Polykastron in Macedonia.

42. By this time the German armoured forces, supported by dive-bombers, advancing Westwards from Bitolj, had overwhelmed the Yugo-Slav Army and had succeeded in joining up with the Italians in Albania. They then advanced Southward from Bitolj to Florina, threatening to isolate the Greeks in Albania from our own forces further East. The Greeks were thus compelled to withdraw from the Northern front of Albania, while our Armoured Brigade and an Australian Infantry Brigade were moved Westwards to close the Florina Gap, where they were joined by a Greek cavalry division from the Koritza area. On 10th April, as the enemy continued his Westward thrust into Yugo-Slavia, Blenheims attacked enemy M.T. columns and A.F.V's. on the Prilep-Bitolj road inflicting heavy damage on them. During the night of 11th/12th April, Wellingtons followed up this effort with further attacks on the enemy at Prilep and Kilkis.

Meanwhile, our forces holding the Florina Gap had been hotly attacked by the Germans on 9th April and compelled, after a strong resistance, to withdraw on 11th April. By the evening of 12th April, our front had been formed roughly on a line extending from the coast near Mount Olympus, along the Aliakmon River to Servia, thence N.W. towards the Albanian lakes. Continued bombing and machine-gun attacks by Blenheims and Hurricanes contributed to the delay of the enemy's advance during the critical periods in which our troops were falling back on new positions. These operations were inevitably accompanied by considerable losses and in one raid on the 13th April, for example, a complete formation of 6 Blenheims of No. 211 Squadron was destroyed by Me.109's. Wellingtons continued to attack more distant objectives. On the night of 13th/14th April a force of 10 Wellingtons from Nos. 37 and 38 Squadrons made a further effective attack on the railway goods yard at Sofia, destroying a large number of trucks containing explosives. At the same time other Wellingtons bombed and machine-gunned M.T. convoys at Yannitsa and Gorna Djumaya. In operations on the following night Wellingtons destroyed the bridge over the Vardar River at Veles and Blenheims dropped bombs on enemy columns on the road from Ptolomais to Kozani. Our aircraft continued to attack similar objectives during the night of 15th-16th April and throughout the following day, to impede the enemy's advance on Katerini and Kozani.

43. Meanwhile the Army had stubbornly held the Mount Olympus-Aliakmon Line until 14th April when it was turned by the Germans forcing the Kleisoura Pass. Our forces started to fall back on the Thermopylae Position on 15th April, completing the withdrawal by the 20th April. This new situation necessitated the withdrawal of all R.A.F. Squadrons to the Athens Area on 16th April and from that date onwards they were controlled directly by H.Q., B.A.F., Greece. Eastern and Western Wings were consequently disbanded.

Continuous enemy attacks on our aerodromes, coupled with losses from enemy fighter action, had by this time considerably reduced the effective striking power of our Squadrons. In a series of attacks on one day alone, the enemy destroyed 10 Blenheims on the ground at Niamata and damaged several other aircraft which had to be subsequently destroyed and abandoned. Several such attacks were made, during which many aircraft were destroyed or rendered unserviceable, but owing to the loss in several instances of unit records during the ultimate evacuation, full details of enemy raids are not available. Towards the end the repeated enemy attacks on our aerodromes in the Athens Area caused further heavy losses, and as a final blow a force of Hurricanes retained at Argos to cover the evacuation was almost wiped out when 13 of them were destroyed on the ground during intensive enemy air attacks on 23rd April.

In turn our aircraft attacked the German occupied aerodromes on the Salonika and Larissa Plains in an endeavour to reduce the scale of the enemy's air effort. Thus between 15th and 22nd April Blenheims made effective night attacks on the aerodromes at Sedes, Katerina, Kozani and Larissa, starting several large fires. The effort could not, however, be maintained on a sufficiently heavy scale to cause any material reduction of the enemy's air effort, bearing in mind the comparatively large numbers of aircraft and reserves available to him.

Nevertheless, our Squadrons continued to operate until, in the end, the use of aerodromes was virtually denied to them by constant enemy air attacks. In the concluding stages Blenheims attacked enemy columns advancing on the Larissa Plain, concentrating on road bridges between Kozani, Grevena and Kalabaka to impede the enemy's progress. One particularly successful attack was made when Blenheims bombed a large M.T. convoy concentrated in front of a broken bridge across the Aliakmon River a few miles from Kalabaka. Similarly our fighters continued to engage formidable enemy formations with success. Throughout the campaign they had gained many victories against the numerically superior enemy, but at no time was their skill and high morale more in evidence than in the concluding stages. In a number of combats during the period of intensive enemy air activity on 19th and 20th April, Hurricanes of Nos. 33 and 80 Squadrons destroyed a total of 29 German aircraft and probably destroyed another 15. In addition, Fighter Blenheims of No. 30 Squadron probably destroyed 2 Italian bombers. These successes were achieved with a loss of 7 Hurricanes brought down and 2 damaged, a truly remarkable record in view of the increasing disparity of strength between the R.A.F. and the German Air Force.

44. At the beginning of these operations the combined strength of the German and Italian Air Forces amounted to approximately 1,100 aircraft, of which over 40 per cent. were fighters, a little less than 40 per cent. bombers and dive-bombers, and the remainder reconnaissance aircraft. The total strength of the R.A.F. in Greece with reserves was approximately 200 aircraft, of which about half were bombers. Although outnumbered, our Squadrons operated with success in the initial stages of the German advance. It is probable that unfavourable weather and the lack of forward all-weather aerodromes at that stage prevented the enemy from making the best use of his superior numbers. As the enemy advanced, however, he was able to establish forward aerodromes, at first in the Salonika Area and subsequently on the Larissa Plain, from which he was able to exploit his numerical superiority to the fullest advantage. He was thus able to concentrate an overwhelming force which took an increasing toll of our aircraft both on the ground and in the air. These casualties could not be replaced at that time from the slender reserves available in the Middle East, particularly in view of the dangerous situation which had arisen in the Western Desert. The odds which our Squadrons had to face, therefore, increased disproportionately until the Germans had gained virtual air superiority. With that achieved they were able to concentrate the main weight of their attack against our troops, lines of communication, and ports. By 20th April our much-depleted Squadrons were concentrated at the few remaining aerodromes in the Athens Area, where, as already described, they were exposed to continuous air attack. With the complete collapse of the Greek resistance it became evident that even the shortened Thermopylae front could not be held against the superior weight of the enemy and the decision was made to withdraw all British Forces to the coast and embark them for Crete or Egypt.

45. The scheme for the evacuation of R.A.F. personnel aimed at the removal of air crews and certain key personnel by air in Squadron and transport aircraft and flying boats. The remainder were to be evacuated by sea with other British and Imperial Forces. Wellingtons of Nos. 37 and 38 Squadrons had already flown to Egypt on the 17th and 18th April, the personnel and equipment following by sea on 23rd April. In addition, 14 Blenheim Fighters of No. 30 Squadron flew to Crete on 18th April to provide convoy protection during the projected sea evacuation. The remaining aircraft of Nos. 11, 84, 113 and 211 (B) Squadrons and 208 (A.C.) Squadron, amounting to 24 Blenheims and 4 Lysanders, flew to Egypt on 22nd and 23rd April, the Blenheims having previously made several journeys between Greece and Crete evacuating air crews.

The enemy air attack on Argos on 23rd April, already referred to, had reduced the remaining strength of Nos. 33 and 80 Squadron

Hurricanes to 6. These and 14 Gladiators of Nos. 80 and 112 Squadrons were flown to Crete on 23rd April to defend Suda Bay against enemy air attack and to take part with No. 30 Squadron in providing cover for sea convoys engaged in the evacuation. Sunderlands started to evacuate R.A.F. personnel on 19th April, when they flew a 30 Squadron party to Crete. The previous day they had also carried King Peter of Yugoslavia and other important political personages to Egypt, having taken them off from Kotor (Yugoslavia) on 17th April. Sunderlands continued the evacuation of essential personnel in stages from Greece to Crete, thence to Egypt. The King of Greece and members of the Greek Royal Family were included among other important passengers flown to Crete in Sunderlands on 22nd and 23rd April.

46. On 23rd April the Sunderlands were reinforced by two B.O.A.C. Flying Boats which operated between Crete and Egypt and rendered valuable service. These efforts were further augmented on the same day by Bombays of No. 216 Squadron which took two parties from Eleusis to Bagush, and the following day by Lodestars of No. 267 Squadron which carried three parties from Argos to Bagush. Enemy air attacks rendered Eleusis and Menidi aerodromes unusable after 23rd April, and Argos was similarly out of action from 24th April. The Bombays and Lodestars thereafter continued to carry personnel from Crete to Egypt. The last Sunderland loads to leave Scaramanga were taken off on 24th April and included Lieutenant-General Sir T. Blamey, C.B., C.M.G., D.S.O., and Air Vice-Marshal J. H. D'Albiac, D.S.O., and their respective staffs.

On 24th April 1,700 R.A.F. personnel were at Argos awaiting evacuation by sea but by the next day the majority of these had moved to Kalamata and Gytheon, three Sunderland loads being taken off from the former, and one from the latter and flown to Crete. Subsequently all personnel remaining there were evacuated by sea, many of them crossing in small boats to Kythera whence they were later taken off in destroyers. Further Sunderland evacuations from Greece, were made from Nauplia (Morea), transporting Prince Paul of Greece, the Greek Prime Minister and other important passengers including General Sir Maitland Wilson and Generals Mackay and Rankin.

Meanwhile flying boats of Nos. 228 and 230 Squadrons and landplanes continued the evacuation from Crete to Egypt, the last flight being made by a Sunderland on 2nd May. The total number of personnel evacuated by air from Greece to Crete was over 600, and from Crete and Greece to Egypt 870. Two Sunderlands were lost in these operations, one of which crashed while alighting by night at Kalamata, and the other was destroyed by enemy air action at Scaramanga.

47. The main evacuation from Greece of British and Imperial Forces was effected between 24th and 30th April in convoys of H.M. Ships and other vessels. All available aircraft operated in support to protect the convoys against the heavy enemy air attacks to which they were constantly subjected, and which were causing heavy losses. The forces available in Crete were 14 fighter Blenheims of No. 30 Squadron, 9 fighter Blenheims of No. 203 Squadron (recently sent to Crete from Egypt to take part in this operation) and the remaining 6 Hurricanes and 14 Gladiators of Nos. 33, 80 and 112 Squadrons. At this stage, however, only 6 of the 14 Gladiators were serviceable.

Blenheims usually operating in patrols of six aircraft provided such cover for convoys as was possible in the vicinity of the mainland of Greece, while Hurricanes and Gladiators provided patrols over convoys approaching Crete and during their disembarkation at Suda Bay. At the same time, Sunderlands provided Ionian and Mediterranean reconnaissances to guard against possible raids on our convoys by units of the Italian Navy.

During the six months' campaign in Greece our Squadrons contended throughout with numerically superior enemy air forces, emerging in the end with much credit although sadly depleted in strength. Our total aircraft losses amounted to 209, of which 82 had to be destroyed and abandoned by our own forces during the withdrawal and subsequent evacuation. Many of the latter had been damaged during enemy attacks on our aerodromes and in normal circumstances might have been repaired. Our total losses of aircraft, missing and in combat with the enemy were 72.

As a comparison, the losses inflicted on the enemy totalled 259 aircraft destroyed and 99 probably destroyed, with several others damaged. Of these, 231 were destroyed and 94 probably destroyed in combat with our aircraft.

Our personnel losses in Greece amounted to 148 killed and missing and 15 taken prisoner. Of the total, 130 were aircrews. Such losses cannot be considered unduly heavy, bearing in mind the difficulties of the campaign and the hazards of the subsequent evacuation.

48. I cannot speak too highly of the work of Air Vice-Marshal J. H. D'Albiac, D.S.O., who commanded the British Air Force in Greece during the whole six months' campaign. His initiative, his personality and tact in dealings with the Greek High Command, enabled him, right up to the end, to obtain the maximum results in support of the Greeks from the small force at his disposal.

Of those under his Command, the most outstanding for their valuable services were:—

Group Captain A. H. Willets, Senior Air Staff Officer during the whole period.

Wing Commander P. B. Coote, who commanded the Western Wing (The Albanian Front) and himself took part in many of the fighter patrols and bombing raids of his Squadrons, from the last of which he is missing.

Wing Commander J. R. Gordon-Finlayson, D.S.O., D.F.C., commanding No. 211 Squadron, and later the Eastern Wing. A fine leader and an inspiration to his Squadron, with which he had completed over one hundred raids.

Squadron Leader E. G. Jones, D.F.C., commanding No. 80 (F) Squadron; his leadership maintained the high morale and efficiency of this Squadron whose six months' record in Greece, mostly in Gladiators, was quite remarkable.

Wing Commander Lord Forbes, Intelligence Officer on the Staff, who carried out many special missions in his Q.6 aeroplane, some of which were of an unusual and hazardous nature.

Italian East African Campaign.

49. The successful land operations against I.E.A., which resulted in the complete collapse of Italian resistance in that area except for a small " pocket " in the region of Gondar, were supported by Air forces from Sudan, Aden and Kenya. In deciding on the actual strength of the Air force required to give full support to the Land forces operating from the North and South, it was necessary to take into account the fact that:—

(i) It was still possible for the Italians, and Germans if they so decided, to send reinforcements of aircraft direct by air from Tripoli to I.E.A.

(ii) To meet the commitments in Libya and Greece the release of Air and Mechanised forces from this front was important. There was, therefore, need for speed if the campaign was to be completely successful before the rains started in April.

(iii) The majority of our aircraft were of obsolete or obsolescent type which needed the cover of a few modern fighters to enable them to operate by day in face of the Italian C.R.42 fighters which were still active until towards the close of the campaign.

(iv) Patriot activities required constant air support to maintain enthusiasm and morale.

(v) The Red Sea shipping route still remained potentially a very vulnerable line of communication. Its security was the more important since traffic through the Mediterranean had virtually ceased.

50. In the Sudan, at the beginning of the year the R.A.F. under Air Commodore L. H. Slatter, O.B.E., D.S.C., D.F.C., consisted of five Squadrons and one Flight. No. 1 South African Air Force (F) Squadron—Hurricanes and Gladiators, No. 237 Rhodesian (A.C.) Squadron—Hardys, No. 47 (B) Squadron—Wellesleys, No. 223 (B) Squadron—Wellesleys, and No. 14 (B) Squadron—Blenheim IV's. In addition, " K " Flight's (Gladiators) move to Egypt was cancelled pro tem. and they were retained in the Sudan. These Squadrons were mainly used during the whole period to defeat the Italian Air Force and to support the advance of the Army into Eritrea. Other commitments which were met included the Air defence of Port Sudan, occasional special convoy escort work in the Red Sea, attacks on the harbour of Massawa and support of the increasing activities of the Abyssinian Patriots further South, Haile Selassie having entered Abyssinia on the 20th January, 1941.

51. Pressure by General Platt's force on the Kassala area resulted in the fall of the town on January 19th and the retreat of the Italian Forces into Eritrea. Steady progress by two parallel columns continued, Agordat and Barentu falling on the 1st and 2nd February. Early in March the advance was halted in front of the formidable defences on the Keren heights. Here the Italians made a determined stand until March 27, when they were forced to withdraw Southward.

In these operations at Keren the R.A.F. played a prominent part in the close support of the Army. Wellesleys, Vincents, Lysanders, Gauntlets and Hardys were employed for continuous bombing of targets both in and behind the enemy's battle positions. Without doubt this heavy and continuous bombing, combined with the effect of artillery fire, seriously weakened Italian morale and contributed very largely to the capture of this formidable position.

Meanwhile, the offensive against enemy aerodromes, lines of communication and aircraft in the air was continued by Blenheims, Hurricanes and Gladiators. Enemy fighters, whose appearance became less frequent as time went on, continued to " shoot up " our aircraft on the ground, occasionally with success, but their air effort gradually dwindled until by the time Asmara was occupied on March 31st it had virtually ceased.

The Hurricanes of No. 1 South African Squadron were especially prominent in these operations. In two attacks on enemy aerodromes they destroyed 6 C.A.133's, 4 C.R.42's and 6 S.79's, besides damaging a further 3 S.79's.

During the attack on Keren a particularly successful bombing attack on lines of communication resulted in the destruction of an ammunition train reported to be carrying over 20,000 shells.

52. Further South bombing attacks were made in support of the Patriots to help in sustaining their morale; Gubba, Gondar, Asosa, Burye and Debra Marcos being among the places attacked. Blenheims of the Free French Flight took part in these operations. Pilot Officer R. A. Collis, D.F.C., of No. 47 (B) Squadron (Wellesleys), made a series of 19 flights, up to a distance of 200 miles into Abyssinia, carrying at various times ammunition, money and supplies for the Patriot forces, and on other occasions representatives of the Emperor and Army Officers.

North of Lake Tana the Italians contrived to maintain themselves in the Gondar area, but South of the Lake the Patriots succeeded in capturing Burye and Debra Marcos and in reaching the Blue Nile.

53. After the occupation of Asmara on the 1st April, the advance continued on Massawa. As our threat to that objective developed, five Italian destroyers based at Massawa left harbour in a Northerly direction on 2nd April. This force was located and attacked on 3rd April by Swordfish of the F.A.A. (H.M.S. Eagle) by No. 14 Squadron (Blenheims) and No. 223 Squadron (Wellesleys). The Swordfish torpedoed two of the destroyers, sinking one of them and leaving the second in a sinking condition, the latter being subsequently bombed and sunk by a Blenheim. A further two destroyers were driven aground on the Hedjaz Coast twelve miles South of Jedda, where they were bombed and destroyed by Blenheims and Wellesleys operating in conjunction with H.M.S. Kingston. The surviving destroyer escaped and returned to Massawa, where she scuttled herself.

Our troops occupied Massawa on 8th April. The capture of this Port, combined with the destruction of the enemy naval forces, greatly reduced the potential threat to our Red Sea communications.

The successful progress of the campaign, coupled with the almost complete destruction of the enemy air force on all fronts of Italian East Africa, now enabled the greater part of the Squadrons previously contained in the Sudan to be released to other theatres. Thus, during the early part of April the remaining forces operating there were reduced to No. 47 (B) Squadron (Wellesleys), No. 237 (B) Squadron (Hardys, Lysanders and Gladiators) and the Free French Flight (Blenheims). Other units, consisting of No. 1 Squadron, S.A.A.F., No. 14 Squadron, No. 223 Squadron, " K " Flight and No. 1430 Flight were moved with what aircraft remained to them to Egypt where they arrived about the middle of April. Nos. 14 and 223 Squadrons took part in the action against enemy naval forces described below before their departure.

54. In the subsequent advance from Asmara towards Dessie the greater part of the offensive effort against objectives in the Dessie area was made by aircraft from Aden and East Africa. These operations are referred to later. Wellesleys of No. 47 Squadron and Gladiators, Lysanders and Hardys of No. 237 Squadron nevertheless made attacks on a light scale on objectives in the vicinity of Amba Alagi where our advance from the North was held up. Bombing and machine-gun attacks were made on enemy troops and M.T. at Mai Ceu, Alomata and Amba Alagi and on the aerodromes at Alomata, Cercer and Sifani. The scale of attack in this area was considerably increased after 27th April when our column from the South captured Dessie, Nos. 47 and 237 Squadrons making over 80 bomber and fighter sorties on enemy positions around Amba Alagi between 28th April and 3rd May to break down the remaining resistance. The enemy was still holding out, however, at the end of the period under review, although the forces there, under the Duke D'Aosta, subsequently capitulated on 16th May.

Operations at Gondar and in the Lake Tana area were continued throughout this period, 27 medium bomber sorties being made by Free French Flight Blenheims and Wellesleys of No. 47 Squadron, the former providing more than half the total effort. The main weight of this attack was against enemy positions and M.T. at Gondar, while other attacks were made on similar objectives at Bahr Dar South of Lake Tana, at Chelga, Gorgora and on the Gondar-Adowa Road.

It appeared likely at the end of this period that, with our troops held up in the Volchit Pass, Gondar would be the last serious military objective in Italian East Africa.

55. Great credit is due to the A.O.C., Air Commodore L. H. Slatter, O.B.E., D.S.C., D.F.C., for his most efficient handling of the R.A.F. and for his excellent team-work with the Army. No praise can be too high for the pilots and aircrews for their accomplishments. Many were flying in obsolescent single engine aircraft. The country was difficult, and much of the flying had to be done at low heights over hostile positions. Great devotion to duty and a high standard of skill were needed to achieve success under these exacting conditions.

56. In Kenya, under the command of Air Commodore W. Sowrey, D.F.C., A.F.C., the Air Force consisted of six South African Squadrons and one Flight of Glenn Martins, No. 2 (F) Squadron—Furies and Gauntlets, No. 3 (F) Squadron—Hurricanes, No. 11 (B) Squadron—Battles, No. 12 (B) Squadron—J.U.86's, Nos. 40 and 41 (A.C.) Squadron—Hartebeestes; a total of 94 aircraft all told.

During January the establishment of advanced landing grounds was completed as far forward as possible on the fronts facing Abyssinia and Italian Somaliland. The advance of General Cunningham's Force started on 10th February and met with some opposition from Italian aircraft operating from Afmadu and Gobwen, but the destruction of 7 C.A.133's and 3 C.R.42's in the first two days went a long way towards establishing the. complete air superiority eventually achieved, and which, without doubt, affected the whole course of future operations.

57. On the 11th February, Afmadu was captured and after a further rapid advance Kismayu was occupied on 14th February.

After the fall of Kismayu our aircraft assisted the turning operations which resulted in the forcing of the River Juba and the dash on Mogadiscio. Gobwen, Afmadu, Jelib, Bardera and Dolo were among the targets attacked, also Ischia, Baidoa and Bur Agaba further North.

By the middle of March the forces had reached Gabredarre, having advanced 755 miles in 39 days.

During the remaining operations in March against Harar and Diredawa intense air attacks were made on these places, on military targets in the Jijigga area and on the railway and stations of the Addis Ababa-Djibuti line. Direct hits by bombs were scored on several trains as well as on M.T. on the roads, and traffic was largely immobilised.

Hurricanes of No. 3 S.A.A.F. Squadron " ground-strafed " Diredawa aerodrome on 15th March, damaging 2 S.79's and 5 G.R.32's. Other enemy fighters were shot down in the air over Diredawa.

At this time enemy bombers made a number of attacks on our forward troops at Marda Pass near Jijigga, but did no damage.

On 28th and 30th March enemy fighters machine-gunned Jijigga aerodrome. damaging four of our aircraft on each occasion. Two of the raiders were shot down.

Glenn Martins of the S.A.A.F. did regular long distance reconnaissances in the Addis Ababa direction. Further South in the Boran Area the rains set in early in March, hampering operations. Our bomber aircraft attacked enemy positions at Yavello, Neghelli, Moyale and Mega in support of the Army, and Neghelli was occupied in March. Thus, by the end of March, our forces were firmly established within the Southern boundaries of Abyssinia and further North were already threatening Addis Ababa along the railway.

On this front alone did the enemy show any activity in the air, but it was only spasmodic, and in no way hindered the advance of the Army.

58. After occupying Diredawa on 29th March our forces resumed their advance and after a brief check at Awah moved on to Addis Ababa which surrendered on 6th April. From

Addis Ababa our forces advanced in three directions. One column moved North East towards Dessie, a second column advanced North West towards Debra Marcos to join forces with the Patriots, while a third column moved South West on Gimma to engage the considerable enemy forces in the Galla Sidamo. In the Gojjam the Patriots achieved much success, capturing Debra Marcos, the principal town, on 7th April. By the end of this period the Gojjam was practically cleared of the enemy.

Squadrons of the S.A.A.F. continued to operate in support of our troops, their activities consisting largely of offensive reconnaissances during which bombing and machine-gun attacks, the latter chiefly by fighters, were made on various enemy objectives.

During the advance of our forces on Addis Ababa effective attacks were made on enemy positions and M.T. in the Awash area, and on the aerodrome at Addis Ababa where some of the few aircraft remaining to the enemy were concentrated.

With the advance of the three columns from Addis Ababa in diverging directions, air operations in support of our troops were continued over widely separated areas. The main military objective at this time was Dessie which our troops were approaching from the North and South. The main effort of the S.A.A.F. at this stage was, therefore, against objectives in that area, bombing and machine-gun attacks being made by S.A.A.F. Battles, J.U.86's and Hurricanes on enemy troops and M.T., and against Combolcia (Dessie) aerodrome. Our forces advancing from the South captured Dessie on the 26th April but the enemy still retained his positions at Amba Alagi, holding up our advance on Dessie from the North.

Operations by Nos. 40 and 41 Squadrons, S.A.A.F. (Hartebeestes) and No. 11 Squadron S.A.A.F. (Battles), were carried out against widely scattered groups of the enemy in the Gojjam and the Lakes area and North East of Yavello.

In the Galla Sidamo, operations were concentrated largely against the Gimma area where No. 41 Squadron (Hartebeestes) and No. 3 Squadron (Hurricanes) attacked the aerodrome, enemy troops and M.T. Engagements with the enemy fighters were few at this time, but on the 10th April a formation of No. 3 Squadron Hurricanes attacking Gimma aerodrome encountered two of the remaining enemy fighters and shot them down over their own aerodrome.

59. As was the case in the Sudan, the general success of the campaign in Italian East Africa enabled two Squadrons to be released from the East African Command. No. 2 Squadron, S.A.A.F., and No. 14 Squadron, S.A.A.F., the latter subsequently re-numbered No. 24 Squadron, were therefore transferred to Egypt during the latter part of April, where they awaited re-equipment.

The South African Air Force are to be congratulated on the important and successful part they played in this campaign. They were operating over difficult country and under conditions which tested their initiative, stamina and technical efficiency to the utmost. They contributed largely to the complete defeat of the Italian Air Force in I.E.A. and to the destruction of 300 aircraft, which is the estimated total of enemy aircraft destroyed on the ground or in the air in that theatre of war.

60. At Aden, under the command of Air Vice-Marshal G. R. M. Reid, C.B., D.S.O., M.C., there remained the following Squadrons at the beginning of the year:—

No. 8 (B) Squadron—Blenheims and Vincents, No. 203 (GR/L) Squadron—Blenheim IV's, and No. 94 (F) Squadron—Gladiators (not complete).

Though the Italian Air Force was within easy striking distance of convoys passing up and down the Red Sea they made no attempt to interfere with this line of communication, which was of vital importance to our Forces in Egypt. Whilst they were still capable of such attacks it was necessary to provide Red Sea reconnaissance, and a certain degree of air protection both to convoys and to Aden. The principal effort, however, of these Aden Squadrons during the period under review was in support of the campaigns from North and South into Abyssinia.

Repeated raids were made on Assab, Dessie, Diredawa, Addis Ababa, Alomata and Makalle. Besides damage to buildings, depots and repair shops, numbers of aircraft were destroyed on the ground in the course of these raids, 8 S.A.133s being set on fire at Alomata in one raid by two Blenheims.

In support of the operations, which resulted in the recapture of Berbera by landings from the sea on 16th March, 21 sorties were made against Diredawa aerodrome, 10 enemy aircraft being destroyed on the ground and 8 others damaged. Offensive reconnaissances were also carried out to neutralise possible enemy air action.

61. In April, operations in support of the Army in Italian East Africa were carried out almost entirely in the Dessie area and on the Assab-Dessie Road. Blenheims made a number of successful attacks on M.T. concentrations and troops in these areas and, in addition, attacked the aerodromes at Combolcia (Dessie) and Macaaca (Assab). The scale of effort at this stage was not heavy, only 31 offensive sorties being made during the period, including a number of machine-gun attacks by No. 203 Squadron (Blenheims) engaged on offensive reconnaissances.

Prior to the action on the 3rd April, already described, when four Italian destroyers were sunk or disabled, the considerable force of destroyers and other Italian Naval units at Massawa was a constant threat to our Red Sea communications. Regular reconnaissances of Massawa, Dahlak Island and Assab and the Eritrean Coast were therefore maintained, and a constant check kept on the movements of Italian ships and Naval units. After the occupation of Massawa on the 8th April this threat was greatly reduced, since Assab was the only port then remaining to the enemy. Thereafter operations in the Red Sea were largely confined to reconnaissances of the port.

The reduction of Red Sea reconnaissances, combined with the general success of the campaign in Italian East Africa, enabled No. 203 Squadron to be transferred to Egypt on the 16th April, 1941.

Malta.

62. Early in January, the arrival of the German Air Force in Sicily and Southern Italy changed the situation at Malta very considerably. Whereas the Italian air effort against Malta had been half-hearted, the Germans made determined and persistent attacks on the Grand Harbour, aerodromes and flying boat anchorages.

As these attacks by day, and later more frequently by night, became more numerous and intense, the defence of the Island and of the aircraft base there became more difficult. Some of our aircraft were damaged on the ground, as also were hangars and buildings, although casualties to R.A.F. personnel were fortunately light.

At the beginning of January there were operating from Malta:—

No. 261 (F) Squadron—Hurricanes, No. 228 (F/B) Squadron—Sunderlands, No. 431 G.R. Flight—Glenn Martins and No. 148 (B) Squadron—Wellingtons.

The aircraft strength of these units varied, but seldom, if at any time, were they up to establishment. Moreover, repair and maintenance under conditions of constant bombing became extremely difficult. Flying boats at their moorings were particularly vulnerable. Also, a certain amount of congestion resulted at times on the aerodromes when reinforcing flights which used Malta as a " stage post " arrived from England en route to Egypt. It was necessary to pass them on without delay in spite of enemy interference.

63. Under these circumstances I considered it advisable, after discussion with A.O.C. Malta, temporarily to reduce the number of aircraft based on the Island. In deciding which units to retain, the needs of the Navy had to be considered as well as the requirements of local Fighter Defence. The spirit of the garrison and the morale of the Maltese reacted remarkably to the Hurricanes' successes in air combats over Malta. This was a most important consideration, and it was obvious that as many fighters as possible should operate whilst the " game " remained plentiful and enterprising.

Next in importance came the reconnaissance of enemy ports, their approaches, and of the Eastern Mediterranean itself. The former was done by the Glenn Martins at Malta, within their limited capacity—there were seldom more than three serviceable. A P.R.U. (Photographic Reconnaissance Unit) Spitfire, which was at Malta for special photographic work, proved invaluable for this port reconnaissance, but after its loss, through a forced landing in Italy, no replacement was made available from home. The Sunderlands of Nos. 228 and 230 (F/B) Squadrons on their Ionian Sea and Eastern Mediterranean reconnaissances could still carry on from Alexandria and Suda Bay, and the work of the Wellington Squadron operating against objectives in Italy, Sicily and North Africa could still be done, though on a reduced scale by Wellingtons " on passage ". Thus, No. 228 (F/B) Squadron returned to Alexandria and the Wellingtons of No. 148 (B) Squadron moved to Egypt, detachments being left behind to maintain such Sunderlands as occasionally used Malta, and the Wellingtons on passage to Egypt.

64. In spite of these reductions it was still found possible to operate " passage " Wellingtons occasionally from Malta. An especially successful attack was made on Catania aerodrome on the night of 15/16th January, when 35 German aircraft which had recently arrived were reported to have been destroyed on the ground by 9 Wellingtons.

The Glenn Martins of No. 431 G.R. Flight reconnoitred and photographed Sicilian and Italian Harbours and aerodromes as far North as Naples and Brindisi. They also searched the sea for enemy shipping between Malta, Tunis and Tripoli as well as the West Ionian Sea, supplementing the wider strategical reconnaissance of No. 228 Squadron.

During the period of our occupation of Cyrenaica, Tripoli had remained within range of Wellingtons and Blenheims operating from Benghazi area which reduced the calls on Malta in that direction. However, after the Italian-German counter-offensive in Cyrenaica, which led to our withdrawal to bases outside the range of Tripoli, it became essential to resume operations against that objective from Malta. A detachment of No. 148 Squadron (Wellingtons) was accordingly sent back to Malta during early April, and aircraft of this detachment made 34 night sorties against Tripoli between 13/14th and 24/25th April, dropping upwards of 50 tons of H.E. and incendiary bombs on harbour facilities and shipping with successful results. Fleet Air Arm Swordfish also made torpedo and bombing attacks on convoys off the Tunisian Coast and against shipping at Tripoli.

Towards the end of April Malta was reinforced from home by Blenheims of No. 21 (B) Squadron which made two very effective attacks on enemy shipping. On 1st May, 6 Blenheims of this Squadron bombed and obtained several direct hits on a destroyer and a merchant ship of 3,000 tons near the Kerkenna Islands off the Tunisian Coast. On the following day four Blenheims made another effective bombing attack on a convoy of Italian Naval and merchant ships South-west of Malta, obtaining direct hits on a destroyer and three merchant ships.

65. During the whole period under review the enemy continued to make persistent and heavy scale air attacks at frequent intervals on the Island. The enemy's main objectives appeared to be the Grand Harbour and naval dockyards, as well as the three aerodromes and flying boat anchorage. Especially severe fighting took place over the Island during the repeated dive-bombing attacks on the Grand Harbour and aerodromes on the 16th, 18th and 19th January, and on the Aircraft Carrier H.M.S. " Illustrious " and convoy ships which had arrived in the Harbour on 10th January. The first attacks were recklessly pressed home, and the enemy suffered heavy losses from our fighters and A.A. Batteries. It is reckoned that between the 10th and 19th January, 196

enemy aircraft were destroyed or damaged, including 44 destroyed in two raids by Wellingtons on the Catania aerodrome.

Another heavy attack, this time mostly by night, took place over a period between 28th April and 1st May when 9 enemy aircraft were destroyed and a "probable" 6, for a loss of 6 Hurricanes.

It is noteworthy that once the German Air Force was established in Sicily, Italian bombers scarcely again appeared over Malta. C.R.42's continued to act as escorts and to make a few low machine-gun attacks, but the Germans clearly preferred escorts of their own Me.109's or 110's for their dive-bombers.

To deal with these attacks the number of Hurricanes of No. 261 Squadron was gradually increased to 34 aircraft, partly by reinforcement from the Middle East and partly as a result of operations by Aircraft Carriers from the Western Mediterranean, in which Hurricanes were "flown off" to Malta. In addition, pilots were double-banked to cope with the increased raids and larger number of enemy aircraft taking part in them. This Squadron was in action almost every day and on many nights. Though losses of our own aircraft were serious, a fair proportion of pilots were saved.

66. At the end of the period under review, despite the enemy's persistent air effort, Malta could still be regarded as an effective air base for fighters for a limited offensive against enemy communications in the Mediterranean and as a "stage post" for the reinforcing aircraft en route for Egypt. The damage done to buildings and hangars made conditions of life and work uncomfortable and repair work was difficult.

In spite of these drawbacks, the fact that operations had been carried on throughout this testing period is a great tribute to the spirit and determination of the pilots, aircrews and ground personnel under the very able direction of Air Vice-Marshal F. H. M. Maynard, A.F.C. Amongst those under his Command who rendered valuable service during this period may be mentioned the Senior Air Staff Officer, Group Captain A. C. Sanderson, D.F.C.; Group Captain R. G. Gardner, D.S.C.; Wing Commander A. D. Messenger, the Senior Signals Officer; Squadron Leader P. S. Foss, No. 148 Squadron, and Flying Officer A. Warburton, D.F.C., of the Glenn Martin Reconnaissance Unit.

Palestine and Trans Jordan.

67. During the period covered by this Despatch there is little to record of the activities in this area. No further enemy raids took place on Haifa, or elsewhere. Aqir aerodrome was completed and opened early in the year. Gaza was developed and Lydda taken over as an R.A.F. Station. These aerodromes were prepared for and subsequently occupied by the Squadron personnel evacuated from Greece, for the purpose of re-forming and re-arming them.

Iraq.

68. The political situation described in my previous Despatch continued to deteriorate, particularly after the coup d'état by Raschid Ali and the subsequent removal of the Regent Emir Abdulla Ali. We were at this period more than fully occupied in Greece and the Western Desert, and the only aircraft available in Iraq were those of No. 4 F.T.S. at Habbaniya and the Vincents of No. 244 Squadron at Shaibah. Towards the middle of April it became obvious that air reinforcements would be necessary. The training aircraft of No. 4 F.T.S. had as far as possible been placed on an operational footing, but it was not until the 28th April that it was possible to spare some Wellingtons for Iraq. On that date 10 Wellingtons of No. 37 Squadron flew to Habbaniya and 10 Wellingtons of No. 70 Squadron to Shaibah, followed on the 1st May by a detachment of No. 203 Squadron (Blenheims).

By this time a landing of British troops at Basra had been effected and ships with additional troops were nearing Basra. It was at this moment, on the 30th April, that the Iraqis disclosed the result of their Axis intrigue by surrounding Habbaniya with a strong Iraqi force, including artillery.

Egypt.

69. At the beginning of January the Fighter defence of Egypt consisted of No. 252 Fighter Wing under Group Captain C. B. S. Spackman, D.F.C., who had most ably improvised an organisation which operated one Squadron at Amriya and a Sector Headquarters at Helwan, controlling the defensive patrols of the 2 R.E.A.F. Fighter Squadrons at Almaza and Suez respectively. Information was provided by No. 256 A.M.E.S. Wing.

During January, as a result of minelaying attacks on the Suez Canal, it was decided to build up an organisation, on the lines that had proved so successful in the U.K. Nos. 252 and 256 Wings were amalgamated as the controlling authority, the Sectors being at Amriya, Heliopolis, Fayid and Port Said. As an interim measure, a temporary Sector was formed at Ismailia to deal with the Suez Canal Zone.

In March I decided to re-form No. 202 Group, under Air Commodore T. W. Elmhirst, A.F.C., to co-ordinate all operational problems concerning the air defence of Egypt, and to co-operate with H.Q., B.T.E., on problems concerning A.A. artillery and searchlights.

Experience showed that communications in Egypt were so poor that it proved impossible to operate even 3 Sectors efficiently from one controlling authority, and accordingly the decision was taken to divide the Delta into two by a line from Baltim through Mansura, thence approximately South Eastwards to the Gulf of Suez, and to form two separate Wings each with its own filter room. No. 250 Wing formed at Ismailia to control the Sectors at Port Said and Fayid and be responsible for the defence of the Suez Canal Zone and Eastern portion of the Delta Area. No. 252 Wing was then made responsible for the control of the Sectors at Amriya and Heliopolis, and the defence of Alexandria, Cairo and the Western portion of the Delta.

70. During the actual period of this report the enemy's effort against Alexandria, Suez, Port Said and the Canal, was small in comparison to his activities elsewhere considering the many important and tempting targets open to him. There were, however, two or three effective raids on the Suez Canal which resulted in its being closed for periods up to a week or ten days on account of mines. Only one attack

was made on the Fleet Base at Alexandria, and it was not until later that attacks increased in intensity.

A Balloon Barrage was established at Alexandria under the very able control of Squadron Leader G. M. Trundle, who commanded No. 971 Squadron.

71. Mention must be made of the work of No. 267 Communication Squadron, ably commanded by Wing Commander S. F. Wynne-Eyton, D.S.O., and of No. 216 Bomber Transport Squadron. Their respective functions involved long and frequent flights to all parts of Middle East Command, stretching from Libya to Kenya and from Greece to Takoradi. Frequent use was also made of the services of the British Overseas Airways Corporation on their regular air routes. Their efficiency and reliability was of great assistance in meeting the very heavy demands for air transport.

Health and Morale.

72. The general health of the Command as a whole remained good during the period under review. This was especially noticeable during the advance in Libya and during the operations in Greece where climatic conditions were extremely hard. The morale of all ranks, especially flying crews, remained high throughout.

As recorded in my previous Despatch, credit is due to Air Commodore A. E. Panter, the Principal Medical Officer, and to his Deputy, Group Captain F. J. Murphy. Squadron Leader, The Rev. F. D. Morley, continued his active interest in the welfare of the airmen.

Administration.

73. The work of endeavouring to maintain the Squadrons throughout the Command with replacement aircraft, spare engines and equipment of all kinds, proved most difficult in the absence of regular supplies from home. Re-equipment with new aircraft of those Squadrons using obsolescent types was in most cases seriously delayed. In spite of these handicaps, everything possible was done by the Air Officer in charge of Administration, Air Vice-Marshal A. C. Maund, C.B.E., D.S.O., within the means at his disposal.

Air Commodore F. L. Fay, M.C., the Chief Engineer, continued most successfully to press on with the construction of the new aerodromes and landing grounds.

The ever-increasing financial problems were most ably handled by the Command Accountant, Group Captain T. H. Evans, O.B.E., and in connection with which Mr. C. W. Evans, my Financial Adviser, was of considerable assistance.

74. No praise can be too high for the work of the ground personnel, Officers and men alike, who, in their various capacities, maintained the aircraft, usually under the most trying conditions; whether in the winter snow or slush on the Greek-Albanian Front, or the sand and heat of Aden, Egypt and the Sudan, their devotion to duty, cheerfulness and faithful service remained the same. All maintenance units, repair and salvage organisations, worked to their utmost capacity to keep the Squadrons supplied.

Air Staff.

75. Air Marshal A. W. Tedder, C.B., whose arrival on the 9th December, 1940, I recorded in my previous Despatch, gave me most valuable support at all times as Deputy Air Officer Commanding-in-Chief.

Amongst others who continued to function most efficiently under extremely high pressure conditions were Air Vice-Marshal R. M. Drummond, D.S.O., O.B.E., M.C., the Senior Air Staff Officer; Air Commodore H. E. P. Wigglesworth, D.S.C., Plans; Group Captain N. S. Paynter, Senior Intelligence Officer; Wing Commander C. Bray, Senior R.A.F. Press Officer; Wing Commander T. A. B. Parselle Air Communications; Squadron Leader Sir Arthur Curtis, K.C.V.O., C.M.G., M.C., my personal Staff Officer. Great credit is also due to Group Captain W. E. G. Mann, D.F.C., the Senior Signals Officer, and all his Staff, for the efficient signal organisation which met each new increase with complete efficiency.

76. In reviewing the part played by the R.A.F. in the Middle East during the period of my Command (May, 1940-May, 1941), the following is a summary of some interesting and prominent features worthy of being placed on record:—

(a) The unexpected survival of Malta as an operational air base. It started without fighters: after one year of war it had 50. It has continued to function as a link on the air reinforcing route to Egypt and as a base for bomber and reconnaissance Squadrons.

(b) The security of the Red Sea shipping route and its comparative immunity from Italian bombers or submarines; a tribute to the Aden and Port Sudan Squadrons and no compliment to the Regia Aeronautica.

(c) The part which the occupation of territory plays on the Mediterranean Littoral, as elsewhere, in adding to or reducing the potential scale of air attack on ships at sea and on our Naval, Army and Air Bases. Instance the Dodecanese (later of course, Greece and Crete), and particularly the North African Coast.

(d) In this respect, the advantage to the enemy of regaining Cyrenaica and the coastal strip of the territory between Tobruk and Sollum. In contrast, our difficulty in providing fighter defence to isolated Tobruk, and the disadvantage to our bombers and reconnaissance aircraft of the increased distance to enemy bases.

(e) The speed of advance by motorised or armoured forces after breaking resistance in breadth, and the importance of mobility of those R.A.F. Squadrons with short range aircraft which must operate at once from rapidly established forward landing grounds if they are to keep pace with, and continue, effective support of the advanced ground forces. Instance the advance into Cyrenaica, December to February, and also General Cunningham's rapid drive into Abyssinia through Italian Somaliland.

(f) The losses in grounded aircraft sustained during a rapid withdrawal through aerodromes being overrun; also the difficulty experienced by Squadrons in offering effective air resistance whilst the ground personnel are constantly on the move to the rear.

Instance the Italian withdrawal in Cyrenaica, and later our own experience in Greece. It was, however, less marked in the case of our withdrawal from Cyrenaica in April.

(g) Finally, the importance of taking into account the "time lag factor" when accepting Air commitments beyond the immediate capacity of the existing force. The interval, which must inevitably elapse with long lines of communication between the date when a decision is taken at home to despatch aircraft from the U.K., until the time they become operationally ready in the Middle East. Though this was considerably shortened by air deliveries in the case of long range aircraft, and also by Aircraft Carrier reinforcing operations, the spares and ground equipment to maintain these aircraft must still come by sea. The figures given at Appendix "C"* of this report show the state of weakness to which my force had been reduced after the campaigns in Greece, Libya, Eritrea and Italian Somaliland.

77. In concluding this Report, I must again pay tribute to the ready co-operation and support of the Naval C-in-C., Admiral Sir Andrew Cunningham, G.C.B., D.S.O., and of General Sir Archibald Wavell, G.C.B., C.M.G., M.C., with whom it was my privilege at all times to work in the closest accord.

To His Excellency the Ambassador, Sir Miles Lampson, G.C.M.G., C.B., M.V.O., once again my thanks and gratitude for his unfailing help and support in dealings with the Egyptian Government.

ARTHUR M. LONGMORE,
Air Chief Marshal.

1st November, 1941.

* Appendices not reproduced.

LONDON
PRINTED AND PUBLISHED BY HIS MAJESTY'S STATIONERY OFFICE
To be purchased directly from H.M. STATIONERY OFFICE at the following addresses:
York House, Kingsway, London, W.C.2; 13a Castle Street, Edinburgh 2;
39-41 King Street, Manchester 2; 1 St. Andrew's Crescent, Cardiff;
80 Chichester Street, Belfast;
or through any bookseller
1946
Price Sixpence net

S.O. Code No. 65-

Numb. 37838

FOURTH SUPPLEMENT
TO
The London Gazette
Of TUESDAY, *the* 31st *of* DECEMBER, 1946

Published by Authority

Registered as a newspaper

THURSDAY, 2 JANUARY, 1947

The Air Ministry,
January, 1947.

AIR OPERATIONS BY THE ALLIED EXPEDITIONARY AIR FORCE IN N.W. EUROPE FROM NOVEMBER 15TH, 1943 TO SEPTEMBER 30TH, 1944.

The following despatch by the late Air Chief Marshal Sir Trafford Leigh-Mallory, K.C.B., D.S.O., Air Commander-in-Chief, Allied Expeditionary Air Force, was submitted to the Supreme Allied Commander in November, 1944.

On relinquishing my command of the Allied Expeditionary Air Force I have the honour to submit the following Despatch, covering its operations under my command during the period from 15th November, 1943 to 30th September, 1944.

Since this Despatch covers the air support of the assault of Europe and the subsequent land operations, it necessarily includes reference to the strategical operations of the United States Eighth Air Force and the Royal Air Force Bomber Command in addition to the operations of these two Air Forces and the Royal Air Force Coastal Command directed to the tactical support of the assault.

As the period covered by the Despatch extends over ten and a half months of the most heavy and concentrated air war in the history of the world, I have not attempted to deal with the events on a day-to-day basis. Rather I have taken the tasks undertaken in the preliminary and preparatory phases and in the assault and post-assault phase and have attempted to show how these tasks were fulfilled, as well as briefly indicating what I feel are some of the outstanding features of these air operations.

PART I—COMMAND AND CONTROL

Formation of A.E.A.F.

By a Directive (reference COSSAC (43) 81) dated 16th November, 1943, issued by your Chief of Staff, I was informed that the Combined Chiefs of Staff had appointed me Air Commander-in-Chief of the Allied Expeditionary Air Force under yourself as the Supreme Allied Commander, and that I was to exercise operational command of the British and American tactical air forces supporting the assault of Western Europe from the United Kingdom. I was also informed that a United States General would be appointed Deputy Air Commander-in-Chief, Allied Expeditionary Air Force. Major-General William O. Butler was the first General Officer to hold this post. He served in this capacity from 1st January, 1944, to 25th March, 1944, and was succeeded by Major-General Hoyt S. Vandenberg who occupied the position until 8th August, 1944. Major-General Ralph Royce then held this appointment until the disbandment of A.E.A.F. on 14th October, 1944.

Forces available

2. The forces under my command comprised the Royal Air Force Second Tactical Air Force, the United States Ninth Air Force and the forces of the Air Defence of Great Britain. The Royal Air Force Second Tactical Air Force and the formations of the Air Defence of Great Britain passed to my command on 15th November, 1943; the United States Ninth Air Force passed to my operational command on 15th December, 1943, but was not released from its commitment to assist the United States Strategic Air Forces in "Pointblank" operations until 10th March, 1944.

3. You will recall that a definition of the role of the strategic air forces was not covered in the original Directive to me, but was deferred to a later date. However, my plans were made on the assumption that I should be able to count on the full support of the strategic air forces when it was required.

4. On 17th November, 1943, I issued a Directive to the Air Marshal Commanding, Royal Air Force Second Tactical Air Force and to the Commanding General, United States Ninth Air Force, in which I informed them of my appointment as Air Commander-in-Chief and of the respective dates on which their units came under my operational control. I further directed that these forces should proceed, without delay, to prepare for operations in support of two British and two American Field Armies in an assault on the Continent. I also issued a Directive to the Air Marshal Commanding, Air Defence of Great Britain, setting out the functions and organisation of the Air Defence of Great Britain, following on its conversion from Royal Air Force Fighter Command.

5. On 6th December, 1943, I issued a further Directive to the forces under my command, outlining the "Overlord" plan and defining the control that I would exercise as Air Commander-in-Chief. A table showing these forces and the chain of command is at Appendix "A" (not reproduced).

Operation "Pointblank"

6. During the preliminary period of preparation for the assault, in late 1943 and early 1944, the medium and light bomber forces of the Allied Expeditionary Air Force continued to lend support to Operation "Pointblank." This was the name given to the combined bomber plan of the strategical bombing forces which had as its aims, first, the reduction of the fighter forces of the G.A.F., second, the general reduction in the war potential of Germany, and third, the weakening of the will of the German people to continue the struggle. The co-ordination of these operations was effected through a Combined Operational Planning Committee, which was a joint British/American Fighter and Bomber Committee responsible for planning daylight operations when the United States Army Air Force heavy bombers took part. During this preliminary period, the operations by Allied Expeditionary Air Force medium and light bombers in conjunction with, and in support of United States Eighth Air Force were given precedence over any other daylight operations. A second Committee, known as the 11 Group Planning Committee, co-ordinated operations of the medium and light bombers of the Allied Expeditionary Air Force other than those in the support role mentioned above. The activities of the fighter forces of the Allied Expeditionary Air Force as escort to, and in support of, bombing operations were also co-ordinated through these Committees.

Ninth Air Force Released from "Pointblank" Commitments

7. On 10th March, 1944, I forwarded a Directive to Commanding General, United States Ninth Air Force, advising him that you, as the Supreme Allied Commander, had decided that the time had come for the operations of the Ninth Air Force to be directed towards the preparation for Operation "Overlord" and that it would, therefore, operate exclusively under the Allied Expeditionary Air Force and be released from the commitment to assist the United States Eighth Air Force in "Pointblank" operations. As an exception to this ruling, such fighters of the United States Ninth Fighter Command as were suitable and available continued to operate as escort to the United States Eighth Air Force when required.

8. At this time also, I advised the forces under my command that the most important assistance the Allied Expeditionary Air Force could give the Army during the preparatory phase would be by attacking the enemy's rail communications, with the object of so disorganising his railway system that he would find it difficult to supply his divisions in Northern France when the fighting started and still more difficult to bring reinforcements into the lodgment area. Selected rail centres were, therefore, put in the first priority for attack.

Role of Strategic Air Forces

9. Until March, 1944, strategic air forces comprising the United States Eighth Air Force and Royal Air Force Bomber Command, continued to be employed on Operation "Pointblank" under the direction of the British Chief of Air Staff acting as a representative of the Combined Chiefs of Staff. In March, 1944, as the completion of the preparatory tasks for Operation "Overlord" became more urgent, the Combined Chiefs of Staff directed that "Overlord" should have priority over "Pointblank" and that the direction of strategic air forces should pass from the British Chief of Air Staff to yourself as the Supreme Allied Commander, on 14th April, 1944.

10. You instructed your deputy, Air Chief Marshal Sir Arthur W. Tedder, G.C.B., to exercise for you general supervision of all air forces, particularly in the co-ordination of the efforts of heavy bomber forces to be employed on operations "Pointblank" and "Overlord". I was responsible to you for all air operations in connection with the latter plan and I accordingly passed to Air Chief Marshal Tedder my requirements for heavy bomber effort both in the preparatory and assault phases. During May, 1944, the Deputy Supreme Allied Commander decided that all air operations could be more easily planned and laid on at a single headquarters, and the Air Operations Planning Staff of Supreme Headquarters was moved to my Headquarters. The Deputy Supreme Allied Commander and the Commanders of the strategical and tactical air forces then regularly attended my daily conferences at Stanmore, thus enabling all operation orders covering all air forces occupied with "Overlord" tasks, to be co-ordinated and given rapidly to the forces to be employed.

Formation of Advanced A.E.A.F.

11. In order to achieve the most economical and effective employment of the air forces at my disposal for the assault and its subsequent development, I considered it essential that the air operations in immediate and direct support of the land battle should be specially co-ordinated and directed. I, therefore, decided to establish a small operational organisation to be known as Advanced Allied Expeditionary Air Force. Under my general direction, the Commander Advanced A.E.A.F. was given the task of directing and co-ordinating the planning for and operations of such forces of the United States Ninth Air Force and Royal Air Force Second Tactical Air Force as were allotted to him from time to time.

12. Air Marshal Sir Arthur Coningham, K.C.B., D.S.O., M.C., D.F.C., A.F.C., was appointed Commander, Advanced Allied Expeditionary Air Force, and he undertook this responsibility on detachment from the Second Tactical Air Force. The Commander, Advanced A.E.A.F. was the one air commander with whom the Commander-in-Chief, 21st Army Group dealt in his capacity as Commander-in-Chief, Land Forces, during the initial phases of the operation. The Commander, Advanced A.E.A.F. had the necessary authority to implement the requests for air action made by the Army, referring to me any requests for air support beyond the resources of the two tactical air forces. Headquarters, Advanced A.E.A.F. was set up at Uxbridge on 1st May, 1944. Its War Room, where meetings to co-ordinate operations of the tactical air forces were held daily, was adjacent to the Combined Operations Room and the Combined Control and Reconnaissance Centres referred to below.

Machinery of Control of Tactical Air Forces

13. Throughout the preparatory and assault periods, the control of the fighter bombers and the light and medium bombers of the two tactical air forces was exercised through a Combined Operations Room located at Uxbridge. This Operations Room was staffed by representatives of the United States Ninth Air Force and the Royal Air Force Second Tactical Air Force. Also under the direction of the Commander, Advanced A.E.A.F., a Combined Control Centre was set up and operated by the Air Officer Commanding No. 11 Group, Royal Air Force, with the full collaboration of the Commanding General, United States IXth Fighter Command and with authoritative representation of the United States Army VIIIth Fighter Command. This Combined Control Centre was manned by a British/American staff and was, in effect, the Operations Room of No. 11 Group, Air Defence of Great Britain, with the complete static signals system of the old organisation developed over a long period and augmented by additional communication facilities. This Centre planned, co-ordinated and controlled all fighter operations in the initial phases of the operations; it was also responsible for issuing executive instructions for the fighter bombers.

14. A Combined Reconnaissance Centre was also operated under the command of the Commander, Advanced A.E.A.F. to co-ordinate and direct the visual and photographic reconnaissance efforts of both the British and United States reconnaissance forces, during the initial phases.

15. At Appendix "B"* is a diagram, setting out the chain of control and the locations of various Headquarters at the time of the Assault. Modifications in this chain of control were made later as they became necessary. Headquarters, Royal Air Force Second Tactical Air Force and Headquarters, United States Ninth Air Force moved overseas on 4th August, 1944, and Headquarters, Advanced A.E.A.F. moved to the Continent on 9th August, 1944; to economise in communications, this Headquarters was located alongside Headquarters, United States Ninth Air Force. It continued in the field alongside this latter Headquarters (which was located next to 12th United States Army Group), in the advance from the Cotentin Peninsula to the Paris area, where it was located at Versailles. Main Headquarters, A.E.A.F. moved from Stanmore to the Continent on 8th September, 1944, and was located alongside your own Headquarters at Julouville. Communications at that place were quite inadequate to meet the needs of a headquarters of the size concerned, and Main Headquarters A.E.A.F. moved with Supreme Headquarters to Versailles on 19th September, 1944.

16. Plans had been drawn up for the further move of Advanced Headquarters, A.E.A.F. with Advanced Headquarters Ninth Air Force to Verdun. In view of impending developments, chiefly the absorption of A.E.A.F. into S.H.A.E.F., these plans were not put into operation. Headquarters, Advanced A.E.A.F. was therefore merged into Headquarters Main A.E.A.F. at 1200 hours on 23rd September, 1944.

PART II.—POLICY AND PLANNING.

(a) *Operations prior to D-Day.*
Operation "Overlord".

17. Operation "Overlord" was part of a large strategic plan designed to bring about the defeat of Germany by heavy and concerted assaults on German-occupied Europe from the United Kingdom, the Mediterranean and Russia. A Joint Study and Outline Plan for Operation "Overlord" was completed in July, 1943. This plan was elaborated in more detail under the title "Neptune"—Initial Joint Plan and Maintenance Project/Administrative Plan—by the Allied Naval Commander-in-Chief, the Commander-in-Chief, 21st Army Group and myself. Operation "Neptune" provided for the launching of an assault from the United Kingdom across the English Channel, designed to secure a lodgment area on the Continent, from which wider offensive operations could be developed.

18. To cover the operations of all air forces allotted to Operation "Neptune", an Overall Air Plan was evolved, which set out briefly the Joint Plan, the command and control of air forces involved, the principal air tasks and their development through the preliminary and preparatory phases, the assault and follow-up, and air operations subsequent to the assault and securing of the lodgment area. The main features of the Overall Air Plan are more fully dealt with in paragraphs 25 and 26 below.

19. To supplement the Initial Joint Plan for Operation "Neptune", joint instructions and memoranda were issued by the Commanders-in-Chief of the Naval, Army and Air Forces.

Administrative and Signals Planning.

20. To supplement the Overall Air Plan, additional Operational and Administrative Instructions were prepared and issued. In particular, comprehensive Administrative plans were issued for the Royal Air Force formations in A.E.A.F. and the United States Ninth Air Force. These Administrative plans, which were issued separately, were based on three previously agreed fundamental decisions:—

(a) The relative administrative responsibilities of the Army and Air Forces in the field. The division laid down was closely followed and, in practice, worked excellently.

---
* Appendices not reproduced.

(b) Since the United States Army Air Force and the Royal Air Force respectively depended on separate administrative systems, no attempt to combine them should be made, except where advantage was clearly to be gained.

(c) The main base was to be the United Kingdom, and the principal administrative units were not to be moved to the Continent until it was clearly advantageous to do so.

21. These Administrative Plans were supplemented from time to time by additional Administrative Instructions issued by my Headquarters.

22. The completeness of these administrative plans and the accuracy of forecasting which was used enabled the air forces involved to fulfil all of the commitments laid upon them, and in the midst of their heaviest operations, to move across the Channel without any diminution of their effectiveness. This, I feel, constitutes a major triumph of organisation. Some details of the problems involved and overcome in this planning and administration are given in Part IV of this Despatch.

23. A comprehensive Signal Plan for Operation "Neptune" was also issued by my Headquarters. This plan was implemented with success on the whole. I deal with certain features of Signals Communications in Part IV of this Despatch.

24. To supplement the Overall Air Plan as necessary, Air Staff Policy and Operational Instructions were also issued by my Headquarters. Operational Memoranda and Administrative Memoranda were additionally issued by your Headquarters in cases where two or more of the Services were affected.

Overall Air Plan.

25. In the Overall Air Plan I set out the undermentioned principal air tasks for the forces under my command and for the allotted effort of the strategical air forces and Royal Air Force Coastal Command. These tasks were decided upon after discussions with yourself and the respective Commanders-in-Chief as to the requirements of the Army and the Navy from the air forces.

(a) To attain and maintain an air situation whereby the German Air Force was rendered incapable of effective interference with Allied operations.

(b) To provide continuous reconnaissance of the enemy's dispositions and movements.

(c) To disrupt enemy communications and channels of reinforcement and supply.

(d) To support the landing and subsequent advances of the Allied armies.

(e) To deliver offensive strikes against enemy naval forces.

(f) To provide air lift for airborne forces.

26. The co-ordination of the Air Plans with those of the other services was achieved by weekly meetings between the other Commanders-in-Chief and myself, together with our respective Chiefs of Staff and Chief Planners. These meetings, held alternately in the office of the planning centre of each of the three Services, ensured that each service was kept informed of the relative development of planning.

Objects of Preparatory Bombing.

27. I considered that the primary objective of preparatory bombing should be to impose the greatest possible delay in the movement of the enemy reinforcements and supplies, and to this end, the railway bombing plan was designed. The object of this plan was to produce a lasting and general dislocation of the railway system in use by the enemy. By so doing the capacity of the system as a whole would be greatly reduced, and the task of dealing with isolated movement once the battle was joined would be made all the easier. Accordingly, the primary targets planned for attack were the railway centres where the most important servicing and repair facilities of Northern France and the Low Countries were located; the secondary targets were the principal marshalling yards, particularly those which possessed repair facilities. The selection of targets was made difficult in some cases by the necessity of avoiding heavy civilian casualties or damage to historic buildings. Where railway centres were situated in thickly populated areas (as at Le Bourget, for example), alternative centres were chosen in order to isolate them. A further limitation was imposed by the necessity to pinpoint the attacks on these targets; this demanded visual bombing conditions for day attacks and clear weather during moon periods for night attacks. The possibility of unreliable weather, particularly round about D-Day, was one of the major factors which dictated an early commencement of this plan; in fact the weather did seriously hamper its execution. The development of the railway plan and some indication of its success are set out in Part III of this Despatch.

28. Complementary to the railway plan, a further plan was made, covering the destruction of road and rail bridges. This plan which called for the cutting of the Seine bridges below Paris and the bridges over the Loire below Orleans was put into operation at $D-30$.

29. In the formulation and adoption of these plans to cause the maximum overall interference with enemy movements, it was fully appreciated, that the more successful were our attacks, the more embarrassing it would be to the Allied Armies when they came to move through the same area. This disadvantage though serious, was felt by the planners to be outweighed by the advantage of preventing the enemy from bringing in to the assault area sufficient reinforcements to contain the Allied bridgehead. I have dealt with this subject further in the section dealing with post-assault operations in Part III of this Despatch.

30. Other preparatory bombing plans included attacks on coastal batteries, enemy naval and military targets and the Radar chain. It was necessary to remember when making these plans that the enemy should not be given any indication of the area selected for the assault. The principal effect of this on the preparatory air operations was that at least two attacks were made on each type of target outside of the projected assault area to one attack on a target within that area.

Estimation of G.A.F. Capabilties.

31. I was confident that the German Air Force would constitute no serious threat to our operations on land, sea or in the air. However, I could not dismiss the possibility that the enemy was conserving his air forces for a

maximum effort against the Allied assault forces. A bombing plan was therefore prepared which aimed at driving the G.A.F. fighters on to bases as far from the battle as were the Allied fighter forces, by destroying its bases within 130 miles radius of the assault area. Enemy bomber bases even further inland were also scheduled for attack.

32. Moreover, as I considered it possible that an intense air battle might last for anything up to a week following the launching of the assault, it was necessary to have on hand a strong enough force of fighter aircraft to ensure that the enemy would be completely mastered in any such battle. I refer to the constitution and use of this fighter force in Part III of this Despatch.

"*Crossbow*" *Operations.*

33. Throughout the whole of the preliminary and preparatory phases of the operation, I had to take into account the need to maintain a sufficient weight of bombing attacks on "Noball" targets. "Noball" was the code word used to designate the sites being prepared by the enemy for attacks on the United Kingdom with flying bombs and rockets. The operations against these sites carried out under the title of "Crossbow" had begun as early as 5th December, 1943, and constituted a considerable diversion of bomber effort. This bombing, while it did not, of itself, succeed in completely eliminating the menace of the flying bomb, was fully justified, in view of the fact that the original scheme had to be abandoned by the Germans. Details of the effort involved and an indication of the results achieved are given in Part III of this Despatch.

34. The diversion of bombing effort on to "Noball" targets, however, was not wholly unprofitable, even if judged from the point of view of "Neptune" alone. The medium and light bomber crews gained invaluable experience in finding and attacking small and well concealed targets and inevitably improved their standard of bombing accuracy. Moreover, much of the flying in these winter and spring months was carried out in very bad weather conditions. Again the crews gained invaluable experience in instrument flying through bad weather. These were all gains that were to stand us in good stead later in the battle.

(b) *Operations during the Assault.*

35. My plan for the use of air power in direct support of the assault called for the fulfilment of the following principal air tasks:—

(*a*) To protect the cross-channel movement of the assault forces against enemy air attack, and to assist the Allied naval forces to protect the assault craft and shipping from enemy naval forces.

(*b*) To prepare the way for the assault by neutralising the coast and beach defences.

(*c*) To protect the landing beaches and the shipping concentrations from enemy air attack.

(*d*) To dislocate enemy communications and control during the assault.

To accomplish these tasks, detailed plans were produced and a record of the manner in which these plans were put into operation appears in Part III of this Despatch.

(*c*) *Operations Subsequent to D-Day.*

36. The planning of air operations during the post-assault phase of the battle was along two lines. The first part included the continuation and expansion of attacks designed to interfere with the movements of enemy supplies and reinforcements, in addition to other detailed plans covering the operations of the heavy bomber forces in close support. These plans were produced at my main headquarters. The second part of post-assault planning covered the changing needs of the ground situation and this day-by-day planning was co-ordinated and controlled through the headquarters of Advanced A.E.A.F.

37. In the foregoing paragraphs I have set out briefly the main principles which guided the planning of air operations before, during and after the assault. A general picture of these air operations as planned is given in the attached map.* More detailed descriptions of the individual plans evolved to implement these principles will be found in Part III where such descriptions fit in more logically. In the final part of this Despatch I have included some considerations governing our general planning.

38. I should like to emphasise that my Planning Staff, like my Operations Staff, was Allied in the true sense of the word, and that both the American and British components worked together most successfully under the direction of my Senior Air Staff Officer, Air Vice Marshal H. E. P. Wigglesworth, C.B., C.B.E., D.S.C.

PART III—NARRATIVE OF OPERATIONS.

(a) *Preliminary Period.*

Air Superiority essential.

39. Air superiority was the principal prerequisite for the successful assault of Europe from the West. The winning of air superiority was therefore the cardinal point of air planning. Air operations to ensure that the requisite degree of air superiority had been gained by D-Day were begun in the preliminary phase and continued during the preparatory phase. On D-Day itself a series of concentrated attacks was made on the G.A.F. airfields in the pre-selected area; but as a result of the earlier operations, I was confident that the necessary degree of air ascendancy had been gained sometime before D-Day and advised yourself, the Allied Commanders and the Chiefs of Staff to this effect. In the event, the German Air Force was more impotent than I expected.

40. I have set out in the following paragraphs some of the efforts of the strategical bomber forces directed to securing air superiority during the preliminary period. The medium and light bomber forces of the A.E.A.F. were throughout this period engaged in support of the stragetical bomber programme and in meeting the commitment for attacks on flying bomb and rocket sites.

41. The long-term strategic bombing plan directed against enemy centres of production and assembly of aircraft and aircraft components, principally by the United States Eighth Air Force and also by Royal Air Force Bomber Command, and the United States Fifteenth Air Force operating from the Mediterranean, inflicted crippling blows on the supply and maintenance organisation of the German Air Force.

---
* Maps not reproduced.

Moreover, the heavy daylight raids of the United States Eighth Air Force into Germany achieved a steady attrition of the German fighter forces.

Attrition of the G.A.F.

42. How crippling these blows were on German aircraft production is illustrated by information obtained from intelligence sources. A comprehensive picture of the effects of direct air attack in terms of enemy single-engine fighter production during the five months from 1st November, 1943 to 1st April, 1944 can be gained from the estimates below:—*

	Planned	Achieved
November	1,280	600
December	1,335	600
January	1,415	650
February	1,480	600
March	1,555	500
	7,065	2,950

43. The difference between the production planned and achieved totals 4,115 aircraft, an average loss to the enemy of more than 820 single-engined fighters per month.

44. These figures ignore the heavy losses sustained by German Air Force fighters in air attacks on their airfields and in combat; also the effective attacks on the factories producing twin-engined fighters must be taken into account.

45. Parallel with the attacks on production centres by the strategic air forces, a campaign of day and night intruding against enemy airfields, designed to hamper enemy training schedules as well as to destroy the enemy in the air, was carried out by aircraft of A.E.A.F. with very great success. In addition, many heavy attacks were made in the preliminary period on the enemy's airfields, which achieved considerable destruction of airfield facilities.

46. It became evident during this period (November, 1943, to May, 1944) that the High Command of the German Air Force was pursuing a policy of conserving its air forces for the defence of vital targets only. This policy made it extremely difficult to get the G.A.F. to fight. Even large scale fighter sweeps failed to produce any serious reaction. However, in the period from 15th November, 1943, the date of the formation of A.E.A.F., to the 5th June, 1944, the eve of D-Day, the Allied forces accounted for the following enemy aircraft in air combat alone (see foot of page).

47. This enormous attrition of G.A.F. strength is based on claims of enemy aircraft destroyed in combat alone; no account is taken in these statistics of aircraft destroyed on the ground. Of the figures given above no less than 2,655 enemy aircraft were destroyed by Allied Air Forces operating out of the United Kingdom during what I have termed the preparatory period of the assault, namely 1st April to 5th June, 1944. I deal with the planned attacks on the G.A.F. and its bases in France during this preparatory period in para. 129 et seq.

(b) *Preparatory Period.*

Method of Presentation.

48. Since the war began all attacks against enemy targets have, in some measure, influenced the situation prevailing on the eve of the assault. The commencement of the preparatory phase for this Despatch I have, however, fixed at 1st April, 1944, except in so far as detailed co-ordinated plans for attacks on targets of specific importance within the framework of the "Neptune" plan were in operation earlier. In these cases, I have included all the attacks made in accordance with the complete plan.

49. For convenience of presentation, I have dealt with these preparatory operations under the headings set out below. These headings cover the various operations planned and carried out to fulfil the tasks laid on to the air forces (see paragraph 25):—

Dislocation of Enemy Lines of Communication, including Destruction of Bridges.
Neutralisation of Coastal Defences.
Disruption of Enemy Radar Cover and W/T facilities.
Attacks on Military facilities.
Harassing of Coastwise Shipping and Sea Mining.
Attacks on Airfields.
Air Reconnaissance.
Protection of the Assembling Assault Forces.
"Crossbow" Operations.

	Destroyed	Probably Destroyed	Damaged
A.E.A.F.			
Aircraft on offensive operations	711	79	308
Aircraft on defensive operations over the United Kingdom and Channel areas	167	23	39
	878	102	347
Guns of Anti-Aircraft Command	73	5	22
Eighth Air Force—by Bombers	2,223	696	1,188
—by Fighters	1,835	202	705
R.A.F. Bomber Command	201	52	267
R.A.F. Coastal Command	28	3	22
Grand Totals	5,238	1,060	2,551

---

* Subject to modification in the light of information subsequently received.

Strength of A.E.A.F. at 1st April, 1944.

50. Details of the composition of the forces at my disposal at 1st April, 1944, are given at Appendix "C".* The number of operationally available aircraft on hand at that date in these Commands was as follows:—

Type	Ninth Air Force	Royal Air Force
Medium Bombers	496	70
Light Bombers	96	38
Fighter and Fighter Bombers	607	1,764
Transport Aircraft	865	225
Gliders	782	351
Reconnaissance Aircraft	63	156
Artillery Observation Aircraft	—	164
	2,909	2,768

Dislocation of Enemy Lines of Communication.

51. Next to the winning of air superiority, the dislocation of the enemy's lines of communication was the most important task set the Air Force (see paragraph 27). The basic intention of my plan for attack on the enemy lines of communication was to force the enemy off the railways, initially within an area of 150 miles from the battle front. There were two broad plans for doing this; one was a short term policy which involved attacks on certain rail centres during the period immediately before D-Day; the other was a longer term plan of destroying the potential of the railway system in North-Western Europe.

52. The short term policy involved attacks on 17 specially selected rail focal points, plus an extra 7 points as cover. It was claimed for this plan that if the attacks were made immediately before D-Day, the enemy's reinforcements by rail would be adequately delayed. Further, it would allow the bomber forces to continue attacks on "Pointblank" and other strategic targets until just before D-Day. Complete success would, of course, have been necessary with all the 17 primary targets to achieve the desired result; moreover, several of the targets chosen were unsuitable for air attack, either by virtue of their location or their nature as bombing targets. Other disadvantages of this plan were that any failure to achieve complete success on the primary targets would have meant that the enemy could direct traffic through such gaps as would be left; the attacks would have to be made at a time when other demands on the available bomber forces were strongest; the successful outcome of a programme covering such a short period would depend entirely upon favourable bombing weather conditions—such conditions could never be guaranteed even in the summer.

53. The longer term plan involved attacks on a large number of repair and maintenance centres designed to reduce the movement potential and the motive power of the railway system, supported by complementary action in cutting railway lines and bridges on the canalized routes nearer D-Day. There were, however, limitations to this longer term plan. It would take longer to implement and would involve a greater diversion of the total effort of the bomber forces. If successful, it would hamper the Allies as effectively as it did the enemy, when the Allies came to move over the same territory. It was, however, a much more certain way of achieving the primary object stated above in paragraph 51, and was less dependent upon a period of good weather near D-Day.

54. In March, 1944, in consultation with the British Chief of Air Staff, Marshal of the Royal Air Force Sir Charles Portal, G.C.B., D.S.O., M.C., the Commanders of the Strategical Air Forces and the representatives of the land forces, you accepted the longer term plan, and the targets selected for attack were allocated to the respective forces (see paragraph 57).

55. Later, the initial plan was amplified and the area selected for attack was greatly expanded. In fact, finally it had little limitation.

56. Attacks by heavy and medium bombers on railway centres were maintained up to and after D-Day. From D-7 they were supplemented by attacks designed to cut the lines and halt or destroy such traffic as could still be moved. In these tasks, fighter bombers played the major part, although the medium and heavy bombers also cooperated. The principal targets in these attacks were bridges, junctions, cross-overs and tunnels, as well as locomotives and rolling stock. I deal with these attacks in paragraph 74 onwards; but in view of special features involved in the attacks on bridges, I deal with those attacks separately, for the sake of clarity, in paragraph 83 onwards.

57. *Allocation of Targets.* A total of eighty rail targets of primary importance were scheduled for attack by A.E.A.F., Royal Air Force Bomber Command and the United States Eighth Air Force. These targets were finally allocated as follows:—

    A.E.A.F. 18
    R.A.F. Bomber Command... ... 39
    U.S. Eighth Air Force 23

58. In addition to these targets, the United States Fifteenth Air Force were allocated fourteen targets in Southern France and nine targets in Germany. However, this Command did not operate against these targets in Southern France until 25th May, 1944 and then only for three days. The targets allocated to them in Germany were not attacked.

59. A number of railway centres not included in the Directive were also lightly attacked, but I have not included these in the general survey of results which follows.

60. By D-Day, of the eighty targets allocated, fifty-one were categorised as being damaged to such an extent that no further attacks were necessary until vital repairs had been effected; twenty-five were categorised as having been very severely damaged, but with certain vital installations still intact, necessitating a further attack; the remaining four were categorised as having received little or no damage, and needing a further attack on first priority.

---
* Appendices not reproduced.

61. The proportion of successes in this respect was as follows:—

Force	Cat "A"	Cat "B"	Cat "C"
A.E.A.F.	14	2	2
R.A.F. Bomber Command	22	15	2
U.S. Eighth Air Force	15	8	—

62. In the period of the operation of this rail plan, i.e., 9th February to D-Day, a total of 21,949 aircraft operated against the eighty selected targets and dropped a total weight of 66,517 tons of bombs. The scale of effort was as follows:—

Force	Sorties	Bombs
A.E.A.F.	8,736	10,125 tons
R.A.F. Bomber Command	8,751	44,744 tons
U.S. Eighth Air Force	4,462	11,648 tons
	21,949	66,517 tons

63. In the attacks made by the United States Fifteenth Air Force on 25th May, 1944, and the subsequent two days, 1,600 sorties were flown against 14 targets and 3,074 tons of bombs were dropped. Of these 14 targets allocated in Southern France, at D-Day five were Category "A", one was Category "B" and eight were Category "C".

64. The first of the really heavy and damaging attacks on rail centres was that made by Royal Air Force Bomber Command on Trappes on the night of 6th-7th March, 1944.

65. An immediate interpretation of photographs taken after this attack showed extremely heavy damage throughout the yards, the greatest concentration of craters being in the "Up" reception sidings. 190 direct hits were scored on tracks, as many as three tracks having, in several cases, been disrupted by one bomb. Numerous derailments and much wreckage were caused by 50 bombs which fell among the lines of rolling stock with which the yard was crowded. All the tracks of the main electrified line between Paris and Chartres which passes through this yard were cut, several of the overhead standards having been hit, and at the east end of the yard, at least five direct hits were scored on the constriction of lines. To the northeast of the target, the engine shed was two-thirds destroyed.

66. Of the other early attacks carried out in March and early April, some of the most successful were those on Paris/La Chappelle, Charleroi/St. Martin, Paris/Juvisy, Laon and Aachen, at each of these centres the locomotive servicing and maintenance facilities were rendered almost, if not completely, useless and great havoc was wrought in the marshalling yards. At Paris/Noisy le Sec, the whole railway complex was almost annihilated. Other damaging attacks in this early period were made on Ottignies, Rouen, Namur, Lens and Tergnier. Nine of these 11 attacks were carried out by R.A.F. Bomber Command.

67. From the first attacks, the enemy energetically set about endeavouring to make good the damage inflicted, but Trappes, first attacked by Bomber Command on 6th-7th March, 1944, was still under repair at the end of April.

68. For the effort involved, the results of the attack on Charleroi/St. Martin on 18th April, 1944, are worth citing, but this attack is only typical of many of these blows at the enemy communications. A force of 82 Marauders and 37 Bostons of the United States Ninth Air Force attacked the railway centre between 1835 and 1905 hours, dropping a total of 176 tons of bombs on the target. Photographic interpretation after this attack showed that the locomotive repair shop and two locomotive depots were very heavily damaged. The marshalling yard was ploughed up and all through traffic stopped. A single through track was later established on the north side of the yard and was completed by 2nd May, 1944, 14 days later. A double track through the marshalling yard was re-established by 11th May, 1944, but at D-Day (6th June), the marshalling yard was still unserviceable and the repair facilities could not be used.

69. During the last days of April and throughout the month of May, 1944, the same high degree of success achieved by the early attacks was maintained. A growing paralysis was being extended over the rail networks of the Region Nord, west of a line Paris-Amiens-Boulogne and South Belgium. In these areas, all the principal routes were, at one time or another, interrupted. Other centres to the east and south of Paris had also been attacked.

70. In the last week of April, Aulnoye, Villeneuve-St. Georges, Acheres, Montzen, St. Ghislain, Arras and Bethune were all attacked. During May, the heaviest attacks were made on Mantes/Gassicourt, Liege, Ghent, Courtrai, Lille, Hasselt, Louvain, Boulogne, Orleans, Tours, Le Mans, Metz, Mulhouse, Rheims, Troyes and Charleroi.

71. Photographic interpretation continued to show the devastating effect on the centres attacked, and other intelligence sources confirmed this evidence, as well as supplying indications of damage to signals and ancillary services, damage which did not appear in photographs.

72. In order to extend the paralysis inflicted on the regions north and west of Paris, attacks were made in the period immediately before D-Day, on the eastern routes to Paris and the important avoiding routes round the south of that city, and on centres on the Grande Ceinture. Attacks on these centres were considerably restricted by the necessity of avoiding causing heavy civilian casualties or damage to historic buildings. A typical example of this restriction was furnished by the important junction of Le Bourget which, because of the strong probability of bombing causing heavy civilian casualties, was not attacked at all.

73. At D-Day, I believed the primary object of the rail plan had been fully realised. The events which followed confirmed my belief. After the Allied advance, enquiry from the

French railway authorities indicated very clearly that pre-D-Day attacks achieved the purpose intended. The Nazi controlled transport system was very badly disorganised. It had therefore, become extremely vulnerable to the attention of the medium and fighter bombers, which, in the periods just before and after the assault, caused great destruction to immobilised rolling stock.

74. *Attacks on Locomotive Power.*—Attack on repair depots and facilities was the main method of achieving the desired reduction in traction power. It was accepted that these attacks would, at the same time, damage and destroy locomotives. For example, in one such attack, about five per cent. of the locomotives in the Region Nord were put out of service. In addition, however, it was planned to attack directly trains and locomotives on open lines.

75. I first initiated special large scale fighter sweeps against trains and locomotives in Northern France and Belgium on 21st May, 1944. On this day, concentrated efforts were made in certain areas in France, with some attention to connections from Germany and Belgium. Fighters of A.E.A.F. and the United States Eighth Air Force swept over railway tracks covering a very wide area and created havoc among locomotives, passenger trains, goods trains and oil wagons.

76. On this day, 21st May, 504 Thunderbolts, 233 Spitfires, 16 Typhoons and 10 Tempests of A.E.A.F. operated throughout the day, claiming 67 locomotives destroyed, 91 locomotives damaged and six locomotives stopped. Eleven other locomotives were attacked with unknown results and numerous trains were attacked and damage inflicted on trucks, carriages, oil wagons, etc.

77. On this same day, United States Eighth Air Force Fighter Command sent out 131 Lightnings, 135 Thunderbolts and 287 Mustangs against similar targets in Germany. They claimed 91 locomotives destroyed and 134 locomotives damaged. In addition, one locomotive tender, six goods wagons and three box cars were destroyed, whilst seven goods wagons, seven trains, three rail cars, four box cars and thirteen trucks were damaged, and sixteen trains set on fire.

78. From 22nd May to D-Day, A.E.A.F. flew 1,388 sorties with the primary purpose of attacking locomotives. In this period they claimed 157 locomotives destroyed and 82 damaged, as well as numerous trucks.

79. On 25th May, United States Eighth Air Force Fighter Command flew 608 sorties over France and Belgium, with the result that 41 locomotives, 1 troop train with approximately 300 men and 19 trucks were destroyed, and 25 locomotives and 50 trucks were damaged. Though outside the "Neptune" area, it is interesting to record that on 29th May, aircraft of Eighth Air Force Fighter Command flew 571 sorties over Eastern Germany and Poland, attacking 24 locomotives, 32 oil tank cars, 16 box cars and 3 freight trains with unobserved results. In addition to these special attacks, aircraft of Eighth Air Force Fighter Command frequently attacked locomotives and trains amongst other ground targets, when returning from escorting heavy bombers.

80. The total effort by fighters against rolling stock from 19th May to D-Day was as under:—

A.E.A.F.	2,201 sorties
U.S. Eighth Air Force	1,731 sorties
	3,932 sorties

81. With the capacity and flexibility of the enemy rail system destroyed, the enemy armies in the field were denied the freedom of movement necessary to mount decisive counterattacks. Further, the enemy armies and their supplies were forced on to the roads, thus not only slowing up their movement and making them more vulnerable to air attack, but also by compelling the enemy to use motor transport making him draw more heavily on his precious reserves of oil and rubber. Air attacks on these road movements eventually forced the enemy to move mainly by night.

82. During the assault and post-assault phases, this stranglehold on the enemy rail communications was effectively maintained. Details of the attacks involved and some evidence of the delay produced in the enemy build-up are given in Part III (c) of this Despatch.

83. *Destruction of Bridges.*—As I have already explained, complementary to the plan to destroy, by air attack, the enemy's rail motive power, I planned also to endeavour to destroy all the principal rail and road bridges leading into the assault area. If these were destroyed, not only would the enemy's rate of build-up in that area be further checked and his flow of reinforcements and supplies be further impeded, but also his ability to escape rapidly from the assault area in the event of his being forced to retreat would be very seriously impaired. The implications of the attacks on bridges were, therefore, somewhat wider than those of the other attacks on his communications system. In conjunction with these other attacks, the attacks on bridges were designed to seal off the assault area and so force the enemy to stand and fight, and since he could not easily retreat, any defeat would be decisive.

84. A bridge is, by nature of its size, very difficult to hit and, by nature of its construction, even more difficult to destroy completely. Calculation suggested that approximately 600 tons of bombs per bridge would be needed if the task were entrusted to heavy bombers. In fact, it was found that an average of 640 tons of bombs per bridge was needed. What was not at first realised was how effectively, and relatively cheaply, the task could be carried out by fighter bombers. It was learnt from the attacks on bridges by the aircraft of A.E.A.F. that a bridge could be destroyed for the expenditure of approximately 100 sorties, that is between 100 and 200 tons of bombs.

85. In order not to betray a special interest in the "Neptune" area, attention was paid in the preparatory phase principally to the bridges over the Seine, with some others over the Oise, Meuse and the Albert Canal, leaving to the assault phase the task of attacking bridges south of Paris to Orleans and west along the Loire.

86. On 21st April, 1944, the first of a series of attacks against bridges was made by Typhoons. Subsequent attacks were carried

out by formations of fighter bombers which included Thunderbolts, Typhoons and Spitfires and by the medium bombers of the United States Ninth Air Force. The early operations were of an experimental nature, the intention being to explore the possibilities of attacks by fighter bombers and medium bombers against this type of target. The success of the early operations by fighter bombers surpassed expectations. It is probable that in one or two early attacks, a lucky hit exploded the demolition charges that had been set in place by the Germans and in such cases, the destruction caused was out of all proportion to the effort expended. Nevertheless, proof was speedily available that fighter bombers could carry out the task of destroying bridges effectively and relatively cheaply.

87. As D-Day approached, so the intensity of the attacks increased, until a crescendo of effort was achieved over a period of about 10 days prior to D-Day. These attacks were carried out, in the main, by fighter bombers and medium bombers of the United States Ninth Air Force, although Royal Air Force Second Tactical Air Force and the heavy bombers and fighter bombers of the United States Eighth Air Force also provided a contribution to the success of the plan. The marked success of the low level fighter bomber attacks of the Ninth Air Force, as well as the results obtained by the medium bombers is a tribute to the high standard of bombing accuracy developed by this force during the preparatory period. These attacks were often met by heavy anti-aircraft fire, and the resultant losses were not light.

88. The outcome of these attacks was that, on D-Day, twelve railway bridges and the same number of road bridges over the River Seine were rendered impassable. In addition, three railway bridges at Liege and others at Hasselt, Herenthals, Namur, Conflans (Pointe Eifel), Valenciennes, Hirson, Konz-Karthaus and Tours, as well as the important highway bridge at Saumur, were also unserviceable.

89. After D-Day, the assault on bridges of tactical and strategical importance to the enemy was maintained and the results are confirmed in prisoner of war reports of the disruption and delay in the movement of troops and equipment which the enemy experienced. Details of these attacks are given in Part III (d) of this Despatch.

90. The statistical summary below is necessarily incomplete as, in many cases, road and rail bridges were attacked as targets of opportunity by fighter bombers of A.E.A.F. and the Eighth Air Force while engaged on offensive patrols against miscellaneous targets. In these instances, therefore, no separate appreciation of attacks on bridges, is possible.

91. *Attacks on Road and Rail Bridges for period 21st April–6th June.*

Force	Attacks	Sorties	Bombs
(a) Rail			
A.E.A.F.	78	3,897	2,784 tons. 904 × 60-lb. R.Ps.*
U.S. Eighth Air Force	11	201	227·5 tons
(b) Road			
A.E.A.F.	28	987	1,210 tons 495 × 60-lb. R.Ps.*
U.S. Eighth Air Force	1	24	24 tons

92. There can be no doubt that the enemy's transport difficulties after D-Day were the result of the cumulative and combined effects of all the attacks levelled against his communications system. The attacks on nodal points in the railway system, the complementary attacks on bridges and the line-cutting by fighter bombers, all contributed to the restriction placed upon enemy movements.

Neutralisation of Coastal Defences

93. I now come to air operations directed to the support of the landing (see paragraph 25). These operations had to be begun well in advance of D-Day. It was essential, as far as possible, to destroy the enemy's capacity to prevent Allied shipping from approaching the assault area and to blind him to that approach. I deal below, therefore, with air operations during this preparatory period directed to the neutralisation of the enemy's coastal defences and the disruption of his Radar cover.

94. There were forty-nine known coastal batteries capable of firing on shipping approaching the assault area. Included in this number were some batteries still under construction. In the conditions that would obtain at the time of the assault, it would clearly be impossible for the naval forces successfully to engage all the coastal batteries. They, therefore, had to be dealt with before the landing and the air forces undertook this task at the request of the Naval and Army Commanders. I did not consider that aerial attacks against batteries whose casemates were completed were likely to be very effective. Fortunately those batteries in the Cherbourg area were the last to be casemated, and it was possible therefore, to attack many of them while they were still incomplete.

95. To avoid showing particular interest in the assault area, it was planned to attack batteries outside the assault area ranging as far north as Ostend, in the proportion of two outside to one within the area.

96. Interpretation reports revealed that, in a great many instances, the bombing was more successful than I at first expected; by D-Day, the majority of the coastal batteries within the area had been subjected to damaging attack.

---

* R.P = rocket projectile.

97. *Attacks on Coastal Batteries for period 10th April–5th June.*

(a) *Inside Assault Area*

Force	Sorties	Bombs
A.E.A.F.	1,755	2,886·5 tons
		495 × 60-lb. R.Ps.
U.S. Eighth Air Force	184	579·0 tons
R.A.F. Bomber Command	556	2,438·5 tons
	2,495	5,904 tons
		495 × 60-lb. R.Ps.

(b) *Outside Assault Area*

Force	Sorties	Bombs
A.E.A.F.	3,244	5,846 tons
U.S. Eighth Air Force	1,527	4,559 tons
R.A.F. Bomber Command	1,499	6,785 tons
	6,270	17,190 tons

Total for the period 10th April to 5th June, 1944—8,765 sorties, 23,094 tons of bombs and 495 × 60-lb. R.Ps.

98. Of these attacks, one of the most outstanding was that carried out by 64 Lancasters of R.A.F. Bomber Command, with 7 Mosquitoes acting as a Pathfinder Force. During this raid, on the night of 28th–29th May, 356 tons of H.E. bombs were dropped on the coastal battery at St. Martin de Varreville, with excellent results. These results, reported by A.P.I.S. Medmenham, after a photographic reconnaissance sortie made on 29th May, were confirmed by a captured German report made by the troop commander of the battery. The two reports are given below for comparison.

Photographic Reconnaissance Report.

A heavy concentration of craters is seen in the target area with excellent results.

Damage to Casemates:

No. 1. Five very near misses, all within 45 feet. Casemate walls damaged.

No. 2. Damaged by at least five near misses.

No. 3. Destroyed and no longer identifiable; six near misses.

No. 4. Excavation undamaged.

Damage to Command Post:
Demolished by a direct hit and five near misses or probable hits.

Damage to Accommodation:
Personnel shelters in rear of each emplacement all indistinguishable amidst the craters.

Captured German Report.

The position is covered with craters . . . .

Several direct hits with very heavy bombs were made on No. 3 shelter (casemate) which apparently burst open and then collapsed. . . . The rest of the shelters remain undamaged.

. . . . the iron equipment hut which contained signals apparatus, the armoury, the gas chamber and artillery instruments received a direct hit, and only a few twisted iron girders remain.

. . . . the men's canteen received several direct hits and was completely destroyed. The messing huts, containing the battery dining room, the kitchen and clerks' office, were completely destroyed by near misses. A concrete-built hot shower bath was completely destroyed by a direct hit; as well as the nearby joiner's shop.

99. Effective attacks were also carried out by aircraft of R.A.F. Bomber Command against the six-gun battery at Morsalines, and by Marauders of the United States Ninth Air Force on the batteries at Houlgate, Ouistreham and Point de Hoe.

100. Out of forty sites allotted to A.E.A.F., thirty-seven were attacked, sixteen out of eighteen in the assault area and twenty-one out of twenty-two outside. Of these, nine in the area and fourteen outside received hits on one or more emplacements. Forty-eight sites were allotted to R.A.F. Bomber Command, fourteen of which were outside. Hits on essential elements were secured on five batteries in the area and nine outside. Of the fifty-two targets allotted to the United States Eighth Air Force, thirty-two of which were in the assault area, only six sites in the area and sixteen outside were attacked. Some of the batteries were allotted to two commands.

101. In addition to the targets listed in the plan, many other coastal defence targets in and out of the area were attacked as targets of opportunity.

102. During the hours of darkness preceding the actual assault, a tremendous air bombardment was directed on to the batteries which could not be destroyed within the assault area, aimed at neutralising them during the critical assault period. This the attacks succeeded in doing. Details of the effort employed are given in Part III (c) of this Despatch.

Disruption of Enemy Radar Cover and W/T Facilities.

103. The enemy Radar cover on the Western Front was complete from Norway to the Spanish border. This cover was obtained by a chain of coastal stations, each composed of a number of installations. The density of these stations was such that there was a major site, containing an average of three pieces of equipment, every ten miles between Ostend and Cherbourg. This coastal chain was backed by a somewhat less dense inland system and by numerous mobile installations. The attached map* shows the location of the principal enemy Radar sites and the coverage of this Radar Chain.

104. The scale and variety of equipment in this Radar organisation was such that completely to destroy the system by air attack alone would have been a formidable proposition. This, however, was not necessary—the destruction of certain vital Radars and the comprehensive jamming of others could so gravely interfere with the operation of the system as almost to make it useless. I therefore decided to attack Radar stations between Ostend and the Channel Islands in accordance with the following principles:—

(a) Radar installations which could not be jammed electronically, or were difficult to jam, should be destroyed:

(b) Radar installations capable of giving good readings on ships and of controlling coastal guns should be destroyed:

(c) Radar installations likely to assist the enemy in inflicting casualties to airborne forces should be destroyed:

(d) Two targets outside the assault area were to be attacked for every one attacked in the area.

The attacks had a dual purpose. They aided both current air operations and naval operations in the Channel, and they prepared for the assault by blinding the enemy.

105. On 10th May, 1944, a series of attacks was begun against the long range aircraft reporting stations, and on 18th May, on the installations used for night fighter control and the control of coastal guns. On 25th May, 42 sites were scheduled for attack. These sites included 106 installations; at D-3, fourteen of these sites were confirmed destroyed.

106. To conserve effort, I then decided, three days before D-Day, to restrict attacks to the twelve most important sites; six were chosen by the naval authorities and six by the air authorities. These twelve sites, containing thirty-nine installations, were all attacked in the three days prior to D-Day.

107. Up to D-Day, 1,668 sorties were flown by aircraft of A.E.A.F. in attacks on Radar installations. Typhoons in low level attacks flew 694 sorties and fired 4,517 × 60-lb. R.Ps. Typhoons and Spitfires made 759 dive-bombing sorties, dropping 1,258 × 500-lb. bombs and light and medium bombers dropped 217 tons of bombs. In addition, the sites and equipment were attacked with many thousands of rounds of cannon and machine-gun fire.

108. These Radar targets were very heavily defended by flak and low level attacks upon them demanded great skill and daring. Pilots of the R.A.F. Second Tactical Air Force were mainly employed and losses among senior and more experienced pilots were heavy. There is no doubt, however, that these attacks saved the lives of countless soldiers, sailors and airmen on D-Day. The following details of some of the successful attacks made during the last three days before the assault, show the outstanding results obtained by Typhoon and Spitfire pilots in low level attacks pressed home to very close range.

(a) *Cap de la Hague/Jobourg.* This site was attacked by rocket firing Typhoons of 174, 175 and 245 Squadrons, Second Tactical Air Force, on 5th June, and 200 × 60-lb. R.Ps. were fired. The "Hoarding", an installation used for long range aircraft reporting, was destroyed. Three of the attacking aircraft were destroyed by flak.

(b) *Dieppe/Caudecote.* This site was attacked by 18 R.P. Typhoons of 198 and 609 Squadrons, Second Tactical Air Force, on 2nd June. 104 × 60-lb. R.Ps. were fired, with the result that the "Hoarding" was destroyed and the "Freya" and "Wuerzburg" installations, used for medium range aircraft reporting, night fighter control and control of coastal guns, were damaged. One of the Typhoons was destroyed by flak.

(c) *Cap d'Antifer.* This station was attacked several times. On 4th June, 23 Spitfires of 441, 442 and 443 Squadrons, Second Tactical Air Force, dive-bombed with 23 × 500-lb. M.C. instantaneous bombs; nine direct hits were scored. The "Chimney" and one "Giant Wuerzburg" were destroyed, and other installations damaged.

109. In addition to the attacks on the enemy Radar stations, attacks were also made on the most important of his navigational beam stations and on certain special W/T stations.

110. *Navigational Stations.* There were two enemy radio navigational stations important to the assault area, one at Sortosville, south of Cherbourg, and the other at Lanmeur, near Morlaix. Both of these stations were attacked, the first target being destroyed and the second rendered unserviceable, at least temporarily.

111. *W/T Stations.* Four W/T stations of the highest importance were subjected to attack by R.A.F. Bomber Command. These attacks were triumphs of precision bombing and completely achieved their object. Details of these attacks are given below.

(a) *Boulogne/Mt. Couple.* This large installation contained about 60 transmitters. The first attack was unsuccessful, but two nights later, 31st May/1st June, in an attack by 105 heavy bombers dropping 530 tons of bombs, at least 70 heavy bombs were placed on the target, which is some 300 yards long and 150 yards wide. Only a negligible fraction of the transmitters on this site survived the attacks, a maximum of three being subsequently identified in operation.

(b) *Beaumont Hague/Au Feure.* This installation was attacked on the night of 31st May/1st June by 121 aircraft; 498 tons of bombs were dropped and good results were obtained. The main concentration of bombs

---
* Maps not reproduced.

fell just outside the target area, but a number scored direct hits. The station was rendered completely unserviceable.

(c) *Dieppe/Bernaval le Grand.* The attack on this station on the night of 2nd/3rd June was completely successful. 104 aircraft dropped 607 tons of bombs. The majority of the eight or nine blast-wall protected buildings received direct hits, and the remainder suffered so many near misses that their subsequent operational value was negligible. In addition, the aerial masts were all demolished, and the two dispersed sites were also hit.

(d) *Cherbourg/Urville-Hague.* This station is now known to have been the headquarters of the German Signals Intelligence Service in North-Western France. The attack on this important W/T centre was made on 3/4th June by 99 aircraft dropping 570 tons of bombs. The results were remarkable, the centre of a very neat bomb pattern coinciding almost exactly with the centre of the target area. The photographic interpretation report may be quoted verbatim:

"The station is completely useless. The site itself is rendered unsuitable for rebuilding the installation, without much effort being expended in levelling and filling in the craters."

112. The success of this last attack on the Headquarters of the German Air Force Signals Intelligence must have been a major catastrophe for the enemy, and it may well be that it was an important contributory factor to the lack of enemy air reaction to the assault.

113. *Radio Counter-Measures.* On the night of 5/6th June in the opening phase of the assault, counter-measures against such installations as were still active were put into operation. These counter-measures covered five separate and distinct tasks:—

(a) a combined naval/air diversion against Cap d'Antifer:

(b) a combined naval/air diversion against Boulogne:

(c) a jamming barrage to cover the airborne forces:

(d) a V.H.F. jamming support for the first three counter-measures:

(e) feints for the airborne forces.

These various components of the counter-measure plan were inter-dependent and the results can, therefore, best be summarised by giving an indication of the enemy's reactions.

114. The most important fact concerning this reaction was that the enemy appeared to mistake the diversion towards Cap d'Antifer as a genuine threat; at all events, the enemy opened up, both with searchlights and guns on the imaginary convoy. Further, the V.H.F. jamming support which was flown by a formation of aircraft operating in the Somme area apparently led the enemy to believe that these aircraft were the spearhead of a major bomber force, as he reacted with twenty-four night fighters, which were active approximately three hours, hunting the "ghost" bomber stream.

115. The other counter-measures all fulfilled their purpose and it can be stated that the application of radio counter-measures immediately preceding the assault proved to be extraordinarily successful. Only three out of the total number of 105 aircraft employed on these operations were lost, and the crew of one of these aircraft was saved.

116. While it is not possible to state with certainty that the enemy was completely unaware of the cross-Channel movement of the assault forces, the success of the plan to disrupt his Radar cover and W/T facilities both by attacks and by the application of counter-measures, can be judged on the results obtained. In the vital period between 0100 and 0400 hours on 6th June, when the assault Armada was nearing the beaches, only nine enemy Radar installations were in operation, and during the whole night, the number of stations active in the "Neptune" area was only 18 out of a normal 92. No station between Le Havre and Barfleur was heard operating. Apart from the abortive reaction mentioned in paragraph 114, no enemy air attacks were made till approximately 1500 hours on D-Day, and this despite the presence of more than 2,000 ships and landing craft in the assault area, and despite the fact that very large airborne forces had, of necessity, been routed down the west coast of the Cherbourg Peninsula right over the previously excellent Radar cover of the Cherbourg area and the Channel Islands.

117. These results may be summarised as follows: the enemy did not obtain the early warning of our approach that his Radar coverage should have made possible; there is every reason to suppose that Radar controlled gunfire was interfered with; no fighter aircraft hindered our airborne operations; the enemy was confused and his troop movements were delayed.

118. Prior to the launching of Operation "Neptune" each service had almost complete freedom to use radio counter-measures, as desired. To eliminate any clash of interests when very large forces would be employed in confined areas, an inter-Service staff was set up at my Headquarters. The primary concern being to get the Armada safely across the Channel, it was agreed that for the 30-hour period immediately prior to the moment of assault, control should be vested in the Allied Naval Commander-in-Chief; subsequently, control of radio counter-measures became my responsibility. The advisory staff with representatives of the three Services, assisted both the Allied Naval Commander-in-Chief and myself.

Attacks on Military Facilities

119. As well as preparing the way for the assault forces by attacking the enemy's coastal defences and Radar system, it was planned to prepare the way further for the landing by reducing the enemy military potential, both in the assault and rear areas. Certain ammunition and fuel dumps, military camps and headquarters were considered suitable targets for attack, in order to fulfil this purpose.

120. In the period 1st May to 5th June, 1944, the following effort was made on these targets.

Force	Sorties	R.Ps. Fired	Bombs dropped
A.E.A.F.	423	282 × 60-lb.	152 tons
R.A.F. Bomber Command	1,139	—	5,218 tons
	1,562	282 × 60-lb.	5,370 tons

121. The following details of some of these attacks indicate the very great damage done to the enemy supply dumps, and the attacks must also have had considerable moral effect on enemy personnel in addition to the actual casualties inflicted.

122. On the night of 3rd/4th May, R.A.F. Bomber Command attacked in force the tank depot at Mailly-le-Camp. 1,924 tons of bombs were dropped and assessment photographs show the whole target to have been severely damaged. In the mechanical transport section and barracks, 34 out of 47 buildings were totally destroyed. Even more remarkable results were obtained by an attack on an ammunition dump at Chateaudun carried out on the same night. Eight Mosquitoes of R.A.F. Bomber Command attacked with approximately 13 tons of bombs. The bombs were dropped very accurately and caused sympathetic detonation throughout the dump. In the resulting explosion, the entire western wing of the depot, containing 90 buildings, was completely destroyed.

123. The Bourg Leopold military camp in Belgium was heavily attacked on two occasions. On 11th/12th May, aircraft of R.A.F. Bomber Command dropped 585 tons of bombs on this depot. On the night of 27th/28th May, a force of 324 aircraft, also from that Command, dropped 1,348 tons of bombs, and photographic reconnaissance revealed very heavy damage throughout the whole area of the camp. Six large buildings and at least 150 personnel huts received direct hits.

124. Smaller in scale, but very effective, were the attacks made by A.E.A.F. aircraft on other targets of this type. On 2nd June, a force of 50 Thunderbolts of the United States Ninth Air Force attacked a fuel dump at Domfront. 54 × 500-lb incendiaries and 63 × 1,000-lb. G.P. bombs were dropped and severe damage was caused to this dump.

Harassing of Coastwise Shipping and Sea Mining.

125. As a result of the successful attacks on the overland communications of the enemy, his coastal shipping became increasingly important. The task of dealing with this shipping was very largely the work of R.A.F. Coastal Command, but Typhoons of A.E.A.F. also operated on occasions in an anti-shipping role under the operational control of Coastal Command, and Spitfires of A.E.A.F. provided when needed fighter escort to the strike aircraft of Coastal Command. The sea mining programme was carried out by R.A.F. Bomber Command in direct consultation with the British Admiralty.

126. During the period 1st April to 5th June, 1944, R.A.F. Coastal Command flew 4,340 sorties on the anti-shipping and anti-U-Boat patrols in the Bay of Biscay, along the Dutch Coast and in the Channel. During these sorties, 103 attacks were made on shipping and 22 on U-Boats.

127. The minelaying had as its objectives not only the interruption of enemy coastal shipping, but also in the closing stages of preparation for the assault, the laying of minebelts, to afford protection to the Allied assault and naval bombardment forces from attacks by E and R boats, especially those operating from Le Havre and Cherbourg.

128. In the period 1st April to 5th June, R.A.F. Bomber Command flew 990 sorties and laid 3,099 mines in the areas east of Texel and along the Dutch, Belgian and French coasts. Other mines were also sown in German home waters, including many in the Baltic Sea.

Attacks on Airfields.

129. I have already dealt (see paragraphs 42 to 47) with the preliminary operations designed to wear down the G.A.F. and render it powerless seriously to interfere with the assault. As D-Day approached however, it became necessary to ensure that our measure of air superiority was fully adequate to our needs. Plans had accordingly been made for direct attacks upon the enemy air force, particularly in France and the Low Countries. The effect of these plans was to deny the German Air Force the advantage of disposition which its fighter squadrons would otherwise enjoy as compared with our own in the initial stages of the assault. It was, therefore, necessary to neutralise a considerable number of airfields within a radius of 150 miles of Caen. The primary object of these attacks was to destroy the aircraft repair, maintenance and servicing facilities and thereby cause the maximum interference with the operational ability of the German Air Force.

130. I planned that these attacks should start at least three weeks before D-Day, and they actually began on 11th May, 1944. It was necessary to bear in mind in the planning of these attacks that no indication should be given as to the selected area for the Allied landings.

131. *Allocation of Targets.*—Forty main operational airfields were selected for attack. Twelve were assigned to R.A.F. Bomber Command and the remaining twenty-eight to A.E.A.F. and the United States Eighth Air Force.

132. Fifty-nine other operational bomber bases with important facilities located in France, Belgium, Holland and Western Germany within range of the assault area and ports of embarkation in the United Kingdom were also selected for attack, as opportunity permitted, by aircraft of the United States Eighth and Fifteenth Air Forces, the latter based in the Mediterranean area.

133. From 11th May, 1944 to D-Day, thirty-four of the most important airfields were attacked by 3,915 aircraft dropping 6,717 tons of bombs with the result that four airfields were placed in Category "A" and fifteen in

Category "B". Twelve airfields of the second list were attacked by the Eighth Air Force with very satisfactory results.

134. The following categories of airfield damage were used:—

Category "A"—major installations completely destroyed; no further attacks needed.

Category "B"—major installations severely damaged; further attacks warranted.

Category "C"—minor damage; further attacks required.

135. *Statistical Summary of Attacks on Airfields during the period 11th May to D-Day.*

Force	Attacks	Sorties	Bombs
A.E.A.F.			
Ninth Air Force	56	2,550	3,197 tons
Second T.A.F.	12	312	487 tons
R.A.F. Bomber Command	6	119	395 tons
U.S. Eighth Air Force	17	934	2,638 tons
	91	3,915	6,717 tons

136. These attacks on enemy airfields accomplished the desired object of placing the enemy under the same handicap as the Allied fighters by forcing them to operate from airfields a long way from the assault area. They were also largely responsible for the lack of enemy air interference with our landings and undoubtedly contributed much to the ineffectiveness of the German Air Force at the really critical times.

Photographic Reconnaissance.

137. The photographic reconnaissance units of the Allied air forces were the first to begin active and direct preparation for the invasion of Europe from the West. For more than a year, much vital information was accumulated which contributed very greatly to the ultimate success of the assault. The variety, complexity and moreover, the detailed accuracy of the information gathered and assiduously collated was of great importance in the preparatory phase of the operation.

138. Each particular service had its own requirements and individual problems which only photographic reconnaissance could hope to solve. Then again, within each service, specialised sections relied to a great extent for their information on these sources, e.g. as early as possible after each major bombing attack, damage assessment sorties were flown.

139. Photographic coverage of the entire coastline from Holland to the Spanish frontier was obtained to gather full details of the coastal defences. Verticals and obliques were taken of beach gradients, beach obstacles, coastal defences and batteries. Full photographic coverage from Granville to Flushing, both in obliques and verticals, was obtained. This very large coverage also served to hide our special interest in the selected assault beaches.

140. Obliques were taken at wave top height, three to four miles out from the coast, in order to provide the assault coxswains with a landing craft view of the particular area to be assaulted or likely to be their allotted landing spots. Then obliques were flown 1,500 yards from the coast at zero feet, to provide platoon assault commanders with recognition landing points. Further obliques were taken, again at 1,500 yards from the shore, but at 2,000 feet to provide, for those who were planning the infantry assault, views of the immediate hinterland.

141. Inland strips were photographed behind the assault areas, looking southwards, so that infantry commanders could pinpoint themselves after they had advanced. Again, it was necessary to photograph hidden land behind assault areas, so that the infantry commanders would know the type of terrain behind such obstructions as hills or woods.

142. Bridges over rivers were photographed and special attention was paid to the river banks to enable the engineers to plan the type of construction necessary to supply temporary bridges in the event of the enemy blowing up the regular bridges.

143. The prospective airfield sites were selected by the engineers after they had studied the vast quantity of reconnaissance photographs available. The success of the Airfield Construction Units, some details of which are given in Part IV of this Despatch, is testimony to the value of this reconnaissance.

144. It was also necessary to cover all the likely dropping areas for the use of the airborne divisions, and to pay special attention to each area for concealed traps such as spikes, etc. These traps were observed on photographs of many sites chosen and it was necessary to make other plans accordingly.

145. Flooding areas, too, throughout Holland, Belgium and France were all photographed at different periods, thus ensuring to the Army Commander full knowledge of these defences in planning the deployment of his forces. The extent to which army commanders depended upon photographic reconnaissance may be gauged by the volume of cover they received. In the two weeks prior to D-Day, one R.A.F. Mobile Field Photographic Section alone made for Army requirements more than 120,000 prints.

146. Continued photographic reconnaissance was also flown covering enemy communication centres, petrol, oil and lubricant dumps, headquarters, inland defences and military concentrations. These reconnaissances provided invaluable information as to the enemy order of battle and his capabilities.

147. Many small scale sorties were flown for Combined Operations, enabling them to make landings at selected spots, long before the real offensive was launched and to bring back vital information.

148. Another important task undertaken was the photographing of Allied landing craft, equipment and stores in the United Kingdom, to facilitate experiments with the type of camouflage most likely to be effective.

149. The demands of all three services for photographic cover were very varied and so great in number that it was necessary to set up a controlling body to deal with them. Accordingly, the Central Reconnaissance Committee was established at your headquarters. This inter-service committee received requests for photographic cover from all services and allocated the task to the most suitable reconnaissance force. One of the most important functions of this Committee was to watch the security aspect of the reconnaissance effort and by ensuring that this effort was judiciously distributed, conceal from the enemy our special interest in the assault area.

150. The bulk of this invaluable reconnaissance effort was flown by aircraft of A.E.A.F. which, in the period 1st April to 5th June flew no less than 3,215 photographic reconnaissance sorties. Aircraft of other commands, however, including 106 Group, R.A.F. Coastal Command and United States Eighth Air Force, operating under the control of R.A.F. Station, Benson, also contributed notably to this work, flying a total of 1,519 sorties during the same period. The excellent co-operation between British and American reconnaissance units in fact enabled the needs of all services to be fully met by D-Day.

151. If we had had to rely, however, entirely on orthodox high altitude reconnaissance aircraft for this work, not more than a small proportion of these needs could have been met. The weather in Western Europe, never very suitable for high altitude photography, was particularly bad in the early part of the year. There was an urgent need for a medium/low altitude photographic reconnaissance aircraft to supplement high altitude reconnaissance. It was decided, therefore, to convert some Mustang fighters into tactical and strategical medium/low altitude reconnaissance aircraft. They were equipped with oblique cameras, were armed to protect themselves and were fast enough to outpace most German fighters.

152. Low altitude reconnaissance, however, whether visual or photographic was at all times a hazardous business in view of the risk of being jumped by higher flying enemy fighters. None the less, early results achieved by Mustangs were very encouraging and eventually a number of reconnaissance squadrons were partly re-equipped with converted Mustangs to supplement their high altitude aircraft. Their work proved invaluable and the development of this aircraft for photographic reconnaissance work has been one of the outstanding lessons of the air war.

Protection of the Assembling of the Assault Forces.

153. I stated in paragraph 25 that one of the main tasks of the air forces was to support the landing of the Allied armies in Europe. As a corollary, the air force was required to protect the assembling of the assault forces. A.E.A.F. was directly charged with this responsibility.

154. More than 2,000 ships and landing craft were used to lift the initial assault forces and other equipment, and they were supported by task forces of over 100 warships including battleships and more than 200 escorts and other naval vessels. In all, over 6,000 ships and landing craft were employed in the first week.

155. The assembly, preparation and loading of these ships and other special beach installations necessitated the concentration of enormous forces in the ports and harbours of the south coast of England, in the Bristol Channel and in the Thames Estuary, over long periods, with especially heavy concentrations in the final six weeks. Moreover, large scale embarkation had to be practised to ensure that speed and flexibility could be attained. To provide this practice, a series of exercises were staged in which the forces to be employed were brought into the concentration areas and in some cases, embarked and sailed to practice assault beaches on the south coast of England.

156. *Enemy Action against Assault Forces.*—It was estimated by my Planning Staff that the German Air Force would have available 850 aircraft, including 450 long range bombers to use against the Allied assault operation. I anticipated that these bomber forces would be used against shipping in ports and in transit, both in bombing attacks and in sea mining. It was further estimated that this force would be capable of the following scale of effort over a period of three weeks during the assembling and loading periods:—

	Sorties.
Sustained per night	25
Intensive per night for 2-3 nights per week	50-75
Maximum in any one night ...	100-150

157. In fact, the enemy activity did not reach this maximum scale of effort. There were three periods of activity in the six weeks prior to 6th June, and they involved only 377 bombing sorties.

158. On 25th-26th April, approximately 40 aircraft operated against Portsmouth and Havant. On 26-27th April, approximately 80 aircraft again attacked Portsmouth and a triangular area between the Needles, Basingstoke and Worthing. On 29-30th April, approximately 35 aircraft operated over and off Plymouth.

159. The second phase of these attacks took place on the nights 14-15th and 15-16th May, when approximately 100 and 80 aircraft respectively operated against Southampton and along the coast, and against Weymouth.

160. The third phase was during 28-29th 29-30th and 30-31st May; on the first of these nights, approximately 35 aircraft attacked from Dartmouth to Start Point and on the next two nights small forces operated indiscriminately.

161. The night fighter forces of the Air Defence of Great Britain were ready to deal with this activity. Of the total of 377 enemy sorties, night fighters claimed 22 destroyed, 6 probably destroyed and 5 damaged, while a further 2 were destroyed by anti-aircraft fire.

162. A valuable contribution to the defence of the assembly areas for the assault forces was made by balloons and anti-aircraft guns. Units were provided for this purpose by R.A.F. Balloon Command, the R.A.F. Regiment, Anti-Aircraft Command and certain Anti-Aircraft artillery formations of the United States forces. Operational control of these units was in general exercised on my behalf by the Air Marshal Commanding, Air Defence of Great Britain.

163. The work of these units not only in protecting the assembly, but later, in defence

against attacks by Flying Bombs, was of exceptional value to the launching and maintenance of the assault. I deal with certain other features of this work later in this Despatch.

164. It was also of the utmost importance to deny to the enemy, air reconnaissance of Southern England. Special precautions had to be taken to this end.

165. Mastery of the air over the Channel, wrested from the enemy in earlier years by aircraft of R.A.F. Fighter Command (later Air Defence of Great Britain), had done much to ensure this end already. Daylight operations of enemy aircraft overland were almost unheard of and it was appreciated that only dire necessity would prompt the enemy to expose his aircraft and pilots to the heavy risk they would run in attempting to spy out our preparations. None the less, the enemy had now so much at stake that a great effort on his part was to be expected. To deal with possible enemy reconnaissance efforts, therefore, I directed that standing high and low level fighter patrols should be maintained by aircraft of Air Defence of Great Britain during daylight hours over certain coastal belts.

166. In the six weeks immediately prior to D-Day, however, the enemy flew only 125 reconnaissance sorties in the Channel area and 4 sorties over the Thames Estuary and the east coast. Very few of these sorties approached land, most of them being fleeting appearances in mid-Channel. Our fighters rarely got even a glimpse of these enemy aircraft, which could have seen very little and could only have taken back, therefore, information of very small value; but as an extra deterrent, standing patrols were maintained as far out as 40-50 miles south of the Isle of Wight and intruder aircraft were directed to the enemy airfields in the Dinard area, from which it was believed such enemy reconnaissance aircraft as appeared were operating. In the result, the enemy appears to have learnt very little.

167. These defensive measures, coupled with the others to which I have already referred, achieved for the assault a complete tactical surprise on D-Day and did much to ensure the safety of the cross-Channel movement of the assault forces. The weather factor relating to this aspect of the operations is considered in paras. 405 and 406.

168. On many days Allied air forces flew more photographic reconnaissance sorties in one day than the enemy flew in the whole of the vital period of six weeks prior to D-Day. In view of the fact that the enemy was aware, in general terms, of our intention to invade the Continent the small scale of his air reconnaissance effort is, to say the least, extraordinary.

"*Crossbow*" *Operations*.

169. It became known early in 1943 that the enemy was preparing an attack on the United Kingdom with flying bombs and rockets launched from the French coast. Much experimental work on these projectiles had been done in the Baltic Sea area, and it was believed that the enemy would shortly be in a position to begin constructing sites, from which the projectiles could be launched. Construction began chiefly in the Pas de Calais and the Cherbourg areas during the autumn of 1943.

170. Considerable research into the nature of these novel weapons was carried out by Operational Research Sections and by a special Committee set up in the Air Ministry, and it was concluded that they represented a potentially serious menace, both to the United Kingdom and to the preparation and build-up of forces for the projected Operation "Neptune". Accordingly, it became necessary to divert part of the available air effort to attacks on these constructional sites in order to prevent the threat becoming a reality.

171. At this time it was not considered desirable to divert any large part of the heavy bomber effort from the commitment on "Pointblank" targets. I was, therefore, made responsible for taking the necessary countermeasures with the forces of A.E.A.F. In addition, however, a proportion of the effort of the heavy bombers of the United States Eighth Air Force was made available to me for this task on days when weather was unsuitable for deep penetration raids into Germany. The United States IXth Bomber Command was committed, up to 1st April, to assist the strategical air forces with diversionary raids, and therefore, was not always available for these operations. R.A.F. Bomber Command was also originally allotted five sites for attack, but this commitment was subsequently re-allotted to A.E.A.F.

172. As is now known, the menace was not under-estimated, and the air effort prior to D-Day did not succeed wholly in removing it.

173. The sites were classified as follows:—
(a) Ski-sites—(so called because of a big store room construction which from the air looked very like a ski)—designed for launching flying bombs.
(b) Rocket sites—larger constructions designed for the launching of heavy rocket projectiles.
(c) Supply sites.

174. The sites were given the code word of "Noball" and operations against them were carried out under the code word "Crossbow". These operations began on 5th December, 1943, and accordingly the summary of activity in this section of the Despatch is shown from this date to D-Day.

175. On 5th December, 1943, 63 ski sites and 5 rocket sites had been identified. It appeared that the sites in the Pas de Calais area were aligned on London and those in the Cherbourg area on Bristol. It was calculated that the enemy was completing new sites at the rate of three every two days.

176. A schedule of priorities based on the British Air Ministry recommendations was carefully worked out. It was most important to ensure that no more bombs than were absolutely necessary to neutralise one target should be dropped before an attack was made against the next target on the priority list. A system was devised of "suspending" a site from further attack, whereby a Command which considered that it had inflicted sufficient damage to a site to neutralise it temporarily, was authorised to notify any authority concerned that the site was "suspended" from further attack, pending photographic confirmation of the damage done.

177. The attacks on sites prior to D-Day are listed below. At D-Day it was estimated that out of 97 identified flying bomb sites, 86 had been neutralised, and out of 7 identified rocket sites, 2 had been neutralised.

B

178. In addition, heavy attacks were launched on several special supply or storage sites which had been observed under construction.

179. The ski sites were normally well hidden, either in or at the edge of woods, well camouflaged and heavily defended by flak so that low flying attacks on them were costly. In photographs their presence was recognised not only by the shape and layout of the buildings, particularly the comprehensive water supply system, but also by the specially built roads and railways that led to them.

180. It was not appreciated before D-Day that in addition to these specially constructed ski sites, there were modified ski sites with all the facilities of the original sites except for the distinctive ski buildings and the water supply system. After D+7, the day on which the enemy first launched flying bombs against the United Kingdom, photographic reconnaissance revealed the existence of 74 of these modified sites. They were camouflaged more completely than the original sites and made use of existing roads and buildings. Details of attacks on these modified ski sites or launching sites are included in my account of air operations in the post-assault phase.

181. The exact number of flying bombs which the known number of ski sites were capable of launching against the United Kingdom if they had not been attacked by aircraft can only be estimated, but it is thought that some 6,000 flying bombs per 24 hours is a reasonable estimate. The success of the air forces, therefore, in attacking and neutralising Germany's capacity to use this secret weapon may be judged in terms of the figures of actual flying bombs launched after D-Day. These figures are set out in the account of the post-assault phase.

182. *Summary of Attacks on Ski Sites prior to D-Day.*

Force	Sorties	Bombs
A.E.A.F.	22,280	13,515 tons
U.S. Eighth Air Force	4,589	7,968 tons
	26,869	21,483 tons

Summary of Attacks on Rocket Sites prior to D-Day

Force	Sorties	Bombs
A.E.A.F.	434	667 tons
U.S. Eighth Air Force	2,045	7,624 tons
	2,479	8,291 tons

Summary of Attacks on Supply Sites and Dumps prior to D-Day

Force	Sorties	Bombs
A.E.A.F.	852	1,148 tons and 126×60-lb. R.Ps.
U.S. Eighth Air Force	166	479 tons
	1,018	1,627 tons and 126×60-lb. R.Ps.

Statistical Summary of Preparatory Operations

183. The following statistics show the immense scale of the effort of the Allied air forces operating from the United Kingdom against both "Overlord" and "Pointblank" targets during the preparatory phase 1st April to 5th June, 1944. That the achievements referred to in the foregoing paragraphs were not accomplished without considerable cost in skilled manpower is evident from the aircraft casualty figures included. Statistics covering personnel casualties in the preparatory period are included in the schedule at paragraph 408 in Part III (*d*).

Preparatory Operations
Period 1st April—5th June, 1944

Force	Aircraft despatched	Tons of bombs dropped	Aircraft lost in combat	E/A destroyed in combat
A.E.A.F.:—				
Ninth A.F.	53,784	30,657	197	189
2nd T.A.F.	28,587	} 6,981	133	66
A.D.G.B.	18,639		46	111
R.A.F. B.C.	24,621	87,238	557	77
U.S. Eighth A.F.:—				
VIIIth B.C.	37,804	69,857	763	724
VIIIth F.C.	31,820	647	291	1,488
	195,255	195,380	1,987	2,655

Total sorties as above	...	195,255
R.A.F. Coastal Command	...	5,384
		200,639

184. The sorties of Coastal Command included are only those on anti-shipping and anti-U-boat patrols in the Bay of Biscay and Channel areas and off the Dutch coast. The weight of depth charges, bombs, etc., dropped and casualties or claims arising from these sorties are not included.

(c) *The Assault*

Decision to make the Assault

185. After consultations with the Commanders-in-Chief of the three services, during May, you had fixed the date of the Assault for 5th June. The decision as to date had to be taken in good time to permit of the completion of final preparations. Some of the ships in the invasion Armada, for example, had to sail a week before the time planned for the assault.

186. As the date approached, the weather forecasts pointed to very serious deterioration in conditions for D-Day. On 3rd June, you summoned a conference at your Advanced Headquarters at Portsmouth to consider the weather situation. This conference included yourself, the Deputy Supreme Commander, Air Chief Marshal Sir A. W. Tedder, G.C.B., your Chief of Staff Lieutenant General W. B. Smith, Admiral Sir Bertram H. Ramsay, K.C.B., K.B.E., M.V.O., and his Chief of Staff, General Sir Bernard L. Montgomery, K.C.B., D.S.O., and his Chief of Staff, and the Heads of the Naval, Army and Air Meteorological Services. I attended this conference with my Senior Air Staff Officer, Air Vice-Marshal H. E. P. Wigglesworth, C.B., C.B.E., D.S.C.

187. The first meeting took place at 2100 hours on 3rd June. It lasted until after midnight, when you decided to postpone any decision until the meteorological staffs could collect later reports.

188. The second meeting took place at 0400 hours on 4th June, and in the light of weather forecasts then available, you decided to postpone the time of the assault for 24 hours, primarily on the grounds that the air forces would be unable to provide adequate support for the crossing and assault operations, and could not undertake the airborne tasks.

189. The meeting reassembled at 2100 hours on 4th June, and after considerable deliberation a decision was again deferred to enable the meteorological staffs to study later data.

190. The final meeting took place at 0430 hours in the morning of 5th June. Weather conditions forecast for the following day were still far from satisfactory and from the air point of view, below the planned acceptable minimum.

191. Nevertheless, taking into account the fact that the adverse weather conditions imposed an equal handicap on the enemy air forces, I considered, and I gave this as my opinion, that the Allied air effort possible would provide a reasonable measure of air protection and support and that airborne operations would be practicable.

192. After considering also the weather conditions as affecting the land and sea operations, you made the decision that the assault was to take place on the first high tide in the morning of the 6th of June and that the airborne forces were to be flown over and dropped in their allotted zones before dawn of that day.

The Assault is made

193. The assault was on a five divisional front on the east side of the Cherbourg Peninsula immediately north of the Carentan Estuary and the River Orne.

194. The First United States Army landed between Varreville and Colleville-sur-Mer; 1 R.C.T.* landed between Varreville and the Carentan Estuary, 2 R.C.T. between the Carentan Estuary and Colleville-sur-Mer. The Second British Army with five brigades, landed between Asnelles and Ouistreham. These seaborne forces were supported on their flanks by two airborne forces, two United States Airborne Divisions being dropped and landed in the area of St. Mere Eglise, and a British Airborne Division in the area between the Rivers Orne and Dives. The map† facing shows the landing beaches and the positions gained in the first three weeks of the assault.

195. The first airborne forces landed before dawn on 6th June and the landing barges and craft coming in on the first tide, touched down at 0630 hours. Follow-up forces were landed with the second tide, and in the evening, additional airborne forces were flown in.

196. There was no enemy opposition to the original passage of the assault or airborne forces. This fact is all the more remarkable when it is remembered that many of the ships had, of necessity, been at sea for periods of some days.

197. I have set out in Section (*b*) of Part II at paragraph 35, the tasks undertaken by the air forces in support of the assault. For convenience of presentation, these tasks have been dealt with under the five headings shown below:—

Protection of the Cross-Channel Movement,
Neutralisation of Coastal and Beach Defences,
Protection of the Beaches,
Dislocation of Enemy Communications and Control,
Airborne operations.

198. The Order of Battle of A.E.A.F. as at D-Day is set out at Appendix "D",† the strength of aircraft available was as follows:—

Type	United States Forces	Royal Air Force	Grand Total
Medium Bombers	532	88	620
Light Bombers	194	160	354
Fighter and Fighter Bombers	1,311	2,172	3,483
Transport Aircraft	1,166	462	1,628
Reconnaissance Aircraft	158	178	336
Artillery Observation Aircraft	—	102	102
A.S.R. (Miscellaneous)	—	96	96
Powered A/C Total	3,361	3,258	6,619
Gliders	1,619	972	2,591
Grand Total	4,980	4,230	9,210

* R.C.T. = Regimental Combat Team. † Maps and Appendices not reproduced.

Protection of the Cross-Channel movement.

199. The task of assisting the naval forces to protect the passage of the assault armies from surface and U-boat attack, was undertaken chiefly by R.A.F. Coastal Command though aircraft of A.E.A.F. assisted in this task. I deal with these operations in more detail in paragraph 387 et seq. Here I need only mention that on D-Day and D + 1, aircraft of R.A.F. Coastal Command flew 353 sorties on anti-shipping and anti-U-boat patrols. A line of patrols was provided at either end of the Channel. The air protection thus afforded contributed much to the safety of the Allied shipping from both surface and underwater attack by enemy naval forces.

200. Fifteen squadrons of fighters were allotted the task of protecting the shipping lanes. These squadrons flew 2,015 sorties during the course of D-Day and D + 1, the cover being maintained at six squadron strength throughout this period. Owing to the lack of enemy reaction, I was able later to reduce this cover to a two squadron force.

201. For convenience of presentation, I have set out the full plan for the employment of fighter forces during the assault and post-assault phase in the next section. (See paragraph 308 et seq.)

Neutralisation of Coastal and Beach Defences.

202. The task of neutralising as many of the coastal defence positions as possible during the crucial period of the assault was shared by naval and air bombardment. The air bombardment plan called for attacks to commence just before dawn on D-Day.

203. R.A.F. Bomber Command commenced the bombardment with attacks on the following ten selected heavy coastal batteries in the assault area:—

Coastal Batteries	Sorties	Tons of Bombs
Crisbecq	101	598
St. Martin de Varreville	100	613
Ouistreham	116	645
Maisy	116	592
Mont Fleury	124	585
La Parnelle	131	668
St. Pierre du Mont	124	698
Merville/Franceville	109	382
Houlgate	116	468
Longues	99	604
	1,136	5,853 tons

204. As R.A.F. Bomber Command left the assault area, United States Eighth Air Force heavy bombers took over the bombardment role. In the thirty minutes immediately preceding the touch-down hour, 1,365 heavy bombers attacked selected areas in the coastal defences, dropping 2,796 tons of bombs. The result of these operations added to the previous air bombardment and combined with the naval shelling, neutralised wholly or in large part almost all of the shore batteries and the opposition to the landings was very much less than was expected.

205. Medium, light and fighter bombers then took a hand in the attacks on the enemy defensive system by attacking artillery positions further inland and other targets in the coastal defences. The immense scale of this effort may be gauged from the statistics which appear after para. 233.

206. The heavy bombers of the United States Eighth Air Force operated again later in the day, and although cloud interfered with bombing about midday, necessitating the recall of some missions, a further 1,746 tons of bombs were dropped. In all, the Eighth Air Force flew 2,627 heavy bombers and 1,347 escort and offensive fighter sorties during the day.

207. *Spotting for Naval Gunfire.* The naval bombardment took place according to plan. In this bombardment, aircraft of A.E.A.F. played an important role. The Fleet Air Arm had stated early on in the planning that it would be unable to find from its own resources enough aircraft to provide for spotting for the gunfire of all the capital ships it was planned to use. Accordingly, despite the unfortunate diversion of effort from air resources that were far from inexhaustible, I had agreed that two squadrons of Spitfires from A.D.G.B. and two wings (each of three squadrons) of Mustangs from R.A.F. Second Tactical Air Force should be trained for this task. At various times, therefore, well before D-Day, these squadrons had been trained with No. 3 Naval Fighter Wing.

208. The result was that on D-Day and subsequently, we were just able to meet the heavy calls for spotting for naval gunfire that were made on us. On D-Day, no less than 394 sorties were flown on this task, of which 236 were flown by five squadrons of A.E.A.F. Each of the two Spitfire squadrons, No. 26 Squadron and No. 33 Squadron made 76 sorties in the course of the day. In all, during the period of consolidation in the beach-head, that is from 6th June to 19th June, a total of 1,318 sorties on naval gunnery spotting were flown. Of this total, aircraft of A.E.A.F. flew 940. Five aircraft of A.E.A.F. were destroyed on these operations during this period.

209. It may be pointed out here that further calls were made on these same A.E.A.F. squadrons at later stages in the campaign. The gunfire of the capital ships bombarding the isolated German garrisons in the fortresses of Cherbourg in late June, and of St. Malo and Brest in late August, was spotted for by these squadrons. On these duties a further 124 sorties were flown apart from those flown by aircraft of Fleet Air Arm.

Protection of the Landing Beaches.

210. In addition to the cover given to the cross-Channel movement of the assault forces, I provided a continuous daylight fighter cover of the beach-head areas. Nine squadrons in two forces of six squadrons of low cover and three squadrons of high cover continuously patrolled over the British and American beaches. A reserve of six fighter squadrons on the ground were also kept at readiness to strengthen any point if the enemy came up to challenge.

211. On D-Day alone, 1,547 sorties were flown on beach-head cover. Night fighters also patrolled continuously during the hours of darkness over the beach-head and shipping lanes; six squadrons of Mosquitoes were available for these operations. Details of the organisation and control and of the scale of effort of the fighter forces are set out in the next section of this Despatch (see paragraph 308).

212. *Balloon Defence of the Beach-head.*—To supplement the defences provided by fighter aircraft and anti-aircraft guns, it had been decided to provide balloon protection for all beaches and artificial ports (Mulberries). It was thought that balloons would give valuable protection against low-flying attacks and would permit economies in the number of light A.A. weapons that would be needed in the early stages of the assault.

213. Operational control of these balloons was vested in the local A.A. Defence Commander. In practice, balloons flew at 2,000 feet by night and just below cloud base by day. Suitable control funnels, within which balloons were grounded by day, were arranged so as to avoid interference with approaches to air strips.

214. In Part IV of this Despatch I give further details of some of the difficulties experienced and overcome in planning the employment of these balloons. Here I need only comment on the results achieved. The passive nature of balloon defence and the monotonous lack of results make it difficult to compute its value. There were practically no reports of low-level bombing attacks by enemy aircraft during the periods the balloons were flying, and such bombing as did occur was scattered, doing little damage to the beach maintenance and none to the Mulberries. One enemy aircraft was destroyed by a balloon on the beaches in the U.S. sector. Apart from the positive value of balloons as a deterrent to low-flying enemy attacks, I feel that the presence of balloons has, in itself, a definite morale value for both Naval and Army personnel.

Dislocation of enemy communications and control.

215. Air operations to dislocate enemy control of operations in the field were begun on the day before the assault. This dislocation of the enemy control went even further than the previous attacks on his Radar chain. The latter had blinded the enemy to the movement of the Allied assault forces; the air operations now proceeded to impede and disrupt in advance any possible enemy moves to make good his initial setback. To do this I tried during the initial stage of the assault, to break up the enemy machinery of control and signals communications and by so doing to make as difficult as possible the co-ordination of enemy counter-attacks. Chateaux known to house German Corps and Divisional Headquarters and also German Army telephone exchanges were attacked on the evening of 5th June and through D-Day by fighters with bombs and rocket projectiles. These operations undoubtedly seriously embarrassed the enemy, both during the assault and later, when a large number of enemy headquarters were knocked out.

216. The Air Forces also were quite successful in causing casualties among German Generals. Field Marshal Rommel himself was fatally wounded in an air attack and it is believed that a further six to eight Commanders were also casualties. The killing in an air attack of a Divisional Commander during a critical stage of the fighting at St. Lo is thought to have had an important effect on the course of the Battle.

Airborne Operations.

217. The general plan of the airborne operations called for the dropping and landing of three divisions of parachute and gliderborne troops, and for the initial reinforcement and resupply of these formations.

218. Two of these divisions were the 101st and 82nd United States Airborne Divisions and their task was to assist in the capture of the Cotentin Peninsula by aiding the seaborne landing of the First United States Army, and by preventing enemy reinforcements from moving into the peninsula from the south. The particular tasks of these divisions were to capture the areas of St. Mere Eglise and St. Martin and the neighbouring coastal defences.

219. The third division was the 6th British Airborne Division and its task was to operate on the left (eastern) flank of 1st Corps of the Second British Army, in the area between the Orne and Dives Rivers. The particular tasks of this division were:—

(a) to secure intact, and hold, the two bridges over the River Orne-Caen canal at Bonouville and Ranville:

(b) to neutralise an important enemy coastal battery and capture or neutralise a key strongpoint:

(c) to secure a firm base, including bridgeheads east of the River Orne:

(d) to prevent enemy reinforcements (including Panzer units) from moving towards the British left flank from the east and southeast.

To accomplish these objects, 3 and 5 Paratroop Brigade Groups flew in with a limited number of gliders carrying details of the 6th Airborne Division Headquarters on the night of D-1/D-Day, and were followed by the 6th Air Landing Brigade on the evening of D-Day.

220. A limited number of S.A.S. troops were dropped in selected areas before and after D-Day for special missions, by aircraft of No. 38 Group.

221. The airlift of all these forces was provided by the transport aircraft of A.E.A.F.

United States IXth Troop Carrier Command carried the American divisions and No. 38 Group and No. 46 Group of the Royal Air Force, carried the British Force.

222. *U.S. IXth Troop Carrier Command.*—The paratroops of the 101st Division were dropped by aircraft of the United States IXth Troop Carrier Command in the general area of St. Mere Eglise, shortly after midnight on the night of June 5th-6th (Operation Albany). The glider force of the 101st Division went in at dawn of D-Day into the same area, in 58 gliders (Operation Chicago). A re-supply mission was flown for the 101st Division on the night of D + 1 (Operation Keokuk). This re-supply mission was necessary as there had been no contact between the 101st Division and the seaborne assaulting forces.

223. Paratroops of the 82nd Division were flown in in aircraft of IXth Troop Carrier Command and dropped in the general area of St. Sauveur le Vicomte (Operation Boston), shortly after midnight of 5th-6th June. Glider elements of this division were flown in as follows:—

    52 Gliders at dawn of D-Day (Operation Detroit).

    177 Gliders at dusk of D-Day (Operation Elmira).

    98 Gliders at dawn of D + 1 (Operation Galveston).

    101 Gliders at dusk of D + 1 (Operation Hackensack).

Re-supply missions for the 82nd Division were flown on the nights of D + 1 and D + 2 with 148 and 117 aircraft respectively, carrying a total of approximately 432 tons of supplies. (Operations Freeport and Memphis.)

224. *Nos. 38 and 46 Groups, Royal Air Force.* The tasks of these groups were as follows:—

  (a) Dropping of S.A.S. troops—
    (i) D − 1/D-Day:
      Reconnaissance parties to be dropped in each of six areas (Operation Sunflower I).
    (ii) D + 1/2:
      Dropping of task forces in Brittany (Operation Coney).
    (iii) D + 3/4:
      Dropping of base parties in the six areas mentioned above (Operation Sunflower II).
    (iv) Re-supply to base parties as required (Operation Sunflower III).

  (b) Dropping and landing of 3rd and 5th Paratroop Brigade Groups plus a proportion of Division troops on the night of D − 1/D-Day (Operation Tonga).

  (c) Landing of the 6th Air Landing Brigade on the evening of D-Day (Operation Mallard).

  (d) Re-supply of the 3rd and 5th Paratroop Brigade Groups on the night of D/D + 1 (Operation Robroy I).

  (e) Subsequent re-supply mission for the 6th British Airborne Division (Operation Robroy II, III, etc.).

225. All these operations were carried out successfully, and with a remarkably low casualty rate, as will be evident from the statistics following para. 233. Total losses amounted to 3½ per cent. and 2½ per cent. respectively of the British and American sorties flown.

226. These airborne operations constituted the greatest air lift of assault forces that had ever been attempted. Up to date, they are exceeded only by the immense operations of the First Allied Airborne Army in mid-September. The accuracy with which these forces were delivered to the allotted zones contributed greatly to the rapid success of their coups de main.

227. *Provision of Air Support.* All the airborne forces and re-supply missions which were flown in daylight were given adequate fighter cover; in addition, the fighter cover to the assault areas and reserves were held in readiness to assist in the protection of these forces. There were no losses due to attack by enemy aircraft on any formation of troop carriers.

228. In the period D-Day to D + 4, 1,839 sorties were flown by special fighter escort to airborne forces, and a further 419 sorties were flown as escort to later re-supply missions. As additional support, special forces of intruders operated against anti-aircraft positions in the vicinity of the dropping and landing zones and others preceded the main forces across the coast to silence light anti-aircraft batteries on the run-in. The lightness of the casualties, which were much fewer than might reasonably have been expected, is evidence of the effectiveness of these support operations.

Review of Additional Air Operations in Support of the Assault.

229. In addition to the specific tasks set out in the preceding paragraphs, many subsidiary ones were also undertaken by the Allied air forces during the assault period. These operations are briefly reviewed in the next paragraphs.

230. Fighter escort was given to the bombers operating by day and these fighters then went on to attack enemy movements. The fighters of A.E.A.F. flew offensive patrols against all road and rail movement within the tactical area and the fighters of the United States Eighth Air Force continued this work farther afield beyond the boundary of the tactical areas.

231. A large effort was expended on reconnaissance sorties on both D-Day and D + 1. The deep reconnaissances revealed the reactions of the enemy, as shown by his movements of reinforcements to the battle area. The short range reconnaissances were also of invaluable assistance to the Army Commanders.

232. With such large forces operating, the Air/Sea Rescue Service was fully occupied. 198 patrols were flown during the two days and, together with the surface craft, these patrols succeeded in locating and rescuing a considerable number of Allied personnel.

233. The following statistics, covering the air operations in support of the assault, show the great effort of the Allied air forces on D-Day and D + 1. This effort, concentrated over a comparatively small area, surpassed in strength any air operations that had ever before been mounted.

TOTAL AIR EFFORT FOR PERIOD 2100 HOURS 5TH JUNE—2100 HOURS 7TH JUNE

	Heavy Bomber		Medium Bomber	Light Bomber	Fighter Bomber	Tonnage of Bombs	R.P. Fighters	No. of R.P's Fired	Beach-head Cover	Shipping Cover	Offensive Patrol	Defensive Patrol	Reconnaissance			Weather	Escort		ASR	Total Sorties
	Bomb.	Misc.											Shipping	Photo	Visual		Bombers	Transport		
D-Day																				
A.E.A.F.	—	—	693	296	665	1,517	24	192	1,547	496	73	211	20	84	384	25	484	187	87	5,276
R.A.F. B.C.	1,136	199	—	—	—	5,853	—	—	—	—	—	—	—	—	—	—	—	—	—	1,335
U.S. Eighth A.F.	2,627	—	—	—	—	4,542	—	—	—	—	—	—	—	—	—	—	1,347	—	—	3,974
Fleet Air Arm	—	—	—	—	—	—	—	—	—	—	—	—	—	—	158	—	—	—	—	158
	3,763	199	693	296	665	11,912	24	192	1,547	496	73	211	20	84	542	25	1,831	187	87	10,743
D + 1																				
A.E.A.F.	—	—	622	424	1,213	1,557	285	1,255	708	1,519	238	154	34	123	320	26	20	1,658	111	7,455
R.A.F. B.C.	1,097	63	—	—	—	3,966	—	—	—	—	—	—	—	—	—	—	—	—	—	1,160
U.S. Eighth A.F.	1,623	—	—	—	—	2,277	—	—	—	—	—	—	—	—	—	—	1,445	—	—	3,068
Fleet Air Arm	—	—	—	—	—	—	—	—	—	—	—	—	—	—	150	—	—	—	—	150
	2,720	63	622	424	1,213	7,800	285	1,255	708	1,519	238	154	34	123	470	26	1,465	1,658	111	11,833

Total Sorties as above 22,576
R.A.F. Coastal Command anti-U-boat and anti-shipping sorties ... 353
A.E.A.F. Airborne Operations 2,346

                     Grand Total ... 25,275

OPERATION "NEPTUNE"
Air Lift U.S. IXth Troop Carrier Command

Mission	Aircraft						Gliders		
	Despatched	Effective	Abortive	Missing	Destroyed	Damaged	Despatched	Released at DZ	Lost before DZ
Albany	443	433	10	—	13	83	—	—	—
Boston	378	372	6	8	—	115	—	—	—
Chicago	52	51	1	1	1	3	52	51	1
Detroit	52	52	—	1	1	6	52	46	6
Elmira	177	177	—	5	—	92	176	176	—
Freeport	208	148	55	5	3	94	—	—	—
Galveston	100	98	2	—	—	24	100	98	2
Hackensack	101	101	—	—	—	—	100	100	—
Keokuk	32	32	—	—	—	—	32	32	—
Memphis	119	117	2	—	3	35	—	—	—
	1,662	1,581	76	20	21	452	512	503	9

Analysis of Loads Carried

Troops	17,262	Gasoline	1,947 gallons	Ammunition	798,683 lbs.
M/T	281	Bombs	26,652 lbs.	Other Combat	
Artillery Weapons	333	Rations	87,373 lbs.	equipment	1,141,217 lbs.

OPERATION "NEPTUNE"
Air Lift Nos. 38 and 46 Groups, Royal Air Force

Mission	Aircraft						Gliders		
	Despatched	Effective	Abortive	Missing	Destroyed	Damaged	Despatched	Released at DZ	Lost before DZ
Tonga	373	359	14	9	—	7	98	80	18
Mallard	257	247	10	2	6	21	257	247	10
Rob Roy I	50	47	3	9	—	19	—	—	—
Roy Roy II	6	6	—	—	—	—	—	—	—
Rob Roy III	12	5	7	—	—	—	—	—	—
Rob Roy IV	15	15	—	—	—	—	—	—	—
Sunflower I	3	3	—	—	—	—	—	—	—
Sunflower II	2	1	1	—	•	—	—	—	—
Sunflower III	6	6	—	—	—	—	—	—	—
Coney	9	9	—	—	—	—	—	—	—
	733	698	35	20	6	47	355	327	28

Analysis of Loads Carried

Troops	7,162	Tanks	18	Bombs	2,000 lbs.
M/T	286	Bicycles	35	Other	731 panniers and
Artillery Weapons	29	Signals Equipment	12	Equipment	622 containers

(d) *Operations subsequent to D-Day.*

Plan of Presentation

234. As in the previous sections of the narrative part of this Despatch, I propose to deal with the operations in the period D-Day to 30th September, 1944, under types of operations, rather than on a time basis. For this purpose the following headings have been adopted:—

Attacks on Enemy Communications.
Close Support Operations.
Attacks on Coastal Garrisons.
Fighter Cover to the Assault and the Shipping Lanes.
Enemy Air Reaction and the Allied Attacks on the G.A.F. and its bases.
Defence against Flying Bombs and Attacks on "Crossbow" targets.
Operations of First Allied Airborne Army.
Attacks on Naval Targets.
Strategical Bombing—"Pointblank."

Attacks on Enemy Communications.

235. I have dealt with the task undertaken by the air forces (see para. 51 et seq.) of dislocating, prior to D-Day, the enemy rail system. I considered that one of the most important contributions which the air could make to the ground battle, after the launching of the assault, was to continue this work of dislocation. With this view you agreed, as did the other Commanders-in-Chief.

236. In order to gain a clear picture of the state of enemy road and rail communications, as I saw it at D-Day, reference should be made to the two maps* facing pages 14 and 18. The lines in Northern France and Belgium were very seriously disorganised, but the lines south of Paris/Rheims/Luxemburg were not nearly so devastated, nor were the railways south of the Seine. Of the bridges over the Seine below Paris, all except two were cut, and although the Loire bridges had not been cut, the crossings at Tours, Orleans, Angers and Saumur had all been rendered impassable by attacks on the railway junctions. In addition, there had been an enormous reduction in the capacity of the whole rail system in Northern France and Belgium.

237. The interruption of enemy communications during the post assault phase falls naturally into two separate periods:—

(a) From the moment the contending armies had joined battle, it became of paramount importance that the enemy should be denied the freedom of movement necessary to prepare and mount successful counter-attacks, and that the reinforcements he sought to bring into the battle zone should not only be hampered in movement, but also subjected to the severest casualties possible by air attack.

(b) After the break through of the Allied armies, the task of the air forces against communications was to harry the fleeing enemy columns, block the defiles and police the river crossings, thereby removing the possibility of orderly retreat.

In the following paragraphs I try to show how these two tasks were carried out.

238. *Attacks on Rail and Road Systems—June and July.*—In the earlier part of this period I was concerned to impose the maximum delay and to inflict the heaviest casualties on the flow of reinforcements and supplies to the enemy armies. The attacks were carried out according to a prepared pattern. This pattern was necessarily developed as the situation changed, following the information I received from deep and tactical reconnaissance.

239. The weather during June severely hampered operations. Frequently I was denied vital information on the progress and direction of German troop movements. Despite this handicap of weather, however, reconnaissance squadrons operated effectively, and the information they provided proved invaluable to the Army Commander as well as to myself.

240. Immediately the battle started, the enemy began to transfer his immediate reserves to the battle zone over the railways between the Seine and the Loire. Action against this movement consisted of low flying fighter bomber attacks against the trains and of line cutting by fighter bombers. The fighter bombers of the United States Ninth Air Force particularly had developed a very effective technique of line cutting. I also employed medium bombers with excellent results in attacks against sidings being used as detraining points.

241. By D+1, those parts of the enemy close reserves which had escaped these attacks had been committed to the battle. I therefore decided to initiate a series of attacks against railway junctions in the tactical area and thus establish a line beyond which enemy movements by rail to the battle zone could not proceed. R.A.F. Bomber Command attacked Rennes, Alencon, Fougeres, Mayenne and Pontaubault and followed up with attacks on the next two nights, on Dreux, Evreux and Acheres. Within the boundary of the tactical area thus drawn, A.E.A.F. fighter bombers caused such destruction that after three days, all railway and all major road movement by day had been virtually halted.

242. The enemy was forced to travel mainly by night and along minor roads. No. 2 Group of the R.A.F. Second Tactical Air Force, whose crews had been specially trained in night harassing, by the light of flares, operated light and medium bombers, frequently in very difficult weather conditions, with outstanding success against this movement.

243. Outside the tactical areas, both road and rail movements were dealt with by fighters of the United States VIIIth Fighter Command. Their fighter bomber attacks on line cutting and against railway centres, and also in offensive fighter sweeps against road and rail movements were outstandingly successful.

244. On 12th June, I re-drew the boundary of the tactical area as follows—along the Seine to Vernon, thence to Dreux, Chartres, Le Mans, Laval and St. Nazaire. Within that area the tactical air forces policed all roads and railways. Outside that area, the United States Eighth Air Force was busy attacking the Loire bridges to prevent any reinforcement from the south; but due, no doubt, to the threat of Allied invasion on the Mediterranean coast, there were no heavy enemy movements from the south for some time.

245. The principal difficulty in maintaining a complete blockade on all movement in the tactical area was the persistent bad weather which hampered the air operations very considerably. Further, the enemy showed great energy and ingenuity in repairing rail cuts and in running shuttle services between cuts. Because of these factors, the enemy was able to move a certain amount of material by rail within the tactical area itself, though he had to move mainly by night.

246. Apart from the forces in Brittany which it was anticipated would move by road, the main source from which the enemy could draw his reinforcement at this time was the Pas de Calais area. I therefore arranged for R.A.F. Bomber Command to attack centres in that area. On the night of 12-13th June, that Command made heavy attacks on Poitiers, Arras, Cambrai and two rail centres at Amiens. On the following night Douai, St. Pol and Cambrai were the targets. These attacks, together with those of the fighter and fighter bombers harassing movements on the railway lines, effectively delayed the transfer of the enemy reserves into the battle zone.

---
* Maps not reproduced.

247. Since most of the fuel and ammunition dumps in the tactical area were attacked at one time or another by aircraft of A.E.A.F., on armed reconnaissance, the enemy quickly began to run out of immediate reserves and was forced to use dumps further afield. As early as the second week of the battle, he was committed to drawing supplies of fuel and ammunition from dumps in the Marne area. These supply columns also had to run the gauntlet of our air attacks.

248. During the third week in June, I again extended the tactical area, following the attacks I have described in para. 244. At this time the enemy was using two particular routes, one through Strasbourg and the other through Saarbrucken and Metz, to transfer reinforcements and supplies from Poland and Germany proper to the Western Front. How much the movement of traffic on these lines had already been embarrassed may be gauged from the move of the 9th and 10th S.S. Panzer Divisions. These divisions, which had been hurriedly pulled out of Poland, were forced to detrain as far east as Nancy and then move approximately 300 miles by road to reach the battle zone. Others detrained as far east as Mulhouse. To complete the disorganisation on these routes, I laid on attacks, at the end of June, on Metz, Blainville, Strasbourg and Saarbrucken.

249. During July, the enemy was committed to move further formations both from the Pas de Calais and the Low Countries, and some of these he tried to bring to centres in the Paris area for detrainment. Heavy attacks were accordingly laid on these centres as well as on others in the Low Countries. I also extended the tactical area to include Northern France, so that A.E.A.F. aircraft could take in the areas north of the Seine in their operations. The fighters of the Eighth Air Force continued to sweep over the routes east and south-east of Paris.

250. The following statistics show the weight of the air attacks on rail centres in the period I have been reviewing:—

Attacks on Rail Centres, Tunnels and Embankments from 6th June—31st July, 1944

Force	Sorties	Tons of Bombs
A.E.A.F.	7,736	7,147
R.A.F. Bomber Command	5,738	23,440
U.S. Eighth Air Force	1,615	3,842
	15,089	34,429

251. The above figures, however, do not cover the attacks by the fighters and fighter bombers against the enemy rail movements. Their work was made easier in that the general disorganisation resulted in the enemy having at best only one or two circuitous routes open at any one time. This canalisation of traffic presented some excellent fighter bomber targets, and the pilots of A.E.A.F. and the United States Eighth Fighter Command took full advantage of them.

252. As the period of static fighting ended and the Allied armies broke out from their bridgehead, I called off the attacks on rail targets, as they were then more likely to hamper than help the Allied advance.

253. *Attacks on Bridges—June and July.*—The destruction of the bridges leading into the battle zone was also continued after the assault was launched. These attacks, as I have already explained, formed part of the general plan of attack on the enemy's transport system. At D-Day, all the Seine bridges below Paris except two were cut. During June, these two were destroyed as well as the principal bridges, both road and rail, across the Loire. Several important bridges on the lines through the gap between Paris and Orleans were also rendered impassable. The map* facing page 18 indicates the ring thus drawn about the battle area.

254. Briefly, this ring ran along the Seine and Loire. A second line of interdiction further afield had been planned, and to this end a large number of the more important bridges in the rail systems of North-Western France and Belgium were also cut; in addition, a number of minor bridges within the tactical area were rendered impassable.

255. In fact, however, this second line of interdiction was never completed. There were several reasons. Chief amongst them was the weather which curtailed operations. Next were the priority claims on the fighter bombers of the United States Eighth Fighter Command. Finally, there came a time when, because of the speed of our advance, further destruction of bridges was no longer necessary and indeed, would have been to our disadvantage. At this time I sought and secured your agreement, and that of the two Army Group Commanders-in-Chief, to stop these attacks.

256. The attacks on bridges had been mainly the work of A.E.A.F. and the United States Eighth Air Force and in the period D-Day to 31st July, the following effort was expended on these targets:—

Force	Sorties	Tons of Bombs
A.E.A.F.	12,823	14,271
U.S. Eighth A.F.	3,225	9,397
R.A.F. B.C.	260	975
	16,308	24,643

257. *Effect of Attacks on Communications.*—The enemy endeavoured to overcome the restrictions the air attacks placed on him by moving his stores and equipment both by road and by barges down the Seine from the unloading points near Paris to the ferries he had established at Elbeuf and in the neighbourhood of Rouen, as well as along the water-ways of Northern France. Both of these channels were dealt with by air attack, and there is a large amount of intelligence material to testify to the effectiveness of these fighter bomber attacks. Prisoners of war have confirmed pilots' stories of losses and have told of divisions moving very long distances by bicycle and being committed to the land battle piecemeal, without heavy equipment, as a result of Allied air attacks.

---

* Maps not reproduced.

258. The following accounts of the difficulties encountered by German divisions moving to the battle zones in July are of interest in this connection:—

(a) Air reconnaissance indicated, and prisoner of war reports confirmed, that the 363rd Infantry Division began to move from Ghent in mid-July. A number of the entraining stations, the junctions along the route and the trains themselves were attacked. The movement became so disorganised that approximately half the trains were cancelled and the troops moved by road. The division did not reach the front until the beginning of August.

(b) The 331st Infantry Division attempted to move from the Pas de Calais by rail. The route originally chosen was the main line Lille-Arras-Amiens, but as a result of line cutting by fighter bombers, a diversion had to be arranged via Lille-Cambrai-Chaulnes, and later through Eastern France via Valenciennes-Aulnoye-Mezieres. This movement eventually became so involved that the attempt to travel by rail was abandoned altogether. Air reconnaissances revealed that loaded trains which had stood by at entraining stations for 48 hours were finally unloaded without having moved at all.

(c) The 326th Infantry Division was also moved from the Pas de Calais at this time. In this move the Germans were evidently not prepared to risk a full-scale rail movement. Less than half the division travelled by rail, and the remainder moved on bicycles by a very circuitous route.

(d) It has been estimated that, in favourable circumstances, the move of the 1st S.S. Panzer Division from Louvain to the Caen area would have taken about three days. In fact, although detraining took place in the vicinity of Paris, and the move was completed by road, the rail journey alone took as long as a week for some elements, presumably because their trains were committed to a " Pilgrim's Progress " as a result of incidents on almost every route attempted. Stories of delays of from two to seventeen hours as a result of bomb damage to railway tracks, were a feature of the majority of interrogation reports of prisoners from this Division. One unit was delayed for two days at a badly damaged railway junction east of Paris.

(e) As had been anticipated, the move of the 346th Infantry Division from the area of Le Havre was conducted entirely by road. Bicycles were the means of transport and, although there is no evidence of any serious delay caused directly by bombing or strafing of columns, it should be borne in mind that the slow and laborious crossing of the Seine in ferries and motor boats was forced on the division by the previous destruction from the air of road and rail bridges over the river. Prisoners of war report that they were exhausted on their arrival and went into action without rest, food or even halts en route.

(f) The 271st Infantry Division which began to move from Montpellier on 1st July took approximately 19 days to reach the Rouen area. Some of the trains were attacked at Arenes just outside Montpellier before they started and casualties totalling 1,500 were reported; other trains were delayed for several days by air attack in the Lyons-St. Etienne area. The troops which did reach the battle area marched into the Caen area under heavy air attack. The original schedules for the 49 trains in this move are interesting in that they allowed 18 hours 25 minutes for the 285 mile journey from Montpellier to Chalon sur Saone. In fact, several trains took 11 days to pass Lyons and 20 trains were blocked in the Lyons area and finally diverted via St. Etienne and Mouling.

259. *Effect of Weather on Operations.* It is clear, I believe, from the foregoing paragraphs that the Allied air forces succeeded in crippling one of the most dense and complex networks of railways and roads in the world, and in practically denying its use to the enemy. I must emphasise, however, the influence which bad weather had on these operations. Both heavy and medium bombers, because of this bad weather, were prevented time and again from taking part in planned attacks on railways and bridges. We needed weather consistently good enough to permit precision visual bombing in density and co-ordinated attacks of a type most appropriate, as regards aircraft and weapons, to the targets involved throughout the whole of this period. I am convinced that if we had had this weather the enemy would have been prevented from moving by rail at all, and his retreat, disastrous as it was for him, would have been virtually impossible and far more costly in casualties to personnel and equipment than it was.

260. *Attacks on Communications—August and September.*—The second phase of attacks on communications began when the enemy tried to get away, and this became almost entirely a fighter and fighter bomber war. Forced to move by day as well as by night to escape the encircling ground forces, the enemy was constantly harried and destroyed. The roads leading to the Seine, then the Seine crossings, pontoons and barges and finally the roads of Northern France were in turn successfully attacked and became littered with the skeletons of the German Army's transport and equipment.

261. The mounting total of this destruction is evident in the following statistics of pilots' claims of mechanical transport and A.F.V's destroyed. These figures do not include those claimed as probably destroyed or damaged:—

6th-30th June	2,400
1st-31st July	3,364
1st-31st August	4,091
1st-30th September	6,238
	16,093

262. *Value of Reconnaissance.* I cannot stress too strongly the importance of reconnaissance in planning attacks on communications. Although inclement weather interfered with the programmes for both photographic and visual reconnaissances, I was generally well informed of the moves of enemy supplies and reinforcements and was able to deal with them before they reached the battle zone. The valuable information brought back also enabled the Army Commanders to make accurate forecasts of the enemy strength and intentions. This position became completely reversed when the Allied armies moved forward. There is

evidence to show that, because the Allied fighters kept the G.A.F. reconnaissance down to a negligible effort, the German High Command was fighting completely in the dark, unaware of the Allied intentions or of the strength and direction of each thrust.

263. In the period D-Day to 30th September, 1944, the reconnaissance units of A.E.A.F. flew 4,808 sorties on photographic and 14,140 sorties on visual reconnaissances, a total of 18,948 sorties.

Close Support Operations

264. In addition to the contribution made to the success of the land battle by attacks on the enemy's communications, the air forces gave direct support to the Allied armies. These operations were laid on in three ways:—
 (a) armed reconnaissance
 (b) pre-arranged support
 (c) immediate tactical support.

265. The armed reconnaissances were made by fighter bomber aircraft, which with bombs, R.P. and cannon fire, attacked a variety of targets, particularly movement seen on roads or railways. The pre-arranged support was of two kinds—attacks made according to plans prepared some time in advance and which included heavy and medium bombers; and secondly, the more normal form of attacks laid on as a result of conferences between Army and Air staff in the field, when tactical targets for the ensuing day were decided upon. For these attacks, the Army usually undertook to assist the bombers by marking the target by means of smoke signals. Immediate support was provided in the usual way by strike aircraft held in readiness to attack targets requested direct by Army forward positions, or reported by reconnaissance aircraft.

266. Much of the work of the squadrons engaged on armed reconnaissance I have described in the preceding paragraphs dealing with attacks on communications. In addition to the pre-arranged support by medium and fighter bombers (dealt with later in paragraph 284 et seq.), there were six large scale attacks by heavy bombers during the period D-Day to 30th September, apart from certain other attacks on the enemy garrisons left in the Channel ports.

267. *Pre-arranged support using heavy bombers.* The use of heavy bombers in close support to ground forces was an important development in air warfare. A word on the situation prior to the employment of heavy bombers in such a role will not, therefore, be out of place.

268. The initial impetus of the Allied assault had secured a bridgehead extending from the Cotentin Peninsula to Caen, but the enemy had been able to concentrate against this relatively short front. He held strong, well sited defence positions in depth. By stealth, ingenuity and taking advantage of frequent periods of bad weather which made air policing of road and rail in the tactical area impossible, he managed to muster just sufficient reinforcements and warlike supplies to maintain his position.

269. Concentrations of artillery had not succeeded in cracking his defences sufficiently to enable a successful breakthrough to be made without, it was considered, a prohibitive cost in both men and material. A stalemate appeared to have arisen.

270. Neither could an air bombardment sufficiently heavy and concentrated to produce a situation ripe for a successful ground attack be provided by medium, light and fighter bombers.

271. I had already submitted to you a study of the situation in which I had made suggestions as to how the air forces could help the land forces to break out of the Normandy bridgehead. After consideration of this study by the various Commands (both land and air) concerned, it was decided to use heavy bombers in the virtually novel role of army co-operation.

272. The detailed plans for these attacks were worked out at an inter-service level, being finally co-ordinated at your headquarters. The co-ordination of the actual operations of the Air Forces involved in the attacks, however, was exercised by me.

273. The first of the large scale attacks, using heavy bombers in close support took place at 0430 hours on 8th July. R.A.F. Bomber Command employed 467 bombers to drop 2,562 tons of bombs on positions North of Caen. The British and Canadian troops, held up to the North of the town for so long by the enemy, followed up the bombing with a frontal attack. By nightfall they had entered the streets of Caen. The bombing had therefore succeeded in its object and had opened a way for a break through by the ground forces.

274. The second, and largest, of these operations (Operation Goodwood) took place on 18th July, when the combined weight of the United States Eighth Air Force, Royal Air Force Bomber Command and the Allied Expeditionary Air Force supported an advance by elements of the Second British Army in the Caen area.

275. This attack was the heaviest and most concentrated air attack in support of ground forces ever attempted. No less than 1,676 heavy bombers and 343 medium and light bombers were committed to the attack and the total tonnage of bombs dropped reached 7,700 U.S. tons.

276. In view of its interest I set out the plan for this large attack in some detail. The plan provided for the destruction of enemy installations and forces to allow the ground troops to advance along the axis Escoville—Cagny. The ground forces prior to the jump-off, were generally along an east/west line through Herouvillette. R.A.F. Bomber Command were employed to destroy the installations and forces in the areas marked A, H and M on the map* facing. Cratering was acceptable in these areas to prevent the possibility of the enemy making flanking attacks over this ground. Heavy bombers of the United States Eighth Air Force were concentrated on the installations and forces in the areas marked I, P and Q. Cratering was acceptable in the first of these areas, but not in the other two, as our own forces were to pass over this ground. The medium and light bombers of the tactical air forces were detailed to neutralise the enemy forces in the areas marked C, D, E, F and G. Pinpoint targets were given in areas, C, F and G, while the whole areas marked D and E were to be swept with an even pattern of fragmentation bombs. The laying-on of this attack, involving more than 2,000 bombers, meant very careful timing.

---

* Maps not reproduced.

277. The other four attacks by heavy bombers were generally based on the same principle of destroying the enemy strongpoints, and cratering given areas to prevent the enemy from attacking the flanks of our forces while they were advancing through the swept but relatively undamaged centre of the assault area.

278. The third of the large scale attacks involving heavy bombers was launched on 25th July, when 1,495 heavy bombers and 388 fighter bombers of the United States Eighth and Ninth Air Forces dropped 4,790 tons of bombs in a bombardment preliminary to an advance by elements of the First United States Army across the Periers—St. Lo highway. Unfortunately some of the bombs in this attack fell short and caused some casualties to our own ground forces in the area.

279. The fourth attack was in support of the Second British Army south of Caumont. The preliminary heavy air bombardment was launched early on 30th July and 693 heavy bombers of R.A.F. Bomber Command and over 500 light and medium bombers of A.E.A.F. dropped 2,227 tons of bombs.

280. The fifth attack assisted the advance of the First Canadian Army along the Caen-Falaise road on the night of 7-8th August and during the succeeding day. 1,450 heavy bombers of the United States Eighth Air Force and of R.A.F. Bomber Command, and fighter bombers of the Second Tactical Air Force dropped 5,210 tons of bombs on enemy installations, strong points and forces in the area of the advance.

281. The sixth attack, also by R.A.F. Bomber Command, took place on the morning of 14th August and assisted the Canadian forces to advance into Falaise. 811 bombers were employed and 3,723 tons of bombs were dropped in the attack. Again, in this operation, some of the bombs fell short of the targets causing casualties to our own ground forces.

282. In each case, the ground forces were able to move into the bombarded positions practically without opposition. That they failed to exploit fully the break-through is known, but there are doubtless many reasons for this failure. In the second attack, the principal cause of delay was the bottleneck across the Caen bridges which delayed the moving of armoured formations sufficiently long to enable the enemy to remount his screen of guns outside the area which had been bombed. In the third attack, the Army Commander agreed that the "carpet" bombing did put his troops through the enemy positions; difficulties which arose in moving the army forces forward as rapidly as was necessary again prevented a complete exploitation. Nevertheless, these heavy attacks did finally succeed in starting off the break-through of the ground forces across the Periers-St. Lo highway, and it was this break-through which eventually determined the battle of Normandy, which liberated France.

283. I have referred to the lessons learned from this series of attacks in close support in Part V of this Despatch. From an air point of view, the attacks definitely proved that saturation bombing by heavy bombers on a narrow front can enable an army to break through, but they also showed the need for the army to exploit, without delay, the favourable situation created. Further, the heartening moral effect of these large scale air support formations on our own forces and the corresponding shattering of the will to resist among the enemy has been stated by Army Commanders to have been of vital consequence. Air and land action must be closely co-ordinated. The land forces must be ready to step off at least immediately the bombing is over, if not just before, accepting some slight risk of casualties from our bombing, and the artillery programme must be directly related to the bombing plan to ensure economy of effort by both arms.

284. *Pre-arranged Close Support by Medium and Fighter Bombers.*—The operation of medium and fighter bombers on pre-arranged support was often in small formations against targets such as gun positions, tank laagers, chateaux suspected of housing headquarters formations, and defended positions. The effectiveness of the support may be judged from the following extract from a captured document:—

" C.-in-C. West (Von Kluge) in a report to General Warlimont, Hitler's representative, on the position at Avranches says— ' Whether the enemy can be stopped at this point is still questionable. The enemy air superiority is terrific, and smothers almost all of our movements. Every movement of the enemy, however, is prepared and protected by its air forces. Losses in men and equipment are extraordinary. The morale of the troops has suffered very heavily under constant murderous enemy fire.' "

285. *Immediate Support.*—The immediate support of the armies was provided by the fighter bombers of the tactical air forces and in this role the fighter bombers have shown their greatest effectiveness. Never before have they been used in such strength and with such decisive results. I have divided my review of their operations in the following paragraphs into four phases of the land battle, as follows:—
  (i) The period of static fighting.
  (ii) The break-through of the Allied armies.
  (iii) The period of encirclement.
  (iv) The retreat across Northern France and Belgium.

286. In the early period of the operations of offensive fighter and fighter bomber forces, the co-operation between the Commander of the United States IXth Tactical Air Command, General Quesada, and the Air Officer Commanding No. 83 Group, Royal Air Force, Air Vice-Marshal Broadhurst, C.B., D.S.O., D.F.C., A.F.C., was close and effective. Each gave the other assistance as the occasion arose and whenever a good target presented itself, neither hesitated to call on the other to take advantage of it. The development of common methods of control and target indication and reference greatly assisted this British and United States mutual support.

287. *Period of Static Fighting.*—During this phase of the land battle, the tactical air forces concentrated upon the close support of the armies within the tactical boundary. The technique of this form of support was considerably developed. A system of Visual Control Points was perfected by which an experienced fighter controller rode in one of the leading tanks, equipped with the necessary V.H.F. radio-telephony equipment for the control of fighter aircraft. By these means an extra-

ordinary flexibility of control of the fighter bombers on army co-operation was maintained. Another interesting development in technique was provided by the use of the American M.E.W. mobile Radar station, which, because of its ability to locate low-flying aircraft and of its range of detection, proved of great assistance to the fighter forces covering the battle areas. However, I feel that the chief value of the tactical air forces during this first period lay in their ability to smash up the enemy's attempted concentrations of tanks and vehicles before a counter-attack could be launched.

288. *The Break-through of the Allied Armies.*—When the United States armies achieved their break-through which carried them to the Brittany Peninsula and on into the country north of the Loire, the close support work of the air forces took on a new aspect. Continuous fighter cover was provided to the advancing armoured spearheads. This cover, not only protected them from enemy air attack, but also reached out, destroying enemy tanks, M/T and gun positions that lay in the path and along the flanks of the advancing armies. In this respect the work of the United States Ninth Air Force, particularly of the IXth and XIXth Tactical Air Commands, deserves special mention. Fighter pilots of this force destroyed hundreds of enemy tanks and vehicles. They had developed a technique of attacking tanks from the rear, which experience had shown was most vulnerable to their .50 calibre machine gun bullets.

289. It was to hold up this break-through that the enemy, under personal orders from Hitler, attempted, on 7th August, his really large scale armoured counter-attack, launched against Mortain in an effort to reach the sea at Avranches and split the advancing American armies from their main bases. This concentration of armour gave the tactical squadrons of A.E.A.F. a great chance to inflict a crushing blow on the enemy and prove the superiority of their weapons and training. The opportunity was fully accepted, particularly by the Typhoon squadrons of R.A.F. Second Tactical Air Force.

290. On 7th August there were nineteen squadrons of Typhoons operating from French airfields. These squadrons carried out 59 missions, flying 458 sorties in all during that day. 294 of these sorties were in the Mortain area. No less than 2,088 rocket projectiles were fired, and 80 tons of bombs were dropped; and the pilots claimed very large numbers of tanks, A.F.V., and M.T. destroyed and damaged.

291. This tremendous blow at the Nazi armour was achieved at the cost of 5 aircraft lost and 10 damaged, and was one of the most vital factors in defeating the enemy attacks.

292. The scale of effort of these Typhoon squadrons is indicative of the sustained activity of the tactical air forces. The number of missions flown by Typhoons in the five-day period, 7th-11th August, rose to 298, involving 2,193 sorties. 9,850 rocket projectiles and 398 tons of bombs were aimed at enemy targets, and many more enemy tanks and vehicles were destroyed. These results were achieved at the cost of 13 Typhoons destroyed and 16 damaged.

293. After the Typhoon attacks on the first day, the fighter-bombers of the United States Ninth Air Force took over the responsibility for the Mortain area, and in many attacks accounted for many more of the enemy armoured vehicles. By this effort, the air forces broke up and partly destroyed the enemy concentrations of armour, and although a number of spearheads did penetrate our forward positions, they were effectively dealt with by the ground forces. In this counter-attack Hitler threw away the one force of armour which could have enabled him to extricate his army. As a result, the disaster to the Army was complete. Between 8th and 14th August, the IXth Tactical Air Command flew a total of 4,012 sorties; virtually all of them in co-operation with ground action in the Mortain region. On 12th August 673 sorties were flown and 310.8 tons of bombs dropped.

294. To the outstanding success of these attacks on the enemy armour, the weather effectively contributed, not only because it cleared and remained fine during the critical days from 7th to 11th August, but also because it had been so bad earlier. This bad weather had drastically restricted air operations and, there seems reason to suppose, had lulled the enemy into a sense of false security.

295. It is difficult to find any other reason why he should have abandoned first principles and moved his armour head to tail in long convoys over roads in daylight. These convoys, once the weather cleared, gave the tactical air forces their unique chance of scoring an outstanding success.

296. *The Encirclement.*—During the period in which the German 7th Army was rapidly becoming encircled by the sweep of the American ground forces to Alencon and Argentan and by the pressure of the British and Canadian forces towards Falaise, the German Commander had to decide whether to withdraw before the gap was closed or to stay and fight it out. I feel certain that any such withdrawal in the face of the overwhelming air superiority of the Allied air forces would have been disastrous, and it would appear that the German Commander also had serious misgivings as to the practicability of such a withdrawal. In large part, the enemy army stood to fight. While the front was more or less clearly defined, the air forces were able to inflict destruction on the concentrations of enemy troops. However, when the encirclement became complete, the ground position naturally became confused. In these conditions it was inevitable that our air forces should have once or twice attacked our own troops in error. Such misfortune could not be avoided. As a result, however, the Army Commanders eventually fixed bomb lines which automatically severely restricted attacks in close support of the land forces and thus denied to the fighter bombers many excellent targets. I pressed for revision of these bomb lines to allow more freedom to operate closer to the fighting, but the Army Commanders maintained their caution. I am convinced that, as a result of this action, the reasons for which I fully appreciate, the air forces let through a great deal of enemy material and troops that would otherwise not have escaped.

297. *The Retreat across Northern France and Belgium.*—Once the enemy had begun his retreat to the Seine, the fighter and fighter bomber forces of A.E.A.F. were presented with some first-class targets. Low flying attacks inflicted enormous personnel casualties, while skeletons of burnt-out transport littered every road and track and were ample evidence of the effectiveness of these attacks.

298. During this retreat it was reported more and more frequently that very large columns of ambulances were moving to the German rear. I was almost certain that these ambulances were faked and did, in fact, contain fighting soldiers and equipment. It was a critical decision to take as to whether or not these ambulances should be attacked. You finally decided against attacking them. Although we were thereby likely to miss some targets, it was preferable to win the battle without laying ourselves open to criticism, however unjustified. In a number of cases, however, it was found that ordinary vehicles were intermingled with the ambulances and these were attacked. It was significant that whenever this happened, the doors of the ambulances opened and German soldiers poured out in every direction and made for cover with a speed and agility quite remarkable for wounded men. Occasionally too, fire was opened on our aircraft from these ambulances.

299. At this time, reconnaissances began to show what was in the circumstances, a relatively considerable enemy movement on the railways north-east of the Seine, particularly through Rheims. This rail movement was apparently to carry up reserves to stabilise a line, probably on the Seine or the Marne. I therefore directed a proportion of the fighter bomber effort against these movements. The United States Ninth Air Force fighters, and further east, the United States Eighth Air Force fighters, did extremely well against these targets, and this effort, I believe, virtually broke up the enemy's last chance of bringing up sufficient forces to re-form a line in France.

300. Once the remnants of the enemy divisions had crossed the Seine (and in the crossing they had to run the gauntlet of continuous air attacks on their ferries) they dispersed rapidly into a widening area. In consequence there were fewer and fewer large targets offering themselves for attack. In the main, therefore, fighters and fighter bombers reverted to direct support of the Allied columns and attacked the enemy rearguards just ahead of them.

301. In general, I would like to emphasise again the terrific havoc that was created by the air forces during the enemy's withdrawal to and across the Seine. Thousands of vehicles were destroyed and from this onslaught the enemy succeeded in getting away only small sections of his previously very powerful army.

302. The two outstanding days for the tactical air forces in this period were 18th and 25th August. The R.P. fighters and the fighter bombers of R.A.F. Second Tactical Air Force particularly claimed many victims, and the fighter bombers of the United States Ninth Air Force added their quota. The densest congestion of these enemy concentrations was in the Trun-Vimoutieres area, and the wreckage later found in this area is ample testimony to the effectiveness of these air attacks.

303. On 25th August, the G.A.F. attempted in force to protect the efforts of the German Seventh Army to use the river crossing in the Rouen area. They were met by the fighters of the United States Ninth Air Force. 77 enemy aircraft were destroyed in combat and a further 49 were destroyed on the ground. On this and the subsequent three days, approximately 3,000 vehicles were destroyed and several thousand dead German soldiers were found among the wreckage in the area of the Seine crossings.

Attacks on Coastal Garrisons.

304. During the last week in August and through September, strong bombing forces were used to reduce the enemy garrisons holding on to the Atlantic and Channel ports. The attacks on Brest between 24th August and 6th September were shared by the United States Eighth and Ninth Air Forces and R.A.F. Bomber Command. More than 6,000 tons of bombs were dropped on the garrisons of this city. The attacks on Le Havre, Boulogne and Calais were R.A.F. Bomber Command operations, and provided excellent examples of reduction of a town by air bombing. This was especially so in the case of Le Havre. The Allied casualties in the subsequent assault against a strongly fortified garrison of 11,000 defenders totalled only 400. Between 1st and 12th September, 2,042 sorties were flown against Le Havre alone and 11,000 tons of bombs were dropped, 5,000 tons of this total being aimed in one massive daylight attack on an extremely small area.

305. This bombing was undertaken at the express wish of the Army Commanders and undoubtedly it succeeded in paving the way for and in saving the lives of thousands of our soldiers in the final assault. It must be recorded however, that casualties to French civilians shut up with the German garrisons in these ports were inevitably high, particularly so at Le Havre. I feel, that in the broad view, this bombing effort would have been more profitably directed against targets inside Germany, particularly as the disorganisation of her retreating army was most acute at this time. I should have been happier to see it used against focal points in the communications system behind the enemy frontier, in an effort to delay the movement of reinforcements with which the enemy succeeded, in mid-September, in stabilising a line along the Rhine and the Moselle.

306. It must also be remembered that the bombing had to be laid on to suit the Army plan, and in consequence it was sometimes delayed or postponed because the Army could not always be ready to attack at the agreed time or because of unfavourable weather conditions over the target. Bad weather over the target areas coincided sometimes with good weather over Germany. Because the heavy bombers had been committed to, and were standing by for, attacks on the garrison towns, opportunities for using them in good conditions against vital industrial targets in Germany were lost.

307. The following statistics give the weight of effort against coastal defences and gun positions during the month of September. This

effort was very largely made up of the attacks laid on for the reduction of besieged garrisons.

Attacks on Coastal Garrisons during September, 1944.

Force.	Sorties.	Tons of Bombs.
A.E.A.F.	5,567	4,406
U.S. Eighth A.F.	1,327	4,501
R.A.F. Bomber Command	4,510	25,811
	11,404	34,718

Fighter Cover to the Assault and the Shipping areas.

308. In the foregoing paragraphs I have tried to describe the support both direct and indirect which the air forces gave to ground forces after the assault was launched. I come now to the equally important task undertaken by the air forces, the task, namely of protecting the beach-head area and our shipping from attacks by the G.A.F. I have already explained (see para. 32) my reasons for retaining a large fighter force to ensure that the air superiority we had won was maintained on D-Day and afterwards, and in addition, in para. 20 I have briefly mentioned the fighter protection given to the cross channel movement of assault forces. There were, in fact, 171 squadrons of day fighters and fighter bombers available for all the tasks that they were called upon to undertake in support of the invasion. These forces were made up as follows:

Day Fighters—	U.S. Ninth A.F.	U.S. Eighth A.F.	2nd T.A.F.	85 Group	A.D.G.B.	Total
Mustang III	6	12	6	—	—	24
Thunderbolt	39	21	—	—	—	60
Lightning	9	12	—	—	—	21
Spitfire	—	—	27	4	15	46
Tempest	—	—	—	—	2	2
						153
Fighter Bombers—						
Typhoon	—	—	18	—	—	18
						171

309. In addition, A.D.G.B. retained 9 Spitfire, 1 Mustang and 2 Typhoon squadrons for the air defence, by day, of the United Kingdom.

310. The night fighter forces available for the protection by night of the assault area and shipping lanes consisted of 6 Mosquito squadrons. (The defence of the United Kingdom by night was undertaken by A.D.G.B. which had 8 Mosquito and 1 Beaufighter squadrons and a further 2 Mosquito Intruder squadrons.) This force allowed me to operate 30 to 40 night fighters over the assault area and shipping lanes during the night.

311. In order to achieve the most economical and effective use of resources these fighter forces were pooled and placed under the control of a Combined Control Centre. This Control Centre was situated at Uxbridge, where it was able to make full use of the tried and proven static control organisation built up by No. 11 Group, Royal Air Force, which had previously handled the very large air cover given to the Dieppe operation, in August, 1942. This unified control ensured the necessary flexibility to cover the principal tasks allotted to these day fighter forces. The principal tasks were:—

(*a*) continuous cover of the beach-head areas.

(*b*) continuous cover of the main naval approach.

(*c*) direct air support of the ground forces, including close support.

(*d*) escort to day bomber and troop carrier formations.

(*e*) withdrawal cover for night bombers leaving the assault area after first light.

(*f*) to provide a striking force for employment as the air situation required.

312. Initially, the following allocation of squadrons was made for employment in these specific tasks.

Beach Cover	54 squadrons
Shipping Cover	15 squadrons
Direct Air Support	36 squadrons
Offensive Fighter and Bomber Support	33 squadrons
Strike Force and Escort to Airborne operations	33 squadrons
	171 squadrons

313. These squadrons were prepared to operate up to a maximum of 4 sorties per day on D-Day, 3 sorties per day on D+1, and thereafter 2 sorties per day. In fact, because of the lack of G.A.F. reaction, this scale of effort was not necessary. On D-Day, A.E.A.F. fighter and fighter bomber squadrons, including night fighter squadrons, flew 1.44 sorties per aircraft available and on D+1, 2.28 sorties per aircraft available. Owing to the lack of enemy activity and the serious deterioration of the weather, the average sorties per fighter aircraft available during June fell to 1.00 per day. However, in the first three weeks of the operation, more than 30,000 sorties were flown on beach-head and shipping cover. Detailed figures are set out below.

314. *Scale of Effort of A.E.A.F. Fighters and Fighter Bombers.*

	No. of operational aircraft available	No. of sorties flown	Average No. of sorties per available a/c per day
2nd T.A.F. :—			
D-Day...	883	1,266	1·43
D+1 ...	843	2,467	2·93
June (average)	840	988	1·18
Ninth A.F. :—			
D-Day...	1,158	2,139	1·84
D+1 ...	1,049	2,804	2·80
June (average)	1,005	1,022	1·02
A.D.G.B. (including 85 Group) :—			
D-Day...	885	811	0·92
D+1 ...	852	984	1·15
June (average)	838	678	0·81
Total :—			
D-Day...	2,926	4,216	1·44
D+1 ...	2,744	6,255	2·28
June (average)	2,683	2,688	1·00

315. Commencing at 0430 hours on D-Day and continued throughout the daylight hours during the assault period, a continuous fighter cover was maintained at nine squadrons strength over the whole assault area. Of this force of nine squadrons, six Spitfire squadrons provided low cover and three Thunderbolt squadrons, high cover. Of the six Spitfire squadrons, one squadron patrolled over each of the two American beaches with a third squadron on the western flank; two more covered the length of the three British beaches with one squadron on the eastern flank. Of the three Thunderbolt squadrons maintaining high cover, one was disposed centrally over the western area, a second over the eastern area, and the third was positioned between the two areas, but some eight to ten miles inland from the beach area itself. In this position it was readily available to reinforce any particular area or to engage enemy aircraft approaching the beach from the south, south-east or south-west.

316. The high and low cover fighters operating over the eastern area were under the control of F.D.T. 217; the fighters over the western area, under the control of F.D.T. 216. The "free" high flying Thunderbolt squadron operating inland, was also controlled by F.D.T. 217 (see para. 322).

317. The scale of the effort described above was maintained, whenever weather permitted, until 13th June, when the force involved was reduced to three low cover and two high cover squadrons. All these squadrons operated from England. In addition, a reserve of two squadrons from those by then operating on the Continent was maintained at readiness for extra low cover if required. This arrangement continued, again whenever weather permitted, until sufficient fighter squadrons had been moved to the Continent to take over the commitment (see para. 329).

318. Four squadrons of Lightnings (each of 16 aircraft strength) maintained throughout the daylight hours a continuous patrol over the assault forces and the shipping lanes leading to the beaches. They operated normally at between three thousand and five thousand feet or just below cloud base, in four distinct areas, and all were under the control of F.D.T. 13 (see para. 322). This cover was maintained for the first three days, but because of the lack of enemy reaction it was then reduced to three squadrons, and finally to two squadrons on 11th June. Additionally, a reserve of not less than six squadrons was also available for reinforcement of any sector requiring it.

319. It was essential to provide adequate fighter cover over the beach-head and shipping lanes during the critical periods of first light and last light. To ensure that sufficient aircraft could be in the area at these times, twelve British and twelve American fighter squadrons were trained to take off and land in darkness. Thus, with the night fighter operations, fighter cover was maintained, whenever weather permitted, continuously throughout the twenty-four hours.

320. *Control of Fighter Forces.*—I have already dealt with the activities of fighter aircraft on offensive patrols and in direct support, and those of the strike force. The arrangement for meeting the calls for air support during the assault were as follows. A Headquarters ship accompanied each Naval Assault Force: this ship carried an Air Staff Officer who was the representative of the Commander, Advanced A.E.A.F. This officer kept the Commander, Advanced A.E.A.F., informed of the Military and Naval Commanders' intentions and requirements through naval channels to Portsmouth and thence to Uxbridge. These Headquarters ships were equipped for the control of direct support aircraft and also to act as stand-by to the Fighter Direction Tenders (referred to below) for the control of fighter cover forces. In neither case did the need for them to exercise direct control of fighters arise. In addition, each Headquarters ship received reports in the clear from reconnaissance aircraft and relayed this information on targets to Uxbridge. They also provided liaison when needed (and it was frequently needed) between the bombarding warships and their spotting aircraft (see paragraph 207).

321. As stated in paragraph 311, the central control of both the night and day fighter squadrons was exercised by the Combined Control Centre, Uxbridge, using the static organisation of A.D.G.B. Three Fighter Direction Tenders operated as forward controls. One of these Fighter Direction Tenders was placed in each of the United States and British sectors and one in the main shipping lane. This ship later

moved to a position off Barfleur, to counter enemy night operations. Detailed arrangements were also made to ensure that the loss of one or all of these ships should not leave us without control of our fighter forces. These arrangements, briefly, provided for a reciprocal stand-by between these F.D.Ts., certain naval vessels, the Headquarters ships, the G.C.I. Stations landed in France, and the control centres in the United Kingdom.

322. *Fighter Direction Tenders.*—Some details of the operations of the Fighter Direction Tenders follow:—

(i) F.D.T. 216 was at first located five to fifteen miles off shore opposite the "Omaha" section of the beach; later it moved closer in to a position off St. Laurent. The tasks allotted to this F.D.T. were to control the day and night fighter cover over the western assault area. Control was effective on the only occasion the enemy attacked beaches in the United States sector in any strength.

(ii) F.D.T. 217 sailed with the Eastern Assault Forces. It was also placed five to fifteen miles off "Sword" beach, but later moved closer in shore. It controlled the day and night cover to the Eastern Assault Area and co-ordinated the cover over the whole area. The control of the night fighter pool was handed over to the far shore G.C.C. on D + 6 and the day fighter cover on D + 8. The ship then moved to a position off St. Laurent to act as stand-by control and continued to control night fighters until D + 17.

(iii) F.D.T. 13 was located forty to fifty miles off the beach-head to control both day and night fighters protecting the shipping lanes. On 12th June, the control of day fighters in these areas was handed back to a fixed station in the United Kingdom and the ship sailed to a position twenty miles east north-east of Barfleur, where from 15th to 27th June it controlled night fighters protecting shipping.

323. The figures below indicate only partially the excellent work of these Fighter Direction Tenders, and when the low scale of enemy effort and the steady and prolonged deterioration of the weather are considered, the number of enemy aircraft claimed destroyed and damaged by the Allied aircraft controlled by these ships, is high. The figures show the number of aircraft controlled by Fighter Direction Tenders at night, and the number of casualties inflicted by day and night by aircraft actually under the control of a Fighter Direction Tender at the time of the combat:—

Operations of Fighter Direction Tenders

Day (6th–13th June inclusive):—
F.D.T. 216 ... 13 enemy aircraft destroyed.
F.D.T. 217 ... 35 enemy aircraft destroyed, others probably destroyed and damaged.
F.D.T. 13 ... Nil.

Night (6th–13th June inclusive):—

	N/F controlled	Contacts	Friendly	E/A destroyed
F.D.T. 216	62	49	33	3
F.D.T. 217	275	123	67	10, 1 damaged
F.D.T. 13	18	13	10	—

Night (15th–27th June inclusive):—

	N/F controlled	Contacts	Friendly	E/A destroyed
F.D.T. 13	64	195	144	12, 1 damaged

324. The story of the setting up of Fighter Control units on the Continent is dealt with in Part IV. Here it may be recorded that at 2230 hours on D-Day, the first G.C.I. station on the far shore began controlling night fighters and on D + 6 took over the co-ordination of all night fighters from the F.D.T. previously responsible. On D + 8, this G.C.I. station had expanded into No. 483 Group Control Centre, and control of both day and night fighters over the battle zones passed to this centre.

325. *Allied A.A. Gunfire.* The operation of our fighter aircraft was at times rendered difficult by the actions of our own anti-aircraft guns. In fact, I regret to say that engagements of friendly aircraft did occur with some frequency in the initital stages of the operation. I made representations to the Allied Naval Commander about certain instances of promiscuous and uncontrolled fire and both Naval Task Force Commanders decided to prohibit any A.A. gunfire from merchant vessels unless these ships were being directly and individually attacked. From many reports of observers, it would appear however, that the merchant ships were not alone to blame. This gunfire occurred despite the fact that it had been agreed, during the planning stages, that no A.A. gunners should be permitted to engage aircraft unless they were qualified to recognise by their appearance all aircraft, both friendly and hostile, which were likely to operate in the area concerned. Furthermore, the Naval and Army Commanders were charged with the responsibility of nominating the type of personnel or unit which should be allowed to engage aircraft under this rather general classification.

326. It must, however, be admitted that the weather conditions generally were so indifferent that the aircraft providing fighter cover and close support was often forced to operate below the height which had previously been agreed as a minimum, except in pursuit of the enemy. This factor must have caused complications for the A.A. gunners, especially when there was enemy activity at the same time.

327. A complete solution to the problem of using A.A. guns and defensive aircraft together in any amphibious operation has clearly not yet been found, and I am of the opinion that the whole question should be given considerably more scientific and practical study on an inter-service and inter-Allied basis than has been done in the past. I refer again to this problem in Part V.

328. On a limited number of merchant vessels, Royal Observer Corps personnel were provided, and this arrangement has drawn very favourable comments from all concerned. I have already recommended elsewhere that an extension of this use of specialised aircraft recognition personnel deserves further examination with a view to more general adoption by both the Army and the Navy.

329. *Transfer of Fighter forces to the Continent.* It was appreciated that the effort of the fighters and fighter bombers over the beach-head would inevitably be seriously reduced after three or four days if they had to operate at such distances from their bases in the U.K. In the early planning therefore, a high priority had been arranged for naval lift of the stores and equipment which would be needed to operate the fighters and fighter bomber squadrons planned to be flown into bases on the Continent as soon as possible after D-Day. This precaution was fully warranted. The weather throughout June frequently prevented the operations of squadrons based in the south of England. Had the scheduled squadrons not arrived on the Continent as planned, fighter cover over the beach-head and shipping lanes would at times have been impossible, at times, moreover, when weather would have permitted the G.A.F. to operate against us. Nor would fighter bombers have been available to answer calls by the ground forces for urgent support. Actually, the beach-head and shipping lanes were left without fighter cover only when the weather both in England and the Continent made all operations by Allied Air Forces and the G.A.F. impossible.

330. The operations of these fighter squadrons from bases on the Continent were made possible only by the work of the Airfield Construction engineers, of the maintenance personnel, and of the supply organisation which ensured the provision of the necessary stores and equipment. I refer to the work of these sections in more detail in Part IV.

331. The first British squadrons to land in France since 1940 were Nos. 130 and 303 which put down at 1200 hours on D + 4 on a strip on the "Gold" area. They were quickly followed by No. 144 (R.C.A.F.) Fighter Wing, consisting of Nos. 441, 442 and 443 squadrons, which at 1637 hours that same day, were airborne for a sweep. These were the first Allied squadrons to operate from French soil since the evacuation from Dunkirk.

332. The strength of squadrons based on the Continent was gradually built up in the first fourteen days of the operation; eight Spitfire, three Typhoon and three Auster squadrons moved in to, and were operating from, beach-head airfields by the end of this period.

333. During the following week, United States forces began moving in and nine Thunderbolt and three Mustang squadrons arrived. A further British contingent of one Spitfire, three Typhoon and one Auster squadrons arrived to make a total of thirty-one Allied squadrons operating from beach-head airfields three weeks after D-Day.

Enemy Reaction and Allied Counter-action.

334. I have dealt in para. 156 *et seq.* with the activities of the G.A.F. directed against our preparations for the assault. I now turn to the G.A.F.'s operations after the assault was launched.

335. The strength of that part of the German Air Force likely to be committed against the invasion was estimated at 1,750 front line aircraft. This figure included such aircraft of Reserve Training Units as were expected to be operationally used. The total was made up as follows:—

Long Range Bombers	385
Ground Attack	50
Single-engine Fighters ...	745
Twin-engine Fighters—Day ...	55
—Night ...	395
Long Range Recce.	85
Tactical Recce.	25
Coastal Recce.	10
	1,750

336. The disposition of these forces is shown in the map* facing page 70. The Units based in Southern France (Mediterranean area) and in Denmark and Norway are also shown on this map, although I have not included them in the total given above.

337. The enemy air strength on D-Day was considerably greater than its strength in this area six weeks before. Bomber strength had increased by approximately 200, single-engine fighters by 500 and twin-engine fighters by 125.

338. It was estimated that the serviceability of these forces would be 55 per cent. for long-range bomber types and 60 per cent. for all others. The destruction of facilities at airfields in the rear of the assault area and the continued pounding of the fields themselves had forced the Luftwaffe to make extensive use of satellite landing fields, with the inevitable attendant difficulties of maintaining serviceability.

339. After D-Day, there was some reinforcement of units on the Western Front, though not as great as might have been expected. The reasons probably included the following:—

(i) a decision not to denude the Reich proper of its air protection, even at the expense of leaving the German armies in the field relatively uncovered.

(ii) the destruction of airfield facilities, making it difficult to service and operate from the fields at the enemy's disposal forces any larger than those already there.

(iii) the lack of fuel and lubricant supplies in the area and the difficulty of replacement of consumed stocks, owing to the dislocation of transport facilities.

340. The enemy scale of effort throughout the whole period D-Day to 30th September was considerably lower than was expected. As I have already stated, I had expected at the outset a week of fairly heavy air attacks, after which I felt confident that the enemy air effort would dwindle and require much less attention from our own air forces. In fact no serious air battle took place during this period.

341. *Enemy Air Opposition — June.* Throughout June, the squadrons which showed the most aggressiveness were bomber units which operated by night, principally on sea mining in the shipping lanes but also on

---

* Maps not reproduced.

bombing operations against shipping in the approach lanes and against the beaches. The fighter units operated mainly in a defensive role against Allied bomber attacks and principally in the Paris area and south of the Seine, where they tried to provide cover to the reinforcement assembly areas and to the main airfields.

342. The scale of effort by a few enemy units was, however, relatively high. On days when flying conditions were good, many aircraft flew more than one sortie and three and four sorties per aircraft were not unusual. The frequent periods of bad weather gave respite from Allied air attack, rested the pilots and allowed ground staffs to keep up serviceability.

343. Except on isolated occasions during this month, the enemy fighter and fighter bomber formations showed a marked disinclination to engage Allied fighters, and they were often deterred, with relative ease, from carrying out their primary tasks. However, the night fighter activity against Allied bombers continued to be fairly heavy and vigorous.

344. On D-Day, the first enemy air reaction to the assault was a reconnaissance of the Channel areas. At approximately 1500 hours, the first enemy fighters and fighter bombers appeared. This was nine hours after the assault began and fifteen hours after the first of very large formations of airborne transports and of the air bombardment squadrons had arrived over enemy territory. The enemy formations consisted of some FW 190s and one formation of 12 Ju 88s; four of this latter force were destroyed.

345. On the night of D/D + 1, approximately 85 enemy aircraft were active over the beach and shipping lanes. Some of the units operating were known to be specialised anti-shipping units. Activity on this scale was maintained on most nights during June.

346. During the morning of D + 1, a total of 59 enemy aircraft were sighted in the battle area. Ju 88s and Ju 188s were routed by low cover patrols and a formation of 16 FW 190s attempting to dive bomb the area north of Caen was forced by a Spitfire Wing to jettison their bombs. In all, fifteen enemy aircraft were claimed as destroyed by Allied fighters over the battle area during that morning.

347. In the afternoon of D + 1, the main enemy effort was defensive patrolling over assembly and rearward areas. Offensive fighter sweeps of Allied aircraft accounted for sixteen aircraft destroyed and five probably destroyed.

348. The principal enemy gains by air action during June were against shipping, and these were mainly as the result of night attacks. On D + 2, however, attacks against shipping off " Sword " beach resulted in a destroyer being sunk. Another destroyer was sunk by day by an aircraft torpedo attack off Portland Bill on 13th June. Sea mines laid in the shipping lanes and approach waters during the month also caused damage and loss to some ships and involved continuous employment of naval minesweepers. Considering the number of ships employed in narrow waters, these enemy gains were remarkably low.

349. *Enemy Air Opposition—July.*—Throughout July, the enemy air effort continued to be sporadic; in the first few days, a scale of effort of up to 450 day sorties was observed, but this quickly fell away and was not again reached until 27th July. Most of the day sorties were directed against Allied positions in the battle area, particularly at the western end of the Allied line.

350. The aggressiveness of the enemy also fluctuated. On some days, attacks were pressed home, on others a marked disinclination to fight was evident. The reaction to our bomber forces also varied; on some days, there was almost no opposition, while on others, determined defensive efforts were put up. The reaction to R.A.F. Bomber Command's night attacks was, however, sustained and on some occasions produced violent activity. Night offensive operations by the G.A.F., principally against shipping targets, were also maintained.

351. *Enemy Air Opposition—August.*—At the beginning of this month, with the break-out of the Allied armies accomplished, the G.A.F. day forces became even more committed to ground support. It was also evident that the enemy could no longer support his ground forces on both the British and American sectors and for a time he left the British sector alone to concentrate on what he considered the more dangerous threat. At about this time, too, the enemy began to use his long-range bombers by night against land targets, with only occasional attacks on shipping. Another feature of his night activity was the use of single-engine day fighters to support twin-engine night fighters.

352. During the second week of August, when the enemy launched his strongest counter-attack in the Mortain area, the German Air Force again rose to an effort of approximately 400 sorties a day. To counter this activity I laid on heavy attacks on the airfields in use by the G.A.F. I refer to these attacks later. The enemy activity declined steeply after the first two days. The decline was due partly to our attacks and partly to the fact that the G.A.F. was compelled to move most of its units to airfields further east with the consequent need of reorganisation; the enemy shortage of fuel and his need of reinforcements for operationally tired units were additional causes.

353. This shortage of fuel was the result, not only of the air attacks on the various oil installations in Germany, but also of the attacks on the enemy's transport system. The G.A.F.'s problem of distribution of supplies to frequently changing bases had become one of extreme complexity.

354. By mid-August, new G.A.F. units began to appear on the Western Front, but although these units pushed up the average daily effort to nearly 300 sorties, the fighting value continued to deteriorate. An effort was, however, made by the G.A.F. throughout the fourth week in August, to assist the land forces trying to scramble back to the Seine by providing cover and relief from air attack at the Seine crossings, but on very few occasions were the attacks pressed home. The enemy losses mounted steadily all the time. On 25th August, United States Ninth Air Force fighters destroyed 77 aircraft in combat and a further 44 on the ground. On 29th August, there was evidence that the enemy units were in flight back to Germany.

355. *Enemy Air Opposition—September.*—Activity in the first ten days of September was not very heavy, the close support units of the

G.A.F. being still very disorganised owing to their moves back to Germany. Later in the month, however, fighter units staged a very spirited revival of effort against strategical bomber attacks. United States Eighth Air Force suffered fairly heavy losses on two days. About this time also, jet-propelled aircraft began to appear in operations.

356. The landing of airborne troops in the Eindhoven-Nijmegen-Arnhem area in mid-September produced a more violent reaction from the G.A.F. than had been encountered for some time in the battle areas although a tactical surprise was gained and the original landings were made without opposition. During the first three days of the operation, many sightings were made and signals intelligence reported many more enemy aircraft airborne, but in spite of favourable weather on the fourth day, this offensive was not sustained. It can only be deduced that the scale of effort of the three previous days had imposed too great a strain upon the G.A.F. organisation and possibly its crews.

357. From the 20th September to the end of the month, close support of the enemy ground forces in the area of the Allied airborne landings was the chief object of the G.A.F. in the battle areas. The scale of effort was fairly low, probably owing to weather, except on 26th September, when a total of over 200 sorties was put up, chiefly ground attacks, by fighter bombers; the pilots showed little inclination to engage in air fighting. Our claims for this day's fighting were 16 enemy aircraft destroyed.

358. The stiffening of German resistance in the air during September, mainly in the Nijmegen area in Holland was, however, accomplished at high cost. There is reliable evidence that the G.A.F. had to scrape up from its training organisation its older and more experienced pilots, a policy not calculated to produce a long term improvement in its condition. However, the G.A.F. is by no means a spent force yet, and recent technical developments, in jet-propelled aircraft, for example, are likely to make it more formidable. It would be folly to regard the G.A.F. as "down and out". In addition, it is certain that it is working on a policy of conserving effort and building up reserves for the defence of the Reich proper. A reduction in heavy bomber attacks on G.A.F. centres of production after D-Day is a factor to be remembered in this connection. (See para. 401.)

359. *Enemy use of Jet-propelled Aircraft.*—The most important feature of G.A.F. activity during the second half of September was the appearance of jet-propelled aircraft, at first in ones and twos, later in fours and fives. In view of the fact that within the period covered by this Despatch (namely until 30th September) we have had insufficient experience of them to form reliable estimates of their activities or capabilities, I do not propose to comment on them at length. That they are a momentous landmark in the history of the air will not be denied, but final judgment on their value must be reserved for the moment.

360. Within the limits of our present experience, they appear to have been employed chiefly as fighter bombers for ground attack in a close support role, and for tactical reconnaissance. In both these roles their very high speed makes them formidable weapons and presents problems of defence not yet solved. As fighters, they have so far played a less decisive part, though their speed and particularly their rate of climb, would seem to equip them admirably for these duties. From aerial combats that have occurred up to the date of writing between orthodox Allied fighters and these jet-propelled aircraft, it would appear that their lack of manœuvrability puts them under some disadvantage in a "dog fight", but their qualities of speed and rate of climb make them deadly if they are given the chance to "jump" the opposition.

361. When it is remembered that the G.A.F. so often refused to fight and had to be diligently sought out before it could be attacked, the losses inflicted on it are remarkable. The following figures give the victories gained by Allied pilots in air fighting alone, but do not include the destruction of aircraft on the ground or by the anti-aircraft forces of the British and American armies:—

Enemy Losses on the Western Front—6th June–30th September, 1944

	Destroyed	Probably Destroyed	Damaged
A.E.A.F.	1,368	187	18
U.S. Eighth A.F. :—			6
VIIIth F.C.	1,325	50	372
VIIIth B.C.	193	108	208
R.A.F. B.C.	240	33	121
	3,126	378	1,319

362. The losses inflicted on the G.A.F. in the heavy and damaging attacks made on its airfields subsequent to D-Day cannot be estimated with sufficient accuracy to warrant the statement of a figure. It is known they were very heavy. The chief difficulty is that photographic reconnaissance never revealed all aircraft destroyed by the Allied air forces' attacks. There is considerable evidence from the airfields now in Allied hands that the G.A.F. continued to use hangars, even after heavy raiding, for the parking and servicing of aircraft, and it was frequently found that even more wrecks of aircraft were under cover than were at dispersal points. This G.A.F. habit made impossible the exact evaluation of the success of our attacks on its airfields.

363. *Attacks on Enemy Airfields.*—Attacks on airfields after D-Day were not made to any set plan, as they had been before the invasion. They were made as a security measure when it was found that enemy air activity was interfering with the success of our land and air operations. Even so, they were laid on only when intelligence indicated concentrations of enemy aircraft in sufficient strength to justify

attacks or revealed that certain airfields were being used for maintenance and servicing purposes. During July and early August, it proved unnecessary to maintain any serious effort against enemy airfields, but from 13th to 16th August, strong forces of heavy bombers operated against several night fighter airfields in Holland and Belgium, from which night fighters, maintaining a high operational effort, were hampering our heavy bombers on night operations. In these attacks, 1,004 aircraft of R.A.F. Bomber Command and 1,743 aircraft of the United States Eighth Air Force dropped over 10,000 tons of bombs in three days. There was an immediate cessation of enemy activity from these airfields.

364. During the enemy withdrawal from France and the Low Countries, an excellent chance was afforded of making profitable attacks on aircraft on a number of airfields. These aircraft were grounded through lack of fuel. Hitherto the heavy concentrations of flak on G.A.F. airfields had make attacks on them costly and had frequently compelled us to use heavy bombers in high level attacks when medium and fighter bombers could have been better spared for this task. During this period of hasty withdrawal however, the enemy flak defences were weakened. In consequence, our losses were reduced and we were allowed much greater freedom in the selection of method of attack.

365. The following statistics show the weight of bombing attacks on airfields in the period D-Day to 30th September. The chief contribution of the aircraft of A.E.A.F. was, however, in low level strafing and destruction of aircraft on the ground.

Total Sorties against Airfields during the period 6th June to 30th September, 1944

Force	Sorties	Tons of Bombs
A.E.A.F.	310	156·7
U.S. Eighth Air Force	11,118	24,747·0
R.A.F. B.C.	2,433	12,283·7
	13,861	37,187·4

Defence against Flying Bombs and Counter-Action against Flying Bomb Installations.

366. In paragraph 169 et seq. I have briefly described air operations prior to D-Day, against the sites the enemy was preparing for the launching of flying bombs and rocket projectiles against the United Kingdom. It was not fully appreciated at the time, that the enemy was also preparing modified and less conspicuous sites. Air operations against "Noball" targets had been suspended before D-Day in order to release the air forces for the major tasks of "Overlord". It was thought that the operations by then carried out had virtually eliminated the menace; in fact, it is known that these operations, coupled with our attacks on his transport system, oil and manufacturing centres had reduced the enemy's potential capacity to launch flying bombs from a probable 6,000 per day to a relatively very small fraction of this number. Nonetheless, his power to hit us with these weapons had not been entirely destroyed.

367. On the night of 12/13th June, the enemy launched his first jet-propelled flying bomb against England and aimed at London. In the first phase between 0405 hours and 0430 hours on 13th June, seven of these flying bombs were observed, one of which reached London. Later, three more operated over Kent.

368. No further flying bombs were reported until the evening of 15th June, when activity began afresh on a fairly large scale. Long-prepared defence plans were immediately put into operation. Direct responsibility for this defence was allotted to Air Marshal Sir Roderic Hill, K.C.B., M.C., A.F.C., the Air Marshal Commanding Air Defence of Great Britain. Additional guns and balloons were deployed to counter these weapons, whilst airborne and fighter patrols were put up both over the Channel and south of London. The United States forces contributed wholeheartedly to this defence with A.A. guns and fighter patrols. Large scale bombing operations were also undertaken against the launching sites and their ancillary installations. The diversion of effort from "Overlord" tasks now assumed larger proportions.

369. From the commencement of flying bomb activity until 30th September, fighter aircraft flew 24,572 sorties on interception patrols. This commitment was almost exclusively met by the aircraft of A.D.G.B. These patrols accounted for 1,915 flying bombs out of a total of 7,503 launched. The following figures give the results of all types of defence against these weapons:—

Period 12/13th June to 2100 hours 30th September, 1944

Despatched	Made Landfall	Reached Greater London
7,503	5,431	2,421

Flying Bombs Destroyed—period 12/13th June to 30th September, 1944

(a) By Fighter Patrols:—

	Day	Night	Total
Over land	287	388½	675½
Over sea	1,034½	205	1,239½
Total	1,321½	593½	1,915

(b) By all causes:—

Fighter Patrols	A.A.	Balloons	Other Causes	Total
1,915	1,547	278	33	3,773

370. Our rapid advance through France forced the enemy to abandon his launching sites in the Pas de Calais; in consequence there was no flying bomb activity over the United Kingdom after the 9th September for a period of ten days. When it recommenced, the launching was from carrier aircraft, chiefly Heinkel 111, operating over the North Sea. The scale of activity of these air-launched flying bombs was never heavy; nevertheless a fully organised defence scheme, involving nine squadrons of fighters, had to be maintained to combat the menace.

371. The scale of the bombing attacks on the launching and ancillary sites and also on large constructional sites believed to be associated with preparations for launching large rocket projectiles is shown in the figures given below:—

"Crossbow" Operations
Period 14th June to 31st August, 1944

Force	Aircraft attacking	Tons of Bombs
A.E.A.F.:—		
14th–30th June	1,005	1,335
1st–31st July	246	419
1st–31st August	—	—
	1,251	1,754
R.A.F. B.C.:—		
14th–30th June	4,050	17,773
1st–31st July	5,833	26,487
1st–31st August	4,384	21,385
	14,267	65,645
U.S. Eighth Air Force:—		
14th–30th June	1,835	4,709
1st–31st July	1,401	3,639
1st–31st August	869	2,329
	4,105	10,677

372. It is very difficult to estimate the success of these counter attacks; the number of flying bombs launched per day varied considerably, as also did the number and location of the sites used. It can, however, be stated that these attacks hampered and kept in check the launching rate; the average number launched per day over the period 13th June to 31st August was 95 against the estimated possible number of 6,000 per day, had the German plan not been upset by Allied bombing. It has already been noted that the air bombing in the preparatory period was so successful in countering the enemy's preparations for the use of the flying bomb, that it was no longer a direct threat to the preparations for, or the carrying out of the Allied assault and subsequent land operations. In the event, the flying bomb was launched mainly as a "terror" weapon against the civilian population of Southern England and not as a counter to the plans for the invasion of the Continent. I do not propose, therefore, to make any wider comment beyond emphasising the cost to the invasion operations by virtue of the diversion of available air effort that had to be made in order to secure this degree of immunity. An indication of the scale of this diversion is given by the statistics in the paragraphs above. Another less calculable cost was the fact that a number of Tempest and Mustang fighters—which had been allocated to re-arm squadrons in Second British Tactical Air Force—had to be transferred to A.D.G.B. for duties on flying bomb interception patrols. We thus lost the use of these very valuable and latest type of fighters over the battlefront.

Operation "Market"—First Allied Airborne Army.

373. On 17th September, airborne forces of the First Allied Airborne Army, comprising United States 82nd and 101st Airborne Divisions, 1st British Airborne Division and a Polish Parachute Brigade were dropped and landed in the Eindhoven—Nijmegen—Arnhem areas of Holland. The lift of these airborne forces exceeded that made during the initial landings on the Continent. The operation was designed to facilitate an advance by the northern group of armies up to and over the rivers Waal and Lower Rhine. With this end in view, the chief objectives of the airborne troops were the bridges at Arnhem and Nijmegen.

374. The initial drops were successful, being carried out accurately and with very few casualties. During the subsequent nine days, as weather permitted, reinforcements and supplies were flown in to the airborne troops and to the supporting ground troops which had linked up with them. Despite an heroic struggle by the troops of the 1st British Airborne Division the bridge at Arnhem, although secured initially, could not be retained. The bridge at Nijmegen, however, was secured and the operation paved the way for a subsequent advance up to the river Waal and beyond. It provided many lessons for the future and marked a definite step in the evolution of airborne operations.

375. The planning for and execution of these operations, which were carried out under the code name "Market", was the work of the First Allied Airborne Army, to which the opera-

tional control of the United States and Royal Air Force troop carrier forces, previously under my command, had been transferred in accordance with your direction, in August, 1944. A full report on these operations is being issued by the Commanding General of the First Allied Airborne Army, Lieutenant General Louis Brereton, who had relinquished the command of the United States Ninth Air Force to take over this new appointment.

376. Besides the aircraft of the troop carrier air forces, the aircraft of A.E.A.F., United States Eighth Air Force, R.A.F. Bomber Command and R.A.F. Coastal Command were engaged in support of these operations. The co-ordination of the activities of all the air forces concerned in a supporting role was carried out at my headquarters at meetings with representatives of the interested commands.

377. The chief meeting took place on 12th September, and at this meeting the principal tasks of the air forces were assigned. These tasks were:—
    (i) The attacking of airfields and known flak positions by heavy bombers.
    (ii) The dive bombing of flak positions which might be developed by the enemy during the operation.
    (iii) The provision of top cover along the route to be followed by the airborne trains, and a fighter screen east and north of the dropping and landing areas.
    (iv) The provision of night fighter patrols.
    (v) The arrangements for dummy drops.
    (vi) The arrangements for diversions by R.A.F. Coastal Command.
    (vii) The arrangements for re-supply of airborne forces by heavy bombers on D+1.

378. All these operations as planned at this meeting were actually carried out, and in addition, the air forces continued to lend support to the ground operations during the whole period that the intense phase of the operation lasted. I have referred to some of these activities by the air forces at other points in this Despatch, but below is summarised briefly what was actually done.

379. On the night of 16/17th September, R.A.F. Bomber Command attacked with 200 Lancasters and 23 Mosquitoes, four airfields at Leeuwarden, Steewijk-Havelte, Hopsten and Salzbergen. These enemy airfields were those from which fighters could attack the transports and gliders carrying the airborne forces. Nearly 900 tons of bombs were dropped with good to excellent results on these airfields. On the same night, 54 Lancasters and 5 Mosquitoes dropped 294 tons of bombs on flak positions at Moerdijk, also with good results. On the following morning, 85 Lancasters and 15 Mosquitoes dropped 535 tons of bombs on coastal defence batteries in the Walcheren area. For these daylight operations Spitfires of A.D.G.B. provided escort.

380. These operations by R.A.F. Bomber Command were followed up on the morning of D+1 by heavy bombers of the United States Eighth Air Force which attacked 117 flak positions along the routes to be followed and near the dropping and landing zones, just prior to the arrival of the troop carriers. In these attacks, 816 heavy bombers dropped 3,139 tons of bombs with fair to good results in most cases. A further six bombers also attacked the airfield at Eindhoven.

381. During the afternoon of D+1, 18th September, 252 heavy bombers of the United States Eighth Air Force dropped 782 tons of supplies to the ground forces with good to excellent results.

382. The airborne forces were carried in two great trains of troop carrier aircraft and gliders, one following a northerly, the other a southerly route. The plan for the protection of these two trains of troop carriers provided for a high cover of fighters and a force of fighter bombers at low level, ready to dive bomb any flak positions that opened fire. On the northern route, aircraft of A.D.G.B. carried out these two tasks, as far as the turning point near 'sHertogenbosch, employing 371 fighters for this purpose. Fighter aircraft of the United States Eighth Air Force then took over covering the train of troop carriers to the dropping and landing zones. Fighters of this air force also provided top cover to the train approaching over the southern route, and in addition, provided a fighter screen to the east and north of the dropping and landing zones. In these tasks, 548 fighters were employed. In addition, 212 fighters of the United States Ninth Air Force dive bombed flak positions along the southern route between the turning point and the dropping and landing zones.

383. The attacks on the enemy flak positions along the routes were very successful. The great bulk of the land batteries were silenced and in addition, several flak ships and barges off the Dutch Islands were destroyed.

384. The G.A.F. reaction to these very large scale operations was small on D-Day, approximately 30 enemy fighters only being seen, seven of which were shot down. On the second, third and sixth days, however, the German Air Force reacted much more strongly, and up to the end of the operation a total of 159 enemy aircraft were destroyed over the area.

385. Throughout the operations, the Allied air forces continued to cover the airborne forces, to lend direct support to the ground forces and particularly to attack flak positions. In all, the supporting air forces flew over 7,800 sorties in support of Operation "Market". A total of 114 aircraft were lost, in addition to the casualties incurred by the troop carrier forces.

386. The Air/Sea Rescue Service functioned most efficiently during these airborne operations. A string of 17 launches was placed across the North Sea on the northern route and a further string of 10 launches along the southern route. In addition, special reconnaissances were flown, spotting for ditched planes and gliders. Most of the ditching occurred on D+2, when the weather was bad and the towlines of many gliders parted. On this day, one launch picked up all the personnel from five ditched gliders. In all 205 personnel were saved by the Air/Sea Rescue Service during these operations.

Attacks against Enemy Naval Targets.

387. I now turn to the duties of the Air Force in assisting the Allied Navies in dealing with enemy naval units trying to interfere with the landing and the subsequent ferrying of reinforcements and supplies by our ships across the Channel. The following brief review covers these operations from the time of the assault to the end of September, 1944. The main burden was shouldered by R.A.F. Coastal Com-

mand, but R.A.F. Bomber Command continued to implement its extensive sea mining programme (which now embraced "Overlord" requirements) and made heavy attacks, referred to below, on shipping in harbours. Aircraft of A.E.A.F. also made attacks on coastal shipping and on E and R boats. After D-Day, Second British Tactical Air Force took over the commitment previously shouldered by A.D.G.B. to provide "Channel Stop" squadrons. The function of these squadrons was to attack enemy surface vessels attempting to enter the Channel from either end. A.E.A.F. fighters also provided escort for the strike aircraft of R.A.F. Coastal Command. Apart from the sea mining of R.A.F. Bomber Command, all these operations were co-ordinated through my headquarters.

388. *Anti-U-Boat Operations.*—In anticipation of an enemy attempt to move U-boats into the invasion waters, R.A.F. Coastal Command flew anti-submarine patrols from the Scillies to Ushant and from St. Albans Head to Cap de la Hague. Through these barriers the enemy had to try to infiltrate. The first U-boats sighted were approaching from the western entrance to the assault area on the night of D-Day. Six of these U-boats were attacked. During the next day and night, a further ten sightings were made and seven were attacked. Some of these attacks resulted in kills.

389. Because of these continuous patrols, U-boat commanders were forced to remain submerged for very long periods; these tactics restricted their freedom of manoeuvre and from P.O.W. statements, it is obvious they had a most distressing physical effect on the crews. During June, 80 U-boat sightings were made in the approaches to the assault area; 46 were attacked, 3 of these jointly with the Navy, and 18 of the attacks appeared promising. During July, the enemy was forced to continue maximum diving tactics. This made detection and attacks by aircraft more difficult, but at least two U-boats on or near the surface were destroyed. A further 20 conning tower or periscope sightings were made and 13 attacks delivered.

390. With the Allied advance in August, the enemy began to move his U-boats away from the ports of North-Western France to the southern portion of the Bay of Biscay. This movement gave the aircraft of R.A.F. Coastal Command a splendid chance to strike. 24 sightings were made in the Bay during August, and 14 attacks resulted; six U-boats were probably sunk, three of these shared with Naval forces, and two more damaged. From D-Day to 30th September, R.A.F. Coastal Command sunk or probably sunk 12 U-boats in the Channel or the Bay of Biscay, shared the destruction of five more with surface forces and damaged a further 12.

391. *Anti-Shipping Operations.* Attacks against enemy surface vessels, including naval vessels, were made by aircraft of A.E.A.F. and by R.A.F. Coastal Command. The first of these actions took place on the 6th June, when the enemy endeavoured to bring into action three heavy destroyers from the west coast of France. These ships were attacked, west of Brest by R.A.F. Coastal Command. Some damage was caused, one was set on fire and the ships were delayed. On 8th June, they again attempted to move into the invasion waters, but were met by Allied destroyers. One was sunk, one driven ashore and the third forced back to Brest.

392. Other attacks were made against smaller enemy naval vessels and merchant shipping and some of these attacks were very successful; details of two are given below. However, not only these missions which saw and attacked enemy vessels should be reckoned as successful. Continuous patrols by fighters of A.E.A.F. and R.A.F. Coastal Command in the Western Approaches and down into the area of the Channel Islands ensured that no enemy surface vessels were able to support the garrisons holding out in coastal areas. These offensive fighter patrols were co-ordinated with the sorties of the reconnaissance aircraft of R.A.F. Coastal Command.

393. On the night of 7th June, Beaufighters and Albacores attacked a formation of E-boats in the Channel; two E-boats were sunk and a further three damaged. In the early morning of 15th June, a force of 42 Beaufighters, escorted by 10 Mustangs of A.D.G.B. attacked a north-bound convoy consisting of a merchant vessel of 8,000 tons, a naval auxiliary of 4,000 tons and seventeen escort ships off the Frisian Islands. The large merchant vessel and the auxiliary were torpedoed and sank, one minesweeper blew up and sank, another was hit by a torpedo and probably sank, while five more minesweepers were seen on fire and four other escorts were damaged by cannon fire.

394*. A brief summary of the work of R.A.F. Coastal Command shows that over 200 sorties were flown in attacks on surface craft during the month of June in the invasion area and its approaches. In July more than 500 aircraft made anti-shipping attacks in the Channel area, off the Dutch and Belgian Coasts, in the Bay of Biscay and off the Coast of Norway. In July, six merchant ships, 10 escort vessels and five E/R boats were sunk, one merchant ship, 11 escort vessels and two E/R boats were seriously damaged, and a further seven merchant ships, nineteen escort vessels and 6 E/R boats were damaged. August saw an even higher scale of shipping effort. Nightly attacks on E/R boats operating in the Channel, five large scale attacks off the Dutch and Norwegian coasts and numerous attacks on the enemy in the Bay of Biscay produced excellent results. Nine merchant ships plus one shared, seventeen escort vessels, 2 destroyers, and 1 E/R boat were sunk. Eleven escort vessels and 1 E/R boat seriously damaged and a further four merchant ships, 1 destroyer, 4 E/R boats and twenty-eight escort vessels were damaged.

395. These air operations directed against enemy surface forces, including the protective mine-laying by R.A.F. Bomber Command, not only assisted the safe-guarding of the Allied merchant fleets from surface attacks, but also prevented any German attempt to evacuate by sea his beleaguered coastal garrisons.

396. *Attacks on Shipping in Ports.*—The majority of the E and R boats operating against the Allied cross-channel shipping in the early

---

* These figures may be liable to review when enemy documents have been subjected to research.

days of the assault were using the ports of Le Havre and Boulogne. The boats were well protected by large shelter pens. However, R.A.F. Bomber Command, in two attacks, inflicted great damage on the enemy's fleet of small ships.

397. On the evening of 14th June, a force of 335 Lancasters and 18 Mosquitoes attacked the port area of Le Havre, dropping 1,026 tons of bombs. This tonnage included 22 × 12,000 lb. special bombs. On the next evening, the same tactics were used in an attack on the port of Boulogne when 285 heavy bombers and 12 Mosquitoes dropped 1,463 tons of bombs in a concentrated attack.

398. Very great damage was caused to the ports and the pens in these attacks, and in addition, the heavy bombs, bursting in the water, created huge waves which flung the small craft against the quays and the concrete sides of the pens. Photographs revealed twenty-five of these enemy naval vessels destroyed in Boulogne, and this number was exceeded at Le Havre.

399. Other air operations which were of direct assistance to Allied naval activity were the attacks on coastal defences (reviewed in Part III (b) dealing with preparatory operations), and also the co-ordination of fighter bomber attacks on Radar stations to upset the enemy warning system when Allied light surface forces operated against E and R boats.

Strategical Bombing—" Pointblank "

400. In addition to their priority operations, already described, against targets in the tactical area and against flying bomb installations, the United States and British strategical air forces maintained a considerable effort against targets within Germany after D-Day. As these operations were not directed by me, I mention them very briefly and in order simply, to round off the story of the Allied air effort.

401. The chief limitation on their effort was the weather which frequently made it necessary to cancel projected attacks. The main weight of this offensive from June to September was directed against the enemy's oil supplies and oil production centres. These targets were given priority over aircraft production and assembly plants (although attacks on these latter were not entirely suspended) and other industrial objectives as being, at this time, of more critical importance to the enemy. The G.A.F. had, by D-Day, been very seriously weakened by the efforts already directed against it, although the deep penetration daylight raids of the United States Eighth Air Force still provoked violent enemy air reaction on most occasions. In consequence, there was a steady attrition of the G.A.F. in aerial combat as well as a depletion of Germany's oil resources. Heavy and concentrated attacks on these targets have produced an oil situation which, taken with the loss of Roumanian supplies, must be seriously worrying the German High Command. The influence of this situation is already being, and will be increasingly, felt on the battlefield.

402. Other operations against " Pointblank " targets included attacks on aircraft and motor transport manufacturing centres, on several important communication centres and on German cities.

Brief Summary of Air Effort for the period D-Day to 30th September, 1944

403. At 30th September, the Allied armies stood on and in some places, over the borders of the Reich proper. In 117 days since the assault began, France, Belgium, Luxembourg and a large part of Holland had been liberated. These 117 days had also been unprecedented in the scale of air effort employed. The aircraft of A.E.A.F. alone had flown 316,248 sorties, an average of 2,703 per day. The effort of the strategical air forces based in the United Kingdom raised this total to 552,197 sorties, an average of 4,719 per day.

404. The remarkable achievement of such a high rate of effort is due, in no small measure, both to the detailed administrative plans which facilitated the transfer of forces to Continental airfields without interruption to the current operations, and to the work of the ground staffs who supplied, serviced and armed the aircraft and provided the ancillary services.

405. *Weather.*—The weather throughout the whole period was frequently unfavourable for air operations, and on many occasions interfered greatly with my plans. This was especially so in the first days of the assault. Before D-Day it was known that unsettled weather was approaching and there was a distinct possibility that the unsettled period might be prolonged and severe. I was, however, confident of the ability of the air forces to carry out their allotted tasks, and in particular to deal with the German Air Force, despite the weather handicap. In the event, just after D-Day, the weather was nearly as bad as it possibly could be.

406. In making the Assault, despite the bad weather, there is no doubt that the invasion forces won an increased chance of tactical surprise. There is the evidence of a captured senior German meteorological officer that the Germans were in fact off their guard; he has stated that he advised the German Command that owing to the approach of unsettled conditions, no assault would be attempted.

407. The following figures show the effect of the weather on air operations during the period. The A.E.A.F. total of aircraft sorties on D-Day was 7,672, on D + 1 8,283 and D + 2, when the weather began to deteriorate, 5,073 and on D + 3 the total reached 662 only. On one other day in June the total was less than 1,000 and on two further days it was under 2,000 sorties; however, despite this handicap, the average number of sorties per day for A.E.A.F. aircraft throughout the month of June was almost 4,000. Weather also affected the planning and carrying out of bomber operations between D-Day and September 30th. In fact, the lack of weather good enough to permit of high altitude precision and, above all, visual, bombing was one of the chief reasons why the start of the attacks on the enemy's transportation and communications system was planned so early.

408. *Personnel Casualties.* The following statistics of personnel casualties cover the period from 1st April to 30th September, 1944. These figures reveal a grievous loss of highly trained men. Reference, however, to the statistics in paragraph 183, dealing with the

preparatory period and paragraph 403, covering the period from D-Day to 30th September, will show that the overall losses per sorties flown are reasonably low.

Personnel Casualties of Allied Air Forces Operating in Western Europe
Period 1st April–30th September, 1944

	Killed in Action or Died of Wounds	Missing and P.O.W.	Wounded
A.E.A.F.:—			
U.S. Personnel	216	1,839	660
British Personnel	694	1,361	864
R.A.F. Bomber Command	2,318	9,265	1,109
U.S. Eighth Air Force:—			
Bomber	931	15,057	1,716
Fighter	49	959	77
R.A.F. Coastal Command	352	597	239
	4,560	29,078	4,665

PART IV—SPECIAL FEATURES

409. The mounting of air operations of the complexity and scale recorded in this Despatch was only made possible by an adequate ground organisation. I wish, therefore, in this Section to pay some tribute to the background work against which these operations were carried out, and upon which they depended for success.

410. For convenience, comments on some of the special features have been arranged under the following headings:—

(i) Administration.
(ii) Airfield Construction.
(iii) Air/Sea Rescue.
(iv) Air Transport and Evacuation of Casualties.
(v) Employment of Balloons.
(vi) Provision of Maps.
(vii) Signal Communications and Radar Cover.

Administration

411. Although I did not have administrative control of the United States Ninth Air Force, there were many and varied administrative matters affecting all forces in the Allied Expeditionary Air Force which set difficult problems to be solved. Administration, maintenance and the provision of equipment, fuel and ammunition to keep modern air forces fighting all had their peculiar complications.

412. An idea of some of the special problems met and overcome by the administrative and other ground staffs is given in the following paragraphs.

413. On 16th November, 1943, the British forces, Second Tactical Air Force and Nos. 38 and 85 Groups had been built up to about 35 per cent. only of their final strength. The United States Ninth Air Force at this time was only approximately 25 per cent. of its final strength. To develop these forces in the winter and following spring, and to have them suitably deployed in readiness for the opening of the campaign was a race against time which involved, inter alia:—

(i) A comprehensive plan whereby aerodromes and landing grounds in the south of England were progressively evacuated by units not participating directly in "Overlord", and occupied by "Overlord" forces as the U.S.A.A.F. arrived from overseas and by the British forces as they were augmented.

(ii) Providing Second Tactical Air Force with a fully mobile organisation for repair, and for the supply of Royal Air Force equipment, in substitution for the service normally provided by the Royal Air Force Maintenance Command in the United Kingdom.

(iii) Integrating the U.S.A.A.F. and R.A.F. administrative services where necessary.

(iv) Re-equipping 110 Royal Air Force squadrons with the most up-to-date types of aircraft.

(v) Changing Second Tactical Air Force from the home system of personnel administration and accounting, to the overseas systems, including the establishment of a Base Personnel Staff Office and a Base Accounts Office.

(vi) On D-Day the British totalled approximately 232,000 personnel and the Americans 181,000. The organisation of the British part of the force alone involved the formulation and issue of some 250 new type establishments.

414. After D-Day, the principal administrative tasks to be executed, and for which full preparations had been made were:—

(i) By means of the inter-Allied and inter-Service machinery known as BUCO and MOVCO to control the transfer of Air Forces to the Continent, together with the stores for immediate use, and to build up reserves.

(ii) Special arrangements to ensure that squadrons could operate at full effort, whether from the United Kingdom or the Continent, even though their normal maintenance organisation was in process of transfer.

(iii) Arrangements by which United States air forces could re-arm and re-fuel at British air strips and vice versa.

(iv) Rapid replacement of personnel casualties, aircraft and equipment.

(v) The institution, quite early in the operations, of arrangements for salvaging aircraft carcasses and certain other equipment, and for returning this material quickly to the United Kingdom by L.C.T. for use by the production organisation there.

(vi) Finally, maintaining a high state of mobility for the Tactical Air Forces which were taxed to the limit to keep up with the advance.

415. There were over 6,600 operational aircraft in A.E.A.F. at D-Day. These aircraft were composed of ten basic types with a large number of varying marks, each with its own problems in servicing. That the maintenance personnel managed to keep the operational serviceability to the high levels stated below is a remarkable achievement. When it is remembered that throughout June and July most of the squadrons operated from new-made landing strips only a few miles from the front line, and that the dust on these Normandy airfields was, in the opinion of many experienced campaigners, worse than that in the North African desert campaigns, then the efforts of the maintenance personnel become even more outstanding.

416. *Average Strength and Serviceability of Aircraft in A.E.A.F.*

	Fighters			Bombers		
	Average Strength	Average Serviceability	Percentage	Average Strength	Average Serviceability	Percentage
Ninth Air Force:—						
June	1,239	1,010	81·7	717	626	87·4
July	1,341	1,063	79·4	721	631	87·5
August	1,344	1,058	78·7	737	658	89·3
September	1,393	1,120	80·3	753	663	88·0
Second T.A.F.:—						
June	1,156	954	82·5	272	231	85·0
July	1,058	946	89·5	265	232	87·5
August	1,077	930	86·4	277	240	86·7
September	1,250	1,093	87·5	253	214	84·6
A.D.G.B.:—						
June	1,207	957	79·3	—	—	—
July	1,281	1,007	78·5	—	—	—
August	1,335	1,060	79·4	—	—	—
September	1,131	926	82·0	—	—	—

417. The maintenance of operational strength was also the result of a carefully prepared plan for replacement of aircraft. In this connection, it is interesting to note that the forecasting of wastage and casualties by the planning staff was sound, and since the losses were somewhat below those planned, there were never any serious difficulties of supply. The replacement pool and recovery organisation both worked extremely well.

418. The statistics of the average daily consumption and wastage of P.O.L. and ammunition also reveal something of the achievement of the supply organisation. During July, A.E.A.F. expended daily 750 tons of bombs and more than 200,000 rounds of ammunition. The fuel consumption of A.E.A.F. in July reached approximately 30,000,000 gallons of petrol, almost 1,000,000 gallons per day. A large part of this fuel and ammunition had to be transported into the beach-head and up to forward airfields. In this connection the work of Air Force beach squadrons deserves special mention. These parties went in with the follow-up troops on D-Day and due in no small measure to their efforts, the first airfields were stocked ready for operations in the beach-head on D+3.

419. The following story reveals some of the difficulties encountered and overcome in supplying an air force of the magnitude of A.E.A.F. Supreme Headquarters Allied Expeditionary Force Operational Memoranda called for special markings on aircraft in order that they might be clearly distinguished on D-Day. To achieve success the markings had to be applied on D − 1 so that all aircraft should have broad black and white bands painted on them on D-Day, but not before. The total requirements of distemper for this purpose to mark approximately 10,000 aircraft and gliders was 100,000 gallons or 1,500 tons. There was no such amount immediately available in the United Kingdom. Supply action on a high priority was necessary. Supply to civilians was stopped, overtime was worked in pits and factories, Whitsun week-end holidays were forgotten and by Y-Day all was ready; the distemper and 20,000 brushes to apply it were on hand.

Airfield Construction.

420. In combined operations it is obviously advantageous that fighters, fighter bombers and reconnaissance aircraft of the Tactical Air Forces should be able to work from bases in the operational theatre as early as possible, and therefore airfield accommodation is of paramount importance.

421. The extent to which airfield requirements could be met in this operation depended, in the main, on the ability of the field engineers to locate and develop suitable sites. These sites had been previously chosen by experts after a detailed study of the coverage provided by photographic reconnaissance aircraft and available maps. It also depended upon having a sufficiently high priority within the available shipping space for the movement of equipment and material. Naturally these claims must be balanced with others of operational urgency.

422. In the initial stages, the terrain in the British sector was generally more favourable

than that in the American. However, the airfield engineers achieved very fine results in both sectors. The position in the British sector deteriorated because the good area to the east and south-east around Caen was not secured as rapidly as had been planned. Neither did the situation in the American sector greatly improve until the advance had progressed to Le Mans and beyond.

423. The minimum programme for airfields to accommodate the forces allocated was as follows:—

3 E.L.S. (2 American and 1 British) by D-Day.

4 R. and Rs. (2 American and 2 British) by the evening of D + 3 and not later than D + 4.

10 A.L.Gs. (5 American and 5 British) by D + 8 (these A.L.Gs. included 4 of the R. and Rs.).

18 Airfields (8 American and 10 British) by D + 14.

27 Airfields (12 American and 15 British) by D + 24.

43 Airfields (18 American and 25 British) by D + 40.

93 Airfields (48 American and 45 British) by D + 90.

424. Definitions of the terms used above and descriptions of the different types of airfields are given below:—

E.L.S.—Emergency Landing Strip.—A strip having sufficient length of level surface to enable pilots in distress to make a landing. These strips have a minimum length of 600 yards and are not fit for the operation of aircraft, but are of inestimable value when operations are conducted a long way from bases especially when a long sea crossing on the way home is involved.

R. & R.—Refuelling and Re-arming Strip.—A strip possessing sufficient length of level compact surface for landing and taking off, adequate marshalling areas for the rapid turn-round of aircraft and adequate tracking to ensure operation under all normal summer and autumn conditions. These strips have a minimum length of 1,200 yards with the marshalling areas of 100 × 50 yards at each end.

A.L.G.—Advanced Landing Ground.—A landing ground possessing the same facilities as an R. and R. to be brought up to A.L.G. standard by the addition of dispersal facilities and capable of use to capacity by adopting the " Roulement " system.

Airfield.—A field with the same facilities as an A.L.G. but with improved dispersal facilities and on which squadrons are established and not operated on the " Roulement " system, as on an A.L.G.

The minimum lengths for both A.L.Gs. and airfields are 1,200 yards for fighters, with dispersal facilities for 54 aircraft, and 1,650 yards for fighter bombers, with the same dispersal facilities.

All-Weather Airfield.—The same requirements as for an airfield but possessing hard-surfaced runways and fit for operation throughout all seasons and all conditions of weather for the appropriate type of aircraft. Within the limits of operational requirements, it was planned that all enemy airfields with hard-surfaced runways would be reinstated, as and when they were captured, if in the opinion of the airfield engineers, reinstatement could be effected without excessive labour and/or material.

" *Roulement* " *System.*—A means of using landing ground facilities to the maximum capacity by flying in squadrons to replace others as they complete their scale of effort appropriate to the period.

425. The priorities fixed for the construction of these airfields were as follows:—

Priority I—E.L.Ss. for emergency landing of aircraft.

Priority II—R. and R. strips for re-fuelling and re-arming fighter aircraft.

Priority III—A.L.Gs. to become airfields later.

426. The following construction units were available for allocation as required in the beachhead:—

American—16 Aviation Engineering Battalions.
2 Airborne Aviation Engineering Battalions.

British—5 Airfield Construction Groups.
1 Field Force Basis Construction Wing.

427. Because we failed in the initial phases to gain the ground agreed in the optimum plan which was needed in the vicinity of Caen, the development of all of the pre-selected sites could not be started. This naturally caused some delay and made necessary a re-allotment of sites in the beach-head area. As a very high proportion of potential sites selected from air photographs proved to be suitable for rapid construction, the intensive preparation of the beach-head area permitted the leeway to be made up and the Air Staff requirements to be met.

428. Later, when the Allied advance became rapid, the problem of finding space to prepare airfields was eased. It became more a problem of getting the airfields constructed rapidly in the now adequate space available. The system adopted for constructing airfields near the front line was to prepare dirt strips 15-20 miles to the rear of the ground forces. These strips were then visited by transport aircraft, which dumped stores and tools there. As a general rule, fighter strips were 50-70 miles behind the front line, and bomber strips 100-120 miles behind. As the ground forces moved forward, so the dirt strips previously prepared were constructed as airfields and became bases for fighters and later for bombers.

429. The position at the end of June (D + 24) was as follows:—

(i) *In the British Sector.*—10 airfields completed at Bazenville, St. Croix sur Mer, Beny sur Mer, Camilly, Coulombs, Martragny, Sommervieu, Lantheuil, Plumetot, Longues. 1 airfield was under construction at Ellon.

(ii) *In the American Sector.*—7 airfields completed at St. Pierre du Mont, Criqueville, Cordonville, Deux Jamaux, Benzeville, Axeville and Carentan. 4 under construction and 75 per cent. completed at Chippelle, Picauville, Le Moly and Creteville.

430. The position at D + 90 (the end of the planned period) was:—

Type of Field	American Sector		U.S. Total	British Sector.		British Total	Grand Total
	Operational	Under construction		Operational	Under construction		
Fighter ALG	24	8	32	23	5	28	60
Medium Bomber ...	5	1	6	1	—	1	7
Transport	9	1	10	2	—	2	12
Tactical Aerodrome ...	1	—	1	—	—	—	1
Liaison Strip	1	—	1	—	—	—	1
	40	10	50	26	5	31	81

431. In addition to these airfields, which were in use at D + 90, five fields in the American sector and three in the British sector had been abandoned, as being too far from the scene of ground operations. These make the number of airfields actually completed by D + 90, 55 in the American sector and 34 in the British sector, a total of 89, as against the planned total of 93. The IX Engineer Command proved very effective and I feel that the Royal Air Force could well consider the adoption of a comparable organisation to ensure immediate operational facilities in overseas theatres. In particular, I feel that more heavy earth-moving equipment should be provided for British units and that the organisation should be reviewed to allow smaller and more flexible companies than the present Wings. These companies should be under the direct control of the air commander in the theatre and not under a ground commander.

432. The fact that airfield construction was still a little behind schedule at the end of the planned period, was due mainly to tactical reasons in the assault phase and to the consequent lack of adequate and suitable ground area, and to some delay in shipping sufficient material. The men of the American Aviation Engineer Battalions of the IX Engineer Command and of the British Airfield Construction units worked exceptionally well, as was proved by the setting-up of the first three Emergency Landing Strips at Pouppeville, St. Laurent sur Mer and Asnelles by D + 1. These men worked right in the battle area, through shelling and bombing, and as well as constructing the airfields often had to lay down their tools to deal with stray snipers in the area around the airfield strip.

Air/Sea Rescue.

433. Air Defence of Great Britain and Royal Air Force Coastal Command provided the aircraft for searches in the battle area and for the forces engaged in Operation " Neptune".

434. These Air/Sea Rescue forces had been working hard prior to D-Day and had effected many fine rescues of bomber and fighter crews. Their effort was, naturally, intensified from D-Day onwards especially during the early phases before landing fields were available on the French side of the Channel. Constant standing patrols were flown so that immediately a "Mayday" call was received, rescue aircraft could be vectored onto the position. Both Warwick and Spitfire aircraft were used for these standing patrols.

435. The weather was unfortunately extremely difficult for Air/Sea Rescue operations during almost the whole of June and when Walruses were employed on searches, it was frequently impracticable for them to make landings on the water. This laid a greater burden on the high speed launches and other surface craft which, operating in all conditions, did very effective work. Two high speed launches were attached to each of the Fighter Direction Tenders located off the beach-head and achieved a number of rescues which would have been extremely difficult and lengthy for home-based craft.

436. During the first forty-eight hours of the invasion, airborne operations led to many incidents and during this period, Air-Sea Rescue squadrons were either directly or indirectly responsible for rescuing 117 paratroopers, all of whom had been previously trained in the essentials of Air-Sea Rescue. Details of the total numbers of aircrew, paratroopers and others rescued are set out in the statistics at the end of this account. These rescues were, however, not effected without some of the inevitable hazards of war. The following three incidents are typical and illustrate the nature of the work.

437. Two Walruses of No. 275 Squadron were ordered to search for a pilot known to have gone into the sea just north of Cherbourg. On arrival at the scene, they found the pilot, who had not been able to get into his dinghy, floating alive in his Mae West. He was, however, not more than two miles from the Cherbourg coast. In spite of the fire from coastal batteries, the two Walruses landed and the pilot was picked up. When they came to take off, they found they had been hit and therefore set out to taxi back across the Channel; both aircraft subsequently sank when taken in tow, but the rescue was made and no one was hurt.

438. On another occasion, two high speed launches from Portsmouth were ordered to search in the same area for an American pilot. These launches faced concentrated fire from the shore batteries and came away unscathed.

439. The third rescue displays the resource and efficiency of the personnel engaged in Air/Sea Rescue work. Two high speed launches were returning after making a successful rescue of an American crew over 70 miles out to sea. A message was sent by one of the launches that some of the rescued aircrew and some of the boat's crew were seriously injured as a result of an attack by FW 190s further

out. It was decided that medical aid should be flown to these injured personnel. A Walrus of No. 289 Squadron took off with two American Medical Officers, made rendezvous with the high speed launches out at sea and in this way, medical aid was brought to the wounded men three hours earlier than would otherwise have been possible. As a result, at least two lives were saved.

440. *Statistics of Personnel Rescued.*—The following figures show the totals of personnel rescued by the Air/Sea Rescue Services of A.D.G.B. and R.A.F. Coastal Command for the period 6th June to 30th September, 1944:—

Month.	Personnel Rescued.
June	685
July	313
August	247
September	600
	1,845

441. It will be seen from the above data that the Air/Sea Rescue services succeeded in rescuing many hundreds of valuable personnel, including aircrew and airborne troops. Without this organisation, the great majority, if not all of these airmen and soldiers, would have perished. Even more important, perhaps, than this direct saving of life has been the moral effect which the existence and known successes of the Air/Sea Rescue Service has had, particularly on aircrews. The value of such effect in air operations is obviously incalculable, but that it is of the greatest significance there can be no doubt.

Air Transport and Evacuation of Casualties.

442. In addition to the operational flying to carry airborne troops and supplies to their dropping and landing zones, the aircraft of the transport forces have flown many thousands of sorties on supply and evacuation missions.

443. The control of all scheduled and emergency airlift by Allied troop carrier and transport aircraft, other than those for airborne forces, was vested in CATOR (Combined Air Transport Operations Room), which was set up at my Headquarters at Stanmore. The operations section of CATOR allocated aircraft between operational tasks, scheduled and emergency demands, in conformity with the policy I laid down on your behalf. The supply section of this formation arranged for the supply and movement to the loading base airfields of the loads which were demanded.

444. The variety of equipment carried in these operations was extremely wide. It included jeeps, trailers, Radar equipment, picks and shovels, propellers and shafts, explosives, mines, petrol, containers, barbed wire, magazines, books, comforts and medical stores including blood plasma and penicillin.

445. Transport aircraft returning from the Continent were utilised to the fullest extent for the evacuation of the sick and wounded. This was in accordance with my policy that although no additional special ambulance squadrons should be formed, or aircraft specially tied up for air ambulance work, the maximum use should be made of all aircraft returning to the United Kingdom after delivering supplies. This policy was naturally not always popular with the medical authorities, but no relaxation of it was found to be necessary save in conditions of extreme urgency. This policy was fully supported by you. In all, during the period from D-Day to 30th September, 107,115 medical cases were evacuated by air from forward positions.

446. The evacuation of sick and wounded in the aforementioned manner has been a great boon to the medical services and of inestimable value in securing adequate and early treatment for the seriously injured. The following is a good example—a tank trooper who was suffering from severe burns was evacuated from a landing strip on the Continent to R.A.F. Station, Broadwell, at 1815 hours, landing at base at 1945 hours. From Broadwell he was flown to R.A.F. Station, Odiham, and was admitted to the Special Burns Centre, Basingstoke, at 2100 hours, less than three hours after he had left Normandy.

447. The success of this work reflects great credit on all concerned—the doctors, nurses, nursing orderlies, stretcher bearers, aircrew and ambulance drivers. In view of the fact that the aircraft often operated from airfields within range of enemy shell fire, it is a remarkable fact that every evacuation from the Continent by air during the period covered by this Despatch, was carried out without mishap either to aircraft, aircrew or wounded.

448. When the advance of the Allied armies began to outrun the normal supply arrangements, special air supply services had to be instituted. In the critical 25-day period from 9th August to 3rd September, no less than 13,000 tons of supplies were flown to forward positions. Furthermore, during the full month of September, more than 10,000 sorties were flown and a total of nearly 30,000 tons of supplies carried. These supplies comprised principally petrol, ammunition and rations and occupied all and more than all of the available lift of the transport groups.

449. It was decided, therefore, to allocate special forces of heavy bombers, both of the United States Eighth Air Force and R.A.F. Bomber Command, to provide additional lift. This increased lift enabled enough fuel to be taken forward to keep the Armies moving.

450. I feel that in certain cases, air supply is an overriding consideration. This was an appropriate instance. However, the diversion of valuable specialised aircraft and crews from their proper operational tasks needs very grave justification and only vital emergencies such as had occurred at this time can warrant this action.

451. The principal lesson so far learnt from the campaign is that the tactical use of air transport to supply a rapidly advancing army can be of decisive importance, and that the limiting factor in its employment is not so much the availability of suitable aircraft as the availability of sufficient landing strips in the forward area and adequate loading and re-loading arrangements at the terminus. These forward strips are primarily constructed and earmarked for the fighter squadrons operating in support of the ground forces, and their use by transport

aircraft is inevitably detrimental to these operations. I therefore consider that in any future campaign the airfield construction programme should envisage the immediate provision of at least one air transport landing strip per army and that these landing strips should be constructed so as to be capable of handling a minimum of 50-60 aircraft per hour.

452. In order to minimise the influence of the weather factor, consideration should also be given to the launching of air supply missions from forward airfields in close liaison with and, where necessary, under the local tactical air command.

Employment of Balloons in the Assault Phase.

453. I have already referred to the reasons for using balloons for protection of the beaches during the assault phase and to the results achieved by their use. Here I think it proper to mention the reasons for the final choice of the Mk. VI (V.L.A.) balloon and also some of the difficulties experienced during the planning stages.

454. Mk. VI (V.L.A.) balloons flying normally at an operational height of 2,000 feet, were chosen for this work for the following reasons:—

(i) The extreme lightness of the ancillary equipment and the practicability of using a light hand winch which could be carried ashore by crews.

(ii) The economy in operating personnel— only two airmen were required for each balloon.

(iii) No extra initial lift was required as the balloons were transported flying.

(iv) The possibility of transporting replacement balloons unmanned flying from L.C.T. and L.S.T.

(v) The comparatively small hydrogen requirements for maintenance and re-inflation.

455. During the planning stage it was realised there would be some difficulty in the employment of the balloons during the passage of the original assault forces. It was essential that balloons should not be brought in so early or at such a height as to give any premature warning on the enemy's Radar system. Inter-Service agreement was made, permitting balloons to go into the beach-head flying at 100 feet, not less than seven miles behind the assault. This height is the worst possible at which to fly a balloon owing to its inclination to dive on encountering erratic air currents near the ground. It was decided, however, after experiments on exercises that this restriction was acceptable, and in the event, no undue casualties resulted.

456. A further problem solved in the preparatory phase was the manner of transportation of the planned number of 240 balloons for the British area and 145 for the American area. As the Navy proposed to carry balloons for their own protection on one-third of the L.C.T. and all of the L.S.T., it was necessary to devise a method of flying two balloons from each L.S.T. in order to have available the planned number in the beach-heads. After several experiments, this was accomplished.

457. To provide the necessary number of inflated balloons for each craft, to maintain them during the marshalling period and during any possible period of postponement, and to replace casualties during that time, required a large number of small vessels and extensive shore servicing and hydrogen organisations at all appropriate ports. These were comparatively easily provided in England from the resources of R.A.F. Balloon Command and the Admiralty Shore Servicing Section, but it should be remembered that such facilities, if not fortuitously available as in this case, have to be arranged.

Provision of Maps.

458. The design, production and supply of maps for use by the air forces under my Command was the responsibility jointly of the War Department, Washington, and the War Office, London. Shortly after the outbreak of hostilities, the Geographical Section, General Staff, (later the Directorate of Military Survey), War Office, attached an officer to each of the principal Royal Air Force Commands, to study their requirements and to ensure adequate production and distribution of air maps. This practice was adopted for the Allied Expeditionary Air Force, a Deputy Assistant Director of Survey (British) being appointed as Chief Map Officer. Later, an officer of the Corps of Engineers, United States Army was also assigned to the Map Section.

459. Upwards of 120,000,000 maps were prepared for Operation "Neptune", of which a large proportion was used by the air forces. They embraced small and medium scale "Air" maps, maps for use in co-operation with ground forces, and an astonishing number of special maps for planning purposes, which were widely distributed to Staff Officers, mainly of the Operations and Intelligence Branches. Equally important for successful planning was the knowledge that special maps would be available for particular operations, e.g., topographical lattice maps for use in craft fitted with special Radar navigational devices and dropping zone maps for use by pilots towing gliders.

460. Headquarters, A.E.A.F. had its own drafting section and reproduction facilities were readily accorded to it by both United States and British armies. Thus, special maps required to illustrate plans, Operation Orders and Staff Memoranda could be made available, often in a matter of hours.

461. When all the Allied Air Forces were based in the United Kingdom, the normal British channels of supply were used, but once overseas, other methods had necessarily to be devised, and the supply of maps to Commands and sub-formations differed slightly as between United States and British forces.

462. Arrangements were made whereby Royal Air Force Commands should draw maps from the British armies to which they were affiliated, and in accordance with normal United States practice, formations of the Ninth U.S.A.A.F. obtained their maps under arrangements made by the Office of the Chief Engineer, ETOUSA. This provided for the establishment of a Ninth U.S.A.A.F. Map Depot, with an Assistant Deputy Engineer in charge, whose duty it was to supply all elements of that force. Events were to prove that although both systems worked well, modifications to improve the service were necessary from time to time, and on this matter I have made comments in later paragraphs.

463. During the initial phase of operations on the Continent, the Director of Survey, 21 Army

Group, established his Base Map Depot close to Bayeux, and the Chief Engineer, Communications Zone, a depot not far from the two landing beaches " Utah " and " Omaha ". The Assistant Deputy Engineer, Ninth U.S.A.A.F. placed his depot first at Carentan and later at Rennes, in order to be close to the main American Base Map Depot. These depots formed the normal source of supply for the allied air formations then gathering on the Continent. Some loss of maps by enemy action occurred during the stocking of depots, but this loss was made good from reserves held in the United Kingdom.

464. Squadrons of both air forces had carried with them overseas sufficient maps to cover any operations they might undertake during the fortnight after their landing, and ground personnel were similarly equipped. It was expected that the depots would, by that time, be able to meet any demands made upon them. Both British and American systems of map supply had been well practised in the United Kingdom and there was no reason to suppose that they would not work successfully overseas; yet late in August, Headquarters, British Second Tactical Air Force complained of delays in filling their demands, and the map depot of the Ninth U.S.A.A.F. was also unable to obtain all it required from Communications Zone base depots. In both cases the difficulty had to be overcome by flying supplies from the United Kingdom.

465. The rapid advance of the Allied armies through France and Belgium during August and the beginning of September created an embarrassing situation in regard to the supply of maps. In the planning stage, it was not expected that by D+90, the Allied Armies would have passed beyond the River Seine. By that date they were, in fact, virtually along the line of the River Scheldt. Thus there arose, long before the forecast planning date, an immediate demand for maps of all kinds and scales covering Belgium, Holland and Germany, most of which were then either concentrated in the base depots, in the United Kingdom or in transit from America.

466. The problem was acute. To move stocks already in the base depots would have taken too long. To print in the field the full quantity required was not practicable except for certain large-scale topographic maps produced on mobile presses. There was, therefore, no alternative but to draw upon reserve stocks in the United Kingdom and fly them as rapidly as possible to where they were most urgently needed.

467. Moreover, the rapidity of the advance had deprived the printing agencies of three valuable months. Reserve stocks of certain sheets, notably those of Germany on a scale of 1/100,000 were extremely low and since they were being demanded in quantity by armies no less than by air force, new stocks of these sheets most urgently required had to be printed as rapidly as possible in the United Kingdom by as many reproduction agencies as could be pressed into service.

468. The air lift for these maps was arranged by CATOR and the maps were flown to airfields close to Paris and Brussels where they were distributed direct to air formations, often within a few hours of their having been printed, and almost before the ink was dry upon them.

469. Although the crisis was surmounted satisfactorily, I have little doubt that a serious hitch might have occurred, and I feel that very careful consideration should be given to the question of whether some modifications in the map supply organisation should not be made (see paragraph 473 et seq.).

470. By an arrangement between the United States and British forces, the " lion's share " of the design, production and supply of general and special maps for use by the air forces under my command fell to the Directorate of Military Survey, War Office and the various Survey Directorates working in conjunction with that office. Their indefatigable co-operation, and also that of the reproduction agencies of both countries was of the utmost assistance. British resources were augmented in the United Kingdom by those of the 660th Engineer Topo (Avn) Battalion, United States Army and the 942nd Engineer Topo (Avn) Battalion, forming part of the Eighth United States Army Air Force, which produced special maps for all commands within the Allied Expeditionary Air Force.

471. The Map and Survey Section of the G-3 Division of your Headquarters also extended their help to me, and on one occasion supplied additional staff from No. 13 Map Reproduction Section of the packing and distribution of " Top Secret " maps.

472. The theatre policy for the supply of maps to a United States Army Air Force is described in Appendix VIII of the Survey Staff Manual, issued by the Chief of Engineers, United States Army, Washington, dated 1st June, 1944. It stipulates as a requirement, in amplification of United States Army regulations, 300-15, a map depot for an air force, such as the Ninth United States Army Air Force, which would draw its maps in bulk from the Engineer, Communications Zone.

473. In the light of experience it is clear that this depot should have been stocked, before leaving the United Kingdom, with sufficient maps to last for a much longer period of the campaign than its initial phases. It would then have been less dependent upon the ability of the Engineer, Communications Zone, to meet immediately such demands as were made upon him. Alternatively, had some of the bulk stocks held by the Engineer, Communications Zone, been marked before shipment for immediate delivery to the Ninth United States Army Air Force Base Depot, the storage would not have been so great.

474. The British Second Tactical Air Force was dependent for its map supply on the Map Depots controlled by the Director of Survey, 21 Army Group. In particular, Nos. 83 and 84 Groups, Royal Air Force, drew their map stocks from the map depots of the British and Canadian Armies to which they were respectively affiliated. By the middle of August, the Air Officer Commanding British Second Tactical Air Force had decided to form a map depot at his headquarters from which these groups, in an emergency, drew those maps they required, which could not be supplied by the armies. In October, the Director of Survey, 21 Army Group, in conference with all concerned, supported this change of policy, and recommended also that the Groups, too, should

each carry their own reserve of maps, so as to be in a position to meet all immediate emergencies.

Establishment of Signals Communications and Radar Cover.

475. The extent to which efficient signals communications enter into the successful launching and controlling of an air operation is never fully realised until by some chance these facilities fail. That the channels of signals communications satisfied the bulk of our complex needs during the course of the operation was due to the careful preliminary planning, as well as to the training of operating and maintenance personnel. Few difficulties arose until the break-out from the beach-head and the rapid moves forward of the air forces.

476. The planning of the W/T and R/T organisation for point-to-point communications was necessarily undertaken many months in advance of the actual assault, and was on a carefully co-ordinated United States and British inter-service basis.

477. The communications required were divided broadly into two categories:—
 (a) tactical communications, and
 (b) strategical communications.

478. The tactical communications were essentially operational channels required for use mainly during the assault phase, to be operated from the Combined Control Centre and Executive Control Centre to the Assault forces, the Headquarters ships and the Fighter Direction Tenders. The strategical communications were those to be used between Air Force Headquarters on the Continent and in the United Kingdom. These communications included a number of administrative channels.

479. It was decided to plan and to provide sufficient W/T communications to enable all traffic to be handled irrespective of such landline or cable circuits as might be provided. In order to handle rapidly large volumes of signals traffic, a number of high speed auto W/T mobile signals units were formed for operation on the main operational and administrative links between the Continent and the United Kingdom.

480. The British Second Tactical Air Force and the United States Ninth Air Force planned their own communications forward of their Headquarters. The communications rearward from these Air Forces were planned by A.E.A.F. and were the main operational and administrative links to the United Kingdom. As a result of a survey of traffic passed over the main W/T links in the North African theatre, it was decided that operational signals traffic should be handled separately from administrative traffic.

481. The implementation of the signal plan necessitated the building of a number of new W/T stations in the United Kingdom and the development of others. No less than two transmitting and four receiving stations were constructed, while a further five mobile transmitting stations were introduced. In addition, three transmitting and three receiving stations were enlarged and developed.

482. For W/T communications, five static and two mobile R/T transmitting and receiving sites were set up and put into operation at points along the South Coast. On the Continent, the R/T channels were provided by Mobile Signals Units, which worked on both Simplex and Duplex circuits; also Radio/Teleprinter facilities were provided for operation in addition to, and simultaneously with R/T.

483. During the assault, all the forward units, in Headquarters Ships and Fighter Direction Tenders, as well as terminal units on the far shore such as G.C.I. stations and even smaller units, including Beach Squadrons, successfully opened communications as planned. There was some slight interference experienced on some channels early in the operation, but this was quickly overcome and a remarkably high standard of operation was maintained.

484. In addition to the limited Radar cover given by the Fighter Direction Tenders, a plan to provide complete Radar cover over the beach-head was set in motion on D-Day. Two complete G.C.I. stations were among the first equipment to follow the original assault forces ashore.

485. One of these G.C.I. stations was landed at mid-day on D-Day and proceeded to a pre-arranged site. By nightfall, two of its pieces of equipment were working, together with its V.H.F., R/T, Air to Ground and D/F channels, and from 2230 hours on D-Day, night fighters were controlled from this station.

486. The second G.C.I. station suffered severe losses, due to being landed on a beach not cleared of the enemy. There were about 40 casualties, some of which were fatal and most of the unit's communication and Radar equipment was lost. Despite these setbacks, the one Radar equipment salvaged was set up and moved to its correct site, where it commenced operating with borrowed R/T equipment on D + 4. The aircraft controlled during this first night made a number of contacts, most of them friendly, but one enemy aircraft was destroyed and one damaged.

487. By 20th June (D + 14), no less than four G.C.I. type stations, one C.O.L. station, five F.D.P's and five Light Warning sets were in operation in the beach-head area. The Radars had all been set up at pre-selected sites that had been chosen by the Operational Research Section from maps and photographic cover. That these stations were sited so well is not only a tribute to the research workers, but also to the air reconnaissance that supplied the detailed material for their work.

488. One unsatisfactory feature of signals communications arose in relation to the major operational and administrative headquarters after operational units began to move forward behind our advancing troops. On a number of occasions, both Headquarters, Second Tactical Air Force and United States Ninth Air Force lost touch temporarily with some of their units as also did Advanced Headquarters, A.E.A.F., with Stanmore. Moreover, after the move of my main headquarters to Julouville in September, where it set up alongside your Advanced Headquarters, I did not have adequate telephone or signals communications with my Advanced Headquarters or the Headquarters of the two Tactical Air Forces. I was much in the dark about what was going on and the co-ordination of the air effort became extremely difficult. The position did not

materially improve until my Headquarters set up again at Versailles, by which time an almost static situation had again developed.

489. Signals facilities just adequate to service a static headquarters and provide links with its more stationary units cannot be adequate when that headquarters and its units begin to move. Because these moves must be carried out by splitting into two parties, the facilities required will be almost double those needed before. In other words, equipment and operators will be needed at two places instead of at one only.

490. This factor, which raises difficult problems of supply, training and administration for the signals service, has none the less to be reckoned with, and the problem it represents solved, if proper direction of operations is to be maintained in conditions of highly mobile warfare.

491. Some mitigation of the task of signals personnel in tackling these problems would result if the moves of main headquarters particularly were delayed longer than has been the practice in these operations, and certainly not made until the communications are suitable for operational needs. While it is important to keep operational headquarters close to the forward units, this factor must be more carefully related to the practicability of providing adequate signals facilities at the new location of the headquarters. Continuity of service is of overriding importance in air and combined operations.

PART V.—SOME BRIEF REFLECTIONS ON THE CAMPAIGN

492. The extensive air operations which are the subject of this Despatch cannot be summed up in a few paragraphs, nor, without entering fields of controversy, is it possible to discuss all the air lessons which have emerged during the campaign. What can be done, however, is to state, and where useful, to discuss briefly, certain of the more prominent issues which can be discerned in the pattern of air operations seen as a whole. Experience gained in subsequent operations in this and in other theatres may confirm these impressions, or, on the other hand, make their revision necessary.

Preparatory Air Operations

493. Events thoroughly justified our strategic bombing policy and your insistence upon an adequate preparatory period of air operations for Operation " Neptune." As it turned out, weather conditions allowed only a partial use of our air forces in the weeks following the assault, and had these preliminary operations not been started before D-Day the task of the air forces of interfering effectively with the enemy's movement within and to the battle area could not have been achieved in time to have directly influenced the land operations in the initial phases. As it was, and in accordance with the plan, the air had, by the day of the assault, completely disorganised the enemy's dense and complex network of rail lines of communications within France and Belgium. This having virtually been accomplished by D-Day, it was soon possible to seal off the battle area through air action, and in this way the area was prepared for the employment of ground forces, with the enemy at a critical disadvantage.

494. During the initial planning and preliminary operations some doubt—based on experience in other theatres—was expressed as to the efficacy of air action on bridges. Results of the initial attacks in France soon proved that given suitable technique, types of aircraft, and weapons, bridges can successfully be destroyed or rendered impassable, although the cost may be a heavy one in aircraft and personnel due to flak, and also in bombs expended. Weather may, however, frequently preclude attacks as and when planned. To have relied entirely upon the destruction of bridges as the main method of achieving the disorganisation of the enemy's communications system at the appropriate moment in Operation " Overlord," would again have proved unsound in the given conditions. The attacks on bridges formed but an integral part, albeit an important one, of the whole plan of action against the movement organisation of the enemy.

Diversionary Operations

495. Our efforts to mislead the enemy proved most effective, but their implementation, though they provided excellent operational training for crews, placed a great strain upon our air resources. In general, for every target attacked in the assault area, two had to be taken on outside that zone. Although " Crossbow " operations were taken into account in the framing of the programme, the diversion of effort from " Pointblank," communication targets, and other objectives of strategic importance, was very considerable. On the other hand, despite the fact that this great effort was directed against targets having little direct material effect on the achievement of the military object of securing the initial bridgehead, it is reasonable to deduce that these operations must at least have been a factor influencing the German High Command to dispose their reserves in the Pas de Calais area as a central position against possible landings in that area and/or any part of the long coastline from Denmark to Brest. This was obviously most advantageous to ourselves especially as our air offensive against his communications rendered movement of these reserves a lengthy and hazardous operation, particularly over considerable distances.

496. A high cost may have to be paid for diversionary activities of this kind, if they are to be realistic, and this fact must always be borne in mind when estimating the strength of the air forces required for combined operations.

Inter-Service Fire Plan

497. The drawing up of the fire plan for the assault phase was rightly regarded as an inter-Service and inter-Allied responsibility. Throughout such planning care must be taken to ensure flexibility, and it must be accepted by the Air Forces that it may not be possible finally to fix the air tasks until a very short time before D-Day—owing to such factors as changes in information, changes in weather conditions (including likely height of cloud bases), the development of enemy beach defences and gun positions and changes in conditions of light for air and naval bombardment and for fire by assault craft of various types. Moreover, an alternative Fire Plan is essential. There is a tendency on the part of the other Services to expect too much of the

air forces from the point of view of the destruction of prepared gun emplacements, especially when completely concreted; their neutralisation for a critical and limited time is, of course, another matter. At the same time there is a strong inclination among airmen to look more upon the material rather than the morale side of such bombing. The demoralisation of the gun crews through the psychological reaction to bombing contributes as much towards the neutralisation of gun defences as does damage by actual hits or by shock effects.

Spotting for Naval Bombardment

498. The Fleet Air Arm was unable to accept the full responsibility of spotting for naval bombardment either for the assault or for subsidiary operations and in the main, this task fell to Royal Air Force fighter reconnaissance squadrons. The pilots of these squadrons had necessarily to undergo a special course of training in naval procedure. The conversion presented no real difficulty but the prolonged diversion of these units from their normal tasks caused some anxiety as our total resources were limited. In the end, all our reconnaissance commitments were fairly adequately met.

499. There are obvious advantages in training some Royal Air Force reconnaissance units for the dual role of co-operation with both ground and naval forces.

Anti-Aircraft Defences

500. On a number of occasions, our own anti-aircraft guns, both naval and military, shot down friendly aircraft. The claims of fighter aircraft and A.A. guns in air defence have always conflicted because the ideal for the fighter is a field clear of any restrictions, and for A.A. gunfire a sky free of friendly aircraft.

501. In comparatively static conditions, such as the Battle of Britain, it has generally been accepted that the merits of these two claims could best be resolved by an Air Defence Commander (who in the case of the United Kingdom was the Senior Defensive Air Force Commander). It is relevant to note that after much experience the same principle was adopted in the Mediterranean.

502. For Operation "Neptune", however, no one officer was made specifically responsible for Air Defence as such, primarily because in the initial stages it was held that the Army Group Commanders themselves should decide the precise allocation of their resources to the limited number of landing craft allowed them. Also, it was considered that in forward areas the only effective control which could be exercised over A.A. weapons would be by the imposition of standing instructions.

503. From the Air Force point of view, it became clear shortly after the operation had been satisfactorily launched that this policy should be revised in favour of unified control. My request on these lines was not accepted by your Headquarters in August on the grounds that the time was not opportune for a change in this particular policy.

504. I cannot help feeling, however, that if the scale of enemy air attack had in fact been heavier such a change would have been essential in order to bring about a satisfactory degree of security when and where it was really needed. Moreover, I am of the opinion that the knowledge that a well co-ordinated air defence system exists will of itself produce a deterrent effect upon the enemy.

505.* In the absence of serious air attack, the claims of A.A. guns were at times pressed, to my mind, without full regard to the air situation of the moment. Army Commanders declared a considerable area around the majority of river crossings or similar places of importance a " prohibited " area for the operation of friendly aircraft by night. The Tactical Air Force Commanders concerned were approached by the appropriate Army Commander for acceptance of these I.A.Z's and, although they could speak for their own night operations, which were primarily of a local nature, they were in no position to answer for the requirements of the Commanders of the Strategic Bomber Forces or for the needs of S.O.E. operations.

506. The patchwork of these restricted flying areas thereby created imposed upon both Royal Air Force Bomber Command and No. 38 Group tremendous operational difficulties and handicaps which were surmounted mainly by the navigational ability of the crews concerned. These I.A.Z's constituted an unnecessary complication of an air situation already made difficult by the restrictions which had to be imposed on the use of I.F.F.

507. I feel most strongly that the establishment of restricted areas for flying, when part of the Air Defence arrangements, is primarily an air problem and should be solved by the Air Commander, naturally after the necessary consultations with the ground and naval commanders. The issues which are involved have never been faced up to because the scale of enemy air attack has been of such a low order, but it has been our own air forces which have had to suffer unnecessary inconveniences, and at times danger, and the A.A. guns have enjoyed a freedom of action which has been out of proportion to the real defensive requirements.

Aircraft Identification.

508. It was realised for some time before Operation "Neptune" was launched that our mechanical means of identifying aircraft, namely I.F.F., was not a satisfactory type of equipment for aircraft which operate in any numbers. In fact, owing to mutual interference and the probability that no value at all could be gained by the general application of this equipment, it was decided, after consultation with all United States and British services and technical authorities concerned, to limit the use of I.F.F. to a few special types of aircraft in order that these aircraft at least could be adequately tracked.

509. This decision meant that the only remaining means of identifying aircraft was the careful passing of aircraft movements and by

---

* Apart from the operational factors referred to in paragraphs 505, 506 and 507, it is appreciated that there is a " morale " side to this question. On the one hand there are the fighting troops who may be kept awake by the effects of minor air action to which they cannot retaliate, and, on the other, the tired crews returning from missions, whose aircraft cannot avoid the prohibited areas, either because of shortage of petrol or because they have been already badly damaged, and who find themselves fired upon and possibly shot down by friendly A.A. defences.

relating aircraft tracks to notifications of flights previously given. This was clearly an unsatisfactory situation but one which had to be accepted in the circumstances. There is no doubt that every step should be taken to hasten the production of a really effective mechanical method of indicating friendly aircraft, and I consider that a great deal more scientific study should be devoted to this subject in the future.

Balloon Defence.

510. In any future amphibious operation similar to Operation "Neptune" which is mounted from a country in which exists a balloon defence with all its attendant facilities, the cheapness and comparative ease of providing balloon protection unquestionably makes Balloon Defence profitable if there be any likelihood of low-level attacks by enemy aircraft. For an operation despatched from an area in which no such facilities exist, the necessary lift in hydrogen, packed balloons, and ancillary equipment to provide for initial inflation and to meet a high casualty rate would, I consider, be justified only if the enemy air effort was expected to be unusually strong and determined.

Operational Items.

511. The enemy air effort, taken as a whole, was mediocre throughout. The lack of efficiency and the low operational effort of the G.A.F., especially during the critical assault stage, were largely the result of previous attention paid to the G.A.F., his loss of Radar coverage, and of attacks on its bases and installations, which constantly compelled him to change his operational aerodromes and A.L.G.'s and to operate his fighters outside effective range of the assault area and shipping lanes.

512. As was forecasted in our early planning, marked Allied air superiority made it possible to use heavy night bombers by day with outstanding success, and relatively slight losses, since, if necessary, they could be escorted by our fighters.

513. The fighter bomber proved to be a battle-winning weapon. It showed tremendous power in breaking up and destroying enemy concentrations, especially of armour, and contributed greatly to the paralysis of enemy road and rail movement.

514. Heavy bombers can be employed to decisive effect in a tactical role. A special treatise on the principles of their employment in support of the land operations has been issued jointly by 21 Army Group and A.E.A.F., with the blessing of Supreme Headquarters, Allied Expeditionary Force, and is now being considered by the U.S. Army and Air Force Commanders.

515. The enemy's Radar cover was effectively disrupted and neutralised by air attacks, and in consequence the enemy was virtually "blinded" at the time of the assault.

516. Because of the possible risk of bombing our own land forces, Army Commanders in some instances insisted on the bomb line being pushed too far ahead of the line of our forward troops. This often proved a handicap to the effective use of tactical support aircraft. The land forces should accept a bomb line as close as possible to our front line, and be prepared to run some small risk of casualties in order to enable the air to give them the maximum close support. The fixing of the bomb line for pre-determined direct support when heavy bombers are participating in a co-ordinated land/air operation is, of course, a separate issue.

517. Armed reconnaissance of roads, rail lines and the Seine crossing by Mosquitoes of British Second Tactical Air Force during the hours of darkness proved extremely effective and disconcerting to the enemy. Intruder action of this kind could have been most effectively extended had more forces been available.

518. The value of good photographic reconnaissance cannot be overstated. Our resources in normal high altitude photographic reconnaissance were on the whole adequate, but here too the weather adversely affected the fulfilment of the reconnaissance programme after D-Day. There were long periods of inactivity when lack of strategic intelligence relating in particular to movements in rearward areas and to damage inflicted by our bombing, had serious consequences and sometimes even frustrated our plans.

519. The absence of an intermediate and low altitude photographic reconnaissance aircraft became apparent very early on, and a few armed Mustang III had to be converted at R.A.F. Station Benson for this special type of photography. There should be one medium altitude and one high flying flight in each photographic reconnaissance unit.

520. It also clearly emerged that the control of photographic reconnaissance of all types for commitments outside the allotted tactical area must be centralised in one authority. The formation of the Combined Reconnaissance Committee at Uxbridge, which filtered and took action on demands for reconnaissance from all quarters satisfied this requirement.

521. The need for a highly efficient mapping and target section which could turn out the necessary material at the shortest notice was fully appreciated before "Neptune" was launched. Experience proved that the personnel and the facilities at the disposal of the Section were not adequate for the multiple tasks by which it was faced. It is impossible to prepare in advance dossiers of every possible target which the air forces may have to hit. The only solution is to have available as large an organisation as may possibly be necessary for the task of turning out with a minimum of delay the material that might be demanded of it.

522. Modifications to the system of supply of maps were found to be necessary during the campaign. The changes made, as described earlier in this Despatch, indicate the lines along which I feel future plans for map supply should be made.

523. Unless signal facilities are much increased and well planned in advance, and staffs given ample time to develop them, major operational and administrative headquarters, when they move, are likely to get out of touch with each other and with forward headquarters and sources of intelligence. The direction of air operations would at times have been more easily and effectively achieved if the moving of headquarters had been postponed until adequate communications between the Continent and the United Kingdom had been established.

524. Signals security is also all-important. It is of little use having scramblers or other devices unless they work efficiently over considerable distances.

525. The value of scientific research into current operations may also be mentioned here since quite apart from its application to day-to-day technical problems, the information which it provides is of great use in the field of planning. An up-to-date check of bombing accuracy and the effectiveness of the weapons used makes it possible to predict within reasonably accurate limits the amount of effort which is required for particular tasks, and thus one aspect of economies of alternative operations can be assessed in advance. In this way, the cost of the major air operations in "Neptune" was assessed with a relatively high degree of accuracy. At the same time, such studies, once again, demonstrated that too great a value cannot be placed on training, and on the improvement of bombing accuracy. As the latter improves, the potential power of a bomber force also increases, but at a far greater rate.

Relationship of Strategical to Tactical Bomber Operations

526. The concept of strategical and tactical air forces as separate entities frequently breaks down in operations in which the activities of the air are interwoven with those of the ground forces. Phased operations by strategical and tactical air forces are sometimes different and at other times the same points within the same target system and within the same general time limits means that there is an inter-relation of effects throughout the whole period the target system is under fire.

527. The inter-relation of effects becomes evident when one considers the premier part played by the strategical air forces in setting the state for "Neptune", not only for subsequent operations of a tactical nature by the tactical air forces, but also for the ground battle. As we have already seen, this preparatory phase occupied the three months preceding D-Day by which time heavy bomber, and to a lesser extent, medium bomber attacks on rail centres achieved their full purpose of causing a catastrophic decline in the potential of the railways. The ensuing chaos, which is difficult to describe, was accentuated by the subsequent fighter and medium bomber attacks on bridges, on trains, and on open lines. If they had not been aided by the heavy blows which had already been delivered by heavy bombers on the key points of the railway systems, the tactical air forces could hardly have played the successful part they did in bringing organised rail movement to a virtual standstill; nor could the isolation of the battlefield have been subsequently achieved as rapidly as it was. Further, the preparatory bombing of the railway system by the strategical forces at the same time drove the enemy increasingly to the roads in spite of his precarious M.T. and fuel situation, and so fighter bombers and fighters were presented with road targets, which, as the record shows, they were able to exploit to the full. In fact, as we now know, road and rail movement became so hazardous an undertaking that the enemy's forward troops were as frequently as not starved of the means with which to continue the fight. These integrated and phased operations against the enemy's lines of communication were a decisive factor both in the success of our initial landings, in that they slowed down considerably the enemy's build-up and concentration of reinforcement, and in the successful outcome of the whole battle in France.

528. Again, in the sphere of direct Army support, whilst it was the fighter bomber which in general had the last word so far as the Air Forces were concerned in the tactical defeat of the enemy in France and Belgium, it was the heavy bomber and medium bomber which, two months before D-Day, began the attack on the enemy's defences. Thus, although the pre D-Day attacks on coastal batteries were unsuccessful in destroying guns under thick concrete cover, they not only stopped constructional work in half finished batteries, but also caused sufficient general damage to reduce critically by D-Day the efficiency of those which had been completed. In fact, opposition offered by the coastal defences was relatively so slight that there was virtually little opportunity for the employment of the fighter bomber against enemy forces in the landing areas.

529. Moreover, the operations in Normandy again made it clear that heavy bombers when used in support of a land battle can, in addition to their direct assistance to the land forces in the attack, open up to the tactical air forces a wealth of targets normally otherwise denied them when the static battle in consequence of the bombing became a war of movement. Major retreats, or the marshalling of forces for a counter-attack, could be carried out only in the open, and once the enemy was exposed the result of the fighter bomber attacks was a foregone conclusion.

530. In a sense, this fusing of the operation of different components of the air forces is merely an extension of a principle which has already been recognised in attacks on the G.A.F. The destruction by our strategical air forces of the enemy's aircraft factories and of his fuel industry represents only one part of a single comprehensive plan. Apart from the attrition as a result of air fighting, there was also the complementary action—the exploitation in "Neptune" of the bombing of airfields. The latter operations achieved their purpose, in particular by still further reducing the resources the enemy enjoyed in France, both in aircraft and crews, in airfields, and in aircraft maintenance factories.

Unified Control of Air Effort

531. Because of the foregoing considerations, and if the best results are to be achieved in the most economic manner, it is essential that the direction of air operations which call for the employment of air forces from various countries and commands should be placed in the hands of one airman to ensure the necessary unity of command and planning. The need for this is equally apparent when one views the inter-relation of the ground and air forces in operations in which heavy bombers are used in a tactical role.

532. The latter operations are in every sense of the term "Inter-Service Operations". The danger of treating the bomber as merely a component part of a Corps artillery, thrown in merely to add some fire support, can at

present be obviated only by co-ordinated planning between the air and land forces. If this principle were lost sight of, there would be a serious risk of the misuse of heavy bombers in a tactical role, and bombing on a large scale might be expended in profitless destruction which would add little, if anything, to the progress of a land battle. From the operational point of view, the need for unified planning stands out all the more prominently when it is realised that the strategical forces which contributed so much and so directly to the land battle in France were in themselves equivalent in fire power to vast ground forces. It is only through integrated ground and air planning that the air forces can serve usefully in a tactical role.

533. Although the tactical operations in which heavy bombers were used in Normandy were initiated by the ground force commander, there may also be times when the air force commander with his better appreciation of the effects which air effort can achieve, might in future suggest to the Army rich opportunities for a combined air and land operation.

Command and Control.

534. The relationship of Air Forces to the Army and Naval Forces and to the Supreme Command from the point of view of Command and Control is well worth touching upon in view of the great importance of this question in future Combined Operations of the scope of " Overlord ". It raises interesting though naturally somewhat controversial problems.

535. In the early days of planning and preparation for Operation " Overlord " there was a Commander-in-Chief of all Air Forces and a Commander-in-Chief of all Naval Forces each having the necessary integrated operational staffs and Headquarters but separate from those of the allied operational forces. The Commanders-in-Chief and their staffs were also service advisers to COSSAC and later to yourself as Supreme Commander. The organisation was, however, different in respect of the land forces, the direction and control of these operations in the field being undertaken by the Army staff of COSSAC itself.

536. In February, 1944, you appointed the Commander-in-Chief, 21st Army Group to co-ordinate the planning and execution for the assault for both the United States and British Army Groups and thereby raised the Commander-in-Chief, 21st Army Group to the level of Commander-in-Chief of the Land Forces. He naturally used his own staff for both these functions but the Army staff of Supreme Headquarters Allied Expeditionary Force still continued to exercise direction of the land operations from the point of view of general policy and to co-ordinate the activities of all three Services on the high level.

537. The Air Commander-in-Chief and the staff of Allied Expeditionary Air Force were, in consequence, required to work on two levels with two large Army staffs. On the one hand, they had, as your Air advisers, to contribute to the directives and numerous operational and administrative memoranda produced by Supreme Headquarters Allied Expeditionary Force and on the other, and this time on the Commanders-in-Chief operational level to plan, prepare for and execute the assault in co-ordination with 21st Army Group. Further, it was inevitable in these circumstances that the closest contact had also to be maintained with the Commanding General of the American land forces.

538. This arrangement severely taxed the staffs of Allied Expeditionary Air Force and inevitably led to overlapping and complications and at times interference with the planning of the tactical air forces and their opposite Army and Navy formations. The two staffs were, in fact, the same as those with which Allied Expeditionary Air Force itself was, at the same time, planning on a high level.

539. In the post assault period when 21st Army Group reverted to its normal position the situation was greatly eased but certain difficulties still remained in that the Army staff at Supreme Headquarters Allied Expeditionary Force retained a dual function in certain respects.

540. In spite of its inherent difficulties the organisation of Command and Control as developed through the various phases, undoubtedly worked, but I suggest that the creation of a separate Commander-in-Chief of all Allied Land Forces on the level with, and having similar functions to, the Air and Naval Commanders-in-Chief would have facilitated the execution of the responsibilities of the Air Commander-in-Chief and the Allied Air Force commanders, and no doubt also of the other service Commanders-in-Chief and staffs.

541. The geographical relationship of the Commanders-in-Chief and staffs of the Air, Army and Naval forces and the Supreme Commander and his Headquarters also has a direct bearing on the question of Command and Control.

542. In the first period of planning the Commanders-in-Chief and appropriate portions of their staffs, were housed mainly in one building in London and this arrangement naturally worked excellently.

543. Shortly after the formation of Supreme Headquarters Allied Expeditionary Force itself, part of its general staff moved out of London to Bushy Park. This inevitably led to a splitting and to some extent further duplication of my staff, part of which had to move to Bushy Park, part had to remain at Norfolk House to plan with ANCXF and the remainder of SHAEF, and part had to remain at Stanmore for the planning and control of preliminary air operations for " Neptune "—the latter being a function and responsibility which the Army and Naval Commanders-in-Chief had not to undertake prior to the assault. I was forced to keep my main staff at Stanmore if only because of communication facilities which were adequate for the control of air operations at no other Headquarters or centre.

544. A further dispersal of the Combined and Joint Planners of the operational staff resulted from the necessity to work with the Headquarters staff of 21st Army Group, whose location was at St. Pauls School, for the detailed planning of the assault.

545. The situation became even more complicated from the air point of view when, for the execution of the initial stages of the invasion, 21st Army Group and ANCXF, with a

SHAEF Command Post, moved to the Portsmouth area. The operations staff at AEAF had still perforce, to remain at Stanmore and Supreme Headquarters Allied Expeditionary Force Main together with AEAF planners, who formed part of the combined planning staff of Supreme Headquarters, continued to work at Bushy Park. Later, a further echelon of Supreme Headquarters Allied Expeditionary Force Main, i.e., Forward SHAEF, which included the operations staff and planners of Supreme Headquarters with its AEAF complement moved also to the Portsmouth area. This arrangement obviously simplified the co-ordination of Army and Naval operations and plans at the Commanders-in-Chief level, but my own difficulties were proportionally aggravated as a result of these moves of Main Headquarters.

546. Only when the various Headquarters were set up at Julouville in Normandy, did the co-ordination of operations and planning become smooth and easy, although the value derived from all the principals being so closely related geographically was unfortunately to some extent negatived by lack of adequate communications between Main Headquarters and Operational Commands.

547. In my view one of the major lessons learned from " Overlord " is that the staffs of the Supreme Commander and of the Air, Naval and Land Commanders-in-Chief if created, should be located very close together during both the planning and the execution stages, and this principle should be held to be inviolate; in order to achieve this the Services must be prepared to make sacrifices.

548. The communication aspect is all important and particularly must communication facilities be adequate for the conduct of air operations which will almost invariably have to commence weeks and possibly months before those of Land and possibly Naval operations. The latter factor is, I suggest, one which must have the fullest possible consideration when determining the location of the Headquarters of the Commanders-in-Chief. Even at the lower Staff levels it is essential for sound planning and development of operations that the staffs of the three Services should be within easy transportation distance of each other, and I will go so far as to recommend within walking distance of each other.

549. Finally, on the more tactical plane, it is essential to have in the field an operational co-ordinating organisation, similar to A.E.A.F. Advanced Headquarters (which was fully mobile), which can keep in touch at one end and at the same time with army headquarters and headquarters of air formations in the forward areas and with the main operational air headquarters in rear. Particularly is this required for the planning of operations in which heavy bombers are used in a tactical role. Only in this way can the bomber forces involved be adjusted smoothly to such alterations in the plan as may be dictated, often at very short notice, by changes in weather and/or in the ground situation.

PRINTED AND PUBLISHED BY HIS MAJESTY'S STATIONERY OFFICE

To be purchased directly from H.M. STATIONERY OFFICE at the following addresses:
York House, Kingsway, London, W.C.2; 13a Castle Street, Edinburgh 2;
39-41 King Street, Manchester 2; 1 St. Andrew's Crescent, Cardiff;
80 Chichester Street, Belfast;
or through any bookseller

1947

Price Sixpence net

S.O. Code No. 65-37838

Numb. 37846

SUPPLEMENT
TO
The London Gazette

Of TUESDAY, *the* 7th *of* JANUARY, 1947

Published by Authority

Registered as a newspaper

THURSDAY, 9 JANUARY, 1947

Air Ministry,
January, 1947.

AIR OPERATIONS IN GREECE, 1940-1941

The following report was submitted to the Air Officer Commanding-in-Chief, Middle East, on August 15th, 1941, by Air Vice-Marshal J. H. D'Albiac, D.S.O., commanding the Royal Air Force in Greece.

REPORT ON THE OPERATIONS CARRIED OUT BY THE ROYAL AIR FORCE IN GREECE: NOVEMBER, 1940, TO APRIL, 1941.

*Appendix " A "—Memorandum on Air Policy in Greece.
*Appendix " B "—Lessons of the Campaign.

Sir,
I have the honour to forward the following report on the operations carried out by the Royal Air Force under my command in Greece from November, 1940, to April, 1941.

Introduction:

2. In framing this report, my object is to describe the various problems with which we were confronted from time to time and how we attempted to solve them; our reasons for adopting certain definite lines of policy; the difficulties with which we were faced; our successes and failures; and finally to draw attention to some of the lessons we learnt in a campaign which, although perhaps not entirely successful in its highest conception, contributed materially to the prosecution of the war as a whole and formed a chapter in history of which the Royal Air Force may well be proud. I do not propose to compile a day to day record of all the activities of the Command. Apart from the immensity of such a task, an account of this description would not serve any useful purpose and would only tend to obscure those particular points which I wish to emphasise. Nevertheless in order to obtain some form of continuity, it is necessary to deal with the campaign in chronological sequence. I propose, therefore,

dividing it into three periods of two months into which arrangement the campaign conveniently divides itself from the strategical point of view.

NOVEMBER-DECEMBER, 1940.

Declaration of War:

3. At 3 o'clock in the morning of 28th October, 1940, the Italian Minister in Athens handed to the Prime Minister of Greece a note from his Government complaining in strong terms of alleged Greek assistance to the Allies and demanding for the Italians the right to occupy certain strategic bases in Greece. General Metaxas regarded this note as an ultimatum which he promptly refused and a few hours later, Greece was at war with Italy.

Unlike the Italians, the Greek forces were little prepared for war. Their regular Army units were at their peace time stations throughout the country and general mobilisation had not been ordered. On being attacked, the Greek units holding the frontier posts on the mountainous borders of Albania, although fighting with the greatest gallantry, were overwhelmed in some cases by sheer weight of numbers and compelled to give ground. This was particularly the case in regions where conditions were suitable for the employment of Italian mechanised forces. The progress of the Italian army was, however, slow for although Italy had concentrated large forces on the Greek frontier, the firm attitude adopted by the Greek government came as somewhat of a surprise as it had been thought that all Italian demands would be met without resort to arms. It was confirmed also from the reports of prisoners taken in the first few days that the opening of hostilities was quite unexpected by the Italian soldiers themselves, who had been led to expect a diplomatic victory and a peaceful advance into Greek territory.

---

* Not reproduced.

The Greek Problem:

4. It was clear that the problem confronting the Greeks was largely one of time. Could her frontier units hold the Italian forces sufficiently long to enable her armies to be mobilised and concentrated? As is well known, Greece is badly served by communications. Roads and railways on the mainland are few in number and the former are in most cases bad. A number of her reservists had to come from the Greek islands and it was estimated that it would take at least three weeks for the Greek mobilisation to be completed and for sufficient forces to be concentrated in the battle area before she could really consider herself reasonably safe. In the meantime, the Italian air force could, if handled properly, play havoc with their mobilisation and concentration arrangements. This, for some unaccountable reason, the Italians failed completely to do and wasted their comparatively strong air force in abortive attacks on undefended islands and hospitals in Salonika.

The Greek Air Force.

5. The Greek Air Force, although small and outnumbered by the Italian, fought most gallantly during this initial stage. Their pilots, many of whom had attended courses in England at the C.F.S. and elsewhere, were keen and what they lacked in modern war technique they made up for in personal bravery. Their aircraft, like those of most small independent nations not possessing an aircraft industry of their own, consisted of a number of different foreign types, French and Polish predominating, with a limited range of spares.

6. Operationally, the Greek Air Force was controlled by the General Staff and was used almost entirely in direct support of their army. They were quite unable to obtain any degree of air superiority and in consequence they suffered severe casualties. In addition, owing to the difficulty of obtaining spares, an abnormally high proportion of unserviceability soon existed and in a comparatively short time, their effort was reduced to negligible proportions.

Decision to send an R.A.F. Contingent.

7. In response to an urgent appeal for help, the British Government decided to send a contingent of the Royal Air Force to Greece from the Middle East. The force decided upon was to consist of two medium bomber squadrons, one mixed medium bomber and two-seater fighter squadron—all armed with Blenheim aircraft, and two single-seater fighter squadrons armed with Gladiator aircraft. On my arrival in Athens on 6th November, 1940, the advance elements of this force had already arrived and were ready for action.

Air Policy.

8. That evening I attended a conference with the Prime Minister and Commander-in-Chief to discuss the war situation generally. Every pressure was brought to bear on me to employ my force in the same manner as the Greek Air Force, in close support of the land forces. I appreciated, however, that the best help I could give to the Greek armies was to concentrate my small bomber force on the enemy's disembarkation ports in Albania and the important centres in his lines of communication. I argued that such a plan would do far more to delay his advance than if I attacked his forward elements. If, however, the situation deteriorated considerably, and a break through occurred, I would of course devote the whole of my force to the immediate task of stemming the enemy's advance. I finally obtained agreement on this policy and attacks were directed forthwith on the enemy's back areas. These attacks were maintained at maximum intensity with the few day bomber aircraft at my disposal and the detachments of Wellington aircraft sent over from Egypt to operate during the periods of moonlight. By the end of November, the Italian advance had been stemmed and the Greek forces who had by then completed their concentration were able to take the offensive. The Greek General Staff were most appreciative of the prompt and valuable help we had been able to provide for their gallant soldiers who, with ferocious intensity, had disputed every foot of the Greek soil, and they expressed the view that it was largely due to our assistance that the situation had now become satisfactory.

Selection of Aerodromes.

9. One of the main difficulties I experienced in establishing my force and one which was a constant handicap throughout the whole campaign, was the extreme scarcity of aerodromes suitable for the employment of modern aircraft. There were no all weather aerodromes, and on the mainland of Greece there are few areas in which aerodromes of any size can be made. In the Salonika area, the country is flat and a number of dry weather aerodromes already exists. For political reasons, however, I was not even allowed to reconnoitre these grounds, let alone use them. In the Larissa plain, there were many sites possible but by November, the rains had already commenced and, although I did station a fighter squadron in that area on its arrival, it was soon flooded out and aircraft were grounded for a period of ten days before they could be moved. There are few other sites in Greece except an occasional flat stretch on the coast and a certain number of level areas in the valleys, but the heavy rainfall and the prevalence of low clouds and mist make the latter quite unsuitable for operational purposes during the winter months, at any rate for modern bombers. I was forced, therefore, to concentrate my bomber force on the two aerodromes in the vicinity of Athens, and station my fighter squadrons on whatever grounds I could find near the front line, where they had to operate under conditions of the greatest discomfort and difficulty.

10. The main disadvantage of the aerodromes near Athens was that they were a long way from the front and it meant long hours of flying to and from the targets. They were, however, better drained and were only out of action for a few days after heavy rain. Furthermore, being near the sea, they were not so liable to get completely covered in by low clouds. Criticism has been made that the initial force which was sent to Greece was inadequate and many more squadrons should have been provided. I should like to point out, however, that even if these squadrons had been available, which they were not at the time, the lack of suitable aerodrome accommodation would, in my opinion, have prevented us from accepting them. During my first week in Greece, I made a tour of all possible sites and on my return pressed the Prime Minister to undertake immediately the construction of all weather runways at Araxos and Agrinion. I pointed out

to him the operational disadvantages of the existing situation and that, unless suitable runways were provided near the front, the support that we could give to the Greek nation during the winter months would be severely limited. He agreed fully with my recommendations and arranged for the construction of runways to proceed immediately. After consulting with the head of the department concerned, he informed me that the runways would be completed by the end of January, 1941. (NOTE.— Unfortunately, owing to weather conditions and shortages of material, this forecast proved over optimistic, and neither of these was ready for use when I left the country at the end of April.)

Arrival of the Force:

11. Units of the force continued to arrive throughout the months of November and December and by the end of the year the concentration was complete and the whole command functioning smoothly. When the composition of the force was being considered in the Middle East, it was decided that all the ancillary services such as hospital, works, rationing, etc., should be provided by the Army, with appropriate Army officers on my Headquarters staff to deal with them. This arrangement was particularly successful. Although, even in our respective services, few of us had served together before, officers of this combined staff soon settled down and worked with the greatest enthusiasm and co-operation. This happy atmosphere which existed at the top had, I consider, a beneficial effect on the relationship between the operational units and the actual services themselves who at all times provided our requirements in spite of countless difficulties occasioned by weather and terrain. Similarly, the liaison that existed between the British forces in Greece and the Greeks was at all times close and cordial. Every evening I attended a conference with the Commander-in-Chief and the Greek General Staff to discuss the day's land and air operations and to plan the programme of work for my force and for the Greek air force for the following day. These nightly meetings which were attended frequently by His Majesty the King and General Metaxas, when matters of higher policy were freely discussed, were carried on throughout the whole of my stay in Greece and were invaluable from a co-operation point of view.

Progress of Operations:

12. As regards the actual operations themselves, the Greeks had by now taken the offensive on land and, although handicapped by severe weather conditions and shortage of equipment, had managed to drive all the Italian forces off Greek territory and in some sectors had even advanced into Albania. In the air, our continued bombing offensive against the ports of Valona and Durazzo and the focal points on the enemy's rearward system was having a serious effect on his supply organisation. In addition, during moonlight periods, our bomber effort was being extended to targets on the mainland of Italy by means of Wellington aircraft detached from Egypt for the purpose, and considerable damage was being inflicted on ports on both sides of the Adriatic. Similarly, our fighter aircraft were establishing a definite atmosphere of moral if not of numerical superiority in this theatre.

JANUARY-FEBRUARY, 1941.
Operational Difficulties.

13. The new year opened with a deterioration in the weather conditions. Heavy falls of snow and much low cloud made flying conditions difficult and dangerous. A further handicap now appeared in the form of severe icing conditions which were experienced by our aircraft over the mountainous country between their bases and the targets in Albania. To avoid this serious state of affairs, we were forced to route our bomber aircraft by way of the coast. Over the sea, the flying conditions were considerably better, but this longer route limited the operational radius of action of our aircraft and militated against effecting surprise. Furthermore, enemy aircraft opposition was now becoming increasingly stronger, and large numbers of modern enemy fighters were being encountered constantly over the targets. These reinforcements were undoubtedly being brought over in an effort to reduce the scale of our attacks on the enemy's rearward communication system, which were obviously causing him growing embarrassment. Whilst it was comforting to think that our bomber offensive was presumably having the desired effect, this addition to the enemy's fighter strength increased considerably our operational difficulties. It was now necessary to make full use of cloud cover and to adopt a system of fighter escorts for our day bomber raids if heavy casualties were to be avoided. Our lack of modern fighter aircraft and the difficulties encountered in arranging for bombers and their escorts to meet, owing to the distance between our bomber and fighter aerodromes, badly connected by communications, with weather conditions constantly changing, all tended to reduce the operational effort of my bomber force and it became increasingly obvious that, until the fine weather came and more aerodromes were made available, there would be little opportunity for any decisive action on our part.

14. I would here like to pay a tribute to the magnificent spirit in which the pilots and air crews carried out their work during an exceedingly difficult period of operations. Based as they were in the Athens area, every raid carried out by the bomber squadrons involved a preliminary flight of at least 200 miles to the theatre of operations in weather conditions which were at times quite indescribable. Throughout the journey, the pilots and air crews were fully aware that they would meet strong fighter opposition over the targets, and would have to engage the enemy before they were able to deliver their attacks. The number of lucrative targets in Albania was strictly limited and the Italians had by this time been able to concentrate a high scale of anti-aircraft artillery to defend them, and it was seldom that our aircraft came through unscathed. Having carried out their task, the long and arduous journey home had to be completed. Direction finding aids existed but the very nature of the country made their results unreliable and much had to be left to the skill, judgment and determination of the individual pilots. In spite of all these difficulties, however, squadrons cheerfully accepted all the tasks I gave them and maintained a scale of effort far beyond that which is normally expected from Service squadrons working under

more favourable conditions. This same spirit prevailed in the fighter squadrons which were operating from forward aerodromes in conditions of extreme discomfort. Although outnumbered and armed with aircraft inferior in performance to those of the enemy, the pilots never hesitated to give battle whenever the enemy appeared.

Reinforcement Plan.

15. Early in the new year, I visited Cairo in order to discuss the question of reinforcement which was then under revision. Operations in the Western Desert were being brought to a successful conclusion and it was hoped that, by the time the weather conditions had improved in Greece so as to allow occupation of more aerodromes, it would be possible to spare additional squadrons from the Middle East Command. The reinforcement plan envisaged a total force in Greece of fourteen squadrons and I intimated that I would be prepared to start accepting the additional squadrons by 15th January. It was hoped that the whole programme would be complete by 15th April. In planning the reinforcement programme, I again endeavoured to get permission to use the aerodromes in the Salonika area, some of which had remained generally serviceable throughout the winter and could be occupied forthwith. The Germans, however, had commenced their infiltration into Roumania, and the Greek Government were particularly anxious to avoid giving them any idea that we had any hostile intentions in Macedonia which could be directed only against German interests.

The Greek Air Force.

16. As I have stated already in this report, the Greek Air Force had suffered severe casualties in the early stages of the war and by the end of the year, it was reduced to a mere token force of a few serviceable operational aircraft. Promises of the provision of modern fighter aircraft had been received from the U.S.A., and the British Government had agreed also to supply aircraft as and when they became available. Whilst admiring the esprit de corps and enthusiasm of the officers and airmen of the Greek air force, I considered that operationally they had a lot to learn before they would get full value out of really modern aircraft. Similarly, from the maintenance point of view, a considerable amount of re-organisation was necessary before they would be able to maintain a reasonable degree of serviceability. As these American and British aircraft would be provided presumably at the expense of the R.A.F. reinforcement or expansion programme, I was determined to do all I could to ensure that full use was made of them. I had previously discussed the whole problem with H.M. the King of Greece and the Prime Minister and had made the suggestion to them that a British Mission of qualified R.A.F. officers and airmen should be appointed to help them in the reconstruction of their flying service. They welcomed the suggestion and in due course a mission was provided, and the work of re-organising the Greek air force on modern lines was commenced. In addition to their primary role, the Mission undertook also to reconnoitre and supervise the work on all the new aerodromes which it was desired to use in spring, and much valuable work they did in this respect.

Offer of British Expeditionary Force.

17. Early in January, conferences were held to discuss the possibility of sending a British expeditionary force to Greece, but the Greek General Staff, on learning the limited size of the force that could be made available at the time, decided that its presence would only tend to provoke Germany, whilst it was not strong enough to be able to provide any very material support.

Battle for Valona.

18. The Greek General Staff now realised that, if as seemed probable the Germans intended to make a move through the Balkans, they might be faced in the spring with a campaign on two fronts. They therefore considered it essential that every effort should be made to bring the Italian campaign to an end before such an eventuality arose, or at any rate to shorten their front in Albania as much as possible so as to have troops available to strengthen their front in Macedonia. They appreciated that an advance to a line north of Valona would certainly accomplish the latter and might conceivably, in view of the low morale of the Italians at that time, achieve the former. Consequently, early in February, the Greek armies in Albania started a fierce offensive in the direction of Valona. The preliminary attacks were successful and a certain amount of progress was made. Bad weather, however, intervened and, although the Greek soldiers fought with their customary heroic disregard of danger, the Italians were able to bring up reinforcements and the advance was held up just north of Tepelene.

Change of Air Policy.

19. This battle for Valona is interesting from the air point of view inasmuch as a change of policy was forced upon us. Hitherto, my bombing offensive had been directed almost entirely upon lines of communication, ports and aerodromes to the rear, and with the limited means at my disposal was, I think, instrumental in reducing the flow of reinforcements and supplies to the Italian armies in the field. When discussing this new operation both with His Majesty the King and the Commander-in-Chief, they stressed the vital importance of a success, particularly as the morale of the nation had recently been badly shaken by the death of their Prime Minister, General Metaxas. They pointed out that the Greek soldiers on the front had experienced a severe winter and, although full of fight, were not too well off for munitions and supplies. Consequently, it was essential that they should have the utmost encouragement and support that could be provided. This could best be given by my bomber force being used in close support of the Greek attack. I produced all the stock arguments against this form of co-operation, and stressed the fact that by bombing enemy communications leading to the battlefield a greater degree of help would be given to their troops fighting the actual battle. However, they reminded me that the morale of some of the Greek soldiers had been shaken severely by enemy bombing attacks, and that the success of the whole operation might depend on the stimulus afforded by seeing the Italians treated in the same way. I therefore acceded to their requests.

Reorganisation of Command.

20. It was obvious that, if successful close support was to be provided, a certain reorganization of my forces was necessary. It was quite out of the question to attempt to keep in touch with a fluctuating battle in Albania from a headquarters in Athens, and if immediate and constant support was to be given, my aircraft must operate nearer the front. Accordingly, I formed a wing headquarters in the area of operations, and moved part of my bomber force to a landing ground which was found to be sufficiently dry close to the front. For the first few days, until road communication could be established, this landing ground was provisioned by air. I delegated the command and operation of all the bomber aircraft engaged in this operation, and a fighter squadron, to the commander of the wing, who was in constant touch with the Greek commander conducting the land operations. From a purely local and spectacular point of view, this form of co-operation was an instant and complete success. The morale of the Greek soldiers was raised considerably and I received fulsome praise and appreciation of the work carried out by the pilots. I was even approached by one divisional commander who implored me to order my pilots not to fly so low over the Italians for fear they would be shot down. Our efforts were made much of in official communiques, and I think that, during this particular period, the prestige of the R.A.F. was higher in the minds of the Greek nation than at any other period during our stay. I felt the whole time, however, that this high regard was based on false premises for, although we were invigorating our friends, we were misemploying our aircraft. Later events proved this to be the case. If the weather had been kinder, the Greeks might have succeeded in attaining their objective, but heavy falls of snow and rain held up their progress, and early in March, the Italians who had been able to assemble reinforcements, staged a heavy counter attack which, although held by the Greek forces, destroyed all hopes of capturing Valona.

Actually, even if we had employed our bomber force solely on ports of disembarkation in Albania, I doubt very much whether we could have interfered to any great extent with the flow of Italian reinforcements. Our available bomber force was small, the weather was bad, and it was clear that, after their recent defeat in Cyrenaica, the Italians were determined to avoid another reverse which might have had disastrous results on the nation as a whole. Freed from the necessity of supporting their North African front, they had the troops available, and under the conditions prevailing at the time it would have been difficult to prevent their arrival in Albania.

Arrival of Hurricane Aircraft.

21. During the latter part of this period, an event of considerable importance concerning our fighter strength occurred. The first six Hurricane aircraft appeared in Greece. Up till now, the pilots in our two fighter squadrons had been doing grand work with their Gladiators, but with the gradual appearance of faster and better types of Italian aircraft, they were finding themselves at a disadvantage, and their re-equipment with a more modern type was most welcome. The first appearance of these well known fighter aircraft over Athens was greeted with the greatest enthusiasm by the local population and it was not long before they justified fully their reputation of being first class fighting aircraft. On their first sortie over the lines on 20th February, they shot down four enemy aircraft, and on 28th February, in company with a formation of Gladiators, destroyed 27 enemy aircraft without a single loss to themselves. This fight, which was the biggest ever fought in the air in Albania, was staged over the Greek lines in full view of both armies. All the enemy aircraft destroyed were confirmed from the ground and caused the greatest jubilation.

MARCH-APRIL, 1941.

Decision to send a British expeditionary force.

22. The opening of this final phase of the campaign in Greece was notable for the decision taken at long last to send a British expeditionary force to the country. The Germans had by now completed their subjugation of Roumania and were repeating their customary penetration tactics this time into Bulgaria. The usual stories of the arrival of tourists and reports of preparations being carried out on aerodromes and lines of communication had been coming in for some time, and it was all too clear that it was only a matter of time before the German armies would be ensconced on the Greek northern frontier. The attitude of the Yugoslavs, on whom the defence of the northern Greek territory depended so much, was strictly non-committal and unsatisfactory. The Greeks, realising fully the seriousness of the situation, were in no doubts that, if they allowed British fighting troops to enter their country, war with Germany was ultimately unavoidable. To their lasting credit, however, they preferred to accept such a situation rather than have to submit when the time came to a tame capitulation in face of overwhelming force. In consequence of this decision, a British force was rapidly assembled in Egypt and the first troops started to arrive in Greece on the 7th of March.

23. I do not propose to give a description of the dispositions or activities of this force, which presumably are included in detail in the G.O.C.'s. report, except in so far as they affect the air operations in my command. The general role of this force was to support the Greek armies against a German threat from the north, and much discussion took place as to where this help could best be given. It was eventually decided that, owing to the shortage of time available before it was considered that Germany's preparations would be completed, and to the doubtful attitude of Yugo-Slavia, it would be unwise to move up to the Greek-Bulgarian frontier. Arrangements were therefore made for a defensive line to be prepared and occupied in suitable country west of Salonika, covering the Larissa plain.

Preparations for the Arrival of the B.E.F.

24. As time was all important now, everything had to be subordinated to get this defensive position prepared and the force assembled. Engineering works on aerodromes which were not of immediate importance had to be stopped so that camps could be constructed, roads repaired, and all the preparations necessary to receive the force could be made. Similarly, in view of the necessity to avoid congestion at the docks, we were forced to

use all our available transport to move the incoming munitions, stores, etc. On the arrival of G.H.Q., the army services which had hitherto been under my command, together with the appropriate army staff officers, were transferred to Army control. These commitments and re-arrangements meant a certain amount of disorganisation in my command. The weather, however, was now improving and the landing grounds in the plains and valleys drying up. Therefore, no very great delays in our arrangements occurred.

Reorganisation of R.A.F.

25. The arrival of the British expeditionary force and the establishment of a new front meant a further reorganisation of my force and a readjustment of my slender resources. Although very few reinforcements had arrived as yet, and my pilots and air crews were beginning to feel the strain of heavy and continuous operations throughout the winter months, an additional burden was now thrust upon us. I still had to provide air support for the Greeks who were being ferociously attacked in Albania by the Italians, spurred on by the presence of Mussolini himself. I had to provide air escorts for incoming convoys, also some form of air defence for the ports of disembarkation of British troops which were becoming alarmingly congested. I had to deliver occasional attacks on the Dodecanese Islands to reduce the scale of enemy attacks on convoys which were becoming embarrassingly frequent, and finally, I had to allocate a portion of my force to support the position in process of occupation by British troops. I attach as Appendix " A "* to this report a memorandum which I issued on 18th March, pointing out the very parlous condition we were in at that time and describing how I proposed to attempt an almost impossible task. Apart from the fact that all my squadrons were much below strength in serviceable aircraft, due to the heavy casualties we had suffered and the unavoidable inability to keep us supplied with replacements, the re-equipping of my fighter squadrons with Hurricanes was not proceeding as rapidly as I had hoped. Furthermore, the arrival of reinforcing squadrons was not keeping pace with the programme decided upon and those that did arrive were much below establishment in aircraft and equipment. In spite of these difficulties and disappointments, however, I still hoped that time would be on our side and that, when the German attack developed, we would be in a reasonable state of preparedness to meet it.

The Battle of Cape Matapan.

26. On the 28th of March, a refreshing interlude to our troubles on land was afforded by the naval engagement off Cape Matapan. All our bombing squadrons took part and the Mediterranean fleet was able to bring the enemy to battle and inflict on them a smashing defeat.

The Fleet Air Arm.

27. At this juncture it is appropriate to mention the good work carried out by the Fleet Air Arm operating from western Greece. Six Swordfish aircraft of the Fleet Air Arm arrived in Greece on 11th March, and proceeded to Paramythia from where they operated against Valona and Durazzo harbours. Their task was beset by various difficulties. The high country surrounding Valona made a night approach awkward and hazardous, while it was almost impossible to get into the bay undetected. At Durazzo, the water was shallow and the approaches were thereby limited. Pilots reported the presence of night fighters over Valona. However, in spite of all this, several ships were sunk and many more hit and damaged during the period the Fleet Air Arm were with us.

Germany declares War on Yugo-Slavia and Greece.

28. In the meantime, events were moving rapidly in the Balkans. While the Regent of Yugo-Slavia was signing away the freedom of his country, a coup d'etat was staged and we had a new ally. Large German forces had crossed the Danube and were moving into Bulgaria. Time was clearly running short. In spite of every effort, we were only able to arrange one so called " staff conference " with the Yugo-Slavs which did little beyond providing an opportunity for mutual criticism as to our state of unpreparedness for war, before the Germans declared war against both Greece and Yugo-Slavia on 6th April, and commenced invading both countries.

THE GERMAN INVASION.

29. I propose to deal with the air campaign against the German air force in somewhat greater detail than the operations hitherto carried out in Albania. I do this because I believe there are valuable lessons to be learnt which, owing to the great disparity between the British and German air forces in this campaign, are shown up in high relief. In addition, our air force gave support to a British army which may, perhaps, consider that the major cause which forced it to withdraw from its positions and eventually evacuate Greece altogether, lay in the lack of this very air support. I was fully aware that the air forces at my disposal could not give the support which the army desired and which we would like to have given. Although I stressed the fact, the full consequences were perhaps not clearly recognised by the army. I feel, however, that if various aspects of our air inferiority are discussed, a more complete comprehension of the issues which are at stake may be gained, and that we may thereby pave the way to a better mutual understanding between the Services, a state of affairs which is essential for the efficient conduct of modern war.

Organisation of R.A.F. Component.

30. At the time when Germany commenced the invasion, my force was organised as follows:

A Western Wing—consisting of one bomber and one fighter squadron (Gladiator) supporting the Greeks in Albania.

An Eastern Wing—consisting of two bomber and one Hurricane fighter squadrons supporting the Anglo-Greek forces facing the German advance. The squadrons of this wing occupied landing grounds on the Larissa plain which, although still soft after the winter rains, was now drying rapidly.

In the Athens area, I had one bomber squadron and one fighter squadron in process of re-arming with Hurricanes. Expressed in terms of aircraft, my total serviceable strength

* Not reproduced.

in the country was some eighty aircraft, to which were opposed, according to all reports, approximately 800 German aircraft on the Eastern front (Bulgaria and Roumania) and 160 Italian aircraft based in Albania plus 150 based in Italy but operating over Albania and Greece, mainly from advanced landing grounds in Albania.

Disposition of Squadrons in Eastern Wing.

31. The first problem with which I was faced in forming the Eastern Wing was that of disposing the air forces I could make available. My intention was to provide each squadron with a base aerodrome, and at least one and if possible two satellite landing grounds.

The location of the fighter squadron was influenced by its role. This was threefold:

(a) to protect the base area, which included the army L. of C., the port of Volos and our aerodromes in the Larissa plain.

(b) to provide fighter escort to our bombers, and

(c) to deal with enemy fighter aircraft in the battle area.

Larissa aerodrome was the most suitable from the geographical and communications point of view, and was one of the few aerodromes which was serviceable for all but a comparatively short period during the winter. Accordingly, the fighter squadron was based there with a satellite on a piece of suitable ground 7 miles to the west. At Larissa the camp was well dispersed at the opposite end of the aerodrome to the hangars, which would be likely to attract bombing attack. Aircraft pens of sandbags capable of taking Hurricanes, though open at the top, were constructed in dispersed positions.

32. As regards the two bomber squadrons, it was my original intention to station them at Almyros, where I hoped they would be sufficiently far back to be immune from escorted bomber raids and low flying fighter attack. Unfortunately, the Greek Air Force were already in occupation of this ground and I did not consider it safe for reasons of congestion to station more than one squadron there. The other squadron had to be sited temporarily at Larissa, pending the discovery of a more suitable ground. This was found eventually at Niamata, which in spite of a nearby marsh and consequent malarial infection, and in spite of the poor strategical position it occupied in the event of the withdrawal of an army to the Olympus line, was the only other which possessed a satisfactory surface and was suitable for night flying in the whole area north of Attica.

Thus the Blenheim squadrons were located at Almyros and Niamata. At each aerodrome every endeavour was made to gain the maximum dispersion of aircraft and encampments. Except at Larissa, the limits of the squadron camps lay at least a kilometre from the aerodrome. Aircraft were widely dispersed off the aerodrome at Almyros, but at Niamata this was hindered by a dyke and drainage ditch which protected the aerodrome from the marsh and lake beyond.

33. The one army co-operation squadron which arrived as the German attack developed I stationed at Kazaklar, where it was suitably sited for meeting the army needs. Unfortunately, however, this squadron rarely had more than one Hurricane serviceable at a time and, since the remainder of its aircraft were Lysanders, which it was quite impossible to use in the face of enemy air opposition, the squadron did very little useful work.

34. It should be realised that the German invasion of Greece started at a time when very few landing grounds were fit for use on account of rain. They were just beginning to dry, and had the attack been delayed for even a week, we would at least have had several more satellite landing grounds at our disposal. As it was, the change in the weather favoured the Germans.

Position of Eastern Wing H.Q.

35. Considerations influencing the location of the Eastern Wing Headquarters were:

(a) ability of the wing commander to make quick personal contact with force commander.

(b) reliability of communications.

(c) ease of access to operational squadrons under wing control.

(d) reasonable propinquity to aerodrome.

The overriding consideration in locating Wing Headquarters supporting the army on this front was that it should be close enough to Force H.Q. to allow the wing commander and the force commander to be within easy personal touch. It was considered undesirable, however, to locate the H.Q. beside Force H.Q., since the combined encampment would be of excessive proportions, difficult to conceal from the air, marked by deeply worn tracks, congested with vehicles and unwieldy to move.

The fully established wing headquarters failed to arrive in Greece by the outbreak of the campaign and, therefore, after consultation with the force commander, I decided to locate the skeleton wing headquarters beside Force H.Q. at Elason. The wing commander lived in the force commander's mess and so the closest liaison was formed.

Control of Squadrons.

36. At the end of March, the Army Signals detachment attached to wing headquarters was asked to link up all the aerodromes which were eventually used with direct lines to wing headquarters at Elason. This task was far beyond the scope and resources of the Army Signals detachment, with the inevitable result that land line communications were extremely poor. The factors leading to this state of affairs were as follows. The shortage of Royal Signals personnel resulting from the rapid R.A.F. build-up in Eastern Greece, had stretched to the limit the resources of the Signals Company despatched to Greece in July, 1940. Furthermore, priority for such equipment as was available was given to the forces in Libya, and the situation in Greece was acute, particularly as regards landline cable and wire. Technical limitations were a further cause. The trunk landline system was limited to overhead alignments which were frequently out of action as a result of hostile air activity, and reliable maintenance was beyond the resources of the Greek Postal and Telegraph administration. Accordingly the Army was faced with providing the R.A.F. with field cable systems which automatically precluded long distance speech facilities. Thus, although the wing had a direct line to Larissa,

25 miles of it consisted of field telephone wire, and the utmost difficulty was experienced in using this line. The force line or Fullerphone to the main exchange was used whenever possible. Similarly, communication to Almyros was not possible from Elason. It was therefore decided to establish a system of relaying operation orders in code by telephone from the wing commander at Elason to Larissa, where they were further transmitted as appropriate either direct to the fighter squadron at Larissa or by telephone to the bomber squadrons at Niamata or Almyros. For this purpose, an officer was permanently standing by at Larissa to relay operation orders.

Communication from Larissa to Niamata only twelve miles away was reliable, but to Almyros it was most unsatisfactory, largely due to the fact that the Air Defence Centre used the Almyros line for reporting enemy aircraft. As the campaign proceeded, so the demands both of the wing and of the Air Defence Centre augmented until finally it took as much as five to six hours to pass a priority telephone message from Larissa to Almyros. Thus it was decided to use the squadron at Niamata for any fleeting targets which presented themselves, while the squadron at Almyros carried out direct support operations, the need for which could be foreseen some hours previously.

Organisation of Fighter Defence.

37. The Greek observer system consisting of posts with sub-posts radiating from each and linked to air defence centres by telephone, operated with a certain degree of success, and various interceptions of Italian aircraft had been made over the Larissa area.

A fighter operations room was established at Larissa and was run by the squadron stationed there. Depending on alternative duties, aircraft were standing by throughout the hours of daylight. It was, however, inevitable to leave the L. of C. and base area unprotected when the fighters were required for escort duty or protective duties over the forward troops.

The system worked well, although there was little enemy air activity during the first few days of the campaign. When, however, the withdrawal of our troops began, the personnel manning the posts of the observer system had to withdraw and consequently the system broke down.

Liaison with Force H.Q.

38. The wing commander visited the force commander in his office each morning as a routine, and daily discussions were held in the force commander's mess both with him and his B.G.S. The force commander was fully informed of the air situation and made no excessive demands upon our resources. Without exception, the utmost was done to meet the requirements of the army and every request for reconnaissance made by the force commander or the B.G.S. was followed by a faithful endeavour to carry out that task. At the outset, however, weather was a serious hindrance, and in spite of the most frequent and determined attempts, many failures had to be reported

The choice of targets for the bombers, the ways and means of providing fighter patrols over our forward troops, the question of leaving the base area unprotected whilst fighters escorted bombers or patrolled over the line, ground straffing of M.T., reconnaissance, and every other aspect of the air situation were discussed, and complete agreement was expressed with the direction and operations of the squadrons supporting the army. Neither the force commander nor the B.G.S. permitted themselves to indicate more than a general plan, in view of the rapidly changing situation, and they always expressed their agreement in the suggested methods of meeting any particular circumstances.

In addition to the personal liaison between the force and wing commanders, an A.L.O. kept in constant touch with the G. Staff, watching and reporting every development in the situation. It is difficult to know how air forces could be operated in closer co-operation with the military forces than was in fact the case during the opening days of the Balkan campaign. Whatever shortcomings there may have been in the support given by the air forces, they certainly cannot be attributed to lack of co-operation or to lack of the most faithful endeavours of our pilots. At every available opportunity, aircraft of this wing were doing their utmost to carry out the multifarious tasks which were required of them.

6th-9th April—The German Advance.

39. On the morning of the 6th April, the German forces were on the march. The bulk of the enemy moved west from the Struma valley, filtering by all available roads into each valley and gorge, inundating every plain with their swiftly moving forces. The first air reports indicated that an attack was being made upon Mt. Beles and the Rupel Pass. Simultaneously, our reconnaissance aircraft reported movement of M.T., on the road west from Petrich.

It was certain that this movement would be covered by fighter patrols, and the fighters were sent off to carry out a sweep over the road and over the Greeks on Mt. Beles and in the Rupel Pass. Twelve Hurricanes met twenty Me.109s. and our fighters shot down five without loss to themselves. This disposed of any anxiety or over cautiousness which the squadron commander of the fighters had felt about the change over from Italians to Germans. Whereas, at the outset, the squadron commander expressed the view that his aircraft could not operate in formations of less than twelve, he now agreed that formations of six would be able to escort Blenheim formations across the line. This meant that the base area only had to be left completely unprotected when the Hurricanes went off in strength to patrol over our forward troops. In the circumstances, the wing commander considered it a reasonable division of fighter strength.

Meanwhile, reconnaissances of the Struma valley were being carried out. During the course of that night Sofia, Gorna Djumaya, Simitli and Petrich were bombed by Wellington and Blenheim aircraft both from Athens and from the Larissa plain. These raids were most successful, and pilots on their return reported good results. The weather was bad on the following day and no reconnaissance was possible, but it was anticipated that considerable concentrations of enemy M.T. would be found at Strumitsa. Late in the afternoon, in spite of severe weather, some of our aircraft got through and bombed the rich target presented by the heavy congestion of German M.T. confined to the road in this area by marshes and watercourses and the surrounding mountainous country. The escort of Hurricanes destroyed a Dornier. A large proportion of the German forces moving west against the Yugo-Slav armies had to pass through Strumitsa, as well as all the forces advancing on Salonika and those about to deploy themselves before our positions on the Mt. Olympus region. Consequently, as many heavy attacks as possible were made against targets in this area.

On the following day, the bad weather continued but in spite of it, we were able to get some of our reconnaissance machines through, and again in the evening we bombed enemy M.T. in considerable concentration near Strumitsa.

Since the army co-operation squadron was short of aircraft, and since it was considered expedient to avoid sending unescorted Blenheims on long reconnaissances, the fighter squadron was asked to help out with reconnaissance. This squadron was thereafter frequently asked to provide recce aircraft, and although the pilots had had no reconnaissance training, they carried out the most valuable work throughout this period of great stress.

The wing commander had received an appeal to give bombing support to the Greeks who were cut off in the Salonika area. On consulting the force commander as to the relative danger to the army of the various points which the German advance was threatening, the wing commander decided, in view of the limited opportunities for air operations offered by the weather, and in view of his limited air resources, not to dissipate any effort on a front which was already lost in spite of the gallant action still being fought in the Rupel area by the Greeks. Nevertheless, the powerful bombing attacks against Strumitsa were bound to have a direct effect upon the situation in the area of Kilkis and Salonika, since German columns passing through Strumitsa and south to Lake Doiran were attempting to encircle the Mt. Beles position.

On the following day, the weather was again very bad. From the information available, however, it was now clear that very considerable German forces were passing through Strumitsa, some advancing south by Lake Doiran were already in or around Salonika, whilst the greater part continued west and north west and were threatening the Monastir Gap.

The situation was beginning to unfold, contact was expected shortly on the Olympus line but anxiety was felt on account of the ineffectiveness of the Yugo-Slav resistance and the lack of information as to the situation in the north. Every effort was made by our air force to alleviate the pressure on the Yugo-Slav army in order to give them time to withdraw in front of the highly mobile German forces, and to take up strong positions in the mountains and gorges.

9th-15th April—1st Withdrawal.

40. Communications between Force H.Q. and Wing H.Q. to Athens were now becoming extremely poor, and I was virtually out of touch not only with the wing commander but with the G.O.C., with whom it was essential for me to be in constant communication. Accordingly, I sent an officer of air rank to take over operations in the forward area. The air officer took over at a time when, in view of the intention of the army to withdraw to the Olympus line, plans were being drawn up to withdraw the ground party of the squadron of Blenheims at Niamata and to use it only as an advanced landing ground.

During the next few days, until the complete evacuation of the Larissa plain on the 15th, enemy M.T. columns and concentrations on the roads between Prilep and Bitolj and in the Amyntaion Area were bombed successfully by our aircraft. Our army had had little time to prepare strong positions in this area, which they had hoped would be protected for some time by the resistance of the Yugo-Slavs. A heavy burden was therefore thrown upon our air forces which now virtually had to make up for the time lost by the caving-in of the Yugo-Slav forces. No stone was left unturned to delay the enemy and to shield our ground forces. Meanwhile, our army was engaged in fighting a rearguard action in the areas around Amyntaion and Kleisoura.

No sooner was the withdrawal to the Aliakmon line complete when, on account of the threat to its left flank, it became necessary for the army to make a further withdrawal to the Thermopylae line. Consequently, all R.A.F. units on the Larissa plain had to be withdrawn at once with the utmost speed along roads which were already congested. At the same time, the R.A.F. continued to throw all its power into delaying tactics.

On 14th April, the weather improved and German air activity intensified. The Germans had brought their fighters forward to the Prilep and Monastir areas, where their engineers had prepared the necessary landing strips. The German air force was mainly directed in close support of their army, and heavy dive bombing attacks were made against our troops. Our Hurricanes, escorting our bombers in attacking enemy M.T. on the roads near Ptolemais and disorganising his lines of communication, shot down many enemy aircraft.

41. On 15th April, the main effort of the German Air Force was directed against our air force, which had been delaying their military operations and had taken toll of their aircraft. Large numbers of short range fighters made their appearance over the Larissa plain and ground straffed Niamata. In spite of A.A., every aircraft of the Blenheim squadron located there was destroyed. Owing to the breakdown of the Greek observer system, our fighters were at a hopeless disadvantage. When, on one occasion, Me. 109s appeared over their aerodrome at Larissa without any warning, three Hurricanes were attacked whilst taking off and two were shot down. The third shot down one Me. 109. Although, when our fighters were able to get off, they played havoc with the enemy, the situation was obviously untenable. I was present on the Larissa aerodrome whilst this attack was in progress and I ordered the squadrons to withdraw to the Athens area forthwith.

The Albanian Front.

42. Meanwhile, the wide manoeuvre of the German forces advancing swiftly through the mountain passes north west and west of Skoplje was developing. Their intention was to force contact with the helpless Italian forces near Kukes in northern Albania and to threaten the right flank of the Greek armies in Albania from the Lake Ochrida area. The Greeks, who had

fought so valiantly against the Italians throughout the winter months, were hardly in a position to withstand the extra pressure of the German forces. Withdrawal from Albania in the Koritsa area had been considered expedient by British commanders before the German invasion began. However, the Greeks did not take a sufficiently strategic view of warfare to allow such a withdrawal to be carried out without seriously affecting the morale of the army. This was especially the case when wrested from the despised Italian invaders. To give up their acquisition of their own free will and to see it fall once more into the hands of the Italians was for the Greek fighting soldier in the line an intolerable idea. When in fact, the withdrawal was eventually forced upon them, it was too late for the Greeks, reliant upon mule and bullock-cart transport, to conduct an orderly retreat. Morale and organisation collapsed. The Greek army commander at Yannina capitulated to the Germans.

As the situation in this area deteriorated, it became increasingly obvious that it was necessary to withdraw the R.A.F. Western Wing, consisting of one Blenheim and one Gladiator squadron. This was successfully carried out in spite of difficulties which arose as the result of numbers of Yugo-Slav aircraft and personnel arriving at Paramythia aerodrome and requiring fuel and food right up to the last moment.

15th—24th April. 2nd Withdrawal.

43. At this juncture, I decided to abolish the Eastern Wing and take over control of all operations from Athens. I left an R.A.F. officer at Force H.Q. to act as liaison between the army commander in the field and myself. Later, when Force handed over the direction of the withdrawal to Anzac Corps, this officer was attached there. The army commander desired only reconnaissance and fighter protection which we did all we could to provide.

Throughout the withdrawal, the army co-operation squadron carried out what reconnaissance they could. After they had evacuated Kazaklar, north of Larissa, they operated their few aircraft from Pharsala, which by this time was serviceable. Later they operated from Amphiklia, just behind the Thermopylae line. Here there was a Greek Gladiator squadron which was ground strafed and destroyed as soon as the Germans were able to locate their fighters on the aerodromes on the Larissa plain. The army co-operation squadron's Hurricanes were not on the aerodrome at the time of the ground strafing, and so luckily escaped, but I considered it wiser to bring them back to the Athens area.

In view of the complete numerical superiority enjoyed by the enemy, I decided to operate my Blenheim squadrons by night as much as possible in efforts to delay, as far as lay in our power, the enemy's advance. But after the decision to evacuate had been taken, the whole weight of the German Air Force was turned on the Athens area and there was no alternative but to save what air crews and material remained. These squadrons ferried the remainder of the personnel of their squadrons to Crete and carried out their instructions with discipline and courage in the face of great peril.

Direction of Bombing Effort.

44. As far as the direction of bombing is concerned, the operations against the Germans followed four clearly defined phases:

The first phase, lasting for about two days, was the disclosure of the enemy plan prior to gaining contact with our troops. During this phase, bombing was directed at previously arranged targets in the Struma valley, including Petrich, Simitli, Gorna Djumaya and Sofia.

During the second phase, in which the direction of the German advance was recognised and in which every possible effort was made to alleviate pressure thrown against the Yugo-Slav armies in the west and the Greek armies in the Salonika area, bombing was directed against supply columns and concentrations of enemy M.T. at the bottleneck around Strumitsa, where the German forces divided into two columns.

The third phase, in which a serious threat developed against the British armies in the region of the Monastir gap, was devoted to the bombing of bottlenecks, railway junctions, stations, bridges, defiles and concentrations of enemy M.T. on roads leading towards the Monastir Gap, from Skoplje, Veles, Prilep to Bitolj.

The fourth phase was the direction of all our air effort in hindering and delaying the advancing Germans to allow our army to conduct a successful withdrawal. All our resources were thrown into the task of alleviating the pressure on our forces in order to allow them the maximum amount of time to withdraw and to prepare new positions.

Targets were chosen at points where it was calculated that the effect of dislocation would be most widespread amongst advancing German columns, and yet close enough to the rear of the German fighting troops to have the maximum immediate effect upon the progress of their advance.

It is impossible to calculate the degree of success which this policy attained, but German prisoners who fell into our hands told woeful tales of the heavy bombing which they had suffered from the R.A.F. throughout their advance. On the night 14/15th, our Wellingtons created much chaos at Veles and broke the bridge across the Vardar. A glance at the map will at once show the importance of a dislocation in the German L. of C. at this point. It is the hinge upon which one, perhaps the greatest, of the main German drives depended.

The continual bombing of M.T. which presented some of the best targets which our Blenheim pilots, accustomed to such targets as dispersed vehicles in the desert, had ever known, caused much confusion amongst the enemy.

Withdrawal of Fighter Squadrons.

45. The fighters were withdrawn to the Athens area, since no aerodrome north of this was free from ground strafing. The constant lack of intermediary aerodromes made it inevitable that, if our fighters were placed on an aerodrome from which they could give protection to our troops, they were in imminent danger of destruction by ground strafing as soon as they were on the ground. If, on the other hand, they were placed beyond the range of ground straffing, they were unable to protect our troops and the tightly packed columns of M.T. withdrawing along the roads. The utmost efforts were made to give the maximum protection to our continually harassed troops. All our machines were working to maximum capacity. Many of our pilots were working at extreme range, challenging untold odds and at times, after they

had used up their ammunition, pursuing enemy aircraft engaged in ground straffing our troops.

On 20th April, approximately 100 dive bombers and fighters attacked the Athens area; my whole force of fighters of fifteen Hurricanes intercepted them, bringing down a total of 22 enemy aircraft confirmed and eight unconfirmed for a loss of five Hurricanes. Small as our losses were, they were crippling to our small force.

Even after having been shot down, our fighter pilots would immediately take the air in aircraft which had been riddled with bullets and by all normal standards were totally unserviceable. The courage of these men never failed nor looked like failing. Each day their fellows died, each day they stepped into their battered aircraft, not without a sensation of fear but quite undismayed. Each man was aware of his great responsibility in the face of great odds.

Final Evacuation of Air Forces.

46. On 22nd April, I sent the remaining Hurricanes to Argos. From here, I intended that they should cover the evacuation of the British Army, but the German air attack became so concentrated, that after a number of Hurricanes had been destroyed on the ground on 23rd April, the remainder were ordered to leave for Crete. In Crete, Blenheim fighter patrols were organised to cover the ships evacuating the troops from the beaches. These escorts were maintained throughout the evacuation without respite, and I consider it was due largely to their efforts that such a large proportion of the total British forces in Greece were evacuated.

47. A reference to the evacuation would not be complete without a tribute being paid to the flying boats, both of the R.A.F. and the B.O.A.C. These boats carried out magnificent work ferrying parties of airmen and soldiers both from the mainland to Crete and from Crete to Egypt. A number of their flights were carried out in conditions of the utmost danger, and, throughout, the pilots and crews displayed the utmost gallantry and devotion to duty. From the point of view of interest, the record number of personnel carried in one single Sunderland on one trip was 84.

CONCLUSION.

48. The lessons and conclusions to be drawn from a campaign of this description are many, and in Appendix " B "* to this report, I have included those which I consider are of the chief interest. In bringing out the various points that come to my mind, I find it difficult to avoid criticising various aspects of service organisation and doctrines. I would like to point out, however, that these criticisms are made in an entirely constructive sense and in the hope that profit may be gained by our experience.

49. Where we are in possession of totally inadequate air forces, there will always be requests from every direction for the air support which in ideal circumstances we would comfortably be able to provide, and which indeed we would be only too pleased to give. In Greece, we had the minimum, and in order to produce any results at all, it was essential that all available force was directed in accordance with a carefully conceived plan. As our bombing forces were inadequate to deal decisive and instantaneous blows on the enemy, our policy had to be to sustain our small efforts for as long as possible at points where the resultant dislocation caused the enemy the utmost embarrassment. This we were able to do in Albania, for the Italian air strategy was extremely weak, and the numerical odds were only some four or five to one against us. When, however, we had to face the full force of the German onslaught in addition, the odds became too great in spite of the superb gallantry of our pilots and crews.

50. In spite of the strategic and tactical disadvantages under which our air forces laboured in Greece, in spite of the great enemy superiority in numbers, and in spite of the weather conditions which there can be no doubt were the worst in which British air forces have had to operate throughout the world, a considerable offensive effort was developed. During the Albanian and German campaigns in Greece, our fighters destroyed 232 enemy aircraft confirmed, and a further 112 unconfirmed. Our bombers operating by day and night dropped 550 tons of bombs on the enemy. There was no indiscriminate or area bombing. Each bomb was carefully aimed in order to obtain the maximum effect to ensure that the efforts required to overcome the disadvantages which beset our air crews were not in vain.

51. The participation of our land forces in the Greek campaign was dictated entirely by political considerations, and we were fully aware of our weaknesses both in the air and on the ground. I have heard criticisms made that, under these conditions, we should never have sent a land force to Greece. I attended all the conferences held in Greece to discuss this matter and I would like to say without any hesitation, and in the light of subsequent events, that in my opinion the decision made was a right one and in accordance with the best traditions of our race. There was always the chance that, in the first place, Germany would respect the neutrality of Yugo-Slavia and that her advancing armies might be delayed sufficiently long to enable our forces to be strengthened and our position made secure. On the other hand, if Yugo-Slavia threw in her lot with us, which eventually she did, it was reasonable to suppose that her soldiers, renowned for their fighting qualities, would prove a tough nut for the Germans to crack and they would be able to protect our left flank. In any case, we would be containing large enemy land forces and air forces at a time when Britain needed a breathing space to perfect her defensive arrangements.

Furthermore, the assistance which we were considering was to be given to a nation which had sacrificed her all in our cause and was herself quite prepared to face complete extinction rather than capitulate. I suggest that it would have been difficult to refuse her this help and our conduct would have been most reprehensible in the eyes of our countrymen and those of important neutrals had we failed to do so.

52. Finally, I would like to express on behalf of each individual under my command, my sincere appreciation of the generous hospitality and friendship which were unfailingly shown to us by Greeks in every walk of life. We will never forget the brave and courteous spirit of these people, whose kindness and sympathy towards us were as great when we finally had

---

* Not reproduced.

to leave Greece to the occupation of the Germans, as when we arrived in November last in the fever and anxiety of the opening days of the war against Italy. It was with a feeling of deep regret but of profound admiration and affection for this heroic people that we left the shores of Greece.

53. Under separate cover, I have forwarded to you the names of officers and airmen who I would particularly like to bring to your notice for their excellent work and devotion to duty during this campaign. I have nothing but praise for all the officers and airmen whom I had the honour to command, whose conduct was at all times exemplary and who, even during periods of the greatest stress, continued to work with that cool and calm efficiency which we have become accustomed to expect from the members of the Service.

I have the honour to be,
Sir,
Your obedient Servant,
J. H. d'ALBIAC.
Air Vice-Marshal,
Commanding R.A.F. in Greece.
November, 1940, to April, 1941.

LONDON
PRINTED AND PUBLISHED BY HIS MAJESTY'S STATIONERY OFFICE
To be purchased directly from H.M. STATIONERY OFFICE at the following addresses:
York House, Kingsway, London, W.C.2; 13a Castle Street, Edinburgh 2;
39-41 King Street, Manchester 2; 1 St. Andrew's Crescent, Cardiff;
80 Chichester Street, Belfast;
or through any bookseller

1947
Price Sixpence net

S.O. Code No. 65-37846

Numb. 38111

SECOND SUPPLEMENT
TO
The London Gazette
Of TUESDAY, the 28th of OCTOBER, 1947

Published by Authority

Registered as a newspaper

THURSDAY, 30 OCTOBER, 1947

LIBERATION OF EUROPE (OPERATION "OVERLORD") OPERATIONS OF COASTAL COMMAND, ROYAL AIR FORCE, FROM MAY TO AUGUST, 1944.

The following despatch was submitted to the Secretary of State for Air on November 1st, 1944, by Air Chief Marshal Sir Sholto Douglas, K.C.B., M.C., D.F.C., Air Officer Commanding-in-Chief, Coastal Command, Royal Air Force.

I have the honour to submit a despatch on the preparations for and results of operations by my Command for the period May to the end of August, 1944. By September the successful progress of our Armies during the three months that they had been established on the Continent had denied the enemy the effective use of the Bay of Biscay ports as submarine bases from which to conduct his war against our shipping. This marked the end of an important phase in the U-Boat war.

PLANNING AND PREPARATION.
Preparations by the Enemy and Ourselves.

2. At the end of March, 1944, there were signs that the enemy was reducing the number of U-Boats operating in the Atlantic, presumably with the intention of conserving his forces for the forthcoming assault. This was confirmed in April, when the number operating in this area was very small. The lull continued during May, with large concentrations of U-Boats in the Bay of Biscay ports. This policy of the enemy's, while it reduced our opportunities for killing U-Boats, permitted an intensive training programme for the Leigh Light squadrons in the United Kingdom—which I had started at the end of March—to proceed without hindrance. The urgent need for Leigh Light aircraft over the past two years had meant that aircrews turned over to this role had had insufficient time to devote to training, and the standard of homing and Leigh Light manipulation was not as high as it might have been. Ten weeks' intensive training was carried out by the U.K.-based Liberator and Wellington searchlight squadrons, and when D-day came the standard was much improved.

Directive for "Overlord".

3. In April, 1944, I issued to my Groups a directive which set out the tasks of each Group for the OVERLORD operation that was shortly to take place, and outlined the action that the Admiralty anticipated would be taken by the enemy.

ANTI-U-BOAT.
Appreciation of Enemy Intentions.

4. On the assumption that the enemy would direct his U-Boat offensive principally against our cross-channel convoys, the Admiralty appreciated that the bulk of his U-Boats would operate from the Bay ports and endeavour to penetrate the S.W. Approaches to the Bristol, St. George's and English Channels, and that he would maintain only comparatively small forces in the Atlantic to hamper the passage of our convoys. The main focus of our anti-U-Boat operations was therefore to be in the S.W. Approaches, and the effort directed to protecting Atlantic convoys would be drastically reduced. It was also necessary to provide to some extent against the passage of U-Boats through the Northern Transit Area and also against the possibility of the movement of U-Boats through the North Sea. These areas had however to be regarded as of secondary importance when compared with the S.W. Approaches, and it was not intended to provide permanently for more than thin cover in the Northern Transit Area. The North Sea area would be covered only if the situation demanded it, and my plans allowed for four anti-U-Boat squadrons to be drawn from those

allotted to the S.W. Approaches and to be transferred to bases on the East coast should the necessity arise.

Tasks of Coastal Groups.

5. The tasks of my various Groups in the United Kingdom in the anti-U-Boat role were briefly as follows:—

19 *Group (Plymouth).*

(i) To provide adequate air cover in the S.W. Approaches to protect the flanks of the Allied Assault Convoys.

(ii) To provide cover or close escort to Allied Assault Convoys in the S.W. Approaches.

(iii) To hunt and destroy enemy U-Boats attempting to attack Allied Assault Convoys in the S.W. Approaches.

16 *Group (Chatham).*

(i) In the event of a threat by U-Boats to the Eastern flank of the Allied Liberation Forces by way of the North Sea, to hunt and destroy enemy U-Boats attempting to enter the English Channel from the east.

(ii) To provide cover or close escort by Fleet Air Arm Squadrons allocated to the Group to Allied Liberation Convoys on passage between The Nore and Beachy Head.

15 *Group (Liverpool).*

(i) To provide cover to threatened Atlantic Shipping.

(ii) To cover the entrances of the North Channel against the passage of enemy U-Boats.

(iii) To provide A/U cover in the Northern Transit Area.

18 *Group (Rosyth).*

(i) To provide A/U cover in the Northern Transit Area.

(ii) To provide aircraft for Fleet Reconnaissance duties.

The Main Threat.

6. In the main area of the S.W. Approaches, the first principle adopted was that of " the cork in the bottle ", the object being to flood an area of sufficient depth to kill or keep submarines submerged from the Western limits of the St. George's and Bristol Channels and the English Channel up to a point as near as possible to the route of our cross-channel convoys. The patrols were so calculated as to provide a cover of thirty minutes density in the area. By this plan I expected a high percentage of kills if the U-Boats came through on the surface, or, alternatively, it would force upon them maximum caution tactics throughout their passage. In the latter event there would be a zone to the East of the flooded area in which U-Boats would be forced to surface for prolonged periods to recharge their batteries, and in which they could be attacked and hunted by air and surface forces with good prospects of success. Moreover, individual patrol areas were so designed as to be readily removable from one part of the main area to another, so that one portion could be immediately strengthened at the expense of another in the light of the situation as it developed. Further, the " cork " could be pushed home or withdrawn at will. In this way the plan preserved flexibility without detriment to the principle upon which it was based.

The Need for Fighter Cover

7. The extent to which the " cork " could be inserted was considered dependent upon the degree of fighter cover that could be provided by A.E.A.F., since the Southern boundaries of our patrols ran close in to the coast of France along which the enemy was expected to move his U-Boats under cover of his fighters and shore defences. Once the assault was launched it was expected that the enemy fighters would be heavily engaged in the area of the main battle and that no substantial numbers of S.E. fighters would be able to be spared for the protection of U-Boats. The commitment for providing fighter cover was not therefore likely to be a prolonged or heavy one, but it was reasonable to expect from the enemy some early reactions to the preparations in progress and also to any exercises which took place before D-day. One such exercise, known as FABIUS, was considered sufficient in scope to make it possible that the enemy might believe the assault was starting. Should this happen, I considered that it might be necessary prematurely to implement the plans of my Command in full, and in this case the requirement for S.E. fighter cover would become much more serious. I considered, however, that at this stage our fighters would not be heavily committed elsewhere, and Air Commander-in-Chief, A.E.A.F., confirmed that full scale fighter support could be provided any time up to D-day. Provision for the protection of A/U aircraft against enemy long range fighters (Ju 88s) was to be met by allotting Mosquito and Beaufighter aircraft of my own Command for this task.

Convoy Cover

8. In addition to flooding the selected area, plans were made for the protection of our cross-channel convoys sailing along the South coast of England. I allotted this task principally to the Fleet Air Arm Squadrons (eight of which were placed under my operational control for " Overlord "), backed by such 19 Group aircraft as I could spare from their main task.

Operation of Surface Hunting Groups

9. Surface hunting groups were to be operated under the control of the Naval Commanders-in-Chief, Plymouth and Portsmouth. Co-operation between these Groups and aircraft was arranged between A.O.C. 19 Group and C-in-C Plymouth, who co-ordinated his own requirements and those of C-in-C Portsmouth.

ANTI-SHIP OPERATIONS

Tasks of 16 and 19 Groups

10. It was expected that the enemy would launch an offensive with destroyers and light surface craft against our convoys sailing to and from their assembly ports and on passage across the Channel. Air operations to meet this threat were to be conducted by 16 and 19 Groups, whose tasks were as follows:—

19 *Group.*

(i) To hunt and destroy E-Boats and destroyers in the S.W. Approaches and Western Channel.

(ii) To provide anti-E-Boat and destroyer reconnaissance in conjunction with Naval Surface Forces operating in the area in (i).

16 Group.

(i) To hunt and destroy E-Boats and destroyers in the Southern North Sea.

(ii) To provide anti-E-Boat and destroyer reconnaissance in conjunction with Naval Surface Forces operating in the Southern North Sea.

Form of Operations.

11. It was correctly appreciated that anti-ship operations would take place mostly at night and at dawn and dusk, and these were to take the following forms:—

At night.

(i) Operation of Albacore and Swordfish under G.C.I. control of 10 and 11 Groups.

(ii) Reconnaissance by Wellington flare-dropping A.S.V. aircraft operating under 16 and 19 Groups, and the subsequent direction of Naval Surface Craft and/or Coastal Command Beaufighters to the target.

At dusk and dawn.

Beaufighter sweeps with the object of destroying enemy Light Surface Craft when leaving harbour at dusk or returning from patrol at dawn.

12. As in the case of anti-U-Boat measures, I was prepared to implement these plans as a result of enemy reaction to exercises such as " Fabius ", or to any other event which might have led him to believe that the assault was imminent.

Main Battle Zone.

13. In agreement with the Admiralty and the Air Commander-in-Chief, A.E.A.F., I demarcated an area between the lines Portland to Jersey on the West and North Foreland to Calais on the East, as the main battle zone. Coastal Command aircraft were to operate primarily on the flanks of this area and only to a limited extent within it. This was an important point. I expected such a concentration of shipping of all sorts in this zone that even by day I considered it would be difficult to distinguish friend from foe, and at night almost impossible. As it turned out, however, it became possible, by special briefing at Area Combined Headquarters, for my anti-shipping aircraft to operate within the Battle Zone outside the central area containing the cross-channel shipping lanes.

Order of Battle.

14. The Order of Battle, as it stood on 6th June, 1944, shows that, in order to make the flooded area in the S.W. Approaches effective, I deployed no less than 21 of my A/U squadrons together with 4 Fleet Air Arm squadrons in this area. My anti-shipping striking force consisted of seven Beaufighter squadrons, of which I allotted initially five to the east of the main battle zone where the threat of E-Boats was considered greater, and two to the west.

CONDUCT AND RESULTS OF OPERATIONS.

U-Boat Operations in the North.

15. Intensive operations for Coastal Command began in mid-May, although only the Anti-U-Boat squadrons in the North were involved. At this time the enemy decided hurriedly to reinforce his U-Boat flotillas in the Bay of Biscay by moving a number of his Norwegian-based boats into the Atlantic and thence southwards to the Channel and French West Coast ports. The U-Boats were presumably in too much of a hurry to proceed submerged, and their Commanding Officers were apparently confident in the efficiency of their anti-aircraft defences, for they remained on the surface and shot it out with the aircraft to their own detriment. Every opportunity was taken to bring to bear on the enemy the fullest weight of attack without reducing the forces preparing for the vital struggle which was shortly to take place in the S.W. Approaches, and I therefore moved detachments of squadrons from Iceland and Northern Ireland to airfields and flying boat bases in northern Scotland and the Shetlands, to supplement the aircraft at the disposal of the A.O.C. 18 Group. All through June and July these Northern operations went on, and towards the end of July they had extended into Arctic waters, where the enemy seemed to be trying to work round into the Atlantic out of aircraft range. This meant that operations were being conducted at no less than 850 miles from the aircraft's bases. At the end of June, however, I had moved the whole of the VLR* Liberator squadron from Iceland to Tain, and this squadron bore the brunt of the operations conducted in these very far Northern regions.

16. During June perhaps three or four boats in all got through to the Bay of Biscay. The rest were either destroyed or damaged and forced to put back to Norway. In those Northern latitudes at that time of year there was no darkness, and, at the beginning of the battle at any rate, few of the Northern U-Boats had been fitted with " schnorkel ". These two factors were largely responsible for the opportunities for so many attacks.

17. During the period mid-May to the end of July, we sighted seventy-five U-Boats in Northern Waters and attacked fifty-one. Of these sixteen were sunk or probably sunk and twelve damaged. These successes were not achieved without cost. 162 Canadian Squadron sank four U-Boats and lost three Catalinas in June alone. Two Victoria Crosses were awarded to officers taking part in these operations, one posthumously to the Captain of a Catalina of the afore-mentioned 162 (R.C.A.F.) Squadron, and a second to the Captain of a Catalina of 210 Squadron.

U-Boat Operations in the South.

18. Despite the importance of these far away operations, it was inevitable that the main attention should be concentrated on the beaches of Normandy and the English Channel. The preparations for the assault and the large scale exercises during the last few days of May and the beginning of June did not produce any reactions from the enemy, and on 6th June the majority of the enemy's operational U-Boats were still assembled in the Biscay ports. They were not offensively deployed on that date, so there can be no doubt that the enemy had been unable to discover the date of our landing. On D-Day however, he reacted swiftly. It soon became clear that the U-Boats were making for the assault area with the utmost speed—that is, on the surface whenever possible. The air patrols which had been planned to counter this move were already being flown and successes soon materialised. Off the Brest Peninsula and in the mouth of the

---

* Very Long Range.

Channel, thirty-six U-Boats were sighted by Coastal Command in the first four days of the assault and twenty-three were attacked. Six were destroyed and four seriously damaged. Sixteen of the attacks were at night. Two of the U-Boats destroyed were sunk on one sortie within 20 minutes by a Liberator of No. 224 Squadron, piloted by Flying Officer Moore. In almost every case the enemy fought back desperately with his anti-aircraft armament, for in those four days the U-Boats were in too much of a hurry to be able to proceed submerged. They inflicted a high proportion of casualties on our attacking aircraft, but very few got through. Prisoners of war from the U-Boats have told us that the penetration of the Channel was a nightmare.

19. After D plus 4 the enemy was forced to change his tactics. During their sojourn in the Bay ports almost all the U-boats had been fitted with the exhaustible air intake (Schnorkel), and from the fourth day of the assault until the end of June sightings mainly consisted of periscopes and " Schnorkels " of U-Boats trying to get through by remaining submerged continuously and by relying on " Schnorkels " to ventilate the boat and charge batteries. The " Schnorkel " is a most difficult target for airborne radar, and it cannot be denied that the enemy's recourse to this cautious method of approach reduced his losses. At the same time, however, the effect of remaining submerged had an adverse effect on the morale of the U-Boat crews and their achievements were notable by their absence. Between D plus 4 and the end of June forty-seven sightings of U-Boats were made by Coastal Command in southern waters and twenty-four were attacked. During this period at least one more U-Boat was sunk by aircraft and two kills were shared with ships of the Royal Navy, who were taking an ever increasing part in the policing of the Channel and its approaches. In addition, aircraft damaged another four U-Boats and shared with the Navy in damaging a fifth.

20. In July the picture was the same. The enemy was still trying to get in amongst our shipping by making the fullest use of his schnorkel device. In all, twenty-two sightings were made and fifteen U-Boats attacked during this month, of which two were sunk and another damaged.

21. By the end of July there was no doubt that the enemy's threat had been beaten. Only a small number of U-Boats had got through to our shipping lanes, and, in the three months from D-Day to the end of August, of the thousands of merchant ships taking part in the Channel operations, only nine were sunk by U-Boat action.

22. Finally, the steady progress of our armies made it obvious to the enemy that he would soon lose the use of the Bay ports. He therefore began to evacuate them during August and to send U-Boats northward to his Norwegian bases. During the month some ferocious actions were fought in the Bay of Biscay almost within sight of land with U-Boats trying to escape, and six were accounted for by Coastal Command aircraft, three of these being shared with the Navy. By early September, the Biscay U-Boat force had withdrawn and was making its passage, underwater nearly all the time, to the Norwegian ports.

23. In the whole battle in the North and the South from mid-May to the end of August, Coastal Command sank twenty-seven U-Boats, damaged another so badly that when it reached its base it was paid off, shared in five more sunk, and damaged another twenty-nine, including two shared with the Royal Navy.

24. In these operations, where skill counted as much as courage, and where both were indispensable, we lost thirty-eight anti-U-Boat aircraft by enemy action and another twenty-two through the hazards of maintaining our patrols in fair weather and in foul. A high proportion of these aircraft were four-engined heavies with large crews.

Anti-Shipping Operations

25. While the U-Boats were being defeated in the south-west and the north-east, Coastal Command was also in action against enemy surface forces. Soon after the assault began, the enemy tried to reinforce his surface craft in the assault areas by bringing up three destroyers from the Gironde. These vessels were attacked by our aircraft while still south of Brest on 6th June, but the damage inflicted did not prevent the enemy from making port. Two days later the ships tried to round the Brest Peninsula, but were brought to action by the Royal Navy. One Seetier class destroyer was driven ashore, the Tjerk Hiddes was sunk, and the second Seetier was forced back to Brest. The beached destroyer was later attacked by Beaufighters with rockets and bombs, and became a total loss. After this the enemy made no further attempts to reinforce his surface craft from the west, and the only serviceable Seetier and Elbing destroyers were withdrawn to the Gironde.

26. In the early stages, as was expected, the enemy operated his light forces on quite a considerable scale against our assault forces in the assault area. E-Boats were the main weapons. Some thirty of these vessels were based between Boulogne and Cherbourg, but the number was later reduced by air attack, by surface action, and by the outstandingly successful attacks by Bomber Command against Le Havre and Boulogne.

27. The operations of Coastal Command against these light forces consisted mainly of continuous anti-shipping patrols in the Channel. Albacores, Avengers, Swordfish, Beaufighters and Wellingtons made a great many attacks, mostly at night, against E-Boats, R-Boats, " M " class minesweepers and trawlers. Wellingtons did a great deal of reconnaissance work, dropping flares and directing naval forces to their targets. Results were naturally extremely difficult to assess, but we know from prisoners of war that hardly an E-Boat put to sea without being spotted and attacked from the air. In the darkness and in the face of flak from other vessels it is almost impossible to investigate the result of a bombing attack on an E-Boat flotilla, but there is no doubt that the menace of the enemy's light forces was held in check by the operations of the Royal Navy and Coastal Command.

28. The enemy made no use of his major units in the Baltic. Moreover, with the exception of one or two flotillas of E-Boats, he never attempted to reinforce the Channel from the East, in spite of the fact that he had a

number of heavy destroyers and about twenty torpedo boats available in the Baltic. It is probable that he realised our combined sea and air defences made the Southern North Sea and the English Channel a very unpleasant area for operations by the German Navy. In any case, it is certain that, despite the few positive results of our night attacks, the enemy was so harassed by them that he was unable seriously to interfere with our "Overlord" shipping.

29. This success meant that, from the end of June, my anti-shipping aircraft were able to devote more of their time to the second of their two tasks—the interruption of German coastal shipping. In June, I directed the greater part of my effort to the naval targets in the Channel, and only a few attacks were made on convoys. These, however, included some very successful engagements, the most important of which occurred on 15th June north of the Dutch island of Schiermonnikoog, when Beaufighters sank a merchantman of 8,000 tons, a naval auxiliary of 4,000 tons and a minesweeper, besides damaging four more of the escort vessels.

30. In July I kept up the Channel protection, but diverted all but one of the Beaufighter Squadrons to convoy strikes off the coasts of Southern Norway and the Low Countries. There is no doubt that these strikes proved most harassing to the enemy, and he was obliged to divert to this purely defensive task numbers of minesweepers and naval escort craft which he urgently required elsewhere.

31. The beginning of August saw a new phase open in the shipping war. As our tanks swept through North-Western France, enemy coastal craft broke for the comparative safety of the North Sea ports; one night alone saw 70 of them attacked from the air. Moreover, the enemy in the Brest Peninsula was cut off by land. He was therefore obliged to squeeze yet more work from his seaborne supply services. Every available ship in Western France from Brest to Bordeaux was pressed into service to keep the beleaguered garrisons supplied. Coastal Command made the best of this opportunity. Mosquitoes based in Cornwall, Halifaxes, previously operating in an Anti-U-Boat role, and a Wing of Beaufighters which I transferred from the East Coast convoy routes, operated all along the Biscay coast. Merchant ships, sperrbrechers, minesweepers and coasters of all kinds were sunk, and a fitting climax was reached on 24th August when the last of the larger German warships in this area, a Seetier and an Elbing class destroyer, were sunk in the Gironde by the rockets of the Beaufighter Wing.

32. At the beginning of September, the area of anti-shipping activity had moved eastward in the wake of the Allied armies. There were no more attacks in the Bay of Biscay or in the Channel. As the enemy-occupied ports fell into our hands, the night patrols of the Beaufighters, Avengers and Wellingtons moved eastwards along the coast. This happened so quickly that there were no attacks off the Belgian Coast after 7th September, and our attention was turned completely to the intensification of the offensive against the enemy's shipping operating off the Dutch and Norwegian coasts.

33. Thus concluded three months of intensive operations in which the German naval units and merchant shipping in Western Europe had been hammered unmercifully.

CONCLUSION.

34. I wish to end this despatch by paying tribute to all personnel in Coastal Command who by their tireless endeavour and concerted efforts helped to bring about the victory over the enemy sea opposition to the liberation of Europe. In addition to the operations of my Anti-U-Boat and Anti-Shipping aircraft, whose activities have been recounted, the photographic reconnaissance squadrons, the meteorological squadrons and the air/sea rescue air and surface craft all carried out their arduous tasks with skill and resolution.

35. I would like to mention particularly the Fleet Air Arm Squadrons which were incorporated in my Command for operation "Overlord". They performed their varied duties with outstanding keenness and precision.

36. A tribute must also be paid to the Liberator Squadrons of the U.S. Navy, under Commodore Hamilton, U.S.N., which, working under the operational control of 19 Group, did invaluable work, particularly during the "cork in the bottle" operations.

37. Two Norwegian Squadrons, a Czech and a Polish Squadron were also distinguished for their gallantry and enthusiasm in the combined team.

38. Finally, it will not be forgotten that the successes of our operations could not have come about but for the skill in planning and organisation of the Command and Group Staffs who —with the invaluable and enthusiastic co-operation of the Staffs of the Naval Commands —worked long and hard to perfect our preparations; and but for the ceaseless energies of the ground personnel at Stations who provided our aircrews with the means to reap their victories.

I have the honour to be,

Sir,

Your obedient Servant,

SHOLTO DOUGLAS,

Air Chief Marshal,

Air Officer Commanding-in-Chief,
Coastal Command, Royal Air Force.

LONDON
PRINTED AND PUBLISHED BY HIS MAJESTY'S STATIONERY OFFICE
To be purchased directly from H.M. Stationery Office at the following addresses:
York House, Kingsway, London, W.C.2; 13a Castle Street, Edinburgh, 2;
39-41 King Street, Manchester, 2; 1 St. Andrew's Crescent, Cardiff;
Tower Lane, Bristol, 1; 80 Chichester Street, Belfast
OR THROUGH ANY BOOKSELLER
1947
Price Sixpence net

S.O. Code No. 65-38111

Numb. 38183

SUPPLEMENT
TO
The London Gazette
Of TUESDAY, the 20th of JANUARY, 1948
Published by Authority

Registered as a newspaper

THURSDAY, 22 JANUARY, 1948

The War Office,
January, 1948

OPERATIONS IN THE FAR EAST, FROM 17TH OCTOBER 1940 TO 27TH DECEMBER 1941

The following Despatch was submitted to the British Chiefs of Staff on 28th May, 1942, by AIR CHIEF MARSHAL SIR ROBERT BROOKE-POPHAM, G.C.V.O., K.C.B., C.M.G., D.S.O., A.F.C., Commander-in-Chief in the Far East.

I.—FORMATION OF GENERAL HEADQUARTERS, FAR EAST.

1. This despatch covers the period from the date of my appointment as Commander-in-Chief, Far East, the 17th October, 1940, to the date on which I handed over to Lieutenant-General Sir Henry Pownall, the 27th December, 1941.

My original staff consisted of seven, exclusive of my personal assistant. Of these seven, the Chief of Staff, Major-General Dewing, the Senior Royal Air Force Staff Officer, Group-Captain Darvall, as well as my personal assistant, travelled out with me.

The Naval Liaison Officer, Captain Back, met me on my arrival at Singapore, and the Army G.S.O.1, Colonel Fawcett, met me in Burma.

Before leaving England I saw the Chief of the Imperial General Staff, Chief of the Air Staff and Major-General Ismay individually, but did not meet the Chiefs of Staff collectively at one of their meetings.

2. I left London on Sunday, the 27th October, and started by air from Plymouth on the 28th October. I spent two clear days in Cairo, three in Delhi and three in Rangoon, arriving at Singapore on Thursday, the 14th November. General Headquarters, Far East, started to operate on Monday, the 18th November, 1940.

During the journey I was able to see the working of the Headquarters of both the Army and Air Force in Cairo, and to consult with the Commander-in-Chief, Sir Archibald Wavell, on the methods of operating his headquarters, and especially why he found such a big expansion from his original staff necessary.

At Delhi I stayed with the Viceroy, and established contact with the Commander-in-Chief, the Air Officer Commanding-in-Chief, and their respective staffs, and with certain civil officials.

At Rangoon I stayed with the Governor, Sir Archibald Cochrane, and reached agreement over the constitutional problems raised by the appointment of a Commander-in-Chief, Far East. I met the General Officer Commanding, Major-General (now Lieutenant-General) Sir K. McLeod, visited various establishments, including the oil refinery at Syriam, and established contact with many of the civil officials.

Instructions and General Policy.

3. My Directive is given in Appendix A.

On my arrival in Singapore it was agreed that, should I become a casualty, the Commander-in-Chief, China Station, should take my place until my successor was appointed.

With reference to paragraph 2 of my Directive, the meaning of the term "operational control" was explained as being higher direction and control as distinct from detailed operational control.

In addition to this Directive, I had two main guides for action: first, that it was the policy of His Majesty's Government to avoid war with Japan, and, secondly, that, until a fleet was available, our policy in the Far East should be to rely primarily on air power in conjunction with such naval forces as could be made available. The first was confirmed during 1941 in many telegrams, *e.g.,* in March, "Avoidance of war with Japan is basis of Far East policy and provocation must be rigidly avoided," and again in September, "Our policy in the

Far East is still to avoid war with Japan." The second was laid down by the Chiefs of Staff in August, 1940.

4. It was pointed out to me that the requirements of Home Defence, the Battle of the Atlantic, and the Middle East, must take precedence over those of the Far East; at a later date Russia also took precedence, and, at one time, Iraq and Iran. Realising this, it was obviously our duty to be content with the essential minimum, to consider what we could do without rather than what we would like to have, and to make the fullest use of local resources. But we always regarded the strength of 336 aeroplanes as an irreducible minimum. (*See para. 79 below*.) In January, 1941, we were cautioned against over-estimate of the Japanese forces.

I was also informed that the defence organisation in Malaya was apparently not working smoothly or efficiently, and that this would necessitate early investigation and action.

5. To carry out the directions outlined above, it was evident that the following steps were necessary:—

(*a*) To avoid any action that might be deemed provocative by Japan, but at the same time to try and convince her that our strength was too great to be challenged successfully;

(*b*) To strengthen our defences in the Far East, and especially to build up our air forces, not only by obtaining new aircraft but also by making all preparations to ensure mutual reinforcement in the Far East area;

(*c*) To ensure effective co-operation in Malaya, not only between the Royal Navy, the Army and the Air Force but also between them and the civil services;

(*d*) To stiffen the Chinese so that they could contain the maximum Japanese effort (*see paras. 70 and 71 below*); and

(*e*) To establish as close co-operation as possible with the Dutch and Americans, as well as with Australia and New Zealand, the main object being to ensure that, should an attack be made on any part of the Far East area, all the nations concerned would simultaneously enter the war against Japan, thus avoiding the risk of defeat in detail, as had happened in Europe.

6. A very brief study of the area comprised in the Far East Command shows that the defence of the whole area is essentially one single problem. Burma, Siam, Indo-China, Malaya, the Philippines, the Dutch East Indies, Australia and, to a lesser extent, New Zealand, all inter-connect and operations or preparations in any one of these areas affect all the others. In view of the above, I regarded it as one of my principal duties to make personal contacts in these places. During 1941 I visited Australia twice, in February and October, Manila three times and the Netherlands East Indies five times. I also visited Hong Kong in December, 1940, and April, 1941; and Burma in June and September, 1941.

Another point that stands out is that the problem is fundamentally a naval one, and that, although the Army and Air Force in combination may defend areas of land and repel an enemy, his definite defeat cannot be brought about unless control of sea communications is obtained. This control will necessitate air superiority.

The Far East is usually examined on a small-scale map, so people are rather apt to get a false idea of distances. From Singapore to Alor Star at the North End of Malaya is a good deal further than from London to Aberdeen. Rangoon to Singapore direct by air is about 1,100 miles; Singapore to Hong Kong, via Manila, is 2,000 miles, about the distance from Gibraltar to Alexandria; and from Singapore to Melbourne about 4,100, which is only slightly less than the distance from London to Aden, via Malta and Cairo.

Size of General Headquarters Staff.

7. Although it was obvious that Singapore was a key position, and therefore that the defence of Malaya was of the greatest importance, it was evident that, apart from my Directive, the size of my Staff rendered it quite impossible to exercise any form of direct operational control, except in the widest sense. I therefore decided that, although the fact of my headquarters happening to be situated at Singapore would naturally involve my dealing with more details in Malaya than elsewhere, the Commands of Hong Kong, Malaya and Burma must be regarded as of equal status. Each General Officer Commanding would have to control the operations in his own area, and the initiative of the Air Officer Commanding, Far East, must not be cramped; the operational control of my headquarters would be limited mainly to the movement of reinforcements, principally air, within my command and to the issue of directives.

The staff of General Headquarters, Far East, was very small for the work it had to carry out, and immediately on its formation in Singapore it was found necessary to add three duty officers of junior rank in order to ensure keeping a twenty-four-hour watch in the office. Requests for an increase in staff at General Headquarters were made on more than one occasion, and finally it was agreed by the Chiefs of Staff, in August, 1941, that the total establishment should be raised to the following:—

Commander-in-Chief: 1.
Chief of Staff: 1.
Staff Officer, 1st Grade: Navy 1; Army 2; R.A.F. 2.
Staff Officer, 2nd Grade: Navy 1; Army 3; R.A.F. 3.
Staff Officer, 3rd Grade: Navy 1.
Total, 15.
In addition to this, there were:—
Personal Assistant: 1.
Cipher Officers: 2.
Signal Officer: 1.
Chief Clerk: 1.

Making a total in all of 20. This establishment was not completed by the time war broke out.

The result of the smallness of the Staff was that individuals were overworked, and this, in conjunction with the Malayan climate, led to sickness. The most serious case was that of my Chief of Staff, Major-General Dewing, who went into hospital on the 8th April, and remained there until he started for England in May. General Playfair arrived to take his place on the 21st June, but for a period of some ten and a half weeks I was without a Chief of Staff.

This sickness was largely attributed by the medical authorities to the effects of overwork. In addition, Wing-Commander Yarde had to be sent away sick, other officers were in hospital for shorter periods, and when war with Japan broke out Colonel Scott, who had taken Colonel Fawcett's place as the Army G.S.O.1, was in India on sick leave, having been sent there from hospital.

Intelligence.

8. For intelligence I relied almost entirely on the Far Eastern Combined Bureau, known for short as F.E.C.B. This consisted of branches of Naval, Army and Air Force intelligence, and was under the administrative control of the Admiralty, the officer in charge of the Naval Section acting as head of the Bureau. At the date of the formation of my headquarters, F.E.C.B. was somewhat unbalanced in that attention was mostly concentrated on Naval intelligence, while Army and Air intelligence took a minor place, the latter especially being quite inadequate. This, however, was steadily corrected, and I consider that F.E.C.B. fulfilled its functions and showed that a combined intelligence staff of the three Services is a workable proposition. What was needed, however, was a real chief of F.E.C.B., and not merely one whose main duty was acting as head of his own branch. The difficulty was in finding a really suitable individual, and this we had not succeeded in doing at the time war with Japan broke out.

Attachments to General Headquarters Staff.

9. A branch of the Ministry of Economic Warfare known as the O.M. Section, was started on the arrival of Mr. Killery at Singapore in May, 1941. He and his staff were keen and capable, but they had no experience and very little knowledge of how to set about their work. Further, as in the case of intelligence, this is work that requires a great deal of preparation. In consequence of this, but through no fault of Mr. Killery or his staff, the O.M. activities really never got functioning properly by the time that war with Japan broke out. There was also a curious reluctance on the part of many people to have anything to do with these activities, or to help on the work. This was particularly noticeable in the case of intended activities in Siam.

10. Colonel Warren arrived in Singapore early in 1941 to assist in starting Independent Companies. The obvious disadvantage of these Companies is that they form a drain on infantry units, which were already depleted of many of their best non-commissioned officers and officers owing to the expansion and demands of other organisations. As a result, it was finally decided to limit these Independent Companies to two—one for Burma and one for Malaya.

II.—FACTORS AFFECTING THE DEFENCE OF MALAYA AND BORNEO.

11. Air Vice-Marshal Pulford became Air Officer Commanding, Far East, *vice* Air Vice-Marshal Babington on the 26th April, 1941, and Lieutenant-General Percival took over the duties of General Officer Commanding, Malaya, from Lieutenant-General Bond on the 16th May, 1941.

The strength of the Army and of the Air Force in Malaya in November, 1940, is given in Appendices D and I respectively.

In Malaya, as in Burma and Hong Kong, there was a War Committee, which sat under the Governor.

The main reason for the defence of Malaya was to preserve the facilities of the Naval Base at Singapore. The port and rubber and tin production were also important, but on a different plane from the Naval Base. It was, of course, not sufficient to have a close defence of the area round the Naval Base itself. It was of great importance to keep enemy aircraft as far away from the Base as possible, on account of the danger of bombing; this meant extending the defence right up to the Northern end of Malaya. It may be noted that this was not dependent upon the policy of defending Malaya by means of air power. Had the policy been to defend Malaya by means of Army forces, the dispositions might have been different, but it would still have been essential to hold the greater part of Malaya in order to deny aerodromes or their possible sites to the enemy. Singapore Island was to be provisioned for 180 days.

Communications.

12. The main roads in Malaya are well-metalled, and the railways are single-track metre-gauge. Down the centre of Malaya runs a range of hills rising to some 7,000 feet, and there are no east-to-west communications north of latitude 4, *i.e.*, about the latitude of Kuantan. The central backbone of hills dies away soon after crossing the frontier with Siam, and good lateral communications were available in the neighbourhood of Singora, where, also, there were suitable sites for aerodromes. Generally speaking, communications in the west are good and on the east poor.

The defence of the east coast was simplified by the lack of communications, since it was only necessary to hold those places from which roads ran into the interior. This meant that the key points to hold were Mersing and Kuantan. Kota Bharu in Kelantan was held because of the aerodrome at that place and two others a few miles further south, these being necessary in order to enable us to strike, with aircraft, as far as possible into the Gulf of Siam and into Indo China. (*See para.* 52 *below.*)

The only existing land communication between Kelantan and the rest of Malaya is the railway, there being no through road. Attempts were made to use the railway for motor transport, but as the rails were spiked and no chairs were available the damage caused to tyres was so excessive that the project was given up as impracticable. This meant that communications with any force at Kota Bharu were precarious, since everything had to move by the single line of railway, which in many parts was highly vulnerable to bombing. I laid down that the road policy in Kelantan should be not to develop any road on or near the coast, but as soon as practicable to construct an internal road running north and south, following more or less the line of the railway.

The only communication overland with Kuantan was a single road, also very vulnerable in places to air bombing.

Co-operation between the services and with the civil authorities.

13. For some time before November, 1940, the relations between the Army and the Air Force were not happy; there was some jealousy

between them, co-operation left a great deal to be desired, and it was some months before this could be considered satisfactory. Every operation should have been looked upon as a combined operation of two, or very often the three, services; for a long time there was a tendency for one of the services to work out a plan on its own and then see how one or both the other services could come in.

A great step in advance was made by getting the headquarters of the Army and Air Force on the same site. This entailed a good deal of building, but before war started there was a single combined Operations Room functioning and the whole of the Army General Staff were located on the same site as Royal Air Force Headquarters. A naval section joined the Operations Room at the start of the war as planned previously.

14. The local tradition of inter-service jealousy had some effect for the first few months on the working of General Headquarters. Personal relations with Army Headquarters were good, but my staff had to be scrupulously careful in dealing with matters that touched on the province of the General Officer Commanding.

Co-operation between the Navy and Air Force was good, and it continually improved between the Navy and the Army, for instance, on such matters as getting advice from naval officers as to the probable sites of landings from the naval point of view.

15. Relations between the Commander-in-Chief, China Station, and myself were close and friendly throughout. Our offices were adjoining after the move of my headquarters to the Naval Base and I had luncheon with him in his house nearly every day.

Relations between the commanders in Malaya and the Governor were good. I always found the Governor ready to help, and our personal relations were very friendly.

As regards the Colonial Service generally, our relations in most cases were satisfactory, and much help was received from many Departments, especially the Survey and the Government Posts and Telegraphs. But, partly owing to the complicated system of government, delays sometimes occurred and on certain matters it was difficult to get full and accurate information. I feel it would be of great value to the Colonial Service if its officers could attend some college on the lines of the Military Staff Colleges at some time in their career.

There was an interchange of liaison officers with the Dutch, first Navy and Air and later Army as well. Observers from the American Army and Navy were also posted to Singapore.

Borneo.

16. Unless we obtained command of the sea, it was impossible to defend British Borneo as a whole with the forces available. But through communications in the island were practically non-existent; consequently, any defence could be limited to holding the important points. The only place which it was decided to hold was Kuching, the reason for this being not only that there was an aerodrome at that place, but that its occupation by the enemy might give access to the aerodromes in Dutch Borneo at the North-Western end of the island, these aerodromes being only some 350 miles from Singapore, i.e., much nearer than any in South Indo-China.

I informed the Governor of North Borneo that his territory could not be defended, and that the volunteers and police at his disposal were to be utilised for purposes of internal security. No attempt was made to defend Labuan, though it was a cable and wireless station.

The State of Brunei was of some importance owing to the oilfield at Seria in the South, which, in addition to Miri, supplied crude oil to the refineries at Lutong in Sarawak. Although one company of the 2nd/15th Punjab Regiment less one platoon to Kuching, had been moved to Lutong in December, 1940, and two 6-inch guns had been mounted there, it was finally decided that it was useless to attempt to defend the refinery or either of the oilfields. Consequently, a partial denial scheme was carried out before war broke out, whereby the oil output was reduced by some 70 per cent., and only a small number of items were left to complete the denial scheme when war broke out. According to reports, the work was completed satisfactorily.

The 2nd/15th Punjab Regiment, less the one company referred to above, left Singapore for Kuching on the 10th and 11th May, 1941. Steps were also taken to develop local forces, i.e., volunteers and a body of native troops known as the Sarawak Rangers.

III.—Factors Affecting the Defence of Burma.

Authorities.

17. Sir Reginald Dorman Smith replaced the Hon. Sir Archibald Cochrane as Governor of Burma on the 6th May, 1941, and Lieut.-General Hutton took over the duties of General Officer Commanding from Lieut.-General McLeod at midnight the 28th-29th December, 1941.

The War Committee in Burma included Burmese Ministers as well as the two British Counsellors and the General Officer Commanding. The Governor was President and the Premier of Burma Vice-President.

Sir R. Dorman Smith established a military liaison officer on his personal staff. There were obvious advantages in this, and it would doubtless have worked well had the facts and figures always been obtained from the responsible authorities. As it was, information was sometimes sought through other channels, with the result that at times inaccurate or incomplete information was given to the Governor, leading to misunderstandings.

Communications.

18. The main factor affecting the defence of Burma was that of communications. The total length of frontier facing Japanese-occupied territory in December, 1941, was nearly 800 miles. There were good roads, as well as railways, running north and south up the valleys of the Sittang and Irrawaddy. Roads in the Tenasserim Peninsula were bad.

Working north from the southern end of the Tenasserim Peninsula, there were only mountain tracks leading eastwards from Siam until reaching the road from Raheng through Mesod towards Moulmein, which crossed the Burma frontier at Myawadi. Even this road was not continuous, and there was a section of fifty miles reported to be not much better than a pack track. From the Japanese point of view, it had the disadvantages that we should be able to operate from close to our railhead at Martaban, and that, so long as we held command of the sea, advance beyond Moulmein by the Japanese would be open to a British flank attack.

Continuing north, there were again only tracks until reaching the road leading from the Bangkok-Chieng Mai railway, through Chieng Rai and thence via Kentung to Taunggyi. On the Siamese side of the frontier this road was good; on our side it was fair-weather only for part of the way.

There were only tracks leading from Burma into Northern Indo-China, and these involved the crossing of the River Mekong. Into China itself there was a fair track from Kentung to Puerhfu, and, secondly, the main road from Lashio to Kunming. A road from Bhamo joined the latter near the frontier.

Westwards, a start had been made on a road communication with India, but this was by no means complete when war broke out.

Landing grounds had been established in the Tenasserim Peninsula with the object of facilitating the movement of aircraft between Burma and Malaya; the main ones were at Tavoy, Mergui and Victoria Point. The last was very isolated, and it was realised that it probably could not be held for long if war with Japan broke out.

19. It was estimated that the total force which the Japanese could bring against Burma, using land communications only, would be about two divisions, of which one division would be on the road running through Chieng Rai. The Chiefs of Staff considered in January 1941 that, although four enemy divisions could be maintained at railhead on the Bangkok-Chieng Mai railway, it was unlikely that even one division could be maintained on the Burma side of the frontier, owing to the limited road communications. The situation would, however, be completely altered should the Japanese get control of sea communications in the Bay of Bengal. In that case, their capture of Mergui, and possibly Tavoy, would only be a question of time. They would be able to outflank our positions at Moulmein, and our line of communication thence with Rangoon; and, should Singapore fall or be invested, would be able to bring by sea against Burma a force much greater than two divisions.

20. Turning to the Chieng Rai line of advance, owing to the indifferent road on our side of the frontier and the shortage of Mechanical Transport, it was impracticable to maintain a big force east of the Salween. The policy, therefore, was to fight delaying actions as far forward as possible, and to make the Salween the main line of defence.

Owing to the heavy growth of trees along the Japanese lines of advance, conditions were not generally favourable for air reconnaissance. On the other hand, there were certain open defiles against which air bombing would probably have been very effective, and it was hoped that sufficient air force would be available to deter the Japanese advance to a great extent. For this purpose aerodromes were constructed with the object of being able to concentrate either on Central or South Burma, and against either the Mesod road or the Chieng Rai road.

Demolitions were prepared along the enemy lines of advance, especially on the Chieng Rai road.

Engineering Programme.

21. There was a great shortage of engineers, both civil and military. In planning the engineering programme, priority was given first to aerodrome construction and accommodation for the Royal Air Force; secondly, to road construction for strategical and tactical purposes, including ferries; and then accommodation for troops and stores, including ammunition.

In the time available there was no opportunity to complete elaborate concrete defence lines; all that could be done was to construct field defences on the probable lines of approach. There were limitations even to this: first, the difficulty of working and the prevalence of malaria in the rainy season; secondly, the number of troops available; and thirdly, the lack of Mechanical Transport, until the Autumn of 1941, which severely limited the number of men that could be maintained near, and east of, the Salween River.

Strength of Forces.

22. The composition of the military forces in Burma when war broke out is shown in Appendix G, and the situation regarding Anti-Aircraft guns in Appendix F.

As will be seen, the organisation was somewhat complicated from the desire to make every possible use of local resources. Originally, the Burma Frontier Force had been independent of the General Officer Commanding in peace, and only came under him in time of war. His Excellency Sir Reginald Dorman Smith decided to put the Burma Frontier Force under the General Officer Commanding's control in peace as well, thus simplifying the organisation. The change was effected on the 10th November, 1941.

The Independent Company was abolished before war with Japan broke out, the British portion being used mainly for additional squads for Chinese guerillas, and the Burmese returning to their original units.

23. In the Singapore Conference of October 1940 it was recommended that as regards the Army, the force immediately required for the defence of Burma was as follows:—

 5 infantry brigades and two additional battalions;
 1 field regiment and 1 battery;
 2 mountain batteries;
 1 anti-tank battery;
 1 heavy A.A. regiment (24 guns);
 1 light A.A. battery, non-mobile (16 guns);
 1 light A.A. battery, mobile; and
 1 company light tanks.

This was exclusive of the Burma Frontier Force and of the Territorial and Auxiliary forces allotted to internal security duties. It was also stated that an additional requirement for the long-term problem was: one Division, less certain units, which made the fighting portion of this Division as follows:—

 2 infantry brigades, each of 3 battalions;
 1 reconnaissance unit;
 1 field regiment (24 guns);
 1 medium regiment (16 guns);
 1 light A.A. regiment (48 guns);
 1 anti-tank battery; and
 1 machine gun battalion.

In their comments of January 1941, on the Conference, the Chiefs of Staff stated that they considered both the threat of attack, and the demands for land forces, had been overstated.

Comparing the Conference recommendations with the total Army strength available in Burma in December 1941 (*see Appendix G*), and omitting the Burma Frontier Force and the Territorial and Auxiliary forces, the shortages were approximately—
- 3 field batteries;
- 1 anti-tank battery; and
- 1 company light tanks

out of the immediate requirements, and the whole of the additional requirement.

Apart from this, up to the outbreak of the war with Japan, Burma remained short of:—
- Rifles;
- Mechanical transport vehicles;
- Officers for the General Officer Commanding's staff and services; and
- Medical personnel.

24. A Burma Royal Naval Volunteer Reserve under the command of Commander K. S. Lyle, R.N., had been raised in 1940. It had two or three patrol boats operating off the Tenasserim Peninsula, and was also responsible for minesweeping the Rangoon approaches and for examination services. There were several other craft building at Rangoon, but these had been help up mainly owing to the delay in obtaining engines and fittings from England. The force was under the Commander-in-Chief, China, for operations, and under the Governor of Burma for administration. It was not under the General Officer Commanding, though co-operation was very satisfactory.

25. In November 1940, air strength in Burma was practically non-existent. The Singapore Conference had recommended the following:—
- 1 general reconnaissance squadron;
- 2 bomber squadrons; and
- 1 fighter squadron.

No. 60 Squadron, equipped with Blenheim bombers, arrived from India in February 1941; in August 1941, one flight was reorganised as a fighter flight and equipped with Brewster Buffaloes. Later, a complete Buffalo squadron, No. 67, was sent from Malaya in November 1941, and the whole of No. 60 Squadron reverted to bombers. There was a Burma Volunteer Air Unit, but this had not got further than a small training organisation. This merely gave Burma two squadrons, which was admittedly very weak, and, actually, when war broke out, most of the Blenheim squadron, No. 60, was in Malaya for bombing practice.

On the other hand, the American Volunteer Group of the International Air Force started to train in Burma in August 1941, and there was an understanding, amounting practically to an agreement, with General Chiang Kai-shek that, if Burma was attacked, part, or the whole, of this American Volunteer Group would be detailed for the defence of Burma. Actually, two of the American Volunteer Group squadrons were sent to Kunming when war with Japan broke out, and one to Mingaladon, near Rangoon.

It was my opinion that the defence of Burma depended largely upon holding Malaya, and that the defence of the latter must have priority. I also considered it unlikely that the Japanese would attack Burma solely in order to cut the Burma Road to China. They knew that this must involve war with Great Britain, and in all probability with the Dutch and perhaps also the United States. If they were going to face this, they would be much more likely to start attacking Singapore than Burma. Admittedly, we were working on probabilities and not certainties, but, in view of the weakness of our air forces, it was essential to concentrate the maximum effort and not try to be equally strong in two places.

The American Volunteer Group.

26. The American Volunteer Group consisted of three single-seater fighter squadrons which were equipped with Tomahawks up to the time I handed over command.

Doubtless the United States will not forget the help that was freely given to the American Volunteer Group by the Burma Government and by the Royal Air Force. They were given the sole use of the Royal Air Force aerodrome at Toungoo, allowed to use Mingaladon aerodrome, near Rangoon, for testing Tomahawks after erection, and were offered the use of further aerodromes if required. Permission from London was given on the 22nd August, 1941, for the American Volunteer Group to carry out operational training in Burma, and they were given assistance in many other directions.

On the 31st October, 1941, the British Ambassador, Chungking, represented to the Foreign Office that the situation in China was very serious. We were asked what we could do to help, and suggested that we might form a British fighter squadron with volunteers from the Royal Air Force to form part of the International Air Force, and possibly a bomber squadron as well. It was pointed out that this proposal would mean a reduction in our own effective fighting and bombing strength. The suggestion was approved by the Chiefs of Staff, provided I was satisfied they would be able to operate effectively as part of the International Air Force and that I could accept the detachment from the Malaya defences. These squadrons would have been largely dependent on the American Volunteer Group organisation for their maintaintence. Pending a detailed examination of the maintenance arrangements in China, volunteers for these squadrons were not called for and actually they were never formed, but many preliminary steps were taken, including the movement of vehicles, spares and bombs. A telegram to the British liaison mission in Washington, and a personal telegram from me to General MacArthur in Manila, resulted in a very fair stock of spares being received by the American Volunteer Group before war broke out. But for this, it is very doubtful if they could have gone on working for more than two or three weeks.

I found that the pilots of the American Volunteer Group were not satisfied with their Tomahawks when I visited them in September 1941. This was largely corrected before war broke out, partly by giving details of the successes of the Tomahawks in the Middle East, and partly by a test carried out between a Buffalo and a Tomahawk, which showed the latter to be considerably superior in speed, climb and in manoeuvrability over some 10,000 feet.

Aircraft Warning System.

27. There was an air observation corps under General Officer Commanding, organised in five groups, each under an ex-inspector of police, the observers being local Burmans and Anglo-Burmans. This Observer Corps did good work, and, according to later reports, warnings of the attacks on Rangoon were received in time

for the fighters to take off and get up. An R.D.F. set at Moulmein was just starting to operate in December 1941.

With regard to A.R.P., the original policy in Rangoon had been evacuation. Sir Reginald Dorman Smith decided to change this, and to construct air raid shelters. There had been no time to complete these shelters before war broke out.

Political Factors.

28. The internal situation in Burma gave rise to much anxiety, and it was realised that in time of war it might become necessary to reinforce the police with military units. There were doubtless many reasons for this potential unrest, but two were particularly evident. The first was the influence of the Buddhist priesthood, especially from Mandalay. In Burma itself, the priesthood was numerous and powerful; it had been brought largely under the influence of the anti-British political party, and consequently preached the doctrine of Burma for the Burmese and complete independence. Many efforts were being made to counteract this, and were partially successful. Apparently, in the Shan States, the native rulers had kept a tighter control over the Buddhist priests than we did in Burma proper, and had limited their numbers.

The second reason was the anti-Indian feeling. The Indians in Burma were much more clever than the Burmese in business transactions, and, amongst other things, lent money out on mortgage, with the result that they owned a large proportion—about one-half—of the best agricultural land in Burma. We were looked upon to some extent as protectors of the Indians, and consequently attracted to ourselves part of the hatred that was felt by the Burmese for the Indians over this land problem.

Transfer of Command to Commander-in-Chief, India.

29. On the 12th December a telegram was received from the Chiefs of Staff stating that the defence of Burma was to be transferred from Commander-in-Chief, Far East, to Commander-in-Chief, India, including all relations with China. The transfer was effected as from 0630 hours on the 15th December, 1941.

IV.—FACTORS AFFECTING THE DEFENCE OF HONG KONG.

Authorities.

30. In November 1940, General Norton was Acting Governor of Hong Kong. Sir Geoffrey Northcote resumed his post as Governor on the 13th March, 1941, and handed over to his successor, Sir Mark Young, on the 10th September, 1941. Major General Maltby took over the duties of General Officer Commanding from Major-General Grasett on the 19th July, 1941.

General Policy.

31. Hong Kong was regarded officially as an undesirable military commitment, or else as an outpost to be held as long as possible. It must, however, be considered in relation to the whole defence of the Far East, especially China and the Philippines. The withdrawal of our troops from Peking, Tientsin and Shanghai in the summer of 1941 after the collapse of France was recognised by General Chiang Kai-shek and the Chinese as being an inevitable and wise move, but the Chinese interest in the defence of Hong Kong grew as their war developed and their difficulties increased. Hong Kong was very valuable to China as a port of access and had they not been convinced of our determination to stand and fight for its defence, and been taken into our confidence and given opportunities to inspect the defences and discuss plans for defence, the effect on their war effort would in all probability have been serious. A withdrawal of the troops in Hong Kong coinciding with the closing of the Burma Road might have had a marked effect on Chinese determination to fight on. Our policy for the defence of Hong Kong, therefore, in all probability played an important part at a critical period in China's war effort.

As regards the Philippines, according to information available in Singapore, it was doubtful, at any rate up to the middle of 1941, whether the Americans intended to defend the islands, or whether they did not. It is therefore possible, that had we demilitarised Hong Kong, or announced our intention of not defending it, the Americans might have adopted a similar policy with regard to the Philippines. In this case, they might have ceased to take direct interest in the Far East, and confined themselves to the Eastern half of the Pacific. Should this supposition be correct, then the attempted defence of Hong Kong was justified for this reason alone, even though it did ultimately lead to the loss of six battalions and other troops.

Strength of Defences.

32. The strength of the Hong Kong garrison is given in Appendix H. The official period for which Hong Kong was to be provisioned, both in military stores and food reserves, was 130 days.

The main defence of Hong Kong was on the Island. Whilst the enemy were to be delayed as long as possible in any advance over the leased territory on the mainland, the troops had orders to retire if attacked in force, as they were required for the defence of the Island itself. The Gin Drinkers line was naturally a strong one, and much work had been done on it, but it would have required two divisions or more to hold properly.

Two Canadian battalions arrived in Hong Kong on the 16th November, 1941. This extra force was of greater value than the figures would indicate. Whilst there were only four battalions in Hong Kong, only one could be spared for the Gin Drinkers line, which practically meant merely a thin outpost line. As this battalion was also essential for the defence of Hong Kong Island, it would not have been able to put up any resistance, but would have had to retire before the advance of even a weak force, since heavy casualties would prejudice the defence of the Island, and could not be faced. With the arrival of these two Canadian battalions, three could be put into the Gin Drinkers line, and a far stronger resistance could be put up, not merely because of the increased strength, but because casualties would not cripple the subsequent defence of Hong Kong Island. Even a few days' delay in the occupation of the mainland by the enemy was of great value, enabling steps to be completed which it was impracticable to take before the outbreak of war, for instance, the movement of the fishing fleet and waterborne population out of Hong Kong waters.

33. A great deal of work had been done in preparing the island for defence, and the construction and concealment of pill-boxes and obstacles showed much originality and initiative. Preparations were also made for offensive operations against islands near Hong Kong, should the Japanese seize them, and for "left-behind" parties on the mainland. Every advantage was taken of any local resources available for defence.

34. There were two Walrus amphibians and four Vildebeeste aeroplanes at Hong Kong, located at Kai Tak aerodrome on the mainland. The former might have been of some value for reconnaissance; in war it had been intended to operate them from Aberdeen Harbour, on the South side of Hong Kong Island, but this was apparently found impracticable. The latter would have had to remain at Kai Tak since no possible site for an aerodrome could be found on the Island itself. It was realised that these aeroplanes could not last for long in time of war, and that the Kai Tak aerodrome would, in fact, be quite unusable unless the Gin Drinkers line could be held.

Civil Population Factors.

35. One of the main problems in the defence of Hong Kong was the large Chinese population. This had nearly doubled during the three years previous to December 1941, owing to the influx from China. The population in April 1941 was—

Hong Kong	709,000
Kowloon	581,000
Water population	154,000
Total	1,444,000

This is exclusive of the population of what is known as the New Territories on the mainland.

The great increase above the normal population led to many problems, e.g., civil hospital accommodation and medical staff, police control, supply of water, food and firewood. In addition, this increase, combined with the constant movement taking place between the Island and the mainland, rendered it very difficult to keep complete control of the Chinese, and made it easy for the Japanese to acquire information.

36. The reservoirs on Hong Kong Island were partly filled by rain water and partly by a supply from the mainland. It was, of course, realised that this latter supply might be cut, calculations showed that the rain, added to the capacity of the reservoirs, was normally sufficient to meet the essential requirements of Hong Kong Island, so long as the whole Island remained in our hands. If there was a dry spell during the winter, the supply might have been short in February and March, and there might not have been sufficient to supply water to deal with outbreaks of fire. Although fire engines could draw on sea water, the higher levels of the town of Victoria could not be reached in one lift. This difficulty was largely overcome, however, by the installation of service tanks at medium levels, which it was intended to keep filled with sea water by separate pumps.

37. As regards food, rice was a constant anxiety, since most of it had to be imported from Siam or Burma. In addition, what was known as the rice supplement was a problem, since fish would not be available in case of war, and storage of alternatives over a period of months was difficult. In December 1941 the stocks of food were not much short of that required for the period laid down, *i.e.*, 130 days. The local supply of firewood was insufficient, and some was being imported from North Borneo.

38. The A.R.P. organisation in Hong Kong was good, and some 12,000 A.R.P. workers of one sort or another had been enrolled before war broke out. In addition, tunnels were made into the granite hills behind the town of Victoria; these provided admirable shelters which should have been proof against any type of bomb. The limitation here was the number of pneumatic drills that could be obtained to enable the necessary blasting to be carried out. It was a slow process but by the time war broke out there was shelter accommodation in the tunnels, concrete splinter-proof shelters and strengthened houses for about 300,000. Provision was made for the movement of the balance to hutments outside the town.

39. Most of the European women and children had been moved away from Hong Kong by July 1941, the total leaving being approximately 1,680 women and children belonging to the Navy, Army or Air Force, and 1,824 civilian. This left about 918 European women and girls in Hong Kong. Of these, 595 were nurses and medical staff, 60 held key duties in A.R.P. and the majority of the remaining 263 were employed in clerical and other duties. The Governor's order for the movement of women and children away from Hong Kong had been disputed, but was upheld in a test case in the courts.

V.—Problems and Work of General Headquarters, Far East.

Site of General Headquarters.

40. General Headquarters started to function at 0800 hours on Monday, the 18th November. The order issued to the three General Officers Commanding and the Air Officer Commanding outlining their relations to General Headquarters is given in Appendix B.

One of the first problems I had to decide was the site of my Headquarters. The Army Headquarters was at Fort Canning and the Air Force Headquarters was in newly-built hutments about five miles away. The Governor and other civil authorities were in Singapore town. The Naval Commander-in-Chief had his Headquarters at the Naval Base, which was some 35 minutes by road from Singapore. It was important for my Headquarters to keep in touch with all these. I hoped at one time that the Commander-in-Chief, China, would move to Singapore, but he felt very strongly that he had to remain in the Naval Base, where the F.E.C.B. was also located. A compromise might have been possible but would have entailed dividing F.E.C.B. After much consideration, I decided that the dominant factors were to ensure close touch with the Commander-in-Chief, China, and to keep the F.E.C.B. intact. Accordingly, my Headquarters moved to the Naval Base in January, 1941, but I continued to reside in Singapore, which enabled me to have interviews with the General Officer Commanding, Air Officer Commanding and the Governor, either before I went to the office or on my return. This was not a perfect solution, but it was the best one in all the circumstances.

Another factor which influenced me in coming to this decision was the danger of my Headquarters becoming intimately involved in the defence of Malaya if I remained at Singapore, to the neglect of the wider problems of the defence of the Far East.

Relations with Commander-in-Chief, China Station.

41. From about June 1941 onwards an intelligence conference was held at ten o'clock every morning, and was attended by the Commander-in-Chief, China, and myself, and our senior staff officers. Generally speaking, the division of responsibilities was clear, and in other cases they were divided up without any difficulty. The Commander-in-Chief, China, had been dealing with Free French problems, and continued to do so after my Headquarters was formed. As our relations with French Indo-China were largely concerned with economics and shipping, he dealt with most of the problems of that country, whilst my Headquarters dealt mainly with Siam. He also agreed to take over responsibility for control of the Press and continued to do so up to the beginning of December, when Sir Tom Phillips arrived and I took over this responsibility.

Other questions, such as food supplies, we dealt with together. In this case also shipping was largely involved, and as the Commander-in-Chief, China, had a representative on the Food Committee, he generally represented our combined views at meetings of the War Committee.

The Commander-in-Chief, China, took over from me the control of the Miri oil denial scheme. This was found more convenient since the problems of oil supply were more closely connected with the Navy than with the Army or Air Force, and the evacuation of both material and personnel from Miri was essentially a Naval matter.

Agreement was reached in regard to surface sea patrols near the coast, and it was decided that the Naval authorities would be responsible for patrolling in the open sea and the Army would be responsible for similar work on the rivers. One or two estuaries were dealt with as special cases, but generally came under the Naval authorities.

Conferences at Singapore.

42. Many conferences were held in Singapore both before and after the formation of General Headquarters, Far East. These were as follows:—

(*a*) The Franco-British Conference held in June 1939. The report of this conference contained some useful observations on the general problems, but the basic assumption of active French collaboration from Indo-China vanished with the collapse of France.

(*b*) The Singapore Conference of October, 1940, with which should be included the Tactical Appreciation dated the 16th October, 1940, prepared by the Commander-in-Chief, China Station, the General Officer Commanding, Malaya, and the Air Officer Commanding, Far East. (*See paras. 79 and 90 below.*)

(*c*) The conversations with the Dutch in December 1940, the principal object being to obtain information and agreement on certain matters raised in Appendix A of the Report of the Singapore Conference.

(*d*) The Conference between British, Dutch and Australian representatives, with United States observers in attendance, held in Singapore in February 1941, resulting in what is known as the A.D.A. agreement. This agreement included plans for mutual reinforcements, principally of air forces and submarines. (*See para. 44 below.*)

(*e*) The Conference between the Americans, Dutch and British, including Australia and New Zealand, together with representatives of India and the East Indies Station. This was held at Singapore in April 1941, and resulted in what is known as the A.D.B. agreement. (*See para. 45 below.*) It was followed by a shorter agreement between the British and the Dutch, which dealt almost entirely with Naval matters, and was really a modification of the agreement reached in A.D.A., bringing the latter into line with A.D.B. It was known as B.D.

(*f*) Arising out of A.D.B., a detailed plan for naval and air operations, known as Plenaps was drawn up.

No political commitment was involved by these agreements, and A.D.A. and A.D.B. remained subject to ratification by the respective Governments.

43. In the case of the conference leading to the A.D.A. and A.D.B. agreements, I felt that the representation was somewhat unbalanced. In the former, the Naval representation of the Dominions was weak since the Chief of the Naval Staff in Australia, Admiral Colvin, was unable to come, and New Zealand was represented by Australia. In the A.D.B. Conference, the Naval representation was strong but that of the Dominion Army and Air Force was comparatively weak. Further, in A.D.B. the United States representatives were somewhat junior, and there was no representative of the Pacific Fleet, but only of the Asiatic.

44. In A.D.A. the necessity for collective action was emphasised, it being pointed out that Japanese aggression against any one country would be of vital importance to the others. Agreement was reached on the particular actions by Japan which would necessitate the Naval and Military authorities concerned advising their respective Governments to take active military counter-action. A suggestion was made that Commanders-in-Chief on the spot might be allowed to take measures in such circumstances without prior reference to London.

The principle of mutual reinforcement was agreed, the Dutch undertaking to provide submarines for operation in the South China Sea, as well as one Fighter and three bomber squadrons to reinforce Malaya; whilst it was estimated that four Bomber squadrons would be available from Malaya to reinforce the Netherlands East Indies. Australia was prepared to assist by the provision of Army units, and of an air striking force at Darwin to reinforce Ambon and Koepang. The necessary administrative arrangements to prepare for these land and air reinforcements were to be undertaken at once, and progress reports were to be rendered monthly to G.H.Q., Far East. The principles on which sea communications would be defended were outlined, and emphasis was laid on the importance of making the passage of the Northern line of the Dutch possessions as difficult as possible for the Japanese.

The A.D.A. report was approved generally by the Chiefs of Staff, the main exception being that there could be no prior definition of an act of war and automatic reaction without reference to London.

45. In the A.D.B. report it was stressed that the Atlantic and Europe were the decisive theatres of war, so that the forces employed in other theatres must be reduced to a minimum. Our main strategy in the Far East for the time must, therefore, be defensive, but it was recommended that preparations should be made for air operations against Japanese-occupied territory and against Japan herself, both from China and from Luzon.

The necessity for collective action was re-affirmed as well as the particular actions by Japan which would necessitate the Commanders concerned advising their respective Governments to take active military counter-action. The importance of Luzon, especially from the offensive point of view, was emphasised, and a recommendation made that its defence should be strengthened. It was suggested in this connection that Hong Kong might be of value as a subsidiary base. It was also recommended that the British and U.S.A. should support the Chinese Army, especially with finance and equipment, should assist the guerilla operations in China, and organise subversive activity in Japan and Japanese-occupied territories.

It was recommended that the Commander-in-Chief, China Station, should exercise strategical direction over all Naval forces, excluding those employed solely on local defence or operating under Commander-in-Chief, United States Asiatic Fleet. Similarly, it was recommended that the Commander-in-Chief, Far East, should exercise strategical direction of the air forces in the Far East. The areas of responsibility were defined. The basis of a plan for Naval and air co-operation, both as regards reinforcements and reconnaissance, was laid down. This included the movement of surface vessels of the United States Asiatic Fleet from Manila to Singapore if the former were attacked, and the despatch of two or more Dutch submarines to the South China Sea, all operating under the Commander-in-Chief, China.

For purposes of planning, the air forces available for mutual reinforcement were assumed to be:—

From Malaya: 4 bomber squadrons;
From Netherlands East Indies: 3 bomber and 1 fighter squadrons;
From Philippines: all available, but in case of evacuation only; and
From Australia: 2 bomber squadrons for the Ambon-Timor Area.

In telegraphic comments by the Commanders-in-Chief, Far East and China, two points were specially stressed: first, the great importance to the defence of the Far East of offensive operations by the United States Pacific Fleet, a point that was deliberately omitted from the report; and, secondly, the importance of strengthening the defences of Luzon.

The A.D.B. report was, with one or two exceptions, approved by the Chiefs of Staff in London. The exceptions were that, whilst they would welcome any strengthening of the Philippines which could be effected otherwise than at the expense of the United States effort in the Atlantic, they were not prepared to press the point in the United States: and that Hong Kong was unlikely to be of much value as an advanced base for operations by United States submarines and naval aircraft against the Japanese sea communications.

But, although signed by the representatives of the United States, the report was objected to in Washington, mainly on the ground that certain political matters had been introduced. An amended A.D.B. agreement, known as A.D.B. 2, was therefore drawn up in London in August 1941, leaving all the main features of A.D.B. practically unchanged, but putting the political matters into an appendix. This, however, did not entirely satisfy the United States authorities in Washington, and eventually it was decided that a further conference should be held in the Far East to draw up a modified A.D.B. This information was conveyed to me on the 25th November, 1941, but was received too late for any action to be taken before war started.

In spite of this, A.D.B. and Plenaps remained the basis on which we were able to work before, and immediately after, the outbreak of war with Japan, both with the Netherlands East Indies and, to a lesser degree, with the Philippines. (*But see para.* 111 *below*.)

Information from London.

46. I found on arrival in the Far East that there was considerable ignorance of modern war conditions, both in the Army and the Air Force. This could not, of course, be made good entirely by documents; personal experience was essential.

For some months after the formation of my General Headquarters there seemed to be considerable delay in getting information from England with regard to the lessons of recent operations and developments in tactical ideas, both as regards the Army and the Air Force, though A.R.P. pamphlets seemed to arrive regularly soon after issue. The situation improved about July, 1941, but we were always uncertain whether we were being kept up to date. This feeling of being neglected was naturally intensified by the distance of London from Singapore, and the whole position in this respect would have been greatly improved if visits by liaison officers from the War Office and Air Ministry had been made from time to time. This was actually started in the case of the War Office, and the first liaison officer arrived in Singapore in November, 1941. I believe it was intended to do the same in the case of the Air Ministry. It would have been a great help had this been done twelve months earlier.

Training.

47. As regards training, steps were taken to ensure that troops were thoroughly acquainted with the nature of the country in which they would have to operate. This was simple in the case of Hong Kong, where units knew exactly the ground over which they were going to fight. It was more difficult in the case of Malaya, as the nature of the country varied considerably, but here special attention was paid to movements through jungle and the acquisition of jungle lore, and many units reached a high stage of proficiency in this. The Volunteers in Malaya were called up for training during February and March 1941.

Apart from minor Staff Exercises, two were carried out under General Headquarters: the first in December, 1940, to test out communications and co-operation between the Army and the Royal Air Force; and the second, a more ambitious one, in March, 1941, to test out all the stages of a change-over from peace to war for the civil authorities as well as for the three Services. This brought out many useful lessons.

A very successful exercise based on this second one was held in Burma in July, 1941, and Hong Kong carried out two or three on similar lines.

Defensive Preparations.

48. The question of the best method of defending the important sectors of the East Coast of Malaya gave rise to much discussion. One school of thought argued that, as there were insufficient numbers to defend any great length of beach, the enemy would be able to land outside the defended portion, thus out-flanking the defenders and possibly cutting them off. The best course of action was, therefore, to fight on a prepared position in rear where the road leading into the interior could be defended. This school also argued that attempts to hold the beaches would result in a purely linear defence with insufficient troops in hand for counter-attack.

The view of General Headquarters, Far East, was that it was essential to hold the beaches, because it was during the period of landing that the enemy would be most vulnerable, and if the beaches were given up he would be fighting on equality with us. Again, it was during this process of landing that our most effective co-operation between the Army and Air, and possibly the Navy as well, could be effected. Admittedly there was a danger of having a purely linear defence, but this was primarily a question of adjustment between the forces retained in reserve and those detailed for holding the beaches themselves.

Another point was that of all-round defence. It was difficult with the forces available to have units in a group of perimeter posts and at the same time to protect an adequate length of beach. Further, the defenders must be prepared to hold on for a period to be reckoned by weeks rather than by days, even if surrounded by the enemy and cut off. There was but little object in this unless adequate reserves were available in rear to attack the enemy and restore the situation. The 22nd Australian Brigade at Mersing found a satisfactory solution to the problem in that they had perimeter defences for units, mutually supporting each other and primarily defending the beaches. But in their case the 27th Australian Brigade was available in Johore for counter-attack on a large scale. The problem was more difficult at Kuantan and Kota Bharu for the reasons indicated above. (*See para.* 12.)

Although it was my policy to allow the General Officers-in-Command as much freedom as possible, I found it necessary in the case of Malaya to issue orders that the first line of our defence was to be the beaches. Previously, except on Singapore Island and Penang, beaches were going to be occupied only by watching posts, and the first lines of defence were sited inland. This change involved a considerable amount of work and preparation of obstacles and defence posts at Mersing, Kuantan and Kota Bharu.

It was found at one period that the work of preparing positions and putting up obstacles was taking up so much time that the training of the troops was being hampered and, in addition, the wire generally required renewing after about six months. Also, I was always on guard against too much reliance upon water obstacles, barbed wire and pill-boxes, in case this should lead to a Maginot Line complex to the detriment of the offensive spirit. Consequently, a division of available hours was drawn up, allowing a proportion for training, a proportion for renewals, and the balance for new work. As far as practicable, troops constructed the actual defences in which they would normally fight. New works carried out included not only defensive preparations, but facilities for making counter-attacks, *e.g.*, preparation of hidden paths fit for Bren Carriers.

Looking back in the light of what actually happened, it is easy to point out that a lot of the preparation was wasted, and that the energy so taken up should have been expended elsewhere; for instance, a great deal of time was spent on the Mersing area, which was never heavily attacked. Mersing, however, was a very important place, and, had the Japanese established themselves here instead of at Kota Bharu, they would have been at once within a short distance of Singapore; and it is possible that, had these defences been less strong, they might have attacked the Mersing area at an early stage in the operations. I feel, however, that steps should have been taken before war broke out to strengthen the defences on the Northern and North-Western sides of Singapore Island.

49. We also had to be prepared for the possibility of a break-through in the Mersing area, which would have isolated Southern and Northern Malaya from Singapore, and this consideration affected the siting of depots for stores and ammunition. Therefore, preparations were made to enable a force to be supplied, if necessary, by a line of communication running through Kuala Lumpur to Penang, so that they would be able to operate quite independently of Singapore.

Another possibility that had to be considered was that of a sudden descent without warning on a part of Singapore Island with the object either of destroying some important place, such as the main wireless station, or of establishing a footing, awaiting subsequent reinforcements. This possibility was met by having a portion of the Singapore garrison ready to come into action and move at very short notice.

Operation "Matador."

50. The importance of the Southern end of the Kra Isthmus, especially the neighbourhood of Singora, has already been referred to (*see paragraph* 12 *above*). The possibility of an advance into this Isthmus, in order to hold a position North of Haad Yai Junction, was considered soon after the formation of General Headquarters, Far East. Detailed plans for carrying out this operation were prepared, and the code word "Matador" was eventually given to it. It was from the start realised that the essential feature of this operation was forestalling the Japanese on a position near Singora; see, for instance my telegram to the Chiefs of Staff through the War Office, in which it is stated: "The success of this plan would depend on rapidity of execution in order to forestall the Japanese on the Songhla line"; also my telegram from which the following is an extract: "I wish to emphasise the fact that the forestalling of the Japanese in Singora area is essential to the success of 'Matador.'"

This necessitated at least twenty-four hours' start before the Japanese landed, and rapid movement of our force once the order was given. It was realised all along that, if these conditions could not be fulfilled, then the Matador operation would be impracticable. The psychological value of offensive movement at the start of the war and the possibility of thereby upsetting the Japanese plans were fully realised, but had to be weighed against the fact that we should be leaving prepared ground with which the troops were familiar, and that, unless we forestalled the enemy, the fighting would be in the nature of an encounter battle, quite possibly against superior numbers. Further, the attitude of the Siamese was uncertain, and questions of secrecy precluded any attempt to get prior agreement from Bangkok. Orders were issued that, should Matador be ordered, any opposition from the Siamese was to be overcome at once, but we could never be certain in advance how much delay might be caused to our movements by obstacles, destruction of bridges or active resistance. A margin of time was necessary.

A total of thirty officers, two or three at a time, were sent over as visitors to the area in plain clothes in order to collect information, especially on the topography of the country, and to have some individuals familiar with it.

The preparations were completed before the Autumn of 1941 as far as could be foreseen, including maps, arrangements for the distribution of rice to the population, the collection of a quantity of Siamese money, and writing, ready for translation and printing, pamphlets of three varieties to suit the different attitudes which might be adopted by the Siamese Government. For reasons of secrecy, knowledge of the plans was confined to a minimum number of individuals, and for the same reason certain steps could not be taken in advance. For instance, it was considered dangerous to translate or print the pamphlets before the operation was ordered.

51. Up to the 5th December, Matador was not to be carried out without reference to the War Cabinet, but on that date a telegram was sent to the effect that I could order it without reference to London in either of the following contingencies:—

(a) If I had information that the Japanese expedition was advancing with the apparent intention of landing on the Kra Isthmus; or

(b) If the Japanese violated any other part of Thailand (Siam).

A few days earlier it had been impressed on me that carrying out Matador if the Japanese intended to make a landing in Southern Siam would almost certainly mean war with Japan, and in view of this I considered it my duty to be scrupulously careful in acting on the telegram of the 5th December.

Aerodrome Policy.

52. The number and location of aerodromes in Malaya was based on the principle of relying mainly on air power for defence. This also applied, though in a somewhat smaller degree to Burma.

It meant, first having a sufficient number of aerodromes to make use of the mobility of aircraft for concentrating a large proportion of our squadrons in any given area; and, secondly, choosing sites as far forward as practicable so as to enable us to reach out the maximum distance both for reconnaissance and for offensive operations. This was particularly important in the case of attacks on Japanese convoys in order to ensure having sufficient time to carry out more than one attack before they reached our coast.

The total number of aerodromes prepared was based on the figure of 336 Initial Equipment aircraft, and since this figure was never reached we had in some areas more aerodromes than we were able to use, the surplus being a liability rather than an asset. The forecasts of development of our air strength were admittedly uncertain, but in view of the long time taken to construct an aerodrome in Malaya we could not afford to wait until we knew definitely that more aircraft were coming. The Army dispositions were largely influenced by the necessity for protecting Royal Air Force aerodromes. As events turned out, owing to the weakness of the Royal Air Force at the time war started, the defence of Malaya devolved largely upon the Army, which meant that sites for aerodromes were not always the most suitable for operations as they were actually carried out. But it was impossible to have foreseen this, since no one could have known in advance when the Japanese would start the war.

In the autumn of 1941, orders were issued that four of the aerodromes in Malaya and two in Burma were to be extended so as to be suitable for the operation of heavy bombers up to the Boeing Fortress type. This meant runways of 2,000 yards with a surface sufficiently strong to bear the weight of these aircraft fully loaded.

Sufficient attention was not always given to the tactical siting of aerodromes from the point of view of their defence. There was rather a tendency at one time to site them solely with reference to their suitability for flying operations; and in one or two cases they were located too near the coast where they were a definite danger so long as the Japanese had command of the sea. This, however, was corrected, and it was laid down that no aerodrome was to be selected or planned except in conjunction with the staff officer of the Army organisation concerned, a principle also applied to the siting of buildings and aircraft pens. The buildings on some of the original aerodromes in Malaya had been laid out entirely on a peace basis, for they were not dispersed and were in straight lines; this was noticeably the case at Alor Star.

53. We learned a lesson from the Dutch as regards the siting of aerodromes. In Borneo, the communications of which were undeveloped, they worked on the principle of locating aerodromes 25 to 50 miles from the coast in jungle country with only one line of access, generally a road, but sometimes a river. This, of course, considerably simplified the problem of defence against overland attacks. It was practicable only to a limited extent in Malaya, but it was laid down that any future aerodromes required in Sarawak and other parts of British Borneo would be sited on this principle.

Aircraft Warning System.

54. There was no air observation system in Malaya when I arrived, and its organisation entailed a large amount of work. The responsibility was at first placed upon the G.O.C. and was later transferred to the A.O.C. Some R.D.F. sets were received during 1941, and before war broke out an air observation system was working well as regards Southern Malaya and Singapore; it was not good up North, partly owing to the lack of depth from the frontier and partly because we had not sufficient R.D.F. sets to install any in the North. Communications were difficult the whole time.

as we were short generally of signalling equipment, especially material for the construction of land lines; but the Government Post and Telegraph Service was most helpful, and war experience proved that so long as the Japanese were kept out of Southern Malaya, Singapore could always rely on half an hour's warning of hostile aircraft. This was, of course, reduced after the Japanese advance had forced us to leave certain R.D.F. stations.

Other Matters that Required Action.

55. Some special camouflage officers having been sent out from England in the late summer of 1941, a Camouflage Committee was set up in Malaya and camouflage classes formed in Malaya for the Far East. Priority in camouflage work was given to the Naval Base and aerodromes, but work was also being done for civilian establishments which were important to the war effort. All this involved a period of years rather than months and was by no means complete when war broke out.

The formation of Army Labour Units in Malaya was a matter that was delayed for various reasons. Finally, however, it was decided to recruit Chinese in Hong Kong, which had the advantage not only of getting labour, but also of reducing the Chinese population of Hong Kong, but, unfortunately, the project was not executed before war broke out.

Arrangements were made for successive variations in the route to be followed by civil aircraft between Australia and India in the event of war with Japan.

56. In December, 1940, there was a serious deficiency in ammunition, especially for the 4.5 and 3.7 A.A. guns, and in reserves for ordnance stores which were only sufficient for 90 days instead of 180. Anti-tank weapons and mines, 3-inch mortars and ammunition were also short.

Aircraft bombs at this time were also quite insufficient to allow for the expected expansion, and up to the autumn of 1941, .5 ammunition for the Buffaloes was difficult to obtain in adequate quantity.

By December, 1941, some of these deficiencies had been made good. (*See paragraph 92 below.*)

57. Although the Government Post and Telegraph Service was responsible for the communications on the mainland of Malaya, the lines on Singapore Island were mainly in the hands of a private company known as O.T.E.C. This caused some difficulties, *e.g.*, as regards maintenance of stocks of spares. But it was decided that the situation in 1941 was not suitable for making the big changes that would have been involved had the Government taken over this company.

58. I found the Malayan War Committee was not on a satisfactory basis; though the proceedings were recorded in the relevant files, there were no formal minutes, so it was often difficult at a meeting to find out quickly what had been decided previously or who was responsible for taking action. This was corrected, a new Secretary for Defence was appointed, and three civilians were brought into the War Committee with good results. The Commander-in-Chief, China, and I were not members of this War Committee, but had a permanent invitation from the Governor to attend meetings.

Press Relations.

59. It was realised in the Spring of 1941 that some organisation to deal with the Press would be necessary when war broke out, and, further, that it would be important before war during periods of strained relations with Japan. As a result of a conference attended by all concerned, an organisation was worked out and brought into operation in the middle of May, 1941. The essential feature of it was that the Press relations of all three Services were grouped under one head. As has been stated above (in paragraph 41), Commander-in-Chief, China, agreed to be responsible for Press relations, and a Commander, R.N., who was called up from the Reserve, was put at the head of the Services Press Bureau. I was, and still am, of the opinion that this organisation was workable. Unfortunately, there were some discordant personalities, and, finally, after war broke out, a somewhat different organisation was adopted, with Sir George Sansom at the head.

I always found the Press ready to help when they were asked (*see, for instance, paragraph 110 below*) and on many occasions we got good value from them. On the other hand, some representatives of the Press of other countries were difficult and required very tactful handling; and we were undoubtedly hampered in the Far East through lack of officers experienced in dealing with the Press.

Complaints reached the Ministry of Information in London that Press correspondents were not being properly treated; in my reply to one that was passed on to Singapore I stated: " Should be most grateful for any assistance you can give to assure that we get out here officers who have knowledge of the work and can be trusted to work loyally as a team and not for their own individual benefit." I feel that in this matter we should have had more help from England, principally in the way of suitable and experienced personnel from the beginning.

I was reluctant to give Press interviews, but the importance of doing so from time to time was frequently intimated to me. There was one stock question I was frequently asked: " Was I satisfied with the strength of the defences of Malaya or the Far East generally? " I always gave the same reply, that I was never going to be satisfied because defensive preparations could always be improved, and, so far as I could, I was not going to allow any of my subordinates to be satisfied either.

60. One of the steps taken to discourage the Japanese from starting war was to emphasise the growing strength of our defences in Malaya. (*See paragraph 5 (a) above.*) The Chiefs of Staff stated in May, 1941, that they saw no objection to this policy and we were aided by directions from the Ministry of Information in London to their representative in Singapore. The method adopted did not consist merely in extensive advertising of any reinforcements; sometimes when these were obvious they were given only a small notice in the papers or broadcast. On the other hand, when reinforcements of Royal Air Force personnel arrived they were merely referred to as Royal Air Force and no mention was made of the fact that no aeroplanes were with them. It is doubtful if the effect was great, but it was probably not negligible.

In interviews with Press correspondents whom I could trust, I made no secret of the fact that the shortage of aeroplanes caused me great anxiety, but warned them that they were on no account to mention it in their papers. A similar attitude was adopted with regard to tanks, of which we had none when war broke out.

Meeting with British Far East Representatives.

61. At the end of September 1941, Sir Earle Page from Australia, the British Ambassador in Chungking Sir A. Clark Kerr, and the British Minister in Bangkok Sir J. Crosby, were all in Singapore. The opportunity was taken to have a combined meeting together with Mr. Duff Cooper and the Governor of Malaya in order that the two Commanders-in-Chief might discuss with them all the situation in the Far East. A report was sent to the Chiefs of Staff.

The meeting agreed generally with the views expressed by the Commander-in-Chief, China, and myself, that Japan's principal asset in the Far East was her foothold in Indo-China, which might be developed as a springboard from which to attack Malaya. Further, that Japan must be anxious to avoid war in the South for the next few months so the time was opportune for bringing pressure to bear on her to withdraw from Indo-China.

The meeting emphasised that, in the absence of a British fleet based at Singapore, there was little doubt that Japan could strike at her selected moment and stressed the propaganda value of even one or two battleships at Singapore. Various steps were recommended, including the following:—

The issue of a co-ordinated announcement by the British, United States and Dutch Governments that they had a combined plan for action in the event of a Japanese move against any of their interests in the Far East;

Urging the United States to reinforce the Philippines, especially with submarines and air forces;

Development of our aid to, and plans for operations in, China; and

Liaison with Russian forces in the Far East.

VI.—CIVIL DEFENCE PROBLEMS IN MALAYA.

Food and Water.

62. On my arrival in Singapore I found a large number of Civil Defence matters requiring attention. As regards food supplies, a six-months' supply for the whole population, as well as for the Navy, Army and Air Force, had been laid down as the minimum requirement. Rice was a constant source of anxiety. The yield of rice in Malaya was insufficient for the whole population, and so some had to be imported mainly from Burma, and this again was naturally dependent on shipping. As soon as the year's crop was gathered, stocks were plentiful, but the consumption was large and required constant watching. There was difficulty over the storage of rice for more than six months, but this had been solved by the introduction of the method of mixing a small proportion of lime with the rice, which, so far as tests went, preserved it for two years without deterioration. There was also the problem of the distribution of rice, some of the States producing an excess of their own requirements. The custom had been to store this surplus on the spot, and at one time there was some 50,000 tons of rice stored as far North as Alor Star. By the time war broke out, however, distribution was satisfactory.

On two occasions, the War Committee decided that a scheme of food rationing in time of war must be prepared. Committees were formed to carry this out, but on both occasions reported that the difficulties were so great that food rationing was impracticable; and, on one occasion, that if it was necessary from the military point of view, it was up to the military to prepare a scheme. The position was certainly complicated, but I did not believe that the difficulties were insurmountable.

The main source of supply for the water reservoirs on Singapore Island was from the mainland of Johore. It was realised that this might be cut, and the matter was investigated on my arrival. The result of this investigation showed that the rainfall was sufficient, with certain additional water mains, to supply enough water to meet the requirements of the whole of the anticipated population of the island, except that water-borne sanitation would have to be stopped. The necessary steps were taken. A sea-water fire service already existed for part of Singapore City.

Air Raid Precautions.

63. A.R.P. in Singapore had started, and before war broke out I was satisfied that the organisation, as regards fire precautions, demolition squads, rescue parties and first aid, was good. Up to the time I handed over command, A.R.P. functioned well, with one exception. (*See para.* 99 *below.*) Up-country, progress was somewhat slower.

Black-out in Malaya was difficult. Owing to the construction of most of the houses, complete black-out meant shutting off most of the ventilation, which was extremely disagreeable in Malayan climate. Consequently, when black-out was enforced it meant most people living either in darkness or in physical discomfort. In consequence, a system was introduced of having a "brown-out," a black-out being enforced as soon as warning was received of the actual approach of hostile aircraft. The brown-out allowed a certain amount of light, sufficient with care to read by without closing up the room. In my opinion, this worked satisfactorily.

64. The provision of air raid shelters in Singapore was insufficient for the total population, but the construction of these was not a simple matter. The water-level was near the surface, so that in most places the digging of trenches was not only useless, but dangerous because they soon became filled with water and formed breeding places for mosquitoes. Many of the streets were narrow, and there was little room for the building of shelters. Quite apart from the blocking of traffic, the medical authorities definitely advised against the building of shelters in streets, on the ground that the circulation of air would thereby be stopped, thus leading to epidemics.

On the other hand, many of the streets of Singapore had footpaths covered over by the first floors of the buildings, which were supported by pillars from the outside. Provided the houses were of fairly solid construction, filling up the spaces between the pillars with stone or bricks afforded a good type of air-raid shelter. Where none could be constructed, the policy was to provide accommodation in open spaces outside the town, where it was expected that the population would move as soon as bombing started. Compulsory evacuation was not enforced.

Denial Schemes and Evacuation.

65. A denial scheme was prepared early in 1941 for the event of an invasion of Malaya, and necessary instructions issued. This scheme was directed principally to the destruction or removal of everything that might facilitate the movement of invading forces. It included such things as the removal of food stocks, or their dispersal amongst the villages, the destruction of any form of repair workshop, as well as the demolition of bridges and the removal or destruction of all forms of vehicle or boat. The plan did not envisage a complete " scorched earth " policy. (*See para.* 119 *below.*) For instance, in the case of tin mines it was only laid down that essential parts of the machinery of dredges were to be removed and brought away. A plan for the denial of British-owned tin mines in the Kra Isthmus was also worked out by the O.M. Section of the Ministry of Economic Warfare, including arrangements with Commander-in-Chief, China, for the evacuation of British personnel by sea after the denial scheme had been carried out.

66. Originally, civil officials were ordered to remain at their posts in the event of invasion. This, however, was modified in December 1941, enabling those who were suitable, physically and otherwise, for service with military units to be withdrawn, so that they could be used for defence. This also applied to a proportion of the civil medical staff.

67. The problem of British families in Singapore and Malaya generally was somewhat involved. In the case of the Navy, families were permitted for those stationed ashore, *i.e.*, officers in the light cruisers were not allowed to bring their families out to Singapore. In the Army and Air Force, families were allowed in those units which were considered to be the permanent garrison in Singapore, which in practice meant the units existing before September 1939. Units which arrived since that date were counted as reinforcements, and families were not allowed in their case. This gave rise to anomalies, because some of the units, *e.g.*, Headquarters, Malaya Command, and the Royal Air Force Depot at Seletar, had expanded very considerably since September 1939, although they were still counted as part of the permanent garrison. In the case of the families of civil officials and civilians there were no restrictions. Apart from 50 W.R.N.S. at the Naval Wireless Station and a number of nurses, many women were employed in the different services for clerical, cipher and other duties, including intelligence work in F.E.C.B. Had all these been sent away, it would have meant a large increase in the number of men absorbed. As it was, we were short of women to fill suitable posts and thus relieve men for the fighting units.

On the other hand, the presence of large numbers of women and children led, in January 1942, to hurried evacuation, with consequent loss of personal belongings and discomfort, and, later, to casualties. (*See para.* 121 *below.*)

Service and Civilian Communities.

68. Relations between the Services and civilian communities were better up-country than in Singapore.

The view held in the Colonial Office was that rubber and tin output was of greater importance than the training of the local forces; for instance, a telegram, dated the 31st December, 1940, to the Governor, states: " The ultimate criterion for exemption should be not what the General Officer Commanding considers practicable, but what you consider essential to maintain the necessary production and efficient labour management.".

Attitude of Non-British Population.

69. With regard to the other races in Malaya, the most numerous were the Chinese. Many of them had no particular roots in Malaya. There was difficulty in filling the Chinese companies of the Volunteers up to establishment, nor could we get a sufficient number of Chinese motor drivers. This may have been partly the fault of the British, and there was not sufficient contact between the British and the leading men of the Chinese community. My experience of the Chinese under air bombing was that they were calm, and with no tendency to panic.

There were several thousand Indian labourers in Malaya, mostly Tamils, who worked on the rubber estates. So long as they were kept free from agitators, these Tamils were a law-abiding community.

Some probable fifth columnists were marked down at Kuala Lumpur and rounded up at the start of the war, but there was very little fifth column work or treachery. There was no difficulty in recruiting for the two battalions of the Malay Regiment, and young Malays who had been specially trained in technical schools worked well in the aircraft maintenance unit on Singapore Island, and were not unduly worried by bombing.

VII.—NEIGHBOURING COUNTRIES.

China.

70. The late Major-General Dennys was appointed Military Attaché in Chungking shortly after my arrival in Singapore, with the intention that, when war with Japan broke out, he would become head of the British Military Mission with the Chinese, this being known as 204 Mission. Chiefly owing to his work, seconded by Wing-Commander Warburton and backed by the Ambassador, Sir A. Clark Kerr, our relations with the Chinese were very satisfactory, and considerable progress was made in plans for co-operation, and, to some degree, in their execution.

Co-operation as regards air consisted mainly in the preparation of aerodrome sites and the dispatch to China of stocks of aviation petrol and, finally, bombs, all for British squadrons which it was hoped to send up later. (*See para.* 26 *above.*) The aerodrome sites were in three groups: the first in the area north and west of Kunming, the object of which was largely to protect the Burma Road; the second, an area north of Hong Kong, from which it was hoped to assist in the defence of that place; and the third, an area further east, from which it was hoped that one day it might be possible to deliver air attacks on Japan. It was only in the first group that these preparations could be called complete when war broke out. Transport was one of the main difficulties, and it was not until the 13th November, 1941, that permission was given to send up bombs. The petrol and bombs were consigned to the Chinese, who took charge of them.

71. The second form of assistance to China was with their guerillas. It was agreed that fifteen special Chinese guerilla companies should be formed initially, and that each should have a squad of fifteen British and Indian personnel attached to it. These squads would be specially trained in the use of explosives and in carrying out demolitions, and would be kept supplied by us with the necessary material. It was proposed eventually to double the number of guerilla companies, and consequently of the squads. These squads went through a thorough training in Burma, including living under the conditions they would experience when operating with the Chinese guerillas.

72. The whole organisation for the supply to the aerodromes and to the guerilla squads was based on Burma. It was known first as Chi Base and later as Tulip. Lieutenant-Colonel McFeat was in charge; his own headquarters were at Rangoon, the training of guerilla squads was carried out at Maymyo, and stores of all sorts were sent up to Lashio and to Bhamo. A mechanical transport organisation for forwarding stores and supplies was in progress, but by no means complete in vehicles by the 7th December. Signalling and medical facilities were deficient for most of the guerilla squads. Tulip was directly under my headquarters till war with Japan broke out, when it was transferred, as planned, to General Officer Commanding, Burma.

73. On their part, the Chinese promised not only to help in the defence of Burma with the American Volunteer Group (see para. 25 above), but also to send troops to Burma if required, and to threaten the Japanese northern flank should they advance against Burma via Chieng Rai. They also promised to help in the defence of Hong Kong by an advance towards Canton.

They kept their promises.

74. A Chinese Military Mission visited Burma and Singapore in April and May, 1941, and various Chinese officers also paid visits individually, including General Mow, of the Chinese Air Force, who was in Singapore from the 19th to the 25th June, 1941, and stayed in my house. Certain members of my staff visited Chungking.

Siam and Indo-China.

75. The dominating factor influencing the actions of the Siamese authorities was fear. Our attitude towards the Siamese was governed by the desire to keep on as friendly terms as possible, and to encourage them to resist any encroachment by Japan. The latter was somewhat difficult because it was quite impracticable for us to take any effective military action to prevent Japanese penetration of Siam. Further, as the Siamese quite rightly pointed out, they were very short of equipment, especially aircraft and anti-aircraft, tank and anti-tank, so that, if they could not get help from us or the United States, there was little they could do but to comply with Japanese demands. Definite proposals were made in October, 1941, for giving the Siamese a few weapons, but nothing was actually sent.

It was suggested in March, 1941, that we should adopt a strong line with the Siamese. It is, however, at least doubtful whether, if we had done so, the Siamese would have been willing or able to render any effective aid when the Japanese attacked their country. As events turned out, in spite of statements by the Siamese Prime Minister, the resistance offered by the Siamese for us lasted only a few hours at Battambang on the frontier east of Bangkok, whereas British troops advancing into Southern Siam were opposed by the Siamese after the Japanese had landed.

76. At the time of my arrival in Singapore, the Japanese had troops in Tongking, at the northern end of Indo-China. This in itself was no direct threat to Burma or Malaya. To some extent it was a threat to the Chinese section of the road from Burma to China, but there seemed some reason to believe that the original purpose for which these troops were sent there was to extricate Japanese forces in Kwangsi, who were malaria-ridden and in a difficult position.

77. In the latter part of 1940, Siamese Ministers, possibly encouraged by the Japanese, had stimulated their country to demand the return to Siam of certain areas that had been taken by the French some years before. This eventually led to a mild form of hostilities between the two countries concerned. Endeavours were made at Singapore by the Governor, Commander-in-Chief, China, and myself to bring about a settlement without posing as official mediators, but these endeavours were unsuccessful. By the end of January, 1941, the Japanese had been recognised as the mediators, and thus scored a diplomatic success.

78. We had concluded an economic agreement with the Vichy French authorities in Indo-China, and they professed themselves anxious to develop friendly relations. In spite of this an agreement between them and the Japanese was announced on the 24th July, 1941. Its terms allowed the Japanese to maintain forces in the South of Indo-China. A Japanese convoy began to arrive at Saigon on the 26th, and by the end of July the Japanese were well established in that town. More important still, this movement gave the Japanese complete control of Camranh Harbour, and they quickly started to make or improve aerodromes to the South and West of Saigon. As was expected, the Japanese did not limit themselves for long to the terms of the agreement, and the French authorities made practically no effort to oppose either the original terms or the successive encroachments. The effect of this expansion on the defence of the Far East is indicated below (*paras.* 93 et seq.).

VIII.—DEVELOPMENT OF THE BRITISH AIR FORCES IN THE FAR EAST.

General Position.

79. In their paper of the 15th August, 1940, the Chiefs of Staff estimated the air strength necessary for the Far East as 336 first-line aircraft, to which, of course, had to be added reserves.

In the Singapore Conference of October, 1940, the final strength of the Royal Air Force recommended for the Far East was 582 aircraft, an increase of sixteen over that given in the appreciation dated the 16th October,

1940 (see para. 42 (b) above). The Chiefs of Staff agreed that 582 aircraft was an ideal, but considered that 336 should give a very fair degree of security. The figure of 566 aircraft given in the appreciation was stated by the Air Ministry to be far beyond the bounds of practical possibility in the light of total resources and vital requirements in active theatres at home and in the Middle East.

The strength of the Air Forces in Malaya in November, 1940, is as shown in Appendix I, that in Hong Kong and Ceylon was negligible. Of the total of 88 first-line aircraft, only 48, i.e., the Blenheims and Hudsons, could be counted as modern, and the former suffered from lack of range. The Vildebeestes which we had at the beginning of the war with Japan were considered by the Chiefs of Staff in August, 1940, as having become an obsolete type.

The replacement for the Vildebeeste was to be the Beaufort. Manufacture of these had started in Australia and we were to get the first 90. Much of the raw material and certain complete parts of these aeroplanes had to come from England and from the United States, and there was considerable delay in supplying many of the items. The urgency of the matter was represented several times from Australia, and particularly at the beginning of August, when the Prime Minister of Australia sent a special telegram to the Australian High Commissioner in London. In spite, however, of every effort on the part of Australia, Vildebeestes were still in use in December, 1941 (see para. 86 below).

The flying boats were not only obsolete, but badly in need of complete overhaul, and the Wirraways could only be considered as training aircraft.

But the great weaknesses were the absence of any fighters and the small size of the reserves. This latter even necessitated restrictions on the number of flying hours in squadrons towards the end of 1940, and the first months of 1941. The importance of remedying these weaknesses was emphasised very shortly after my arrival at Singapore, and the aircraft situation was elaborated in a telegram three months later. In this latter telegram I estimated that, at the end of 1941, we should be able to reckon, as an absolute maximum, on a total of only 215 aircraft, including anticipated reinforcements of 39 Dutch aircraft, or 176 exclusive of the Dutch.

80. The general deficiencies in aircraft were also emphasised in many other telegrams.

The following are extracts:—

"This means bluntly that at present not only is our ability to attack shipping deplorably weak, but we have not the staying-power to sustain even what we could now do. As our air effort dwindles (as it would if war came now) so will the enemy's chance of landing increase";

and:—

"Nor do I know whether troops or aircraft will be the easier to provide but I have no doubt what our first requirement here is. We want to increase our hitting power against ships, and our capacity to go on hitting."

The need for more aircraft for the attack of shipping had also been emphasised in a previous telegram of the 23rd July, 1941.

81. The Chiefs of Staff fully appreciated my anxiety about the smallness of the air forces at my disposal, but pointed out that they had had to face disappointments in production, had to reinforce the Middle East still further to meet the probable scale of attack in the Spring, and that the necessity for supporting Russia was likely to impose a further strain on British and American resources. Further, that in these circumstances it was clear that neither could the target programme for the Far East be completed, nor, indeed, could any substantial reinforcements be sent before the end of 1941.

82. This Chiefs of Staff's figure of 336 first line aircraft referred to in para. 79 above, was based on the assumption that Borneo would be defended, but took no account of the defence of Burma. Whilst the latter was a greater commitment than the former, I accepted the figure of 336 as the target at which to aim in view of two telegrams from the Chiefs of Staff, in both of which the figure of 336 was confirmed.

Fighters.

83. Single-seater fighter aircraft, known as the Brewster Buffalo, began to arrive in Singapore in cases from the United States in February, 1941, and permission was given by the Air Ministry to form two squadrons in the first instance. These were formed mainly with pilots taken from existing squadrons, who had a good deal of flying experience, and so got up to the operational standard much quicker than the two new squadrons formed later; though not up to establishment, the first two squadrons would have been able to fight by the middle of April, 1941. A total of 167 Buffaloes in all were received in Singapore, and on the 30th May, 1941, permission was given by the Air Ministry to form two further fighter squadrons.

These new squadrons took a long time to become operationally efficient. The majority of the pilots had to be brought from Australia and New Zealand. They all came straight from the Flying Training Schools, and some from New Zealand had never flown anything beyond a Hart, and had no experience of retractable undercarriages, variable-pitch propellors, or flaps. Under these conditions it took over four months from the time that the pilots arrived in Malaya before the squadrons could be considered fit for operations; in fact, they had not been passed as fit when war with Japan broke out. It would have helped a great deal if we could have formed a proper operational training unit in Malaya, but I was informed that neither personnel nor aircraft could be spared for the purpose, and that all the training of pilots would have to be done in the squadrons. As this would have seriously hindered the operational training of squadrons, the nucleus of an O.T.U. was formed from our own resources.

After the formation of the third and fourth Buffalo squadrons had been started, it was found that the re-equipment of the R.A.A.F. Wirraway Squadron was going to be delayed indefinitely, and I was requested by Australia to take any possible steps I could to ensure that this Australian squadron was re-equipped with some form of more modern machine than the Wirraway. The only possible course of action was to re-equip it with Buffaloes. This was sanctioned by the Air Ministry and carried out, but five squadrons were definitely too many for the total number of Buffaloes available, and overstrained the reserves.

84. The Buffalo proved disappointing, at any rate when up against the Japanese Zero fighter. This was due partly to technical reasons and partly to incomplete training of pilots. With regard to the former the performance of the Buffaloes at heights of 10,000 feet and over were relatively poor. (See Appendix " L "). Whilst it had been realised that the Buffalo lacked speed, it had been hoped that, with good warning system and the comparatively small area of important objectives, e.g., the Naval Base, it would be able to reach the height necessary before the arrival of enemy aircraft, and that its better armament would enable our squadrons to give a good account of themselves. Whether deliberately or not, the Japanese appear to have sacrificed armour and armament in their Zero fighters in order to save weight, thereby obtaining the advantage of rate of climb and manoeuvrability at heights. In the case of these two particular types, the technical advantage certainly lay with the Japanese. Attempts were made to improve the performance of the Buffalo by substituting .303 for the .5. In addition some trouble was experienced with the valve gear of the Cyclone engine in the Buffalo, and with the interrupter gear of the two fuselage guns. The Buffalo was unsuitable for night flying owing to the exhaust flames, flame dampers would have been essential for night flying but were not available. Actually this was not serious as I had laid down that the Buffalo was to be used for day work only, and that, by night, reliance was to be placed on the A.A. guns assisted by Blenheim fighters.

Pilots have been referred to in paragraph 83 above. What the R.A.F. lacked in Malaya was a good proportion of pilots with practical war experience. Apart from forming a leaven when operations started, they could have taught the new pilots those niceties of manoeuvre and aiming which just make the difference between missing the enemy and bringing him down, the type of training that can only be given as a result of experience. Again all the Buffalo squadrons were formed in Malaya and there was no squadron with practical war experience to set a standard, and it is possible that in some respects ours was not sufficiently high for modern conditions.

85. Apart from the fighter squadron in Burma, we had in Malaya in December, 1941, a total of four Buffalo squadrons, one Dutch fighter squadron, which arrived on the 9th December, and one Blenheim squadron, the last principally for night fighting. This total was considered adequate both by the Chiefs of Staff and by my own General Headquarters, but results showed that more fighter squadrons were required, largely because the scope of a fighter's duties has widened. One Buffalo squadron was specially trained for Army co-operation, and we really wanted two. I had also agreed with the Commander-in-Chief, Eastern Fleet, that one squadron, which ought to have been a Buffalo, should be trained in the duties of fighter protection for ships. Fighter squadrons are also the most efficient type with which to attack enemy aerodromes. To carry out these functions at all adequately, as well as the normal duties of a fighter, at least seven fighter squadrons were needed in Malaya alone, without allowing for night fighters.

Long-Range Bombers.

86. The need for long-range bombers had been constantly pressed from the time I was first appointed Commander-in-Chief, Far East. At that time I had merely felt that they would be wanted without having any concrete proposals, but as the Japanese advanced into Southern Indo-China, the object for which they would be used became clear and definite. The targets which we wished to reach in Southern Indo-China were just within reach of Blenheim IV's from the Northern end of Malaya, and of Hudsons, but we had too few of the former and the latter were required for overseas reconnaissance.

Six Beauforts were flown from Australia a few days before the war started, but as these aircraft were not operational, and as the crews required considerable operational training in their use, the Air Officer Commanding, with my concurrence, sent all bar one, which was retained in the hope of using it for photographic work, back to Australia in order that they might continue their training under suitable conditions.

Other Requirements.

87. Other requirements which were realised too late were special aircraft for photographic reconnaissance and transport aircraft for facilitating the rapid movement of squadrons. Photographic aircraft were first asked for in August, 1941, after the visit of a special photographic officer. The Dutch were ready to help us in the second requirement, but once war had started were making full use of their transport aircraft for their own purposes, and we felt the lack of having a few of our own available at very short notice.

It was also suggested at one time that a balloon barrage would be valuable for the protection of Singapore, especially the Naval Base. Experiments, however, proved that the climate and meteorology of Malaya were quite unsuitable for the use of kite balloons.

88. The strength and location of the Royal Air Force in the Far East on the 7th December, 1941, are given in Appendix J and a summary of serviceable aircraft in Malaya on different dates in December in Appendix K.

Our most serious deficiency at that time was in reserves, partly of pilots, but principally aircraft. It was not only a stock of reserve aeroplanes we wanted, but also a continuous flow of new aircraft to replace wastage, for aeroplanes must be regarded as expendable material, and there must be a regular, continuous channel of supply. Without these it was impossible to keep the squadrons up to their first-line establishment. Apart from the material weakness, failure to keep up what is commonly known as " a full breakfast table " always has an adverse effect on squadrons' morale.

89. There were several civil flying clubs in Malaya, and the Air Officer Commanding had organised for these an Auxiliary Air Force, which did useful work in communication and assistance to the Army in certain aspects of training.

IX.—ARMY STRENGTH AND REQUIREMENTS, MALAYA.

90. In the appreciation of the situation drawn up by the Commanders in Malaya previous to the Singapore Defence Conference of October,

1940, an estimate was made of the total armed forces required on the supposition that 582 aircraft would be available for the defence of the Far East. The estimate was as follows:—

26 infantry battalions, including 3 for Borneo.
5 field regiments.
3 light tank companies.

In addition anti-tank units, troops for local defence of aerodromes, volunteer units and ancillary troops. This figure of 26 battalions was agreed to by the Chiefs of Staff in January, 1941.

On his arrival, General Percival went thoroughly into the question of the strength of the Army and, in August, 1941, sent his estimate of the strength required, which he summarised as:—

48 Infantry Battalions.
4 Indian Reconnaissance Units.
9 Forward Artillery Regiments.
4 Light A.A. Regiments.
2 Tank Regiments.
3 Anti-Tank Regiments.
2 Mountain Artillery Regiments.
12 Field Companies.

This was based on my forecast of the strength which our Air Forces would reach by December, 1941, namely 186 first-line aircraft as against the accepted figure of 336. I was asked for observations and my general conclusion was that no drastic reduction in General Percival's estimate was acceptable until the strength of the Royal Air Force was materially increased not only in numbers but in quality of aircraft and in reserves of air crews, and aircraft. Also that before General Percival's new target was reached in Malaya, the question of increasing forces in other areas of my command, especially Burma, would have to be considered. The Chiefs of Staff commented: "We accept estimate by General Officer Commanding, Malaya, as reasonable figure for land forces required in present circumstances. Nevertheless, this target cannot be fulfilled in foreseeable future."

91. In December, 1941, while the actual strength of the Royal Air Force (*see Appendix J*) approached very closely to my forecast, the Army strength (*see Appendix E*) fell far short of the figure which it had been agreed was required to compensate for the deficiency in aircraft. The main deficiencies were:—

17 Battalions;
4 Light A.A. Regiments; and
2 Tank Regiments.

The strength in A.A. weapons in the Far East on the 7th December, 1941, is given in Appendix F.

92. The fact that we were entirely without tanks in Malaya was a serious handicap to any offensive land operations, whether on a small or a large scale. There were also very few armoured cars. Many efforts were made to obtain both tanks and armoured cars from various sources. On the 14th August the War Office offered forty light tanks from the Middle East. These tanks were at the time being employed for aerodrome defence, and they were offered to the Far East on the condition that they would be employed in an operational role, and that we could man them from local resources. Some delay occurred at Singapore in finding the best method of meeting the latter condition. Eventually Australia agreed to provide the necessary men and to train them up to a reasonable standard in Australia, this training to be completed by the 1st January, 1942. On the 13th November, 1941, however, Middle East reported to the War Office that they could not provide forty tanks for the Far East except at the expense of operational requirements. After war had broken out, War Office ordered Middle East to send fifty light tanks to India, their subsequent destination to be decided later.

With regard to armoured cars, a model of an armoured vehicle mounted on an American chassis was obtained from the Dutch and six were made in Singapore, chiefly at the Naval Base; drawings were also made and sent to Burma. No more, however, could be made owing to a shortage of boiler plate, which was used for the armouring. By the 24th November, 1941, a total of 84 Marmon-Harrington armoured cars had been shipped from South Africa for Singapore. Some of these arrived a few days before war broke out, and the drivers had not become accustomed to them before they had to go to the front.

The number of anti-tank weapons had improved considerably by the time war broke out, but there was still a shortage of the 0.5 anti-tank rifle in infantry units.

The lack of mobile A.A. weapons was serious, especially in view of the shortage of fighters. A constant anxiety to the General Officer Commanding, also, was the continual drain on the Army for men to protect aerodromes. Indian State troops were brought over to assist, but it would have been a great help if we had had more armoured cars or even tanks of an obsolete pattern for this duty. This would have enabled us to have a mobile defence and to substitute mechanical vehicles for a large proportion of the men required. The reserve of small-arms ammunition was well below the authorised figure. In November, 1941, General Headquarters informed the War Office that, with releases in sight, we should be short of our authorised holding of 150 million rounds by 57 million on the 1st January, 1942. Australia, who were already sending us 3 million rounds per month, agreed to increase this to 8 million.

X.—EVENTS LEADING UP TO THE WAR.

The Problem of Japanese Intentions.

93. As the Japanese spread South into Cambodia and Cochin China, the potential danger to Burma, Malaya, the South China Sea, and even the Philippines, increased; this danger had been realised from the start, and was referred to in a telegram in December, 1940. But it was difficult to judge whether this movement signified definite plans for an offensive against us in the near future, whether it was merely the acquisition of a strategic asset to be used in negotiation, or whether it was the first step towards occupation of Siam. This applied even to the construction of aerodromes, of which we were kept fairly well informed; what we were particularly on the look-out for was any indication of movements of long-distance bombers, or of the Zero-type fighters fitted with detachable petrol tanks. These, of course, could be concentrated on the aerodromes at short notice.

94. Another difficulty in getting any long warning of the Japanese intention was due to the restriction on exports to, and imports from,

Japan. So long as Japanese merchant shipping was being employed on its normal work, F.E.C.B. could keep track of every vessel, and should it be found that an unusual number was being kept in home ports for no good reason, it would indicate the possibility, or even probability, that the Japanese were refitting these ships as transports prior to an overseas expedition. The effect of the embargo, however, was to drive all Japanese shipping off the seas for purely economic reasons, and once in Japanese ports they could be altered as required without our being any the wiser. This applied especially to the fast vessels, *i.e.*, round about 18 knots.

In spite of the preparations going on in Southern Indo-China there were some indications—at any rate up to the end of November—that the Japanese did not intend immediate hostilities. The first was a general one, namely, that if the Japanese intended to attack Malaya, they would have been more likely to have done so in 1940, when our forces were far weaker than they were at the end of 1941. Then the winter months, December to February, were less favourable for an expedition against the East coast of Malaya and the Kra Isthmus than other periods of the year owing to the North-East monsoon. (*See also para.* 134 *below.*) Finally, there was the visit of Kurusu to Washington. It seems now probable that Kurusu, though possibly innocent himself, was sent to Washington with the deliberate object of misleading the United States and ourselves as to the Japanese intentions, and keeping us quiet until their own preparations had been finally completed. But at the time it seemed to us in Singapore that this was a genuine attempt on the part of the Japanese to get relaxation of the restrictions that had been imposed, and possibly to drive a wedge between Britain and the United States. I believe the same view was held in England.

95. In the latter part of November information accumulated to show that the Japanese were probably intending an offensive at an early date. Four Mogami class cruisers with a few destroyers had been despatched from the Japanese Combined Fleet to the South China Sea. Two squadrons of long-range Zero fighters arrived in South Indo-China. The number of aircraft in Indo-China rose from a total of 74 at the end of October to 245 at the end of November. The 5th Japanese Division, which was highly trained in landing operations, was reported by the Chinese to have moved to South Indo-China. There were large movements of motor landing craft from Central China, though there was no definite information as to where they had gone. In addition, a telegram was received from the War Office to the effect that the United States Army commanders in the Far East had been informed from Washington that the Kurusu negotiations might break down at any time and offensive operations be started by Japan against Siam, the Netherlands East Indies or the Philippines; up to the receipt of this telegram we had remained completely in the dark on this matter except for Press reports.

Aeroplanes, almost certainly Japanese, occasionally flew over parts of Malaya in the latter part of November and early December, in all probability carrying out photographic reconnaissance, but owing to the speed and height at which they operated we were never able to make contact and obtain definite identification.

In view of the continued Japanese developments in Southern Indo-China, which gave them the facilities needed to attack Malaya, precautionary steps were taken on the 22nd November, and orders were issued for vulnerable points to be guarded, and on the 1st December the Volunteers were mobilised. Certain movements of air forces were carried out, and reconnaissances over the China Sea were instituted.

During this time we felt great need of aircraft capable of doing high-altitude photographic reconnaissance. This applied not only to the aerodromes in Southern Indo-China, but particularly to Camranh Harbour, on which we got no information whatever. We had no aircraft suitable for the purpose since, though a Catalina could have flown the distance, it had neither the speed nor the necessary ceiling. It seemed highly undesirable to aggravate a strained situation by sending over an aeroplane which would in all probability have been intercepted and definitely identified as British. I asked General MacArthur to carry out a photographic reconnaissance from Manila with one of his Boeing Fortresses, which had the necessary speed and ceiling, but he replied that orders from Washington prevented him from carrying out my request.

96. Near the opposite end of the prospective theatre of operations, the island of Timor was important as being a definite link in the air communications between Australia and the Netherlands East Indies. Its occupation by the Japanese would also be a serious threat to Australia. The importance of Timor was noted in the A.D.A. agreement, and it was referred to in A.D.B. Roughly half the island was Dutch territory and half Portuguese; it was the latter half which gave no small anxiety. The Japanese had a consulate in Dilli, the capital of Portuguese Timor, and by November, 1941, had received permission to run a regular flying-boat service to Dilli, and were gradually getting an economic hold on Portuguese Timor. In November, 1941, a small nucleus of Australian troops was sent to Koepang in Dutch Timor, where there was an aerodrome and a flying-boat base. On the 12th December one infantry battalion, one independent company and a few coast defence troops reached Koepang from Australia. A combined Australian and Dutch force occupied Dilli in the middle of December, 1941. About the 7th December, in accordance with the A.D.A. and A.D.B. agreements, two flights of Hudsons of the Royal Australian Air Force moved to Ambon in the Netherlands East Indies. These were followed later by an infantry battalion.

Order of the Day.

97. The Commander-in-Chief, China, and I had agreed as far back as May, 1941, that it was desirable to prepare an Order of the Day before the war broke out, so that it could reach Burma and Hong Kong in time to be translated into the different languages spoken by the troops in the Far East and be ready for issue on the first day of war. Drafting this Order presented difficulty because it had to appeal to men of varying races and religions, *e.g.*, British sailors and Burmese troops. The main object that I had in view when preparing it was to make an effective appeal to the Indian

troops, as I considered it would be necessary to stimulate them rather than the British. Through information that has reached me subsequent to the outbreak of war I believe it had the effect it was meant to. The order is given in Appendix M.

Approach of the First Enemy Expedition.

98. About 1400 hours on the 6th December I received information that an air reconnaissance had sighted two Japanese convoys escorted by warships about 80 miles East-South-East of Pulo Obi, an island off the Southern point of Indo-China, steaming West. One convoy consisted of 22 10,000-ton merchant vessels escorted by one battleship, probably the *Kongoo*, five cruisers and seven destroyers; the other of 21 merchant ships escorted by two cruisers and ten destroyers. Further West, one Japanese cruiser and three 10,000-ton merchant ships had been sighted steering North-West. I consulted with Admiral Sir Geoffrey Layton and Admiral Palliser, Sir Tom Phillips' Chief of Staff, and we concluded that the probability was that the convoy would not continue its course due West, which would have brought it on to the Kra Isthmus, but that it would follow the first four vessels and round Cambodia Point. It was pointed out that there was a good anchorage on the West Coast of Indo-China at Koh Tron, which they might be making for as the next step towards Siam.

Bearing in mind the policy of avoiding war with Japan if possible—a policy which had been reaffirmed by the Chiefs of Staff as recently as the 29th November—and the situation in the United States with the Kurusu talks still going on in Washington, I decided that I would not be justified in ordering "Matador" on this information, but orders were issued to bring all forces to the first, *i.e.*, the highest, degree of readiness. I also impressed upon the Air Officer Commanding the urgent necessity for maintaining contact with the convoy, a point which he had already realised.

The location of these forces by Hudsons of No. 1 Royal Australian Air Force Squadron, based on Kota Bharu, was a particularly good piece of work in view of their being at the limit of their patrolling range, over 300 miles from the Malayan Coast. This same factor of distance, however, made it impossible for them to remain in contact until relieved, but a Catalina Flying-boat was despatched to shadow the convoy during the night. The Air Officer Commanding also ordered a reconnaissance by Hudsons starting early on the 7th December, fanning out from Kota Bharu on to the last known bearings of the convoy. No signal was received from the Catalina, and, from information received later, it is almost certain it was shot down. A second Catalina failed to make contact with the convoy. On the morning of the 7th December, visibility East and North-East from Kota Bharu was good. The reconnaissance found no ships in the area between Kota Bharu and the Southern end of Indo-China, thus confirming the supposition that the convoy had rounded Cambodia Point, and had followed the four leading ships North-North-West into the Gulf of Siam. In this Gulf the visibility was very bad and no positive information was received from this area until the evening, when a report was received that a Hudson had seen, through low clouds, three small Japanese ships which were then passing Singora and heading south. This information reached me about 2100 hours. I met General Percival and we proceeded together to the Naval Base; I decided not to order "Matador"; the main reason being that at least 24 hours start was required before the anticipated time of a Japanese landing and this was most unlikely to be available, should the 3 ships seen turn out to be part of a Japanese expedition. Further, the conditions for reconnaissance were bad, on the information then available there could be no certainty that the Japanese were about to open hostilities, and on more than one occasion the British Minister to Thailand had stressed the serious consequences that would ensue should we be the first to break Thai neutrality. (*See also paragraph 51 above.*)

It is pertinent to record that, until the Japanese had committed some definite act of hostility against the United States, the Dutch or ourselves, permission had not been given to attack a Japanese expedition at sea.

XI.—THE START OF HOSTILITIES.

The Opening Day.

99. Clear evidence that the Japanese had, in fact, taken the plunge into hostilities was soon forthcoming when, at 0130 hours on Monday, the 8th December, the Japanese started to land from about ten ships at Kota Bharu. I received this news at about 0200 hours in my office at the Naval Base, Singapore, and the necessary steps were at once taken to put everything on a war footing, including the internment of Japanese. Later on, reports were received that the Japanese were landing large forces at Singora and Patani in the Southern part of the Kra Isthmus.

At 0300 hours on the 8th December Singapore was attacked by Japanese bombers, which, in all probability, came from Southern Indo-China. In one case, at any rate, they came over in a formation of nine at a height of between 12,000 and 14,000 feet, without dropping any bombs, apparently with the object of drawing the searchlights and A.A. guns away from a few other aircraft which, flying at 4,000 to 5,000 feet, attacked objectives on Singapore Island, mainly aerodromes, with practically no results. An attack was also made on the Eastern part of Singapore Harbour, possibly in mistake for the aerodrome at Kallang; this attack caused a number of casualties, killing about sixty, mostly Chinese.

The observation system worked satisfactorily, and thirty minutes' warning of the approach of Japanese aircraft was received at my headquarters. For some reason that I never ascertained, the Headquarters of the A.R.P. organisation had not been manned, and it was only a few minutes before bombs were dropping on Singapore that contact was made by Fighter Group Headquarters and the sirens sounded giving the warning for black-out. In my opinion, the absence of black-out had but little effect, since there was a bright full moon, and the coastline and most of Singapore must have shown up very clearly.

Apart from this failure in Civil A.R.P., there was no tactical surprise, since as has been stated above, the troops were all in readiness, and the black-out was carried out at all Naval, Army and Air Force establishments.

100. In the morning of the 8th December the weather was clear over the land and close to the coast, but out to sea there were clouds down to 500 feet. No. 1 Squadron, Royal Australian Air Force, at Kota Bharu, aided by the Vildebeestes of Nos. 36 and 100 Squadrons, carried out a vigorous offensive against the Japanese vessels and landing craft. Reports showed that these attacks had a considerable measure of success, many landing craft in the Kota Bharu River being sunk, and a ship reported to have contained tanks being sent to the bottom.

No. 62 Squadron from Alor Star also went out to attack the same target, but, owing probably to being ordered too far from the coast, failed to locate the enemy ships near Kota Bharu and proceeded to the neighbourhood of Patani on the Kra Isthmus. Here it was met by a greatly superior force of Japanese Zero fighters, and though Japanese ships were located there and bombs dropped on them, the attack was probably ineffective.

On the Western side in Kedah reconnaissance forces of the 11th Division crossed the Siam frontier in the afternoon of the 8th December and made contact with the enemy, who were already employing 10 A.F.Vs. After inflicting casualties, our forces withdrew in the afternoon, demolishing bridges on their way to the frontier. Further South a force known as Krohcol also crossed the frontier beyond Kroh in order to take up a position on the Siamese side of the border as originally planned. Both these forces met with some opposition from the Siamese.

Meanwhile, in spite of resistance on the beaches and further back, the enemy had made progress at Kota Bharu, until by 1600 hours the aerodrome was so threatened by Japanese troops that our aircraft had to leave and fly to Kuantan.

101. A feature of the opening day of hostilities was the enemy air attack upon our Northern aerodromes. Gong Kedah, Machang, Penang, Butterworth, Alor Star and Sungei Patani aerodromes were all attacked, the total scale of enemy effort for the day being estimated at some 150 aircraft, of which probably 65 per cent. were fighters. Of these attacks, the most damaging were against Alor Star and Sungei Patani, several aircraft on the ground being rendered unserviceable in both cases and most buildings at Sungei Patani destroyed. Both aerodromes were henceforth unable to operate and had to be vacated.

The attack on Alor Star was made by a formation of 27 twin-engine bombers of the Army type 97, and started about twenty minutes after the return of No. 62 Squadron from their attack at Patani and whilst the aircraft were refuelling. The Japanese attacked from a height of about 13,000 feet and used pattern bombing, the bombs being partly high-explosive, mostly about 150 lb., and partly incendiary. The attack was very effective; some ten of our Blenheims were put out of action, four being completely written off. The fuel dump and some buildings were set on fire, and, as the water supply was put out of action, the fires were not extinguished till dusk. Casualties were small, only seven men being killed. Alor Star was defended by four 3-inch 20-cwt. guns, but they failed to bring down any Japanese aircraft, possibly owing to the height at which they were flying.

9th-11th December.

102. Broadly speaking, assaults on our aerodromes, coupled with fresh landings in Siamese territory, continued to be the main feature of the Japanese operations for the first two days of the war. The enemy was greatly helped in them by the prompt use to which he put Siamese aerodromes, our reconnaissances on the 9th and 10th December revealing concentrations of some sixty aircraft at Singora and eighty to a hundred aircraft at Don Muang, Bangkok. On the 9th December eleven Blenheims attacked Singora aerodrome, but they were met by a greatly superior force of enemy fighters and five of our aircraft were brought down; the results of our bombing were not observed. Aircraft of No. 62 Squadron, which had moved back to Butterworth at dawn on the 9th December, were also ordered to attack Singora, starting at 1700 hours the same day. Butterworth was attacked by Japanese aircraft just as ours were about to take off, and, although Buffaloes were up, considerable damage was caused, with the result that only one Blenheim left. The pilot, Flight-Lieutenant Scarf, reached and attacked Singora, but was badly wounded; he flew his aeroplane back, landed at Alor Star and died a few minutes later.

On the 9th December our aircraft were forced to vacate Kuantan owing to enemy bombing, though it was still used for refuelling. Already by this date it was clear that the success of the enemy's attack on our Northern aerodromes would considerably handicap our own air action, and that this in turn would unfavourably prejudice our fortunes in the fighting on land. Interference with Singora landings was made difficult, once our Northern aerodromes had succumbed, by our lack of bombers of adequate range. In a telegram to London from General Headquarters a warning was given that it was unlikely we should find it practicable to maintain the existing air effort for more than two or three weeks.

Dutch air reinforcements arrived in Singapore Island on the 9th; they consisted of three squadrons of Glenn Martin bombers, total 22 aircraft, and one squadron of nine Buffalo fighters. It was found necessary to send eight of the bombers back to the Netherlands East Indies to complete the training of their crews in night flying.

103. The 8th Brigade, defending Kota Bharu, was pressed back on the 9th, demolition being carried out before the aerodrome was evacuated. By the end of the day it was forced back to a line in Kelantan running Peringot-Mulong. The enemy was employing infiltration tactics and working round the flanks of our forces wherever possible. The 8th Brigade had put up a stout resistance round Kota Bharu, and its commander, Brigadier Key, was faced with a difficult problem in deciding when retreat would become necessary. (*See para.* 138 *below.*) The decision having been made, the Brigade was disengaged skilfully.

Japanese Army reinforcements meanwhile arrived on a considerable scale. A large force, consisting of transports escorted by a battleship, three cruisers and eleven destroyers, was sighted by our aircraft between Kota Bharu and the Penhentain Islands on the 9th December. North of Kuantan the Japanese landed in small numbers at Beserah during the night

9th-10th December. These were driven off, and by 0845 on the 10th December all was quiet there. The general situation in regard to Japanese landings was thus that all successful landings took place North of the Malaya-Siam frontier, except that at Kota Bharu, which, as already stated in para. 12 above, had no road communications to Southern Malaya, and depended for reinforcements from the South on the railway alone.

By the 10th December it was evident that the enemy's primary object was the establishment of air superiority in Northern Malaya, whilst at the same time he was testing our defences on a wide front. It was estimated that the Japanese were now employing about 30 Zero-type fighters from Patani and about 70 aircraft, mainly Zero fighters, from Singora. All but about 50 of the Japanese bombers previously based in Southern Indo-China had presumably been moved to Siam.

A complication of the situation which gave some anxiety at this date was that our efforts might be impeded by lack of support, or even actively hostile measures, among native elements. Native labour tended to disappear for days after bombing, and non-British railway employees, including engine-drivers, deserted temporarily on a large scale; the Army was able to replace the drivers to some extent.

104. By the 11th December the 8th Brigade, in Kelantan, retiring along the road which meets the railway at Kuala Krai, was in a position covering Machang. In Kedah a new threat was opening in the form of enemy infiltration from Siam, especially in the Chaglun area. This advance into Kedah, coupled with the heavy air attacks on Penang, indicated that the Japanese main attack would be down the road communications of Western Malaya. Advanced troops of the 11th Indian Division were in position South of a line Chaglun-Kodiang, while Krohcol sought to hold off the enemy in this more central region. Some of the demolitions that had been prepared in Northern Kedah failed to be effective; this was not due to any failure to act in time, but to some technical fault either in the fuses or explosives. All our serviceable aircraft had now been withdrawn from Northern Malaya. It was estimated that by the 11th December the Japanese were employing in Malaya at least two divisions, supported by 250-300 aircraft.

H.M.S. Prince of Wales and Repulse.

105. H.M.S. *Prince of Wales* and *Repulse* arrived at Singapore on Tuesday, the 2nd December, 1941, Admiral Sir Tom Phillips having arrived by air two days before. He and I had no opportunity for full consultation over the situation before war broke out, partly because he was taking over from Sir Geoffrey Layton as Commander-in-Chief, Eastern Fleet, and partly because he visited Manila by air to meet Admiral Hart.

H.M.S. *Repulse* left to pay a visit to Port Darwin on the 5th December, and it was agreed she should proceed for the first 48 hours at comparatively slow speed. She was recalled as soon as the air reconnaissance report of the 6th December was received, and arrived back in Singapore on the 7th December. The naval forces at Singapore on the 7th December are given in Appendix C.

106. Admiral Phillips decided to take action with his two capital ships. So far as my Headquarters was concerned he was put into direct touch with the Air Officer Commanding with regard to the air co-operation required, and asked for three things:—

(a) Reconnaissance 100 miles to north of the force from daylight, Tuesday, the 9th December;

(b) Reconnaissance to Singora and beyond ten miles from the coast starting at first light on the 10th December; and

(c) Fighter protection off Singora at daylight on the 10th December.

The Air Officer Commanding gave tentative replies that he could provide (a), hoped to be able to provide (b), but could not provide (c). It was decided that he should go thoroughly into the problems involved and give definite replies to the Chief of Staff, Eastern Fleet, Rear-Admiral Palliser, who was remaining behind. Air Officer Commanding later confirmed his tentative replies and this information was sent on by signal to Commander-in-Chief, Eastern Fleet, in the evening of the 8th December. The doubt about (b) was due to the fact that the reconnaissance would have to be provided by Blenheim IV's based on Kuantan aerodrome, and it was uncertain whether this would be out of action or not. Actually, both the reconnaissances were carried out, though one of the Blenheims doing (b) had wireless troubles.

The reason why (c) could not be provided was mainly that the northern aerodromes were either untenable or else had been badly damaged by bombing; this meant that the fighters would have to operate from aerodromes at considerable distance from Singora, and, owing to the short endurance of the Buffalo, they would have been able to remain only a very short time over that area before having to return to refuel. The Dutch fighter squadron had not arrived by the 8th; it was uncertain whether it would be available by the 10th and thus there was a shortage of fighter aircraft. These factors meant that a short patrol might possibly have been provided at intervals at Singora, but that it was impossible to guarantee continuous fighter protection.

107. The *Prince of Wales* and *Repulse*, accompanied by four destroyers, left Singapore in the afternoon of Monday, the 8th December. Early on the 10th December a signal was made to Singapore indicating that the ships would return earlier than originally planned. Except for this, no communication was received and their position remained unknown until, shortly after twelve noon on Wednesday, the 10th December, a signal was received from *Repulse* that she was being bombed in a position about 60 miles East-South-East of Kuantan. On receipt of the message a fighter squadron was at once despatched and reached the position of the ships in commendably quick time, but only to see the *Prince of Wales* go down. No enemy aircraft were spotted. Fighter cover, though only a weak one, was provided for the destroyers that picked up the crews from the sunken ships.

108. I had been asked by Rear-Admiral Palliser to give an indication of the strength of the air force that the Japanese might bring against these two ships from Indo-China, and gave an estimate of between 50 and 60 bombers.

which might be expected to arrive five hours after the ships had been first located by reconnaissance. Whether this information was ever received by the Commander-in-Chief, Eastern Fleet, I do not know.

109. The ships were attacked by high-level bombers and torpedo bombers, the latter being by far the more effective. It is possible that the high-level bombers were used with the object of attracting any of our fighters that might have been with the ships away from the torpedo bombers. The Japanese would probably have expected that such fighters would be flying high, and that they would naturally attack high-level bombers in the first instance, thus giving sufficient time for the torpedo bombers to get in their attack before our fighters could get down to them. Admittedly, this is conjecture, but it is on similar lines to the bombing attack carried out on Singapore Island early on the 8th December. It also indicates the value of the dive bomber as a third alternative method of attacking ships, thereby giving greater facilities for surprise.

110. The psychological effect on Malaya of the loss of these two ships was somewhat mitigated by the fact that shortly after they arrived I had summoned a Press conference, and talked to those present on the following lines:—

"The arrival of the two capital ships in no way reduced the need for continuance of every effort being made to improve the defences of Malaya and Singapore; indeed, it enhanced the importance of this effort. Warships must not be tied down to their base; they must be free to operate to the full limit of their range of action and know that they can still return to a safe base when necessary. These ships would be of value to the Far East as a whole, but must not be regarded in any sense as part of the local defences of Malaya and Singapore. Further, in the same way as these ships had arrived from distant stations, so, if the situation changed and they became needed elsewhere, we had to be prepared for them to be ordered away."

Based on this, the local papers published good leading articles, bringing out the particular points I made. In addition, Mr. Duff Cooper, at my request, gave an excellent broadcast on the evening of 10th December, pointing out that the loss of these ships must not lead to despondency, but merely to a determination to fight all the harder and so avenge their loss.

Japanese Command of the Sea.

111. From the point of view of the defence of the Far East as a whole, what was more serious was the Japanese attack on the United States Pacific Fleet in Pearl Harbour. In appreciations of the situation we had always relied on the deterrent effect of the existence of this Fleet, even if the United States were not in the war from the start. It was expected that this deterrent would prevent the Japanese from allotting more than a limited number of warships for escort duties, which fact would limit the number of convoys sent into the South China Sea, and that it would also stop them from sending an expedition round the East side of the Philippines towards the Netherlands East Indies, especially the Eastern islands.

An indirect result of the Pearl Harbour attack was to prevent the surface ships of the Asiatic Fleet from Manila co-operating with British and Dutch ships in the Java and South China Seas in accordance with the A.D.B. agreement. This Asiatic Fleet was, by orders from Washington, limited to operations between Sourabaya and Port Darwin.

As a final result, the command of the sea acquired by the Japanese was greater than we had ever anticipated. We were, in fact, fighting under conditions of which the British Empire had very little previous experience.

Penang.

112. Penang Island was of no small importance for three reasons:—
   (a) Very fair port facilities.
   (b) Stocks of ammunition and stores.
   (c) The point of departure of two Overseas cables.

It was decided that the true defence of Penang was on the mainland and that, should the forces in Kedah be driven south, direct defence of Penang would be of no value. This enabled most of the garrison of Penang to be released to reinforce the mainland. One of the great weaknesses of Penang lay in the fact that there were no A.A. guns, which was entirely due to shortage of weapons. It had been laid down that the Naval Base, Royal Air Force aerodromes, Singapore Harbour and Kuala Lumpur had to have priority above Penang, and there were not enough to go round.

There was no analogy between Penang and Tobruk. Even had the garrison of Penang held out for some weeks, it would have been entirely isolated both by land and by sea, and could not have carried out any attacks against the Japanese line of communications except possibly an odd spasmodic raid. Any troops that might have been utilised for a garrison under these conditions would have been more valuable elsewhere.

113. The first attack on Penang was at 1100 hours on the 8th December, when the aerodrome was bombed by Japanese aircraft, the effect generally being small. At 1000 hours the 11th December, Georgetown was bombed and heavy casualties caused among the native population; these were due not so much to any inadequacy of A.R.P. as to the fact that the native population turned out into the streets to watch the sight, presumably under the impression that another attack was about to be made on the aerodrome. As a result nearly the whole native population left the town and the labour problem became acute. Next day the military authorities had to take over many civil duties, including burial of the dead, and the naval authorities had to work the ferries between the Island and the mainland.

114. In view of the situation in Kedah, it was decided to move women and children, other than Malays and Chinese, from Penang on the 13th December. This was intended to apply to Indians as well as Europeans, but owing to some misunderstanding the Sikh Police were not given the opportunity to send their women and children away, and in the end only the Europeans left, the total numbers being about 520.

At 2030 hours, the 15th December, orders were received by the Military Commander at Penang to destroy all military stores, etc., that could not be moved and to come away with the remainder of the garrison and British civilians. About half a dozen British residents were left as they did not wish to move. The native Volunteers were given the option of moving, but most of them decided to remain with their families in Penang; the British personnel of the Volunteers were brought away.

The coast artillery denial scheme was carried out and all 6-inch guns destroyed. Approved armament was withdrawn and most first-line transport. Electrical machinery and the oil fuelling system of the Eastern Smelting Company were smashed, the river house, telephone exchange, cable and wireless station and aerodromes destroyed. The Singapore-Colombo and the Singapore-Madras cables were, however, connected by binding screws and left working in the hope that the Japanese might not discover them—a hope that proved vain. A reserve of food was opened for the civil population, which had suffered some 600 killed and 1,100 wounded in air raids during the last week.

The destruction of material was incomplete, the most notable example being certain vessels that were left intact. Efforts were made by the naval authorities to immobilise these by laying mines in the Southern Channel, the Northern already having been mined by the Japanese. Presumably this was not effective for long.

XII.—THE RETREAT FROM NORTHERN MALAYA.

12th-18th December.

115. By the 12th December enemy pressure on the Kedah front was becoming very severe. The Kroh forces were being forced backwards over the frontier, while our right in Northern Kedah was also driven back, necessitating the 6th Indian Infantry Brigade withdrawing on the left to conform and hold a line River Bukit (north of Alor Star) to Penang. Penang was the subject of daily air attacks at this period. Two days of heavy fighting then saw our forces pushed back twenty miles south of Alor Star, the 11th Division taking up a position in the Gurun area. Some of the infantry units in this division reported losses up to 50 per cent., but this included missing, many of whom rejoined later.

The immediate preoccupation on our part at this moment was to co-ordinate the movement of the 11th Division with that of Krohcol. Unless this was done there was serious danger of the Japanese cutting off one of the two forces. Krohcol was now back in Kedah just east of Baling and under the command of the 12th Indian Infantry Brigade, which had been sent up from the south as reinforcements. But on the 16th December the enemy drove in between the Kroh forces and the 11th Division, and counter-attacks by two battalions of the 28th Indian Brigade proved unavailing to restore contact. It was now that the lack of adequate reserves to relieve troops who had been fighting continuously for a week began to be felt. The enemy were pressing home their attacks in spite of heavy losses. Troops from Penang were sent up as reinforcements, while the 6th and 15th Indian Infantry Brigades had been so weakened in the fighting that they were ordered to re-form into one composite Brigade.

The Japanese were now employing Kota Bharu aerodrome, reconnaissance revealing some forty of their fighters on the ground. To attack Kota Bharu, Singora and Patani aerodromes with the object of reducing the scale of Japanese air effort was part of our general air policy at this period, but our bomber effort was painfully limited by our lack of aircraft. Apart from deficiency of adequate A.A. weapons, the defence of our aerodromes was handicapped by lack of adequate warning in the North. (*See para. 54 above.*) These formed two causes of our heavy losses of aircraft on the ground. The retention of our main fighter strength for the defence of Singapore (*see para. 142 below*) was a contributory cause and also reacted directly on our bombing effort, since it was impracticable to provide fighter escorts.

Two Buffaloes had been specially fitted for photographic reconnaissance. To allow of extra petrol being carried, and at the same time to reduce weight, all guns were taken out. Even then the Buffaloes were inferior in performance to the Japanese Zero fighters. The pilots of these specially fitted aircraft carried out useful work under very difficult conditions.

From the start of hostilities the Dutch submarines had been very active. On the 12th December one of them reported sinking four enemy troopships at Patani Roads.

116. The difficulty of combating the Japanese attacks on our aerodromes resulted on the 16th and 17th December in the evacuation and demolition of Butterworth, Taiping and Kuantan aerodromes, and our aircraft were forced further South. Ipoh, too, was now being bombed, and the aerodrome petrol dump was hit.

On land, the enemy, having advanced in Kelantan (as far as the Sungei Nal) and in Kedah, was now also attacking detachments of our troops in Perak round about the Grik area. The 3rd Indian Corps was accordingly authorised to withdraw behind the line of the Perak River to protect the communications of our forces North of Kuala Kangsar. The 11th Indian Division began withdrawing from the line of the River Muda Southwards behind River Krian, linking up with the 28th Indian Infantry Brigade and protected all the time on the right flank by the 12th Indian Infantry Brigade. During this period the Argyll and Sutherland Highlanders made counter-attacks with gallantry and skill. This withdrawal was carried out successfully, the enemy being repulsed with loss at his first attempt to cross the river.

Inter-Allied Conference, 18th December.

117. On the 18th December a conference of inter-Allied representatives took place at Singapore, in accordance with proposals made by President Roosevelt. Owing to the time factor, China was not represented. Results of the conference were telegraphed to England. The main conclusions were as follows:—

(*a*) The importance of Singapore to the war in the Far East, and to the world war, could not be exaggerated;

(*b*) The immediate plan was to dispose our combined forces then available in the Far East so as to—

(i) Keep the enemy as far North in Malaya as possible and hold him in the Philippines; and

(ii) Prevent the enemy acquiring territory, and particularly aerodromes, which would threaten the arrival of reinforcements;

(c) Our urgent and immediate need was for reinforcements, which must be on a scale not only to meet the present scale of attack, but also that likely to be put in the field against us;

(d) It was recommended that the United States convoy at present directed to Brisbane should proceed to Sourabaya, where aircraft would be assembled and flown on to destination;

(e) It was desirable that the Chinese should be asked to maintain the maximum pressure on the Japanese in order to contain as many divisions as possible, and subsequently to provide bases for long-distance bombing attacks on Japan.

Finally the conference considered that the situation, though serious, need not give rise to undue pessimism provided the necessary reinforcements were supplied in the available time, but time was the essential feature.

Reinforcements.

118. From the 8th December, 1941, onwards many requests for reinforcements had been made from General Headquarters, Far East. The time factor meant that reinforcements had to come from the Middle East, India and convoys already at sea rather than from the United Kingdom. Complicated quadrangular references between Malaya, India, the Middle East and London were hence entailed, but Commander-in-Chief, India, was most helpful in appreciating the need for diversion to Malaya of forces originally intended for his own command. A sub-committee of the Inter-Allied Conference, having considered all the previous requests for reinforcements, agreed on the following immediate requirements for Malaya to stabilise the situation:—

Air—
4 Fighter Squadrons;
4 Bomber Squadrons;
1 Photographic Flight;
1 Transport Flight; and
Reserves at 100 per cent. for fighters and 50 per cent. for bombers, plus aircraft to complete existing squadrons and their reserves.

Land—
1 Brigade Group;
1 Division;
Reinforcements for 9th and 11th Divisions;
3 Light A.A. Regiments;
2 Heavy A.A. Regiments;
1 Anti-Tank Regiment;
50 Light tanks;
350 Anti-tank rifles;
Bofors ammunition; and
500 Tommy guns and ammunition;
Further large forces would be required later in view of probable Japanese reinforcements.

By the 27th December the following had been definitely promised:—

Air—
51 Hurricanes. (One fighter squadron ex convoy W.S. 12.Z with 18 additional pilots);
24 Blenheims. (One squadron from Middle East);
52 Hudsons (from United Kingdom);
While measures were in hand aiming at the release of a further 3 fighter squadrons from the Middle East, and for 80 4-engined United States bombers.

Land—
2 Infantry Brigade Groups } Reinforcements for 9th-11th Divisions } ex India

85th Anti-Tank Regiment complete
6th Heavy A.A. Regiment (16 guns)
32nd Light A.A. Regiment (24 guns)
} ex Convoy W.S. 12.Z.

Light tank squadron (17 Light tanks and reserves) ex India;

53rd Infantry Brigade (18th Division), guns and transport of which were to follow after arrival of personnel;

1 Machine Gun Battalion and reinforcements for the A.I.F. Brigades ex Australia;

Provision of further tanks was under discussion, while General Headquarters, Far East, was also pressing strongly for the complete 18th Division.

Five Blenheims from the Middle East and four Hudsons from Australia arrived in Singapore on the 23rd December, 1941.

19th–25th December.

119. In accordance with instructions from London, a scorched earth policy was ordered at this period instead of the denial scheme referred to in para. 65 above.

The general situation on land by the 19th–21st December was that our troops were trying to keep the enemy West of the River Perak, while at the same time preventing him advancing further South than the River Krian. To this end the 11th Indian Division, which it was considered essential to maintain as a fighting formation, was holding a line along the River Kuran with the 28th Indian Infantry Brigade, and also protecting Kuala Kangsar with the 12th Indian Infantry Brigade, a detachment of which was also further North along the Grik road. The Division as a whole was suffering from exhaustion, damaged feet and loss of equipment. The 6th and 15th Indian Infantry Brigades were now re-formed at Ipoh as the composite 15th Infantry Brigade, while a composite battalion of the 2nd/16th and 3rd/16th from these two Brigades was in Corps Reserve. The Kelantan forces, 8th Indian Infantry Brigade, 9th Indian Division, had suffered about a hundred casualties in each battalion, and were now along the railway at Manik Orai. Of elements not thus far engaged in the main operations, the 22nd Indian Infantry Brigade (9th Indian Division) was at Kuantan, while the Australian 22nd and 27th Brigades were responsible for Johore, and the 1st and 2nd Malay Infantry Brigades for Singapore Fortress. None of these last four Brigades could be despatched North to relieve the hard-pressed 11th Indian Division, for the reasons given below. (*See para.* 138 *below.*)

120. Heavy enemy air attack was now falling on Ipoh aerodrome, and our own fighters were driven further South to Kuala Lumpur (Selangor). Attacks on our road and rail communications were becoming an increasing feature of the Japanese air operations. Reconnaissance revealed that the enemy was now making use of Sungei Patani aerodrome, where thirty fighters were discovered. Our aircraft were making night and dawn attacks on enemy

aerodromes, and were very valuable for reconnaissance; reconnaissances were regularly being made—
    (a) 350 miles N.N.E. of Singapore;
    (b) along the East coast of Malaya;
    (c) over the Rhio Archipelago; and
    (d) to the Miri and Kuching areas—from Sinkawang;
in addition to those over the fighting area.

By the 21st-22nd December Kuala Lumpur was coming in for heavy air attack, though little damage was at first inflicted. Against an attack by Ju. 87's on the 21st December the Buffaloes were more successful, causing the Japanese bombers to break formation in disorder, but to deal with the Zero fighters it was apparent that only the speedy arrival of Hurricane reinforcements, while we still held sufficient air bases, could turn the tide.

The land situation in the next few days (21st-23rd December) witnessed further advances by the enemy in all areas. Pressure along the Grik road was heavy, in spite of severe losses inflicted during a successful clash on the night of the 19th-20th December.

The Japanese floated troops down the Perak River by night, and on the 22nd December the 12th Indian Infantry Brigade was forced back South of Kuala Kangsar. The 28th Indian Infantry Brigade was also pressed in the same direction, small detachments only being left North of Kuala Kangsar and West of the Perak River. Bridges were destroyed as the troops retired. While this was taking place on the Perak front, the Kelantan withdrawal was also continuing, the 8th Indian Infantry Brigade retiring South of Kuala Krai along the railroad. A problem similar to that of Krohcol and the 11th Division referred to above (see para. 115) now arose in regard to 8th Indian Infantry Brigade and the main body of III Corps in Perak, and, to a lesser degree, in regard to the force at Kuantan and the 8th Indian Infantry Brigade. It was therefore decided to withdraw this 8th Brigade much further South into Central Malaya, and it took up completely new positions in the Kuala Lipis-Raub area. A small party known as "Macforce" was left with an armoured train at Dabong to withdraw down the railway, demolishing it as they went. The Kuantan force was ordered to prepare to withdraw Westwards at short notice. On the 23rd December all our fighters on the mainland were withdrawn to Singapore, Kuala Lumpur and Port Swettenham being kept as advanced landing grounds. The enemy was also occupying various points down the East coast of Malaya, and had proceeded from Kuala Trengganu to Dungun. By the 25th December it would be true to say that something like one-half of Malaya had passed from our control.

121. With the object of maintaining the morale of the civil population of Malaya I held a meeting on the 22nd December, attended by members of the Legislative Council, leading men of the different communities and the Press, the total number being about 120. The main points I stressed were that the available strength had proved inadequate; we had to remember that the aircraft, A.A. guns and tanks that might have come to Malaya were not being wasted, but were being used with great effect in Libya and Russia; that there was every reason for confidence that, now the requirements of the Far East had become pressing, those responsible were taking steps to ensure the despatch of adequate reinforcements of men and material; and that it was up to everyone to ensure that no effort was spared to hold up the enemy until the necessary forces arrived.

On the 22nd December, a telegram was sent to Mr. Duff Cooper to the effect that useless mouths were to be evacuated from Singapore without racial discrimination and on a voluntary basis so far as the general population were concerned.

The total number of British women and children evacuated from Malaya from the beginning of the war with Japan to the 31st January, 1942, was as follows:—

    7,174 European;
    2,305 Indian; and
    1,250 Chinese.

According to a Japanese report, the number of British women and children left in Singapore at the time of capitulation was about 200.

XIII.—THE ATTACK ON, AND FALL OF, HONG KONG.

122. On the 8th December, at 0800 hours, hostilities began with the launching of a Japanese air attack on Kowloon. Frontier demolitions were accordingly blown and our troops withdrew according to plan as the Japanese crossed the frontier on a broad front during the course of the morning. It was estimated that the enemy were employing a force of one division, with the possibility of increasing this to two divisions with the troops then in the area.

There was no enemy action from the air or sea during the night of the 8th-9th December, but heavy pressure was exerted against our forward troops along the Taipo Road. During the day of the 9th December these troops were compelled to withdraw within the Gin Drinkers' line in consequence of their left flank being turned. Enemy air attacks during the day, directed mainly against the south coast of the island, did little damage. Leaflets, too, were dropped. The day closed unfortunately, since the Shing Mun Redoubt, held by The Royal Scots, was suddenly captured at 2300 hours—an unexpected blow in view of the difficulty of approach over such country at night. It was considered that local fifth columnists must have guided the Japanese in this attack. One company of Winnipeg Grenadiers was now despatched to reinforce the Kowloon Brigade.

It was soon found necessary, in view of enemy pressure, to readjust the line south-west of the Jubilee Reservoir, where the enemy was making progress, and to vacate Kai Tak aerodrome, after the two remaining aircraft had been demolished. During the morning of the 11th December, however, after the two left Companies (Royal Scots) at Kowloon had been driven in, and reserves (including Winnipeg Grenadiers) had failed to effect more than a temporary halt, it was decided to withdraw from the mainland, with the exception of Devil's Peak. This withdrawal was successfully carried out, beginning at dusk on the 11th, and included howitzers, mechanical transport and armoured cars. Some interference by Kowloon Chinese fifth columnists was experienced. Stonecutter's Island, which had been heavily bombarded and had suffered damage to the military barracks, was also evacuated during the night of the 11th-12th. Hong Kong Island itself was now also the subject of bombardment, both from the air and by artillery, the main target being the naval dockyard.

123. During the night the 12th-13th December, troops were withdrawn from Devil's Peak, our last post on the mainland. Coast defence guns were now used landwards for counter-battery work against the Japanese. It was noted that the evacuation of Kowloon had considerably disturbed the morale of the Hong Kong civil population, and defeatist elements came to the fore. It became necessary to organise rice distribution. The Japanese Commander-in-Chief demanded the surrender of Hong Kong, which was refused.

During the 14th December the Japanese shelling of the island increased in severity, and several of our gunposts were hit, as a result of which some Chinese gunners deserted. The enemy was now enjoying the use of Devil's Peak as an observation post. On the same day Aberdeen was bombed from high-level, and the generating station was hit, though not put out of action. Considerable trouble was still being experienced with the civil population, the police were unable to prevent robbery by armed gangs in the A.R.P. tunnels, and rice distribution was a difficulty. Propaganda was accordingly circulated about the proximity of a Chinese advance to relieve Hong Kong; the Chungking Government's representative was most helpful in maintaining order.

During the night of the 14th-15th December, the Japanese continued their systematic shelling, and gathered together a collection of small craft in Kowloon Bay. The Thracian entered the Bay and sank two river steamers, while a special agent succeeded in blowing up a third ship. The Thracian, however, in view of damage, had to be beached and dismantled the following day.

On the 16th December, Aberdeen was heavily bombed, eight times in all, with resulting loss of one Motor Torpedo Boat and damage to the dock. Most of our Auxiliary Patrolling Vessels were now useless in view of desertion by Chinese crews. The enemy landed parties on Lamma Island, and started concentrations of troops on the mainland at Customs Pass and Waterloo Road, but these were dispersed by our artillery. During the night of the 16th-17th mortar fire damaged some of our machine guns along the water-front.

On the 17th December, Hong Kong Island was twice raided by fourteen Army light bombers, coinciding with heavy bombardment by artillery. After this raid the Japanese again came across with proposals of surrender, which were rejected.

124. The night of the 17th-18th was very quiet, but on the 18th decisive events took place. The North face of the Island was subjected to continuous artillery, mortar and dive-bombing attack, some of our infantry defence posts being struck three or four times. Hospitals were badly hit and much damage was done to water mains, roads, cables and signal communications, also rice stores. Stanley and Murray Barracks were bombed in two raids by nine and six bombers, roughly 100 bombs being dropped—the largest number to that date. Much of the transport of the 2nd Battalion Royal Scots was destroyed, and C Battery Plotting Room O was demolished by a direct hit. The civil Government centre was also dive-bombed. It was following this intense activity that, after dusk, the Japanese effected landings at Quarry Bay and at Lyemun in the north-eastern corner of the island.

The following day the Japanese infiltrated over the hill to the Wong Nei Cheong and Tytam Gaps with pack artillery and mortars. Our artillery from the Collinson and D'Aguilar areas (east and south-east of the Island) were successfully withdrawn to Stanley (south of the Island), but were compelled to destroy their heavy guns and equipment. Our line ran now from Stanley Mound northwards, Stanley Mound itself being held by one battalion of Canadians, two companies of Indian infantry and some miscellaneous artillery and machine guns.

During the afternoon of the 19th a counter-attack was attempted, with the help of motor torpedo boats, to regain possession of Mount Parker and Mount Butler, but broke down through heavy enemy shelling, failure of intercommunications and the exhaustion of our troops. Our motor torpedo boats were successful in destroying landing craft in Kowloon Bay, but two were lost in the operations.

125. On the 20th our line was still roughly North from Stanley Mound. A communiqué was again issued to inspire civilian morale with belief in near relief by Chinese forces. By the 21st the enemy was attacking strongly across Mount Nicholson through Middle Gap, and our troops were suffering greatly from exhaustion, the wet and cold of the night-time, and isolation from food and ammunition stores. Counter-attacks on the enemy rear by the Royal Rifles of Canada came to nought, and Winnipeg Grenadiers were also unsuccessful in an effort to retake Wong Nei Cheong Gap. The enemy still paid attention from the air to the Dockyard area, and practically all Naval personnel were now ashore and took their place in the land fighting. Japanese naval forces blockading the Island consisted of two cruisers, two destroyers and two torpedo boats.

It was during the 21st that the "Resist to the end" message from the Prime Minister was received, followed by instructions from the Admiralty to wreck all oil installations and storages.

The 22nd December witnessed a fresh enemy landing on the north-east coast of the Island. Part of our force was now cut off in Stanley, while various remnants were still holding out in isolated positions. The Japanese were now virtually surrounding Victoria, where a great deal of damage had been inflicted by bombing and shelling. Oil installations were destroyed, but it was found impossible to do so at Lai Chi Kok, since a large hospital would have been endangered. A telegram was received from the Admiralty giving the full text of Mr. Churchill's message, but also leaving to the Governor the discretion of surrender when resistance could no longer be usefully continued.

126. By the 23rd December the principal reservoirs were in the hands of the enemy, and the connections of those that remained under our control were damaged through shell-fire. Great efforts were made to effect repairs, but, in the absence of any substantial success in this direction, only one day's supply of water remained to the beleaguered city. Food stores, too, were greatly depleted. Our troops had become more or less exhausted, though Royal Marines managed to recapture ground on Mount

Cameron (protecting the South of Victoria), which had been heavily bombarded by the Japanese, and the Middlesex Regiment beat off an attack on Leighton Hill. The enemy, however, penetrated through the A.R.P. tunnels and street fighting began at Wanchai. The conduct of the civil population, which had thus far suffered some 4,000 casualties (1,000 killed), was, however, good and had become increasingly so since the first depression after the evacuation of the mainland.

On the same day the forces isolated in the South of the Island made an effort to counterattack towards Stanley Mound, but to no avail.

On the 24th December the Royal Scots, following heavy enemy attacks, were driven off the top of Mount Cameron, and Leighton Hill was captured after bombardment. The position in the South of the Island was unchanged.

On the 25th December, in the early hours of the morning, street fighting took place as the enemy fought his way towards the centre of the town, but another Japanese demand for surrender was refused. Two hours later, however, the Governor was advised by the Military and Naval commanders that further effective resistance could not be made, and, after carrying out a series of demolitions, our forces were ordered to lay down their arms. The Chinese kept their word and had endeavoured to assist the defence of Hong Kong by advancing on Canton, but their force was not strong enough to produce any serious effect on the Japanese.

XIV.—OPERATIONS IN BURMA AND SARAWAK.

Burma.

127. A fresh field of operations opened in Burma on the 9th December, when a landing was reported at Prachuabkhirikun, a clear threat to Mergui and the Tenasserim Peninsula.

On the 11th December, Tavoy was bombed. A further enemy landing at Chumporn (Siam) gave access to the southernmost tip of Burma, and an advance on Victoria Point threatened. In the next two or three days the Japanese advance materialised and coincided with raids on Mergui by about fifty aircraft, propaganda leaflets being dropped as well as bombs. An effort was made to cut off the Japanese advance southwards by crossing the Siam frontier to demolish the railway a few miles south of Prachuabkhirikun, but the strength of the opposition and the heavy rains proved too great for the success of this expedition. The situation was still in an undeveloped stage, but with a clear threat to Southern Burma, when on the 15th December Burma reverted to the province of the Commander-in-Chief, India. (*See para. 29 above.*)

Sarawak.

128. The general problem of the defence of Borneo was indicated in para. 16 above. The oil denial scheme was put into operation at the outbreak of war and completed by the 11th December. The landing ground at Miri was also demolished and the forces at Lutong evacuated by sea to Kuching in H.M.S. *Lipis*.

The Company of 2/15 Punjab Regiment rejoined the rest of its Battalion, which formed the regular garrison of Kuching and the remaining individuals—from the 2nd Loyals and S.S. Police—were brought on to Singapore.

Considerable anxiety and uneasiness was felt by the authorities in Kuching owing to the absence of Naval and Air Forces. It was pointed out to them, however, that many places in England had stood up to bombing without any direct defence, and that they would be expected to do the same. It was evident, however, that the morale of the population of Kuching was in a bad way. This, in my opinion, was partly due to the fact that the ruler, Rajah Brooke, was absent—actually in Australia. He had a great deal of influence with the natives, and in view of the situation he should have returned to his country immediately on the outbreak of war, if not before. As it was, the Sarawak Rangers proved quite unreliable, and the 2/15 Punjab Regiment were left to carry out the defence by themselves.

The complete control of the South China Sea exercised by the Japanese reduced the problem of the capture of Kuching to a mere calculation of the strength necessary to overcome the resistance that they would probably meet. They appear to have attacked it with the equivalent of one Brigade Group.

129. Japanese naval forces were not long in appearing in strength before Miri. By the 16th December, some ten warships had been sighted in company with a tanker off Miri and Lutong, and these ships became the object of our attacks. On the 17th December, 6 Glenn Martins and 5 Buffaloes of the Netherlands East Indies Air Force delivered an attack from Sinkawang, but scored neither hits nor near misses. The same day, Dutch bombers from Samiuwkoa located and attacked this force, a Dutch navy Dornier scoring a direct hit on a destroyer. Encounters between Dutch Buffaloes and the Navy Zero fighters revealed the clear superiority of the Japanese aircraft. Reports of a Japanese landing at Lutong and Baram Point were received, and on the 18th December renewed attacks on enemy shipping in this area were made, without success, by a mixed force. Eight Glenn Martins from Sinkawang had to return without delivering their attack owing to the bad weather. The following day 6 Netherlands East Indies Glen Martins claimed a hit on a cruiser and some near misses. The 19th December, however, was also marked by Japanese air attacks, Kuching aerodrome and town being bombed by about 15 heavy bombers and one seaplane. Civilians suffered approximately 100 casualties, while the main material damage was the destruction of the Borneo Company Benzine Stores. The air war was also carried to Dutch Territory by a heavy attack on Pontianak, much of the city being destroyed.

An expedition clearly aimed at Kuching was then sighted on the 23rd December, and 5 Blenheim IVs, attacking this on the 24th December, scored one hit on a transport and some near misses. Air support from Sinkawang was no longer possible in view of the damage to the aerodrome from a Japanese attack, and the Dutch aircraft were withdrawn to Palembang.

The 2/15 Punjab Regiment carried out demolitions on the aerodromes, held up the Japanese for a time, and eventually moved in accordance with orders, along a jungle path, to join up with the Dutch, though this necessitated abandoning practically the whole of their equipment.

It was noteworthy that Malay labour at Kuching disappeared as the course of operations approached the area.

According to later reports, some 800 of the 2/15 Punjab Regiment joined the Dutch and were still fighting with them at the end of January, 1942.

XV.—SPECIAL FEATURES OF THE OPERATIONS.
Changes in Commands.

130. A large number of changes took place shortly before or shortly after the war with Japan started. These were as follows:—

(a) Admiral Sir Tom Phillips replaced Admiral Sir Geoffrey Layton on the 6th December.

(b) On the 10th December, after Sir Tom Phillips had gone down with the *Prince of Wales*, Sir Geoffrey Layton—who was then actually on board his ship about to start for Australia on his way home—resumed command.

(c) On the 6th November I was informed that " owing to recent developments in the Far East, it had been decided that the duties of Commander-in-Chief should be entrusted to an Army officer with up-to-date experience." My successor was to be Lieutenant-General Paget. This prospective change became generally known in the Army and Air Force in Malaya by the end of November.

(d) On the 29th November a signal was received from Whitehall to the effect that General Pownall had been substituted for General Paget.

(e) On the 15th December the responsibility of the defence of Burma was transferred from the Commander-in-Chief, Far East, to Commander-in-Chief, India.

(f) On the 29th December General McLeod was replaced by General Hutton as General Officer Commanding, Burma.

(g) On the 10th December Mr. Duff Cooper was appointed as Cabinet representative in the Far East, and instructions were received by him that a War Council was to be formed under his leadership.

These changes may have been inevitable, and it could not, of course, have been foreseen that they would coincide so closely with the start of the war, but they did add to the difficulties of the situation.

War Council.

131. The composition of the War Council, the formation of which was started on the 10th December, was as follows:—

Mr. Duff Cooper, *Chairman;*
H.E. the Governor of Malaya;
C.-in-C., Far East;
C.-in-C., Eastern Fleet;
G.O.C. Malaya;
A.O.C., Far East;

and later, Sir George Sansom, as being responsible for Propaganda and Press control.

The War Council did useful work in several directions, but as it was not formed until after the war began there had been no time to work out its correct functions. Actually, the composition led to its dealing rather too much with the details of what was happening in Malaya, whilst it would have been more useful if it had concentrated on the wider problems.

On the 16th December a Civil Defence Committee was set up to review and deal with all measures affecting the defence of Singapore other than those of a purely military character. Its composition was:—

Mr. Duff Cooper, *Chairman;*
Fortress Commander;
Inspector-General of Police; and
One civilian.

Intelligence.

132. Turning to intelligence, perhaps the most serious error was one involving the broadest aspect, namely, the intention of the Japanese Government. From the tactical point of view in Malaya there was no surprise, but from the wider point of view there was. Whilst in General Headquarters we always realised the possibility of the extreme military party in Japan forcing their country into war, we did not believe, till the end of November, that Japan might be actually on the verge of starting war. (*See paras.* 61 *and* 94 *above.*)

As indicated in paragraph 75 above, there was also some error regarding the intentions of the Siamese Government.

133. As regards the more local intelligence, the forces that the Japanese would have at the beginning for an attack on Malaya were estimated with a fair degree of accuracy, but there was an under-estimate of the power of the Japanese to attack several places simultaneously. Before the war it was considered that the Japanese might attack in force either the Philippines (with or without Hong Kong), or Malaya or the Netherlands East Indies. It was not anticipated that they would attack in force both the Philippines and Malaya simultaneously; still less that they would also attack Pearl Harbour. So far as I could gather from telegrams, this opinion was also held in England, at any rate up to the last few days before war started, though I believe the Embassy in Tokio held a more correct view of the Japanese power to attack several places simultaneously.

134. There was also an under-estimate of the efficiency of the Japanese Army and Air Force, particularly in the following points:—

(a) Their disregard of weather conditions, especially their ability to land on beaches in bad weather. Also they appear to have been but little hampered by the flooded state of the country in the Southern end of the Kra Isthmus;

(b) Their mobility. This was due to several causes. The Japanese Army seemed generally to depend less on mechanism than ours and to be content with a smaller proportion of artillery. The men needed only simple food and were able to live largely on the country and apparently required nothing in the way of comforts. In some cases they used lighter weapons including a mortar that was lighter than our 2-inch mortar. As a result the Japanese Army was able to operate with less mechanical transport than ours and so was less dependent upon roads. The whole organisation could be kept less complicated than ours and more flexible;

(c) The individual initiative of the Japanese soldier;

(d) The performance of the naval single-seater fighter known as the Zero type. This had a detachable petrol tank under the fuselage and the Japanese got much value from the long range thus given to it. In spite of this complication, its speed and manoeuvrability at heights of 10,000 feet and over were remarkably good; and

(e) The rapidity with which repairs were carried out, in particular of bridges and aerodromes. This last affected the strength of the Japanese air force in the Singora area at the South end of the Kra Isthmus in the early days of the war.

These under-estimates were not attributable solely to errors on the part of F.E.C.B., but also to those of other bodies, including my own General Headquarters.

Japanese Army Tactics and Training.

135. With regard to tactics, in general the Japanese endeavoured to infiltrate or outflank. They made use of certain novelties such as:—

(a) A type of light infantry screen acting in advance of their main body. The men were very lightly clad, had but little equipment and were armed with a light automatic weapon, the calibre of which was something under 0.3; they carried only about forty rounds of ammunition and a few hand grenades. These light infantry parties used to work individually, would get round to the rear of our advance troops, and resorted to such expedients as climbing trees from which to fire their automatic or throw hand grenades. Our men frequently mistook these light troops for Malays or Chinese, but it is doubtful if the Japanese soldiers were deliberately disguised as Malayan natives;

(b) The use of noise, including Chinese crackers and strange cries at night; these tricks, though laughable when one knew about them, had a certain amount of moral effect, especially on young Indian troops at the commencement of the campaign; and

(c) Inflatable rubber belts to enable men to cross creeks and small rivers.

To combat these tactics the General Officer Commanding, Malaya, stressed the importance of discipline and steadiness, the necessity for alertness and cunning on the part of the individual, and that the way to defeat the enemy was to attack or counter-attack him on every possible occasion. "Essentially war of movement and attack, and too much digging creates defence complex."

136. An anti-white campaign had started in Japan in 1936, and it was evident that for long before the commencement of the war the spirit of hatred of Europeans, particularly the British, had constantly been inculcated into the Japanese soldiers. They appear to have been taught that the killing of Europeans by any method was a patriotic action.

It is possible that had we adopted the same course some men might have fought harder at the start, but it is difficult to inculcate the spirit of hatred into the Englishman. This is partly due to his peculiar faculty of seeing a jest in the most depressing circumstances, and partly to the fact that hatred is ultimately based on fear, which is not a natural characteristic of our race.

Factors affecting Morale of our Forces.

137. The majority of the Indian regiments laboured under some disability on account of the inexperience of most of their British officers. As a rule, there would be two or three senior officers, with fifteen or more years' experience, then a gap until we came to officers who had joined after September, 1939. Somewhere about half these officers had experience in India and could talk the language, but having only from one to two and a half years' service they did not carry the weight which more experienced officers would have done.

In both British and Indian units there was only a small leaven of war-experienced officers and men, and it was under these conditions that young soldiers had to meet the first shock of the Japanese attack.

138. A factor which had some effect on morale generally was that, strategically, we were on the defensive; everyone knew that it was to our interests to avoid war with Japan, which meant that the initiative and especially choice of moment for opening hostilities rested with them.

As stated above, the Matador plan provided for a tactical offensive, provided adequate warning could be obtained. As events turned out, the execution of Matador was impracticable, and later events confirmed that the decision not to carry out this operation was correct.

Then, owing to the comparative weakness of our forces in Malaya we could neither afford heavy losses up North nor send up there more than limited reinforcements, because of the necessity for retaining a force to defend Southern Johore and in the last resort the island of Singapore itself. This was not the result of a sort of fortress-complex, but because the essential factor was preservation of the repair and other facilities in the Naval Base. The opinion held in London on this point was made perfectly clear in the latter part of December when the Chiefs of Staff telegraphed: "His Majesty's Government agree your conception that vital issue is to ensure security of Singapore Naval Base. They emphasise that no other consideration must compete with this."

Holding Northern Malaya was not an end in itself; it was with reference to the Naval Base that Northern Malaya acquired its importance. This meant that Commanders in the North had to bear in mind the possibility of withdrawal in the face of superior forces, their action—at any rate until Johore was reached—being mainly a delaying one to gain time for the arrival of reinforcements from overseas. This applied particularly to the Kelantan area, and to a lesser extent, to Kuantan, since in both cases (as stated in para. 12 above) the line of communication was a single one and vulnerable to air bombing.

139. It is easy to talk of the lack of an offensive spirit and of a "retreat complex," but under the conditions described above withdrawals from the North were necessary; and the adverse effect induced by having to carry out a continuous retreat over some hundreds of miles starting from the early days of the campaign must be attributed to the general situation rather than to any fault in the original morale of the troops themselves.

It is possible however, that the need for offensive action even during a retreat had not been so stressed during the training of officers and men as to become a second nature. For instance, there appeared to be a tendency to use reserves for supporting a weak portion of a defensive position rather than retaining them at all costs for bringing about a counter-attack. Again, up to the time I handed over command, there was a tendency to use the Independent Company in Malaya as a reinforcement and not to carry out the functions for which it was specially intended. Further, officers and men must be taught that occasions will arise when some parties have got to hold on to the last man, even though the main body of the force may be moving back.

Royal Air Force problems.

140. With regard to the Air Force, reference has already been made in paras. 79 and 88 above to the obsolescence of our Vildebeeste aircraft and to the effect of lack of reserves. Apart from this, the necessity for rapid evacuation of the Northern aerodromes had some effect on the ground personnel, many of whom were young and inexperienced. There were insufficient rifles or Thompson guns to equip all Air Force personnel, but they must be prepared to fight, and, if necessary, sacrifice themselves in the same way as the infantry; and further, must spare no effort to ensure that all material than can possibly be moved is despatched, or in the last resort destroyed, to prevent its being of value to the enemy.

141. The Royal Air Force suffered from lack of staff. It was not so much that more officers were required at headquarters as that sufficient should have been available to form another Group Headquarters. A Fighter Headquarters had been formed and operated well, but the rest of the operations had to be carried out direct by Royal Air Force Headquarters, with the result that practically all the headquarters air staff officers had to be employed in the operations room, and, including the Air Officer Commanding, were fully occupied in working out details of bombing and reconnaissance, leaving no one to plan and think ahead. This condition would have been improved had it been possible to form another group to operate the bombing squadrons, or, possibly, naval co-operation and overseas reconnaissance as well as all bombing.

142. As aerodromes in Northern Malaya became untenable there was a danger of those in the South becoming too few to allow of adequate dispersal of the Royal Air Force Squadrons. The possibility of this had also been foreseen some months before war broke out and it had been decided in such an eventuality to move the bombing squadrons to Dutch aerodromes in Sumatra, retaining most of the fighter squadrons on Singapore Island. Up to the time that war broke out this remained little more than a project owing to the Royal Air Force staff being fully occupied with other work. At the end of December, however, the plans were well advanced, not only for the move of these squadrons but also for the possible establishment of an erecting depot in Java.

143. The need for preserving an adequate force for the protection of the Naval Base (*see para.* 138 *above*) applied especially to the Royal Air Force. This accounts for the comparative weakness of the fighter strength in Northern Malaya at the start of the war and for fighter escorts not being available for our bombers. From the last week in December air protection for reinforcement convoys absorbed most of our fighter strength.

Defence and Denial of Aerodromes.

144. As indicated in para. 103 above, the primary object of the Japanese appears to have been to get command of the air, principally by the attack on our aerodromes by aircraft, or by their capture. The weakness of our aerodrome defence is referred to in para. 115 above. In regard to A.A. weapons, as a result of the experiences in Crete, I laid down that the defence of aerodromes was to take precedence over everything else except the A.A. defence of the Naval Base. It was decided that the full scale of the defence would be eight heavy and eight light A.A. guns; this was altered after war broke out to four heavy and twelve light, a scale that was hardly every approached.

145. When our aerodromes had to be abandoned, steps were naturally taken to render them useless to the enemy, particularly by explosives in runways and other parts of the landing area. The effect of this action was generally of disappointingly short duration. The Japanese were certainly quick in carrying out repairs, but, even allowing for that, the results of many of the demolitions as carried out seem hardly to have repaid the energy expended and the adverse moral effect on troops of hearing explosions behind them. A system of delay-action mines would probably have been effective provided they could have been properly concealed; preparations would have been necessary for this at the time the aerodromes were constructed. A heavy tractor drawing some form of deep plough or scarifier and working in between craters would have been a very useful addition; it could not have gone on working to the last moment, unless it was intended to abandon the tractor, since these could only move very slowly and were likely to block roads if left to the last.

At aerodromes located in wet or low-lying areas, mines should be located with reference to the drainage system with the object of dislocating it and so putting the aerodrome out of action for a long period. Aerodromes in our possession were occasionally rendered unserviceable for about twenty-four hours by Japanese bombing of runways; this would have been much more effective had delay-action bombs been used.

Left-Behind Parties.

146. An attempt was made to organise left-behind parties in Northern Malaya with the object of obtaining information and carrying out sabotage of all sorts in the enemy's rear. This duty was entrusted to the O.M. Section of the Ministry of Economic Warfare under Mr. Killery. It was, however, started too late and there was no time to organise it thoroughly. This was in no way the fault of the O.M., but was due to the factors mentioned in para. 9 above.

Question of a Military Governor.

147. The appointment of a Military Governor might have been desirable for Singapore Island during the later stages, but I was of the opinion that such an appointment for the whole of Malaya at the start of the war was not a practicable proposition. The main reason was that the organisation of the Colony, with the Federated and the Unfederated States, was very complicated and that it was not a practical proposition for anyone to take it over at short notice. It would have been found far more practicable for Hong Kong.

Australia's Assistance.

148. The Australian Government fully realised the importance of Singapore to the defence of the Far East and especially to Australia and did everything in their power to help. In November, 1940, there were three squadrons of the Royal Australian Air Force

in Malaya. In December, 1940, the Australian War Minister visited Singapore. Largely as a result of his representations, the Australian Government despatched the 22nd Brigade, Australian Imperial Forces, to Singapore in February. The 27th Brigade followed later, and arrived on the 20th August. Besides these valuable reinforcements, Australia supplied officers for the Royal Air Force Volunteer Reserve for administrative work on aerodromes, men for two reserve mechanical transport units in the spring of 1941 and for the forty tanks which we had hoped to get from the Middle East. The situation regarding Beaufort aircraft has been mentioned in para. 79 above, and small arms ammunition in para. 92. In addition to this, Australia also supplied many items of signalling equipment and special radio sets for coast defence guns. After the war started four Hudsons from Australia reached Singapore on the 23rd December and Army reinforcements were promised. (*See para.* 118 *above.*)

The Dutch.

149. The Dutch in the Netherlands East Indies faithfully executed their share of the agreements and, indeed, went beyond them, and co-operated wholeheartedly with us in every way. They sent three bomber squadrons and one fighter squadron in the early days of the war in Malaya, although, owing to technical troubles they were having at the time with their engines, the bomber squadrons consisted of only six aircraft, the whole three, therefore, being equivalent to little more than one British bomber squadron. Their submarines operated with great gallantry in the Gulf of Siam. They also gave me three of their reserve flying boats to make good our losses, and sent over a guerilla band to Northern Malaya to operate in the Japanese rear.

At a later stage in the operations I believe they were somewhat critical of the amount of assistance we were able to send to the Netherlands East Indies, and of the length of time before it arrived; should this give rise to any acrimony in the future, I hope that the prompt and whole-hearted assistance they rendered to us will not be forgotten.

Work of General Headquarters.

150. In Malaya the operations of my own Headquarters were limited to the issue of certain directives to the General Officer Commanding and Air Officer Commanding. These laid down such matters as the withdrawal from Kelantan and Kuantan, and priority of tasks for the Royal Air Force. Apart from that, the main work was to secure the proper co-ordination of air operations with the Dutch and Australians.

A great deal of the time of my small staff was taken up at the beginning by the drafting of Sitreps telegrams and communiqués, as well as preparing appreciations demanded from England. One of the problems regarding the two former was the fact that they had to be sent to Australia as well as to England; their timing was, therefore, a matter of fine adjustment, since it was necessary to ensure, for instance, that a communiqué should not be printed in Australian newspapers before the Sitreps telegrams arrived in England. Eventually, it was found simpler to hand over most of this work to the combined Army and Air Force Operations room, in so far as Malaya itself was concerned, and General Headquarters Sitreps communiqués were confined to the situation as a whole.

Although my General Headquarters operated at the Naval Base at the beginning of the war, it was found that, after the loss of the *Prince of Wales* and *Repulse* and the formation of the War Council, it was more convenient for my Headquarters to be located near the Combined Operations Room. Preparations had been made for this some months before, and the necessary accommodation was available. The move was carried out about the 15th December.

151. After the transfer of the defence of Burma to Commander-in-Chief, India, and the fall of Hong Kong, it was felt that the location of General Headquarters should no longer be in Malaya, since to keep it there would not only hamper its own work but cramp the initiative of the General Officer Commanding and Air Officer Commanding and make the organisation in Singapore too top-heavy. It was decided before I left that the correct location of General Headquarters would be in Java, preferably near Bandoeng, and steps were already in hand to effect this move. The possibility of a move away from Singapore becoming necessary had been foreseen many months before.

152. The results of the campaign in the Far East naturally gave rise to some speculation as to the advisability of forming what may be called Strategic Headquarters, devoid of all responsibility for direct operational control or administration. Commander-in-Chief, Middle East, at the time I passed through Cairo in November, 1940, stated that, in his opinion, such a General Headquarters was impracticable. My view is that, under special conditions such as existed in the Far East, a strategic General Headquarters was a workable proposition, provided its limitations are fully recognized.

In para. 5 above were indicated the measures which it was expected to achieve by the creation of a General Headquarters, Far East. We failed to convince the Japanese that our strength was too great to be challenged with success; the limitation of the forces, especially aircraft, that could be sent to the Far East was imposed by prior requirements elsewhere.

Co-operation in Malaya and co-ordination of effort with neighbouring countries, including plans for mutual reinforcement, were achieved.

Farewell Order.

153. I handed over Command of the Far East to Lt.-General Sir Henry Pownall on the 27th December, 1941, and left Singapore, in accordance with instructions, on the 31st December.

I end with my farewell order which was published on the 28th December, 1941.

To ALL RANKS OF THE ARMY AND AIR FORCE, MALAYA.

On relinquishing the Far East Command I send to you all in the Army and Air Force in Malaya a message of farewell, of admiration for the way you have faced danger, fatigue and hardship, and of all good wishes for 1942.

I know my successor well, and I turn over the command to good hands.

Remember that upon the issue of this war depends the welfare of the whole world, including our own families. Their eyes are upon you. Do your Duty unflinchingly, knowing that the resources of the Empire and of our Allies are behind you, confident that, however hard the struggle now, our cause will triumph in the end.

R. BROOKE-POPHAM,
Air Chief Marshal.

APPENDICES

A.—Directive to the Commander-in-Chief, Far East ... ...

B.—Instructions issued to General Officers Commanding and Air Officer Commanding, Far East ... ...

C.—His Majesty's Ships based at Singapore and Hong Kong, December 7, 1941

D.—Summary of Army Strength, Malaya, November, 1940 ... ...

E.—Order of Battle, Malaya, December 7, 1941, and Summary ... ...

F.—Anti-Aircraft Position, December, 7, 1941 ... ...

G.—Order of Battle, Burma, December 7, 1941, and Summary ... ...

H.—Order of Battle, Hong Kong, December 8, 1941 ... ...

I.—Strength of Air Force in Malaya, November, 1940 ... ...

J.—Strength and Dispositions of the Royal Air Force, December 7, 1941 ...

K.—Summary of Operationally Serviceable I.E. Aircraft in Malaya ... ...

L.—Performance of the Buffalo Single-Seater ... ...

M.—Order of the Day issued December 8, 1941 ... ...

APPENDIX A.

DIRECTIVE TO THE COMMANDER-IN-CHIEF, FAR EAST.

1. You are appointed Commander-in-Chief, Far East.

2. You will be responsible to the Chiefs of Staff for the operational control and general direction of training of all British land and air forces in Malaya,* Burma and Hong Kong, and for the co-ordination of plans for the defence of these territories.

You will also be responsible for the operational control and general direction of training of British Air Forces in Ceylon and of the general reconnaissance Squadrons of the Royal Air Force which it is proposed to station in the Indian Ocean and Bay of Bengal for ocean reconnaissance in those areas.

3. For these purposes, the following will be under your command:—

General Officer Commanding, Malaya.
General Officer Commanding, Burma.
General Officer Commanding, Hong Kong.
Air Officer Commanding, Far East.

---
*Including the Straits Settlements, the Federated and Unfederated Malay States, Brunei, Sarawak and North Borneo.

4. It is intended that you should deal primarily with matters of major military policy and strategy. It is not the intention that you should assume administrative or financial responsibilities or the normal day-to-day functions at present exercised by the General Officers Commanding and Air Officer Commanding.

These Officers will continue to correspond as at present with the War Office, Air Ministry, Colonial Office and Burma Office, on all matters on which they have hitherto dealt with these departments, to the fullest extent possible consistent with the exercise of your Command; keeping you informed as and when you wish.

5. Your staff will consist of the following only, and no expansion of this staff is contemplated:—

A Chief of Staff (an army officer of the rank of Major-General),
A Senior Royal Air Force Staff Officer,
A Naval Liaison Officer,
An Army Officer of the rank of General Staff Officer, 1st Grade,
An officer from each Service of the equivalent rank of General Staff Officer, 2nd Grade, together with the necessary clerical and cypher staff.

6. You will, where appropriate, consult and co-operate with the Commander-in-Chief, China, the Commander-in-Chief, East Indies, and the Commander-in-Chief in India. You will also communicate direct with the Defence Departments of the Governments of the Commonwealth of Australia and New Zealand on all routine matters of interest to them, but on matters of major policy you will communicate to these Dominion Governments through the appropriate Service Department of His Majesty's Government.

7. You will keep the Governor of the Straits Settlements and High Commissioner for the Malay States, the Governor of Burma and the Governor of Hong Kong closely and constantly informed and will consult them as appropriate.

8. The General and Air Officers mentioned in paragraph 3 above remain, subject to your general direction and supervision, in touch with the Governor of the Straits Settlements and High Commissioner for the Malay States, the Governor of Burma and the Governor of Hong Kong. In the case of Burma you will ensure that the constitutional relations between the Governor and the General Officer Commanding are not affected. This is of particular importance with regard to any movement of troops which might affect internal security.

9. You will, where appropriate, maintain touch with His Majesty's representatives in Japan, China, the United States of America and Thailand, and with His Majesty's Consuls-General in the Netherlands East Indies and Indo-China. The maintenance of touch with His Majesty's representatives and Consuls-General in these countries will rest with you exclusively and not with the General and Air Officers referred to in paragraph 3.

10. The Far East Combined Intelligence Bureau, in addition to keeping you informed of current intelligence, will be charged with the duty of collecting such special intelligence as you may require. The Bureau will remain under the control of the Admiralty.

11. You will normally communicate as necessary with the Chiefs of Staff, the Air Ministry being used as a channel of communication for telegrams, and letters being addressed to the Secretary, Chiefs of Staff Committee; but you have the right to correspond direct with an individual Chief of Staff on matters particularly affecting his Service.

APPENDIX B.

INSTRUCTIONS ISSUED TO GENERAL OFFICERS COMMANDING AND AIR OFFICER COMMANDING, FAR EAST.

Headquarters of Commander-in-Chief, Far East, will open at Singapore at 0800 hours on the 18th November.

(2) A prime function of staff of Commander-in-Chief, Far East, will be to prepare, in conjunction with Staff of Commander-in-Chief, China, all joint plans that may be required either by Chiefs of Staff organisation in London or by strategic situation in Far East. The Authority for such plans will be either Chiefs of Staffs in London or two Commanders-in-Chief.

(3) There will be no alteration in channels by which you correspond War Office, Air Ministry, Colonial Office or Burma Office on any matters other than questions of policy affecting strategy or operations. On these questions of policy you will correspond direct with this Headquarters, sending copies of your communications to appropriate Governor. Similarly, all communications from Commander-in-Chief, Far East, to you on these questions will be repeated to appropriate Governor.

On other questions you will repeat to Commander-in-Chief, Far East, such of your communications to War Office, &c., as you judge of sufficient importance.

(4) You will ensure that intimate touch now existing between yourself and Governor in your command is maintained.

(5) You will submit to Commander-in-Chief copies of your most recent appreciations and plans which are now in operation and will keep him fully informed of any changes in situation by signal if of immediate importance, otherwise by periodical liaison letter.

(6) You will submit location statement showing present location of all forces within your command. You will subsequently report major changes in location as they occur.

(7) The Commander-in-Chief requires to be kept informed of general administrative conditions of forces under your command, including position in respect of reserves of essential commodities. Any major administrative difficulties which you may now be experiencing, or which arise subsequently, will be reported at once, in order that both extent to which they may affect operations or policy may be accurately gauged, and that representations may be made direct by him to higher authority, if such a course appears to be required.

(8) You will submit short report of present state of training of units under your command and your programme of training for coming months. Further instructions will be issued on method by which Commander-in-Chief is to be kept informed of progress of training.

(9) Chiefs of Staff have made Commander-in-Chief, Far East, responsible for maintaining touch with His Majesty's representatives in Japan, China and Thailand, and with His Majesty's Consuls-General in Netherlands East Indies and Indo-China. Your direct touch with His Majesty's representatives or Consuls-General in these countries should therefore be restricted to matters immediately affecting your commands.

APPENDIX C.

H.M. SHIPS BASED AT SINGAPORE AND HONG KONG ON 7TH DECEMBER, 1941.

Singapore—
  Capital Ships—
    Prince of Wales.
    Repulse.

  Cruisers—
    Danae.
    Dragon.
    Durban.

  Destroyers—
    Jupiter.
    Electra.
    Encounter.
    Express.
    Tenedos.
    Thanet.
    Scout.
    Stronghold.

Ships from other Stations refitting at Singapore.
  Cruiser—
    Mauritius (E.I. Station).

  Destroyers—
    Isis (Mediterranean Station).
    H.M.A.S. *Vampire* (Australian Station).
    H.M.A.S. *Vendetta* (Australian Station).

  Submarine—
    Rover (Mediterranean Station).

Hong Kong—
  Destroyer—
    Thracian.

This list does not include auxiliary minesweepers, patrol vessels and small craft.

APPENDIX D.

SUMMARY OF ARMY STRENGTH, MALAYA, NOVEMBER, 1940.

Infantry—
  17 Battalions, viz.—
    British ... ... 6 (including 1 M.G. Battalion).
    Indian 10
    Malay 1

Mobile Artillery—
  1 Mountain Regiment, R.A.

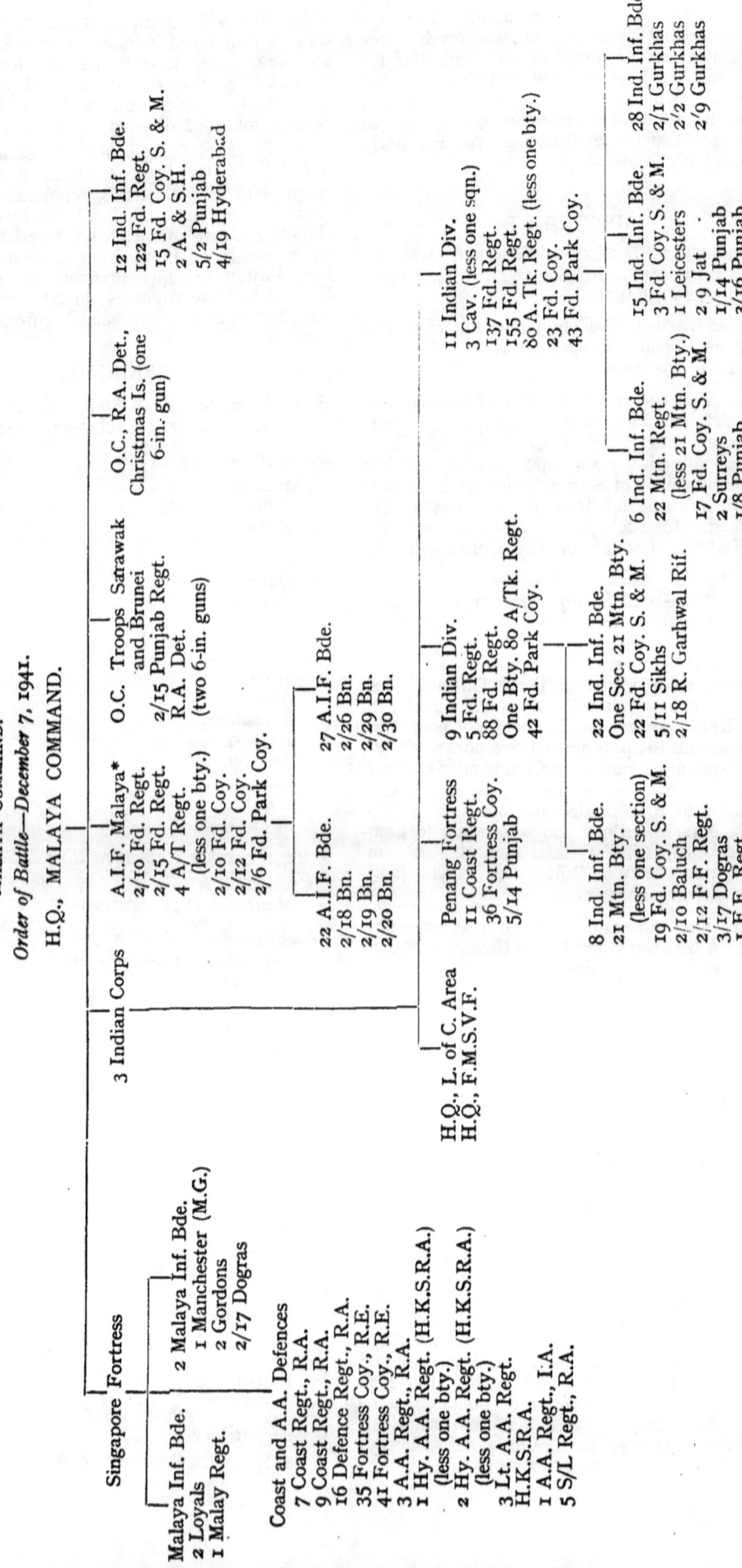

Summary of Strength of Army in Malaya, December 7, 1941.

(Royal Engineers, Mechanical Transport, Signals and Ancillary Units not included.)

Infantry Battalions—
    British ... ... 6 (including 1 M.G. Btn.).
    Indian 18
    Australian 6
    Malay 1
            Total 31
    Volunteer Battalions 10
    Johore Military Forces ... 1
    Indian State Forces 5

Artillery—
    Field Regiments ... ... 7 (5 of 24 guns; 2 of 16 guns).
    Mountain Regiments ... ... 1 (24 guns).
    Anti-Tank Regiments ... ... 2 (1 of 48 guns; 1 of 36 guns).
    Anti-Tank Batteries ... ... 2 (1 of 8 Breda guns; 1 of 6 2-pounders).

Total Strength—
    Regulars—
        British 19,391
        Australian 15,279
        Indian 37,191
        Asiatic 4,482
            Total 76,343
    Volunteers—
        British 2,430
        Indian 727
        Asiatic 7,395
            Total 10,552

            Grand Total 86,895

APPENDIX F.

FAR EAST.

Anti-Aircraft Position, December 7, 1941.

	Approved Scale.	Holdings.	En route.	Allocated but not shipped.
Malaya—				
Heavy	176	70	12	20 ⎫ (b)
Light	100 (plus 144 field force)	78	28	52 ⎭
3-in. Naval	Nil	24	Nil	
Burma—				
Heavy	24	8 ⎫ (a)	8	
Light	68	16 ⎭	8	
Hong Kong—				
Heavy	32	14	4	
Light	30	2	8	
3-in. Naval	Nil	2		

(a) Of these 4 heavy and 8 light had only just reached Rangoon and had not been installed.
(b) A proportion was to be allocated to Burma by Commander-in-Chief, Far East.

APPENDIX G.

BURMA.

Order of Battle at Commencement of Hostilities.

(1) 1st Burma Division—
consisting of—

    Maymyo Brigade — 2nd K.O.Y.L.I.
1st Burma Rifles.
6th Burma Rifles.
7th Burma Rifles.
12th Mountain Battery.
56th Field Company (S. and M.).

    Tenasserim Brigade — 2nd Burma Rifles.
4th Burma Rifles.
5th Burma Rifles.
8th Burma Rifles.
2nd Mountain Battery.
Sec. Field Company.

    13th Indian Infantry Brigade — 5th/1st Punjab.
2nd/7th Rajputs.
1st/18th R. Garh Rifles.
23rd Mountain Battery.
5th Field Battery R.A., B.A.F.

(2) Rangoon Brigade — 1st Gloucesters.
3rd Burma Rifles.
Coast Defence Battery.

(3) 16th Indian Infantry Brigade — 1st/9th Jat.
4th/12th F.F. Regiment.
1st/7th Gurkha Regiment.
5th Mountain Battery.
Headquarters, 27th Mountain Regiment.
50th Field Company (S. and M.).

(4) Burma Frontier Force — Bhama Battalion.
Chin Hills Battalion.
Myitkyina Battalion.
Northern Shan States Battalion.
Southern Shan States Battalion.
Kokine Battalion.
Reserve Battalion.

(5) Garrison Companies — 1st Garrison Company.
2nd Garrison Company.
3rd Garrison Company.
4th Garrison Company.
5th Garrison Company.

(6) Burma Rifles (Territorials) — 11th Burma Rifles.
12th Burma Rifles.
13th Southern Shan States
    Battalion Burma Rifles.
14th Burma Rifles (forming).

(7) Burma Auxiliary Force — Rangoon Battalion.
Upper Burma Battalion.
Burma Railways Battalion.
Tenasserim Battalion.
1 A.A. Regiment (forming).

(8) Burma Rifles — 9th and 10th Battalions (forming).
Six Anti-Tank Troops.
One Field Battery.

(9) Field Company — Forming.

(10) Armed Police — Three Battalions.

SUMMARY OF STRENGTH OF ARMY IN BURMA, DECEMBER 7, 1941.

Infantry—
British	2 battalions.
Indian	6 battalions.
Burma Rifles (Regulars)	8 battalions (4 of these just formed).
Burma Rifles (Territorials)	4 battalions.
Garrison Company	5 battalions.
Burma Auxiliary Force	4 battalions.
Burma Frontier Force	6 battalions, 1 reserve battalion.

Artillery—
Indian Mountain Batteries	3
Burma Auxiliary Force	1 field battery, 18-pounders.

Five mobile detachments Burma Frontier Force.

APPENDIX H.

HONG KONG.

Order of Battle at Outbreak of War.

At the outbreak of hostilities on the 8th December, 1941, the garrison comprised:—

Hong Kong Infantry Brigade—

	Arrived.
1st Battalion Middlesex Regiment (M.G.)	August, 1937.
1st Battalion The Winnipeg Grenadiers	November, 1941.
1st Battalion The Royal Rifles of Canada	November, 1941.

Kowloon Infantry Brigade—

2nd Battalion The Royal Scots	January, 1938.
2nd 14th Punjab Regiment	November, 1940.
5th 7th Rajputana Rifles	June, 1937.

Headquarters Fortress, R.E.—

1 E. and M. Company.
1 Field Company (3 British, 1 Chinese section).
1 Bomb Disposal section.
1 Medium Regiment, H.K.S.R.A.
8th Coast Regiment, R.A.
12th Coast Regiment, R.A.
5th A.A. Regiment, R.A.
Ancillary Units.
Hong Kong Volunteer Defence Corps (strength about 2,000).
A Chinese machine-gun battalion was in process of being formed, but had not progressed beyond the cadre stage.

Appropriate strengths of all personnel mobilised at the 8th December, 1941, were:—

British	3,652
Canadian	1,982
Indian	2,254
Local Colonial	2,428
Hong Kong Volunteer Defence Corps	2,000
Auxiliary Defence Units	2,112
Nursing Detachment	136
Total	14,564

APPENDIX I.

STRENGTH OF AIR FORCE IN MALAYA.

November, 1940.

Bombers: 2 squadrons Blenheim I—24 aircraft.
Reconnaissance: 2 squadrons Hudsons (R.A.A.F.)—24 aircraft.
Torpedo Bombers: 2 squadrons Vildebeestes—24 aircraft.
General Purpose: 1 squadron Wirraways (R.A.A.F.)—12 aircraft.
Flying Boats: 1 squadron Singapores—4 aircraft.

Total: 88 first-line aircraft.

APPENDIX J.

STRENGTH AND DISPOSITIONS OF THE R.A.F., DECEMBER 7, 1941.

Malaya.

Aerodrome.	Squadron No.	Type.	Strength in Aircraft.
Alor Star	62	Blenheim I (B)	11
Sungei Patani	21 (R.A.A.F.)	Buffalo	12
Sungei Patani	27	Blenheim I (F)	12
Kota Bharu	1 (R.A.A.F.)	Hudson	12
Kota Bharu	36	Vildebeeste	6
Gong Kedah	100	Vildebeeste	6
Kuantan	60 (a)	Blenheim I (B)	8
Kuantan	8 (R.A.A.F.)	Hudson	8
Kuantan	36	Vildebeeste	6
Tengah	34	Blenheim IV	16
Kallang	243 and 488	Buffalo	32
Sembawang	8 (R.A.A.F.)	Hudson	4
Sembawang	453	Buffalo	16
Seletar	100	Vildebeeste	6
Seletar	205	Catalina	3
			158

(a) No. 60 Squadron had arived from Burma for Bombing practice, and was retained in Malaya on the start of the war with Japan. About the middle of December the personnel were sent back to Burma by sea, the aeroplanes being retained in Malaya to replace wastage in other squadrons.

There were two maintenance units, No. 151 at Seletar and No. 153 at Kuala Lumpur.

Reserve Aircraft.

Blenheim I and IV	15
Buffalo	52 (b)
Hudson	7
Vildebeeste	12
Catalina	2
Total	88

(b) Of these, 21 were temporarily out of action owing to trouble with the engine valve gear on a new mark of engine.

Burma.

Aerodrome.	Squadron No.	Type.	Strength in Aircraft.
Mingaladon	60	Blenheim I (B)	4
Mingaladon	67	Buffalo	16

Reserve Aircraft.

Blenheim I	Nil
Buffalo	16

Of the total of 32 Buffaloes in Burma, 24 were temporarily out of action owing to trouble with the engine valve gear on a new mark of engine.

Ceylon.

Catalina	2

Total in Far East.

Initial Equipment	180
Reserves	104
Total	284

Of these aircraft, the Vildebeestes were obsolete, and if these are deducted the figures become:—

Initial Equipment	156
Reserves	92
Total	248

Requirements as laid down by the Chiefs of Staff were 336 Initial Equipment. Reserves for these on the basis of 50 per cent. for flying-boats and 100 per cent. for all other aircraft should have amounted to 327, a total of 663.

Omitting the Vildebeestes, the total deficiency in aircraft was 415.

The Dutch sent over a total of 22 bombers and 9 fighters. If these are included, the net deficiency becomes 384.

The figure of 100 per cent. for reserves of land-based aircraft was laid down in an Air Ministry telegram of the 23rd February, 1941.

APPENDIX K.

SUMMARY OF OPERATIONALLY SERVICEABLE I.E. AIRCRAFT IN MALAYA.

	Dec. 7.	Dec. 12.	Dec. 17.	Dec. 19.	Dec. 22.	Dec. 24.
Bombers (including Torpedo Bombers)	59	45	59	58	49	61
Fighters	72	53	58	53	45	50
Reconnaissance	24	7	12	11	12	13
Flying Boats	3	3	4	4	3	3
Total	158	108	133	126	109	127

The above figures do not include Dutch aircraft in N. Sumatra or in Borneo, which were stationed North of the Equator and thus came under the command of the Air Officer Commanding, Far East, under the terms of the A.D.B. Agreement. Nor do the figures include Immediate Reserves with Squadrons, Reserves in the Maintenance Units nor Aircraft in the A.A.C.U.

APPENDIX L.

PERFORMANCE OF THE BUFFALO SINGLE SEATER.

A report on the tests of a Buffalo was sent in from the A. & A.E.E., Boscombe Down, dated the 3rd July, 1941. Comparison of this with the official intelligence figures of the Japanese Naval fighter, Zero type, showed that the Buffalo was much inferior at heights of 10,000 feet, and over, viz. :—

	Zero Fighter.	Buffalo.
Rate of climb to 13,000 feet	4·3 minutes	6·1 minutes
Speed at 10,000 feet	315	270 (Approx.)

At 20,000 feet the performance, as indicated by the official figures, is more nearly equal, i.e. :—

	Zero Fighter.	Buffalo.
Speed at 20,000 feet	295	292

Actual experience in Malaya, however, showed that this speed of 292 for the Buffalo could not be obtained. Whether this was due to the aeroplane, to the climate or to the pilots I cannot say.

APPENDIX M.

MALAYA.

Order of the Day issued December 8, 1941.

Japan's action to-day gives the signal for the Empire Naval, Army and Air Forces, and those of their Allies, to go into action with a common aim and common ideals.

We are ready. We have had plenty of warning and our preparations are made and tested. We do not forget at this moment the years of patience and forbearance in which we have borne, with dignity and discipline, the petty insults and insolences inflicted on us by the Japanese in the Far East. We know that those things were only done because Japan thought she could take advantage of our supposed weakness. Now, when Japan herself has decided to put the matter to a sterner test, she will find out that she has made a grievous mistake.

We are confident. Our defences are strong and our weapons efficient. Whatever our race, and whether we are now in our native land or have come thousands of miles, we have one aim and one only. It is to defend these shores, to destroy such of our enemies as may set foot on our soil, and then, finally, to cripple the power of the enemy to endanger our ideals, our possessions and our peace.

What of the enemy? We see before us a Japan drained for years by the exhausting claims of her wanton onslaught on China. We see a Japan whose trade and industry have been so dislocated by these years of reckless adventure that, in a mood of desperation, her Government has flung her into war under the delusion that, by stabbing a friendly nation in the back, she can gain her end. Let her look at Italy and what has happened since that nation tried a similar base action.

Let us all remember that we here in the Far East form part of the great campaign for the preservation in the world of truth and justice and freedom; confidence, resolution, enterprise and devotion to the cause must and will inspire every one of us in the fighting services, while from the civilian population, Malay, Chinese, Indian, or Burmese, we expect that patience, endurance and serenity which is the great virtue of the East and which will go far to assist the fighting men to gain final and complete victory.

R. BROOKE-POPHAM, *Air Chief Marshal,*
Commander-in-Chief, Far East.

G. LAYTON, *Vice-Admiral,*
Commander-in-Chief, China.

LONDON
PRINTED AND PUBLISHED BY HIS MAJESTY'S STATIONERY OFFICE
To be purchased directly from H.M. Stationery Office at the following addresses:
York House, Kingsway, London, W.C.2; 13a Castle Street, Edinburgh, 2;
39-41 King Street, Manchester, 2; 1 St. Andrew's Crescent, Cardiff;
Tower Lane, Bristol, 1; 80 Chichester Street, Belfast
OR THROUGH ANY BOOKSELLER
1948
Price 2s. 0d. net

S.O. Code No. 65-38183

THIRD SUPPLEMENT
TO
The London Gazette
Of FRIDAY, the 20th of FEBRUARY, 1948

Published by Authority

Registered as a newspaper

THURSDAY, 26 FEBRUARY, 1948

REPORT ON THE AIR OPERATIONS DURING THE CAMPAIGNS IN MALAYA AND NETHERLAND EAST INDIES FROM 8TH DECEMBER, 1941 TO 12TH MARCH, 1942.

The following report was submitted to the Secretary of State for Air on July 26th, 1947, by Air Vice-Marshal Sir PAUL MALTBY, K.B.E., C.B., D.S.O., A.F.C., Assistant Air Officer Commanding Far East Command, Royal Air Force, from January 12th to February 10th, 1942, and Air Officer Commanding Royal Air Force in Java from February 11th to March 12th, 1942.

FOREWORD.

A report on the operations in Malaya and the N.E.I. would be incomplete without a survey of the situation in the Far East before war broke out there. A convenient date for beginning such a survey is 1st June, 1941, soon after the date, 24th April, 1941, on which the late Air Vice-Marshal C. W. Pulford became Air Officer Commanding R.A.F. Far East Command.

A number of other newly posted Senior Officers also took up their new duties about the same time, the more important amongst them being Lieut.-Gen. A. E. Percival (G.O.C. Malaya—16th May, 1941), Air Commodore C. O. F. Modin (A.O.A. at A.H.Q. 10.6.41), Group Captain A. G. Bishop (Group Captain Ops. at A.H.Q. 1.6.41) and the late Group Captain E. B. Rice (Fighter Defence Commander of Singapore and Co-ordinator of Air Defences of Malaya, both newly established appointments, 10.7.41).

Although 1st June, 1941, has been chosen as the datum line from which to start the survey, full recognition is given to the large amount of preparatory work which was done by the predecessors of the officers whose names are mentioned above. Some reference is necessarily made to matters which occurred during the time they were in office, but in general the survey deals with the period between 1st June, 1941, and the outbreak of war. It indicates the energetic measures which were taken immediately beforehand to prepare the Command for war, and points a picture of the situation as it existed at the outbreak of hostilities.

The narrative contains only brief reference to developments in Hong Kong, Burma and the Indian Ocean, operational control of which passed out of the hands of the A.O.C. Far East Command soon after the Japanese had landed in Malaya. Their presence in the Command during the pre-war period did, however, appreciably divert attention and work from pressing matters of local application, and to this degree affected preparation for war in Malaya.

Some reference is necessary to sources of information on which the report is based.

Official records from the Far East are few and incomplete. Most of those which were maintained there had to be destroyed to prevent their capture by the Japanese. The few which survive consist of brief situation reports and a few files of important signals and correspondence, now with the Air Ministry. To make good the loss of the destroyed documents, reports have since been obtained from a number of officers who held important appointments in the Far East Command. But these are far from authoritative. Most of them were written in December, 1945, and January, 1946, nearly four years after the events which they describe had taken place, during which years their authors had been prisoners-of-war in Japanese hands, or alternatively had been actively employed in other theatres of war. A number of important individuals who could have given valuable evidence, I regret to report, died in captivity or during subsequent operations. Discrepancies have been slow and difficult to reconcile between sources of information now scattered thoughout the world, despite the ready help I have received from the authors of such reports.

On the other hand valuable information has been freely supplied to me from the Cabinet War Library, the Air Ministry, the War Office, the Colonial Office and by the authors of several other despatches relating to the War in the Far East. To them also I am much indebted.

For the sake of brevity only those matters are mentioned in the report which are necessary for establishing important events, for elucidating the factors which governed action at the time, and for compiling before it is too late a reasonably comprehensive narrative of what happened in the Far East.

Within these limitations every effort has been made to ensure accuracy, and the report, as a whole, is believed to give a reasonably true picture of the campaign from the air aspect— although doubtless it may display inaccuracies of detail brought about by the circumstances in which it has been compiled. It should, however, contain the necessary data from which correct deductions can be drawn. In order, however, that inaccuracies may be corrected, readers are invited to call attention to them through the Air Ministry.

The whole report has been written under my direction, the first two sections on behalf of the late Air Vice-Marshal Pulford who held his command until 11th February, 1942, two days before he left Singapore. In my opinion there is nothing in these sections, or in Section V, with which he would not agree.

I myself took over my duties at his headquarters on 12th January, 1942, from which date the report is written on my responsibility, and largely with my personal knowledge. This part of the report continues in the third person for the sake of continuity in the narrative.

P. C. MALTBY,
Air Vice-Marshal
Royal Air Force.

London.
July 26th, 1947.

LIST OF ABBREVIATIONS USED IN THE REPORT.

G.H.Q.—General Headquarters of the Commander-in-Chief, Far East.
H.Q.M.C.—Headquarters of the General Officer Commanding, Malaya Command.
A.H.Q.—Air Headquarters of the Air Officer Commanding, R.A.F. Far East Command.
Norgroup—Code name for Group H.Q. controlling air operations in Northern Malaya.
Abdacom—Code name for Supreme Allied Headquarters, S.W. Pacific, which formed on 15th January, 1942, and absorbed G.H.Q.
Abdair—Code name of the Air Section of Supreme Allied H.Q., S.W. Pacific.
Westgroup—Code name allotted to A.H.Q. on the formation of Supreme Allied H.Q., S.W. Pacific.
Recgroup—Code name for the Allied Air Reconnaissance Group responsible for seaward reconnaissance of whole sphere of Supreme Allied Command, S.W. Pacific.
Britair—Code name for A.H.Q. in Java after the dissolution of Supreme Allied H.Q., S.W. Pacific.
A.A.C.U.—Anti-Aircraft Co-operation Unit.
A.H.K.—Headquarters of the Dutch Commander-in-Chief at Bandoeng, Java.
A.I.F.—Australian Imperial Forces.
A.L.G.—Advanced Landing Ground.
A.M.E. Station—Air Ministry Experimental Station (Radar).
A.O.A.—Air Officer in charge of Administration.
A.S.P.—Air Stores Park.
(B)—Bomber.
D/F—Radio Direction Finding.
(F)—Fighter.
(F.B.)—Flying Boat.
F.E.C.B.—Far East Combined Bureau—a combined service intelligence organisation for obtaining intelligence, under Admiralty administration, throughout the Far East.
(G.R.)—General Reconnaissance.
I.E.—Initial Equipment.
I.R.—Immediate Reserve.
M.U.—Maintenance Unit.
M.V.A.F.—Malayan Volunteer Air Force.
N.E.I.—Netherlands East Indies.
[N.F.]—Night Fighter.
O.T.U.—Operational Training Unit.
P.R.U.—Photographic Reconnaissance Unit.
R.T.—Radio Telephony.
R. & S.U.—Repair and Salvage Unit.
S.A.O.—Senior Administrative Officer.
S.A.S.O.—Senior Air Staff Officer.
(T.B.)—Torpedo Bomber.
V.H.F.—Very high frequency radio.

SECTION I.

PRE-WAR PREPARATIONS.

SCOPE AND FUNCTIONS OF THE ROYAL AIR FORCE, FAR EAST.

By mid-summer 1941 the geographical area of the Far East Command, Royal Air Force, included Hong Kong, Borneo, Malaya and Burma; then, embracing Ceylon, it stretched across the Indian Ocean to Durban and Mombasa.

2. The main functions of the Command were firstly to protect the Naval Base in Singapore, and secondly, in co-operation with the Royal Navy to ensure the security of the trade routes in the Indian Ocean and South China Sea. The Headquarters of the Command was in Singapore.

3. In November 1940, Air Chief Marshal Sir Robert Brooke-Popham was appointed Commander-in-Chief, Far East. He was responsible for operational control and general direction of training of all British land and air forces in Malaya, Burma and Hong Kong; for coordinating the defences of those territories; and for similar responsibilities for additional British Air Forces it was proposed to locate later in Ceylon, the Indian Ocean and the Bay of Bengal. He set up his headquarters at the Naval Base in Singapore where he was provided with a small operational staff, but no administrative staff.

4. The formation of G.H.Q. in no way relieved the Air Officer Commanding, Royal Air Force, of his responsibility (which was now within the policy laid down by the Commander-in-Chief) for ensuring the effective co-operation

of his Command with the Naval and Military Commands throughout the area, nor did it alter his position vis-à-vis these Commands or the Air Ministry and the several Civil Governments with which he dealt.

The Basis of Defence in the Far East.

General Plan.

5. The general defence plan was based on an appreciation written by the Chiefs of Staff in July 1940. Briefly stated, this paper laid down that defence was to rely, in the absence of a Fleet, primarily on air power.

The Chiefs of Staff recognised that, for the defence of the Naval Base, it was no longer sufficient to concentrate upon the defence of Singapore Island but that it had become necessary to hold the whole of Malaya. Their intention now was to replace, by the end of 1941, the existing establishment of 88 obsolete and obsolescent aircraft by an air strength of 336 modern first-line aircraft backed up by adequate reserves and administrative units. This strength was allocated to the defence of Malaya and Borneo and to trade protection in the N.E. half of the Indian Ocean; it did not include aircraft necessary for the defence of Burma.

6. On the basis of this C.O.S. paper, the three Services in Malaya produced a tactical appreciation, which became the agenda of a conference held at Singapore in October 1940 attended by representatives from all Commands in the Far East. This conference recommended that the C.O.S. figure of 336 aircraft should be increased to 582, which it considered the minimum strength of Air Forces required to meet defence commitments in the Far East. The Chiefs of Staffs' reply on this point stated " we agree that 582 aircraft is an ideal, but consider 336 should give a fair degree of security taking into account our experiences in Middle East, Malta, and Air Defence of Great Britain ". The conference also recommended that until the additional air forces were provided, the Army in Malaya should be substantially reinforced.

7. Meanwhile, talks had been initiated between the British, U.S.A. and Dutch Staffs with the object of obtaining concerted action in the event of war breaking out with Japan. After the appointment of the Commander-in-Chief, Far East, in November 1940, further Allied conferences were held in Singapore. By April 1941 agreed general plans had been drawn up.

Allied Air Plans.

8. For the purpose of planning, it was assumed that the Japanese would not be able to attack simultaneously at several widely dispersed places in the Far East, in particular that they would not challenge the combined British, American and Dutch might. It was assumed, therefore, that Allied air forces would be able to reinforce one another. Preparations for mutual help were to be made as follows:—

(*a*) For Malaya to reinforce the N.E.I.—4 Bomber Squadrons, R.A.F.

(*b*) For N.E.I. to reinforce Malaya—3 Bomber and 1 Fighter Squadrons, Dutch Army Air Service.

(*c*) For the Philippines to reinforce Malaya —All U.S. Army and Navy Air Service Units available, but only if the Philippines were evacuated.

Each service accepted responsibility within its own territory for providing the necessary bases, where stocks of bombs, petrol and lubricants, peculiar to the respective air forces which might use them, were to be laid down.

9. Further matters of importance which were settled at these conferences were:—

(*a*) Responsibility for air reconnaissance over the South China Sea; this was co-ordinated and defined.

(*b*) Allied cypher and signal procedure.

(*c*) Allied. Naval/Air recognition signal procedure.

10. Concurrently with the above, the Far East Command R.A.F. was authorised to provide the means for operating general reconnaissance aircraft in the Bay of Bengal, Ceylon and the Indian Ocean.

Implications of the Plans.

11. Here it is opportune to stress the implications of the expansion programme authorised by the Chiefs of Staff; for the mere statement that the strength was to be raised from 88 obsolete or obsolescent aircraft to 336 modern types conveys no true impression of the extensive preparatory measures required before this force could be accommodated and operated.

12. It should be remembered that until the new policy had been decided by the Chiefs of Staff, defence had been largely confined to the vicinity of Singapore Island: thereafter it included the whole of Malaya.

13. The first step was the construction of bases. Sixteen new ones had to be found and built in Malaya, a country largely covered with secondary jungle remote from human habitations. Of the bases in existence in the colony 5 needed modernisation and 2 reconstruction. Concurrently, construction of new maintenance, repair and storage units was necessary, also throughout the colony.

Fighter defence had to be built up *ab initio;* none whatever had existed hitherto. In addition to bases for fighter squadrons, provision was necessary for an extensive radar system, for a modernised Observer Corps expanded on a primitive one already existing, for communications throughout the colony, and for Fighter Headquarters to control the whole.

At the same time, 8 new bases had to be built in Burma and 3 in Ceylon. Refuelling bases for flying boats were needed at numerous islands in the Indian Ocean from the Andamans to the coast of Africa.

14. The second step was to provide the authorised increase—the new units, the new aircraft; the ancillary services and the staffs for operating them on modern lines; and finally the modern equipment, supplies and local reserves for all.

15. The third step was to train the whole Command in conjunction with the Navy, Army and Civil Defences under the circumstances existing in the Far East, and concurrently to introduce up-to-date methods of operating.

16. The whole presented a truly formidable expansion programme, made still more formidable by the fact that time was short. The end of 1941 was the date by which the Chiefs of Staff planned for the expanded force to be ready for war. A combination of circumstances was, however, to result in realisation falling far

short of the mark, dominating all being the prior and acute claims of the war in Europe and the Middle East.

ACTION TAKEN IN MALAYA TO IMPLEMENT PLANS

Development of Air Bases

Problems of construction

17. The siting of aerodromes in Malaya was mainly influenced by the topography of the country. A rugged, heavily forested mountain chain runs down the centre of the peninsula cutting off the eastern and western coastal belts from each other until Johore is reached at its southern end. Much of both coastal belts is covered by a medley of broken hills; the rest consists of plains planted with rubber and paddy, or of potential mining sites. Rainfall is heavy throughout the year, increasing as the central mountain range is approached. Constant cloud over this range handicaps flight from one side of the peninsula to the other. Consequently, in order to provide reconnaissance over the South China Sea, from which direction the threat to Malaya by sea was greatest, a number of aerodromes had to be sited on the East Coast.

18. Workable sites were difficult to obtain. Every effort was made throughout 1941 to accelerate construction, but progress was not as rapid as had been hoped, despite the fact that, in some cases, sites involving a minimum of work were selected at the sacrifice of operational requirements.

19. There were 11 separate provincial government authorities in Malaya concerned with the acquisition of land; negotiations with each had to be separate. In the earlier stages, delay occurred owing to misunderstanding of the land acquisition legislation; later, emergency powers of acquisition were invoked and this source of delay ceased.

20. Mechanical plant was very short. That which was available was in poor condition, whilst there were few personnel qualified to operate or maintain it, a combination which constituted a primary handicap to progress.

21. Labour generally throughout Malaya was insufficient to meet the needs of the defence expansion programmes of the three Services, and later of the Civil Government. A permanent Labour Committee existed but its function was, in practice, mainly limited to controlling wages in order to eliminate expensive and wasteful competition between the three fighting Services and Government departments. The powers of this Committee were limited; all labour was voluntary, not conscripted, and no control could be exercised over the rates paid by civilian firms. By mutual agreement, however, it was possible to arrange a certain priority of employment of the labour available; and this was exercised to the benefit of the Royal Air Force in Kelantan State (in N.E. Malaya).

To improve the labour situation, negotiations were opened with the Civil Government in May, 1941, for forming locally enlisted works units to be clothed in uniform and officered by Europeans. Approval was obtained in August, 1941, and the matter was then put to the Air Ministry, but by the time final sanction was given it was too late to be effective. Fortunately an aerodrome construction unit arrived from New Zealand at the end of October, 1941. It did excellent work.

22. Most R.A.F. sites were in remote and sparsely populated spots to which it was necessary first to build roads. Native labour had to be collected, conveyed to the spot and housed. When this had been done it was still necessary to carry to the area almost all the building material required.

23. Much effort was necessarily diverted to anti-malarial measures, which had to be put in hand concurrently with construction in order to protect labour from epidemic. On completion, drained areas had to be maintained and oiled.

24. Supplies of material fell far short of the total needs of the services and civil departments. A Joint Priorities Committee was established in the Spring of 1941. It sat regularly and allocated supplies in accordance with the priorities decided from time to time. During the latter half of 1941, some shortages became particularly acute. Metalling material for runways was also always particularly short, a serious matter on aerodromes constantly subjected to tropical rainfall, which in itself was a major handicap to rapid construction.

25. It is clear, therefore, that the problems which confronted the Air Ministry Works Department were as numerous and complicated as any encountered in other theatres in war time. That it did excellent work does not alter the fact that it was severely handicapped in executing quickly a very large and urgent programme of expansion by the absence, particularly during the early stages, of the accelerated administrative procedure which the situation demanded.

State of Construction, 1st December, 1941

26. The locations of R.A.F. Stations and Establishments in Malaya and Singapore Island, together with remarks about their state of completion a few days before war broke out in the Far East, are shown in Appendix "A."

27. Of the occupied bases in Malaya, both Alor Star and Kota Bharu were old civil grounds with little room for dispersal. The buildings at Alor Star had been constructed on the old R.A.F. peace-time layout and were congested and too near the runway. This station was high in the priority list for reconstruction when opportunity offered. Both stations were in the forefront of operations in the first days of the war; their deficiencies proved a great handicap.

28. The old bases, and the first of those built on the new programme, had no form of camouflage. The ground had first been deforested and no attempt had been made to use natural surroundings or irregular outlines to obtain concealment. They stood out stark and bare, against the surrounding country. This was largely due to failure before 1940 to realise, not only in the Far East but in Europe also, the need for dispersal and camouflage on the scale which war experience proved to be necessary. In later bases, excellent concealment was obtained by retaining natural surroundings, avoiding straight lines and using a type of construction which, amongst the trees, was indistinguishable from the native huts. Financial considerations, however, continued to prevent the acquisition of sufficient land for effective dispersal.

29. Dispersal areas and splinter-proof pens at aerodromes in Malaya were arranged on what was then thought to be an adequate scale based on:—

(a) The scale of attack in accordance with the information then available about the Japanese Air Services.

(b) The ultimate scale of A.A. defences to be provided at each aerodrome.

(c) The development of a fighter defensive system.

By the 1st December, 1941, however, neither time nor resources had permitted satisfactory development of the fighter system, and few anti-aircraft weapons were available. The Commander-in-Chief, Far East, had laid down that each aerodrome was to be protected by eight heavy and eight light A.A. guns. At no aerodrome in Malaya was this scale approached; on the outbreak of war, some aerodromes had no A.A. guns at all (for details see Appendix A, Column 5 (b)).

30. Each base was provided with a supply of road metalling and labour for the repair of aerodrome surfaces in the event of damage by enemy attack. The reason for mentioning this apparently trivial point will become clear later.

Ancillary Construction

31. In addition to aerodromes the following important works were either completed or in hand on the 1st December, 1941:—

(a) Combined Army/Air Operations Room: This was completed and occupied by H.Q. R.A.F. Far East Command (A.H.Q.) and H.Q. Malaya Command (H.Q.M.C.) at Sime Road, Singapore.

(b) Alternative Combined Army/Air Operations Room: Provided because of the above-ground vulnerable position of the main Combined Operations Room.

(c) Fighter Control H.Q. in Singapore: This was ready for occupation. It had an operations room, a filter room, a W.T. station, etc.

(d) A.M.E. Stations: The ultimate intention was to have 20 Radar Stations throughout Malaya. Six stations only, all in the vicinity of Singapore Island, were completed by the 1st December, 1941.

(e) Radio Installation and Maintenance Unit: This was partially completed at Ponggol, Singapore.

(f) Ammunition Park: Construction at Batak Quarry, Singapore; it was occupied although extensions were in progress.

(g) Storage of Petrol:

(i) Reserve storage accommodation for 6,500 tons of aviation petrol was under construction at Woodlands North, Singapore.

(ii) Reserve storage accommodation for 7,500 tons of aviation petrol at Port Dickson was more than 50 per cent. complete.

(iii) Reserve storage accommodation for 930 tons at Kuantan was completed.

(h) Universal Holding Unit: This was completed and was occupied by 152 M.U. at Bukit Panjang, Singapore; extensions were in progress. This reduced the congestion and concentration of stores held at Seletar.

(i) Engine Repair Depot and Universal Holding Unit: This depot was completed at Kuala Lumpur, provided with its own railway siding and occupied by No. 153 M.U. It was designed to service squadrons based in North Malaya and so to reduce further the congestion and concentration which had hitherto persisted at Seletar.

Allied Reinforcement Arrangements

U.S.A. Reinforcements from the Philippines

32. The actual number of aircraft that might be expected in Malaya, should the evacuation of the Philippines occur, was of necessity indefinite; so was the amount of equipment peculiar to the U.S. Naval and Army Air Services which might accompany them.

33. Reconnaissances were carried out and dispersed moorings planned for a total of 20 reinforcing Catalinas of the United States Naval Air Service. A provisional plan for maintaining them was also prepared.

34. The Commander-in-Chief ruled, in September, 1941, that four bases were to be prepared for accommodating B.17's of the United States Army Air Corps; two in the North and two in the South of Malaya. Gong Kedah and Butterworth in the North, Tebrau and Yong Peng in the South, were selected. Extensions of the runways to 2,000 yards at each were put in hand but only those at Gong Kedah were completed by the time war came.

Dutch Reinforcements from N.E.I.

35. In the mutual reinforcement programme arranged with the Dutch Army Air Service, it was assumed that:—

(a) Three Bomber Squadrons (27 Glenn Martins would be based at Sembawang:

(b) One Dutch Fighter Squadron (9 Buffaloes) would be based at Kallong:

and plans were made accordingly.

36. The Dutch Squadron and Flight Commanders concerned visited these stations, toured Malaya and were given a short course in R.A.F. operational methods. Appropriate stocks of Dutch bombs were procured.

37. The Dutch Naval Air Service had been allotted, in the initial seaward reconnaissance plan, responsibility for the area Kuantan-Great Natunas-Kuching (B. Borneo). To execute this task, it had to base a Group (3 Catalinas) of Flying Boats at Seletar. Provision was made for this; and stocks of petrol and moorings were also laid down at Kuantan. The Group remained under Dutch operational command.

38. Liaison Officers of the Dutch Army Air Service and the Royal Air Force were interchanged and were attached to A.H.Q. in Singapore and at Dutch Army Air H.Q. in Java respectively.

Preparations within R.A.F., Far East Command.

Role of Squadrons in War.

39. In July, 1941, a memorandum was circulated outlining the role of squadrons in war, and training syllabi were issued. Strict supervision was imposed to ensure that the fullest training value was obtained in all exercises and that the maximum number of practices of different kinds was arranged whenever a training flight was undertaken.

Preparation of Initial Reconnaissance Plan.

40. Seaborne invasion from the N.E. constituted the main threat to Malaya. A reconnaissance plan was therefore drawn up to detect its approach at the maximum distance, responsibility for its execution being divided amongst the Allies. R.A.F. Far East Command was allotted responsibility for the area Kota Bahru-Southern tip of Indo-China-Great Natunas-Kuantan. A reconnaissance plan was prepared accordingly. Its execution necessitated the employment of one G.R. (Hudson) Squadron based on Kuantan and one based on Kota Bahru. The use of two Catalinas was superimposed to ensure an overlap with the Dutch area immediately to the South. Squadrons were exercised in this plan from their war stations.

41. When the Japanese occupied Indo-China in July, 1941, A.H.Q. queried the fact that this reconnaissance plan made no provision for searching the Gulf of Siam, but G.H.Q. confirmed that the limited reconnaissance force available must be concentrated initially upon the more likely area of approach.

Concentration of Squadrons in War.

42. In accordance with the principle that squadrons were to be concentrated in the defence of whatever area was threatened, alternative locations for squadrons, dependent on the axis of attack, were prepared.

Transition to a War Footing.

43. In the past, a considerable number of code words had been issued, each governing the action of units in various kinds of emergency. As a whole, they were most confusing and liable to result in unco-ordinated action. To rectify this situation, G.H.Q. instructed all Commands, in May, 1941, to prepare for three " degrees of readiness " and laid down the general principles governing each. A.H.Q. took the opportunity to issue Units with an exact description in detail of the action to be taken on promulgation of these degrees of readiness. The transition to a full war footing was thereby made smooth and rapid.

Co-ordination of Night Flying Arrangements.

44. Before the autumn of 1941, arrangements for night flying had not been co-ordinated, each Unit employing its own method of laying out a flare path and other lighting. A standardised procedure was drawn up in November, 1941, as it was essential to ensure that all squadrons could operate by night with confidence and could use any aerodrome in the Command.

Establishment of Air Corridors.

45. Air corridors " in " and " out of " Singapore were established and promulgated, whilst a standardised procedure for " approach " to all aerodromes in the Command was issued in July.

Establishment of Operations Rooms.

46. Operations rooms were opened at each base as it became available for use, the ideal aimed at being that squadrons on arrival should find the same layout, information and procedure as that which existed at their parent aerodromes. This was designed to avoid the delay and disorganisation caused by the necessity of transferring material and documents: it speeded up the efficiency of operations.

Mobility of Squadrons.

47. A high degree of mobility was necessary for squadrons to fulfil their laid-down role as the primary defence of the Far East in general, and of Malaya in particular. But the composition of the forces allotted to the Far East included no transport aircraft; and although A.H.Q. drew attention to the deficiency on several occasions no aircraft could be provided. The Dutch Army Air Service had a fleet of some 20 Lodestars and promised assistance, provided their own circumstances permitted. In the autumn of 1941, some Lodestars were borrowed, and selected squadrons were practised in the organisation required for moving.

48. A shortage of M.T. in Malaya made the position more serious. Orders for the M.T. required were placed in the U.S.A. but they could not be met in time. There was no M.T. unit in the Command nor were there sufficient spare vehicles to form a Command pool. Individual units were themselves below establishment in M.T.

DEVELOPMENTS IN HONG KONG.

49. No Air Forces were allotted for the defence of Hong Kong. There was a station flight at Kai Tak on the mainland for target towing purposes, but apart from local reconnaissance no war role was envisaged or arranged for this flight.

50. In the summer of 1941, an urgent request was received from Hong Kong pressing for some fighter aircraft because of the great support they would give to civilian morale. This request could not be met. In case it should prove possible later to meet the request for fighter aircraft, a Fighter Sector Control room and Radar Stations were sited and plans were prepared for the provision of a fighter defensive system.

DEVELOPMENTS IN BRITISH BORNEO.

51. Facilities for land planes in British Borneo were confined to one aerodrome and one landing ground, at Kuching and Miri respectively. The former was not large enough for bomber aircraft but its extension was in hand when war broke out. Flying boat moorings were also laid in the river nearby. There were no A.A. defences, but a battalion of the Indian Army, with H.Q. in Kuching, was located in Borneo for the protection of the aerodrome and landing ground areas and the Miri oilfields.

DEVELOPMENTS IN BURMA.

52. As a result of the Singapore Conference in the autumn of 1940 (para. 6), the findings of which were generally endorsed by the C.-in-C. Far East on his arrival, the Government of Burma co-operated actively in constructing and developing the eight air bases, and additional satellite strips, considered necessary for air operations from Burma. These bases stretched from Mergui on the Tenasserim Coast in a half circle round the Siamese frontier to Lashio in the Northern Shan states. In anticipation of approval, Flight Lieutenant C. W. Bailey, Inspector of Landing Grounds at A.H.Q., had been sent by A.H.Q. to Burma in November, 1940. He had drawn up plans for extending old, and constructing new, aerodromes. Further, in co-operation with the Government of

Burma, arrangements had been made for re-organising the Public Works Department so that it could undertake supervision of construction, which was immediately begun.

53. In March, 1941, H.Q. No. 221 Group (Commander, Group Captain E. R. Manning) was established at Rangoon to develop these bases and to command the Air Forces located in Burma. Although the Group staff was very small, progress was so good that all bases were completed by the end of 1941 with accommodation at each for some 450 all ranks. Facilities for dispersal were reasonable, pens being provided, as were some satellite strips. There was a measure of A.A. protection in the Rangoon area but none elsewhere.

54. Co-operation with the Army in Burma was excellent. Army H.Q. in Burma and No. 221 Group R.A.F. were in close proximity and the G.O.C. and his staff could not have done more to assist the R.A.F. in its preparations. From the outset of planning in November, 1940, the G.O.C. was in the picture of R.A.F. development. The raising and training of aerodrome defence troops was consequently conducted in parallel with construction.

55. During 1940, an air observer system was developed by the G.O.C. under the active direction of the Postmaster-General. From the outset, its functions were made clear and, despite difficulties of training, it developed and operated usefully on the outbreak of hostilities; control of it passed to the R.A.F. on the formation of 221 Group Headquarters. One Radar Station was completed at Moulmein and two others in the Rangoon area were nearing completion when war broke out. A Fighter Control Operations room was designed and constructed in Rangoon.

56. No. 60 (B) Squadron (Blenheim I's) ex India, was located at Rangoon from February, 1941. G.H.Q. considered it important to ensure some measure of fighter defence at Rangoon; consequently, pending the availability of an established fighter squadron, half of No. 60 was re-equipped with Buffalo fighters for the period August-October, 1941, somewhat handicapping the squadron's operational efficiency. As soon as No. 67 (F) Squadron (Buffaloes) in Malaya was fully trained it was transferred to Rangoon; the transfer took place in October, 1941.

Heavy demands on No. 60 (B) Squadron for communication flights occupied much of its flying effort; and although it had a very high standard of flying in monsoon conditions over Burma, it became desirable to transfer the squadron to Malaya to bring it operationally up-to-date in practice. All its aircraft and crews were therefore sent to Kuantan, the new Air/Armament Station of the Command, where they arrived shortly before the Japanese attacked Malaya.

57. In addition there was a flight of six Moths used for training Burma's Volunteer Air Force. The aircraft of this flight were allotted the role of maintaining communications and carrying out certain limited reconnaissance.

58. A plan was drawn up in co-operation with the Army in Burma, the object of which was to destroy communication facilities in the Siamese Isthmus. Land forces were to advance across the isthmus and conduct a "burn and scuttle" raid on port, rail and air facilities at Prachuab Kirrikand. Their arrival was to synchronise with air attack from Malaya under A.H.Q. arrangements.

59. The question of the Command of the forces in Burma had been raised on more than one occasion. Those who considered it from the angle of India's defence recommended that control should be by India. A.H.Q. supported the opposite view, namely the retention of Burma in the Far East Command, because it considered that effective co-ordination of the air forces operating from Burma and Malaya in defence of the Far East could only be achieved by unified command. This view was accepted. In the actual event, however, the control of Burma had to pass to India seven days after war broke out—at 0630 hours on 15th December, 1941.

60. Finally, reference must be made to the American Volunteer Group under Colonel Chennault, who was given all possible assistance, particularly in relation to maintenance, training and accommodation. R.A.F. Base, Toungoo, the training aerodrome for the Force, was visited by the A.O.C. and Staff Officers from A.H.Q.; officers who had had fighter experience in Europe were sent to lecture and to assist in training. Excellent work was later done by this Force, in co-operation with the R.A.F., in the defence of Burma.

DEVELOPMENTS IN N.E.I.

Dutch Borneo.

61. In accordance with the mutual reinforcement plan, the Dutch allocated Sinkawang and Samarinda in Dutch Borneo for use as bases for four R.A.F. bomber squadrons. Each of these bases was to be provided with accommodation for two bomber squadrons and to be stocked in peace with supplies peculiar to the Royal Air Force. Their only method of supply was by means of transport aircraft provided by the Dutch, who deliberately avoided making roads to them through the dense jungle in which they were situated, and which thus remained an undisturbed defence. By December, Sinkawang was ready and had been inspected by the C.O. and Flight Commanders of one of the squadrons allocated to it. Samarinda was not ready.

Sumatra.

62. Permission was also obtained from the Dutch in the summer of 1941, to reconnoitre all aerodromes in Sumatra. This was required because A.H.Q. anticipated that, in the event of war, Sumatra would be required for:—

(a) An alternative air reinforcement route from India owing to the vulnerability of the old route to Singapore via Burma and N. Malaya once the Japanese had penetrated into Siam.

(b) Potential advanced landing grounds for operations against the flank of a Japanese advance down Malaya.

The main preoccupation was therefore with those aerodromes which were situated in the Northern half of Sumatra.

63. As the result of this reconnaissance, extensions to the grounds at Lho'nga and Sabang were put in hand to make them suitable for modern aircraft.

64. Assistance was also given to B.O.A.C. to organise facilities at Sabang for the operation of an alternative seaplane route Rangoon—Port Blair—Sabang instead of the normal one via Bangkok.

Java.

65. Visits were paid to Java by a number of staff officers from A.H.Q. who thus gained useful information about Dutch maintenance establishments and resources generally.

DEVELOPMENTS IN INDIAN OCEAN AND BAY OF BENGAL.

66. A memorandum was prepared about June, 1941, and issued by A.H.Q. detailing the bases to be developed in this area; their status was defined and priority of provisioning was laid down. By December, 1941, the position was as follows:—

Andamans and Nicobars—at Port Blair and Nancowrie, moorings and petrol had been laid, and limited accommodation constructed for operating flying boats. Port Blair was also prepared by B.O.A.C., with R.A.F. assistance, as an alternative to the route Rangoon—Penang.

Ceylon—H.Q. No. 222 Group was established, with a joint Naval/Air Ops. Room, at Colombo.

China Bay—one flight of Vildebeestes was located here for target towing and local reconnaissance. This station was being developed as a permanent base for one G.R. Squadron and one F.B. Squadron, the accommodation for which was practically completed.

Ratmalana—Aerodrome was being constructed for one G.R. Squadron.

Koggala—was being developed as the main base for flying boats operating in the Indian Ocean. Accommodation for one Squadron was nearly ready.

Christmas Island	
Cocos Islands (Direction Island).	Fuel and moorings had been laid and limited accommodation provided for operating flying boats at each of these places.
Maldives (Male)	
Seychelles (Mahe)	
Chagos (Diego-Garcia).	
Mauritius ...	
Tanganyika (Lindi).	
Durban ...	Were being developed as permanent bases for one F.B. Squadron each.
Mombasa ...	

Much credit is due to the Air Ministry Works Department for the great volume of construction which had been carried out in these outlying parts of the Command, as well as for that executed in Malaya, in a relatively short space of time despite many and considerable handicaps.

OPERATIONAL EFFICIENCY OF UNITS IN MALAYA.

Intelligence Organisation.

67. In June, 1941, A.H.Q. had no Intelligence Organisation of its own. All air intelligence personnel and records in the Far East had been centralised in the Combined Intelligence Bureau (F.E.C.B.) which functioned under the control of C.-in-C. China Station. Theoretically it served, inter alia, the needs of A.H.Q. In practice, however, its means for obtaining air information throughout the Far East was totally inadequate; its staff was insufficient to cope fully even with G.H.Q. Air Intelligence requirements; and although the information it possessed was always available to A.H.Q., F.E.C.B. had not the means of supplanting the missing intelligence machinery at A.H.Q.

Representations were therefore made by A.H.Q. of the need for a thorough intelligence system throughout the Command. About July, a conference was held with G.H.Q., who wished to create a second Combined Intelligence Centre to serve the joint needs of A.H.Q. and H.Q.M.C. A second joint organisation of this nature would not, however, have been suitable for building up the Intelligence organisation required throughout the Command at all levels from A.H.Q. downwards. This view was accepted.

An establishment for an Intelligence organisation for the whole Command was drawn up and submitted to the Air Ministry, and in late autumn, in anticipation of approval, personnel were made available locally and were appointed to H.Q. and Units. The nucleus organisation thus formed was fortunately in being when hostilities broke out, but its development was backward, and in particular the information it had collated for briefing crews was scanty.

68. According to intelligence current in the Command, the efficiency of the Japanese Naval Air Units was known to be good, but that of their Army Air Units was not high despite the fanatical valour of their personnel.

This wrong assessment of their Army Air Units was partly due to the fact that the system for collecting intelligence throughout the Far East was only sufficient to enable F.E.C.B. to obtain incomplete air information; and the reliability of most of this was far from high. And it was partly due to the fact that A.H.Q., stations and squadrons possessed only the embryonic intelligence organisation already referred to: the result was that such intelligence as the Command received was not effectively digested, promulgated or acted upon.

A particular outcome of this state of affairs, which was destined to have far-reaching consequences in Malaya, was that the personnel of the Command remained unaware up to the outbreak of war of the qualities of the Japanese fighter squadrons, whose Zero fighters were to prove superior in performance to our own fighters. This naturally affected training in our squadrons, particularly in the tactics to be adopted by our fighters.

The need for an Operational Training Unit.

69. The Air Ministry had been unable to approve requests made during the year to establish an O.T.U. in Malaya. But in September, 1941, owing to the fact that large numbers of personnel required operational training, A.H.Q. established a makeshift O.T.U. at Kluang from the resources available in the Command. Its role was:—

(*a*) To train pilots for Fighter Squadrons who had been, for some time, arriving from

New Zealand direct from Service Flying Training Schools, and who therefore lacked operational training.

(b) To convert personnel of No. 36 and No. 100 (T.B.) Squadrons from Vildebeestes to twin-engine aircraft in anticipation of their re-equipment with Beauforts.

(c) To train pilots from New Zealand on twin-engine aircraft to fill vacancies in Bomber Squadrons.

Training aircraft were provided from Wirraways thrown up by No. 21 (F) Squadron when it re-armed with Buffaloes, and by Blenheims borrowed from No. 34 (B) Squadron. The Wing Commander Training at A.H.Q. (Wing Commander Wills-Sandford) was appointed Commanding Officer. The Unit had to be disbanded on 8th December, on the outbreak of hostilities, but it had completed most valuable work.

Lack of Armament Training Facilities.

70. Up till October 1941, the only armament training facilities in the Command were on Singapore Island, and at an improvised air range near Penang. Maximum use was made of the Singapore ranges, but they were very insufficient to meet requirements. In October 1941, the new Command Armament Training Station at Kuantan was opened, but there was time for one squadron only to complete a course before the outbreak of war.

71. The air firing situation was particularly unsatisfactory. There was an acute shortage of target towing aircraft, and the few available were slow.

Lack of Transport and Communication Aircraft.

72. The lack of transport and communication aircraft was acutely felt during the pre-war period when training was all important. G.H.Q. and H.Q.M.C. had frequently to ask for communication flights, aircraft for which had necessarily to be found, mainly by G.R. Squadrons. Although such requests were pruned and co-ordinated, flights were nevertheless sufficiently frequent to interfere seriously with the training of squadrons, many of whose vital flying hours were thus expended. Furthermore, visits to subordinate units by A.H.Q. staff had to be correspondingly curtailed.

Fighter Squadrons.

73. In June-July 1941 a Fighter Group Operational Cadre was formed to take over the training and operation of all fighter aircraft in Singapore: the Senior Officer (Group Captain E. B. Rice) at the same time being appointed Air Defence Co-ordinator, Malaya.

74. The following Fighter Squadrons, with an establishment of 16 I.E. and 8 I.R. Buffaloes, were formed on the dates shown:—

No. 67 (F) Squadron, formed at the end of March 1941. The Squadron and two Flight Commanders to be appointed from U.K., the remaining pilots from bomber squadrons within the Command. Establishments were completed with pilots from New Zealand F.T.S's. The Squadron was transferred to Burma in October 1941, shortly after it had been passed as operationally efficient (para. 56).

No. 243 (F) Squadron, formed in April, 1941. Personnel were found as in the case of No. 67 Squadron, but a slightly higher proportion were F.T.S. personnel.

No. 453 (F) Squadron, formed October 1941. The Squadron and two Flight Commanders were appointed from U.K. This was an R.A.F. " infiltration " squadron* filled from F.T.S's in Australia. Some of the personnel were not entirely suitable for a Fighter Squadron, and the Squadron Commander was in Australia selecting replacements when war broke out.

No. 488 (F) Squadron, formed in October-November 1941. The Squadron and two Flight Commanders came from U.K. This was an R.N.Z.A.F. infiltration squadron and was filled from F.T.S's in New Zealand with excellent material; but their standard of flying on arrival was backward. This squadron had taken over the aircraft on which No. 67 (F) Squadron had trained, and many of these were in poor condition.

No. 21 (F) Squadron, R.A.A.F., which had formed as a General Purpose Squadron in Australia and moved into the Command in 1940, was in October 1941 re-equipped with Buffaloes and converted into a Fighter Squadron, with 12 I.E. and 6 I.R. aircraft. The Squadron had been previously equipped with 2-seater Wirraways, some of which were returned to Australia, the remainder being retained to assist in training Nos. 453 (F) and 488 (F) Squadrons. It will be observed, therefore, that the pilots of this squadron had not been selected originally for fighter aircraft, and some were not in fact entirely suitable for this role.

75. The main role of the Buffalo Squadrons was " day defence " only, primarily of the Singapore area, but night flying training was instituted to ensure that pilots could take off before dawn and land after nightfall.

76. Except for No. 488 (F) Squadron all the above squadrons were considered operationally trained by the outbreak of war. No. 488 (F) Squadron was deficient in squadron and flight training and was not passed as operationally ready until the latter half of December 1941. Training and assessment of operational readiness had, however, been based on an under-estimation of the enemy. The tactics thus taught and practised proved unsuitable and costly against the Japanese Navy " O " fighter, which was greatly superior to the Buffalo in performance. Moreover, advanced training had suffered because, prior to the formation of an O.T.U. in September 1941 (see para. 69), all pilots had joined their squadrons without having received individual operational training.

77. The standard of gunnery in all squadrons was low because:—

(a) Towing aircraft were very slow and there were very few of them,

(b) Cine gun equipment was lacking,

(c) Continual trouble was experienced with the .5 gun and synchronising gear. This was largely overcome by local modification by

---
* *i.e.*—an R.A.F. as distinct from a Dominion squadron but manned by Dominions personnel.

October 1941. Nevertheless, pilots were still not confident about their armament when war overtook them.

78. The Buffalo had a disappointing performance. It was heavy and underpowered and had a slow rate of climb. Maintenance was heavy, which meant a low standard of serviceability. Wastage during training was high, and many of the aircraft in Squadrons suffered from rough handling. The Buffalo had no V.H.F. radio, and the maximum range of R.T./W.T. was 9 miles, being frequently less when atmospherics were bad. Intercommunication between aircraft was unreliable.

79. There was one multi-seat fighter squadron in the Command, No. 27, a night fighter squadron equipped with Blenheim I's. Aircraft were old and in poor condition and were thus of limited value in a night-fighting role. Its conversion into a bomber squadron, for which personnel were available, came up for consideration but could not be adopted owing to the need for retaining a night fighter unit.

Observer Corps.

80. In July, 1941, control of an existing Observer Corps system was transferred from the Army to A.H.Q. It had been organised chiefly as part of the civil air raid warning system, and needed a great deal of development for use in an active air defence system. The personnel were enthusiastic, but unfortunately little time was available to train them in their new duties. It was found impossible to establish the necessary Observer Posts in the jungle-clad mountainous country of Central Malaya where there was, therefore, a serious gap in the warning system. Observer Corps Operations Rooms were established at Kuala Lumpur and Singapore, and were linked up to the Dutch system in the Rhio Archipelago to the South, but difficulty was experienced in organising the whole through lack of existing telephone communications in Malaya and to an acute shortage of telephone material and equipment.

Radar Stations.

81. The approved policy of priority for the development of radar facilities was:—
   (a) Singapore Island.
   (b) The East Coast of Malaya.
   (c) Penang and the West Coast.

All Stations were to look seaward with only restricted overland cover behind, the hinterland being covered by the Observer Corps.

82. By December, 1941, four stations were operating—Mersing, Tanah Merah Besar (in East of Singapore Island), Bukit Chunang (S.E. tip of Johore) and Tanjong Kupang (S.W. tip of Johore). A further station, Kota Tingi, in Johore was nearly ready and was being accelerated partly to close the gap down the central portion of Malaya. A sixth, at Kota Bahru, the most northerly point on the East Coast of Malaya, had been built but no radar had yet been installed.

The general position was, therefore, that there was fair cover for Singapore but little elsewhere.

Fighter Operations Room.

83. A Fighter Group Operations Room in Singapore was designed, constructed and occupied by December—almost too late to do more than break the ice of training its staff and fighter squadrons in the intricate art of fighter defence. It had an operational staff only, no administrative branches: it was in fact an offshoot of the Air Staff of A.H.Q.

Fighter considerations in general.

84. Thus an Air Defence system had been organised by the time war came. Whilst it was by no means as efficient as it would have been if the resources, time and equipment had not been so short, yet it provided Singapore with a scale of defensive effort which was by no means insignificant. Great credit is due to those who achieved this result with so short a time for preparation, outstanding amongst whom was the late Group Captain E. B. Rice.

Bomber and G.R. Land-based Squadrons.

85. There were two light bomber and two landplane G.R. squadrons in Malaya:—

   No. 62 Squadron (Blenheim I)—Alor Star.
   No. 34 Squadron (Blenheim IV)—Tengah.
   No. 1 (R.A.A.F.) Squadron (Hudson II)—Kota Bahru.
   No. 8 (R.A.A.F.) Squadron (Hudson II)—Sembawang.

These two types of squadron, Bomber and G.R., are bracketed together because, owing to the small size of the total force, specialisation was impracticable. Although the Hudson squadrons were the main oversea reconnaissance force, the Blenheims had also to be trained in these duties. Similarly, both types of squadron had to be trained in all types of bombing over the sea and over the land, both by day and by night.

86. From May, 1940, until the Spring of 1941 there had been severe flying restrictions imposed on Blenheim Squadrons owing to the lack of spares in the Command. During this period, flying hours were restricted to 5 hours monthly per I.E. aircraft. In Spring, 1941, selected pilots had to be withdrawn from these squadrons to assist in the formation of the first two fighter squadrons in Malaya.

87. Nos. 1 and 8 (G.R.) Squadrons R.A.A.F. had reached a higher standard of training, but it was necessary for the Australian Air Board to withdraw crews as they became fully trained and to replace them by untrained crews, the former being required for the further expansion of the R.A.A.F. in Australia.

There was, therefore, in both types of squadron a wide variation between crews in the degree of their training, and especially in their efficiency in night flying, in which a high degree of skill was desirable for operating through the violent tropical thunderstorms which prevail over Malaya at night during the monsoons.

Torpedo/Bomber Squadrons.

88. There were two Torpedo/Bomber Squadrons, Nos. 36 and 100, both based on Seletar, the personnel of which were highly trained and of long experience. But their aircraft, Vildebeestes, which had a speed of 90 knots and an action radius of 180 miles, were obsolete. With modern aircraft these highly trained squadrons would have been invaluable, especially in the first days of the war. But their approved rearmament programme, with Beauforts, had been delayed by technical complications in production in Australia. In their training more emphasis was placed on the torpedo than the

bomb, because their main role was to attack enemy convoys well out to sea. Facilities for them to operate with torpedoes from Kota Bahru had been established.

Flying Boat Squadron.

89. There was one Flying Boat Squadron in the Command, No. 205 Squadron, based at Seletar with a detachment in Ceylon.

90. The squadron did not have sufficient trained crews. When its establishment was raised from 4 I.E. Singapore III's to 6 I.E. Catalinas, no additional crews were available. These were therefore trained by the squadron. One or two trained crews were based in Ceylon for work in the Indian Ocean, where, unfortunately, two crews were lost in accidents in September/October, 1941.

Photographic Reconnaissance.

91. Long-range Hurricanes had been requested for photographic purposes but were not available. In November, 1941, a P.R.U. with 2 I.E. (later raised to 4) aircraft was formed in Singapore with Buffaloes drawn from local resources, and personnel were trained in photographic reconnaissance. By stripping all armament and non-essential equipment and providing additional tankage, the Buffaloes range was increased to 1,400 miles. The formation of this flight proved a most valuable asset to the resources of the Command. Concurrently a Photographic Interpretation Unit was formed.

Malayan Volunteer Air Force

92. The Malayan Volunteer Air Force had flights located in Singapore, Kuala Lumpur, Ipoh and Penang. Its miscellaneous collection of about 30 aircraft comprised two Rapides, one Dragonfly, and a number of Moths and Cadets. Flights were organised for transport duties under A.H.Q., and for communication and reconnaissance in affiliation with Army formations. Moths were fitted with 20-lb. bomb racks and pilots were trained in their use, but none of the aircraft could be fitted with defensive armament. The enthusiasm of the unit was most marked and it made excellent progress.

Elementary Flying Training School

93. An E.F.T.S. had been established at Kallang in 1940 from local resources: instructors and technical personnel were obtained from units stationed in Malaya, and from the M.V.A.F., whose club aircraft were made available for its use. It did excellent work. A number of pilots were trained by it, some subsequently serving in other theatres of war and some in Malaya.

Signals Organisation

94. Signals organisation was generally backward. There was a shortage of W/T equipment, particularly of mobile sets.

Teleprinter lines existed between A.H.Q. and aerodromes on Singapore Island, but not between A.H.Q. and aerodromes up the peninsula.

There were two telephone lines from Singapore to N.W. Malaya and one to the N.E. and East. These were quite insufficient for joint needs, Army, Air Force and Civil, and all passed through civil exchanges. Secraphones were very few and were apportioned between the services in a strict order of priority.

There was no V.H.F., which limited the effective control of fighters to about 10 miles; this was still further limited by atmospherics during thunder periods.

Centralisation of Work at A.H.Q.

95. Appendices A and C will show how many, and scattered, were the units in the Far East Command and how varied were their duties by land, sea and air: their administrative problems were correspondingly numerous and varied.

A degree of decentralisation of work from A.H.Q. was achieved by:—

(a) forming, in March, 1941, No. 221 Group H.Q., with a small staff in Rangoon, to which all work of formations in Burma was decentralised,

(b) forming, in March, 1941, No. 222 Group H.Q. in Ceylon for controlling flying boat operations based on Ceylon: this Group had no administrative staff, so that A.H.Q. continued to administer direct all its bases throughout the Indian Ocean.

(c) forming, in August, 1941, No. 224 (Fighter) Group H.Q. in Singapore, for supervising fighter training and air defence arrangements within Singapore Island: this Group also had no administrative staff (see para. 83) so that A.H.Q. dealt direct with its stations and units on administrative matters.

But this was the limit of decentralisation. It resulted in a heavy load of centralised work at A.H.Q. This was particularly felt once the expansion programme began to take effect. It fell heavily enough on Air Staff, but still more so on the Administrative Staff and on that of the Air Ministry Works Department.

The need for an A.O.C. Malaya, with an appropriate staff to whom to decentralise local problems in Malaya, became increasingly apparent during 1941, but it was not found possible to meet this need.

This state of affairs was complicated by a shortage of qualified officers—(see next paras.) —caused by the demands of the war in Europe.

Supply of Officers for Staff and Administrative Duties

96. Officers for filling vacancies on the staff of the greatly expanded A.H.Q. and at the new stations were largely found by enrolling personnel from Australia and New Zealand. More than 140 were obtained from this source. It was possible to give them only a short disciplinary course combined with a brief survey of their duties. Their average age was 45. They naturally varied much in their qualifications. The remainder, more than 50 in number, were obtained by commissioning local business men in Singapore; most of them just before, but some after the outbreak of war in the Far East. For them no training was practicable. The majority of these officers were willing and able, but their value was limited owing to their unavoidable lack of service knowledge, experience and training.

97. Of the regular officers, there were few with Staff experience; and the brunt of the work consequently fell on the few. The work of A.H.Q. was increased by the inexperience of officers at stations, which needed more "nursing" than is normally the case.

98. The strain fell particularly heavily upon the A.O.C., who despite the great increase of work which was caused by the expansion of his Command, undertook much supervisory staff work which he would have delegated to others in normal circumstances. He did so in order to ensure that it was properly carried out. This reacted unfavourably on his health, which was poor even when he arrived. He overtaxed his strength, and was a tired man when war descended on Malaya.

Equipment Problems

99. The equipment position was bad in many important items. Except for Buffaloes there were no reserve aircraft whatsoever in the Command. There was an acute shortage of spares, especially for Blenheims and even more for Hudsons, and also of all tools. M.T. was very short, with an effect on mobility that has already been noted. Small arms were insufficient to arm more than a proportion of R.A.F. personnel. All these were items which were badly needed during 1941 in Europe and Africa, and the requirements of the Far East had necessarily to take second place.

On the other hand, stocks of petrol and bombs laid in with G.H.Q.'s particular assistance were good.

Personnel Problems.

100. The following major personnel problems affected the efficiency of the Command:—

(i) There were no reserve aircrews.

(ii) The strength of the Command in airmen was doubled during the last six months of 1941, but most of these reinforcements came direct from training establishments in the United Kingdom and needed further training. At the same time, a number of time-expired airmen were relieved, with the result that at the outbreak of war three-quarters of the strength was new to Malaya.

(iii) A number of the reinforcements were posted to the Command in anticipation of the completion of the expansion programme. They arrived faster than the expansion programme could absorb them. A surplus was therefore built-up, which was employed partly as infantry guards on Singapore Island to relieve the Army of such duties.

(iv) Special courses were organised in musketry and, in the expectation of the defection of native employees, in cooking and M.T. driving.

Other Measures.

101. The following preparatory measures were also put in hand:—

(i) An Air/Sea Rescue Service was organised. It was given six launches, and some light aircraft of the Malayan Volunteer Air Force. It commenced operations in mid-December, 1941, and altogether saved the lives of 24 aircrew. Five of the launches were provided locally.

(ii) A Bomb Disposal Unit was formed in June, 1941, to serve all Services, including Civil Defence.

(iii) Welfare Services were organised. Holiday facilities were provided at Butterworth and Malacca. A fund of 20,000 dollars was raised and used by a central welfare committee. Mobile canteens were made and equipped locally.

(iv) Arrangements were made for hospitalisation and evacuation of R.A.F. sick and wounded; these facilities were provided by the Army everywhere except within the bounds of R.A.F. stations, where they were provided by the R.A.F.M.S.

RELATIONS WITH G.H.Q.

102. The Commander-in-Chief, Far East (Air Chief Marshal Sir Robert Brooke-Popham) being an Air Force officer naturally took a keen personal interest in the R.A.F.; and relations between G.H.Q. and A.H.Q. were correspondingly close.

103. But G.H.Q., had no administrative staff, only an operational one. It was felt at A.H.Q. that the lack of the former prevented the latter from fully appreciating the day-to-day impacts of the multitude of administrative problems which arise in the subordinate command during the period of preparation for war. Without this full experience the operational staff must have found it hard to grasp in their full significance the difficulties which faced the subordinate command. This statement is made in no critical spirit of G.H.Q.'s staff, who were sympathetic and helpful about matters which came their way, but merely to disclose the weakness of an organisation which is vested with operational responsibility but which has no administrative branches of its own through which to keep its finger on the pulse of the administrative problems arising at the level of the subordinate command.

104. The difficulty which G.H.Q. experienced in obtaining full and accurate intelligence about air matters in the Far East has already been referred to (paras. 67 and 68). Its estimation of the Japanese Naval Air Arm was high. Its estimation of the Japanese Army Air Forces was that, although numbers were great and they were known to possess long-range fighters, efficiency was low and that, despite their fanatical bravery, reasonable opposition would turn them from their targets.

105. To turn to the enemy's probable actions. For most of 1941, G.H.Q. was in doubt about the date and place Japan would challenge the Allied position in the Far East. The chance that she would do so early was reduced when in the late summer of 1941 the U.S.A. decided to reinforce the Philippines. Further support for this view came from the Chinese, who, in the early summer of 1941, considered that the next major Japanese effort would be made on the line Hanoi-Kunming to cut the Burma road.

Nevertheless, throughout the summer, G.H.Q. stressed the need for pressing on with all preparations necessary for meeting an attack, realising that Japan could strike at her selected moment so long as no British fleet was based on Singapore.

Early in November, 1941, the C.-in-C. re-affirmed the opinion that Japan was unlikely to attack Malaya now that the N.E. monsoon had set in, because the heavy surf, which beats upon the beaches of the East coast of Malaya throughout the season, would make it difficult for assaulting troops to land. It was reckoned that the attack, although possible, was unlikely before February, 1942, by which time the monsoon would be over.

By 22nd November, however, the Japanese intention of further aggression had become clear to the C.-in-C. (para. 140).

106. Meanwhile, during the autumn, preparations were initiated for giving air support to the Chinese, on the assumption that the next Japanese move would probably be towards Kunming. It was the intention to form an International Air Force, consisting of R.A.F. bombers and fighters and of an American Volunteer Group under Col. Chennault, to operate in South China. Administrative preparations were begun, petrol stocks were sent to the Chinese airfields, and bombs and components were prepared for despatch. Early in November, 1941, an R.A.F. Commission was sent from the Far East to investigate operational conditions: it included several senior staff officers of A.H.Q. and the station commander of Tengah, who were still away when the Japanese landed in Malaya. The project was no small commitment for A.H.Q., as G.H.Q. had insufficient staff to undertake all the detailed planning and administration which would normally have been done at the level of the higher command: much of this had necessarily to be done by the staff of A.H.Q., which was already insufficient for dealing with its own work (paras. 96-98).

CO-OPERATION WITH NAVY.

107. A.H.Q. had advocated a combined Naval/Air Operations Room in Singapore to co-ordinate and control the seaward air operations of the Command with the naval forces of the Commander-in-Chief, China Station, but it was decided that such co-operation would be better conducted on a G.H.Q./C-in-C. China Station level. To ensure liaison, however, a Naval liaison officer was attached to A.H.Q., for some months before war broke out: later a Naval air-maintenance officer was added.

108. It was recognised that should a full scale Eastern Fleet be based on Singapore, many detailed arrangements for liaison would become necessary. But a full Eastern Fleet staff could not be assembled owing to a shortage of naval officers; indeed, it was considered unwise to assemble one in Singapore before the situation cleared, namely until a fleet arrived in Singapore and its future role could be estimated.

Five days after the outbreak of war, however, a staff of junior Naval officers was provided for watchkeeping in the Army/Air Combined Operations Room, a step made possible when additional officers were thrown up by the loss of H.M.S. Prince of Wales and Repulse. They proved adequate for subsequent needs, but had the Far Eastern Fleet remained in being in Singapore it would have been necessary to strengthen them in order to provide the close co-operation which would have been then essential.

109. Co-operation with the C.-in-C., East Indies was close, and a Combined Operations Room had been established at Colombo. There was real understanding of the problem facing the R.A.F., particularly the difficulty, owing to shortage of flying boats, of assisting in the control of sea communications in the Indian Ocean. There were never more than two Catalinas, often only one, available in Ceylon for this work.

110. Invaluable memoranda about Naval/Air matters, obtained by G.H.Q. from Coastal Command and other sources, were available at A.H.Q. These were collated and revised to suit local conditions and a Far East Command handbook was printed. It was issued in August, 1941, to R.A.F. Units and Naval Commands for guidance in carrying out all types of operations over the sea.

CO-OPERATION WITH ARMY IN MALAYA.

Close Support.

111. Co-operation with the Army in Malaya had not been highly developed or exercised in the past. No. 21 Squadron, R.A.A.F., when it was equipped with Wirraways, had been regarded in part as an A.C. Squadron, and had carried out some limited exercises with troops in the field. The methods of co-operation which had been practised were, however, not in line with recent developments in Europe and the Middle East.

112. There was much material available at A.H.Q. of the experience gained in other Commands but, owing to lack of staff, the lessons had not been digested. Active steps were taken to remedy this, and instructions for the joint information of Army and Air Force Units to cover the operations of bombers in support of troops were produced and issued in September, 1941, with the concurrence of the G.O.C., Malaya Command. Similarly, instructions were compiled and issued for joint information to cover the operations of fighter aircraft employed on tactical reconnaissance.

113. Classes were started for training aircrews in Army organisation and tactics. Each bomber and fighter squadron in the Command was affiliated to an Army formation and was allotted so many flying hours per month for combined training. But owing to lack of signals equipment, communications were improvised and primitive, which severely restricted the type of support which could be given.

Aerodrome Defence.

114. For some years before war broke out, considerable difference of opinion had existed between the Army and the R.A.F. about the siting of aerodromes on the peninsula of Malaya.

Until 1937 the army's policy had always been to have the East Coast undeveloped as far as possible because insufficient forces were available to defend the long coast-line.

The need then arose for aerodromes on the peninsula well forward of the Naval base at Singapore. Sites for them on the eastern side of the mountainous backbone of the peninsula, hitherto undeveloped, were essential for two reasons. Firstly to obtain maximum air range over the sea to the east, from which direction the threat to Malaya was greatest. Secondly in order to avoid the cloud-covered mountainous backbone which, in those days, effectively prevented aircraft based on aerodromes on the west side from operating over the sea on the east, the threatened, side.

Unfortunately there had been insufficient co-operation on the spot in Malaya between the two interests involved, with the result that some of the sites selected were tactically weak to defend. But in the Spring of 1941 the necessary full co-operation was established between the services on the spot, in this important matter of selecting aerodrome sites.

115. However, those aerodromes that were located in the Singapore fortress area were well sited for defence. They were, furthermore,

covered by the fortress A.A. umbrella. Sabotage was regarded as the main threat, particularly during the initial stages of war.

116. The defence of aerodromes on the mainland was a more difficult problem. There were three areas of major importance:—
   (i) *N.E. Malaya*—Kelantan aerodromes.
   (ii) *E. Coast Malaya*—Kuantan.
   (iii) *N.W. Malaya*—Kedah aerodromes.

It was some of these aerodromes which had been sited in tactically weak positions for the reasons given in para 114. Some were even in exposed positions close to favourable landing beaches. The desirablility, from an administrative view-point, of selecting sites close to existing communications and sources of labour had contributed to this dangerous situation.

It meant that the Field army on the west coast, down which the main enemy thrust on land was expected to develop, had to make large detachments to protect aerodromes on the east coast.

117. On the east coast, the direct defence of aerodromes was the prime function of the Army. Accordingly, the Brigadiers at Kota Bahru and Kuantan were, by agreement between the A.O.C. and G.O.C., appointed Aerodrome Defence Commanders in their respective areas. The arrangement, with certain safeguards, worked well and resulted in good co-ordination of the resources available for defence.

118. The training, experience, quality and numbers of the forces manning the defences of the aerodromes other than those at Kota Bahru and Kuantan were much under requirements. They were mostly Indian State troops, who had had little opportunity for training in this specialised work. A further handicap was a general paucity of weapons of all kinds, particularly A.A. guns and their equipment.

119. Every effort was made to improve the defences of aerodromes against ground attack. Old tanks, armoured cars and any form of weapons were sought from other Commands and from the U.S.A. H.Q.M.C. did its best, but the men and weapons required could not be made available. Assistance was also given by the Naval Base and later by the Dutch. Financial authority was given by the A.O.C. in the autumn to put in hand urgent work on defence schemes of mainland aerodromes without the necessity for prior reference to A.H.Q.

120. Joint Army and R.A.F. Aerodrome Defence Boards were set up about July, 1941, throughout Malaya to co-ordinate defence schemes; and thereafter care was taken to ensure that the defence aspect was considered at the outset when new aerodrome construction was put in hand.

121. Full instructions were prepared and issued to guide local Commanders in preparing denial and destruction schemes, and arrangements were made for obstructing airfields not in use.

122. The first two major aerodrome defence exercises were held in the late summer in the presence of large numbers of Army spectators for instructional purposes: one was held at Tengah with the co-operation of Fortress troops, and one at Kluang in Johore with the Australian Division.

123. Finally, in conjunction with A.H.Q. and H.Q.M.C., G.H.Q. produced about this time a handbook on aerodrome defence which detailed the probable scale of attack to which each would be subject, the minimum defences required, and the priority of their provision.

Co-operation with A.A. Defences.

124. During the latter half of 1941, A.A. equipments rapidly increased in number, in Singapore especially, and demands for air co-operation for the training of A.A. crews multiplied accordingly. Special aircraft for the purpose were few, so A.A. defence exercises were combined with other forms of training in order to make full use of flying hours. Nevertheless, this resulted in many flying hours of operational units, which were all too precious for their own training, being expended on this work; yet the A.A. Defence Commander's requirements were never approached.

Photographic Survey.

125. Photographic survey of large areas in Malaya for both the Army and the Civil Government was another commitment which had to be met. It necessitated the allotment and training of a special flight.

Joint Army/Air Planning: Operation "Matador".

126. During July, 1941, a staff conference was held at H.Q. Malaya Command which was attended, it is believed, by representatives of G.H.Q., H.Q.M.C., III (Indian) Corps and A.H.Q. It was called to consider a War Office project for the occupation of the Kra Isthmus by a joint Army/R.A.F. force from Malaya, the object of which was to deny to the Japanese the port and aerodrome facilities in it (which, if exploited, constituted the main threat to Malaya) by meeting and defeating him on the beaches.

127. It was evident that the development of the aerodromes there by the Siamese could only be linked up with the spread of the Japanese over Indo-China and their increasing influence in Bangkok. It appeared obvious that they would soon contain all the facilities required by Japanese aircraft, particularly fighters, which would then be able to support effectively landings in Southern Siam and Northern Malaya. The A.H.Q. representative was consequently in favour, at the least, of a raid to destroy these facilities.

128. The conference finally adopted a plan for seizing and holding the Singora area and "The Ledge" position on the Patani Road, but only if:—
   (a) a minimum of 24 hours' start of the enemy was available;
   (b) the opportunity occurred during the North-East Monsoon (October/March), i.e., when the Japanese would not be able to employ tanks off the roads.

This plan was known as "Operation Matador". The A.H.Q. representative was strongly pressed to state definitely what squadrons would be available to take part in it, with particular reference to breaking the railway running south from Bangkok, along which it was presumed a Japanese advance would come concurrently with any attack from seaward. An offer was made of a Singapore III flying boat to carry a demolition party to some suitable stretch of railroad near the Siamese coast, but it was not taken up. Otherwise, no definite allotment could be made because of the meagre air strength in Malaya and its many commitments. The force available would have to depend on the situation at the time and on the priority of tasks allotted by G.H.Q. to the R.A.F. as a whole. From the Army point of view this was a most unsatisfactory reply.

129. At this conference the chances of executing this operation successfully appeared remote, dependent as it was upon most accurate timing for forestalling the Japanese in the Singora-Patani area and for doing so without precipitating war with Japan or appearing to be the aggressors. Moreover, there seemed some doubt whether sufficient Army resources would be available to carry it out. However, the benefits deriving from it, if it were successful, were held by G.H.Q. to outweigh the risks involved. Careful and comprehensive plans were therefore drawn up with the Army to move elements of the IIIrd (Indian) Corps by road and rail to Siam, with the R.A.F. supporting from aerodromes in Northern Malaya with such units as the situation at the time permitted.

Control of Army/Air Operations.

130. For the control of operations in support of the Army in the north of Malaya A.H.Q. formed a nucleus Operations Group H.Q. It was designated Norgroup. Its functions were:—

(i) to command such air forces as A.H.Q. might allot to it from time to time;

(ii) to advise G.O.C. IIIrd Corps on air matters and to control such air forces as might be allotted to IIIrd Corps. A Combined IIIrd Corps/Norgroup Headquarters was established at Kuala Lumpur with an advanced H.Q. close to Butterworth.

Norgroup Headquarters was formed in July, 1941, was exercised in its functions, and was then disbanded. But it was held in readiness for mobilization when required.

131. On Singapore Island, under G.H.Q. orders, a combined Army/Air Operations Room was constructed alongside A.H.Q. in Sime Road, Singapore. It was ready for use just before war broke out. (As it was very vulnerable the construction of an alternative Operations Room was put in hand.) It functioned at the level of A.H.Q. and H.Q.M.C. Thus G.H.Q. and C.-in-C. China Fleet were not represented in it. Five days after the outbreak of war, however, the latter provided a staff to represent him in it.

SUMMARY OF SITUATION, 22ND NOVEMBER, 1941.

General pre-war situation.

132. Enough has been said to paint a pre-war picture of the Command and, it is hoped, of the vigorous efforts which were made to carry out the expansion programme authorised by the Chiefs of Staff. But the fact remains that by December, 1941, the R.A.F. Far East Command was not yet in a position to fulfil its responsibility of being the primary means of resisting Japanese aggression. The calls of the war in Europe had allowed it to develop only a fraction of the necessary strength.

133. Re-equipment of squadrons had not taken place and was not likely to do so in the near future; Vickers Vildebeestes were still our main striking strength. Buffalo fighters had arrived, it is true, but their performance and armament were disappointing, and inexperienced pilots were still being trained to man them.

134. The aerodromes in Northern Malaya on which so much was to depend, especially during the early stages of the war, had none of the pre-requisites of secure air bases for occupation in the face of the enemy. The number of fighters available was very inadequate for providing effective fighter cover. Both heavy and light A.A. guns were quite insufficient. Dispersal arrangements for aircraft and their protection from blast were not as complete as was planned. And, in the absence of an adequate air raid warning system the aerodromes were open to surprise attack.

135. But the role of the Command remained constant. It was not practicable to alter it. It was:—

(a) To find the enemy at sea as far away from Malaya as possible: then

(b) to strike hard and often,

(c) to continue attacks during the landing operations: and

(d) in co-operation with the Army to delay his advance.

While real progress had been made in fitting the Command for its allotted tasks, deficiencies were still apparent in almost every aspect of its functions.

136. The Army in Malaya was also still weak: its additional interim strength considered necessary to ensure security until such time as the air strength had been built up was not present in the Colony. It was over-extended in its dispositions, a state of affairs forced upon it by its many and widely scattered commitments.

137. In a country like Malaya it was not difficult for the enemy to obtain information about our forces. He was well served by a long-established system of agents.

138. For their part the Japanese had already occupied Indo-China. While no certain information could be obtained by F.E.C.B. it was patent that they were building up their forces there and were preparing operational facilities in Siam. Japanese reconnaissance flights over Borneo and Malaya had become so frequent by October 1941 that a section of Buffaloes had been stationed at Kota Bahru to curb those over Malaya.

Deterioration of the Political Situation.

139. During 1941, relations with Japan became increasingly strained. The attitude of the Siamese Government was doubtful. It professed great friendship for Britain and sent two goodwill missions to Singapore to cement this friendship. Nevertheless, the Japanese continued to reconnoitre Siam and to make preparations for utilising that country as a Base: they accelerated the provisioning of the aerodromes at Singora and Patani, which they also extended to make them suitable for modern aircraft. As November 1941 progressed, evidence of Japanese activities increased until, on 22nd November, 1941, the information at G.H.Q's disposal was sufficient to indicate that Japan was about to embark upon a further major

venture in South-East Asia. The resultant action initiated by G.H.Q. is dealt with in Section II.

Section II.

NARRATIVE OF OPERATIONS BASED ON MALAYA.

Events from 22nd November to Midnight 7-8th December, 1941.

G.H.Q. Appreciation of the Situation—22nd November, 1941.

140. On 22nd November, 1941, G.H.Q. issued their appreciation of the situation. Briefly, this appreciation considered that any further major action by Japan in the near future would take place from South Indo-China against Siam, rather than from North Indo-China against the Burma road. G.H.Q. did not, however, disregard the possibility of Japan making a " gambler's throw " against Malaya or even against Singapore itself. G.H.Q. concluded that the most likely operation which would be called for on our part in the immediate future would be to the set plan " Matador," namely an advance by our land forces into South-East Siam. A.H.Q. was accordingly instructed to make all preliminary moves and to be ready to support " Matador " at 72 hours' notice, and was informed that this support for " Matador " was to take precedence over the preparations then being made for an International Air Force to operate in South China. A.H.Q. was also warned that the full reconnaissance plan for detecting the approach of a sea expedition against Malaya might be ordered later.

141. The Order of Battle of the Far East Command in Malaya at this stage is shown in Appendix " C ".

Action taken by A.H.Q. to implement Operation " Matador ".

142. A.H.Q. immediately adopted the following measures for reinforcing N. Malaya.

(a) Formed Headquarters Norgroup which assembled on 24th November at Kuala Lumpur alongside Headquarters IIIrd Indian Corps. The Commander appointed was Wing Commander R. G. Forbes, Station Commander, Alor Star, in the absence of the Commander designate, Group Captain A. G. Bishop, who was away in South China. (See para. 106.)

(b) Ordered No. 21 (F) Squadron, R.A.A.F., to move to Sungei Patani: move to be completed by 25th November.

(c) Put No. 34 (B) Squadron (Blenheim IV) at short notice to move to Alor Star.

(d) Made provisional arrangements for the move of No. 60 (B) Squadron aircraft (7 Blenheims) out of Kuantan to Butterworth. This move would be necessary if the reconnaissance plan were to be brought into force because No. 8 (GR) Squadron, R.A.A.F. would require the accommodation at Kuantan for carrying out that plan.

(e) Instituted certain other precautionary measures, including the warning of our fighters at Kota Bahru, Sungei Patani and Singapore of the action they were to take if unidentified aircraft were sighted. Training was allowed to proceed with certain restrictions.

143. Commander, Norgroup, was informed that the following squadrons would support Operation " Matador ":—

(a) No. 62 (B) Squadron (Blenheim I) from Alor Star.
(b) No. 34 (B) Squadron (Blenheim IV) from Alor Star.
(c) No. 21 (F) Squadron, R.A.A.F. (Buffaloes) from Sungei Patani.
(d) No. 27 (NF) Squadron (Blenheim I) from Sungei Patani.

Further G.H.Q. Appreciation—28th November, 1941.

144. On 28th November, 1941, G.H.Q. informed A.H.Q. of a report received from Saigon that the Japanese intended landing troops in South Siam on 1st December, 1941. G.H.Q. stated that the Japanese had adequate forces to carry out such a move but placed no great credence in the report. They assumed that if such a convoy did leave Saigon it would travel at 15 knots or less and anchor off Nakwan or between Singora and Patani on the S.E. coast of Siam on the morning of either the 30th November or 1st December. G.H.Q. ordered A.H.Q. to despatch air reconnaissances daily with a view to locating this Force, but in view of the danger that the Japanese might, by holding out a bait, induce us to strike the first blow and thus appear to be the aggressors, with consequent loss of American sympathy, stated that " a striking force will not be ordered to attack the convoy if found ". From this day until 3rd December, reconnaissances proceeded without event except that on the 3rd December two large cargo boats were sighted.

145. On 29th November, 1941, the notice for Operation " Matador " was shortened by G.H.Q. from 72 hours to 12 hours.

Assumption of No. 2 Degree of Readiness.

146. On 1st December, 1941, G.H.Q. ordered the Command to be brought to " No. 2 degree of readiness ". The promulgation of this degree informed the Command that " the international situation was deteriorating " and brought it into a position to operate at short notice. Inter alia it meant that the full air raid warning system was to be brought into being.

Arrival of Naval Reinforcements.

147. On the 2nd December, H.M.S. " Prince of Wales " and H.M.S. " Repulse " arrived in Singapore as a counter-measure to continued Japanese encroachment in the South-West Pacific. The former wore the flag of Admiral Sir Tom Phillips, the new C.-in-C., Eastern Fleet.

Initiation of full Air Reconnaissance Plan.

148. On 3rd December, 1941, orders were issued by G.H.Q. for the full reconnaissance plan to be put into force on the following day. As a result, in the afternoon of the 3rd, a Dutch group of three flying boats arrived at Seletar in accordance with prearranged plans (see para. 37). The reconnaissance areas

allotted to the Dutch and British respectively were:—

Dutch: Kuantan - Gr.Natunas - Kuching (British Borneo).

British: Kota Bahru-Southern tip of Indo-China-Gr.Natunas-Kuantan.

An extension of the reconnaissance area into the Gulf of Siam as part of routine reconnaissance was not possible owing to a shortage of aircraft.

The task of executing the British section of the reconnaissance plan was allotted to Nos. 1 and 8 (GR) Squadrons, R.A.A.F., based on Kota Bahru and Kuantan respectively. Their effort was reinforced by Catalinas of No. 205 (FB) Squadron to fill in gaps and to ensure overlapping the Dutch.

The initiation of the full reconnaissance plan cancelled the special reconnaissance which had been carried out hitherto, and involved the movement of No. 8 (GR) Squadron, R.A.A.F. from Sembawang to Kuantan. Owing to lack of transport aircraft and inadequate land communications, the ground personnel and equipment of this squadron proceeded there by sea.

Reconnaissance period 4th-6th December, 1941.

149. On the 4th December, owing to bad weather, aircraft at Kota Bahru (No. 1 (GR) Squadron, R.A.A.F.) were unable to operate, but those at Kuantan (No. 8 (GR) Squadron, R.A.A.F.) carried out their part in the reconnaissance plan, as did the Dutch, with nothing to report. Reports of the sightings of strange submarines in the reconnaissance area had been received, so a special reconnaissance was carried out by No. 60 (B) Squadron from Kuantan; but it was negative. On this day a Catalina took Admiral Sir Tom Phillips, Commander-in-Chief Eastern Fleet, to Manila.

On 5th December, 1941, bad weather still prevented No. 1 (GR) Squadron, R.A.A.F., at Kota Bahru operating, but again the Dutch Reconnaissance Group and No. 8 (GR) Squadron, R.A.A.F., at Kuantan gave negative reports. On this day a special anti-submarine patrol was maintained by three Vildebeestes ahead of H.M.S. " Repulse " which proceeded at slow speed en route from Singapore to Australia.

On the 6th December, 1941, three crews were despatched to Sourabaya to collect three Catalinas loaned by the Dutch. The anti-submarine patrol in co-operation with H.M.S. " Repulse " was also maintained.

First sighting of Japanese Expedition—6th December, 1941.

150. On December 6th Kota Bahru aerodrome was serviceable and the full reconnaissance plan was operated. The N.E. monsoon was blowing; its tropical downpours periodically made unaided navigation and accurate ship recognition matters of considerable difficulty.

A Hudson of No. 1 (R.A.A.F.) Squadron, Captain F/Lieut. J. C. Ramshaw, was the first to sight the enemy. He located two approaching convoys:—

(a) at 12.12 1 Motor vessel, 1 minelayer and 1 mine sweeper in a position 185 miles, and on a bearing of 52°, from Kota Bahru, steering a course of 310°.

(b) at 12.46 1 battleship, 5 cruisers, 7 destroyers and 25 merchant vessels in a position 265 miles, and on a bearing of 86°, from Kota Bahru steering a course of 270°.

Another Hudson of the same squadron shortly afterwards reported another convoy:—

(c) at 13.00 2 cruisers, 10 destroyers and 10 merchant vessels in a position 260 miles, and on a bearing of 76°, from Kota Bahru steering 270°.

151. Information about the latter convoy was subsequently amplified to the effect that it contained 21 merchant vessels which were cruising in two lines astern. This amplification was received by telephone at A.H.Q. at 1517 hours.

152. The position of the first of these convoys was such that it had the appearance of having recently rounded Cape Cambodia and was now headed N.W. into the Gulf of Siam. The position of the other two convoys was about 80 miles S.S.E. of Cape Cambodia, the Southern tip of French Indo-China; both were steering west, one slightly ahead of the other. They might, or might not, be following the first small convoy and in turn head N.W. into the Gulf of Siam.

One of the Hudsons had been chased by an enemy aeroplane and there could be no doubt that the Japanese knew that they had been spotted.

153. In the meantime, reports were received of aircraft, apparently Japanese, taking photographs at various points. G.H.Q. confirmed that no offensive action was to be taken by fighters against them, although A.A. defences were given authority to open fire on unidentified aircraft.

154. As a result of the enemy sighting reports, Kota Bahru was instructed to send Hudsons from No. 1 (GR) Squadron, R.A.A.F., to shadow the convoys. Catalinas of No. 205 (FB) Squadron from Seletar were ordered to take over this shadowing from the Hudsons, and to maintain it during the night 6/7th December until relieved by Hudsons again in the morning of 7th December.

155. On receipt of sighting reports, the Command was put by G.H.Q. at " No. 1 degree of readiness " which meant that it was to be " ready for immediate operations and prepared for enemy attack without prior warning."

Action taken by A.H.Q. on Enemy Sighting.

156. The following action was taken by A.H.Q. as a result of the reconnaissance reports received:—

(a) 7 Vildebeestes of No. 36 (TB) Squadron were despatched from Seletar to Kota Bahru. (9 were ordered but only 7 could proceed). Aircraft were armed with torpedoes on arrival at Kota Bahru.

(b) Norgroup was informed that No. 62 (B) Squadron at Alor Star was removed to A.H.Q. control.

(c) No. 34 (B) Squadron was retained at Tengah at short notice to move to Alor Star.

(d) The one Beaufort* still in the Command was moved to Kota Bahru to stand by there for a special photographic reconnaissance required by G.H.Q. (see para. 162).

---

* 6 Beauforts had recently been delivered, but 5 were sent back to Australia owing to "teething" troubles with the aircraft. Nos. 36 (TB) and 100 (TB) Squadrons were due to be rearmed with this type.

Attempts to maintain contact with Enemy.

157. On the afternoon of the 6th December, Hudsons despatched at 1620 hours from Kota Bahru to shadow were unable to contact the convoys, and bad weather prohibited relief aircraft being sent. The first Catalina of No. 205 (FB) Squadron left Seletar at 18.30 hours according to programmes to shadow the convoy during the night.

158. During the late evening of the 6th, scrutiny of reports and records revealed that the Japanese convoys were probably one hour ahead of the positions reported. It was assumed, therefore, that the convoys on rounding Indo-China had turned to the N.W. into the Gulf of Siam, thus passing out of the reconnaissance area (vide para. 152). This, perhaps, appeared at the time to explain why Hudsons despatched to shadow had not contacted the enemy; visibility conditions, however, had been poor.

159. No reports having been received from the first Catalina despatched to shadow the convoys, orders were issued to a second Catalina, before it took off to relieve the first, that if no contact was established, a search was to be made off the West Coast of Cambodia.

This was done because G.H.Q. considered the convoy had probably anchored at Ko Kong, for which it might be making as the next step towards Siam. The second Catalina left Seletar at 0200 hours on 7th December. After it was airborne it was ordered to keep 10 miles away from the coast of Siam. No report was ever received from this second Catalina, which was afterwards confirmed as having been shot down by the Japanese.

Reconnaissance Plan for 7th December, 1941.

160. For the 7th December, 1941 the Dutch flying boat "Group" and No. 205 (FB) Squadron at Seletar, and No. 8 (GR) Squadron, R.A.A.F., at Kuantan were instructed to continue the set reconnaissance plan covering the more direct line of approach to Singapore in case a further invasion convoy should attack from that direction. Such an attack would have been most dangerous, particularly if it were directed against the beaches in the Mersing/Endau area, where a successful landing would have gravely jeopardised the field army in Northern Malaya and might even have threatened Singapore itself before the same field army could come to its defence.

But the G.R. Squadron at Kota Bahru was detailed to carry out a special reconnaissance sweep into the Gulf of Siam with the object of re-establishing contact with the Japanese convoys known to be in it.

Vildebeestes were despatched to maintain an anti-submarine patrol ahead of H.M.S. Repulse which had been recalled from Australia.

Events on the 7th December, 1941.

161. Owing to bad weather, it was not until 0645 hours on the 7th that the reconnaissance aircraft from Kota Bahru, of which there were three, were able to take off for a sweep into the Gulf of Siam. Shortly afterwards, owing to rain, low clouds and bad visibility, two of them returned; the third proceeded alone.

162. At 1025 hours the C.-in-C., Far East, visited the Combined Army/Air Operations Room and stated that he:—

(a) Wished B.O.A.C. to continue using Bangkok until the last possible moment, and confirmed that flights on the 8th December were to go through Bangkok.

(b) Was considering allowing our aircraft to fire at aircraft not established as friendly.

(c) Would issue orders shortly for the reconnaissance of Ko Kong anchorage, which he wished the P.R. Beaufort, now at Kota Bahru, to carry out.

163. Shortly afterwards, G.H.Q. issued their orders for the reconnaissance of Ko Kong. The aircraft left Kota Bahru at 1220 hours, but returned at 1445 hours owing to bad weather. During the morning, the Catalina with Admiral Sir Tom Phillips on board returned from Manila.

164. Meanwhile at 1345 hours on the 7th December, A.H.Q. was informed that air reconnaissance from Kota Bahru had sighted a 6,000-8,000 ton cargo vessel in the Gulf of Siam steaming west, and this was followed by a further sighting at 1545 hours, by a Hudson of No. 8 (R.A.A.F.) Squadron, of one other Japanese merchant vessel steering south. This latter vessel was stated to have a large number of men on deck in khaki.

165. Two Hudsons from Kota Bahru were immediately directed on a diverging search north of that place and 10 miles off the Siamese coast. At 1750 hours one merchant vessel and one cruiser steaming 270° were sighted about 112 miles north of Kota Bahru. The cruiser opened fire on the aircraft. At 1848 hours, under conditions of very bad visibility, four Japanese naval vessels, perhaps destroyers, were seen 60 miles north of Patani steaming south.

166. Owing to subsequent destruction of records, the exact positions of some of the ship sightings mentioned above cannot now be given with any certainty.

Resulting Action.

167. In consequence of these reports, G.H.Q. decided, late on 7th December, not to put "Operation Matador" into effect that night, and issued orders for B.O.A.C. aircraft to avoid Bangkok and to use the West coast route.

168. Conditions at midnight 7th-8th December, 1941 were therefore:—

(a) Contact with the main Japanese convoys located on the 6th had not been re-established.

(b) Conditions for air reconnaissance in the Gulf of Siam had been bad, but in the late evening four ships had been sighted off Singora steaming south.

(c) "Norgroup," with Nos. 21 (F) R.A.A.F., and 27 (NF) Squadrons at Sungei Patani, was standing by in support of IIIrd Corps, but Operation Matador had not been ordered.

(d) The following aircraft under the command of the Officer Commanding Kota Bahru were fully armed and ready to take the offensive:—

(i) No. 1 (GR) Squadron R.A.A.F., and one Section (2) Buffaloes of No. 243 (F) Squadron at Kota Bahru.

(ii) Seven Vildebeestes (No. 36 (TB) Squadron), with torpedoes, at Gong Kedah, to which they had been transferred owing to congestion at Kota Bahru.

(e) The remainder of the squadrons were under A.H.Q. control as follows:—

(i) Reconnaissance:—
No. 8 (R.A.A.F.) Squadron at Kuantan.
No. 205 (F.B.) Squadron at Seletar.
Dutch (F.B.) Group at Seletar.

(ii) Bombers:—
No. 60 (B) Squadron at Kuantan (N. Malaya).
No. 62 (B) Squadron at Alor Star (N. Malaya).
No. 34 (B) Squadron at Tengah (Singapore).
No. 100 (T.B.) Squadron at Seletar (Singapore).

(iii) Fighters:—(decentralised to 224(F) Group for the direct defence of Singapore).
No. 453 (F) Squadron at Sembawang.
No. 243 (F) Squadron at Kallang.
No. 488 (F) Squadron at Kallang.

The Command was at the fullest degree of readiness, but there was no undue alarm owing to G.H.Q's view that the Japanese expedition was directed against Siam.

169. A.H.Q. decided to send at first light on the 8th December a coastal reconnaissance to the Lakon Roads, north of Singora, to identify whether or not the Japanese had landed in S.E. Siam as forecast in the G.H.Q. appreciation (para. 140).

OPERATIONS FROM 8TH TO 23RD DECEMBER, 1941.

Japanese landing at Kota Bahru.

170. At midnight 7th–8th December, the weather at Kota Bahru cleared, but the aerodrome surface was extremely boggy owing to heavy rains. About 0030 hours on the 8th, O.C. Kota Bahru rang up A.H.Q. and stated that three ships had been seen by the beach defences. This message was followed by another at 0100 hours confirming the presence of these ships, stating that shelling was taking place and that Brigade H.Q. were being asked to clarify the situation. On this, A.H.Q. ordered the despatch of a single Hudson with flares to see what was happening. Before this could be done, at 0115 hours definite information came through from Kota Bahru that landing on the beaches by the Japanese had started from 3–5 ships lying three miles off shore.

Orders issued by A.H.Q.

171. O.C. Kota Bahru was immediately ordered to take offensive action with all available Hudsons, and to order the Vildebeestes at Gong Kedah to deliver a torpedo attack at first light. It must be remembered that the orders issued to O.C. Kota Bahru as a result of G.H.Q. instructions (para. 144) specifically stated that no offensive action would be taken against the convoy when sighted. He could not, therefore, initiate the first offensive action of the campaign without further orders.

172. A.H.Q. also issued orders to Nos. 8 (GR), 27 (NF), 34 (B), 60 (B) and 62 (B) Squadrons to take off at first light and attack shipping in the Kota Bahru area whilst No. 100 (TB) Squadron was ordered to proceed to Kuantan on the following morning and stand by for orders.

173. Norgroup was informed that No. 27 (NF) was also to revert to A.H.Q. control, leaving only No. 21 (F) Squadron (R.A.A.F.), for co-operation with IIIrd Corps.

174. The Beaufort at Kota Bahru was instructed to carry out the photographic reconnaissance at first light to Lakon Roads (para. 169).

First Operations against enemy landings at Kota Bahru.

175. At Kota Bahru the first seven Hudson sorties of No. 1 (GR) Squadron R.A.A.F. had taken off to oppose the landing, and by 0300 hours the two available Buffaloes had been despatched against landing barges entering the river which flows into the sea within the frontage of the beach defences guarding the aerodrome.

176. At 0730 hours on 8th December, the O.C. Kota Bahru gave a résumé of the night's operations. 17 Hudson sorties had been carried out, one transport had been destroyed and two others damaged and perhaps sunk. Landing barges en route to the beaches had been attacked and casualties had been inflicted amongst the troops in them. Intensive A.A. fire had been experienced, particularly accurate from a cruiser covering the landing. Two Hudsons had been shot down and a third badly damaged, leaving him still six. One Buffalo had also been hit. The Vildebeestes from Gong Kedah were in the air.

177. Apparently some 8 transports covered by one cruiser and several destroyers had been involved, and O.C. Kota Bahru thought all vessels had now retired to the north. He intended to carry on using the Hudsons for mopping up small craft and beach parties still visible. At 0800 hours, he confirmed that all vessels had retired to the north and that he was mopping up the few small craft left with bomb and machine-gun fire. He added that there had been some infiltration into the Brigade area.

178. Meanwhile the Vildebeestes of No. 36 (TB) Squadron from Gong Kedah, in heavy rain, found the cruiser, delivered an attack with torpedoes which it evaded, and landed at Kota Bahru on their return.

179. Nos. 8 (GR) R.A.A.F., 27 (NF), 34 (B) and 60 (B) Squadrons also arrived on the scene and found little to attack in the area; a signal sent them whilst they were airborne to search further north was not received by all units. One flight of No. 8 (GR) Squadron at least received it but was unable to find the enemy owing to a very heavy rainstorm. Nos. 8 and 60 Squadrons returned to Kuantan, No. 27 to Sungei Patani, whilst No. 34 Squadron landed at Butterworth. All squadrons were ordered to refuel and re-arm.

180. No. 62 (B) Squadron which had also been ordered to attack, not finding any target, proceeded north to Patani to bomb transports there. This squadron (11 Blenheim I's) encountered fighter opposition and fairly intensive A.A. fire. It carried out its attack from 8,000 ft. but the results obtained were not seen.

First Air Attack on Singapore.

181. Whilst the first landings had been taking place at Kota Bahru, Singapore had its first

air-raid shortly after 0400 hours on the 8th December. Radar detected the approaching raid at a distance of 130-140 miles from Singapore (giving more than 30 minutes warning). Its approach was promulgated from the Fighter Control Operations Room. Unfortunately the staff of this room was unable to obtain any response from the H.Qs. of the Civil A.R.P. organisation, with the result that the civil population received no effective warning, nor was the Civil Air Defence Scheme put into effective action until it was too late. Some 17 aircraft took part in this raid, the majority of the bombs falling at Seletar and Tengah. At the latter place 3 Blenheims of No. 34 (B) Squadron were damaged and the aerodrome was cratered.

Japanese attacks on Northern Airfields.

182. Between 0730 and 0800 hours, Kota Bahru, Gong Kedah and Machang aerodromes were attacked by bombers and low-flying fighters; except for dummy aircraft, the latter two were unoccupied at the time. These attacks were repeated throughout the day mainly by low-flying fighters, with little effect save in delaying the refuelling and re-armament of aircraft at Kota Bahru.

183. Sungei Patani, Penang and Butterworth in N.W. Malaya were also attacked throughout 8th December by formations of from 27 to 60 bomber aircraft, with serious results. The Japanese used light bombs only, directed against aircraft and personnel; they studiously avoided damaging aerodrome surfaces. Personnel on the spot noted that for the next few days Japanese attacks in this area frequently synchronised with aircraft landing or getting ready to take off. This indicated a leakage of information to the Japanese, but it was never definitely proved that such a leakage actually occurred.

184. There was a particularly serious attack against Alor Star, delivered immediately after No. 62 (B) Squadron had landed after its attack at Patani (para. 180). The aerodrome was first bombed by 27 Japanese aircraft, which then came down low and machine-gunned aircraft on the ground. As a result No. 62 (B) Squadron had only two serviceable aircraft left.

185. Nos. 21 (F) R.A.A.F. and 27 (NF) Squadrons at Sungei Patani also suffered badly and were each reduced to 4 serviceable aircraft; and in consequence of the repeated low attacks on this airfield both squadrons, with their personnel, were withdrawn to Butterworth. It was later learnt that the guns in the Buffaloes had given trouble and were all unserviceable from lack of solenoids. The serviceable Blenheim fighters of No. 27 Squadron had carried out periodic patrols over N.W. Malaya without result. No. 34 (B) Squadron at Butterworth was also seriously reduced.

Ground Situation in N.W. Malaya.

186. Aircraft losses from enemy attack thus gravely weakened the air forces available in N.W. Malaya for supporting the army, where the main enemy advance on land was expected to develop. On the 8th there was little enemy air activity against our own ground forces, owing to the enemy's concentration on the bombing of our aerodromes.

187. "Matador" had been cancelled during the morning, and the Army was taking up positions forward of a partially prepared line at Jitra. Covering forces were advancing north and north-east from Kedah province: one to make contact along the line of advance from the Singora area, the other (Krohkol) to occupy what was known as the Ledge, an important tactical feature across the Siamese frontier on the Kroh-Patani road, which protected the communications of the force in North Kedah.

The first of these covering forces made contact with the enemy at 2130 hours on the 8th, at Ban Sadao, ten miles inside Siam. The other (Krohkol) reported some opposition from Siamese forces, but continued its advance.

Enemy landings in Singora and Patani area.

188. At 0915 hours on the 8th December the P.R. Beaufort returned from its reconnaissance of the Lakon Roads (para. 174). En route, it had been heavily attacked by fighters and landed in a badly shot up condition, subsequently having to be destroyed. The pilot reported verbally that a large concentration of vessels was landing troops in the Singora-Patani area. His photographs were flown back to Singapore by the remaining Buffalo fighter. Shortly afterwards, Norgroup, under orders from IIIrd Corps, despatched 3 Buffaloes of No. 21 (F) Squadron R.A.A.F. on a tactical reconnaissance to Singora. This reconnaissance confirmed the presence of the main convoy in the Singora area and also revealed a force of about 60 Japanese aircraft, mainly fighters, on Singora aerodrome.

Squadrons driven out of aerodromes in N.E. Malaya on 8th December.

189. It is now necessary to return to the Kota Bahru area. Heavy fighting had been going on on the beaches all day, and reserves had been put in to try and regain the beaches by counter attack. At 1245 news was received at A.H.Q. of the landing of further troops from one transport covered by a cruiser and several destroyers. The Station Commander at Kota Bahru had at 1200 hours despatched 4 Hudsons and 3 Vildebeestes to deal with this threat. It transpired later that the report of this further landing was false, but aircraft continued mopping up barges and machine gunning beaches. At 1530 a Hudson from Kota Bahru bombed the railway bridge across the South Golok River west of Kota Bahru, but with doubtful success; the crew, however, observed that the line itself had been partially destroyed already at a point further eastward.

190. Towards 1600 hours reports received at A.H.Q. indicated that the situation on the ground had become serious. The Station Commander reported that penetration had been made up to the aerodrome boundary, and that aircraft and personnel had come under sporadic fire. On his representation A.H.Q. approved the evacuation of the aerodrome. All aircraft were ordered to Kuantan, personnel and stores to proceed by train, whilst the denial scheme was to be put in operation. This was successfully achieved, and 5 Hudsons and 7 Vildebeestes arrived at Kuantan. This withdrawal as far south as Kuantan was unavoidable because Gong Kedah, the only aerodrome in the Kota Bahru

area that might have been used, was virtually undefended and was in a very exposed situation near the coast.

191. During the day, various reports of suspicious vessels off the East coast had been received, necessitating reconnaissances which, however, were all negative.

Summary of situation on the evening of the 8th December, 1941.

192. That night (8th-9th December) the situation was, therefore:—
   (a) The Japanese expedition to capture the Kota Bahru aerodrome area was succeeding; and the use of aerodromes in this area was now denied to the R.A.F. Our troops in the area were thus without close air support.
   (b) The Japanese main forces were landing unimpeded in the Singora-Patani area, covered by air operations against our aerodromes in N. Malaya. Their advance towards the north-west frontier of Malaya had already begun, and our forward troops had made contact. The shipping at Singora had not been attacked; partly because the aircraft at Kota Bahru were fully engaged locally by the time it was reported, and partly because heavy Japanese air attacks against our virtually undefended aerodromes in N.W. Malaya had seriously reduced the squadrons available on them.
   (c) The Japanese Air Force was already operating in strength from Singora aerodrome. From the narrow view point of the Royal Air Force, it was apparent that the cancellation of Operation "Matador" was to have a far-reaching influence on air operations in Northern Malaya.

Air Operations in North West Malaya—9th December, 1941.

193. In the N.W. aerodrome area, enemy air attacks continued, and early on the 9th No. 62 (B) Squadron was forced to withdraw from Alor Star to Butterworth.

194. To counter these attacks, it was decided to destroy the Japanese fighters based on Singora. Two attacks against this aerodrome were planned. The first was to be made by the aircraft of No. 34 (B) Squadron still located at Tengah, reinforced by No. 60 (B) Squadron, which had by now moved there from Kuantan. No. 34 Squadron was ordered to land at Butterworth, re-arm and take part in the second attack. The second attack was to be made by all available aircraft of Nos. 34 and 62 Squadrons, from Butterworth. A.H.Q. issued orders that both attacks were to be escorted by the maximum strength of Buffaloes from No. 21 (F) Squadron, R.A.A.F.

195. The first attack, consisting of 6 Blenheims of No. 34 (B) Squadron, three of which were manned by crews of 60 (B) Squadron, was made in the early afternoon of the 9th. Heavy fighter opposition was encountered, and 3 of our aircraft were shot down. Results of the attack were not observed, but returning crews claimed that, at least, a congested aerodrome had been hit.

196. No fighter escort had been available. No. 21 (F) Squadron, R.A.A.F., had two aircraft serviceable only, which were on tactical reconnaissances for IIIrd Corps. It may be noted here that these aircraft on the morning of the 9th reported the presence of Japanese light tanks, which were observed at Ban Sadao moving south.

197. The second attack—a mixed force of Blenheim I's and IV's from Nos. 34 (B) and 62 (B) Squadrons—due off from Butterworth at 1700 hours, was never launched. Just before the time of "take-off," Japanese bombers carried out a high bombing attack followed up by machine-gunning aircraft on the ground. One aircraft only of No. 62 (B) Squadron—Captain, Flight Lieutenant A. S. K. Scarf—took off as the attack was developing; the remaining aircraft on the ground were all rendered unserviceable. Flight Lieutenant Scarf circled the aerodrome until it became apparent that no other aircraft were joining him. He then proceeded to Singora and pressed home his attack. During his approach to the target and subsequent get-away, A.A. fire and heavy fighter opposition were encountered, and Flight Lieutenant Scarf was mortally wounded. This very gallant officer felt unable to make the longer journey back to Butterworth, but managed to retain consciousness until he reached Alor Star, where he crash-landed without injury to his crew. He died in hospital that evening. He was subsequently awarded the Victoria Cross.

198. As a result of this day's operations against Singora, A.H.Q. decided that no more bombing by day should take place over land until such time as fighter escort could be provided.

Preparations for withdrawal from the N.W.

199. At 0900 hours on the 9th, Adv. H.Q. Norgroup opened at Bukit Martajim (near Butterworth), but it became evident that the evacuation of the N.W. bases could not long be delayed. Up till this time there had been no A.A. defences at Butterworth. Eight Bofors guns arrived on the afternoon of the 9th but their presence was not, of course, any deterrent to high flying bombers.

200. A.H.Q., therefore, issued instructions that all airfields on the mainland to the southward were to be got ready for immediate operational use. At the same time, orders were issued to do everything possible to improve dispersal arrangements at aerodromes on Singapore Island.

Evacuation of Kuantan Aerodrome on 9th December.

201. During the night of the 8-9th there were many reports of further landings on the East coast, fears of which were to persist throughout the brief campaign and cause many hours to be spent on coastal reconnaissance.

202. On the 9th, two pairs of Vildebeestes were sent at 0300 hours to sweep the coast north and south of Kuantan. During the day, 6 Hudsons were employed on similar duties whilst Catalinas extended the search area into the South China Sea. The remainder of the aircraft at Kuantan stood by to attack whatever might be found. Confirmation was obtained of the large concentration of ships of all natures unloading in the Singora-Patani area, but no threat of further seaborne attack was discovered although 3 Vildebeestes were despatched on a false report to attack a ship 60 miles east of Kuantan.

203. However, with the destruction of aircraft on the ground in N.W. Malaya in mind, it became evident to A.H.Q. that a dangerous congestion of aircraft existed at Kuantan, particularly vulnerable because there was no A.A. protection there at all. Orders were issued to O.C. Kuantan, early on the 9th, to retain 12 Vildebeestes and the 13 Hudsons of Nos. 1 and 8 (GR) Squadrons, R.A.A.F., and to despatch the remainder to Singapore.

204. At noon the expected attack took place, and Kuantan was subjected to its first experience of high bombing, followed up by the bombers flying low and shooting up at will. A.H.Q. thereupon decided to evacuate Kuantan, the surviving 10 Hudsons and 8 Vildebeestes returning to Singapore. The withdrawal of the ground party from Kuantan might have been better controlled. From then on Kuantan was available as an A.L.G. for refuelling only.

Reports of a landing at Kuantan—9-10th December, 1941.

205. During the night 9-10th, reports were received of a landing north of Kuantan. Six Vildebeestes and 3 Hudsons were ordered to attack. The Vildebeestes found 3 small ships and bombed them with doubtful results, but the Hudsons which arrived later found no target although they prolonged their search of the area past daylight. There is reason to believe that the beaches at Kuantan had been fired on during the night, but that the enemy force was only a light reconnaissance to test the defences, and its size had been magnified in the telling.

206. Further bombing of Kuantan aerodrome on the morning of the 10th added to the uncertainty of the situation and all available bombers in Singapore were put at short notice to await developments. Sharks from the target-towing flight carried out reconnaissance of the approaches to Singapore, whilst Blenheim IV's from No. 34 (B) Squadron, using Kuantan for refuelling purposes, continued reconnaissance of the east coast up to 50 miles north of Singora, confirming once more the large concentration of shipping off the Siamese coast.

207. The false report of a landing at Kuantan proved to have a vital bearing on the movements of H.M.S. " Prince of Wales " and H.M.S. " Repulse ", and it is now necessary to turn to the events leading up to the sinking of these two vessels.

Sinking of H.M.S. " Prince of Wales " and " Repulse "—10th December, 1941.

208. The C.-in-C. Eastern Fleet, Admiral Sir Tom Phillips, decided to sail on the 8th December, 1941, with H.M.S. " Prince of Wales " and H.M.S. " Repulse " accompanied by four destroyers, with the object of attacking the concentration of Japanese transports reported between Singora and Patani. He intended to arrive in the target area at dawn on the 10th December.

209. Before leaving on the 8th December (p.m.) the C.-in-C. asked for the following:—

(a) Reconnaissance 100 miles to north of the force from daylight, Tuesday, the 9th December:

(b) Reconnaissance to Singora and beyond, ten miles from the coast, starting at first light on the 10th December:

(c) Fighter protection off Singora at daylight on the 10th December.

The A.O.C. gave tentative replies that he could provide (a), hoped to be able to provide (b), but could not provide (c). It was decided that he should go thoroughly into the problems involved and give definite replies to the Chief of Staff, Eastern Fleet (Rear Admiral Palliser), who remained at the Naval Base in close liaison with G.H.Q.

210. The doubt about the reconnaissance required in (b) above was due to the fact that the reconnaissance would have had to be provided by Blenheim IV's based on Kuantan, and it was uncertain whether this aerodrome would be out of action or not.

211. The reason why the fighter protection asked for in (c) could not be provided was mainly that the northern aerodromes were either untenable or else had been badly damaged by bombers; this meant that the fighters would have to operate from aerodromes at considerable distance from Singora, and, owing to the short endurance of the Buffalo, would have been able to remain only a very short time over the Singora area before having to return to refuel. These factors meant that a short patrol might possibly have been provided at intervals at Singora, but that it was impossible to guarantee appreciable fighter protection.

212. On the evening of the 8th December the A.O.C. confirmed his tentative replies to the Chief of Staff, Eastern Fleet, and this information was passed by the latter to the C.-in-C. The signal as received on board " Prince of Wales " expressly stated that no fighter protection could be provided on 10th December, 1941. The words " off Singora " did not appear in the text of the signal, but were implied in the light of Admiral Phillips' request (para. 209 (c)).

213. The agreed air reconnaissances were carried out on both the 9th and 10th December.

214. In the early hours of 10th December a signal was received at Singapore indicating that the Fleet might return sooner than was originally planned. Apart from this no communication was received from the C.-in-C. and his position was unknown.

215. Suddenly, shortly after 1200 hours on the 10th December, a signal, originating from H.M.S. " Repulse ", was received in the Operations Room at A.H.Q. of enemy air attacks on H.M.S. " Prince of Wales " and " Repulse " in a position some 60 miles Eastwards of Kuantan. No. 453 (F) Squadron (11 aircraft), which was standing by specifically to provide protection for these ships in case of their return to Singapore, left six minutes later, only to arrive in the area, 165 miles away, to find destroyers picking up survivors from these two great vessels. For the rest of the day a number of sorties by flying boats and fighters was carried out in connection with the return of these destroyers to Singapore.

216. It subsequently transpired that the Fleet had been located by Japanese reconnaissance p.m. 9th December, and that later the

same day the C.-in-C. received news of a landing at Kuantan (in para. 205). These two events must have decided the C.-in-C. to abandon the Singora operation and to close Kuantan on the 10th December.

217. Had the C.-in-C. notified his change of plan, it is conceivable that A.H.Q. might have moved No. 453 (F) Squadron to Kuantan where it could have stood by at call: R/T inter-communication between the two ships and the squadron aircraft had already been arranged. Some effective support might then have been given. Actually no call for assistance was sent until the Japanese attack had been pressed home, by which time intervention from Singapore was impossible.

218. It also transpired later that the ships had been attacked by a force of high level bombers backed by a large number of torpedo-bombers, that both ships had suffered a number of hits by torpedoes and had thus been sunk. The sinking of these two ships was a serious shock to the morale of everybody in the Far East. Their loss, combined with the American losses at Pearl Harbour, gave the Japanese an undisputed command of the sea in Malayan waters. The reactions of this state of affairs upon the subsequent dispositions of air units, with particular reference to the share they were able to take in the land battle, will become clear later in the narrative.

Arrival of Dutch Reinforcements.

219. During the morning of 9th December the three Dutch Bomber (22 Glenn Martins) and one Fighter (9 Buffaloes) Squadrons arrived at Sembawang and Kallang respectively in accordance with the mutual reinforcement plan. It was found that the Dutch bomber crews were not trained in night flying, and so one squadron (9 aircraft) was sent back to the N.E.I. to train; the intention being, on its return, to send back the other squadrons in succession for the same purpose. As A.H.Q. had already decided not to use British bomber squadrons in their bombing role by day until fighter escort or cover could be provided (see para. 198), it was obviously essential to apply the decision to the Dutch bomber squadrons, particularly as their Glenn Martins were slower and no better protected than the British Blenheims.

Air Forces driven out of Aerodromes in N.W. Malaya.

220. Meanwhile in Northern Malaya it was evident that the main line of advance by the Japanese Army was from Singora across Malaya to the Alor Star area. The advanced troops of the 11th (Indian) Division were still holding a position near the frontier but the vital Ledge position on the Kroh-Patani road had not yet been secured.

221. Bombing of our aerodromes in N.W. Malaya continued during the 10th December and A.H.Q. decided that the area must be evacuated. From Butterworth No. 62 (B) Squadron (reduced to 2 aircraft) was evacuated to Taiping: No. 21 (F) Squadron R.A.A.F. (6 repairable aircraft) to Ipoh, where 8 Bofors guns had by now been installed, leaving No. 27 (NF) Squadron (nil serviceability) still at Butterworth. All the unserviceable aircraft of Nos. 27, 34 (B) and 62 (B) Squadrons which were capable of flying were flown to Singapore for repair.

222. The withdrawal of the ground parties was carried out under difficult circumstances.

Units had been subjected to severe and constant bombing and machine gun attacks on scantily defended aerodromes where they saw no effective means of hitting back, and aircraft were remorselessly destroyed on the ground without replacement. The apparent opportuneness of the enemy's attacks (see para. 183) and pernicious rumours of disaster in the land fighting added their influence. There was no senior officer at Butterworth with sufficient weight to take control, and some of the personnel of No. 21 (F) Squadron R.A.A.F. and No. 27 (NF) Squadron R.A.F., both of which had already been driven out of Sungei Patani, did not behave at all steadily. Other units, however, maintained their order.

223. The difficulties of all units was intensified by the wholesale, but understandable, disappearance of unenlisted native followers— cooks, M.T. drivers, sanitary personnel etc.— and only improvised arrangements were possible for replacing them by European personnel at the dislocation of the latter's normal work.

The defection of labour spread to the railway area.

224. Withdrawals were nevertheless effected successfully and, in the case of units other than those mentioned above, in good order. It was due to the untiring energy of a small party headed by Flight Lieutenant R. D. I. Scott, who himself drove a locomotive, that much R.A.F. equipment was removed south.

225. In an endeavour to improve repair and maintenance facilities in N.W. Malaya, an R. & S.U. was formed at this time from No. 151 M.U. at Seletar and was ordered to Taiping; on arrival it detached a Mobile Salvage Section to Butterworth to assist in the work of salving material.

226. Meanwhile, during the commencement of the denial schemes at Alor Star on 10th December, the sight of large fires and the sounds of explosions in their rear had caused some concern amongst our forward troops. Orders were therefore issued to the Commander, Norgroup, that no fires were to be started and no demolitions by explosives carried out. Buildings were to be damaged only, petrol and oil run to waste, and the demolition of aerodromes with the help of explosives was to be left to Corps Royal Engineers to co-ordinate with the operations of our troops.

Scale of Enemy Air Effort.

227. It was computed that on the 8th, 9th and 10th December the Japanese had used a daily average of over 120 aircraft in N. Malaya, mostly against R.A.F. aerodromes. Fighters and some bombers were based on S.E. Siam, the majority of bombers on Indo-China. It was estimated that over 100 aircraft were based in the Singora—Patani area and at least 280 in Indo-China. Types identified were:—

Fighters—Navy " O ".
Twin-Engine Bombers—Navy 96 and Army 97.
Dive Bombers—Junkers 87N (Japanese version).

Formation of War Council, Malaya.

228. On the 10th December Mr. Duff Cooper, whose ministerial duties had taken him to Singapore, formed a War Council, the composition of which was as follows:—

Mr. Duff Cooper, Chairman;
H.E. the Governor of the Straits Settlements;
C.-in-C., Far East;
C.-in-C., Eastern Fleet;
G.O.C., Malaya;
A.O.C., Far East;

and later, Sir George Sansom as being responsible for propaganda and Press control, and the late Mr. Bowden as representative of the Australian Government.

This War Council met daily for deliberation, mainly in connection with the conduct of the war in Malaya.

Events on the 11th December, 1941.

229. On 11th December the squadrons in N. Malaya were not in a position to take offensive action. Coastal reconnaissance, however, to the north of Kuantan by sections of Hudsons, continued. Catalinas extended the search into the S. China Sea, whilst P.R. Buffaloes continued to register Japanese activities off the South Siamese coast. Enemy submarine reports necessitated the despatch of sections of Vildebeestes without result.

230. No. 21 (F) Squadron, R.A.A.F. at Ipoh had no aircraft available for tactical reconnaissance for IIIrd Corps, and so A.H.Q. issued orders that the squadron was to be brought up to strength (16 I.E.) immediately with a proportion of new pilots.

231. Eighty Japanese aircraft attacked Penang Town; no aircraft were available for its protection.

232. On the ground, in addition to advances in the N.E. and N.W., the Japanese had infiltrated down the east coast as far as Trengannu. In the north-west, where the main Japanese forces were advancing, there was considerable pressure on the 11th (Indian) Division, but no major action had been fought. Attacks from the air on our forward troops increased in weight on the 11th, though the enemy air effort was still being expended chiefly on our aerodromes.

233. To assist in the defence of Borneo the Dutch placed at Sinkawang under A.H.Q. operational control one squadron of (9) Glenn Martins and one flight of (4) Buffaloes.

Consideration of Bomber Policy.

234. On the evening of the 11th December it was decided to attack Singora aerodrome once more, the arrival over the objective to be just before first light on the 12th. Eight aircraft of No. 34 (B) Squadron at Tengah were detailed. The attack was unsuccessful: few aircraft got through the bad weather and others were lost as a result of it.

235. This raid was carried out as part of the current policy for bombing Japanese aerodromes in order to reduce the scale of their air activity against our ground forces. The Air Staff at A.H.Q., however, favoured the view that the correct employment of air forces was in the attack of the shipping and troop concentrations in the Singora area, where the main landing had taken place, and through which reinforcements were still entering. They felt that the time had not yet come to concentrate on co-operation with the Army to delay the Japanese advance on the ground. Furthermore, the resources available for the bombing of aerodromes were not sufficient to produce any real effect on the Japanese effort. This was the view of the A.O.C., but he considered that he could not alter the policy which was selected to meet the wishes of the G.O.C., Malaya, who was anxious that action should be designed to reduce the scale of air attack on our troops. The G.O.C. was approached again at about this time, but reiterated that "bomber policy must give immediate relief to his troops" which, in his view, could only be achieved by bombing aerodromes. (See next paragraph.)

236. *Note by Lieut.-General A. E. Percival.*

"I have no recollection of this approach. In any case I am quite certain that there was no strong difference of opinion on the subject between the late Air Vice Marshal Pulford and myself. I would point out that there had been practically no air attacks on the ground troops up to that time, so it was very unlikely that I should press for immediate relief of the troops. At the same time I have always held, and still do, that the first essential in any campaign is to obtain some measure of control in the air. By 11th December the Japanese fighters, most of which were based on Singora aerodrome, had established control of the air over Northern Malaya. As long as they held that control the chances of our aircraft doing damage to Japanese shipping and troop concentrations in the Singora area was remote. Before that could be done it was necessary to regain some measure of air control. The only chance of doing this was to destroy a number of enemy fighters on their congested and weakly defended aerodrome. Therefore, if I did press for an attack on the aerodrome, it would have been for that reason and not to provide immediate relief for the ground troops."

237. The G.O.C.'s point of view was confirmed by G.H.Q. who, on 12th December, issued a War Instruction, the relevant paragraph of which read:—

"For the present, assistance to the 11th Ind. Division is to take precedence over other R.A.F. offensive tasks."

On the 12th December the C.-in-C. visited A.H.Q. and re-emphasised the importance of providing support to the Army in the north-west.

Provision of Support for the Army.

238. On the 11th/12th December the land position in the north-west worsened. The 11th (Indian) Division was attacked in and forced to evacuate the Jitra position, and Krohcol came under heavier attacks. The withdrawal of the latter force would have had grave consequences as it would have exposed the communications of the 11th Indian Division and thus necessitated a general withdrawal out of Kedah province.

239. The only aircraft still available in the area for direct support of the Army were two or three Buffaloes of No. 21 (F) Squadron, R.A.A.F., at Ipoh; the rest of the squadron was being re-equipped at Singapore. The

A.O.C. decided, therefore, to send the aircraft and pilots of No. 453 (F) Squadron from Singapore to Ipoh where they would be serviced by the ground crews of No. 21 Squadron. It was intended to return them to Singapore when the rest of No. 21 Squadron had been re-equipped.

240. No. 453 (F) Squadron arrived at Ipoh on the morning of the 13th and began operating from there, using Butterworth as an advanced landing ground. Connection was established with the Observer Corps Operations Room at Kuala Lumpur in the hope of obtaining at least a short warning of attacks upon the station.

241. Operations were vigorously undertaken from Ipoh between the 13th and the 15th December. Japanese convoys were attacked on the road Simpang—Alor Star—Kepala Bantas. Tactical reconnaissances were carried out, and enemy bombers and reconnaissance aircraft in the area were engaged with some success, notably on the 13th when five enemy aircraft attacking Penang were claimed by the squadron. As a result, it was reported that the morale of our troops sharply appreciated.

242. On the 15th December No. 21 (F) Squadron, R.A.A.F., left Singapore to reinforce Ipoh, but owing to bad weather five aircraft force-landed and crashed and only six aircraft got through.

243. Operations in support of the Army seriously reduced the serviceability of No. 453 (F) Squadron, and further losses were caused by the intensive bombing of Ipoh aerodrome, which now started. In consequence, on the 15th December, G.H.Q. issued an instruction that the role of the Ipoh fighter force was primarily reconnaissance for IIIrd Corps: it was not to be used against ground targets, and wastage was not to be made good at the expense of the squadrons allotted to the defence of Singapore. In practice, the squadrons in the north functioned mainly in the defence of the Ipoh area, carrying out such tactical reconnaissance as was required by IIIrd Corps. They continued in this role at Kuala Lumpur, to which enemy air attacks drove them on the 19th December.

Demolition of Aerodromes.

244. The salvage of equipment from aerodromes in north-west Malaya continued. Sungei Patani, Butterworth and Taiping were successively cleared, and all stores and personnel sent back to Kuala Lumpur by road and rail for sorting.

245. Experience was to show that the demolition of aerodrome surfaces had little more than nuisance value, and only slightly retarded the Japanese efforts to bring them into service for their own forces. Speedy repairs were possible because:—

(a) large stocks of road-metal had been accumulated on each aerodrome for repairs, and it proved too bulky for removal and denial to the enemy (para. 30);

(b) occupation by the Japanese followed demolition so quickly that the heavy rains had no time to take effect;

(c) the abundant native labour was forcibly impressed by the enemy for repair work.

Air Forces driven out of North-West Malaya.

246. As early as the 20th December Japanese bombers and fighters were using aerodromes in the north-west, particularly Sungei Patani, and the scale of attack in the Kuala Lumpur area correspondingly increased By the afternoon of 22nd December these attacks had reduced the combined strength of Nos. 21 (F) R.A.A.F. and 453 (F) Squadrons to four operationally serviceable aircraft.

247. In view of the enemy's great numerical superiority, further attempts to reinforce these squadrons only meant dissipating aircraft from their main role—the defence of Singapore. It was decided, therefore, to withdraw the force to Singapore, and this was done on 23rd December. It meant that operations in support of the Army in the north-west could be undertaken only by using Kuala Lumpur and other airfields to the south of that place as advanced landing grounds.

248. These two fighter squadrons had been forced to operate under very difficult conditions. Maintenance and servicing facilities had been necessarily primitive, whilst the warning system gave little, if any, notice of attack.

249. However, the unexpectedly high calibre of Japanese aircraft and pilots, and the superior numbers of the enemy, had proved too much for them.

250. Nevertheless, the work of these squadrons had had a good effect on the attitude of our troops to the air, although the number of enemy aircraft shot down was only small.

251. With the withdrawal of the R.A.F. from the north-west, Norgroup was disbanded, and a Liaison Officer was left at H.Q. IIIrd Corps.

Army Situation.

252. While these operations and moves of air forces had been taking place the Army had been compelled to give more ground. On 15th December the Japanese forced the 11th (Indian) Division to evacuate the Gurun position, and threatened to push through the gap between the division and Krohcol. A big withdrawal had therefore to be made out of Kedah province to the Krian river. Penang was thus left isolated and was evacuated on the night of 16th/17th December.

253. Between the 17th and 26th December our forces fought for the Taiping—Ipoh area, preparatory to taking up positions in the Kampar district, which offered the best possibilities for prolonged defence in this part of Malaya.

254. The prospects of stabilising the situation, however, were not good; and as early as 16th December the sole Command reserve, consisting of a Brigade Group, had been committed to the fighting in the north-west.

255. In the rest of Malaya were:—

(i) A Brigade Group which was in process of being withdrawn from the State of Kelantan.

(ii) A Brigade Group at Kuantan which was already threatened by Japanese infiltration down the Trengganu coast.

(iii) A Division (2 Brigades) of the Australian Imperial Forces in Johore, whose particular role was to guard against landings in the Mersing area on the east coast of Malaya.

(iv) The garrison of Singapore Fortress.

All these formations were either already committed actively or potentially. Adequate reinforcement for the main battle area therefore depended upon the safe arrival of reinforcements from outside Malaya. But before dealing with this aspect it is first necessary to dispose of some other matters.

Preparations for basing squadrons in the N.E.I.

256. The evacuation of the northern aerodromes had been foreseen, and as this would eventually result in congestion of aerodromes on Singapore Island, A.H.Q. issued orders as early as the 14th December for stocks of bombs together with refuelling and re-arming parties to be sent to aerodromes in Sumatra. Shortly afterwards, two staff officers from A.H.Q. and an officer of the A.M.W.D. were ordered to Sumatra to accelerate work in connection with:—

(a) providing facilities for the transit of reinforcing aircraft;

(b) the operation of bombers from Sumatra, including the selection of a Bomber Group H.Q.

257. For these movements it was possible to call upon an Air Transport service from Singapore-Sumatra-Java which had been instituted by the Dutch Army Air Service. The number and capacity of the transport aircraft were limited, but they enabled the movements to Sumatra to be carried out rapidly. They illustrated the value of transport aircraft. It was considered inadvisable to operate these aircraft in Northern Malaya where little fighter protection could have been provided for them.

258. A warning order was also issued on the 22nd December for moving No. 153 M.U. from Kuala Lumpur to Java. By that date the Japanese had advanced as far south as Taiping, and Kuala Lumpur was threatened. Thus it was felt that the work of the unit could be more satisfactorily carried out in Java.

Japanese Attack on Borneo.

259. It is now necessary to revert to operations off the East coast of Malaya leading up to the Japanese attack on Borneo.

On the 13th December G.H.Q. received information from a reliable source that a large convoy of well over a hundred ships was heading S.S.W. from the direction of Saigon. Its destination was not known for some days. It constituted a serious threat to Malaya, on the east coast of which existed several good landing beaches with little or no defence, where a successful landing would have seriously jeopardised our army formations still closely engaged with the enemy on the western side of the peninsula.

260. Accordingly, reconnaissance activity from Malaya was materially increased, and during the period 13th to 24th December most of the available bombers stood by to attack the enemy convoy in the event of its approach.

261. An average of 2 Catalina, 6 Hudson and 6 Glenn Martin sorties was sent out daily from Malaya to locate the expedition, whilst Dutch Glenn Martins from Sinkawang in Dutch Borneo were similarly employed. On the 14th, 6 cruisers were reported south of Saigon, and on the afternoon of the 16th a landing was reported at Miri, in British Borneo. The ships in the area were attacked by the Dutch in bad weather on the 17th, 18th and 19th. Hits were claimed on a cruiser and transports, and several near misses against transports.

262. The reconnaissance activity continued, spreading south-east to the Rhio Archipelago, and on the 23rd December an expedition heading towards Kuching was detected. Both Kuching and Sinkawang aerodromes had been attacked by Japanese aircraft on the preceding days, and the former had been " blown ". The Dutch aircraft at Sinkawang were withdrawn to Palembang in Sumatra on the 24th, though before they were transferred they were able to carry out a few attacks against the enemy convoy.

263. This same convoy was attacked on the 24th by 3 Hudsons and also by 5 Blenheim IVs of No. 34 (B) Squadron. Several near misses were claimed but no positive sinkings. A Dutch submarine claimed to have sunk 3 transports and 1 tanker in the area.

Increased Air Reconnaissance activity.

264. Seaward reconnaissance at this time absorbed almost all the G.R. and bomber aircraft in Malaya. In addition to major Japanese expeditions east of Malaya, Japanese forces were still infiltrating southwards down the East coast towards Kuantan; and on the 15th December a flight of M.V.A.F. was established at Kahang to carry out local coastal reconnaissance for the Australian forces in Johore who were responsible for guarding against landings in the Mersing-Endau area. Reconnaissance up the West coast also became an increasing commitment during the second half of December. Regular reconnaissances were instituted from 22nd December, as the Japanese were already showing signs of infiltrating in small boats by day and night down the West coast behind our Army's left flank. The discovery and attack of these infiltrations was difficult because the boats moved in waters flanked by luxuriant tropical undergrowth. By day the Japanese protected their movements with fighter patrols.

265. The possibility that the Japanese might spread across from Malaya to Sumatra had also to be faced, thus a squadron of Dutch Glenn Martins at Pakenbaroe in Sumatra were employed on reconnaissance to detect any such movement with effect from 15th December.

Minor Reorganisations.

266. Meanwhile, certain reorganisation of squadrons had taken place. One flight of Wirraways (6) was formed at Kluang on the 18th and training in dive-bombing commenced. The aircrews of No. 60 (B) Squadron were sent back to Burma by sea by B.O.A.C. to join their ground personnel at Rangoon: the squadron's aircraft were taken over by No. 62 (B) Squadron.

Order of Battle—24th December, 1941.

267. At this stage of the campaign the disposition of squadrons and their approximate strengths in serviceable aircraft were as follows:—

Bomber Squadrons:

Type	Squadron	Aircraft	Location
Blenheims	No. 34 Squadron	10	Tengah
	No. 62 Squadron	9	Tengah
Dutch Glenn Martins	Two Squadrons	15	Sembawang
Wirraways	One Flight	6	Kluang

T.B. Squadrons:

Type	Squadron	Aircraft	Location
Vildebeestes	No. 36 Squadron	16	Seletar
	No. 100 Squadron	13	Seletar
Albacores	One Flight	5	Seletar

Fighter Squadrons:

Type	Squadron	Aircraft	Location
Buffaloes	No. 21 Squadron R.A.A.F.	...	reorganising
	No. 453 Squadron	...	Sembawang
	No. 243 Squadron	15	Kallang
	No. 488 Squadron	14	Kallang
	Dutch Squadron	9	Kallang
Night Fighter (Blenheims)	No. 27 Squadron	...	reorganising Kallang

G.R. Squadrons:

Type	Squadron	Aircraft	Location
Hudsons	No. 1 Squadron R.A.A.F.	5	Sembawang
	No. 8 Squadron R.A.A.F.	8	Sembawang
	No. 205 Squadron	4	Seletar

Miscellaneous:

Type	Unit	Aircraft	Location
No. 4 A.A.C.U. Swordfish	One Flight	4	Tengah
Sharks	One Flight	4	Tengah
M.V.A.F. (Various)	Recce. Flight	—	Kahang
M.V.A.F. (Various)	Comm. Flight	—	Kallang
Dutch Squadron (Glenn Martins)	One Squadron	9	Pakanbaroe (Sumatra)

Reinforcement Situation

268. From the 8th December onwards many messages had been interchanged between the Air Ministry and the Far East on the subject of reinforcements, which, commencing with a long-range policy of supply, developed, with the steady advance of the Japanese Army, into an emergency arrangement of diverting to the Far East squadrons from other Commands which it was hoped could arrive in time. By the 25th December, the position as understood by A.H.Q. was:—

Hudson II's—6 arrived from Australia on 25/12 to reinforce Nos. 1 and 8 (GR) Squadrons, R.A.A.F.

Hudson III's—52 to be flown out from England commencing about 20/12.

Blenheim IV's—12 from Middle East—7 arrived by 25/12: remainder en route.

Hurricanes—51 in crates with 24 pilots en route by sea due on or about 8th January, 1942. These had left England as reinforcements for the Middle East but were diverted to Singapore whilst at sea.

Catalinas—4 en route with 2 spare crews.

The Plan for their disposition was:—

Hudson III's—to (a) re-equip No. 62 (B) Squadron: and
(b) reinforce Nos. 1 and 8 (GR) Squadrons R.A.A.F.

Blenheim IV's—to be absorbed into No. 34 (B) Squadron.

Hurricanes—to be used from Kallang and Johore in defence of Singapore: it was anticipated Buffalo Squadrons would be whittled away by the time these Hurricanes arrived.

Catalinas—One to remain at Ceylon, remainder to reinforce No. 205 (FB) Squadron at Seletar.

Thus some air reinforcements, urgently wanted, were now on their way despite the still critical state of the war in Europe from which they had had to be diverted to Singapore.

NARRATIVE FROM 25TH DECEMBER, 1941, TO 30TH JANUARY, 1942

Changes in Higher Command

269. Before proceeding further with the narrative, it is appropriate to mention some changes in the Higher Command in the Far East which were about to take place during the next few weeks.

On 27th December, General Sir Henry Pownall relieved Air Chief Marshal Sir Robert Brooke Popham as Commander-in-Chief, Far East. The former's instructions differed from those of the latter, as described in para. 3. General Pownall was instructed to deal with " matters of major military policy and strategy ", but that it was not the intention that he should " assume operational control ". These instructions were given before the outbreak of the Japanese war, which occurred however whilst he was en route. As their consequence, the system described in para. 3, under which G.H.Q. was responsible for the control of operations, now came to an end.

270. On 1st January, 1942, the small Fighter Control H.Q. in Singapore was expanded, albeit on a restricted scale. It became known as No. 224 (F) Group. Group Captain E. B. Rice remained in command. Circumstances, however, did not permit full administration of its units and stations being transferred to it from A.H.Q.

271. On 4th January, Air Vice Marshal P. C. Maltby arrived in Singapore as Chief-of-Staff

designate to the newly appointed C.-in-C. Far East. He remained in Singapore to assist the A.O.C., being attached to A.H.Q. on 12th January for the purpose.

To resume the narrative of events

Arrival at Singapore of Reinforcement Convoys

272. With effect from the 26th December, arrangements for the reception of reinforcement convoys at Singapore became of overriding importance, not the least factor being the urgent necessity to maintain the secrecy of their arrival. This was successfully accomplished, it is believed.

273. In view of the importance of these convoys to the defence of Malaya, G.H.Q. issued an instruction on the 27th December that " air protection for convoys bringing reinforcements will now take precedence before the other tasks ".

274. Reinforcements were, if anything, more important to the Army even than to the R.A.F. All the fighting since the beginning of the campaign had fallen on the IIIrd Corps, particularly the 11th (Indian) Division, and the troops badly needed a rest; and as the reinforcements contained a complete fresh Division (18th) as well as anti-aircraft regiments, it was vital from the Army point of view that the Air Force in Malaya should do everything in their power to ensure that the convoys got through.

275. Air protection for these convoys was provided by means of widespread reconnaissance sweeps into the S. China Sea, close anti-submarine patrols from the Banka Straits onwards and fighter escort for the final approach to Singapore. An extremely vulnerable part of the route was that which lay through the Banka Straits off E. Sumatra. For the protection of the convoys in this area, the Dutch Fighter Squadron based at Kallang was moved to Palembang on the 29th December, and again on the 9th January. Apart from the fighters, operations for shepherding these convoys, for periods of three days for each convoy, employed at least 2 Catalinas, 6 Hudsons and 4 Glenn Martins daily. In addition, during these 3-day periods, all other available aircraft in the Command were kept at short notice in case the convoys were attacked by enemy naval or air forces. In this situation the absence of effective Naval strength in Malayan waters was aggravated by the insufficiency of air forces to reinforce the Navy, and at the same time to meet the needs of the battle on the land. In these circumstances there was no alternative but to withdraw appreciable numbers of our aircraft, and to make them stand by for the protection of convoys when they might otherwise have been participating in the battle on land.

276. The task was successfully accomplished. The first convoy arrived in Singapore on 3rd January and a second on 13th January. The latter included the first brigade of the 18th Division to arrive. It also contained 51 crated Hurricanes accompanied by more than 20 Hurricane pilots.

It is difficult here adequately to convey the sense of tension which prevailed as these convoys approached Singapore, and the sense of exultation at their safe arrival. The feeling spread that at least the Japanese were going to be held on the ground if not driven back, whilst many confidently expected that the Hurricanes would sweep the Japanese from the sky.

Withdrawal of the Army to Johore

277. But by the time that the first reinforcements arrived the position of the Army had seriously worsened. On the West coast a withdrawal from the strong Kampar position had been forced upon IIIrd Corps by an out-flanking landing at Telok Anson on the West coast.

278. The forcing of a line on the Slim river and further landings in the Kuala Selanger region led to the evacuation of Kuala Lumpur and Port Swettenham on the 10th January; and by the middle of January the bulk of our forces were back to the northern frontier of Johore, little more than 100 miles from Singapore.

279. On the East coast, the Brigade that had originally held the Kota Bahru area had fallen back, without serious losses, to Central Malaya. The Brigade Group defending Kuantan, which had been attacked from the north on 30th December, had also to be withdrawn to prevent its communications being cut as the result of the West Coast withdrawal.

280. Thereafter, the Japanese on the East coast began to move steadily down towards Mersing. There had been no attacks in this area up to the middle of January, but a major Japanese landing was expected daily.

281. Thus the progress of the Japanese Army was quicker than had been anticipated, chiefly as the result of its possession of an armoured component, its superiority in jungle warfare, its superiority in the air, and its ability to pass parties in boats down the West coast round the left flank of our Army. Infiltrating Japanese frequently got behind our forward troops and formed road blocks on their lines of communication which proved difficult, and sometimes impossible, to clear. Our own demolitions were swiftly repaired or circumvented by the enemy; and in general the speed and aggression of his follow-up came as a surprise.

Co-operation with the Army on the West coast

282. The heavy commitments of the air forces for reconnaissance, convoy protection and the air defence of Singapore, reduced the number of aircraft available for the direct support of the Army during this period. But, within the limitations thus imposed, air action was carried out on both West and East coasts, increasing in quantity as the battle area came within range of aircraft based on aerodromes in Singapore.

283. In response to requests from H.Q.M.C. and IIIrd Corps, action was taken against Japanese landing parties on the West coast. Daily offensive reconnaissances were carried out by 4 to 6 Glenn Martins or Blenheims, unescorted at first, but later, after 4 aircraft had been shot down in one day, with fighter protection. Five Shark aircraft were moved up to Batu Pahat on 2nd January: they also took part in this type of operation.

284. Barges off Port Swettenham were attacked by Blenheims on the 2nd, 3rd and 4th January: several near misses were observed but no definite sinkings.

285. As Japanese activity against the West coast increased, so, from 15th January, air attacks were made on an increased scale:—

15th Jan.—by 6 Hudsons, 6 Glenn Martins and 3 Blenheims escorted by 12 Buffaloes attacked barges in the Linggi River: two barges were sunk and three damaged by the Hudsons.

16th Jan.—15 Buffaloes attacked transport and movements on the road Tampin/Gemas whilst 9 Blenheims and 6 Glenn Martins followed by 4 Buffaloes attacked barges in the Muar River where further landings were taking place.

17th Jan.—9 Vildebeestes escorted by 6 Buffaloes continued attacks on barges in the Muar River, whilst fighter cover was provided for a move by road of the A.I.F. in the area.

18th Jan.—Attacks on barges in the Muar River and on troop concentrations in the Gemas area continued—a total force of 6 Blenheims, 5 Hudsons and 14 Buffaloes being employed.

286. In addition, tactical reconnaissance by one or two sections of Buffaloes was carried out for IIIrd Corps, chiefly in the Seremban-Tampin-Gemas area. Special bombing attacks were carried out by Blenheims on 10th January to destroy trains full of Army stores, which, owing to the congestion and dislocation of the railway system, had been stranded at Malacca. The attacks were at least partly successful, as were others made on 12th January against some oil tanks which had been left intact at Port Swettenham.

287. Part of our offensive effort continued to be made against Japanese-held aerodromes in order to meet the wishes of G.O.C. Malaya for reducing enemy air action against our forward troops, which had been carried out concurrently with attacks against our aerodromes both in Malaya and on Singapore Island and against our road and rail communications behind the battle front.

288. Daily flights over Northern Malaya by our P.R. Buffaloes revealed that aerodromes "blown" in the withdrawal were quickly repaired and occupied. Gong Kedah was occupied by the enemy on the 31st December, Ipoh on the 4th January and Kuantan on the 9th January.

289. Consequently our aircraft made attacks on aerodromes in Northern Malaya at frequent intervals during the latter part of December and the first half of January. They entailed long flights by night, often in the face of violent tropical thunderstorms. Altogether, between 20th December and 15th January, some eighty sorties were carried out against this type of target. Sungei Patani was attacked six times, Gong Kedah twice, Ipoh and Alor Star once. Good results were achieved by Blenheims of No. 34 (B) Squadron at Sungei Patani on 27th/28th December: photographic reconnaissance on the following day confirming that at least 7 fighters had been destroyed and 5 fighters and 3 bombers damaged.

290. Good results were also obtained at Gong Kedah on 1st/2nd January by Catalinas. These aircraft had by this time largely been withdrawn from reconnaissance work, which was instead carried out by Hudsons, owing to the vulnerability of the Catalina to fighter attack. The range and bomb load of the Catalinas proved very useful for night bombing operations. Twice in January they attacked the main enemy base at Singora, a target which by this time was beyond the range of any other aircraft in the Command.

291. In addition, two attempts were made to carry out strong fighter attacks against Kuantan aerodrome; but tropical thunderstorms on each occasion forced our fighters to return.

292. That these operations inflicted losses upon the enemy is certain. It is equally certain that he had more than sufficient reserves to replace his losses without delay.

Air Activity off the East coast.

293. Off the east coast there was considerable reconnaissance and activity. On 27th December, photographic reconnaissance confirmed the arrival of 34 ships at Singora, which were proved subsequently to have brought a reinforcing Division. Further reports of enemy shipping necessitated sweeps by Hudsons to the Natunas on the 3rd and 4th January.

294. Daily East coast reconnaissances to the north from Endau beyond Trengannu occupied at least 6 Glenn Martins or Hudsons, whilst the M.V.A.F. continued close reconnaissance for the A.I.F. in the Endau-Mersing area.

295. On the 8th January, 9 Glenn Martins and 4 Hudsons bombed and scored direct hits on a ship anchored in the South China Sea, believed to be used by the Japanese as a navigational aid for their aircraft. On 9th January, 9 Glenn Martins bombed with success ships unloading at Kuantan.

296. Meanwhile, Kuantan had been occupied by the Japanese on the 9th January. Infiltration down the coast towards Endau and Mersing immediately commenced. By the 13th January A.H.Q. became convinced of the possibility of a landing in this vital area, and a general direction was therefore issued to all squadrons governing their action in such a contingency. A daily reconnaissance by 6 Hudsons was instituted to detect the approach of any convoy from Indo-China; reconnaissance northwards up the east coast, although restricted, was still maintained.

Capture of Borneo.

297. Borneo had been lost by this time. Kuching had been captured on 26th December, and its garrison of one Indian Battalion forced to retreat. It was located by our reconnaissance as it made its way to Sinkawang, where supplies were dropped for it by three aircraft on 31st December. Apart from a further reconnaissance on 9th January to ascertain the state of Kuching aerodrome, no further air action in the Borneo area was possible.

Japanese air operations against Singapore.

298. During the first half of January the Japanese extended their air attacks to Singapore Island, directing them mainly against its aerodromes, with the evident intention of neutralising our squadrons. Tengah, on which the Blenheim force was based, received particular attention. Night raids were a constant occurrence, but these were mainly of a nuisance value and little damage was done by them. No. 27 (NF) Squadron, which had been reorganised at Kallang, and which now had 5

Blenheim I's serviceable, was used in an endeavour to intercept these attacks, but without success owing to the poor performance of their aircraft.

299. Day raids by the enemy took place with increasing intensity, at first by bombers alone, and later by bombers escorted by fighters. On the 1st January the first serious attack against Tengah took place, as a result of which native labour disappeared. This was to happen at all aerodromes as they became attacked, necessitating the replacement of domestic personnel by Europeans and making it increasingly difficult to repair damage to aerodrome surfaces. At all Stations on the Island dispersed accommodation was provided for personnel normally quartered at them, mobile kitchens were improvised, and, in the case of Seletar, married families were moved to alternative quarters.

300. Tengah was attacked again on the 6th January, 9th January, 12th January, 13th January and 14th January. On the 15th, the naval base was attacked, and on the 16th, aerodromes and the docks. The 17th was a particularly bad day. Attacks on aerodromes were carried out by escorted bombers, and, under their cover, low flying fighters slipped in and attacked Sembawang and Seletar. At Seletar, 2 Catalinas at their moorings were burned out and another 2 damaged. Six Blenheims at Tengah were damaged to a varying degree, whilst at Sembawang 3 Buffaloes on the ground were destroyed and 4 damaged. Attacks were carried out by some 80 bombers, of which 2 were brought down and another 4 damaged. The attack was repeated on the 18th against the naval base and the docks, and again 2 were brought down and possibly 6 damaged for the loss of 8 Buffaloes.

301. The absence of a first-class fighter aircraft prior to the second half of January was a handicap. An attempt was made to improve the performance of the Buffalo by reducing its petrol load and replacing the unsatisfactory .5 guns, which were heavy and possessed faulty interrupter gear, by .303 machine guns, but it remained inferior to the Navy O particularly in " dog-fighting ".

302. Moreover, owing to the short warning of enemy raids, our fighters were frequently still climbing to meet the enemy when they were themselves attacked. A warning of at least thirty minutes was required to enable the Buffalo to reach 24,000 feet, which was the height at which the enemy formations often flew. But the successive evacuation of Observer Corps Posts on the mainland as the Japanese advanced, and the inadequate radar cover available, meant that the period of warning was almost always insufficient.

303. The Dutch Fighter Squadron in Singapore was transferred in the middle of January to Palembang (para. 357), leaving only 2 squadrons of Buffaloes—Nos. 243(F) and 488(F)—for the defence of Singapore, because Nos. 21(F) R.A.A.F. and 453(F) Squadrons based at Sembawang were used primarily for Army co-operation and for escorting bombers operating by day on the West coast. Apart from other handicaps, therefore, defending fighters were outnumbered in the air by the Japanese fighters in varying degrees between 6-1 and 15-1.

304. The A.A. defences of the Island were of limited effect in countering air attacks. Bofors guns gave protection against all but a few surprise low level attacks. But the great majority of the enemy's bombing was carried out from altitudes of over 20,000 feet, where they were well above the effective range of the 3-in. guns which formed one-third of the heavy A.A. defences. At such heights only the 3.7-in. guns, of which there were only 40 for the defence of the many targets on the Island, could reach them.

Further changes in the Higher Command.

305. At the beginning of January it had been decided by the Allied authorities to unify the command of all their forces in the South West Pacific under a Supreme Allied Commander. General Sir Archibald Wavell was appointed to this post. He arrived in Singapore on 7th January and commenced to form his staff, absorbing into it the Commander-in-Chief, Far East, and his staff. On 11th January he moved to the site selected for his Supreme Allied Headquarters, South West Pacific Command, namely to Bandoeng in Java. There on 15th January he assumed command of operations throughout the S.W. Pacific, and G.H.Q. as such ceased to exist. The code name for General Wavell's H.Q. was Abdacom.

306. It is unnecessary for the purpose of this report to describe the organisation of Abdacom. Suffice it to say that it included a department, the code name of which was Abdair, whose head functioned in the dual capacity of Chief-of-the-Air-Staff at General Wavell's H.Q., and of Commander of all the Allied air forces in the S.W. Pacific. This appointment was temporarily filled by Major General Brereton, U.S. Army Air Corps, pending the arrival of Air Chief Marshal Sir Richard Peirse, R.A.F., who was appointed to it and who took up the duty during the last days of January.

307. To facilitate control of air operations within the S.W. Pacific Command, the area was divided by Abdair into six Groups, of which only two need be mentioned in this Narrative:—

(i) *Westgroup*—consisting of R.A.F. Far East Command, including Units in Malaya and those in process of being transferred to the Netherlands East Indies.

(ii) *Recgroup*—consisting of all seaward reconnaissance units in S.W. Pacific Command, British, Dutch and American. Its Headquarters was in Java.

Directive to Air Forces in Malaya.

308. On the 18th January Abdacom stressed the importance of Singora as a target and issued a general directive to govern the operations of the Air Forces in Malaya. This directive stated that " protection of convoys at present takes precedence over action against other Japanese forces. If, however, new expeditions are located threatening the east coast of Malaya or endeavouring to pass south of Singapore, all available air effort should be directed to destroying such targets ". The directive also stressed the importance of slowing up the Japanese advance on land by attacking Singora, intervening in the land battle, and of reducing the scale of Japanese air attack.

Relative Strength of Air Forces in Malaya.

309. To carry out efficiently all these tasks was beyond the strength of the Air Forces available. On the afternoon of 18th January, the serviceability state of the Air Forces in Malaya showed 74 bomber and G.R. aircraft and 28 fighters, all based on Singapore with the exception of a small detachment at Kahang. Moreover, many of these aircraft were obsolete or obsolescent. Against these it was estimated that the Japanese were maintaining in Malaya at this time a force of 150 fighters and 250 bombers. Concentration was therefore made, in general, on one task at a time in the order of priority indicated in the directive, but influenced by the situation.

Arrival of Further Convoys and of Air Reinforcements.

310. Special attention, as the directive instructed, continued to be paid to the provision of protection for reinforcing convoys arriving at Singapore. Further convoys came in on 22nd, 24th and 28th January, bringing the remainder of the 18th Division, except for a few units, a Brigade Group from India, two to three thousand troops from Australia, and more anti-aircraft units.

311. Five Hudson sorties were made daily over wide areas around the convoys to detect the approach of Japanese naval forces. One Catalina was maintained on anti-submarine patrol, and during the final approach to Singapore a fighter escort of six aircraft was maintained. All other aircraft were kept at short call as the convoys approached, in case the enemy should attack them.

312. Three reinforcing Catalinas arrived on 7th January and were allotted to No. 205 (FB) Squadron.

313. During the third week in January, the 51 Hurricanes which had arrived on the 13th January (para. 276), were being assembled preparatory to joining Buffaloes in the defence of the Island. Spares were ample but tool kits were scarce.

314. On their arrival they were immediately unloaded, and the majority dispersed to previously selected concealed positions, where they were erected and wheeled to nearby airfields for test; the remainder proceeded direct to No. 151 M.U. for erection at other dispersed points. The speed with which these aircraft were erected was a very remarkable achievement (see Postscript).

315. Twenty-four pilots from Nos. 17, 135 and 136 (F) Squadrons had arrived with them: some had had experience in the Battle of Britain. When A.H.Q. first heard of their diversion to the Far East, it had been planned to give aircrews a spell before employing them in operations. This spell was obviously desirable, not only because of the length of their sea voyage, but also because of the need for acclimatising pilots to local conditions. However, events had moved too fast and the stake was too high for delay to be acceptable. The Hurricanes had to be used immediately they had been erected and tested. They were in action as a squadron by the 20th January, exactly a week after they had been landed in crates.

316. The aircraft were accompanied by some ground personnel of No. 232 (F) Squadron, deficiencies being made good by personnel from the transit camp. They were based at Seletar and Kallang, and the whole operated as No. 232 (F) Squadron.

317. Sixteen Hudson III's arrived in Singapore from the United Kingdom, the first of them during the third week of January. They were allotted to 62 (B) and No. 8 (GR) R.A.A.F. Squadrons. They came at somewhat scattered intervals, and as long as the air route to the Far East remained open, i.e., until mid-February. The balance of the 52 which had been expected were unable to get through before the enemy cut the air route from India.

318. Two reinforcing bomber squadrons, Nos. 84 (B) and 211 (B) Squadrons, began to arrive on 23rd January from the Middle East. They were diverted to Sumatra, for reasons which will be related in due course. They, too, arrived at scattered intervals and were far from complete when the enemy cut the air route. Their ground crews and equipment were to follow by sea (para. 417).

A.H.Q. was notified that a further 48 Hurricanes, over and above those mentioned in para. 313, would be flown into Singapore from H.M.S. Indomitable about the end of January, and that 39 more in crates were en route by sea.

Further withdrawal of the Army—to Singapore Island.

319. Despite the arrival of reinforcements the position on land continued to develop adversely during the second half of January.

320. On the west coast, the Japanese took full advantage of their command of the sea to land behind the Army positions. Between the 16th and 18th January there was a succession of landings on the Johore coast between Muar and Batu Pahat, which, combined with heavy frontal attacks, forced our troops to withdraw to the line Batu Pahat—Mersing.

321. On the East coast, the long expected landing in the Mersing—Endau area took place at Endau on 26th January. The lateral communications available in north Johore permitted a junction between the Japanese forces in the east and west of the peninsula, while a Japanese advance from the Endau area threatened the communications of the main British forces in the west.

322. Our losses in the west coast battle and the new threat from the East dictated a general withdrawal of our forces to Singapore Island itself, a decision which was taken on the 27th January. The withdrawal was achieved in good order. Nevertheless it had been hoped that the arrival of reinforcements would permit the holding of a bridgehead in Johore, but this now proved to be impossible.

Air Action against the Japanese Advance: West Coast.

323. The Japanese exploitation of their superiority at sea led, on the west coast as well as the east, to a number of air reconnaissances and sweeps being undertaken over the left flank of the Army. Attacks against Japanese-held aerodromes in Central Malaya were also carried out.

324. On the 19th January the situation at Muar was reported to be serious. Twelve Buffaloes carried out an offensive sweep of the area, using surplus ammunition on barges during their return. The latter were also attacked twice during the day by 3 Hudsons escorted by Buffaloes. That night, 19th/20th January, 9 Vildebeestes bombed the aerodrome at Kuala Lumpur, where some twenty fighters had been observed by Buffaloes of No. 488(F) Squadron.

325. On the 20th January two Blenheims made an offensive reconnaissance against shipping off the coast. Later, 6 Buffaloes carried out an offensive sweep of the Muar—Gemas area where the Army reported heavy dive bombing against troops of IIIrd Corps. They met a formation of 6 Army 97's, destroyed one and forced the others to jettison their loads. That evening, at last light, 7 Blenheims bombed and machine-gunned Kuala Lumpur with great success, claiming the destruction of over 20 fighters. 6 Hudsons attacked Kuantan at the same time. These attacks were followed up that night by 24 Vildebeestes, 12 bombing each aerodrome.

326. From the 21st to 24th January, many requests for support of the Army in the Muar area were received, but these were days during which the protection of convoys took precedence, and little was available with which to meet them. On the 21st January, 6 Buffaloes carried out sweeps in the morning and afternoon in the Parit Salong—Batu Pahat area; 2 Albacores and 2 Buffaloes attacked small boats near Batu Pahat; and 2 Albacores dropped supplies successfully for troops who had been cut off, and thus assisted them to extricate themselves.

327. On 22nd January the Japanese were infiltrating from Muar to Batu Pahat. This road was attacked by 2 Albacores, 1 Shark and 6 Buffaloes. More supplies were dropped by Albacores of No. 36 Squadron to troops cut off in the Parit Salong area. That night, 22nd/23rd January, 21 Vildebeestes again bombed Kuala Lumpur.

328. On the 23rd January, 5 Buffaloes patrolled over the withdrawal of troops from the Yong Peng area (N.NE. of Batu Pahat) and engaged 12 Navy 'O' fighters which were harassing them. All available Sharks, Albacores and Wirraways attacked enemy troops on the road leading south from Muar. That night, 23rd/24th, 12 Vildebeestes bombed Kuantan aerodrome.

329. On the 24th January, 6 Vildebeestes attacked troops on the bridge at Labis on the Segamat—Singapore road, whilst 3 others bombed oil tanks left standing at Muar.

330. On the 25th January, 12 Buffaloes carried out sweeps, morning and evening, in the Kluang—Gemas—Batu Pahat area, whilst that night 24 Vildebeestes and 3 Albacores carried out 2 sorties each to cover the sea evacuation of a battalion which had been cut off in the Batu Pahat area. During that day 5 U.S.A. Fortresses from Java bombed Sungei Patani under Abdair direction. At night, 3 Hudsons attacked Kuala Lumpur.

331. By the evening of the 25th January, the airfields at Kahang, Kluang and Batu Pahat became untenable and were demolished, as were also the strips which had been prepared in S. Johore. Their loss was a severe blow, as it had been hoped they would be available for the reinforcing Hurricanes; they had been specially prepared and equipped for that purpose. Seletar, which had now to be used instead, was not so well equipped with dispersal points.

Air Action against the Landing at Endau.

332. To turn to the East coast. On the 26th January, at 0930 hours, Hudson reconnaissance sighted 2 cruisers, 11 destroyers and two 10,000 ton vessels accompanied by barges, 10 miles off the coast approaching Endau. (para 321). They were being protected by Japanese fighters based on Kuantan.

333. The forces available for opposing them were:—

    9 Hudsons of Nos. 1 and 8 (GR) Squadrons, R.A.A.F.
    21 Vildebeestes, 3 Albacores of Nos. 36 and 100 (TB) Squadrons.

334. The attack was organised in two waves. The first wave comprised 9 Hudsons and 12 Vildebeestes and was escorted by 15 Buffaloes and 8 Hurricanes; the second, 3 Albacores and 9 Vildebeestes, escorted by 4 Buffaloes and 8 Hurricanes.

335. Unfortunately, as the Vildebeestes and Albacores of Nos. 36 and 100 (TB) Squadrons had been operating throughout the whole of the previous night (para. 330), the first wave of attack could not be launched until the early afternoon. By this time most of the Japanese troops were probably clear of their transports.

336. However, the first wave, consisting of 9 Hudsons and the Vildebeestes of No. 100 (TB) Squadron, was able to press its attack home, being helped by rather cloudy conditions. 5 Vildebeestes were lost. It was claimed that one cruiser and two destroyers were sunk, both transports were hit (one set on fire), and casualties were caused to troops in barges and on the beaches.

337. With the arrival of the second wave, the Vildebeestes of No. 36 (TB) Squadron, the weather in the area suddenly cleared and enemy fighters intercepted the squadron before it could attack. 6 Vildebeestes and 2 Albacores were shot down and other aircraft damaged and aircrews wounded. Later, 5 Hudsons of No. 62 (B) Squadron from Sumatra arrived in the area and attacked barges.

338. The fighter escort problem had not been easy owing to the slow speed of the T.B. aircraft and the distance of the target from their aerodrome. During these two attacks, 12 Japanese Navy "O" fighters were shot down and 4 damaged for the loss of 2 Hurricanes and 1 Buffalo, one Hurricane pilot personally accounting for 4 Japanese fighters.

339. No. 36 & 100 (TB) Squadrons suffered very heavily. More than half their aircraft were shot down, including those of both Commanding Officers. The remainder were badly shot about, and a number of aircrews in them were wounded. Both were withdrawn to Java on 29th/30th January for reorganisation after their very gallant effort.

Sustained Japanese Air Attacks on Singapore

340. During the second half of January the Japanese carried out air attacks on targets on Singapore Island with increasing intensity.

Two, and sometimes three, attacks were delivered by formations of 27 to 54 enemy bombers escorted by fighters. The main targets were our aerodromes, but a number of attacks were delivered against Singapore harbour, the naval base and other military objectives. Raids were made in perfect formation despite A.A. fire, and the accuracy of bombing from heights over 20,000 feet was marked.

341. This continual pounding made it difficult to keep aerodrome surfaces serviceable. Kallang was built on reclaimed salt marsh, which oozed up through the bomb craters. The drainage at Tengah had never been satisfactory. Effective repairs were thus difficult. Rainfall at the time was exceptionally heavy, which in itself was a further handicap to repair work.

342. To complicate matters further, practically all native labour, which had many disabilities to face under air bombardment, disappeared. On the 7th January the Director General of Civil Defence had appointed a Director of Labour who was to organise and control all labour, allotting it to the services in accordance with an arranged priority programme.

There was also an acute shortage of M.T., without which labour, and the material for labour to use, could not be transported to the places where it was needed. The collection and allocation of M.T. was also placed under the Director General of Civil Defence.

Both these measures had become acutely necessary—to provide and organise labour in the face of repeated air raids, and in order to make the best use of limited supplies of motor transport.

343. First priority for what labour there was, was given to the repair of aerodromes. The G.O.C. Malaya diverted some of his reserves, at the expense of the construction of defence work, to reinforce R.A.F. labour parties. Later, parties of 100 sailors, survivors from H.M.S. " Prince of Wales " and " Repulse ", were stationed at each of the 4 airfields in the Island.

344. Heavy attacks on our aerodromes on the Island had been anticipated some weeks beforehand by A.H.Q. In order to augment the number of airfields on the Island, six sites for landing strips had been selected, and work on them was put in hand on various dates during the latter half of December. Labour difficulties slowed up their construction, and, as will be narrated later, they had all to be demolished before they could be brought into use.

345. A considerable number of aircraft was destroyed, or rendered unserviceable on the ground largely because dispersal points had not been widely enough scattered in the first instance, whereas, time and labour had not been sufficient afterwards to rectify this shortcoming.

Operations by Fighters in the defence of Singapore

346. During the second half of January our depleted fighter squadrons did their utmost to ward off the enemy's attacks. No. 21 (F) Squadron R.A.A.F. and 453 (F) Squadron were mainly employed in operations in support of the army (paras. 323-330), leaving Nos. 243 and 488 (F) Squadron in a defensive role. To their assistance now came the newly arrived squadron of Hurricanes (paras. 314-316).

347. The Hurricanes' first day, 20th January, was most successful. Twenty-seven bombers came over unescorted and 8 were shot down without loss. It appeared as if confidence in their decisive influence was to be justified. This was the last occasion, however, on which Japanese bombers came over unescorted. The following day 5 Hurricanes were shot down, including the C.O., S. L. Landells and a Flight Commander, against no loss to the Japanese.

348. From then on the Hurricanes were constantly airborne, carrying out 3 to 5 " scrambles " daily. Owing to their being constantly outnumbered by the escorting fighters, which were well handled, bombers could seldom be attacked. But with the realisation that " dog-fighting " did not pay, the revised " in and out " tactics adopted gradually gave increasing success.

349. The Hurricane pilots had been informed of the characteristics of the Navy " Os " and particularly warned of the inadvisability of getting involved in " dog-fighting " owing to the Navy " O's " small turning circle. Despite this, some of them had become involved in " dog-fights ", which led to casualties.

350. The limitations of the warning system for Singapore have already been described (para. 302). Some help was obtained at this stage from Army G.L. sets; but the short time of warning, 10-15 minutes, remained a great handicap to efficient fighter defence. Operational control remained restricted owing to the lack of V.H.F. and to the unreliability of R/T.

351. These new aircraft were Hurricane IIs. They were fitted with desert oil filters because their original destination had been the Middle East. These deprived them of some 30 m.p.h. They were not quite so fast as the Navy " O " near the ground, but as height increased the Hurricane gradually overhauled the Navy " O " until at 20,000 feet it had an appreciable advantage in speed and climb. The Hurricane could always dive at higher speeds, but at all heights the Navy " O " was the more manoeuvrable.

352. It must be admitted here that too much had been expected of this handful of Hurricanes. Civilians and the armed forces alike had anticipated that these modern aircraft would carry all before them. That this was not achieved was no fault of the pilots, who under S/L. R. E. P. Brooker, D.F.C., achieved, in the face of overwhelming numbers, results which stand greatly to their credit. Nevertheless the false hopes which had been placed in them reacted keenly when they were not realised.

353. The average daily serviceability of Hurricanes from the 21st January to 28th January was 16, and by the latter date the position as regards the 51 crated aircraft was:—

17 destroyed (some of them at their bases).
2 repairable at Unit.
7 repairable at Depot.
21 available + 4 more in 24 hours.

On the 29th and 30th January, 20 were available.

354. During this period the Buffaloes of Nos. 21 R.A.A.F. and 453 (F) Squadrons were employed mainly on operations in support of the Army. Nos. 243 and 488 (F) Squadrons had continued in their role, in co-operation

with the Hurricanes, in the defence of Singapore. By the 30th January, the number of Buffaloes had so dwindled that all (6) were concentrated in No. 453 (F) Squadron. Nos. 21 R.A.A.F. and 243 (F) Squadron personnel were evacuated, whilst No. 488 (F) Squadron was retained to service the Hurricanes, together with a few of the pilots of all these squadrons to replace casualties.

Effect of Japanese Advance on R.A.F. dispositions.

Decision to Transfer Units to N.E.I.

355. The advance of the Japanese into Johore meant that our aircraft had to operate from the four aerodromes on Singapore Island. Thus a dangerous congestion of aircraft on the ground had come about. The dangers of congestion increased as enemy air attacks steadily grew in violence during January. When expected aircraft reinforcements should begin to arrive from the United Kingdom and the Middle East during January there were prospects of still greater congestion. Dispersal beyond the confines of Singapore Island would then become imperative.

356. During December, the first preparations had been made for operating R.A.F. Units in the N.E.I. (paras. 256-258). On 4th January No. 153 M.U. was moved to Java, and on 16th January No. 225 (B) Group Headquarters was formed in Singapore and moved to Sumatra two days later in order to make preliminary arrangements for operating bombers from aerodromes in that island.

357. By mid-January it was clear to A.H.Q. that the transfer of Units must be accelerated even though facilities for their operation and maintenance in Sumatra were not yet ready. In accordance with a prior agreement made with the Dutch Army Air Force, that Dutch Units should be moved first, a progressive withdrawal now took place from Singapore:—

19th January—Dutch Buffalo Squadron at Kallang was withdrawn. On arrival in the N.E.I. it reverted to Dutch control. Its main function was to maintain, as requisite, fighter cover required for future convoys through Banka Straits.

22nd January—2 Dutch Glenn Martin Squadrons withdrew to Java and reverted to Dutch control.

23rd-27th January—Nos. 27 (NF), 34 (B) and 62 (B) Squadrons, except for small aircraft handling parties, were transferred to Sumatra, as were also the main parties of Nos. 1 and 8 (GR) Squadrons, R.A.A.F.

358. Concurrently with the above moves:—

(a) No. 151 M.U. was ordered to prepare to move to Java, less a party approximately 100 strong who were to remain and salvage and pack equipment.

(b) Base Accounts and Record Offices were ordered to Java.

(c) Station H.Q. Sembawang was ordered to Sumatra.

359. Each Unit was instructed to proceed with 30 days' rations, certain barrack stores and 28 days' pack-up of aircraft equipment. All ground personnel proceeded by sea. It will be seen later that, owing to confusion at the Singapore docks caused primarily by bombing, and owing to enemy attacks on shipping en route, the arrangements made for the transfer of our units to the N.E.I. were badly disorganised. Dutch Lodestars helped in these moves. Their assistance was invaluable.

360. When the decision was taken on 27th January that it would be necessary for the army to withdraw to Singapore Island, it became evident at once that one aerodrome only, Kallang, would shortly be available for use. The other three on the Island, Tengah, Sembawang and Seletar, were sited on its northern coastline and would soon be exposed to observed artillery fire from Johore at ranges as close as 1,500-2,000 yards: it would not be practicable to operate aircraft from them for long. Unfortunately Kallang itself was rapidly becoming of limited use. Its surface, a crust of marl laid on a salt marsh, was pock-marked with bomb craters which were most difficult to fill. Extension was impracticable, huddled as it was between the sea and the built-up area of Singapore Town. Consequently, further transfer of squadrons to the N.E.I. now became inevitable.

361. On the 27th January No. 8 (GR) Squadron, R.A.A.F., was sent to Sumatra, and No. 205 (FB) Squadron on the 28th to Java. The latter on arrival in Java, was placed by Abdair under Dutch control as part of Recgroup. No. 205 Squadron left 1 Catalina at Seletar until the 30th January in connection with the arrival of a further convoy. On the 29th and 30th January the remaining G.R. Squadron (No. 1, R.A.A.F.) was transferred also to Sumatra.

362. Thus by the end of the month the whole of the bomber force had been compelled to withdraw to air bases in Southern Sumatra, where they were now organising with the intention of providing air support from that quarter to the army invested in Singapore.

363. On the 31st January, apart from fighters, there were left in Singapore only 3 Swordfish. They were still under Army control for coast defence spotting purposes, as H.Q.M.C. at this stage still did not rule out the possibility of a landing from the sea on Singapore Island itself.

Changes in appointments in the Command.

To digress for a moment from the narrative:—

364. With the arrival of reinforcements a reorganisation of senior appointments became practicable in the second half of January.

365. About 17th January Group Captain G. E. Nicholetts replaced Group Captain A. G. Bishop as Group Captain, Operations, at A.H.Q., the latter having been appointed to command the Bomber Group (No. 225) in Sumatra.

366. About 19th January Air Commodore W.E. Staton arrived and began taking the duties of S.A.S.O. from Air Commodore B. J. Silly. His recent and personal experience of air operations over Europe was to prove of great value to the Command

367. On the 29th January Air Commodores S. F. Vincent and H. J. F. Hunter arrived from the U.K. They had been sent by the Air Ministry as Commanders designate of Fighter and Bomber Groups respectively. Air Commodore Hunter was sent to Sumatra on 1st February, to command No. 225 Group which had already formed at Palembang.

368. By the 30th January, owing to the transfer of units to the N.E.I., the A.O.C. decided to make preparations for establishing of a rear A.H.Q., in the N.E.I. Air Commodore Silly was sent to Sumatra as Deputy A.O.C. in order to select its site and begin its organisation

NARRATIVE—30TH JANUARY UNTIL THE FALL OF SINGAPORE.

Situation of the Army.

369. It will be remembered that the Army withdrew into Singapore Island on a programme to be completed on 31st January. This was successfully carried out.

Early in February a reinforcing convoy arrived in Singapore. It brought the few remaining units of the 18th Division.

370. But the position of the Army, now invested on the Island, was jeopardised by the presence of four aircraft landing strips which were being constructed to augment the airfields of the Island (para. 344). There was real danger that the Japanese might use them for establishing airborne troops behind the frontal defences of the Island in order to accelerate the reduction of the garrison, a danger which could only be averted so long as they remained serviceable, by means of large detachments of troops who could not be spared for the purpose. On 30th January it was therefore decided to blow them, and also to accelerate the obstruction of other open spaces.

Reduction of the Fighter Force in Singapore.

371. This action restricted our fighters to the four main aerodromes of the Island, and negatived any possibility of their further dispersal. These aerodromes were under constant bombing, and considerable difficulty was being experienced in maintaining serviceable strips upon them. Further, three of them—Tengah, Sembawang and Seletar—were sited on the northern side of the Island and were therefore likely to be usable for a short time only (para. 360).

372. On the 30th January, therefore, Sir Archibald Wavell approved A.H.Q. plans to maintain in Singapore only a fighter strength of 8 Hurricanes reinforced by the remaining Buffaloes. It was agreed that the further reinforcing Hurricanes now arriving in H.M.S. " Indomitable " should be based on Sumatra, and from there not only maintain the strength at Singapore but also reinforce it as opportunity permitted.

373. To implement this policy A.H.Q.:—

(*a*) decided to retain in Singapore for the maintenance of the Fighter Force—an Air Stores Park, a Repair and Salvage Unit and an Ammunition Park.

(*b*) formed No. 226 (F) Group with H.Q. in Palembang and appointed Air Commodore Vincent the Group Commander. The staff for this Group H.Q. was to be provided partly from the reductions now possible in the Staff of the existing Fighter Group in Singapore and the remainder from H.Q. No. 266 (F) Wing, known to be arriving by sea in the N.E.I.

(*c*) issued orders for the move to Java of No. 151 M.U. less the repair and salvage party referred to in para. 358(*a*).

374. Concurrently with this reduction in strength, General Wavell approved the A.O.C.'s proposal that, consequent on the transfer of the bulk of the strength of the Command to the N.E.I., he should proceed himself with the main body of A.H.Q. to the N.E.I, whence it would be possible to control more effectively the conduct of further air operations. It was intended to leave in Singapore a small advanced A.H.Q. to maintain liaison with H.Q.M.C. H.Q. No. 224 (F) Group was also to remain to control fighter operations.

375. A.H.Q. was reduced in accordance with this plan, personnel being despatched to Palembang in Sumatra for attachment to H.Q. No. 225 (B) Group pending the decision about the site for the rear A.H.Q. which Air Commodore Silly had been instructed to find.

376. On 5th February Abdair expressed disapproval of the transfer of A.H.Q. to the N.E.I., being of opinion that A.H.Q. should remain in close contact with the G.O.C. Malaya, to ensure that future air operations were planned in relation to the best means for the defence of Singapore. The A.O.C., after an exchange of signals with Abdair on the subject, cancelled the transfer on 6th February. He decided to remain himself with A.H.Q. in Singapore, despite another signal he had received on 5th February which instructed him to proceed temporarily to Java when it was convenient for him to do so: he was badly in need of a rest. But circumstances moved fast, and he declined to go until the last of his subordinates had been evacuated (para. 394).

377. By the 5th February it had become clear that no suitable site for a Rear H.Q. existed in Sumatra, and so Air Commodore Silly was instructed to proceed to Batavia and take administrative charge there.

378. Not only were personnel and equipment from Singapore now arriving at that port, but also the ground personnel of the reinforcing squadrons. It was also anticipated that the site for a Rear A.H.Q. would best be located in the Batavia area.

Dislocation at Singapore Docks.

379. There was a scarcity of suitable shipping for conveying equipment, particularly M.T., to the N.E.I.: a difficulty aggravated because some vessels had to be loaded at their moorings by means of lighters. Those which did come alongside, of which there were many, deserve great credit. Owing to enemy air bombardment, ships had to be dispersed, which further delayed loading. Air bombardment also caused dock labour to disappear; its replacement by Service personnel could not be on a scale adequate to meet requirements. Conditions at the docks became confused as the scale and intensity of air attack increased. Plans made for the embarkation of personnel and stores were disorganised. Units became split up and personnel became separated from their equipment. Much equipment, urgently required by the Bomber Force in Sumatra, could not be loaded at all. In some instances, owing to air attack, ships sailed before being fully loaded.

Severe losses were inflicted by the Japanese air attacks on ships en route from Singapore during the final 14 days of evacuation. Considerable quantities of equipment, including some 200 M.T. vehicles, were lost, all of it urgently needed in the N.E.I.

Final Air Operations from Singapore.

380. Except for a small number of Hudson sorties for convoy protection, and a sweep by Buffaloes over the Batu Pahat area on 28th January to cover the evacuation of troops cut off by the Japanese advance, air operations from Singapore itself from the last days of January to the fall of the Fortress were nearly all carried out by fighters for the defence of the Island. Bomber operations from Sumatra for the support of the defence of Singapore are narrated in Section III.

381. An attack was carried out on the night of 2nd February by the Swordfish flight, released by the Army for the purpose, against the aerodrome at Kluang, where the Japanese had by now established a strong fighter force. Subsequently this Flight had to be destroyed, as its aircraft were in no condition to be flown to Sumatra.

382. The P.R. Buffalo Flight, which had functioned almost daily with outstanding success under the command of Squadron Leader Lewis since the beginning of the campaign, finally lost its aircraft by enemy air attacks on the 7th February. This Flight had carried out over 100 sorties, the majority of which had proceeded as far north as Singora. Aircraft were intercepted by Japanese fighters and hit on numerous occasions, although none was shot down. Throughout, no armour or guns had been carried: pilots had relied entirely upon evasion in order to fulfil their missions. The greatest credit is due to them for the valuable work they did.

Final Fighter Operations from Singapore.

383. On the 31st January the fighter strength of Singapore was 8 Hurricanes of No. 232(F) Squadron and 6 Buffaloes taken over by No. 453(F) Squadron. The small Buffalo force gradually wasted away and 453(F) Squadron was evacuated to Java about 4th February. The Hurricanes were maintained from Sumatra at an average daily strength of 10 aircraft. This average was maintained firstly by the arrival on 29th January of No. 258(F) Squadron with 15 Hurricanes. This squadron was one of several which had been convoyed from the Middle East (where they had just arrived as reinforcements from England) to the Far East in H.M.S. Indomitable. They had been " flown off " south of Java and had proceeded by air via Batavia and Sumatra, No. 258 thence flying on to Seletar. They had had a long and varied passage from England, involving a sea voyage to Sierra Leone, followed by a long flight across the whole breadth of Central Africa to Port Sudan, where they had embarked in H.M.S. Indomitable. They came into action on 1st February after a delay caused by the necessity for removing all guns to clear them of anti-corrosion grease with which they had had to be protected for the journey. This squadron was relieved by 232(F) Squadron on 3rd February, also ex H.M.S. Indomitable. The latter remained in Singapore until the withdrawal of the last of our aircraft.

384. These fighters were far too few in number to affect materially the scale of enemy attack. But they put up a stout fight, and throughout the first ten days of February they were almost constantly airborne throughout the hours of daylight, attempting to ward off the constant Japanese attacks.

385. Most of their sorties were for the defence of the Island. Fighter cover was provided on 30th January for the final withdrawal of the Army across the Johore causeway; and a few sorties were also flown against aircraft attacking our troop positions on the Island. On 9th February, the day following the Japanese landing on the Island, Hurricanes took off at the request of the Army and engaged enemy dive bombers, shooting down at least one.

386. A number of patrols were made for convoy protection. One convoy reached Singapore on 5th February. It had been shepherded through the Banka Straits, and during its onward passage towards Singapore, by reconnaissance and protective patrols from Sumatra. Fighters from Singapore covered its final approach. The "Empress of Asia" was attacked and set on fire, but that was the only loss incurred by reinforcing convoys. They escaped unscathed partly because of the protection they were given, but partly also because, it must be admitted, the Japanese made no very determined attacks against them. In contrast, many ships leaving Singapore during February were heavily attacked and there were many losses amongst them.

387. The devotion to duty of the fighter pilots and of the ground crews who serviced their aircraft and maintained landing strips during these last few days was exemplary. Warning of attack was short, and on occasion the Japanese bombers had dropped their bombs and were withdrawing before our fighters could reach them. But with experience of the enemy's tactics results steadily improved; and on the final day of operations, (9th February), 6 enemy aircraft were shot down and a further 14 seriously damaged for the loss of 2 Hurricanes and 1 pilot. It was significant that by 5th February the surviving pilots were mostly experienced men who had had previous battle experience before coming to the Far East.

388. On the 4th and 5th February, Seletar, Sembawang and Tengah came under steady observed shell fire, and all operations had then to be carried out from Kallang. The Japanese bombers concentrated their attack on this station, and the landing area was soon so riddled with craters that only by constant and arduous labour was a landing strip 750 yards long maintained in operation. Even so, by 6th February our pilots experienced very great difficulty in avoiding craters when taking-off and landing.

389. On the 10th February, by which time the Japanese were established in strength on the Island, all aircraft were withdrawn to Sumatra. G.O.C. Malaya concurred in this decision, which was also endorsed by C.-in-C. South-West Pacific who visited Singapore the same day. A few Buffaloes were left, owing to their condition, and had to be destroyed.

Results of Fighter Operations in Malaya.

390. Total results of the fighting in the air over Singapore are difficult to assess with any accuracy, as definite confirmation of successes was in most cases impossible. Group Captain Rice, who commanded the Fighter Force during

the whole of its operations over Malaya, estimated that 183 Japanese aircraft were destroyed, exclusive of others lost by them during our attacks on their aerodromes.

391. It is felt that this claim may be excessive, though not by much. Reports which have been received from all sources appear to establish that the Buffalo Squadrons shot down a total of 30 Japanese aircraft: others were damaged and a proportion of them probably crashed during their return to base.

It is probable that the Hurricane force destroyed, or so seriously damaged that they failed to return to base, a total of 100 Japanese aircraft. For this total, 45 Hurricanes were lost from all causes, including flying accidents and enemy air bombardment. In view of the odds which were faced these figures speak for themselves.

Final transfer of R.A.F. to Sumatra.

392. On 8th February the Japanese launched their attack on Singapore Island and rapidly obtained a firm foothold. It now became essential to transfer A.H.Q. to Sumatra in order to take control of the Command, whose combatant units were already there, for the purpose of carrying on the fight in the N.E.I.

A nucleus staff, including the S.A.S.O. (Air Commodore Staton) proceeded by air to Palembang on 10th February by order of the A.O.C.

Sir Archibald Wavell again visited Singapore the same day, 10th February. He ordered the immediate evacuation to the N.E.I. of all remaining R.A.F. personnel, which was commenced the following day. At the same time he instructed Air Vice Marshal Maltby, hitherto Assistant A.O.C. at A.H.Q., to take charge in the N.E.I. as soon as possible, that officer proceeding there by air the same afternoon accompanied by an addition to the nucleus staff which had preceded him. He was appointed by Abdair A.O.C. Westgroup in the N.E.I. with effect from 11th February.

393. Aerodrome surfaces were ploughed up. Bomb components, large stocks of petrol and much equipment which could not be got away was destroyed or rendered ineffective. But the volume of the whole was so great that neither time nor circumstances permitted its transfer or destruction, particularly a large quantity salved from Malaya which was housed in the town of Singapore where its destruction by fire was impossible. Special action was taken to destroy secret equipment e.g. radar apparatus, signals installations etc. It is believed that little of immediate value to the enemy was left to him.

394. On 13th February Air Vice Marshal Pulford, who had declined to leave until all R.A.F. personnel, who could be, had been evacuated, left Singapore. He did so at General Percival's instigation. He accompanied a party under the orders of Admiral Spooner, R.A. Malaya. When they sailed they were unaware that the Japanese fleet had interposed itself between Singapore and their destination, which was probably Batavia in Java. They were detected, attacked from the air and their boat was stranded on an island of the Tuju or Seven Islands Group some 30 miles north of Banka Island. There the whole party, some 40 in number, lived as best they could, the fishermen inhabitants having deserted it. It was malarial, unhealthy and contained little food. The party had few stores, practically no medicines and no doctor. After remaining at large for more than two months the survivors were compelled to surrender. By then 18 had died, including Air Vice Marshal Pulford and Rear Admiral Spooner. The remainder were in a bad way. Thus it was that these gallant officers lost their lives and that the former was unable to rejoin his Command in the N.E.I.

Fall of Singapore.

395. On the 15th February Singapore Fortress was compelled to surrender.

SECTION III.

SUMMARY OF OPERATIONS BASED ON SUMATRA.

INTRODUCTION.

396. As has already been narrated in Section II of this Report, by the 16th January, 1942, all Air Force units in Malaya had been driven back to Singapore Island. Even with the existing strength, aerodromes on the island were already congested; they would become more congested when reinforcements, now well on their way, arrived. The scale of Japanese air attack against these aerodromes was increasing. It had become imperative to disperse more widely. Extra elbow room was particularly desirable because H.M.S. "Indomitable," with 48 Hurricanes on board, was due to arrive at the end of January. If bomber units could be transferred to Sumatra, not only would they be dispersed more safely, but fighter squadrons could then be distributed to all the aerodromes in Singapore. It was not realised at the time how soon three of those aerodromes —Tengah, Sembawang and Seletar—would become untenable (para. 360).

General Conditions in Sumatra.

397. Sumatra, an island nearly 1,000 miles long, lies west of and runs parallel to the west coast of Malaya, but extends far to the southward. Its main features are a mountain range running down the west coast throughout the whole length of the island, and a relatively low-lying belt of country eastward of it, consisting mainly of jungle and swamp, which is intersected by many rivers with a west to east trend. It is developed in scattered areas only.

Roads are few, and although there are railway systems in the north and south, they are not connected, and communications are consequently poor. From the Allied point of view the chief economic importance of Sumatra was the oil field and refinery near Palembang, of which the normal outlet is to the east via Palembang river to the sea, though there is a single track railway running to the Port of Oesthaven in the extreme south. There was a radio telephone system inter-connecting the principal towns in Sumatra with an external connection to Java. This telephone system was open and insecure.

398. At the time this Section of the Report opens, the monsoon was still in progress over Sumatra. A feature of this monsoon was the prevalence of torrential thunderstorms, both by day and night. These thunderstorms are very violent indeed, and they completely black out

all visibility from aircrews flying through them, whose skill and endurance they test to the utmost: navigation through them is fraught with great risk. Unfortunately at this season several such thunderstorms were certain to be encountered during the course of every long flight.

State of Aerodromes.

399. Up to this date, 18th January, the policy of A.H.Q. had been to develop aerodromes in Northern Sumatra as refuelling grounds for reinforcements arriving by air from India, and as advanced landing grounds for operational use on the flank of Malaya. In consequence of this policy constructional work on them had been given priority over that at aerodromes in the south, and it was the aerodromes in the south of Sumatra which would now be wanted for our squadrons to use as their main bases. By the middle of January small refuelling and re-arming parties of varying strengths, up to 50, had been established at the following places:—

(a) Sabang (also for Flying Boats);
(b) Lho'nga.
(c) Medan Civil Aerodrome (a large military aerodrome was also being constructed in this area);
(d) Pakanbaroe;
(e) Padang;
(f) Palembang—at the civil aerodrome known as P.I.;
(g) a secret military aerodrome 20 miles south of Palembang known as P.II.

In addition there was a strip at Lahat, and a field under construction by the Dutch at Oesthaven. Wing Commander Duncan, Squadron Leader Briggs and Squadron Leader Wightwick (A.M.W.D.) were already located at Palembang for liaison with the Dutch in connection with the development of these aerodromes.

DEVELOPMENT OF R.A.F. ORGANISATION IN SUMATRA.

400. A.H.Q. therefore decided, on the 16th January, that the time was becoming imminent when bomber units would have to be transferred to Sumatra. For this reason H.Q. 225 (B) Group was formed at Singapore on this date, and was sent to Palembang in Sumatra on the 18th January, 1942. Initial appointments made by A.H.Q. were:—

Group Commander	Group Captain A. G. Bishop.
S.A.S.O.	Wing Commander K. Powell.
S.A.O.	Squadron Leader Briggs.
A.M.W.D. ...	Squadron Leader Wightwick.

Instructions to No. 225 (B) Group.

401. On formation of the Group Headquarters, the A.O.C. instructed the Group Commander:—

(a) to establish a Bomber Group H.Q.;
(b) to accelerate, to the maximum, arrangements for operating bomber units from Sumatra; such arrangements not only to provide for all bombers then in Singapore but also for the following reinforcements:—
  (i) Nos. 84 and 211 (B) Squadrons (Blenheim IV) then en route from Middle East;
  (ii) Hudson III's en route from U.K. which were to re-equip in succession No. 62 (B) Squadron, and Nos. 1 and 8 (GR) Squadrons, R.A.A.F.

402. The A.O.C. also decided that, dependent on the situation, when bomber units were located in Sumatra, either Group H.Q. would be responsible for the selection of targets (within the policy laid down by A.H.Q.) and for the briefing of squadrons, or alternatively squadrons would proceed to bases in Singapore and be briefed there under A.H.Q. arrangements. To provide for this latter arrangement, refuelling and re-arming parties for bomber units would be maintained at aerodromes on Singapore Island. At this time it was fairly confidently anticipated that the situation on the ground in Malaya would be stabilised and that a bridgehead would be held of sufficient area for the deployment of reinforcements preparatory to a counter-offensive being undertaken (para. 322). That it would be necessary later to transfer fighter squadrons from Singapore was not at this time " on the cards ".

Development by No. 225 (B) Group H.Q.

403. Group Captain Bishop, on arrival at Palembang on the 18th January, decided to:—

(a) Establish Group Headquarters at Palembang.
(b) Expand and accelerate the provision of accommodation at P.I and P.II aerodromes, and improve aircraft dispersal at each.
(c) Develop Lahat for use by bombers.
(d) Reconnoitre the area to the south of Palembang for the selection and development of further landing strips.

At the same time he put in hand reconnaissance for siting an Ammunition Park, an Air Stores Park and an R.S.U., which were to be provided for the maintenance of the Force.

A.H.Q. were informed and approved of these decisions.

404. P.I. was, at that time, a large 'L' shaped aerodrome with two hard runways. It possessed dispersal arrangements which were at once considerably developed by Dutch Engineers. There was no accommodation for personnel nearer than the town, 8 miles away.

P.II was a huge natural field about 10 miles in perimeter with good natural cover for aircraft. It was not visible from the road, and its construction had been successfully kept secret from the Japanese. Similar clearings in the neighbourhood made it difficult for air crews to locate it from the air, even by those who had been briefed as to its location. Great care was taken to preserve its secrecy and, although at one time more than 100 aircraft were based on it, Japanese reconnaissance, which frequently flew over it by day and night, never located it. Communications between Palembang and P.II were handicapped because there was no bridge over the Palembang river, on the north of which lay Palembang town and P.I; the river had to be crossed by a small ferry which had a limit of 4 to 6 vehicles. The Dutch put in hand the construction of huts for accommodation of personnel at P.II aerodrome.

405. There was a single line telephone linking each aerodrome with Group H.Q's., but instruments and wire were not available for developing an internal telephone system on either aerodrome.

For point to point communication a W/T set was improvised which was able to link up with A.H.Q., and with Sabang and Lho'nga on the air reinforcement route.

406. A civil Dutch Observer system existed at Palembang, consisting of two concentric circles of posts round Palembang, at 50 and 100 kilometers radius. There were a few posts still further out—one on the north end of Banka Island, one at the mouth of the Palembang river and one on Tanjong Pinang Island, just south of Singapore. Posts on the outer circle were unavoidably somewhat widely spaced: most warnings came from the 50 kilometre circle only. Communication between posts and the centre was by W/T or telephone. No radar was available to supplement the observer system, whose volunteer operators were most enthusiastic but unfortunately had had little experience in aircraft recognition. Warnings were consequently erratic.

407. With the most willing and energetic co-operation of the head of the Observer Corps, steps were immediately taken to improve the system. Additional posts were selected, manufacture of W/T sets began and additional personnel were trained. But events moved too fast for these measures to take effect. The original system only was available during the actual events which followed.

408. The Dutch army in the N.E.I. had no A.A. artillery, having been unable to obtain guns from the belligerents in Europe or from the U.S.A. Thus the aerodromes in Sumatra had no A.A. defences. The Dutch had already had aircraft destroyed on the ground at Medan and Pakenbaroe by Japanese low flying fighters.

409. By the end of January, however, Abdacom was able to allot A.A. defences to P.I. and P.II., 6 heavy and 6 Bofors guns to each aerodrome, and 4 of each type to the oil refinery at Palembang. Ships carrying ammunition for these guns were unfortunately sunk and there was little ultimately available. There were two Dutch armoured cars and 150 native Dutch troops allotted to the defence of each aerodrome. With the arrival of R.A.F. ground personnel, aerodrome defence parties were organised to reinforce them.

410. There was one Dutch native regiment for the defence of the whole Palembang area, but there were no defences on the river leading to the town. On the 23rd January representations were made both to the Dutch naval and military authorities, and to Abdacom, on the inadequacy of the defences in the Palembang area, but no reinforcements were available. It is thought that plans were in hand to strengthen the defences, as General Sir John Laverack, Commanding 1st Australian Corps, visited Palembang about 25th January and indicated that an Australian division might be expected in the near future. Presumably, owing to the general situation in the Far East, the move was cancelled.

411. In short, the aerodrome defences were very weak and few troops were available for the defence of the area against invasion.

Arrival of R.A.F. Units from Singapore.

412. However, Japanese progress in Malaya was quicker than had been anticipated. The transfer from Singapore had to be accelerated and expanded beyond what had first been contemplated. In the event, all aircraft had to be based on P.I and P.II, although the personnel of one bomber squadron moved to Lahat on 10th February, Group Captain Noble being appointed Station Commander. But events moved too quickly for that aerodrome to come into use.

413. This Report has already narrated the plans made by A.H.Q. in Singapore for transferring and re-organising in Sumatra and Java, and how these plans were largely frustrated by the speed of the Japanese advance in Malaya and by the dislocation caused at the docks in Singapore by air attack. These plans were further frustrated by Japanese action against shipping at sea en route to the N.E.I. Many ships were sunk and others re-routed at sea to other ports. The cumulative effect was disastrous. Practically all equipment destined for Sumatra went astray. In particular no M.T. arrived except some light motor cars about the 8th February and a few bomb trailers. There were only three refuellers available. Most important of all on the domestic side, few rations arrived and no tentage and field equipment. On aerodromes which were practically without accommodation, the last was a serious loss during the prevailing monsoon weather.

Aircraft spares were also scarce, particularly those for Blenheims, with which type the two reinforcing squadrons, Nos. 84 and 211(B) Squadrons, were also equipped.

Three month's anticipated requirements in petrol, oil and lubricants had arrived at each aerodrome. A limited number of bombs also came across and these were distributed to P.I. and P.II.

414. Local buses were requisitioned and gradually came into service. An organisation for the local purchase of supplies was set up and contracts already placed for the manufacture of domestic equipment were expedited and expanded.

415. By the end of the first week of February personnel were reasonably fed and accommodated. But later when large numbers arrived, many unexpectedly, from Singapore, accommodation had to be found at short notice. Thus 1,500 were provided for in P.II, where provision was ready for only 250, whilst 2,500 were housed in schools and cinemas in Palembang town.

Throughout, however, operational and maintenance facilities remained primitive in the extreme. The aerodromes in Sumatra were virtually landing grounds " in the blue ".

All the problems which faced the staff and units were tackled with energy and spirit, and the praiseworthy results which were achieved in the face of every handicap are a great credit to both.

The Dutch gave magnificent assistance in all these local preparations, headed by the Resident Palembang, who personally inspired and directed the civil authorities in their efforts.

416. From the 22nd January onwards, personnel and aircraft started streaming in. The former were in some disorder owing to loss of

kit and a splitting up of units through the confused conditions of embarkation at Singapore. The situation was further aggravated because the arrivals included units destined for Java, which had been re-routed at sea to Palembang. All had to be sorted and re-organised, and units for Java entrained for Oesthaven and shipped thence to Batavia.

417. On the 23rd January Blenheim IV's of Nos. 84 and 211 (B) Squadrons began to arrive from the Middle East. Their ground personnel, who came by sea, landed at Oesthaven about 14th February. The arrival of the latter coincided with the Japanese attack on the Palembang area (which will be related in due course), and they had to be re-embarked for Batavia before they could join their squadrons, which thus never had their own ground staffs with them in Sumatra. Each squadron had 24 aircraft when it left the Middle East. Sixteen of No. 84 Squadron arrived at P.I. 18 of No. 211 Squadron arrived on different days between 23rd January and 14th February (para. 318). Unfortunately the change of route from Singapore to Palembang resulted in the loss of 3 aircraft of No. 84 Squadron as a result of wrong briefing given to them on leaving Burma about the location of landing grounds in Sumatra.

Dispositions arranged for Units.

418. On the 23rd January P.I aerodrome received its first air attack. Twenty-seven unescorted bombers dropped their loads from 22,000 feet with great accuracy, but caused only slight damage to the surface of the aerodrome. The Dutch Buffalo Squadron on the aerodrome established contact with the formation and damaged at least two Japanese bombers without loss to themselves. It was now evident that our aerodromes in southern Sumatra were about to be bombed in their turn, in all probability with increasing severity. It was therefore decided to dispose our squadrons accordingly. Fortunately it was possible to take advantage of Japanese habits which by this time were well known; complete confidence could be placed in the fact that no daylight attack would take place before 0830 hours or after 1700 hours. Other factors which were taken into consideration were:—

(*a*) that P.I. was best adapted to the use of fighters, and it was soon realised that part of the Hurricane force, which was known to be arriving in H.M.S. Indomitable, would want to use it: thus it would be advisable to minimise the number of bombers on it.

(*b*) that P.II was suitable for all types of medium bombers, that its existence was believed to be unknown to the Japanese. Moreover it had good facilities for dispersal, and cover from view in the scrub jungle which surrounded it.

419. Squadrons were, therefore, to be disposed on them as follows:—

P.I. M.V.A.F., Nos. 84 and 211 (B) Squadrons, serviceable aircraft moving to P.I during Japanese raid hours.

P.II. Nos. 1 (GR), 27 (NF), 34 (B) and 62 (B) Squadrons, whose aircraft strength when they arrived from Singapore would be low.

It will be remembered that the ground parties of Nos. 84 and 211 (B) Squadrons had yet to arrive by sea from the Middle East. Provision for servicing them was therefore made from amongst technical personnel who had been evacuated from Singapore. Those surplus to requirements were sorted out and despatched to Java.

420. Aircraft and personnel began to arrive from Singapore earlier than had been anticipated, so Wing Commander Powell, S.A.S.O. of the Group, was appointed Station Commander of P.II until the arrival of Group Captain McCauley on 29th January. The former then took over command of P.I from Wing Commander Duncan, the latter being placed in charge of the refuelling party at Pakenbaroe.

OPERATIONS CARRIED OUT BY No. 225 (B) GROUP.

22nd January-14th February.

421. No. 225 (B) Group was responsible for reconnaissance northwards from the Sunda Straits to cover several convoys that went through to Singapore during the last week in January and the first in February. During the passage of a convoy through the Banka Straits on the 27th January, Blenheim IV's maintained a fighter escort over it because no fighters were available in Sumatra; the Dutch Buffalo Squadron had by this time been withdrawn to Java. All other available bomber aircraft stood by during these periods in case convoys were attacked by Japanese naval forces. The whole resources of the Group were directed towards the protection of these convoys during the two-day periods each took to traverse the area for which it was responsible.

422. On the 26th January the Endau landing took place (paras. 332-339) and No. 225 (B) Group was ordered to despatch all available aircraft to the scene. A force of 6 Hudsons from No. 62 (B) Squadron and 5 Blenheim I's of the same squadron but manned by No. 84 (B) Squadron aircrews was scraped up. The Hudsons arrived on the scene during the late afternoon, and landed at Sembawang for the night, returning to Palembang on the 27th January. The Blenheims arrived too late to participate, and so were ordered to land at Tengah and await orders from A.H.Q. This force was used on the night 27th-28th January to bomb Kuantan, returning to Palembang on 28th January.

423. On 26th January 6 Blenheim IV's of 34 (B) Squadron and 6 Hudsons of No. 8 (GR) Squadron R.A.A.F. were withdrawn from operations and were sent to Java under orders of A.H.Q. in connection with the arrival of H.M.S. Indomitable with 48 Hurricanes on board. This carrier was met at a point some distance to the Southward of Java by the bombers or G.R. aircraft, on which the Hurricanes were flown off in Squadron formations and were navigated to Java by the former aircraft. Meanwhile a Catalina provided antisubmarine patrols for the carrier's protection. The Hurricanes were again navigated during their onward journey to P.I, one squadron No. 258 (F) Squadron onward again to Singapore. The bombers and G.R. aircraft returned to P.II on 2nd February and became available again for operations.

424. On the 30th January Air Commodore H. J. F. Hunter, who had been appointed by the Air Ministry as Commander designate of a Bomber Group in the Far East, arrived in Sumatra and took over Command, Group Captain Bishop becoming S.A.S.O. of the Group.

425. Incidentally, Air Commodore Silly, Deputy A.O.C., also arrived in Palembang on the 30th January with orders from the A.O.C. to site a Command H.Q. in Sumatra. In this he was unsuccessful and left on 6th February to organise the R.A.F. Base, Batavia.

426. By the 30th January Singapore was clear of all but fighter aircraft. The strengths of bomber squadrons in Sumatra then were:—

No. 1 Squadron, R.A.A.F. ...	16 Hudson II	Many overdue for inspection and showing signs of wear and tear.
No. 8 Squadron, R.A.F. ...	6 Hudson III	} Not available until 2nd February.
No. 34 Squadron	6 Blenheim IV	
No. 62 Squadron	10 Hudson III	
No. 62 Squadron	5 Blenheim I	} Particularly poor condition.
No. 27 Squadron	3 Blenheim I	
No. 84 Squadron	10 Blenheim IV	} Most aircraft required inspection and minor repairs, after their long flight from the Middle East.
No. 211 Squadron	4 Blenheim IV	
M.V.A.F.	Mixed Flight	

427. From the 30th January–5th February, as convoy duties permitted, the following attacks were carried out during the nights shown:—

30th January–31st January.
  6 Blenheims—Ipoh aerodrome—using Pakenbaroe for refuelling.

31st January–1st February.
  6 Hudsons—Alor Star aerodrome—using Medan for refuelling. Hits were scored on the runway and aerodrome buildings.

1st February–2nd February.
  5 Blenheims—Penang aerodrome—using Medan for refuelling.

2nd February–3rd February.
  7 Blenheims, 3 Hudsons—Singora docks—using Medan for refuelling.

4th February–5th February.
  5 Blenheims, 4 Hudsons—Kluang aerodrome—using Singapore for refuelling.

5th February–6th February.
  8 Blenheims—proceeded Medan en route Singora: cancelled owing to bad weather.

12th February–13th February.
  12 Hudsons—Kluang aerodrome.

The policy was for aircraft to arrive at the advanced landing ground just before dusk, refuel and rest. Then after delivering their attacks aircraft either returned direct to base, or alternatively refuelled again at the appropriate advanced landing ground and returned to base at first light. On account of Japanese fighter patrols, aircraft could not remain on undefended grounds in Northern Sumatra during daylight hours.

428. These long flights in themselves imposed great strain on crews; it was still the wet monsoon season in Sumatra and torrential thunderstorms were prevalent, particularly at night. Not all the crews of reinforcing squadrons were up to the standard of night flying required for such conditions, particularly in the absence of radio aids to navigation: those that were showed outstanding determination and skill, and of them Wing Commander Jeudwine, C.O. of No. 84 (B) Squadron, was pre-eminent. It was only rarely that results of bombing could be observed in any detail owing to the bad conditions of visibility.

429. Up to the 6th February No. 225 (B) Group had maintained daily reconnaissances across the South China Sea to Borneo to detect any Japanese movement southwards.

On the 6th February there were reports of a Japanese force assembling in the Anambas. This was located by Hudson sorties; it was attacked on the night 7th–8th February by 9 Blenheims in most adverse weather conditions, and again on the 11th–12th February by 10 Blenheims.

430. Throughout this period many transit flights to and from Singapore were carried out by Hudson aircraft either escorting Hurricanes or assisting in the evacuation of personnel.

Serviceability in all units was low.

The M.V.A.F. at Palembang were invaluable throughout in maintaining communications between P.I. and P.II. and Lahat, providing a twice daily reconnaissance of the river approaches, and locating crashed aircraft.

ORGANISATION—No. 226 (F) GROUP.

431. It will be remembered that it had not been the intention until quite a recent date to operate any of our fighters on aerodromes in South Sumatra, but that the unexpectedly rapid Japanese advance right up to the confines of Singapore island had made it impracticable for them to use the aerodromes on the island except Kallang. It now became necessary, therefore, to make arrangements for them in Sumatra. On the 1st February, 1942, Air Commodore Vincent arrived in Palembang and formed H.Q. No. 226 (F) Group. For this purpose he brought with him personnel drawn from No. 224 (F) Group, Singapore, and absorbed those of H.Q. 266 (F) Wing which was now arriving in Sumatra from U.K. (para. 373 (b)).

432. In anticipation of the formation of a Fighter organisation, and with the energetic co-operation of the Dutch, a Fighter H.Q. Operations Room had already been established at Palembang on the 25th January by H.Q. 225 (B) Group. This Operations Room was connected to a naval transmitter in the docks some distance away, for communicating with aircraft. At first, orders from the Operations Controller had to be relayed to aircraft: later this arrangement was improved and the Controller was connected direct to the transmitter.

Arrangements were made for the Gun Operations Room to be in the same building. It was also connected with the Dutch Civil Observer System, which was in course of being improved (paras. 406 and 407).

433. The role of the Group was:—
(a) Defence of the Palembang area:
(b) Protection of shipping in the Banka Straits, by means of escort patrols and offensive sweeps:
(c) Up till the 9th February 1942 maintenance of a token force of fighters in Singapore.

434. V.H.F. was not available, nor was D/F for assisting homing aircraft. The absence of the latter was a serious handicap because intense thunderstorms were frequent and fighter pilots were apt to lose their bearings when negotiating them.

All aircraft of the Fighter Group were based on P.I. aerodrome, the administrative shortcomings of which have already been related. It had a telephone from the Operations Room in Palembang but no instruments were available for dispersal points round the aerodrome, which slowed down the speed with which fighters could get away to intercept an enemy raid.

Strength of Fighter Squadrons.

435. About 50 Hurricanes were available when the Group formed, the majority direct from H.M.S. "Indomitable." The remainder were part of the original consignment which had arrived in crates in Singapore on the 13th January.

436. Forty-eight flew off H.M.S. "Indomitable" on 26th January. All flew off with their guns protected with anti-corrosion grease with which they had been provided for the journey. Fifteen flew via Batavia and P.I. to Singapore, arriving on the 29th January. Their guns were cleaned at Seletar. The remainder remained at P.II to have their guns cleaned before transfer to P.I. Cleaning of these guns was a slow operation owing to lack of all the usual facilities, and considerable delay occurred before squadrons were able to go into action.

437. Pilots were drawn from Nos. 232, 242, 258 and 605 (F) Squadrons and operated as two composite squadrons—Nos. 232 and 258. Most pilots, with the exception of the Commanding Officers and Flight Commanders, were straight from O.T.U's., and deserve credit for the spirit with which they went straight into action. They had experienced a long sea voyage, but once again no time could be spared for acclimatization or training.

438. When they first arrived their aircraft were serviced by personnel from Buffalo squadrons. From the 6th February onwards, however, ground personnel of No. 266 (F) Wing began to arrive via Oesthaven, including advanced parties and stores with an Air Stores Park and an R.S.U. There was a deficiency of Hurricane tool kits, few battery starters for aircraft, and no battery-charging facilities were available at the aerodrome: factors which contributed to a low standard of serviceability.

439. To improve the climb and manoeuvrability of the Hurricane the four outside guns were removed, as it was considered that eight guns were ample against the unarmoured Japanese aircraft.

OPERATIONS CARRIED OUT BY No. 226 (F) GROUP.

440. From the 2nd-5th February many sorties were carried out escorting shipping proceeding north and south through the Banka Straits. On the 3rd February, nine aircraft of No. 258 Squadron left for Singapore to co-operate with a bomber force in a combined attack on Kluang aerodrome, returning the following day. They landed at Tengah, but owing to an error on the part of that Station, the squadron was not ready to take off at the appointed time, and the attack was a failure.

441. Meanwhile, Japanese reconnaissance was maintained daily over Palembang, and was quick to note our activity. Air attacks on P.I. aerodrome took place on 6th, 7th and 8th February by formations of bombers escorted by fighters.

442. On the 6th February warning was short, and the Hurricanes, caught at a tactical disadvantage, lost four and claimed one Navy "O". No. 232 Squadron were away at Singapore on this day conducting operations from the Island.

443. On the 7th February warning was even shorter, and results were serious. The Japanese combined a high bombing attack with a low attack by fighters. Three Hurricanes were destroyed and 11 others damaged on the ground, whilst three were shot down in the air. In addition four unserviceable Blenheims on the ground, and one Hudson, which arrived as the attack was in progress, were destroyed. Only one Navy "O" fighter could be claimed.

444. On the 8th and 13th February fresh attacks on the aerodromes took place, but more warning was received: on the 8th an inconclusive interception took place, but on the 13th, three Navy "O" fighters and two Army 97 bombers were shot down for the loss of one Hurricane.

445. On the 12th February the Group was reinforced by Wing Commander Maguire and eight aircraft. These were part of a reinforcing Wing, No. 226 (F) Wing which included 39 Hurricanes, a pool of 15 pilots, and the ground crews of Nos. 232, 258 and 605 Squadrons: it had arrived at Batavia by sea on the 4th February.

446. On the 13th February a further nine aircraft from Batavia arrived at P.I. Unfortunately they did so while the attack on the aerodrome was in progress. They were short of petrol, and in ensuing engagements six were either shot down or crashed.

447. It was quite evident that the Japanese already realised that we were endeavouring to establish our squadrons on P.I. and that they were devoting a very considerable effort, particularly with strong forces of fighters, to prevent it.

It is opportune at this juncture to digress for a moment.

Control of operations in Sumatra assumed by Abdair.

448. It will be realised that A.H.Q. in Singapore had, by the end of January, much depleted its staff in forming the staffs of the two new Groups, Nos. 225 and 226, in Sumatra, which were themselves much under requirements. This depletion particularly affected the

signals organisation. Firstly because its numbers were reduced at a time when signals traffic was on the increase consequent upon the splitting up of the Command between Singapore and Sumatra. Secondly because it was just as this time that the trained and experienced lady cypher staff had to be evacuated. The result was acute congestion of, and increasing delays in, signals traffic. This had reached such a pitch on 6th February as to constitute a breakdown between Palembang and A.H.Q. in Singapore. Abdair therefore assumed operational control of all R.A.F. units in Sumatra with effect from 7th February.

Formation of Westgroup H.Qs. in the N.E.I.

449. Air Vice-Marshal P. C. Maltby and Air Commodore W. E. Staton arrived in Palembang on the 10th February, and on the following day the former became A.O.C. and the latter S.A.S.O. of Westgroup, which comprised all R.A.F. and R.A.A.F. Units of the Far East Command now located in Sumatra and Java. Whilst in Palembang they picked up a nucleus staff and moved with it on 12th February to Java, having first reconnoitred South Sumatra and ascertained that no suitable site for a H.Q. existed in that area. It was arranged that, pending the establishment of H.Q. Westgroup in Java, Abdair would continue in direct control of all operations carried out by Westgroup Units.

FURTHER OPERATIONS BY 225 (B) GROUP—
12TH TO 14TH FEBRUARY.

450. From the 7th February onwards, all reconnaissance by No. 225 (B) Group had been discontinued under orders from Abdair, who wished to economise air effort by centralising all reconnaissance under the Reconnaissance Group in Java and thereby increasing the size of the striking force available in Sumatra.

451. On the 13th February, however, the shipping situation as known at H.Q. 225 (B) Group appeared most confused. Reconnaissance reports made by Reconnaissance Group and received through Abdair showed that Japanese naval forces were in strength south of Singapore. These reports were 5-7 hours old by the time they reached 225 (B) Group owing to bad communications; locations of convoys had by then completely changed. To confuse matters still further, a stream of shipping of all kinds was at the same time passing south from Singapore to Java despite the presence of Japanese forces; friend was difficult to distinguish from foe.

452. By the 13th February (p.m.) it was felt at H.Q. 225 (B) Group that, despite orders to the contrary, a reconnaissance must be carried out to clear the situation and ascertain whether or not there was an immediate threat to Sumatra. One Hudson of No. 1 (GR) Squadron, R.A.A.F., was sent in the afternoon and reported a concentration of Japanese shipping north of Banka Island, which confirmed impressions that a landing at Palembang was imminent. All available Blenheims were immediately despatched to attack the enemy force, but results were difficult to assess owing to darkness and rainstorms.

453. On the 14th February an offensive reconnaissance of 5 Hudsons was despatched so as to be over the area at first light. This located and attacked a convoy consisting of 25-30 transports, heavily escorted by naval vessels, at the northern entrance of the Banka Straits, heading towards the Palembang river. The convoy was protected by fighters believed to be from one or two aircraft carriers which were not, however, located. This was followed up by attacks by all available Hudsons and Blenheims, during which at least 6 transports were sunk or badly damaged. All of these attacks, except the first, were unescorted and carried out in the face of heavy A.A. fire and strong fighter defence. Six to eight of our aircraft were shot down or destroyed on landing in a damaged condition, whilst the majority were hit to a varying degree. Nevertheless, the successes already achieved more than balanced those losses and during the night of the 14th everything possible was done to prepare for further attacks the following morning.

454. The reason why no fighter escort had been available except for the first attack was because the Japanese had, in co-ordination with the approach of their convoy, staged a parachute attack on P.I. aerodrome, on which our fighters were based. It was the only occupied aerodrome which they had located in Sumatra. Presumably by attacking it they hoped to neutralize all air resistance to the convoy. As events will show, their failure to locate P.II and neutralize it as well was to prove costly. However, before proceeding further it is now necessary to turn to describe events at P.I.

*Parachute attack on Palembang I Aerodrome—
14th February.*

455. On 14th February all serviceable Hurricanes were airborne, escorting 225 Group's bombers which were attacking enemy shipping in Banka Straits. At about 0800 hours the approach of a large hostile formation was reported by the Observer Corps. Attempts to divert our Hurricanes to intercept it failed because they were beyond R/T range.

456. Shortly afterwards P.I. was attacked, first by bombers with light bombs, then it was well shot up by the large escort of fighters, and finally troop carriers dropped 2 groups of parachutists, each 150-200 strong, at two points 400-800 yards to the S. and W. in the scrub jungle which surrounds the aerodrome. Simultaneously 300 more were dropped on the oil refinery a few miles away near Pladjoe.

457. The aerodrome defences (8 heavy and 8 Bofors British A.A. guns, 150 Dutch infantry with 2 old armoured cars and about 60 R.A.F. ground defence gunners of 258 and 605 (F) Squadrons) warded off an attempt to rush the aerodrome, a number of casualties occurring on both sides.

458. Our absent fighters, now with empty tanks and guns, were diverted to P.II. and were subsequently employed against the main enemy attack in the Palembang river. Some landed at P.I, not having received the diversion order, were refuelled and sent on to P.II.

459. Shortly afterwards the A.A. guns, having by then almost exhausted their small stock of ammunition, were withdrawn to Palembang Town. Wing Commander Maguire organised the withdrawal of unarmed R.A.F. personnel at the same time. He remained himself with about 60 R.A.F. personnel and some Dutch native infantry to deny the aerodrome to

the enemy. One paratroop party had, however, reached the road leading to Palembang and ambushed part of the withdrawing parties, subsequently making a road block with overturned vehicles.

460. Two subsequent attempts from Palembang Town to reinforce the aerodrome were driven back at the road block after close quarters fighting. The first, at about 1100 hours, was by an R.A.F. party under F.L. Jackson and P.O. Umphelby who pressed their attack with determination: some of the party succeeded in reaching the aerodrome through the scrub and assisted in evacuating some wounded and unarmed personnel. The second, at 16.30 hours, was by a Dutch contingent which also was able to get some small assistance and information to the aerodrome.

461. Wing Commander Maguire's party, by now much reduced, was running out of ammunition, and had no water or food. Thus, this handful of men was in no position to continue their gallant denial of the aerodrome to the enemy in face of an attack in force which was certain to come at night. He therefore destroyed all material, including some unserviceable aircraft, and withdrew. Being cut off from Palembang Town the party made its way to the West Coast of Sumatra after an arduous trek of seven days, during which they destroyed a number of stocks of petrol and some rubber factories. They there rejoined their units in Java.

462. Our aircraft at P.II meanwhile were too busy dealing with far greater a threat to be in a position to help recover P.I aerodrome, as will now be related.

Events from 14th February (p.m.)— 18th February.

Attacks on Japanese Convoy off Palembang, 15th February.

463. By 14th February (p.m.) therefore, the total Air Forces located in Sumatra were at P.II aerodrome. The strength consisted of:—

22 Hurricanes.

35 Blenheim I's and IV's—many of which were unserviceable.

3 Hudsons (the remainder of the Hudson force was flown to Java for repairs on the 14th February).

The whole was placed under the command of the Station Commander P.II, Group Captain McCauley, who was instructed by the A.O.C. No. 225 (B) Group to continue attacks on the Japanese convoy entering the Palembang River from first light on the 15th (paras. 452-4).

464. Reconnaissance on the 15th pin-pointed the position of transports and barges, and revealed approximately 20 naval vessels and transports steaming through the Banka Straits, whilst other transports and landing craft were in the river mouth.

465. The first attack, off at 0630 hours, was made by 6 Blenheims escorted by Hurricanes. It met strong fighter opposition but pressed home the attack. From then onwards until 1530 hours a constant stream of our aircraft proceeded to attack the convoy, and, as all enemy fighter opposition had ceased, Hurricanes were employed in shooting up barges whilst bombers similarly expended their ammunition after dropping their bombs. The limiting factor in the number of attacks was the speed with which re-armament and refuelling could be carried out. The Japanese in barges and transports fought back for a time with A.A. and small arms fire but by 1100 hours this opposition ceased. By 1530 hours all movement on the river was stopped and surviving barges and landing craft had pulled in to the thick undergrowth. Troops had dispersed on to the river bank, and against them attacks continued.

466. It is difficult to assess the damage done. All pilots reported upon its extent. Thousands of troops in barges were caught in the open by machine gun fire, particularly by the Hurricanes, and very heavy casualties were inflicted upon them. Bombing accounted for many more, whilst in addition, 3 transports were sunk, a number of others were hit and an unknown number of landing craft were also sunk.

467. As a fitting finale to the day, a number of Navy 'O' fighters were located on a strip on the beach on Banka Island and were destroyed by Hurricanes. It is probable that these fighters were those which had been encountered during the initial sorties of this day.

468. Air action thus brought the landing to a standstill. The Japanese were punished heavily for their failure to locate P.II aerodrome. Unfortunately, there were no troops or naval light craft available in the area to take advantage of the situation.

Withdrawal from Sumatra.

469. On the evening of the 14th February, A.O.C. 226 Group returned to Palembang from P.II. Both he and A.O.C. 225 Group were informed by the local Dutch Territorial Commander that the situation was well under control and that he had every hope of eliminating the paratroops. He gave the impression that a drive was to take place that night to clear the area. Contrary orders evidently were received later by him, because a start was made during the night in burning oil and rubber stocks in the town, and in the destruction of the oil refinery area.

470. When A.O.C's. Nos. 225 and 226 Groups saw the Dutch Territorial Commander early on the morning of the 15th, they found that the Dutch H.Q. had closed and that the Territorial Commander himself considered it too late to restore the situation. He was himself about to leave for Lahat in the South.

471. The Dutch Territorial Commander also stated that the ferries across the river and the railhead facilities would be blown in one hour's time, with the object of embarrassing the Japanese advance towards the South. In consequence, A.O.C. No. 225 Group ordered the immediate evacuation of the town by all remaining R.A.F. personnel. This was effected by road and rail to Oesthaven.

472. A further paratroop landing took place at P.I. later during the morning of the 15th, and the Japanese established themselves in the vicinity of Palembang town. There was thus a distinct possibility that P.II. aerodrome might be over-run during the night 15th/16th February. Also by 15th February (p.m) stocks of bombs and ammunition at P.II were almost expended, whilst food supplies were cut off.

473. In view of these factors and the lack of any supporting troops, Abdair approved the

evacuation back to Java of all R.A.F. units, and this was effected by road and rail on the evening of the 15th via Oesthaven. All flyable aircraft were flown to Java, the remainder destroyed. Aircraft of Nos. 84 and 211(B) Squadrons, which had borne the brunt of the attacks during the day, finished their last sorties too late to proceed that evening. They remained on the aerodrome, flying to Java on the morning of the 16th February.

474. Personnel at landing grounds in N. and Central Sumatra were instructed to proceed by road to west coast ports for evacuation in accordance with pre-arranged plans.

475. Special mention must be made here of the valuable services rendered by the General Manager, Sumatra Railways. Despite orders received from his superior authorities he delayed destruction of rail facilities and personally arranged for the trains required during the night 15th/16th February. He himself did not leave until after the departure of the last train conveying R.A.F. personnel.

Credit is also due to Group Captain A. G. Bishop for the part he played in Sumatra. He put our squadrons on their feet and organised the staff despite primitive circumstances. He contributed in no small degree to the success of the operations which were conducted in Sumatra, and finally he personally supervised the successful withdrawal of the force from the Palembang area when its position there was no longer tenable.

476. At Oesthaven on the 16th February, it was found that the Dutch had already fired the bazaar and destroyed all military property. At the docks the British Military Embarkation Commandant stated that he had been given orders that all personnel were to be clear by midnight; personnel only were to be evacuated, not M.T. or equipment. As a result, essential and vital aircraft equipment, including that brought from Palembang, was left behind. This was particularly unfortunate because spare engines and other urgent stores for the Hurricanes which had been landed at Oesthaven with No. 41 Air Stores Park, of No. 266(F) Wing, were left behind. No. 266(F) Wing's R.S.U. similarly lost valuable equipment. A.A. guns and ammunition which had been brought to the port from P.I. and P.II aerodromes had also to be abandoned. Section IV of this Report will show that the loss of this R.A.F. and A.A. equipment had serious results during operations conducted later in Java. Fortunately the light tanks were re-embarked, and all personnel, Army and R.A.F., were evacuated.

477. The evacuation of the port was covered by a screen of R.A.F. personnel from No. 84 (B) Squadron acting under the command of Group Captain G. E. Nicholetts, who had been appointed R.A.F. Base Control Officer about ten days previously.

478. It was unfortunate that Oesthaven was evacuated so hastily. Two days later Group Captain Nicholetts, with a party of 50 volunteers of No. 605(F) Squadron, returned from Batavia to Oesthaven by sea in H.M.S. "Ballarat" which was commanded by a Royal Australian Naval Reserve officer specially appointed for the voyage owing to his knowledge of Oesthaven Harbour. On arrival, early on the 18th, twelve hours were spent by the party loading the ship to the gunwales with R.A.F. equipment and some Bofors ammunition. At the same time the railway track was damaged, loaded rolling stock and petrol dumps were fired, and the water by the dockside was obstructed by pushing into the sea abandoned heavy M.T. and other vehicles.

479. That this work of salvage and destruction proceeded unhampered by the enemy must not detract from the spirit shown by both the R.A.F. party and the crew of H.M.S. "Ballarat," who volunteered for the adventure with a full knowledge of the hazards involved.

As it happened, air reconnaissances from Java had made it clear that the casualties and disorganisation caused as a result of our air attacks on the convoy off Palembang during the 14th and 15th February had been so severe that the Japanese were in no state to run through from Palembang to Oesthaven at the speed which had been anticipated when the port was evacuated, but Group Captain Nicholetts and his party were unaware of this fact.

SECTION IV.

SUMMARY OF OPERATIONS BASED ON JAVA.

INTRODUCTION.

Early Days of War in the N.E.I.

480. Before hostilities had broken out in the Far East the Dutch considered that their best interests lay in co-operating with the British from the outset with the object of repelling a Japanese attack in its early stages. They felt confident that, by joint means, an attack could be halted in the north and that war would never reach Java itself.

481. Dutch air units, therefore, operated from the first day of war in Malaya, Borneo and the northern islands of the N.E.I. There they suffered considerable casualties. Dutch naval units also played an early part and suffered considerably.

482. Early reverses caused apprehension but acted as a spur to Dutch co-operation. Their will to help was most marked although their resources were very limited.

Formation of H.Q. S.W. Pacific Command (Abdacom) in Java.

483. On 15th January, 1942, Sir Archibald Wavell arrived in Java to take control of all Allied Forces in the S.W. Pacific and formed his H.Q. (Abdacom) near Bandoeng. Confidence was raised by this and by the news of expected reinforcements—British, Australian and American—and still further by the actual arrival, towards the end of January and early February, of the first of them. More were on the way.

484. Even when the British forces in Malaya were, by 31st January, invested on Singapore Island, it was believed that that fortress, the key of the Far East, would hold out for some while. This would provide the necessary time for adequate forces to be built up in the N.E.I. for the successful defence of the rest of the Far East.

Then came a series of unpleasant events.

Effect in the N.E.I. of Japanese Capture of Singapore and Sumatra.

485. On 8th February the Japanese secured a foothold on Singapore Island and within a couple of days its imminent capitulation became evident.

486. On 14th February they attacked and overran South Sumatra, admittedly at heavy cost. The British forces, mainly air units, had to withdraw to Java.

487. Between 12th and 18th February large numbers of personnel, evacuated from Singapore and Sumatra, arrived in considerable confusion in Western Java: amongst them were approximately 10,000 R.A.F. of all ranks. They augmented considerable numbers of refugees who had preceded them in a steadily growing stream from the same places and from other N.E.I. Islands.

488. At this time, mid-February, Abdacom was still established in Bandoeng, reinforcements were arriving and more were expected. Nevertheless it was evident now that Java would be attacked in the near future. A civilian exodus from Java on a grand scale replaced the small stream which had been leaving for some time through Sourabaya and Batavia.

Congestion in Batavia.

489. At Batavia the exodus became confused with incoming reinforcements and evacuees from Singapore and Sumatra. For several days the harbour of Batavia, and the roadstead outside, were congested with shipping. This unloaded as best it could. The result was that quays, warehouses and the roads leading from them rapidly became blocked with an inextricable confusion of merchandise, equipment, M.T., abandoned cars and goods of every description. The town of Batavia became congested with personnel—outgoing refugees, incoming reinforcements, incoming evacuees and Dutch troops mobilised for defence of the locality.

490. Into this confused area the R.A.F., evacuated from Singapore and Sumatra, arrived, for the most part between 12th and 18th February.

491. Those from Singapore had embarked there under heavy air attack on shipping of all kinds as it came to hand, and amongst a number of civilian refugees. Units had become much mixed, many personnel were separated from units and many had become separated from their equipment. It had proved impracticable to embark much equipment owing to conditions at Singapore docks, and some of what had been embarked had been lost at sea through enemy action.

492. Units from Sumatra had also suffered loss of their equipment by reason of the hasty withdrawal from aerodromes near Palembang, and still more so by circumstances at the port in South Sumatra, Oesthaven, at which they had embarked: such small amount of equipment as they had possessed in Sumatra, and which they had succeeded in removing to Oesthaven, could not be embarked and brought with them (para. 476).

493. An appreciable number of bombers and fighters had, however, reached aerodromes in the Batavia district, though a high proportion of them were unfit for operations.

494. Such was the situation in Batavia on 16th February. It was from personnel and equipment so placed that a maximum air fighting strength with ancillary services had to be evolved, and surpluses evacuated from Java. Twelve days were destined to be available for this work before the Japanese landed in Java.

R.A.F. Re-organisation in Java.

Situation on 16th February.

495. On the 16th February, the date of the evacuation of Sumatra, the position in Java was as follows:—

(*a*) *H.Q. Westgroup* (A.O.C.—A.V.M. P.C. Maltby)—A.O.C. and a nucleus staff had arrived at Soekaboemi on 14th February and were organising a H.Q. there; this was still known as Westgroup. Soekaboemi was chosen because it is centrally located in Western Java, where all Westgroup units were being located. Westgroup assumed administrative responsibility for its units on 16th February. As it was not yet ready to take operational control, this was retained by Abdair, which had assumed it on 7th February whilst units were still operating in Sumatra (para. 448).

(*b*) *No. 205 (F.B.) Squadron*—(Wing Commander Councell in Command) had arrived in Batavia on 1st February and was operating as part of the Allied Reconnaissance Group (Recgroup), using anchorages at Batavia and Oesthaven.

(*c*) *Nos. 36 and 100 (T.B.) Squadrons*—(Squadron Leader Wilkins in Command). Aircraft had arrived on 29/30th January from Singapore for re-organisation. After being based on various aerodromes they were rejoined by their ground personnel on 15th February at Tjikampek.

(*d*) *No. 153 M.U.*—(G/Capt. Ridgway in command) had arrived in Java on the 9th January and moved to Djocjacarta, where it was ready to start work on 15th January.

(*e*) *No. 152 M.U.*—(Squadron Leader S. G. Aylwin in command) had arrived in Batavia on 14th February and moved on the 17th to Poerbolinggo to form a transit store.

(*f*) *R.A.F. Base, Batavia* (Group Captain Ridgway in command until 18th February 1942 when Air Commodore Silly relieved him). This base had been established in Batavia on the 24th January to organise the reception, sorting and despatch of personnel arriving by sea from Singapore and Sumatra and of air reinforcements from the Middle East and the United Kingdom. It also organised the reception and erecting of a number of boxed Hurricanes. By 18th February this base was administering 5 transit camps in Batavia and one at Buitenzorg. Personnel of all other units not mentioned in (*a*) to (*e*) above passed through this base for re-organisation and disposal, a total of over 12,000 being handled.

(*g*) *Certain A.M.E. Units* were installing radar facilities in the Batavia and Sourabaya areas.

(*h*) Thirty-nine crated Hurricanes had been erected in Batavia during the first ten days of February. Seventeen had proceeded to No. 266 (F) Wing in Sumatra, where a number of them were lost. Twelve were handed over by Abdair to the Dutch

Army Air Force. For diplomatic reasons they could not be withdrawn in spite of the losses which our fighter squadrons had just sustained in Sumatra. Thus only 10 were left as replacements for our squadrons.

Allocation of Aerodromes.

496. On the evacuation of Sumatra, on 16th February, Abdair allocated aerodromes as follows:—
  (a) All Hudsons to Samplak:
  (b) All Blenheims to Kalidjati:
  (c) All fighters to Tjililitan.

These aerodromes had not been highly developed, dispersal being limited, aerodrome ground defence weak, internal signals and night flying arrangements lacking. No. A.A. defences were available.

497. On the 18th February, in view of the reduced strength of squadrons and the fact that no further bomber reinforcements could be expected, A.O.C. Westgroup decided to concentrate all aircraft by types into selected squadrons as follows:—

(a) *Semplak:*
  Station Commander—Group Captain Brown, No. 1 (GR) Squadron, R.A.A.F.—Commander, W/Cdr. R. H. Davies. Strength 14 Hudson II's and 12 Hudson III's (about 12 operationally serviceable).

(b) *Kalidjati:*
  Station Commander—Group Captain Whistondale (pending availability of Group Captain Nicholetts) No. 84 (B) Squadron—Commander, W/Cdr. Jeudwine. Strength 26 Blenheims (about 6 operationally serviceable).

(c) *Tjikampek:*
  No. 36 (TB) Squadron—Commander, S/Ldr. Wilkins. Strength 9 Vildebeestes and 1 Albacore. (No torpedo facilities were available in Java.)

(d) *Tjililitan:*
  No. 232 (F) Squadron—Commander, S/Ldr. Brooker.
  No. 605 (F) Squadron—Commander, S/Ldr. Wright.
  Total strength of 25 Hurricanes (about 18 operationally serviceable).

The former had been in action since its arrival in the Far East, in Singapore and Sumatra, and had been kept up to strength by absorbing No. 232 (F) Squadron proper which had arrived in H.M.S. Indomitable. It was now very depleted again, and in turn absorbed practically the whole of No. 242 (F) Squadron also from H.M.S. Indomitable—but the original designation of the squadron, No. 232 (F) Squadron, was retained.

No. 605 (F) Squadron had hitherto been mainly employed in erecting Hurricanes for No. 266 (F) Wing. But it was now armed with a small quota of aircraft and came into action on 23rd February.

The decision to retain two fighter squadrons in Java was taken in expectation of the arrival of U.S.S. "Langley," a U.S.A. aircraft carrier, with a consignment of P.40 fighters on board, with which it was hoped to arm one of them, the other retaining Hurricanes. Unfortunately the "Langley" was later sunk when approaching Java and the expectation was never realised.

Re-formation of Bomber and Fighter Groups.

498. On 18th February H.Q. Nos. 225 (B) and 226 (F) Groups were re-formed in skeleton to assist Westgroup in re-establishing their squadrons in Java.

No. 225 (B) Group, under Air Commodore Hunter, re-formed in Bandoeng. Bomber aerodromes were visited and assistance given, in co-operation with the Dutch, to units to solve their acute problems of housing, rationing and transportation. Air Commodore Hunter was absorbed into Abdair on 19th February to act as A.O.A.; the remaining members of Group H.Q. were absorbed into H.Q. Westgroup on its arrival in Bandoeng on the 23rd February.

No. 266 (F) Group, under Air Commodore Vincent, took charge of Nos. 232 (F) and 605 (F) Squadrons, and of a fighter operations room in Batavia and its local warning system. This had made good progress during the preceding few days, thanks largely to the initiative of Wing Commander Bell, previously Station Commander at Kallang, Singapore. Owing to the highly developed nature of communications in Java, efficient operations and filter rooms were quickly connected to the Dutch Observer Corps, the fighter aerodrome, the A.A. defences of Batavia, and Abdair's (later Britair's) operations room in Bandoeng. Two R.D.F. and two G.L. sets were quickly erected in the Batavia district and were also connected with them. The Dutch provided the utmost assistance, including the provision of many volunteer Dutch youths and women to man the filter and operations rooms; their alertness and enthusiasm could hardly have been bettered.

499. To maintain this Force it was decided to retain:—
  (a) No. 153 M.U. (already organised for work at Djocjacarta).
  (b) No. 81 R.S.U.
  (c) No. 41 Air Stores Park for Unit supply.
  (d) An improvised Air Stores Park for collection and sorting of equipment.

500. Establishments were drawn up and issued; and instructions were given that all personnel surplus to establishment were to be evacuated via the R.A.F. Base, Batavia, as shipping became available and as far as possible with their original units. Preference was to be given in the following order, after women and children evacuees—formed units, aircrews, technical personnel and selected details.

501. Aircraft serviceability for various reasons was low: the Hudson and Blenheim Squadrons had about six serviceable each, the two fighter squadrons not more than 18 in all. For the next few days minor operations only were carried out (under Abdair orders), and all efforts were directed towards improving the condition of aircraft and to getting ready generally for the serious operations to come.

AIR OPERATIONS 18TH TO 24TH FEBRUARY.

502. While re-organisation described above was progressing under Westgroup direction, the following operations were carried out under the directions of Abdair.

503. On the 18th February, one Hudson reconnoitred the port of Oesthaven and the road to Palembang. No signs of Japanese activity were observed.

504. On the 19th February all available (5) Blenheims attacked shipping at Palembang. On this day a bombing attack was launched by the Japanese against Semplak and 6 Hudsons were destroyed. Semplak had no A.A. defences and dispersal facilities were poor.

505. On the 20th February 4 Hudsons and 3 Blenheims again bombed shipping at Palembang in the face of severe fighter opposition from aircraft based on P.1. The following day 2 Hudsons and 5 Blenheims continued these attacks. On this occasion it was possible to observe results; hits were obtained and one 10,000-ton ship was set on fire.

506. On the 22nd February, Semplak, which had no A.A. defences, sustained low flying attacks by some 20 fighters. Six Hudsons were burnt out and three others damaged beyond repair. As a result of this raid Abdair approved the move of the remains of No. 1 (G.R.) Squadron R.A.A.F. to Kalidjati where a light battery (8 Bofors) had by 20th February been located as part of the aerodrome defence. Six aircraft were transferred the next day, a rear party being left at Semplak to repair the unserviceable aircraft on the aerodrome and to strip the rest of serviceable parts. Whilst they were there, another attack was sustained on 24th February, and more aircraft, unserviceable, were destroyed.

507. On the 23rd February, 3 Blenheims bombed 4 submarines off the coast and claimed that one had been sunk.

508. On the 24th February, Kalidjati was bombed by the enemy, and again twice on the 26th. The Bofors guns successfully prevented a low flying attack from developing on the latter date.

509. Four Blenheims attacked P.1 on the 25th February. By this time there were only 2 Hudsons operationally serviceable, with 9 others repairable: the Blenheim position, however, was slowly improving.

SUPREME ALLIED H.Q. S.W. PACIFIC LEAVES JAVA.

510. The enemy's unexpectedly rapid advance had frustrated the hopes, originally entertained, of building up a large Allied strength in the S.W. Pacific under the direction of Abdacom in Java, which was by now under imminent threat of invasion. Being without appropriate forces to handle, Abdacom could serve no useful purpose by remaining in the island: on the contrary such action could only result in the loss of a valuable Allied staff, the capture of which would have given great prestige to the enemy. On 22nd February its withdrawal was ordered.

511. It was decided that the British forces remaining in the island should in future operate under the Dutch Naval and Army Commanders-in-Chief in the N.E.I. In conformity with this decision H.Q. Westgroup moved on 23rd February from Soekaboemi and took over the H.Q. in Bandoeng vacated by Abdair. It took over operational control of its squadrons from Abdair on 24th February and was renamed Britair. It was placed under the orders of Maj.-Gen. van Oyen, the Dutch A.O.C., whose staff was already installed in Abdair's operations room. Command passed to the Dutch Authorities on 25th February, and personnel of Abdacom left Java on 25th and 26th February.

512. Before he left Java Sir Archibald Wavell issued his instructions to the A.O.C. Britair (Air Vice Marshal Maltby). They were to the effect that:—

(a) He was to command all R.A.F. units left in Java.

(b) He would exercise Command under the orders of General van Oyen, the Dutch A.O.C. in Java, who, in turn, was under Command of the Dutch C.-in-C., General ter Poorten.

(c) The British Army troops left in Java were under command of Major-General H. D. W. Sitwell who would receive his orders from General ter Poorten.

(d) To co-operate with the Dutch and to go on fighting as long as they continued effective resistance.

(e) Thereafter to do the utmost to evacuate remaining personnel.

(f) To ensure that no undamaged equipment fell into enemy hands.

(g) As senior British Officer in Java to act as signals link between all British forces in the island and their service departments in London, Delhi, Washington and Melbourne.

(h) That no help from outside could be expected for a long time.

513. Gen. van Oyen issued instructions that the operations room, vacated by Abdair, was to be maintained for the combined use of his H.Q. and of Britair, and that it was to be organised for covering all operations in the S.W. Pacific. This necessitated a last minute augmentation of Britair's staff.

514. As the Japanese invasion fleet began its approach to Java, from bases in and around Borneo, on 25th February, energetic action was essential for collecting and organising the necessary personnel and material, and for establishing the contacts with the various Dutch, American and British authorities with whom Britair was now to deal.

515. During the following days encouraging messages were received from the Prime Minister, the Secretary of State for Air, and from the Chief of the Air Staff, emphasising the importance of every day which could be gained by resistance in Java. These were promulgated.

FORCES AVAILABLE AND DUTCH PLAN FOR DEFENCE OF JAVA.

516. Before proceeding further with the narrative of events it is advisable to give a brief description of the outstanding topographical and climatic features of Java, of the Dutch naval, army and air resources, and of the Dutch plan of defence.

Topography and Weather.

517. Java is approximately 650 miles long with an average width of 80 miles. Its northern coast, the one most exposed to Japanese attack, affords innumerable landing beaches throughout its length. The western end is dominated by aerodromes in South Sumatra. Highly developed road and rail communications cover the Island, the main arterial lines of which run east to west: these are exposed at many points throughout their

length to attack by landings on the northern coast. An outstanding feature of the island is its mountainous southern coast, parallel to which run a series of mountainous massifs along the centre of the island. During the season under consideration, S.W. winds pile up tropical thunderstorms on them from midday until far into the night. Whilst these are raging, aircraft based on aerodromes in the southern (mountainous) half of the island are, for the most part, seriously handicapped by them.

Squadrons based on aerodromes along the northern coastal strip are, on the other hand, not so severely handicapped: although heavy cloud and rain occur throughout the afternoon and night, aircraft can effectively operate at all hours. Mornings are usually bright and cloudless. Aerodromes in the northern coastal strip are, however, sited not far from exposed landing beaches. Their occupation was, therefore, not unattended by risk.

Naval, Army and Air Resources.
High Command.

518. Bandoeng, in central western Java, was the wartime seat of the Dutch Government, and of Naval and Military Headquarters. The latter was known as A.H.K. (The Dutch have no separate air force—their navy and army having their own air contingents.)

The High Dutch Commanders were:—

Governor-General of N.E.I.—Jonkheer Dr. A. W. L. Tjardo van Starkenborgh Stachouwer.

C.-in-C. Royal N.E.I. Navy—Admiral Helfrich.

C.-in-C. Royal N.E.I. Army—Lt.-Gen. ter Poorten.

Navy.

519. A Combined Allied Fleet was based on Sourabaya, with a subsidiary base at Batavia. It consisted of 8 cruisers (3 British, 2 Australian, 1 American, 2 Dutch), 11 destroyers (5 British, 4 American and 2 Dutch) some Dutch submarines and other auxiliary craft, and was commanded by Vice Admiral C. E. L. Helfrich, Royal Netherlands Navy, as Commander of Naval Forces. He had assumed command on the 11th February.

Army.

520. (*a*) The Dutch had approximately 25,000 regular troops, made up of four regiments of infantry (native) with artillery, garrison and ancillary units. They had a few obsolete A.F.V.'s, having been unable to obtain modern tanks from the Allies. Units had been heavily depleted of white personnel for various reasons, from a proportion of one white to five native to a proportion of one to about forty. An attempt to re-arm and to re-organise on modern lines had failed because modern armaments were unobtainable for the new units which had been formed for handling them.

(*b*) In addition there was a Home Guard of about 40,000. They were static in role, and necessarily poorly armed and trained. Those in west Java were reported to be the best, particularly those in the vicinity of Soebang near Kalidjati aerodrome (eventually to be occupied by British bombers) where there were about 1,000 men with twelve armoured cars.

(*c*) To the Dutch Army was added a small British force under the direction of Major-General H. D. W. Sitwell. It consisted of a squadron of light tanks, two Australian infantry battalions (one a machine-gun unit without its machine guns) and a number of small administrative units. The whole was organised hastily into a mobile striking force for operation in western Java, and was under the command of Brigadier A. S. Blackburn, V.C. (Australian Imperial Forces). To it were added later an American Field Battalion much under strength, and a contingent of 450 R.A.F. airmen hastily armed and trained as infantry under Wing Commander Alexander. It was called " Blackforce ". It co-operated closely with the Dutch troops (under the command of General Schilling) located in western Java for the defence of the Batavia area.

(*d*) Certain British A.A. batteries were concentrated on aerodrome defence in Western Java as follows:—

Tjililitan—12 Bofors guns soon after 15th February. Also one battalion Australian Infantry relieved on 25th February by 15th Heavy A.A. Battery armed as infantry. The former were relieved from aerodrome defence duties because they were required as part of " Blackforce ".

Kalidjati—10 Bofors guns soon after 15th February. Also some Dutch Infantry relieved on night 28th February/1st March by 12th Heavy A.A. Battery hastily armed as infantry. The former were wanted for service with the Dutch field army.

Thus there were no Heavy A.A. guns for the defence of these aerodromes. The few available on the island were wanted at more vulnerable places, including the Naval base at Sourabaya.

Air Forces.

521. (*a*) The Dutch had about 5 Bomber, 3 Fighter and 2 Observation Squadrons in Java, most of which were much depleted as the result of protracted operations in the north. Serviceability of aircraft was low. They and their administrative units operated under Dutch control decentralised from Bandoeng.

(*b*) There were 12 to 15 American heavy bombers (believed to be B.17's) and a few fighters (P.40's). Whole serviceability was low. These were located under American control in east and central Java.

(*c*) There was also a mixed Dutch, American and British Reconnaissance Group based in Java for seaward reconnaissance, which operated under a Dutch Commander. No. 205 (F.B.) Squadron formed part of it.

(*d*) To this force was to be added the British Air Contingent under Westgroup, alias Britair, whose re-organisation has already been described.

During the time that Abdair remained in Java, all the above air formations acted under its direction, control of the first two being exercised through the Dutch A.O.C., General van Oyen. When Abdair left Java, the latter took command of them all.

Strategy.

522. An invasion of Java was considered most likely to approach down the east or west sides of Borneo, or both. The Dutch High Command feared simultaneous landings at both

ends of the islands, near Sourabaya in the east and in the Sunda Straits on the west: this was the most difficult form of attack to parry, and it was to be expected that the enemy would adopt it. A landing in central Java was not thought to be likely. The Dutch defence plan was laid accordingly.

Dutch Plan.

523. This was:—

(a) To watch, by means of air reconnaissance, as far northwards as possible on both sides of Borneo, and the whole of the Java Sea—this being undertaken by the Reconnaissance Group. Submarines supplemented this watch.

(b) An invasion was to be opposed as far out to sea as possible by air action: all bomber and reconnaissance aircraft were to be used for the purpose when occasion arose.

(c) A Combined Allied Naval Striking Force of 5 cruisers and 9 destroyers was based at Sourabaya and would engage the main threat when it appeared.

(d) Finally, should the enemy land, he was to be resisted on the beaches at certain points only. Suitable landing beaches were so numerous that only a few of the most obvious could be defended. Elsewhere the plan was to keep troops in local reserve and to counter-attack landings with them, the Army falling back if necessary on to previously prepared positions covered by demolitions.

(e) As a successful invasion was all too probable it was decided that there should be two centres for a final stand, a decision which was enforced by a shortage of troops and by the great length of the island. The two chosen centres were Malang Plateau in the east and Bandoeng volcanic plateau in the west.

APPROACH OF ENEMY CONVOYS.

524. On the 25th February air reconnaissance on the east side of Borneo reported that shipping, which had been collecting for some time past in ports in the Macassar Straits, was forming up at Balikpapan, evidently in preparation for putting to sea. The invasion of Java was imminent.

525. On 26th February a convoy of more than 50 ships and transports, accompanied by a strong naval escort, was located in the southern end of the Macassar Straits steaming south.

526. On the 27th February it was again located, now in the Java Sea, on a course and speed which would bring it to the north coast, westward of Sourabaya, at midnight 27th/28th February.

527. The Allied Fleet put to sea and fought an engagement with the escort of heavy cruisers and destroyers during the night 27th/28th February. The latter was very superior in numbers, weight and metal. The Allied ships were either sunk or disabled. This gallant action afforded the land defences another 24 hours' grace, because the transports turned away northwards at the beginning of the sea action and steamed towards Borneo during the night.

528. On 28th February the transports were again located steaming south at a speed which would bring them to landing beaches westward of Sourabaya about midnight 28th February/1st March.

529. Meanwhile the situation on the west side of Borneo had not developed so clearly. Invasion forces had been suspected in the Natuna or Anambas Islands and possibly at Muntok on Banka Island. Reconnaissances had failed up to 26th February to clarify the situation.

530. On the 27th February, a small convoy with escort was located about 50 miles south of the southern tip of Banka Island steaming slowly on a north-easterly course. This might or might not be part of an invading convoy "marking time" before turning south towards Western Java.

531. On the 28th February about noon, the situation became clearer. A convoy was sighted at that hour approximately 100 miles north-east of Batavia steaming on an easterly course at high speed. It consisted of 11 transports; one cruiser and three destroyers were disposed some 30 miles to the south and on a parallel course. Another and larger convoy was located to the north-west: strength, course and speed were not clear. Both were at a distance which would make landings possible at two points in western Java about midnight.

532. The moon was one day past full, wind off shore, ideal conditions for landing. All was evidently set for simultaneous landings—one at the eastern end of Java probably just west of Sourabaya, and two at the western end of Java in the vicinity of Batavia.

BOMBER OPERATIONS 27TH FEBRUARY TO 1ST MARCH.

533. To revert to the night of 27th/28th February. It then appeared that the major threat would develop against Eastern Java. It was therefore decided to move No. 36 (T.B.) Squadron (9 Vildebeestes and 1 Albacore) at once to Madioen (near Sourabaya) to co-operate with American B.17's in resisting it. No. 36 (T.B.) Squadron arrived at Madioen on the afternoon of 28th February, and during the night 28th February/1st March carried out two sorties per aircraft, the first against transports, the second against landing barges. The first attack entailed a long search because reconnaissance information with which they had been briefed proved inaccurate. A convoy of 28 ships was eventually found 5 miles off the Coast, north of Rembang, some 100 miles west of Sourabaya. Most pilots claimed hits on transports, and execution amongst the barges. Subsequent reports received from American H.Q. in the area stated that attacks had been most successful and that No. 36 (T.B.) Squadron had sunk 8 ships—the Americans themselves claimed 7 others: but it has not been possible to verify this seemingly very high rate of success. On completion of the second attack, No. 36 (T.B.) Squadron returned direct to Tjikampek, less three aircraft which had been shot down including that of the C.O., Squadron Leader J. T. Wilkins, an outstanding leader who was unfortunately killed. Each aircrew of this squadron, operating from a strange aerodrome, thus carried out two night attacks in 24 hours, involving over 15 hours, flying in open cockpits—an excellent achievement.

534. In the meantime, during 28th February, the threat to western Java had crystallised

(para. 531) in the form of two Japanese convoys approaching from the north with the evident intention of landing on both sides of Batavia.

535. All available Blenheims and Hudsons were directed against that convoy, which was approaching the beaches eastward of Batavia. During the night 28th February/1st March, 26 Blenheim and 6 Hudson sorties were carried out against it from Kalidjati. The first attack found it 50 miles north of Eritanwetan, a point on the north coast about 80 miles east of Batavia: it was steaming south at high speed. Weather conditions were bad and by this time only one narrow strip was serviceable on the aerodrome. Not all pilots were sufficiently well trained to cope with the conditions: of those that were, some carried out three sorties each. There is no doubt that attacks were successful and were pressed home from a low level with great determination. When attacks began, 15 ships formed the convoy: early on 1st March, only 7 were seen anchored off the disembarkation beach which was at Eritanwetan. At least three, perhaps more of its ships, are believed to have been sunk. The larger figure may be an exaggeration, as other Japanese ships were seen on 1st March lying off some miles N.W. of the main convoy.

536. Disembarkation at Eritanwetan began at about 0100 hours on 1st March and continued during the rest of the night, despite a number of attacks by our aircraft while landing was in progress.

537. During the night, the Dutch A.O.C., General van Oyen, advised Air Vice Marshal Maltby that the bomber force at Kalidjati would be more favourably placed for opposing the enemy landings if it remained there than if it were withdrawn to aerodromes further inland amongst the hills. He did not appear to have much confidence in the weak detachments of Dutch Home Guard which were watching the river crossings on the roads leading from the enemy landing at Eritanwetan to Kalidjati, a distance of more than 50 kilometres. But he placed more reliance upon the Home Guard of about 1,000 strong, supported by about 10 armoured cars, which were located at Soebang, a town on the road leading to the aerodrome. He also stated that a Dutch battalion at Cheribon had been ordered to counter-attack the landing. The British A.O.C., therefore, decided to keep the bomber force at Kalidjati where it was best placed to resist the enemy.

538. It was decided to "stand down" bombers at Kalidjati at the end of the night's operation because:—

(a) Crews had been on a stretch for 36 hours, standing by during much of the night of 27th-28th February, and then operating at high pressure throughout late afternoon and the night of 28th February-1st March. They had worked splendidly, had achieved good results, and needed a rest.

(b) There would be plenty for the crews to do at high pressure for several days to come.

(c) Previous experience had shown that Blenheims and Hudsons were particularly vulnerable if employed in the cloudless conditions which prevail during the mornings at this season, because the Japanese normally provided their landings with strong Navy 'O' fighter cover. It was therefore decided to employ bombers daily during the late afternoons (when cloud cover could be relied upon) and under cover of darkness, and to use all available fighters, which could look after themselves, to continue the opposition during the cloudless mornings.

539. On completion of the night's work, the Station Commander at Kalidjati, Group Captain Whistondale, was instructed at 0700 hours, 1st March, to disperse his aircraft and to prepare them for further operations later in the day.

Shortly after daybreak the Dutch squadrons withdrew from Kalidjati aerodrome, under General van Oyen's orders as it later transpired, although no information that they were going to do so was given to the A.O.C. or his staff. Nor were the latter kept informed that the Dutch counter attack had failed or that the Dutch defences between the beaches and Kalidjati had not been able to put up the resistance it had been understood they would offer. It is probable that this failure was due to the fact that time had been insufficient for the wheels of co-operation of the recently established staffs (see para. 514) to get run in, and that there was a similar unestablished close touch between the aerodrome and the local Dutch Commander in Soebang. It had a disastrous sequel.

540. About 1030 hours the aerodrome was overrun by Japanese light tanks supported by infantry in lorries—part of the force which had landed at Eritanwetan some hours earlier—and the aerodrome was captured. The whole force of Blenheims, by now reduced to 8 serviceable aircraft, being fully dispersed, was captured. 4 Hudsons which were dispersed on the aerodrome managed to take off under fire of light tanks, which were by now on the aerodrome, and to reach Andir near Bandoeng.

541. Subsequent inquiry made it clear that the aerodrome defence party, a combination of Army and R.A.F. personnel, put up a stout fight and covered the withdrawal of the ground personnel of the squadrons, the majority of the Bofors guns adopting an anti-tank role. It is believed that there are no British survivors of the aerodrome defence party. The Japanese appear to have given no quarter. Later the Japanese testified to the gallant and protracted defence the aerodrome defences put up, and this was supported by the number of bodies, both British and Japanese, which were found near the aerodrome and in the woods around it by the British salvage parties employed by the Japanese after the capitulation of Java. The Dutch aerodrome defence contingent, although it had been relieved during the night by the newly arrived British defence party, remained to assist in the defence. It located posts on the roads leading to the aerodrome on the N., E., and W., the two former of which were overrun by the enemy's armoured vehicles, to deal with which it had no anti-tank weapons. The number of Dutch bodies which were later found on both sides of the roads along which the Japanese attack came, testify to the opposition it put up.

542. It has been impracticable as yet to obtain a clear picture of what exactly happened at Kalidjati. Surviving British witnesses of

consequence are few. Much still remains unsatisfactorily explained. It is hoped that time may reveal the full facts.

543. The captured aerodrome was only a few miles from Tjikampek, the aerodrome on which No. 36 (T.B.) Squadron was also resting after having operated throughout the night (para. 533). The latter aerodrome had no defences whatever and was in considerable danger of being overrun by the same troops which had already captured Kalidjati. The Squadron was, therefore, immediately withdrawn to Andir, and was later moved to Tjikamber in S.W. Java, Group Captain Nicholetts being placed in command of the Station.

FIGHTER OPERATIONS IN BATAVIA AREA—
1ST FEBRUARY TO 3RD MARCH 1942.

Consolidation of Fighter Strength.

544. Before proceeding further it is necessary to turn to earlier operations of the Fighter Force.

545. It will be remembered that Nos. 232 (F) and 605 (F) Squadrons were operating at Tjililitan under a Sector Control (a skeleton of No. 226 (F) Group) whose operations rooms and warning systems were installed in and around Batavia.

546. From 17th to 27th February this force was continually in action in its role of the air defence of Batavia. Normal odds met in air fighting were in the vicinity of 10-1. Its operations were handicapped, particularly during the earlier part of the period, by insufficient warning of approaching enemy aircraft.

547. A Fighter Group H.Q. became redundant by 27th February, its squadrons and overhead controlling organisation being established by that date. The Group Commander, Air Commodore Vincent, and several members of his staff, were ordered on that date by the A.O.C. to leave Java, which they subsequently did by sea.

548. By noon on 28th February the combined strength of the two fighter squadrons was less than that of one. The U.S. aircraft carrier "Langley" had been sunk by the Japanese when bringing in a full load of P.40 fighters, with some of which it had been hoped to re-arm one of the squadrons. Thus the last prospect of keeping two fighter squadrons at reasonable strength had gone. It was decided to retain No. 232 (F) Squadron which, under Squadron Leader Brooker's leadership, volunteered to remain in Java. Vacancies in it were filled from volunteers in No. 605 (F) Squadron. No. 605 Squadron, except the volunteers who could be employed, was withdrawn for evacuation after it had handed over its remaining aircraft to No. 232 (F) Squadron on the afternoon of 28th February.

Fighter Operations 1st—3rd March.

549. In accordance with the decision (para. 538 (c)) not to employ bombers during the cloudless mornings, but to oppose the landings during these hours by means of fighters, instructions were issued to No. 232 (F) Squadron to employ all its Hurricanes throughout the forenoon of 1st March, in co-operation with 10 Dutch Kittyhawks and 6 Buffaloes, in attacking two Japanese landings which had occurred simultaneously during the night in Western Java.

550. One of these landings was that which had been made at Eritanwetan (para. 536). Twelve Hurricanes took part in opposing it, and in doing so encountered intense A.A. fire. They pressed home their attacks at low height, inflicting severe casualties amongst troops in landing craft, and set on fire at least six landing craft and three motor vehicles. Several later attacks against the same targets also produced good results.

551. The other landing in Western Java had occurred simultaneously with the foregoing one, but on the extreme western beaches on either side of Merak in the Sunda Straits. It was in greater strength. The remaining Hurricanes of No. 232 (F) Squadron made several sorties against it during the morning at the request of the Dutch Army: they successfully engaged enemy columns, including cavalry and M.T., advancing along the roads from the landing beaches towards Batavia.

552. After the British bombers had been overrun at Kalidjati the fighters continued their attacks against the landing at Eritanwetan. Shortly after midday they brought to a standstill a cyclist column proceeding westwards towards Batavia. In addition three Japanese flying boats were destroyed on the water.

553. All No. 232 (F) Squadron aircraft suffered damage in varying degree from A.A. fire during these operations, which were all carried out at low level.

554. On 2nd March Tjililitan aerodrome was under constant attack by the enemy, and the squadron was in action all day defending it and carrying out road reconnaissances in western Java for the Dutch Army. The aerodrome was also becoming somewhat exposed to overland attack by Japanese forces which had disembarked at Eritanwetan; these were, by the afternoon, reported to be approaching Poerwokerto and the river crossings thirty miles or so to the north-east of the aerodrome. Withdrawal along the road which passes through those places was already out of the question. Moreover, these places were held by Dutch troops on similar lines to Soebang and the river crossings protecting Kalidjati aerodrome; a repetition of the Kalidjati debacle, involving the only remaining British fighter squadron, was distinctly possible during the night or following morning. The A.O.C. therefore, when visiting the aerodrome on this day, ordered No. 232 (F) Squadron, now 10 Hurricanes, to move back to Andir near Bandoeng, the move of the ground parties and aerodrome defence troops to be completed along the Buitenzorg road by the following day. Group Captain Noble was appointed Station Commander at Andir.

555. In the early morning of 3rd March the squadron returned to Tjililitan from Andir under orders issued by General van Oyen. It was airborne throughout the morning repelling Japanese air attacks. At noon it was finally withdrawn to Andir, en route to which it made a successful attack on Kalidjati aerodrome destroying several enemy aircraft. A running fight took place with Japanese fighters from Kalidjati to Bandoeng.

Withdrawal from Batavia.

556. As the Dutch announced on 3rd March their intention of declaring Batavia an "open" town, the operations and filter rooms, together

with the radar stations in the vicinity, were destroyed, and their staffs were ordered to Bandoeng on the 3rd March.

OPERATIONS BY NO. 205 (F.B.) SQUADRON— 1ST FEBRUARY TO 3RD MARCH.

557. No. 205 (F.B.) Squadron during the whole of its stay in Java operated as a unit of the Allied Reconnaissance Group which was responsible for all seaward reconnaissance throughout the S.W. Pacific Command. This Group, under Dutch Command, took its orders first from Abdair and then, after Abdair left Java, from General van Oyen, the Dutch A.O.C. Britair was responsible for administration only of 205 (F.B.) Squadron.

558. Based on Batavia and Oesthaven, 205 (B) Squadron carried out reconnaissances between Borneo and Sumatra, and also undertook anti-submarine patrols in the Sunda Straits.

559. When the Japanese descended upon the Batavia area on 1st March it was ordered to transfer its base to Tjilitjap, an unserviceable flying boat having to be destroyed when it left. The Squadron operated from Tjilitjap on anti-submarine patrols until 3rd March, by which time it could no longer be usefully employed. The squadron was then ordered out of the island, two boats going to Ceylon and one, with a damaged air-screw, to Australia.

FINAL AIR OPERATIONS—4TH MARCH TO 8TH MARCH 1942.

560. The position on the morning of 4th March was:—

(a) H.Q. Britair—Bandoeng.
(b) No. 1 (GR) Squadron, R.A.A.F., 7 Hudsons (3 serviceable)—Andir.
(c) No. 232 (F) Squadron, 10 Hurricanes (all in dubious condition)—Andir.
(d) No. 36 (T.B.) Squadron, 5 Vildebeestes (4 just serviceable)—Tjikamber.
(e) About 450 armed R.A.F. personnel under Wing Commander Alexander operating as infantry with " Blackforce " in the Buitenzorg area.
(f) About 1,900 unarmed personnel awaiting evacuation near the port of Tjilitjap, and a further 600 at Djojacarta; many other personnel now surplus to squadron requirements were under orders to move to the area as accommodation became available near the port.

561. The Army situation on 4th March was:—

Eastern Java: The enemy had made a successful landing on 1st March west of Sourabaya and was pressing the Dutch forces in two directions—those originally in the Sourabaya district towards the S.E. extremity of the island, and those in central Java westwards towards Poerwokerto.

Western Java: The enemy after landing at Eritanwetan had captured Kalidjati aerodrome, on which strong Japanese fighter forces were by now well established. The enemy had repulsed Dutch attempts on 2nd March to recapture Soebang (from the direction of which the enemy was by now pressing towards Bandoeng) and on 3rd March to recapture Kalidjati aerodrome.

The enemy force, which had landed in the Sunda Straits, had forced the evacuation of Batavia, and the Dutch garrison of extreme western Java was in the Buitenzorg-Soekaboemi vicinity, falling back on the final Bandoeng " stronghold."

562. *No. 36 (T.B.) Squadron* based at Tjikamber attacked Kalidjati aerodrome, now full of enemy aircraft, on the nights of 2nd-3rd and 3rd-4th March. On 4th March it was moved to Tasik Malaja because of reports (subsequently proved to be false) of landings in S.W. Java which threatened the aerodrome, and because the rapid advance, authentic, of the enemy towards Soekaboemi threatened to cut the only road available for withdrawal from it.

563. From Tasik Malaja the squadron continued attacks on Kalidjati during the nights of 4th-5th and 5th-6th March, doing two sorties per aircraft on the former night. Large fires were caused and considerable damage was done.

564. On 6th March, by which date an early capitulation had been forecast by General ter Poorten (See para. 577), two aircraft only remained serviceable, and orders were given for these to be flown north in an endeavour to reach Burma. They left on the 7th March but unfortunately both crashed in Sumatra and the crews were either killed or captured.

565. *No. 1 (G.R.) Squadron, R.A.A.F.,* was ordered to fly its three remaining flyable Hudsons to Australia carrying operational records and as many spare aircrews as possible. The first left on the night 4th-5th, the others on the nights of 5th-6th and 6th-7th—all reaching Australia.

566. *No. 232 (F) Squadron,* now at Andir, was given the role of carrying out periodic offensive sweeps against Kalidjati aerodrome. It was instructed also to take advantage of any particularly favourable targets presented by the Japanese Army attacking Bandoeng from the north. For the latter purpose the squadron established a liaison officer at the Dutch H.Q. responsible for defences on that front.

567. By this time no warning of impending attack could be obtained, and the aerodrome was subjected to almost continuous attack throughout each day. The squadron was repeatedly in action and considerable success was achieved.

568. By the 7th March the squadron was reduced to 5 aircraft. On this day it was transferred to Tasik Malaja, and by the evening only two aircraft remained. These two carried out a tactical road reconnaissance on the morning of the 8th March, and on completion of this they were destroyed under orders from Britair.

Operations of No. 266 (F) Wing.

569. Whilst No. 266 (F) Wing was in action in Sumatra and Java it is believed to have inflicted the following losses on the enemy:—

In Sumatra, 2nd-16th February.

About 8 enemy aircraft were shot down. In co-operation with the bombers of No. 225 (B) Group, very heavy casualties were inflicted on troops in boats and barges moving up the Palembang river on 15th February.

In Java, 17th February–8th March

About 32 enemy aircraft were shot down (8 by No. 605 Squadron and 24 by 232 Squadron) of which about 15 were destroyed during the closing days in Java, 2nd to 8th March. Heavy casualties were also inflicted on enemy troops which landed on Java at Eritanwetan and Merak, particularly the former.

During the combined periods about 60 Hurricanes were lost, chiefly on the ground, by enemy attacks on our inadequately defended aerodromes.

Progress of Evacuation.

570. Throughout the period under review, evacuation of surplus R.A.F. personnel proceeded as fast as shipping permitted. Units were concentrated for evacuation as they became surplus to requirements. They were kept together as units as far as possible, and as shipping accommodation allowed. Towards the end, when accommodation became extremely limited, priority was given to aircrews and technical personnel whose value in other theatres of war was greatest.

571. On the 23rd February, owing to enemy action, Batavia was closed as a port and the R.A.F. Base, Batavia, with its ancillary transit camps, was progressively transferred to Poerwokerto, adjacent to Tjilitjap in South Java, the sole port still open. Tjilitjap was also subjected to air bombardment, and ships leaving it to attack by Japanese light naval forces. On the 27th February, S.S. "City of Manchester" was torpedoed off Tjilitjap whilst approaching the port to assist in the evacuation.

572. From the 1st March onwards, little movement from the port took place. It was finally closed on the 5th March leaving on the island about 2,500 R.A.F. personnel whom it had been intended to evacuate, but for whom no shipping was made available.

573. On 5th and 6th March about 8 seats were allotted to the R.A.F. in Dutch Lodestars; the Dutch had been using these aircraft to evacuate personnel to Australia. The Lodestar service ceased on the 6th March, thus closing the last evacuation channel from Java.

574. A handicap experienced throughout the evacuation of surplus R.A.F. personnel was the difficulty which many of the Dutch had in understanding the necessity for sending out of the island, at a time when it was about to be invaded, personnel who appeared to them to be soldiers: they could not realise that our airmen were untrained as such and were of great value in their real role as airmen for prosecution of the war elsewhere. Informed Dutch authorities appreciated the matter, but many failed to grasp its truth. This is said in no critical spirit; the Dutch outlook is easily understood. But it must be stated in part explanation of the loss in Java of a number of surplus airmen.

575. During the period 18th February onwards, nearly 7,000 R.A.F. personnel were evacuated, leaving a total of about 5,000 in Java.

Events leading up to Surrender of Java.

576. *Conference at Dutch Headquarters.* At 1800 hours on the 5th March, the Dutch Commander-in-Chief, Lieut.-Gen. ter Poorten, convened a conference at his H.Q., A.H.K. in Bandoeng. The Air Officer Commanding, Britair, and the General Officer Commanding British Military Forces in Java, Major-General H. D. W. Sitwell, and representatives of their staffs, were summoned to this conference. It was also attended by senior officers of the Dutch C.-in-C's. staff.

577. At this conference the Dutch Commander-in-Chief stated:—

(a) That the situation was grave: the enemy had practically overcome the northern defences of Bandoeng and was also rapidly closing in from the west.

(b) That morale was at a low ebb and that it was possible Bandoeng might fall very soon. When the enemy penetrated the outer defences, the C.-in-C. did not propose to defend that town, which would be declared an open city. It was full of refugees and could not in any case hold out for long.

(c) That no guerilla warfare was possible or would be attempted by the Dutch. There was great hostility amongst the native population towards the whites, and without the help of the natives guerilla warfare could not possibly be successful. All his staff were emphatically agreed that such warfare was out of the question.

(d) That owing to difficulties of communication, Dutch G.H.Q. could operate only from Bandoeng. They could not exercise control from elsewhere and so would not move from Bandoeng.

(e) That resistance was to be carried on elsewhere under the direction of local commanders if possible and in accordance with an order issued by Queen Wilhelmina of Holland that there should be no surrender to the Japanese. He then added an unexpected rider—that he had instructed his troops to disregard any order that he might subsequently issue to them to cease fighting: they were to disobey it and to go on fighting.

578. In subsequent discussion the Commander-in-Chief was informed by General Sitwell that the British would certainly continue to fight on as long as any of the Dutch did so. When Dutch resistance ceased, then he must reserve to himself the right to decide his actions in accordance with the circumstances at the time. The Commander-in-Chief also informed the A.O.C. that A.H.Q. and Andir aerodrome in Bandoeng must not be defended in the event of the Japanese entering the town. The Commander-in-Chief was then asked to allot an area in the hills in which the British Forces could concentrate and continue resistance. After some discussion he allotted an area near Santoso to the southward of Bandoeng. Its choice appeared to be influenced more as a means of escape to the south coast than as a stronghold; emphasis had to be laid on the fact that it was wanted for the latter purpose.

British move into the Hills.

579. In consequence the G.O.C. and the A.O.C. British Forces went to Santosa at first

fight on the 6th March to reconnoitre. The remainder of A.H.Q. and other Army and R.A.F. personnel in the area of Bandoeng, except the ground party at Andir, were moved to Tasik Malaja the same day.

580. The distribution of Air Force personnel on the 6th March (p.m.) was:—

(a) Tasik Malaja, preparing for defence, with Army Units also ordered there 900
(b) Contingent with " Blackforce " 450
(c) Andir area, aerodrome staff and units 850
(d) Poerwokerto area awaiting evacuation, under Air Commodore Silly's orders 2,500
(e) Detached from units, stragglers, escape parties, etc., in south central Java 400

Total 5,100

581. The orders issued to the various contingents on the 6th March were:—

(a) The Andir contingent was to surrender because Bandoeng was being declared an " open " town, and on that day there was no transport to move them.

(b) The Poerwokerto contingent was to place itself under the orders of the local Dutch Commander, stand fast and surrender. There was no alternative as the men were unarmed and had very slender rations and other resources. They would have been an embarrassment to a final stand in the hills, yet would have had to share its hardships and any retribution which might be meted out. They were therefore less likely to come to harm if they were not associated with further resistance.

(c) The Tasik Malaja contingent was to defend to the last the aerodrome area, where the G.O.C. and A.O.C. would rejoin them if a better place for continuing the fight was not found.

582. Reconnaissance of the Santosa area on 6th March drew a blank. Not only was the terrain unsuited for defence by a small force, but the local Dutch had no defence plan, obviously did not want fighting to occur there, and were only too ready to assist the British to the coast.

583. As the result of a suggestion from General Schilling, who was most helpful to the British in their wish to continue resistance, the area south of Tjikadjang was reconnoitred on 7th March. It was found more suitable for protracted defence. It was therefore decided to concentrate all army units and all armed R.A.F. personnel in the defence of that area.

584. In conformity with this decision orders were issued to the following to move to the area on 8th March:—

(a) The Andir contingent, for whom transport was now available; and

(b) the Tasik Malaja contingent.

Both of these contingents were armed. In addition, " Blackforce " and all other British Army Units in Java were also ordered to the area. The total combined force was about 8,000 strong.

585. At the same time it was confirmed that the remainder of the personnel, who were unarmed, were to stand fast and surrender. The Dutch G.O.C. of the Poerwokerto area, under whose direction Air Commodore Silly had placed the Poerwokerto contingent in accordance with his instructions, ordered them to move further west because unarmed forces would be an embarrassment in a locality where he intended to resist the Japanese advance. This was done under his arrangements and the contingent arrived at Tasik Malaja on 8th March (p.m.). It had suffered severe casualties owing to its rail convoy having been ambushed en route.

586. On 7th March (p.m.) A.H.K. declared Bandoeng, Tasik Malaja and Garoet " open " towns. This action had been anticipated for Bandoeng but in respect of the other two it came as a complete surprise, and it did not assist the concentration of the British Forces in the hills, which was by now in progress.

587. Early on 8th March moves to the concentration area in the hills began. A combined Army/Air H.Q. was established at Tjikadjang with W/T station alongside to communicate with the Air Ministry, etc.

Order to Surrender received from Dutch H.Q.

588. At about 0900 hours 8th March, a rough translation of a broadcast by the Dutch C.-in-C. was received at British H.Q. at Tjikadjang. It had been promulgated in the name of all the Allied Forces in Java as well as in that of the Dutch. At about 1030 hours it was telephoned through in English by, it is believed, Colonel Gulik the Dutch Air Staff Officer at A.H.K., who had come for the purpose to Garoet at the foot of the hills. It was to the effect that " all organised resistance " in Java had ceased and that troops were to offer no further resistance to the Japanese. Colonel Gulik said that the Dutch C.-in-C. had cancelled his instructions about disregarding surrender orders and that he intended this order to be obeyed. The last was quite unexpected.

589. The A.O.C. received this message and, in the absence of the G.O.C., who was reconnoitring the area and allocating defence positions, he first sent a despatch rider to inform the G.O.C., and then, feeling that further clarification was desirable, went himself to Garoet to make further enquiries.

590. At Garoet the Dutch Resident, Heer Koffman (the District Civil Administrator) who had on the previous day, 7th March, strongly emphasised the difficulties of local supplies and accommodation, and had been apprehensive about the prospects of a " massacre of whites " if guerilla warfare was attempted particularly amongst the difficult natives of the Garoet district, now on 8th March re-emphasised his belief in the dangers of a native rising if fighting in the hills was attempted. He called in other authorities to support his opinion—amongst them the District Regent (Native District Administrator).

591. The A.O.C. rang up A.H.K. and spoke (it is believed) to Colonel Gulik who confirmed that the Dutch C.-in-C. had cancelled his order, and that he intended his latest instruction, namely for fighting to stop, to be obeyed. He said that all Dutch troops were complying. The A.O.C. then telephoned to several other Dutch centres and found this to be so in each instance.

592. Whilst he was so engaged, A.H.K. again rang him up at the Resident's House. The Staff Officer doing so specifically enquired whether the British were going to fight, whether General Sitwell had full control of "Blackforce", and whether the last could be persuaded to stop fighting. To these questions he was given non-commital answers except an assurance that "Blackforce" would definitely obey any orders General Sitwell might issue. The A.O.C. was given a further urgent message from the Dutch C.-in-C., which it is understood was telephoned through from Kalidjati, where at that time the Dutch C.-in-C. was negotiating terms with the Japanese C.-in-C. The message pressed for action to be taken to stop "Blackforce" blowing up any more bridges to cover their withdrawal to the hills, as this action was handicapping the negotiations. It is not known how the information about blowing the bridges south-east of Bandoeng reached the Japanese at Kalidjati many miles to the north. This information made it clear that the Japanese already knew our intention and whither we were withdrawing into the hills.

593. The A.O.C. then returned to Tjikadjang where he met the G.O.C. and Brigadier Blackburn at 1330 hours, when the situation was as follows:—

(a) Troops were arriving in the concentration area, the last being due during the night. They possessed small arms and ammunition and a few Bofors guns, but as had been expected, no mortars, aircraft or artillery. Although personnel were tired and many were poorly clad and kitted, particularly R.A.F. personnel evacuated from Singapore, morale appeared on the whole good.

(b) Administrative arrangements were, however, grave. Only $3\frac{1}{2}$ days' rations had so far accompanied the force. Army convoys had experienced considerable obstruction when collecting stores, and the dump in Bandoeng was reputed to be destroyed (news later to prove false). There might be time to collect some more, but this was not certain. Petrol was limited to what vehicles had in their tanks. The combined British/Australian Field Hospital in Bandoeng could not be moved to the hills because it was already overloaded with patients. Hospitalisation was therefore totally impracticable, and medical supplies limited to those carried by units, which were few and of a first aid nature only. Water was everywhere polluted by reason of native habits, water carts were few and effective sterilization was impracticable. Stomach troubles were already in evidence.

594. Given local co-operation and time these handicaps could have been overcome, but there appeared to be prospect of neither. The Dutch had ceased fighting everywhere and, to say the least, were not being helpful. The natives might, or might not, turn against the whites: warning about them had been received, and in any case they were unlikely to assist. And time had suddenly become unexpectedly short now that the Japanese knew about the movement. Much had still to be done in reorganising, in preparing positions for defence and in solving administrative difficulties. Time was now particularly short for training the R.A.F. contingent, which comprised about one-third of the force, in its new and future role, namely in infantry fighting about which it knew nothing, particularly of jungle fighting. Indeed, many A.A. gunners recently rearmed as infantry were in little better case.

595. Yet something might have been done but for the quandary in which the British had now been placed by reason of the Dutch C.-in-C's. broadcast (para. 588). This had been promulgated on behalf of the British forces, as well as on that of the Dutch, but without consultation with the A.O.C. or G.O.C. and although the British intention to continue resistance was well known to the Dutch C.-in-C. The broadcast contained the phrase "All organised resistance having now ceased." This phrase had an important bearing. It was believed to have the effect in international law of placing those who continued to resist outside the protection of belligerent rights and subject to summary execution if captured. The Japanese were likely to exercise their rights in the matter. The problem which now faced the A.O.C. and G.O.C. was how to sort out the force, now in a state of movement over a wide area, into those who were willing to face such consequences and those who were not. The latter could not be given legal orders to continue fighting under such conditions as bandits against their will. The next problem was to reorganise the former into a fighting force well clear of the latter and of the 2,900 unarmed R.A.F. contingent which had by now moved unpleasantly close, although still in the plains. (para. 585). One alternative was to send the "bouches inutiles" down to the plains to surrender and for the former to fight where they were. But Japanese revenge on those who submitted themselves under such circumstances was already too well known to permit adoption of such a course. The other alternative was for the volunteer contingent to move to, and reorganise in, a new defence area. But this was impracticable. The Japanese already occupied Bandoeng, through which led all roads to the hill country in the S.W. extremity of Java, where lay the only other remote spots which might be suitable for guerilla resistance: the country elsewhere was too highly developed and too well served by numerous roads. The Japanese quite clearly knew where the British had withdrawn and their intention, and were free to follow up quickly, as was their habit. It was thus impracticable by now to reorganise anything effective.

596. In these circumstances the A.O.C. and G.O.C., regretfully decided that they must comply with the order to surrender. The order as received from A.H.K. was accordingly issued to units about 1430 hours.

Orders were also issued:—

(a) To destroy arms and warlike stores likely to be of value to the enemy, except a limited amount of transport.

(b) For all ranks to observe absolute reticence if questioned for military information by the enemy.

A signal was sent to the R.A.F. H.Q. Signal Section for transmission to the Air Ministry to the effect that the orders to surrender were being complied with. The reasons why this signal did not get through are contained in paras. 610-613.

Escape Organisation.

597. Col. van der Post, a British officer believed to be of South African Dutch descent, had remained in Java in order to organise a means of escape after the foreseen occupation of the island by the Japanese. He initiated plans for assembly points in the mountains to the southward of Batavia and tried to organise shipping and boats for surreptitious evacuation from the mountainous S.W. coast. Lack of time prevented his plans maturing. Great credit is due to this officer for his activities, attended as they were by considerable personal risk at the hands of the enemy, a fact of which he was well aware. In anticipation of Col. van der Post's plans succeeding, authority was given by the A.O.C. for the issue from public funds of 2,000 guelders to each of twenty individuals to finance the attempt; action was to be taken by Air Commodore Staton to select them.

598. Despite the necessity for abandoning the organised escape scheme, many still wished to make an attempt to leave Java. The hazards involved by the doubtful attitude of the natives and the malarial nature of the country were pointed out; if nevertheless they wished to persevere in their attempts they were assisted by advice and the advance of money from the funds already drawn for the organised escape scheme.

POST-CAPITULATION PERIOD, 8TH—30TH MARCH, 1942.

8th—10th March.

599. By 2200 hours 8th March the concentration in the hills, as ordered, was complete. Distribution of Royal Air Force personnel was:—

In Tjikadjang area, in the hills, armed	2,200 (approx.)
Tasik Malaja and other areas, in the plains, unarmed	2,500 (,,)
Stragglers, detached and in hospital in Bandoeng ...	400 (,,)
	5,100 (,,)

600. On 9th March a second order was received from A.H.K., containing instructions to collect arms, to display white flags and to make surrender arrangements with the nearest Japanese General. The A.O.C. accordingly went to Bandoeng on 9th March and on 10th March contacted Lieut General Maruyama, the Japanese Commander in the Bandoeng district. From him were received instructions about collecting arms and troops and handing them over to Japanese representatives. Accommodation and promises to help with supplies were also obtained. He forbade communication with outside countries, but implied when pressed, without committing himself fully, that prisoners would be treated in accordance with the Geneva Convention of 1929.

11th—12th March.

601. On 11th March the four Senior Officers (British A.O.C. and G.O.C.: Australian—Brigadier Blackburn: American—Col. Searle) were summoned to Garoet. They were conducted during the night from there to Bandoeng. The true reason was not told them. After being kept waiting all night they were assembled at 0730 hours 12th March for the formal signing of the surrender terms before General Maruyama.

602. In front of a number of Japanese witnesses General Maruyama undertook that prisoners would be treated in accordance with the terms of the Geneva Convention of 1929, an undertaking which was recorded in writing.

603. An undertaking that the British and American troops would obey all orders of the Japanese was also included. An attempt to introduce the word "lawful" before the word "orders" was refused by General Maruyama who stated that it was unnecessary since he was giving P.O.W's. the protection of the Geneva Convention, under which no unlawful orders by the Japanese Army would be possible. It was evident that further insistence on the inclusion of the word "lawful" might lose the grant of the terms of the Geneva Convention. It was, therefore, erased from the original Instrument of Surrender, which was retained by General Maruyama.

13th—20th March.

604. Arms and equipment were subsequently surrendered at Garoet, all equipment and weapons in possession of the R.A.F. except some M.T., a number of rifles and bayonets, some field glasses and minor equipment, having been destroyed. Some difficulty arose about this, but an explanation that it was a point of honour with the British not to let arms fall undamaged into the enemy's hands was accepted.

605. On 17th March all senior officers were summoned to Garoet for the first cross-examination by the Japanese Intelligence Staff: a few other officers who happened to be nearby also became involved. So far as the G.O.C. and A.O.C. were concerned, it was conducted entirely correctly. Refusals to answer questions, based on the Geneva Convention of 1929, were generally accepted.

606. Brigadier S. R. Pearson was, however, faced by a firing party but, on still refusing to speak, was pardoned. Pilot Officer R. L. Cicurel was threatened with mutilation but, still refusing, was also pardoned.

607. On 20th March occurred a further deliberate and flagrant violation of the Geneva Convention. General H. D. W. Sitwell, Air Commodore W. E. Staton, Brigadier S. R. Pearson, Group Captain A. G. Bishop and Colonel A. E. Searle, U.S. Army, went to Bandoeng ostensibly to attend a conference. They were, instead, subjected to interrogation for military information by Major Saitu, an Intelligence Staff Officer. The first four were subjected to a month's rigorous imprisonment, which in Japanese hands is truly rigorous, for refusing to answer questions, after which they were released. Whether or not representations made by the Dutch Representative of the International Red Cross in Bandoeng and by Col. E. E. Dunlop, C.O. of the Australian Hospital in Bandoeng, to General Maruyama's H.Q. had any effect in bringing about their release will never be known, but there is reason to believe that this may have been the case, because these events coincided in time.

608. The Japanese subsequently endeavoured to extract information from aircrews of Nos. 232 (F) Squadron and No. 1 (G.R.) Squadron,

R.A.A.F., and from other individual officers and airmen, with almost complete lack of success, in spite of protracted brutal treatment in many cases. They then gave up all attempts to obtain it. More than once, their Intelligence Officers afterwards stated that the British had proved obstinate and stupid about the matter and had suffered accordingly. Credit is due to the above named individuals, who were the first to set an example of compliance with orders to observe complete reticence in spite of brutal treatment, as it is due to those who subsequently followed their lead.

609. The later treatment of P.O.W.'s, with little regard to the terms of the Geneva Convention of 1929 which had been accorded to them on surrendering, is too well known to need further elaboration in this report.

Breakdown of Signals Communication with Air Ministry.

610. The original site chosen on 7th March (p.m.) for the Signals Station near Tjikadjang proved unsuitable for communication with outside countries, screened as it was by the surrounding mountains. It was, therefore, moved about noon 8th March towards the coast, in an attempt to find a suitable position.

611. A technical breakdown, caused by contamination of the Diesel fuel of the T. 1087 high power transmitter, followed by a road accident which damaged the transmitter itself, prevented this set being used again.

612. Attempts were made that evening to come into action with another, a low power, set were at first forbidden by the Commander of the Dutch troops into whose area the station had by now moved, and who by this time, was strictly obeying the terms of surrender. These orders forbade further communication with the outside world. Despite them a T. 1082/R. 1083 Vanette set was brought into action but it failed to establish communication with Melbourne, Ambala or Air Ministry. Several signals were broadcast by this means for three hours on the morning of 9th March in the hope that they would be picked up. Amongst them was the signal which informed the Air Ministry that the orders to surrender were being complied with (para. 596).

It subsequently transpired that these signals were not picked up although at the time the operator believed that they had been.

613. Subsequent attempts by the Signal Station to contact H.Q. and reciprocal attempts by H.Q. to find the new position of the station, failed to establish touch before the staff of this station had to destroy their equipment because:—

(a) It was believed that the last signals for despatch had been sent:
(b) Current reports of the imminent arrival of Japanese troops (subsequently proved to be false) made it necessary to destroy compromising documents and the set itself, to avoid capture in accordance with strict instructions which the A.O.C. had issued a few days previously on the subject of preventing the capture of cyphers and secret equipment.

These were the circumstances in which the report of the final surrender of the British troops in Java was not received by their respective Governments.

REFLECTIONS ON THE FAR EAST CAMPAIGN, DECEMBER, 1941, TO MARCH, 1942.

SCOPE OF REPORT.

614. This paper reports on only one aspect of the campaign of 1941/42 in the Far East— the air aspect. Weaknesses are admitted where they are believed to have existed.

The air aspect was, however, only one of several. An account which discloses its weaknesses, but not those of the other aspects, is liable to leave an impression that the air was primarily responsible for the downfall of Malaya. This was not the case.

615. In order to counteract this tendency it is necessary, therefore, to refer to weaknesses elsewhere which played their part. This is done hereunder in no carping spirit, but in recognition of their causes and of the efforts made by those who endeavoured to overcome them. It is done for one reason only—to counterbalance a one-sided examination and to throw the whole into perspective. Weaknesses lay in many places. Failure in Malaya was a combined failure brought about firstly by the unpreparedness of the Empire as a whole for war, and then, when war came, by the needs of far more vital theatres of war on the other side of the world and in the seas which served them.

WEAKNESSES IN THE FIGHTING SERVICES.

616. In Malaya, the old policy of restricting the defence of Singapore to the immediate vicinity of the Island had been replaced by one of defending the whole of Malaya. In conformity with this policy the Chiefs of Staff had authorised large army and air force increases. In the absence of the Fleet, defence of the Far East was to depend primarily on a mobile air defence. Pending provision of the increased air-strength, the army needed additional interim strength, over and above its ultimate total, to ensure security in the meantime.

617. The Japanese attacked whilst this policy was being implemented. The air force and the army had by then received only a part of the modern equipment and reinforcements which had been estimated to be necessary. The vital and pressing needs of the war in Europe and the Middle East, which had passed through a long and very critical period, had proved of overriding importance. The result was that the forces in the Far East were attacked in positions which could only have been defended if the full strength planned by the Chiefs of Staff had been available.

Mutual Naval and R.A.F. Support.

618. The Air Force in Malaya was not yet in a position to deny the waters off Malaya to a seaborne invasion. It possessed neither the necessary aircraft nor secure aerodromes, and the enemy proved altogether too strong in the air once he had obtained a footing in South Siam and North Malaya.

619. The "Prince of Wales" and "Repulse" were lost in a gallant attempt to help the army and air force in their predicament in North Malaya. The attempt was made in the face of a strong shore-based Japanese Air Force but without the corresponding air support, either carrier-borne or shore-based. Thereafter it was progressively impracticable for the

Navy, other than the lightest units, to remain in Malayan waters, particularly in the absence of such support.

620. The freedom of the seas which the enemy gained by his use of air power both at Pearl Harbour and off the coast of Malaya, was such that he was virtually free thereafter to hit when and where he liked. The consequences to the army and air force dispositions and operations in Malaya were profound. No criticism is levelled; the war against Germany and Italy had stretched our resources as never before. The small forces which were available in the Far East were faced with overwhelming circumstances and were too weak to overcome the advantages which the enemy gained in the first and most vital days of the campaign. In short, neither the Air Force nor the Navy was in a position to support the other.

Mutual Army/Air Support.

621. The enemy army proved to be more effective than had been expected: our army had a number of shortcomings. It is not for this paper to say what they were or to expand upon them: it is appropriate only to say that they existed and that the army, in consequence, was unable to play its part adequately in the provision of secure air bases for our air forces. The root cause was the same, namely the over-riding calls of the war in Europe and the Middle East.

622. When war came, the construction of aerodromes in Malaya had outstripped the provision of air forces to occupy them. But the aerodromes had had to be defended—a factor, amongst others considerably more important, which led to the army adopting a forward policy. The army had insufficient troops for the purpose, particularly in the absence of the additional interim strength it required pending full Air Force expansion. It became widely scattered in trying to meet all its commitments, and was defeated in detail.

623. The R.A.F., although inadequate for the task, had to occupy these forward and ineffectively defended aerodromes. There it suffered severe losses which could not be replaced, and it was driven out.

624. Thereafter the army had to fight in northern and central Malaya without any air support, and to face an enemy whose air support was constant and strong. It was not until the Japanese advance brought the land battle within effective range of aerodromes on Singapore island, that our army could be supported from the air. Even then this support fell far short of the scale demanded by the situation, although it was the maximum available. The enemy's air support remained undiminished. Neither service was in a position to support the other or to fulfil its commitments: both suffered severely in attempting to do both.

Mutual Support between Japanese Forces.

625. The Japanese, on the other hand, had sufficient forces to support one another. Their naval and air forces were adequate to cover the initial landings of their army, and to give its subsequent expeditions virtual freedom of action to strike where and when they liked. Their army was strong enough to hold the countryside as it was overrun, and in particular to defend the aerodromes it captured. Their air forces were able to fill those aerodromes with aircraft, maintain them there at full strength, and from them gain and fully exploit the advantages of air superiority in the land, sea and air battles.

They possessed what we had not—balanced harmony by land, sea and air, their forces in which elements were strong enough to play their respective parts and to support one another fully.

Joint Navy/Army/Air Co-operation.

626. Two lessons emerge from the foregoing factors:—

Firstly, that only by full co-ordination of the fighting services—in strength, organisation and methods of operating—can success be achieved.

Secondly, that the issue of a modern war largely depends on the struggle for secure air bases, which all three fighting services have a joint responsibility for obtaining, defending and maintaining.

That side which is successful, and which denies its opponent the advantage of secure air bases, dominates the whole theatre of war within air striking range. It has then every prospect of success, while its opponent has but little.

THE CIVIL COMMUNITY.
Shortages of Labour and Material.

627. Civil interests and the fighting services competed keenly for labour, M.T., constructional material and equipment, all of which were in short supply (see paras 21 and 24). Before war came it was difficult to obtain access to land for the construction of aerodromes and other installations (see para. 19), particularly if its acquisition affected the production of rubber or tin, which were Malaya's most important contribution to the war in Europe and which her administrators had been enjoined to raise to a maximum.

628. The complicated administrative machinery in Malaya, which comprised numerous states with varying constitutions, was slow to produce results. Speed was further handicapped by the multiplicity of nationalities—Chinese, Malay, Indian and European—who populated Malaya and whose interests and outlook varied widely.

Native Labour.

629. Experience confirmed the unreliability of unenlisted natives employed as domestics, as M.T. drivers and for construction and repairing damage to aerodromes. They disappeared en bloc, as did many native employees of the railways, whenever bombing started or the siren sounded. At critical moments dislocation occurred to the domestic life of R.A.F. stations, and to road and rail movements.

630. It is imperative in these days of air warfare to enlist all native personnel on whom dependence is to be placed in war. If enlisted, and officered by trained leaders, the natives in the Far East proved to be most reliable. This was demonstrated by the R.A.F. Special Technical Corps of enlisted Chinese, Malays and Indians, whose service in Malaya and Java during the war was exemplary.

Outlook in Malaya Towards War.

631. A word on this subject is necessary because it had its effect upon preparation for war in the Far East.

Considerable criticism, much of it unjust, has been levelled against the civil population of Malaya, although, unfortunately, there was justification for much of it. But it must be remembered that Malaya had been enjoined to spare no effort to raise business output to a maximum in support of the war in Europe, particularly of rubber, tin and of dollars for financing foreign exchange. It was thus natural that many in Malaya should have felt that Malaya's best contribution to the war in general lay in this direction—and no one will deny that the response they gave was a great contribution to the war in Europe.

Nevertheless their efforts in this direction had its effect on Malaya's preparations for her own defence, because the calls of the latter could only be met by diverting effort from the former. It must have been most difficult at times for those in responsible positions, in administrative and business circles alike, to hold the correct balance between these diametrically opposed interests.

In short, the calls of the war in Europe had its effect upon the civilian side of preparation for war in Malaya as it had on the fighting services.

632. Despite these difficulties much was done on the civil side towards preparing for war. Yet much remained to be done when war came. Shortages of equipment and, still more important, lack of thorough training resulted in voluntary organisations not being ready, some more some less, when war broke out. Credit is due to those who volunteered to play their part and who, when war overtook them, played it despite many a handicap. But it is unfortunate to have to state that there were appreciable sections of the community, particularly amongst its Asiatic element, which might have been more interested and might have done more towards putting Malaya's defences on a sound footing.

In this respect a belief was widely held that Singapore defences were in reasonably good order, and that war was not imminent in any case. More than one official pronouncement on the subject had the unintentional effect of fostering a false sense of security and of supporting the view that business output came first, despite other official pronouncements which were made with the express object of combating complacency. Again that statement is made in no critical spirit. The former pronouncements were made for very good reasons. But they must be mentioned because of their effect on civilian and service personnel alike. The general atmosphere inevitably affected the latter, who had to live in it from day to day. Only the more informed and imaginative of both communities could be expected to foresee the future with accuracy and to remain unaffected. Nevertheless there were many, amongst the civil community as well as in the services, who foresaw the danger and who strove to accelerate readiness for war. To them the greatest credit is due. But despite their efforts the general atmosphere militated against the progress of which they aimed and had a grave effect upon preparations for war.

633. Two lessons were learned:—

Firstly, the most drastic and comprehensive measures are necessary to shake up a community which has long lived in peace into a realisation of the dangers of war and of the need to take timely action to prepare for it. This is particularly true if a community is of such a complex political and economic structure as that which existed in Malaya.

Secondly, the success of the fighting services is largely dependent upon the wholehearted, thoroughly organised and, where necessary, trained support of the civil community.

UNITY OF COMMAND.

634. In the Far East the Higher Direction of War, and of preparation for it, was not unified until the formation, in January, 1942, more than a month after war had broken out, of H.Q. Supreme Command, S.W. Pacific, under General Sir Archibald Wavell.

635. Before this date many and complicated channels of control had existed between Ministries and the Chiefs of Staff in the United Kingdom on the one hand, and, on the other, the Civil Government and Service Commanders in Malaya. They varied in degree. G.H.Q. had operational but not administrative responsibility for the army and the air forces; while in the case of the navy its responsibility was limited to co-operation with the naval C.-in-C. in the Far East. G.H.Q. had no administrative staff, which handicapped its operational staff in appreciating in full detail the true state of affairs in the subordinate commands (para. 103). The situation was further involved by additional channels of communication with the Australian and Dutch Governments, and by varying control of the forces which they contributed to the defence of Malaya.

636. Such complicated machinery is unlikely to work efficiently during times of emergency when speed in preparing for war is paramount. It has even less chance of success in war itself.

637. From this emerges the lesson that responsibility for the defence of any region which is exposed to attack is better centralised in a Higher Command, both during the preparatory period before war and during war itself. This Higher Command should have full operational and administrative authority over the three fighting services, and also strong representation in all matters affecting the civil population.

638. In short, control should be comprehensive, and, in particular, administrative responsibility should not be divorced from operational responsibility. The outcome of war is likely to be in proportion to the observance of this lesson. Unity of Command enhances the prospect of success: lack of it invites failure.

POLITICAL CONSIDERATIONS BEFORE OUTBREAK OF WAR.

Handicap imposed on Air Striking Force.

639. At the outbreak of war, political circumstances, which made it imperative for us to avoid any action that might precipitate war, or that might make us appear to be the aggressors, were partly responsible (but only partly —see paras. 641 and 671) for preventing the small air striking force that was available in Malaya being used in the role for which it had

been primarily trained—to hit the enemy convoys at sea, as far away and as often as possible. The consequence was that the enemy was able to establish himself firmly ashore in a neutral country before action could be taken against his convoys.

Operation Matador.

640. The political factor was also partly responsible for preventing the initiation of the planned British advance into Siam. The consequences were far-reaching: those affecting the Air Force were immediate. The enemy was able to establish his squadrons in strength in Siam within easy striking distance of our virtually defenceless aerodromes in northern Malaya. Many of our aircraft were thus destroyed with little accomplished, and our squadrons were driven out. Thereafter they were unable to give air support to the army in its battles in northern and central Malaya.

641. In passing, it is legitimate to reflect that had the reconnaissance into the Gulf of Siam been greater on 6th December after the Japanese convoys had been sighted, and on 7th December (paras. 150-169 and 671), and had the object of the Japanese expedition been disclosed thereby, it might well have had an influence on the decision to initiate operation "Matador", or brought about its cancellation earlier than was the case.

Japanese Action.

642. The Japanese, on the other hand, chose the moment for attack that was most opportune for themselves. In doing so they brushed aside political hindrances—as indeed they had done whenever it suited them during their successive encroachments into the South-Western Pacific.

Lesson.

643. The lesson which emerges is that when the initiative lies in the hands of a prospective enemy, as it did in the Far East, it is highly dangerous to depend upon a plan of defence which may be frustrated by political considerations.

WEAKNESS OF ALLIED INTELLIGENCE.

Under-estimation of Japanese Strength.

644. Put bluntly, the enemy's true value was much under-estimated. Although he was known to possess some good military (the word is used in its widest sense) qualities, conspicuous amongst which was a fanatical valour, it was believed that he would display weaknesses, hitherto undisclosed, when he came face to face with the modern forces of the British Empire and the U.S.A.

645. There is reason to believe, from the experience of those who underwent military interrogation as prisoners-of-war in Japanese hands, that the enemy took deliberate steps in peace-time to mislead her potential enemies into under-estimating her fighting forces. They themselves on the other hand were not deluded about our true value: they were too well informed by a long-established organisation of agents.

Japanese Air Forces.

646. The qualities of the Japanese Air Force came as a complete surprise—in numbers, performance and quality of equipment, training and experience of its personnel, and in its mobility. Its fighters displayed unexpected all-round qualities. They and the Japanese medium bombers had ranges of 1,500 to 1,600 miles which enabled them to operate from bases out of our reach. Their normal operational height was 20,000-24,000 feet where they were immune from any of our A.A. gun defences. Japanese torpedo-bombers proved to be unexpectedly effective.

647. It is difficult to assess the precise air strength the enemy deployed against Malaya. At the time, it was thought that he had 700 first line aircraft based in South-Indo-China, with adequate immediate reserves, as against our 158 obsolete and obsolescent types with practically no reserves.

Japanese Army and Naval Forces.

648. It is not for this paper to explain the extent to which these were under-estimated, except to say that his army proved to be more effective than it was believed to be, and that the Japanese ability to strike so strongly and simultaneously in several directions in the Pacific had not been anticipated.

Need for an Intelligence Corps.

649. It is therefore appropriate to suggest here that our mistakes can only be attributed to lack of an adequate Intelligence organisation. True, a combined services intelligence organisation was in existence for obtaining naval, military and air information throughout the Far East (F.E.C.B.—see para 67) but it was inadequate for the purpose. In the East an Intelligence system of any real value takes years to build up and requires considerable funds at its disposal. That it should be a combined organisation to serve the needs of all the defence Services goes without saying. It is suggested that a specialised Intelligence Corps will be essential in the future: that only by this means can continuity of knowledge, experience and contact be maintained: and that the appointment of individuals, as an incident of their service careers, can no longer be relied upon to fulfil requirements.

WEAKNESS OF JOINT ARMY/AIR FORCE INTEREST.

Army/Air Force relations.

650. There has been much exaggerated talk about the poor relations which existed between the Army and R.A.F. in Malaya. That there was foundation for it in limited quarters is unfortunately true during the time immediately before the arrival of the late Air Vice-Marshal Pulford and Lieut.-General A. E. Percival, who quickly took steps to put matters right. Unfortunately, honestly held differences of opinion about defence matters between their predecessors had led to weaknesses which had not been fully rectified by the time war came. The two chief matters are hereunder (paras. 651 and 652).

Army/Air Support.

651. Organisation of, and training in, air support for the army was in a primitive state of development in both services. There was a marked lack of specialised equipment for the purpose, and there were but few persons in both services who had had appreciable experience in co-operation between air and ground forces, particularly modern experience. The result was

that neither party in Malaya knew much about the technique of co-operating with the other when war came.

Siting of Aerodromes in N. Malaya.

652. Unfortunately the selection of several aerodrome sites in Malaya had been made with insufficient regard to the needs of their tactical defence. Until the middle of 1941, sites had been chosen without sufficient consultation between the army and air force authorities concerned. Sited as they were, in positions tactically difficult to defend, these aerodromes imposed an unnecessary strain on the army in the ultimate event. It is only fair to point out, however, that they were strategically necessary if the R.A.F. was to fulfil its allotted role in the defence of Malaya.

Insecurity of Aerodromes.

653. Our aerodromes, particularly in N. Malaya, were far from being the secure air bases which could properly be occupied in the face of a strong enemy. There were neither the fighter aircraft, nor sufficient A.A. defences, nor an effective warning system to ensure reasonable defence against air attack. The enemy could, and did, destroy our aircraft on the ground in N. Malaya almost at will, and our squadrons were driven out of the aerodromes there within a matter of days.

654. These same aerodromes were invaluable to the enemy. He had the necessary air forces to occupy them as they were captured, and he had the means of defending them from all forms of attack.

655. From this emerges the lesson that aerodromes may be a liability rather than an asset unless there are sufficient forces, both air and ground, available to prevent the enemy capturing and using them. In other words—provision of defences must go hand in hand with aerodrome construction.

WEAKNESSES IN AIR FORCE MATTERS.

Over-centralisation in A.H.Q.

656. A.H.Q. had to deal directly with eight superior and collateral authorities. The area it controlled stretched from Durban to Hong Kong. The majority of its units were located in Malaya. (See Appendices A and C).

657. When war came in 1941 the formations in Burma and the Indian Ocean were transferred to another Command. Nevertheless, A.H.Q. still had to handle a large number of units with many different functions, and to do so simultaneously in a land battle, in seaward operations and in air defence. It had to administer direct the operational units engaged in them as well as a large number of administrative units, many of which were unexpectedly involved in mobile operations for which they were not fully prepared. It had no intervening bomber, coastal or administrative groups to which to decentralise in Malaya.

658. Even if the staff had contained an adequate number of experienced staff officers, such a high degree of centralisation would have been difficult to exercise efficiently. But most of the staff were inexperienced, although they were willing and many were able men. The load had consequently to be carried by a few able and experienced officers whose numbers were quite inadequate to cope with the situation —either before war broke out or after. Here again the war in Europe had its effect: its urgent needs absorbed all but a few experienced officers.

659. These faults demonstrated the weakness of an over-centralised organisation and of a Command which lacks a sufficient percentage of trained staff officers. A Headquarters which suffers from either fault cannot withstand the strain of war.

Allied Air Forces.

660. The British air striking force which was available in the Far East was in numbers far below that which the Chiefs of Staff considered necessary to ensure a reasonable degree of security, even against the calculated Japanese strength which, as already shown, was underestimated.

661. In quality our aircraft were obsolescent or obsolete. Squadrons had not been modernised. Their signals and navigational aids were primitive or out of date. Radar warning was limited to the immediate vicinity of Singapore. Their armament was in some respects poor.

662. Several fighter squadrons had formed shortly before the war broke out and were not adequately trained. Others had recently re-armed and were still unfamiliar with their aircraft. A high proportion of fighter pilots had joined their squadrons straight from F.T.S.'s without O.T.U. training.

All were troubles which would have been put right but for the war in Europe.

Change of Personnel.

663. A sweeping change of personnel by posting and drafting occurred during the summer and autumn of 1941. Those who were relieved had been over-long in the Far East and it was time they went. A high proportion of those who replaced them came straight from training establishments without having had unit experience. No criticism of those responsible is intended: it was assumed that there would be time for them to settle down before war broke out. When war unexpectedly came the Command contained a high percentage of personnel who had much to learn about the application of what they had been taught or about their new duties in service units. Many were new to the tropics. Much credit is due to them for the manner in which they strove to play their part. It is unfortunate that circumstances in Europe had prevented the change being spread over a longer period by being started sooner.

Inadequate Training.

664. Personnel were willing, but the means for training them were inadequate because the demands elsewhere had drained resources. Many courses of instruction were improvised locally, during the summer and autumn preceding the war, to make good short-comings in training of aircrews, administrative and other personnel of all ranks, but they were too late to produce the results required.

665. In particular there were weaknesses in the training of fighter squadrons which had been based on the assumption that the enemy was of poor quality.

666. The imperative necessity for personnel to be fully trained in their duties before they have to face a trained enemy needs no further emphasis.

Reserves.

667. Reserves of aircrews and aircraft were inadequate; even the first casualties could not be fully replaced. Spare parts, for engines, airframes, armament, and M.T. in particular were short. Squadron strengths consequently became abnormally low at the outset and remained so.

The need for adequate reserves in a theatre of war cannot be over-emphasised. Unfortunately it had been impossible to build up reserves in Malaya because supplies had been absorbed in supplying critical theatres in Europe, particularly in the Middle East and Russia.

Morale.

668. As perhaps is liable to happen when a force is confronted by an unexpectedly superior enemy, there was a loss of morale by a small section of the Command in the early days of the war. Trials had been severe, and had come before those concerned had had time to adjust themselves to their unpleasant and unforeseen circumstances. Lack of sufficient experienced officers undoubtedly contributed to the trouble, many of whom were newly commissioned and were not versed in their responsibilities.

Such incidents were few, and should not be exaggerated. But they serve to emphasise the need for giving all ranks that vital training which alone enables inexperienced troops to withstand their first novel shock of war. Such incidents also serve to enhance the credit of those who did maintain their morale, and who did their duty as was expected of them, and they comprised the great bulk of the force.

Mobility.

669. Few units were properly organised for mobile warfare. M.T. was very scarce and there were no transport aircraft. Each move involved appreciable interruption in operations, caused loss of valuable equipment and subsequent reduction of efficiency. The lack of transport aircraft was particularly felt when squadrons had to be transferred from Malaya to Sumatra, and thence later to Java: they suffered considerable loss and disorganisation during the enforced sea passage in the face of the enemy and without naval cover, the provision of which was quite impossible at the time.

670. The lesson was demonstrated that ability to take part in mobile operations, without loss of operational efficiency, is dependent on correct organisation and provision of suitable transport. A liberal scale of air transport is essential in those cases where long distances, sea crossings or other natural obstacles are involved.

INCIDENTS DURING THE CAMPAIGN.

Air Reconnaissance of approaching Japanese Convoy, 7th/8th December.

671. Contact with the Japanese expedition at sea was lost on 6th December and was not regained, except for a few ships sighted on the afternoon of 7th December. Admittedly weather conditions were bad in the Gulf of Siam during this vital period. Nevertheless only a small air reconnaissance effort was made for re-establishing contact. No. 8 (R.A.A.F.) Squadron at Kuantan had to be directed to continue its initial rôle of searching in an area far to the south and eastward of the probable position of the lost Japanese expedition for fear of a still more dangerous but possible attack, namely one directed against southern Malaya where a successful landing, particularly on the Endau/Mersing beaches, would have been very dangerous indeed. It is impossible to resist the inference that reconnaissance dispositions were strongly influenced by a conclusion at the time that the lost Japanese expedition might be proceeding against the Bangkok area of Siam. It is easy to be wise after the event, but the reconnaissance effort which was directed into the Gulf of Siam appears to have been small, bearing in mind its great area and the possible courses open to the Japanese convoys which were known to be in it.

Initial Action at Kota Bahru.

672. Only those who have given insufficient thought to the matter could venture to criticise the station commander at Kota Bahru for not having launched his aircraft to the attack on receipt of the news, at 0030 hours on 8th December, 1941, that ships were lying off the coast. It is equally easy to criticise the A.O.C. for ordering away only a reconnaissance to clear up the situation. But that both were correct in doing as they did, in the circumstances which existed at that particular moment, is beyond doubt. War had not broken out: Pearl Harbour had not been attacked and the U.S.A. was still neutral: there was grave risk that the Japanese might stage a bait in order to induce us to strike the first blow, and by doing so reinforce that section of the American Public which was then strongly opposed to America entering the war, a danger against which all in Malaya had been warned emphatically by G.H.Q. Admittedly 45 minutes were lost before the first air action was taken, but it is merely academic to conjecture what might have happened if it had been taken at once.

Main Japanese Landing at Singora not attacked.

673. It may fairly be asked why the initial Japanese landing at Singora was not attacked on 8th December, as this was the best target for our air striking force. The answer is that it was not realised, until too late, that it was in fact the enemy's main effort, although Singora had long been recognised as the area in which a Japanese expedition against Malaya was likely to be landed. The enemy, moreover, achieved a tactical surprise because our air reconnaissance failed to maintain contact with the main Japanese convoy, which was not found again until landings at Singora were well under way. By the time that the situation was fully realised, all our available aircraft had been launched against the Kota Bahru subsidiary attack. Before their objective could be changed to Singora, our own aerodromes in Northern Malaya were undergoing so heavy a scale of air attack that another effective force for opposing the Singora landing could not be launched from them.

Attempt to Neutralise Enemy Air Bases.

674. As soon as our Squadrons had been driven out of the aerodromes in Northern Malaya, our army was in turn subjected to

heavy air attack. Its A.A. protection was quite inadequate and it had no fighter cover. Our own aircraft were therefore employed in the early stages of the campaign against enemy aerodromes, in an effort to give immediate relief to our troops. This was not successful. The enemy's reserves were sufficient to replace at once the small casualties which our attenuated squadrons could inflict. Moreover, he had the means to repair rapidly the damage our squadrons inflicted on his aerodromes.

675. The lesson was again learnt that little relief can be obtained by attacking the aerodromes of an enemy who has the means for replacing or repairing damage, particularly if such attacks are of little weight.

Reinforcements.

676. The reinforcements which the R.A.F. received arrived too late to save the situation. By the middle of January, when the first few came on the scene, the aerodromes which they had to use in Singapore were already under constant and heavy bombing. Reinforcements which came later had to use aerodromes in Sumatra which were little more than clearances in the jungle, for by this time, namely late January and early February, the enemy was in possession of the whole of the mainland of Malaya, and three out of the four aerodromes on the Island of Singapore were under observed artillery fire.

677. Hurricane reinforcements arrived in batches at intervals, and had to be thrown into the battle against greatly superior numbers and at tactical disadvantage caused by the lack of effective warning or efficient R/T control. The great majority of their pilots had never been in action before, and some had been at sea for as long as three months.

678. About half the bomber reinforcements that were despatched reached Malaya. They arrived in driblets of two and three aircraft at a time—the result of circumstances along a lengthy and insufficiently developed air reinforcement route. They had to be used piecemeal, without their own ground crews, and not as complete units. No time could be allowed for acclimatising and training them in local conditions. Extremes of weather caused navigational difficulties to which crews were strange. Adequate ground and radio aids, to which many were accustomed, were lacking.

679. The very important lessons were demonstrated that reinforcements must, in order to be effective, arrive as complete units, with aircraft, aircrews, specialised equipment, servicing crews and sufficient stocks and reserves. They are merely frittered rapidly away if they arrive piecemeal. They must have adequate bases from which to work, and they gain much if they are given time to obtain experience of local conditions before being engaged in battle. In short, the more orderly and methodical their arrival and their preparation for battle, the greater their chances of success —and vice versa.

Postscript.

The Army in Malaya.

680. I wish to pay a tribute to the help which the R.A.F. received from the army in Malaya. Despite its own acute needs and shortages it gave ungrudging help—in defence of aerodromes at cost to its vulnerable points; in working parties and native labour to repair aerodromes at cost to the construction of military defences; in maintaining signals communications and in many other ways. In particular, thanks are due to Lieutenant-General A. E. Percival for all that he did, in conjunction with the late Air Vice-Marshal Pulford, during the months immediately before war broke out, to re-establish good relations between the two services. Had the latter officer survived I know how strongly he would have expressed these views.

The Royal Navy in Malaya.

681. The R.A.F. owes much to the Royal Navy also. Nothing that was requested was refused if it was available; frequently it was given at cost to itself—working parties for aerodrome repair, for replacing stevedores and labour which had deserted the docks under bombing: facilities in the dockyard workshops, and in many other ways. Thanks are particularly due to the late Rear Admiral Spooner, R.N., who lost his life in attempting to escape with the late Air Vice-Marshal Pulford, and whom the latter would wish to commend to your notice for all that he and his subordinates did for the R.A.F. in Malaya.

The Merchant Navy.

682. Much credit is due to the Merchant Navy. It rendered the R.A.F. devoted service in bringing into Singapore reinforcements and supplies at a critical time, in transferring units to the N.E.I., and in evacuating several thousands of personnel from Singapore and later from the N.E.I. This work was done at great hazard in waters exposed to surface, submarine and air attack. A number of ships and seamen were lost in the doing of it. I wish to record our deep appreciation to the masters and crews who did so much for us at such cost to themselves.

Civilians in Malaya.

683. A tribute is also due to the civilians, men and women, who put themselves and their means at the disposal of the R.A.F. Of them there were many—nurses, business men, clerical staffs, tradesmen, welfare workers, contributors of material and money, and others. Their assistance and good-will were invaluable at a most difficult time. To them the R.A.F. owes a real debt of gratitude.

The Dutch in the Far East.

684. It must be remembered that the Dutch pinned their faith to collective Allied resistance in the Far East, and that they lost part of their Air Force and of their Navy to the common cause before the Japanese reached Java at all. When their hopes of successful resistance disappeared, and only a small British force remained to replace the forces the Dutch themselves had sacrificed, their isolated position came home forcibly to them.

685. Moreover, everything that the Dutch community possessed was in the N.E.I. Towards the end it was obvious to them that the whole of it, including their families, must inevitably fall into the hands of the Japanese. They had already experienced incidents of

Japanese savagery in Borneo. They were consequently reluctant to continue guerilla resistance in Java in the circumstances in which they finally found themselves. It was only then, when the British wanted to go on fighting after the general capitulation in Java, that differences arose as to the best line to pursue.

686. Nevertheless, I want to express my thanks to the Dutch. Their wish to help was unbounded. They fulfilled their planned undertakings to the full. Special recognition is due to those of them who, as a result lost their lives in Malaya's defence. When arrangements had to be made to transfer the R.A.F. to the N.E.I., their Army, Air Force and Civil Administration placed everything at our disposal. As a community the Dutch refused the British nothing—labour, materials, money and help of every kind were ungrudgingly given—frequently at considerable sacrifice. The devotion of their doctors and nurses to our sick and wounded was outstanding. The Royal Air Force owes a debt of gratitude to these people.

Recommendations for meritorious service.

687. I have already reported to the appropriate branch of the Air Ministry the names of those whose services were particularly meritorious, and whom I recommend for honours, awards and mention in despatches. But I want to bring to your notice here the units mentioned hereunder, and also to name a few individuals who rendered particularly meritorious service but who, I regret to report, are no longer alive.

Air Vice-Marshal C. W. Pulford, C.B., O.B.E., A.F.C.

688. This officer, despite ill health, worked unceasingly and uncomplainingly to overcome the many difficulties with which he was faced when preparing his Command for war and after hostilities had broken out. He never flinched from meeting an overwhelming situation with very inadequate means. No man could have striven more wholeheartedly to carry a burden which was far beyond one man's capacity. All his decisions were reached with complete disregard for self and entirely in the interests of what he felt to be his duty according to the situation and to his instructions.

689. He refused to leave Singapore himself until all his men had been evacuated. He lost his life in a last-minute attempt to follow his Command to the N.E.I. (see para. 394). His selfless devotion to duty and his loyalty to all those around him, both senior and junior, were an inspiration to all.

Personnel of the R.A.F. Far East Command.

690. I am confident that the late Air Vice-Marshal Pulford would wish me to place on record the praiseworthy manner in which the personnel, of all ranks, under his Command carried out their duties. I know how deeply he appreciated the loyal support they gave him.

Aircrews.

691. The aircrews of our squadrons, of the Royal Air Force, Royal Australian Air Force and Royal New Zealand Air Force alike, consistently met the calls that were made upon them despite the enemy's great superiority in numbers and equipment, especially in the matter of fighters. Their own aircraft, on the other hand, were many of them obsolete and old, and were difficult to maintain owing to technical shortages and poor facilities for overhaul work. Their aerodromes possessed little protection against air attack, sometimes none at all. They flew long distances by night over jungle-clad country in the face of violent tropical thunderstorms with the help of only rudimentary navigational aids; towards the end with none at all. It is difficult to overstate the cumulative effect of the hazards which they faced. They deserve the very greatest praise for the way in which they consistently carried out their missions despite these hazards and despite casualties.

692. At the risk of selecting examples which may prove invidious to other units, against whom no reflection is intended, I would particularly mention the following:—

Fighter Defences of Singapore.

693. Credit is due to the spirited leadership of the late Group Captain E. B. Rice, Fighter Defence Commander of Singapore, and of the late Wing Commander R. A. Chignell, his Chief Air Staff Officer. Both were outstanding in their selfless devotion to duty. They were primarily responsible for the good morale which the small fighter force at Kallang maintained throughout the campaign in the face of a numerous and better armed enemy. The steadiness of the ground personnel of this fighter station is also worthy of mention.

No. 4 Photographic Reconnaissance Unit.

694. This flight, flying unarmed and unarmoured Buffaloes, unfailingly carried out their photographic missions deep into enemy territory dominated by a very superior enemy fighter force. Its service throughout the Malayan campaign was most valuable.

No. 232 (F) Squadron.

695. This unit, under the leadership of the late Squadron Leader R. E. P. Brooker D.S.O., D.F.C., who volunteered to take command at a critical moment, was in constant action from the time it arrived in Singapore in mid-January 1942 until fighting ceased in Java. It inflicted severe casualties on the enemy in the air, in landing craft and on the ground. It volunteered to remain in Java as the last fighter squadron. Great credit is due to all ranks of a magnificent squadron, drawn as they were from the ranks of several different fighter units.

Nos. 36 and 100 (TB) Squadrons.

696. These two squadrons attacked the enemy landing at Endau on 26th January, 1942, covered as it was by numerous Zero fighters, whereas their own fighter escort was unavoidably small. They pressed home their attacks on their obsolete Vildebeeste torpedo-bombers regardless of casualties, amongst whom I regret to report were lost the Commanding Officers of both squadrons, the late Squadron Leaders R. F. C. Markham and I. T. B. Rowland. After being reorganised into a composite squadron in Java, and after having patched up their old aircraft, they again pressed home attacks against the enemy convoys which were invading that island, this time at night, again suffering casualties and the loss of their squadron commander, the late Squadron Leader J. T. Wilkins. Such gallant conduct speaks for itself.

No. 84 (B) Squadron.

697. This unit arrived as a reinforcement much strung out after a long flight from the Middle East. Its crews set a fine example of throwing themselves into the fight at once under many handicaps. Particular credit is due to the Commanding Officer, the late Wing Commander J. R. Jeudwine D.S.O., O.B.E., D.F.C., whose leadership and courage were a great inspiration to others. He led a small party which escaped from Java in an open boat across the 1000 mile crossing of the Timor Sea to Australia, a typical example of his spirit.

M.V.A.F.

698. At a critical time of the fighting in Southern Malaya, a number of successful reconnaissances were carried out by this unit to locate bodies of our troops who had been cut off by the enemy, and to locate the enemy's infiltrating forces. These reconnaissances were performed in unarmed Moth aircraft (originally the property of Malaya's flying clubs) at tree top height over a battle field dominated by Japanese Zero fighters. Their value was great to the Army, then closely engaged with the enemy. Pre-eminent in this work was the late Flight Lieutenant Henry Dane, M.V.A.F., whose qualities as a leader and a man were a byword amongst those who knew him. His example was largely responsible for the excellent work done throughout by the M.V.A.F.

Technical Personnel.

699. A word of recognition is due to the Technical Personnel of the Command.

700. Before war broke out they handled great quantities of stores and equipment which arrived in Malaya greatly in excess of the new stations' power, and that of the Command's backward maintenance organisation, to absorb them. Many aircraft were erected and rapidly passed into commission and many others were overhauled during the period of the Command's expansion.

701. During the war itself, technical personnel worked untiringly in most difficult circumstances. Aircraft and equipment had to be dispersed as a protection against bombing, mostly to improvised dispersal points in rubber plantations or scrub. There they were erected, overhauled and serviced with little or no protection against tropical downpours.

702. An example of such work was the erection of the first 50 Hurricanes which arrived in Singapore in mid January 1942; it was a particularly fine feat. Within a few days all were ready to take the air, the first in under 48 hours: during that time they had been unloaded in crates at the docks, conveyed many miles by road to scattered hide-outs in rubber plantations, and there rapidly erected despite tropical rain, blackout conditions at night and a great shortage of specialised tools.

703. It would be invidious to select any particular unit for special mention. Suffice it to say that most meritorious technical work of all kinds was performed by units throughout the command at all stages of the operations in Malaya and the N.E.I. under very severe conditions. Not least of these handicaps was an almost complete breakdown of the backward maintenance organisation of the command which was brought about by circumstances that first overloaded and then disrupted it.

704. I will mention only one name, that of the late Wing Commander E. B. Steedman, whose unflagging efforts did much to inspire others to overcome their difficulties. He subsequently lost his life as a prisoner of war for refusing, it is believed, to divulge technical information about Spitfires. His spirit remained unbroken to the end.

Personnel in the N.E.I.

705. Those who landed in unavoidable disorganisation in the N.E.I. were required to reorganise into a fighting force within a few days with very limited resources indeed. I wish to express my gratitude to them for the very loyal manner in which they gave their best services, in particular to our squadrons who had to face a well organised enemy in overwhelming numbers. Their behaviour is particularly creditable, coming as it did after many reverses, and was in the best tradition of the Service.

Finally, I am indebted to all those who, at the end, were willing, despite shortage of arms, lack of training, and lack of most essentials, to fight in the hills in a form of warfare about which they knew nothing, namely in infantry warfare and in the jungle at that, and to do so against an enemy whom they knew to be well-equipped and highly trained in this form of fighting. That they were unable to put their willingness to the test was no fault of theirs. I wish to place on record my gratitude for the loyal response they gave to the call made upon them. Their conduct deserves the highest praise.

SUMMARY.

706. One can summarise in a few words the reason for the initial reverses in the Far East.

707. We lost the first round there because we, as an Empire, were not prepared for war on the scale necessary for the purpose. When war broke out in Europe it absorbed the Empire's resources to such an extent that only a fraction of the strength could be deployed which had been calculated to be necessary for withstanding Japanese aggression in Malaya—navy, army, air force and civil organisation alike being much below the required mark. When Japan attacked she proved to be even more formidable than had been expected, the result being that she swamped our underdeveloped defences before they could be supported.

708. Mistakes undoubtedly occurred, as they always do in war when the unexpected happens on the scale that it did in the Far East. But credit should be given to those on the spot who did their best to take the first brunt of the enemy's overwhelming strength with inadequate means, and who gained thereby the necessary time for other forces to be collected to prevent his further advance towards Australia and India.

P. C. MALTBY,
Air Vice-Marshal.

London,
26th July, 1947.

APPENDIX "A".

To Report on R.A.F. Operations in Malaya and N.E.I., 1941-2.

SITUATION AT R.A.F. STATIONS IN MALAYA—8TH DECEMBER, 1941.

Location	(a) Peace Scale of Accommodation (b) Concentration Scale of Accommodation	Runways	State of Accommodation	Defences (a) Aircraft shelters (b) A.A. Guns (c) Troops	Bombs (Approx. weight)
NORTH-WEST MALAYA					
Alor Star	(a) 1 B Squadron	Hard 1—1,400 yds.	1 Squadron.	(a) Yes. (b) 4—3" guns. (c) 1 Coy. Infantry (Bahawalpur).	250 tons.
Butterworth	(a) 1 GR Squadron.	Hard 1—1,600 yds., being extended to 2,000 yds. 2nd in hand.	Hutted. 2 Squadrons. Occupied.	(a) Yes. Incomplete. (b) None until 10.12.41. Then 8 Bofors. (c) Bahawalput Inf. Btn. (less 2 Coys.).	250 tons.
Jabi	(b) 1 B Squadron	Hard 1,400 yds. Graded but not surfaced.	1 Squadron only, just commenced.	(a) — (b) — (c) —	Nil.
Kuala Ketil	Satellite for *Sungei Patani*.	Tarmac 1,400 yds.	Guard Room; Petrol, oil and bomb stores.	(a) Nil. (b) Nil. (c) 1 Coy. Bahawalpur Inf.	Nil.
Lubok Kiap	(a) 1 B Squadron	Hard: 1—1,600 yds. 1—1,200 yds. partly graded.	Hutted—2 Squadrons nearing completion. Partly occupied.	(a) — (b) Nil. (c) Nil.	Nil.
Malakoff	Satellite for *Lubok Kiap*.	1,600 yds. Grading not complete.	No buildings completed.	Nil.	Nil.
Panang	Civil Airfield	Limited grass airfield.	Nil.	Nil.	Nil.
Sungei Bakap	Satellite for *Butterworth*.	2,000 yds. (1,400 yds. soled but not surfaced).	No buildings completed.	Nil.	Nil.
Sungei Patani	(a) 2 F Squadrons	Grass: 1—1,400 yds. 1—1,200 yds.	Hutted: 2 Squadrons. Partly occupied.	(a) Not quite finished. (b) 7—3.7" guns. (c) Btn. HQ. and 1 Coy. Indian State Troops.	250 tons.
NORTH-EAST MALAYA					
Gong Kedah	(b) 1 B Squadron	Hard: 1—2,000 yds.	Hutted: 1 Squadron. Ready and partly occupied.	(a) Yes: nearly 100% (b) 2—3". (c) 1 Pltn. Mysore Inf.	250 tons.
Kota Bahru	(a) 1 B Squadron	Grass: 1—1,600 yds. Being extended.	Hutted: 2 Squadrons. Being extended.	(a) Yes: nearly 100% (b) 4—3" guns. (c) 1 Btn. Inf. (less 1 Coy.).	250 tons.
Machang	(b) 1 F Squadron	Hard: 1—1,600 yds. 1—1,200 yds. in hand.	Hutted: 2 Squadrons partly completed.	(a) Just started. (b) Nil. (c) 2 Coys. Mysore Inf.	50 tons.
EAST MALAYA					
Kuantan	(b) 1 B Squadron, 1 GR Squadron.	Grass: 1—1,500 yds. 1—1,200 yds.	Hutted: 2 Squadrons. Complete.	(a) In hand. (b) Nil. (c) 3 Coys. 5th Sikhs.	100 tons.
CENTRAL MALAYA					
Ipoh	(b) 2 B Squadrons	Grass plus tarmac. 1—1,400 yds.	Hutted: 2 Squadrons. Nearly completed. Partly occupied.	(a) Nil. (b) Nil. (c) 1 Coy. Indian State Troops. 1 M.G. Platoon.	Nil.
Sitiawan	Civil Airfield	Grass: 1—1,000 yds. 1—800 yds.	Guard Room only.	(a) Nil. (b) Nil. (c) 1 Coy. (less 1 Pltn.) Indian State Troops.	Nil.
Taiping	Satellite for *Ipoh*	Grass plus tarmac. 1—1,400 yds.	Requisitioned cottages. Hutments in hand.	(a) Yes. (b) Nil. (c) 1 Coy. and 1 M.G. Pltn. Indian State Troops.	Nil.
SOUTH MALAYA					
Batu Pahat	Civil Airfield. Satellite for *Kluang*.	Grass: 1—1,400 yds.	Petrol and oil stores only.	(a) Nil. (b) Nil. (c) 1 Pltn. A.I.F. Inf.	50 tons.
Bekok (Labis)	(a) 1 Squadron	2,000 yds. 1,400 yds. surveyed only.	Nil.	Nil.	Nil.
Kuala Lumpur	Civil Airfield	Grass: 1,315 yds.	Completed. Occupied by 153 M.U.	(a) Nil. (b) Nil. (c) 1 Coy. Indian State Troops. 1 M.G. Pltn.	50 tons.
Kluang	(a) 2 F Squadrons, 1 F Squadron (Dutch).	Grass: 1—1,200 yds. 1—1,600 yds. Hard runway commenced.	Hutted: 2 Squadrons. Nearing completion. Mostly occupied.	(a) In hand. (b) Nil. (c) 1 Btn. (less 1 Coy. and 1 Pltn.) and Johore Military Forces Details.	50 tons.

Location	(a) Peace Scale of Accommodation (b) Concentration Scale of Accommodation	Runways	State of Accommodation	Defences (a) Aircraft Pens (b) A.A. Guns (c) Troops	Bombs (approx. weight)
*SOUTH MALAYA—cont.					
Kahang	(b) 1 GR Squadron.	Grass: 1—1,400 yds. 1—1,300 yds.	Hutted: 2 Squadrons. In hand.	(a) In Hand. (b) Nil. (c) 1 Coy. A.I.F. and Johore Military Forces Details.	50 tons.
Port Swettenham	Civil Airfield	Grass (tarmac in centre). 1—1,000 yds.	Nil.	(a) Nil. (b) Nil. (c) 1 Coy. and 1 MG Pltn. Indian State Troops.	10 tons.
Tebrau		Hard: 1—1,200 yds. 1—2,000 yds. in hand.	1 Squadron only. 2nd Squadron in hand.	(a) In hand. (b) Nil. (c) A.I.F. Infantry in vicinity.	Nil.
SINGAPORE ISLAND					
Kallang	(a) 1 B Squadron	Complete (Civil Airfield). Grass: 1,400 yds.	2 Squadrons	(a) Yes. (b) Under cover of A.A. defences Singapore Town. (c) 1 Coy. Jind. Inf.	10 tons (plus ammunition).
Seletar	(a) 2 TB Squadrons. 1 FB Squadron.	Complete. Grass: 1,400 yds.	3 Squadrons and M.U. Dispersed hutted accommodation partly completed.	(a) Yes. (b) 8 Bofors. Within defended zone of Naval Base A.A. cover. (c) 1 Btn. (less 1 Coy) Kapurtala Inf.	500 tons.
Sembawang	(a) 2 B Squadrons	Grass: 1,380 yds. Construction of 2 hard runways deferred.	2 Squadrons. F.A.A. adjacent.	(a) Yes. (b) Nil. Within defended zone of Naval Base A.A. cover. (c) 1 Coy. Kapurtala Inf.	1,000 tons
Tengah	(a) 3 B Squadrons 2 GR Squadrons (for Borneo).	Grass L.G. 1—1,400 yds. Concrete runway.	2 Squadrons.	(a) Partly finished. (b) Nil. Under extended A.A. cover of Island defences. (c) 1 Btn. Jind. Inf.	750 tons.

NOTE: 1. Aerodrome Operational Equipment—serious shortages existed at Stations in North and Central Malaya, other than Alor Star and Kota Bahru, despite local manufacture and purchase.
2. Adequate stocks of P.O.L. were in position at the Stations where required.

RADAR UNITS—FAR EAST COMMAND—8TH DECEMBER, 1941

Location (1)	Unit No. (2)	Type (3)	Degree of Completion on 8th December, 1941 (4)
MALAYA EAST COAST:			
Kota Bahru		C.O.L.	Not technically complete.
Kota Bahru		T.R.U.	Some construction done.
Kuantan			Under construction.
Endau			Under construction.
Mersing	243	M.R.U.	Operational.
Bukit Chunang	511	C.O.L.	Operational.
Ayer Besar		T.R.U.	Under construction.
MALAYA: WEST COAST			
Penang			Three stations. One partly complete.
Batu Phat		C.O.L.	Partly completed.
Tanjong Kupang	512	C.O.L.	Operational.
MALAYA: JOHORE			
Kota Tinggi	518	C.O.L.	Operational late December, 1941.
Bukit Dinding			Crews on site. Not quite complete } Did not function.
Sungei Kahang			Work nearing completion } Over-run by enemy.
SINGAPORE ISLAND			
Seletar		R.I.M.U.	Operational.
Tuas	243	T.R.U.	Operational 15.1.42.
Tanah Merah Besar	250	M.R.U.	Operational.
Serangoon	308	T.R.U.	Operational December, 1941.
Changi Jail		LD/CHL	Operational December, 1941.
JAVA: WEST			
Batavia (East)		T.R.U.	Operational February, 1942.
Batavia (West)		T.R.U.	Operational February, 1942.
Angelov		Army G.L.	Operational February, 1942.
Lebuan		Army G.L.	Operational February, 1942.
Tanara		Army G.L.	Operational February, 1942.
JAVA: EAST			
Modong		American G.L.	Operational 22.2.42.
Parmakassen		American G.L.	Operational 24.2.42.
Sitoebondo		American G.L.	Operational 24.2.42.

SUPPLEMENT TO THE LONDON GAZETTE, 26 FEBRUARY, 1948

APPENDIX "C"

to Report on R.A.F. Operations in Malaya and N.E.I. 1941-2

R.A.F. ORDER OF BATTLE IN MALAYA
22nd November, 1941
AIR HEADQUARTERS, SINGAPORE

A. OPERATIONAL UNITS

SINGAPORE ISLAND

1. *Seletar* Station Commander—Group Captain H. M. K. Brown.
   - (a) No. 36(TB) Squadron—Commander—Wing Commander R. N. McKern.—12 Vildebeestes.
   - (b) No. 100(TB) Squadron—Commander—Wing Commander A. W. D. Miller.—15 Vildebeestes.
   - (c) No. 205(GR) Squadron—Commander—Wing Commander L. W. Burgess.—3 Catalinas.
   - (d) P. R. Flight—Commander—Squadron Leader C. G. R. Lewis.—2 Buffaloes.
2. *Sembawang* Station Commander—Group Captain J. P. J. McCauley (R.A.A.F.).
   - (a) No. 8(GR) Squadron, R.A.A.F.—Commander—Wing Commander F. N. Wright.—8 Hudson II.
   - (b) No. 21(F) Squadron, R.A.A.F.—Commander—Squadron Leader W. F. Alshorn.—10 Buffaloes.
   - (c) No. 453(F) Squadron—Commander—Squadron Leader W. J. Harper.—12 Buffaloes.
3. *Tengah* Station Commander—Group Captain F. E. Watts.
   - (a) No. 34(B) Squadron—Commander—Wing Commander G. P. Longfield.—17 Blenheim IV.
   - (b) No. 4 A.A.C.U.—Commander—Squadron Leader N. W. Wright.—5 Sharks, 5 Swordfish, 2 Blenheim I.
4. *Kallang* Station Commander—Wing Commander R. A. Chignell.
   - (a) No. 243(F) Squadron—Commander—Wing Commander G. B. M. Bell.—12 Buffaloes.
   - (b) No. 488(F) Squadron—Commander—Squadron Leader W. G. Clouston.—9 Buffaloes.
5. *Fighter Control* in Singapore—Group Captain E. B. Rice.

MAINLAND OF MALAYA

6. *Kota Bahru* Station Commander—Wing Commander C. H. Noble.
   No. 1(GR) Squadron, R.A.A.F.—Commander—Wing Commander R. H. Davis.—7 Hudson II.
7. *Kuantan* Station Commander—Wing Commander R. B. Councell.
   No. 60(B) Squadron—Commander—Wing Commander R. L. Vivian. (From Rangoon for training at Armament Practice Camp)—7 Blenheim I.
8. *Alor Star* Station Commander—Wing Commander R. G. Forbes.
   No. 62(B) Squadron—Commander—Wing Commander J. Duncan.—10 Blenheim I.
9. *Sungei Patani* Station Commander—Squadron Leader F. R. C. Fowle.
   No. 27(NF) Squadron—Commander—Squadron Leader F. R. C. Fowle.—10 Blenheim I.
10. *Butterworth*—Care and Maintenance.—i/c—Flight Lieutenant R. D. I. Scott.
11. *Kluang* Station Commander—Wing Commander W. R. Wills-Sandford.—Improvised O.T.U.
12. *Kuala Lumpur* Norgroup H.Qs.—Wing Commander R. G. Forbes.

NOTES:
- (a) Aircraft shown are those serviceable as at 22nd November, 1941.
- (b) A further 40 Buffaloes were repairable within 14 days.
- (c) For other Squadrons, there was an average of 2 or 3 aircraft per Squadron repairable within 14 days.

B. MAINTENANCE UNITS.

13. No. 151 M.U.	*Seletar*		Group Captain C. T. Walkington.
14. No. 152 M.U.	*Bukit Panjang, Singapore*		Squadron Leader S. G. Aylwin.
15. No. 153 M.U.	*Kuala Lumpur*		Group Captain M. W. C. Ridgway.
16. No. 81 R. & S.U.	*Kluang*		Wing Commander H. Stanton.
17. "Z" M.U.	*Batak Quarry, Singapore*		Flight Lieutenant J. H. Cocks.
18. R.I.M.U.	*Seletar*		Squadron Leader T. C. Carter.

C. MISCELLANEOUS UNITS

19. Radar Units (Four operational)	Wing Commander N. Cave.
20. R.N.Z.A.F. Aerodrome Construction Unit	Squadron Leader Smart.
21. Transit Camp, Singapore	Squadron Leader O. G. Gregson.
22. S.S. "Tung Song"	Pilot Officer G. T. Broadhurst.
23. S.S. "Shenking"	Pilot Officer C. E. Jackson.

LONDON
PRINTED AND PUBLISHED BY HIS MAJESTY'S STATIONERY OFFICE
To be purchased directly from H.M. Stationery Office at the following addresses:
York House, Kingsway, London, W.C.2; 13a Castle Street, Edinburgh, 2;
39-41 King Street, Manchester, 2; 1 St. Andrew's Crescent, Cardiff;
Tower Lane, Bristol, 1; 80 Chichester Street, Belfast
OR THROUGH ANY BOOKSELLER
1948
Price 3s. 0d. net

S.O. Code No. 65-38216

Numb. 38229

SECOND SUPPLEMENT
TO
The London Gazette
Of FRIDAY, the 5th of MARCH, 1948
Published by Authority

Registered as a newspaper

THURSDAY, 11 MARCH, 1948

AIR OPERATIONS IN BURMA AND BAY OF BENGAL, JANUARY 1ST TO MAY 22ND, 1942.

General Headquarters, India,
New Delhi, India,
28th September, 1942.

From:
General Sir Archibald P. Wavell, G.C.B., C.M.G., M.C., A.D.C.

To:
The Chiefs of Staff, London.

I forward herewith two copies of a report by Air-Vice-Marshal D. F. Stevenson on Air operations in Burma and the Bay of Bengal from January 1st (the date on which Air-Vice-Marshal Stevenson assumed command) to May 22nd, 1942 (the date when the forces from Burma completed evacuation to India).

Air-Vice-Marshal Stevenson's report emphasises the remarkable work performed by a small air force in defence of Rangoon, and the difficulties which the Air Force, in common with the Army, suffered through lack of the necessary resources for the defence of Burma. I have already commented on these in my Despatch* of July 1st, 1942, on the Burma operations and I have nothing further to add.

In paragraphs 122 to 131 Air-Vice-Marshal Stevenson refers to certain telegrams addressed to ABDA Command to which he received no reply. From the records of ABDA Command it appears that both these telegrams were received with very considerable delay, and not until instructions had been received transferring Burma back from ABDA Command to the command of the C.-in-C. India. Also Air-Vice-Marshal Stevenson had included the proviso that "failing immediate instructions am putting this plan into action commencing today". By the time, therefore, that these telegrams were received command had passed from ABDA and Air-Vice-Marshal Stevenson had presumably already taken action. No reply was therefore necessary.

Please pass one copy of this report to Air Ministry.

A. P. WAVELL,
General.

Despatch on Air Operations in Burma and the Bay of Bengal covering the period January 1st to May 22nd, 1942, by Air Vice-Marshal D. F. STEVENSON, C.B.E., D.S.O., M.C.

AIR OPERATIONS IN BURMA AND THE BAY OF BENGAL, SPRING, 1942.

INTRODUCTION.

1. The following is a report on the air operations carried out by a small Allied Air Force (American Volunteer Group, Royal Air Force and Indian Air Force) against the Japanese Air Force in Burma and the Bay of Bengal and the subsequent movement of the R.A.F. and I.A.F. to India whence operations against the Japanese continue.

2. In reading this Despatch the following chronological summary may be of assistance:—
1941.
Dec. 9th—War declared by Japan.
Dec. 23rd—Struggle for air superiority over Rangoon commenced.
1942.
Jan. 18th—Mergui and Tavoy evacuated.
Jan. 29th—Japanese thrust through Tenasserim towards Rangoon commenced.
Feb. 15th—Singapore fell.

---
* General Wavell's despatch appears as a supplementary London Gazette No. 38228 of the 11th March, 1948.

Feb. 25th—Last Japanese effort failed to establish air superiority over Rangoon.

March 7th—Demolitions at Rangoon commenced, Rangoon evacuated and General Alexander's Army commenced withdrawal up Prome Road.

March 21st—Japanese inflicted severe reverse on R.A.F. Wing at Magwe.

April 12th—Air operations based in India and Assam in support of the Army commenced.

May 20th—General Alexander's Army withdrawn to India and Air operations against the enemy in Burma continue.

3. On the 12th December, 1941, I was informed by the Air Ministry that I was to take over Command of the Air Forces in Burma. It was proposed to reinforce Burma with a force of 4 Fighter Squadrons, 6 Bomber Squadrons and 1 G.R. Squadron with the object of making a front in Burma should the Japanese campaign against Malaya prove successful. On the 14th December I left England. I met the Commander-in-Chief in India, General Sir Archibald Wavell, and the Air Officer Commanding-in-Chief, Air Marshal Sir Patrick Playfair, on the 28th December in Delhi, where the land and air situations were explained to me.

PART I—AIR SITUATION ON MY ARRIVAL IN BURMA AND CONSEQUENT REQUEST FOR REINFORCEMENT.

4. On the 1st January, 1942, I flew to Rangoon to take over command from Group Captain E. R. Manning. He met me at Mingaladon aerodrome and I proceeded to Group Headquarters. It was necessary to make an appreciation of the air situation as a first step.

5. During the first seven days of January I visited the airfields in Burma, the Station, Squadron and Detachment Commanders and met the Military and Civil Authorities. The Governor of Burma was H.E. Sir Reginald Dorman Smith, G.B.E., the Army in Burma was under the command of Lieutenant-General T. J. Hutton, C.B., M.C., while the Senior Naval Officer at Rangoon was Commodore C. Graham, R.N.—Commodore Burma Coast—who succeeded Capt. J. Hallett, R.N., up to that time N.O.I.C. Rangoon.

6. I found that the air garrison of the country comprised one Squadron of the American Volunteer Group, armed with P.40's at a strength of 21 I.E. based at Mingaladon, and No. 67 R.A.F. Buffalo Squadron of a strength of about 16 aircraft, also based at this Sector Station. Apart from the personnel of 60 Squadron—whose aircraft had been retained in Malaya—and the Communication Flight equipped with aircraft of the Moth type belonging to the Burma Volunteer Air Force, there was at that time no further aircraft in the country. Reinforcing aircraft for the Far East were, however, flying through Burma to Malaya and the Dutch East Indies.

7. The American Volunteer Group, whose primary role was the defence of the Burma Road, under the command of General (then Colonel) C. L. Chennault, was based at Kunming. A Squadron of the A.V.G. had been detached by the Generalissimo Chiang Kai-Shek for the defence of the Port of Rangoon, the only port through which supplies for China could be passed.

8. Control of the R.A.F. in Burma had been somewhat chequered. Up to the 15th December, 1941, it was organised as Burgroup—later 221 Group—under A.O.C. Far East. On the 15th December 1941, this Group was transferred to the command of the C.-in-C. India. Almost immediately after my arrival in Burma 221 Group became Norgroup under the command of General Wavell, Supreme Commander South-Western Pacific Command, though remaining under the C.-in-C. India for administration. After the fall of Java, Norgroup reverted again to the Command of C.-in-C. India.

9. *Airfield lay-out and topography.*—Geographically, Burma is a cul-de-sac with a long tongue of jungle escarpment reaching South from Moulmein to Victoria Point. The Port of Rangoon therefore provided the only means of maintaining an Air Force in Burma, since on the West, Burma is cut off from India by the dense jungle escarpments of the Arakan Yomas, in the North by the Naga Hills, in the East by the Karenni Hills, while the Pegu Yomas, a mountain range, divides the waters of the Sittang and the Irrawaddy which flow almost their entire distance through Burma to Rangoon and the Gulf of Martaban. Thus there were two Valleys in which airfields could be made.

10. The main line of airfields ran from Victoria Point to Moulmein, to Rangoon and Mingaladon and then up the Valley of the Sittang through Toungoo to the East, through Heho and Namsang and up to Lashio in the North, a total distance of some 800 miles. This line of aerodromes faced the enemy air force based in Thailand and because the territory to the East and South East of this line of air bases was mountainous country covered by jungle, through which there were few if any communications, it followed that situated here adequate R.D.F. and telephone warning of the approach of enemy aircraft attempting to attack our bases was impossible. Had Toungoo, Heho and Namsang been situated with their attendant satellites in the Irrawaddy Valley, warning would have been possible and satisfactory as long as the communications in the Sittang Valley remained in our hands. This fact gravely influenced the air campaign.

11. In general, the aerodrome development and construction undertaken on behalf of the Far East Command by the Government in Burma showed an extremely good state of affairs. Indeed, remarkable. All airfields had one or two all-weather runways fit for modern aircraft of the heaviest type. Accommodation for personnel, P.O.L. and bombs and ammunition were available and all-weather satellites were provided for most airfields. Moreover, at this time of the year the paddy fields were hard and, provided labour was available, a runway suitable for fighter or bomber aircraft could be prepared in a week. Thus airfield accommodation for a considerable air force was available in Burma. The weakness of the lay-out, however, was, as already stated, that the four main airfields between Toungoo and Lashio (inclusive) had little or no warning.

12. *State of Warning of Air Attacks.*—It was hoped, however, to develop our telephone system in the Karenni Hills and the Valley of the Salween, and with R.D.F. to bring warning to a state where it would be practicable to base bombers and fighters at all these airfields. We asked India for the necessary equipment and personnel, including a W/T screen of 35 posts.

13. *Airfield Accommodation.*—Consequently, from the point of view of airfields, there was nothing to prevent the reception of considerable reinforcements as long as we held Rangoon.

14. As regards communications, a good telephone system connected all our airfields, while point-to-point wireless was in course of being put in to parent Stations.

15. *Burma Observer Corps.*—I found the Burma Observer Corps under the command of Major Taylor to be, over the area covered, an efficient warning system. As long as main centres of communications and telephone lines were not closely threatened by land attack the system functioned devotedly and satisfactorily.

16. In respect of aerodrome defence I found that outlying Station airfields such as Tavoy and Mergui had garrisons while detachments of troops for land defence and anti-sabotage precautions had been provided at occupied airfields.

17. *A.A. Defence.*—A.A. defence was weak, with an initial strength of but one battery of locally raised troops, whose equipment had only arrived at the end of December, 1941. The later arrival of British and Indian light and heavy batteries rendered it possible to organise a weak scale of defence for the important vital points. Although the A.A. defence did yeoman service they were never in sufficient strength to provide adequate defence for all the vital points and areas—let alone our airfields. Except for a weak airfield detachment the A.A. Artillery was deployed in defence of vital points in Rangoon and of our troops so that some cover against enemy bomb attacks in forward areas could be provided. Later during the withdrawal they provided such close protection as was practicable for our columns. General Alexander has remarked upon this phase of the operations in his Despatch.

18. *L.A.A. Defence.*—For light automatic defence against low-flying aircraft, detachments of the B.A.F., each equipped with 10 to 12 .5 Browning machine guns on A.A. mountings, were stationed at Mingaladon and Zayatkwin and later at Magwe. They were manned entirely by Burmese personnel mainly of the 12th Burma Rifles. Their training was of necessity hurried and their numbers were generally much under strength. Elements of the R.A.F. regiment arrived too late to be of much service although they were in action at Akyab.

19. *Headquarters' Staff.*—The position as regards Headquarters and Station Staffs was not good. Only a nucleus H.Q. staff existed and Mingaladon was the only airfield having a Station H.Q. All other airfields had care and maintenance parties.

20. A store holding unit and an explosives depot existed but there was no repair organisation.

Air Appreciation—Strength of the Air Force in Burma.

21. On the 14th January I completed my appreciation of the situation. Copies of this paper were forwarded to Headquarters, ABDA Command, India and the Air Ministry. The object of this paper was to appreciate the likelihood of a determined attack being made by Japan on Burma and from this to deduce the form and scale of air attack; and thus the fighter force necessary to secure our interests against this attack and the bomber counter-offensive force that would also be necessary. From this it will be noted that I considered that the Japanese Air Force would attempt a "knock-out" blow against Rangoon in the event of the fall of Singapore and that the scale of attack might reach as much as 600 aircraft a day at maximum intensity.

22. *Air Defence.*—The air defence system necessary to secure our interests in Burma against an attack of this kind required that the fighter force should be on a 14 Squadron basis—9 beyond the 5 Squadrons already on programme. (These 5 Squadrons were 67 Squadron and the 4 Squadrons of 267 Wing, which had been allocated in the first place to India for Burma—Trooper's telegram 57543 of 12.12.41.) One of these Squadrons—232 Fighter Squadron—was later diverted from Burma. The fact that the Hurricane force comprised only 3 (which only reached a strength of 2 Squadrons) instead of 4 Squadrons during the initial phase of the campaign, had a serious effect on the operations.

23. Further heavy and light A.A. Artillery was necessary together with a Balloon defence for the City and Port of Rangoon. More R.D.F., G.C.I. and Observer Corps and W/T. posts were required for strengthening the warning system.

24. *Bomber Counter-offensive.*—As regards the Bomber offensive, I considered that the 7 Squadrons on programme would be sufficient (i.e. 60 Squadron already in Burma plus 6 reinforcing Blenheim Squadrons promised from the Middle East—Trooper's telegram 58315 of 16.12.41) until vigorous attacks against Japan from bases in China became necessary.

25. *Security of Sea Communications.*—The 1 Hudson Squadron on programme, provided we had a force of 2 Torpedo Bomber Squadrons to call on at seven days' notice would, I considered—together with the Bomber force—go a long way to secure our line of sea communications from attack by Japanese war vessels in the Northern portion of the Bay of Bengal and the Gulf of Martaban. Apart from one or two patrol craft there were none of H.M. ships present in these waters. Thus the burden of anti-submarine protection, anti-bomber security and the attack of enemy surface vessels in the Bay and the Gulf would rest for some time on the Bomber, G.R. and Fighter aircraft of my command.

26. *Reinforcement requested.*—After agreement in the Joint Commanders' Sub-Committee I accordingly telegraphed ABDA Command and the Air Ministry requesting reinforcements to the scale (A.418 of 18/1) recommended in

my appreciation. On the 20th January ABDA Command (00186 of 20/1) informed the Air Ministry that while the reinforcements asked for were undoubtedly required, it was not known whether they would have to be found from the aircraft allotted to the South Pacific theatre. The full position was asked before agreement to allocate from the total pool was possible—since the need in the Southern Malayan theatre was more immediate than that in Burma.

27. *Proposals for immediate Fighter reinforcement.*—On the 2nd February the Deputy Chief of the Air Staff telegraphed the Air Ministry's proposals for reinforcements for Burma in the immediate future (Webber W.446 of 2/2). This approved an immediate reinforcement of 2 further Hurricane Squadrons, bringing the programme to 6 Hurricane Squadrons in all, but assumed that we should be able to re-equip 67 Squadron with Hurricanes. There were never enough Hurricanes to do that. After the fall of Singapore on February 15th the Chiefs of Staff diverted these 2 Squadrons (30 and 261 Fighter Squadrons) to Ceylon. Thus the total Fighter force actually available throughout the air campaign in Burma was reduced to 3 Hurricane Squadrons.

28. *Initial Equipment of Hurricane Squadrons and the Hurricane Flow.*—The inability adequately to equip our Squadrons with Hurricanes and to maintain them during air action had a serious effect on the air campaign. For example, it led to a situation in which it was only possible for 6 Hurricane II's to take the air against the first heavy attack on our air base at Magwe on 21st March—and except for 1 aircraft every Hurricane II in the Command was present at Magwe on that day.

29. The requirement initially to equip 17, 135 and 136 and to re-equip 67 Squadron was a total of 80 Hurricanes (i.e. 16 I.E. plus 4 I.R. per Squadron). Additionally, a flow of at least 24 per month was necessary to meet minimum war wastage. Therefore over the campaign which lasted three months, the total requirement was at least 128. During this period a considerable number of our Hurricanes due for Burma were diverted to Singapore. Thus of this total requirement only a proportion arrived in Burma and of these a number were obsolescent, worn-out Hurricane I's.

30. *Hurricane Effort.*—Consequently the maximum number of Hurricanes reached in action with the enemy was about 30 Hurricanes, i.e. the equivalent of 2 instead of 4 Squadrons. This strength, moreover, fell away rapidly due to lack of reinforcing aircraft, proper operational facilities and absence of spares, and was on 11th February 15 serviceable Hurricanes, and on 5th March only 6.

31. *Maintenance, Spares and Tool Situation.*—With the exception of 2 Hurricane "pack-ups," no spares for the Hurricane II's arrived in the country before the fall of Rangoon. Consequently, aircraft becoming unserviceable for lack of small parts remained so unless requirements could be provided from the cannibalisation of other unserviceable aircraft. There was a great shortage of tools and rotol kits, while the lack of air screw blades was serious. Moreover, since the equipment of our R.S.Us. and A.S.Ps. did not arrive before the fall of Rangoon, there was no proper organisation for the repair and salvage of aircraft. This factor exercised a considerable influence on our small fighter force and contributed towards the critical shortage of serviceable Hurricanes at Magwe on the 21st March.

32. *A.V.G. Maintenance.*—The A.V.G. Squadron at Rangoon usually had 21 P.40 aircraft of which about 15 would be serviceable. Later in March this figure fell to 10 or 7. But here again the shortage of replacement aircraft, spares, and proper maintenance for the A.V.G. reduced the effort available. The maintenance crews of the A.V.G. did remarkable work in maintaining their aircraft, often under bombing attack. As the A.V.G. were short of trained personnel, R.A.F. personnel were attached to them.

33. *Bombers.*—As regards Bombers, the D.C.A.Ss. telegram indicated that of the 7 Squadrons promised, we should only have 3 in the immediate future. This assumed that Blenheims would be available to equip 60 Squadron. There were never enough Blenheims to do that. The aircraft, personnel and "pack-up" of 113 Squadron arrived in January and early February. The aircraft of 45 Squadron (Blenheim) also arrived but were unaccompanied by personnel or "pack-up." There was a great shortage of tools and spares. Additionally, the R.S.U. and A.S.P. organisation did not arrive in time. Consequently, the average daily bomber effort of the combined Blenheim force stood at about 6 aircraft a day. Thus throughout the campaign, we had the equivalent of one Bomber Squadron available for operations instead of 7.

34. *General Reconnaissance.*—In respect of G.R. aircraft, No. 4 Indian Flight equipped with Wapiti and Audax aircraft arrived in Burma at the end of December. This was later replaced by No. 3 Indian Flight which was armed with an I.E. of 4 Blenheim I's. After the fall of Singapore, 139 Squadron en route for Java was held up in Burma and, equipped with Hudsons commencing at 6 I.E., undertook our G.R. requirements. There were no personnel or Squadron equipment and the Hudsons were maintained by No. 3 and No. 4 Indian Flights.

35. *Army Co-operation.*—2 Squadrons armed with Lysanders, No. 1 Indian A.C. Squadron and No. 28 A.C. Squadron, were made available for operations in Burma.

36. Constant requests were made for the re-equipment of these Squadrons with modern aircraft. The Mohawks, however, were not available and the Lysanders were retained until the Squadrons returned to India.

37. *Indian Air Force.*—The units of the Indian Air Force referred to above proved their war efficiency and gallantry on active service. In addition to a number of tactical reconnaissances, No. 1 Indian Squadron's Lysanders provided 41 bomber sorties against enemy aerodromes and direct support targets. The standard of accuracy achieved in bombing was satisfactory. No Lysanders were shot down by enemy fighters. The G.R. aircraft and, in particular the Blenheim I's of No. 3 Flight, carried out a considerable number of reconnaissances in the Preparis Channel and the Gulf of Martaban.

38. *P.R.U.**—Up to half-way through January there were a few Buffaloes in 67 Squadron with the necessary range. They undertook long reconnaissance. When these were finished we were without long reconnaissance until in the first week of February 2 P.R.U. Hurricanes en route for Java remained in Burma. These were attached to Hurricane Squadrons and met our P.R.U. requirements on an outline basis only.

39. *Balloons.*—An advanced party of 274 Balloon Wing arrived and reconnaissance of sites commenced. The Balloon Wing, which was diverted from Basra, did not arrive in time and, in consequence, balloon defence was not available.

40. *R.D.F. Warning.*—Of the considerable programme of R.D.F. in Burma (3 chain stations 2 C.O.L. and 2 G.C.I.) only one C.O.L. set was in the country, the balance not having arrived. This one was at Moulmein, but its arc of observation there was ineffective. It was therefore moved out for the defence of Rangoon. It was later moved to Magwe. No spares of any kind existed for this set but local arrangements were possible to keep it in action until it left Rangoon. The lack of adequate R.D.F. equipment of the M.R.U. or Chain Station and C.O.L. type exerted a critical influence on the air battle in Burma, since *early warning* of low flying fighter attack and high flying bomber attack was an essential quality of successful air operations. Without such warning an air force inferior in numbers —as ours constantly was—faced annihilation as indeed later happened at Magwe.

41. To summarize under this heading: Of the Air Ministry programme of 6 Fighter Squadrons, 7 Bomber Squadrons, 2 A.C. Squadrons and 1 G.R. Squadron for the defence of Burma—for various reasons— principally that of time—only the mixed equivalent of 2 Fighter Squadrons, 1 Bomber Squadron, 2 A.C. Squadrons and one-third G.R. Squadron joined action with the enemy in the campaign. Of 7 R.D.F. Stations only 1 existed.

42. As regards other units, the following arrived:—

H.Q. 267 (Fighter) Wing.
No. 60 R.S.U.
No. 39 A.S.P.
No. 7 S. and T. Column.
No. 258 A.M.E.S.

The R.S.U. and A.S.P. had no equipment, and the A.M.E.S. arrived so late that it was turned round at Rangoon, sited to defend Akyab, and finally withdrew to Calcutta where for many critical weeks it remained our primary means of warning for oversea attack.

43. Personnel for Group H.Q. Staff gradually arrived and Station H.Qs. Zayatkwin, Toungoo and Magwe were formed.

Co-operation.

44. *Co-operation between the Services.*—As regards the co-operation between the four Services, I have to record that Sir Reginald Dorman Smith, H.E. the Governor, was always ready to assist me with wise advice and his Government was at my service with active and energetic help so long as was practicable.

---
* Photographic Reconnaissance Unit.

45. General Hutton's Headquarters and mine lay close together at Rangoon. I gratefully record the good feeling and understanding he extended to the R.A.F. which made possible close co-operation. We usually met each morning and evening to review the situation and to agree action. At these meetings there was an interchange of important telegrams which had been received or despatched by us. The same cordial relations continued when General Alexander took over on the 5th March.

46. Our co-operation with Commodore Graham, R.N., and earlier Capt. Hallett, R.N., was all that could be desired. Although there were none of H.M. ships present in the close defence of Rangoon and Tenasserim, there were many maritime tasks to be undertaken from day to day by aircraft and the few patrol craft that were available.

47. *Co-operation with A.V.G. and the American Air Force.*—I took the earliest opportunity of meeting Colonel (now Brigadier-General) Chennault in Kunming on the 31st January. At this meeting we discussed and agreed the principles on which the A.V.G. Squadron in Burma would be used in air battle. As always, his primary requirement was good warning. He was quite clear that if I was unable to provide this for the A.V.G. the Squadron would have to be withdrawn to China. I have to record my appreciation of the way in which General Chennault wholeheartedly maintained the Squadron at the highest practicable level in pilots and P.40's from his fast dwindling resources in China. On the 18th January so bad were these that he issued instructions for the Squadron to be withdrawn to China. The Supreme Commander was informed and the Generalissimo, Chiang Kai-Shek, after the representations of the combined Chiefs of Staff, agreed to the retention of the A.V.G. in the defence of Rangoon. Elsewhere I have remarked upon the admirable gallantry and fighting characteristics of the 3 Pursuit Squadrons of the A.V.G.—who fought over Rangoon in turn—an admiration felt not only by the R.A.F. but by the Army also. The co-operation between the A.V.G. and the Hurricanes was close and cordial.

48. When bombing operations in Burma were later carried out from India, a small force of American Army Air Corps long range bombers closely co-operated.

49. *Co-operation with the Chinese.*—I took the first opportunity of visiting the Generalissimo, Chiang Kai-Shek, on the 30th January. The Generalissimo very kindly gave me an interview on this day at which he promised to maintain 1 Squadron of the A.V.G. in the defence of Rangoon as long as this was possible. It is a matter of great regret to the R.A.F. that towards the end of the campaign in Burma it was impracticable on account of shortage of aircraft and the effect of the air battle for the R.A.F. to give adequate support to the Chinese Armies deployed in Burma.

PART II—STRENGTH AND EQUIPMENT OF THE JAPANESE AIR FORCE ENGAGED IN BURMA.

50. *Enemy Air Effort.*—In the opening stages, from the 1st January onwards, P.R.U. reconnaissance and information from other sources put the enemy air force within close

range at 150 plus, bomber and fighters—an effort of (say) 100 plus. They were disposed as follows:—

Prachaub Girikhan	10
Mesoht } Tak }	40+
Bangkok	70+
Lampang } Chiengmai }	30+

Our effort on the 31st January was 35 plus.

51. Reinforcement of the enemy air force took place during February. The strength of the enemy air force which joined action with up rose to 200 plus—an effort of (say) 140 plus —disposed at:—

Bhisanuloke	20+
Bangkok	30+
Nagorn Sawan	20+
Tak and Mesoht	20+
Moulmein	30
Chiengmai	40+
Lampang	40+

Our effort on February 14th was 53 plus.

52. Singapore fell on the 15th February and Rangoon on the 7th March. During this period and up to the 21st March the enemy had again brought up reinforcements, bringing his total air force, based largely on our airfields in the Rangoon area South of Tharrawaddy and Toungoo, to 400 plus—an effort of (say) 260 plus. This was the opinion of the Intelligence staff at Burwing. I considered it on the high side.

53. Some corroboration for this, however, is provided by the fact that intelligence from China and other sources has since indicated the presence in Burma and Thailand of some 14 air regiments of the Japanese Army Air Force. This would comprise a force of 420 to 500 plus aircraft.

Our total effort on March 21st when the Magwe action commenced was 42, of which 14 were at Akyab.

54. *Japanese Fighter equipment.* — Of Japanese fighter equipment there were three types: the Army 97 with a fixed undercarriage; the Army 0.1 (an Army 97 with slightly improved performance and a retractable undercarriage) and the Naval "O" fighter. The former two were manœuvrable with a top speed of 270 miles an hour at 15,000 feet and a climb of 2,500 feet per minute. Armament consisted of 2 machine guns. No self-sealing tanks and no armour were fitted. Similarly, the Navy "O" had neither armour nor self-sealing tanks. It had, however, two 20 millimetre machine guns in addition to 2 machine guns of the Vickers' type. This aircraft was much superior in performance to the Army 97, having a top speed of 315 miles an hour at 10,000 feet, a good climb and good manœuvrability. It was, however, slightly inferior to the P.40 and the Hurricane II, particularly at medium heights. At heights above 20,000 feet the Hurricane II was definitely superior.

55. All three types were convertible to long range fighters with a radius of over 500 miles. Two jettisonable petrol tanks were fitted. Even without such tanks both types were superior in range to our short range interceptor fighter having a radius of action of over 250 miles instead of the 135 miles of the Hurricane II.

56. *Japanese Bomber equipment.*—In respect of bombers, the Army 97 heavy bomber was mostly employed. It had a cruising speed of about 200 miles an hour, a radius of action of 700 miles and a service ceiling of 25,000 feet. With a full load of petrol its lift was $1\frac{1}{2}$ tons of bombs—a formidable bomber. Indeed such range and bomb lift placed great flexibility in the hands of the enemy air command. This type was used for day bombing and occasionally for night bombing operations, and had a crew of 7. No self-sealing tanks nor armour were fitted.

57. Although air fighting frequently took place over scrub or jungle country, 32 crashed enemy fighters and bombers were located on the ground up to the fall of Rangoon. Technical examination of these—although many were burnt or otherwise destroyed beyond recognition—established the quality of equipment about which little was previously known.

58. *Effect of equipment.*—Thus the enemy with their long range fighters were able to reach out over great distances and to destroy our first line aircraft on the ground. There were decisive instances of this kind in the Malayan campaign. Consequently unless airfields, both for bombers and fighters, had a good warning system—i.e. a time warning the equivalent of at least 50 miles—the enemy fighters, achieving surprise, would come in and by deliberate low flying attacks and good shooting could be relied upon to cause great damage to first line aircraft, if not indeed to destroy them all. This form of attack could well be met by a good ground defence, including an adequate number of Bofors (predictor controlled), automatic weapons and P.A.C., but in the campaign in Burma we were extremely weak in these forms of defence.

59. As regards bombers, such range and bomb lift gave the enemy a wide choice in the selection of objectives and great flexibility. If warning of such attacks, particularly those carried out at high altitude, was not adequate, a bomb lift of considerable weight, accurately aimed, could be expected on the objective. Operating in formations of not less than 27, such a pattern of some 27 tons of small light A.P. and H.E. bombs causes great damge to first line aircraft and P.O.L., even though dispersal and anti-blast protection has been provided. If such protection is not provided results may well be decisive and the provision of such protection requires time and labour—two needs that in the hurried movement of war may not be available.

60. *Comparison of Air equipment.*—Thus we were much inferior to the enemy; in the first place in numbers, in the second place in the vital factor of restricted range in our fighters, in the third place range, bomb lift and speed of our bombers. The enemy, on the other hand, suffered the grave disadvantage of not having armour and self-sealing tanks, both characteristics of all our types, while from the point of view of the air battle, the Hurricane II was a much superior fighter to the Army 97, slightly superior to the Naval "O" and quite decisive against such ill-defended bombers as the Army 97. The P.40 was comparable to the Hurricane II, particularly in medium altitude fighting. With its fine clean dive and armament of .5's it could be relied upon to do as much

damage or more to the enemy than the Hurricane II—especially as the air battle usually took place at medium altitude heights below 19,000 feet.

61. As regards bombers, the Blenheim with its power-operated turret gave a good account of itself against enemy fighters—only on one occasion was a Blenheim known to be shot down by enemy fighters. This, however, was mostly due to the provision of fighter escort to bombing raids or careful routeing which would give the bomber formation the best chance of avoiding enemy fighter interception.

62. *Conclusion.*—To sum up on equipment, fighter for fighter we were superior and it was only when heavily outnumbered, and without warning and proper airfield facilities, that the enemy were able to get a decision. Their bombers were " easy meat " for our fighters if interception took place, while our bombers were satisfactory for their task, though light on range and much inferior to the enemy in bomb lift and numbers.

PART III—THE AIR SUPERIORITY BATTLE OVER RANGOON.

63. *Situation.*—From the initial attack carried out by the Japanese air force on the 23rd December against Rangoon and the second attack which followed 48 hours afterwards, in which the bomber formation on both occasions numbered between 70 and 80, with escort of some 30 fighters, it was obvious to me that I had against me at close range a Japanese air force of about 150 plus. A severe set back had been inflicted on the enemy in these two attacks by the P.40's of the A.V.G. and the Buffaloes of 67 Squadron and not less than 36 enemy first-line bombers and fighters were claimed as destroyed on these two days. The situation, therefore, that faced me on my arrival on 1st January was that I must with my small but growing fighter force defend the base facilities at Rangoon, the docks, the convoys arriving and departing and the air bases at Mingaladon and Zayatkwin. If these could be preserved from a damaging scale of day bombing attack, we should be enabled to secure our interests hereabouts and to get in our land and air reinforcements and maintenance. Additionally, I should have to be prepared to aid the Army in any operations they undertook with both fighter and bombing action.

64. *Plan.*—Thus my general plan was to keep my fighter force concentrated in the Rangoon area, to accept such enemy bombing attacks as might be made on any other objectives in Northern Burma, to fight the enemy in the defence of the base and lean forward to hit the enemy wherever and whenever I could with my small but total force.

65. To achieve this, against a numerically superior and constantly growing air force, I must do all I could to reduce the scale of air attack on the Rangoon area, yet still be able to meet attacks on the bases in sufficient force to inflict a high casualty rate proportional to the scale of attack—thus making such attacks in this area abortive and wasteful for the enemy.

66. *Reduction of the scale of attack.*—To reduce the scale of attack I therefore commenced to lean forward with a portion of my fighters, and by using advanced air bases like Moulmein, Tavoy and Mergui to attack enemy aircraft wherever found. Further to weaken him I must spread my bombing action in daylight to widely dispersed but important objectives such as Chiengmai, Mehohngsohn and Chiengrai in the North and in the South his aerodrome and railway communication system running down the Eastern coast of the Malaya Peninsula from Bangkok to Singora. As Singora was a main base for Japanese operations in Malaya this action was especially favourable. Thus I hoped to make him disperse his fighters by forcing protection for these widely separated points and so weaken him in the central sector opposite Rangoon. I gave instructions accordingly on 2nd January.

67. *Offensive Fighter and Bomber action.*—Such enemy airfields as Chiengmai, Mehohngsohn, Lampang, Rahong, Mesoht, Prachuab Girikhan, Jumbhorn and Kanchanburi were searched and attacked if enemy aircraft were present. Later when in enemy hands Moulmein, Mingaladon and Highland Queen were attacked and loss inflicted on the enemy. Hangars, M.T., launches, enemy troops and trains were also attacked.

68. *Results.*—Attacks in pursuance of this policy during the campaign resulted in the P.40's and Hurricanes and Buffaloes claiming 58 enemy bombers and fighters destroyed on the ground. In addition, a large number were damaged but could not be computed. Furthermore, attacks by bombers taking part in the air superiority battle also accounted for a considerable number. Such, however, is the difficulty of assessing results by bomber attack that no claims were made; but from the strike of the bomb lift and its position either amongst or close to enemy aircraft concentrations on the ground, further considerable losses must have been inflicted on enemy first-line aircraft.

69. This was a handsome contribution towards the air superiority battle in Burma and reduced the scale of air attack against Rangoon and our troops.

70. But this form of action was later reduced in effort, since General Chennault at this time was not anxious to undertake offensive operations with the P.40's against ground targets on account of the shortage of equipment. The Buffalo Squadron was reduced to two or three serviceable aircraft with engines too worn out to permit of flying far over jungle country. The Hurricanes with an effective range of 135 miles were unable to reach anything but the closest enemy objectives.

The Air Battle.

71. The air battle over Rangoon lasted from 23rd December, 1941, until 25th February, 1942. The weight of enemy attack was directed intermittently against air bases at Rangoon with the object of destroying our growing fighter force and achieving air superiority over Rangoon to the point where it would be possible for him to undertake unrestricted day bombing operations on a destructive scale.

72. During this period of about 8 weeks, 31 day and night attacks were made—one in great weight. After sustaining serious losses—38 claimed destroyed—in the first 3 attacks terminating on the 4th January, the enemy resorted to night bombing, his scale of effort varying between 1 or 2 heavy bombers up to 16.

73. *Scale of attack brought to rest.*—Between 23rd and 29th January a second attempt was made to overwhelm our small fighter force, the enemy putting in a total of 218 plus— mostly fighters. In the air battle of those 6 days our fighter force claimed a total of some 50 enemy bombers and fighters destroyed. He at once went back to night operations and continued these until his third and last attempt to achieve air superiority over Rangoon on the 24th and 25th February. On those two days, when he put on a scale of attack of 166 bombers and fighters, he sustained the heavy loss of 37 fighters and bombers which were claimed destroyed with 7 probably destroyed. On the second day, the 25th, the P.40's of the A.V.G. claimed no less than 24 aircraft shot down. This terminated the air superiority battle over Rangoon.

74. Such wastage had been inflicted on the enemy that thereafter he never attempted to enter our warning zone round Rangoon until the city was captured and the air bases in his hands.

75. *Result.*—This had a critical influence on the course of our land operations and on the security of our convoys bringing in final reinforcements. These and the demolition of our oil and other interests in the port and the final evacuation by land or sea were completed without interference from enemy bomber or fighter aircraft.

76. Thus up to the last moment the P.40's of the A.V.G. and the Hurricane force were able to provide a state of absolute air superiority over this wide and vital area against a considerable weight of air attack.

77. *Conclusion.*—To sum up on the air superiority battle over Rangoon, for a force of 1 Squadron of P.40's of the A.V.G., a half Squadron of Buffaloes and the equivalent of 2 Squadrons of Hurricanes commencing to arrive in January and continuing to half-way through February, a claimed loss of 130 enemy bombers and fighters was inflicted on the enemy with 61 claimed as probably destroyed—the greater proportion falling to the guns of the A.V.G. Counter-offensive action by our fighters and bombers to reduce the scale of attack had inflicted a loss of not less than 28 enemy aircraft destroyed on the ground, not counting those destroyed by our bombing attacks. Air superiority was achieved over Rangoon and maintained until it fell on 8th March. The A.V.G.—first in the field—fought with ready devotion and resolute gallantry.

Fighting Tactics.

78. In regard to the major tactics employed in the air battle over Rangoon, in the first place the warning was good. As long as the telephone lines remained in our hands the Burma Observer Corps provided this with high war efficiency. The R.D.F. set from Moulmein had been sited in Rangoon looking over the main avenue of enemy approach. Thus enemy plots were accurate and frequent until the line of the Sittang was threatened.

79. *Fighter deployment.*—Fighters in the correct proportion could be deployed against the enemy scale of attack. The A.V.G. and the Hurricanes fought together. The Wing leader system was introduced. The pilots of the A.V.G. had considerable flying experience. Some of the pilots, particularly the leaders in the Hurricane force, had considerable war experience against the G.A.F. Consequently, the force fought well together. In the operations room there were two R/T. sets for the control of the air battle on different frequencies—one for the American fighters and one for the Hurricanes.

80. The general principles of fighting the air battle were agreed between myself, the Wing leader and the Commander of the A.V.G. Pursuit Squadron, and the major tactics employed were those generally exercised in the Western theatre; the single point of difference being that on account of the manoeuvrability of the Japanese fighter (which was the only advantage it had over our aircraft), the best method of attack was a dive, taking advantage of height and the sun, breaking away in a half roll or aileron turn before resuming position to carry out the attack again.

81. Enemy escorted bomber raids were met on first interception, the bombers were attacked with a suitable proportion of our forces while the fighters were attacked and drawn off by the remainder. Against the fighter formations of (say) 40 to 60 plus, which so frequently appeared at height with the object of drawing up our fighters and shooting them down before they got their height, the P.40's and the Hurricanes leant back on Rangoon and delivered their attack when the enemy fighters either lost height, with the object of carrying out a ground attack, or turned for home.

82. Throughout this air action from the 21st January onwards the fighter force in addition to defending Rangoon had also to meet its commitments over the battle area, providing security for our bombers and carrying out ground attacks on enemy concentrations in support of the Army.

83. *Night Fighting.*—As regards night bombing, there were no facilities for night interception. Although the enemy bombers were operating without flame dampers, and at first with navigation lights burning, the P.40's and Buffaloes were not able to intercept. On the arrival of the Hurricanes, trained in night fighting, however, some success was achieved. On the first night an enemy bomber was shot down in flames at 9,000 feet over the aerodrome at Mingaladon, the aircraft, with bombs, exploding close to the airfield. Two further successful night interceptions were made, both enemy aircraft being shot down in flames. With pilots at constant readiness throughout the hours of daylight, however, it was impossible in view of our limited resources to put the Hurricanes up each night.

84. I have no doubt that on moonlight nights —and the enemy bombed on no other—considerable success would have been obtained from the "fighter night" system, had Rangoon held.

85. *Assessment of Fighter Results.*—There was a little feeling in the A.V.G. on the assessment of results. Consequently I held a meeting with the A.V.G. Squadron Commander, and the Wing leader and Squadron Commanders, at which it was agreed that the standard of assessment should be that obtaining in Fighter Command at home. Colonel Chennault was informed. Combat reports by pilots were

initialled by Squadron Commanders. The claim was then admitted. Previous claims by the A.V.G. for aircraft destroyed in the air were agreed at this meeting.

PART IV.—THE LAND BATTLE—AIR OPERATIONS IN SUPPORT OF THE ARMY IN TENASSERIM.

86. *Situation at Sea.*—After the fall of Singapore and Java the Japanese had command of the sea in these waters. There was no effective naval force of ours based in the Bay of Bengal. Thus the littoral of Burma was thereafter under the threat of sea-borne invasion unopposed by the Navy. Consequently, reinforcement by sea of the Japanese Army in Burma took place unmolested after the fall of Rangoon. This was a vital factor in the defence of Burma.

87. The Joint Commanders' Committee telegraphed on several occasions pressing for the provision of ships and material to provide some further local defence at least for the Port of Rangoon and for light craft to support our operations on the coast of the Gulf of Martaban and Tenasserim. No ships were, however, available and none arrived—except those which escorted our convoys.

88. *The Land Situation.*—The land situation, which influenced air operations, has been fully described in the Despatches of Lieutenant-General Hutton and General Alexander. It is not proposed further to remark on this except in so far as it is necessary in order to make clear the influence of air superiority fighting and bombing action on land operations and vice versa. I should, however, make the point that until Mergui and Tavoy fell on January 19th, I assumed the security of Burmese territory from attack by the Japanese Army based in Thailand.

89. *Daily Planning of Close Support Operations.*—Bomber and fighter action in support of the Army during the land campaign up to the fall of Rangoon was decided each evening at a general staff and air staff Conference held at my Headquarters. General Hutton and I met morning and evening to agree joint action and review the changing situation. Subsequently, the programme was adjusted according to the requests made by the 17th (Indian) Division, to which an Air Liaison Officer had been attached. Communication was by W/T and telephone. In general, the system worked satisfactorily.

90. *Tenasserim unsatisfactory for Bombing Operations.*—Close support bombing operations in the close jungle country in Tenasserim and to the East of the River Sittang was an unsatisfactory task for the R.A.F. At the request of the Army we undertook bombing operations in jungle country where it was impossible to see the enemy or to see our troops— indeed difficult to see anything except the tops of the trees. In such circumstances not only is the objective not seen but it is impossible for navigators to pin point their target with accuracy since there are no suitable land marks. The situation is made more difficult still by the knowledge in the mind of the crew that our positions were frequently outflanked by the enemy and therefore there was always the chance that our troops and the enemy were intermingled near the objective. When attempts were made to give bombing objectives in forest clearings, crews often found on arrival that such clearings were overgrown with scrub and consequently the same difficulties arose. As, however, our forward troops in the jungle on the Kawkareik position and during the battle of Tenasserim had reported the enemy's promiscuous bombing of the jungle to be effective and as having considerable moral effect, I did not hesitate, while realising the risk to our own troops of bombing in such densely wooded country, to continue the task in order to do our best to help the Army.

91. Further obvious difficulties arose from the bombing point of view. For example, the enemy was frequently disguised in captured uniforms and native dress. This made recognition difficult. Moreover, they captured some of our transport during actions, while the native bullock carts, launches and private cars left behind and other vehicles were used freely. This made it difficult, and sometimes impossible, for crews to recognise the enemy in the open. Unsatisfactory, therefore, as the "bomb line" method was in such circumstances of cover, communications and moving battle, it had to be adopted as our primary security against the risks of attacking our own troops.

92. *First requirement—Army support.*—The fundamental requirement for the support of the Army in Tenasserim was the maintenance of air superiority over the Port of Rangoon, and the bases and supply depots in this vicinity. This secured the line of communication from serious bombing attack in the form and scale best calculated in this campaign to bring about a critical if not disastrous situation. Consequently I kept my small fighter force concentrated in the defence of Rangoon with the satisfactory results noted above.

93. *Security of Bombers and Fighter support for Army.*—From day to day, however, security for our bombers acting in support of the Army was necessary, since few as they were their destruction by enemy fighter action would have brought about a serious situation. Consequently, each day a careful appreciation of the air situation was made and a portion of the fighter force was thrown off from the Rangoon defence to undertake the Army support role. Indeed, when a particularly favourable ground target presented itself, I accepted the risk of an attack on Rangoon, and all fighters, with what bombers were available, were thrown in to support the land battle. The point here is that where the command of the fighters and bombers is undivided, such operations are practicable and close co-ordination between fighter and bomber operations can be readily achieved.

94. *Bombing of Bangkok.*—The aircraft and crews of 113 Squadron had arrived during the first week in January. The night of their arrival the enemy base at Bangkok, the main enemy base in Thailand, was attacked by 10 low flying Blenheims. 11,000 lbs. of bombs were dropped on the dock area in the centre of the town and fires were started. The Squadron was then withdrawn to Lashio to enable aircraft inspections to be carried out after its long desert flight. Owing to the shortage of tools and spares, it was the 19th January before the Squadron was in action again.

Japanese Offensive begins.
Mergui and Tavoy.

95. On the afternoon of the 18th January the situation at Mergui and Tavoy suddenly deteriorated and I was informed by the B.G.S. Burmarmy that instructions had been issued for the evacuation of Mergui. I accordingly ordered the withdrawal of our refuelling parties from both aerodromes, and as Tavoy was closely invested, an attempt was made to evacuate our detachments by air. On arrival of the aircraft the following morning the aerodrome was, however, in the hands of the enemy. Both detachments were safely evacuated by sea.

Action at Kawkareik.

96. Concurrently with this, reconnaissance beyond the Kawkareik position on the track through Mesoht and Raheng had disclosed some, but not unusual activity. We had also destroyed a number of enemy bombers and fighters on both these forward landing grounds. The country was densely covered with jungle and unsuitable for air action since movement on the ground could not be seen from the air.

97. On the 20th the enemy commenced their attack on the Kawkareik position. Air action in support of the troops holding this position was difficult, since no clear picture of the whereabouts of the enemy or our own troops was possible. Accordingly the enemy forward landing ground and base depots at Mesoht was attacked by bombers and fighters. Two enemy aircraft were destroyed on the aerodrome. Reconnaissance was carried out over this position and towards Tavoy in the South with the object of locating our own troops and the enemy.

98. The withdrawal from the Kawkareik position to Moulmein took place on the 22nd January. On the 21st and 22nd the Blenheims attacked Raheng aerodrome and village and Mesarieng, dropping some 6,000 lbs. of bombs on each raid. Fighter escort was provided with the object of clearing the air for short periods over the Army front and providing support for the bomber operations. Moulmein was bombed by a strong formation of enemy escorted bombers which was intercepted by the escort of our bomber raid on its outward journey—an occasion on which our attempt to choose the right time proved correct. Seven enemy bombers and 9 fighters were destroyed in this air action. Reconnaissance was continued over the battle area.

The Action at Moulmein.

99. On the 30th January the Japanese attacked Moulmein. Our forces were disposed holding Moulmein and the right bank of the Salween from Pa'an, southwards, with one Brigade in the Bilin area. During the period between the 23rd January and the 30th, frequent low visual reconnaissance by fighters was carried out covering the battle area and the coast of Tenasserim together with Japanese lines of communication. Information obtained, however, was sketchy owing to the nature of the country and the fact that, in open country, the enemy lay close in the day time and moved by night. Our available bomber force—an average of about 6 a day—with the aid of such fighters as could be spared from the defence of Rangoon, acted in support of our land forces in the area.

100. Our bombers and fighters attacked enemy aerodromes, M.T., and the enemy line of communication, through Kawkareik, Myawaddy and Mesoht, while the enemy main base at Bangkok was attacked again on the nights of the 24th, 27th and 28th. In these operations a total of 42,100 lbs. of bombs were dropped.

101. Limited escort to our ships coming into Rangoon, anti-submarine patrols and G.R. reconnaissance in the Gulf of Martaban were carried out from day to day.

102. The fighter support which was provided over the Army forward positions each day on a limited scale had accounted for at least 7 aircraft shot down and 13 damaged (to end of January). Our losses were slight.

103. The main objective of the Japanese air force, outside the Rangoon area, during this period, was Moulmein, which was attacked on 7 occasions between the 3rd and 22nd January. The first attack was carried out by 9 fighters, and the later ones by bombers, in pairs by night, and in formations up to 27 in number by day with fighter escorts of up to 15 aircraft, the chief target being the aerodrome.

The Action on the Bilin.

104. From the 30th January until the 15th February, when the 17th Division took up a line on the Bilin River, all available bombers were employed in direct Army support with the maximum number of fighters it was practicable to spare each day. Bombing operations took the form of support to our hard pressed detachments. Attacks were made on river craft on the River Salween and off Moulmein with both bombers and fighters. The fighter effort available was employed in attempting to intercept at this great distance from its base the enemy raids on our forward positions, and providing security for our bombing operations. During this period river craft, batteries, enemy concentrations, troops, landing stages, railway stations and barracks and stores were attacked. A total weight of 70,136 lbs. of bombs were dropped on these objectives with successful results. Most of the bombing was carried out from a low altitude and, in consequence, the results could be seen, provided objectives were not in the jungle. The raids were carried out on such places as Kado, Martaban, Pa'an, Moulmein, Minzi, Heinze, the Thaton Road and the Dunzeik Road. The fighter effort diverted from the Rangoon defence in support of the Army and bombing operations was usually from 6 to 12 per day and sometimes sorties were repeated.

105. During this period the Japanese air force continued night activity against Rangoon on a small scale up to the 8th February. Daylight operations, apart from support of their land forces, comprised 4 attacks on Toungoo aerodrome by raids of 6 to 15 bombers on the 3rd and 4th February. From the 8th to the 12th enemy bombers attacked our troops between Pa'an and Thaton, but generally with little effect.

The Battle of the Sittang.

106. The withdrawal to the Bilin River commenced on the 15th February, and this position was attacked by the Japanese on the 17th. On the 18th the River had been crossed and the

withdrawal to the Sittang position commenced. On the 22nd our forces had reached the right bank of the Sittang.

107. During this period air operations continued at the maximum intensity practicable in support of the Army. The air battle of Rangoon still continued. With the loss of Moulmein we lost our forward air base in this area. Consequently, air operations, both fighter and bomber, were carried out from the main air base at Rangoon. Furthermore, with the capture of territory by the enemy, our warning system in Tenasserim was rapidly rolled up. Now warning of the approach of enemy raids over Tenasserim was impossible. For the defence of Rangoon we still had observer posts to the East of Rangoon, while our R.D.F. set provided some warning. But the interception of enemy aircraft supporting the Japanese Army was impracticable unless such attacks took place when our fighters were present over the line.

108. The Supreme Commander, General Sir Archibald Wavell, visited the command during the last week of January and on the 5th February. At these meetings I explained the air situation and our urgent need for reinforcements, particularly the acceleration of the 2 reinforcing Hurricane Squadrons which had been promised and for an allocation of 24 Hurricanes per month from the flow. As regards bombers, I asked for 2 further reinforcing Blenheim Squadrons, for 16 Blenheims to equip 60 Squadron and for 12 Blenheims a month from ABDA Command flow of maintenance aircraft, and additionally for the Mohawks to re-equip the 2 Lysander Squadrons. General Wavell said that he would do what he could to meet these requirements, but explained the pressing need for air support in Malaya and the N.E.I.

109. During the period 16th to 23rd February the maximum effort that could be put forward by the bombers was 102 sorties, in which 89,992 lbs. of bombs were released in low flying attacks on the enemy, accompanied by machine gun fire. Such objectives as the railway station at Moulmein, troop concentrations and M.T., river traffic and aerodromes were bombed. Direct hits on such things as trains and paddle steamers in Sittang were observed. Fighter support for the Army and the security of our bombers continued.

Air Action on the Bilin-Kyaikto Road.

110. For the first time in the campaign the enemy provided a satisfactory bombing target. On the 21st an enemy column of some 300 or more vehicles, ox-carts and M.T. was reported on the road between Bilin and Kyaikto. The "bomb line" ran North and South through Kyaikto. The total fighter effort of the Rangoon defence and what bombers were at readiness were ordered to attack at 16.25 hours. The first sortie off was one of 12 P.40's at 16.30, closely followed by 8 Hurricanes at 16.40. A total of 38 fighter sorties and 8 Blenheim sorties were engaged in the attack. Direct hits were reported on M.T. and horse transport accompanied by many fires. The village of Kyaikto through which the column was passing was also set on fire. At 16.25 hours the Army Headquarters moved the "bomb line" to a line running North and South 2 miles West of Kyaikto.

111. The enemy had during the afternoon of the 21st penetrated through the village of Kyaikto and moved along the road running North to Kimmun. That afternoon their infantry were seen by the Duke of Wellingtons West of this road (and North of the Kyaikto Road). Their thrust that night at the Sittang Bridge took place up this road when they worked round our left flank and attacked the Bridge in the rear of the 16th and 46th Brigades. It is evident that although our air attack in some weight on the enemy's main column could not have entirely prevented his attack from developing, it must have reduced its scale and intensity.

Alleged bombing of own Troops.

112. There was an incident reported on this day and remarked upon in Army reports. It is alleged that our troops at Mokpalin were bombed and machine gunned by some Blenheim aircraft between 12.00 and 15.00 hours. The facts are that at the request of Army Headquarters 8 Blenheims bombed Kawbein (near Bilin) in the morning and landed back at their base after mid-day. After an exhaustive enquiry, in which I have taken the opinion both of Officers who were in the air and on the ground, I have failed to reach a firm conclusion that our aircraft did, in fact, bomb our own troops at this time and place. The enquiry is complicated by such statements as "the attacking aircraft were identified by roundels on the underside of their wings"—our Blenheims have roundels on the upper side of the wing but certainly not on the underside, and the possibility that the Japanese used captured Blenheims during this campaign should be considered. There is, moreover, a great similarity between the plan silhouette of the Japanese Army 97 medium bomber and the Blenheim, and there must have been a number of enemy bombers flying over Mokpalin about this time because the enemy effort was concentrated on the Sittang area, a few miles to the West of Mokpalin. Since, however, the country between the Rivers Sittang and Bilin is closely covered in jungle, I consider it not improbable that some crews by mistake may have bombed the wrong objective. The enemy effort reached on this day a total of 90 fighters and 12 bombers in action in the Sittang area. The Sittang Bridge was the scene of the heaviest attacks.

113. In the meantime, Mandalay had its first attack by 10 bombers on the 19th.

114. *G.R. Escort for Shipping.*—Such escort to shipping, G.R. reconnaissance and coastwise search in the Gulf of Martaban as was practicable was carried out with the slim effort available. Fighter support against bomber attack was provided once our convoys came in range.

115. To extend the range of our reconnaissance for this purpose and to give forewarning of enemy naval movements in the direction of the Andaman Islands, it was decided to locate reconnaissance aircraft at Port Blair. The construction of a landing ground in the Andaman Islands presented some difficulty, but after considerable work it was possible to construct a runway of 800 yards at Port Blair. The only type of reconnaissance aircraft available that could be operated from such a base was the Lysander and 2 of these aircraft were fitted

with long range tanks and flown over escorted by Hudsons on the 11th February. These aircraft were able to carry out reconnaissance until the Andamans were evacuated.

116. Daily coastal reconnaissance was also carried out throughout the campaign against possible Japanese attempts to attack our Army by landing behind them. Such an attack did happen on one occasion—at night.

117. This concludes the air operations carried out in support of the Army in Tenasserim.

Air Directif—ABDA Command.

118. On the 17th January air directif 0087 from Headquarters, South Western Pacific, was issued to Norgroup. This gave our primary tasks as:—
(a) To secure the arrival of reinforcements and to protect the Port of Rangoon, and
(b) To reduce the scale of air attack on Malaya.

Subsequent directifs received from ABDA Command related more to the battle in the South Western Pacific than to operations that could be based in Burma.

PART V—AIR OPERATIONS COVERING THE EVACUATION OF RANGOON.

119. In February it seemed to me that the troops available in Burma might be unable to hold the country against the form and scale of land attack which the Japanese were exerting through Tenasserim. This question was discussed in the Joint Commanders' Committee on several occasions. Our forward air bases at Mergui and Tavoy had fallen. The Moulmein airfields had been captured. Our warning system East of the Sittang was in enemy hands.

120. At this time the fighter force and bomber squadrons building up in Burma comprised the only Allied air force between the Japanese and India, indeed between the Japanese and Middle East. Had we had time to establish and consolidate the forces in passage from the U.K. and Middle East comprising personnel, equipment, maintenance and warning system, there would have been a good chance of presenting a firm front to the enemy air force with their inferior equipment. On the other hand, if the Port of Rangoon fell into enemy hands in March or April, the flow would stop, and there was a grave possibility that our air force might well be destroyed piece-meal in Burma before it was strong enough and had time to organise. Such a defeat in detail could be of no help to the Army in Burma and would uncover India at a critical time.

121. The question therefore arose as to whether plans should not be prepared to prevent the annihilation of our force by moving our base to India and providing it with strong mixed Wings in Burma maintained from India. Thus dispersed, air support could be given to the Army in Burma and bombers based in India could support operations in Burma. Such action, moreover, would contribute to the air defence of India in her critical and naked sector.

122. On the 12th February I therefore telegraphed ABDA Command, A.677 of 12/2, indicating that in the unlikely event of the loss of Rangoon administrative plans might be necessary to enable fighter equipment to be withdrawn, and requesting a directif as to whether the R.A.F. units should proceed with the Army North towards China or whether they should proceed in the direction of India for the defence of Calcutta and North Eastern India. I pointed out that if they were withdrawn to the North there was no adequate warning on the airfield line Toungoo-Heho-Namsang-Lashio and that the forces there located would therefore be open to fighter attack without warning when on the ground. If withdrawn to Calcutta they could provide a strong defence. R.D.F. cover could be provided. Once separated from Rangoon (the only point through which maintenance for an air force could pass) the force instead of building up to its planned size would become a wasting force. In China there were few or no facilities for operating our bombers and fighters, whereas with lay-back bases in India and forward bases and strong detachments in Northern Burma, bomber and fighter action in support of the Army could continue. No reply was received to this telegram.

123. On 15th February Singapore fell.

124. On the 18th February, General Hutton sent off his telegram 0.749 of 18/2 which indicated the possibility that the enemy might penetrate the line of the Sittang and that the evacuation of Rangoon might become an imminent possibility. Consequently, in view of this serious situation, I telegraphed my appreciation in which I set out the factors of the air situation and indicated three courses of action. Firstly, to remain with the Army during the move northwards towards China. In these circumstances the R.A.F. units would have become a wasting force, since maintenance would be difficult if not impossible once Rangoon had fallen, while heavy losses for small return would be inevitable in the event of reinforced enemy scale of attack. Secondly; to withdraw the air force to India when Rangoon was closely threatened. The final course was to leave a mixed force of 1 Hurricane Squadron, 1 Blenheim Flight and 1 Army Co-operation Flight, withdrawing the remainder of the force to India. No reply was received to this telegram.*

125. On the 20th February instructions were given for the withdrawal of the 17th Division behind the River Sittang. A meeting was held at Government House at which General Hutton and I were present. The G.O.C. stated that he had instructed the Commander of the 17th Division to fall back behind the Sittang. He outlined the steps that he proposed to take in this situation in regard to commencing the evacuation scheme of Rangoon and the establishment of Rear Headquarters at Maymyo.

126. Our Rangoon air bases were closely threatened. The warning facilities except for limited R.D.F. and Observer Corps observation had practically gone. As a result of this meeting the G.O.C. despatched his telegram 0.792 of 20/2.

Decision to organise base landing grounds in India with mixed Wings in Burma.

127. I therefore telegraphed Headquarters ABDA Command indicating the situation described at this meeting. There was no time to be lost. General Hutton agreed with me

---
* See covering letter from General Wavell.

that the only course open to us to maintain our effort in support of the Army in Burma—once our airfields and warning at Rangoon had been lost—was to establish base landing grounds in India, operational landing grounds at Akyab and Magwe with advanced landing grounds in the Rangoon area to provide what fighter and bomber support could be given. Failing immediate instructions to the contrary, I proposed in my telegram putting this plan into action.

128. Arrangements were accordingly made to leave a mixed Wing one Hurricane Squadron, one Blenheim Squadron and half an Army Co-operation Squadron, organised as a mixed Wing, with one Squadron of the A.V.G. in Upper Burma, based at Magwe, one mixed Wing of one Hurricane Squadron, one Bomber Squadron and one G.R. Squadron at Akyab and to build up and feed these two Wings from a base organisation in India.

129. The decision which set the size of the Wing left at Magwe was based on the amount of maintenance in the country on the 20th February. It was calculated by the staff that there was sufficient maintenance in this mixed Wing for a period of three months. As regards Akyab, access by sea was still open and maintenance therefore would be satisfactory. There was no overland communication between Magwe and Akyab. The route from India in the North down the Manipur Road had not been completed.

130. The decision to base the force in Northern Burma at Magwe was made because it lay behind two lines of observer corps telephone lines, one down the Valley of the Salween towards Rangoon and the other down the Valley of the Irrawaddy. It was proposed to attempt to evacuate the R.D.F. set if Rangoon fell. By this means it was hoped to provide sufficient warning at Magwe to secure the base against anything but the heaviest scale of attack. Since Singapore had fallen on the 15th February the weight of the Japanese air force could now be turned towards Burma. I therefore expected that if Rangoon fell, with the considerable number of airfields now prepared in the Rangoon area, heavy reinforcement of Japanese aircraft would be flown in at will to Burma. The enemy would have control of the communications and the free use of the Port of Rangoon and thus a large air force could be maintained.

131. I received no reply to my telegram.* Action was commenced. I had received a personal telegram from Air Headquarters, India on the 19th in which the A.O.C.-in-C. informed me that if the necessity arose he had prepared a plan for the withdrawal of my force to India. On the 20th we requested air transport to be flown to Magwe, whence it would work a shuttle service between Magwe and Akyab. Onward transport of personnel from Akyab would be by sea. The personnel to be evacuated numbered some 3,000, the majority of whom were in the Rangoon area. A proportion were moved by sea, the remainder by air.

132. On the 21st the Postmaster General reported to me that the telephone system in Rangoon would cease functioning at 18.00 hours that day. Except, therefore, for our single R.D.F. set—worn-out and of the wrong kind—there would be no warning for the defence of Rangoon and our airfields. Arrangements were at once made to man the observer centre in the Central Telegraph Office with R.A.F. personnel. This limited warning continued until within a few days of the fall of Rangoon.

133. Beyond the general statement by the Army that in the event of the evacuation of Rangoon they would proceed to the North and generally in the direction of China, there was always the element of doubt as to whether they would proceed to China or fall back towards the Manipur Road and so towards India. Rear Headquarters had been established at Maymyo and stocks were being back-loaded up country to the Mandalay-Maymyo area. The initial line of withdrawal, I had always been informed, would be along the Prome Road, a road 150 miles in length.

134. Our air bases in general lay on the other main route to the North—up a Valley of the Sittang. The main railway system ran through this Valley to Mandalay and branched to Myitkyina in the North, and Lashio in the N.E. The Burma Road lay along the same route to Mandalay and Lashio.

135. In consequence, from the air point of view the Prome route was unsatisfactory since there were no air bases of any kind of withdrawal between Rangoon and Mandalay suitable for the operation of modern fighters and bombers with high wing loading—except Magwe, and that had no accommodation, no pens and no dispersal. Indeed the only other aerodromes were at Myitkyina, 600 miles to the North (runway incomplete) and Meiktila—our depot of the future—where a runway was finished. But Meiktila was rather too much to the North and East to be effective in the initial stages and had only slight warning facilities.

136. I had foreseen the possibility of having to operate my mixed fighter and bomber effort in what might well be—and later proved to be—a tense situation, in which the Army would be attempting to withdraw along this single line of communication. There would be no opportunity of dispersing off the road and no cover from air attack. Accordingly, I had a series of strips cut into the hard paddy land along this line of communication and on the 1st March, when the C.-in-C., India, visited Rangoon, I was able to report that I was prepared to operate on this route.

137. But operating a numerically inferior force from such landing grounds against a weight of air attack without adequate warning was a risky and fortuitous operation. Thus I had grave doubts about our ability to maintain ourselves in being. But when and if this situation arose we should have done our best to secure the Army against enemy air action.

138. Against this threat, therefore, the location of our " kutcha " strips had been kept as secret as possible and a very useful number had been prepared in the vicinity of Mingaladon and towards the North and West up the Irrawaddy to Prome.

139. At night all first-line aircraft, bombers and fighters, were flown off the parent airfields at Mingaladon and Zayatkwin to " kutcha " strips. Thus the location of our fighting force, when based on such temporary airfields, was not readily obvious to the enemy. Pilots and

---
* See covering letter from General Wavell.

air crews were motored into their accommodation. They arrived at the "kutcha" strip before dawn the next morning to fly their aircraft. This we found the only method of ensuring secrecy of the strips and the security of equipment from the damage caused by night bombing. With large numbers of small bombs the enemy's night bombing of Mingaladon was accurate and effective. If Rangoon were to be evacuated when the warning had entirely gone, I proposed to guard the security of my fighters by the use of these strips, and evacuate the parent airfields. The bombers on account of their range could operate from Magwe and refuel and rearm in the forward area, but the fighters with an extreme fighting range of 135 miles would have to be brought back along the Prome Road in steps of some 50 miles so that security could be provided for our retiring columns.

140. All preparations practicable were made to improve the warning system at Akyab and Magwe, but with the time and resources available this proved to be a hopeless task. Furthermore, much work was necessary at Magwe to make it a satisfactory base, and labour was difficult to get. The provision of satellite "kutcha" strips was, however, undertaken to provide dispersion. Magwe, although it had a runway still under construction, had been a civil air port and, since it lay in the back area of Burma, was not intended in the general plan to be an operational aerodrome. Anti-blast protection in the way of pens or dispersal arrangements had not been started. Had, for example, Toungoo been situated where Magwe was, it would have been a different story and the situation in regard to P.A.D. measures would have been much more satisfactory for the operation of a mixed Wing.

141. Final preparations to continue to fight the battle over Rangoon, and for the withdrawal to the North, were taken in hand at once. Rear Headquarters was opened up at Magwe on 22nd February with forward Headquarters in Rangoon.

Formation of "X" Wing.

142. To control the fighter action and the bombing offensive action in support of the Army throughout this phase, I formed an "X" Wing Headquarters under the command of Group Captain Noel Singer, D.S.O., D.F.C., with a strong staff, reasonable communications, and good mobility. The role of "X" Wing was to maintain air superiority over Rangoon until the demolitions of the oil interests at Syriam and Thilawa, the docks, power stations, munitions and stores had been completed and until the Army had withdrawn from the area and thereafter to provide air superiority over the area in which the Army was moving, until it reached Prome.

143. The detachments on Toungoo, Heho, Namsang and Lashio would continue in operation to enable limited air action to take place in support of the Chinese, while a landing ground was prepared at Mandalay to serve Rear Headquarters at Maymyo. A scheme was drawn up to enable detachments to be withdrawn from forward aerodromes should the situation necessitate—with preparations for the evacuation of equipment, stores, etc. Arrangements had been made with Army Headquarters that in these circumstances all petrol and oil would be handed over to the Army for the use of the Armoured Brigade and M.T. columns.

144. On the 23rd February the Sittang Bridge was blown. Except on the days on which the enemy had thrown the weight of his attack against the Rangoon defence, his bombers and fighters flew over their forward troops advancing through the jungle. Air action was carried out against our troops intermittently on most days. As explained previously, we did the best with the slim fighter resources available to support the Army in this respect.

145. On the next two days, the 24th and 25th, the final attack was made by the Japanese Air Force on the Rangoon defence system with the object of attaining air superiority over the area. As noted elsewhere, this failed in a signal manner and severe casualties were inflicted on the enemy. Thereafter, until the fall of Rangoon, his fighter force was occupied purely defensively over the area in which his advance was taking place, formations of up to 40 plus operating each day. When possible, therefore, in order to keep them on the defensive, bombing operations were carried out in the area in which the enemy fighters were working. We attempted to make interceptions but with no great success, since their fighter effort was only over the area of operations at certain times. On the 23rd, however, a message was received from the 17th Division and interception did take place in which 2 enemy aircraft were shot down.

146. Our fighter effort which had built up to no less than 44—Hurricanes and P.40's—on the 17th February, dwindled away after the air battle on the 24th and 25th and after our air operations over Tenasserim to a low mark of under 10 on the 28th February, due to the lack of maintenance, spares and the number that were "shot up" in the air battle. The figure, however, gradually increased again to 27 on the 4th March, but fell to an average of about 17 aircraft from this date until the 10th March.

147. As regards bombers, the effort built up to 16 on the 17th February and fell away during the battles in Tenasserim to a low mark of under 5 on the 25th February for exactly the same reasons as described above. It built up, however, to 12 aircraft on the 28th February and to an average of about 10 serviceable from that time until the 10th March.

The Battle of Pegu.

148. On the 23rd February I visited the 17th Division at Pegu with General Hutton. The Armoured Brigade had now arrived and was mostly deployed in this area. The enemy used the hours of darkness to cross the Sittang and pressure was exerted against our forces at Waw on the 26th February. Between this time and the 5th March the battle developed.

149. On the 4th March General Alexander arrived at Magwe. He flew down with me to Rangoon. I accompanied him on his visit with General Hutton to the 17th Division at Pegu. The enemy had engaged our forces round Pegu and an infiltration in strength, accompanied by light tanks, had taken place to the North through the jungle country of the lower Pegu Yomas in the direction of the Prome Road— our line of communication. This movement

was observed by low flying Hurricanes on reconnaissance. The 63rd Brigade had been accepted and General Alexander planned the last stand in the defence of Rangoon. Throughout this action which terminated on the 8th March with the completion of the demolition and the final evacuation of the Port of Rangoon, an interesting air situation arose.

150. It was of paramount importance that the last vital demolition on a big scale should be completed without the interference of hostile aircraft and that the movement of the Army which was disposed astride the Pegu Road and in Rangoon should be enabled to give last cover to demolition parties and to withdraw as planned through the cross-road at Taukkyan and North up the Prome Road. The Army was tied to the road on account of the nature of the country and the fact that it was mechanised.

151. As already noted, the air actions over Rangoon on the 24th and 25th had inflicted severe casualties on the enemy air force. From that day until the evacuation of the Army from Rangoon had been completed, until all our convoys and ships had left the Port in security and until our demolition parties had been withdrawn, no enemy bomber attempted to enter what had previously been our warning zone round the airfields of Rangoon, i.e., roughly a circle 40 miles in radius from the centre of the town.

152. I can only assume that when their last effort to establish air superiority failed, the enemy air force were determined not to incur further wastage until Rangoon fell. Consequently the demolitions and the withdrawal of our forces from Rangoon took place in a state of absolute air superiority.

153. As regards the enemy effort in the battle of Pegu, air attacks took place against Maymyo, Toungoo and Bassein, whilst considerable activity was maintained over the battle area.

154. On the 2nd March I gave instructions for the R.D.F. station, which had been made mobile to move to Magwe, to provide some R.D.F. warning for our new air base. Consequently, when the telephone observer corps system collapsed there was no warning in the area except that provided by observation from military points and airfields.

155. To offset this to some extent a " Jim Crow " Hurricane was kept over Rangoon by day.

156. During this critical phase, fearing that my fighter force might be caught on the ground and destroyed by surprise low flying fighter attack, I had moved them out to a newly prepared " kutcha " strip at Highland Queen from which offensive fighter patrols were maintained. To give the impression that the force was still at Mingaladon, wrecked aircraft fuselages and dummies were parked in the readiness position on the runways.

157. During this critical phase to the 7th March, the bomber effort was directed against the enemy wherever he could be found. The fighters accompanying the bomber raids came down to shoot up enemy objectives. 96,800 lbs. of bombs were released, and a considerable number of fighter offensive and protective sorties carried out. Such objectives as enemy troop concentrations, trains, boats on the Sittang and M.T. columns were attacked with satisfactory results. The bombers operated from Magwe aerodrome using Highland Queen and John Haig as advanced bases.

158. General Sir Archibald Wavell, now Commander-in-Chief, India—to which Command Norgroup had reverted—visited Burma on the 1st and 2nd March. A meeting was held at Magwe on the morning of the 1st March in which the Commander-in-Chief reviewed the land and air situation. At this meeting H.E. the Governor, General Hutton and myself were present. I described the air situation and the need for reinforcing Hurricanes and Blenheims. With Rangoon now closely threatened, with our warning non-existent, with a slender fighter force of 20 serviceable Hurricanes and a few Buffaloes, with the A.V.G. force standing at 4 serviceable aircraft at Magwe, it was a position in which I said we should be unable to deny the enemy fredom of air action; while our bombing effort in support of the Army would be limited to the efforts of our quickly dwindling force of 16 bombers.

Attack on Highland Queen.

159. On the 6th, an enemy formation of about 20 plus aircraft which was flying over the Japanese troops advancing through the jungle towards the Prome Road over-shot its mark and, by accident and without warning, arrived flying low over Highland Queen where our fighters, some bombers and some G.R. aircraft were on the ground.

160. Fortune attended us on this occasion. The enemy shooting was bad and some Hurricanes were able to take off. Although no claims were made there were indications that 2 enemy fighters were damaged or destroyed. Two aircraft of ours were destroyed on the ground. The anti-aircraft defence of the aerodrome went into action satisfactorily. This was a raid which might well have been a decisive end to our small air force.

161. I immediately issued instructions for all aircraft to fly in from Highland Queen to Mingaladon, whence our last sorties were carried out.

162. Infiltrations by boat had taken place up the River Rangoon. Offensive action by our fighters was taken but movement continued by night. On the afternoon of the 6th March I left Wing Headquarters, Rangoon, and flew to my Headquarters at Magwe.

163. Our fighter force had for some days been split between Magwe and the forward bases round Rangoon, Highland Queen and Mingaladon. The Hurricane force which was then standing at about 15 aircraft was a mixed one comprising commanders and pilots of 17, 135 and 136 Squadrons, and operating from the forward bases was maintained from Magwe, where maintenance inspections were carried out. The P.40's of the A.V.G. which had done such sterling work were now suffering from acute unserviceability due to lack of spares and replacement aircraft. I therefore placed them in the defence of the air base at Magwe. This made good my promise to General Chennault that I would not employ them at airfields without adequate warning.

Evacuation of Rangoon.

164. I had been with General Alexander until 14.00 hours. He had told me of his decision to evacuate Rangoon, and the code word for blowing demolitions and evacuation was issued just before midnight on 6th March. With his agreement I moved Headquarters "X" Wing from Rangoon to Zigon, the first "kutcha" strip from which we would operate in support of the Army's withdrawal along the Prome Road. A small party of Officers and airmen were left behind to complete the demolition of the operations room and the facilities at Norgroup Headquarters. They were then to go on to Mingaladon and help to complete the demolitions at this airfield. This party came out with the Army.

PART VI—AIR OPERATIONS COVERING WITHDRAWAL UP THE PROME ROAD.

165. There was a heavy haze on the 7th and 8th, which interfered with observation by fighters, made worse by the great pall of smoke from the burning oil which rose to a height of 15,000 feet and was blown North over the area of operations as far as Tharrawady. General Alexander's force failed to dislodge the road block at Mile 22 on the 7th, but on the morning of the 8th was able to overcome this resistance, and the withdrawal of our Army commenced North up the Prome Road.

Operations from Zigon.

166. The rough surface of Zigon proved unsatisfactory for Hurricanes. I had to decide whether to risk damaging Hurricanes—which when damaged might not be repaired—or to operate the fighters from Magwe where their range would not have enabled them to provide security over our troops. The following day from Zigon the fighter effort was maintained.

167. The column of our withdrawing Army was reported by aircrews to be some 40 miles long, mostly M.T. vehicles and tanks—an admirable target for enemy bomb action in country where there was little or no cover from air attack and no possibility of getting off the long straight tarmac road.

168. But the state of air superiority finally established on 25th February still continued. Fighter patrols were carried out over the line from Zigon to Rangoon. The Army, without molestation from the enemy air force, was thus able to take up and consolidate its position on the Petpadan-Tharrawaddy line.

169. As regards fighter sweeps to secure the withdrawal, the Hurricanes at Zigon carried out about 12 to 18 sorties a day until "X" Wing had withdrawn from Prome to Magwe on the 11th March. It was then disbanded on the formation of Burwing at Magwe. Group Captain Singer, who arrived on the 12th March, took over the command of Akwing, which was then in formation at Akyab.

170. Operations from Zigon resulted in the tail unit of a Hurricane giving way on an average of 1 in every 5 landings. A bamboo skid was fitted to the tail of the Hurricane which then took off and landed at Magwe for repair. 2 Buffaloes were badly wrecked by the aerodrome surface and were eventually burnt. 1 Blenheim and 1 Lysander were also rendered unserviceable, but were repaired and flown out before the airfield was left.

171. The sole Japanese air attack driven home at this time was directed against the town of Tharrawaddy, where the bomb lift of 10 bombers was disposed of on civilian quarters causing a number of civilian casualties.

172. G.R. Reconnaissance in the Gulf of Martaban and the Bay of Bengal continued and escort was provided for the last convoy which carried detachments and demolition parties. All ships got safely away.

Operations from Park Lane.

173. The range for fighters was now shortened and, consequently, "X" Wing moved to Park Lane, a "kutcha" strip North of Prome. This move was completed on the night of the 9th March. The enemy did not locate and attack the fighters at Zigon or Park Lane.

174. Fighting continued and on the 25th March the Army had taken up their position on the Prome line, with the 1st Bur. Division's move from Toungoo to Allanmyo in progress.

175. During this period, from the 7th March to the 21st March, the bomber force was either held in readiness for close support of the Army or attacks were made in order to reduce the scale of air attack and so aid the fighters in their task of security. Attacks on enemy objectives in support of the Army were also carried out. A total of 31,500 lbs. of bombs was released with good results on such objectives as troop concentrations, aerodromes, road and railway communication and river craft. Constant reconnaissance was carried out over the entire front towards Rangoon and in the Valley of the Sittang, while a close watch was kept on our old air bases in the Rangoon area and at Moulmein for signs of the arrival of the enemy air force and reinforcements. Some effort, however, was wasted because bombers available were held standing by for objectives which the Army did not provide.

176. The enemy attacked Toungoo on the 17th March and carried out reconnaissance of our airfields up the Burma Road, Tangan, Namsang, Nyaumglebin and Meiktila—obviously searching for our air force.

Formation of Burwing.

177. Burwing, comprising No. 17 Hurricane, No. 45 Bomber Squadron, the elements of an Army Co-operation Flight, 1 weak A.V.G. Squadron and the R.D.F. Station, had been formed at Magwe under the command of Group Captain Seton Broughall. This was a fully mobile mixed Army support force which, by instructions from Air Headquarters, India, was placed under the operational control of General Alexander on the 18th March.

Air Directif—9th March.

178. On the 9th March I flew to Akyab to meet Air Marshal (now Air Chief Marshal) Sir Richard Peirse, the Air Officer Commanding-in-Chief, Air Forces in India.

179. The Air Officer Commanding-in-Chief issued a Directif in which I was told to maintain my two mixed Wings at Magwe and Akyab and to support the Army in Burma and to organise the air defence of Calcutta, Asansol and Tatanagar in India, and of Digboi oil installation in Assam; also to continue from India offensive bombing operations in support of the Army in Burma. Additionally, a further

role of the force was reconnaissance and the attack of enemy surface vessels in the Bay of Bengal in aid of the security of our sea communications.

Formation of Akwing.

180. My Headquarters were moved from Magwe to Akyab on the 12th March, where I commenced forming Akwing. On the 17th this Wing comprised 135 Squadron, armed with obsolete Hurricane I's and 1 Hurricane II, a G.R. Flight and a small air communications detachment. It was proposed to make good the warning (R.D.F.) and to build the Wing up with 1 Bomber Squadron (113 Squadron) when Blenheims became available from flow and 1 G.R. Squadron (139 Squadron) when Hudsons became available.

181. On the 17th March I flew to Calcutta to meet the Commander-in-Chief and the Air Officer Commanding-in-Chief. My Headquarters was in process of opening in Calcutta.

PART VII—REVERSE INFLICTED ON MIXED WING AT MAGWE.

182. On the 22nd March I returned to Burma to inspect Akwing at Akyab and Burwing at Magwe. On landing at Akyab I received a telegram from Group Captain Seton Broughall to say that the enemy had attacked Magwe in force the previous day. This was immediately followed by a signal telling me that heavy attacks had recommenced and closing the aerodrome to approaching aircraft. He reported that nearly all the first-line aircraft had been written off or damaged and asked for approval to move to Lashio and Loiwing to refit. I telegraphed agreement and flew on to Mandalay where I arranged for Group Captain Seton Broughall to meet me.

The Bomber Attack at Mingaladon.

183. Examining this action in full detail:— On the 20th March reconnaissance carried out by Burwing had disclosed concentrations of the enemy air force taking place in the Rangoon area. More than 50 aircraft were reported on our old airfield at Mingaladon. Group Captain Seton Broughall decided to attack the following morning in an effort to reduce the scale of attack in Burma which his intelligence staff had put at 400 plus in all. A raid of ten Hurricances and nine Blenheims of 45 Squadron accordingly took off. The Blenheims were intercepted by enemy Naval "O" fighters 40 miles North of Rangoon and fought their way in to Mingaladon. The bomb lift of 9,000 lbs. with stick adaptors was dropped on the runways among the enemy aircraft. The formation fought their way back to Tharrawaddy. During this gallant engagement in which 18 enemy fighters were encountered the Blenheims shot down two enemy fighters and claimed two probably destroyed and two damaged. Most of our aircraft were shot up but none were shot down. There were no casualties to personnel except one pilot wounded.

Low Flying Fighter Attack on Mingaladon.

184. The Hurricanes carried out a low flying attack. Nine enemy fighters were claimed as destroyed in air combat while 16 enemy bombers and fighters were destroyed or damaged on the ground. This was a magnificent air action. Some Hurricanes were badly shot up while one crashed on our side of the line through lack of petrol, following combat. O.C. Burwing intended to repeat the attack that afternoon, but while final preparations were being made for this sortie, the enemy commenced their considerable attack on the air base at Magwe.

185. It should be appreciated that on this day at Magwe all serviceable operational aircraft, fighters and bombers, of my command were present with the exception of one Hurricane II and nine worn-out Hurricane I's, ex O.T.U., at Akyab.

Enemy Attack on Magwe Begins.

186. Over a period of some 25 hours, commencing at 13.23, Magwe was attacked in force by the enemy. In all, the scale of attack reached about 230 fighters and bombers, which included 166 Army 96 and 97 medium and heavy bombers. It is calculated that a great weight of bombs, some 200 tons, were accurately released in patterns during this attack.

187. Similar attacks had been carried out against Rangoon without decisive effect. But at Rangoon there was good warning and the number of fighters available against such attacks was usually 20, rising on occasion to the high figure of 45.

Fighter Effort.

188. 21 fighters were present at Magwe when attacked, but as a direct result of the air action which had been fought over Mingaladon in the morning, *the number of serviceable aircraft at readiness to take to the air was only 12*. It should here be mentioned that the leaders and many of the fighter pilots at Magwe had been at two minute readiness day after day, from dawn to dusk, for a period of some eight weeks.

Warning.

189. The only observer corps system remaining to the East and South-East was the observer post belt as far South as Toungoo and Prome on the main line of communication, reporting through Mandalay, and a chain of posts on the railway line Pyinmana-Kyaukpadaung which reported direct to Magwe operations room over an R.A.F. W/T. link. There was no observer corps system to the West and North-East of Magwe—an outflanking avenue used by the enemy during this attack. The R.D.F. set was of wrong type; its arc of observation was to the South-East. The equipment had given three months hard service and no spares had been available. The warning was weak and unreliable.

The Enemy Air Action.

190. At 13.00 hours on the 21st March, a report was received of a single unidentified aircraft approaching and two Hurricanes were sent off to intercept, but were unable to make contact. At 13.23 hours the approach of an enemy formation was confirmed and all available fighters took off. But they numbered only four Hurricanes and six P.40s. At 13.30, 21 bombers escorted by ten fighters attacked, bombing and machine gunning the airfield. Our fighters intercepted and destroyed four enemy aircraft with one probable and one damaged, but the weight of the attack got home and considerable damage resulted in which communications were destroyed.

191. The enemy followed this up with further raids at 14.10 and 14.30. In all the scale of attack was 59 bombers and 24 fighters that day.

192. On the 22nd March, plots of movements were received from the R.D.F. set at 08.04 and 08.11 hours. Immediately afterwards there was a temporary breakdown of the W/T link which, combined with interference, prevented the reception of plots in the operations room until the enemy attack had developed at 08.45 hours. Two Hurricanes had been sent off to intercept a high flying enemy reconnaissance aircraft heard over the airfield at 08.30. They had not yet made contact when at 08.47 hours 27 bombers with an escort of ten plus fighters appeared over the aerodrome, followed a quarter of an hour later by a second wave of 27 bombers also with fighter escort. As no warning of these raids had been received, no further fighters were sent off to engage. The two Hurricanes already in the air engaged the Japanese formation and damaged two.

193. Considerable damage was sustained. The runways were rendered unserviceable, communications were broken down and a number of aircraft, both bombers and fighters, were destroyed on the ground.

194. Immediately afterwards, the Commander of the Second Pursuit Squadron, A.V.G., reported to Group Captain Seton Broughall that in view of the absence of warning and the scale of attack he was compelled by the terms of his instructions from General Chennault to withdraw his remaining flyable aircraft to refit. At this stage of the action only three P.40s and three Hurricanes remained flyable, the Hurricanes alone being operationally serviceable. The A.V.G.'s P.40s withdrew to Loiwing that afternoon followed by their ground party.

195. At 13.30 hours reconnaissance aircraft were again reported approaching and two of the three remaining Hurricanes were sent up but failed to intercept. While they were returning to land at 14.30 the enemy again commenced his attacks with two waves of 27 and 26 bombers respectively, each accompanied by fighter escort. This terminated the enemy's attacks.

196. Great damage had been done and 9 Blenheims and at least 3 P.40's were destroyed on the ground, 5 Blenheims were unserviceable, while 3 Hurricanes had been destroyed in air combat. The remaining 20 aircraft (6 Blenheims, 3 P.40's and 11 Hurricanes) were flyable but unserviceable due to normal unserviceability or damage from enemy action. These aircraft, except the P.40's, were flown out to Akyab.

197. This grave reverse to Burwing—the R.A.F. detachment in Upper Burma—was the result of our weakness in fighters, the weakness of the warning system at Magwe and the complete absence of aircraft pens and bad dispersal arrangements at this airfield so hurriedly occupied. There has been a good deal of criticism of the subsequent hasty move of Burwing from Magwe, while it had an adverse effect on the morale of both the Army and the civil population.

198. The convoy left Magwe for Lashio and Loiwing early on the morning of the 23rd. Salvage and refuelling parties were left behind.

199. On the nights of the 22nd and 23rd respectively, I met General Alexander and Group Captain Seton Broughall at Maymyo. It was confirmed that Burwing would be withdrawn to Lashio and Loiwing—the only remaining aerodrome where fair warning existed—for refitting.

200. In the meantime it was proposed to try and make good the warning at Magwe, to put it into a proper state of defence and fit for Burwing to return there for operations. As the convoy had already left Magwe I issued instructions for the R.D.F. set to be turned round and sent back to Magwe and for the salvage and working parties at Magwe to be strengthened.

201. Loiwing was the only airfield left with reasonable warning and therefore the proposal to leave Magwe and to refit at Loiwing was not unsound despite the great distance of the latter airfield from the area in which the Army was operating. By use of the advanced landing grounds, limited support could be given to the Army until the defence at Magwe was satisfactorily completed and the aerodrome reoccupied. At Lashio warning was weak.

202. As events turned out it would not have been possible to reoccupy Magwe since the airfield fell into enemy hands 3 weeks later and the organisation of the warning system and the provision of works—for which only limited labour then existed—could not have been done in time. Additionally, the observer corps belt in the Sittang Valley and the Valley of the Irrawaddy was gradually being rolled up and with it any warning from this source.

Enemy Action—Akyab

203. The enemy had also found our small force at Akyab. A similar action took place which commenced on the 23rd, was repeated on the 24th and on the 27th. Our fighters intercepted on 2 occasions inflicting a loss of 4 enemy aircraft destroyed and 3 probably destroyed for a cost of 6 Hurricanes.

204. Although warning was received on the 27th, low flying enemy fighters caught our small force unprepared on the ground on this occasion. 2 Hurricanes got into the air and engaged, 1 being shot down. 7 Hurricanes were destroyed on the ground and a Valencia. Instructions had already been issued by Air Headquarters, India, to withdraw Akwing from Akyab to Chittagong as warning was so weak. Akyab would continue to be an advanced landing ground for refuelling aircraft and to enable our Hudson reconnaissance to reach the Andaman Islands. A small R.D.F. set with a limited range of 20 miles, had been flown in and was operating, but the observer corps warning for Akyab was poor. The posts were few, only the outlines of communication existing owing to the difficult nature of the country.

205. These two actions—at Magwe and at Akyab—in effect terminated the R.A.F. activities based in Burma. The supply of aircraft now became the critical factor. The necessity to build up our defence in North Eastern India and Ceylon brought about a decision by the Commander-in-Chief, India, not to re-equip Burwing. The maintenance of a small force in Burma was uneconomical in view of the lack of warning and increasing weight of attack.

Indeed, such air forces of ours operating in these circumstances would be destroyed piecemeal, giving but small returns for considerable losses.

206. Burwing continued, however, as an organisation, and although bombers were flown in to Lashio and Loiwing to operate for a few days and return to Calcutta, very little could be achieved. Eight Hurricanes that were flown in on 6th April lasted only a few days in the face of Japanese attacks on Loiwing.

207. With the reverse that the Chinese 5th Army sustained on the Southern Shan front on 20th and 21st April which led to the rapid advance of the Japanese to Lashio, Burwing was withdrawn to China to provide British refuelling parties at main Chinese air bases. The personnel of 17 Squadron were withdrawn via Myitkyina to take their part—re-equipped with Hurricane II's—in the Calcutta defence.

208. But using the depth towards India, our bomber operations were continued on a slight but growing scale. Much remained still to be done for the support of the Army and the evacuation of our wounded and civilians.

PART VIII.—WITHDRAWAL OF BURMA ARMY TO INDIA.

209. General Alexander's Army moved from the oil field area through the dry zone of Upper Burma to Mandalay with Headquarters at Shwebo, the final withdrawal taking place across the River Chindwin through Kalewa and over the Manipur Road through Tamu. The Army passed through the forward screen of 4th Corps troops on the Lochao pass on the 18th May and General Alexander's force finally reached Imphal on the 20th May.

210. The enemy air force now extended their patrols over a wide area in Northern Burma and carried out attacks on Lashio, Mandalay, Loiwing and Meiktila. Support was given to their forces operating against our Allies in the Taunggyi and Mawlaik areas whilst flying boats based on the Andaman Islands commenced attacks on shipping in the Bay of Bengal between 28th March and 5th April.

211. The Japanese reinforcement of Burma took place during the first week in April. Under the cover of a vigorous attack on Ceylon and on our shipping in the Bay of Bengal on 6th April a convoy of ships reached Rangoon. We were powerless to prevent this. Fortress aircraft of the U.S.A.A.C., however, attacked with five and a half tons of bombs an enemy force in the Andamans and straddled a cruiser and a transport. Further night flying attacks were carried out on the enemy convoy at Rangoon with useful results—fires and explosions being seen in the dock area.

212. During the eight weeks from 21st March, when the Magwe action took place, until May 20th, when the Burmarmy was finally withdrawn to India, action with bombers and fighters continued against the Japanese in Burma.

213. The fighter action was limited to such fighter sorties as could be carried out within the range of the Mohawk Squadron based at Dinjan. Bomber action was exerted either from aerodromes in Assam—Tezpur and Dinjan—or from bases in the Calcutta area, using Chittagong as a forward landing ground. One hundred and three tons of bombs were released on the enemy in these attacks. On arrival in Eastern India Squadrons were reformed and aircraft reconditioned slowly but as quickly as possible.

214. On the 12th April the first attack was made in support of General Alexander's right flank, when 9,000 lbs. of bombs were dropped on Japanese troops at Nyaungbintha. The enemy and his transport were also attacked at Singbaungwe, Allanmyo, Magwe, Sandoway and Taungup. In all 15,000 lbs. of bombs were released.

215. Attacks, helped by some long range bombers of the U.S.A.A.C., continued on objectives of all kinds. In all 58 raids took place in support of the Army's withdrawal, some to reduce the scale of air attack and the remainder in direct support of the Army. Most of the bombing took place on General Alexander's right flank, although three raids were directed against such places as Mongpawn, Laikha and Kongchaiping on the Chinese front.

216. Such airfields as Mingaladon, Akyab and Myitkyina were kept under a harassing scale of attack. Operations against Akyab and Myitkyina were particularly effective and when the enemy attempted to establish himself there on forward bases, bomber action made these untenable by the destruction of his first-line aircraft on the ground.

217. Of the 58 raids, 13 were undertaken by aircraft of the U.S.A.A.C. and 45 by the R.A.F. A total of 231,900 lbs. of bombs in all were dropped, mostly followed by low flying machine gun attacks.

218. The enemy were using river craft to outflank the Army in Burma. This line of communication was continuously harassed by our aircraft and a total of some 30,000 lbs. of bombs were released on steamers, barges and wharves while the attack on a concentration of river craft at Monywa on the 4th and 5th May was, by its delaying action, largely instrumental in preventing the Japanese encircling movement of the right flank of our forces, then withdrawing from Yu to Kalewa, a movement which if successful would have proved embarrassing to our Army.

219. A single Blenheim which had attacked Akyab on the 22nd May was engaged by 4 Army o.1 fighters. The fight lasted 20 minutes and was broken off by the remaining 3 fighters when 70 miles out to sea the aircraft of their leader, the Japanese air ace Lt.-Col. Takeo Kato, was shot down in flames. No other Allied aircraft attacked Akyab on that day.

220. Requests for bombing action and tactical reconnaissance were made by General Alexander to Headquarters in Calcutta. Reconnaissances continued, 55 being completed for Burmarmy.

221. No. 31 air transport Squadron had been placed at my disposal equipped with D.C.2 and later some D.C.3 aircraft. This Squadron did magnificent work. Their daily effort was about 3 aircraft and considerable air transport requirements had to be met. Food had to be dropped on the 3 routes along which the evacuation of civilians from Burma was taking place. These routes ran from Shwebo-Kalewa-Tamu

to Imphal, from Myitkyina-Mainkwan-Shingbwiyang to Ledo and from Katha-Indaw-Homalin/Tonhe to Imphal. Evacuees travelling along these routes required supplies of food and medical stores to maintain them during their march to India. Additionally, many of our wounded were evacuated by air from Magwe, Shwebo and Myitkyina in turn as the battle moved northward. Civilians were also evacuated when there were no wounded to move.

222. In all a total of 8,616 persons, which included 2,600 wounded, were flown out to India and 109,652 lbs. of supplies were dropped for victualling refugees and troops. In carrying out this task we had the help of D.C.3 aircraft of the American Air Force—I have to record the good work carried out by these crews.

223. About the middle of March a serious situation had risen in the Bay of Bengal. In the Port of Calcutta there was some one-quarter of a million tons of shipping. It was not known how long the enemy naval force would remain within striking distance of our line of sea communication between Calcutta and Ceylon. There were none of H.M. ships available at this time to provide the necessary cover to secure this shipping now also within the range of attack of the enemy long range bombers based at Mingaladon and Magwe.

224. Instructions were issued for the Port to be cleared. There were two courses of action —either to sail convoys close in shore and to provide what fighter protection against bomb attack—and bomber protection against attack by surface units—as was practicable or to use diversional sailing which would spread the ships over a large area in the Bay of Bengal. The latter course was chosen.

225. It seemed possible that the attacks of our coast-wise shipping on the 6th April were an offensive move covering the arrival of the large convoy of troops in Rangoon. Consequently it was likely that if enemy air reconnaissance could be prevented—the sailing of this large tonnage of shipping over a short period might be secured from enemy surface and air attack, since the enemy would be unaware of the operation.

226. We knew where the enemy reconnaissance force was. Nine four-engined and two-engined reconnaissance flying boats had been located at Port Blair. On the 14th April this figure had risen to 13. Moreover, there were indications that the enemy had developed the aerodrome at Port Blair and that local fighter defence had been put in. Two out of the 3 serviceable Hudsons of 139 (now 62) Squadron, the only aircraft that could (refuelling at Akyab) make the range, were instructed to carry out an attack with the object of destroying and damaging all aircraft of this reconnaissance force. A determined low-flying attack was carried out in which 2 twin-engined boats were left burning, 1 four-engined flying boat left sinking and all the other flying boats were believed to be damaged. This attack was repeated on the 18th, when 2 Hudsons again attacked 12 four-engined flying boats. Two of these were destroyed and 3 severely damaged. On both occasions the enemy were moored in lines and the Hudsons carried out a number of mast-height runs on them using their turret guns. On the 18th, Navy "O" fighters engaged our 2 aircraft—1 failed to return and the second was hit by cannon shell and machine gun fire. After these attacks this enemy reconnaissance force remained inactive. Not only during the critical time when some 70 of our ships made the passage through the Bay of Bengal, but until the end of July no activity by it was recorded.

PART IX.—CONCLUSION.

227. To summarize, during this air action which commenced on the 23rd December, a small Allied air force, consisting of 1 Squadron of the A.V.G., the equivalent of 2 Hurricane Squadrons, the equivalent of 1 Bomber Squadron, 2 Army Co-operation Bomber Squadrons and the equivalent of half a G.R. Squadron, engaged the Japanese air force in the defence of Rangoon and in the support of our Army in Tenasserim and Burma. But the early fall of Rangoon, diversion of reinforcements and the shortage of aircraft equipment prevented the air force building up to 16 Squadrons (6 Fighters, 7 Bombers, 2 Army Co-operation and 1 G.R.) and full maintenance promised on programme. Up to the fall of Rangoon—by which we lost our warning system and our organised airfields in this vicinity—air superiority over Rangoon had been maintained and after its fall continued until the Magwe action on the 21st March.

228. During this period the enemy, finally unable to subject the base of Rangoon to unrestricted day bombing, which would have given him the best chance of surrounding and destroying the Army, turned his effort to defend his troops and aid their advance. In Tenasserim, enemy day bombing attacks were carried out on our forward troops and Headquarters. Although support was given, our attempts to prevent this bombing were not successful, it being impossible in the circumstances of poor warning and shortage of fighter equipment.

229. It is a remarkable fact that from February 25th—when the enemy's last attack to achieve air superiority over Rangoon failed —he would not face our fighter force until Rangoon was in his hands and considerable reinforcements had been flown into the country after the fall of Singapore. Consequently, this absolute state of air superiority remained over Rangoon at this critical time—and no "Namsos" here took place.

230. On March 21st he began his determined attack to stamp out our now fast dwindling air force at Magwe and Akyab. Having achieved this, although good bombing objectives were constantly present as our Army withdrew to India, he did not follow up his success by attacking our moving columns. Thus the casualties to our Army from enemy air action during withdrawal over great distances with poor cover from air attack were small. This may well have been because the enemy did not know the temporary success that he had achieved. The main weight of the enemy bomber attack was directed on such places as Prome, Mandalay and Maymyo, where great damage resulted with considerable moral effect on the civil population. The bases at Toungoo, Heho, Namsang, Lashio and Loiwing were constantly searched and attacked, though except at the latter there were no aircraft present.

231. Norgroup was then using the depth to India, and with its base organisation being hurriedly prepared in the Calcutta area and up the Valley of the Brahmaputra, was able with what resources were available, to continue a harassing scale of bombing attack in Burma with some fighter action in the North. By the nature of the campaign and the shortage of warning, of aircraft, of equipment, and of maintenance, we were unable to maintain our 2 mixed Wings in Upper Burma and Akyab.

232. In the Burma campaign the main brunt of the fighting was borne by the P.40 Squadrons of the A.V.G. They were the first in the field with pilots well trained and with good fighting equipment. Their gallantry in action won the admiration of both services.

233. According to the records available in the Intelligence staff of Norgroup, 233 enemy fighters and bombers were claimed destroyed in the air in this campaign, of which the A.V.G. claimed 179 and the R.A.F. 54. Fifty-eight were claimed destroyed on the ground, 38 by the A.V.G. and 20 by the R.A.F. Seventy-six were claimed probably destroyed, 43 by the A.V.G. and 33 by the R.A.F. One hundred and sixteen were claimed damaged, 87 by the A.V.G. and 29 by the R.A.F.

234. From January 1st the cost in losses was 38 fighters shot down by the enemy in air combat. Of these 16 were P.40's and 22 Buffaloes and Hurricanes, but the majority of pilots were fortunately saved. I regret to report that there were 2 substantiated incidents when Japanese figher pilots attacked and killed our fighter pilots while descending by parachute.

235. As regards bombers, 8 failed to return from operations.

236. Our losses on the ground due to enemy action were 51 aircraft, 17 fighters, 23 Blenheims, 4 Hudsons. The remainder were transport and communication aircraft.

237. Comparable with the total of 233 enemy fighters and bombers claimed to have been shot down in air combat by the A.V.G. and the R.A.F., the Allies' losses were 46. Thus an average of slightly more than 5 enemy aircraft were claimed shot down for each of our aircraft lost.

238. We destroyed more of the enemy's aircraft on the ground than the enemy destroyed of ours. We made no claim moreover in respect of enemy aircraft destroyed on the ground by bombing attack, the number of which must have been considerable.

239. The bomber action in close support of the Army has been described. Slight as the effort was, valuable results were achieved. Counter offensive bombing action to reduce the scale of attack made an effective contribution towards the maintenance of air superiority over Rangoon.

240. The evacuation of R.A.F. personnel from Burma by air and sea, with small parties by land, was completed without loss.

241. As regards stores, much valuable equipment was back loaded at the last moment from Rangoon. The majority of stores remaining in Burma were moved to the Lashio area, whence on the sudden and unexpected Japanese thrust in that region as much as possible was moved into China. The remainder was destroyed except for some large bombs which were rendered useless.

242. The task of supporting General Alexander's Army terminated on May 20th when it was withdrawn to India. Air operations based in Eastern India continue against the Japanese in Burma.

LONDON
PRINTED AND PUBLISHED BY HIS MAJESTY'S STATIONERY OFFICE
To be purchased directly from H.M. Stationery Office at the following addresses:
York House, Kingsway, London, W.C.2; 13a Castle Street, Edinburgh, 2;
39–41 King Street, Manchester, 2; 1 St. Andrew's Crescent, Cardiff;
Tower Lane, Bristol, 1; 80 Chichester Street, Belfast
OR THROUGH ANY BOOKSELLER
1948
Price 1s. 0d. net

S.O. Code No. 65 38229

SUPPLEMENT TO The London Gazette

Of TUESDAY, the 14th of SEPTEMBER, 1948

Published by Authority

Registered as a newspaper

THURSDAY, 16 SEPTEMBER, 1948

AIR OPERATIONS BY FIGHTER COMMAND FROM 25th NOVEMBER 1940 TO 31st DECEMBER 1941

The following report was submitted to the Secretary of State for Air on 29th February, 1948, by Marshal of the Royal Air Force Sir Sholto Douglas, G.C.B., M.C., D.F.C. (now Lord Douglas of Kirtleside), former Air Officer Commanding-in-Chief, Fighter Command, Royal Air Force.

PART I: OPERATIONS.

Night Operations.

(a) *The Situation on 1st November, 1940*

1. At the beginning of November, 1940, the most urgent problem confronting the air defences was that presented by the night bomber. For the first ten months of the war the Luftwaffe had undertaken only minor operations against this country; but in June, 1940, the enemy began a series of small-scale night attacks on ports and industrial towns. During the next two months, while the daylight battle of Britain was being fought, this night offensive gathered momentum. On September 7th London became its main objective, and the scale of attack increased once more. By the end of October the night offensive had become in many respects a bigger threat to the kingdom than the day offensive, which, for the moment at least, had been successfully beaten off.

2. At that stage London had been raided on every night but one for the last eight weeks. On every night but four during those eight weeks at least a hundred tons of bombs had fallen on or around the Capital; Coventry, Birmingham and Liverpool had all suffered attacks of some weight. So far no intolerable harm had been done to industry or the public temper, although many people had been killed and much material loss and hardship had been caused. But there was every reason to expect that the attacks would continue and perhaps grow heavier; for during the last two months the defences had claimed the destruction of only 79 night bombers—a number equivalent to about a half of one per cent. of the number of night sorties that the Germans were believed to have flown in that time. Obviously, losses of this order were not likely to act as a deterrent.

3. The directive by which I found myself bound when I assumed command on 25th November, 1940, required me to give priority to the defence of the aircraft industry. No formal variation of this directive was needed to make it clear that the defeat of the night bomber must be one of my main tasks.

4. It would be wrong to give the impression that hitherto this problem had been ignored. On the contrary, it had long been foreseen that if the enemy found day attacks too expensive, he would probably turn to night bombing on a substantial scale. But with limited resources it had been necessary to place the emphasis on high-performance, single-seater fighters capable of defeating the enemy by day. Before the war, and in the early stages of the war, it was hoped that, with the help of searchlights, these aircraft would also be effective at night.

5. This hope had proved vain. Except at the beginning of the night offensive, when the enemy flew at 12,000 feet or lower, the searchlights were incapable of doing what was required of them. This was partly because they relied on sound locators, which were unsuited to modern conditions, and partly because very often cloud or moonlight prevented pilots from seeing the searchlight beams at the height at which they had to fly.

6. A method of night interception which did not rely on searchlights had been under development (although not continuously) since 1936. This method rested upon the installation in twin-engined, multi-seater aircraft of the radar equipment known as A.I.

7. On November 1st, 1940, the Command had possessed six squadrons of aircraft fitted with this equipment. All were Blenheim Squadrons;

but as the Blenheim was too slow and too lightly armed to take full advantage of its opportunities, Beaufighters were being substituted for the Blenheims as fast as the Air Ministry and the Ministry of Aircraft Production could make them available.

8. But at best the provision of A.I. solved only half the problem. This airborne Radar had a restricted range which could not be greater than the height of the aircraft, subject to a maximum of 3½ miles. Before the A.I. could detect an enemy bomber in the darkness, the fighter had therefore to be brought to within three miles of it at roughly the same height. If searchlights were ruled out, this could only be done by means of directions given to the pilot by a Controller on the ground. It was vital that this controller should have accurate knowledge of the bomber's position. Under my Command, I had No. 60 (Signals) Group, which controlled a chain of some 80 Radar Stations round the coasts, used for giving early warning to the controller of the approach of enemy aircraft across the sea. Over land, information on the raider's position was given by the Observer Corps. Although these sources had proved sufficiently accurate for daylight interceptions, they were not precise enough for successful night fighter operations.

9. Only Radar could provide the answer—special ground search radar stations for the direct control of A.I.-equipped night fighter aircraft. Such stations, termed G.C.I. (Ground Control of Interception), were under development when I assumed Command. Nevertheless, the tactics of their employment in conjunction with A.I. night fighters had yet to be evolved from practical experience as and when the G.C.I. stations became available.

10. The Radar Stations used for detecting the approach of enemy aircraft across the sea had only a limited application to this problem; but another kind of ground radar equipment, designed for gun-laying and known as G.L., promised to give good results. Although other varieties of radar equipment were under development, the defects of both ground and airborne search radars were not the most important factors in the establishment of an efficient night fighter defence. Any success A.I. was likely to achieve depended initially on the skill of the ground controller and then on the operational ability of the aircraft A.I. observer. There was an acute shortage of personnel for both of these highly specialised tasks.

11. It was clear that many problems of method, maintenance and supply would have to be solved before all this delicate equipment could be expected to yield concrete results, and that their solution was likely to take some months. In the meantime, the Air Ministry were anxious that some immediate attempt should be made to improve the situation.

12. A step in this direction had already been taken in the late Summer, when it was decided that the two Defiant Squadrons in the Command, together with a third Defiant Squadron which was about to be formed, should be turned over from day to night duty. Despite its early successes as a day fighter, the Defiant had proved too slow and too vulnerable to attack from below to be effective against the Me109, but it was still likely to prove a useful weapon against bombers.

13. In addition, three Hurricane Squadrons had been turned over to night duty, in the middle of October, 1940.

14. Thus when I assumed Command, the night-fighter force comprised the following squadrons:—

Squadron	Equipment	Station
No. 23	Blenheim	Ford
No. 25	Blenheim and Beaufighter.	Debden
No. 29	Blenheim	Digby and Wittering.
No. 219	Blenheim and Beaufighter.	Redhill
No. 600	Blenheim	Catterick and Drem
No. 604	Blenheim	Middle Wallop
No. 141	Defiant	Gatwick
No. 264	Defiant	Rochford
No. 73	Hurricane	Castle Camps
No. 85	Hurricane	Kirton-in-Lindsey
No. 151	Hurricane	Digby

15. In addition to these first-line units, the Fighter Interception Unit at Tangmere had the task of developing methods of night interception with twin-engined fighters; and sometimes provided aircraft for active operations; No. 422 Flight had been formed recently at Gravesend to study the problem of night interception with single-engined fighters; while a new Defiant Squadron, No. 307 (Polish) Squadron, was forming at Kirton-in-Lindsey, No. 420 Flight (later No. 93 Squadron) had just begun to form for the purpose of sowing and trailing mines in front of German bombers. Finally, the formation of No. 54 Operational Training Unit, to specialize in night training, had been ordered.

16. I also had operational control of the guns and searchlights of Anti-Aircraft Command, under Lt.-General Sir Frederick A. Pile, Bart., K.C.B., D.S.O., M.C., and the balloon barrages of Balloon Command under Air Vice-Marshal O. T. Boyd, C.B., O.B.E., M.C., A.F.C. (succeeded on 1st December, 1940, by Air Marshal Sir E. L. Gossage, K.C.B., C.V.O., D.S.O., M.C.).

17. In the early stages of the attack, except in conditions of good visibility, the A.A. guns had to rely on one of three methods of directing their fire. These were: illumination of the bomber by searchlights, which were controlled by sound locators; a combination of rather rudimentary radar and sound locator; or a system of prediction which depended entirely on sound locators. The shortcomings of these sound locators were a great handicap to A.A. gunnery, and the gunners deserve great credit for their achievements at a time when night fighters were almost powerless. By 25th November, 1940, radar equipment for gun-laying was beginning to arrive, and a variant intended for controlling searchlights (S.L.C. or "Elsie") was on the way.

18. Other means of frustrating enemy bombers included measures designed to jam or otherwise interfere with the directional beams that they used to find their targets, and various kinds of dummies and decoys which were intended to attract bombs. With the exception of decoy and dummy airfields, these were not under my control, but liaison was maintained with those responsible for their operation.

(b) *Operations, November and December, 1940.*

19. During the first two weeks in November, London had continued to be the enemy's main target, and was visited by at least 100 German bombers nearly every night. Then, in the middle of the month, came a change. On the night of 14th November, by the light of the full moon, nearly 500 German aircraft delivered an attack on Coventry which lasted from about eight o'clock in the evening until half-past five the following morning. The attack began with the dropping of large numbers of incendiary bombs by a Unit called K.Gr.100, which was known to specialize in this form of target marking. More incendiaries, hundreds of high explosive bombs and a number of parachute-mines followed. The raid wrought great havoc in the centre of the city, severely damaged 21 important factories, wrecked gas and water-mains and cables, blocked the railways, and put four or five hundred retail shops out of action. Three hundred and eighty people were killed and 800 seriously injured. The Civil Defence Services did excellent work, and, though shaken, the citizens of Coventry remained undaunted.

20. The defences were not unprepared for this move. The A.A. guns put up a tremendous volume of fire, and 123 fighter sorties were flown, day squadrons as well as night squadrons taking part. A few enemy aircraft were seen and some of them were engaged, but none of these combats was conclusive. The A.A. gunners claimed the destruction of two bombers.

21. Another such raid on Coventry soon afterwards might have created a serious situation. Fortunately the Germans did not consider a second raid necessary, and on the next night London was once again their main objective. But, for the rest of the month and throughout December, provincial towns and cities, including Southampton, Bristol, Plymouth, Birmingham, Sheffield, Liverpool and Manchester, competed with London for their attention. Clearly they had passed to a new stage in their programme and were now seeking to dislocate our means of production and supply.

22. Although this phase of the offensive did not come as a surprise, the ability of the Germans to reach and find their targets in wintry conditions was disturbing. With the help of radio beacons, directional beam systems, and blind-landing devices, the bombers were able to operate effectively in weather which seriously hampered and sometimes precluded fighter operations. As yet the new methods of interception which depended on radar were not perfected, and the less elaborate methods which we had hoped would tide us over this intervening period were largely defeated by this factor of bad weather. Inasmuch, however, as the enemy bomber crews were mainly reliant upon radio beams and beacons for navigation and bomb aiming in conditions of bad visibility, they were correspondingly vulnerable to radio counter-measures against those aids. There had grown up since the beginning of the war an extensive organisation which had developed a most effective technique for interfering so subtly with radio beams and beacons as to leave the enemy almost unaware of the fact that his own aids were leading him astray.

This organisation had been consolidated shortly before I assumed command, in the form of No. 80 Wing, whose invaluable services were almost entirely at my disposal. Operating in association with other forms of decoy, No. 80 Wing was responsible for deflection of a great number of enemy bombers from their targets, while the information it gathered as to the orientation of enemy radio beams from time to time proved a valuable guide to the air defences as to the enemy's intentions. Indeed, until our night fighters were to become a weapon of any significance against the enemy bombers in March of the following year, radio counter-measures were to contribute as much as any other defensive arm towards reduction of the impact of the enemy bomber offensive.

23. On the night of 19th November, a pilot and crew of No. 604 Squadron, using their A.I. in conjunction with searchlight indications and instructions from their Sector Controller, had succeeded in engaging a large aircraft over Oxfordshire. The crew of a Ju88 which crashed later in Norfolk reported that they had been attacked by a fighter on their way from the South Coast to Birmingham; and it seems probable that this was the aircraft engaged over Oxfordshire. If so, this was the first enemy aircraft whose destruction was attributable to a fighter carrying A.I. and belonging to a first-line squadron, although as long ago as July a success in active operations had been claimed by the Fighter Interception Unit.

24. Up to the end of the year fighters claimed the destruction of only three more night bombers, and none of these successes was attributable to A.I.

25. Many novel and unusual means of dealing with the night bomber were suggested about this time and subsequently. The more practicable of these included the release of a free balloon barrage, other forms of aerial mining, and the use of searchlights carried by aircraft. These are dealt with below under the appropriate headings.

26. On a number of occasions I arranged for fighters carrying equipment which responded to the "beam" transmissions which the Germans used to find their targets to be sent to "hunt in the beam," but the German crews seem to have anticipated this move and were wary. Fighters sent to patrol the points at which the bombers were expected to cross the French coast on their homeward journey, burning their navigation lights, were no more successful.

27. On the night of 11th December, I tried out for the second time, a measure which had previously been given an inconclusive trial over Bristol. Twenty Hampden bombers were sent to patrol at various specified heights over Birmingham during a concentrated attack on that city. The crews reported seeing a large number of enemy aircraft, but the Hampdens were too unwieldy to bring any of them to action. This experience proved, however, that in suitable circumstances interception by purely visual means was possible.

28. Meanwhile we were taking every possible step to improve the chances of interception by more orthodox means. Up to this time such G.L. sets as were available to assist the fighters had been grouped close together in the Kenley Sector. In consultation with General

Pile, I now arranged for them to be more widely spaced to form a "G.L. Carpet," designed to extend over the whole of Southern England from Kent to Bristol and ultimately, we hoped, over a still wider area. I also arranged with General Pile that the searchlights should be grouped in clusters of three, instead of singly, in order to provide a stronger illumination. In addition, I earmarked a number of airfields as night-fighter bases and took steps to equip them with every available aid to night flying.

29. It became clear in December that for the adequate defence of the Kingdom more specialist night squadrons were needed, and I therefore asked the Air Ministry to provide, as soon as possible, a total of 20 such squadrons, to include twelve twin-engined squadrons. Although it was some time before this figure was achieved, substantial additions were made to the night-fighter force during the ensuing months.

30. In the second week of December I was informed that the Air Ministry wished me ultimately to accept responsibility for the "Security Patrols" which had hitherto been flown by aircraft of No. 2 Group, Bomber Command, over airfields in Northern France and the Low Countries.

31. The use of fighters for this work had already been discussed by my Staff with No. 2 Group, and arrangements were being made for aircraft of No. 23 Squadron to supplement the efforts of No. 2 Group's Blenheims. On receipt of the Air Ministry's letter, I ordered that the whole of No. 23 Squadron should be turned over to this duty, to which the name "Intruder" was now applied. The A.I., whose capture could not be risked, was removed from the squadron's aircraft, navigators were posted to the squadron, and some crews were sent to one of No. 2 Group's Stations to learn all that they could about the operation. The squadron was ready to operate by 18th December and the first patrols were flown on the 21st.

32. A further account of operation "Intruder" is given below, under a separate heading. (Paras. 68 to 72.)

33. On 29th December, the Capital suffered one of its worse raids of the war when a determined attempt was made to destroy the cities of London and Westminster by the dropping of large numbers of incendiary bombs. Nearly 1,500 separate fires were started, some of them of vast dimensions. The weather was poor and the night-fighter force had no success.

(c) Operations, January to May, 1941.

34. Early in the New Year the efforts made to apply the principles of Radar to the special problems of night defence began to yield results. Radar equipment began to be available in increasing quantities, although it was some time before the S.L.C. sets needed by the searchlights arrived in anything like sufficient numbers. The performance of the heavy A.A. guns at night, measured by the number of rounds required to bring down one enemy aircraft, quickly improved and soon surpassed the standard achieved in daylight at the end of the 1914-1918 war.

35. For the fighter force an important step forward was the arrival of G.C.I. sets—hitherto only in the development stage—which enabled a ground controller to follow on a fluorescent screen the track in the horizontal plane both of a selected bomber and of the fighter sent to intercept it.

36. At first these sets could not read height with any accuracy, but their performance in this respect was soon improved.

37. For some time progress was slow, but by March substantial results were being achieved by the night-fighters, and indeed in that month their claims exceeded those of the A.A. gunners for the first time since June, 1940. Of the 43 night bombers whose destruction was claimed that month, 22 were claimed by the night-fighter forces, and half of these by twin-engined fighters using their A.I.

38. From this moment the A.I. fighter became the principal weapon of the night-fighter force. Unlike the single-engined fighter, it was not dependent on moonlight or artificial illumination and could therefore be used in weather which put the single-engined fighter out of court. From March onwards the steadiest results were claimed by A.I. fighters. On the other hand, a number of clear moonlit nights in Spring, on which German aircraft were to be found in large numbers over their target and along the route thereto, gave the single-engined fighters opportunities which enabled them to surpass, for short periods, the performance of their twin-engined rivals.

39. From that moment, too, the fighter rather than the A.A. gun became the chief means of inflicting casualties on the night bomber. But it would be unwise to draw any hasty conclusion from this fact. Although there was always a friendly rivalry between guns and fighters, it was recognised throughout the war that together—and in conjunction with the balloon defences—they formed a team of which all the members were indispensable. The value of what may conveniently be called the static defences was not to be measured solely, or even mainly, by the casualties which they inflicted on the enemy. Their deterrent effect, not only in causing some bombers to turn away before reaching their target, but in preventing leisurely and methodical bombing from low altitudes by the remainder, was always of inestimable value. The experience of the "Baedeker" raids (which came after the end of the period now under review) proves that if important objectives had been deprived in 1941 of their gun and balloon defences, they could very quickly have been destroyed, regardless of any action by night-fighters. Moreover, it must be remembered that the limitations of Radar at this time made interception at low altitudes extremely difficult. If the guns had not helped to keep the enemy up, successful interceptions at night would have been rare.

40. On the other hand, the guns and balloons were equally incapable of acting as a complete defence in themselves, but required the co-operation of the more mobile fighter, which was capable of harrying the bomber wherever he flew.

41. In January and February bad weather frequently defeated all the enemy's attempts to make his bombers independent of extraneous circumstances, by rendering many airfields unserviceable. Chiefly on this account, the German effort declined considerably. March

brought a revival, and in April and May the Germans increased their scale of attack still further in an attempt to conceal their intentions with respect to Russia.

42. Early in 1941, the Germans began to show an increasing tendency to concentrate on ports and shipping. There were other signs that an attempt to strangle our sea communications was contemplated, and at the end of February, I was instructed by the Air Ministry to provide additional "watch and ward" for coastwise shipping, and warned that the German bomber force might be expected to pay special attention in future to ports on the West Coast.

43. Early in March this was followed by a formal directive which required me to give priority to the defence of the Clyde, the Mersey and the Bristol Channel, which were now to rank above the aircraft industry in this respect.

44. I immediately took steps to strengthen the A.A. defences of these areas, partly by moving guns from other parts of the country and partly by pledging a substantial part of the anticipated production in March and April. By the middle of March, the move of 81 additional heavy A.A. guns to the West Coast ports had been ordered, and shortly afterwards further increases amounting to another 104 heavy A.A. guns were arranged. Actual increases exceeded what had been planned: 58 guns were withdrawn from the Midlands in March, and 24 guns came from the factories: by 1st June a further 106 new guns had been deployed.

45. I also modified the deployment of the night-fighter force in order to give increased protection to the Clyde and the Mersey. I considered that the Bristol Channel was already adequately defended by the squadrons deployed to cover the Southern approaches to the Midlands.

46. In spite of the enemy's growing tendency to attack ports and shipping, his attention at this stage was by no means exclusively devoted to such objectives. Many attacks were made on London and provincial towns, and the operations of German long-range fighters against our bombers and their bases caused some concern.

47. On the night of 10th May the enemy made the most ambitious attack on London that he had attempted up to that time, or indeed was ever to attempt. Although contemporary estimates were lower, it is now known that the German bomber force flew more than 500 sorties on this night. Visibility was good and the results were eminently satisfactory. A total of 60 single-engined fighters were sent to patrol at various heights over London, twenty over Beachy Head, and smaller numbers over the other approaches to the Capital, while twin-engined fighters were used to intercept the bombers as they came and went. These defensive fighters claimed between them the destruction of 23 enemy aircraft, of which the single-engined fighters claimed nineteen. A Defiant on an "Intruder" patrol over Northern France claimed one more, making 24. The A.A. gunners, although their fire was restricted by the presence of our fighters, claimed another four, making a grand total of 28 enemy aircraft, or roughly five per cent. of the enemy effort.

48. Perhaps the most remarkable feature of this night's operations was the success of the Hurricane and Spitfire flying in the Bomber Stream. On various other nights in April and May, aircraft on "Fighter Night" patrols claimed the destruction of twenty enemy aircraft in the aggregate. The impression that "Fighter Nights" was an unprofitable operation is widespread, but these figures show that, given good weather, moonlight, and a substantial concentration of enemy aircraft, these patrols could achieve satisfactory results. It was, however, only at periods when the moon was above the horizon that any success was achieved.

49. Operation "Fighter Night" was, of course, always regarded with disfavour by the A.A. gunners, whose chances of success it diminished. When it was first put into effect, the guns in the target area were forbidden to fire; but it was argued that their silence might cause apprehension amongst the public, and later they were allowed to fire up to heights safely below that of the lowest fighters. Such a restriction of A.A. fire was only justified, of course, when the conditions were particularly favourable to fighters; but the figures just quoted show that in these conditions its justification was beyond dispute. It is interesting to note that, despite the limitation imposed on them, the guns in the target area were not always barren of success on these occasions. While generally the guns kept the German bombers up to the heights at which the fighters could most conveniently engage them, it would seem that on occasions the fighters must have forced individual bombers down into the A.A. belt.

50. A night of scattered raiding on 11th May brought to an end the intensive phase which had begun eight months before. Thereafter, until the end of the year, the scale of attack was much smaller. Although a few more raids were made on London and the Midlands, the Germans devoted most of their attention for the rest of the year to targets near the coast or at sea, and to minelaying.

51. Undoubtedly the main reason for this change was a new strategic conception by the Germans. Having decided to attack the Russians, they withdrew most of their bombers from the West, leaving behind only a small force to second the German Navy's attempt to blockade the British Isles. To what extent this decision was due to the realisation by the enemy that his night offensive was failing as surely (though not so spectacularly) as his day offensive had failed in the previous Autumn, I do not know. But that the "Blitz" did fail to achieve any strategic purpose is clear enough. In eight months of intensive night raiding, the German bomber force did not succeed in breaking the spirit of the British people or preventing the expansion of our means of production and supply. Moreover, the cumulative effect of the ever-increasing losses which the Germans incurred as the defences got under way cannot have been a negligible factor, even though these losses were not sufficient in themselves to have brought the offensive to a standstill. To the country as a whole, and everyone in it, the end of the night battle was a great relief; nevertheless there was a sense in which it came to those under my command, and indeed to myself, as something of a disappointment. An

enemy over whom we felt that we were gaining the mastery had slipped out of our grasp. All arms of the defence were working better than they had ever done before; the first five months of 1941 had seen a steady and striking improvement in the results achieved. We were confident—I am confident still—that if the enemy had not chosen that moment to pull out, we should soon have been inflicting such casualties on his night bombers that the continuance of his night offensive on a similar scale would have been impossible.

(d) *Operations, June to December, 1941.*

52. As it was, the minor operations which formed the staple of the German night offensive during the second half of 1941 gave few chances to the defences. Minelaying aircraft, which flew low and could usually avoid gun-defended areas, were particularly hard to shoot down, and although we made many attempts to evolve means of intercepting them, it was not until 1942 that we had much success. But when the enemy did venture overland, the improvement which had been made since the beginning of the year was well maintained. When the Medway towns were attacked in June, for example, the defences claimed the destruction of seven enemy aircraft out of less than 100 operating; on two successive moonlit nights in July, eleven out of about 170 were claimed; and on the first night of November, when some 50 aircraft operated against Merseyside, the defences claimed the destruction of six.

(e) *The Free Balloon Barrage.*

53. Towards the end of 1940, I made arrangements to release Balloons carrying lethal charges in the path of German bombers approaching London. The intention was to use this free barrage on nights when the conditions were unsuitable for fighters; but it did not follow that whenever conditions were unsuitable for fighters they would be favourable for the Balloon Barrage, which had certain positive requirements of its own. These were by no means easy to satisfy. A disadvantage of the scheme was that deployment of the equipment had to be begun many hours in advance, on the strength of a difficult meteorological forecast, and on the chance that when the time came the character of the enemy's operations as well as the weather would favour release.

54. The first release was made on the night of 27th December. Imperfect communications caused a delay of 35 minutes between the issue of the order to release and the ascent of the first balloons. Shortly afterwards the enemy attack died away and the order to stop releasing the balloons was given. So far as is known the comparatively small number of balloons released had no effect on the enemy.

55. A further release on the night of 11th January, 1941, went much more smoothly. The weather turned out as predicted and 1,252 balloons were released over a period of three hours. Some 60 German bombers flew through the area in which the barrage was operating but appeared to be quite unaffected by it, mainly, perhaps, because the balloons were too widely spaced to give a good chance of success.

56. Although arrangements were subsequently made to improve the equipment and system of release, the scheme never achieved any practical success and was eventually abandoned.

(f) *No. 93 Squadron.*

57. No. 93 Squadron was formed in the late Autumn of 1940 for the purpose of trailing and sowing aerial mines in the path of German bombers. During its life of rather less than a year the squadron claimed a number of successes, and the destruction of two enemy aircraft—one in December, 1940, and one in the following April—was officially credited to it.

58. As time went on, however, the performance of orthodox night-fighter squadrons using A.I. improved so much that I came to the conclusion that the comparatively modest results achieved by No. 93 Squadron did not justify the manpower and effort involved in its continued existence. In November, 1941, therefore, I obtained authority to disband the squadron.

(g) *Airborne Searchlights.*

59. The idea of a searchlight carried in an aircraft is an old one, but the practical difficulties involved are considerable, because of the great weight of the equipment needed to produce a sufficiently powerful light.

60. In 1941 this problem seemed to have been solved, thanks to the skill and ingenuity of Air Commodore W. Helmore. Aircraft carrying searchlights were now a practicable weapon and I was ordered to form the equivalent of five squadrons of Havoc aircraft so equipped.

61. In trials these aircraft succeeded in illuminating and holding their targets while attendant single-engined fighters intercepted them. The crews of the target aircraft reported that the effect when the Havoc suddenly switched on its searchlights and held them in its blinding glare was extremely disconcerting, and hopes ran high.

62. By the time that the Havocs were ready for active operations, however, the enemy effort had dwindled to very small proportions, so that the scheme had no chance to prove its worth in 1941. When, after the end of the period now under review, the Havocs were given their opportunity, they proved too slow to compete on level terms with the orthodox A.I. squadrons against the faster bombers with which the German bomber force was then equipped.

(h) *Deployment of Ground Searchlights.*

63. Reference has been made to the siting of the searchlights in clusters of three during the winter of 1940-41.

64. This arrangement was found to be no solution to the problem, and, in the autumn of 1941, I arranged with General Pile for the searchlights to be re-sited singly.

65. Their primary function was now to help fighters to intercept, since the heavy A.A. guns were no longer dependent on them, and the basis of the new system was what was called the "fighter box."

66. It was found by calculation and experiment that the area within which a fighter pilot could hope to pick up and intercept a bomber with the aid of searchlights alone was a rectangle 44 miles long and 14 miles wide. Accordingly, we divided the whole of the area to be covered by searchlights into rectangles of this size. The searchlights were then so arranged that in the centre of each rectangle

there was a stationary vertical beam. Round this beam the fighter circled until an enemy bomber entered the "box." Other searchlights were disposed at intervals of 3½ miles near the centre of the box and wider intervals near its borders. As soon as the bomber entered the box the beams of the outlying searchlights (belonging to the "Indicator Zone") began to converge on it, thus indicating its approach to the fighter pilot, who thereupon set a course which would put him in a position to intercept it in the central "Killer Zone."

67. This system was not working with full efficiency by the end of 1941, but ultimately proved very effective and remained substantially unchanged until the end of the war.

(j) *Operation "Intruder".*

68. The circumstances in which No. 23 Squadron began to fly "Intruder" patrols on 21st December, 1940, have been described above.

69. It was not until the early spring that the squadron had many opportunities of successful action. With better weather and increased enemy activity it was then very successful, claiming the destruction of three enemy aircraft in March, 1941, two in April, and eleven in May. Thereafter, opportunities were again limited. Nevertheless, it was decided that a second "Intruder" Squadron should be added to the Command, and No. 418 (R.C.A.F.) Squadron, equipped with Bostons, began to form in the autumn.

70. No. 23 Squadron, originally equipped with Blenheims, re-armed with Havocs in March and April, 1941, and received a few Bostons later in the year.

71. Between 21st December, 1940, and 31st December, 1941, operation "Intruder" was carried out on 145 nights and 573 sorties were flown, of which 505 were by Blenheims, Havocs and Bostons of No. 23 Squadron, and 68 by Hurricanes and Defiants of Nos. 1, 3, 87, 141, 151, 242, 264, 306 and 601 Squadrons, which were employed on this work occasionally on moonlit nights. The destruction of 21 enemy aircraft was claimed, 290 separate bombing attacks on airfields were reported, and ten of our aircraft were lost.

72. Throughout this period the executive control of this operation was something of a problem. To secure the best results, it was essential that the "Intruder" aircraft should arrive at active enemy bases just as returning bombers reached them. This could only be achieved by a close study of information from intelligence and raid-reporting sources on the part of those responsible for ordering the despatch of the "Intruder" aircraft. In accordance with the normal practice in my Command, control of the operation was delegated at the outset to No. 11 Group, from whose stations No. 23 Squadron was operating. The executive orders were issued by whichever of the Controllers at No. 11 Group's Headquarters happened to be on duty at the time, in consultation with the Officer Commanding No. 23 Squadron. It was a matter for consideration whether these Duty Controllers, with their numerous responsibilities, could be expected to give that constant specialized attention to the changing data provided by the Intelligence and Raid-Reporting services which was essential for success. The suggestion that control of the operation should be exercised directly from my Headquarters was made more than once and from more than one quarter in 1941. I did not think it desirable to make any change at this stage, but later, when the necessity of co-ordinating the work of the "Intruder" Squadrons closely with the operations of Bomber Command made a more centralised control almost essential, this solution was adopted.

Day Operations.

(a) *Defensive.*

(i) *Forces Available.*

73. At the end of the Battle of Britain, that is to say at the beginning of November, 1940, the strength of the day fighter force amounted to 55½ squadrons, including three and a half squadrons in the process of formation. On paper this was a substantially larger force than the Command had possessed at the beginning of the battle; but really the force available was weaker. Many of our best pilots had been killed, and quantitatively the casualties had proved greater than the training organisation could make good, so that despite such expedients as the transfer of pilots from other Commands, the squadrons were short of their proper establishment of pilots.

74. The long-term measures taken within the Command to ameliorate this situation are described in Part II. In the meantime the position was such as to give some ground for anxiety. Of the 52 operational day squadrons in the Command at the beginning of November, only 26 were, in the most strict sense, first-line squadrons. Another two squadrons were being kept up to operational strength so that they could act as reliefs in an emergency. The remainder, apart from a half-squadron employed as "spotters," had only a few operational pilots apiece and were suitable only for employment in quiet sectors.

75. The practice of stripping some squadrons of most of their experienced pilots in order to keep others up to strength is clearly indefensible except in a grave emergency, if only because of the invidious distinctions thus created. It had been adopted by my predecessor in the late Summer only because, in the circumstances of that time, it seemed the sole alternative to "telescoping" or disbanding squadrons. As soon as conditions permitted, I abandoned this system, with its categorisation of squadrons as class "A," "B" or "C," and all squadrons in turn were given their chance in the more active Sectors.

76. Although the Battle of Britain is now regarded as having ended on 31st October, 1940, no sharp break was noticeable at the time. Not until some weeks later was it evident that, for the time being, the Germans had abandoned the idea of defeating the Command by a series of mass attacks in daylight. Even then a resumption of these mass attacks in the following Spring or Summer was regarded as inevitable; and in December I asked for a force of 80 day fighter squadrons to meet this situation.

77. The Air Ministry were unable to accept the dislocation of their plan for the expansion of other Commands which the attainment of

so large a fighter force by the Spring or early Summer would have entailed, and eventually the strength to which the day fighter force was to expand by April, 1941, was fixed at 64 squadrons.

78. When April came, this figure had been duly reached. However, once again the position was less strong than it appeared on paper. Of the 64 day squadrons shown in the Order of Battle, two and a half were still in process of formation and two, although formed, were temporarily out of the line. The effective strength amounted, therefore, to $59\frac{1}{2}$ squadrons. Many of them had considerably less than their established complement of pilots, and the general level of experience was substantially below that of the previous Autumn.

79. On the other hand, the opposing forces had been weakened numerically by the withdrawal of Units to the Mediterranean and Balkan theatres, and were soon to be reduced still further by withdrawals to Eastern Germany and Poland in preparation for the campaign against Russia.

80. In the event, of course, the mass attacks made by the Germans in the Summer of 1940 were never to be repeated on a comparable scale, so that after the opening of the Russian campaign, the day fighter force, although still charged with important defensive duties such as the protection of coastwise shipping and the interception of bomber reconnaissance aircraft flying singly, became largely an instrument for containing enemy forces in Northern France and attempting to compel the return of Units from the Eastern Front.

81. But even then the strength of the Russian resistance could not be foreseen; it still seemed likely that the Germans might bring the Eastern campaign to a successful conclusion within a measurable time and then renew their daylight offensive in the West. Accordingly, further additions were made during the second half of 1941 to the day fighter force, which, despite the despatch of seven squadrons overseas in December, reached the end of the year with a strength of 75 squadrons.

(ii) *Operations, November, 1940, to February, 1941.*

82. It has been said that, although October 31st, 1940 is now regarded as the last day of the Battle of Britain, the fact that the battle had ended on that day was not apparent at the time.

83. Indeed, the first few days of November, far from constituting a lull, were days of exceptional activity. Nevertheless, 1st November did appear to mark the beginning of a new phase of the offensive. For on that day the Germans turned to a form of attack with which they had opened the battle some months earlier, by sending over bombers and dive-bombers with fighter escort to attack our shipping in the Thames Estuary and the Dover Strait.

84. Before this no mass attacks on shipping had been made for many weeks. The Ju87 dive-bomber, which appeared in substantial numbers on that day, had not been reported in action since 18th August although it now appears that, unknown to the Command and apparently also to the Air Ministry, these aircraft may have been used against shipping at least once in September. When further attacks followed on the next day, it seemed clear that a new stage of the battle had been reached, and on 4th November the Air Officer Commanding No. 11 Group issued orders which detailed the tactical measures required to defeat this new move.

85. Both before and after the issue of these orders the fighters reported excellent results, especially against the German dive-bombers and the Italian aircraft which took part in a few of the attacks. Doubtless for this reason, the mass attacks on shipping ceased on 14th November and from that date the Ju87 virtually ceased to be employed in daylight operations on the Western Front.

86. Despite its brevity this phase was important, for it brought to a head a conflict between the claims of shipping and the aircraft industry, which had long been a source of anxiety to my predecessor.

87. Since the beginning of the War the primary task of the Command, as laid down in a directive issued by the Air Staff and endorsed by the Chiefs of Staff, had been the defence of the aircraft industry. The Command was, of course, responsible for the air defence of the United Kingdom as a whole, and it also had a somewhat ill-defined responsibility for the fighter protection of shipping close to the coast; but the directive made it quite clear that the aircraft industry had the first claim on the Commander-in-Chief's resources.

88. So far as action by fighters was concerned the defence of the aircraft industry and the general air defence of the country were practically inseparable tasks, for it was an axiom of air defence—though one which the Minister of Aircraft Production was reluctant to accept—that the best way of defending an objective such as a factory was to deploy fighters over the approaches to it rather than concentrate them near the objective itself.

89. This principle did not apply to the protection of shipping. The ships moved mostly on the perimeter of the air defence system and it was seldom possible to be sure of intercepting aircraft which might attack them except by detailing specified fighter units to protect them, either by flying standing patrols near the ships or the adjacent coastline or by assuming an advanced state of readiness at airfields near the coast.

90. The inherent extravagance and relative inefficiency of standing patrols has always been recognised by students of air defence problems; nevertheless there are occasions in which they constitute the only practicable method of defence, and in this case they were the form of protection which the Naval authorities preferred and for which they constantly pressed.

91. It was not always possible, however, to place our fighters on standing patrol near a convoy without exposing them to the risk of being caught at a tactical disadvantage by the enemy. Another difficulty was that regulations imposed for the benefit of the ships themselves forbade our pilots to come close to the ships, virtually on pain of being fired at.

92. In spite of these difficulties and uncertainties, loyal attempts were made from the beginning of the War to give every practicable

assistance to the Royal Navy in their task of safeguarding the convoys whenever they were within range of our fighters. At the same time, attempts were made to place the matter on a more satisfactory basis, and in particular to obtain from the Air Ministry a clear statement of the Command's duties in respect of shipping and the degree of priority to be accorded to them. These attempts culminated at the end of October and beginning of November, 1940, in the receipt of a series of communications from the Secretary of State for Air which gave renewed sanction to the Command's existing practice of protecting convoys whenever possible by holding fighters at readiness rather than flying standing patrols; confirmed that the defence of the aircraft industry was still the primary task of the Command; but added that convoys, and also flotillas and minesweeping craft, must be protected so long as their protection was practicable.

93. This pronouncement did not end my predecessor's perplexities, since—perhaps inevitably—it neither defined the practicable nor assisted him to determine how much of his resources he would be justified in diverting from his primary task to what was clearly a secondary—and yet, apparently, essential—one.

94. The difficulty of the problem will be the more easily grasped if it is borne in mind that, at this stage of the war, practically the whole resources of the Command could have been expended on either of these rival tasks, without glutting the appetite of the Minister of Aircraft Production in the one case or the Naval authorities in the other.

95. The renewal of mass attacks on shipping at the beginning of November brought fresh demands from the Naval authorities. Accordingly, my predecessor again asked the Air Ministry, this time by means of a formal letter, to clarify their policy in regard to the fighter protection of shipping. In this letter he placed before the Air Ministry a series of proposals based on the practice which had grown up gradually within the Command.

96. No reply to this letter had been received when I took up Command, and I therefore assumed the Air Ministry's tacit consent to the proposals. Henceforward three degrees of fighter protection for shipping were recognized, namely *close escort*, to be given only in special cases and by prior arrangement; *protection*, which meant that specified fighter units were detailed to defend specified shipping units in a given area and over a given period, either by flying patrols or remaining at readiness; and *cover*, which meant that note was taken of the position of the shipping, and arrangements were made to intercept any aircraft which appeared to threaten it.

97. Fortunately the scale of attack against coastwise shipping declined considerably after the middle of November. In the circumstances the Naval authorities remained, to all appearances, reasonably contented with a standard of protection which would probably not have satisfied them had the attacks of early November continued.

98. Only four ships were sunk by air action within fighter range in December 1940, and only two in January 1941, as against eleven in November.

99. Apart from operations against shipping, the enemy continued in November to make the fighter and fighter-bomber sweeps over Kent and Sussex which had been a feature of his operations in October. But in November these sweeps were made at less extreme altitudes than in October, perhaps to avoid causing condensation trails or to reduce the strain on pilots. Consequently they were rather easier to counter. Heavy casualties were inflicted on the enemy's fighters as well as his dive-bombers, and in this month No. 11 Group claimed the highest proportion of enemy aircraft destroyed to their own pilots lost which had yet been recorded.

100. The fighter sweeps virtually ceased in the middle of December and were resumed on a reduced scale in February. In the meantime the Germans made a number of so-called "pirate" raids on aircraft factories and similar objectives. These raids were made by single aircraft, flying over carefully prepared routes, often in cloudy weather. The German pilots showed great skill in taking advantage of every favourable circumstance of topography and weather to elude the defences. Although the raids were too infrequent to do much harm to our war potential, they caused some anxiety and resulted in great pressure being put on me to provide local fighter protection for the threatened factories.

101. The unsoundness of this method of defence, which, if carried to its logical conclusion, would have been impossibly extravagant and would have exposed our fighter force to defeat in detail, needs no elaboration. Nevertheless the Minister of Aircraft Production was so insistent that eventually I devised a scheme whereby a number of aircraft factories were to be allotted fighters for local defence, these to be piloted by the firms' own test pilots. Although put into effect later in the year, the scheme achieved little practical success and was eventually allowed to fall into abeyance. As to its thorough unsoundness from the military viewpoint there can be no doubt; but I think that it may have been worth while at the time simply for its moral effect. Workers who, seeing no fighters in the immediate neighbourhood of their factory, were unaware of the protection that they were receiving from the general air defence system, may have been and probably were heartened by the knowledge that there was a fighter on the factory airfield expressly for the purpose of defending them.

102. A more important measure taken at this stage concerned the flying of Balloon Barrages. On the outbreak of War the intention had been to fly the balloons at all times. This practice proved so expensive, chiefly because of the large number of balloons carried away or damaged by bad weather, that it soon gave way to a system whereby balloons were close-hauled in doubtful weather and raised only on the approach of hostile aircraft. The disadvantage of this system was that the weather conditions in which balloons were likely to be close-hauled were precisely those in which a "pirate" raider might hope to approach its target undetected, or at least without its purpose being divined in time for the barrage to be raised. Thus, if the barrage commanders interpreted their freedom to close-haul the balloons too liberally, there was a risk that

the barrages would be out of action just when they were most needed.

103. The experience of the "pirate" raids revealed this danger. In consequence I overhauled the machinery which had been set up to inform barrage Commanders of the approach of hostile aircraft, and laid down the principle that some risk of damage to balloons by bad weather must be accepted and that all barrages must be kept flying by day unless there were really strong grounds for close-hauling them.

(iii) *Operations, March to December,* 1941.

104. At the end of February a decision was reached at the highest level to give absolute priority to the defence of shipping in the North-Western approaches, which was now dangerously threatened by a combination of U-boats and long-range aircraft.

105. The measures taken in consequence of this decision included the transfer to Northern Ireland of some Units of Coastal Command which had hitherto shared with my Command the task of protecting coastwise trade off the East Coast. Consequently, when announcing this decision on 28th February, the Air Ministry instructed me to provide additional "watch and ward" for this traffic, at the expense, if necessary, of other tasks. At the same time I was warned of the possibility of increased attention by the German bomber force to West Coast Ports.

106. These instructions were followed on 9th March by a directive which made the defence of the Clyde, the Mersey and the Bristol Channel my primary task.

107. As has been seen in discussing night operations, I made arrangements in consequence of these instructions to increase the A.A. and night-fighter defences of the West Coast Ports. At the same time, I increased the day-fighter defences of the Bristol Channel and the Mersey by bringing into operation Nos. 118 and 316 (Polish) Squadrons, which had been training for some time past at Filton and Pembrey, and by moving the newly-formed No. 315 (Polish) Squadron to Speke. I did not consider that any addition was necessary to the day-fighter defences of the Clyde, as No. 602 Squadron was already at Prestwick, while Nos. 43, 603 and 607 Squadrons at Turnhouse and Drem could quickly be made available as reinforcements.

108. On 5th March I gave instructions to all the Fighter Groups to allot a greater proportion of their effort to the protection of shipping and ports. The system of giving "escort", "protection" or "cover" to convoys, according to circumstances, remained in force, but I arranged that "escort" should be given more generously than hitherto in specially dangerous areas, and that, where attacks were likely to be made without warning, fighters giving "protection" should be kept airborne while the risk continued.

109. The practical effect of these instructions is best shown by a few statistics.

110. In February 1941, my Command devoted to the protection of shipping 443 sorties, or eight per cent. of its total defensive effort by day; in March 2,103 sorties, or eighteen per cent.; and in April 7,876 sorties, or 49 per cent. During April several Squadrons in No. 10 Group each spent more than 1,000 hours of flying time in the discharge of this task. In no ensuing month of 1941 was the proportion of the total defensive effort of my Command by day which was devoted to the protection of shipping less than 52 per cent., the highest proportion being 69 per cent. (in August and again in September). The smallest number of daylight sorties expended on this duty in any month after March was 3,591 (in December) and the largest 8,287 (in May).

111. Besides providing this vastly increased scale of fighter protection, I surrendered from the resources under my operational control, a number of light A.A. weapons for installation in merchant vessels. Other forms of armament now provided for these vessels included rocket projectors and parachute-and-cable projectors.

112. In consequence of these measures the Germans were forced to make an increasing proportion of their attacks under cover of darkness or twilight. After rising to a peak of 21 ships in March, the number of ships sunk by air action in daylight within the radius of fighter action fell to negligible proportions.

113. Various means of protecting ships at night as well as by day were tried, but after dark fighters were at a disadvantage, since their presence tended to confuse the ships' gunners and thus do more harm than good. On the whole the best form of protection for merchant vessels after nightfall proved to be a combination of the A.A. weapons carried by the ships themselves and their escort vessels, and the orthodox use of night-fighters to intercept enemy bombers wherever they could be most conveniently engaged. On the other hand it was important not to withdraw escorting fighters too early, since the Germans were quick to seize opportunities of attacking ships at dusk. At the end of the last patrol of the day, therefore, fighters had to be landed in the dark. Conversely it was necessary for the earliest patrols to take off long before dawn in order to be in position by "first light."

114. A word of tribute is due to the pilots who undertook these unspectacular and often tedious duties. Convoy patrols gave pilots comparatively few chances of distinguishing themselves in combat with the enemy, yet they constituted an essential, often exacting, and sometimes hazardous task, since the possibility of a sudden deterioration in the weather, which might render the handling of a high-performance fighter a business requiring all the pilot's skill, was always to be reckoned with.

115. There remained the problem of protecting shipping outside the radius of action of the short-range fighter. Hitherto my Command had not been concerned with this; but in the Spring of 1941 the Air Ministry announced a decision to equip a number of merchant vessels as "Catapult Aircraft Merchant Ships". At least one of these "C.A.M. Ships" would form part of every Atlantic convoy. Each would carry a Hurricane fighter, which could be launched by rocket-catapult on the approach of an enemy aircraft. On completion of his patrol the pilot would either bale out, alight on the sea, or, if near the coast, make for an airfield on land.

116. In order to provide the necessary complement of pilots, the formation of the Merchant Ship Fighter Unit began at Speke, in No. 9 Group, early in May 1941. I also made arrangements to train a number of Naval Officers as

"Fighter Directing Officers". The latter were to sail in the C.A.M. ships and, making use of radar and radio-telephony equipment, direct the fighters towards approaching German aircraft. The Merchant Ship Fighter Unit absorbed the equivalent of approximately two fighter squadrons.

117. The Unit despatched its first pilots and maintenance crews on operational service early in June. In August a detachment opened at Dartmouth, Nova Scotia, to administer a pool of replacement aircraft on the Western side of the Atlantic.

118. German aircraft continued to make occasional "pirate" raids on factories and other objectives in the Spring, but thereafter activity by day, apart from operations against shipping, consisted almost entirely of reconnaissance flights and occasional "tip-and-run" attacks on coast towns in England and Scotland. Offensive operations by German fighters virtually ceased in the early Summer. On a few occasions in the Autumn Me109 fighters were seen over Kent and Sussex, but the only offensive action worthy of the name which was taken by German fighters in the second half of 1941 was on Christmas Day, when two aircraft appeared off the South Coast and opened fire on buildings near Hastings. This was the prelude to a new low-level fighter and fighter-bomber offensive which was to take place in 1942.

119. The interception of "pirate" raiders and other aircraft flying singly was a difficult task, especially in cloudy weather, when problems arose similar to those which surrounded night interception. As early as December 1940, the principle of using Beaufighters fitted with A.I. by day in bad weather was established, and as experience grew it became evident that in such conditions the only reasonable chance of success was offered by the same combination of A.I. in the aircraft, and G.C.I. on the ground, as was used at night.

120. The next step was the use of G.C.I. by day for controlling fighters without as well as with A.I. In August 1941, I made provision for this to be done throughout Nos. 10 and 11 Groups, although at this stage G.C.I. Stations in No. 11 Group were not required to keep watch by day in good weather.

121. Another step taken about this time was the development of a plan for intercepting aircraft capable of flying at very great heights, which it was thought that the Germans might be planning to use against us. After fighters of No. 10 Group had practised making very high-altitude G.C.I. interceptions of Fortresses of Bomber Command, my staff devised a system of control whereby the country was divided into a number of regions each containing an "area control" connected with a "central control" designed to co-ordinate their activities. This scheme was to prove useful in 1942 when the Germans sent a number of high-flying Ju86 P reconnaissance aircraft over this country.

122. With the decline in the volume of overland activity by the Luftwaffe towards the end of 1941, I considered it reasonable to contemplate a relaxation of the principles of balloon-barrage control which had been re-affirmed in the Spring. Technical improvements which made it possible to raise balloons to their operational height more quickly than hitherto favoured a change which seemed called for by an increased volume of flying by our own aircraft, to which the barrages were in some circumstances an impediment. In November trials were made with a system whereby a large number of provincial barrages were grounded throughout the 24 hours except when German aircraft were known to be about. It was not until 1942, however, that this system was finally adopted.

(b) *Offensive.*
(i) *Operations up to 13th June*, 1941.

123. During the Battle of Britain the initiative in daylight operations lay with the Germans. Nevertheless, even before the battle was over a time was foreseen when our fighter squadrons would seize the initiative and engage the German fighters over the far side of the Channel. The necessary operational instructions were drawn up as early as the third week in October, 1940, and revised in the first week of December.

124. By the latter date it was possible to contemplate something more ambitious than a mere pushing forward of fighter patrols, and on 29th November, I instructed the Air Officer Commanding No. 11 Group to look into the possibility of combining offensive sweeps with operations by Bomber Command.

125. In the middle of December the German fighter force, which had suffered heavy losses since the Summer, virtually abandoned the offensive for the time being. Clearly, the moment had come to put our plans into effect and wrest the initiative from the enemy.

126. Broadly speaking, the plan which we now adopted visualized two kinds of offensive operations. In cloudy weather, small numbers of fighters would cross the channel under cover of the clouds, dart out of them to attack any German aircraft they could find, and return similarly protected. In good weather fighter forces amounting to several squadrons at a time, and sometimes accompanied by bombers, would sweep over Northern France. The code-names chosen for these operations were respectively "Mosquito" (later changed to "Rhubarb," to avoid confusion with the aircraft of that name) and "Circus"; but in practice it was necessary to restrict the name "Circus" to operations with bombers, and fulfilling certain other conditions which will become apparent as this account proceeds.

127. "Rhubarb" patrols were begun on 20th December, 1940, and provided valuable experience alike for pilots, operational commanders, and the staffs of the formations concerned. I encouraged the delegation of responsibility for the planning of these patrols to lower formations, and many patrols were planned by the pilots themselves with the help of their Squadron Intelligence Officers.

128. It was obvious from the start that in many cases pilots engaged on these patrols would not succeed in meeting any German aircraft, and they were authorised in this event to attack suitable objectives on the ground. Nevertheless, I considered it important that the primary object of the operation—namely, the destruction of enemy aircraft—should not be forgotten, and discouraged any tendency to give undue emphasis to the attacks on ground objectives.

129. Between 20th December, 1940, and 13th June, 1941, 149 " Rhubarb " patrols, involving 336 sorties, were flown, of which 45 were rendered abortive by unsuitable weather or other extraneous circumstances. German aircraft were seen in the air on 26 occasions, to a total of 77 aircraft, and on 18 occasions were engaged. The destruction of seven enemy aircraft was claimed for the loss of eight of our pilots, and 116 separate attacks were made on a variety of surface objectives, including ships, road vehicles, airfield buildings, grounded aircraft, artillery and searchlight posts, German troops and military camps.

130. Operations on a larger scale began with a sweep off and over the coast of France by a total of five squadrons of fighters on 9th January, 1941. The first operation with bombers followed on the next day, when dispersal pens serving landing grounds on the edge of the Foret de Guines, South of Calais, were attacked. Altogether eleven of these " Circus " operations were executed up to 13th June, the objectives for the bombers including the docks at Dunkirk, Calais and Boulogne, a number of airfields and one industrial plant known to be working for the Germans. In addition more than forty sweeps were made during this period by fighters without bombers.

131. After the first three " Circus " operations an inevitable difference of view between Bomber and Fighter Commands as to the primary object of these attacks became apparent. The principal aim of my Command was to shoot down enemy aircraft, while Bomber Command, naturally enough, attached more importance to the bombing. It was, however, the view of the Chief of the Air Staff that the bombing of objectives in France with the resources available for operation " Circus " could have no decisive military effect at this stage of the War, and that it would be a pity to spoil the chances of the fighters by making them conform to the requirements of a bomber force bent exclusively on inflicting material damage by bombing, and prepared to linger over the target area for that purpose. On his instructions, the Air Officer Commanding-in-Chief, Bomber Command, and myself, held a conference at my Headquarters on 15th February, 1941, when we agreed that the object of operation " Circus " was to force the enemy to give battle in conditions tactically favourable to our fighters. To compel the Germans to do so, the bombers must do enough damage to make it impossible for them to refuse to fight.

132. The early " Circus " attacks were not always successful in producing these tactically favourable conditions, even after agreement on this point had been reached. This was largely because, in practice, there was still a tendency for our forces to operate too low down. There is no doubt that ideally our lowest fighter squadron should never have flown at less than about 18,000 feet, the highest being somewhere about 30,000 feet. To achieve this it would have been necessary for the bombers invariably to fly at 17,000 feet or more. This was not always practicable, if only because of the time required by the Blenheim bombers then used for these operations to reach that height. Nevertheless, it was thought advisable to lay down this principle as a *desideratum,* and this was done when I issued fresh instructions for operation " Circus " during the third week in February. In the next three operations the bombers flew at heights between 15,000 and 17,000 feet and in the following two at 10,000 and 12,000 feet respectively.

133. Towards the end of May the weather declined, and between 22nd May and 13th June no " Circus " operations were attempted. Up to this point no major fighter battle had occurred, the enemy having been content, on the whole, to pounce on stragglers or otherwise attempt to exploit any favourable tactical situation which might develop. In the absence of such favourable circumstances he had usually avoided combat. In this sense the operations had proved slightly disappointing. On the other hand, statistically the results were fairly satisfactory so far as they went, the destruction of 16 aircraft and probable destruction of a substantial number of others being claimed for the loss of 25 of our pilots; and much valuable experience had been gained. Moreover, by a combination of " Circus " and " Rhubarb " operations our ultimate object, which was to seize the initiative, harass the enemy, and force him on to the defensive, had undoubtedly been achieved.

134. Besides these " Circus " operations, fighter sweeps, and " Rhubarb " patrols, a series of bombing attacks on shipping and what were called " fringe targets " by aircraft of Bomber and Coastal Commands, with fighter escort, were made between 5th February and 12th June, 1941. These operations differed from " Circus " operations inasmuch as the primary object was not to force enemy fighters to give battle, but to damage or destroy the target. The fighter force therefore conformed to the requirements of the bomber force and did not seek battle unless attacked.

135. Sixteen such operations were undertaken during the period stated, the size of the bombing force ranging from three to eighteen aircraft, and that of the fighter escort from one flight to eight squadrons. A number of combats with German fighters developed, in which we claimed the destruction of one German aircraft for approximately every one of our pilots lost. A considerable volume of fighter-reconnaissance was carried out in connection with these operations.

(ii) *Operations, 14th June to 31st December, 1941.*

136. On 14th June an improvement in the weather permitted the resumption of the " Circus " offensive, and an operation which had been planned towards the end of May was put into effect. A similar operation on 16th June was followed on 17th June by the most ambitious " Circus " yet attempted. This involved an attack on a Chemical Plant and Power Station near Bethune by eighteen Blenheim bombers, escorted by no less than 22 squadrons of fighters. The enemy fighter force reacted vigorously, and although we lost nine pilots, those who returned reported a very favourable outcome of their combats. It seemed that the long-expected " fighter battle on terms tactically favourable to ourselves " had come at last.

137. On the same day the Chief of the Air Staff instructed me to devise, in consultation with my colleagues at Bomber and Coastal

Commands, the most effective means possible of checking the withdrawal of Luftwaffe Units to the East—where the German attack on Russia was imminent—and, if possible, forcing the enemy to return some of the Units already withdrawn.

138. A meeting to discuss this question took place at my Headquarters, on 19th June, and was attended by the three Commanders-in-Chief and members of our staffs and by the Air Officer Commanding No. 11 Group and two of his staff.

139. We came to the conclusion that the best plan would be to attack objectives within range of escorting fighters—in other words, to intensify the " Circus " offensive. Since the enemy had reacted most energetically so far to the " Circus " against a target near Bethune on 17th June and another against a target in that area on 21st May, we concluded that the industrial area which included Bethune, Lens and Lille was probably his most sensitive spot. By attacking this area it was hoped to induce him to concentrate in North-East France such fighter units as he still had in the West. Bombers without escort might then hope to reach West and North-West Germany in daylight round the flank of the defences, and this in turn might force the enemy to bring back fighters from the Eastern Front in order to defend the Fatherland.

140. As a corollary to this offensive, night attacks would be made on communications in the Ruhr, and shipping attempting to pass through the Straits of Dover would also be attacked. This two-pronged offensive would, we thought, constitute a threat to communications between France and Germany which the enemy could not afford to ignore.

141. These proposals met with the approval of the Air Ministry, and an agreed list of " Circus " objectives was drawn up. It was arranged that aircraft of No. 2 Group, Bomber Command, should attack them in co-operation with fighters of my Command, and, as a secondary task, should also attack shipping and " fringe targets."

142. On 3rd July, the Air Ministry informed me that the formula defining the object of operation " Circus," which had been agreed upon in February, must be abandoned and that the object must now be " the destruction of certain important targets by day bombing, and incidentally, the destruction of enemy fighter aircraft."

143. Two days later Stirling bombers of No. 3 Group were used in these operations for the first time instead of Blenheims of No. 2 Group. This change, together with the tactical adjustment which the new policy laid down by the Air Ministry made necessary, imposed a slight and temporary handicap on the fighter force. As soon as experience had been gained under the new conditions, a small formation of Stirlings was found to suit the fighters better than a larger formation of Blenheims. Towards the end of the month the Stirlings ceased, however, to be available for " Circus " operations, as Bomber Command required them exclusively for other purposes.

144. During the first few weeks of the intensive period, which may be regarded as beginning on 14th June, our pilots reported outstandingly good results in combat, and early in July it seemed that something like complete ascendancy had been gained over the opposing fighter force. For a short time in the middle of June the German fighter-pilots had offered determined opposition, but they now seemed, as in the Spring, reluctant to engage unless specially favoured by circumstances.

145. The results reported by our pilots during the next few weeks were not quite so good, although still much in our favour, and at the end of July the Air Ministry decided to review the results achieved up to this time.

146. To assess these results with any approach to accuracy was a matter of great difficulty. Our pilots had reported the destruction of enemy fighters in large numbers; but in operations on this scale there is room for much honest error, and even if the claims were accepted at their face value, it was impossible to know how many German pilots had baled out of their damaged aircraft, descended safely by parachute, and lived to fight another day. We believed that our information about the enemy's Order of Battle was good—as, indeed, it subsequently proved to be—but our knowledge of his capacity to replace losses was scanty. We had good reason to think that so far our attempt to force the Germans to bring back units from the Eastern Front had failed, but suspected that towards the end of July some experienced individual pilots had returned in order to stiffen up the mass. We also had information which suggested that reserve training units in France had been called upon to replace losses. The effect of the bombing attacks was virtually unknown.

147. As for our own losses, so far as Fighter Command was concerned these had been heavy, but not so heavy as to cause serious embarrassment. Our losses in pilots during the first two weeks of the intensive period had been far lighter than at the height of the Battle of Britain; and our losses in aircraft over the same period not beyond our capacity to replace. Bomber Command had lost fifteen aircraft in " Circus " operations since 14th June, and in the course of a daylight attack on German capital ships at Brest and La Pallice had suffered the rather more serious loss of sixteen bombers out of 115 despatched.

148. Losses like this, incurred when attacking an objective on the left flank of the German defensive system, suggested that attacks round the right flank into Germany might not prove such a practicable undertaking as had been hoped.

149. It was in these circumstances that a conference was held at the Air Ministry on 29th July to decide whether " Circus " operations should continue. It was agreed that some of the conceptions formulated at the conference of the Commanders-in-Chief on 19th June had been too sanguine; the daylight bombing of Germany, in particular, no longer looked like being practicable on any appreciable scale for some time to come, and it was agreed that for the medium and heavy bombers of Bomber Command night operations should normally take precedence over day operations. On the other hand it was equally clear that, if anything was to be done to contain the enemy fighter force in the West, offensive operations by Fighters must not cease; and it seemed to

me that the co-operation of a bomber force was necessary to make these operations effective. The Chief of the Air Staff upheld this view; and it was decided that the "Circus" offensive should continue.

150. Up to this time 46 "Circus" operations had been carried out since 14th June. In those six weeks escort and support had been given to 374 bomber sorties and over 8,000 fighter sorties flown. We had lost 123 fighter pilots but it was hoped that many more German fighters than this had been destroyed. In addition, over 1,000 fighter sorties had been flown in support of 32 bomber operations against shipping, including the operations against the German capital ships on 24th July and an attack on the docks at Le Havre on 19th June. Fighter sweeps without bombers accounted for approximately another 800 sorties, and operation "Rhubarb"—resumed on 16th July after a month's pause—for a further 61. Altogether the six weeks' intensive effort had meant the expenditure of nearly 10,000 offensive sorties by my Command. This was an impressive total, but to preserve perspective it must be remembered that the effort devoted to defensive purposes was still greater, approximately this number of sorties being expended during the same period on the protection of shipping alone.

151. The "Circus" offensive was resumed on 5th August and 26 operations were carried out during the month. Blenheims of No. 2 Group provided the striking force for 24 of them and Hampdens of No. 5 Group for the other two. As the enemy gained experience in repelling these attacks his opposition grew more effective, and the balance of advantage showed a tendency to turn against us. This being so, it was for consideration whether the scale of the offensive should be reduced, if not at once, at any rate as soon as there was any sign of a more stable situation on the Eastern Front.

152. Apparently the same considerations occurred simultaneously to the Chiefs of Staff. Consequently, the problem was studied at the end of August and beginning of September in the Air Ministry as well as at my Headquarters and at Headquarters No. 11 Group. The outcome was that, although it was now clear that the offensive had not succeeded in forcing the return of German Units, at any rate in substantial numbers, from the Eastern Front, and could not now be expected to do so, it was generally agreed that it ought to be continued, although on the reduced scale which the declining season was likely to impose in any case. A suggestion made by the Air Officer Commanding No. 11 Group, which I endorsed, was that, instead of being largely concentrated against the French departments of the Nord and Pas-de-Calais, the attacks should now be delivered over a wider area so as to induce the Germans to spread their fighters more thinly along the coasts of France and the Low Countries.

153. Accordingly, twelve "Circus" operations were carried out in September and two during the first week of October. The objectives attacked by the bombers included two targets at Rouen, one at Amiens, one at Le Havre and one at Ostend.

154. By this time it was clear that demands from other theatres of war were likely to cause a shortage of fighter aircraft at home for some time to come. For this reason, and also because the weather was growing less favourable and the situation on the Eastern Front had reached a stage at which it was unlikely to be materially affected by the "Circus" offensive, on 12th October I instructed the three Group Commanders concerned with offensive operations that in future "Circus" operations must only be undertaken in specially favourable circumstances, but that a rigorous offensive should be continued against shipping and "fringe targets".

155. Early in October the Hurricane bomber, which had been under development for some time, became available for active operations, and armed with this weapon the Command assumed responsibility for what was called the "Channel Stop". The object of this operation, which hitherto had been performed mainly by Blenheims of No. 2 Group with fighter escort, was to close the area between the North Foreland, Ostend, Dieppe and Beachy Head to all hostile shipping by day.

156. When the Air Ministry decided to reduce the scale of the "Circus" offensive in September, I made arrangements at their instance to increase the scale of scope of operation "Rhubarb". Hitherto pilots had seldom been lucky enough to meet German aircraft, so that their only alternative to inaction had been to make rather aimless attacks on surface objectives. I might have taken advantage of this situation by imposing a rigid "target policy," but up to the present I had judged it inadvisable to lay down any rule which might give the impression that attacks on surface objectives were as important as the destruction of enemy aircraft. Pilots were therefore given a free hand in this matter so long as they observed the general bombardment instructions which reflected the attitude of H.M. Government to questions of humanity and international law.

157. Although the relative importance of enemy aircraft and surface objectives as objects of attack had not changed, my staff and I felt that the time had come to subordinate the ideal to the real by recognizing that on nine occasions out of ten our pilots were not likely to see any German aircraft and must either attack surface objectives or do nothing.

158. Accordingly, new instructions for operation "Rhubarb" were issued in October. Pilots were now to proceed to a selected surface objective, and if they met no German aircraft on the way, that would be their target. If they did meet German aircraft, then the destruction of those aircraft would take priority.

159. Categories from which the surface objectives were to be selected were drawn up by my staff in consultation with the Air Ministry; they included canal barges, railway tank wagons, electrical transformer stations and, for a season, factories engaged in distilling alcohol from beet. On 20th October, H.M. Government withdrew a long-standing ban on the attack of moving goods trains, so that we could now attack tank wagons on the move as well as in sidings.

160. Factories distilling alcohol and a number of other targets on land were also attacked in November by fighter-bombers with fighter escort. The fighter-bombers, which attacked from heights below 5,000 feet, suffered rather heavy losses from A.A. fire in these operations and also in some of their attacks on shipping. In the past the Blenheim bombers used by No. 2 Group for these " shipping strikes " had come up against the same difficulty, despite attempts by accompanying fighters to silence the German gunners by attacks with cannon and machine-guns.

161. Meanwhile, on 21st October, I carried the reduction in the scale of the " Circus " offensive a stage further by imposing on No. 11 Group, as the Group principally concerned, a limit of six such operations a month.

162. In practice there was only one " Circus " after this date. This was carried out on 8th November in conjunction with a high-level fighter sweep and a low-level attack by fighters and fighter-bombers on an alcohol distillation plant. An unexpectedly high wind added to the difficulties of the undertaking, which resulted in the loss of sixteen fighter aircraft and thirteen pilots. Later in the day another aircraft and its pilot were lost in the course of a fighter sweep.

163. Although not by any means disastrous, losses on this scale were unwelcome in view of the shortage of aircraft that was expected to make itself felt during the next few months. I therefore decided to restrict No. 11 Group to three " Circus " operations a month in future instead of six.

164. A few days later the Air Ministry informed me that the War Cabinet had called attention to the desirability of conserving resources in order to build up strong forces by the Spring of 1942. Since the wording of the letter in which the Air Ministry conveyed this information made it clear that no risks must be taken by pressing attacks in unfavourable weather, I now imposed a still more stringent limitation on the Air Officer Commanding No. 11 Group, who was asked to undertake no more " Circus " operations without reference to me.

165. The outbreak of War between the United States of America and Japan in December provided still further grounds for conservation, since it was clear that the supply of aircraft from America was likely to cease or at least be greatly reduced for some time to come. Consequently the constant drain imposed by even minor operations could no longer be afforded.

166. In point of fact, wintry weather was already upon us, and after 8th November no more " Circus " operations were carried out. The intensity of our other offensive operations was also substantially reduced as the year drew to its close.

167. A word must be said here about some of the special offensive operations, outside the normal " Circus ", anti-shipping, fighter-sweep and " Rhubarb " categories, in which the Command participated between 14th June and the end of 1941.

168. Reference has already been made to Bomber Command's attack on the German warships at Brest and La Pallice on 24th July. In connection with this operation six squadrons of fighters from No. 11 Group provided escort for two diversionary attacks on Cherbourg and another fourteen took part in a " Circus " against Hazebrouck, while the equivalent of nine squadrons from No. 10 Group gave support over Brest and the Western end of the English Channel. Since only five squadrons of single-seater fighters with long-range tanks were available, the degree of support that could be given over Brest was necessarily disproportionate to the size of the bomber force, which suffered accordingly.

169. On 12th August a force of 54 Blenheims of Bomber Command attacked two Power Stations at Cologne in daylight. A squadron of Whirlwinds accompanied them on the first 135 miles of their outward journey, and on their return journey a wing of long-range Spitfires met them near the Dutch Coast, while another Spitfire wing made a sweep over Flushing in support. Two " Circus " operations over France by a total of nineteen fighter squadrons and twelve Hampdens of Bomber Command were carried out as diversions. Eleven aircraft of the bomber force despatched against the Power Stations were lost, but Bomber Command expressed themselves as well satisfied with the results achieved. In the light of our subsequent knowledge of the enemy's system of deploying and controlling fighters at that time, it now appears unlikely that diversions so far from the scene of the main attacks could have had any effect on the opposition in that area.

170. On 18th December and again on 30th December, Bomber Command made further attacks on the German warships at Brest. Fighter support was provided by ten and nine squadrons of the Command respectively. As before, the results were satisfactory from the fighter aspect, but once again the bombers suffered substantial losses.

(iii) *Results Achieved by the Offensive.*

171. It would be unwise to attach too much importance to statistics showing the claims made and losses suffered by our fighters month-by-month throughout the offensive.

172. The experience of two wars shows that in large-scale offensive operations the claims to the destruction of enemy aircraft made by pilots, however honestly made and carefully scrutinized, are a most inaccurate guide to the true situation. Moreover, the results achieved by an offensive can rarely be judged by a mere statistical comparison of casualties suffered and inflicted. Except when an operation has been launched purely for the purpose of procuring the attrition of the opposing force, a broader view than this must be taken of the strategic purpose and the extent to which it has been achieved.

173. In the present case the original object was to wrest the initiative from the enemy for the sake of the great moral and tactical advantages bestowed by its possession. Later the Command was entrusted with the task of co-operating with Bomber and Coastal Commands in order, first to prevent the enemy from withdrawing any more flying units from the Western Front after the middle of June, and secondly to induce him to return some of the units already withdrawn by that time. These may be

designated respectively objects numbers one, two and three.

174. Object number one was achieved within a few months of the opening of the offensive. By the Spring of 1941 the initiative in major daylight operations had passed from the Germans, who did not subsequently regain it.

175. Objective number two was also achieved, inasmuch as the Germans did in fact retain on the Western Front throughout the second half of 1941 approximately the same first-line fighter force as was present in the late Spring. In particular, two Geschwader of particularly high quality, which might have been usefully employed elsewhere, remained in Northern France to oppose the "Circus" offensive and our other offensive operations. It is, of course, most unlikely that, even without the offensive, the Germans would altogether have denuded the Western Front of fighters: so long as even the threat of an offensive was present, a substantial defensive force would doubtless have been retained in the West in any case. Still, the fact remains that throughout the Summer and Autumn of 1941 roughly one third of the total establishment of German first-line single-engined fighters was contained on the Western Front.

176. Object number three was not achieved. Such moves between East and West as occurred were by way of exchange rather than reinforcement.

177. To turn to subsidiary achievements, the offensive against shipping went far to deny the Dover Strait to the enemy in daylight, so that the Germans were induced to pass more and more of their shipping at night. This produced favourable conditions for the employment of naval forces. Furthermore the offensive as a whole, and particularly the "Circus" offensive, brought about a substantial attrition of the German fighter force in Northern France during the Summer, at a substantial cost to ourselves. Such an effect could not, by its very nature, be other than transitory so long as the enemy's means of replacement remained intact; for any slackening of the offensive, whether caused by bad weather or our own losses, would enable him to restore the situation more or less quickly. One of the clearest lessons which was later seen to emerge from this experience was that fighters operating from this country over Northern France could, at a sufficient cost, inflict such losses on the opposing fighter force as would bring about a local and temporary air superiority. But this achievement could, of itself, have no decisive military value: the ability to create this situation was valuable only if means were to hand of exploiting it by some further move capable of producing a decision.

178. This condition was not fulfilled in 1941. Consequently the operations just described, although they achieved two of the three objects for which they were undertaken, and also provided valuable experience, were necessarily indecisive. This was, indeed, recognized as inevitable when the intensified offensive was begun, for its underlying strategy rested upon the assumption that the decisive theatre lay, for the moment, in the East. Nevertheless these operations pointed the way to the events of 1943 and 1944, when the temporary reduction of the opposing fighter force was to be deliberately and successfully undertaken as a necessary prelude to the decisive military gesture which was to lead to the defeat of Germany.

PART II: STRENGTH, FIGHTING VALUE AND ORGANISATION.

(a) *Expansion of the Operational Training System.*

179. At the beginning of November 1940, the first-line strength of Fighter Command stood nominally at 67½ squadrons. Outwardly, therefore, the Command was stronger than at the beginning of the Battle of Britain, when only 58 squadrons were available. In reality it was weaker. After several months of intensive fighting some of the squadrons had only a few pilots fully up to operational standards, and the first-line strength was backed by insufficient depth. At the height of the battle the supply of new pilots had failed to keep pace with losses and it had been necessary to improvise measures to avert a crisis.

180. Superficially this weakness was due to the inability of the operational training organisation within the Command to keep pace with our losses. In reality the trouble went deeper. It is true that if there had been a larger reserve of pilots in the Operational Training Units the decline in the effective strength of the first-line squadrons could have been avoided or postponed. But such a reserve could only have been accumulated in the first place either by withholding pilots from the first line or by increasing the supply from the Flying Training Schools. Neither course was practicable in the circumstances of the time. The real "bottleneck" was the restricted capacity of the Flying Training Schools, and it was not within my competence to remedy this shortcoming, which was perhaps an inevitable consequence of the change from peace to war.

181. Nevertheless, this experience pointed to the desirability of expanding the operational training organisation so that full advantage might be taken of the increased supply of pilots from the Flying Training Schools which would eventually become available. On 1st November 1940, three Operational Training Units were in existence and the formation of another had been ordered. On 5th November my predecessor proposed to the Air Ministry that two more should be added and that all six should be incorporated in a Fighter Operational Training Group within the Command.

182. The sequel was the formation in December 1940 of No. 81 Group under the Command of Air Commodore F. J. Vincent, D.F.C. On 31st December, No. 81 Group assumed control of the six O.T.U.s then in existence or being formed. During the succeeding twelve months the number of O.T.U.s was increased to eleven. In the course of the year No. 81 Group did 263,604 hours flying and turned out 4,242 pilots—an average of more than 350 a month.

(b) *Pilot Strength of Squadrons.*

183. Nevertheless, the supply of pilots continued to be a source of anxiety during the greater part of the period covered by this account. The nominal establishment of a fighter squadron stood on 1st November 1940 at 26 pilots. In practice the average strength was

a little over 22. Heavy calls were already being made on the Command to send pilots to the Middle East, and it was also necessary to find instructors for the expanding operational training organisation and for Flying Training Command. In these circumstances there was little prospect of raising the strength substantially within a measurable time. For this and other reasons I agreed soon after assuming Command that the establishment of a fighter squadron should be reduced to 23 pilots.

184. In practice even this lower figure was not achieved for many months. By the beginning of January 1941, the average strength had fallen to 21 pilots a squadron, and it remained at this level until well into the Spring. Since it was thought that the Germans were likely to resume mass attacks on the United Kingdom in the Spring or Summer, this situation caused me some anxiety. The view taken by the Air Ministry was, however, that the general strategic situation and the requirements of other theatres of war justified a reduction in the strength of Fighter Command below the level postulated in the previous Winter.

185. I believe that if the Germans had delivered a second daylight offensive in 1941 with such forces as they could then have mustered, Fighter Command would have given as good an account of itself as in the previous Summer. But no second Battle of Britain was fought. Instead, the Germans turned their attention mainly to other theatres, and the initiative in the daylight battle passed to ourselves.

186. As the year went on, the benefit of the expanded operational training organisation and an increased flow of pilots from the Flying Training Schools began to be felt, so that in spite of substantial losses in offensive operations and the posting of many pilots to other Commands, Fighter Command reached the end of 1941 with a surplus of pilots in the squadrons. The proportion of seasoned veterans was, however, inevitably somewhat low, for of those who had survived, many had been claimed by other theatres and others had been assigned for the time being to other duties.

(c) *Number of Squadrons and Fighting Value.*

187. Of the 67½ squadrons in the Command on 1st November 1940, twelve were specialist night squadrons and the rest were primarily day squadrons. Shortly after this, one of the night squadrons—No. 73 Squadron—was transferred to the Middle East.

188. In December 1940, I estimated that for the adequate defence of the country in the coming Spring, 20 night and 80 day squadrons would be required.

189. The Air Ministry were unable to contemplate the provision of so large a force by the Spring. Instead, an immediate target of 81 squadrons was set and was reached by the beginning of April. This force comprised sixteen orthodox night squadrons (including one " Intruder " Squadron), one aerial mining squadron, and 64 day squadrons. Some of the squadrons had considerably fewer pilots than their establishment, but even so the force was numerically a good deal stronger in first-line and depth than that which had resisted the German onslaught in the previous Summer. On the other hand the general level of training and experience was somewhat lower. A high proportion of the pilots who fought in the Battle of Britain were seasoned men who had fought successfully at Dunkirk or elsewhere over France and Belgium. The majority of these had now been killed or posted away and had been replaced largely by pilots who had been hurried through the O.T.U.s in the Autumn or whose operational training had been hampered by Winter weather.

190. In respect of equipment the Germans seemed at the time to be drawing ahead. Of the 64 day squadrons in Fighter Command at the beginning of April, 1941, one was equipped with the Spitfire VB and 29 had Spitfires II or Hurricanes II. The rest were equipped with types that were not altogether a match for the Me109F which the Germans were now using. However, it seems that only about half the opposing fighter force was equipped with this aircraft by the early Spring; the other half still had the Me109E. In reality, then, there was probably little to choose between the two forces in this respect.

191. On the other hand we had made a good deal of progress in the practical application of Radar to the problems of night defence, and although we were not yet capable of inflicting prohibitive casualties on the night bomber, we were in a much better position to deal with this menace than in 1940.

192. At this stage the Command was called upon to provide six squadrons as reinforcements for the Middle East, while one squadron—No. 232—was temporarily withdrawn for training in Combined Operations. Before Midsummer, however, the formation of seven new squadrons was begun, so that when, in the middle of June, I was required to intensify my offensive campaign over Northern France, the strength was back at the old figure of 81 squadrons.

193. A further expansion during the second half of the year had always been contemplated by the Air Ministry, although from my point of view it would, of course, have been preferable to have the extra squadrons in the Spring or early Summer. It was now decided that the aim should be to build up the Command, if possible, to a strength of 89 day and 25 orthodox night squadrons by the end of 1941. There was also a new requirement for units to carry airborne searchlights to assist in night interception; for this an additional ten flights, or the equivalent of another five squadrons, were required.

194. In practice the needs of other theatres made it impossible to carry out this programme in its entirety. A decision by the Air Ministry to send Beaufighters overseas, although doubtless justified in the circumstances, reduced the supply of these aircraft at home and so hampered the expansion of the night-fighter force. Again, the desirability of guarding against a German break-through at the Eastern end of the Mediterranean made it necessary for Fighter Command to surrender to the Middle East Command six more day squadrons as a contribution to a force which was to be built up for this purpose. These squadrons left England in December and after they had sailed were diverted, because of events in Malaya, to the

Far East. With them went No. 232 Squadron, which had returned to the Command in July after being absent for training in Combined Operations earlier in the year.

195. The outcome was that the Command reached the end of 1941 with a strength of 100 squadrons—comprising 23 night defensive squadrons, two "Intruder" Squadrons, and 75 day squadrons—in addition to ten "Turbinlite" Flights (as they were called), whose function was to carry airborne searchlights. In the event these "Turbinlite" Flights, despite the skill and enthusiasm of those concerned with them, were to accomplish little, for by the time they were used in substantial numbers the enemy had virtually ceased to send over the slower bombers with which they might have coped successfully.

196. Thus by the end of the year, the Command had achieved approximately the strength which I should have wished to have at my disposal in the Spring and Summer. The squadrons had, however, been drained of most of their more seasoned members, and the general level of experience was not so high as I could have wished. But since the size of the opposing force left in the West after the opening of the German campaign against Russia in June was only about a third of that which had opposed us in 1940, there is no doubt that at this stage the country was adequately defended.

197. On the other hand, the enemy was working on internal lines of communication and could have moved back units from Poland or the Mediterranean more quickly than we could have brought squadrons from overseas. It would be a mistake, therefore, to conclude that we were needlessly strong.

198. From August to December two Hurricane Squadrons were detached for service on the North Russian Front in No. 151 Wing under the command of Wing Commander H. N. G. Ramsbottom-Isherwood, A.F.C.

(d) *Expansion of Group and Sector System.*

199. During the period covered by this account a considerable expansion of the Group and Sector system took place, mainly in accordance with plans laid before the period began.

200. The need for new Fighter Groups on the flanks of Nos. 11 and 13 Groups had become apparent at an early stage of the War. Indeed, a Group in the West of England was visualised in the Command's tentative plans even before war broke out. Accordingly, Nos. 10 and 14 Groups had been formed during the Battle of Britain. Thus by the beginning of November, 1940, there were five Groups and 23 Sectors in existence, as against the three Groups and eighteen Sectors required by the approved pre-war programme.

201. Furthermore, on the fall of France it had become necessary to plan a further extension of the air defence system up the West Coast. Clearly another Group would be needed to take charge of the Sectors which were to be formed in Wales and the West Midlands. Accordingly, No. 9 Group began to form at Preston early in August, 1940, and on 16th September its first Air Officer Commanding, Air Vice-Marshal W. A. McClaughry, D.S.O., M.C., D.F.C., took up his appointment.

202. At the beginning of November, 1940, the development of this Group had not yet reached the operational stage, mainly because the necessary airfields and communications were not yet ready. Consequently, such specific fighter defence as it was possible to allot to the area for which the Group would ultimately become responsible was still being provided by No. 12 Group.

203. In the middle of October special measures had been set in train to bring No. 9 Group to the operational stage as rapidly as possible. These efforts continued, with the result that on 1st December the Group was able to assume operational control of two of the four Sectors (later increased to five) which were allotted to it. By the middle of March, 1941, No. 9 Group had assumed responsibility for all its Sectors in daylight, although No. 12 Group, with its better night-flying facilities, continued to defend one Sector at night.

204. Before this a Sector, planned before the War, had been established in Ulster, where one fighter squadron was established in the Summer of 1940. At the same time improved facilities for operating fighters under the control of No. 13 Group were set up in South-Western Scotland.

205. These measures, of which some had been executed and all had been planned when the period under discussion opened, now bore fruit, and the twin problem of providing adequate defences in the West and protecting shipping between the Rhinns of Islay and the Bristol Channel was much eased in consequence.

206. In the Spring of 1941, there were six operational fighter Groups and 29 Sectors in existence. On the outbreak of war the flanks of the air defence system had stood on the Firth of Forth and Spithead, although there was an outlying detachment at Filton for the defence of Bristol. In a little over eighteen months the system had been so expanded that the Command was now able to operate short-range fighters, under close control, over almost every part of Great Britain and Northern Ireland and adjacent waters, with the exception of North-West Scotland.

207. Towards the end of 1940 the Command was asked to form two new Sectors in this last area in order that shipping in the Minches and objectives in the Western Highlands and the Hebrides might be brought under the shelter of the Fighter Command "umbrella". Although this desire was natural, its accomplishment was far from easy. There were no airfields suitable for short-range fighters on the mainland, and the nature of the country made it impossible to construct them. From a practical viewpoint there was much to be said for placing the responsibility for this distant area on Coastal Command, whose long-range fighters could operate in safety from airfields in the Hebrides. However, the Air Ministry rejected this solution, and eventually a compromise was adopted, whereby short-range fighters to be provided by Fighter Command would be supplemented by long-range fighters, which would be provided by Coastal Command. The latter would operate under Fighter Command when used for controlled interception.

208. The arrangements necessary to put this scheme into effect were not completed until

1942, and it may be noted that in the sequel, although two fighter Sectors were duly set up with Headquarters at Stornoway and Tiree, and remained in being until 1944 and 1943 respectively, it never became necessary to base there any flying units of Fighter Command.

209. In the Summer of 1941 I was instructed to provide an increased scale of defence for certain Naval anchorages in Northern Ireland and it was decided that the number of Sectors in Ulster should be increased to three. This necessitated the formation of a new Fighter Group and accordingly on 25th September, No. 82 Group under the command of Air Commodore G. M. Lawson, M.C., and with its Headquarters at Belfast, assumed operational control of these three Sectors.

210. As a result of these and other developments, the Command comprised, at the end of 1941, seven operational Groups and 33 Sectors—ten more than had existed at the beginning of the period covered by this account.

(e) *Adoption of Section of Two Aircraft and Three-Squadron Wing as Standard Tactical Units.*

211. During the Battle of Britain it became clear that from the tactical viewpoint there was much to be said for sections consisting of two or four aircraft rather than three, which was then the standard number. When a formation broke up in a dog-fight it was desirable that it should break into pairs, so that individual pilots could give and receive mutual protection. A section of three aircraft could not do this.

212. Since administrative arrangements were based on the sub-division of a squadron into two flights each comprising two sections of three aircraft, there was a conflict here between operational and administrative interests. But the tactical superiority of the section of two or four was so clear that some sacrifice of administrative convenience was obviously justified. Accordingly, it was decided that the section of two aircraft should be adopted, and in the Spring of 1941 a new sub-division of the squadron into two flights each comprising three sections of two aircraft was standardized throughout the Command.

213. Another change which arose out of experience gained in the Battle of Britain concerned the use of Wings consisting of three or more squadrons. Such wings had sometimes claimed exceptionally good results in combat with large enemy formations, and there was a body of opinion which favoured a more frequent use of them. Against this it was argued that in many cases, if time were consumed in assembling large wings, it would be impossible to attack the enemy formations before they reached their targets.

214. A conference to discuss this point was held at the Air Ministry in October, 1940. At this meeting it was confirmed that Wings of three or more Squadrons were the proper weapon to oppose large enemy formations when conditions were suitable; but as to what constituted suitable conditions for their employment no definite decision was reached. A more concrete suggestion was that some of the squadrons in the Command should be disposed and organized in such a way as to facilitate their employment as wings when occasion called for it.

215. It was my view that the best way of defending an objective was not so much to interpose a screen of fighter squadrons between that objective and the enemy, as to shoot down a high proportion of the enemy force sent to attack it, irrespective of whether the objective was bombed on a particular occasion or not.

216. On assuming Command, therefore, I adopted the suggestion made at the conference. Provision was made to operate three-Squadron Wings from a number of Sectors in South and South-East England, and in February, 1941, the sanction of the Air Ministry was obtained for the appointment of Wing Commanders second-in-command at fifteen of the principal Stations in the Command. I arranged that these Officers should concern themselves with the operation and training of the day squadrons in their Sectors and, where there were three-Squadron Wings, Sector Commanders were encouraged to rely on them to lead the wings in battle on important occasions.

217. By that time we had turned to the offensive, and it was as an offensive weapon that I had begun to visualise the wings. If there had always been some controversy as to their practical usefulness in defensive warfare, their advantages for offensive use were clear enough. It so happened that no opportunity was to arise in 1941 to test them on the defensive, since the Germans did not resume their mass attacks of 1940. The wings became, however, an essential weapon of our own daylight offensive, which began to gather weight early in the year and was greatly intensified after the middle of June.

(f) *Growth and Development of Artillery and Balloon Defences.*

218. The development of the Group and Sector organisation in Fighter Command was accompanied by a considerable expansion of the artillery and balloon defences.

219. I exercised general operational control over these defences and was responsible for their disposition and co-ordination with other means of defence. I was not responsible for their administration nor, in the case of the artillery defences, for training or technical development, apart from the provision (during part of the period) of aircraft for anti-aircraft co-operation and exercises.

220. It is therefore necessary to mention here only a few of the more important organisational and technical changes, such as had a close bearing on the operation or disposition of the defences.

221. One of the chief of these was the reorganisation of A.A. Command which occurred at the end of 1940. Three A.A. Corps were created, the number of A.A. Divisions was increased from seven to twelve and these formations were re-grouped so as to facilitate co-operation with the formations of Fighter Command. Co-operation at the Command level had always been and remained excellent, but

to secure effective co-ordination at lower levels was more difficult. Inevitably the requirements and interests of guns and fighters must sometimes conflict, and to achieve a satisfactory adjustment between them through two different chains of command was not an easy problem. This change did not prove to be the final answer to it, but it was a step in the right direction.

222. Other important changes belonging to this period concerned the deployment of searchlights.

223. At this stage of the War searchlights were used to illuminate enemy aircraft for the benefit of both guns and fighters. In 1940 they gave disappointing results in both capacities, partly because they relied on sound locators which could seldom cope satisfactorily with the speed of the modern bomber and partly because clouds and haze often made them ineffective. As a means of overcoming the second difficulty, recourse was had to the expedient of siting them in clusters of three so as to provide a stronger illumination. This arrangement was found in practice to confer no advantage sufficient to compensate for the drawback of wider spacing, and in September, 1941, General Pile and I decided that the lights should be resited singly. In the meantime calculations had been made to determine the size of the area in which a single night-fighter aided by searchlights could hope to effect an interception, and the pattern in which the searchlights were deployed was based on this conception. The method of operating this "fighter box" system of searchlight-aided interception has been described above. (See Part I, paragraphs 63-67.)

224. The following table shows the numbers of heavy and light A.A. guns and searchlights deployed on various dates, together with the approved scale on the outbreak of War:

	Heavy A.A.	Light A.A.	Searchlights
Scale approved before War	2,232	1,200	4,128
Outbreak of War	695	253	2,700
End of 1939	850	510	3,361
July, 1940	1,200	549	3,932
May, 1941	1,691	940	See below
December, 1941	1,960	1,197	

225. Although the approved scale of searchlight defence on the outbreak of War stood at 4,128, a total of 4,700 lights was recommended. Early in 1941 the figure of 4,532 lights actually deployed was reached, but subsequently the need for economy in manpower led to a reduction.

226. It was hoped that the introduction of the "U.P." A.A. rocket projector would do much to remedy the shortage of heavy A.A. guns, but the effective use of this weapon by A.A. Command was delayed by a number of factors, including shortages of ammunition. It was not until the crisis had passed, therefore, that they could be used for home defence in substantial numbers.

227. The total number of balloons authorized to fly and actually flying in the various barrages at the beginning of the period covered by this account was 1,958 and 1,741 respectively. In the Spring of 1941 it was 2,191 and 2,115. Subsequently a further expansion brought the number of balloons, actually flying at the end of 1941 up to 2,340—some 900 more than the total initial equipment of the barrages on the outbreak of War.

(g) *Expansion of the Raid Reporting Radar Organisation.*

228. In common with other forms of Home Defence, the Radar Chain of coastal stations of No. 60 (Signals) Group in my Command entered into a phase of intensive expansion to complete early warning radar cover to our Western sea approaches and also to face the problem of the enemy low-flying raiders. During 1941 the constructional programme involved nearly 100 radar stations—equivalent to setting up all the stations of several B.B.C.s within a period of a few months only. The War Cabinet had instructed that the highest priority should be accorded to this effort. The burden of this work fell heavily on the No. 60 Group organisation. Short of technicians for installation, calibration, and maintenance duties, an acute shortage of the crews of radar operators to man the new stations also had to be faced. No. 60 Group nevertheless proved equal to the task, despite the fact that officers, airmen and airwomen in the Group were almost exclusively non-regular personnel of the R.A.F.V.R. without any previous service experience. 1941 was certainly the most hectic year of its existence.

229. The expansion of the Group and Sector organisation in my Command permitted a decentralisation of the radar reporting system. Originally all radar information had been reported to a Filter Room at Command Headquarters at Stanmore, the tracks of aircraft being passed on to the Operations Room. At the end of 1940 it was possible to decentralise the Stanmore Filter Room and split it between Fighter Groups throughout the country. This was also in accord with a decision to delegate the Air Raid Warning control from my Command Headquarters to the Headquarters of each Fighter Group. Owing to the heavy telecommunications re-arrangements involved, the complete decentralisation of radar reporting was not achieved until September, 1941.

230. Together with the great expansion of the radar chain and the decentralisation of the reporting system, there was an equivalent technical progress, not only with regard to equipment, but also in the handling and filtering of the radar information. The Operational Research Section of scientists at my Headquarters, working in conjunction with No. 60 Group, made many improvements to extract the maximum benefit from the available radar information. This application of the scientific method to the use of weapons through the medium of Operational Research Sections began first on problems within Fighter Command and subsequently spread throughout all Royal Air Force Commands.

(h) *Organisation to resist Invasion.*

231. Any account of the activities of the Command during this period would be incomplete without some mention of the preparations made to resist an invasion of the United Kingdom.

232. The roles to be played by the Home Commands in this eventuality had been laid down in broad terms by the Air Ministry in the Summer of 1940. It was then assumed that an invasion would fall into three distinct phases, beginning with a large-scale offensive against Fighter Command, continuing with an airborne invasion, and culminating in the seaborne invasion by which alone the Germans could hope to bring about our final defeat. It was thought that the third phase might in turn fall into three sub-phases, namely the preliminary concentration of shipping, the voyage across, and the attempt to establish a bridgehead. The Air Staff plan laid down the functions to be performed by the Command in each of these phases and sub-phases.

233. On consideration it seemed doubtful whether all these phases and sub-phases would be distinguishable in practice, and in devising arrangements to carry out the spirit of the plan, it was thought inadvisable to allot different roles to the squadrons during the voyage across on the one hand and the attempt to establish a bridgehead on the other. Instead, the various tasks which might devolve upon the fighter force in consequence of these activities by the enemy were grouped together in order of importance. Priority at this stage was given to the protection of our Naval forces against enemy bombers.

234. As experience grew, other modifications were made, and throughout the period it was necessary to keep constantly under review an elaborate complex of operational and administrative arrangements. It would be tedious to describe these arrangements in detail, more especially since, after the success of the Command during the preliminary phase of the German invasion plan in 1940, it never became necessary to repeat the experience or deal with subsequent phases.

235. One aspect of these preparations called, however, for something more concrete than planning. This was the defence of airfields against various forms of attack.

236. Before the War the necessity for providing for the local defence of our airfields against anything more than sabotage or low-level air attack had not been grasped. Consequently, when it was realised that airfields in this country might be seized by airborne troops or landing parties, measures had to be improvised.

237. The general defence of the country against enemy troops, whether airborne or seaborne, was, of course, the responsibility of the Army. On the other hand it had always been recognised as a principle in the Royal Air Force that Station Commanders were responsible for the local defence of their Stations. At the same time it was obviously essential that local defence schemes should fit into the general defence plan and be approved by the appropriate military Commander.

238. On the outbreak of War the resources of the Royal Air Force were insufficient to give adequate protection even against the dangers that were then foreseen, and help had to be obtained from the Army. Detachments of troops were supplied to undertake Station defence duties jointly with Royal Air Force personnel.

239. The consequence was a bewildering division of responsibility for defence against the various forms of attack that might be made; and it was quite clear that in many cases Station Commanders, who were answerable to their Group Commanders for the local defence of their Stations, would in practice be unable to exercise effective control over the miscellaneous units nominally at their disposal.

240. This problem was common to all Home Commands, but it was particularly urgent in Fighter Command, since fighter stations were a vital element in the defence system and some were peculiarly vulnerable by reason of their geographical position.

241. In the Spring of 1941 the experience of Crete focussed attention on this problem, which was already causing me grave anxiety, and various means of improving the situation were suggested. Few of these were of practical value, for although the necessity of securing the fighter bases was now generally recognised, the resources at my disposal were not adequate or suitably organised to effect the desired object.

242. It has already been pointed out that the local defences of Stations were manned partly by Army and partly by Royal Air Force personnel. This in itself was a source of weakness, particularly since there was a tendency for the Army detachments allotted to these duties to be changed at frequent intervals. The creation of a Royal Air Force defence force had begun in 1940, but towards the end of that year a halt was called to the scheme, pending a decision as to whether the War Office or the Air Ministry should ultimately bear the responsibility for defending the Stations.

243. To enable Station Commanders to dispose their resources to the best advantage, each was given the services of a Station Defence Officer. Many of the Officers appointed by the Air Ministry to fill these posts were past their first youth and lacked the resilience of mind and body required for service in the field.

244. There was a great need, in addition, for officers to be attached to the Staffs of the Fighter Groups for the purpose of inspecting Station defences and supervising training. After repeated requests, the services of one Army Officer at each Group were obtained; but the instructions given to these officers by the military authorities limited them, in effect, to the performance of liaison duties for which they were not needed.

245. Finally, there was in many cases a fundamental difference of view, which written orders seemed powerless to adjust, between Station Commanders and the Army Officers responsible for the general defence of their area, as to their respective duties and responsibilities in relation to their superiors and to each other.

246. There is no doubt that the problem was a difficult one, involving many issues which it lay outside the competence of a Commander-in-Chief to decide and on which even now no opinion can be properly expressed. The solution eventually adopted, which led to the formation of the R.A.F. Regiment, did not become effective until after the close of the period with which this account is concerned. In the meantime the system of divided responsibility continued with all its evils. Consequently, despite much hard work at all levels, many Stations in my Command were far from impregnable throughout those months of 1941 when enemy landings by sea or air were at least a possibility.

LONDON
PRINTED AND PUBLISHED BY HIS MAJESTY'S STATIONERY OFFICE
To be purchased directly from H.M. Stationery Office at the following addresses:
York House, Kingsway, London, W.C.2; 13a Castle Street, Edinburgh, 2;
39-41 King Street, Manchester, 2; 1 St. Andrew's Crescent, Cardiff;
Tower Lane, Bristol, 1; 80 Chichester Street, Belfast
OR THROUGH ANY BOOKSELLER
1948
Price 1s. 6d. net

S.O. Code No. 65-38404

SUPPLEMENT TO
The London Gazette
OF TUESDAY 19th OCTOBER, 1948
Published by Authority

Registered as a newspaper

WEDNESDAY, 20 OCTOBER, 1948

AIR OPERATIONS BY AIR DEFENCE OF GREAT BRITAIN AND FIGHTER COMMAND IN CONNECTION WITH THE GERMAN FLYING BOMB AND ROCKET OFFENSIVES, 1944—1945.

The following report was submitted to the Secretary of State for Air on 17th April, 1948, by Air Chief Marshal SIR RODERIC HILL, *K.C.B., M.C., A.F.C., Air Marshal Commanding, Air Defence of Great Britain, Royal Air Force, from 15th November, 1943, to 15th October, 1944, and Air Officer Commanding-in-Chief, Fighter Command, Royal Air Force, from 15th October, 1944, until the end of the war in Europe.*

PART I: PRELIMINARY

(a) *Command and Higher Organisation of A.D.G.B. and Fighter Command.*

1. Towards the close of 1943 the Allied fighter, tactical reconnaissance, and tactical bomber forces in the United Kingdom began to assemble under the command of Air Chief Marshal Sir Trafford Leigh-Mallory, K.C.B., D.S.O., in readiness for the landing in north-west Europe which was to take place in the spring. The name of the Allied Expeditionary Air Force was given to this combination, part of which was set aside, under my command, for the defence of the British Isles.

2. The Force that I commanded was functionally a successor to Fighter Command. For the time being, however, that name was abandoned, and the old name of Air Defence of Great Britain was revived.

3. I commanded Air Defence of Great Britain from its inception on 15th November, 1943, until 15th October, 1944, when the Allied Expeditionary Air Force was disbanded. My Command then became an independent one and the name Fighter Command was restored. Thereafter, I held the post of Air Officer Commanding-in-Chief, Fighter Command, until the end of the war with Germany.

4. Throughout the life of Air Defence of Great Britain, and especially after the landings in Europe had begun, the control over my handling of operations which was exercised by Air Chief Marshal Leigh-Mallory in his capacity as Air Commander-in-Chief was little more than nominal. His energies were engrossed by offensive tasks. As the Armies in France pushed on, these tasks made it necessary for him to spend more and more of his time on the Continent. I was obliged, therefore, with the Air Commander-in-Chief's knowledge and consent, to deal directly with the Air Ministry, the British Chiefs of Staff, and governmental bodies on many points of operational policy. On the other hand, Air Chief Marshal Leigh-Mallory continued to exercise, through his staff, a close supervision over certain aspects of administration, especially those affecting personnel.

5. On 17th November, 1943, I received from Air Chief Marshal Leigh-Mallory a directive which defined the functions of my headquarters " under the general direction of the Air Commander-in-Chief " as follows:—

(a) To be responsible for the air defence of Great Britain and Northern Ireland.

(b) To command Nos. 9, 10, 11, 12, 13, 60 and 70 Groups and exercise operational control of fighters in Northern Ireland.

(c) To control operationally the activities of A.A. Command, the Royal Observer Corps, Balloon Command, " and other static elements of air defence formerly controlled operationally by Fighter Command ".

(d) To conduct " defensive and offensive operations which involve the use of squadrons of both A.D.G.B. and T.A.F. as heretofore under instructions issued to both headquarters until fresh instructions are issued ".

(e) To develop air interception methods and apparatus for eventual use in A.D.G.B. and other theatres.

6. The reference in article (d) to offensive operations by squadrons of the Tactical Air Force was hardly more than a convenient fiction. Its purpose was not so much to place these operations under my control, as to prevent them from prematurely absorbing the energies of the Air Officer Commanding and staff of the Tactical Air Force, to the detriment of their more important task of preparing for the coming events in Europe. Although the operations were planned and their execution ordered from the headquarters of No. 11 Group, which was part of my command, they were supervised until the 15th March, 1944, by the Air Commander-in-Chief himself. Thereafter they were directed by the Air Marshal Commanding, Second Tactical Air Force (Air Marshal Sir Arthur Coningham, K.C.B., D.S.O., M.C., D.F.C., A.F.C.). This arrangement was typical of a series of complex relationships brought about by the special circumstances of the time. In effect it meant that the Air Officer Commanding, No. 11 Group (Air Vice-Marshal H. W. L. Saunders, C.B., C.B.E., M.C., D.F.C., M.M.), while he never ceased to be constitutionally my subordinate, acted for certain purposes as the agent first of Air Chief Marshal Leigh-Mallory and later of Air Marshal Coningham.

7. My real task, then, was that set out in articles (a), (b), (c) and (e) of the directive, and as much of article (d) as related to operations by formations under my own command. In short, it was primarily a defensive one. Although squadrons of A.D.G.B. were to play their part in operations over France during the assault phase of the European operations, the Overall Air Plan issued by the Air Commander-in-Chief showed that my most significant responsibility even in that phase would be to stand guard over the base. Obviously, we were approaching a stage at which the needs of the offensive must have priority. The directive of the 17th November emphasized the need for economy in defence " in order to make greater provision for offence ", and called upon me to suggest changes in organisation with this need in mind. My problem, in fact, was to ensure, with limited resources, that the United Kingdom was securely defended from air attack as a base for the great operations by land, sea, and air which were being planned.

(b) *Resources Available.*

8. In the circumstances some " rolling up " of the Group and sector organisation seemed clearly justified. No. 14 Group, in the north of Scotland, had already been amalgamated with No. 13 Group before the time of my appointment. During the next few months I secured approval for further reductions. By 6th June, 1944 (D Day) the number of operational fighter Groups had been reduced to four and the number of active sectors from 19 to 14 —less than half the number in existence at the end of 1941. Still further reductions were made later.

9. Plans for translating the Air Commander-in-Chief's directive into practice were worked out by my staff and his in consultation. The basic strength of A.D.G.B. was fixed at ten day-fighter and eleven night-fighter squadrons. In addition six night-fighter squadrons earmarked for allotment to No. 85 Group—a Group formed for the purpose of defending the overseas base after the land forces should have advanced beyond the lodgment area—were to be put under my command for the time being. So long as I retained them I should be responsible for the night-fighter defence of the lodgment area as well as the United Kingdom and the waters between. Similarly, six day fighter squadrons intended ultimately for No. 85 Group were to be put at my disposal to enable me to keep German reconnaissance aircraft at bay, and perform a number of other tasks arising directly out of the situation created by the coming assault. Finally, another fifteen day-fighter squadrons were to remain nominally in A.D.G.B., but be lent to the Second Tactical Air Force for the duration of the assault phase. Only in an emergency would these squadrons revert to my operational control before the end of that phase. It was agreed, however, that if a serious situation should arise, the Air Officer Commanding, No. 11 Group, would be justified in using any part of his uncommitted resources (other than American units) for the daylight defence of his Group area. A few aircraft of the Royal Navy would also operate under my control.

10. Thus, the maximum number of Royal Air Force, Dominion and Allied squadrons on which I was expected to call—including the fifteen squadrons lent to the Second Tactical Air Force—would be 48: rather less than half the number that had been considered necessary for the defence of the United Kingdom at the end of 1941, when the main theatre was in Russia.

11. However, since 1941 much progress had been made in the technique of fighter interception, especially at night. The German Air Force, on the contrary, was known to have lost a great deal of its hitting power since those days, and its offensive spirit had declined. Furthermore, great advances had been made in the technical methods and equipment on which the " static " elements of the air defence system relied. Against this I had to reckon with the psychological difficulty of maintaining the fighting spirit of men placed on the defensive while their opposite numbers were fighting an offensive battle. But despite this handicap, and despite the numerical limitations of the forces under my operational control, it was my opinion that the air defences would give a good account of themselves against any attack by orthodox weapons that the German Air Force might deliver.

(c) *Appreciation of the General Situation before the start of the German Flying Bomb Offensive.*

12. From the time of my appointment until the beginning of the flying-bomb offensive a

week after D Day, coming German air operations against the United Kingdom were expected to consist of attacks by both orthodox bombers and "secret weapons". The two kinds of attack might be delivered either at different times or, more probably, together.

13. Numerically the capabilities of the German bomber force could be judged with a fair degree of accuracy from our knowledge of its strength and disposition. To foresee how this potential hitting power would be used in practice was more difficult. For planning purposes we assumed that orthodox opposition to the landings in France might take the form of minor daylight attacks along the south coast before D Day, and attacks on the beaches and anchorages thereafter. Night attacks on a scale of 50 long-range-bomber sorties a night for two or three nights a week, increasing to 150 sorties a night for very short periods, seemed likely to occur during the weeks preceding D Day. Ports, concentration areas, and concentrations of shipping would be the most probable targets. Slightly heavier attacks would be possible if the enemy should decide to punctuate nights of maximum activity by comparatively long intervals of quiet.

14. Whether the German bomber force would operate on a major scale in daylight on D Day or the succeeding days was problematical. If it did, the enemy would doubtless choose the most favourable tactical conditions by attacking targets on his own side of the Channel.

15. All this was theoretical. But our estimates were based on practical experience. While our plans were going forward, the enemy came to our assistance by disclosing part of his hand. Early in 1944 the German bomber force delivered the series of night attacks on London and other towns which has been called the "baby Blitz" Thanks to the watch which we were able to keep on its movements, these attacks did not take us by surprise. The defences were ready. Although the Germans used their fastest bombers, which stayed over England only for brief periods, we were able to inflict a higher rate of casualties than the German night defences could inflict on our bomber forces during their long flights over Europe. Moreover, the navigation, target-marking, and bombing of the Germans when faced by our defences proved to be very poor. Thus the attacks were extraordinarily ineffective. After this experience, I felt confident that we should be able to deal with any attempt by the German bomber force to interfere with the concentration of the Anglo-American land, sea, and air forces in preparation for the assault.

16. The threat from "secret weapons" was harder to assess and more disturbing. By the autumn of 1943 a mass of information collected over a long period was beginning to convince even the most sceptical that the Germans were preparing novel means of air attack. When I took up my appointment in the early winter, few men in responsible positions doubted that those means included both a long-range rocket of some kind and also some form of flying missile, or pilotless aircraft. Evidence received a few weeks later made us virtually sure that certain new constructions in northern France, which we called "ski sites"* were meant for the launching of missiles of the latter kind against this country.

PART II: THE FLYING BOMB CAMPAIGN.

(a) *Appreciation of the Threat up to "D" Day and Plans to meet it.*

17. Against a flying missile launched from the ground two methods of defence were possible. We might conduct a "defensive offensive" against the places where the missiles were made or stored, the constructions required for their launching, or the means of communication between those places. Some or all of these objectives might be attacked either separately or in combination, provided that we were able to locate them. Alternatively, or in addition, we might try to render the missiles harmless once they had been launched.

18. Early in December, 1943, the Chiefs of Staff decided to pursue the first method while exploring the possibilities of the second. Accordingly, on the 5th December the Second Tactical Air Force and the American Ninth Bomber Command began a series of bombing attacks on the "ski sites". The Strategic Air Forces, in the shape of our own Bomber Command and the American Eighth Bomber Command, also contributed their quota. By the end of the year, 3,216 tons of bombs had been dropped on the sites—about the weight that fell on London in an average fortnight during the night "Blitz" of 1940-41. So far as the Air Ministry could judge, the effect of these attacks was to "neutralize" twelve sites and seriously damage another nine. But since 88 "ski sites" had been located by this time, and the existence of another 50 was suspected, the neutralization of all the sites with the bombing resources that could be spared from other tasks seemed likely to prove a long-drawn business.

19. Meanwhile, early in December the Air Commander-in-Chief, at the instance of the Air Ministry, had instructed me to study the problem of defending the country against attack by pilotless aircraft and draw up plans accordingly. By way of assistance I was given an "appreciation" which embodied what was known at the time about the missiles that the Germans were getting ready to use against us. According to this document, these missiles flew at something between 250 and 420 m.p.h. and a height which might be anything from 500 to 7,000 feet. I was to assume that an attack by two missiles an hour from each of 100 sites might begin in February, 1944.

20. These estimates of speed and height were so broad as to make detailed planning difficult; but on 20th December, in reply to a questionnaire from my staff, the Air Ministry committed themselves, with reservations, to the opinion that the missiles would probably fly at an average speed of 400 m.p.h. and a height of 7,500 feet. Later these estimates were reduced to 350 m.p.h. and 7,000 feet, and still later to 330 m.p.h. and 6,000 feet. The views of the

---

* They were so called because on each site stood a number of buildings shaped like a ski laid on its side. The buildings seem to have been meant to provide blast-proof shelter for the missile while they were being stored and serviced.

Chiefs of Staff as to when the attacks were likely to begin were also modified from time to time, as our bombing offensive against the "ski sites" got under way.

21. In devising measures to deal with pilotless aircraft, my staff and I worked in close touch with General Sir Frederick A. Pile, Bart., G.C.B., D.S.O., M.C., General Officer Commanding, Anti-Aircraft Command, and his staff, who helped in the preparation of all detailed plans which involved guns and searchlights as well as fighters.

22. It was clear at the outset that to prepare a detailed plan of defence would take several weeks. I therefore decided to submit a preliminary outline plan. I took as my point of departure the fundamental proposition that a pilotless aircraft was still an aircraft, and therefore vulnerable to the same basic methods of attack. Of course, as there was no crew, such an aircraft could not be made to crash by killing the pilot; on the other hand, it would be incapable of retreat or evasion, except, perhaps, to a very limited extent.* Nevertheless, if the missile should prove in practice as fast as was believed at first, the performance of the fighters on which we normally relied would be inadequate.

23. However, on balance, and considering the uncertainty of our knowledge, it would clearly have been unjustifiable to exclude any of the normal methods of defence which we were accustomed to use against piloted aircraft. Accordingly, I recommended in my outline plan, which I submitted to the Air Commander-in-Chief on the 16th December, that aircraft, guns, searchlights, and balloons all be deployed against pilotless aircraft in such a manner as to avoid causing mutual interference. I pointed out, however, that the missiles might well prove too fast for our fighters, and in any case would make difficult targets for A.A. gunners. I recommended, therefore, that the bombing offensive against the installations in France be continued with the utmost vigour. I also asked to be kept informed of the progress made by two committees which had been set up at the Air Ministry to investigate the possibility of radio and electro-magnetic counter-measures.†

24. During the second half of December General Pile and I completed our detailed plan on these lines. On the 2nd January I submitted the plan to the Air Commander-in-Chief, who approved it and submitted it in turn to higher authority. Meanwhile, the Allied bomber offensive against the "ski sites" was achieving good results and the likelihood of imminent attack seemed to be receding. On 22nd January the Chiefs of Staff came to the conclusion that the date by which we must be ready for attacks by pilotless aircraft to begin could safely be put back until the 1st March; later they postponed it still further, until the middle of the month. Since intensive preparations for the European operations were due to begin on the 1st April, we were thus faced with the possibility that the first use of pilotless aircraft by the Germans might coincide with these preparations, or even with the assault itself.

25. Hence, by the time the Chiefs of Staff came to examine the detailed plan it had been overtaken by events. Circumstances now called for a modified plan which would provide simultaneously for defence against pilotless aircraft and the needs of the offensive. Early in February the Chiefs of Staff asked that such a plan should be prepared. In the meantime, General Pile and I received authority to proceed with the administrative arrangements which would have to be made before any deployment on the lines laid down in the existing plan could be ordered.

26. During the next few weeks, therefore, we overhauled our plan and devised a modified version of it which aimed at meeting the threat from pilotless aircraft mainly with resources not directly required for the European operations. We called this modified version the '"Concurrent Air Defence Plan for 'Overlord' and 'Diver' "', or, more briefly, the " 'Overlord'/'Diver' Plan "*. I submitted it to the Air Commander-in-Chief towards the end of February. After receiving his approval, it was approved in turn by the Supreme Commander and the Chiefs of Staff. On 4th March I gave instructions for copies of the plan to be sent to the Commands and Groups which would be directly concerned if it were ever put into effect.

27. With minor amendments, this was the plan on which we acted three months later, when the attacks began. Some account of it, and of its relationship to the earlier detailed plan out of which it grew, must therefore be given at this stage. Such an account may provide, perhaps, an insight into the conditions in which a major defensive operation of this kind has to be contrived. For in such cases a Commander must not only take into account a number of factors, political as well as military and logistic, which are governed by the capabilities of his own side; he must also reckon, first and last and all the time, with what the enemy may have up his sleeve.

28. Both the "Overlord/Diver" Plan and the earlier plan were based on the fundamental principles postulated for the first outline plan of the 16th December. But some of the assumptions which had been made when the original outline and detailed plans were made were modified by altered circumstances or fresh intelligence by the time the second plan was made. For example, as I have already pointed out, estimates of the performance of the weapon which we had to counter differed from time to time. Again, as the bombing offensive against the "ski sites" began to achieve its purpose, the Air Ministry revised their estimates of the probable scale of attack. But the broad concepts which determined the general nature of our defensive measures remained substantially unchanged.

---

* At that time we believed that the missile could be made to turn in the air. In point of fact this effect was limited to the first few moments of flight, during which it had to be directed on to its calculated course by an adjustment of the automatic control mechanism made beforehand.

† Later it was established that the missiles were not controlled by radio. To divert them by means of an electro-magnetic field was theoretically possible, but would have needed so much copper and electric power that it was quite impracticable. Thus neither investigation produced any positive result.

* "Overlord" was the code-name for the European operations and "Diver" that for pilotless aircraft.

29. Much, therefore, remained common to both plans. Both plans, for example, relied on the ability of our existing radar chain stations to detect pilotless aircraft in the same way as they detected ordinary aircraft. After taking expert advice I had come to the conclusion that the stations would be able to do this, and that we should be able to tell pilotless from piloted aircraft by " track behaviour "—that is to say, the characteristics of their flight as interpreted by the radar responses. Similarly, members of the Royal Observer Corps would, presumably, be able to recognise pilotless aircraft by their appearance and the noise they made.* All that was required under this head, then, was to lay down a procedure for reporting pilotless aircraft by the means already in existence, and instruct all concerned in its use. For this both plans provided.

30. Again, at every stage the principal object that General Pile and I had in mind was the defence of London, which was the target threatened by the vast majority of the " ski sites ". Secondly, we had to provide for the defence of Bristol, which was threatened by a smaller number of " ski sites " near Cherbourg. Thirdly, we had to bear in mind the possibility that, as a counter-measure to our preparations for the European operations, pilotless aircraft might be used against assembly areas on the south coast, and particularly round the Solent.

31. In each case, fighter aircraft were to be the first line of defence. For the defence of London the arrangement envisaged in both plans was that whenever an attack in daylight seemed imminent, fighters of No. 11 Group would patrol at 12,000 feet on three patrol lines, 20 miles off the coast between Beachy Head and Dover, over the coastline between Newhaven and Dover, and between Haywards Heath and Ashford respectively. Once an attack had begun, additional aircraft would patrol these lines at 6,000 feet. At night, fighters would patrol under the control of G.C.I., Type 16, and C.H.L. radar stations, and would be reinforced, if necessary, by further aircraft under Sector control.

32. At Bristol and the Solent the facts of geography promised a longer warning and more room to manoeuvre as well as a lighter scale of attack. Consequently I did not propose to fly standing patrols for the defence of those places. Should attacks appear imminent, however, fighters would be held ready to intercept by normal methods.

33. Under both plans, guns and searchlights would provide the next line of defence, and would, of course, become the first line of defence if at any time the state of the weather or any other factor prevented the fighters from operating. For the defence of London, General Pile and I proposed under the first plan to deploy 400 heavy A.A. guns in folds and hollows on the southern slopes of the North Downs, where their radar equipment would be liable to the minimum of interference from " jamming " by the enemy. We also proposed to use 346 light A.A. guns, to be deployed largely on searchlight sites, and 216 searchlights. In front of Bristol we proposed to put 96 heavy A.A. guns and 216 light A.A. guns, with 132 searchlights. Thirty-two heavy A.A. guns, 242 light A.A. guns and a smaller number of searchlights would defend the Solent.

34. It was here that the most important differences between the two plans lay. The original plan called for the deployment of a grand total of 528 heavy and 804 light A.A. guns and more than 350 searchlights. Clearly, to muster as many guns and searchlights as this would not be easy. General Pile and I proposed to find half the required number of heavy A.A. guns from within Anti-Aircraft Command by depleting the defences of places not directly threatened by pilotless aircraft; the other half would have to come from the resources of 21 Army Group and Home Forces, and thus would consist very largely of guns already earmarked for the European operations. In the case of light A.A. guns and also of searchlights, 21 Army Group would have to provide an even higher proportion of the total.

35. Some risk would, of course, be involved in removing guns from places like Oxford, Birmingham, and the Clyde to defend London, Bristol, and the Solent against flying bombs. But the risk was one that I felt we should be justified in taking, since otherwise there was no possibility of finding the resources required for adequate defence against the threat from pilotless aircraft as we conceived it in December, when the plan was made.

36. By February, when we came to draw up the revised plan, the position had changed. Virtually every gun and searchlight that could be spared would shortly be needed for the European operations; and it was essential that the " Diver " defences should make the smallest inroad on the " Overlord " resources that was compatible with an adequate scale of defence. Fortunately, the success of the bombing attacks on the " ski sites " held out the hope of achieving an adequate scale of defence on cheaper terms than had seemed possible two months earlier.

37. Accordingly, General Pile and I carefully reviewed this part of our original plan. We came to the conclusion that substantial savings in both guns and searchlights could and must be made. We therefore proposed to reduce the number of heavy A.A. guns to be deployed on each of the sites in the belt defending London from eight to four. This would save 208 guns. We hoped that by the time the attacks began 128 American 90 mm. guns, using electrical predictors and a new type of radar called S.C.R.584, might be available to replace a corresponding number of our 3.7-inch guns with their mechanical predictors and G.L. Mark III radar; for there was every indication that the S.C.R.584 and electrical predictors would be particularly effective against pilotless aircraft. But as this equipment had yet to arrive from the United States and crews be trained in its use, we dared not count on it: we therefore prepared alternative plans to cover either contingency. We also proposed to reduce the number of light A.A. guns in front of London from 346 to 246.

38. No reduction in the number of heavy A.A. guns defending Bristol seemed possible, and we decided to leave this figure at 96. In view of the great need of light A.A. guns for " Overlord " we proposed, however, to reduce

---

* All these assumptions proved correct.

the strength of these from 216 to 36. We also proposed to do without searchlights in this area, other than those provided by the normal layout. Under the revised plan, all the Bristol guns, both heavy and light, would have to be withdrawn by "D" Day; but we hoped that by that date the threat to that city, never very serious, would have been neutralized by bombing.

39. As for the Solent, fortunately that area would, in any case, be heavily defended against orthodox air attack during the final stages of preparation for "Overlord". In these circumstances no special "Diver" deployment would be needed there, apart from a few searchlights. We visualized, however, a possible re-disposition of the "Overlord" guns to fit them for a dual role. Here, again, there would be a substantial saving.

40. Under the original plan, balloons would provide a third line of defence for London. For this purpose I had originally proposed to put a permanent* barrage of 480 balloons immediately behind the guns on the high ground between Cobham (Kent) in the east and Limpsfield in the west. It so happened that I was already seeking authority from the Chiefs of Staff to reduce the balloon defences of the country by 500 balloons: by appropriating this saving to defence against pilotless aircraft the problem of providing the "Diver" barrage could be solved. As these balloons were not needed for "Overlord" there was no need to alter these proposals in the revised plan.

41. It was, then, with the revised plan ready for action that we awaited the beginning of the German attacks. To say that this plan represented a compromise between the requirements of "Overlord" and those of "Diver" would not be strictly true; for the defence of the base against "Diver" was itself an essential "Overlord" requirement. But it provided at once the largest appropriation that could be spared for the job, and the smallest that was likely to be effective against the threat which was then foreseen. The number of guns to be deployed, in particular, was no more than a bare minimum. In the circumstances it was impossible for us to budget for more guns; but we took care to frame the plan in such a way that the numbers could easily be increased if further guns should happen to become available. I also took the precaution of pointing out that if the pilotless aircraft should fly between 2,000 and 3,000 feet instead of at the greater altitude expected by the Air Ministry, the guns would have a very awkward task, for between those heights the targets would be too high for the light anti-aircraft guns and too low for the mobile heavy guns which at that time could not be traversed smoothly enough to engage such speedy missiles.

42. In the event, the threat which materialised in the summer was to prove a very different one from that foreseen in February when the plan was made. This was not only because the height at which the pilotless aircraft flew had been over-estimated, but also because the forecasts of the enemy's capabilities with which the Air Ministry provided us were based on knowledge which was incomplete in one important respect. Consequently, when the attack developed we soon found that we needed not only more than the 288 heavy and 282 light A.A. guns postulated in the revised plan, but more than the 528 and 804 respectively for which we had budgetted in our original, superseded plan.*

(b) *The Eve of the Attacks*

43. Ironically enough, the emergence of this undiscovered factor which upset our calculations was due to the very success with which we had bombed and neutralized the "ski sites". By the end of April most of the sites had been rendered unfit for use. Although the Germans repaired some of them, from that time onwards there were never at any time more than ten "ski sites" in a state to fire.

44. Fortunately for them, the Germans soon realised how vulnerable the "ski sites" were, and began to build other launching sites which were more carefully hidden and harder to destroy. By simplifying the plan of construction and using pre-fabricated parts, they were able to complete these new sites very quickly.

45. Since the armistice the Germans have told us that they began this new programme of construction in March 1944. However, it was not until the 27th April that the first of the "modified sites", as we called them, was seen on a reconnaissance photograph. By the middle of May twenty such sites had been located, and by the 12th June the number had risen to 66. Forty-two were aligned on London and the rest on Bristol or south-coast ports.

46. The "modified sites" made difficult bombing targets. When Typhoon bombers carried out an experimental attack on one of them on the 27th May the site proved hard to find and the results were poor. Besides being small and well concealed, the sites comprised few buildings at which bombs could be aimed. Unlike the "ski sites", they seemed to be intended as launching points and nothing more. The conclusion was that any stocks of pilotless aircraft held locally would not be kept on the sites themselves, but stored elsewhere or dispersed in the wooded country amongst which all the sites were placed.

47. At least partly for these reasons, we made no further attacks on the "modified sites" until after the Germans had begun to launch missiles from them. Meanwhile, the officers at the Air Ministry and elsewhere who were responsible for offensive counter-measures were debating whether to attack certain other constructions, usually referred to as "supply sites". They believed that these constructions had something to do with the storage or maintenance of pilotless aircraft; but they were not sure. Nevertheless, two attacks on one of the sites were made about the end of May. From that time onwards, little was done to hinder the enemy's final preparations for the offensive.

48. This state of affairs was a natural consequence of the awkwardness of the "modified sites" as bombing targets, and our uncertain

---

* At that stage lack of communications and manning difficulties were expected to make the usual system of control impracticable

* The weapons actually deployed in the middle of August, 1944, when the campaign was in full swing, comprised 800 H.A.A. and 1,100 40 mm. L.A.A. guns, over 700 rocket barrels, and some 600 light guns (mostly 20 mm.) manned by the R.A.F. Regiment and the Royal Armoured Corps.

knowledge of the enemy's plans. I believe, however, that aligned with these causes was a psychological factor. It must be remembered that for many months past the chief threat had seemed to come from the " ski sites ". The use of our bomber forces against the " ski sites " had therefore been felt as a necessary, but still an unwelcome, diversion of effort at a time when interest was focussed on the coming European operations. To the officers responsible for directing offensive operations the success of the attacks on the " ski sites " must have come as a great relief. In the circumstances, they would have been hardly human if they had not been more reluctant than perhaps they realised to recognise that the neutralization of the " ski sites " had not averted the menace after all.

49. I think, therefore, that at the end of May and in the first half of June the threat from the " modified sites " was under-estimated, not in the sense of a failure to apprehend it intellectually, but in the sense that it was not felt as keenly as the original threat from the " ski sites " six months earlier. If it had been, I do not doubt that the " modified sites " would have been attacked as vigorously then—despite their shortcomings as targets—as they were a few weeks later, when " Diver " had begun.

50. Whether this would have had much effect on the subsequent course of events is another matter. The question is one to which no final answer is possible. My own opinion is that a well co-ordinated series of attacks on the " modified sites " during the weeks immediately preceding the " Diver " campaign would have been worth making, but that nothing short of the destruction of all the sites would have prevented the Germans from using their new weapon sooner or later. Nor does my belief that the menace of the " modified sites " was under-estimated necessarily imply that I think the omission to attack the sites was wrong in the light of the knowledge available at the time. Even if their dangerousness had been fully realised, there would still have been strong arguments against attacking them. And while it is easy to be wise after the event, at the time there was no means of knowing how imminent the danger was. On the contrary, until some 36 hours before the first pilotless aircraft was launched, such intelligence as was available suggested that the " modified sites " were not likely to be used for several weeks.*

51. The fact remains that during the first half of June the Germans were able to press on with their preparations to bombard us with pilotless aircraft, virtually unmolested by our bomber forces.

52. At that stage, one of the tasks of my Command was to prevent German reconnaissance aircraft from approaching the areas where our forces were concentrating. In this we succeeded even beyond our expectations. Partly on this account, the landings in Normandy early on the 6th June achieved complete tactical surprise. Even on subsequent days, when the Germans had had time to appreciate what we were doing, air opposition was far from energetic. Naturally enough, the Air Commander-in-Chief and his staff were jubilant, and had little time or inclination to think of pilotless aircraft.

53. It was equally natural that my staff and I, with our defensive preoccupations, should not entirely share this optimism. It seemed to us that things were going almost too well. So much was at stake for the enemy that we dared not believe he would let us have everything our own way. We could not help suspecting that he still had something up his sleeve.

(c) *The Attacks: First Phase (13th June to 15th July).*

54. Events were soon to substantiate our doubts. Shortly after midnight on the night of the 12th-13th June the German long-range guns opened fire across the Channel. In this there was nothing novel; what was unusual was that for the first and last time during the war, a town some miles from the coast was shelled. Eight rounds fell at Maidstone, one at Otham, two-and-a-half miles to the south-east, and twenty-four at Folkestone. The bombardment doubtless achieved its purpose, inasmuch as it gave some people the impression that a novel weapon was being used and tended to create an atmosphere of uncertainty and rumour. At least one Me.410 flew over the London area during this phase and was shot down by anti-aircraft fire near Barking.

55. At 0400 hours the shelling stopped. A few minutes later an observer on duty at a Royal Observer Corps post in Kent was passed by an aircraft which made " a swishing sound " and emitted a bright glow from the rear. In common with all his colleagues, he had been briefed to recognise pilotless aircraft; and in accordance with his instructions he shouted " Diver ". The missile continued over the North Downs " making a noise like a model-T Ford going up a hill " and fell to earth with a loud explosion at Swanscombe, near Gravesend, at 0418 hours. During the next hour three more of the missiles came down at Cuckfield, Bethnal Green, and Platt (near Sevenoaks) respectively. No casualties were suffered except at Bethnal Green, where six people were killed and nine injured; in addition a railway bridge was demolished.

56. The attack then ceased for the time being. I came to the conclusion that so small an effort did not justify the major re-disposition of the anti-aircraft defences required by the " Overlord-Diver " Plan. The Chiefs of Staff agreed. I therefore gave orders that the plan was not to be put into effect until we could see more clearly what was going to happen. In the meantime the existing defences were authorised to engage pilotless aircraft on the same terms as ordinary aircraft. I had already arranged that a visual reconnaissance of the most likely launching areas should be flown; and at the instance of the Air Ministry several attacks were made on three of the so-called " supply sites " on the 13th, 14th and 15th June. These absorbed the whole of the bombing effort that could be spared from other

---

* On the 11th June, however, the Air Ministry received a report which stated that a train loaded with missiles had passed westwards through Belgium two days earlier. On the same day photographic reconnaissance revealed unusual activity at six of the " modified sites ". This information did not reach my headquarters until after the German offensive had begun; but little or nothing would have been gained if I had received it earlier, for the defence plan had been ready since March, and I should not have ordered deployment merely on the strength of these two reports.

tasks. Accordingly the "modified sites" still went unmolested, although it is now known, and was strongly suspected at the time, that the missiles had been launched from sites of this class.

57. At 2230 hours on the 15th June the attacks were resumed on a much heavier scale. During the next twenty-four hours the Germans launched over 200 pilotless aircraft—or, as we soon began to call them, flying bombs or "doodle bugs"—of which 144 crossed the coasts of Kent and Sussex and 73 reached Greater London. Thirty-three bombs were brought down by the defences, but eleven of these came down in the built-up area of Greater London.*

58. Clearly we were confronted on the morning of the 16th June by a situation very different from that of the 13th. I was of the opinion that the time to execute the "Overlord-Diver" Plan had now come; and in the course of the day the Chiefs of Staff agreed that this should be done. That afternoon I attended a "Staff Conference" over which the Prime Minister and Minister of Defence presided. One of the decisions then reached was that, in consultation with General Pile, I should redistribute the gun, searchlight, and balloon defences "as necessary to counter the attacks". Another was that for the time being the guns inside the London area (as well as those outside) should continue to engage flying bombs. We abandoned this arrangement two days later, after experience had cast doubt on the assumption that most of the bombs that were hit exploded in the air.

59. Before going to the conference I had given orders for deployment of the "Diver" defences to begin. By the early hours of the 17th June the first A.A. regiment to move had taken up its new positions and the deployment of the balloon barrage had also begun. When drawing up the plan we had calculated that deployment would take eighteen days to complete and that it would be wiser to allow twenty-five days; the Air Ministry had expected to be able to give us a month's warning. In the event we had received no warning at all, apart from that provided by the Germans themselves on the 13th June. In the circumstances it was imperative that we should get the job done quickly. The original time-table went by the board. Thanks to the administrative arrangements which had already been made and to remarkable feats by both Anti-Aircraft Command and Balloon Command, the whole of the planned deployment was virtually complete by the 21st June, only five days after the issue of the order to deploy.

60. All this time the attacks were continuing at the rate of about 100 flying bombs a day. Our fighters were bringing down about thirty per cent. of the bombs and the static defences some eight to ten per cent.; but more than half the bombs which crossed the coast were getting through to Greater London. I soon realised that a scale of static defence which might have been adequate against such attacks as eight or ten "ski sites" could have delivered was not going to suffice against the effort of which the "modified sites" were showing themselves capable. In consultation with General Pile, therefore, I arranged for the gun defences to be substantially reinforced. By mid-day on the 28th June 363 heavy and 522 light A.A. guns were in action. Further weapons, including light guns manned by the Royal Air Force Regiment, anti-aircraft tanks of the Royal Armoured Corps, and rocket projectors, were either in position or on the way. I also arranged for the strength of the balloon barrage to be doubled.

61. Meanwhile Tempest V, Spitfire XIV, Spitfire XII, Spitfire IX, Typhoon, and at night Mosquito aircraft of No. 11 Group had been in action against flying bombs since the beginning of the main attack. As we have seen, their rate of success at this stage amounted to about thirty per cent. of all the bombs which crossed or approached the coast. On the 16th June I had issued orders defining their area of patrol as the Channel and the land between the coast and the southern limit of the gun-belt, and prohibiting them from passing over the gun-belt except when actually pursuing a flying bomb. I soon found that in good weather the fighters were much more successful than the guns, which were badly hampered by the fact that the flying bombs did not fly at the height of 6,000 or 7,000 feet previously estimated by the Air Ministry, but at that very height of 2,000 to 3,000 feet which we had always realised would make the gunner's task most difficult.* On the other hand, when the weather was bad, poor visibility hampered the fighters, and in these conditions the guns were likely to prove the more effective weapon. Accordingly, I arranged on the 19th June that in very good weather the guns should abstain from firing in order to give the fighters complete freedom of action. Conversely, when the weather was bad, the guns would have freedom of action and no fighters would be used. In middling weather fighters would operate in front of the gun belt and enter it only when pursuing a flying bomb. When a fighter entered the gun belt for this purpose the guns would, of course, withhold their fire; otherwise the guns inside the belt would be free to fire up to 8,000 feet. Outside the gun belt gunfire was prohibited in these circumstances, except that light A.A. gunners linked to the communications network might open fire on targets they could see, provided no fighters were about.

62. These rules for engagement, which I ordered to be codified and issued to those concerned on the 26th June, were intended to prevent mutual interference between guns and fighters. For reasons which I shall explain later, they did not altogether achieve this aim. But before coming to this question it will be appropriate to review the progress of the German attacks and of our counter-measures up to the date in the middle of July when the question of an important change in our defence plan came to a head.

---

* The figures were:

	Brought down outside London	Brought down inside London
By fighters alone	7	—
By guns alone	14	11
By fighters and guns jointly	1	—
Totals	22	11

* Originally the Germans meant the bombs to fly higher, doubtless so as to minimize the effect of light A.A. fire. This proved impracticable, and without the knowledge of the Air Ministry they changed their plans.

63. The scale of attack for the first two weeks was, as I have said, of the order of 100 bombs a day. After a period of deliberation at the outset, the authorities responsible for offensive counter-measures embarked on a series of bombing attacks on the "modified sites". A number of sites were neutralized, but the number remaining was always sufficient to have launched a scale of attack several times greater than that which we actually experienced. In other words, the factor limiting the German effort was not the number of sites available, but something else—most probably the rate at which the flying bombs could be supplied to the sites. It was therefore arguable that the attacks on the "modified sites" amounted to locking the stable door after the horse had been stolen, and were a waste of effort. The authorities decided to continue the attacks, however, in order to harass the launching crews and thereby reduce their efficiency. I cannot say how far that object was achieved, since my staff were never able to establish any statistical relationship between the bombing attacks on the "modified sites" and the rate or quality of the enemy's fire. The Germans have told us since the armistice, however, that the bombing of the "modified sites" made little difference to them.

64. At the same time the authorities responsible for offensive counter-measures appreciated that the factor limiting the scale of attack was probably supply. Information from intelligence sources cast increasing doubt on the relevance of the so-called "supply sites" and showed that the key-positions were probably certain underground storage depots situated in limestone quarries in the valley of the Oise and an abandoned railway tunnel in Champagne. Successful bombing attacks were made on several of these depots, and in two instances were followed by a noticeable decline in the scale of attack. In both cases, however, the effect was only temporary. Apparently the Germans were able to improvise other channels of supply. Hence, while I was much relieved by the offensive counter-measures undertaken by the Tactical and Strategic Air Forces, I realised that they were not likely to put a stop to the German attacks. The loss or preservation of thousands of lives, much valuable property, and a substantial productive capacity, would turn on our ability to provide an effective system of defence for London with the resources under my operational control. At that time our land forces in France had not advanced beyond the lodgment area: the capture of the launching sites in the imminent future seemed very doubtful. The flying-bomb attacks might well go on for many months.

65. And in fact the attacks continued at the same rate of roughly 100 flying bombs a day until the end of the first week in July, when the effort fell for about ten days to an average of less than 70 a day. This decline may have been partly due to good weather, for the Germans usually saved their biggest efforts for days when the weather was likely to hamper the defences. But I incline to the view that it was largely the result of a specially successful attack on one of the main storage depots which was made by Bomber Command on the night of the 7th July. Except during this same second week in July, when both good weather and a reduced scale of attack helped our fighters to shoot down a higher proportion of the bombs than usual, about half the bombs that crossed the English coast went on reaching Greater London. In sum, during the five weeks which ended at sunrise on the 15th July, just under 3,000 flying bombs came within the compass of the defensive system.* Our fighters shot down rather more than a tenth of them into the sea, and a few were brought down into the sea by A.A. fire or fell into it of their own accord. Of the remaining 2,500 odd which crossed the coast, fighters, guns, and balloons respectively destroyed or brought down about half over the land, fighters claiming ten and guns four casualties to every one claimed by the balloon defences.

66. Outwardly these results were not too bad. Nevertheless, I was far from satisfied that the defences were working properly. In the first place, an average of 25 bombs a day was still reaching Greater London. The overall average since the beginning of the attacks amounted to nearly 40 bombs a day. London had endured heavier bombing than this in 1940; but for various reasons an intermittent drizzle of malignant robots seemed harder to bear than the storm and thunder of the "Blitz". Nor were the material results of the bombardment inconsiderable. Between the 13th June and the 15th July it killed about 3,000 people, seriously injured 10,000, and irreparably damaged 13,000 houses. Although no objectives of vital importance to the war effort were hit, many public buildings such as churches, hospitals, and schools appeared in the casualty list.

67. Secondly, although the performance of the defences as a whole had improved continuously since the beginning of the attack, and although the fighters had done particularly well during the last two weeks, I saw many signs that the limit of improvement with our existing methods had been reached. I was reluctantly convinced that unless some radical change was made, the future was more likely to bring a slow decline than further progress.

68. The circumstances which led me to this view can only be understood by reference to the special problems of the various arms of the defence. In order to gain an intimate knowledge of those problems I had decided early in the attack to share in the fighter operations as a pilot, using various aircraft in turn. Personal experience convinced me that the first problem confronting the fighters was the speed of the bombs, which was rather greater than we had expected before the attacks began.† The fastest aircraft I had were a wing of Tempest Vs and a wing of Spitfire XIVs. These could not be everywhere at once. One of my first moves, therefore, was to obtain the Air Commander-in-Chief's consent to my borrowing at first a flight and later a wing of Mustang IIIs from the Second Tactical Air Force. These aircraft were very fast at the height at which the bombs flew and made a valuable contribution

---

* This figure does not include "abortive" bombs which fell in France or into the sea on the French side of the Channel. It seems that the Germans launched five flying bombs for every four that came within the compass of the defences.

† Most of the bombs seem to have left the launching sites at about 200 m.p.h. Their speed increased throughout their flight, reaching about 340 m.p.h. at the English coast and 400 m.p.h. or thereabouts over London.

to the improved results achieved by the fighters after the first week in July. By the 15th July I was using a total of thirteen single-engined and nine twin-engined (Mosquito) squadrons against flying bombs. Six of the Mosquito squadrons alternated between this work and operations over the lodgment area, two of them doing bomber-support work as well. I found that, while some pilots took readily to the work of shooting down flying bombs, the majority preferred shooting down enemy aircraft over France. To instil enthusiasm for the novel and impersonal business of shooting at pilotless missiles, and ensure that pilots were not kept long enough at the task to make them stale, was not the least of my anxieties.

69. In order to get as much speed as possible, I arranged that aircraft which were to be used exclusively against flying bombs should be stripped of their armour and all unnecessary external fittings, and that their paint should be removed and their outer surfaces polished. The engines were modified to use 150-octane fuel and accept a higher boost than usual. In this way we managed to increase the speed of some of the single-engined fighters by as much as 30 m.p.h.

70. Even with these modifications the fighters had only a small margin of speed over the flying bombs. Nevertheless they did have a margin. It was reported that a demonstration by a German pilot with a captured Spitfire had convinced Hitler that our fighters could not catch the flying bomb. This was true of the Spitfire V, and almost true of the Spitfire IX; but it was not true of the Spitfire XIV or the Tempest. Even so, these aircraft had no more than a fractional superiority. Hence the problem was essentially one of time and space. For interception over the sea we used a method of close control from radar stations on the coast, or alternatively a method of running commentary. At best the radar chain could give about six minutes' warning before the flying bombs reached the coast; but in practice the time available to the fighters over the sea was always less than this, not only because of inevitable time-lags but because we dared not risk our modified aircraft on the far side of the Channel, where they might be surprised by German fighters. Later the Royal Navy were to come to our assistance by providing a chain of small craft which operated at three mile intervals seven miles off the French coast, carrying observers who warned our pilots by means of signal rockets and star-shells that flying bombs were on their way. This improvised system was in the final stages of development about the time when the main attack came to a close.

71. Over the land we used the method of running commentary from radar stations and Royal Observer Corps Centres, supplemented by various devices such as signal rockets, shell-bursts, and searchlight beams, for indicating the approach of flying bombs to patrolling pilots. The weakness of this method was that sometimes several pilots would go after the same flying bomb, leaving other bombs to slip through unmolested. However, there was nothing else we could do, for the absence of low-looking radar made close control over the land impracticable.

72. The majority of the flying bombs crossed the coast between Cuckmere Haven and St. Margaret's Bay. The distance thence to the southern edge of the gun belt was in most places about 30 miles. The flying bombs covered this distance in five minutes. Five minutes, then, was the time available to the pilot of an overland fighter to select his target, get within range of it, and shoot it down, unless gunfire had been restricted or he took advantage of the rule which allowed him to enter the belt in pursuit of his quarry. In this case he would have an extra minute or so before he reached the balloon barrage. Thus there was rarely time for a stern chase unless the pursuer started with a substantial advantage in height. On the whole the most effective procedure was to fly on roughly the same course as an approaching bomb, allow it to draw level, and fire deflection shots as it passed, being careful not to fire when it was closer than 200 yards lest it should explode in the air and blow up the attacker.* The hot gases emitted by a bomb immediately in front of the fighter made a steady aim difficult, so that short bursts and frequent aiming corrections were required. Usually several bursts were needed to inflict enough damage to explode the bomb or bring it down. Another method useful on occasions but hardly suitable for general adoption, was to get close beside the target and tip it over by inserting the wing of the fighter underneath that of the bomb and then raising it sharply.

73. Thus, in many respects the fighters had a stiff task. That which faced the guns was, if anything, more awkward still. Theoretically, pilotless aircraft ought to have made ideal targets for anti-aircraft artillery, since they flew on courses which could be accurately predicted from the data on which the technical devices normally employed had been designed to work. For the first time in the war, the gunners were presented with targets that could not dodge. In practice this advantage was outweighed by the speed of the missiles and the critical height at which they flew. They were too high and went too fast to make good targets for light A.A. guns, but were too low and crossed the field of vision of the heavy A.A. gunners too swiftly to give adequate time for the radar and predictors to be used and the guns be laid by hand. These difficulties could be minimised so far as the heavy guns were concerned by replacing the mobile guns used in the original "Diver" deployment by static guns which could be electrically elevated and traversed and were fitted with improved fuse setters and other devices which made them quicker to operate and more accurate. Unfortunately the static guns required concrete emplacements which took some time to instal. A steel mattress, known as the "Pile Mattress," which was devised by the R.E.M.E. detachment at Anti-Aircraft Command provided a way out of the difficulty; and the task of replacing the mobile guns by static guns was started towards the end of June.

---

* During the first six weeks of the attacks alone, eighteen fighters were substantially damaged and five pilots and one Navigator/Radio Operator killed in this way. Even though the flying bomb could not hit back deliberately, "Diver" patrols were by no means unattended by risk.

74. Another change which General Pile found necessary at an early stage was the removal to higher ground of the radar sets belonging to the heavy guns. At the start these were placed in hollows because the "Overlord/Diver" Plan had been made in anticipation of attempts at "jamming" by the enemy. Successful bombing attacks during the "Overlord" preparations had, however, virtually deprived the Germans of this resource, and so it was possible to move the sets to more exposed positions in which the contours of the ground caused less interference.

75. Another variation from the plan concerned the light guns. Originally these were to have been deployed on searchlight sites, but after the attacks had begun, General Pile came to the conclusion that better results would be achieved by concentrating them in front of the heavy gun belt. He also found that by linking troops of four guns each to a heavy-gun predictor and G.L. radar set he could use the light A.A. guns against "unseen" as well as "visual" targets.

76. Towards the end of June we began to receive the S.C.R. 584 radar sets and improved predictors which we had been eagerly expecting since February. These two items of equipment were destined to contribute very largely to the ultimate success of the guns. An intensive training programme which had to be organised with such resources as could be spared from operations was, however, indispensable before they could be used on any considerable scale.

77. With the balloon barrage the problem was largely the arithmetical one of achieving a sufficient density to give a reasonable chance of success. We found, however, that in practice the theoretically computed rate of success was not always attained: somehow more bombs slipped through the barrage than should have done so according to the laws of probability, if our assumptions were correct. One difficulty was that the "double parachute links"* used to arm the balloon cables in normal barrages had not been designed to cope with aircraft travelling much faster than 300 m.p.h. For this reason we did not arm the cables of the balloons deployed during the first few days of the attack. But we soon came to the conclusion that an imperfect arming device was better than none; and by the 21st June all cables were armed. I received a large number of suggestions for increasing the effectiveness of the barrage in other ways, such as by adding "whiskers", nets, kites, and other forms of drapery. Many devices of this kind were tried, and some were of value, but as most of them increased the physical difficulty of handling the balloons in one way or another, I had to adopt a somewhat cautious attitude lest the best should prove the enemy of the good.

78. A slight re-disposition of the barrage proved necessary in order to prevent bombs which penetrated to its northern edge from being brought down in built-up areas. The notion of keeping the balloons up in all weathers—which was contained in the original "Overlord/Diver" Plan but afterwards abandoned—was considered a second time after the attack had begun, but once more found impracticable. We therefore used a system of control which was less flexible than that used for normal barrages, but served its purpose adequately. In order that our pilots should not lose their lives by colliding with the barrage we perpetrated a pious fraud on them by allowing them to believe that the balloons would fly continuously.

79. So much for the problems that confronted the individual arms of the defence and the chief measures taken to solve them. There were, of course, many smaller problems with which I have not space to deal. But the biggest problem of all was not confined to one arm: it was of wider consequence and consisted in securing the right kind and degree of co-operation between guns and fighters. Since in a sense these were rival weapons, the task had always been a troublesome one from the early days of the war; nevertheless, so far as operations against orthodox aircraft were concerned, with experience a satisfactory working solution had been found. During the "Baby Blitz," for example, the co-operation between guns and fighters had been most satisfactory. I found, on the other hand, that as the Germans must have intended, the novel problem presented by the flying bomb created a host of new difficulties. For example, it was sometimes hard for a pilot to realise that he was approaching the gun belt in time to avoid infringing the rule against entering it. Conversely, gunners in the belt who were engaging a flying bomb did not always realise in time that a pilot was legitimately entering the belt in pursuit of this or another missile, and would go on firing to the peril of the pilot's life. The crews of the guns on the coast and elsewhere outside the gun-belt were in a still more difficult position, for except in bad weather they always bore the onus of ensuring that no fighters were about before they could open fire. In the excitement of the moment, when the attention of the gunners was concentrated on their targets, it was only too easy for a fighter travelling at six miles a minute to slip unnoticed into the field of fire. Consequently numerous infringements of the gun-belt by fighters, and many unintentional engagements of our fighters by the guns, were reported, especially in middling weather when guns and fighters were simultaneously in operation. Charges and counter-charges mounted; and with deep misgiving I began to sense a rising feeling of mutual distrust between pilots and gunners.

80. I felt very strongly that this state of affairs could not be allowed to continue. If the causes of friction were not removed, the situation would inevitably grow worse. As the first four weeks of the attack went by, the overall achievement of the defences improved. To all appearances, the machine was growing more efficient. But this improvement brought me scanty satisfaction. I knew that the point would soon be reached at which this friction would become the limiting factor, and no further improvement would be possible. Looking further ahead, I realised that, whatever temporary advantages our existing practice might bring, we could not afford to sacrifice the spirit

---

* The "double parachute link" was a device whereby, as soon as a balloon cable was struck, it was automatically severed near the top and bottom, so that the aircraft which struck it carried away the central portion. Parachutes then opened at each end of this portion and exercised a drag intended to make the aircraft stall.

of co-operation between gunners and pilots which had been steadily built up in the past.

81. I came to the conclusion that the only solution was to give guns and fighters freedom each in their own sphere. On the 10th July, therefore, I decided to prohibit fighters from entering the gun-belt, whatever the circumstances, after the 17th July. At a conference held to discuss this change, General Pile pointed out that an obvious corollary to it was to move all the guns inside the belt, so as to have them all in one place and provide both guns and fighters with clearly-defined spheres of operation. The logic of this argument was irrefutable; and I agreed to examine detailed proposals for moving all the guns into the belt except a few which would remain on the coast to act as " markers ".

82. The great advantage of the principle of separate spheres of operation for guns and fighters was that it would lessen the chances of misunderstanding by creating a clear-cut situation. It would also ease the task of the gunners by giving them a free hand in their own territory. Not the least important point was that when not in action they would always be free to train, whereas under the existing arrangements when gunfire was restricted and fighters were operating they were condemned by the presence of our aircraft to an enervating inaction. At the same time the change would reduce the field of action open to the fighters. In order that the necessity for making this sacrifice might be clear to pilots, I instructed my Deputy Senior Air Staff Officer, Air Commodore G. H. Ambler, C.B.E., A.F.C., to prepare an explanation which could be circulated to lower formations At this stage no question of changing the geographical position of the gun-belt had been raised.

(d) *The Re-deployment of the Guns (mid-July).*

83. Nevertheless, there were strong arguments in favour of such a move. Originally we had deployed the guns on the North Downs largely because the " Overlord/Diver " Plan had been drawn up at a time when jamming of our radar by the Germans was a threat which could not be neglected. The desire to reduce this threat or minimise its effects if carried out had done much to dictate this choice of situation. Now, as we have seen, by D-Day successful bombing of German wireless and radar stations had virtually removed the possibility of jamming. This fact and its significance had not become fully apparent until after deployment had begun.* Consequently we had carried out the deployment as planned, though shortly afterwards, as already related, General Pile had taken advantage of the absence of jamming to move some of the heavy-gun radar sets to better and more exposed positions within the original deployment area.

84. By the middle of July what had been a reasonable hope a month before had become a practical certainty. Clearly, little danger from jamming need be feared. Consequently there was no need to hide the guns and their radar sets away in folds of the Downs if a better position could be found for them. Was there such a better position, and where was it?

85. These questions were far from simple. The guns could not really be considered in isolation; they were part of a defensive system which also included fighters, searchlights, and balloons. If, nevertheless, the subject was approached from the sole viewpoint of the operational effectiveness of the guns, there was much to be said for moving the gun-belt away from the Downs and putting it on the coast. In this position the gunners would get a better view of their targets; the hampering effect of ground echoes on their radar sets would be reduced to a minimum; and they would be able to use shells fitted with " proximity fuses ", which were potentially more effective than normally-fused shells, but could not be used inland because they were dangerous to life and property. Added to this was the important point that if the guns were on the coast the majority of the bombs that they brought down would fall harmlessly into the sea.

86. From a more general aspect there was one weighty argument against moving the guns to the coast. To do so would split the operational area of the fighters into two, and thus, to all appearances, infringe the principle of separate and clear-cut spheres of operation for guns and fighters which I was anxious to establish. Up till then the fighters had been by far the most successful weapon against flying-bombs; out of 1,192 bombs which had been destroyed or brought down up to sunrise on the 13th July, they had accounted for 883. No move which threatened to impair their effectiveness was to be undertaken lightly. Still, to a great extent interception over the sea and interception over the land were already separate problems. Hence in practice the disadvantage of having three spheres of operation for guns and fighters instead of two would not be so great as it looked at first sight.

87. These considerations struck Air Commodore Ambler with great force when he sat down to write the explanation of the new rules for engagement which I had instructed him to prepare. The correctness of the decision to banish fighters from the gun-belt was not in question; nor did he dissent from the proposal to put all the guns in one place. But he felt that to bring this about by moving the guns already on the coast to the North Downs was only going half-way. What was wanted was to put all the guns together in the place where they could function best. In his considered view this meant adopting the opposite course, and sending forward the guns already on the Downs to join those on the coast. The disadvantage of splitting the operational area of the fighters would, he thought, be more than outweighed by the increase in effectiveness of the guns in the latter position.

88. To clarify his mind, Air Commodore Ambler incorporated his arguments in a formal appreciation. Armed with this document, he came to see me on the morning of the 13th July and put his views before me.

89. His arguments convinced me that unless discounted by some faulty technical assumption, the tactical theory behind the case for

---

* It is true that by D-Day at the latest we knew that heavy damage had been done to the German transmitters. But until experience had shown that in consequence the Germans were manifestly unable to jam, General Pile and I would not have been justified in departing from the plan on that account.

moving all the guns to the coast was sound. At the same time I learned that Sir Robert Watson-Watt, the Scientific Adviser on Telecommunications to the Air Ministry, had made an independent study of the problem and reached substantially the same conclusions as Air Commodore Ambler. Sir Robert's opinion, coming from such a distinguished pioneer of radar, carried all the more weight since better conditions for the radar equipment of the guns was one of the main advantages claimed for the proposed change.

90. On the other hand the matter had necessarily to be considered from many aspects besides that to which Air Commodore Ambler, as an Air Staff Officer, had properly confined himself. Even if I accepted the argument that the material and moral effect on pilots of splitting their sphere of operation into two would be no worse than that of excluding them from the existing gun-belt, many practical and administrative factors had still to be taken into account. Hundreds of guns, with all their equipment, were now in position on the Downs. Great reserves of ammunition had been collected there. Thousands of miles of telephone cables had been laid over a period of six months. Accommodation had been found or improvised for the gunners. The best positions available for the guns themselves and their equipment had been selected. In short, a small city was spread out between Redhill and the Thames. The proposal was that we should pick up this city bodily and transport it thirty or forty miles further south. On top of this, for the last two weeks men had been busy building permanent emplacements for the guns among the apple orchards and on the slopes of the chalk hills in Kent and Surrey. The organism was taking root. To transplant it might still be possible, but would not long remain so. Air Commodore Ambler's proposal, with all its consequences, must be endorsed or rejected without delay.

91. I decided to think the matter over during the day and hold a conference late that afternoon, primarily for the purpose of discussing it with General Pile. In the meantime I took steps to acquaint him with the proposal so that he might be in a position to give a considered opinion when the time came. My reflections were punctuated by the intermittent clatter of the bombs, which continually reminded me of the hourly toll of lives and property. The attack that day was the lightest we had had yet; nevertheless sixteen flying bombs crashed into Greater London.

92. General Pile came to the conference with three of his staff. At my request, Sir Robert Watson-Watt also attended, as did the Air Officer Commanding, No. 11 Group, with two of his staff, a representative of the Air Commander-in-Chief, and several of my own staff officers.

93. I opened the conference by outlining the situation. I then asked General Pile whether he supported the proposal to move all the guns to the coast, leaving the balloons where they were, and creating two areas for fighters, one between the balloons and the new gun-belt, and the other in front of the gun-belt, over the sea. He replied that he was in full agreement with it: and in fact, the merits of siting the guns along the coast had been under consideration in A.A. Command for some time.

From the gunners' point of view, such a deployment would present notable advantages. General Pile now proposed that the guns be deployed between St. Margaret's Bay and Beachy Head, and asked that they be given freedom of action inside a strip extending 10,000 yards out to sea and 5,000 yards inland.

94. Air Vice-Marshal Saunders, the Air Officer Commanding, No. 11 Group, might have been expected to demur, since the plan would throw a barrier across the area in which his fighters operated. On the contrary, he welcomed the proposal, which he said was " certainly the most satisfactory plan that had yet been produced ". Sir Robert Watson-Watt also spoke in favour of the plan, and undertook to produce improved radar equipment for controlling fighters over the sea.

95. On hearing these opinions, which confirmed the conviction that had been growing in my mind throughout the day, I decided to adopt the plan. This left two courses open to me. On the one hand, since the forces which I intended to re-dispose had already been allotted to me for the defence of London against flying bombs, and no move of guns from one defended area to another was involved, I might regard the change as a tactical one and act at once on my own responsibility. On the other hand, bearing in mind that no move involving so many guns had ever been made on purely tactical grounds before, I might adopt a more proscriptive attitude and refer the matter to higher authority first, as I should have done, for example, if I had proposed to move guns from, say, Manchester to the " Diver " belt, or from Birmingham to Bristol.

96. I decided in favour of the former course. I felt that the situation had reached such a point that no delay could be accepted. If the work on the gun-emplacements on the Downs were allowed to proceed even for another week, the opportunity to shift the guns would be lost. They must be shifted now, or anchored where they were. It seemed to me, rightly or wrongly, that if I were to pause and consult higher authority at this juncture, controversial questions of such magnitude might arise and the further authorities who might claim to be consulted would be so numerous, that I should not reasonably be able to count on a decision before it was too late. Time was running out. It was now or never.

97. I therefore gave instructions before the meeting closed for the new arrangements to be set in train forthwith. General Pile returned to his headquarters, and within a few hours advance parties were on their way to the coast.

98. During the following week vehicles of Anti-Aircraft Command travelled an aggregate distance of two-and-three-quarter million miles in consequence of this decision. Stores and ammunition weighing as much as two battleships, as well as the guns themselves and 23,000 men and women, were moved to the coast, and telephone cables long enough in the aggregate to have stretched from London to New York were laid. By dawn on the 17th July all the heavy guns were in action in their new positions, where they were joined by the light guns two days later.

99. After the conference I acquainted the Air Commander-in-Chief with its outcome. He asked me whether we could not make a trial

deployment on a small stretch of the coast. I replied that half-measures would be worse than useless, and that, taking the view that no more than a tactical re-orientation of resources already at my disposal was involved, I had decided to order the complete move on my own responsibility, and in fact had done so. In accordance with his custom where purely defensive measures were concerned, he did not question my judgment and made no further comment.

100. I was greatly relieved to hear that evening that the move had begun without a hitch, for I was convinced that, whatever the risks involved, we were now on the right track. I had made my decision in full knowledge of the issues at stake and the responsibilities which I was incurring. I was aware that the immediate effect on the performance of the fighters was bound to be adverse, and that if improved results from the guns did not counterbalance this loss within a few weeks, and things went wrong, I alone should be held to blame.

101. In the event, I did not have to wait so long. Within a few days the Air Ministry informed me officially that the Air Staff considered that I ought not to have ordered a major re-deployment of the guns without prior reference to themselves. The move itself was not explicitly disapproved, but I was left in no doubt that thenceforward I should be held personally responsible for the outcome and that any blame or credit that might accrue would be laid upon my head.

102. Despite this intimation the Air Staff continued to give me full support; and I found that at the price of incurring a formal stricture I had purchased an appreciably greater degree of operational freedom than I had hitherto enjoyed. This was to be invaluable in subsequent operations. Happily the performance of the guns in their new positions vindicated the change of plan before many weeks were out, thus proving incontestably the soundness of the deployment which had grown out of Air Commodore Ambler's proposal. The Air Staff were as good as their word in the matter of responsibility for the decision to move the guns; and the effect of the move on the operational results eventually obtained received notice in a letter of approbation sent by the Air Council to my Command at the close of the main attack.

(e) *The Attacks: Second Phase* (17th *July to 1st September*).

103. Nevertheless the next few weeks were an anxious time. The new system went into effect at dawn on the 17th July. During the following six days 204 bombs reached Greater London out of 473 that came within the compass of the defences. These figures reflected a substantially lower rate of destruction than that achieved during the last week under the old system, although a somewhat better one than we had obtained during the first four weeks of the attacks, before the defences had got into their stride. Analysis of the week's figures showed that—as critics of the new plan had predicted—improved results from the guns and from an expanded and denser balloon barrage had not sufficed to outweigh a sharp decline in the achievement of the fighters.

104. Still, it was encouraging that the performance of the guns had improved at all during a week which had begun with a major upheaval and afforded little time for the gunners to get used to their new positions. As for the decline in the performance of the fighters, this was no more than I had expected. I was not disheartened. Thanks to the energy and skill of the operational and administrative staffs of all Services concerned, the change from the old system to the new had been made without any serious setback. The machine had been brought safely to its new position. It was in running order, as witness, for example, the bringing down of sixty bombs between sunset on the 20th and sunset on the 21st July.* Already the gunners were showing that they knew how to make good use of their opportunities. I felt that one of my main tasks must now be to ensure that the forces directly under my command were made thoroughly familiar with their part in the new plan.

105. I realised that this was a task I must undertake myself. My own staff had their hands full: to devise and apply measures which would ensure that the safety of our own aircraft was not endangered by the "Diver" defences was only one of many duties that called for much careful staff work and painstaking liaison. The Air Officer Commanding, No. 11 Group, and his staff were preoccupied with matters arising out of the operations in Normandy. Realising that this would be so, I had arranged that the Sector Headquarters at Biggin Hill should become a co-ordinating centre for "Diver". I found, however, that the practical, hour-to-hour supervision of operations left the Sector Commander and his staff with little time for other work; and it seemed to me that, in any case, the study and dissemination of tactical doctrine and the promotion of disciplined enthusiasm amongst pilots faced with a novel weapon ought to proceed from a rather higher level than that of a Sector Headquarters.

106. I daresay that, if the circumstances had been slightly different, the best answer to this problem might have been the creation of a Task Force commanded by an officer of air rank answerable to myself for all fighter operations against flying bombs. It would have been necessary to make such an officer responsible for studying tactical methods and the technique of improvised training under operational conditions, as well as for the actual conduct of operations. This would have meant giving him a small staff. I had not the resources to do this, nor the smallest chance of persuading the Air Ministry to provide them. Indeed, in the circumstances this hope would have been quite unreasonable, and I did not entertain it. I felt that this was a case where I must give a direct lead to the Station and Squadron Commanders concerned with flying bombs.

---

* This figure was made up as follows:

Bombs brought down by

Guns alone	23
Fighters alone	19
Guns and fighters jointly ...	1
The balloon barrage	17
	60

107. Here my practice of sharing actively and frequently in the fighter operations stood me in good stead. Trying to shoot down a missile travelling at six miles a minute while flying at the same speed and a height of perhaps a thousand feet across a narrow belt of undulating country bounded by balloons and guns was a business whose subtleties were not readily appreciable from an office chair. I found that a practical acquaintance with this business had its uses. Not only did it help me to acquire a fund of tactical knowledge that I could hardly have gained in any other way; above all it enabled me to talk on a basis of common understanding and endeavour with the pilots whose devotion it was my task to foster.

108. An incidental advantage of the abolition of the inland gun-belt was that it gave the searchlights, which remained when the guns had gone, more scope to assist night fighters. Another unlooked-for benefit of the move was that it brought the headquarters of the A.A. Batteries close to the bases from which our fighters were operating. Immediate and personal contact between Battery Commanders and Station Commanders suddenly became possible and even easy. I found during my first visits to stations after the move that advantage was not always being taken of this proximity. I was shown—as I had been shown for the last five weeks—aircraft whose pilots alleged that the guns had fired at them; I was shown marks of damage said to have been thus inflicted, and fragments of shell-casing which appeared to have entered aircraft or fallen on airfields. In each case I suggested that the Station Commander concerned should pocket the more portable of these exhibits and, armed with this evidence, go and discuss his grievances, real or imaginary, with the local Battery Commander.

109. The hint was taken. The consequences were profound and striking. As a result of these meetings between Station and Battery Commanders, the first requisite of understanding between two parties whose interests must occasionally conflict—the realisation that the other side also has a viewpoint—was attained. The mists of suspicion whose gathering had troubled me so much were dispersed almost overnight. On subsequent visits to the same stations I was again shown aircraft that had suffered minor damage from anti-aircraft fire. But this time, instead of having to listen to grievances against the gunners, I was told of pilots who had flouted discipline and good sense by venturing too near the guns. In short, pilots and gunners were beginning to understand one another's problems and work together. Unity was restored. The process reached its climax towards the close of the main attack. Flying towards the south coast on the 28th August, I could see over Romney Marsh a wall of black smoke marking the position of the "Diver" barrage. From time to time a fresh salvo would be added to repair the slow erosion of the wind. On the far side of the barrage fighters were shooting down flying bombs into the Channel; on the nearer side more fighters waited on its fringe to pounce on the occasional bomb that got so far. The whole was as fine a spectacle of co-operation as any commander could wish to see.

110. That day 97 bombs approached these shores. The defences brought down 90* and only four reached London.

111. Some weeks before this the fact that we were gaining mastery over the flying bomb had become clear to ourselves and also to the Germans. During the second week after the re-deployment of the guns, the defences brought down a higher proportion of the bombs that came within their compass than in any previous week; and only a little more than a quarter of the total got to London.

112. In the following week there was a spell of bad weather, and the fighters did not do so well; but the gunners, whom this factor affected much less, again did better than before. For the first time since the beginning of the attack they maintained a higher rate of destruction than the fighters over a full week. About this time the Meteor, our first jet-propelled fighter came into service, and I decided to match jet against jet by trying it out against the flying bomb. At first only a few of these aircraft were available, and various problems, including that of limited endurance, had to be overcome before we could get the full benefit out of the Meteor's great speed.

113. As the month went by, all concerned gained further experience and new equipment began to yield results. Soon the overall performance of the defences, and that of the gunners in particular, surpassed all previous achievements. In the middle of August we reached the stage of being sure that, whatever the weather, we could bring down from one-half to three-quarters of all the bombs that approached this island. Indeed, it has been calculated that during the last three weeks of this phase only one out of every seven bombs that the enemy launched actually reached London. Shortly afterwards the enemy High Command permitted the publication in the German press of the significant pronouncement that the Allies had found a counter-measure to the flying bomb. In the last few days of August only an occasional bomb eluded the defences and got through to its target. Thus it is fair to claim that almost complete ascendancy over this novel and ingenious weapon had been gained when, at the beginning of September, the capture of the launching areas by our Armies ended the main attack.

(f) *Attacks with Bombs launched by Aircraft from Holland (9th July to 5th September).*

114. Meanwhile, as early as the 8th July, flying bombs had started to approach London from a new direction, namely from the east. No launching sites were known to exist in Belgium; and after a few weeks it was established that these bombs, which came only at night, were being launched by specially-equipped He. 111 aircraft operating wholly or mainly from bases in Holland.

---

* This figure was made up as follows:

Shot down by fighters		
over sea	13	
over land	10	
	—	23
Shot down by A.A. guns		
over sea	46	
over land	19	
	—	65
Brought down by balloons ...		2
		—
		90

115. To meet this new threat I arranged with General Pile that the gun-belt should be supplemented by a gun "box" situated in the quadrilateral Rochester-Whitstable-Clacton-Chelmsford.* By the middle of August 208 heavy, 178 40 mm., and 404 20 mm. guns, besides 108 rocket barrels, were deployed in the "box". I also took steps to extend the balloon barrage to Gravesend,† and fly standing patrols over the mouth of the Thames.

116. During July and August 120 flying bombs were seen or detected approaching this country from the east: the number actually despatched from that direction was doubtless much greater, for launching the bombs from aircraft was a tricky business which must have resulted in many premature descents. There followed a lull that lasted until the early hours of the 5th September—four and a half days after the last bomb had come from northern France—when at least another nine bombs approached London from the east. The "battle of the bomb" was not yet over; but these nine missiles were Parthian shafts, which marked the end of one phase rather than the beginning of another. They were a postscript to the main attack.

(g) *Attacks with Bombs launched by Aircraft from Germany (16th September, 1944, to 14th January, 1945).*

117. The further lull that followed the launching of the last bomb by aircraft operating from Holland lasted the best part of a fortnight; and to many it seemed that "the battle of the bomb" was over. Our Armies were advancing rapidly. Before long they had driven the Germans from every part of the Continent where launching ramps within the existing range of London could be built. The German flying unit responsible for launching the bombs from the air was known to be leaving its bases in Holland and moving northeast. Not only the uninformed, but many in positions of authority concluded with relief that London's long ordeal was ended.

118. This belief was too sanguine. Further attacks with long-range weapons could not be ruled out. Lacking ramps within the existing range of the bomb, and without using their old bases in Holland, the Germans might still send flying-bombs against us. They might increase the range of the bomb and build ramps further back. They might—and certainly could—launch bombs from the air by using airfields in Germany. In the event they were to do both. Moreover, the flying bomb was not their only long-range weapon. They were known to possess a rocket capable of covering more than 200 miles and which was expected to be ready for use against us during the first fortnight in September. Despite some hopeful statements by men in responsible positions, my staff and I felt that, so long as the Germans continued to hold the western provinces of Holland, we ought to be prepared to meet attacks by the rocket.*

119. That the Germans might still launch flying bombs from aircraft was not disputed by the Air Ministry or the Chiefs of Staff; and I secured authority to keep the existing "Diver" defences in being.

120. By the middle of September the German flying-bomb air-launching unit had completed its move and was installed at bases in western Germany. Towards dawn on the 16th September the attack was resumed. The first bomb fell in Essex at 0549 hours. A few minutes later another came down at Barking. During the next half-hour five more bombs approached this country; one reached Woolwich, one fell at Felsted, and the remaining three were brought down by fighters, one of them into the sea. Two bombs not included in these figures were destroyed at sea by the Royal Navy.

121. After a night of inactivity the attack continued on the evening of the 17th September. Only three bombs came within range and two of them were shot down—one by a fighter and one by gunfire. More bombs followed on the succeeding nights.

122. Countering this phase of the offensive presented special difficulties, because the enemy was no longer tied to fixed ramps. Hitherto he had exploited the mobility of the kind of aerial launching-platform provided by an aircraft only to a limited extent: more than nine-tenths of all the bombs seen or detected up to the beginning of September had come from ramps. Nevertheless the few bombs launched from the air had sufficed to turn the left flank of the defences and compel us to extend it by creating the eastern "box".

123. The advance of the Allied Armies had now forced the enemy back on bases further to the north and east.† Clearly, he intended to make a virtue of necessity by attempting a further turning movement which entailed launching his bombs well out over the North Sea.

124. To meet this move General Pile and I decided to extend the defences northwards by adding to the "Diver Belt" and "Diver Box" a "Diver Strip" extending from the left flank of the "box" at Clacton up to Great Yarmouth. We had already taken some guns from the "belt" to strengthen the "box". We now carried this process a stage further. Between the 16th and 19th September orders were issued to sixteen heavy and nine light anti-aircraft batteries to move from the "belt" to the coast between Clacton and Harwich. As the month went on further moves were

---

* An alternative deployment envisaging the mounting of guns on ships moored in the mouth of the Thames, as well as on land, was considered, but rejected because General Pile preferred a deployment that would allow of continuous engagement of bombs by cross fire as they flew up the river, and also because, in any case, not enough ships could have been found to make the plan fully effective. Nevertheless, a few guns mounted on forts and small vessels were eventually included in the eastern "Diver" defences.

† In addition, 1,250 possible balloon-sites north of the Thames were reconnoitred; but I decided not to fly any balloons in that area unless it became essential to do so, since General Pile feared that their cables would hamper the defence of London against orthodox air attack by interfering with the radar sets belonging to the guns.

* For an account of the rocket campaign, which was to start on the 8th September, 1944, see Part III.

† There were airfields in northern and central Holland which he might still have used; but tactically they would have been no more convenient than bases in Western Germany, and to supply them with bombs and fuel would have been no easy matter.

ordered; and by the middle of October no less than 498 heavy and 609 light guns were deployed in the " box " and " strip ".*

125. The changed direction of attack brought new problems. For various reasons, of which the chief were the intermittent character of the attacks and the geographical position of our own bomber airfields, I could not give the gunners the same freedom of fire as they had enjoyed in the south-east during the summer. Although I was able to establish the principle that flying over the " box " or " strip " below 6,000 feet should be prohibited in normal circumstances during the hours of darkness, I was forced to defer to the needs of Bomber Command to the extent of permitting their aircraft to fly over the " strip " (though not over the " box ") at any height they pleased provided they gave prior warning to my headquarters. This concession entailed a corresponding restriction of gunfire; and I also had to reserve the right to restrict gunfire at any other time in order to safeguard friendly aircraft which, for one reason or another, were unable to avoid flying low over the " strip " to reach their bases.

126. Another problem for the guns arose out of the fact that, instead of maintaining a height of 2,000 or 3,000 feet during the greater part of their flight, the bombs launched from aircraft often approached the coast as low as 1,000 feet. A new type of equipment for controlling low-angle fire was coming into service, but only in small quantities; consequently General Pile had to get over the difficulty by siting the rest of his equipment so as to give the best results against low-flying targets. This meant sacrificing some of its capacity to give early warning.

127. Despite these limitations, the performance of the gunners was beyond all praise. Out of 576 bombs which approached the coast between the 16th September, 1944, and the 14th January, 1945, without being shot down into the sea by fighters or the Royal Navy, 321 were brought down by anti-aircraft fire. One hundred and ninety-seven of these fell into the sea and the remaining 124 on land.

128. For the fighters the chief problem arose out of the fact that all activity was now at night. There was a natural tendency to suppose that interception at night would be easier than in daylight simply because the tongue of flame emitted by the bomb was so conspicuous in the dark. Unfortunately, seeing the bomb was not enough: pilots had also to estimate its range, and this proved extremely difficult, as anyone who has tried to judge his distance from a light on a dark night will understand. Sir Thomas Merton, the distinguished spectroscopist, designed a simple range-finder which eventually proved of great value to pilots; but individual skill and experience remained the biggest factor in overcoming this difficulty. Some pilots showed remarkable aptitude for this work, so baffling to many; for example, one Tempest pilot, Squadron Leader J. Berry, shot down more than 60 bombs at night before being himself shot down while on an offensive sortie.

129. During this third phase of the attack we used two types of fighters against flying-bombs at night: Mosquito night fighters in front of the guns, and Tempest day fighters piloted by specially-trained night-fighter pilots between the guns and London. Although the Mosquito was too slow to catch a flying bomb except in a dive, these aircraft brought down a total of 21 bombs during this phase. The Tempests, which had been outstandingly successful during the main attack in the summer, now operated with the aid of a searchlight belt extending from Saffron Walden and Sudbury in the north to Southend and Brightlingsea in the south.* They brought down 50 bombs, most of which fell harmlessly in open country. Thus, throughout the four months of this phase, only 205 bombs eluded the defences out of 608 seen or detected on their way to the capital; and of these only 66 reached Greater London.

130. To supplement these orthodox measures of defence my staff worked out a scheme whereby Mosquito night fighters were sent to the area from which the He. 111 aircraft of the German air-launching unit despatched the bombs, in order to shoot these aircraft down. This was not a simple undertaking. The German aircraft flew low, rising to a height of 2,000 feet or so for only a short time while they released their bombs. Thus the night fighters, too, had to fly only a few hundred feet above the sea. For the fighter as for the bomber this was a hazardous proceeding; and at such low altitudes the radar normally employed by night fighters to make contact with their targets was not at its best. Furthermore, the radar stations on land which were used for controlling the fighters were often unable to detect the bombers except when the latter gained height to launch their bombs.

131. As a step towards overcoming some of these difficulties we modified the equipment of several radar stations and also tried the experiment of controlling the fighters from the naval frigate H.M.S. Caicos and from an aircraft equipped with A.S.V. Mark VI. But these measures bore little fruit until the air-launched attacks were nearly over. All the more credit is due, therefore, to the skill and perseverance of the night-fighter crews, who claimed the destruction of sixteen launching aircraft, the probable destruction of another four, and damage to four more, between the 16th September, 1944, and the 14th January, 1945. There is evidence that these losses, coming on top of the natural hazards incurred by heavily laden aircraft operating almost at sea-level, imposed no little strain on the German unit responsible for air launching.

132. Nevertheless, the Germans seem to have remained unaware how small a proportion of the bombs launched were reaching London, or else to have resigned themselves to receiving a poor return for their efforts so long as some sort of offensive could be continued against this country. For they not only persevered with the operations, but even took steps during the winter to increase their scope. This fact, of which our intelligence service was aware,

---

* The permanent defences of towns like Harwich and Lowestoft were incorporated in the " strip " and are included in these figures.

* At first these searchlights were deployed at intervals of 3,000 yards. Experience showed that so thick a spacing tended to dazzle pilots and we altered the interval to the normal 6,000 yards.

caused me some anxiety. Although the defences were doing so well, the air-launched flying bomb was still a dangerous weapon because of its mobility. We could not deploy guns everywhere at once; and the bomb might be used against other targets besides London. At that time the country was being bombarded with rockets as well as flying bombs: a simultaneous increase in the scale of attack by both weapons was a contingency against which I felt bound to provide.

133. On the transfer of the Air Commander-in-Chief's main headquarters to the Continent in the autumn of 1944 I had acquired at least a nominal responsibility for directing and co-ordinating offensive as well as defensive counter-measures against flying bombs and long-range rockets. So many authorities whose interests alternately coincided and conflicted were concerned in this matter that my responsibilities were inevitably somewhat indeterminate. Moreover, I was in an even less favourable position than the Air Commander-in-Chief had been to discharge such a responsibility. Like him, I could not help knowing that our striking forces had many tasks to perform besides that of attacking "crossbow" targets. Unlike him, I could not call at my discretion on the tactical, let alone the strategic, air forces for this work. The area from which rockets were being fired against London was within fighter range, and I was able to send fighters and later fighter-bombers to intervene. But the bases of the flying-bomb air-launching unit in north-west Germany were beyond the reach of all my aircraft except those used for long-range "Intruder" work.

134. Thus, so far as offensive counter-measures to the flying bomb were concerned the only thing I could do in practice was to make representations. My staff kept a close watch on the activities of the air-launching unit, and as soon as it was plainly seen to be expanding I urged that its bases be attacked. That the response was not more active was perhaps an inevitable consequence of the multiplicity of calls upon the strategic and tactical air forces, and of the very success which the defences had achieved against the flying bomb up to that time. Even so, a number of attacks on the bases were made by our own Bomber Command and the American Eighth Bomber Command.

135. As a further precaution against a possible extension of the flying bomb campaign General Pile and I took steps to counter any attempt that the Germans might make to turn the northern flank of the defences. A scheme was worked out whereby 59½ batteries of guns could be rapidly deployed between Skegness and Whitby if an attack should develop in that area.

136. This eventuality was realised, without any specific warning on Christmas Eve, 1944. Early on that day about 50 He. 111s—almost the entire operational strength of the air-launching unit—launched bombs in the direction of Manchester from a position off the coast between Skegness and Bridlington. Thirty bombs came within range of the reporting system, and all thirty crossed the coast. Only one of them reached Manchester, but six came down within ten miles of the centre of the city and eleven within fifteen miles. Thirty-seven people were killed and 67 seriously injured.

137. This was one of the few occasions on which the Germans showed resource in exploiting the capacity of the air-launched flying bomb to outflank the defences. Happily for us they were seldom so enterprising; for however carefully our plans were laid, we could not deploy the defences on every part of the East Coast at once, and if more such attacks from novel directions had been tried, they would inevitably have achieved at least a fleeting success, as on this occasion.

138. Immediately after this attack I ordered that deployment north of the Wash should begin. Shortly afterwards I secured the approval of the Chiefs of Staff to a more comprehensive scheme for the defence of the coast as far north as Flamborough Head. I also arranged that plans should be worked out for the defence of the areas Tees-Tyne and Forth-Clyde. But here again, as in the case of Manchester, I could not afford to order deployment in these areas, at the expense of others, merely on the ground that the enemy might attack them at some future date. Consequently, if he had followed up his attack on Manchester with a series of carefully-spaced attacks at other points north and south of the Wash on succeeding nights, he would undoubtedly have scored some success and set us something of a problem.

139. However, either this did not occur to the Germans, or such an enterprise was beyond the capabilities of an organisation whose spirit was shaken and which was running short of fuel. No more bombs came from north of the Wash; and three weeks later the air-launching unit ceased operations. The last air-launched flying-bomb to reach this country came down at Hornsey at 0213 hours on the 14th January, 1945.

(h) *Attacks from Ramps in Holland (3rd to 29th March, 1945).*

140. This was not the last of the flying bomb. In the meantime the Germans had been working on the problem of increasing the range of the weapon. Fragments of some of the bombs fired from Germany into Belgium in February showed that they were adopting methods of construction which might solve this problem and enable them to attack London from ramps in south-west Holland. Reconnaissance photographs of that area were taken, and showed that two launching sites were being constructed, one at Ypenburg, near the Hague, the other at Vlaardingen, six miles west of Rotterdam. In addition the German built a third site near the Delftsche Canal; but of this we were not aware till later.

141. To meet this new threat General Pile and I decided to reinforce the gun defences between the Isle of Sheppey and Orfordness by transferring 96 heavy guns from the northerly part of the "strip" and adding a number of batteries then under training to the remaining defences in the latter area. Instructions for the move to begin were given on the 27th February and by the 6th March nine batteries out of twelve had taken up their new positions.

In the event, owing to the modest dimensions of the attack, only one further battery was deployed.

142. I also earmarked six Mustang squadrons for operations against the bombs in daylight, and arranged that their engines should be specially boosted. Three of them, together with a squadron of Meteors which I arranged to borrow from the Second Tactical Air Force, were to operate between the guns and London; the other three forward of the guns, over the sea. At night two Mosquito squadrons would patrol over the sea and a squadron of Tempests behind the guns. A direct link with the radar stations of the Second Tactical Air Force in Belgium was set up to assist in giving warning of the approach of flying bombs from the general direction of the Scheldt.

143. The attack began in the early hours of the 3rd March. The first bomb to reach this country got through the defences and fell at Bermondsey at 0301 hours. The next six bombs were all destroyed by anti-aircraft fire: five of them exploded in the air and the sixth fell into the sea. After a lull of nine hours the attack was resumed in the afternoon of the same day and continued intermittently until noon on the 4th, when there was another lull. Ten bombs came over during this second burst of fire: four of them were destroyed by the guns and only two reached London.

144. The second lull came to an end late in the morning of the 5th March. Thereafter, until activity finally ceased on the 29th March, there was spasmodic activity punctuated by intervals of quiet. The performance of the guns during this phase was outstanding.

Indeed, it was so good that, in view of the unexpected lightness of the attack, I was able to dispense with the Meteors and five of the six Mustang squadrons, which returned to their former duties. During the whole of this last phase of the flying bomb campaign 125 bombs approached this country. Eighty-six were shot down by anti-aircraft guns alone, one by the Royal Navy and shore guns jointly, and four by fighters. Only thirteen bombs reached London.

145. Typhoon fighter-bombers of the Second Tactical Air Force attacked the launching-site at Vlaardingen on the 23rd March, Spitfire fighter-bombers of my Command that at Ypenburg on the 20th and again on the 23rd March. At both sites essential components were destroyed. Presumably the missiles launched during the last few days of the attack came from the third site, of whose existence we had not previously been aware.

146. The attacks ended with a bout of intermittent firing between half-past nine on the evening of the 28th March and lunch-time on the 29th. During this period 21 bombs approached this country: 20 were shot down, and the twenty-first came ignominiously to earth at Datchworth, a village of some seven hundred inhabitants twenty-five miles from London Bridge. This was the last bomb of the whole campaign to fall on British soil.

(j) *Summary.*

147. The following table summarises the progress of the campaign and the results achieved by the defences in its various stages:

	Phase 1 (a) 12/6– 15/7/44	Phase 1 (b) 16/7– 5/9/44	Phase 2 16/9/44– 14/1/45	Phase 3 3/3– 29/3/45	Total 12/6/44– 29/3/45
(i) No. of bombs reported	2,934	3,791	638	125	7,488
(ii) No. of bombs in target area	1,270	1,070	67	13	2,420
(iii) Percentage of (ii) to (i)	43·3	28·5	10·5	10·4	32·3
(iv) No. of bombs brought down					
(a) by fighters	924$\frac{1}{3}$*	847	71$\frac{1}{2}$	4	1,846$\frac{5}{6}$
(b) by guns	261$\frac{1}{3}$	1,198$\frac{1}{2}$	331$\frac{1}{2}$	87	1,878$\frac{1}{3}$
(c) by balloons	55$\frac{1}{3}$	176$\frac{1}{2}$	—	—	231$\frac{5}{6}$
(d) by all arms	1,241	2,222	403	91	3,957
(v) Percentage of (iv) (d) to (i)	42·3	58·6	63·2	72·8	52·8

* The fractions relate to claims shared between different arms of the defence.

PART III: THE ROCKET CAMPAIGN.

(a) *Intelligence and Countermeasures, 1939 to November, 1943.*

148. The German long-range rocket, known to the enemy as the A-4 and to us as "Big Ben," was a rival to the flying bomb. There is no doubt, however, that if circumstances had permitted, the Germans would have conducted simultaneous campaigns with the two weapons from northern France.

149. The first hint that the enemy intended to use a long-range rocket for military purposes was contained in a report received in this country soon after the outbreak of war. More was heard of the project towards the end of 1942, when agents reported that trial shots with such a missile had been fired shortly beforehand on the Baltic coast. Early in 1943 a connection was established between this activity and the German experimental station at Peenemünde.

150. From that time onwards a stream of intelligence about the rocket reached this country. Not until more than a year later, however, did we receive conclusive evidence about the characteristics and performance of the weapon. During part of the intervening period responsibility for investigating the new threat was taken out of the hands of the intelligence staffs and placed in those of a governmental committee created for the purpose. A number of distinguished scientists and ordnance experts were invited to speculate about the nature of the rocket, and some hypotheses were advanced which ultimately proved wide of the mark. The prevailing impression in responsible quarters during the earlier months of the investigation was that the enemy was forging a titanic weapon which weighed seventy or eighty tons and carried a warhead containing some ten tons of explosive, which would descend upon London with little or no warning. The problem of defending the capital against so disobliging a projectile was naturally a source of some anxiety to my predecessor.

151. Towards the end of 1943 a fresh approach to the problem was adopted. In November, responsibility for investigating the nature of the rocket and devising countermeasures was transferred to the Air Ministry. Thereafter, as information from intelligence sources accumulated, a conception of the weapon which was based on reports of what the Germans were doing gradually replaced the earlier conception, which had leaned more towards our own ordnance experts' ideas of a suitable rocket. We shall see that ultimately —although only a week or two before the beginning of the campaign—the intelligence staffs were able to show that the alarms of the previous year had been exaggerated as well as premature, and that the rocket was very much smaller than had been supposed.

152. Meanwhile, by the summer of 1943 the authorities who were then responsible for countermeasures had come to the conclusion that, whatever the dimensions of the missile, radar would probably be able to detect its flight. By the time I took up my appointment in the early winter, five radar stations between Ventnor and Dover had been modified to detect rockets fired from northern France, and operators had been trained to identify the characteristic trace which a rocket was expected to produce. As a further precaution, artillery units in Kent were told to look out for visible signs of ascending rockets and a Survey Regiment of the Royal Artillery was deployed there to take care of audible signs.*

153. These measures had a two-fold object. In the first place, if all went well, the radar, backed up by flash-spotting and sound-ranging troops, would tell us when rockets were fired, and perhaps enable us to give the public a few minutes' warning by firing maroons in London or elsewhere by remote control. Secondly, the information obtained by these means might help us to locate the places from which the rockets were coming, so that we could attack the firing sites and the troops who manned them.

154. To complement these purely defensive countermeasures, an attack, which proved successful, was made by Bomber Command on the experimental station at Peenemünde. Afterwards the Germans transferred part of their activities to Poland. This move somewhat eased the difficult task of our intelligence services in keeping a watch on the rocket trials.

155. During the summer and autumn of 1943 the Germans were observed to be building a number of extraordinary structures in northern France, which we called "large sites".† Agents persistently reported that these sites had something to do with "secret weapons". Their impressive dimensions, taken in conjunction with the exaggerated idea of the rocket which prevailed at the time, led to the notion that the sites were intended for the storage and firing of the missile. Ultimately they proved to have little direct connection with the rocket.

156. At this stage Bomber Command and the American Eighth Bomber Command made a number of attacks on one of these "large sites" at Watten. Bomber Command also attacked, as part of their normal programme, several production centres in Germany which were suspected of manufacturing components of the rocket or fuel for it.

(b) *Intelligence and Countermeasures, November, 1943, to August, 1944.*

157. Thus the situation when I assumed control of the air defences in the middle of November, 1943, was that the Germans were known to be experimenting with some kind of long-range rocket.* The intelligence officers on whom the responsibility for establishing the precise nature of this missile would normally have rested had insufficient evidence on which to base any reliable estimate of the date when it might be used against us or the weight of the explosive charge which it would carry. A special investigation had, however, led to much *a priori* speculation about these matters. In consequence the impression had arisen that the Germans were preparing to bombard London with gigantic projectiles each capable of killing hundreds of people and flattening buildings over a wide area. The experimental station at which the weapon was being developed, and where objects some forty feet long which were evidently rockets had been photographed in the summer, had been successfully bombed, as had the first of a series of mysterious constructions in northern France and a number of production centres in Germany. No firm connection between the rocket and the targets in either of these latter classes had, however, been established. Besides taking these offensive countermeasures we had made dispositions which, we hoped, would give us a few minutes' warning of the arrival of individual rockets and also help to tell us where the rockets came from.

158. Soon after I assumed command the discovery of the original flying-bomb launching sites, or "ski sites",† in northern France, taken in conjunction with other evidence, convinced us that the pilotless aircraft or flying bomb was a more imminent threat than the rocket. For the time being, therefore, the latter receded into the background. Early in 1944 I received authority to relax the continuous watch for rockets which had been maintained at certain radar stations since the previous summer. I arranged, however, that the operators who had been trained for this work should remain at the stations and train others, so that the watch could be resumed, if necessary, at short notice. When flying-bomb attacks began next June, I gave orders for the resumption of this watch. Two special radar stations were added to the five whose equipment had been modified.

159. Meanwhile the Allied bomber forces continued to attack the "large sites" as occasion arose and opportunity afforded. At the same time the intelligence staffs at the Air Ministry were gradually piecing together a picture of the enemy's activities at Peenemünde and later also at Blizna, in Poland.

---

* These activities, which were an extension of those normally conducted in respect of artillery fire, were accordingly known as "flash spotting" and "sound ranging" respectively.

† They were at Watten, Wizernes, Mimoyecques (near Marquise), Siracourt, and Lottingham in the Pas de Calais, and at Martinvast and Sottevast near Cherbourg. The constructions had few features in common apart from their great size.

* There were, however, some distinguished disbelievers in the rocket, who continued long after this to argue that the story was a hoax.

† See paragraphs 16–18, above.

Although our ordnance experts continued to believe that anything but an outsize long-range rocket was out of the question, as time went by the evidence began to point more and more clearly to a warhead of relatively modest size.

160. Notwithstanding this evidence, the conception of a huge, earth-shaking projectile persisted. Accordingly much effort was spent on a vain search for the massive launching devices which were believed to be necessary to start so large a missile on its flight.

161. Yet, as the summer of 1944 wore on, the case for the lighter rocket grew stronger. Evidence was obtained that the firing process called for nothing more elaborate than a slab of concrete, on which a portable stand was erected and from which the rocket rose under its own power. By the last week in August all the main characteristics of the A-4 had been established. We knew that it was approximately forty-five feet long and that its all-up weight was less than fourteen tons. We knew that the standard warhead weighed about a ton, but were prepared for the possibility that, by reducing the maximum range from about 200 to 160 miles, the Germans might be able to fit a heavier warhead, weighing up to two tons. We knew that before being fired the rocket was placed upright on the firing platform and there fuelled and serviced—a process which would probably take about two hours. Furthermore, we knew that the Germans had planned at least two methods of storing the missiles, namely in underground pits or tunnels, and in wooden bunkers dispersed in woods. Finally, we had some reason to suspect that active operations would begin during the first half of September.

162. What we did not know was how (if at all) the rocket was externally controlled once it had left the ground. Misleading evidence on this point led to wasted efforts to forestall, detect and hamper non-existent radio transmissions which were expected to be used for this purpose. Not until some time after rocket attacks had begun was the conclusion reached that control of the rocket under operational conditions was entirely internal and automatic, apart from the use of a " beam " to control the line of shoot in certain instances.*

163. The Allied Armies, during their advance through Normandy, discovered a number of sites which the Germans had clearly intended for the firing of rockets. Far from resembling the " large sites ", these consisted merely of rough concrete slabs let into the surface of roads. We were bound to assume that similar firing sites existed in areas still in German hands; but their location was unknown to us, and there was not the slightest chance of our detecting them on air reconnaissance photographs.

(c) *The Eve of the Rocket Campaign* (30th August to 7th September, 1944).

164. Such, then, was the state of our knowledge towards the end of August, 1944, when we found ourselves faced with the possibility that rocket attacks might begin at almost any moment. For many months past a system for detecting the firing of rockets had existed, and a programme of bombing attacks on the " large sites " and other objectives suspected of a connection with the rocket had been carried out. In addition the Air Staff at the Air Ministry had devised and kept up to date an elaborate scheme of countermeasures which was to be put into effect as soon as the first rocket was fired.

165. One of the provisions of this scheme was that as soon as attacks were seen to be imminent, fighter aircraft should be held ready to fly armed reconnaissance sorties over the firing areas.* These operations were to be conducted within the " tactical area "† by the Tactical Air Forces, and elsewhere by my Command.

166. Towards the end of the month the stage of imminent attack appeared to have arrived; and the Air Staff decided that we should go a little further than had been contemplated in the paper scheme, by starting to fly the armed reconnaissance sorties without more ado.

167. I had already taken the precaution of authorising my operations and intelligence staffs to issue instructions and memoranda which would enable us to start these operations at short notice; and on the 30th August the sorties began. Since we did not know the location of any firing sites in enemy territory, all we could do was to brief our pilots to recognise anything they might see, and despatch them over the general area from which we expected to be attacked.

168. A few days later, on the 4th September, the rapid advance of the Allied troops into the Pas de Calais and Flanders obliged us to discontinue the sorties. Thereupon I learned that the Chiefs of Staff considered that, since the whole of the Pas de Calais was or shortly would be ours, the threat to London from the rocket could be regarded as over.

169. My intelligence staff felt unable to assent to this opinion without a reservation. They pointed out that the rocket, having a range of 200 miles or more, could still be fired at London from western Holland. Western Holland was still in German hands, and part of it would remain so if the Germans stood on the lower Rhine and the Siegfried Line. True, we had no evidence that the Germans had prepared any firing sites on Dutch soil; but the sites could be so quickly built and were so hard to spot that this proved nothing. While recognising that the Chiefs of Staff were better able than ourselves to foresee the effect of future operations, my intelligence officers felt, therefore, that as things stood at the moment we ought to be ready to meet rocket attacks from western Holland within the next ten days.

170. The logic of this argument was irrefutable; and I was relieved to learn next day that a review of the situation by the Vice-Chiefs of Staff had led to the conclusion that the immediate relaxation of all defensive

---

* In the later stages of the campaign the Germans did, however, use radio for control of range in certain cases. They do not seem to have perfected this technique, which gave less accurate results than their usual methods.

* " Armed reconnaissance " is defined as " air reconnaissance carried out by offensively-armed aircraft with the intention of locating and attacking suitable enemy targets ".

† This was an area, defined from time to time by the Air Commander-in-Chief, in which the conduct of all air operations devolved upon the Tactical Air Forces.

measures would be precipitate, not because the Vice-Chiefs thought that there was any threat to London, but on the ground that the Germans might still fire rockets at other targets.

171. I mention this divergence of opinion, not to claim superior prescience for myself or my staff, but because the factors involved were so delicately balanced as to give the point some interest. The argument for caution was sound so far as it went, and indeed was shortly to be justified by events; yet there was much that might have been urged on the other side. The disorganisation of the enemy's transport services at this stage must have been so great that he might well have shrunk from the task of diverting the rocket-firing organisation from France to Holland. Again, there was a time during those first few days of September when the possibility that Allied troops might reach Germany in one bound seemed not at all remote; if the Germans had appreciated this, would they have thought an attempt to fire rockets from Holland worth their while? Yet when all this has been said, the fact remains that an area from which rockets could reach London was to remain in German hands for more than seven months to come, and that during this time over a thousand rockets were to fall on British soil.

(d) *The Attacks: First Phase (London, 8th to 18th September, 1944)*

172. In the event, only a few days elapsed before brute fact justified the argument for caution. At approximately twenty minutes to seven on the 8th September Londoners on their way home from work or preparing for their evening meal were startled by a sharp report which sounded almost, but not quite, like a peal of thunder. At 1843 hours a rocket fell at Chiswick, killing three people and seriously injuring another ten. Sixteen seconds later another fell near Epping, demolishing some wooden huts but doing no other damage.

173. During the next ten days rockets continued to arrive intermittently at the rate of rather more than two a day. On the 17th September the Allied airborne operation against the lower Rhine at Arnhem was launched. Thereupon the German High Command ordered the rocket firing troops to move eastwards, and on the following day attacks on London ceased for the time being.

174. Up to that time 26 rockets had fallen in this country or close enough to its shores to be observed. Thirteen of them had landed within the London Civil Defence Region. The higher figure does not represent the total fired during the period, which was certainly not less than 29 and probably well over 30; for we know that a substantial proportion of the rockets despatched habitually miscarried.

175. Early in this opening phase two things about the functioning of the technical devices deployed to detect rockets became apparent. One was that radar stations chosen to detect rockets fired from France were not, on the whole, well placed to detect rockets fired from Holland. Accordingly we arranged to increase the number of stations keeping watch between Dover and Lowestoft from three to six, and to deploy additional radar, sound ranging, and flash spotting equipment on the Continent. No. 105 Mobile Air Reporting Unit was formed within my Command in the middle of September and despatched to Malines, near Brussels, to correlate and transmit the information obtained from technical sources across the Channel. In the meantime the War Cabinet decided that for the moment the public-warning system should not be put into effect. This decision was based on a number of considerations, some of which lay outside my province; but there is no doubt that it was justified on operational grounds alone. If the technical devices had worked perfectly, we could at best have warned the public on any given occasion that the Germans had just launched a rocket which, if it did not miscarry and was not aimed at some other target, would come down somewhere in southern or eastern England in a minute or two. And since at that stage the technical devices were far from working perfectly, our attempts to give even so rudimentary a warning as this would have led, in practice, to many false alarms and the arrival of some rockets unheralded by any warning at all.

176. The other point which emerged during this phase was that, even when the results obtained from the technical devices were good, the calculations based upon them did not, by themselves, enable us to locate the firing points with the accuracy required for the effective briefing of pilots despatched on armed reconnaissance. At best this method told us the position of a site within a mile or two; and until opportunities had arisen of adjusting the assumptions on which the calculations were based by reference to the known location of sites, as established by other means, some of the estimates obtained in this way were manifestly incorrect. Such difficulties were inevitable in the development of a new technique. They did not prevent the radar and sound ranging equipment from giving us useful information from the start. A combination of the data furnished by these two sources confirmed, for example, that the first two rockets to arrive had come from south-west Holland, as our deductions from first principles had led us to suppose they would; and within a few hours "intruder" aircraft of my Command were on their way to that area.

177. After the first day or two, however, we did not depend on technical devices to locate the firing points. One of the first measures taken by the Air Ministry when the attacks began was to brief the Dutch Resistance Movement, through the appropriate channel, to provide intelligence on this subject. A speedy method of getting this information to the Air Ministry was devised. There it was scrutinized by intelligence officers who passed all reports of probable value to my headquarters with the least possible delay. The information contained in these reports was then correlated by a member of my intelligence staff with that based on the data furnished by the technical equipment, as well as that derived from the observations of pilots on armed reconnaissance and of the many flying personnel in the Royal Air Force and the United States Army Air Forces who reported seeing the trails made by ascending rockets. Within a few days the fruits of this process pointed to a number of fairly well-defined areas, all in wooded country in the neighbourhood of the Hague, from which most

of the rockets fired at London seemed to be coming.* By keeping a close watch on the information pointing to these "suspected areas" and ensuring that it was passed to the Fighter Groups concerned by means of frequent and full reports from my intelligence staff, I was able to satisfy myself that our armed reconnaissance effort was employed to the best advantage. During the ten days which this phase lasted, pilots of my Command carried out approximately 1,000 sorties of this kind. They attacked a variety of targets, including road, rail, and water transport vehicles and installations, suspicious constructions, and German troops. On one occasion when Tempests attacked a suspected firing point an explosion occurred so violent as to wreck the leading aircraft. Afterwards a large, shallow crater was seen, such as might have been caused by the detonation of a rocket in the firing position.

178. At this stage I was made responsible for directing and co-ordinating all operations by air forces based in the United Kingdom against the rocket-firing area as well as the bases of the German flying bomb air-launching unit.† This meant that besides using my own aircraft for such tasks as were within their power, I could ask Bomber Command or No. 2 Group, Second Tactical Air Force, to bomb any objectives which seemed to me to call for attack by heavy, medium, or light bombers. But there was nothing mandatory about these requests, and I had no means of ensuring that they were carried out, save that of making representations to higher authority if direct appeals should prove unavailing. My relations with Bomber Command and No. 2 Group left nothing to be desired; but since both had many calls on their resources, mere reiteration on my part and goodwill on theirs were not enough to ensure that my demands should always receive neither more nor less than their due. These difficulties become more intelligible if the requirements for rocket counter measures which preoccupied my attention are fitted into the vast perspective of air operations at that time. In the circumstances it would have been too much to expect a series of firm and favourable decisions on the part of a well-informed and competent higher authority, by means of which alone detailed and adequate response to my special needs could have been ensured. As it was, the Air Commander-in-Chief was busy with the offensive battle, and in any case had no power to direct Bomber Command in matters of this nature; while the Air Staff at the Air Ministry were naturally reluctant to give other than very broad directions to operational commanders.

179. Soon after the rocket attacks had begun, intelligence was received which suggested that the Germans had made preparations to store rockets on three properties situated at Wassenaar, just outside the Hague, and named respectively Terhorst, Eikenhorst, and Raaphorst. At the first two there were comparatively small wooded areas, which for various reasons seemed eminently suitable for the purpose; Raaphorst was a rather extensive property, and we were not sure which part of it was meant. In any case we had no proof that any of the storage shelters which were said to have been constructed on the three properties were actually in use. Nevertheless, I concluded that the Germans must be storing their equipment somewhere, and presumably also supplies of fuel and rockets, unless they were living entirely from hand to mouth. Accordingly, after weighing the probabilities carefully, I invited Bomber Command to bomb given aiming-points at Terhorst and Eikenhorst. Meanwhile, as early as the 14th September, and before receiving my request, they had sent a small force to attack Raaphorst. An aiming point close to the main road bordering the property was chosen. A few days later fresh intelligence gave us the probable location of three supposed storage areas on the Raaphorst estate, one of them close to this aiming point.

180. The first attack carried out by Bomber Command in response to my request was made on the 17th September, when a small force attacked Eikenhorst, dropping 172 tons of bombs. The bombing was well concentrated and a large explosion was seen to occur in the course of it. No further attacks were made during the first phase of the rocket offensive, which ended on the 18th September.

(e) *The Lull* (19*th to* 25*th September*, 1944).

181. During the next week no rockets arrived in this country. Towards the end of that period secret informants reported that the firing troops had received orders on the afternoon of the 17th September to leave the Hague, and been seen departing with their equipment towards Utrecht. We know now that this information was correct; but the arrival of a rocket at Lambeth on the evening of the 18th, coupled with a report that rockets had been fired from Wassenaar on that day and the next, made us a trifle disinclined to give it credence at the time.* I decided that for the present armed reconnaissance sorties over the Hague and its neighbourhood should be continued, and the suspected storage sites at Wassenaar be left on the list of "Crossbow" targets which I wished to see attacked by Bomber Command. If no more rockets should come from the Hague or Wassenaar within the next few days, the sites would lose their value as targets and be taken off the list.

182. Accordingly, aircraft of my Command continued to fly armed reconnaissance and "intruder" sorties over the Hague and its environs during the period from the 19th to the 25th September, so far as the weather and the demands of the Arnhem operation allowed. On the 19th, three whole squadrons from No. 12 Group—to which I had delegated responsibility for supervising the conduct of air operations a few days previously—were sent to attack objectives in an area south-east of the racecourse at the Hague, from which we believed the Germans had been firing rockets. Troops, transport vehicles, and buildings there were all attacked. On the previous night (as on two other nights about this time) "intruder" aircraft bombed a railway station at Woerden which an agent had mentioned in connection with the supply of rockets to the Hague.

---

* During the first phase a few rockets were fired at London from the Island of Walcheren as well.
† See paras. 133–134, above.

* The rocket fired on the 18th must have been a parting shot from a rear detachment of the departing troops. The report that firing occurred on the 19th was doubtless a mistaken one; or perhaps the message was misconstrued.

Neither Bomber Command nor No. 2 Group attacked any rocket targets during the week. Indeed, the latter were not asked to attack any, for up to this time none suitable for the method of precise bombing in which No. 2 Group specialised had been discovered.

183. All this time aircraft of No. 100 Group, Bomber Command, were flying special patrols with a view to intercepting and jamming any radio transmissions which might appear to be used to control the rocket. Aircraft of my Command provided fighter escort for these missions both at this stage and subsequently. In addition, thousands of reconnaissance photographs were being taken and interpreted. This procedure was in accordance with the scheme which the Air Staff had prepared before the attacks began.* One of the provisions of that scheme was that every area indicated by the radar, sound-ranging, and flash-spotting complex as a suspected firing-point should be photographed as soon as possible. My staff pointed out, however, that since many of the estimates based on these data were manifestly incorrect,† and since experience had quickly shown that the firing-points could not be seen on reconnaissance photographs,‡ the procedure served no useful purpose. At our suggestion the Air Ministry agreed to a modification which saved much effort on the part of skilled pilots and interpreters: henceforward only areas in which we expected reconnaissance to reveal something of interest were photographed. We also took advantage of the lull to perfect arrangements for the rapid provision of the "target material" which was used in briefing bomber crews, and to discuss our problems with Bomber Command.

(f) *The Attacks: Second Phase (Norwich, 25th September to 12th October, 1944).*

184. On the evening of the 25th September the lull came to an end. At 1910 hours a rocket fell near Diss, in Suffolk. Neither the flash-spotting nor the sound-ranging troops could give us any useful data about its origin, and at first the radar stations were equally reticent. Even the objective which the Germans had meant to hit remained unknown. Hence the rocket might have come from any area in German hands which was within 230 miles of the point of impact—for this, as we had reason to believe, was the maximum range of the A-4. Thus we were reduced to this hypothesis: that if the rocket had been aimed at London, then it must have come from the Hague or somewhere near it; but if at some other target, then it could have come from another part of Holland, from the Frisians, or even from a part of Germany near Cleves.

185. On the following afternoon another rocket landed in East Anglia—this time about eight miles from Norwich, which subsequently proved to be the target. Once again the technical devices were silent; but five minutes before the rocket fell, chance observers flying over a point about fourteen miles west of Arnhem saw a trail rise, as they supposed, from a wood some twenty miles away, called the Speulder Bosch and adjoining the village of Garderen. Immediately afterwards the wood appeared to catch fire over an area of perhaps two acres and remain alight for about five minutes. The trail, or one like it, was also seen by chance observers who were flying well north of the Frisians, and thought it came from Ameland or Schiermonnikoog.

186. Now, Garderen lies between Amersfoort and Apeldoorn, in the direction which the firing troops were said to have taken when they left the Hague. Moreover, a secret informant had mentioned Apeldoorn as the apparent destination of a trainload of rockets and fuel which he claimed to have seen a week before. That the rocket which had fallen near Norwich originated from the Speulder Bosch was thus a plausible hypothesis, especially as a trail ascending from that area might well look to observers over the North Sea as if it came from the Frisians.

187. Meanwhile the films which should have recorded any data obtained by the radar stations about the rocket that fell near Diss had been scrutinized without success. They were scrutinized again; and this time faint traces were found on them. These traces showed that the missile had come from a point more remote from the stations than had the rockets observed during the earlier phase of the attacks. Armed with this evidence, the specialist whose task it was to calculate the location of firing points from such data went to work. After some delay he gave an "estimated position" which coincided with the village of Garderen.

188. Superficially the case for Garderen as the new firing area now looked stronger than, perhaps, it really was. The specialist, who was frankly giving an estimate and not the result of a purely objective calculation, may have been influenced by the knowledge that the next rocket was supposed to have come from the Speulder Bosch. If so, the whole case really rested on a single item of positive evidence—the trail seen from a distance of twenty miles. Yet one thing was certain from the impartial testimony of the radar traces: the Suffolk rocket had not come from the Hague or Wassenaar but from some more distant spot. Accordingly I authorised the removal of the suspected storage sites at Terhorst, Eikenhorst, and Raaphorst from the list of "Crossbow" targets which we had furnished to Bomber Command.

189. On the 27th September No. 12 Group sent four Tempest pilots to make an armed reconnaissance of the area between Amersfoort and Apeldoorn. They saw signs of military activity at two points in and adjoining the Speulder Bosch and a third point just south of the neighbouring railway; but there was no proof that this activity had anything to do with rockets. However, on the same day and the two following days six more rockets fell near Norwich and one off the Norfolk coast. In four of these seven cases the information furnished by radar suggested or was consistent with firing from the area between Amersfoort and Apeldoorn. Whether our suspicions of the Speulder Bosch were justified or not evidently

---

* See paragraph 165, above.

† On several occasions areas under water or otherwise unsuitable for rocket-firing were indicated.

‡ During the previous few weeks nearly 100,000 photographs of western Holland had been examined by interpreters. Not a single firing point had been found.

the rockets were coming from an area so remote that armed reconnaissance of it could not be performed with maximum efficiency by fighters operating from this country. Unfortunately the airfields on the Continent which had fallen into Allied hands were already so congested that facilities for my aircraft to operate from them could not be provided. I could not resist the conclusion that the task must now be done by a force based on the Continent. Accordingly, at the end of September the Second Tactical Air Force assumed responsibility for armed reconnaissance of the firing areas. Air Marshal Coningham's headquarters in Brussels was not well placed, however, for the detailed work of collating intelligence on this subject, which came from a variety of sources; and we arranged that this should continue to be done at my headquarters, where good communications existed. From the 1st October onwards, therefore, my intelligence staff transmitted to Brussels a daily signal—for which we coined the name "Benrep"—containing a brief appreciation of the most recent information and a note of the areas in which armed reconnaissance seemed most likely to be fruitful.

190. Rockets continued to fall near Norwich during the first half of October, but on the 3rd October, as we shall see, London also became a target once again. Thereafter little evidence of firing from Garderen was forthcoming, and most of the rockets apparently aimed at Norwich seemed to come from northern Holland. The evidence of the radar pointed to the shores of the Zuyder Zee and the islands of Vlieland and Terschelling; and secret informants confirmed the presence of firing points in wooded country near Rijs, in the former area.

191. Altogether, from the 25th September onwards, some 36 rockets apparently aimed at Norwich fell on land or close enough to the shore to be reported. Not one fell inside the city, although the enemy's shooting against Norwich was actually somewhat better than that against London, inasmuch as the rounds that reached this country were more closely grouped. The last round of this phase fell on a farm in Norfolk soon after half-past seven on the morning of the 12th October.

192. Meanwhile fighters of the Second Tactical Air Force visited a number of suspected firing areas in the course of the operations of wider scope which they were conducting in support of the campaign on land. Apart from a few trails, however, their pilots saw nothing that threw much light on the activities of the firing troops. But by the end of the attack on Norwich a number of fresh factors had combined to produce a new situation, which ultimately led to a further change in the allocation of responsibility for armed reconnaissance.

(g) *The Attacks: Third Phase* (*London, 3rd October to 18th November, 1944*).

193. Among the most important of these factors was the resumption of attacks on London. On the 3rd October an agent reported that the firing troops might be in the process of returning to the Hague. Sure enough, late that evening a rocket fell at Leytonstone—the first in Greater London for a fortnight. More followed on the 4th and 7th. By the middle of the month—when attacks on Norwich ceased— the new phase of activity against the capital seemed to be settling down to a rather unsteady average of two or three rounds a day. The degree of concentration achieved was about the same as in September, but the mean point of impact was further east.

194. So far as we could judge, the Germans were now firing at London from some half-dozen wooded parks and open spaces within the built-up area of the Hague and on its southern outskirts. Possibly a few sites elsewhere were being used as well. The firing troops were said to have taken over a lunatic asylum in the suburb of Bloemendaal and to be storing rockets and equipment in the grounds and neighbouring woods. In addition, informants who had usually proved reliable in the past reported that vehicles and equipment were stored in a wooded park adjoining the Hotel Promenade, in the centre of the town. We were told that supplies were reaching the Hague by way of the goods station at Leiden, and that laden railway trucks were often parked at the main railway station in that town.

195. All this information, and much more besides, we passed to the headquarters of the Second Tactical Air Force by means of the daily "Benreps". Officers from my headquarters visited Brussels to give Air Marshal Coningham's staff the benefit of such experience as we had gained in the first three weeks of the campaign. Both in the "Benreps" and verbally we stressed the desirability of confirming by visual reconnaissance the intelligence obtained from other sources. More than this we could not do. The responsibility for conducting the armed reconnaissance sorties which alone enabled visual observations to be made now rested solely on the Second Tactical Air Force; and according to a recent decision of the Air Commander-in-Chief, this situation was unaffected by the resumption of firing from the Hague.

196. Whatever the merits of this decision, as far as I was concerned the situation to which it led had one grave disadvantage: Air Marshal Coningham, with his many commitments in the battle area, could spare few aircraft for subsidiary tasks. Instead of making sorties over the Hague expressly for the purpose of observing and harassing the firing troops, as my forces had been able to do, the Second Tactical Air Force was obliged to rely on its general programme of armed reconnaissance over the enemy's lines of communication. This method of tackling the problem was probably right in the circumstances; but from my point of view it had several shortcomings. It left us without any means of judging the effect of so indirect a counter-measure; nor did it throw any light on what the enemy was doing at the Hague or meet our demand for visual reconnaissance of suspected areas. Indeed, from the date when the Second Tactical Air Force assumed responsibility for armed reconnaissance up to the 17th October—when this issue came to a head —we were without any report to say that pilots of that Command, while engaged on these duties, had seen or attacked anything on the ground which could be associated with long-range rockets.

197. Another factor which helped to give a new aspect to the problem created by the A-4 was an increasing scale of attack on Continental cities. By the middle of October well over 100 rockets were known to have fallen on the Continent; and with the capture of Antwerp,

whose potential value to the Allies was great, the problem of defending such objectives against both flying bombs and rockets was beginning to exercise the minds of the Supreme Commander and his staff. The likelihood that Antwerp and Brussels would become the main targets for the rocket during the coming winter —possibly to the exclusion of London and Norwich—doubtless contributed to the Air Commander-in-Chief's decision to leave the responsibility for armed reconnaissance with the Second Tactical Air Force even after attacks on London had been resumed.

198. As a result of this quickening of interest in "Crossbow" weapons at Supreme Headquarters, the Supreme Commander directed on the 11th October that the Chief of the Air Defence Division of Supreme Headquarters, who was responsible for co-ordinating terrestrial air defence measures in the north-west European theatre, should also assume responsibility for co-ordinating countermeasures against flying-bombs and rockets in that theatre.

199. The decision to entrust this task to a staff division of Supreme Headquarters itself, and not to the Allied Expeditionary Air Force, foreshadowed the imminent demise of the subsidiary formation. Now that the Allied Armies were firmly established on the Continent, that body, which had been formed primarily to plan and supervise air operations in support of the assault and build-up, was considered to have fulfilled its purpose. On the 15th October, therefore, the Allied Expeditionary Air Force was formally disbanded. Consequently my Command—re-named Fighter Command—and the Second Tactical Air Force became independent formations. Thereupon the constitutional responsibility for the air defence of the United Kingdom which had hitherto rested on Air Chief Marshal Leigh-Mallory devolved upon me, with this difference: I had no control over the Second Tactical Air Force. A situation in which I was responsible for defending the country against long-range rockets while responsibility for conducting the only countermeasure open to a fighter force was exercised by another Command, not under my control, was no longer merely inconvenient; it was clearly untenable.

200. I therefore negotiated with Air Marshal Coningham and with the Deputy Supreme Commander and the Air Ministry a new arrangement, whereby Fighter Command resumed responsibility for the armed reconnaissance of all known or suspected rocket-firing or storage areas in Holland west of a line running north and south through a point approximately 45 miles east of the Hague. At the same time steps were taken to assist the Air Defence Division of Supreme Headquarters in discharging their responsibility in respect of rockets fired against Continental cities. The Supreme Commander had already asked that the 10th Survey Regiment, Royal Artillery, which had been deployed on the Continent in September to undertake sound-ranging and flash-spotting on my behalf, should return to its normal duties in the field. Meanwhile, experience had suggested the possibility of doing without a Survey Regiment in Kent, where the 11th Survey Regiment, Royal Artillery, was deployed. Accordingly arrangements were now made to move the 11th Survey Regiment to the Continent and place it at the disposal of Supreme Headquarters. No. 105 Mobile Air Reporting Unit, too, was likely to be more useful to Supreme Headquarters than it was to me; and we agreed that this, too, should be handed over. Since the accurate detection and reporting of rockets aimed at Continental targets was of direct as well as indirect benefit to my Command—for without this information we could not be sure of distinguishing the reports that related to rockets aimed at the United Kingdom or assessing their reliability—I readily assented to these changes. I also agreed to lend a number of officers to Supreme Headquarters to assist in setting up the organisation on the Continent.

201. Under the terms of these new arrangements, during the third week in October No. 12 Group once more assumed the responsibility for operations over the Hague with which I had charged them in September. From the 18th October onwards, No. 12 Group, instead of the Second Tactical Air Force, were the primary recipients of the daily "Benrep"; but we continued to keep in close touch with Air Marshal Coningham's headquarters, and reached an understanding whereby the Second Tactical Air Force undertook to do its best to reconnoitre the Hague on my behalf on any day when the weather made flying possible from Continental airfields but impossible from airfields in this country.

202. In the meantime my staff had been making a close study of the intelligence bearing on the disposition of the rocket-firing complex, and had selected five objectives at or near the Hague which seemed worth bombing. Three—the goods station and the railway yard of the main station at Leiden, and the suspected store near the Hotel Promenade at the Hague —were small targets situated close to built-up areas in places whose inhabitants were well-disposed to us and were, indeed, our Allies. On the information I had at the time, these targets seemed eminently suited to the kind of precise attack in which the Mosquito bombers of No. 2 Group specialised. Accordingly we asked that Group to attack them.* The other two—the first consisting of living quarters and storage areas at Bloemendaal, and the second of the storage site at Raaphorst, which was credibly reported to be in use again—were larger and stood in more open situations. We therefore suggested them to Bomber Command as targets for a less precise form of attack. Further enquiry cast some doubt on the validity of our most recent information about Raaphorst, and on the 19th October we withdrew that target from Bomber Command's list, thus leaving them with Bloemendaal as their sole "Big Ben" objective.†

---

* Air Marshal Coningham, of whose Command No. 2 Group formed part, had agreed to my making such requests direct to the headquarters of the Group in England.

† Strictly speaking, there were two objectives at Bloemendaal, with separate target names and numbers. The storage area round Bloemendaal church was known as "The Hague/Bloemendaal"; the neighbouring lunatic asylum in which firing troops were quartered and whose grounds were said to be used for storing and possibly for firing rockets was known as "The Hague/Ockenburg Klinier". Our suggestion was that the two should be regarded as a single complex, whose internal and external communications could be disrupted at the same time as the living quarters and equipment were destroyed, by bombing two given aiming points.

203. Urgent as these requests were, the entire attention of Bomber Command at the time was being absorbed by tasks to which greater importance was attached. The proposed targets at Bloemendaal were, therefore, not attacked, and after further discussion with No. 2 Group, the goods station and railway yard at Leiden and the storage site near the Hotel Promenade at the Hague were ruled out as not being suitable as precision targets for low level Mosquito attacks. Consequently the Germans were able to develop their offensive, unhampered save by such punishment as fighter-pilots could inflict in the course of armed reconnaissance sorties over an area heavily defended by anti-aircraft weapons.

204. And in fact, as October gave way to November the scale of the German attack rose sharply. During the first three weeks in October an average of two-and-a-half rounds a day reached this country. The average over the next three weeks was four a day; and the week after that it rose to six a day. Six rockets a day was not an intolerable weight of attack, for an individual rocket was not appreciably more destructive than a flying bomb. Yet I became uneasy about the fact that the scale of attack was rising and that comparatively little was being done to check it.

205. On the 17th November I expressed my concern to the Air Ministry in a formal letter. I pointed out that armed reconnaissance was clearly not an adequate method of limiting the German offensive unless supplemented by other measures. Yet no bombing attack on any rocket target at the Hague had been made for two months. Since the Tactical and Strategic Air Forces were not, at the moment, in a position to undertake such tasks, I should have to rely on my own resources. Now, the Spitfire aircraft which I was using for armed reconnaissance had recently begun to carry bombs; but their pilots were precluded from dropping their bombs in circumstances which involved any risk at all to Dutch civilian life or property. I suggested that this injunction should be relaxed to the extent of permitting pilots to bomb such targets as could be accurately located and were situated in areas from which the inhabitants were known to have been removed. In these circumstances the risk to civilian life, at least, would be small; and what we had to do was to balance the off chance of injury to life and property at the Hague against its certainty in London. I asked that this question should be carefully considered, in consultation with the Dutch civil authorities if this were thought fit. Such a concession would also apply, of course, to any attacks that the Mosquito aircraft of No. 2 Group might make.

206. Finally, I asked that consideration should also be given to the desirability of allotting a higher degree of priority to the bombing of rocket targets by Bomber Command. At that time an increase in the scale of attack by air-launched flying bombs was also causing me concern; and I took the opportunity of asking that the bases of the air-launching unit should be attacked as well.*

207. This letter, as I have said, was signed on the 17th November. On that day four rockets fell in London, killing 14 and seriously injuring 36 people. A gas-holder was set on fire and nine factories were damaged. Only two days earlier ten rockets had landed in this country within 24 hours—six of them in London. Altogether, since the start of the campaign on the 8th September some 200 rockets had arrived in the United Kingdom— an average of three a day.

(h) *The Attacks: Fourth Phase (London, 19th November to 31st December, 1944).*

208. The suggestion made in my letter of the 17th November that the Dutch authorities be consulted was adopted; and on the 21st of the month this point and others raised in my letter were discussed at one of the Deputy Supreme Commander's conferences at Supreme Headquarters. Thereupon, with the concurrence of the Air Staff, I was authorised to undertake fighter-bomber operations on the lines I had laid down. On the other hand, I was given clearly to understand that for some time to come any assistance I could expect to receive from the Second Tactical Air Force would be virtually limited to that provided by their current rail interdiction programme.* I was also informed that, unless the enemy increased his scale of attack considerably, the Combined Chiefs of Staff would not be likely to countenance the diversion of any part of the strategic bomber effort from the attack of the German petroleum industry and communications to that of rocket targets. The Air Staff assured me, however, that if the scale of attack by "Crossbow" weapons did increase, the matter would be reconsidered.

209. No time was lost in taking advantage of the concession regarding fighter-bomber operations. My staff drew up a list of storage sites and similar objectives all situated at least 250 yards from the nearest built up area; and from the 21st November onwards the four squadrons in No. 12 Group which were assigned to this duty† took every opportunity of attacking them with bombs and machine-gun and cannon fire. The general prevalence of bad weather made these opportunities few, especially in November and the latter half of December. As a result, these squadrons had plenty of time for intensive training in pin point dive-bombing, of which they took full advantage, and during the first half of December, when the weather temporarily improved, more frequent attacks were made. Altogether, between the 21st November and the end of the year No. 12 Group made 470 fighter-bomber sorties against rocket targets

---

* This programme included attacks on railway bridges at Deventer, Zwolle, and Zutphen, which some competent judges considered the most promising form of countermeasure to the rocket offensive from western Holland.

† The squadrons were:
No. 453 Squadron   Spitfire XVI
No. 229 Squadron   Spitfire XVI
No. 602 Squadron   Spitfire XVI
No. 303 Squadron   Spitfire IX

The Spitfires XVI were each capable of carrying two 250 lb. bombs and an overload tank which enabled them to fly to and from their bases in England without refuelling on the Continent. By refuelling in Belgium—which became possible on a strictly limited scale at the end of November—they could dispense with the tank and carry twice the load of bombs. The Spitfire IX could carry at most one 500 lb. bomb and that only by refuelling in Belgium. At this stage, therefore, we did not normally use No. 303 Squadron to carry bombs.

---

* See paragraph 134, above.

and dropped 54 tons of bombs in the course of them. In these operations no effort was spared to ensure that the bombs were dropped with a skill and precision rivalling that displayed by the picked crews of No. 2 Group in some of their spectacular attacks on buildings used as headquarters by the Germans. A characteristic attack delivered during this phase was one made by Nos. 453, 229 and 602 Squadrons, on Christmas Eve, on a block of flats near the centre of the Hague, which the Germans were using to house the firing troops in that district. The building was so badly damaged that the Germans had to leave it.

210. To all appearances the influence of these operations on the rate and quality of the enemy's fire was considerable. The scale of attack declined from an average of nearly seven rockets a day at the end of November to four a day in the middle of December and three-and-a-half at the end of the month. Moreover, the enemy took to doing most of his firing at night, and the apparent accuracy of the shooting decreased. A statistical analysis of the rocket effort and our counter-measures led to the belief that sustained attacks on the firing areas by day and night would exercise a cumulative effect on the enemy and hence on the number of rockets that reached London.

211. At the time I was not altogether prepared to accept this conclusion. In the light of subsequent experience I feel quite sure that to do so would have been to claim too much for our efforts. The chief factor in limiting the scale of attack was almost certainly the rate at which supplies could be brought to the firing areas; and this in turn must have been mainly determined by the frequency and success of the armed reconnaissance and rail interdiction sorties flown by the Second Tactical Air Force over the enemy's lines of communication. Preparations for the German offensive in the Ardennes—which was accompanied by an increased scale of rocket attack on Antwerp—may also have helped to diminish the attack on London towards the end of 1944. The simultaneous decline in accuracy is not so easily accounted for; and its significance in view of the comparative smallness of the figures analysed is open to question.

212. On the other hand the enemy's new tendency to fire most of his shots at night was definite and unmistakable. For this change of habit by the Germans our fighter-bombers may perhaps claim the credit, since it cannot readily be explained on any other grounds than a desire to evade their attention. Admittedly the gain was an indirect one, seeing that fire at night was no more inaccurate than by day; in fact, as a general rule a higher proportion of the rounds fired in darkness hit the target than of those fired by day; but casualties were generally lower after dark, when most people were at home, than in the daytime, when they were massed together in factories and offices and in the streets. Thus, from our point of view the preponderance of night firing was definitely favourable.

(j) *The Attacks: Fifth Phase* (London, 1st January to 27th March, 1945).

213. However, the respite was short-lived. In the New Year the scale of attack went up again. During the first half of January an average of more than eight rockets a day reached this country. Thereafter the rate of fire declined a little, only to rise again early in February, until an average of ten rockets a day was attained in the middle of the month. Moreover, the Germans again took to doing more than half their firing in daylight, and their accuracy improved. In an average week in January and the first half of February, twice as many people were killed or seriously injured by rockets as in a corresponding period in December.

214. Clearly, our fighter-bomber programme was not such an effective deterrent as we had hoped. This was not to say that our methods were wrong: without the fighter-bomber attacks, the rate of fire might have risen still more sharply. But evidently something more was needed if the German offensive was to be kept down.

215. What form that something more should take was not so obvious. In December the Air Ministry had asked the Foreign Office and the Ministry of Economic Warfare to investigate the possibility of curtailing supplies of fuel for the A-4 by attacking factories where liquid oxygen was made. The experts reported that there was no means of knowing which of the many factories in German hands or under German control were supplying liquid oxygen for that particular purpose. There were, however, eight factories in Holland, five in western Germany, and five elsewhere in Germany which might fill the bill. As a sequel to this investigation, the Air Ministry invited me to consider attacking three factories in Holland. One of them, at Alblasserdam, near Dordrecht, was successfully attacked by the Second Tactical Air Force on the 22nd January. Another, at Ijmuiden, consisted of two buildings so closely surrounded by other factories that the prospect of a successful attack with the means at my disposal was remote. The third, at Loosduinen, on the outskirts of the Hague, was adjoined on three sides by Dutch civilian property. Hence I was reluctant to attack it, especially as there was no certainty that its destruction would cause the Germans to fire even one less rocket at this country. However, in view of the Air Ministry's request and my desire to leave nothing undone which offered a chance of hampering the enemy, I agreed to do so. In order to reduce the risk to civilian property to a minimum, the pilots chosen for the job were instructed to use methods which can best be described as "trickling their bombs towards the target". This technique necessitated five separate attacks of which all but one were made from the direction in which there were no houses adjoining the factory. Two attacks were made on the 3rd February, two on the 9th February, and one on the 8th. After the last attack on the 9th we judged that the target had suffered enough damage to be left alone in future.

216. In January bad weather limited the number of fighter-bomber sorties that we could make to a little more than half the number made in December. In February the weather was better and during the first half of the month we made more fighter-bomber sorties than in the whole of January. Besides delivering the five attacks on the oxygen factory at Loosduinen to which I have alluded, we made six attacks on the Haagsche Bosch, a

wooded area in which rockets had been seen on reconnaissance photographs taken in December. The Hotel Promenade was attacked on three occasions, and attacks were also made on other suspected storage areas at the Hague, Wassenaar, and the Hook of Holland, as well as on railway targets. The Second Tactical Air Force continued to attack communications, as hitherto, in the course of their armed reconnaissance and rail interdiction programmes.

217. Meanwhile, in consequence of the rise in the scale of rocket attack, towards the end of January the Air Ministry had begun to press me to intensify my efforts against the firing and storage areas. Nevertheless they were still unwilling to see any part of Bomber Command's effort diverted to the attack of such targets. On the 26th of the month, however, the Defence Committee agreed to invite the Air Ministry to ask Supreme Headquarters to sanction the precise attacks on selected targets by the light bombers of No. 2 Group, which I had been urging since the previous autumn. Shortly before this I had arranged to raise the strength of the force earmarked for exclusive use against rocket targets from four squadrons to six, and to equip and use all six squadrons regularly as fighter-bomber squadrons.* I now negotiated a new agreement with the Second Tactical Air Force whereby my area of responsibility was extended as far east as Amersfoort. On days when the weather was unsuitable for precise attack on objectives at the Hague, our fighter-bombers were now attacking rail targets; and the inclusion of Amersfoort in our area would enable us to bomb the railway junction there—a bottleneck through which all traffic from Germany to the firing areas in western Holland passed. Under the terms of the new agreement the Second Tactical Air Force would use any light or medium bombers that they could spare from the battle on land to attack rocket targets chosen from lists provided by my staff.

218. The full effect of the expansion of the "Big Ben" fighter-bomber force was seen in the second half of February, when Fighter Command made 548 sorties and dropped 108 tons of bombs—precisely the same weight in two weeks as in the previous six. At the suggestion of my Chief Intelligence Officer, who recommended that we should try the effect of concentrating our efforts on a single target for at least a week, nearly three-quarters of this bomb tonnage was aimed at the Haagsche Bosch, where severe damage was done, particularly on the 22nd February, when a film studio which the Germans used for storage was gutted. An almost complete cessation of rocket fire over a period of more than sixty hours followed this attack; and on the 24th February photographic reconnaissance failed to reveal a single rocket anywhere in the square mile or so of wooded parkland that the Haagsche Bosch comprised. Other evidence strengthened the inference that the Germans had been driven from the Haagsche Bosch, at least for the time being, and suggested that they had been forced to improvise facilities in the racecourse area at Duindigt, further to the north.

---

* The additional squadrons selected were Nos. 451 (Spitfire XVI) and 124 (Spitfire IX, modified for bombing).

219. So far as they went, these results of our new policy of concentrating on one area were encouraging; but events soon showed that no lasting effect on the Germans had been achieved. When firing was resumed (apparently from Duindigt) on the 26th, no appreciable decline in its quality or quantity was apparent. Nor did the first of No. 2 Group's long-awaited bombing attacks, which was delivered on the 3rd March, have any better effect. The attack was delivered by 56 Mitchells, and the target chosen—not without some misgivings since the continued presence of the Germans and their gear was doubtful—was the Haagsche Bosch. Unfortunately the bombing was not sufficiently accurate, in consequence of which casualties occurred among Dutch civilians and their property was damaged. After this unhappy experience, Air Marshal Coningham decided to make no more attacks on targets at the Hague.

220. Another counter-measure considered at this stage was the use of anti-aircraft artillery to fire at approaching rockets and explode them in the air. If only because the rockets travelled many times faster than the fastest bomber and completed their parabolic flight from Holland in less than five minutes, the problems involved seemed formidable. Indeed, proposals in this sense had been carefully considered before the attacks began and found impracticable. General Pile raised the subject again in December, 1944, when he asked permission to make an operational trial of a scheme designed to ensure that the rockets would pass through a curtain of shell-fragments as they approached the earth. An essential requirement of the plan was accurate and timely warning that a rocket was on its way. Although there were still difficulties in the way of disseminating such warnings to the public, for operational purposes reliable information of this kind was now available. There were some obvious drawbacks to the scheme: for example, the expenditure of rounds required to explode even one rocket was likely to be extravagant and possibly alarming to the public. Nevertheless, I was satisfied that it contained the germ of a successful countermeasure, which might become important in the future, and that on purely operational grounds a practical trial was desirable. I made recommendations to this effect when submitting General Pile's proposal to higher authority. The committee before whom the scheme was laid, after taking the opinion of eminent men of science, one of whom put the chances of a successful engagement at one in a hundred and another at one in a thousand, decided that an operational trial would be premature. They invited those concerned to seek ways of improving the scheme, and promised to consider it again in March.

221. Accordingly General Pile repeated his request for an operational trial towards the end of that month. He pointed out that time was clearly running out: the opportunity of testing the scheme in practice would soon have passed. In response, on the 26th March a panel of scientists were asked to prepare a theoretical estimate of success. They reported on the same day that if 400 rounds were fired against any one rocket the chance of scoring a hit would, at best, be one in thirty. After a further statement by General Pile, who said

that he would endeavour to increase the chance of success by trebling the rate of fire, the proposal went before the Chiefs of Staff, who decided on the 30th March that the likelihood of success was too small to outweigh the objections to the scheme. But in any case, by that time the campaign was over.

222. Meanwhile we had been continuing our fighter-bomber offensive against the rocket-firing organisation and its communications. After the 3rd March we made no further attacks on the Haagsche Bosch, but turned our attention to the adjoining racecourse area at Duindigt, along with other storage and firing areas and a group of buildings belonging to the Bataafsche Petroleum Company, which apparently the Germans were using as billets and offices. As before, we selected railway targets for attack when conditions were unsuitable for attacking our primary objectives. During the second week of March alone we dropped some 70 tons of bombs at Duindigt. By the middle of the month we had evidence that the Germans had abandoned the area, which was by that time so pitted with craters that, in the words of a contemporary report, "it looked as if Bomber Command, not Fighter Command, had been attacking it". This success was accompanied by another temporary decrease in the scale of rocket attack on London; and what was, perhaps, more significant was that about this time the Germans took to doing more and more of their firing in the early hours before dawn. We concluded that our efforts had spoilt their arrangements for storing rockets in the forward area and that they were being forced to bring the missiles up at night and fire them off as soon as possible. Accordingly, during the second half of March we paid little attention to storage areas and devoted most of our fighter-bomber effort to communications. Altogether we made more fighter-bomber sorties in March than in the previous four months put together, and dropped more than three times the weight of bombs dropped in February.

223. The German offensive came to an end at 1645 hours on the 27th March, when the one thousand, one hundred and fifteenth rocket to fall in this country or within sight of shore fell to earth at Orpington, in Kent. The campaign had lasted seven months. During that time the Germans had fired at least 1,300 rockets at London and some 40 or more at Norwich. Of these 518 had fallen within the London Civil Defence Region and none at all within the boundaries of the latter city. Altogether, 2,511 people had been killed and 5,869 seriously injured in London, and 213 killed and 598 seriously injured elsewhere. These figures would have been substantially smaller but for a number of unlucky incidents, in which rockets chanced to hit crowded buildings. Among the worst of these incidents were three which occurred at New Cross Road, Deptford, on the 25th November, 1944, and at Smithfield Market and Hughes Mansions, Stepney, on the 8th and 27th March respectively. Deplorable as these occurrences were, their rarity is a measure of the random quality of the long-range rocket in the stage to which the Germans had developed it.

224. Yet the A-4 rocket cannot be dismissed as a mere freak. Practically, it was a new weapon, which brought new hazards to the lives of millions, and set new problems of defence. Its significance, and that of the flying-bomb, when posed against the wider background of the war as a whole, remain to be considered.

PART IV: A SUMMING UP.

225. In describing our countermeasures to the flying bomb and A-4 rocket, I have been at pains to point out that these measures were only a part of operations of much wider scope, ultimately extending over the greater part of Europe. Perhaps a balanced view is best preserved by remembering that although defence against these two weapons formed the main task of the air defences during a period of nearly ten months, operations directly concerned with the bomb and rocket absorbed only a fraction of the total Allied air effort, offensive and defensive. From the time when attacks on "Crossbow" targets began, in August, 1943, until the end of the war with Germany, these operations accounted for about eight per cent. of the total weight of bombs dropped by the tactical and strategic air forces in the western theatre. On the other hand, the number of guns and balloons concentrated in south-east England that summer as part of our defences against the flying bomb was certainly the greatest ever assembled in a comparable area for the purpose of air defence. The fighter squadrons deployed in this role were limited in number by geographical conditions; but they included some of our fastest aircraft, which had to be withheld from operations in the tactical area.

226. This leads naturally to the question: to what extent did this expenditure of effort prevent the Germans from doing what they set out to do? An answer calls for a few comments on what the German intentions seem to have been. When accelerated development of the A-4 rocket began in 1942, the Germans cannot have known very clearly what they meant to do with it. Not only had the capabilities of the weapon yet to be established, but in any case the formulation of precise strategic aims does not seem to have been the enemy's strong suit. In the OKW* the Germans possessed what the Allies sometimes accused themselves of lacking—namely, a permanent and fully equipped organ for the supreme direction of the war. In practice, however, it failed to come up to expectations. For this there seem to have been two reasons. For one thing, Keitel, the head of the OKW, lacked a forceful personality. For another, the selection of his staff was entrusted to the General Staff of the Army, who were not so innocent as to put a rod for their own backs into the hands of men remarkable for their vigour. Hence the OKW worked less as an authoritative body than as a kind of secretariat to the Fuehrer. Hitler was thus the only man in Germany really in a position to settle problems of overall strategy.

227. Hitler, we are told, had little taste or aptitude for long-term planning, though his intuitive judgment of immediate issues was phenomenal. Such qualities as this were not enough to ensure a consistent aim or policy. When firm direction from above was lacking, the three fighting services pursued separate and

---

* *Oberkommando der Wehrmacht*, or Supreme Command of the Armed Forces.

sometimes divergent courses. "Because of the impotence of the OKW," says Albert Speer, the former Reichsminister of Armaments and War Production, "I had to negotiate and make decisions separately with the three Services."

228. According to the same authority, the development of the flying bomb was begun towards the end of 1942 because the German Air Staff grew jealous of the success achieved by the Army in developing their own long-range missile, the A-4 rocket. Thus, from the outset the two weapons seem to have been competitors. An attempt to co-ordinate their use at the operational level was, however, made in December, 1943, when a military formation called LXV Army Korps was given overriding control over both weapons. The efficacy of this measure is doubtful, since the staff of LXV Army Korps seem to have had an imperfect understanding of the flying bomb, and were sometimes at loggerheads with Flakregiment 155 (W), the Luftwaffe formation immediately responsible for its operation. I daresay there was something to be said on both sides.

229. Despite these disagreements and uncertainties, by the spring of 1944 the notion of using the two long-range weapons to remedy the shortcomings of the bomber force seems to have been generally accepted. Outwardly the odds against a German victory had become so great that those in the know could hardly have found the will to go on fighting if they had not been sustained by the mysterious promise of new scientific marvels, reinforced by the hope of driving a wedge between the Allies. Koller, the last Chief of the German Air Staff, has said that "the final role of the flying bomb and the A-4 rocket was to replace the bomber arm of the Luftwaffe entirely." Hitler expressed a similar intention when addressing representatives of Flakregiment 155 (W) at Berchtesgaden soon after the flying bomb campaign had begun. Yet even at that stage inconsistencies of aim and viewpoint were evident. Only a few months earlier the aircraft industry had been directed to continue the production of bomber types; while LXV Army Korps, true to its tradition of conflict with Flakregiment 155 (W), envisaged the simultaneous use of flying bombs and bombers. Finally, Goering, who as head of the Air Ministry and Commander-in-Chief of the Luftwaffe was ultimately responsible for the decision to adopt the flying bomb, is said to have had little faith in the weapon; while Speer, who was ultimately responsible for its production, was certainly not unaware of its defects.

230. On one further point, at least, the Germans were agreed: the time to use the long-range weapons was *before* the Allies could set foot in north-west Europe, in order to postpone the day and gain time for dissension to spring up between the United Kingdom, America and Russia. The A-4 rocket was an ill-favoured monster, slow to reach maturity; but tests of the flying bomb in the summer of 1943 were so promising that the commencement of active operations before the end of the year was ordered. Whether attacking London with flying bombs was a good way of upsetting Allied plans for the assault is arguable; but very likely the Germans clung to the hope that opposing views about the diversion of our resources to the defence of the capital would split the western Allies, and the consequent delay in opening the new front detach us both from Russia.

231. The bombing of the "ski sites" and other factors led to a postponement of this programme. The landings in Normandy on the 6th June, 1944, took the Germans tactically by surprise and found them still not ready to use the flying bomb. Thereupon LXV Army Korps, apparently on Hitler's instructions, peremptorily ordered Flakregiment 155 (W) to begin operations on the 12th June. The precise grounds of this decision are never likely to be known. The opportunity to use the long-range weapons to delay the Allied assault had gone, if indeed it had ever existed. But the Germans may still have hoped to gain time by exploiting the harassing effect of the bomb and hampering the flow of reinforcements and supplies. Moreover, it is improbable that we need look very far for the motive that prompted such a natural reaction to events. At moments of crisis the impulse to retaliate against an England which had upset all Hitler's plans by perversely refusing its allotted role was never far below the surface. The Germans quickly publicised the flying bomb as "revenge weapon No. 1": and their propaganda may well have contained a hint of their real purpose. With the "west wall" in jeopardy and defeat on the horizon, Hitler may have seen no more than the need to strike back and hope for a miracle.

232. In any case such hopes as the Germans may have entertained were bound to be disappointed. During the next ten months they were to launch well over 10,000 flying bombs at London, thereby squandering about a million and a half gallons of sorely-needed petrol and a productive effort which, according to Speer, would have been better employed in turning out 3,000 fighters. Whether Germany would have gained anything decisive if every one of those peevish darts had found its mark is open to question. But for us the effects would certainly have been embarrassing. As it was, our casualties in the two V-weapon campaigns included 8,938 persons killed and 24,504 seriously injured, while over 200,000 houses were destroyed or severely damaged and over a million more suffered less important damage. We may therefore be thankful that the number of bombs which reached the London Civil Defence Region was not 10,000 but 2,419.

233. I fancy that Londoners in particular will readily acknowledge their debt to the gunners, fighter crews, balloon crews, and a host of others whose skill, devotion, and unfailing toil brought about the premature descent of far more bombs than reached the target. Nor will they forget the involuntary but cheerful contribution of their neighbours in Kent, Sussex, Surrey, and other counties surrounding London, whose fields and gardens were graveyards for buzz-bombs stricken by the way. Despite the care that we took to bring the bombs down away from houses whenever we could, the path of damaged or defective bombs was sometimes unpredictable. Like their neighbours in London, some of the dwellers in "bomb alley" met their deaths in the front line. It is right that I should record, however, that our efforts were so far successful that the casualties caused by the bombs which failed to reach the target were only a fraction of the total.

234. In this battle the part played by gunners and fighters was so conspicuous and important that it tends to monopolize attention, perhaps unduly. I am conscious that in writing the foregoing account of the flying bomb campaign I have not resisted the natural tendency to bring out those features which make for easy narrative and positive statement. I wish, therefore, in this summing up, to emphasize that victory over the flying bomb was gained by the joint efforts of thousands of men and women of the different Services, working in every variety of unit and at all levels of responsibility. As an example of this co-operation I may cite the mutual trust and unity of purpose that always existed between General Pile's staff and mine. So far as the work of the gunners and fighter crews is concerned, the bare chronicle of their achievements requires no embellishment. Nothing need be added, therefore, except perhaps a word of tribute to those whose work was done outside the limelight. The contribution of Balloon Command, too, speaks for itself, although perhaps in too modest a tone for its true value to be apparent. Every one of the 232 bombs brought down by the balloons was one which had eluded the other defences and would almost inevitably have hit the target if it had been allowed to continue on its way. To the administrative skill and practical efficiency which enabled the deployment of the initial barrage to be completed in less than a third of the time originally forecast, I can give no higher praise than by comparing this feat with those performed by Anti-Aircraft Command at the same time and in July. The part played by the Royal Observer Corps—the Silent Service of the air defences—was an epic in itself. Together Anti-Aircraft Command, Fighter Command, Balloon Command and the Royal Observer Corps made up a team in whose play I am proud to have had a share.

235. Of the helping hand extended by many who were not members of the team, limitations of space forbid that I should say much. A hint has already been given of the technical advice and assistance rendered by distinguished men of science. Acknowledgement must also be made of the important part played by the Royal Navy and the Admiralty, especially in connection with the problems of obtaining and utilising early warning of the approach of flying bombs over the sea, and also that of helping pilots to " pinpoint " their position off the coast. In particular, the heroism of those who sailed in the small craft which operated off the French coast, under the noses of the Germans and exposed to attack by land, sea, and air, deserves to be remembered.

236. Teamwork, aided by such help as this, won the " battle of the bomb ". Indeed, it is not too much to claim that the flying bomb was prevented from achieving even a secondary purpose; for although we suffered casualties and damage, the flow of supplies to the Allied Armies across the Channel went on unimpeded by the worst the flying bomb could do.

237. Such, then is the answer to our question, so far as it concerns the flying bomb.

238. I turn now to the A-4 rocket. This was in some ways a more disturbing menace than the flying bomb. Not that it was more destructive; but it was difficult to counter, and fore-shadowed further developments which still loom ahead of us. Albert Speer, one of the ablest and most far-seeing of our enemies, remarked soon after the German surrender that, whereas the flying bomb had had its day, the rocket must be considered the long-range weapon of the future. On the other side of the scale must be set the complication and high cost of such missiles. Delivering approximately the same explosive charge as a flying bomb, the A-4 rocket required twenty times the productive effort, or as much as six or seven fighters.

239. That the German rocket attacks of 1944 and 1945 were conceived with a well-defined military object in view is open to doubt. I fancy that if the situation had been less desperate the Germans might have postponed active operations until further trials enabled them to attain a higher standard of accuracy. Their plight was such, however, that in September, 1944, they found themselves constrained to improvise a rocket offensive from Holland in order to cushion the shock resulting from the obvious failure of the flying bomb. This does not mean that if northern France had remained in their hands, and our countermeasures to the flying bomb been less successful, they would not have used both weapons together; but that in such circumstances the use of the rocket would have been equally premature. The standard of accuracy attained, the many misfires, and the inconsistency of method adopted by different firing units, all point in the same direction.

240. To an even greater extent than the flying bomb campaign, then, the rocket offensive must be regarded merely as a harassing attack. In the outcome it was not particularly successful in that capacity. Why was this? The contribution of the defences, as I have related, was practically limited to tracking the missiles, trying to locate the firing points, and attacking these and other targets more or less frequently and more or less effectively with fighters and fighter-bombers. As I urged at the time, these measures were not, by themselves, enough to interfere seriously with the rate or quality of the enemy's fire. The ineffectiveness of the A-4 rocket was due rather to the inaccuracy of the weapon and to the restricted scale of attack, reduced as it was by the enemy's insistence on dividing his efforts between Antwerp and London, probably from propagandist motives. But to say this does not imply that no effective countermeasure to the rocket would have been possible in any circumstances. In one sense its very lack of weight was what made the attack so hard to counter. For if the enemy had begun to fire at a much greater rate, he could no longer have lived from hand to mouth. He would have been obliged to store rockets and fuel in bulk near the firing area. Valuable bombing targets would then have been offered to us; and in such a case the Chiefs of Staff would doubtless have considered lifting their virtual ban on the use of the strategic bomber forces against rocket targets. I have little doubt that if this had been done and the diversion of part of our bomber effort been accepted, we should soon have been able to restore the scale of rocket attack to its original proportions.

241. Accordingly, so far as the rocket was concerned the answer to our question is that, although in the circumstances the effect of the

defences was small, potentially we had the means of keeping the situation in hand if the scale of attack had risen.

242. On the broader issue of the extent to which the Germans were right, in the military sense, to develop their two long-range weapons and put them into operation, a number of questions naturally arise. Would several thousand fighters have been worth more to the enemy than the 20,000 flying bombs and 3,000 rockets, or thereabouts, which he aimed at England and Continental cities? Put thus, the issue is misleadingly simple; the fighters would have been no use without pilots, ground crews, bases, and supplies of aviation spirit greater than the Germans could command. If this effort had been put into the production of bombers instead, the Germans would still have been no better off: the crews and the aviation spirit would not have been forthcoming. And indeed, since by the time the most important decisions were taken the Luftwaffe had lost much of its striking power, the devotion of so much skill and manpower to the flying bomb and the A-4 is at least understandable. The former was an ingenious weapon, which we might not have overcome if we had been less well prepared; the latter a notable advance on anything that had gone before, and a source of problems with which the nations are still grappling. The sponsors of these engines of destruction may be pardoned for a certain lack of judgment if they fancied themselves on the brink of changes comparable to those which followed the rifled barrel and the machine-gun.

243. Whatever the pros and cons of the German policy which lay behind the operation of the flying bomb and the A-4 rocket, it is probable that, as the end approached, the German measures to stave off general defeat became less well co-ordinated and more involuntary. I have tried to show why I think it more than doubtful whether Hitler could have developed a decisive attack with the flying bomb and the rocket in 1944, whatever targets had been chosen. I have suggested that in fact he was confronted with the peremptory need of a sign which would show his followers that England was being attacked, and so mitigate to some degree the terror that was coming upon them. Where action is taken under forces of overwhelming compulsion there can hardly be a question of fastidious strategic judgment. None the less, in the complex and often tangled web of German strategy one important thread was missing. Though hidden at first by reason of the great number of aircraft deployed to lead off the German land campaigns, its absence became more obvious as operations went on. I refer to the German failure to think consistently in terms of air power. The Luftwaffe was allowed to run down, and no big enough measures were set in train for its continuous replenishment, especially in respect of competent bomber crews. The result of this neglect was a progressive loss of air superiority, at first over the occupied territories and finally over the "living space" of Germany.

244. If, as Koller had said, the flying bomb and the A-4 rocket were to be regarded as a substitute for the strategic bomber force, the cardinal mistake was to suppose that these novel weapons could be used effectively in the absence of air superiority, which alone could have provided reasonable immunity from air attack. Only air superiority could ensure that the places where the missiles were stored, serviced, and fired, the crews who fired them, and the vehicles which carried them by road and rail would not be subject to systematic interference.

245. By the time the flying bomb and rocket campaigns were got under way, the Allies had gained a high degree of air superiority over all the areas from which the weapons could be fired. Hence we were in a position to conduct a counter-offensive at will, and without serious hindrance from enemy aircraft, wherever targets might present themselves and whenever the scale of attack by the Germans was sufficient to warrant the diversion of Allied bombers from their main task. Sometimes—as with the rail interdiction programme of the tactical air forces—operations conceived with the main task in view served a dual purpose, and no diversion was involved.

246. Moreover, this vital condition of air superiority, for which we had fought without respite since the Battle of Britain, enabled us constantly to improve the system of air defence whose application to new threats I have endeavoured to describe. Because we had air superiority we found ourselves free to adapt the system to novel circumstances and keep it in action day and night, with scarcely a rap from the German bombers not an hour's flying away.

247. The problems of air defence which have been described will not remain static. They may recur in new forms in the future. The scientific advances which the Germans used so spectacularly, if unsuccessfully, gave us a foretaste of hazards against which it is our business to provide. As science goes forward, and fresh discoveries lead to changes in the apparatus and methods of air defence, fertility in research and skill in engineering will provide better tools and weapons; but these are only raw materials of progress. What we need to do, above all, is to give rein to the qualities of mind and imagination which can take the growing mass of technical knowledge and mould what it brings forth to fit the shape of things to come.

LONDON
PRINTED AND PUBLISHED BY HIS MAJESTY'S STATIONERY OFFICE
To be purchased directly from H.M. Stationery Office at the following addresses:
York House, Kingsway, London, W.C.2; 13a Castle Street, Edinburgh, 2;
39-41 King Street, Manchester, 2; 1 St. Andrew's Crescent, Cardiff;
Tower Lane, Bristol, 1; 80 Chichester Street, Belfast
OR THROUGH ANY BOOKSELLER
1948
Price 2s. 0d. net

S.O. Code No. 65-38437

Numb. 39173

THIRD SUPPLEMENT TO
The London Gazette
OF TUESDAY, 13th MARCH, 1951
Published by Authority

Registered as a Newspaper

MONDAY, 19 MARCH, 1951

AIR OPERATIONS IN SOUTH EAST ASIA 16TH NOVEMBER, 1943 TO 31ST MAY, 1944.

NOTE.—A set of maps for this despatch is on separate sale at 1s. 0d. net. This set of maps also covers the operations described in the other Air and Army despatches of the Burma campaign from 16th November, 1943 to 12th September, 1945.

The following despatch was submitted to the Secretary of State for Air on 23rd November, 1944, by AIR CHIEF MARSHAL SIR R. E. C. PEIRSE, K.C.B., D.S.O., A.F.C., Allied Air Commander-in-Chief, South East Asia.

PART ONE

INTRODUCTORY

1. As a result of the formation on 16th November, 1943, of South East Asia Command, I assumed operational control of all Air Forces in the South East Asia theatre, with authority to employ them in conformity with the policy of the Supreme Allied Commander, Admiral The Lord Louis Mountbatten, G.C.V.O., C.B., D.S.O., A.D.C. Thus I had at my disposal what had constituted R.A.F. India Command, and those American units in this theatre which comprised the 10th U.S.A.A.F. It was my task to ensure that these forces operated as a coherent body and that the best use was made of the potentialities of each.

2. In addition it was my continued responsibility to develop India as a base for future air operations, as a supply centre, and as a training area for R.A.F. and I.A.F. personnel. Such activities absorb a considerable proportion of the energies of the Command, and constitute a task of which the importance and results are not immediately apparent. I have therefore devoted Part Four of this Despatch to the progress that has been made in this direction.

3. Responsibility for operations on the North West Frontier and for the Indian Air Force was relinquished to the formation which replaced the Inspectorate-General of the I.A.F. and to which was bequeathed the name Air Headquarters, India.

* * * * * *

4. To ensure the integrated operational control of Units in Bengal and Assam, a new Headquarters was set up under Major-General G. E. Stratemeyer, U.S.A.A.F., designated Eastern Air Command and located initially at Delhi. This formation, which had previously existed under the title Headquarters, U.S.A.A.F., India-Burma Sector, China-Burma-India Theatre, had administered and controlled the 10th U.S.A.A.F. and provided in addition base facilities for the 14th U.S.A.A.F. The new Headquarters consisted basically of the Operations Section of the old organisation with the addition of an R.A.F. element. This Command, and all those comprising the 10th which had formerly come under Bengal Command and all those comprising the 10th U.S.A.A.F. in the same area. These forces were subdivided into a Tactical Air Force under Air Marshal Sir John Baldwin, and a Strategic Air Force under Brigadier General Howard C. Davidson, U.S.A.A.F. I was authorised to effect such re-grouping of operational units that I considered necessary to achieve maximum operational efficiency, and as a result R.A.F. and U.S.A.A.F. transport units were merged on 15th December into one organisation which was given the title of Troop Carrier Command. This new formation was commanded by Brigadier General D. Old, U.S.A.A.F. Similarly R.A.F. and American photographic reconnaissance units were incorporated into one command which assumed the title of

Photographic Reconnaissance Force. Wing Commander S. G. Wise, R.A.F., was appointed Air Commander from the date of formation.

5. In exercising operational control of these forces, the integrity of U.S. Groups and R.A.F. Wings was retained and administrative control and responsibility remained with the respective American and British Commanders. The Chiefs of Staff agreed to the integration with the qualification that in view of American commitments to China, it might become necessary to transfer units from the 10th to the 14th U.S.A.A.F.

6. The chain of command and the conduct of operations by the merged forces almost without exception worked well, and mutual concessions and adjustments were made by each element. In ancillary services, examples of co-operation were most notable in the sphere of maintenance, signals and flying control. Major General G. E. Stratemeyer has said in his report on operations during this period—" The various obstacles which might be expected to arise as a result of combining U.S.A.A.F. and R.A.F. units have been overcome as a result of integration of staffs at Headquarters, Eastern Air Command, Strategic Air Force, Third Tactical Air Force, Troop Carrier Command and Photographic Reconnaissance Force. Such a revolutionary change in staff organisation might well have produced many difficulties and misunderstandings, but such has not been the case, and we have undoubtedly derived mutual benefit, not only on the staff side, but in the tactical operating of air forces ". With these and other evidences of the working of integrated forces I have dealt in detail in the appropriate sections of the narrative.

THE TASKS TO BE ACCOMPLISHED.

7. The tasks which lay before the combined Air Forces were:—

(a) To conduct a strategic air offensive in conformity with the general plan to destroy enemy air forces and installations, selected rail, road and river communications, and depots and maintenance facilities.

(b) To ensure the air defence of the U.S. Air Transport Command airfields in North-East India and to provide for the defence against air attack of Calcutta and adjacent industrial areas.

(c) To provide support for the operations of Fourteenth Army.

(d) To provide support for the Chinese-American forces under command of General J. W. Stilwell which were operating from bases in the Ledo area.

(e) To support the operations of Long Range Penetration forces, and

(f) To conduct photographic reconnaissance and survey.

8. The prosecution of the first of these tasks was not only the best method of maintaining a favourable air situation, which was my principal charge, but would also force the enemy on the defensive and thus provide the best protection for the air route to China, for the Calcutta area and for sea communications in the northern Bay of Bengal.

9. Offensive fighter operations were to be undertaken to the greatest possible extent and it was proposed to use long range fighters in particular in the offensive against enemy airfields and air installations. Moreover, in order to overcome the wide dispersal of my available fighter strength, it was necessary to maintain at the highest pitch of efficiency the early warning system.

10. I planned to employ the strategic bomber force against targets in the following order of priority: enemy occupied airfields and installations, shipping, railways, oil installations in Burma and suitable objectives in Bangkok. The course which the battle took, however, made a readjustment of these priorities necessary and a considerable proportion of the total bomber effort was directed to tactical targets in support of the Army and later, to carry supplies to the garrison at Imphal. Another task which assumed increasing importance during the period was the evacuation of casualties. Much had to be done to build up a successful organisation which could deal with the transhipment of sick and wounded from battle areas and casualty clearing stations to better equipped hospitals in the rear.

THE FORCES AVAILABLE.

11. To accomplish these tasks there was a total of forty-eight R.A.F. and seventeen U.S.A.A.F. squadrons deployed for operations. By May these totals had increased to sixty-four and twenty-eight respectively.

12. The disposition of tactical units in Bengal and Assam was designed to provide defence and support over the three main areas of land operations; in the Arakan, along the line from Tiddim to Homalin, and the Ledo Sector in Northern Burma; they were under the control of 224 Group, 221 Group and the U.S.A.A.F. Northern Air Sector Force respectively. Strategic units continued to be stationed further to the west since the marshy areas of the Sunderbunds and the poor lines of communication in that area made the construction of airfields east of the Brahmaputra up to heavy bomber standards a matter of extreme difficulty which neither the labour, transport nor supply position would allow me to undertake except as a relatively long term plan.

THE SITUATION IN NOVEMBER.

13. Facing the enemy from India there was a more modern, more powerful, and numerically stronger air force than had hitherto been available in this theatre. Moreover, during the monsoon much had been achieved to give the units comprising this force greater striking power. Communications, although overstrained were now better geared to carry war supplies than at any time since the outbreak of hostilities. Advanced landing grounds which had been constructed afforded short-range aircraft a greater radius of action, both offensive and defensive, during the dry weather that was to come and the warning system was now able to give ample notice of the approach of hostile aircraft.

14. The enemy for his part disposed of a force of approximately 250 aircraft concentrated in the airfield groups at Heho, Anisakan, Rangoon and Chiengmai with the remainder at lay-back bases in Siam and the Netherlands East Indies. His ground forces faced ours along a front of 700 miles. In Arakan he held the line from Maungdaw to Buthidaung and was opposed by XV Corps, thence north-west across the inhospitable Chin Hills to Kalemyo and northwards up the Kabaw Valley where

IV Corps was deployed. Further north still he was confronted by two Chinese Divisions based on Ledo, and beyond this we held positions as far as the River Salween with a small force based at Fort Hertz. The enemy's bases and lines of communication stretched for 900 miles from Bangkok to Myitkyina, over the whole length of which it was possible to attack him.

15. The security of sea communications meant that General Reconnaissance aircraft had to cover an area ranging from South Africa to Sumatra. The patrol of this vast expanse of sea contributed a problem that could only be met by the careful husbanding and disposition of the small forces available.

* * * * * *

16. The account of a campaign covering such a wide area and diversity of activities does not admit of chronological treatment. I have therefore dealt separately with each strand of the pattern of operations, commencing with the primary task, the maintenance of air superiority, and placing air transport operations next in view of the importance they were to assume.

* * * * * *

PART TWO

OPERATIONS

I.—THE MAINTENANCE OF AIR SUPERIORITY

17. The advent of Spitfires in Bengal early in November had already begun an era of successful interceptions in which the enemy discovered for the first time in this theatre the efficacy of modern fighter aircraft backed by a well developed system of warning and control.

18. The first squadrons (Nos. 615 and 607 A.A.F.) were based on Chittagong in order to protect and cover that vital port and to cover the Arakan front which was to be the scene of the first major battles of the campaign. Within the month the Spitfires destroyed four enemy photographic reconnaissance aircraft of the Dinah type whose excellent performance had hitherto allowed them to range with impunity over our forward bases at a height and speed which Hurricanes could not equal. The enemy reacted by sending out fighter sweeps to test the new arrivals and whittle down our Spitfire strength in order that he could once again range over the Arakan suffering only the minor casualties that Hurricanes could inflict. In both these objects he was unsuccessful, and by the end of December had lost twenty-two aircraft, probably lost seven and had suffered damage to twenty-six against our loss of thirteen. The greatest success scored in these raids was by No. 136 Squadron who, on the last day of the year, scored 12 destroyed, 3 probably destroyed, and 8 damaged against a mixed force of bombers and fighters which were attempting to attack light Naval forces off the Arakan coast. As a result of this victory the Secretary of State for Air signalled his congratulations and commented that the newly arrived Spitfires had come into good hands.

19. The one occasion the enemy could claim as a success at this time was a bold strike aimed at Calcutta with the double object of damaging port installations and demoralising the city. He divined that over a front of 700 miles, defence in depth could not be so uniformly effective and that in the rear areas which included Calcutta, he would probably be met with Hurricanes. On 5th December he sent a mixed force of approximately sixty bombers and fighters in two waves which succeeded in bombing Calcutta for the loss of 2 destroyed, 1 probably destroyed, and 4 damaged, while the three and a half Hurricane squadrons (the half being night fighters) suffered five destroyed and six damaged. That the enemy put his maximum effort into the attack is evidenced by the fact that the second wave included Naval aircraft.

20. During January the Spitfire squadrons gained valuable experience in air fighting and tactics that was to stand them in good stead in the greater battles to come. The enemy continued to send fighter sweeps over the Arakan, but Spitfires were able to inflict casualties upon them in the ratio of eight to one. By this time two squadrons of Spitfire VIIIs (Nos. 81 and 152) had arrived from Middle East, and I now had at my disposal in the forward areas of Bengal four squadrons of Spitfires and nine of Hurricanes for fighter operations; the stage was thus set for the opening of the battle in Arakan on the 4th February. Anticipating our own ground offensive by four days the enemy launched an attack with the object of annihilating the 5th and 7th Indian Divisions and pressing on to capture Chittagong. This ambitious plan was attended by the most impressive measure of air support afforded by him in this theatre, sweeps by formations of fifty plus aircraft being reported daily. The objects of the J.A.F. appear to have been firstly to intercept our aircraft engaged on close support, secondly to increase the morale of his own troops and thirdly to give some measure of ground support by attacks on our positions and forward bases. As the battle developed, one other task assumed overriding priority for the enemy air forces. The 7th Indian Division, cut off from its supply bases, was being supplied wholly by air. It was of vital importance to the enemy that our supply-dropping aircraft should not succeed in this task, but the air superiority which we had established, the provision of standing patrols —particularly in the Kaladan Valley where, owing to the intervening hills, no radar cover below 10,000 feet was available—and resort to supply dropping by night enabled transport aircraft to maintain the beleaguered forces for the loss of only one Dakota (C.47) to enemy fighters.

21. The tactics which were employed to gain this dominance over the Arakan battle front centred around the three forward squadrons equipped with Spitfire Vs and a few Spitfire VIIIs. Hurricanes were used for airfield cover when Spitfires were re-fuelling and re-arming, and for standing patrols over possible target areas during hostile raids in case of a missed interception. The enemy countered by introducing the Tojo, whose performance exceeded that of the Oscar, adopting the defensive circle and splitting into small groups when the circle was broken. This brought them a relative measure of success inasmuch as their losses decreased whilst those of the Spitfires gradually increased.

22. The advantages of the Spitfire VIII in this battle were not immediately apparent, for

the enemy continued to operate at his best performance height, that is 10,000 feet. No. 136 Squadron, who re-equipped with these aircraft in February, could not effectively employ their high overtaking speed against an enemy who exploited the manoeuvrability of his aircraft to the full. At first attacks were delivered at too high a speed with a resultant falling off in marksmanship.

23. When the battle switched to the Chindwin front in the second week in March and it became clear that the main Japanese ground effort was to be aimed at Imphal and the railway to the north, 243 Wing and eight squadrons were moved into the area from 224 Group. Spitfires did not immediately repeat their successes of the Arakan campaign for the following reasons. Firstly, although the three Ground Control Interception Stations were excellent and brought off fine interceptions against Dinahs (No. 81 Squadron scored their first successes in this theatre by destroying two in four days at the beginning of March), the rugged nature of the terrain produced technical difficulties in the way of echoes which left many blank spots in the radar coverage. Secondly, the substitution of Indian Mobile Wireless Observer Companies for R.A.F. Wireless Units resulted in a lower standard of reporting. Thirdly, squadrons which had already lost a number of experienced pilots in action were now losing many more as operational tours were completed. Moreover, the sudden influx of personnel, both Army and R.A.F. could not be met with a similar growth of transport, accommodation and communications. Finally, as the Japanese advanced, more and more of our early warning system was overrun, and the Army Corps Commander decided that he could not employ troops on local protection of airfields and the warning net. Squaddon personnel became exhausted through disturbed rest, and guard duties by night combined with operations by day. Certain squadrons were therefore withdrawn from the Imphal Valley whilst others were flown out every night.

24. Once again the problem of protecting transport aircraft operating so near to Japanese bases asserted itself. Deteriorating weather and absence of warning made it increasingly difficult to ensure interception, but that our superiority was never lost is shown by the fact that between the opening of the battle and the end of May, thirty-one enemy aircraft were destroyed, twenty probably destroyed and sixty-six damaged in air combat over the Manipur area, for the loss of seventeen. Of this number, three were destroyed by No. 176 (Beaufighter) Squadron operating at night from advanced airfields near Imphal.

25. Meanwhile the accretion to the Command of long-range American fighter aircraft enabled tactics to be developed which were to have most damaging results for the Japanese Air Force. Already Mustangs (P.51) had proved their worth, notably in a combined victory with Kittyhawks (P.40) against an enemy formation in the Digboi area on 27th March, claiming 26 destroyed and 4 probably destroyed, for the loss of two. The Army reported finding twenty-two crashed enemy aircraft in the area after the interception. At the same time, No. 459 (U.S.) Squadron, equipped with Lightnings (P.38) began to operate under 224 Group. Thus, it was possible to employ Lightnings (P.38) and Mustangs (P.51) to supplement the work of the Spitfires which were still in short supply, and had to be husbanded for purely defensive work. The serious contraction of the warning system around Imphal could now be partly offset by sending the American long range fighters to intercept the enemy on his return to the Central Irrawaddy strips.

26. The first success of the policy of intrusion fell to No. 1 Air Commando Force, which surprised a large concentration of aircraft on the Shwebo group of airfields on 8th March, and destroyed 46 of them. Three days later, the Lightnings (P.38) squadron scored 15 against the enemy at Heho. The primitive nature of the Japanese warning system in the area augured well for the successful continuance of the operations. Pilots became increasingly familiar with the details of those airfields which were within range, and photographs and models aided quick identification of dispersal areas and anti-aircraft posts. In early strikes of this nature the enemy were not airborne and awaiting attack, and it was possible to make more than one run over the target, the first run being utilised to locate aircraft in their dispersal pens.

27. In May, an improvement in the enemy's warning system became evident, since often fighters were airborne and awaiting the attack. However, losses remained low, since No. 459 Squadron discovered that if they maintained an indicated airspeed of 300 m.p.h. and refused to enter into combat with the slower and more manoeuvrable Oscars and Tojos, they were still able to deliver their attacks at aircraft on the ground, perhaps fire one burst at any fighter which attempted to intercept and make their withdrawal without loss. The prospect of combat during the intrusion therefore proved no deterrent. In this manner No. 459 Squadron destroyed 121 enemy aircraft on the ground or in the air in March, April and May. The enemy was forced in consequence to discontinue the use of the Shwebo group of airfields and even Heho and Meiktila became practically untenable. By the end of May, the J.A.F. had been forced into the humiliating position of providing such support as their army, 600 miles away in the northern mountains, could receive from the comparative safety of airfields around Rangoon.

28. To sum up, the extent of Allied superiority in the air throughout the period can be seen by a comparison of the effort and losses of the opposing forces. The enemy scale of effort amounted to 2,700 sorties sighted or plotted, or less than three per cent. of the Allied effort. To achieve this, the J.A.F. lost 402 aircraft destroyed in the air or on the ground, or some 14 per cent. of their effort, while the comparable total for British and American forces amounted to 230 or less than one-third per cent. of the effort. The air superiority maintained over the period needs no further emphasis.

* * * * * *

II.—AIR TRANSPORT OPERATIONS

29. Throughout the period under review the number of transport squadrons under my command steadily increased, though their growth was by no means out of proportion

to the continually increasing importance of their task in the operational areas. Indeed, it is not too much to say that their services were instrumental in preserving the existence of the Fourteenth Army as a striking force on the Burma frontier. Operations on the Eastern front made calls upon them at an ever increasing rate, so that despite reinforcement, transport squadrons worked at a high rate of effort from the moment they became operational. In consequence, crews underwent a period of considerable strain, for not only does supply dropping in this theatre involve intricate low flying over the dropping zone for as much as an hour in a hot aircraft interior, but the crews were normally responsible for the arduous work of unloading 6,000 to 7,000 lbs. of freight.

Development of Troop Carrier Command.

30. In November, the only R.A.F. transport squadron operating was No. 31, an experienced and pioneer unit, but the 1st and 2nd Troop Carrier Squadrons U.S.A.A.F. had begun to work over the northern sector of the front and there were other squadrons both British and American, either in training or on their way. Unified operational control of these forces was effected by the institution in December of Troop Carrier Command, Eastern Air Command, under Brigadier General W. D. Old, U.S.A.A.F., administrative control remaining in the usual British or American channels. Headquarters was established at Comilla on 2nd January, 1944, in close proximity to the Headquarters of Fourteenth Army and of the Third Tactical Air Force, as well as to main Army supply bases. Subsequent operations illustrated the dependence of air transport operations upon the tactical air situation, and in order to combine final responsibility for the former with the exercise of our air superiority—as well as to integrate air transport with army policy—Troop Carrier Command was placed under the control of the Air Commander, Third Tactical Air Force, from 1st May. Subsequently Troop Carrier Command was dissolved as from 4th June, by when its component squadrons numbered 8—4 R.A.F. and 4 U.S.A.A.F. Moreover, in February the Air Transport Command had loaned to me twenty-two Commandos (C.46) to meet the emergency in the Arakan, and when it became necessary to return these in April, five U.S.A.A.F. Troop Carrier squadrons and the larger part of 216 Squadron R.A.F. were detached to work with my Command from M.A.A.F. Upon their return to the Mediterranean theatre in June, aircraft and crews from the Strategic Air Force were attached to the Third Tactical Air Force to fill the gap until the first of the U.S.A.A.F. Combat Cargo Groups became operational. During its short but eventful life of little over six months, Troop Carrier Command had thus increased more than four-fold in size, and even more in significance.

31. The routine supply dropping missions of No. 31 Squadron over the Chin Hills and Arakan were being continued at the time of the formation of South East Asia Command. The first additional need was that of 81 (West African) Division which already in December received supplies landed for it at Chiringa by U.S.A.A.F. It then moved eastwards over the mountains to the Kaladan Valley at Daletme and began its advance southwards, being dependent throughout for its maintenance upon air supply. From 7th January, 1944, onwards, this became a commitment of No. 62 Squadron R.A.F. At the same time U.S.A.A.F. aircraft came to the help of No. 31 Squadron in building up a large reserve of supplies at Tiddim, while further north, Nos. 1 and 2 Troop Carrier Squadrons U.S.A.A.F. in addition to maintaining the air warning centres screening the Assam Valley, began to supply on a much larger scale the two Chinese Divisions advancing south-east from Ledo down the Hukawng Valley. They also gave help to the Kachin levies waging guerrilla warfare in the Fort Hertz district, as well as to the Gurkha garrison of Fort Hertz itself.

The Arakan Battle—February, 1944.

32. When the Japanese offensive in the Arakan opened on 4th February, the needs of the 14th Army for air supply greatly expanded with only a few days' warning. The land communications of 7th Indian Division were soon cut and those of 5th Indian Division in danger, and it was only by supply dropping that the encircled forces could be expected to stand their ground and turn a potential catastrophe into a decisive victory. Japanese preparations for an offensive had been observed, however, and the possibility of encirclement envisaged, so that when supply by air was called for on 8th February, there was no delay.

33. On the first day some of our transport aircraft encountered an enemy fighter sweep and one was shot down. Such was our air superiority that throughout the Arakan operations this was the only loss sustained by transport aircraft from enemy fighters, although many aircraft were damaged by fire from the ground. Later, as a measure of protection, much of the supply dropping was done by night with but little falling off in efficiency. The operation while it lasted was of such unexpected magnitude that I was compelled to request the loan of a number of Commandos (C.46) from the India-China Wing of the U.S. Air Transport Command. These aircraft were promptly and unstintingly supplied. The critical period from the 8th February to 6th March inclusive involved the delivery of 2,010 short tons of supplies of all kinds, including rations, animals, ammunition and P.O.L.* With such large scale help, ground forces were able to break out of their encirclement and inflict a decisive defeat on the enemy—significant in that it pointed the way towards the neutralisation of the long familiar Japanese offensive tactics. By the end of the month, air supply to the Arakan, though it still continued, was no longer of an emergency nature.

Operation "Thursday".

34. The major offensive action planned and carried out by 14th Army before the onset of the monsoon, was a penetration of enemy-occupied territory by columns of Special Force under Major General O. C. Wingate. Its purpose was to disrupt enemy communications and thereby aid the recapture of northern Burma and create a favourable situation for the 14th Army to exploit. The operation as

---

* Petrol, Oil, Lubricants.

finally planned involved the large scale use of transport aircraft to fly in and supply the brigades, and the energetic employment of close support aircraft to make up the mobile columns' deficiencies in artillery. The First Air Commando Unit under Colonel Cochran, U.S.A.A.F., had been specially created and sent to this theatre to fill these needs, and acted as a task force in support of General Wingate. I have dealt with the activities of this force separately.

35. The long range penetration brigade which was making its way across the Chindwin overland towards Katha received its first airborne supplies on 10th February, and its maintenance thereafter became a continuous commitment. The remaining two brigades were landed on two strips improvised in the jungle during the nights of 5th/6th and 10th/11th March, and a fourth and fifth brigade were flown into another landing ground during the nights of 24th/25th March and 5th/6th April. The successful accomplishment of the air side of this operation was shared directly by the First Air Commando Unit and by the British and American Transport squadrons which participated, although the whole operation was only made possible by the high degree of air superiority gained by the tactical air forces in the preceding months.

36. The initial fly-in was the work of gliders which carried an American airfield engineer company whose task it was to receive Dakotas (C.47) on the following night, and also a sufficient number of combat troops with equipment to defend the locality meanwhile. Although this preparatory operation was a complete success, it was twice in danger of being compromised. The first occasion was when at the last moment it was discovered by photographic reconnaissance that one of the jungle clearings earmarked for use and called "Piccadilly" had been deliberately obstructed by the enemy. The commanders on the spot decided to continue with the operation and divert the aircraft intended for "Piccadilly" to the other landing zone—"Broadway". Secondly, the towing of gliders in pairs proved impracticable under the difficult flying conditions encountered; tow ropes snapped and a number of gliders failed to reach their destination. Moreover there existed in the clearing a number of undulations not visible on air photographs, so that even on making the best of landings the earlier gliders frequently crashed, and each wrecked glider became a source of danger for its successors. Worse confusion and damage was avoided by the airfield control improvised by Lt.-Col. Allison of the U.S.A.A.F. who was able to stop the arrival of additional gliders. Despite these difficulties, by the next night the American airborne engineer unit and British troops had levelled "Broadway" sufficiently for Dakotas (C.47) to land. The Air Commander 3rd T.A.F. commented particularly on the quality of the airfield control and the excellent flying discipline that were features of the operation, which enabled the strip to be used almost to saturation by a constant stream of transport aircraft in the short hours of darkness available. His report remarks as follows: "Nobody has seen a transport operation until he has . . . watched Dakotas coming in and taking off in opposite directions on a single strip all night long at the rate of one landing or one take-off every three minutes".

37. By D plus 6 day there had been flown in 9,052 personnel, 175 ponies, 1,183 mules and 509,083 pounds of stores.

38. The element of surprise which had accompanied the entry of these forces and which had been aided by diversionary bombing around Bhamo and Indaw was maintained throughout. Even when the enemy divined our intentions, our air superiority was instrumental in rendering his attacks ineffectual. It was not until 11th March and 13th March that the enemy attacked the two landing grounds which had been first extemporised—by which time one had already been evacuated and a detachment of Spitfires of No. 81 Squadron had been installed on the other. Other landing strips were contrived as the occasion arose, though for the most part the thirty columns of the division were supplied by dropping. Much of the effectiveness of this air supply depended upon the standard of training of the Dakota crews. The dropping zones were continually being changed as the columns moved from place to place. Delivery normally took place by night and there was often no other guide than navigational skill supplemented by pre-arranged light signals which became visible only when the aircraft arrived in the vicinity of the dropping zone. Danger from ground fire whilst dropping was a frequent and accepted risk. This was no less true of occasions on which Dakotas were able to utilise a landing ground, for enemy detachments were often in the neighbourhood. The strip opened in the later stages of the operation at Hopin was evacuated because of small arms fire through which our aircraft had unavoidably to pass before landing.

39. Before the advent of the rains made the use of fairweather landing grounds impossible, one Brigade (No. 16) was flown back to its base in India. The others subsequently joined the Chinese-American forces advancing upon Myitkyina under General J. W. Stilwell, and participated in the operations around Myitkyina, to whose success their columns, supplied entirely by air, had contributed.

First Air Commando Unit.

40. This unit came to my command with the specific duty of assisting the fly-in of Special Force, the initial maintenance of its columns and the evacuation of casualties. These functions were extended to include direct support of the ground forces and sustained attacks on installations and communications to hinder the eventual mobilisation of the enemy against these forces. The Bomber-Fighter component was engaged from the 3rd February onwards in attacks on railways and airfields and, as soon as the fly-in had been accomplished, in direct support when called for by the columns. In these tasks the Mustangs (P.51) flew 1,482 sorties and the Mitchells (B.25) 422. Their claims against enemy aircraft destroyed on the ground and in the air amounted to ninety. The glider component of the force carried out fourteen separate operations involving the release of 99 gliders which took into Burma a variety of equipment ranging from bulldozers to rivercraft.

41. An important part was played in the operation by the hundred light communication aircraft which the Air Commando possessed.

These aircraft (L.1s and L.5s) could land more or less at will even in bad country to convey messages and supplies of small bulk, to carry commanders from one unit to another, evacuate casualties and perform a host of miscellaneous services without the risks attendant upon wireless silence or employing heavy aircraft. I consider their widespread use in future comparable operations essential.

42. The record of the small force of selected personnel with first-class equipment, which constituted the Air Commando, was naturally good, but that record cannot be advanced in support of extending the principle of Air Commando Units. Such a principle gives rise to the danger of tying down fighter and bomber aircraft permanently and exclusively to one particular Army formation with the consequent risks of duplication and lack of flexibility.

43. Such units have a place as spearheads for airborne and air transit operations, but as soon as normal supply can begin, fighter cover and air support, as requisite, should be provided by the tactical air forces as a whole under the direction of the appropriate air force Commander.

* * * * * *

The Siege of Imphal.

44. Concurrent with the heavy claims on Troop Carrier Command from Special Force and General Stilwell's forces arose an emergency that surpassed in importance all other transport operations, and on whose successful solution by air supply depended the fate of Imphal and the continuance of support to China.

45. On the 7/8th March the enemy crossed the Chindwin in force with the three-fold object of occupying Indian soil, capturing our main base at Imphal, and cutting the Bengal-Assam railway which fed the airfields from which supplies were flown to China.

46. Before the end of March, the enemy had cut the Tiddim-Imphal and Imphal-Kohima roads, occupied Tiddim and part of Kohima and swept round to the Bishenpur area west of Imphal. From the air point of view, the over-running of our warning system and the loss of advanced landing grounds on the perimeter of the Imphal plain were a serious inconvenience. The encirclement of the IV Corps divisions at Imphal, however, had immediate and heavy repercussions upon the transport situation, since I was forthwith confronted with unprecedented demands for the large scale delivery of reinforcements and supplies, not merely to the beleaguered forces in the Imphal Plain, but also to the garrisons holding out at Kohima and elsewhere. These demands were met, though not without considerable strain upon an already hard-worked force.

47. It was clear that the needs of our ground forces could not long be satisfied by the existing number of transport aircraft under my command. Thus, when the threat of a Japanese offensive westwards from the Chindwin had become apparent, although before it actually materialised, I made strong representations for further reinforcements of transport aircraft. As a result I received on loan from M.A.A.F. the services of the 64th Troop Carrier Group, U.S.A.A.F., consisting of five squadrons and a detachment of No. 216 Squadron, R.A.F. These six squadrons were all operating on the Burma Front by the second week in April. In addition, I was permitted to retain for a further period the Commandos (C.46) temporarily withdrawn from the India-China Wing of the Air Transport Command for supply dropping in Arakan.

48. The needs of our forces in the Manipur area were many and pressing. No. 50 Parachute Brigade was flown from the Punjab to reinforce the garrison at Imphal, and a little later No. 5 Indian Division was moved by air complete from the Arakan in 758 sorties. Between 10th/15th April, an infantry brigade was flown from Amarda Road, south-west of Calcutta to Jorhat in Assam. 99 Commando (C.46) and 189 Dakota (C.47) sorties lifted 3,056 all ranks, 937,000 pounds of stores and the following equipment: 50 motor-cycles, 40 jeeps, 31 jeep trailers, 16 25-pounders and eight 3.7 howitzers. An Army Air Support Control unit was taken by air from Poona to Jorhat for service with 33 Corps. The movement by air of the servicing echelons of tactical squadrons became a matter of routine. In regard to the maintenance of our troops, the most varied articles were delivered to the forces momentarily engulfed within the flood of Japanese infiltration. At Kohima, for instance, owing to the enemy seizure of the wells, it was necessary to drop drinking water as well as routine supplies and medical necessities. Three hundred and seventy tons of bitumenised hessian were delivered by air at Tulihal to make the airfield there all-weather. On the return journeys all transport aircraft brought out with them casualties or troops not needed for active combat.

49. The 79 aircraft borrowed from the Middle East were due to be returned at the beginning of May. If this arrangement had been adhered to the consequences might well have been disastrous. General Stilwell's forces would have been forced to withdraw to their Ledo base, the Imphal Plain would have become untenable, the air route to China threatened, the morale of the Fourteenth Army troops encircled in the Imphal Plain would have been considerably affected and the all-weather airfields and warning system in the Surma and Brahmaputra Valleys would have been lost. Moreover, the major victory the enemy might have won would have had serious repercussions in India.

50. I was compelled to represent that these vital aircraft must stay until the reinforcements envisaged by the Chiefs of Staff arrived and became operational. Agreement was obtained, and I instructed the Air Commander, Eastern Air Command, to employ aircraft of the Strategic Air Force in a transport rôle should there be any gap between the departure of the M.A.A.F. squadrons and the new reinforcements becoming fully operational.

51. On 15th April my commitment for air supply to the besieged garrison at Imphal was established at the figure of over 400 short tons per day—which even then entailed the occupants going on short rations. The fulfilment of this contract depended upon a modicum of fair weather and upon the speedy loading of aircraft at Army supply bases. Neither of these conditions was entirely fulfilled, and it was only by reorganisation of the ground

elements of the air supply system and the unstinted efforts of the U.S.A.A.F. and R.A.F. transport squadrons available that the target figure was reached and surpassed in June. But by the end of May it was clear that the enemy's disregard of air transport as a major factor in the battle was to render his ambitious and costly offensive a failure.

The Advance from Ledo.

52. Throughout the whole period the supply of the Chinese-American forces operating from Ledo under General Stilwell had been proceeding. These troops were advancing down the Hukawng and Mogaung Valleys and thereby gradually bringing the opening of an overland route to China nearer realisation. Each advance took them further from their bases, and consequently their calls for air supply were increasing, necessitating up to 100 sorties per day. Landing grounds were constructed wherever possible along the path of the advance, and light aircraft were employed with good effect. The Dakota (C.47), however, remained as the greatest single factor in maintaining the advance. In April the entire 50th Chinese Division, numbering almost eight thousand men, was flown from Sookerating to Maingkwan, while by then all the combat troops in North Burma, both American and Chinese, had become dependent upon air supply. In May, a fast moving column of American troops, known as Galahad Force and supported entirely by air, made a considerable detour and caught the enemy unawares, seizing the main airfield at Myitkyina on 17th May. All units of Troop Carrier Command in the north had been standing by to carry in those forces which General Stilwell believed adequate to defeat the expected enemy counter attack. Brigadier-General Old was waiting at Shinbuiyang to conduct the initial glider operation in which troops and engineering equipment were to be conveyed, and himself towed the first glider into Myitkyina. Transport aircraft followed the gliders almost at once. In the course of thirty-six hours of intensive operations by both day and night, during which ground fire was continually encountered, and one enemy air attack was successful in shooting down a Dakota (C.47) and destroying others on the ground, there were landed a complete Chinese Regiment, six light anti-tank batteries, twelve Bofor guns and crews, one airborne engineer company and a Chinese mortar company. Many loads of ammunition, food and stores were also conveyed. Before the end of the month further troops, in numbers equivalent to a division, had been taken by air to Myitkyina, and the first stage of the reconquest of Burma and the reopening of the Burma Road was completed.

Evacuation of Casualties.

53. It would be incomplete to close this account of the operations of transport aircraft under my command without some mention of a further aspect of their work. During the first five months of 1944 the aircraft of Troop Carrier Command flew no less than twenty-three thousand sick and wounded back to safety. It may safely be said that but for the provision of air transport the greater proportion of these would have had little hope of survival. The alternative was many days' journey by sampan, mule and ambulance, and perhaps rail, to the nearest base hospital. Moreover, a proportion of the casualties evacuated were from the columns of Special Force fighting in enemy occupied territory. The 2,126 casualties evacuated from the division by the end of May would have been a total loss had they not been flown out by air.

54. Although evacuation of casualties by air was no new phenomenon in this theatre of war, nevertheless it first assumed considerable proportions during the Arakan battle in February and reached its peak during the struggle for Imphal in April. Transport aircraft, when they landed to deliver supplies frequently received casualties for the return journey. When, however, supplies were dropped, the intervention of light aircraft was necessary for the journey from a small advanced landing ground to a strip further back where a Dakota might land. But since neither heavy nor light aircraft could be spared throughout this period specifically for the evacuation of casualties, the removal of sick and wounded remained an "ad hoc" matter arranged on a basis of expediency and improvisation. R.A.F. medical personnel at airfields were insufficient to deal with the load of casualties which, due to operational exigencies, might be entrusted to them with little or no warning by a flight of transport Dakotas. And so, although the care of all wounded at airfields was officially an R.A.F. responsibility, nevertheless help in this matter was gladly accepted from the Army.

CONCLUSION.

55. Thus air transport played a decisive part in the three great battles of the period. By the end of May the reconquest of portions of northern Burma was in sight, and the garrison of Imphal was still an offensive force. The events related above make a reiteration of the importance of transport aircraft unnecessary. In connection with the operations, however, certain lessons were learned which I would emphasize. First, it is essential that Army Commanders should not be allowed to regard air transport as an auxiliary arm upon which they can call without reference to the appropriate Air Force Commander. Secondly, the Army must be impressed with the necessity for the quick turn-round of aircraft; during intensive operations loads must be ready for the aircraft as they land. Too often crews wasted valuable hours waiting at an Army Supply Base because their freight had not been assembled ready for loading. Thirdly, when the Army are the main customers of air transport forces, the fullest day-to-day liaison and discussion of problems must be combined with clear statements as far in advance as possible of what they require in the way of air transport, and for what purpose, in order that priorities may be allotted.

56. It is to be noted that the inadequacy of the Army ground organisation for supply by air operations became recognised by the Army as and when these operations became large-scale undertakings. Steps were taken to improve the ground organisation in the light of the experience gained during the operations. The first step was to provide Indian Air Supply companies at supply loading airfields. A further important development was to create Army staff organisations both to control the

activities of the Army elements on the airfields, and to organise the flow of Army supplies both from base to airfield and from airfield to aircraft. These developments did not, however, reach completion during the period covered by this despatch.

* * * * * *

III.—STRATEGIC AIR FORCE

57. Operations by heavy and medium bombers sought to accomplish the following tasks:

(i) Denial and destruction of *the enemy's lines of communication.*

(ii) Destruction of *airfields and other military installations.*

(iii) Destruction of *industrial and stores areas.*

58. In addition to these, the Strategic Air Force was often called upon to furnish direct support to ground forces and to provide aircraft and crews for transport operations.

59. For the transhipment of sea-borne supplies to Burma, there were available to the enemy the ports of Rangoon, Moulmein, Tavoy and Mergui; the three latter are all connected by rail or road to Rangoon. In addition to these, the enemy could use the port of Bangkok and two lesser ports in the Gulf of Siam, Koh Sichang and Sattahib, both with adequate communications to Bangkok. From here the vital Burma-Siam railway, which was completed about the beginning of the period under review, could transport supplies to Moulmein, thence across the Salween by ferry to Martaban, rail again to the Sittang River where the bridge was down, once again a ferry, and so to all points of use by rail. Among the measures designed to deny these facilities to the enemy was the laying of a total of 89 mines in the harbours of Rangoon, Moulmein, Tavoy and Mergui, and, further afield, at Bangkok and the Gulf of Siam ports. Though the number of mines laid was not large, the results exceeded expectations. Moreover, it must be remembered that the effort involved was considerable, sometimes necessitating flights of 2,300 miles. The enemy's lack of efficient minesweeping equipment caused much delay in the clearance of harbours, and intelligence reports show that considerable dislocation and damage was caused to shipping.

60. Attacks against rail communications accounted for almost 25 per cent. of all operations. Destruction of the larger installations was allotted to the heavy bombers, with particular emphasis on Rangoon, Bangkok and Mandalay. Wellingtons operating by night were directed mainly against railway centres. The Mitchells' (B.25) performance and characteristics made them particularly suitable for railway sweeps and the destruction of bridges. In this connection, the spiked bombs that came into use in March proved invaluable and were used to tear up stretches of the permanent way at intervals over many miles of track. Bridges of strategic importance were attacked continuously and attacks were repeated each time the enemy completed repair work. An excellent example of this was the Sittang Bridge at Mokpalin. Destroyed during the evacuation from Burma, the bridge was repaired after long and arduous work by the enemy. The progress of the work was carefully followed by reconnaissance, and as soon as it was completed the bridge was wrecked once more in a single operation. It has not been repaired since this attack.

61. The overall strategy of rendering each part of the railway system ineffective was exemplified in the spirited low-level attack on the Burma-Siam railway by American Liberators (B.24), the series of attacks on marshalling yards at Bangkok and Moulmein, and the mining of the ferry crossings at Martaban and Mokpalin. At shorter range, the railway from Rangoon to Myitkyina was subject to continuous attacks, with the result that throughout its length there was always one bridge or more out of action. Amongst these bridges which were put out of action were the Mu River, Myittha, Meza, Kyungon, Zawchaung, Budalin, Songon, Natmauk, Tantabin, Swa, Tangon, Ye-u, Sinthe, Pyu, Bawgyo, Pyawbwe, Myingatha, Natkyigon, Daga and Myothit. Whenever intelligence indicated that enemy troops or supplies were moving in quantity, sweeps were undertaken along the stretches of track approaching the battle fronts.

62. Attacks on road facilities and communications began in earnest in April 1944, when the threat to the Imphal Plain assumed serious proportions. One enemy division moving north from the Tiddim area had, as its main line of supply, the motor road leading from Ye-u. Two other divisions attacking from the east across the Chindwin were largely dependent upon the road from Wuntho. Mitchells (B.25) and Wellingtons began on the 18th April an almost daily assault upon these vital arteries and the supplies moving along them. While the former carried out low-level daylight sweeps, the latter took up the rôle of intruders by night, replacing Beaufighters which Third Tactical Air Force considered could not be usefully or economically employed on moonless nights. The sum of these attacks, other aspects of which I have described elsewhere in this Despatch, contributed greatly to the constant shortage and slow transit of men and supplies which dogged the enemy throughout his offensive.

63. The effort by strategic bombers to neutralise the Japanese Air Force was directed primarily to the destruction of airfield installations and supplies. At the beginning of February a large-scale operation by night was undertaken against the Heho group of airfields in conjunction with Beaufighters, who were to follow up the attack at dawn. From the Strategic Air Force point of view, the operation was highly successful, photographs revealing many bomb patterns in vulnerable areas. The Beaufighter attacks were hampered, however, by early morning mist.

64. Of industrial targets, oil installations were one of the primary objectives. A concentrated bombing programme was carried out against facilities at Yenangyaung in which American daylight bombers demonstrated their accuracy to such an extent that twice Beaufighters operating in the area the following night reported large fires still burning. In late 1943 this plant was producing 600 barrels of crude oil daily, from which were extracted 5,000 gallons of petrol. By May, 1944, the daily processed yield had been reduced to 1,680 gallons. Installations at Chauk, Lanywa, and Thilawa were dealt with in a like fashion. Attacks against other industrial areas were reserved for the few large towns where targets

of a reasonable size presented themselves, notably Rangoon, Moulmein, Bassein, Insein and Prome. The Aircraft Factory and Arsenal at Bangkok received many hits from the 106 tons of bombs aimed at it. When considering the relative lightness of the attack, allowance must be made for the distance involved, which is equivalent to a return flight from London to Tunis.

65. While I had not originally planned to use strategic bombers in close support of ground troops, the Commanders on all three sectors of the front requested their help and were accorded it. I have dealt with these operations in more detail in the section devoted to Army Support, where it will be seen that the greater proportion were in direct support of IV Corps in front of Imphal. Wellingtons were initially employed on this task by daylight, with fighter escort, since the Mitchells (B.25) could more usefully be employed on sweeps along the various Lines of Communication. Subsequently, when Wellington crews had to be withdrawn for air supply duties, the Liberators (B.24) were used in a similar daylight rôle. This method of employment of strategic bombers was all the more acceptable to me since monsoon conditions made night bombing wellnigh impossible. The frequency of these attacks increased, and by the end of May No. 231 Group alone had been able to achieve the creditable total of 646 short tons of bombs dropped on Army Support targets.

66. The above duties of Strategic Air Force involved the dropping, from January onwards, of 6,741 short tons of bombs, of which R.A.F. and U.S.A.A.F. dropped almost equal proportions. The distribution of this effort was as follows:

	Per cent.
Military installations, dumps, etc.	54.7
Railroad communications	22.6
Airfields and landing grounds	10.2
Bridges	5.5
Shipping	3.5
Jettisoned	3.5

67. The Strategic Air Force carried out one more duty during the period, the reinforcement with crews and aircraft of the transport squadrons maintaining the life-line to forces cut off on the Imphal Plain. On 19th May forty Wellington crews were attached to Troop Carrier Command to help the over-worked crews there, and five aircraft and crews were detailed to carry 250-lb. bombs to the tactical squadrons operating at high pressure in the Imphal Plain. Despite bad weather, 544 bombs were delivered by 31st May. In the same period, No. 490 U.S. (Mitchell) Squadron delivered 380 tons of ammunition to the forces defending Imphal. The offensive power which these loads represented contributed to the eventual breaking of the Japanese offensive and enabled the normal transport aircraft to concentrate on delivering other supplies of which the Army was in urgent need.

* * * * *

IV.—SUPPORT OF GROUND FORCES

68. Operations on land were renewed and maintained on a large scale during this period, so that there were greatly increased opportunities for giving support to our land forces. The fact that we possessed and held air superiority enabled full advantage to be taken of these opportunities, and throughout the big battles—first in Arakan and then in Manipur and around Myitkyina—ground support reached dimensions which absorbed a large part of the total effort.

69. The successful provision of direct support to our armies in this theatre is faced by two great difficulties. The first of these is the nature of the terrain over which the fighting was taking place. Much of it is close, densely wooded, or covered with thick undergrowth, so that the recognition of targets presents a problem to even the most experienced crews. The second is the nature and characteristics of the enemy as a fighter on the ground. Three things distinguish him: his tenacity and stamina, which enable him to take great punishment from the air and still retain his fighting spirit; his skill in camouflaging his positions and dumps, which makes it very difficult to locate them from the air or the ground; and his beaver-like propensity for digging himself into the ground by excavations that range from a number of shallow foxholes to hold one or two men to an elaborate system of bunkers unharmed by all but direct hits from heavy bombs. By virtue indeed of the nature of each, the terrain and the enemy are strikingly suited to each other.

70. The difficult nature of the terrain and the enemy's complementary skill in camouflage were overcome, to a great extent, by the intimate knowledge that aircrews came to have of the country over which they were operating. Another aid to target recognition was the use of artillery or mortar smoke shells. The enemy, however, on several occasions put down diversionary smoke to mislead our aircraft. One remedy to this ruse is the employment of coloured smoke which has recently arrived in the theatre.

71. The enemy's capacity for absorbing punishment from the air without losing his will to continue fighting was countered by the application to his positions of a fire-power or a bomb-load of such a magnitude as would seem in a European theatre to be out of all proportion to the objects it was hoped to achieve, having regard to the forces available.

72. Such a concentration of bombs over any area held by the enemy also helped in finding an answer to the gift of the enemy for camouflage and to the fact that the terrain lends itself to concealment. An area was often found to contain more bunkers than even the most careful and thorough reconnaissance had disclosed. If these attacks were confined to pinpoint bombing of those bunkers whose existence was known, then when the bombing ceased and ground troops followed up, other enemy positions were found untouched by the bombardment. For instance, at Kyaukchaw, attacked on 17th January by heavy bombers, it was thought even after bombing had taken place that there were only three bunkers, whereas there were actually eight. Only complete saturation of an area can ensure a chance of all bunkers being hit or the troops in them being at least held down.

73. The problem presented by the strength and depth of many of the enemy's bunker positions was never properly solved. The

bombs carried by light bombers and fighter-bombers did little damage unless they made direct hits, and the use of medium and heavy bombers for the task was of necessity restricted. Moreover, when heavy attacks were carried out with the help of the Strategic Air Force no really decisive success was achieved, and as yet the Army has not been able to make an effective assault in conjunction with these attacks. What advantage medium and heavy bombers have in the weight of their blow is offset by their greater margin of bombing error, which makes it necessary to allow a safety margin and so forces troops to start their assault at a greater distance from their objective than is the case with light bombers and fighter-bombers. A good example of the difficulty of co-operation between heavy bombers and ground forces is given in the operation at Razabil, which is described later. Of such attacks, the Air Commander, Third Tactical Air Force, noted in his report for this period: "The Army have not yet been able to carry out an effective assault in conjunction with these attacks.... However, the accession of Mitchells in a forward location and under Third Tactical Air Force is expected to be a very considerable help in enabling us to put an adequate and timely weight of attack on ... strongpoints".

74. Another way in which such bombing assisted ground forces was in disclosing the enemy's positions by clearing thick undergrowth from around them. This tactic was of great assistance to our artillery and tanks, but was inclined to be a double-edged weapon in the opinion of the infantry, since not only was the enemy exposed to view, but their own line of advance was also stripped of cover so that they were forced to attack either at night or by a flanking movement.

75. The technique of air attack was determined by the nature of the terrain in which the target lay. Where thick jungle made approach necessary at a height sufficient to locate the target by reference to its surroundings, then dive or shallow-dive-bombing was used. When the location of targets, as for instance on the lines of communication, was not so difficult, then low-level attacks could be carried out. Dive-bombers therefore and fighter-bombers were used principally against pin-points and specified areas, the ground attack fighters against concentrations of troops and supply dumps immediately to the rear.

76. The results of attacks made in ground support could not always be observed from the air, but an analysis of the reports of Army units that followed up the attacks or watched them as they took place, testifies to their effectiveness in terms of men and animals killed and positions weakened, if not destroyed. Although great destruction of life was not necessarily the primary object of these attacks and was not always achieved, the Army was unanimous in its belief that the air support given helped it to advance when the initiative was ours and to hold out and later counter-attack when the enemy were attacking. Army formations repeatedly expressed their thanks to the air force units that had helped them, and further tribute to the effectiveness of this support is to be found in many reports. One of these may be quoted as being typical of many others: "10th May air strike on Japanese in Lynch position (near Tengnoupal) reported by forward troops to be most successful. Bunkers were seen to be blown in and bodies flying about". This was the work of twelve aircraft of No. 42 Squadron.

77. A more intangible result of direct support was the effect that it had on the morale of our troops. It was the opinion, for instance, of the Commander of the garrison at Kohima in April, that the audible and visible evidence of the arrival of air support on the two critical days, the 15th and 18th April, put new heart into his men towards the end of the siege. The obverse side of the picture is given by prisoners of war who bore complete witness to the effectiveness of our bombing and machine gunning.

* * * * *

78. In November and December, squadrons gave the limited scale of support called for by Fourteenth Army, which was then occupied in regrouping for forthcoming operations.

79. In the 4 Corps area the enemy advanced into the Chin Hills and occupied the line Fort White—Falam—Haka. They were held south of Tiddim, and both sides spent the rest of the year consolidating their positions. During this phase Nos. 45 and 110 Vengeance Squadrons did good work in direct support and in destroying supply dumps particularly around the area of Milestone 52 on the Tiddim—Kalemyo road.

80. During the same period in the Arakan, 15 Corps was also regrouping in preparation for an advance, and many attacks were made on enemy positions in order to inflict casualties and disperse enemy troops. Among the targets successfully attacked were the Headquarters of the Japanese 55th Division at Rathedaung.

81. In January the rate of effort increased to support the several intended thrusts forward. 4 Corps took the offensive during this month, and on the 25th occupied Kyaukchaw in the Atwin Yomas, an enemy fortress that blocked their line of advance from Tamu to Yuwa on the Chindwin. From the air point of view this was the most interesting operation of the month, since the first ground assault was preceded by an air attack in which aircraft of both the Strategic and Tactical Air Forces took part. Eighteen U.S. Liberators (B.24) and nine Mitchells (B.25) escorted by R.A.F. fighters, dropped thirty-five tons of bombs including depth-charges; twenty-four Vengeances and twelve Hurricanes dropped eighteen tons. The bombing was accurate and the whole area of jungle and undergrowth was covered. On the other hand there were no direct hits on bunker positions, and the near misses did little damage to personnel or to positions. The attack took place at 16.30 hours in the afternoon, but the Army did not advance until 08.30 hours the next morning, by which time the effect of the bombing had mainly worn off. The unintended result of the operation, therefore, was that the Army's advance was made more difficult by the lack of cover where blast had laid the undergrowth flat.

82. Meanwhile in Arakan, 15 Corps had begun to move forward shortly before Christmas towards the line Indin—Kyauktaw. At the beginning of January, Maungdaw was taken and the approach towards the Maungdaw—Buthidaung road was continued till the

end of the month. The major part of the available direct support effort was now being expended on this front, and our advances at Buthidaung and Maungdaw were both preceded by intensive dive-bombing of enemy strongpoints. More than once the two Vengeance squadrons, Nos. 82 and 8 I.A.F., mounted nearly fifty sorties between them in a day. In the Arakan too this month, the Strategic Air Force took part in direct support bombing to clear a salient in anticipation of the general advance. The target was a position near Razabil, another enemy fortress, three miles east of Maungdaw. The attack was carried out by sixteen American Liberators (B.24) and ten Mitchells (B.25), with an escort of R.A.F. Spitfires and Hurricanes, preceded by twenty-four R.A.F. and I.A.F. Vengeances which indicated the target. The majority of the bombs fell in the area, one 2,000-lb. bomb obliterating the top of a small hill containing enemy positions, but again there was an appreciable time lag before the Army moved to the assault, and the enemy appeared to have suffered no appreciable or lasting damage from the bombardment. The area of attack was 1,000 by 600 yards and the bomb load 145,250 pounds. The target area was too large for the weight of the bombardment, and it is clear that, to be really effective, future attacks will have to be more concentrated.

83. Early in February, the enemy, anticipating our intended offensive by four days, himself attacked in the Arakan. His plan was to separate 5 and 7 Indian Divisions, cut off their overland communications, and then destroy them in detail. 224 Group, therefore, instead of assisting this offensive, found itself involved in a very grim defensive battle. The enemy's move to outflank 7 Indian Division reached as far as Taung Bazaar, harried the whole time by the two Vengeance squadrons. Although there was some difficulty in finding targets in the battle areas, every opportunity was taken to attack reported concentrations, bunkers and lines of communication. Over 600 Vengeance and 800 Hurricane sorties were directed to this end during the month.

84. At the height of the battle, additional weight was lent to the support given the ground troops by the employment of Wellingtons, carrying 4,000-lb. bombs, from Nos. 99 and 215 Squadrons in a tactical rôle. Targets included enemy headquarters at Godusara and Rathedaung, and enemy-held villages were reported completely devastated. In addition one operation with R.A.F. fighter escort was carried out, with excellent results, by nine Mitchells (B.25) of No. 490 U.S. Squadron against the entrances to the tunnels on the Maungdaw-Buthidaung road.

85. By the 4th March the battle in Arakan had been brought to a successful conclusion. There is little doubt that our overall air supremacy was largely responsible for this, since it enabled transport aircraft to drop food and ammunition to 7 Indian Division, which could not otherwise have maintained the fight, the Strategic Air Force to lend its weight against tactical targets, and the close-support squadrons to break up many attacks, to maintain a constant harassing of the enemy's line of communication, and to pin him down in his bunkers while our own troops moved in deployment or attack. Air Commander, Third Tactical Air Force, commenting on operations in this area, says "It is interesting to note that in 15 Corps support was allied with artillery rather more than infantry H.Q. This was considered by the Corps to be more satisfactory in that gunners are more used to thinking in terms of supporting fire. . . ."

86. In the first few days of March the enemy launched an offensive across the Chindwin on the 4 Corps front. This was not unexpected. During February he had shown increased activity on the east bank of the river, and attacks had been made by Vengeances and fighter-bombers on enemy storage areas along the river as far north as the Uyu river and upon small vessels and concentrations of rafts on the Chindwin. The battle in Arakan had precluded any large reinforcement of the Imphal Plain, although during the preparations for operation "Thursday" it became evident that the enemy's preparations threatened Imphal and the Assam railway. It was indeed a question which only events would resolve, whether the fly-in or the enemy's offensive would start first. As it happened, although the first enemy units crossed the Chindwin on the night of the 7/8th March, the fly-in was begun on the 5/6th, in sufficient time to release important air resources for dealing with the new situation. Had the reverse been the case, the demands of defence and counter-attack against the enemy's thrust and of support for the fly-in could not both have been fully met. The brunt of air support was now switched from the 15 Corps to the 4 Corps front.

87. The Army's intention was, in the event of Long Range Penetration Brigades creating a favourable situation, to push forces across the Chindwin. To give air support to these forces airfields had been developed in forward areas, including one as far forward as Tamu. Now, however, instead of fighting in support of an offensive, direct support squadrons again found themselves taking part in a defensive battle, and Tamu itself was overrun.

88. Having crossed the Chindwin the enemy pushed onwards towards Imphal by the Tamu and Tiddim roads, and towards Kohima through the Somra hill tracts and from Homalin via Ukhrul. Air support to meet the threat was provided to the maximum from the resources available, the two Vengeance squadrons already on this front being joined by No. 82 Squadron from the Arakan and, towards the end of the month, by No. 7 I.A.F. Squadron. There was also at this time a welcome increase in the number of Hurricane squadrons equipped to carry bombs. No. 42 Squadron had been so equipped since January, No. 34 since the end of February; now, at the end of March, No. 60 and No. 113 Squadrons, too, began to carry out bombing operations.

89. In April Kohima was seriously threatened as well as Imphal, and support was consequently divided between 4 and 33 Corps, although till May the greater part of the effort was centred around Imphal. The four Hurricane fighter-bomber squadrons flew over 2,200 sorties, the majority of which were in the Churachandpur area, on the Imphal-Tiddim road, against the road block set up at Kangla-tongbi on the Imphal-Kohima road, against concentrations of enemy troops attempting to

open the Tamu-Palel road westwards, and against 31 Division which was operating against Kohima. The four Vengeance squadrons flew over 2,000 sorties during this month. Their bombing was extremely accurate, and in addition to direct support tasks they attacked enemy dumps and camps. On the 8th April No. 82 Squadron carried out its last operations on this front and then rejoined No. 224 Group. Over 750 sorties were flown by Hurricanes in offensive sorties against fleeting targets and troop positions.

90. In May, direct support operations centred around Kohima, where the town itself and the Aradura Spur to the south were eventually cleared of the enemy after intensive attacks by Vengeances and Hurricane fighter-bombers against bunker positions and slit trenches. To the south of Imphal, where the enemy made several attacks on the Tiddim road from the west and also on Bishenpur, fighter-bombers and ground-attack fighters attacked concentrations of enemy troops and vehicles. Further south on the Tiddim road, Moirang was also attacked by fighter-bombers and Vengeances. During this month Vengeances flew over 1,000 sorties on the 4 and 33 Corps fronts and Hurricane fighter-bombers 1,693.

91. In this battle the Strategic Air Force again assisted with its heavier striking power. In May the Wellingtons of Nos. 99 and 215 Squadrons flew 125 sorties against tactical targets, American Liberators (B.24) 12, and Mitchells (B. 25) 106. Apart from one attack on the Mintha-Tamu road, the whole of this effort was made against targets on the Imphal-Tiddim road, especially in the neighbourhood of milestones 120 and 87, two points of great tactical importance in preventing enemy reinforcements from coming up the road. Attacks against enemy strongholds included one against the village of Ningthoukhong, which was accurately bombed by forty-eight Wellingtons and Mitchells (B.25) on the 9th May. Once again, however, the enemy withstood the effects of the bombardment and was able to repulse the subsequent assault by ground troops.

92. The enemy's efforts to deploy in the Imphal Plain during the month were decisively defeated by the Hurricanes and Vengeances which attacked at extremely short intervals any concentrations in the foothills reported by ground troops through the Army Air Support Control operating at a high standard of efficiency. By the end of the month, Fourteenth Army were going over to the offensive and it was possible to predict that the threat to Imphal had been averted. Constant attacks on the tracks through the jungle which served as his Lines of Communication had prevented the enemy bringing his full potential strength up to the perimeter of the plain, and the effectiveness of air attack in thick jungle had impressed on him the futility of advancing over open country without overwhelming forces. The attacker was becoming the attacked; the period of attrition and defence was over, and the squadrons supporting 4 and 33 Corps could look forward to the prize for which all air forces hope—the annihilation of an enemy in retreat.

93. Positive results in the form of men killed, storage areas devastated, and transport destroyed are hard to achieve against an enemy with such a high standard of camouflage and concealment who, when on the offensive, moves in small groups with little impedimenta. No army can maintain its standard of camouflage in retreat, however, and as this despatch is being written, the air forces in this theatre are proving again what has been and is being demonstrated in every other theatre of war, that an enemy experiencing overwhelming pressure from advancing ground forces provides the best targets for air attack. The experience gained by Army Commanders, who have come to realise the limitations and possibilities of air support during the period of trial, is now paying full dividends, the results of which should form an impressive achievement during the monsoon operations now beginning.

94. During these six and a half months the American squadrons of the Northern Air Sector Force had, as their primary task, the maintenance of the air superiority necessary to guarantee the safety of the air route to China and of the bases of the Air Transport Command. They were also, however, responsible for giving air support to General Stilwell's Chinese-American Forces in their advance down the Ledo Road, which culminated in the assaults on Kamaing, Mogaung, and Myitkyina.

95. By February the ground forces had successfully advanced as far as Maingkwan in the Hukawng Valley, and the Mustangs and Kittyhawks comprising the force had given valuable support in the form of attacks against camps, concentrations of troops, M.T. and stores, both in the valley and along the road from Kamaing to Mogaung. The work of ground attack squadrons in sweeps along the flanks of the road was reported by prisoners of war as particularly effective. Liberators (B.24) and Mitchells (B.25) were also used in attacks on this sector of the front, dropping 155 tons of bombs on Kamaing, 93 on Mogaung and 40 on Myitkyina. This support continued when the Hukawng Valley had been left behind, and by the end of the period covered by this despatch Mogaung was being invested by ground forces and the main strip at Myitkyina, taken on 17th May, was in the hands of the N.A.S.F., forming a potential advanced all-weather base.

* * * * * *

V.—ATTACKS ON COMMUNICATIONS

96. The comparative lack in Burma of large static targets suitable for heavy bombers has been offset by the extreme vulnerability of the Japanese lines of communication. No. 27 Squadron, R.A.F., has been operating on Beaufighters against these communications since January, 1943, and No. 177 Squadron, R.A.F., similarly equipped, from September of the same year. As a result of their persistent and ubiquitous attacks, both by day and by night, the enemy has been driven to remove the main weight of his transport from road to river and from river to rail. His major movements have been restricted to the hours of darkness, and for protection during daylight he has been compelled to resort to an ingenious and complex system of camouflage coupled with the establishment of an extensive network of gun posts as a supplement to his more orthodox anti-aircraft defences. The Taungup Pass road, the shipping on the Irrawaddy, the Ye-u and Myitkyina railway lines, as examples, have long

afforded daily targets for Beaufighters and, latterly, Lightnings (P.38) and Mustangs (P.51). In November, 1943, there occurred an event of prime importance as regards the supply problem of the enemy troops in Burma—the opening of the Burma-Siam railway. This did not diminish the importance of the routes of Northern and Western Burma, but it did bring into strategical prominence their relationship to these routes from the south and east. New objectives such as the railway junction at Thanbyuzayat, the ferry termini at Moulmein and Martaban, the bridge over the Sittang river at Mokpalin and in general the railway system north, south and east of the all-important junction at Pegu became of cardinal significance.

97. The armament of the Beaufighters of Nos. 27 and 177 Squadrons, consisting of four 20 mm. cannon and six machine guns, proved very suitable weapons for attacking the rivercraft, motor transport, rolling stock and locomotives on these routes. They first reached Moulmein on 27th February; thereafter they regularly attacked targets as far south and east as the Burma-Siam railway itself, and the terminus of the main Siamese railway to Bangkok at Chiengmai.

98. In January, 1944, a third squadron of Beaufighters (No. 211) began to operate under my command using rocket projectiles (R.Ps.). The enemy had by this time instituted a system of pens and shelters to protect his locomotives, and although a target thus protected was immune from cannon and machine-gun fire, it was often vulnerable to R.P. attacks. Another development rendered the advent of rocket projectiles even more timely. The opening of the Burma-Siam railway now allowed the Japanese to bring replacement engines into Burma by this quick and easy route. Accordingly, the emphasis of attack was moved to the more permanent installations on Burmese and Siamese railway systems, since the destruction or damaging of locomotives was not now so serious to him. In attacks on stations, water-towers, curved portions of the track which could not easily be replaced, and bridges, the rocket projectile proved a valuable supplement to existing weapons.

99. The delay fuse which was all that was available with which to arm R.P.s was soon found to be unsuitable for attacks on bridges, and their destruction was left more and more to bomb-carrying aircraft of both the Strategic and Tactical Air Forces. I have dealt in more detail with this aspect of strategic bombers' work in the section devoted to their activities. In attacks by tactical aircraft the long range of Mustangs (P.51) and Lightnings (P.38) was exploited to the full. The Shweli suspension bridge for example had often been attacked by bombers but its position rendered bombing from any height difficult. Fighter-bomber attack was not possible until the long-range Mustangs (P.51Bs) of No. 1 Air Commando Unit arrived. Immediately after their arrival the bridge was destroyed by them in April and its emergency replacement a fortnight later. Other attacks on communications by Mustangs (P.51) and Lightnings (P.38) included many against the vital Mandalay-Myitkyina railway particularly on the section between Shwebo and Wuntho which fed both the divisions attacking Imphal and the forces opposing Special Force.

100. Although not primarily intended for attack on rivercraft, the 40 mm. cannon, with which the Hurricane IIDs of No. 20 Squadron were fitted, did great damage to hundreds of assorted craft with which the enemy supplied his forces dispersed among the waterways of the Arakan coast. This squadron began to operate in December, 1943, using A.P. shells. In February, H.E. ammunition became available and the rate of destruction increased. Craft when holed could no longer be beached, but disintegrated in the water, with the inevitable instead of occasional loss of their cargo. When, finally, aircraft with additional internal tankage arrived, the effective radius of attack was extended south of Akyab, and the rate of destruction reached a peak which seriously hindered the reinforcement and supply of all Japanese forces occupying the coastal region from Cheduba Island northwards to the front line, a distance of roughly 150 miles.

101. The damage and hindrance that the enemy suffered from these widespread attacks are hard to assess, but one criterion of their effectiveness was the energy with which the Japanese attempted to defend their communications. The statistics show that in 1,276 effective sorties by R.A.F. long-range fighter aircraft, 35 were destroyed by enemy action or did not return from operations, and 29 were seriously damaged by enemy fire, but no statistical summary can adequately record all the damage and delay that the enemy suffered. For example, it was estimated that in April reinforcements travelling from Bangkok to Manipur took six weeks to reach their destination.

* * * * * *

VI.—GENERAL RECONNAISSANCE

Control and Planning.

102. The vast areas of ocean for which aircraft in this Command were responsible in November precluded the density of patrol that was desirable. Moreover, it was difficult to maintain a sufficiently close liaison with those formations responsible for the security of sea communications in neighbouring areas. In December, however, a new directive from the Chiefs of Staff enabled a more clear-cut policy to be introduced and better defined the system of control and responsibility. The boundaries of the Naval C.-in-C.'s Command were extended to include Aden. This facilitated co-operation with coastal aircraft there, which were, in the interests of consistency, to come under my command. I thus became responsible for all flying boats, G.R. landplane and coastal striking force units allotted for operations in the Indian Ocean, the Mozambique Channel, the Gulf of Aden, the Gulf of Oman and the Bay of Bengal. Day-to-day operational and administrative control remained with the A.O.C. in whose command the aircraft were located. Broad control was normally to be exercised through A.O.C. 222 Group, who was to work in close liaison with the appropriate Naval authorities and South African Air authorities. Thus A.O.C. 222 Group had a dual responsibility, combining with the command of his own Group the organisation and direction of all G.R. operations in the Indian Ocean. To aid him in this latter task a new body was formed—Indian Ocean G.R. Operations, or "IOGROPS"—with a Deputy A.O.C. and separate staff.

103. In order to make the best use of the relatively few aircraft available to patrol these areas, a new policy was introduced with the object of making G.R. forces as mobile as possible and to concentrate in areas where submarines were known or suspected to be. In addition, the generous allotment of air escort to convoys in areas where no threat existed was reduced to the minimum, and flying hours were thereby conserved for concentrated action where necessary.

104. C.-in-C. Eastern Fleet is in complete agreement with this policy and co-operates to the fullest extent.

105. The concentrations of aircraft needed to implement the policy and carry out intensive patrols when necessary demand considerable shuttling of aircraft between bases. These movements are used to good effect by routeing the aircraft over shipping lanes so that they may carry out traffic patrols while in transit.

106. One of the first tasks carried out by "IOGROPS" was an investigation of the practical application of the system used in the Atlantic, by which air cover is given to shipping in accordance with the degree of risk and the value of the convoy. By the standards of this procedure—known as "Stipple"—the wastage in flying hours during May was assessed as follows:

		Per cent.
(a) Aden area	... ...	17
(b) East Africa	... ...	59
(c) 225 Group	... ...	55
(d) 222 Group	... ...	$2\frac{1}{2}$

107. Negotiations are now proceeding with C.-in-C. Eastern Fleet to introduce the procedure, modified to suit local conditions, in this Command.

108. Finally, all operations by Indian Ocean General Reconnaissance aircraft are in process of coming under the control of five Naval Air Operations Rooms at Bombay, Vizagapatam, Kilendini, Aden and Colombo. The resultant cohesion over the areas controlled, and closer liaison with the Navy of which these N.A.O.R.s will permit, promise well for future control of coastal aircraft in this theatre.

* * * * *

Operations.

109. A decrease in enemy submarine activity in November permitted a reduction in air escorts and a subsequent saving in aircraft hours.

110. The lull was utilised to carry out a more intensive training programme as a necessary initiation for No. 203 Wellington Squadron, newly arrived at Santa Cruz; and as a refresher for the other squadrons already operational but in need of training to fit them for their more versatile work in the revised policy of mobility and aggression then being introduced. Otherwise, traffic patrols and shipping escorts were the main features of G.R. activity.

111. Survivors of a tanker torpedoed in the Seychelles area were located and rescued as a result of continuous sorties flown from the 28th January to 30th January. One Catalina crew flew for forty-two hours on the 29th-30th and was particularly mentioned in the telegram of congratulation from C.-in-C. Eastern Fleet. The sinking of this tanker was the only one of the month in either 222 or 225 Group areas.

112. December opened with considerable activity and movement of G.R. aircraft in order to protect large shipping movements in the Bay of Bengal. To relieve the congestion on the Bengal communications system, Fourteenth Army were to be reinforced from east coast ports, and extensive patrols were provided to cover the entire eastern approaches to the Bay of Bengal. This involved a large-scale and rapid movement of forces over distances varying from 1,000 to 1,400 miles to concentrate suitable aircraft in strategic positions.

113. Round-the-clock patrols began at first light on the 6th and finished at midday on the 9th as the ships reached Chittagong. The redeployment between Groups, and the conduct of the operation were notable for the high state of efficiency and serviceability maintained. During the operation there was only one sighting of a submarine, thought to be a Japanese of the "I" class. Unfortunately the Catalina was not positioned for an immediate attack and further searches failed to locate the enemy again. Two enemy aircraft were sighted over the Bay of Bengal but were not allowed to come within range of the surface vessels.

114. On the 23rd December the enemy torpedoed the s.s. Peshawar in convoy off the south-east coast of India. The attack was made in perfect weather at midday and while a Catalina was escorting. This was the first example of such an attack while escort was provided. Continuous day and night cover and a hunt to exhaustion was instituted, but apart from a report from the same convoy on the 25th, which caused an extension of the air cover, no other sightings were made.

115. On the 27th, H.M.I.S. BERAR (escort vessel) carried out a submarine attack near the south-west tip of India without any known result. A Catalina of 225 Group witnessed the attacks, and the detailed report and photographs taken by the aircraft's crew were of great value in assessing the results. Further south-west, on the same day, a merchant vessel was torpedoed, and to counter the threat to the many convoys in these waters, Catalinas were moved from Ceylon to Kelai, and Addu Atoll was reinforced.

116. Since commitments in 222 Group were heavy, especially in affording air cover to units of the growing Eastern Fleet, Beauforts were used to escort coastal convoys, and long-range aircraft reserved for the forward island bases and the Australia-Colombo convoys.

117. During this month No. 354 Liberator (B.24) Squadron took over the G.R. patrols previously flown by Wellington medium-bomber squadrons, and extended them to cover the N.E. Bay of Bengal, and the Arakan coastal areas. No sightings of enemy surface or underwater forces were made during these patrols, but this did not detract from their value as negative reconnaissance. Several small craft off the Arakan coast were attacked and sunk with bombs and gunfire.

118. The early part of January was conspicuous for the dearth of enemy activity in southern and eastern waters, in spite of the

increased number of convoy sailings and movements of naval forces. One U-boat was known to be in the Maldives area, and on the 16th another made an attack off Pondicherry, sinking one vessel. A Catalina assisted in the rescue work, but the offensive anti-submarine search which was immediately instituted proved fruitless. What was probably the same submarine was sighted and attacked by a Catalina of No. 240 Squadron returning from a convoy escort on the 22nd. Probable damage was done in spite of the difficult conditions of light and angle of attack, and a hunt to exhaustion was immediately initiated using Catalinas of both 225 and 222 Groups. The enemy was not destroyed, although depth-charges were dropped on a possible sighting, and no further attacks were made on convoys in the area.

119. 225 Group aircraft continued to search for the submarine until after dawn on the 25th, but the 222 Group detachment returned to Ceylon to provide cover for units of Eastern Fleet. Beauforts carried out anti-submarine sweeps in front of Trincomalee harbour, while the Catalinas escorted the arriving ships to port.

120. In spite of defensive air patrols, one independently routed merchant vessel was sunk in the Maldives area, but aircraft again located survivors and guided a cruiser to the spot.

121. Considering the great amount of shipping activity, the month witnessed comparatively few attacks. It is probable, however, that enemy submarines were being employed on reconnaissance, particularly of the growing concentration of naval forces. There is no doubt that the provision of patrols and escorts of the greatest density possible with the forces available was responsible for denying to these enemy reconnaissance submarines much useful information.

122. In February the number of enemy submarines estimated to be in the Indian Ocean rose to ten, and patrol activity was intensified to meet the threat. It became necessary to augment air cover for the threatened areas around Ceylon with Catalinas and Wellingtons from 225 Group. Sinkings were heavy during the month, but one submarine was destroyed by escort vessels with the co-operation of the covering aircraft, and another, after it had sunk H.M.T. KHEDIVE ISMAIL, by H.M. destroyers who were guarding the troopship in such a strength that no air escort was deemed necessary.

123. The sinkings necessitated many rescue operations by aircraft, and the survivors of three ships were located and covered while surface craft were guided to them. The outstanding rescue was that of survivors of a ship torpedoed fourteen days earlier 800 miles from the mainland.

124. The other major operation of the month, which absorbed a considerable number of aircraft hours, was the cover given to a slow-moving floating dock from Bombay to Trincomalee—cover which would probably not have been afforded had the "Stipple" procedure been in force.

125. Towards the end of February there arose a potential threat to the east coast of India from the move of a considerable portion of the Japanese Fleet to Singapore. Plans were laid for the assembly and despatch of air striking forces including all heavy bomber squadrons should the occasion arise. Bases in Southern India and Ceylon were prepared and stocked for the possible advent of large forces from Bengal, and No. 200 (Liberator G.R.) Squadron from West Africa and No. 47 (Torpedo) Beaufighter Squadron from the Mediterranean arrived as reinforcements. No. 27 (Coastal Fighter) Beaufighter Squadron was detached from Bengal to work with No. 47 Squadron at Madras. The threat did not materialise but the organisation built up has been retained in skeleton form.

126. March witnessed a peak of activity which began on the first of the month with a hunt to exhaustion following the sinking of a merchant vessel twenty-five miles south-west of Galle. In the forty-fourth hour of the search a Catalina sighted and attacked a surfaced submarine by moonlight. The enemy U-boat was not seen after the attack, and although it was probably damaged the search was continued for two more days.

127. Further enemy attacks resulted in two sinkings in the Arabian Sea, four in more southerly waters, and one of a troopship in the northern Bay of Bengal, an area hitherto almost completely immune from submarine attacks. There were regrettable delays in reporting the sinking, and thus the assembling of forces to search for the submarine, but the limited number of aircraft available to 173 Wing which controlled the area, eked out by Beaufighters from 224 Group, carried out a modified search until the arrival of reinforcements. The flying effort and quick turn round of the few aircraft available, however, was particularly creditable, one Liberator of No. 354 Squadron being airborne again forty-seven minutes after landing.

128. No. 230 (Sunderland) Squadron arrived in the Command during March, but it did not begin to operate fully until later, since lack of spares kept its serviceability low.

129. In April the number of submarines operating in the Indian Ocean fell to an estimated two. One was believed to be in the Maldives area and the other to be operating on the trade routes between Freemantle and Colombo, out of range of aircraft operating from the Maldives. Beaufort aircraft were thus employed on coastal convoy escort, and long-range aircraft were held at Ceylon in readiness for a threat further afield. No ships were sunk in the waters around India during the month, and the gradual change-over from the defensive to the offensive was symbolised in this month by the successful escort provided to Eastern Fleet in their strike with carrier-borne aircraft against Sabang in North-West Sumatra.

130. In May, Eastern Fleet was again covered during its journey to and from Sourabaya. During the month, it became possible to discontinue the Arakan coast patrols. No sightings of any importance had been made in the six months that the patrols had been carried out, and the continued absence of a threat in this area now allowed of a diversion of these aircraft to more positive work.

131. The loss of Liberators (B.24) engaged on photographic reconnaissance of the Andamans, Nicobars and North Sumatra led

to the investigation of enemy radar by two specially equipped Liberators allotted to my Command. Twenty-six sorties were flown from Ceylon to the Andaman Islands, Car Nicobar, Simalur, and Northern Sumatra. Conclusive evidence was obtained on these flights that the enemy employ in this theatre beam-swept radar of the type found on Attu and Guadalcanal. At the end of April the aircraft were transferred from Ceylon to Bengal in order to operate along the Burma coastline and in the Bangkok area, but the results of their investigations have not been sufficiently conclusive to be included in this despatch.

132. Searches carried out by coastal aircraft during the period assisted in the location and rescue of a total of 535 survivors from torpedoed vessels in the waters around India.

133. The results of coastal activity are seldom tangible, and an account of the work of forces engaged on this work must of necessity draw attention to those occasions when the enemy's positive attacks overcame the efforts of negative reconnaissance. Such attacks in the area patrolled by India and Ceylon-based aircraft did not and could not meet with sufficient reaction to provide a continual deterrent to the enemy's intrusions, nor was the rate of destruction of submarines high enough to prove a serious obstacle to him, since the maximum forces available in India and Ceylon during the period consisted of ten long-range and three medium-range squadrons.

* * * * * *

VII.—PHOTOGRAPHIC RECONNAISSANCE

134. In November it was the intention that No. 681 and 684 P.R. Squadrons should eventually come under the control of Strategic Air Force. To this end No. 171 Wing, which had originally been formed as a Tactical Reconnaissance Wing, was moved from Southern India to take over administrative and operational control. The 9th P.R. Squadron, U.S.A.A.F., was still under the control of 10th U.S. Army Air Force.

135. No really long-range reconnaissance had been carried out by this time, since No. 684 Squadron had only recently received Mosquitoes, and there had not been time to explore the potentialities of this aircraft under tropical conditions. The radius of P.R. cover on the 1st December, excluding the Andaman Islands, was only 680 miles. On 15th December the first cover of Bangkok was obtained and provided much valuable information regarding Japanese dispositions and their use of lay-back airfields. Although Bangkok is now a routine target, the sortie was at that time an outstanding achievement, since the range of the Mosquito in this climate was still undetermined.

136. At this time the main rôle of the two squadrons was to provide airfield cover for aircraft counts, to photograph communications and areas indicated by the Army, and to cover potential target areas for attacks in Burma. Twice weekly sorties were flown to Port Blair in the Andamans to secure information on the enemy's anti-shipping activities. In January one of the few Mitchells (B.25) belonging to No. 684 Squadron photographed Mergui on the Tenasserim Coast for the first time, involving a journey of 1,600 miles. Survey photography was also begun during the month to meet a long-felt need for accurate and up-to-date maps of Burma. By the end of May, not only immediate battle areas had been surveyed, but also approximately 57 per cent. of the whole of the country. The remainder of the effort was absorbed in assessing the extent to which communication facilities were being used and the damage inflicted upon them. The record number of eighty airfields were covered in one day, as was the greater part of the Burma railway system, allowing of an accurate aircraft count and a reliable estimate of the engines and rolling-stock in the country. Another valuable result of the large-scale airfield cover was the issue of target mosaics to long-range fighter squadrons, which proved of great assistance, especially when airfields were attacked.

137. Meanwhile, the American P.R. squadron equipped with Lightnings (F.5) was still working independently. This often resulted in duplication of effort, and closer coordination was clearly desirable. Thus on the 1st February, Photographic Reconnaissance Force was formed, incorporating No. 171 Wing Headquarters. This month and March were notable for many sorties to obtain airfield information and to assess the damage to communications by aircraft of Third Tactical Air Force and No. 1 Air Commando Force. Survey work was also carried out, together with regular flights to the Andamans and the vast area bounded by a line joining Kentung, Sittang, Mergui and Koh Si Chang Island (South-East of Bangkok).

138. Small country-craft were now being increasingly used by the enemy, and the waterways of the Arakan and Central Burma were also frequently photographed to assess the density of traffic and staging points. On 27th March the longest flight yet, of 1,860 miles, was achieved by a Mosquito of No. 684 Squadron when a large stretch of the Bangkok-Singapore railway was covered.

139. In April a substantial increase in the number of Army requests entailed numerous sorties over the battle and reinforcement areas. A Mosquito improved upon the record flight of the previous month by photographing many stretches of railway in the Malay Peninsula, flying 2,172 miles to do so.

140. The advent of the monsoon affected photographic reconnaissance work perhaps more than any. In May, instead of concentrating on the programmes laid down, it became a question of finding areas where the weather was best and photographing the highest priority targets in them.

141. The outstanding achievement of the month was the photography of islands in the Great Nicobar group. The flight was intended to discover if it were possible to reach these islands, but on arrival there was sufficient fuel remaining to take photographs before returning. Short-range squadrons during May obtained routine cover wherever possible and were also instructed to bring back as full a weather report as possible, which proved valuable in planning the next day's sorties. Only three of the twenty-three sorties flown on survey photography were wholly successful. An idea of the achievement in the field of survey photography before the bad weather is shown by the following figures, which represent the

photographing of an area three times the size of England in four and a half months:

Net area covered ... 152,000 square miles (approx.)

Made up of:
6 in. cover ... 134,000 square miles
12 in. cover ... 18,000 square miles

In addition:
12 in. cover of areas photographed on a smaller scale ... 38,000 square miles

142. The foregoing account will give an indication of the great advance in the regularity and extent of the cover obtained. Targets as far away as Rangoon, Bassein and Lashio came to be regarded as routine even by Lightnings (F.5) and Spitfire aircraft, while the ranges achieved by Mosquitoes were little less than phenomenal. A high standard of photography and technical work was maintained.

* * * * *

PART THREE

SURVEY OF RESULTS AND LESSONS LEARNED

143. Although territorial gains in the campaign until the end of May were small, the ground won back from the enemy in Northern Burma marked the first step towards the re-opening of overland communications with China. The advance of the Chinese-American forces, and the disruption of enemy communications by Special Force which aided it, would have been impossible without the air superiority which had been gained, allowing the free use of transport support aircraft and of fighters and bombers in close support. The same is true of both the less positive achievements of the campaign, the breaking of two large-scale enemy offensives—one aimed at Chittagong and the other at Imphal. Of the attack on Imphal, C.-in-C. 11 Army Group stated: "There is absolutely no doubt that had we not had air supply we should have lost the Imphal Plain, and the position on the eastern frontier of India would have been very grave". He might with equal truth have said "Had we not had air superiority".

144. The campaign established that the employment of air transport in this theatre is capable of indefinite expansion, and yields dividends that could not be gained by any other agency. Moreover, there is scope for a wider range of transport aircraft than obtains in Europe, where thick jungle and high mountain barriers do not impede swift communication. Light aircraft which can land in a space too small for Dakotas are able to carry out a multitude of tasks for commanders, and, by eliminating the feeling of isolation brought on when fighting so far from established bases, have a beneficial effect on the morale of the forces engaged.

145. Close support of ground troops in such terrain has proved the value of accurate bomb and gun attacks in a locality where pin-points are few and targets difficult to identify, requiring a thorough knowledge of the sector. Such knowledge is clearly of special significance in this theatre. Air liaison officers when briefing crews can give targets that would often be refused in other theatres as too difficult for identification. The same is true of dropping zones for supply-dropping aircraft. Crews and staff officers from the European theatre of operations state that the dropping points given here would be considered impossible there. Thus, complete familiarity with the area over which they have to operate has been found essential for crews engaged in ground or transport support work.

146. I have discussed the complexities of close support in Burma in the section dealing with that type of operation. Certain conclusions follow that are worthy of note. First, unless used in overwhelming strength, the heavy bomber is no more the answer against an entrenched enemy than has been found in other theatres. Secondly, if air bombardment on a heavy scale is used, the infantry must follow the attack immediately in order that the limited effect on the enemy is not lost before the attack goes in. Thirdly, specialised trials are necessary to determine the best types of bombs for use against jungle targets. These are now being carried out in this Command. Finally, the fighter-bomber and the dive-bomber, with their extreme accuracy, proved excellent aircraft in close support in difficult terrain. The Hurricane, for example, could be employed against targets in valleys hemmed in by cloud, conditions that demanded high manoeuvrability if the target was to be reached at all. Comparable aircraft of higher performance and with the ability to carry a greater weight of bombs should prove an even more decisive weapon.

147. In combating the Japanese Air Force, the lack of long-range fighters was acutely felt until Mustangs (P.51) and Lightnings (P.38) of the U.S.A.A.F. became available. Once our air superiority was established in the forward areas the enemy utilised bases too far away for normal-range aircraft to reach them. I have recounted later how it was that pressurised long-range tanks were not yet ready for the Spitfires, which could not therefore be used in the rôle of long-range counter air offensive. In this theatre, where distances are so great and the enemy so widely dispersed, long-range fighters are essential both for escort and offensive operations.

148. Finally, it has been proved in this theatre as in others that air power is co-equal with land power, and that Army and Air Commanders should work from a Joint Headquarters if they are effectively to implement the principles of command required by a combined Army/Air Plan. It is according to this broad principle, which has been agreed with the General Officer Commanding-in-Chief 11 Army Group and approved by the Supreme Allied Commander, that future air operations in South-East Asia will be conducted.

* * * * *

PART FOUR

EXPANSION AND DEVELOPMENT

I.—ORGANISATION, REINFORCEMENTS AND BASES

149. The remoteness of this theatre of war from centres of control at home, together with the obligation of developing so economically backward a country as India as a supply base, has inevitably led to the assumption by my Headquarters Staff of functions which rightly

belong to an Air Ministry, a Ministry of Aircraft Production, a Ministry of Labour, a Ministry of Economic Warfare, and perhaps even a Board of Trade. Estimated at its lowest, Air Command, South-East Asia, exercises the powers at least of Deputies to such bodies.

150. The formation of South-East Asia Command resulted in extensive developments in organisation, and a whole hierarchy of Headquarters has been called into being. Headquarters, Supreme Allied Commander, South-East Asia, moved from Delhi to Kandy in March, 1944. It was not possible to move my Headquarters to Kandy at this time, as the expansion and development of my Command necessitated maintaining the closest contact with G.H.Q. India, and so it was necessary to form an Advanced Headquarters, A.C.S.E.A., consisting of a Planning and Liaison Staff, to accompany H.Q. S.A.C.S.E.A. in its move to Kandy. Air Headquarters, India, was set up as an autonomous unit to control operations on the North-West Frontier and assume responsibility for the I.A.F., directly responsible under its own A.O.C. to C.-in-C. India. Eastern Air Command was established to co-ordinate air operations on the Burmese frontier. Its Headquarters moved on 15th April to Calcutta in order to maintain closer touch with its subordinate units—the Strategic Air Force, Third Tactical Air Force, Troop Carrier Command and Photographic Reconnaissance Force. Thus administrative control of American units also gravitated to Calcutta, since this remained the responsibility of Major-General G. E. Stratemeyer in his other capacity, that of Commanding-General of the U.S.A.A.F. in the India-Burma Sector of the China-Burma-India Theatre.

151. In December, 1943, three new R.A.F. Groups were formed—Nos. 229 (Transport) Group, 230 (Maintenance) and 231 (Bomber). Within the period covered by this despatch eleven R.A.F. and I.A.F. squadrons were added to my command either by formation or on transfer from another theatre. In addition, a second flight has been added to Nos. 681 and 684 P.R. Squadrons, whilst at the height of the defence of Imphal, No. 216 Transport Squadron was operating under my command on detachment from the Mediterranean. A further eight squadrons were held in back areas for re-equipment, and seven others changed their battle rôle. The conversion programme has been mainly bound up with the further infusion of Mosquitoes and Spitfires into the Command, while Thunderbolts are also arriving, and plans to re-equip the Hurricane squadrons with them have been formulated. The flow of aircraft in support of this modernization has been steady, though the R.A.F. in South-East Asia remains, as far as aircraft types are concerned, at least a year behind other theatres. Parallel to this expansion and re-equipment has been the rationalisation of the areas for which Groups in India are responsible to correspond with the boundaries of Army Commands.

152. The large programme of airfield development has been continued, with the ultimate purpose of providing accommodation for the approved number of squadrons included in my long-term target. Save for certain new sites in the forward areas and in Ceylon, all development has been of existing airfields. Five airfields west of Calcutta have been developed for the U.S.A.A.F. as bases for V.H.B. aircraft. The need for pressing forward our offensive and air transport operations has been responsible for the expansion of a number of airfields in the Fourteenth Army area east of the Brahmaputra. In Ceylon, work has begun on the development of two new airfields at Kankesanturai and Negombo for heavy aircraft, while, for special operations, runway extension and strengthening of taxitracks has been undertaken at China Bay. Work is being started on a plan for reinforcement route development. In this field of development effective use has been made of bituminised hessian—" bithess "—for both runways and apron hardstandings. The serviceability of this experimental material under monsoon conditions is being closely observed.

153. The procedure of implementing works projects was altered slightly in January, 1944, though the difficulties and delays remained as before. In the Fourteenth Army area, priorities awarded to the R.A.F. services have been liable to alteration by Army commanders without any reference being made to the Air Commander concerned, and without any appreciation of the effect of such alterations on the future of the air offensive. Labour and material has been diverted and moved without giving any notification to the R.A.F. authorities concerned; frequently the first intimation that they receive of such action is the complete cessation of work upon some R.A.F. project.

154. The expansion of establishments connected with the formation of new Headquarters units and the preparation of cadres for the reception of future reinforcements has aggravated the manpower shortage. The overall Command deficiency of effective strength against current establishments has throughout the period been approximately 12 per cent.; but although this deficiency may not appear unduly in excess of the global R.A.F. shortage, nevertheless there has been very severe lack of personnel in individual trades. Since reinforcements in the period reached this Command in only negligible quantity, various alternative sources of supply to meet the deficiencies have been tried. An extensive scheme has been inaugurated for remustering British other ranks from lower trade groups into the more severely deficient higher trade groups, but this, besides merely transferring the shortage from one trade to another, has also meant a loss to effective strength of the airmen undergoing conversion training. The recruitment of Indians both as officers and men to fill the vacancies has also offered some solution, but this has continued only at a diminished rate and it has been very difficult to find suitable officer candidates. Further, some months must elapse even after the period of formal training before such reinforcements can be counted on as fully effective. The question of substitution by women has also been given special attention. The W.A.A.F. mission from the Air Ministry led by Air Chief Commandant Dame Trefusis J. Forbes arrived in February. As a result of her investigations discussions have been begun with the Government of India. Meanwhile W.A.C. (I) recruiting for the Air Forces in India has been at a standstill. It may be added that with the

advent of the decentralised system of establishment control introduced at the end of 1943 manning has been placed on an entirely new basis. Personnel are now demanded against ceiling establishment figures as fixed by the Asian Establishments Committee after consultation with my Headquarters.

* * * * * *

II.—MAINTENANCE AND REPAIR

155. I referred in my last despatch to the uphill task confronting the maintenance organisation in this Command. Without actual knowledge of the conditions, however, many of the inherent difficulties cannot be fully appreciated and deserve further emphasis.

156. The low standard of industrialisation in India throws a heavy burden on the shoulders of Service maintenance personnel, who receive none of the assistance from contractors' working parties that is available at home establishments. Even when it is possible to sub-contract work to civilian firms, the quality of the products leaves much to be desired. Secondly, the vast distances involved call for a wide dispersal of existing stocks and make A.O.G. procedure extremely slow. Thirdly, there is a case for stating that it is not sufficiently realised that more manpower is needed per unit of output than in other theatres of war where spares are more readily available, the sickness rate lower, and base repair not rendered so difficult by the distances between depots and the operational areas, with the inevitable deterioration of damaged aircraft in transit. It is in the light of these and similar difficulties that the work of maintenance and repair should be considered.

157. Expansion during the period was directed mainly to preparations for dealing eventually with the load of 156 squadrons envisaged under the Long Term Target for the Command. Additional civilian capacity has been mobilised; one unit—No. 2 Command Maintenance Unit Trichinopoly—is in process of being doubled in size, and three new C.M.U.s have been formed. No. 322 M.U. at Cawnpore is now in operation, constituting the largest service base repair depot in India. When it reaches full capacity it will be able to deal with major repairs to about 55 large aircraft and with the overhaul of nearly 500 engines per month.

158. A comprehensive organisation has been built for holding reserve aircraft at Aircraft Storage Units and Reserve Aircraft Pools so disposed as to cover the whole of India in three zones. The A.S.U.s hold a two-months' reserve, while the R.A.P.s hold a fortnight's reserve of aircraft ready for immediate issue. This organisation has contributed in no small measure to the high rate of serviceability in squadrons, since it is generally possible to replace aircraft within twenty-four hours.

159. Lack of storage accommodation for holding main stocks has been due to poor progress in the erection of new buildings planned long since, and is a most serious problem at the present time, when approximately 30,000 cases of R.A.F. stores have had to be stored in the open.

160. Often in this Command an aircraft which has crashed or force-landed away from an airfield has to be written off because of the fundamental and ineradicable shortcomings of the transport system. Even if a damaged aircraft can be taken to the nearest railway, the journey thence to a repair depot generally causes so much further damage that a machine that was capable of repair is fit only for write-off when it reaches its destination. One remedy, which is having encouraging results, was the formation of an Airborne Salvage Section in November 1943 to fly to the scene of a crash in a specially fitted transport aircraft which can carry spares, tools and engines. On reaching the site, patch repairs are effected and the damaged aircraft nursed to the nearest depot. The Airborne Salvage Section was given one of the first Dakotas it salvaged, and in that aircraft mainplanes of large aircraft and complete Spitfires have been carried. Up to date, the Section has salvaged eighteen aircraft; the possibility of forming further similar sections is under consideration.

161. An example of the shortage of manpower to meet emergencies arose in April when transport operations necessitated the maximum output of Dakotas both from major inspections and repair. By diverting all available resources, the time taken on the floor was progressively reduced until it became half of what it had been at the end of 1943. This rapid turnover was only achieved, however, by concentrating maintenance personnel on Dakotas at every stage of their travel, with a consequent reduction of work on other types. The output of Dakotas from repair rose from two in December to ten in April and eleven in May. The later figures would have been higher still but for the complete lack of certain spares in this Command which had to be demanded from America.

162. Attempts to produce locally jettison tanks exemplify the difficulties and delays experienced in indigenous production. The tanks were requested in October/November 1943 to implement the long-range fighter policy. The most suitable firm for their manufacture was chosen, but found that it could not work to the required limits laid down in the standard Vickers' drawings, and more generous tolerances had to be permitted. In spite of this, one difficulty after another arose, and metal tanks are still not available for issue. I have already indicated the urgency with which they were needed in the Third Tactical Air Force. As an alternative, a plywood tank was developed and successfully flight tested in December 1943. There were, however, the inevitable delays in getting it into production, and they were not actually available for operational use until May.

163. Simple types of equipment more suited to the manufacturing resources of the country have been produced to the fullest extent, and British production thereby relieved of a considerable burden. The monthly output of supply-dropping parachutes increased from 35,000 to 144,000, and it is anticipated that this figure will be increased to 250,000 by the end of the year.

164. Very close liaison has been maintained with the U.S. Air Service Command. There is a free and complete exchange of technical information and liaison officers are established at both Headquarters. At the time when the Dakota position was acute, the Air Service Command released to the R.A.F. one-third of

their total stocks of Dakota spares in the country.

165. Despite the increased operational effort, the serviceability of squadrons has been well maintained. To some extent the higher wastage of aircraft has had to be met from reserve stocks, whilst the number of airframes and engines under or awaiting repair has increased. It is not certain that this back-log will be fully eliminated during the monsoon, because of shortage of personnel in the various trades and the inherent shortcomings of an organisation of rapid growth working with inadequate local resources.

* * * * * *

III.—SIGNALS, COMMUNICATIONS AND RADAR

166. One of the major problems of the Command has always been the provision of efficient communication facilities over long distances. Trunk telephone and telegraph systems give poor and unreliable service, nor can any appreciable improvement be expected until the Indian Posts and Telegraphs Department is reinforced by Military signals units. Meanwhile the construction of long-distance overhead carrier systems is proceeding, although the maintenance problems that will arise when they are complete cannot be solved without additions to personnel. The six Air Formation Signals units within the Command have worked well in view of their deficiency of seven Officers and 270 British Other Ranks on the 1943 target. Indeed, shortage of personnel has been the greatest single limiting factor in the expansion of signals facilities. The situation was further aggravated by the need to supply to Special Force 185 Wireless Operators and Mechanics and eight Officers. These personnel are still with the Division.

167. The formation of Eastern Air Command resulted in a high degree of co-operation and exchange of technical information between American and British forces, particularly in the sphere of radar. Two G.C.I. stations were sited to cover American bases in the Brahmaputra Valley and another was sited at Shinbuiyang in May to provide early warning for the Chinese-American forces advancing down the Hukawng Valley. Further British and American Light Warning sets were also deployed in the area. Another G.C.I. set has been modified in order that it may be carried by air and made available to U.S. forces. New American Light Warning sets have been tested jointly by R.A.F. and U.S.A.A.F. officers. Moreover, with the prospect of Loran stations for the use of A.T.C. aircraft proceeding to and from China being installed, the operational use of this device by the R.A.F. in the Command has come nearer to realisation. Information on Radio Counter Measures has been provided to XXth Bomber Command and to other American units. Finally, all American units in this theatre have adopted the R.A.F. callsign procedure.

168. All signals planning for future operations has been undertaken with mobility as the keynote. Specialist signals vehicles have been produced within the Command and are designed to meet needs peculiar to this theatre. Moreover, static establishments in operational units in the Third Tactical Air Force have been replaced by mobile units with the result that Group and Wing Headquarters will in future be self-contained and fully mobile as regards signals requirements. The formation of No. 5 Base Signals Unit provided the cadre for operational training under field conditions. Personnel thrown up by the substitution of Wireless Observer Units by Indian Mobile Wireless Observer Companies were among the first to use these training facilities. It has thus been possible to establish No. 4 Group Control Centre and 104 Mobile Air Reporting Unit which will replace the existing organisation in the Tactical Air Force of Group Operations Rooms, Filter Rooms, etc. The installation of Radar units in barges has been used to good effect already. In November, the most advanced units were those along the Cox's Bazaar—Ramu Road and the terrain in front of these was unsuitable for more extended siting. As soon as the Army had advanced to Maungdaw, an Air Ministry Experimental Station (A.M.E.S.) was anchored off St. Martin's Island. This station, together with a G.C.I. and Mobile Radar Unit (M.R.U.) sited at Maungdaw, provided most useful cover and assisted in successful interceptions off the Arakan coast. G.C.I. sets have also been installed in a jeep, amphibious jeep and an amphibious DUKW.

169. There has been an overall increase of 30 per cent. in navigational aids since November. The installation of static H.F. D/F* stations is practically completed and the delivery of V.H.F. D/F† equipment permitted a start to be made on its erection at all airfields along the main transport and reinforcement routes within India. An up-to-date map is issued quarterly giving details of all aids to navigation, and the combining of R.A.F. and U.S.A.A.F. facilities has been of great value.

170. Details of the airborne investigations of enemy Radar have been given in Part Two of this Despatch.

171. Signals traffic saw a large increase with the creation of Advanced Headquarters, Air Command, South East Asia, in Ceylon, and of Eastern Air Command, Strategic Air Force, No. 230 and 231 Groups in Bengal. Cypher traffic increased from $11\frac{1}{4}$ to $15\frac{1}{2}$ million groups per month, and a High Speed Automatic W/T channel was installed to handle the increased traffic between Delhi and Colombo arising from the move of the Supreme Allied Commander's Headquarters to Ceylon. To offset the increase rendered inevitable by the creation of many new Headquarters, an airgram service has been started within the Command. That such a step was necessary is an apt comment on the vast distances over which messages have to travel in this theatre.

* * * * *

IV.—FLYING CONTROL

172. Although the value of Flying Control facilities has always been recognised in the Command, development has been hampered by the continued shortage of trained personnel and necessary equipment. An efficient Flying Control organisation has become more and more essential in this theatre where bad weather, a lack of land-line communications, and widely dispersed landing grounds make diversion a

___
* H.F. D/F—High Frequency Direction Finding.
† V.H.F. D/F—Very High Frequency Direction Finding.

complicated task. Moreover, air transport operations into the Imphal Valley could have been intensified but for the low standard of proficiency among the inexperienced controllers on the few airfields available. Within these limitations, however, much has been done, and its value is evidenced by the fact that at the only two airfields in 221 Group which could be provided with proper flying control, there were in February no avoidable accidents among the four squadrons accommodated there.

173. In November there were only thirty trained British Flying Control Officers in the Command. This small body was reinforced by forty resting aircrew and thirty I.A.F. officers. There were forty main airfields along the reinforcement routes and in Ceylon, with no airfield controllers, no trained airmen and very little equipment, among which these personnel were distributed.

174. In anticipation of the arrival of trained controllers from England, plans were made to institute a full Flying Control organisation in the operational areas and along the reinforcement routes by February. Unfortunately the flow from U.K. was stopped in January and the plan could not be implemented. The urgent needs of operational airfields had to be met by stripping other areas below the safety margin and diluting their establishment with too high a proportion of I.A.F. officers. At the end of May deficiencies on current establishments amounted to 150 officers and 100 airfield controllers.

175. One of the most encouraging features of the development is the progress made towards complete integration with the U.S.A.A.F. Liaison has been pursued since September 1943, and in March of this year a joint conference proposed the setting up of one system of Air Traffic Control throughout the Command. A committee was set up to examine the technical problems involved and make recommendations. These included a Joint Flying Control Board which will meet at intervals and, it is hoped, maintain the unanimity achieved by the initial committee. Application was made to U.S.A.A.F. H.Q. to send to the Command officers trained in the joint system now working in U.K.

176. I therefore anticipate that a unified system of Flying Control will soon be operating throughout the Command, and that every crew will receive standard briefing and standard aids on all flights.

* * * * *

V.—ARMAMENT

177. The slow receipt and dissemination of up-to-date information on armament matters, as indeed in all technical branches, has hindered the work of making the best use of weapons and developing the striking power of the Command. New publications take two months to arrive and an even longer period to reprint and distribute. One remedy has been an extensive use of the microgram service to hasten the process of keeping technical personnel informed on all current developments.

178. Operational failures have been reduced in spite of the fact that fighter squadrons do not possess Armament Officers. It has been found that the stoppage rates on squadrons more than twenty miles from their Wing Armament Officer are from 1.5 to 2.5 times those on squadrons less than twenty miles from the wing. In spite of the fact that there are established posts for only ten squadron Armament Officers in the Command, which are naturally allotted to the bomber squadrons, and that there are many establishment vacancies which have not been filled because of the serious shortage of armament officers, .303 gun failures have fallen from 0.11 to 0.08 and 20 mm. from 2.07 to 1.48 per thousand rounds. Bomb failures have similarly fallen from 0.47 to 0.25 per hundred bombs. The measures which contributed to this improvement were a decentralisation of the training and maintenance branches, a better system of check on failures, and careful distribution of available manpower. To aid in this distribution a certain dilution of I.A.F. personnel has been accepted. These have proved suitable and efficient tradesmen at certain tasks and have enabled the following dilution to be effected:

	per cent.
(i) I.A.F. Squadrons	100
(ii) M.U.s	50
(iii) Other non-operational units	25
(iv) Operational R.A.F. Squadrons	25

(provided British Other Ranks are substituted when available.)

179. A number of new weapons have arrived in the Command and come into use, operationally, during the period. Hurricane IID aircraft armed with 40 mm. cannon first operated in No. 20 Squadron in December, 1943. The initial A.P. ammunition was supplemented in February by H.E. which has proved very effective against rivercraft. R.P. has been used by No. 211 Squadron since January. It was at first employed against bridge targets, but the delay fuse was found to be unsatisfactory for this type of attack and no proper facilities were available for modifying it. In view of this, R.P. attacks have been directed against rolling stock, transport convoys, oil installations, factories and rivercraft with good effect. 500 lb. M.C. bombs came into use early in the new year, and in addition to the supply to Bengal, stocks have been built up at selected stations in Southern India and Ceylon should action become necessary against a Japanese Naval Task Force. 2,000 lb. A.P. bombs have been distributed for the same purpose.

180. A 4,000 lb. bomb was dropped on Burma for the first time in November, 1943, against railway targets at Sagaing; its employment since then has been extended both by day and night. Among American weapons which have been introduced since November are parachute fragmentation bombs, 300 lb. spike bombs for use against railway lines, the noses being of indigenous manufacture, and the rocket-gun employed in the same manner as the R.A.F. rocket-projectile.

181. Close liaison between British and American Armament Staffs resulted in much inter-change of information and resources. American aircraft used R.A.F. flares and the R.A.F. used American mines, incendiaries and drift lights.

* * * * *

VI.—Training

182. The re-orientation of the training organisation early in the period allocated responsibility on a geographical basis, and No. 227 Group was no longer regarded primarily as the training group. From January onwards, each group supervised and administered training within its own area.

183. Much of the available resources have been absorbed by the need to convert crews to the latest types of aircraft, since reinforcements arriving in the Command have not been familiarised with these types, and many existing squadrons are re-equipping. The change-over from Vengeances to Mosquitoes, from Wellingtons to Liberators and from Hurricanes to Thunderbolts are the outstanding examples. As a result, it is hoped that there will be five trained Liberator and nine Thunderbolt squadrons by November, and two Mosquito squadrons by October. Wastage replacement crews are trained concurrently and provide a valuable reserve without calling upon outside assistance.

184. Refresher flying training was provided at Poona for 614 aircrew either newly arrived in the Command or returning to operations after a period of rest. Air Gunner Instructor courses, I.A.F. ab initio W/Op. A.G. courses and R.A.F. Pilot Refresher courses have been carried out continuously at Bairagarh in Bhopal where two I.A.F. squadrons (Nos. 3 and 9) also completed armament and gunnery training. The Air Fighting Training Unit gave advanced courses on tactics and gunnery control, through which 71 pilots and 83 gunnery leaders passed, and which were attended by many U.S.A.A.F. personnel. No. 22 Armament Practice Camp carried out six bomber and fighter refresher courses, one of which was attended by No. 459 Squadron U.S.A.A.F. whose results improved markedly during the course. No. 231 Group Navigation School passed 420 aircrew through its courses.

185. I.A.F. G.D. recruiting did not come up to expectations. The following table of output during the period indicates the scale of I.A.F. production and wastage:

From I.T.W.	...	...	224
From E.F.T.S.	...	...	101
From S.F.T.S.	...	...	80
From O.T.U.	...	...	113

186. Ground training was mainly of I.A.F. personnel, of whom 8,049 were admitted to Recruit Training Centres. A fraction over 9,000 I.O.R.s were under training of all kinds at the end of the period. One important task, the training of flight mechanics, was taken over from the Director of Civil Aviation, and as a result the civilian schools were closed or taken over as Schools of Technical Training.

* * * * *

VII.—Internal Air Routes

187. The formation early in December of No. 229 Group of Transport Command enabled me to introduce a stricter supervision of internal transport flying, passenger and freight services, and of the movement of aircraft in India and Ceylon. The need for this had long been apparent but the means had been lacking. One of the more positive results of the decentralisation of control I was able to make was a reduction in the accident rate for the aircraft which came under No. 229 Group's control from 46 per 10,000 in December, 1943, to 13 in May, 1944.

188. The number of aircraft available for internal services continued to be small in comparison with requirements and the distances involved. Since it was necessary to earmark nearly all Dakotas for the replacement of wastages in squadrons operating at pressure on the Eastern frontier, the formation of another transport squadron (the sixth) had to be continually postponed, and the conversion of No. 353 Squadron from Hudsons to Dakotas delayed. This squadron, based on Palam at Delhi, together with the B.O.A.C. and the few aircraft belonging to Indian civil air lines, was all I could make available for the Air Routes. No. 229 Group's task was thus no easy one. In the six months from December to May, Hudson aircraft of No. 353 Squadron flew 7,570 hours on transport work. The age of the Hudsons makes this a creditable figure. It was only achieved by a high standard of maintenance and by using as engine spares such parts from obsolete Mohawks as were available. Six Dakotas were also made available to the squadron in April and May as a detached flight based on Dum Dum. They flew 860 hours in these two months on services between Calcutta, Colombo and Bombay. This flight was given concurrently two Dakotas to maintain a service to China which had formerly been carried out by No. 31 Squadron. Thus this one squadron was operating services extending from Ceylon to Kunming and Calcutta to Bombay.

189. Ferrying and the movement of reinforcing aircraft accounted for an average of over 1,300 aircraft deliveries a month within the Command. These flights were used to the fullest extent to supplement the internal air services. By this means, over 1,060 passengers and 500,000 pounds of freight were flown from Karachi alone.

190. I am glad to say that trunk routes to the United Kingdom have been vastly increased. The weekly R.A.F. Liberator service from Karachi has been doubled and a weekly service by R.A.F. Dakota from Colombo has been started. In May a B.O.A.C. Sunderland began to ply twice weekly from Calcutta. For communications with the Mediterranean there has been since March a B.O.A.C. Ensign service three times a week between Cairo and Calcutta. The establishment of No. 229 Group in my Command, followed by a personal visit of the A.O.C.-in-C. Transport Command and many representatives of his staff has been amongst the happiest auguries for the future that I have to record in this Despatch.

* * * * *

VIII.—R.A.F. Regiment

191. The strength of the R.A.F. Regiment throughout has been insufficient to justify the acceptance of full responsibility for the local defence of Royal Air Force Stations and to meet the threat of infiltration by enemy ground raiding parties to airfields and Radar stations. A remedy was sought in November, 1943, whereby the Army agreed to withdraw all static garrisons from R.A.F. stations in areas remote from enemy action, and to provide them at stations where attack was possible. The R.A.F. was to have made a contribution

192. By December, 1943, R.A.F. Regiment personnel had been organised into units with independent establishments. It was possible to form only five field squadrons, the remaining personnel being organised into A.A. flights armed with light machine-guns, since there were not enough officers nor the requisite equipment to allow larger units to be formed. These units functioned with considerable efficiency and, in addition, station personnel instructors drawn from the Regiment trained in defence a large percentage of all personnel in threatened areas.

193. By January, 1944, Army garrisons west of the Brahmaputra had been withdrawn, but no static garrisons had been provided for the more vulnerable stations in either the 4 or 15 Corps areas. The local defence of these stations depended entirely upon the few R.A.F. Regiment Units and the station personnel. Despite repeated representations, the reduction of the Regiment to nearly half its initial strength was insisted upon by Air Ministry, and in February action to remuster personnel to other trades was initiated. The results were seen when in April the Air Commander, Third Tactical Air Force, was obliged to withdraw a number of operational squadrons from the Imphal Valley. I had no alternative but to direct that further reduction of the Regiment, already down to 3,434 all ranks, should be suspended. My Command Defence Officer was sent to England in May to explain the circumstances and to request, not only that the suspension of the Regiment reduction should be confirmed, but that a force adequate for the task of defending airfields and ancillary stations in the battle areas should be provided.

194. I append a comment by the Air Commander, Third Tactical Air Force, upon the Regiment units under his control:—

"Units of the R.A.F. Regiment have proved themselves of the greatest value in this campaign, of which the insecurity of airfields and warning establishments in forward areas has been a feature. When Radar Stations were established at St. Martin's Island and later in the Maungdaw area, the unusual situation existed of Radar Stations being actually well in advance of the front line and within range of the enemy's guns and night patrols. It says much for the R.A.F. Regiment personnel that the Radar crews enjoyed undisturbed conditions in which to carry on their work under such trying conditions. It has proved to be quite unsound to rely on the Army maintaining troops for local defence in times of crisis when the land situation deteriorates. This is the time when they are really needed by us, but this is the time when they are invariably withdrawn to take part in the land battle".

* * * * *

IX.—AIR SEA RESCUE

195. The Air Sea Rescue organisation in this Command has been based on that of the United Kingdom, with the necessary adaptations for local conditions and the scale of equipment that is available. The responsibility for operations has been delegated to the A.Os.C. of Groups, to whom in turn the Group Controllers of Naval Air Operations Rooms, keeping constant watch, are responsible for initiating such operations.

196. Officers responsible to their respective A.Os.C. for the efficient arrangement of Air Sea Rescue and for keeping squadrons informed of any new developments in methods of search and ancillary equipment have been established in Commands and Groups as follows:—

Eastern Air Command—One Squadron Leader.
Third T.A.F.—One Flight Lieutenant.
No. 225 Group—One Squadron Leader; One Flight Lieutenant.
No. 222 Group—One Squadron Leader.

197. Twelve Warwicks have now after some delay arrived in India and are undergoing major overhaul at Karachi, Allahabad and Jessore. Seven Sea Otters are being off-loaded at Karachi and crews have been detailed to take a conversion course as soon as the aircraft become serviceable. When they are ready for operational flying, these aircraft will join No. 292 Squadron, the Headquarters of which will be at Jessore.

198. Meanwhile searches have been carried out by the four Walruses already in the Command, and by operational aircraft, which, whenever possible, carry the Lindholme Dinghy Gear. Experiments are being made to fit this gear to Liberators.

199. Little progress has been made in the formation of A.S.R. marine craft and Units. This is chiefly due to the slow rate at which launches have been delivered. By July, 1943, there were nine in the Command. Between this date and January 1944 no more arrived, and as a consequence no additional units could be formed. With the improvement, however, in the shipping position, four launches have recently arrived from the United Kingdom and four from the U.S.A. There has also been notification of another seventeen being shipped to this Command.

200. Air Sea Rescue Units have been formed or are now in the process of forming at the following places: Chittagong, Maiakhal Island, Calcutta, Dhamra River, Vizagapatam, Madras, Cochin, Bombay, Karachi, China Bay, Colombo, Galle, Kayts (Jaffna), Jiwani and Jask (Iraq). The craft, however, allocated to most of these units have not yet arrived in the Command, or are still being fitted out and so are not yet operational.

201. The maintenance of these craft has been a difficult problem owing to the limited supply of spares and special tools, to the great distances between operational areas and the overhaul workshops, and to the lack of transport that prevails. The problem has been met by using naval facilities where possible for shipping and engine overhauls and by locating rescue craft by types, so that they are within as easy reach as possible of the workshops capable of doing the overhaul of their respective types of engines.

202. Thirty-seven aircraft in all were searched for. The number of aircrew personnel in these aircraft was 168, of which 102 were saved. An American amphibious Catalina, based on Calcutta, was responsible for two ocean landings and the saving of twenty-one

aircrew, both R.A.F. and U.S.A.A.F., in the Bay of Bengal.

203. The demand made upon the marine craft has on the whole been light, except in the Chittagong area where some lone sorties have been made off enemy-controlled coasts, and where an advanced rendezvous position off Katabdia Island was manned day and night for several months. This position has now been superseded by an advanced base established on Maiakhal Island.

* * * * *

X.—BALLOONS

204. Balloons were flown subject to weather conditions at six sites : at Calcutta for the protection of the docks and Howrah Bridge; at Jamshedpur, defending the vital iron and steel works; at Colombo and Trincomalee to protect harbour installations and naval anchorages; at Chittagong to protect dock facilities and the Janali Hat Bridge; and, since 12th May, at Kharagpur airfield to protect the Very Heavy Bomber base established there.

205. There were no impacts with balloon cables by enemy aircraft, but two by Allied aircraft. During the enemy attack on Calcutta in December, many bombs were dropped in the area occupied by No. 978 Squadron, killing two and wounding ten other ranks. Some equipment was destroyed and buildings damaged, but the efficiency of the unit was unimpaired.

206. Indianisation of Balloon Squadrons has continued and by the beginning of May there were 1,246 I.A F. other ranks compared with 971 B.O.R.s. There are now no surplus R.A.F. Balloon Operators in the Command, and all those rendered redundant by the Indianisation are being absorbed into other trades. When the process is carried further it should be possible to release another 400 to 450 British airmen.

* * * * *

XI.—PHOTOGRAPHY

207. Photographic reconnaissance and survey commitments in India have produced a high quality of photographs, and the speed of reproduction has been good considering the many technical difficulties involved. The construction of mobile photographic processing vehicles is progressing, and a plan to construct two self-sufficient photographic units each comprising eleven vehicles will be begun in the near future.

208. Experiments in night photographic reconnaissance by Ceylon-based Liberators of 160 Squadron are proving satisfactory. Cameras and storage for 28 flashes have been installed in aircraft, together with the means of releasing the flashes at variable intervals to obtain line-overlaps. Other trials have proved the practicability of obtaining stereo pairs at night using two F.24 cameras installed in tandem. Plans to use carrier-borne aircraft for long-range reconnaissance have been implemented to the extent of installing and testing equipment in Hellcat aircraft. Experiments now wait upon the provision of American and British cameras.

209. R.A.F. and U.S.A.A.F. processing and interpretation in Eastern Air Command have been integrated at Photographic Reconnaissance Force Headquarters at Bally Seaplane Base, Calcutta, where British and American staffs work together and have achieved a high degree of co-ordination.

* * * * *

XII.—MEDICAL: WELFARE

210. The health of the Command as a whole shows only a slight improvement compared with the analogous period for the preceding year. The sickness rate for malaria and dysentery, although lower than that for 1943, has since February maintained the seasonal rise; that for venereal disease alone has steadily declined. The rate of invaliding in the Command has risen gradually. In 1943 the incidence was 1.44 per thousand, whilst in 1944 the rate has increased steadily from 2.00 in January to 2.50 per thousand in May; these figures are doubtless connected with the increasing average length of the sojourn spent by personnel in the Command. Malaria has continued to be the most important single cause of lost service days through sickness, and measures have been actively taken in hand further to combat it. A Deputy P.M.O. (Malariology) has been appointed to re-organise the plan for malaria control and to give the necessary technical directions. Action has been initiated to raise, by propaganda and instruction, the standard of personal anti-malaria discipline, and plans have been prepared for forming anti-malaria units. A further step has been the experimental spraying from aircraft of areas where malaria-carrying mosquitoes are known to breed, and a flight of No. 134 Squadron has been detailed for this purpose.

211. It is hoped to increase the liaison with the Army and the U.S.A.A.F., which has hitherto not been as close as desirable. Arrangements are being made to increase hospital accommodation to meet the potential needs of the eighty-five squadrons accepted as the short-term target. Work is now proceeding on the conversion of the buildings of La Martiniere School, Calcutta, to serve as the 500-bedded General Hospital, the first R.A.F. Hospital in the Command, for whose opening sanction was given in April. When open, the existence of this hospital should not only obviate to a very large extent the present necessity for sending R.A.F. casualties in the forward areas to army hospitals, with all the consequent administrative difficulties, but should also put the four R.A.F. Mobile Field Hospitals in a much stronger position with regard to the supply of stores and equipment. They have been frequently overcrowded, and on occasion it has been found that essential equipment for which they had vainly been asking was nevertheless being made available to neighbouring Army hospitals.

212. At the beginning of the year a representative of the R.A.F. Physiological Laboratory, Farnborough, toured the Command and investigated flying conditions, including such matters as oxygen needs, flying clothes, flying rations and length of operational tour. A report on his visit has since been received and action is being taken where necessary.

WELFARE

213. The provision of amenities for airmen has continued to be a pressing and difficult problem. The greater proportion of R.A.F.

personnel live in scattered communities on the eastern marches of India, housed in bamboo huts or tents, often widely dispersed in small groups of less than a hundred, and generally at least a day's journey from the nearest centre of what to them represents civilisation, and perhaps even from the nearest R.A.F. unit. To ameliorate as far as possible the drab and lonely life inevitable under these circumstances, 170 gramophones and 363 wireless sets have been made available during the period and distributed at special rates to units. It is the aim ultimately to provide a wireless set for every hundred men. Special arrangements have also been made for the distribution of books and the supply of sports gear. Correspondence courses which have been made accessible for airmen at a specially low fee have been meeting a heavy demand. Six mobile cinemas have been set up in Bengal to which the average attendance is 15,000 weekly, and touring concert parties have visited many units.

214. No single factor has conduced more to ill-feeling between the airman and the people of the country in which he is living than the uncontrolled operation of the laws of supply and demand at a time when so many men whose standards of self-respect and personal cleanliness are high were arriving, and stocks of tooth-paste, shoe polish and razor blades were short. The rise in the price of such essential goods was aggravated by the fact that there is in India no N.A.A.F.I. to cater for the essential needs of the serviceman, the Government of India preferring to retain the contractor system. Thus the only possible obstacle to the exploitation of the airman by bazaar store-keepers has been a progressively more rigid supervision of local canteen contractors. The problem has been made easier during the last few months by the provision from abroad of large stocks of essential articles which are disseminated through service channels and sold at controlled prices in canteens. The problem is now one of distribution rather than supply and in general it may be said that the airman can buy essential commodities at fair prices in his canteen—though not yet at all times or in all units.

215. Without the services of N.A.A.F.I., the provision of entertainment parties from England proved impossible for a long period. The Government of India have finally been prevailed upon to allow E.N.S.A. parties to perform in this country, and G.H.Q., India, has partly defrayed the cost from excess canteen profits.

216. Other advances which may be mentioned include the improved scales of accommodation and furnishings which have been sanctioned for Hill Depots, and the development of airmen's clubs. The number of beds available for personnel on leave has practically doubled during the past year, and Hill Depots have been made as informal as possible with no parades at all and a minimum of restrictions. In spite of this, approximately 70 per cent. of airmen still prefer to spend their leave in towns. I cannot see any alteration in this proportion until travelling facilities on Indian railways vastly improve, and proceeding to distant leave centres becomes less of an ordeal. The unhealthy nature of most large Indian towns makes this improvement even more desirable.

217. Assistance has been given by my Welfare Staff to 915 airmen in need of advice or undergoing avoidable hardship, in addition to the many cases handled by the welfare officers in subordinate formations. The provision of amenities has continued with grants from the Amenities, Comforts and Entertainments for the Forces Fund, while the Royal Air Force Welfare Grant has been received from 1st April onwards. To deal with the growing scope of welfare duties, six selected airmen have been commissioned in the A. & S.D. (Welfare) Branch and five welfare officers with the rank of Squadron Leader have arrived from the United Kingdom.

XIII.—INDIAN OBSERVER CORPS

218. In November, 1943, the Indian Observer Corps consisted of three control units, six mobile companies in Bengal, static units in four main areas, Calcutta, Chittagong, Vizagapatam and Madras, and fourteen other mobile companies under training. These together with Care & Maintenance companies and training centres made up a total strength of 10,851 personnel. In December it was decided to break down the static organisation and certain Care and Maintenance formations, and form from them seven additional mobile companies. By May, 1944, the number of control units had increased to four, and that of operational mobile companies to seventeen with ten others under training or in process of formation.

219. During the battle in Arakan, four companies were involved, and re-deployment of a number of posts was necessary. Such posts as were forced to retire succeeded in destroying their equipment before retreating. Similarly, when the enemy advanced towards Imphal, nearly 50 posts had to be evacuated or re-deployed. The posts east and south of Imphal naturally lost much equipment, but a high percentage was saved and all abandoned equipment was denied to the enemy. Casualties, too, were light in view of the little or no warning provided, consisting of some six missing and six others wounded.

220. Experience gained during the period led at the end of April to the substitution of Mobile Control Units for the Base and Forward Control Units, with resultant closer supervision and greater flexibility. Ultimately there will be seven of these to control the seventeen companies, and each of the latter will control fifteen observer posts.

R. E. C. PEIRSE,
Air Chief Marshal,
Allied Air Commander-in-Chief.

23rd November, 1944.
Air Command, South East Asia.

LONDON
PRINTED AND PUBLISHED BY HIS MAJESTY'S STATIONERY OFFICE
1951
Price 2s. 0d. net.
PRINTED IN GREAT BRITAIN

S.O. Code No. 65-39173

THIRD SUPPLEMENT TO
The London Gazette
OF FRIDAY, 6th APRIL, 1951
Published by Authority

Registered as a newspaper

THURSDAY, 12 APRIL, 1951

AIR OPERATIONS IN SOUTH EAST ASIA FROM 1st JUNE, 1944, TO THE OCCUPATION OF RANGOON, 2nd MAY, 1945

NOTE.—A set of maps for this despatch is on separate sale at 1s. net. This set of maps also covers the operations described in the other Air and Army despatches of the Burma Campaign from the 16th November, 1943 to 12th September, 1945.

The following despatch was submitted to the Secretary of State for Air on 16th November, 1945, by AIR CHIEF MARSHAL SIR KEITH PARK, K.C.B., K.B.E., M.C., D.F.C., Allied Air Commander-in-Chief, Air Command, South East Asia.

PART ONE.
FOREWORD.

1. This Despatch is a review primarily of air operations in Burma during the last year beginning in June, 1944. During this period a fanatical and over-confident enemy has been driven back from his foothold in India at Imphal over 800 miles, which included the complete rout of the enemy's field army in the open plains of Burma and culminated in the occupation of Rangoon by our forces on 3rd May, 1945.

2. The primary cause was the defeat of the Japanese Army. This achievement has been made possible by air power, which not merely took an intimate share in the ground attack, but also isolated the enemy's forces in the field. Confronted by overwhelming air power, the enemy's air forces withered away, and this same air power helped to undermine the stability of his land forces, so that after their decisive defeat at Imphal, although they made a tenacious stand on a number of occasions, they were no match for our well-equipped field army—well equipped in large measure by the unstinted effort of air supply to provide their daily needs. Though air supply did not and could not supplant all other means which themselves involved a great effort to maintain, without it the campaign could not have been successfully fought. Regardless of weather, climate, and distance, the air supply line was maintained unhindered by enemy air opposition, which had been driven from the skies.

3. The Burma campaign should make its mark in the annals of history as a triumph of air power and air supply and as a feat of endurance of Allied land forces.

COMMAND.

4. In June, 1944, the Allied Air Forces in South East Asia were under the command of Air Chief Marshal Sir Richard Peirse, K.C.B., D.S.O., A.F.C. Upon his relinquishment of the appointment on 26th November, temporary command was assumed by Air Marshal Sir Guy Garrod, K.C.B., O.B.E., M.C., D.F.C., until my arrival on 23rd February, 1945.

The Position in June, 1944.

5. Two events mark the beginning of the period. The major Japanese offensive against Imphal had been blunted and was in process of being broken by means of air supply on a hitherto unprecedented scale to the forces cut off from land communications with their base; and second, the south-west monsoon was reaching its full intensity over the operational areas. It remained to be seen whether air forces could materially influence the land battle in weather which had in preceding years prohibited their effective employment, and whether the enemy defeat in Manipur was to prove the turning-point in South East Asia strategy which would

enable the primary tasks of the Command, the re-opening of the land route to China and the clearance of Burma, to be accomplished.

6. The dry-weather campaign which was drawing to a close had brought few positive results. Only in the north-east had any territorial gains been made, and here General Stilwell's forces had cleared the Hukawng Valley and were in possession of Myitkyina airfield. In the Fourteenth Army sector, Imphal was still invested, though 33 Corps was driving the Japanese from the Kohima-Imphal road, and 4 Corps was attacking the Japanese in the Imphal plain. In Arakan, although one enemy offensive had been frustrated, the Japanese still held the Mayu peninsula and the rice port of Akyab. The other British forces operating on the offensive were the long-range penetration groups of Special Force.

7. The Air Forces, having just completed a period of intensive operations, were envisaging some retrenchment, a "reculer pour mieux sauter". An extensive programme of re-equipment was in train which would convert nine squadrons of Hurricanes to Thunderbolts, the two Wellington squadrons to Liberators, and four squadrons of Vengeances to Mosquitos. The relative sparsity of all-weather airfields in the forward areas entailed a withdrawal of these squadrons to bases in India for their conversion, and the monsoon campaign was undertaken with a total of 17 squadrons out of the line, re-equipping, resting or training. Having regard to the nature of monsoon conditions and of the fighting in progress, the forces remaining in the line were ample, nor indeed could any more be deployed. The net result was that the air component conducting tactical operations that culminated on all three sectors in the capture of springboards for a dry-weather assault, was a moderate, well-balanced force of experienced squadrons, versed in the ready identification of jungle targets and trained in close co-operation with the formations whom they were supporting.

* * * *

Plans for 1944-5 *Operations.*

8. The broad mission of S.E.A.C. was formulated at the Octagon conferences as . . . "the destruction or expulsion of all Japanese forces in Burma at the earliest date. Operations to achieve this object must not however prejudice the security of the existing air supply to China, including the air staging post at Myitkyina and the opening of overland communications with China".

9. The plans that were prepared to this end during the monsoon of 1944 envisaged an elaborate series of airborne assaults that did not appreciate the reliability and self-sufficiency of an army supplied unstintingly from the air. Indeed, had it then been suggested that Rangoon could be reached by an army travelling overland and supplied largely by air, the proposal would not have received serious consideration. The overall strategy can best be judged from the four main plans which were formulated during the 1944 monsoon:—

(i) *Plan "X"* involved an overland advance from the Mogaung-Myitkyina area to Katha and Bhamo, co-ordinated with another advance from Imphal to the Chindwin and an airborne operation in the vicinity of Wuntho. The furthest penetration that was envisaged was the occupation of territory north of a line stretching between Kalewa and Lashio.

(ii) *Plan "Y"* intended to employ airborne troops in the seizure of Kalewa, and a second air landing at the point of debouchment into the Mandalay plain to exploit the confusion that would be caused.

(iii) *Plan "Z"* entailed an airborne assault in strength with all transport aircraft in the theatre immediately north of Rangoon, to capture the city.

(iv) *General Stilwell's plan* was for British forces to press forward towards Shwebo-Mandalay, while N.C.A.C.* profited by the diversion to occupy Bhamo, whence they could mount an airborne operation to capture Lashio.

10. The part that the Air Forces were to play in these operations was given in an Operational Directive in which the order of priorities was interesting, putting as it did close support and transport operations very low in the scale. In the event, a reorientation of tasks took place which gave greater emphasis to the work of close support and air supply. The results of such a shift in the centre of gravity to a machine geared to the classical form of air warfare involved changes in organisation, control, supply and maintenance which are discussed at more length in the appropriate context.

11. Plans "Y" and "Z" were approved in principle by the Chiefs of Staff in July and August, and called "Capital" and "Dracula" respectively. In point of fact, however, operations in Central Burma progressed more quickly than anticipated. Continually outflanked by Allied forces, to whom the manna of air supply gave an unprecedented degree of mobility, and continually harried by our close support aircraft, the enemy was never allowed to consolidate the new positions that he occupied along the line of his retreat. Thus by January, the airborne aspect of "Capital" had been rendered unnecessary, a fact which caused great relief to the Allied Commanders, for it was increasingly evident that the transport aircraft to train for and launch the operation, scheduled for mid-February, would be difficult to find from existing resources.

12. Operation "Dracula" was to be the greatest airborne operation yet conceived, involving a fly-in over a distance of 480 miles by some 900 transport aircraft and 650 gliders. The necessity for retaining these forces in Europe, and their high attrition rate in operations there, precluded their re-deployment in this theatre as planned, and in October "Dracula" was postponed with the prospect of not being mounted until the winter of 1945-46.

13. The emphasis now lay on Central Burma operations. An advance to the Monywa-Mandalay area was considered to be the furthest point that could be reached before the 1945 monsoon. Exploitation further south was not thought to be practicable in view of the difficulties of supply. In the event, the

---

* Northern Combat Area Command.

advances made exceeded all planned expectations. This can be attributed to the following main causes:—

(i) The magnitude of the Japanese defeat at Imphal, which was not realised until much later.

(ii) The virtual elimination of enemy air opposition resulting in complete predominance and liberty of action of our offensive and air transport forces.

(iii) The steady growth of air supply resources and improvements in their organisation.

(iv) The occupation of Akyab and Ramree, which had been decided upon to provide advanced air supply bases. This enabled us to reorient and shorten the supply lines in relation to the advance southward of Fourteenth Army.

14. By February, 1945, the possibilities of a more ambitious plan were becoming evident, and Fourteenth Army and 221 Group submitted a plan for vigorous exploitation of the favourable set of circumstances then obtaining. G.O.C. Fourteenth Army considered that if the enemy elected to stand and fight around Mandalay, there was every hope of destroying the Japanese Army in the open plains of Central Burma, thereby opening the route for a swift advance upon Rangoon by highly mobile columns. The plan aimed at encirclement of the enemy forces on the Mandalay Plain to be completed by air attack on such lines of communication as remained open to him. In conjunction with a direct thrust by 33 Corps towards Mandalay, 4 Corps were to carry out a wide encircling movement directed towards Meiktila which would cut the main line of communication southwards. Meiktila itself was to be secured by a small air transported force who would consolidate our position athwart this vital route.

15. This bold plan was highly successful, and as a result the Japanese Army in Burma suffered heavy casualties in a costly and bloody killing match to which the Air Forces contributed in large measure. Notwithstanding its success, the battle of extermination took longer than had been contemplated, and the time-table for the dash to Rangoon by 4 Corps was in jeopardy. The prospect of a race against a reduced time limit caused considerable anxiety in the mind of C.-in-C. Allied Land Forces, South East Asia (A.L.F.S.E.A.). In his opinion the overland advance by highly mobile forces might not have the necessary impetus to overcome opposition en route, together with the final opposition estimated from the defenders of Rangoon, reinforced by the remnants of field formations extricated from Central Burma. Upon his urgent recommendations, the capture of Rangoon before the monsoon was made more certain by the mounting of a modified " Dracula " by sea and air.

16. To carry out this operation, it would be necessary to utilise forces which were earmarked to seize concurrently with the capture of Rangoon a springboard on the Malay Peninsula. In the event, this modified " Dracula " proved to have been unnecessary, as the following pages will show. Nevertheless the capture of Rangoon entailed such a large expenditure of effort and resources that planning has had to be conducted since then on the premise that large-scale refitting, redeployment and marshalling of forces is necessary before the next step is undertaken. The occupation of Rangoon therefore constitutes a milestone in the history of South East Asia, marking the end of a well-defined period.

* * * *

PART TWO.

THE OPERATIONAL BACKGROUND, JUNE, 1944—MAY, 1945.

17. When, on 22nd June, 1944, an overland junction was effected on the Imphal-Kohima road between the garrison of the Imphal plain and the relieving ground forces which had advanced from the north, a major crisis had been resolved, and our land forces, despite the monsoon, were able gradually to turn more and more both tactically and strategically to the offensive.

18. The Fourteenth Army, with its headquarters beside those of the Third Tactical Air Force at Comilla, controlled the Allied units on the southern two-thirds of the front. On its coastal section, 15 Corps held the port of Maungdaw and a monsoon line along the Maungdaw-Buthidaung road; its left flank was thinly covered by the Lushai Brigade which operated in guerilla fashion over the desolate hill country as far north as Haka and the valley of the Manipur River. In the Imphal Valley, although 4 Corps had linked up with 33 Corps advancing from Assam, the Japanese were still holding tenaciously to their positions among the hills east of Palel overlooking the plain; further to the north-east, however, the position was more favourable, and elements of 33 Corps were pressing forward towards Ukhrul.

19. Beyond the operational area of the Fourteenth Army, Special Force, which had been boldly launched into the heart of enemy held territory in March, was fighting both the weather and the enemy in the general area of the railway corridor east and south-east of Lake Indawgyi. It was controlled by the Northern Combat Area Command under General Stilwell, and had effected a junction with the Chinese and American forces now investing the Japanese garrison of Myitkyina, where the main airfield had passed into their hands. Further still to the north-east, a Chinese army based on Yunnan was fighting in the upper Salween valley.

20. The front remained static, during the period of the monsoon, only in the coastal area. On the Imphal sector, 33 Corps—which took over from 4 Corps when the latter was withdrawn from the line for four months—remained on the offensive. In the course of July the enemy was finally driven by combined air and ground bombardment from his tenaciously held positions on the perimeter of the Imphal plain, and with the capture of Tamu in early August the Allied forces had re-established a foothold in the Kabaw Valley and were ready to push southwards towards Yazagyo and Kalemyo and eastwards to the Chindwin.

21. On the right flank, a series of Japanese delaying positions on what was euphemistically called the Tiddim Road, was overcome during

August and September, the "Hurribomber" again proving itself a most effective weapon for close support in jungle country, as the wreckage along the Tiddim Road testified. Tiddim itself fell on 18th October, and the way was now open for a double thrust towards Kalemyo from the west and north. Japanese resistance in the Kennedy Peak area, albeit grim, proved no match for the experienced Allied troops and the accompanying air bombardment, and Kalemyo fell on 15th November. With the capture of Kalewa on 2nd December the chapter of mountain warfare was closed and the Fourteenth Army was ready to debouch upon the plains of Central Burma.

22. Comparable progress had also been made in the Northern Combat Area Command sector, where the enemy garrison at Myitkyina had been reduced early in August. In the railway corridor, 36 Division, which had replaced Special Force, made steady progress; it captured Hopin on 7th September and by 10th December had reached the junction at Indaw. A drive southwards from Myitkyina carried Chinese units to Bhamo at approximately the same time. Thus by the end of the monsoon period the forces of the Northern Combat Area Command were in a position seriously to threaten the right flank of the enemy elements facing the Fourteenth Army.

23. Before the opening of the campaigning season proper, a certain number of changes had been made in the organisation of the ground forces facing the Japanese in Burma. Since with the converging advances of both the Fourteenth Army and the Northern Combat Area Command the opening of a continuous front in Central Burma seemed probable in the near future, Lieut.-General Sir Oliver Leese, Bart., K.C.B., C.B.E., D.S.O., was allotted command of all the Allied Land Forces in Burma. This Headquarters absorbed that of 11 Army Corps, and was set up at Barrackpore outside Calcutta, while an off-shoot was maintained at Kandy. 15 Corps, operating in Arakan, was removed from the control of Fourteenth Army and placed directly under his command—a step which enabled Headquarters, Fourteenth Army, to move forward and establish itself beside 221 Group on the Imphal plain. With the return of 4 Corps to the field in early November it thus retained command of two army corps, for 33 Corps remained in control of the operations developing against Kalemyo. Such was the general organisation of the ground forces when the new campaign fairly opened in November, 1944.

24. In the coastal sector, 15 Corps had begun the preliminaries to its offensive at an early hour and before the end of October, 81 (West African) Division, supplied entirely by air, had crossed into the Kaladan valley from its monsoon quarters at Chiringa and was beginning to advance southwards against some opposition. The main offensive was opened west of the Mayu Hills in mid-December; its purpose was to secure air bases on Akyab and Ramree Islands, from which support could be mounted for future operations in southern Burma, and also by driving the Japanese from the coastal strip west of the Arakan Yomas to liberate the considerable Allied forces they had contained there. It met with even less resistance than had been anticipated. Forward units of 15 Corps reached Foul Point before Christmas, and an Allied landing on Akyab Island on 3rd January was unopposed. A further landing on Ramree Island on the 21st met with only slight opposition. The core of Japanese resistance was, however, met along the coastal road from Myohaung to Taungup, and a number of amphibious landings which were effected in January and February at various points along the coast provoked fierce fighting (whose issue was beyond doubt due to the heavy and accurate air support that was given), and gradually the enemy was driven towards the two routes leading eastwards from An and Taungup towards the Irrawaddy valley. With the capture of Taungup in the middle of April the coastal campaign was virtually over.

25. The climax of the main battle in central Burma was meanwhile not long delayed. During December the Fourteenth Army struck eastwards, and with the occupation of Wuntho by 4 Corps on the 20th, secured its left flank by laying the basis for a continuous front with the Northern Combat Area Command. The railhead at Ye-U was occupied by 33 Corps on New Year's Day, and the Japanese stronghold at Monywa was finally reduced on the 21st, by when 33 Corps had reached the general line of the Irrawaddy, on which it was evident that the enemy had resolved to make a stand. Bridgeheads had however been secured by 20 Division on the left bank of the river at Thabeikkyin and Singu, and in the great bend of the Irrawaddy the Japanese stoutly defended the approaches to Sagaing on the right bank. In these two sectors, where the contending forces were not separated by the river, bitter fighting continued throughout the second half of January and the first half of February. To the north-east, the Northern Combat Area Command forces were moving southwards across the Shweli valley and towards Lashio; Hsenwi was taken on 19th February, and Namtu on the 23rd.

26. While these events were taking place in the Irrawaddy valley and to the north-east, the main strategy of the campaign was beginning to take shape. 4 Corps was removed from the left flank of the Fourteenth Army as soon as the junction with the Northern Combat Area Command was assured, and with two divisions was given the task of pushing southwards from Kalemyo along the Gangaw valley towards Tilin and Pauk. The natural obstacles on this wild route were every bit as great as those prepared by the enemy, who did not appreciate the threat to his left flank that was thus being unfolded. His ignorance of the situation was due to the fact that his reconnaissance aircraft dared not cover the area, and to his tardy realisation of the new mobility of the Allied armies with which air supply endowed them. His defences at Gangaw were overwhelmed on 10th January after an air bombardment to which the Army paid full tribute, and by the 27th the forward units of 4 Corps had reached Pauk. Early in February they established themselves on the right bank of the Irrawaddy below Pakokku. The stage was now set for the crowning blow of the campaign.

27. After a few days' pause, a series of concerted crossings at various points of the Irrawaddy below Mandalay began on the night of 12th-13th February. A new bridgehead was established by 33 Corps opposite Myinmu, in the teeth of determined opposition on the part of the Japanese, who took it to be part of a major encircling movement against Mandalay in conjunction with the forces in the Singu bridgehead to the north. They accordingly threw in most of their available reserves to combat it. A feint crossing was made far to the south, opposite Seikpyu, while the main thrust was made a little upstream, opposite Myitche, where 4 Corps was able to establish a foothold against comparatively light opposition from the enemy, who still underestimated the threat to his left flank. When this bridgehead had been consolidated, a motorised brigade was concentrated behind its lines.

28. On the 23rd, this Brigade moved swiftly eastwards, reaching the railway at Taungtha the next day. It then turned south-east along the line towards the junction of Meiktila, a nodal centre in the communications of central Burma, in the neighbourhood of which there were also several good airfields. The enemy was completely taken aback by this thrust into his rear areas, and although his line of communication troops fought hard, they were unable to do more than delay slightly our advance. By the afternoon of 3rd March, the garrison of Meiktila had been annihilated and 4 Corps had thus placed a brigade, which our air transport speedily built up into a division, squarely athwart the main enemy line of communication from his base at Rangoon to the fighting zone.

29. It was in March that the battle which was to decide the fate of most of Burma north of the Gulf of Martaban was fought. The Japanese reacted speedily to the major strategic thrust whose significance they had grasped too late, and hastily moved southwards all their available forces, in an effort, first, to break our stranglehold on their communications, and, when this failed, to withdraw to safety as many as they could of their troops in the Mandalay-Meiktila noose. Mandalay itself fell to our troops advancing from the north by the middle of the month.

30. Meanwhile the whole area Mandalay-Myingyan-Meiktila had been transformed into a vast battlefield, in which the Fourteenth Army and No. 221 Group attacked from three directions the disorganized forces of the enemy, whose casualties were heavy. A number of scattered units made their escape, but by the beginning of April it might fairly be estimated that Japanese military power in Burma had been shattered. In the Northern Combat Area Command sector, the course of events in central Burma had helped to quicken the pace of the Japanese withdrawal; Lashio was captured by a Chinese division on 8th March, and the enemy soon broke contact, retreating southwards into the Shan States.

31. The Fourteenth Army resumed its large-scale offensive on 12th April, after a short period for regrouping its forces. 4 Corps, supplied by air, struck along the main Mandalay-Rangoon axis; by the end of the month it had covered some 250 miles and had reached the outskirts of Pegu, less than 50 miles from Rangoon, which the Japanese were known to have evacuated two or three days earlier. 33 Corps had moved south-west to Magwe, which was captured on the 18th, and thence advanced down the Irrawaddy valley; its forward elements reached the railhead at Prome on 1st May. Nowhere was the enemy able to bar the advance by a frontal stand. Such were the circumstances when the combined operation for the capture of Rangoon from the south was put into execution at the express wish of C.-in-C. A.L.F.S.E.A.

32. As already explained, Operation "Dracula" met with little or no opposition. It was a copy-book operation, and the troops advancing into the city from the south partook more of the nature of a triumphal procession than an assault force. They were met by the commanding officer of No. 110 Squadron R.A.F., Wing Commander Saunders, who on the previous day, perceiving no signs of the enemy at Mingaladon airfield, had decided to land and reconnoitre the city. He took formal possession of Rangoon on behalf of the Allied forces. It was fitting that the vital part the Air Forces had played in the campaign should be symbolically rounded off by the occupation of Rangoon by the Royal Air Force.

* * * *

Part Three.

ALLIED AIR DOMINANCE.

33. Until October, 1944, when the enemy began to withdraw aircraft from this theatre to reinforce his garrison in the Philippines, the overall strength of the Japanese Air Force in this theatre remained at some 450 aircraft in operational units. Normally about 150 aircraft, 70 per cent. of which were fighters, were disposed in Burma and Thailand for immediate use. The majority of the remainder were retained in Malaya and Sumatra, and comprised bombers and floatplanes for shipping escorts and anti-submarine duties, fighters for the defence of the Sumatra oilfields, and operational echelons refitting or training. With General MacArthur's invasion of the Philippines, when up to 100 aircraft left S.E.A.C., a steady decline in strength set in, aggravated by the constant attrition caused by our fighters, for which full replacement was not forthcoming, until in May, 1945, the enemy could muster but 250 aircraft in the S.E.A.C. area, of which over 100, stationed in Malaya and Sumatra, were for most purposes ineffective by reason of their distance from the battle areas.

34. Following the sharp lessons he received between March and May, 1944, the enemy's warning system became somewhat less embryonic, so that it was difficult to achieve complete surprise in any part of the theatre. By listening to Allied W/T and R/T, and by supplementing a skimpy radar system with observation posts and sound locators, a comprehensive albeit somewhat thin warning-system had been established around the whole of the Western Perimeter, and it was only a question of time before growing technical proficiency rendered the task of Allied aircraft in search of all too rare targets, even more difficult.

35. By comparison, the strength and composition of the Allied fighter force was most satisfactory. Spitfires, Lightnings, and latterly Thunderbolts and Mustangs, completely transformed the situation which had obtained until November, 1943, when our Hurricanes were outclassed and out-manoeuvred by the enemy. Backed by a warning and control system of high standard, Allied fighters had without fail rendered the enemy's incursions into our defended areas costly and ineffectual. During the eleven months covered by this despatch 165 enemy aircraft were destroyed on the ground or in the air, together with 47 probables and 152 damaged. This destruction was achieved against a total enemy effort, offensive and defensive, of 1,845 sorties. One enemy aircraft was destroyed for every eleven sighted; that the air superiority established before the period of this narrative was well maintained over the year, needs no further proof.

36. This virtual dominance of the air over Burma was the result of hard work with small dividends upon the part of our fighter organisation. Freed from the necessity of establishing superiority, the major problems remaining to Allied fighters by the time this despatch opens were the interception of sneak raids, usually undertaken by the Japanese Air Force under the protection of cloud-cover, and the searching-out and destruction of a meagre enemy air force dispersed upon a generous network of rear airfields. Initially, the greatest danger was to the stream of transports hauling supplies to the Imphal Plain, which offered the best prey ever presented to any air force. Some one hundred unarmed aircraft flew daily in and out of the area, and fighter patrols laboured under the handicaps of extensive cloud conditions and a shortage of P.O.L.* at their bases.

37. Moreover, the mountainous terrain to the east precluded efficient early air raid warning, and the enemy could at will come unannounced through the valleys. To minimise the danger, traffic was routed along a corridor from the Khopum Valley to Palel under a fighter umbrella. Ground signs were displayed en route to indicate the presence of enemy aircraft which was also broadcast by R/T. The sight of a stream of transports flying into the Imphal Valley with a screen of Spitfires circling overhead was a most heartening sight to the garrison, who thereby received constant assurance that their aerial life-line was unbroken. The precautions taken and the impotence of the enemy resulted in only two transports being destroyed by enemy action during the whole of the siege, a remarkable achievement.

38. The danger to transport aircraft persisted during the whole of the advance, since they were continually operating in front of the warning screen, and fighter bases were not always established as far forward as was tactically desirable. For this there were two main reasons; in the early stages of the advance through hilly jungle no airstrips could be constructed near the front, and second, having debouched on to the plains, the Army were not willing to devote supplies and resources to

* Petrol, Oil, Lubricants.

establish fighter bases in the area of dropping operations.

39. On two occasions, therefore, our transport aircraft were victims of enemy sneak raids; on one day in November while dropping along the Tiddim Road, five aircraft were destroyed by the enemy, and on the 12th January four were shot down while supply dropping near Onbauk, an airfield recently recaptured from the enemy which, however, had not by that time been prepared for defensive fighters. Even when during the temporary halt around Mandalay, and Spitfires were able to occupy the Shwebo and Monywa airfield groups, air supply was proceeding over a hundred and thirty mile front which the four available squadrons of Spitfires were hard pressed to cover in conjunction with their other defensive commitments. It is a lesson of the campaign that the air supply of ground forces depends on the immediate deployment as far forward as possible of fighter squadrons to patrol the Lines of Communication. Had the enemy used his fighters effectively instead of frittering away their effort on infrequent low-level attacks against forward troops, he would have been able to do great execution among our Dakotas and Commandos, thus seriously impeding the advance.

* * * *

40. Since it was not always possible to engage the enemy in the air, it was necessary to search out his aircraft on the ground. To this end, intruder raids were undertaken at frequent intervals, and paid a dividend of 80 destroyed, 25 probably destroyed and 78 damaged aircraft on enemy airfields. In October, a series of raids were undertaken against the Rangoon airfields with the additional motive of hindering the transfer of units to the Philippines. In this operation, many types of aircraft were employed, including Beaufighters, but, as aircraft resources became more suited to operational requirements, intrusion was progressively left to the Mustang squadrons of the Air Commandos, who on more than one occasion in the spring of 1945, made the 1,500 mile round trip to the Japanese base airfields in Siam with good results totalling 38 destroyed, 10 probably destroyed and 21 damaged aircraft.

41. The problem of destroying an enemy intent on conserving his forces and possessing a wide choice of airfields containing many revetments (Meiktila airfield disposes of over a hundred) is not an easy one. In addition, the enemy's skill with light anti-aircraft and machine-gun fire is well-known, and low-level "strafing" runs are apt to be costly. It was found uneconomical to make a preliminary reconnaissance run to discover which revetments were occupied, and often only a quick snap-shot at a target seen late in the "strafe" was possible. In view of these factors it will be seen that the result achieved is more than creditable.

42. Early attempts to ground or destroy the enemy by bombing his airfields were ineffective and were discontinued in favour of more worthwhile targets.

* * * *

43. The enemy's offensive effort was so ineffectual as to be hardly worth mentioning except to recount the losses he sustained. In

late September the Japanese Air Force began a series of reconnaissances with disastrous results. Cover was attempted of the Manipur Road, Silchar, Chittagong and battle areas. Four Dinahs were destroyed during this brief spell and since then no reconnaissance over the India border has been attempted. On Christmas night three bombers attempted to penetrate to the Calcutta area; of these, two were destroyed by Beaufighters and the third returned in a damaged condition. Enemy attempts to interfere with shipping off Akyab in January were decisively dealt with by the Spitfire squadrons who moved in five days after its occupation, No. 67 Squadron destroying five out of six attacking Oscars in one day.

44. Thereafter, the enemy effort degenerated into a series of sporadic and infrequent attempts to disrupt our forward columns. The ineffectual nature of these attacks was evident to all who flew over the battlefield and noted, on the enemy side no signs of activity, but, behind the British lines, long lines of transport moving in uncamouflaged safety, supply-dropping parachutes in use as tents, and all the apparatus of war left in full view by troops whose immunity from air attack was scarcely ever violated even by fast-flying fighters, for the enemy dared not send a bomber over the Allied lines by daylight.

* * * *

45. It is unnecessary to recount in detail the enormous advantages accruing to both ground and air forces when the enemy air arm is small and misemployed, and when our own squadrons are superior in performance, training and control. It is, however, worth pausing to consider the results had enemy aircraft been allowed unrestricted use of the sky. The air supply on which the whole land campaign hinged would have been impossible, the attrition rate of our close support squadrons, which worked with accuracy and effect, would have been prohibitive, and the disuption caused by our strategic bombers to the enemy's communications far to the rear could not have been such as to have materially influenced the battle.

* * * *

Part Four.

TRANSPORT SUPPORT OPERATIONS AND DEVELOPMENT.

46. The Burma campaign has proved beyond all doubt that once air superiority has been achieved, the air maintenance and supply of forces in the field is governed primarily by the availability of airfields and of transport aircraft. The supply and maintenance of the Army, in the field and engaged in intensive operations together with a tactical air force in support, is a major problem under most favourable conditions. It should be borne in mind, however, that supply bases were some 250 miles distant, and that the intervening country comprised vast stretches of impenetrable jungle and a formidable mountain barrier rising up to 10,000 feet. In addition, weather conditions were by no means favourable, and experience has shown that monsoon cloud develops a degree of turbulence which has been the cause of a number of fatal accidents.

47. Despite these many difficulties, the success of the air supply operations in the Burma campaign has been fully testified. It is fair to say that without air supply the Burma campaign could never have been fought on its present lines. It was in fact a decisive factor of the land campaign. Admittedly mistakes occurred, sometimes due to miscalculation but more often due to unforeseen contingencies. Even so the air supply operations in Burma will probably rank as one of the greatest, if not the greatest, of air supply achievements in this war.

48. The organisation and operation of air supply is a problem which calls for mutual understanding of each other's difficulties by the respective Services. In this respect it cannot be too strongly emphasised that it is the operators and not the consumers who determine the most efficient method of delivering the goods. Moreover, it is up to the consumers to state precisely what is required, in a given order of priority. It is their responsibility also to deliver these goods in the required quantities and at the right time to the air supply heads. The swift and unco-ordinated growth of the air transport organization did not allow of a full appreciation, by either the Army or the Air Force, of the importance of the ancillary services necessary to promote the full effectiveness of the machine. As the campaign advanced, this tendency has been progressively eliminated, and the situation is now that only a lack of resources prevents the air transport organisation from incorporating all the lessons that have been learnt, and giving it the full effectiveness with which experience can endow it. From this observation, the air supply organization that has developed within the area of Northern Combat Area Command and Tenth Air Force is excepted. There, a realisation of the importance of firm backing to the supply system was evident from the outset, and resulted in a very high standard of operating efficiency.

* * * *

49. In June, 1944, there were in Air Command eleven transport squadrons engaged on air supply, four British and seven American. By May, 1945, these figures had risen to nine and sixteen respectively, an increase which still left the air supply force with little or no margin of reserve. The growth of air supply during the period can well be imagined.

50. At the beginning of the period, attention was still centred upon the critical position of 4 Corps besieged in and around the ancient capital of Manipur. There were still twenty-three days of June to go before the road to Imphal was to be re-opened. Working to supply the garrison and to build a stockpile to exploit the anticipated Japanese retreat, as much as 700 tons were being flown in on a single day under monsoon conditions. When the road was re-opened, effort was not allowed to drop and for the remaining days of June the squadrons flew at maximum effort in order to build up stocks and ascertain the peak air lift that could be achieved. The wisdom of this was doubtful; all concerned were already exhausted, and experience has illustrated the value of retaining a margin of effort in reserve, and of not over-straining a complicated machine without urgent necessity.

51. However, by the end of the month, the enemy was in retreat, and food and munitions were available to speed his withdrawal. The threat to India and to the China life-line had been removed, and a grim defence, sustained solely by air supply, was becoming a vigorous offensive, whose progress was also fed from the air. From July until November, 33 Corps fought its way eastwards to the Chindwin, southwards along the Kabaw valley and down the Tiddim Road, provided entirely with munitions and food by our transport squadrons. Until the end of the monsoon, supply was carried out under conditions of unbelievable difficulty. In July the commander of 33 Corps sent the following signal to No. 194 Squadron: "Your unflagging efforts and determination to complete your task in spite of appalling flying conditions are worthy of the highest praise." In August, another squadron summarised its efforts as follows:—"It has taken on occasion six to seven days of battling through torrential rain, strong winds and 10/10ths cloud down to 200 feet to achieve one mission, but it has been done."

52. In August and September it was becoming clear that the planning and day-to-day control of air supply operations required an organisation separate from Third Tactical Air Force, whose responsibility air supply operations had been since the dissolution of Troop Carrier Command. This was rendered all the more necessary by the large part that it was proposed airborne operations should play in the coming dry season. Thus, in October, Combat Cargo Task Force (C.C.T.F.), an integrated U.S.A./British Headquarters, was formed and became responsible for the day-to-day control and the planning of air transport operations in support of Fourteenth Army and 15 Corps.

53. One of the first measures undertaken by H.Q.C.C.T.F. was the reorganisation of the allocation of tasks, whose importance when demand is always outrunning supply cannot be stressed too strongly. The original procedure had been that, prior to the beginning of each month, Fourteenth Army submitted to Third Tactical Air Force its planned air supply requirements, which were based on the assumption that the Army's advance in the various sectors would invariably be strongly opposed. Consequently, demands were always high and supplies were occasionally fifty per cent. below the planned figure but withal more than sufficient for current requirements. The Rear Airfield Maintenance Organisation (R.A.M.O.) received its day's tasks direct from the headquarters of the Corps which it was supplying, and at the same time asked the Air Forces for the requisite number of aircraft. If, as often happened, the Army's daily requirements exceeded the air resources available, considerable confusion resulted, since no proper system of allocating priorities had been evolved.

54. This problem was solved by forming, alongside C.C.T.F., the Combined Army-Air Transport Organisation (C.A.A.T.O.) which received and collated daily requests, assessed their urgency and, having a full knowledge of aircraft states, allotted the tasks accordingly. The organisation was thus more in line with current European practice, with two notable exceptions, the lack of signals and telephone communications was such as to clog any air supply machinery no matter how well-planned, and second, there were crippling deficiencies of personnel in such ancillary bodies as Staging Posts and Casualty Air Evacuation Units.

55. On December 20th, the first strip for landing-on of supplies was opened at Indaing-gale. Others followed in quick succession, Taukkyan near Kalemyo, Kawlin and Indaw trans-Chindwin as soon as the river had been crossed, and Kan in the Myittha Valley where 4 Corps had returned to the line, replacing the Lushai Brigade and representing another and growing commitment to our transport forces.

56. Thus, by January, the increasing demands of mobile warfare, which did not accord with the plans on which resources had been allotted and organisation developed, and the engagement of larger forces, witnessed a gradual and sustained rise in the demands of Fourteenth Army for air supply. Many unforeseen difficulties were now coming to light, and when the Supreme Commander visited the forward areas he was informed that the Air Forces were not carrying enough supplies. C.-in-C. A.L.F.S.E.A. circulated a memorandum calling for more resources in transport aircraft, without which, he stated, not only would the advance to Mandalay and beyond be arrested, but due to the impossibility of supplying forces in front of the roadhead he might be forced to withdraw beyond the Chindwin for the monsoon. This view of the situation (which in my opinion was unduly pessimistic) caused an urgent request to the Chiefs of Staff for additional transport squadrons, and as a result Nos. 238 and 267 Squadrons arrived in March. Actually a better organisation of existing ground transport resources would have met every commitment, and for this reason Air Marshal Garrod undertook a tour to investigate the working of the system.

57. It is as well here to outline, for the sake of comparison, the working of air supply in the N.C.A.C. area, to which but little reference has so far been made.

Air Supply in the Northern Combat Area Command.

58. The most striking feature of this organisation was the high standard of co-operation achieved by all agencies concerned—N.C.A.C., Service of Supply, Tenth Air Force, Air Service Command and all ancillary formations. Collective responsibility for the task of aid supply was rated higher than service allegiance; each body trusted the ability of the others to carry out their part of the work and did not attempt to dictate on matters outside its own sphere. The second great advantage was the abundance of good signal communications; every link in the chain, organisational, supply, squadrons, co-ordinators, being linked by a teletype and telephone network which allowed of a quick dissemination of the next day's tasks and priorities as allotted by the collating agency in N.C.A.C., and of speedy re-adjustment if necessary. A last-minute change in location of a Dropping Zone could be signalled back by a Division and retransmitted to an aircraft already airborne for another objective. Moreover, the packing and loading processes were organised on a moving-belt principle whose

efficiency eliminated a multitude of small delays; these ancillary organisations worked with the industrial efficiency of a large commercial factory.

59. A comparison between the American packing loading agencies at Dinjan and the R.I.A.S.C. Air Supply Companies at Hathazari reflected no credit on the British ground organisation. Here it should be emphasised that no reflection is intended on the personnel involved; British Officers and Indian Other Ranks were strained to breaking-point, and often had to work seventy-two hours at a stretch to complete their tasks; the fault lay in the fact that the importance and nature of the work demanded a much more generous scale of personnel, facilities, and organising ability than could be allotted by the Army.

* * * *

60. An examination of the data gathered on Air Marshal Garrod's tour brought to light the differences of organisation and procedure between the two air supply systems, and revealed a crying need for improvement in the organisation operated by C.A.A.T.O. and C.C.T.F. Too numerous to recount here, these points did have the effect of initiating action to improve the operating procedure. Meanwhile, Air Command was pressing for the speedy development of the recaptured bases along the Arakan Coast at Akyab and Ramree whose employment would shorten the haul into Central Burma. Journeys from the established bases at Chittagong, Comilla and Tulihal were now becoming so long that in order to complete three trips in a day, aircraft had to take off at first light and perhaps not finish until after dark. The strain on technical maintenance, flying and loading personnel can well be imagined.

61. It was in February that an overland advance to Rangoon supplied entirely by air was first put forward as a serious proposal. Fourteenth Army prepared a plan which envisaged two parallel drives southwards along the axes of the River Irrawaddy and of the Mandalay-Rangoon railway, while a large force from 33 Corps, of up to three and a half divisions, struck east to Takaw with the object of containing and destroying all enemy forces cut off north of Meiktila.

62. Air Command reactions to the plan were

(i) a re-orientation of supply lines, using Akyab and Ramree as advanced air supply heads which would result in substantial reduction in length of the air supply line as the force advanced south of Mandalay.

(ii) We doubted the soundness of the plan which aimed at a total destruction of the enemy in addition to the capture of Rangoon if the former necessitated a drive eastwards to cut off and destroy the enemy in the hills. This would inevitably involve a supply problem in that direction in addition to sustaining a main advance southwards.

63. A study of the situation after the fall of Rangoon shows that these reactions were fully justified. Apart from this, the plan had many advantages, and at a major conference in Calcutta on 23rd February which heralded my arrival as Allied Air Commander-in-Chief, it was approved in principle and the target for tonnage to be hauled in its execution decided. The maximum lift was assessed at 1,887 tons per day between 20th March and 1st April and 2,075 tons per day between 1st May and 15th May. I emphasised that these figures would entail a very high rate of effort from the squadrons involved, and would entail considerable retrenchment during the monsoon to pay off the mortgage in maintenance and overstrain we would have contracted in its achievement.

64. Meanwhile, the air lift was still increasing. In February, C.C.T.F. hauled 51,210 short tons of supplies into the operational area. In addition, at the end of the month, a small though vital airborne operation took place to consolidate the capture of Meiktila, which had been seized following an armoured dash from their bridgehead on the Irrawaddy by 17 Division.

65. Troops were landed to reinforce the flying column which had seized the airfield and was now being fiercely attacked on all sides by the enemy. Transport aircraft landed and discharged their loads under fire, many suffering damage while so doing. One aircraft taking on wounded for its return journey had a shell explode inside it, causing further injuries to the casualties who were already emplaned. Thus, within very few days, landing became impossible, and it was necessary to resort to the less economical practice of dropping, which still further increased the load on our transport squadrons.

66. The Meiktila operation was a success, and a captured Japanese Staff officer assessed it as the turning point in the battle for Burma. It was not accomplished without mistakes, however, which rendered it far more hazardous than it might otherwise have been. It should be established that aircraft will not land until the possibility of the airfield being subjected to heavy fire is ruled out. Planning should be carried out on this premise. Secondly, the R.A.M.O. that was established on the airfield was pitifully inadequate, the officer in charge having to guide aircraft to unloading points instead of being free to organise their quick turn-around under fire. In a critical operation, such points might make all the difference between success and dismal failure. They merit much greater consideration in combined planning than has hitherto been accorded them.

* * * *

67. By the beginning of April, Meiktila was again safe for landing, although shells were still bursting less than 200 yards from the strips. Preparations were immediately commenced to build up stocks to maintain Fourteenth Army in the final dash which was to carry them 250 miles southward in the second half of the month. On the 20th, the main airfield at Lewe was captured and speedily prepared for light aircraft and gliders, which began landing on the morning of the 21st. Toungoo, 50 miles further south, was occupied on the 22nd and, in spite of bad weather, over 100 Dakotas and Commandos landed on the 24th. Within five days, Pyuntaza, another airstrip 70 miles further south, was also receiving supplies, and a battalion group was flown in to cut the enemy escape route eastwards from Pegu. The enemy was still active on both sides of the narrow strip along the Mandalay-Pegu railway which had formed our

corridor, and while the capture of Rangoon was left to an assault from the south, transport squadrons continued with unabated activity the supply of Fourteenth Army, who but for these outstanding efforts would not have been able to hold the ground they had won.

* * * *

Casualty Evacuation.

68. Throughout the period, the saving of lives, the morale of the fighting troops and the mobility of our ground forces has been materially assisted by the work of light aircraft and Dakotas flying out sick and wounded from the battle areas. The total of men thus saved from avoidable pain and suffering, from many days' journey by sampan, mule and ambulance, and from dying for lack of hospital facilities was formidable.

69. The flexibility of air power, by no means lessened when used in the interests of humanity, was well illustrated by a unique operation carried out by Sunderlands of No. 230 Squadron, which landed on Lake Indawgyi behind the enemy lines and flew out 537 wounded men of Special Force, whom General Wingate's columns would otherwise have been forced to abandon to the mercy of the Japanese.

70. This operation was, however, exceptional. The normal procedure was for light aircraft of the R.A.F. Communication squadrons and the U.S.A.A.F. Liaison squadrons to bring in the sick and wounded from extemporised landing strips to grounds where Dakotas and Commandos were discharging their cargo, and whence they would take them to base hospitals on return journeys. It was proposed at one time to attach light aircraft to the transport squadrons, and form one co-ordinated flying unit to undertake the whole process of casualty evacuation, but such a scheme would either have impaired the mobility of the light aircraft components or would have left them continually detached from their parent squadrons with no administrative or domestic backing for the difficult conditions under which they live and operate. Accordingly, as the American light aircraft are withdrawn from this theatre and the R.A.F. take on the whole of the work, it is proposed to form independent self-sufficient flying units to reinforce the Group Communication Squadrons in casualty evacuation. The resultant organisation will be sufficiently elastic to cover the whole front and yet be capable of concentration where casualties are heavy.

71. Casualty evacuation has been a regular part of the Air Forces' work in this theatre since the middle of 1943. It is unfortunate that with the increase in traffic which intensified operations have caused, there has been insufficient parallel growth of resources. Nursing Orderlies are 11 per cent. below establishment, and the buildings and accommodation for the reception of wounded at base airfields are not of the standard which good hygiene and humanity demand. If the Royal Air Force is to maintain the high reputation it has built in this sphere, far more generous scales of equipment and personnel must be authorised.

* * * *

Conclusions on Air Transport.

72. The first essential for air supply is good ground organisation. One weak link in the chain can vitiate the work of the aircrews and maintenance personnel, the estimates of the planners and the efforts of the fighting troops. It is worth outlining some of the faults that have occurred in order that they may be avoided in the future.

(i) Dropping Zones should always be located where a drop is feasible. This might sound a platitude to anyone who has not flown on supply-dropping operations in Burma and found dropping areas continually located in narrow valleys whose negotiation after each run is a major hazard.

(ii) The system of communicating information on dropping areas, on the composition of loads, on changes of location, on enemy interference and all other aspects of air supply must be such that the one small and vital item of knowledge which might make the difference between a successful or an abortive sortie is available at all links in the chain.

(iii) The British Army-Air supply system in South-East Asia has been continually marred by the failure to provide for meticulous organisation in a sphere where great efforts can be rendered nugatory by inaccuracy in minor details.

The following are some of the lessons learnt:—

(a) Adequate distributing facilities must be made available by the land forces at landing grounds to ensure that perishable goods are quickly distributed when unloaded from aircraft.

(b) Aircraft should not be detailed to convey food to areas in which the same commodities can easily be obtained by local purchase.

(c) Packing of goods must be strong enough to ensure that containers do not burst in transit.

(d) Adequate facilities must be provided for feeding and resting aircrews engaged on this arduous flying, as they are often absent from their bases for as long as ten hours at a time.

(e) An efficient supply of re-fuellers and facilities for night maintenance must be arranged, otherwise aircraft which could otherwise be making an effective contribution to the battle will be grounded.

(iv) Forward airfield commanders and flying control personnel took a long time to realise that air supply traffic is as vital as any other. Cargo aircraft should not be kept circling an airfield while tactical aircraft take off on a routine operation whose delay by half an hour is immaterial.

(v) Each part of the planning and assessment of air lift must be carried out by the Service in whose province it lies. Much confusion has been caused here by the Army attempting to quote and work on flying hours per aircraft with no knowledge of the implications of U.E. and I.E.*, aircraft serviceable

---

* U.E. = Unit Equipment.
  I.E. = Initial Equipment.

or aircraft on strength. Moreover it was consistent practice for the Army to require full data on the performance of our aircraft and explanations for any short-fall that might occur, while never giving equivalent information upon their own short-fall in overland or inland water transport.

73. Air supply depends on so many agencies, and is affected by so many imponderables, that the allocation of resources and good brains to ensure efficiency, speed and good liaison can never be too generous. The campaign in Burma would have been rendered easier had the engineering resources that were poured into less profitable projects been directed towards timely building of forward airfields, more efficient supply depots and stronger lines of communication to the air haulage centres. The Ledo Road, for example, is surely the longest white elephant in the world. Had the wealth of ability and material that went to its building been employed in strengthening the air supply system, the recapture of Burma could probably have been advanced by an appreciable period.

* * * *

PART FIVE.

TACTICAL SUPPORT OF THE GROUND FORCES.

The Organisation of Tactical Support.

74. Air forces operating in tactical support of the Allied Land Forces in Burma comprised Nos. 221 and 224 Groups R.A.F. and 10th U.S.A.A.F. all under the command of Headquarters, Eastern Air Command. Each worked in close association with a corresponding army headquarters—the Tenth U.S.A.A.F. with the Northern Combat Area Command, 224 Group with 15 Corps and 221 Group with 33 Corps and 4 Corps, and finally from the beginning of December onwards with the Fourteenth Army. 221 Group and Fourteenth Army remained together at Imphal only until the end of December, when the latter moved forward to Kalemyo, being accompanied by the A.O.C. and his air staff. The two headquarters were again united fully at Monywa from 9th February until the middle of April, when they moved to Meiktila, their final staging post before Rangoon. The mobility of 221 Group headquarters had a less active counterpart in that of 224 Group, which remained with the headquarters of 15 Corps first at Cox's Bazar and later at Akyab. In both cases the close relationship of the headquarters of the two Services was an essential element in their successful co-operation.

75. In the campaign in central Burma, just as all the ground forces came under the Fourteenth Army, so all the aircraft engaged in close, as distinct from tactical, support of the former were controlled by Headquarters, 221 Group. There were however two exceptions. The two Air Commando Groups operated directly under Eastern Air Command, and the Mustangs of the Second Air Commando Group, which played so important a role in the operations of 4 Corps which led to the seizure of Meiktila, were for the crucial period of these operations controlled by an advanced headquarters of the Combat Cargo Task Force located with 4 Corps headquarters.

The second exception was provided by the Thunderbolt squadrons of 905 Wing, for which, owing to administrative reasons, there was no room east of the Lushai Hills and which were therefore located in Arakan under 224 Group.

76. In this connection the very difficult problems of administration confronting 221 Group must be recalled. Its wings and squadrons operated from bases covering a front of some two hundred miles, and a depth which at the beginning of the campaigning season in November was no less, and which by the end of April had expanded to some six hundred miles, from the Mosquito wing at Khumbigram to the fighter squadrons on forward strips near Toungoo. Most were on a highly mobile basis, with personnel reduced to the minimum; the separation of squadrons from servicing echelons which was generally effected towards the end of 1944 contributed materially to the mobility of units in the group. Fighter squadrons moved forward in pace with the advancing front as quickly as the army were able to prepare landing grounds and forego air transport for them; the squadrons of 906 Wing, for instance, were operating from airfields near Ye-U by the middle of January, a fortnight after the occupation of the district by 33 Corps, and before the end of April no less than nine fighter squadrons were located at Toungoo, which had not been captured until the 22nd, and another four at Magwe, which fell on the 18th, in preparation for the assault upon Rangoon. These moves were effected with the aid of transport aircraft, overland communications being almost non-existent. There was, however, some feeling among the squadrons that in the matter of motor transport and indeed of supplies generally the army was at a distinct advantage.

77. The enormous area over which the squadrons of 221 Group were scattered, together with the meagreness of communications by land and telephone, also precluded the wholesale adoption, for the operational control of fighter aircraft in close support, of the organization which had been evolved in the European theatre of war for army-air co-operation. The former system of Army Air Support Units was replaced in the closing months of 1944 by the establishment of Air Support Signals Units with Visual Control Posts (V.C.Ps.), Air Advisers being also provided for both corps and divisional headquarters. A Combined Army/Air School for training V.C.P personnel was set up at Ranchi, and it was soon found that the greatest difficulty in the establishment of Visual Control Posts was the provision of personnel, particularly of Controllers, who it was agreed must be chosen from experienced junior officers of the General Duties branch. Ten teams were however operating by the end of 1944 and by the beginning of May, 1945, their number had risen to thirty-four. The special value of the V.C.Ps lay in the extra flexibility and accuracy which they lent to air operations planned in conjunction with the ground situation; the former device of indicating targets by smoke shells, always liable to inaccuracies in both place and time as well as to counterfeiting by the enemy, was now needed only when the target lay in flat jungle country, invisible from the air and not determinable in relation to any obvious feature of the landscape.

78. Of the general success of the V.C.P. system there can be no doubt, from both air and ground points of view. It contributed materially to that close and efficient co-operation of ground and air forces which was so marked a feature of the campaign of 1944-45. It led however to a tactic of less unquestionable value in the employment of the "cabrank" method, by which aircraft patrolled continuously over selected areas, maintaining touch all the time with the V.C.P., who as opportunity offered would call them down to attack any fresh target revealed by the progress of the battle. This tactic was very popular with our own troops, as the continued presence overhead of our own air support had excellent morale effect. Furthermore, air support was available to engage any target at a moment's notice. It was however wasteful of flying hours and reduced petrol stocks, in that the aircraft were liable to be kept waiting and targets could not always be provided, while it diminished the weight of air attack, since in order to maintain a continuous patrol the aircraft could seldom operate in more than pairs. If the army requires direct air support to be available at such short notice, it is considered that their desires could more economically be satisfied by providing the air forces with airfields as close behind the front line as the reasonable security of the ground installations will warrant.

* * * *

Close support of the Fourteenth Army.

79. The aircraft employed in close support operations were of various types. In June, 1944, there were still four squadrons of Vengeances operating, two on the Imphal and two on the Arakan front; they had done excellent work in the 1943-44 campaign, but had soon to be withdrawn. In September, the first R.A.F. Thunderbolts began operations; Thunderbolts had already been in use for some time with the Tenth U.S.A.A.F. which had also occasionally employed its Lightnings (P.38) in close support work. As the new campaign developed, and it became clear that the enemy was in no position seriously to challenge the Allied air superiority, Spitfires were increasingly diverted to the ground-attack role, particularly in the Arakan sector.

80. But the backbone of direct air support was always provided by the Hurricane, with or without bombs. The "Hurribomber" had well proved its worth in the 1943-4 campaign, and some in particular of the "Hurribomber" squadrons enjoyed an immense reputation for their accurate pin-pointing of targets within a comparatively few yards of our own positions. Their value in this was particularly evident during the period of mountain warfare that ended at the beginning of December, 1944, and subsequently in the interval of semi-static fighting that was marked by the battle of the bridgeheads in late January and February, 1945. In conjunction with fighter-bombers as well as independently, ground-attack fighters also frequently operated in close support, doing particularly effective work in attacks upon gun sites and patrols over areas in which enemy artillery was suspected to be located.

81. Heavier aircraft were also taken into service in support of ground attacks. Mitchells (B.25) had already been employed for this purpose in the 1943-4 campaign, but the four squadrons of the Twelfth Bombardment Group were now withdrawn from the Strategic Air Force and placed under the operational control of first 224 Group and later 221 Group, so that their work might more simply be dovetailed into the general tactical pattern. They operated sometimes independently, but in close support more frequently in conjunction with fighter-bombers, and added greatly to the weight and effectiveness of large-scale close support operations; the term "Earthquake" which was ultimately taken into official use to describe these concerted attacks upon Japanese bunker positions originated among these Mitchell squadrons, who earned for themselves the name of "the Earthquakers."

82. An outstanding "earthquake" operation, for instance, was the air contribution to the combined army and air attack directed on 10th January against the enemy stronghold at Gangaw in the Kabaw Valley, where an extensive and well-defended system of bunkers and gun emplacements was holding up the advance of 4 Corps southwards in its vital thrust against the Japanese left flank. Four Mitchell squadrons participated in this operation, as did some thirty-four "Hurribombers," defensive cover being supplied by Spitfires and Thunderbolts. It turned out to be a highly successful day; the bombs were dropped at approximately 1430 hours and within ninety minutes five out of the six main Japanese positions were in Allied hands. The subsequent withdrawal of the enemy from the whole neighbourhood during the next few days was attributed by 4 Corps to be due in great measure to a lowering of his morale as a result of this air attack. But the participation of so large a number of aircraft in a single operation was not usual, and as the campaign wore on it was realised that Mitchells operating in numbers as low as two or three could do effective work in accurately winkling out small enemy parties from their lairs.

83. Heavy bombers of the Strategic Air Force were also employed on "earthquake" operations from time to time, mainly in support of the Fourteenth Army during the battle for the bridgeheads in January and February, 1944, though they also intervened effectively in support of 15 Corps during the struggle for the possession of the coastal road at Kangaw at the end of January. But well-marked targets suitable for their employment in direct co-operation with the ground forces were of necessity few, owing to the Japanese skill in camouflage, and the heavy bombers were therefore of most assistance to land operations in their attacks upon targets not in the immediate battle-zone.

* * * *

Indirect Support of the Fourteenth Army.

84. On numerous occasions the ground forces requested the help of the Strategic Air Force, and nominated targets some distance behind the battle area though still in the tactical zone of land operations. These targets were, in the main, supply centres or nodal communication points or built-up areas in which the enemy was believed to be living. A notable attack of this type was mounted on

13th January against Mandalay, the keystone of the whole Japanese defensive system in central Burma and directly threatened in two directions by the advance of the Fourteenth Army. Fifty-four aircraft attacked the Japanese-occupied district and a further 12 the suburb of Sagaing on the opposite side of the river, the operation being preceded by attacks by Thunderbolts upon anti-aircraft gun sites in the neighbourhood, and accompanied by fighter sweeps over the airfields at Aungban and Meiktila. Photographic evidence confirmed the destruction of some 70 major buildings in the Japanese quarters, while intelligence reports variously estimated Japanese casualties alone at 600 and a 1,000, in addition to those inflicted upon Burmese puppet troops.

85. Such operations undertaken at the request of the Allied land forces reached their zenith in February, during which month nearly two thirds of the total number of sorties flown by Liberators of the Strategic Air Force were directed against targets in or near the battlefront as requested by the Fourteenth Army. These included, for instance, the stores dumps near the railhead at Madaya, from which the enemy forces fighting to contain the Singu bridgehead were supplied, which was attacked by forty-five heavy bomber aircraft, and the garrison districts at Yenangyaung, which were attacked by 50. Later in the month, heavy bomber targets included objectives designated by the Army at Myittha, Mahlaing and Myingyan—all towns lying on or close to the path being followed by the armoured columns of 4 Corps in their thrust towards Meiktila. To take a final example, the climax of the air attacks upon the potential stronghold of Toungoo, where the enemy was expected to make a serious effort to stop the drive of 4 Corps southwards towards Rangoon in the second half of April, was supplied by over 40 Liberators, which bombed the garrison area there on the 21st, when the nearest Allied troops were already within striking distance, and indeed entered the town the following day.

86. Very effective operations against targets in the immediate rear of the enemy were carried out by ground-attack fighters throughout the period; their most vulnerable objectives were to be found along the lines of communication, where animal and motor transport units were carrying to his troops in the field, and also along the waterways where miscellaneous rivercraft served the same purpose. In these operations varied aircraft were employed, from Hurricanes and Spitfires to Beaufighters, Lightnings, Thunderbolts and Mosquitos, while Mitchells also participated, particularly by night. Armament included rocket projectiles and bombs, as well as 40 mm. cannon, also guns of lesser calibre.

87. Some small foretaste of the weight and pattern of this tactical support of the army was given in July, when the enemy was endeavouring to withdraw from the perimeter of the Imphal plain, and good toll was taken of his transport forced to brave the open road to Tiddim and the other routes eastward to the Chindwin. Direct attacks upon vehicles, mainly by Hurricanes, were varied by successful efforts to block the Tiddim road by causing landslides, and to break the bridges both along it and in the Kabaw Valley—achievements for which Lightnings and Vengeances were responsible. In all, over 75 motor transport units were successfully attacked in this area during the month. These operations, though invisible to the army, were controlled with the military situation always in view, and evidence was subsequently forthcoming in plenty from captured diaries of enemy officers and men of their effectiveness in hindering the passage of supplies and the movement of personnel, and in aggravating the conditions of disease and undernourishment under which the Japanese ground forces laboured.

88. In August the tactical picture on the Fourteenth Army front came to centre round the Chindwin river, which for two or three weeks became of considerably enhanced importance as a supply route. It had long been in use by the Japanese as a line of communication, and the riverine ports, particularly Monywa and Kalewa, were active points of supply. The still worsening military situation continued to impose upon the enemy the necessity for emergency movements of men and supplies behind the Manipur sector of the front. Since the capacity of the Sagaing—Ye-U railway had been greatly reduced by air action, and the other overland routes were more or less unusable owing to the monsoon, they were forced to have increased resort to the Chindwin as a line of communication.

89. Early in the month the toll of rivercraft successfully attacked began to increase and it became apparent that something was afoot. The Spitfires and Hurricanes which had hitherto been covering the river were reinforced by a detachment of Beaufighters from 224 Group. "Hurribombers" were joined by Wellingtons, and later by Mitchells, in a series of attacks upon riverside targets. In addition, mines, both magnetic and ordinary, were laid in the Chindwin by Mitchells so as to catch traffic attempting to move under cover either of cloud or darkness. The total number of rivercraft successfully attacked on the Chindwin during the month was not far short of five hundred, and included seven launches; of this total the Beaufighters accounted for slightly over half, together with five of the launches.

90. Attacks upon road transport vehicles continued throughout the campaign, their effectiveness being increased with the advent of better weather at the close of the monsoon. In particular, the periods during which a major Allied advance was in progress and the battlefront was therefore fluid, were marked by the presence of transport targets in otherwise unusual quantity. This was so during the advance to the Irrawaddy in December, the thrust towards Meiktila during late February and early in March, and above all during the final advance of 4 Corps towards Rangoon in the second half of April. Ox-carts belonging to the local population had long been habitually pressed into service by the Japanese, and were attacked at all times. But lorries moved mainly under cover of darkness, and the Beaufighters which lit upon a convoy of forty to fifty vehicles travelling westwards along the road from Meiktila to Kyaukpadaung on the afternoon of February 5th and successfully strafed them made an exceptional discovery. But it was probably no coincidence that on the night of February 15th/16th, just after the Fourteenth Army had

made its decisive crossing of the Irrawaddy below Mandalay, another Beaufighter located some fifty vehicles all moving eastwards along the Chauk—Meiktila highway.

91. A little later, on the night of the 27th/28th, a Mitchell on intruder patrol discovered a convoy of over a hundred vehicles, together with some armoured cars and six tanks, travelling northwards along the road from Taungdwingyi to Myothit, doubtless to be thrown into the attempt to stem the advance of the Fourteenth Army. The aircraft delivered attacks by both bombing and strafing for the space of an hour. It then attacked another smaller group of vehicles some distance to the south-east, after which it returned to the large convoy and was able to observe that some forty units had been knocked out by its previous attacks; finally it delivered one more strafing attack, setting three more vehicles on fire.

92. In the second half of April, with the final stages of the advance southwards in progress, such targets became unprecedentedly plentiful. A Hurricane squadron, for instance, caught over forty vehicles on the 19th standing nose to tail, heavily loaded and camouflaged, off the road a little south of Pyinmana, and was subsequently able to count seventeen in flames and many more severely damaged. The same squadron located an even larger number near the site of the bridge over the Sittang at Mokpalin on the 30th, when a total of forty-three lorries finally was counted in flames. Both Mustangs of the Second Air Commando Group and Beaufighters of 224 Group had each already made a haul similar in size and nature in this escape corridor on the 26th. In all, during this second half of the month, approximately three hundred and fifty motor vehicles were successfully attacked behind the enemy's lines throughout Burma. The analogous figures for the whole period covered by this despatch may conservatively be assessed, on the basis of visible evidence, at 3846 M.T. vehicles.

93. One operation in tactical support of the Fourteenth Army is worthy of special mention, namely the achievement of a Hurricane IID squadron, firing rocket projectiles, which on February 19th—in the course of a single day—put out of action twelve tanks which the Japanese were about to throw into the battle for the bridgehead opposite Myinmu. These belonged to the single tank regiment of which the Japanese forces in Burma were known to dispose, and it was a measure of the importance attached by the enemy to the outcome of the struggle in the Myinmu bridgehead that he now sought to commit them in the field for the first time since they had been withdrawn from the Imphal front in the previous June. They were, however, destroyed before they came within range of infantry weapons, their destruction being shortly afterwards verified by advancing Allied troops who inspected their remains.

94. Somewhat different in character from the harassing of Japanese road communication was the interdiction of the railways used by the enemy in supplying his troops in Burma. Already, before the opening of the period covered by this despatch, the operation of ground-attack fighter aircraft over these lines had become a difficult and expensive undertaking. Trains had practically ceased to run by day, their component parts generally being camouflaged and dispersed until sunset with the locomotives hidden in specially constructed shelters, often at the end of long sidings deep in the jungle. All obvious railway targets were guarded by efficient anti-aircraft defences, dummy or derelict locomotives being placed to decoy the aircraft into traps or at least to draw their fire. Nevertheless, some three hundred and ten locomotives were successfully attacked by day, Beaufighters accounting for one hundred and eighty-seven. Most of the remainder were claimed by Mosquitos, Mustangs, Lightnings and Thunderbolts.

95. Of the number of rolling stock destroyed it would be unsafe to give any estimate, but in any case there were always more than enough waggons available in Burma to satisfy Japanese military needs—in contrast to the position in regard to locomotives, which, as a result of past Allied air attacks were always in short supply, the Japanese going so far as to import them from Siam and to use petrol-driven cars to haul railway waggons. Water-towers always presented a vulnerable target, difficult to hide, and thirty-nine were holed during the period. It should be noted that these day attacks by ground-attack fighters reached as far as the northern extremities of both the Burma-Siam and the Bangkok-Chiengmai railways.

96. A further one hundred and twenty-two locomotives were put out of commission as a result of night attacks, thirty-seven being contributed by Mosquitos and thirty-seven by Mitchells. These attacks were of course delivered upon trains in full employment, and were not infrequently accompanied by spectacular results, with engine boilers exploding, trucks aflame and a series of secondary explosions. They may be reckoned as having inflicted greater material injury upon the enemy than a numerical comparison between the numbers of locomotives damaged by day and by night would suggest.

97. Concurrently with attacks upon locomotives, key points in the Burmese railway system, such as the junctions at Thazi and Pyinmana, were bombed, mainly by Mitchells and Lightnings. But the main weight of attack continued to be directed upon bridges, which were so numerous that it was impossible to provide anti-aircraft defences for more than the most important. The enemy pursued his established policy of erecting by-pass trestle bridges to serve as temporary substitutes for the permanent structures wrecked or menaced by air attack.

98. In all, about three hundred bridges were put out of commission by medium, light and fighter bombers; of this total, one hundred and twelve were railway bridges. So great, however, was the success of the bridge destruction policy, that in connection with the unexpectedly rapid advance of the Fourteenth Army it provoked the query whether we were not destroying our own future land line of communication in advance, and agreement was reached by which, from February onwards, the indiscriminate destruction of bridges was abandoned in favour of a policy of keeping specified major bridges unserviceable. When, in course of time, the sites were occupied by Allied

troops, Bailey bridge sections flown in by transport aircraft were available to mend the broken thoroughfare.

99. Attacks on watercraft in Burma were pressed home by ground-attack fighters of all types throughout the campaign, particularly along the Irrawaddy, always an important Japanese line of communication, and also on the Arakan coast and the waterways of south-west Burma, though, as along the land routes so on the waterways, the enemy moved mainly by night. A rough estimate of the total number of inland or coastal watercraft in enemy use successfully attacked is 11,822 of which 302 were power-driven units. Towards the end of the campaign, the Irrawaddy tended to become less a line of communication for the Japanese than a hindrance to their lateral mobility, so that boats collected for ferrying rather than supply craft provided the main targets. At the same time, air reconnaissance and attack was maintained at a high rate over the Bassein-Henzada district in order to discourage the enemy division located there from moving eastwards to reinforce the main battle-front in central Burma. In the course of April, the motor launches supplying this garrison formation were successfully attacked on a number of occasions, notably on the 25th, when their hiding-place south-west of Rangoon was located and bombed and strafed with rocket projectiles by a mixed force of twenty-seven Beaufighters and Mosquitos.

100. A word must be added in connexion with the patrols flown by Beaufighters to intercept enemy shipping in the Gulf of Martaban. Owing to the reduction through air attack of the carrying capacity of the overland routes of entry into Burma, the Japanese had increasing resort during 1944 to the shipment of goods northwards along the Tenasserim coast and thence westwards across the Gulf of Martaban to Rangoon, employing for this a number of coasters of wooden construction eighty to one hundred and twenty feet in length. A daily patrol was maintained by Beaufighters, whose base at Chiringa lay not far short of five hundred miles distant from the Gulf at its nearest point, and resulted in the sinking of twenty-eight coasters, many of which were destroyed at dawn or dusk soon before ships reached or after they had left the nooks in which they hid during the day.

101. Attacks by all types of aircraft likewise continued, throughout the campaign, to be directed against enemy bivouac and barrack areas and against storage points from small stacks of petrol drums near the front line to the great dumps north of Rangoon mentioned elsewhere in this despatch. Despite the undoubted accuracy of operations against this type of target, more particularly by Lightnings, Mosquitos and Mitchells, difficulties of terrain often forbade the assessment of results, even with the aid of photographs, and in default of the subsequent occupation of the target area by our own troops it has often only been a reference in a Japanese diary or an intelligence report which has arrived weeks or even months later which served to clinch the evidence of success. To take one instance out of many, it was not until several weeks after the event that the full success of the heavy raids of 8th February on targets at Yenangyaung was confirmed, when two prisoners of war agreed that they had been most terrifying, and stated that one bomb had destroyed thirty-four motor vehicles parked under shelter, and that another had landed in a trench in which some thirty Japanese were sheltering, killing all the occupants.

* * * *

Tactical Support of 15 Corps.

102. Tactical support of 15 Corps followed lines closely parallel to those on which air support was furnished to the Fourteenth Army. There were, however, certain special characteristics which deserve mention. After the initial advance down the Kaladan Valley, the major forward moves of the ground forces were marked not by overland offensives leading to a break-through by mechanised formations, but by a series of amphibious landings at half-a-dozen points on the coast. Of the three island landings, those on Akyab and Cheduba were completely unopposed, while that on Ramree met only with slight opposition; few or no targets presented themselves and the air support on these occasions was therefore akin to a peace-time exercise. The mainland landings each achieved tactical surprise, but were all followed shortly by bitter fighting when the enemy entrenched himself in characteristic fashion and attempted to prevent the exploitation of the initial landing. Fierce battles then developed on the same general pattern as those for the Irrawaddy bridgeheads.

103. Two developments confined to operations by 224 Group deserve mention. The first was the use of Spitfires in the fighter-bomber role. The second was the employment, from February onwards, of airborne Visual Control Posts, whose success was undoubted. From a light aircraft they were able to discern targets in the coastal jungle that were well concealed from ground observation, and so to pass directions to the aircraft waiting to attack. Two of these teams were operating by the end of the campaign.

104. Indirect support of 15 Corps centred largely around the maintenance of air attacks upon the long supply line on which the Japanese depended for the existence of their troops in Arakan. Its forward end among the coastal waterways and along the parallel road southwards to Taungup was covered by ground-attack fighters of all types, while the eastward track from An to Minbu—whose existence had been established by Beaufighters on reconnaissance—and the mountain road from Taungup to the railhead at Prome, also yielded valuable targets. Stress was laid by the army in March and April, 1945, upon the need for maintaining a continuous interdiction of the latter road by cratering its surface or precipitating landslides by bombing, even at the cost of denying ourselves the future use of a much needed supplementary land line of communication to the Irrawaddy valley, and fighter-bombers and also heavy bombers of the Strategic Air Force were accordingly diverted to this purpose. Targets along the Prome-Rangoon railway were attacked as elsewhere in central Burma; in this, the destruction of its bridges by Lightnings of the 459th Squadron in February was especially

notable. The stores areas at Taungup and Prome were watched and bombed from time to time.

* * * *

Tactical Support of the Northern Combat Area Command.

105. On the north-eastern sector of the front, direct air support to Special Force and later to Thirty-six Division together with the Chinese divisions and the American Mars Task Force further to the east, was provided by the P.47s., P.38s. and also by the B.25s. of the Tenth U.S.A.A.F. The general principles of army/air force co-operation were as on other sectors of the front, the Visual Control Post being known as the "air party". There were, however, two directions in which the technique of close air support as practised by the Tenth U.S.A.A.F. was more advanced than on the 221 and 224 Group sectors. The first was in the more highly developed signals methods used in R/T communications between the "air party" on the one hand and the attacking aircraft and also the light aircraft—L.5s.—used for observation on the other.

106. The second lay in the special use made in the N.C.A.C. area of photography for tactical operations. Photographs of all sorts were used—low level verticals, reconnaissance strips, obliques and pin point shots. A simple method was worked out by which a common photograph grid was accepted by both ground and air forces for marking photographs; this was all the more necessary in that the country through which the N.C.A.C. forces were advancing consisted of an expanse of jungle-clad hills with few natural features by reference to which a target could be simply identified. The effectiveness of close air support was acknowledged by the ground forces in this sector no less than elsewhere, despite the considerable obstacles offered by the wild terrain to an exact collaboration.

107. It was no doubt in part the very success of air support operations in the N.C.A.C. area that led to their comparatively early cessation. The country through which the land forces advanced with a continually growing momentum offered few or no sites for the construction of forward landing-grounds, and the leading army units tended more and more to draw away from the available air bases as a consequence. Enemy opposition also dwindled, and, from the end of March onwards, contact was lost with the Japanese. Thenceforward, the air effort was thus inevitably restricted to long-range attacks upon the transport routes, supply centres and bivouac points along the enemy line of retreat through the Shan States southwards into Siam.

* * * *

PART SIX.

STRATEGIC AIR FORCE.

108. Operations by heavy bombers in this theatre were conditioned by the restricted nature of the targets available and by the vulnerability of the all-important Japanese lines of communication. To understand the pattern of attack, and to assess its results, demands some knowledge of these circumstances, which are discussed in some detail hereunder.

109. The factors of climate, topography and the occupation of large areas of China combined to make the Japanese grip on Burma one which, it was early realised, the Allies would have great difficulty in prising loose. Notwithstanding his seemingly inviolable front, the enemy possessed an Achilles' heel in his poverty of natural resources and his consequent dependence on seas that he has never actually controlled. A high percentage of everything upon which his industry thrives must cross the sea in crude form to be processed in the homeland; thence it must recross the seas to arrive at the fighting line. From Japan to Burma the sea lanes stretch for some 4,000 miles, of which more and more were open to attack by Allied bombers as strength, experience and air bases developed. The railways which carried his supplies thence to the front were at the mercy of Allied bombers to an even greater degree.

110. Communications by sea were not disputed during 1942 and much of 1943. It was simple to follow the normal channels of commerce to the ports of Siam and Malaya in the east, Singapore in the south, and Mergui, Tavoy, Ye, Moulmein and Rangoon in the west. But Japan herself had proved by the sinking of the "Prince of Wales" and "Repulse" that control of the sea demands control of the air above the sea. In her early victory lay the seeds of her own defeat, for Allied aircraft disputed with her, and won, control of the air over all her lines of communication in Burma and Siam.

111. From the nodal ports, the railways of Burma and Siam constitute a system of strategically connected lines with a total length of approximately 5,000 miles. From Phnom Penh, north-west of Saigon, the railway goes west and north-west through Bangkok, Pegu and Mandalay, where it forks into two lines terminating at Lashio and Myitkyina with branches to Rangoon, Bassein, Kyaukpadaung, Myingyan and Ye-U. The tactical importance of all these railheads was reinforced by their strategic positioning on the lines of supply. Their function was not only to feed forward material from Japan, but to shuttle within the occupied territories the natural resources whose employment would ease the load on Japanese shipping—rice, tungsten, oil, tin and rubber. It has been estimated that at least 50 per cent. of the Japanese Army's requirements in Burma were produced locally.

* * * *

112. In June, 1944, the Strategic Air Force underwent changes in organisation and composition that materially reduced its strength and effectiveness during the monsoon months. The Twelfth Bombardment Group, comprising four squadrons of Mitchells, was transferred to Third Tactical Air Force, a step for which Air Marshal Baldwin had long pressed, and the Seventh Bombardment Group of four squadrons of Liberators was diverted to haul petrol to China. This was considered more remunerative employment for them than the conduct of bomber operations under active monsoon conditions. Strategic Air Force therefore retained only its British component, totalling three Liberator and two Wellington squadrons, excluding the Special Duty and Air Sea Rescue element. In consequence of the

reduction in strength, and with the monsoon at its height, a change in policy was necessary, and a new Operational Directive (No. 10) declared that objectives would be tactical targets best calculated to assist Fourteenth Army; communications, shipping and railways, with particular attention to the Martaban—Pegu, Pegu—Mandalay and Bangkok—Nampang sections.

113. In October, the Seventh Bombardment Group returned to Strategic Air Force, and in the following month, Nos. 99 and 215 Squadrons returned to the line having been re-equipped from Wellingtons to Liberators. With one more accession to its strength (No. 358 Squadron formed within the Command and operating by January), Strategic Air Force reached its full power for the vital six months to follow. Its operational function was accordingly expanded from October onwards to include all the duties of strategic bombers, including mining, and the Force was ready for the decisive campaign which lay ahead.

* * * *

114. Operations fell into well-defined categories, the first of which was the effort against shipping and harbour installations; the second, and most important, was the interdiction of the overland supply routes into Southern Burma; and the third the destruction of the enemy's powers of resistance in Burma by disorganising his internal communications, razing his dumps, and denying him the use of his airfields and military installations.

(I) *Attacks against Shipping and Harbours.*

115. Although the main weight of attack fell upon railways, some effort was directed towards the furtive and well-camouflaged shipping which plied the coasts, seldom moving by day and never venturing far within the radius of action of strike aircraft. Such operations were carried out with the purpose of deterring the enemy from committing his supplies to the perils of the sea rather than of sinking the ships en route. It was a policy of denial rather than of destruction. This choice was necessary since shipping was never frequent enough to justify intensive search for it, and the most remunerative targets were therefore harbours, docks and port facilities. Of these Mergui, Martaban, the new port of Khao Huagang, and Bangkok were most often attacked, and considerable destruction achieved. A typical intelligence report on a raid against Bangkok in March, for example, was—" Concentrated and successful attack causing destruction of forty per cent. of the storage units; sixty Japs killed ".

116. Accepting that enemy shipping was hard to search out, Strategic Air Force had resort to the policy of hindering what it could not destroy. Mining was already proved by photographic reconnaissance as being a profitable method of delaying the passage of supplies, for in harbours already mined there had been a serious curtailment of Japanese shipping, and such craft as continued to approach the harbours anchored outside so that cargoes had to be lightered ashore.

117. Thus from August onwards plans and technique for very long-range mining were developed and soon bore fruit. In September the Pakchan river, housing the newly constructed port of Khao Huagang, was heavily mined and the flow of coastal traffic seriously disrupted. Similar operations against Bangkok, Goh Sichang and Tavoy followed. In October a remarkably successful flight was carried out to the inner approaches of Penang harbour. Fifteen Liberators each laid four 1,000 lb. mines " precisely in the positions ordered ", with no mishap or failure although the round trip was over three thousand miles. Such operations continued throughout the campaign against all ports and anchorages along the Tenasserim Coast and from March onwards against those in the Gulf of Siam. Mining was the special and exclusive province of No. 159 Squadron R.A.F. who throughout the period laid the impressive total of 1,953 mines at ranges which a year before would have been considered impossible. The following results were observed from reconnaissance:

(i) Jap launch and passenger steamer sunk near Victoria Point (February).

(ii) 3,000 ton tanker Kuisho Maru sunk at Bangkok (January).

(iii) 200 ft. M.V. sunk at Bangkok (March).

(II) *The Interdiction of the Southern Burma Supply Routes.*

118. If the anti-shipping effort was intangible in effect, that against railways was spectacular, and its results immediately apparent. By far the greatest attention was paid to the Bangkok-Moulmein railway on which an overall total of 2,700 tons of bombs were dropped. With the interdiction of nearly all alternative routes, this railway was of paramount importance to the Japanese to supply and maintain their forces in Burma. Approximately two-thirds of the railway pursues a winding course in jungle hill-covered country, and it is not suitable for low-level attack, in addition to providing first-rate concealment. But as the strength and efficacy of the bomber force grew and the Burma—Siam railway became more vital, techniques were developed for its neutralisation. No precise date can be given for the introduction of these methods. A modus operandi was hammered out and in use before it became a doctrine, but its broad principles were as follows:—

(i) Bridges were the best targets because they were the most vulnerable and the most difficult to repair.

(ii) The underlying motive was to isolate segments of the line, and then to destroy at greater leisure the rolling stock and locomotives stranded thereon.

(iii) Diversity of attack was necessary to confuse the enemy.

(iv) Close photographic reconnaissance was maintained to detect any abnormal build-up at sidings or stations which would repay attack.

119. These principles were followed to such good effect that between January and April the average number of bridges unserviceable at one time was 9.2 over the stretch of railway from Pegu to Bangkok. It has been estimated that this reduced the traffic from 700-800 tons to 100-200 tons a day. The value of the attacks needs no further emphasis.

120. Operations similar in concept but less in intensity were maintained against the Bangkok—Chiengmai line, the Kra Isthmus railway, and the Bangkok—Singapore line. In all cases, the enemy reacted by placing the strongest A.A. defences he could muster along such a dispersed network of lines, by rebuilding and repairing bridges with beaver-like zeal, and by constructing as many as four by-pass structures at one crossing to counter or anticipate our attack.

(III) *Destruction of the Enemy's Powers of Resistance within Burma.*

121. To sever the external supply routes was not enough, for the enemy held at least six months' reserves of supplies that were contained in vast dumps, mainly dispersed in the Rangoon area. Therefore, during March and April, systematic destruction was initiated on the Rangoon Dumps in conjunction with XXth Bomber Command. Their destruction was vital, since with the stores contained therein the enemy might have been able to delay our advance and even halt it above Toungoo. The Dumps contained about 1,700 storage units well dispersed in revetments, and of these, photographic evidence alone showed 524 destroyed, and ground observers reported that well over 50 per cent. destruction was achieved.

122. The attacks on Japanese Headquarters and concentration areas can be illustrated by a strike on 29th March against the Japanese Burma Area Army Headquarters located in Rangoon. Reports indicate that four hundred Japanese, with a high proportion of officers, were killed. News of the attack spread to the Allied prisoners in Rangoon, and was the cause of considerable encouragement to them. The enemy's evacuation of the city a month later is much more understandable in the light of these attacks, which made Rangoon such a dangerous area even before ground forces were within striking distance. Mandalay had already suffered such attacks, notably one in January when it was reported by agents that six hundred Japanese were killed. The part played by such air blows in persuading the enemy to abandon his strategic positions earlier than anticipated must surely have been great.

* * * *

"*Special Operations.*"

123. Air operations in connection with intelligence and guerilla raising activities in this theatre have increased greatly during the past year. From a strength of two squadrons totalling 15 U.E. aircraft in June, 1944, resources were increased by the end of April, 1945, to three squadrons and one flight totalling 61 U.E. aircraft. The dividend that has been paid definitely justified the effort involved. From a handful of informants supplying skimpy information at great risk, the organisations grew, by the end of the campaign, into a powerful force capable of exerting a considerable influence on the course of the battle, and the air effort to support them reached a total of 372 sorties in the lunar month 18th April to 17th May. Between November, 1944, and May, 1945, over 1,350 sorties were flown, in which 2,100 tons of stores and 1,000 liaison officers were dropped behind the enemy lines. The effort for the preceding comparable period resulted in 34 tons of stores and 35 bodies being parachuted in.

124. One of the major results of the great effort involved was the prevention of the Japanese Fifteenth Army from taking any part in the defence of Toungoo during our advance, and rendering unnecessary the major battle which Fourteenth Army anticipated in front of the town. Other guerillas killed up to seven hundred Japanese, including a General, in the Toungoo-Rangoon area alone.

125. From the Air Force point of view, the great value of the Special Duty effort flown by Strategic Air Force was the provision of targets for the tactical Groups. During the final fortnight of April almost the whole of the long-range Fighter-Bomber resources of No. 224 Group were employed on Force 136 targets. Troop trains were caught at rest and a pagoda reported as a petrol/ammunition dump blew up with a huge explosion.

126. Special Duty operations in this theatre are of vital interest to the Air Forces in view of the difficulty of locating targets without the help of informants. Thus the diversion of effort to secret work has not been grudged, and current developments, foreshadowed in the R.A.F. Airborne Commando, will make the information supplied by operators behind the lines of even greater value. It is emphasised that parties should be thoroughly briefed in the limitations and potentialities of air strikes and that they should develop a speedy and accurate method of reporting if a full harvest is to be reaped from the information whose garnering depends so much upon the operations of our S.D. squadrons.

* * * *

Part Seven.

PHOTOGRAPHIC RECONNAISSANCE.

127. At the opening of the period, photographic reconnaissance was carried out mainly by the aircraft of the Photographic Reconnaissance Force commanded by Group Captain S. G. Wise, D.F.C. These included the Spitfires, Mosquitos and Mitchells of 681 and 684 Squadrons, R.A.F., operating from Alipore, and the Mustangs, Mitchells and Liberators of three U.S.A.A.F. squadrons, the last of which specialised in mapping. A fourth U.S.A.A.F. squadron flying Lightnings, began to operate in September.

128. The dense cloud banks habitually shrouding the operational area of South East Asia during the period of the monsoon interfered greatly with photographic reconnaissance, but advantage was taken of the northward passage of the monsoon in August to procure the first large-scale and survey cover of northern Sumatra by Mosquitos detached to operate from Ceylon. Other detachments were later sent eastwards to operate with the forward tactical air force headquarters from Tingawk Sakan (where at the beginning of September an American tactical reconnaissance squadron was placed under the P.R. Force), Imphal, Comilla and Chittagong in preparation for the forthcoming campaign, and these were later reinforced and moved forward in step

with the ground forces. From the beginning of September onwards, a considerable measure of decentralisation in the planning and conduct of operations was introduced, with the purpose of giving squadron commanders more latitude in the allotment of sorties.

129. With the return of fair-weather conditions in October, the effort of the photographic reconnaissance squadrons rose to its former level, and during this month the daily average of sorties represented over a third of the total aircraft available in the whole force. The methodical cover of enemy airfields, communications and other targets was resumed, survey photographs being supplied as required by Headquarters Air Command, and Headquarters Allied Land Forces, South East Asia. In proportion with the increased flying, the photographic work of the photo sections of the P.R. Force was expanded, nearly 354,000 prints being produced during January, 1945, the peak month. Technical photographic developments included the introduction of the moving film camera on operational sorties, and the fitting into Mosquito aircraft of forward facing oblique cameras. The latter were first used on 14th February, when a set of stereoscopic pairs covering the Burma-Siam railway was thereby secured.

130. An exceptionally valuable photographic reconnaissance of the Burma rice areas was carried out by Squadron Leader C. Fox during 1944. The results shown by an analysis of the pictures were subsequently checked up on the ground, and were found to be correct within 5 per cent.

131. The main hindrances to the operations of the P.R. Force continued, even in the campaigning season, to be factors inseparable from flying in the tropics rather than the opposition of the enemy, which remained slighter than was usual in other theatres of war. Successful cover of the waterfront at Akyab, for instance, was secured in November, 1944, by two Spitfires flying at from 50 to 200 feet, at neither of which a shot was fired. But the lengthening range of Mosquito sorties month by month bore witness to the mastery of climate and terrain. It was in December, 1944, that the first cover of Puket Island was obtained, in the course of a flight involving a round trip of 2,100 miles, which marked the furthest penetration to be made in this area. This record was, however, eclipsed by another aircraft which in January flew 2,431 air miles in eight hours and 20 minutes to cover Moulmein and the railway from Bangkok to Phnom Penh. Finally on 22nd March a Mosquito XVI broke the long distance record for this type of aircraft in any theatre of war with a flight of 2,493 air miles in eight hours forty-five minutes, covering the Bangkok-Singapore railway to a point south of the Malayan frontier. It was thus that the Mosquito made amends for the structural defect which had seriously curtailed its use during November and December, 1944.

132. The work of the P.R. Force was co-ordinated at one end with the short-range photography of the tactical reconnaissance squadrons, while at the other end, long distance survey work over Malaya was undertaken by the Superfortresses of XXth Bomber Command, U.S.A.A.F. The P.R. Force was responsible, for instance, for all the workaday survey and mapping required by the Fourteenth Army. As the Officer Commanding, No. 11 Indian Air Survey Liaison Section, R.E., reported in February, 1945, 684 Squadron, R.A.F. alone had achieved, in twelve months, three-quarters of the basic cover for the whole campaign and 1/30,000 cover for maps, photomaps and artillery block plots over the battle lines from Dimapur nearly to Rangoon and Moulmein. The work of photographic reconnaissance in general in this theatre has, of course, been of all the greater importance owing to the comparatively meagre intelligence available from ground sources; for air force purposes alone it provided an indispensable factor in the maintenance of Allied air superiority by providing speedy evidence of the location of enemy aircraft, while the work of the Strategic Air Force would have been unprofitable without the coverage of targets it furnished.

* * * *

Part Eight.

GENERAL RECONNAISSANCE.

133. As the period under review opened, a deal of uncertainty existed as to whether the Indian Ocean U-boat warfare would be intensified by the arrival of long-range German U-boats. Such a possibility was not improbable, and had the contemplated threat materialised then, all General Reconnaissance air power in this theatre would have been harnessed under the co-ordinating and supervising control of IOGROPS.*

134. The period from June to August witnessed a decided increase in enemy U-boat warfare, although at no time can it be said that the threat reached alarming proportions. During these three months the enemy (operating with considerable wariness) sank thirteen ships of the medium-sized merchant vessel class, and, in turn, suffered the loss of one submarine as a result of a combined attack by aircraft and Naval Force 66.

135. In July, a concentration of enemy units in and around the shipping lanes to the east of the Maldives—resulting in the loss of five ships—portended a possible menace. In this connection it is worthy of comment that Catalina aircraft employed on rescue searches co-operated in the location and eventual rescue of 244 survivors.

136. Having regard to the amount of shipping in the Indian Ocean, and the fact that during August there were possibly five German units operating in these waters, the enemy's achievements might be considered singularly paltry. This is a tribute to the constant vigilance of General Reconnaissance aircraft in the flying of anti-U-boat sweeps and patrols. Such a policy might not have produced many sightings and kills—a consideration of the immense expanses of ocean to be guarded will clearly show the difficulty of locating enemy units—but it kept U-boats submerged and out of range of our shipping.

137. With September came a falling-off in U-boat operations, and this was continued during October and November. A slight in-

---
* Indian Ocean G.R. Operations.

crease during November was considered as a parting shot of little weight and trifling importance. As an explanation of this it is reasonable to assume that American aggressiveness in the China Seas and the Pacific was absorbing the attention of Japan, as was the European war the attention of Germany. Thus the expected threat did not develop but rather declined, and as a consequence the need for an over-all centralised control as vested in the organisation of IOGROPS diminished with the declining U-boat threat.

* * * *

Offensive General Reconnaissance.

138. The second half of the twelve months under review opened with No. 222 Group still being primarily concerned in supplementing the hunting and striking powers of the East Indies Fleet in anti-U-boat warfare. But it was becoming apparent that the U-boat threat no longer existed. Therefore, in the due consideration of alternative employment was conceived the undertaking of an offensive role. The mining of enemy waters in the Malacca Straits and the Chumphorn, Singora, Padang, Singapore areas ; anti-shipping operations to deny the waters of the Andaman Sea to enemy shipping—this was to be the future employment of General Reconnaissance aircraft.

139. Mining operations were the first to commence, on the 21st January. From that date until 3rd May, 1945, 833 mines have been carried to enemy waters by No. 160 Squadron, the high percentage of 86.9 being successfully laid. The success of these operations, although not immediately apparent, will be revealed with the broadening of the operational scene in this theatre.

140. Only a short period of training was necessary to prepare No. 354 Squadron for its new assignment of low-level anti-shipping strikes, which were commenced early in February. A second Liberator squadron—No. 203—began to augment the anti-shipping effort in March. A statistical summary of the material damage inflicted as a result of these operations proves that these two squadrons played no small part in complicating the enemy's acute problem of shipping shortage.

* * * *

The Development and Control of Offensive General Reconnaissance.

141. The last four months had seen General Reconnaissance changing the nature of its operational function with deftness and adaptability. The reinforcement and development of this new offensive role was envisaged during March, when No. 346 Wing was formed at Akyab, to provide escort for " forward area " convoys and to make easily available a striking force against enemy shipping off the Arakan and Burmese Coasts.

142. One squadron of Sunderland aircraft based on the depot ship S.S. " Manela " constituted a significant part of 346 Wing. This vessel ultimately proceeded from Colombo to Rangoon via Akyab, and her advent to these waters was an important milestone in offensive General Reconnaissance. Should a situation develop wherein it was necessary to conduct anti-shipping and similar operations in a theatre where the scene of operations might be constantly and rapidly changing (with a consequent paucity of adequate land-bases) then a mobile flying boat base would be an invaluable asset. If this situation did not develop, then the inherent mobility of such a unit could be usefully adapted to the requirements of Air Sea Rescue and Transport operations, where, as always, the lack of immediate land-bases establishes a major problem.

143. The period closed on an encouraging note. General Reconnaissance had already struck a worthwhile blow at enemy shipping, and plans were in hand for an intensifying of these operations in the months to come. In considering the strategic plan of anti-shipping sorties, mention should be made of the invaluable contribution of those General Reconnaissance Liberator and Mosquito aircraft based on Ceylon, in their day and night photographic reconnaissance over the Andamans, Nicobar Islands, Northern Sumatra and parts of Malaya. Meteorological flights were also flown regularly, and materially assisted weather forecasts for aircraft flying over vast expanses of water.

* * * *

PART NINE

ADMINISTRATIVE AND OTHER ASPECTS

(I) *Administration.*

144. Administrative development of Air Command, South East Asia, during the year was dictated by the following factors:—

(i) The move of Command Headquarters to Kandy.

(ii) The need for identifying group administrative areas inside India with the geographical boundaries of the Indian Army Command.

(iii) The traditional problem of administering units spread over vast areas with insufficient resources.

(iv) The desirability of removing from operational formations extraneous administrative burdens.

(v) The necessity for providing operational units with greater mobility.

(vi) The planning of the administrative network to sustain and control units advancing into Burma.

(vii) The formation of new units in anticipation of future operations, while hardly meeting present commitments with existing resources in manpower and material.

(viii) The development on an unprecedented scale of air supply for the Allied forces advancing into Burma.

145. The primary British interests in South East Asia were the re-conquest of Burma, the Federated Malay States and Singapore, the Netherland East Indies, Thailand and French Indo-China. British air responsibilities in South East Asia also included the air defence of India and of Allied shipping in the Indian Ocean, the Arabian Sea and the Bay of Bengal. With these somewhat diverse objectives

and geographical vagaries in mind it was essential to evolve an administration covering Royal Air Force commitments which would effectively meet the situation in South East Asia.

146. The extensive re-organizations which took place during 1944-45 were effected against a background of strict and cumbrous control of expenditure by the Government of India, and of dependence upon India through the organization known as the War Projects Co-ordination and Administrative Committee for the provision of resources. There was, too, a crippling shortage of manpower in precisely those trades which make for good administration—non-flying officers (notably signals and maintenance staffs), clerks G/D., equipment assistants, cooks and the like. Moreover, the growing body of Air Command continually bumped its head against the Command manpower ceiling. It is not intended to infer that the R.A.F. in South East Asia was badly served in relation to other commands, for it was well understood that the allocation of manpower had to be assessed in relation to theatre requirements. Nevertheless, it was considered that perhaps the incidence of and the remedies for the growing pains experienced were not fully recognised at home.

* * * *

The Move of Headquarters, Air Command, to Ceylon.

147. The move of the Command Headquarters to Kandy was compelled by the insistence of the Supreme Allied Commander that his Commanders-in-Chief should work beside him. It was, however, rendered the more acceptable to Air Command on account of the growing need for divorcing operational and higher administrative control from the extensive and complicated negotiations necessary with the Government of India and with G.H.Q., India, relative to administrative services, which had tended to hamper the primary tasks of the Allied Air Commander-in-Chief.

148. The institution of H.Q. Base Air Forces at New Delhi had, therefore, many advantages. It liberated the Air Commander-in-Chief and his staff from direct day to day responsibilities for developing India as a base, and thus enabled him to address his attention more closely to the general problems of planning and policy control.

149. Before Base Air Forces was established and re-organisation was under consideration, it was generally supposed that a vertical split between the Air Staff and Administrative Branches offered the best solution to a complex problem. This meant that operations sections of the staff would move with the Air Commander-in-Chief to Kandy while the administrative sections remained at New Delhi. It was intended that administrative representation at Kandy should be effected by the provision of small cells or projections of the administrative branches concerned, which would work in an advisory and liaison capacity. This at the time, was broadly the view of Air Chief Marshal Sir Richard Peirse.

150. Difficulties ahead if such an administrative set-up was adopted at New Delhi as suggested, were foreseen by Air Vice-Marshal Goddard. The reins of higher administrative control and policy, he considered, must in the first instance, be held firmly at Air Command in order to effect perfect co-ordination with the Air Commander-in-Chief and the operational branches at Kandy. Beside, the geographic factor was an important consideration, for Delhi was fifteen hundred miles from Kandy.

151. A new scheme which would more effectively meet the situation once re-organisation was established and yet ensure the retention of higher administrative control at Air Command, was brought up for consideration during the visit of Air Vice-Marshal Goddard to London in July, 1944. This revised project was, in the main, largely adopted when, at the beginning of October, Headquarters Air Command moved to Kandy and Headquarters Base Air Forces was formed at New Delhi.

152. The essence of the new arrangement lay in the retention at New Delhi of an administrative staff competent to deal with all questions, save the important policy matters, direct with the analogous departments of General Headquarters, India, and the Government of India. This ensured adequate Air Force representation at the centre of political power in India and, at the same time, avoided the creation of a duplicate headquarters under Air Command for which neither the men nor the means were to hand. The administrative services, whose heads remained in Delhi were, nevertheless, represented at Kandy by responsible and independent skeleton staffs under a senior officer competent to inform and advise on his own specialist topic as required, so that broad policy might properly be formulated at the Headquarters of Air Command.

153. During October and November, 1944, there persisted a considerable amount of uncertainty as to the basis on which the administrative machinery would ultimately rest. For instance, as matters of high policy were decided at Kandy, it was decided by the Air Commander-in-Chief that he must have by his side the head of the service primarily concerned. This applied successively to the Principal Medical Officer, the Command Accountant, the Command Welfare Officer and the Command Catering Officer, and finally to the Air Officer in charge of Training.

154. The situation was finally crystallised and clarified in October, when a revised directive was issued to the Air Marshal Commanding Base Air Forces. For all day to day matters affecting administrative services, the heads of those services were solely responsible to the Air Marshal Commanding Base Air Forces. But when matters of administrative policy affecting the Command as a whole arose, then the heads of the administrative services were responsible to the Allied Air Commander-in-Chief through the Air Officer (Administration) (A.O.A.), Headquarters, Air Command. Similarly, when matters of new Command policy came under discussion and the agreement of the Government of India was required, the heads of the administrative services concerned were empowered by the Air Commander-in-Chief, through the A.O.A. Air Command, to deal with their opposite numbers in G.H.Q. India, on behalf of the Air C.-in-C.

155. As a corollary to this arrangement, the staff officers under the A.O.A., Air Command at Kandy were not established as mere liaison

officers. Their allegiance and responsibility was towards the A.O.A. Air Command, who looked to them for staff work, for records and for facts. They were not, however, his advisers in the formulation of new policy—these continued to be the heads of the services in New Delhi, who might if they wished send their own staff officers from Delhi or come themselves to make representations to the A.O.A., Air Command, on matters of Command policy external to the responsibility of the Air Marshal Commanding, Base Air Forces. This was not a normal system. But the separation of the Supreme Allied Commander and the Headquarters of his Commanders-in-Chief from the seat of the Government of India and duality of channels to the United Kingdom Government—either through the Government of India or direct—constituted an abnormal situation.

156. The value and effectiveness of the base organisation thus created was endorsed by the Air Member for Supply and Organisation (A.M.S.O.) during his visit in February, 1945. Air Chief Marshal Sir Christopher Courtney was impressed by the extent of the negotiations which were necessary in New Delhi with the numerous organisations concerned with the conduct of the war from India. He counselled a progressive decentralisation of functions to Base Air Forces and its gradual endowment with a greater measure of autonomy; this was of course in keeping with the original scheme and was accordingly pursued.

* * * *

Disbandment of Third Tactical Air Force and Formation of H.Q., R.A.F., Bengal-Burma.

157. Eastern Air Command, from its formation in December, 1943, onwards, was an exclusively operational Headquarters with no administrative responsibilities. When its Headquarters moved to Calcutta in March, 1944, administrative services for the area of Eastern (Army) Command were being provided by Headquarters No. 231 Group, and this Headquarters also administered the R.A.F. element of Eastern Air Command. But it was clearly anomalous that a Bomber Group engaged in active operations should continue to be saddled with the wide responsibilities for administration which were of no concern to the Strategic Air Force.

158. This, and other considerations pointing towards a re-organisation of the groups in India, was discussed with the A.M.S.O. in August, 1944. The logical course would have been to confer administrative responsibilities upon the R.A.F. Element of Eastern Air Command and to form a new Group Headquarters under it to exercise them. But owing to the manpower shortage it was impossible to create a new headquarters altogether distinct from Headquarters, Eastern Air Command, and it was therefore agreed that H.Q. No. 231 Group should give up its extraneous administrative responsibilities, and that the administrative staff so released should be reconstituted as Air Headquarters, Bengal. At the same time, the Deputy Air Commander, Eastern Air Command, was to become Air Officer Commanding, Bengal, with administrative responsibilities extending eastwards as far as the Brahmaputra. They could not be further extended, since this would have meant that the Air Marshal Commanding, Third Tactical Air Force, would have been administratively subordinated to the the Air Vice-Marshal, A.O.C. Bengal.

159. It was therefore decided to propose the disbandment of Headquarters, Third Tactical Air Force. For such a course there were other good reasons outside the administrative sphere—operationally, the title was now a misnomer, since in June, 1944, the Tenth U.S.A.A.F. had been reconstituted as an independent formation under Eastern Air Command, and the Headquarters of the Fourteenth Army was due after the opening of the new campaign to move forward to Imphal, where Headquarters, No. 221 Group had long been established, leaving XV Corps in the Arakan to operate independently under the G.O.C.-in-C., Allied Land Forces. Authority for the disbandment of Headquarters, Third Tactical Air Force was given in October, 1944.

160. The disbandment of Third T.A.F. involved also the expansion of Headquarters, No. 221 Group and the allotment to Eastern Air Command of direct operational control of all its subordinate operational formations. The date of this further re-organisation was timed to synchronize with the move of Headquarters, Fourteenth Army to Imphal beside Headquarters, No. 221 Group, and the establishment of Advanced Headquarters, Allied Land Forces, alongside Eastern Air Command at Calcutta. This move took place on 4th December when the Air Marshal Commanding, Third Tactical Air Force, became Deputy Air Commander, Eastern Air Command and Air Marshal Commanding, R.A.F., Bengal-Burma.

161. Headquarters, R.A.F., Bengal-Burma was the name given to the administrative formation now brought into existence to combine the functions of R.A.F. Bengal and the administrative responsibilities previously wielded by Third T.A.F. Geographically, its responsibilities covered both the base area of Bengal and the more easterly marches, bit by bit being extended into Burma with the advance of the Fourteenth Army. The military suzerain of the former was G.H.Q., India, and of the latter, Headquarters Allied Land Forces. Headquarters, Bengal-Burma was accordingly built up on a dual basis commensurate with the existence of two sets of army authorities with which it would have to deal, and also with an eye to future development whenever the reconquest of Burma should compel it. This stage was reached in February, 1945, when it became possible to carry out the anticipated divorce between Bengal and Burma components of the Air Marshal Commanding's province. R.A.F. Bengal was then expanded into Headquarters, No. 228 Group and returned to Base Air Forces, though the filling of its establishments proved a slow process.

* * * *

Administrative and Training Groups.

162. In order to ensure better co-ordination of administrative services, to facilitate combined training, and to ensure close liaison on internal security measures, the groups in India underwent a rationalization of their areas to coincide with those of the army formations.

This measure was brought to its logical conclusion by the formation of No. 228 Group in February, 1945, to provide functional and/or administrative control of all units of Base Air Forces within the area of Eastern (Army) Command, and to provide R.A.F. administrative services within that area. As Eastern (Army) Command extends its boundaries to the Burma frontier, the area of responsibility of No. 228 Group will expand. R.A.F. India is thus split up between four administrative and training groups.

* * * *

Introduction of Wing H.Q. and Servicing Echelon Organisation.

163. In the Far East more than in the metropolitan air force, the administrative problems confronting junior operational commanders are such as to hinder them in the performance of their primary tasks. In recognition of this and to improve the mobility and flexibility of the wing organisation, it was decided to introduce the principle of wing headquarters and servicing echelons for single-engined and light twin-engined aircraft. The scheme came into effect by the end of September, 1944, with the wing headquarters based on certain major airfields, and the servicing echelons became responsible for the upkeep of the squadron aircraft. The squadrons were thereby relieved of the responsibility for their own administration and most of their first-line maintenance.

164. In anticipation of a more mobile kind of warfare, it became necessary in December, 1944, to remove the geographical restriction implied by naming the wing according to its current location. The wings were accordingly given numbers, and their attitude to mobility thus greatly enhanced, as evidenced by the advance of No. 906 Wing from Imphal to Rangoon in six months, in a series of well-organized moves. The scheme has been successful, and its principle has been extended to other squadrons in order to centralize control of resources and administration and to economise in overheads.

165. Perhaps one factor has marred full advantage being taken of the inherent mobility and flexibility which the organisation would afford. The provision of more servicing echelons than squadrons would allow of peak periods of operational effort at very short notice from advance airfields, for an additional servicing echelon could be flown in to supplement the existing maintenance personnel. This lesson was learned at Akyab where the providential presence of a servicing commando allowed of a much higher rate of effort from the island during the early days of the occupation than would otherwise have been possible.

* * * *

The Manpower Situation.

166. The Command has been continually hampered by an ill-balanced allotment of manpower, whereby shortages have been concentrated in certain vital trades, rendering the administrative machine extremely difficult to operate efficiently.

167. In June, 1944, the establishment and strength of the Command for ground British personnel were as follows: —

	Establishment	Strength	Shortage
Officers	6,277	5,170	1,107
Other ranks	88,636	80,967	7,669
	94,913	86,137	8,776

The deficiency of 18 per cent. in ground officers was concentrated principally in such important branches as Admin. G., Tech. (E), Code and Cypher and the like. The airman deficiency of 9 per cent. more seriously affected the clerical trades.

168. By May, 1945, the position had changed, but not improved, as the following figures and illustrations will show: —

	Establishment	Strength	Shortage or Surplus
Officers	8,103	7,573	530 Shortage
Other ranks	105,470	110,459	4,989 Surplus
Total	113,573	118,032	4,459 Surplus

169. The 6½ per cent. deficiency in ground officers affects principally the following branches, Admin., Code and Cyphers, Tech. (E), Catering, etc. The shortages in the Technical Branch have caused particular difficulty. The overall 5 per cent. surplus in airmen does not give a true picture of the situation, for there are very serious deficiencies in clerical and domestic personnel which are hampering the development of the Command. Clerks G/D are below establishment by no less than 36 per cent., Equipment Assistants by 29 per cent. and Cooks by 28 per cent. The surplus was concentrated in the technical trades and amounted to 7,100. Such a surplus was more of a liability than an asset, since it created additional work for the already overburdened administrative and domestic personnel and could not be used to offset the shortages elsewhere.

170. Since February, 1945, very strenuous efforts have been made to disband redundant units and prune such establishments as can conceivably be reduced. The diminishing air threat to the east coast of India and Ceylon has made it possible to thin out the early warning Radar system, and considerable economies have been effected. Much has been done to distribute the shortages where they could more easily be borne, and it was Command policy to make the strongest where it was most effective, that was nearest to the enemy.

* * * *

Conclusion.

171. The administrative network covering the vastness of India is now as complete and rational as present resources allow. It cannot be said, however, that the administrative problems of the Command are now solved. As the armies advance, the area to be controlled grows, and the net is in many places thin.

This is particularly so in those areas vacated by the advancing tactical groups, and extra provision must continually be made to administer those formations left in the backwash of the advance. It has even been necessary to graft additional administrative responsibilities on to the air supply group in the forward areas (No. 232), for lack of personnel to set up the requisite administrative framework. The conflicting factors of function and distance have called for an organization far more complex than would be the case in a more compact theatre. For this the only solution is a realization at home that additional personnel and transport facilities to maintain India as a base, and conduct an energetic campaign in Malaya and beyond, must be allotted on a more generous scale than previously.

* * * *

(II) *Maintenance.*

172. The maintenance organisation in South East Asia embraces supply, servicing, repair and salvage of all air force material in India, Ceylon and Burma; an area approximately the size of Europe. It was realised at an early stage that it was impossible to have the same maintenance system operating throughout the Command, since the extensive topographical diversities encountered necessitated that the ultimate systems adopted be dictated by the geography of the country. Broadly speaking, therefore, one system applies in Ceylon and India as far eastwards as the Brahmaputra, and an entirely different one was evolved to operate throughout Assam and Burma. In the former area conditions are more or less static, the ground communications, although greatly inferior to those of Europe, are reasonably good with no considerable land or water barriers. Here, a large and efficient base maintenance organisation has been built up which provides adequate backing for the air forces far beyond the Brahmaputra; it is in this base area that the Base Repair Depots, Equipment Depots and Aircraft Storage Units are to be found. In Assam and Burma, however, the situation bears a vastly different appearance, parsimonious communications from Calcutta to the railhead at Dimapur and thence by road over the Naga and Chin Hills to Central Burma prohibited the use of a maintenance organisation which was possible in England and which, to a limited degree, has also been found possible in India.

173. From the time of the siege of Imphal to the capture of Rangoon, air lift, the principal means of supply to our combat Army and Air Force formations, was restricted to essential needs and could not be provided to support avoidable maintenance at forward airfields. As a result, a policy was agreed of flying aircraft back to India for comparatively simple servicing requirements such as periodical inspections and engine changes. This obviated the necessity for flying spare engines and to some extent, equipment and spares, into the forward areas; at the same time it increased the mobility of squadrons and reduced their maintenance personnel requirements. Aircraft which crashed away from airfields had normally to be written off charge, while those which crashed on airfields, provided the damage was not too great, were repaired on the site. Surface movement back to India was restricted to a minimum, since damage to an aircraft during transit in this part of the world is normally so great that it is beyond economical repair on arrival at its destination. On occasions, damaged fighter aircraft were dismantled and flown back to India, the servicing personnel becoming so expert that they were able to pack the whole of a fighter aircraft and its components into one Dakota fuselage.

174. Owing to the speed and intensity at which the campaign was being fought, and the vital need to capture the strategic base of Rangoon before the onset of the monsoon, I decided that all the normal rates of effort must be exceeded, and all our Air Force resources were thrown into the battle. During one month of 1945, no less than 700 aircraft passed through the Aircraft Storage Units and Reserve Aircraft Pools in order to provide replacements for the 75 squadrons operating east of Calcutta. During the early stages of the campaign, the small number of combat losses introduced a major maintenance complication, since low wastage rates, giving aircraft a long life, placed upon the repair organisation a storage commitment which had not been foreseen. A further strain was caused by severe deterioration owing to climatic conditions, such as to subject aircraft to monsoon rains accompanied by sudden bursts of sunshine. This had an adverse effect upon the timber, fabric, rubber and electrical parts of aircraft. In the autumn of 1944, for instance, Mosquito aircraft had to be grounded as a result of such defects, until extensive repairs had been effected.

175. The maintenance organisation in the forward areas consisted of the Repair and Salvage Units (R. and S.U.) supporting squadrons at their airfields, and taking on all work which the flying units could not complete within forty-eight hours. Air Stores Parks held sufficient stocks of spares and equipment for three months supply, and the Forward Repair Depots which were located far enough forward to undertake major inspections and repairs beyond R. & S.U. capacity. In addition Motor Transport Light Repair Depots were deployed in the forward areas, and the importance of their work can be measured by the fact that in traversing the tortuous line of communication from Calcutta through Dimapur and Imphal to central Burma, mechanical transport vehicles had expended the major part of their useful lives before reaching their destination. Thus a great deal of ingenuity and inventiveness on the part of M/T servicing personnel was necessary in order to keep vehicles running, vehicles which in base areas would have been scrapped.

176. The maintenance effort in Burma can best be summarized as a triumph of improvisation to overcome bad climate and worse terrain, the paucity of spares, tools and equipment which was designed for the European theatre of war and not designed to be flown over, driven through or manhandled in the cruel country of Assam and Burma. The overloading of home production, and the overriding need to finish off the western war first, were adequate reasons for this situation, and the maintenance effort during the period which culminated in the capture of Rangoon was very

largely dissipated in a desperate struggle to keep the units of the maintenance organisation abreast of the operational flying units. That this was achieved speaks volumes for the tenacity, skill and loyalty of the maintenance personnel.

* * * *

(III) *Internal Air Lines.*

177. The growth of air routes during the past year is best illustrated by the following figures:—

	Passengers	Freight	Mail
May, 1944	2,103	166,313 lbs.	99,435 lbs.
April, 1945	11,514	1,579,119 lbs.	777,944 lbs.

178. This rapid increase was attributable to a greater intensity of operations, and better planning followed somewhat tardily by a growth of resources. At the beginning of the campaign, one squadron (No. 353) shouldered the whole burden while still largely equipped with Hudsons. In July, 1944, No. 52 Squadron was formed, and by flying 19,000 hours without an accident, speedily gained an excellent reputation for its high standard of operating and freedom from accidents over routes that include the hazardous flight over the Hump to China. In April, 1945, a flight of No. 232 Squadron, equipped with Liberator C-87 aircraft, began to operate on the longer routes, forming the most recent addition to a force the strength of which has grown to two and a half squadrons.

179. Parallel action to build up a ground organisation to handle greater traffic and more complex problems was necessary. To this end, static transport wings have been established at Delhi, Karachi and Calcutta; that at Delhi was intended eventually to move to Rangoon. Located at nodal points on the trunk routes, these wings also gave advice on all matters affecting air transport and ferrying to the group in whose area they were located. When their establishments were fully implemented, 229 Group Headquarters was relieved of a great deal of day to day work in administering some sixty units spread over India.

180. Even now, internal air communications within the theatre are not adequate. This fact cannot be fully realised by anyone who has not appreciated the vastness of India from a railway carriage or travelled over roads on which the twentieth century has barely left its mark. Moreover, in a sub-continent whose urban centres are so distant from one another, it is often necessary to plan an operation eight hundred miles from its mounting base, while the allocation of resources may be effected from another centre which may be fifteen hundred miles from the controlling headquarters. Furthermore, the major base for the prosecution of a campaign in southern Burma, Malaya or Java, is still India, and the need for swift communication between base and combat area is another continually growing commitment for squadrons who serve an area ranging from Karachi to Kunming and from Peshawar to Ceylon.

181. At times, local operational tasks have made the diversion of aircraft from internal routes to air supply a tempting solution to a pressing problem. This temptation has always been resisted, and it is a first principle that the vital arteries of South-East Asia Command shall remain open. The mobility of the staffs, the despatch of urgent freight, close contact with the battle areas, and the building up of India as a base, must always be a prime consideration when assessing priorities for air transport resources in this theatre. Not only is the work of all three services dependent upon speedy communication over long distances; it is on the air routes that the Air Force can reap a dividend from the transport aircraft which are so frequently operated for the benefit of others. The R.A.F. should also use the speed and flexibility of its transport squadrons to improve the efficiency of its own organisation.

182. Air Command has derived great benefit from the Transport Groups allotted to this theatre, which has made possible a closer study of transport problems and a more effective supervision of this specialised type of flying. The improvement in operating standards is well illustrated by the accident rate. In October, 1943, there were 49 accidents per 10,000 hours of transport and ferry flights. By April, 1945, the rate had been reduced to 9 per 10,000 hours. Such an improvement reflects the greatest credit on all concerned and demonstrates the close co-operation which has been achieved between South-East Asia and Transport Command.

* * * *

(IV) *The R.A.F. Regiment.*

183. Until mid-1944 the strength of the R.A.F. Regiment was deployed to the extent of rather more than two-thirds in machine gun anti-aircraft units, and the remainder in field squadrons designed for an infantry role. Events then forced a fundamental revision of the part for which the R.A.F. Regiment in South East Asia was cast. It had become apparent that advanced airfields, radar sites and other air force installations would not necessarily be guarded if their locations did not happen to fit into the tactical schemes adopted by the local army formations, and that unless the air forces were to withdraw everything to a safe distance behind the front lines they would themselves have to provide the necessary defence force. For this purpose the R.A.F. Regiment during the later months of 1944 was expanded and re-organised into ten wing headquarters, twenty field squadrons, three armoured (holding) squadrons and ten anti-aircraft squadrons, so as to provide tactical defence for air force units as required. The balance of functions in the Regiment as between air and ground defence was thus completely reversed.

184. The wisdom of this re-organisation was abundantly proved in the course of the 1944-45 campaign. As has already been explained, the essence of the tactics by which the re-conquest of Burma was achieved lay in the rapid advance of mechanised units thrusting through or around enemy positions, the strength of which had been weakened by air bombardment. The fighter bombers which provided the backbone of the latter, and also the fighters required for air defence, could only operate effectively from airfields close behind the advanced army units. The supplies on whose delivery the maintenance of the Army's advance depended were

likewise landed at airstrips as close as possible to troops in the line. Allied transport aircraft were often being unloaded on captured airfields within a few hours of their being seized. But as the army units advanced, it frequently proved impossible, despite the presence of enemy troops lurking in the neighbourhood, to leave garrisons behind to protect the airfields they had overrun. The defence of the latter thus fell to the squadrons of the R.A.F. Regiment. On their shoulders there thus rested the defence of the army lifeline and also of the air bases indispensable for air support and defence, and they were accordingly moved forward step by step with the progress of the campaign, sometimes by air.

185. The main airfield at Meiktila for instance, was occupied early in March, 1944, and was speedily transformed into a forward base for the supply of the Fourteenth Army, whose units had forged ahead both southwards and eastwards, leaving numerous organised parties of the enemy in their rear. The defence of the airfield thus fell mainly upon two field squadrons of the R.A.F. Regiment, which went into action on a number of occasions against Japanese parties attempting to dig themselves in within the airfield perimeter. For a short period indeed, the landing strip used to change hands twice daily, the enemy infiltrating by night only to be expelled the next morning when, as soon as all was clear, the transport aircraft would begin to land. The Regiment casualties in the course of these engagements included two officers and twelve other ranks killed.

* * * *

PART TEN.

CONCLUSIONS, RESULTS, AND LESSONS LEARNED.

I. *Operations.*

186. One of the major difficulties under which an Air Force works is the impracticability of ever drawing up a full balance-sheet which will give in detail the full results of air action. Unless a detailed examination of enemy records is made, air forces must rely upon the disjointed accounts of the ground forces, the reports of informants, and photographic reconnaissance, for an assessment of their results. This has been particularly the case in Burma, where so much of the effort has been expended upon fleeting targets, reported troop concentrations, or objectives obscured by thick jungle. Notwithstanding the vagueness of the information, it is certain that the number of casualties inflicted upon the enemy as a direct result of air action has undoubtedly been large, the isolation of the battlefield by the interdiction of the supply lines has been almost complete, and prevented the enemy from deploying his full strength in every major engagement that has taken place, while the new mobility given to armies by the unstinting use of air transport has undoubtedly been the major factor in the expulsion of the enemy from Burma.

187. There have at times been grounds for a belief that the effort of our close support squadrons has not been used to full advantage because of a lack of experience on the part of Army commanders of the relative efficacy of certain types of air attack against the varied objectives. A more scientific application of the fire-power afforded by ground-attack aircraft might have led to an economy of effort thus made available to apply to other targets. Whether the attack by twelve fighter-bombers against a well-camouflaged single machine-gun is justifiable, must always be a moot point until machinery is devised to assess the debit and credit side of the picture. It is not difficult in a staff study to deduce that the effort is unprofitable, but the same point of view may not be held by the troops making the actual assault. The results of the air bombardment may be just what was needed to make the action successful. It is certain that the high standard of accuracy developed in our tactical squadrons during 1944-45 has had an enormous effect upon enemy resistance.

188. The low incidence of casualties during assaults by our own troops also bears this out, as do the unvarying tributes paid by battalions and divisions to the work of the squadrons who supported them. Recently, further evidence has come to light from informants on the efficacy of attacks. With the co-ordination of Visual Control Post teams and other sources, an even more efficient direction of fire-power on to targets and better observation of results will be possible. If analysed, the plans compiled from these sources would provide valuable proof of the decisive part that can be played by close support squadrons properly trained and handled.

II. *Planning.*

189. The amount of planning that has been necessary to bring the campaign to a close has been large, due in part to some misappreciation of Japanese intentions and to frustration imposed by non-arrival of resources. There was a tendency also on the part of ground forces to formulate a plan of operations without consulting the Air Commander in the early stages of planning. In consequence, much effort was expended in the recasting of operational plans to take advantage of the striking power of air forces.

190. Much of this could have been avoided had the Army Commander been able to remain alongside the Supreme Commander and the Allied Air Commander-in-Chief instead of having to base himself at an Advanced Headquarters in Calcutta. Not only was proper liaison at C.-in-C. level impossible, but the full flow of information and views between the staffs was rendered difficult. The Burma campaign proved that no plan of operations is complete unless it represents the views of the air as well as of the ground forces at all stages.

* * * *

III. *Maintenance.*

191. South East Asia Air Forces have a background of three years' development under trying conditions with insufficient resources. The organisation became vast and was spread over a wide area. The first phase for which this organisation was designed is now completed; the flow of supplies has become secure, and the necessity for tying down large numbers

of men and stocks of essential equipment in India has decreased. A more fluid and economical base organisation should be possible as the war progresses.

192. Energetic action has been taken, now that the pipe line is secure, to reduce the reserve holdings of aircraft and equipment which clog the machinery of supply and absorb so much of the Command resources in manpower and storage space in India. An extensive reorganisation to undertake more maintenance in the field is contemplated, and, it is hoped, will do much to avoid the bottlenecks to which centralised maintenance is prone. Such a reorganisation is only possible if the scales of ground equipment, hand tools and other servicing facilities are adequate and fully maintained. For an Air Force working in the field a generous scale of equipment is essential, and the lack of it was largely responsible for the uneconomical base maintenance organisation which events forced upon South East Asia in its early stages. The saving in man-hours that results from a generous scale of ground equipment is vast. This should always be taken into account in campaigns in tropical countries where sickness and lack of communications militate against units possessing their full establishment.

* * * *

IV. *Administration.*

193. The standard of unit administration in the operational areas was not high. With formations spread over wide areas, and deficiencies in ground officers also in the majority of vital trades, notably among clerical and signals personnel, much of this has been inevitable. Nevertheless a very real need exists for the indoctrination of service personnel in overseas theatres of war with the principles of self-reliance and better improvisation.

194. The principles of mobility and self-help have only resulted from the perception of those on the spot to train personnel in the rudiments of active campaigning. In so doing they have made the best use of local resources to achieve that standard of morale and well-being which are the prerequisite of good discipline. The posting of a squadron commander from a well-established bomber base at home to an overseas appointment with no preliminary training in his changed circumstances cannot but have an adverse effect upon the well-being of the Unit. The setting-up of Junior Commanders' Courses within the theatre is the best immediate remedy, but the problems of accommodation, and the time absent from units, rendered it little more than a palliative in this theatre.

* * * *

V. *Air Transport.*

195. Finally, the Air Forces, having given a new-found mobility to land warfare, must also take advantage of it. When assessing bids for air transport and air supply, the highest priority should be given to the rapid movement of spares, personnel, and indeed whole R.A.F. units, in order to keep the force working at maximum efficiency. It is bad economy to keep the 15 serviceable out of 20 available aircraft supplying the ground forces when the diversion of one aeroplane to collect A.O.G.* spares would raise the serviceability rate to 18. If full advantage is taken of air transport, the striking radius of the Air Force can be still further extended, and the application of air power to any situation made more rapid and more decisive than hitherto.

K. R. PARK,

Air Chief Marshal.

Allied Air Commander-in-Chief, South East Asia.

Kandy, Ceylon.

October, 1945.

---

* Aircraft on Ground.

LONDON
PRINTED AND PUBLISHED BY HIS MAJESTY'S STATIONERY OFFICE
1951
Price 2s. 0d. net

Numb. 39202

SUPPLEMENT TO
The London Gazette
OF FRIDAY, 13th APRIL, 1951
Published by Authority

Registered as a Newspaper

THURSDAY, 19 APRIL, 1951

AIR OPERATIONS IN SOUTH EAST ASIA 3RD MAY, 1945 TO 12TH SEPTEMBER, 1945

NOTE.—A set of maps for this despatch is on separate sale at 1s. 0d. net.
This set of maps also covers the operations described in the other Air and Army despatches of the Burma Campaign from 16th November, 1943 to 12th September, 1945.

The following despatch was submitted to the Secretary of State for Air in August, 1946, by AIR CHIEF MARSHAL SIR KEITH PARK, G.C.B., K.B.E., M.C., D.F.C., Allied Air Commander-in-Chief, South East Asia.

FOREWORD.

1. Air Power's contribution to the overthrow of Japanese land forces during the closing stages of the war in South East Asia, is reviewed in this Despatch, which opens with the period following the Allied Forces' victorious entry into Rangoon on 3rd May, 1945, and culminates in the official surrender of the Japanese Southern Army to Admiral The Lord Louis Mountbatten, at Singapore, on 12th September, 1945.

2. During this period, squadrons of the Royal Air Force played a conspicuous rôle in the last battle against the enemy land forces on Burmese soil. More than ten thousand Japanese troops, ill-equipped, sick and demoralised, were annihilated by our air and ground forces while attempting a mass escape from the Pegu Yomas across the Sittang River and south to Moulmein. Their Air Force had already been eliminated from Burma.

3. August 1945 brought with it Japan's realisation of defeat and her decision to surrender. It forestalled by only a few weeks the planned invasion of Malaya in which over 500 aircraft of the Royal Air Force and about 200 carrier-borne aircraft of the Royal Navy would have demonstrated again the power of air superiority.

4. Instead, squadrons of the Royal Air Force re-directed their energies to the most extensive mission of mercy by bringing relief and liberation, in the initial stages, to tens of thousands of Allied prisoners-of-war and internees in the many Japanese prison camps scattered throughout the vast territories of South East Asia.

5. The successful accomplishment of this task made a fitting conclusion to Air Power's participation in a war against a ruthless and fanatical enemy whose years of aggression in these territories ended with crushing and complete defeat.

PART I.

RANGOON AND AFTER.

THE SITUATION IN MAY, 1945, AFTER THE FALL OF RANGOON.

1. With unconditional surrender of Germany on 8th May, 1945, the conflict in South East Asia and in the Far East against the last remaining of the Axis Powers took on a new significance, with the balance weighted heavily in favour of the Allies against Japan.

2. The only outcome of the war in the East, like the one prescribed for Germany, could be complete and unconditional surrender of Japan.

3. Decisively beaten in Burma, and with Rangoon recaptured only five days before the surrender of Germany in Europe, Japan, fighting alone, faced almost certain invasion of her homeland in the coming months. The systematic loss of territories throughout South East

Asia which she had invaded during her orgy of conquest some three years before, was now inevitable.

4. A redeployment of manpower and material resources from Europe for the war against Japan was scheduled to begin, which would thus quicken the tempo of operations. But long before the collapse of Germany had taken place in Europe, the plans for the reconquest of Malaya and Singapore had been prepared. With the other Commanders-in-Chief in this Theatre, I shared the conviction that the second half of 1945 would bring the reinforcements promised by London.

5. On the entry into Rangoon on 3rd May, 1945, theatre strategy was directed to the liberation of Singapore at the earliest possible date with a view to opening up the sea-route to Indo-China and the East Indies, and to liberating enemy-occupied countries. Thereafter, strategy subsequent to the re-occupation of Singapore would depend upon the march of events in the Western Pacific Theatre.

6. It had been the contention, hitherto, that the capture of Singapore would involve at least two intermediate operations before the final goal could be achieved. Firstly, it was considered that an initial operation would be necessary to establish an advanced air and naval base. Through this base, aircraft and assault craft could be staged and operated in support of the next operation for the seizure and occupation of a bridgehead on the Malayan Peninsula. Occupation and development of this bridgehead on the mainland was considered an essential prelude to the final overland advance on Singapore itself.

7. Hastings Harbour was originally selected as the initial objective, but this was postponed to take place after the Monsoon. Further examination by the Joint Planning Staff at Headquarters, S.A.C.S.E.A., however, indicated that a stepping-stone still further south than Hastings Harbour was not only desirable in relation to the time margin, but also a practicable proposition as regards the fly-in of single-engined fighters and close support aircraft. It was essential, however, from the aspect of resources available, that such an operation should be a limited commitment as a military operation and also as regards the shipping lift. These limitations, therefore, narrowed down the selection of this objective to a lightly defended island. Puket Island fulfilled this requirement. Its occupation was therefore planned for June, 1945.

Puket Operation or "Roger".

8. The Puket operation—("Roger")—was approved in principle by the Chiefs of Staff in February, 1945, but they reserved judgment as to its timing in relation to the fall of Rangoon. A plan for the operation was nevertheless prepared by the Joint Planning Staff and Force Commanders' Staffs were appointed.

9. Force Planning began in Delhi on February 2nd, but it became apparent that the occupation of an island so close to the mainland would involve a greater military commitment than had been envisaged earlier. The Army concept of this operation demanded one Division for the assault and initial occupation of the island, including a small bridgehead on the mainland, and one follow-up Division to consolidate the position. The Japanese garrison of this island was reported to be approximately one battalion, but other land forces could have been assembled on the mainland once the attack was disclosed.

10. Owing to the distance from our own mainland bases, air cover and support would have to be given by carrier-borne aircraft initially until the capture of the first airstrip, when the Air Forces would accept full responsibility for all air operational requirements. I suggested that the Army demands, both in manpower and material, were excessive for so small an operation (the same opinion being expressed by the Supreme Allied Commander and the Naval C. in C.). I felt that if such demands were persisted in, it might mean that the operation (which would have given vital air bases to support a major operation) would have to be dropped. These fears were well-founded, as the proposed operation was subsequently abandoned, mainly for this reason.

11. Development of the air base at Puket envisaged the completion of three runways to all-weather standard, with an initial force of three Single Engine Fighter Squadrons and an ultimate build-up to:—

    3 S.E.F. Squadrons.
    1 Fighter/Recce Squadron.
    3 Light Bomber Squadrons.
    2 Heavy Bomber Squadrons.
    Detachments of Air Sea Rescue and Photographic Reconnaissance Unit.
    Staging facilities for air transport and other types of air traffic.

12. In addition to this, the base would also require to be capable of staging airborne operations in relation to future requirements of the campaign in Malaya. The air base, too, would require to be fully operational by D plus 100 days, while its development to full capacity was so timed as to provide the necessary air support and cover for the next stage of operations comprising re-occupation of the Ports Swettenham and Dickson areas, and a bridgehead for the final overland advance on Singapore. The occupation of this bridgehead was planned to take place some four months after the initial occupation of Puket with a view to the final assault for the capture of Singapore.

13. Events in Burma, however, had forced a change of plan, which envisaged the necessity to capture Rangoon from the sea before the monsoon broke, and open it as a port to relieve the other overworked supply routes.

14. In this connection, it can now be put on record that a R.A.F. Mosquito aircraft, carrying Wing Commander Saunders, made a low reconnaissance of Rangoon the day before the British Armada disembarked. Finding the city empty of Japanese, and Allied flags flying over P.O.W. camps, he landed at the nearest airfield, hitchhiked into Rangoon and released some of our P.O.W's. Wing Commander Saunders then borrowed a native boat and rowed down the river to tell the British Commander that Rangoon was unoccupied by the enemy, and offered his services as guide to the Expedition. This unusual incident revealed that the enemy forces in Rangoon itself had departed between the times of departure and arrival of the sea convoy. It was later revealed

that the Japanese Commander of the Burma Area Army had been ordered to hold Rangoon to the end, but on his own initiative decided to withdraw in the face of the Fourteenth Army's pressure.

15. It was realised after Rangoon's capture that to postpone the Puket operation later than mid-June, 1945, would inevitably retard the progress of subsequent operations timed progressively for the capture of Singapore by the end of the year. The Puket operation was therefore abandoned. With it, there vanished a stepping-stone to Singapore which the British Air Forces could well have utilised to great advantage.

Effect of Delay upon Future Strategy

16. The importance of accelerating the Allied Malayan offensive had been emphasised. In the first instance, it necessitated planning for the occupation and development of Puket approximately one month after the Monsoon had set in. Any further delay than this incurred a steady deterioration in weather conditions and a heavy swell on exposed beaches. The cumulative effect of rain was also calculated to cause a steady increase in the saturation of the ground and proportionately greater difficulty in airfield and road construction.

17. It was estimated that the closing stages of the campaign in Burma, involving at the eleventh hour a mounting of the amphibious operation "Dracula" to make doubly certain Rangoon's capture, had imposed a minimum of nine weeks delay in the initiation of the operation to capture the weakly held Puket. It followed, therefore, if Malayan strategy was to be implemented to meet the proposed time schedule for the capture of Singapore that this initial delay must be made good quickly.

18. To achieve this there were three courses open for consideration, each of which involved much planning:—

(1) To select an alternative objective where airfield development was an easier proposition in relation to weather conditions and time available, or where airfields already existed.

(2) To retain the existing objective but on a less ambitious scale of airfield development and military occupation, thereby speeding up development.

(3) To abandon any project for development of a stepping-stone, and to embark upon the second phase of our overall strategy which envisaged a bridgehead on the Malayan Peninsula as a prelude to the final advance on Singapore.

19. Course 1, on examination, revealed that areas more suitable for airfield development did not fulfil the operational requirements, while the occupation of existing airfields in suitable areas was likely to require a major military operation.

20. As regards Course 2, if some reduction in the scale of effort was acceptable, particularly as regards the requirements of heavy bombers, then a substantial reduction in runway development could be achieved. This, however, would reduce the overall period of development to the extent by which the base could be fully operational to provide the necessary air support and softening up operations on a lighter scale in relation to the next phase of Malayan operations as timed. Furthermore, if reduction in base development were accompanied by a decrease in the scale of military effort required to occupy the island, this would result not only in saving time, but also in a general economy in resources and shipping. The Army, however, would not agree to any reduction in strength of assault and garrison forces.

21. Course 3, when considered, had the great advantage of making up the total time lost, which, for reasons which have already been stated, was of paramount importance.

22. It was obvious, however, that without intermediate air bases, close support by land based aircraft could not be provided either as a prelude to or during the initial occupation of the bridgehead.

23. For this purpose, complete reliance had therefore to be placed upon air support and air cover by carrier-borne aircraft until suitable airstrips could be prepared within the bridgehead. Furthermore, the degree of heavy bomber support would be severely limited by distance and weather. Even on the most optimistic assumption that one or more heavy bomber airfields would be available in Burma by September, air bombing involved a distance to targets of 1,000 miles with a consequent reduction in bomb load and intensity of effort.

24. It was obvious, therefore, that operations at such a range could not afford the required support for the initial occupation of the bridgehead. The lack of an advanced air base also introduced difficulties as regards the fly-in of aircraft for the build-up, and a routine service for aircraft replacement.

25. When the problem was examined, the Joint Planning Staff recommended Course 3, provided that carrier-borne air forces could be assured.

26. Course 3 was therefore adopted, and the operation which, in planning, became known as "Zipper", envisaged the occupation of a bridgehead in the Port Dickson—Swettenham area. The assault, it was intended, should be carried out by two Divisions of No. 34 Indian Corps, with 15 Corps in the following-up rôle. The amphibious operation would be undertaken by a naval task force.

27. It was planned that air cover and support would be provided initially by carrier-borne air forces, presupposing that at least three light fleet carriers would be available for the operation in addition to the escort carriers already in the Theatre. The R.A.F. Squadrons of 224 Group, which had given outstanding service in Burma, were to be flown into the bridgehead as soon as strips were available.

28. As complementary to operation "Zipper", planning was also initiated for the occupation of Singapore Island under planning code word "Mailfist".

29. The initial assault for "Zipper" was timed to take place in early September, 1945, and subsequent exploitation southwards in Malaya was so timed as to permit of the final assault on Singapore by the end of December.

30. From the air point of view I consider the "Zipper" plan for the assault on Malaya possessed one distinct disadvantage—its great

range from established air bases, principally in Burma. Had it not been for the diversion of considerable military resources to the capture of undefended Rangoon, I would have preferred an intermediate step to Singapore which would have permitted adequate air support and staging of aircraft. Time, however, was not on our side. In view of the Army's commitments at Rangoon, and of the naval disinclination to make an assault without a suitable anchorage nearby, the prospects of any intermediate operation completely faded away.

31. The "Zipper" plan, on the other hand, gave the recently occupied Cocos Islands a new and important rôle as an offensive air base in addition to its primary function as a staging post to the South West Pacific. Originally, it was intended that the garrisoning Air Forces to be based in the Cocos should comprise one Single-Engined Fighter and one Coastal Torpedo Fighter Squadron. The inclusion of the Coastal T.F. Squadron was mainly on account of a possible threat of enemy sea-borne attack. This threat, however, had steadily declined. In consequence, the operational rôle of the T.F. Squadron virtually disappeared, while the limited range of T.F. aircraft precluded them from employment offensively against targets within and beyond the Netherlands East Indies barrier. Therefore, I decided to substitute one Long Range General Reconnaissance squadron in the Cocos in place of the T.F. Squadron, thus enabling General Reconnaissance Liberator aircraft to carry out strikes from the Cocos on targets along the coast of Malaya and N.E.I. An additional advantage of the Cocos was the certainty of more favourable weather conditions during the monsoon.

32. In short, the R.A.F. developed the Cocos Islands into a most valuable offensive air base, and air staging post.

THE AIR BUILD-UP IN BURMA FOR FUTURE OPERATIONS.

33. From the review of strategy and planning for the impending assault of Malaya, it was evident that the air forces would be called upon to fulfil commitments extending over a vast area from Central Burma southwards to Southern Malaya and around N.E.I., until the defeat of the enemy in the South East Asia Theatre.

34. As the result of this trend in future operations, the problem of command and control of the Air Forces became far wider in responsibility than that which had obtained hitherto. Accordingly, it was decided that operational command and control of all R.A.F. Groups other than those serving in Burma should be exercised directly by Headquarters, Air Command, South East Asia, through the respective Group Commanders. Air power, it was realised, would soon embark upon a large-scale intensification of operations against the Japanese, not only in South East Asia, but also in the South West Pacific Theatre.

35. While the tempo of air operations had eased off considerably after the capture of Rangoon, the immediate task nevertheless facing the Air Forces was to secure bases and all weather airfields for the future redeployment and reinforcements of the squadrons in Burma and Malaya in the quickest possible time.

36. The decrease in air operations which coincided also with the arrival of the monsoon, was, in every respect, a welcome relief for squadrons. The task of the preceding six months in supporting and supplying the Allied land forces in the non-stop advance to Rangoon had exhausted R.A.F. personnel to a degree never experienced in the Middle East or North West Africa or the Central Mediterranean during 1942-1945. Headquarters S.E.A.C. required our squadrons to operate at maximum effort for a longer period than called for in other Theatres. Aircraft, too, had withstood the gruelling test of climate and semi-developed airfields. In the race through Burma to beat the Jap and the monsoon, No. 221 Group Headquarters had moved four times; moves of Wing Headquarters totalled twenty-five, and squadrons made no less than 112 movements. These moves by the Air Forces in Burma through a tortuous country whose roads and communications were notoriously bad, had meant some disorganisation and much discomfort, but hardly an operational sortie had been lost owing to any forward movement. Neither the men, nor the aircraft, however, could go on indefinitely. For the former a period of rest was necessary; for the latter, re-equipment was in many instances, already long overdue.

37. It was during this lull in operations that certain of these squadrons in Burma were rested and re-equipped before the next phase in the campaign in South East Asia was due to begin. The "Battle of the Break Through" by thousands of Japanese forces trapped in the Pegu Yomas of Southern Burma had still to come—a battle in which the Air Forces had conspicuous success.

38. At this time there were ominous signs that the Japanese Empire was beginning to reel under the fury of American air attack, which was now directed upon it without pause.

39. With the next blows in South East Asia about to descend upon Malaya, the trend of the Air Forces was a movement to the south—as far south as possible with Southern Burma as the springboard for the major operation which was to come.

40. The plan required a gradual movement of squadrons of fighter bombers, light and medium bombers and indeed, heavy bombers, to Southern Burma. It was hoped that by August, 1945, Mingaladon Airfield, Rangoon, would be capable of providing facilities for 100 aircraft, Toungoo with a capacity for 70 aircraft; Pegu 70 aircraft; Zayatkwin 48 aircraft; Pabst 50 aircraft; Myingyan 70 aircraft; and Meiktila 70 aircraft.

41. This phased build-up was by no means firm, for there was a decided lack of engineers' information on the eventual ability of certain of the more important and vital airfields. In face of Army representations that the original plan for the net of airfields in Southern Burma could not be met without diverting Army engineers from other tasks in Rangoon, I had to agree, most reluctantly, to a much reduced constructional programme in the Rangoon area.

42. On entry into Rangoon, speed in airfield construction was absolutely essential. Delivery of bithess, for servicing the only airstrip, was,

however, retarded owing to the land communication difficulties within the area, and I had to give orders that No. 96 (Dakota) Squadron should be given the task of flying-in bithess from Bengal to Mingaladon. The task was completed to scheduled time.

43. I regret that the Air Forces should have had to call upon the Army for airfield construction in Burma owing to the absence of R.A.F. airfield construction units and Air Ministry Works Supervisory personnel in this Theatre. There is no doubt that the American system of providing aviation engineer battalions in Burma proved better and more satisfactory. It might also be noted that some fifteen thousand R.A.F. constructional personnel were allocated by Air Ministry to the Tiger Force Operation in the Pacific, although South East Asia Command was deplorably short of engineers, and it must have been evident that this new Air Force was most unlikely to operate before the defeat of the Japanese.

Hastening Construction of Burma Airfields.

44. Early in June, my Air Marshal Administration visited Rangoon to obtain first-hand details of the problems being encountered, and to hasten construction of airfields as much as possible. On my own visit to Rangoon on June 15th, I was assured by Major General Administration, Headquarters, A.L.F.S.E.A., that all points brought up by my Air Officer Administration were receiving attention.

45. The enormous increase in the Air Forces' radius of action which the new airfields under construction would afford was foreshadowed in June, when R.A.F. heavy bombers, operating from bases in Bengal, attacked and sank a 10,000-ton Japanese tanker in the Gulf of Siam. One aircraft damaged by flak was forced to land at Mingaladon Airfield, Rangoon, which was not yet completed, and over-ran the available length of the runway, killing the crew.

46. The continued pressure by Air Command on the Army for more speedy construction brought better results, and it was a little more heartening, on June 28th, to be given dates estimated for the various stages in the completion of the following airfields in the Rangoon area:—

    Zayatkwin—1,750 yards. A/W runway by July 20th.
    Zayatkwin—2,000 yards. A/W runway by July 31st.
    Mingaladon—1,750 yards. A/W runway by July 31st.
    Mingaladon—2,000 yards. A/W runway by August 15th.

47. By October 1st, it was estimated that Mingaladon Airfield would be capable of accommodating a total of 150 aircraft for operational purposes. The airfield at Zayatkwin was expected to handle 130 Thunderbolts or Mosquitos, and would be staging through the Squadrons for "Zipper" by 1st October. Pegu was also being developed as quickly as possible as a heavy bomber airfield.

48. While it was expected that squadrons would be able to move into the new airfields by the end of July, No. 224 Group, which had been linked with Lieutenant-General Sir Philip Christison's 15 Corps in some of the fiercest fighting in Burma, was preparing to leave the Arakan with its units and to proceed to India for training and re-equipment in preparation for the mounting of "Zipper".

49. The move of 224 Group squadrons was greatly delayed and handicapped on account of the shortage of shipping and the inadequate land transport facilities in Burma. The fact that Army units were also leaving Burma at the same time did not make the position easier for the movement of Air Force personnel and their equipment. June, indeed, ended with the move of 224 Group far from complete, and it soon became apparent that units would not succeed in clearing from the Arakan before the third week in July.

Withdrawal of U.S.A.A.F. from Air Command, South East Asia

50. On June 1st, 1945, because of our air dominance, the narrowing front, and the fact that the tactical situation after Rangoon permitted no offensive action by the 10th U.S.A.A.F., the British and American Air Forces reached the parting of the ways in South East Asia Command. The American commitment in Burma had ended with the capture of Northern Burma and removal of the enemy threat to the supply line to China.

51. Each Air Force was now to prosecute the air war against the Japanese in neighbouring Theatres. For the Royal Air Force, the offensive now headed down the Malay Peninsula to Singapore. For the U.S.A.A.F., however, the route lay across the Himalayas to China, since the sphere of the American Command was designated the China-Burma-India Theatre. Yet another reason for the withdrawal of the 10th U.S.A.A.F. was the critical air supply situation in the Northern Combat Area Command, due mainly to the high rate of effort at which the 10th Air Force Transport Squadrons had been operating and which was now beginning to tell on personnel and aircraft alike. At the same time, the American squadrons required refitting and rest before their impending move to China.

52. The withdrawal of American Squadrons for service in another Theatre did not affect the strategic situation in South East Asia Command. The only aircraft which could have been retained with advantage were (*a*) the transports which were being phased out gradually to bridge the gap until the arrival of our Stage 2 aircraft, and whose withdrawal could not be further delayed on account of the urgent need in China, and (*b*) the photographic Liberators of the 24th Combat Mapping Squadron.

53. The period of integration between British and American Forces in South East Asia had shown a very real spirit of close co-operation —a fact which I emphasised in a special Order of the Day published on June 1st, announcing the withdrawal from Air Command, South East Asia, of the United States Army Air Forces under Major General George E. Stratemeyer, Eastern Air Command, Calcutta.

54. In my Order of the Day, which I sent to General Stratemeyer, I revealed how air power had followed the basic principle in modern warfare—that the air battle had first been won before embarking on the land battle. Once the air battle was decided, air power was then able to provide the ground forces with direct forms of assistance.

55. "Having taken a vital part in the defeat of the Japanese in Burma", I said, "the U.S.A.A.F. units are being withdrawn from Eastern Air Command to fight the Jap in another Theatre. The closing down of the fully integrated Eastern Air Command Headquarters is, therefore, an important milestone in the war against Japan.

"Eastern Air Command was formed on 15th December, 1943, at a critical time in the Battle of Burma, in order to weld into one Command the British and American Air Forces on this front.

"The British Army was hanging on to the western fringes of Burma, having stemmed the Japanese advance into Bengal.

"When the British Army was besieged in Imphal due to Japanese infiltration resulting from their superior mobility, the first task of the newly formed Eastern Air Command was to obtain air superiority in order to enable our close support squadrons to assist the land forces.

"Within a short time air superiority was obtained, due in no small measure to the long range fighter squadrons of the U.S.A.A.F. It enabled the Allied Transport Squadrons to supply and reinforce the beleaguered Army; also, it gave them the mobility which previously the Japanese had monopolised. From this time, until the capture of Rangoon in May, 1945, the Allied Land Forces enjoyed all the benefits of air supremacy which, in turn, kept inviolate the air supply lines and endowed the Allied Army with the mobility and striking power to forge ahead to Mandalay, followed shortly by Rangoon. It made possible the isolation of the Japanese Army in Burma by Allied aircraft, thus preventing the arrival of reinforcements and supplies from Siam and Malaya.

"In Northern Burma, the Tactical and Transport Squadrons of the 10th U.S.A.A.F. played a decisive part in the repulse of the enemy from the Chinese border and in the reopening of the overland route to China.

"A Japanese officer who was captured in Burma attributed the defeat of the Japanese Army to the superior mobility of the Allied Army. This mobility was almost entirely due to the air supply provided by the Allied Air Forces, whose record tonnage exceeded 2,900 tons per day in April, 1945. Due mainly to their superior numbers and operating at maximum effort, the American Transport Squadrons carried the greater portion of the air lift in support of the land forces in Burma.

"In conclusion, it is fair to say that without the support of the American Air Forces in Burma, we could not have defeated the Japanese Army as rapidly and as decisively in 1945. All British Forces, both land and air, are deeply grateful for the whole hearted support and complete harmony that existed between the American and British Air Force units in this Theatre.

"I am exceedingly proud to have had these American Air Force units in my Command, and, together with all members of the British Air Force in South East Asia, wish them good luck, and good hunting."

56. In my Order of the Day announcing disintegration of Eastern Air Command, I did not make especial mention of units of the Air Service Command, but, instead I wrote to Lieutenant General D. I. Sultan, Commanding General, India-Burma Theatre, U.S. Army, and expressed the valuable and splendid work which the Air Service Command had performed under Major General T. J. Handley, Jnr. Without this help, we should have failed to carry through the intensive operations of the previous 12 months.

57. While it was necessary to sever the British and American Combat units of Eastern Air Command, and Air Command, South East Asia, there was, however, no break as yet with the Air Service Command.

58. With disintegration of Eastern Air Command, the air offensive in South East Asia now passed in its entirety to the Royal Air Force, and an exceedingly active period in the deployment of squadrons in Burma began. Thus, the integration ordered by the Supreme Commander in December, 1943, had been fulfilled in so far as it concerned the integration of British and American Air Forces employed in the defeat of the Japanese in Burma.

The Impact of "Tiger Force" on Air Command

59. For some time after the capture of Rangoon in May, there were indications that Tiger Force was going to be favoured by London in men and material resources previously promised to South East Asia Command.

60. The Supreme Allied Commander, Admiral Mountbatten, showed his reliance on the Air Force in this Theatre, by a strong signal to the Chiefs of Staff expressing his intense disappointment at the contemplated step since he considered it would delay his carrying out their directive to open up the Straits of Malacca and to recapture Singapore at the earliest possible date.

61. I also communicated the concern felt by the Supreme Allied Commander to the Chief of Air Staff, emphasising that future strategy and operations in this Theatre had been based on the agreed rate of build-up of the British Air Forces and especially of British Transport and Heavy Bomber squadrons. Moreover, the withdrawal programme of the U.S.A.A.F. forces for China which had now begun, had been agreed and phased in with the rate of build-up of the British Air Forces.

62. The question of airfields in South East Asia for staging Tiger Force through to the Far East also presented some difficulties, since the most suitable area was Rangoon where insufficient bases for our own aircraft were available. In the United Kingdom it was thought that Chittagong and Cox's Bazaar were too far from Manila, and they were not accepted as alternatives.

63. It became clear that Air Command, South East Asia, must accept the situation wherein the air war in the Pacific against Japan received higher priority than ourselves. This was finally confirmed by a signal from the Chief of Staff in London on June 22nd, part of which read:—

"In case you are in doubt, 'Zipper' and 'Mailfist' have been approved by the Combined Chiefs of Staff with the proviso that these operations are conducted without prejudice to the preparation and execution of operations for the invasion of Japan and other operations directly connected therewith."

64. At the beginning of July, Air Vice-Marshals Sharp and Satterly arrived at Air Command on their return from the West Pacific where they had been making preliminary arrangements for air bases of Tiger Force.

65. I then learned that, owing to the lack of airfields, operations by the V.H.Bs. (Very Heavy Bombers) were not expected to begin until the end of 1945. This delay greatly simplified the problem of providing staging posts for Tiger Force aircraft through India and Burma since, by the time Tiger Force could be in transit, both the monsoon and "Zipper" would have finished, leaving fair-weather airfields available for Tiger Force in the Rangoon area.

66. It was indicated by the visiting Air Vice-Marshals that A.C.S.E.A. were expected to provide staging facilities, not only for the initial aircraft, but also for the reinforcement flow and for a daily transport service of three aircraft each way. They further expressed the hope that the maintenance of their reserve aircraft would be accepted by this Command.

67. I consider it worthy of note that while Air Command South East Asia was barely making do with transport resources of Dakotas which still constituted the major life-line of the 12th Army, engaged with the Japanese at bay in the Sittang area of Southern Burma during July, the representatives of Tiger Force assumed that Yorks and C.87s would be forthcoming as a matter of course, for their transport requirements.

68. Other examples of this clash in priorities were not lacking, for it was disappointing to learn from Air Ministry by signal on July 21st that, owing to prior needs of Tiger Force, no Lancasters or Lincolns could be expected save for Air/Sea Rescue before mid-1946.

69. My appeal to Air Ministry for Lancasters and Lincolns had been for no other reason that I was concerned about the future heavy bomber supply situation in the Command. I took the long view that we could not expect to rely upon U.S. supplies of Liberators and, as the result of the difficulties which were already arising over spares and maintenance backing, I was, therefore, anxious to start the re-equipment of the heavy bomber squadrons and to introduce Lancasters vice Liberators into Air/Sea Rescue, Meteorological and several training units.

PART II.

THE AIR WAR IN BURMA AND BEYOND.

AIR SUPERIORITY.

Won and Maintained after Air Battles over Arakan in 1943-44.

70. Allied air superiority in South East Asia was won and maintained in the Theatre after the air battles over Bengal and Burma late in 1943 and the Spring of 1944, and remained almost unchallenged until the final surrender of the Japanese.

71. This air superiority is not always given its full value when the fortunes of war in Burma are weighed. Without it, the history of the indomitable 14th Army might well have centred around a fighting force, justly capable of defence, but not capable of sustained offence. Air superiority too, meant a "safe conduct" for the air transport fleets engaged upon air supply and reinforcing of the advancing troops. At one time no single Dakota in Burma could with safety have taken the air on any supply mission had not the air lanes been protected by our short range fighters.

72. Air superiority, whether used for the close support of the ground forces, or the interdiction of lines of communication far beyond the battle area, or in air supply or in casualty evacuation, was indisputably ours, a fact which Japanese Army Commanders themselves confirmed after their surrender in August, 1945.

73. In the Japanese Army, one Commander had said, there had never been any real plan to develop the Military Air Forces. The air weapons he said, had been neglected from the beginning in favour of ground weapons. Ever since the China Incident, however, there had been a growing feeling that Japanese air power must be developed at all costs, but this realisation had come too late, and even then, the Army's claims had over-ridden the long term policy which recognised the absolute necessity of a wide expansion of air power and the production of aircraft.

74. Another Japanese officer, after fighting against us in South East Asia, said that almost always the Japanese Army had left the construction of airfields until the last, having concentrated firstly upon its own ground defences.

Few Airfields left to J.A.F. in Burma.

75. While the main Japanese Army had retreated to Moulmein after the fall of Rangoon in May, it still preserved enough strength to make a spirited stand during July at what came to be known as "The Battle of the Sittang Bend."

76. The Japanese Air Force, on the other hand, had been driven out of Burma completely broken. No attempt, indeed, was made to alleviate the distress in which the thousands of trapped Japanese forces in Burma found themselves during July.

77. Only twelve months earlier, the Japanese Air Force in South East Asia had made 333 sorties in May of 1944 in their last bid to tip the scales in their favour at the siege of Imphal, but had failed. For them, this air effort was a record for the Japanese Air Force for any single month when the targets were Allied airfields and troop concentrations in the Manipur Valley.

78. The enemy had behind them at that time the important air bases at Shwebo, north of Mandalay, and, in Central Burma, they possessed the airfields at Meiktila, Magwe, Pyinmana, Prome and Toungoo. Their most southerly bases were those which comprised the Rangoon group of airfields.

79. The Allies' sweep through Burma and the capture of Rangoon however, had taken all these airfields from the Japanese. All that remained to them in Southern Burma were three serviceable airfields located at Tavoy, Mergui and Victoria Point, on the Tenasserim Coast, and these soon became the regular targets for our aircraft based at Rangoon.

80. In June, 1945, yet another indication of the weakness of the Japanese air power in South East Asia in face of air superiority was

the withdrawal of R.A.F. fighter protection for the air transports—a protection which had been maintained consistently from the beginning of the Allied advance through Burma after Imphal in 1944, and had involved fighter cover over a front extending many hundreds of miles.

81. When Fourteenth Army marched a thousand miles through Burma in six months they achieved a great military feat in a country which had been deemed hitherto to be almost physically impassable and medically disastrous for the mass movement of men. With that Army, the Air Forces went every mile of the way—scouting, supporting, reinforcing, supplying, evacuating wounded and striking ahead of the advancing troops, to disrupt Japanese lines of communication and supply bases.

82. The same air-ground co-operation which brought about the fall of Rangoon and the re-conquest of Burma would have been repeated on a grand scale for the assault planned on Malaya—forestalled only by Japanese surrender. Even then the flexibility of Air Power was such that, in the emergency which followed the cessation of hostilities, it was able to re-direct its energies in one of the greatest relief and liberation operations of World War II.

83. In any final analysis of the war in South East Asia, air superiority is of paramount importance, and an indispensable factor upon which maintenance and supply of all our Forces in the Theatre depended.

TACTICAL AIR OPERATIONS.

After Rangoon.

84. When the Japanese pulled out of Rangoon, and the remnants of the main army succeeded in reaching Moulmein after the disastrous retreat down the Central Corridor in April, hostilities in Burma were by no means over.

85. There was no question of the enemy's capacity to stage a serious comeback; his supply lines were no longer reliable and the Japanese Air Force was out of the race.

86. But there was one aspect of the campaign which was not yet complete and one which began to assume greater importance now that the Allied Forces had established themselves firmly in Southern Burma and Rangoon. It was the presence of the large isolated forces of Japanese troops in Central and North Burma, estimated at over 50,000 men. While the Allied advance down the Central Corridor during March and April had driven a wedge through a crumbling enemy defence, it had, at the same time, forced a considerable strength of Japanese troops into the hill regions of Eastern and Western Burma, isolating them from the main Japanese army as it retreated on Moulmein.

87. The Air Forces, principally those of No. 221 Group, and the Allied ground forces deployed in Southern Burma, swung round to face these large concentrations of Japanese troops in the north between the Irrawaddy and the Mandalay railway corridor in Central Burma and the railway corridor and the Sittang and Salween Rivers to the east. Their object was to close the principal escape routes which these Japanese forces must pass through to get out of Burma.

88. Few factors sustain the morale of fighting men more than the knowledge that supplies of provisions and equipment are assured. The isolated Japanese forces in Burma, however, as the result of disruption and disorganisation of their rear lines of communication, were ill-equipped, and certainly denied any possibility of supply by air. They suffered considerably through shortages of food, also medical supplies, and took to eating attractive looking but dangerous fruits.

89. So long as these trapped Japanese forces remained on Burmese soil, however, they required considerable effort from the air to watch their movement and to destroy them as opportunity arose.

The Competitive Spirit of Squadrons.

90. The task of hunting and destroying these isolated pockets of Japanese forces, in co-operation with the Allied ground troops, fell largely upon the squadrons of No. 221 Group, since No. 224 Group, after its fine record of achievement in Burma, was now in the process of pulling out for training and re-equipment in Southern India prior to the assault on Malaya.

91. The competitive spirit among squadrons soon produced keen offensive patrols in seeking out the enemy with Mosquitos, Beaufighters, Hurricanes, Spitfires and Thunderbolts covering wide areas of country—in spite of Monsoon weather—and succeeding in driving parties of Japanese troops off the main escape routes and forcing them to seek the cover of jungle or scrub.

92. In this offensive drive by the squadrons during May and June, a total of 4,813 sorties was flown by our aircraft in monsoon weather to bomb and strafe the enemy.

93. It was during this period that a return was made to jungle warfare in Burma, as grim and fierce as anything experienced by the air and ground forces during previous months. The air forces faced the considerable hazards of monsoon flying conditions as they attacked enemy troop concentrations attempting to regroup and reach appointed regrouping areas.

94. The effectiveness of these R.A.F. jungle strikes was not only substantiated in appreciative messages by the Army, but also by Japanese officer prisoners-of-war captured at this period. Of the air forces operating against them, a Japanese officer, a L/Cpl., and a Superior Private had said during interrogation:—

"Dawn found us heading towards a village on the opposite shore. Later, we found that it was near Mumbu. We cooked some rice and afterwards all went to sleep in a bamboo clump on the bend of the river. Sleep, however, was not so easy, for the enemy 'planes were roaring overhead, and we would awake in a cold sweat in the midst of a horrible nightmare."

95. There could be no doubt that the enemy had a healthy respect for our British Air Force and sought the cover of undergrowth when surprised by our fighters, which strafed them incessantly. A Japanese Private of the 82nd Air Field Battalion, captured in Burma, when shown a collection of silhouettes of Allied aircraft, picked out the Spitfire as the aircraft most feared by the Japanese.

Closing the Net around the Enemy in Burma

96. By the end of June, the net was gradually tightened around the isolated Japanese land forces holding out in the Pegu Yomas in Central Burma. The monsoon continued. The heavy rains made the movement of Allied troops and their supporting arms exceedingly difficult on the fringes of the Pegu Yomas and along the Mawchi Road east of Toungoo.

97. The Japanese, however, got no nearer to escape. Whenever weather permitted, the squadrons of 221 Group were overhead endeavouring to locate the enemy in the most difficult of wooded country, and bombing on every occasion whatever targets presented themselves. For days, aircraft continued to search for heavily laden animal transports which the enemy were pressing into service to carry accoutrement of every description. Even lumber elephants, taken from their work in the famous Teak Forests of Burma, were employed in carrying light guns and other heavy equipment for the enemy. If the monsoon proved a handicap to the Allied Forces it was worse for the Japanese, who were completely cut off from sources of supply. In the Pegu Yomas, the plight of the enemy, as a result of the vigilance of air power and the movement of Allied ground troops, became desperate as they struggled against malaria and starvation, or suffered foot-rot and stomach and skin troubles. Some, indeed, were like skeletons when captured, while the remainder, still imbued with fanaticism of glory and death, rather than disgrace in surrender, struggled on.

98. In their jungle strikes and "hunting" expeditions, the squadrons obtained a large number of good results in spite of the difficulties of weather and thick ground cover. If the enemy looked for a lull in operations as a result of the monsoon, thus giving them an opportunity to regroup, they got none from the R.A.F. squadrons and ground forces.

99. In the Mokpalin area, where No. 20 Squadron had damaged much enemy transport, a message sent by Headquarters, 4 Corps, after the strike, said:—

"Thanks for the magnificent efforts yesterday on the Mokpalin road."

100. When Mosquitos of 47 Squadron went out on a strike, they bombed a village north east of Nyaunglobin, where it was reported that the Japanese, moving south, had taken cover during the day. The Mosquitos dispersed their bombs well among the bashas and on dumps of packing cases seen on either side of the roadway, while many low flying attacks made across the area did extensive damage.

101. An Army report which reached 221 Group Headquarters stated that during an air attack in the Meprawse area, some 30 to 40 bullock carts carrying food were accounted for, two petrol dumps destroyed and 50 to 70 Japanese troops killed.

102. Up the Mawchi Road, Hurricanes went after a number of guns or tanks stated to be moving in the district. Two attacks which they made on heavily camouflaged objects, revealed large guns with limbers or tractors. They left the targets in flames.

103. The plight of the enemy as a result of these jungle strikes worsened. A report brought in, following an air strike by No. 11 Squadron, said that "the villagers reported that they carried away 30 Japanese corpses after the strike."

104. Some time earlier, a strike by Nos. 79 and 261 Squadrons brought the following message from Headquarters, 20 Indian Infantry Division:—

"One 75 mm gun, one 70 mm gun, one 77 mm A/T gun, one 20 mm A/T rifle, six pistols, six swords, approximately 100 rifles, three stacks of ammunition and much artillery ammunition,"

were found by ground forces after a successful air attack.

105. In the last week of June, the main concentration of Japanese forces in Central Burma, was opposite Nyaunglobin, with protective forces north west of Pegu and south west of Pyu, which gave R.A.F. Thunderbolts opportunities for attacks. During one raid, six aircraft of 79 Squadron bombed the village of Thaingon. Some days later it was learned that 170 Japanese and 40 mules had been killed.

106. On the Sittang river too, where movement by the enemy became more active, Spitfire aircraft undertook patrols down the river, damaging and sinking small river craft of every description almost daily, thus helping our ground forces to interrupt enemy efforts in that area to escape across the river.

"*Force 136*" *and Sittang River Air Patrol.*

107. There were other major difficulties which stood in the way of the trapped Japanese forces in escaping from Burma. The guerilla tactics of "Force 136", which later played a conspicuous part in the slaughter of the enemy on the Sittang River, helped to seal this stretch of water against any large scale enemy crossing.

108. The forces of Burmese guerillas, which began to assume considerable importance at this time in Burma, had caused the utmost concern to small parties of Japanese stragglers, who suffered severe losses at their hands. These guerillas had been operating with success during the latter weeks of March, and throughout April, but they were even more active during June and July, as the Japanese casualty figures testified.

109. Organising the Burmese patriots was the work of the British Organisation in Burma known as "Force 136". It was an independent body which operated both with the Air Forces and the Army. The Force consisted of trained and specially picked officers who were dropped by parachute into enemy-occupied areas to organise Burmese levies and to wage surprise attacks against the Japanese. This guerilla warfare demanded the closest liaison with the Air Forces. Supplies, including arms and ammunition, were air dropped once the parties of levies had been organised.

110. It was through the machinery of "Force 136" too, that much valuable information on enemy dumps, troop movements, headquarters, and concentrations of transport carrying food, stocks and equipment, was passed by W/T to Army Headquarters, and special air-strikes quickly organised for the squadrons of 221 Group, R.A.F. These tasks were carried out eagerly by pilots, and many profitable and successful strikes were made against the

enemy. The Japanese casualties showed a sharp rise as a result of these sudden air attacks.

111. The air patrol on the Sittang River, on the other hand, consisted of three standing patrols daily—dawn, midday and dusk. The duration of the patrols up and down the river was so varied that the Japanese could never be certain of escape.

112. During one such patrol in June, two Hurricanes of 28 Squadron came upon 50 river craft of all types in the Suppanu Chaung and, after damaging them by strafing, went on to Letpan and there strafed several boats drawn up on the bank of the river near some villages.

113. There could be no doubt that the vigilance maintained by aircrews engaged on offensive patrols over the Sittang River was a contributory factor to holding up any river crossing in strength, which the Japanese may have contemplated during June.

Disaster overtakes the Japanese in Burma.

114. Disaster overtook the Japanese during July, when their final bid to break through the Allied net and escape from Burma ended in a debacle.

115. It was one of the blackest periods for the enemy throughout their ill-fated campaign. More than 10,000 men were killed in the month's operations. Those who succeeded in getting away and joining the main Japanese forces at Moulmein, took with them a picture of the punishing they had faced from the British air forces, the warring guerillas, and the newly-formed 12th Army under Lieutenant General Sir Montague Stopford.

116. Operations by the air and ground forces in this last major battle in Burma took on an entirely new character from the mobility and speed which had so characterised the pursuit of the enemy down the central railway corridor during April and May. Instead, the lull period in June had given the squadrons and ground forces a better opportunity to deploy at strategic points in Southern Burma, so that the enemy break-through from the Pegu Yomas, when it ultimately took place, developed into a wholesale killing. The monsoon forced R.A.F. Squadrons to base themselves at airstrips other than they would have preferred, but, even so, the operations were maintained.

117. The squadrons of 221 Group, R.A.F., accounted for at least 2,000 Japanese casualties. Throughout the campaign it was always difficult to assess with accuracy the number of actual casualties inflicted by the air forces and our own artillery.

118. Four separate phases characterised the July battle.

(a) There was a sudden flare-up of enemy activity on the Sittang Bend at the opening of the month where the Japanese, firmly established at Mokpalin, succeeded in making a bridgehead across the river and, after some grim fighting, succeeded in holding on the right bank, an area of approximately one square mile of country, encompassing the villages of Nyaungkashe, Abya, and Myitkye.

(b) Up country, on the Sittang, taking in an area between Shwegyin and Kyaukkye, parties of Japanese troops, as they endeavoured to escape by crossing to the left bank of the Sittang, continued to fall into the hands of organised guerillas.

(c) Yet further to the north 19 Indian Division and Patriot Burmese Forces in the worst of monsoon weather, were struggling along the Mawchi Road from Toungoo in an effort to reach Mawchi, and cut the main escape route of large Japanese forces retreating southwards down the road from Loikaw, and Kemapyu, on the Salween River, and then south by valley tracks which led to Papun and Kamamaung. From Papun, one escape route continued south-west to Bilin with easy access by road and rail to Moulmein. The second escape route from Papun went south-east to Kamamaung, thence by ferry down the Salween to Shwegun, and there joined a track leading through Pa-An to Moulmein.

(d) The final, and major phase, was the large scale attempted break-through across the railway corridor from the Pegu Yomas, starting on July 21st, by Japanese troops whose strength had now been estimated to be about 18,000, of which about 1,000 were left behind sick in the Yomas and could not take part in the breakout operations.

119. Squadrons which played such a conspicuous part in these operations were deployed as follows:—

(a) When the sudden flare up at the Sittang Bend began, No. 906 Wing with Nos. 273 and 607 Squadrons; one detachment of night Beaufighters, and the H.Q. and one flight of No. 28 Fighter Recce Squadron, were based at Mingaladon, Rangoon, thus within easy reach of this enemy force.

(b) Based at Kinmagon was No. 908 Wing with Nos. 47 and 110 Mosquito Squadrons, which were able, weather permitting, to afford valuable support to the parties of guerillas in their successful attacks on the Japanese in the Sittang river area.

(c) No. 910 Wing was based at Meiktila with four Thunderbolt squadrons, Nos. 34, 42, 79 and 113, ready for action at the first sign of the break-through from the Pegu Yomas.

(d) Assisting 19 Indian Infantry Division on the Mawchi road, was 909 Wing at Toungoo, with No. 155 Spitfire Squadron, and later strengthened by No. 152 Spitfire Squadron which moved down to Thedaw for a short period, and, at other times, staged through Toungoo.

120. When the break-through by the Japanese from the Pegu Yomas started on July 21st, the whole of the air support was switched over to this area and, for eight or nine days, the bewildered enemy was strenuously harassed by the squadrons supporting the 12th Army.

Battle of the Sittang Bend.

121. In an attempt to create a large scale diversion of the Allied ground forces, the Japanese, at the opening of July, launched an offensive at the Sittang from the bridgehead which they tenaciously held on the right bank opposite Mokpalin.

122. It was flat, open country with scattered scrub, and some very fierce fighting took place in appalling weather at Nyaungkashe, Abya, and Myikye. The village of Nyaungkashe, indeed, changed hands several times.

123. Air support thrown in by 221 Group, included the Spitfire and Thunderbolt squadrons operating continuous patrols or "Cabranks" in the Nyaungkashe area. The enemy took exceedingly heavy punishment. His determination to hold this area, at all costs, however, until the large Japanese forces to the north got down past Bilin, with the strategic town of Mokpalin on their right, safeguarded by the Sittang troops, was obvious.

124. Day after day, gun positions, troop concentrations, and river craft of all descriptions were subjected to intensive attacks by the air forces, bringing sincere thanks from the Army. On July 4th, No. 42 Squadron's Thunderbolts had a most successful day, when a 105mm gun was wrecked and two other guns silenced at Nyaungkashe.

125. It was at this time that some forces of 7 Indian Infantry Division found themselves in a precarious position as a result of the determined Japanese thrust, but, assisted by air attack, succeeded in extricating themselves.

126. "With the help of excellent air support quickly given," wrote Lieutenant General Messervy to Air Vice-Marshal Bouchier, A.O.C. 221 Group, "I have been able to extricate some four hundred men, including sixty wounded, from a difficult situation with good knocks to the Japs at the same time."

127. It was noted throughout these air operations, and further substantiated by ground reports, that a considerable number of Japanese troops were killed as a result of air attacks.

128. By July 11th, the Japanese offensive at the Sittang Bend had been contained, though the enemy still retained their foothold on the right bank of the Sittang, opposite Mokpalin.

Air Power Assists the Guerillas.

129. As the month advanced, a notable movement of enemy troops endeavouring to cross the Sittang River in parties at various points between Shwegyin and Kyaukke, kept the Spitfire squadrons on continuous patrol over the Sittang River exceedingly active. Thunderbolt squadrons, too, came down from the Meiktila area to attack forces of Japanese numbering, in some instances, one thousand strong, as they made their way eastwards. The large scale break-through from the Pegu Yomas had not yet started.

130. It was in this area of the Sittang, and also in the east, on the right bank of the Salween, that the organised guerillas, which had been brought under the control of 12th Army, ambushed hundreds of escaping Japanese troops moving down from Loikaw to Papun, and literally massacred them. No enemy party was safe from these guerillas under Force 136 who, with portable W/T, kept base informed of the enemy's movements and as a result provided the Mosquitos and Spitfires with definite targets, which they bombed and strafed untiringly.

131. The guerillas' flag was seen regularly by pilots heading for their targets. They were assisted by large indicator arrows on the ground, and even cryptic messages which the levies had conceived. On one occasion, pilots, correctly interpreting a message, "In M", located a Japanese force in a marsh.

132. Following a heavy raid on Pa-An, one of the principal staging villages used by the Japanese while moving down the Salween valley, a message sent from our land forces to 273 and 607 Squadrons on July 1st said:—

"More than five hundred Japs killed in last heavy raid on Pa-An. Did not tell you before as awaiting confirmation. Congrats to pilots."

133. An earlier report had described this whole area after the raids as covered in dust and smoke, with Japanese soldiers seen running about in panic and rushing for shelter as aircraft came down to strafe them. The Mosquito Squadrons got equally effective results for, during a strike at Kawludo, an enemy staging post in the Salween valley, north of Papun, a ground report stated that over one hundred Japanese troops had been killed.

134. Thunderbolts and Spitfires carried out a very successful attack on July 15th and 16th, in the Shwegyin Chaung area of the Sittang, and a message from Kyadwin to 113 Squadron and 607 Squadron said:—" Tell R.A.F. strike great success."

135. North East of Kyadwin, at Paungzeik, Mosquitos of 47 Squadron, on July 16th, made a bombing and strafing attack in the Paungzeik valley and 51 dead Japanese were counted after the attack. Yet another attack by aircraft on the 19th, at Shanywathit, resulted in two direct hits being made on a house which was full of Japanese troops, and over eighty are believed to have been killed.

136. The reports of successful air strikes against the escaping enemy were many and varied. In the credit for their success the guerillas of Force 136 must equally share. Their daring in approaching large enemy parties and making sudden furious assaults on them with gunfire and grenades before retiring to their hideouts to plan further surprise raids, was outstanding in this final killing of the Japanese in Burma. The risks, too, which they ran, while blatantly guiding aircraft on to enemy concentrations, frequently involved them in hazardous escapes. Many escapes were only made possible indeed, by aircraft swooping in between the levies and the enemy, strafing the Japanese pursuers. If caught, guerillas were tortured cruelly by the enemy.

Tribute to R.A.F. from Guerilla Leader.

137. A tribute paid to the Royal Air Force in Burma came from the leader of one of these courageous parties operating in the Okpyat area of the Sittang.

"Both I and every guerilla would like to make it known to every pilot who took part in the battle of the Okpyat area just how much all the brilliant offensive action of the R.A.F. fighter-bomber pilots was appreciated," wrote Captain J. Waller, British Officer in charge of Force 136 Guerillas, Okpyat. "From our point of view on the ground, we wished that we had more air ground strips so that we could write in full —' Hats off to the R.A.F. pilots. You are killing hundreds of Japs and your perfect co-ordination and patience in reading our crude signals is saving the lives of many thousands of defenceless civilians.' "

138. Whilst these exploits revealed the magnificent work of aircrews, they illustrated at the same time the confidence and daring of the British-led irregular, for whom the pilots of 221 Group squadrons felt most strongly that it was a case of "Hats right off" to the guerillas.

139. "From Letpangon we were attacked by two hundred Japs at 23.30 hours. We only killed fifteen of them, but we kept them there for you to attack next day when you put in two good strikes. They cleared out after dark, and went on to Yindaikaein where you were able to attack them again," said Captain Waller.

140. The combined attacks on the Japanese aircraft and guerilla parties constituted a war of attrition on the enemy. They could never be sure of safety in any village they passed through, and roads, planked with thick scrub, were a perpetual nightmare. The guerillas were masters in the art of ambush. With the air forces to supply and assist them they seemed to be everywhere, and to know the enemy's next move. This was evident from the casualties they inflicted against the Japanese.

141. It was after an attack by air forces on a large concentration of Japanese troops at Letpangon, that the Okpyat Guerilla party, which had been pinning down the enemy until the aircraft arrived, went out in a most successful mopping-up task.

142. Captain Waller reported to the R.A.F., "We only killed 15 of them but you killed 105 in three cracking good air strikes. You also saved the lives of almost three thousand occupants and evacuees in Okpyat who were completely cut off."

Japanese Break-through from Pegu Yomas Fails

143. The desperate and last bid by the 28th Japanese Army to escape across the Sittang began on July 21st, when some 15,000 to 18,000 enemy troops, sick and demoralised, moved out of the jungle and scrub shelter of the Pegu Yomas.

144. The moment for which the squadrons and Allied ground forces had been awaiting had now come. The ground forces of 17 Indian Infantry Division, ranged in groups along the 100 miles stretch of roadway between Toungoo and Pegu, which formed part of the railway corridor, engaged the enemy, bursting over the road at several points simultaneously, and slaughtered them.

145. The squadrons of 221 Group were switched over to this battle area in support of 17 Division, and for almost nine days air assault was directed on the wretched Japanese as they made desperate attempts to reach the Sittang River.

146. From a captured enemy document it was revealed that the main break-through from the Pegu Yomas had been delayed by the enemy to allow the move of the Japanese 28th Army to co-ordinate. The greater part of the Mayazaki Group (Lt.-Gen. G.O.C. 54 Division) had planned to attempt to cross the Sittang between Nyaungbentha and Pyu. Coinciding with this move, Koba Group (Major-General Koba) had planned another major break out, and while the area of the move was not determined, it was anticipated that it would take place north of Toungoo in 19 Division area where troops were deploying along the Toungoo-Mawchi Road.

147. The enemy's plan was to form road blocks at selected points and to pass through them assisted by "Jitter Squads" to create diversions. All movements were to be made by night and the keynote of the break-through was to be "speed" so that the maximum time would be available for the collection of boats and rafts from the Sittang river in order to complete the crossing before daylight. The enemy had planned, on reaching the Sittang, to cross on a wide front using barges, rafts, logs, bamboo poles and even petrol tins to assist the buoyancy of escapees in the water.

148. It would be invidious to state that one squadron, more than another, inflicted the greatest punishment on the escaping enemy. All squadrons thrown into the "Battle of the Break-through," overcoming monsoon with low clouds and heavy rain for long periods, did what was expected of them with credit. The keenness of squadron ground personnel was equal to the occasion. They worked hard and ungrudgingly. All, indeed, in the air, as well as on the ground, felt that something substantial was being accomplished in this last show-down with the Japanese in Burma.

149. The July killing lasted until the 29th. The Thunderbolt squadrons, carrying three 500 lb. bombs on each aircraft, played havoc among concentrations of moving Japanese troops. The Spitfires too, carrying one 500 lb. bomb on each aircraft, pursued the enemy relentlessly, strafing them as they ran for cover. As many as 62 sorties were flown on July 23rd by Nos. 152 and 155 Squadrons.

150. The extent of the full air effort by the R.A.F. squadrons in this battle cannot be adequately measured in the many squadron reports which told of the effectiveness and killings made during their strikes. The confusion and disruption caused among the Japanese forces, amounted to almost chaos. More convincing, perhaps, were the reports sent by 12th Army Divisional Commanders to H.Q. 221 Group, who were not slow to express their gratitude for the support given to their troops.

151. After almost nine days of intense fighting, the attempted break out by the Japanese from the Pegu Yomas ended in utter and complete failure. More than 10,000 men were killed, as against only three hundred odd casualties sustained by the Allied forces. Out of approximately 1,300 Japanese troops who succeeded in crossing the Sittang between Meikthalin and Wegyi, it was estimated that 500 of their number had been killed during air strikes by Spitfires and Thunderbolts.

152. The whole Japanese plan for organised escape petered out in the closing days of July, and the air and ground attacks were then transferred once more to the Sittang Bend, where the other Japanese forces, to their credit, had held out bravely in their struggle to keep open the last doorway leading out of Burma. In the July battle, R.A.F. squadrons had flown a total of 3,045 sorties—92 per cent. of which were offensive strikes in support of ground troops, while a total weight of 1,490,000 lb. of bombs had been dropped.

153. As the last few hundreds of exhausted Japanese were making their escape to Moulmein with bitter recollections of the ordeal they had passed through, Lieutenant-General Sir Montague Stopford, G.O.C. 12th Army, when recalling the severity of the weather, its flooding, rains and cloud, showed his appreciation of the R.A.F. in these words:—

"Grateful if you would accept and pass on to all ranks under your command my most grateful thanks for the admirable support given during break-out battle and my congratulations on splendid results achieved. Flying conditions must have been most difficult but on all sides I hear nothing but praise of the keenness and determination of pilots to get through. You have all played a great part in the Twelfth Army's first big operation."

154. Over and above the R.A.F. contribution, our victory was won by our superiority over the Japanese in training, fighting ability and weapons; the accurate intelligence which was obtained before the battle began; the fine work of the guerillas, and above all the high morale and fighting efficiency of the troops.

STRATEGIC AIR OPERATIONS.

A Well Sustained Offensive against Enemy Supply and Communications.

155. With the capture of Rangoon and the disbandment of the integrated Anglo-American Strategic Air Force on June 1st, the R.A.F. heavy bombers of 231 Group were left to carry out the next phase of the battle against the enemy's communications leading to Singapore, and on other important targets.

156. The partnership which had been forged between heavy bomber units of No. 231 Group, R.A.F., and the 7th Bombardment Group, U.S.A.A.F. had, over a period, produced a striking force so effective that it brought about a serious disruption to Japanese strategic communications in this Theatre, with a critical decline in the quantity of supplies intended for their ground forces in Burma.

157. The departure of the 7th Bombardment Group had one important significance. The Group had operated twelve aircraft fitted with "Azon" equipment, consisting of a radio transmitter in the aircraft and a radio receiver on the bomb which, once released, could be guided in such a way that line errors could be eliminated. Throughout the series of "bridge-busting" missions on the Burma-Siam railway, which, on account of anti-aircraft defences could not be attacked from low level by Liberators, the Azon equipment was used with great success.

158. The destruction of bridges in Burma and Siam, notably on the Bangkok-Pegu railway, which was one of the principal tasks of the Strategic Air Force, was a vital factor in crippling the enemy's land communications.

159. In a six-month period between December 1944 and May 1945, there was photographic confirmation of bridge destruction as shown hereunder:—

	Destroyed	Damaged
Rail	96	36
Road	13	4
Total	109	40

160. Feverish efforts made by the Japanese engineers, who worked with great energy repairing and rebuilding bridges, failed to keep open many of the vital communications upon which the Japanese in Southern Burma depended.

Greater Distances Flown to Target Areas.

161. On the Allied occupation of Rangoon, R.A.F. Liberators carried the heavy bomber offensive much further afield into the enemy-occupied territories of South East Asia, involving frequent flights of over 1,000 miles radius from their Indian bases in Bengal. This was inevitable, as the newly occupied airfields in Southern Burma, after the capture of Rangoon, were not yet big enough to take heavy bombers. The long distance flights undertaken by these aircraft across the Bay of Bengal in difficult monsoon weather were most hazardous.

162. From Moulmein, at the mouth of the Salween River, to Victoria Point, the southernmost tip in Burma, is nearly 500 miles. This coastal tip, known as the Tenasserim, together with Japanese bases in the Andaman Islands, came in for attention by the heavy bombers after our entry into Rangoon. Nearly 1,000 tons of bombs were dropped by the R.A.F. squadrons during May, which reflected the determination of the crews to carry on their heavy bombing work in the disruption of the enemy's communication system. Indeed, what was to have been a V.E.-Day celebration in May, was spent by crews of the squadrons standing by for an attack on shipping in the Andamans. This culminated in a bombing raid on May 17th against the most westerly Japanese base in the Bay of Bengal—Port Blair. The bombing force on this occasion concentrated on important harbour installations, including marine workshops at Phoenix Bay, while buildings at Hope Town, the main coaling point, were destroyed. A large orange red explosion, with flames rising up to 1,500 feet, was seen by the crews after they had hit their target. The enemy had fortified the whole area of Port Blair with shore batteries and A.A. guns, which succeeded in shooting down one of our aircraft.

163. But the main battle against the enemy's communications—notably those affecting Singapore—was now on. The same air strategy which had disrupted the Japanese supply line between Bangkok and Rangoon was applied in the succeeding months with equal effectiveness to the line linking Bangkok with Singapore.

164. Communications on this mountainous peninsula, embracing territory of three States—Burma, Siam and Malaya—had, for the most part, been seaborne, though, as the Japanese advance in 1941 showed, Singapore still had a backdoor by means of the rail route to the north.

165. With the sea lanes in the Strait of Malacca made more and more hazardous for Japanese shipping through the effectiveness of our mine-laying from the air and the vigilance shown by R.N. submarines, the enemy was forced to fall back steadily on the use of the Bangkok-Singapore railway for the movement of supplies. This line snaked for a thousand miles up the narrow neck of land between the Gulf of Siam and the Andaman Sea.

166. Not all the stretch of railroad was within range of the R.A.F. Liberators. With persistence, however, they succeeded in getting as far south from their bases in India as the Bay of Bandon at the Isthmus of Kra, to inflict heavy damage on the important railway junction of Jumbhorn at the narrowest part of the Isthmus.

Enemy's concern over Systematic Damage

167. I must express most sincere admiration for the aircrews who flew these Liberators such abnormally long distances, frequently through atrocious monsoon weather, to bomb their targets in Siam and Malaya.

168. Crews of Bomber Command in Europe flew 1,200 mile round trips to Berlin when attacking targets in the capital of the Reich, but the R.A.F. Liberators in South East Asia flew from their bases in India round trips well over 2,000 miles to bomb objectives at Bangkok, and other targets on the Isthmus of Kra. This is equal to a flight from London to Naples or well to the east of Warsaw—flights, it should be noted, which the R.A.F Liberators in my Command carried out regularly against the Japanese.

169. The concern of the enemy over the systematic damage to, and destruction of, their lines of communication in Siam and Malaya was revealed in a document which came into our hands entitled " Protection of Communications ". This document called upon Japanese Unit Commanders to overhaul their A.A. defence methods as " enemy aircraft are carrying out continuous and unceasing attacks on our rear communications and planning to cut our rear lines altogether. We must perfect our counter-measures."

170. The enemy's increased vigilance, however, appeared to make no material difference to the preservation of their rail bridges, dumps, water towers, locomotives, rolling stock and shipping.

171. On June 5th, seven Liberators attacked railyards at Surasdhani on the Bangkok-Singapore line. Surasdhani was an important supply post for the Japanese and, to reach it, our bomber crews flew for 17 hours, mostly across the Bay of Bengal, and through some of the worst weather which the monsoon during 1945 had produced. This flight of 2,400 miles was one of the longest undertaken, up to that time, on a heavy bombing mission in this Theatre. The bombing was well concentrated, and the results were good. Subsequent reconnaissance confirmed all claims made by the crews.

Liberators sink 10,000-ton Japanese Tanker.

172. A shipping strike in Siamese waters on June 15th, when a 10,000-ton Japanese tanker was set on fire and left sinking by the stern, was one of the most noteworthy operations of its kind during the closing stages of the war against Japan in South East Asia.

173. To effect this strike, aircraft had to make a round trip of approximately 2,500 miles to the expected anchorage, the route being almost entirely over the Bay of Bengal and the Andaman Sea.

174. The tanker was the largest enemy vessel reported in Siamese waters for many months, and was believed to be one of the last of its size remaining to the Japanese in the Southern Area. It was sighted by a Sunderland aircraft of 222 Group when it was apparently trying to make a northbound run through the Gulf of Siam and along the east coast of the Malay Peninsula. The tanker had an escort.

175. The Air Forces at the disposal of 231 Group for this strike were four heavy bomber squadrons—Nos. 99, 159, 355 and 356, equipped with Liberator Mark V aircraft. A detachment of six aircraft from No. 159 Squadron, based in India, moved down temporarily to Akyab, on the Arakan, for the operation. This enabled the aircraft of the detachment to load up during the night and to take off at 0900 hours on the day of the strike. They were, therefore, the last squadron in to attack.

176. Due to exceedingly bad weather encountered by all aircraft on the route to the target, a number of the aircraft were forced to abandon the operation and returned to base. The master bomber and deputy master bomber were, unfortunately, included in this number. The remaining aircraft, which pressed on, came upon their target in the early afternoon as the tanker was moving past Samui Island. An escort was some distance away.

177. Three aircraft of 99 Squadron attacked the tanker at low level but did not succeed in securing hits. All three aircraft were damaged by A.A. fire from the escort vessel and the tanker itself. One aircraft had a fin shot off. After delivering its attack, it eventually reached Mingaladon Airfield, Rangoon, where it crash-landed. The second aircraft, also damaged, by A.A. fire, crash-landed at Akyab.

178. The battle against the tanker was continued later with three aircraft of 356 Squadron attacking at low level, and a direct hit produced fire and a series of explosions. The tanker still fought back fiercely, and all three aircraft were damaged by A.A. fire, one of which crashed when landing at Salbani in Bengal. The fight continued with the arrival of three further aircraft from 159 Squadron which pressed home the attack, claiming four and possibly six hits. With smoke billowing to 7,000 feet, the tanker was left burning from stem to stern and sinking. The tanker's escort succeeded in making its escape.

179. Subsequent reconnaissance showed that the tanker was sunk, the funnel and mast were seen showing above the sea.

180. Loss of so vital a supply vessel as an oil tanker of 10,000 tons, particularly at a time when supply meant everything to the enemy in South East Asia, added further to the embarrassment of the Japanese.

181. For this outstanding success I sent a message of congratulation to Major-General J. T. Durrant, S.A.A.F., who, on June 15th, had assumed Command of 231 Group, vice Air Commodore F. J. W. Mellersh, C.B.E., A.F.C., repatriated to the United Kingdom.

182. The attack on the Japanese tanker ended a month of most successful shipping strikes by the air forces of 231 Group during June, for, on June 1st, Liberators had surprised enemy vessels at Satahib in the Gulf of Siam, when a 335-foot submarine depot ship—" Angthong "—was sunk.

183. The stranglehold on the Japanese supply and communications system was further tightened on June 24th, when Liberators destroyed two important bridges at Kanchanaburi, eighty miles west of Bangkok. The raid on these bridges across the Meklong River at Kanchanaburi was a disruption of serious consequence on the Burma—Siam railway. The ultimate result of this attack was that three spans were demolished and one span displaced.

184. Strategic bombing by the air forces of this Command drastically cut down the use of the enemy's railroads, compelling the transfer of more and more supplies to road and sea transport, which inevitably slowed up the enemy's war supply machine.

185. When the A.C.S.E.A. Command formed in December, 1943, our heavy bomber effort was only 449 tons dropped by Liberator aircraft. In 1944 the figure had risen to 3,846 tons, and by August, 1945, it had again risen to a total of 9,441 tons.

186. Behind these tonnages is evidence of the contribution by the heavy bomber aircraft of this Command to the overall strategy of the Supreme Allied Commander, South East Asia, in bringing about the disruption of Japanese supply and road, rail and sea communications.

AIR SUPPLY

A Testing Period for Squadrons During Monsoon

187. Although the capture of Rangoon brought an end to the more intensive Army-Air co-operation in Burma, the day by day air supply for ground troops concentrated in Southern Burma, and still engaging large isolated forces of the enemy, was still maintained.

188. There was no alternative. Air supply, it was realised, would have to meet the Army's demands until seaborne supplies began to function, and road and rail communication inland from Rangoon were re-established.

189. Much was being done to hurry forward rehabilitation in Rangoon generally and to get port facilities working, but this was no easy task. Looting of property and bomb damage to those essential services which are the mainspring of a busy commercial port were extensive. Entry of larger ships into the harbour was also delayed until dredging of the river channel was completed, while there was the additional task of repairing docks, wharves, and badly disrupted road and rail communications. All these were vital factors which indirectly affected supply to a vast Allied ground force which had pushed its way into Rangoon.

190. The period May to August, 1945—covering the re-entry of the Allied forces into Rangoon, and later the surrender of Japan—cannot be termed spectacular in air supply operations, when reckoned against such efforts as persisted during the Allied advance down through Burma earlier in the year, and the supply tonnage record was broken in April, 1945, with 2,900 tons on one day. But it was, nevertheless, an exacting period for squadrons and personnel alike, for the following reasons:—

(a) The period of the monsoon had set in, making flying exceedingly hazardous in so mountainous a country as Burma.

(b) With the disintegration of the British and American Air Forces after 1st June, 1945, American Transports were withdrawn, leaving R.A.F. squadrons of No. 232 Group to continue air supply operations unaided.

(c) Supply demands made by H.Q. Allied Land Forces were not immediately reduced after entry into Rangoon. On the contrary, the Army persisted in a continuance of air supply on a scale which it was not always practicable to meet in face of atrocious weather and fewer available aircraft.

191. The departure of the American transport squadrons towards the end of May, 1945, resulted in a corresponding reduction in air supply to the ground forces. With hostilities in Burma virtually over, this was only to be expected. What air supply did not anticipate was the enormous concentration of Allied ground forces which had pushed into Rangoon at the last minute to ensure its speedy capture. These troops had still to be fed and supplied, as had the Allied ground forces engaging the remnants of the Japanese main Army trapped in the Pegu Yomas of Southern Burma as the result of the rapid Allied drive to Rangoon.

192. Throughout the campaign in Burma it had been the practice to pool the air resources for the mutual benefit of the British and American elements of Eastern Air Command. The result had been a building up of a balanced organisation known as Combat Cargo Task Force, capable of operating at an intensive rate of air supply.

193. The operational achievement of Combat Cargo Task Force, covering the period October, 1944 (the date of its inception) to the end of May, 1945, when disintegration took place, is best indicated by the following figures:—

Total hours flown	386,283
Supplies carried (short tons)	332,136
Number of persons carried	339,137
Number of casualties carried	94,243
Total tonnage carried, including weight of persons and casualties	379,707

Forecast for Air Lift after Rangoon.

194. From the examination of results achieved during the advance through Burma, and the lessons learned, it was possible, in the middle of May, to agree that each transport squadron's effort as from 1st June, 1945 to 31st July, could be 125 hours per aircraft for the month. This demanded an effort of 156 hours per aircraft on the squadron strength.

195. A better flow of reinforcement aircraft was expected, which would thus greatly help towards making the new transport effort possible, also a stepping-up and increase in efficiency of maintenance organisation, with consequent increased monthly output and quicker turn-round of aircraft undergoing repair, was taking place.

196. On the assumption that two R.A.F. squadrons were made available for airborne training by 1st June, that internal airlines requirements were met, and that U.S.A.A.F. transport squadrons were all out of the Theatre from 10th June, it was calculated that the

following transport aircraft would be available:—

1-10 June—
  8 R.A.F. Squadrons—240 C-47
  4th C.C. Group—100 C-46
11 June-31 July—
  8 R.A.F. Squadrons—240 C-47

197. On such a basis, the capacity for the daily lift on long tons of squadrons was estimated as under:—

1-10 June—
  1,474 long tons
11 June-31 July—
  800 long tons

198. This capacity measured against the Army's requirements of 14th May, 1945, showed the following situation in tons:—

Period	ALFSEA requirement tons	Capacity to Deliver tons
1— 8 June	1,310	1,474
9—10 „	1,070	1,474
11—18 „	1,070	880
19 June—8 July	840	880
9—31 July	600	880

199. On calculation, therefore, a total surplus capacity of 2,120 tons existed from 1-10 June, and a deficiency of 1,520 tons from 11-18 June, giving a surplus airlift. The surplus airlift from 1-10 June, it was calculated, could be stock-piled to offset the deficiency from 11-18 June. From these calculations, therefore, it was considered that the transfer of the U.S.A.A.F. squadrons could be accepted without detriment to any foreseen operations. Unfortunately, a variety of factors militated against this target which had been so carefully planned.

Some Difficulties with the Army over Supply.

200. On 11th June, Advanced H.Q. A.L.F.S.E.A. signalled direct to the Supreme Allied Commander that the short fall in air transport for the first nine days in June totalled 955 long tons, and asked, therefore, for the retention of No. 238 Squadron already overdue to go to the Pacific.

201. I proceeded to Rangoon to discuss this matter more fully with Lieutenant General Sir Oliver Leese, C.-in-C., A.L.F.S.E.A. and Major-General Bastyan (Major-General Administration), A.L.F.S.E.A.

202. The Army had come fully briefed, and it was obvious that any detailed discussion in Rangoon without a full knowledge of all factors would place the Air Force at a disadvantage. Accordingly, I signalled Air Command to take all possible measures to lessen the short fall and, for this purpose, to allocate 22 additional Dakotas at once. Upon my return to Command, at Kandy, I held a full discussion on the problem.

203. The varied aspects of the problem are worth detailing since they illustrate the many links upon which air transport depended at the time, and also the strong disinclination of the Army to accept responsibility for breakdowns in air supply. Factors which had upset the air supply target planned in the middle of May included the following:—

(a) The reinforcement flow had not been sufficient to equip the squadron up to a Unit Equipment of 24 plus 6 as planned and, in consequence, aircraft strength was 12 per cent. deficient.

(b) Ramree airfield, which had been built by the Army for the express purpose of monsoon air supply operations, was often so waterlogged that aircraft could not get off.

(c) There had been an epidemic of main bearing failures in Dakota aircraft engines which had caused an appreciable drop in serviceability; one squadron needed 26 new engines.

(d) Although we had a margin of surplus lift available in May, the Army could not take advantage of it in June, owing to shortage of transport.

(e) Army demands remained high because they could not withdraw sufficient troops through Rangoon due to shipping and communication difficulties.

204. It was decided to take the following steps:—

(i) Inform B.A.F.S.E.A. that the allotment of 24 aircraft to each squadron was of the greatest urgency.

(ii) Press the Army for better drainage of Ramree airfield.

(iii) Transfer as soon as possible one or two transport squadrons from Ramree to Akyab.

(iv) Give the squadrons a target of 100 short tons per day. This was desirable, for it provided a goal that could be reached, and prevented the frustration that had so often been felt in the past at being given a target impossible of achievement. Any margin above the stated figure would be in the nature of a bonus and have a stimulating moral effect.

(v) Withdraw one of the two squadrons engaged from airborne training and employ it on transport. This would give a total of 810 long tons a day against the Army requirements of 880. The difference was so small that it could surely be made up by inland water transport or other means and would certainly entail no drastic cut in rations or amenities.

205. Even then, air transport problems were not solved. There were still in Burma tactical squadrons whose speedy withdrawal for refit and training in preparation for "Zipper/Mailfist" Operation could not be effected through the overloaded land and sea lines of communication. The only method of withdrawing these units in sufficient time was to fly them out. I decided, therefore, that such a task held priority over the airborne training 96 Squadron was accomplishing at that time, and accordingly I received the Supreme Allied Commander's agreement to 96 Squadron's temporary withdrawal to enable air lift to be provided for R.A.F. personnel and equipment of the units already mentioned.

Transport Preparations for "Zipper/Mailfist".

206. An important step was taken in July when I directed that Air Force representation should be made available for Army planning bodies in order to prevent the Army supply authorities from budgeting for airlift which

could not possibly be met. By means of closer liaison it was hoped that the Army would make bids for air transport which would be practicable, so that there would be no need for the Air Forces to overwork their squadrons in order to make good the backlog. In addition, it was possible, in planning, to leave some airlift for domestic requirements such as the carriage of A.O.G. spares, etc.

207. For the coming months air transport commitments could be divided into the following categories:—

(i) The requirements of "Zipper/Mailfist" Operation.

(ii) The supply of 12th Army fighting in Burma.

(iii) The maintenance and expansion of internal airlines.

(iv) The continuance at a higher rate than hitherto of airborne training.

208. In order to meet requirement (i) it had been anticipated that there would be a sharp diminution in the supply of 12th Army in Burma as the port of Rangoon became cleared. It became apparent in the first week of July, however, that the requirements of the Army in Burma were going to be very considerably in excess of the figures that had been estimated at the time when aircraft had been allocated for "Zipper/Mailfist."

209. A complete review of air transport plans was thus once again necessary. The Army suggestions for meeting the new situation were given in a signal from H.Q., A.L.F.S.E.A., which, however, could not be agreed. The Army was accordingly asked to await recommendations which would be available with all data at the next meeting of the Supreme Allied Commander, when the whole question of air transport requirements would be reviewed and priorities adjusted.

Hazards of Weather in Monsoon.

210. Weather was the one dominant factor which affected air supply operations throughout Burma after the breaking of the monsoon. It is no exaggeration to state that the transport aircraft, probably more than any other aircraft employed in the Burma Theatre, had to wage a day to day battle against the elements.

211. During the crucial months, while the Allied advance down through Central Burma was in progress, transport aircraft had been able to fly long hours, often in good weather, which greatly contributed to the successful completion of their commitment.

212. The proposition, however, was different in May, after the arrival of the monsoon. Not only did weather make flying hazardous and difficult, but it was frequently impossible for meteorological staffs to determine in advance what weather the transport aircraft were likely to encounter en route to their destination.

213. The monsoon in Burma is at its worst during June and July, when cumulo nimbus cloud, the greatest enemy of aircraft flying over Burma, builds up frequently from low level to above aircraft ceiling.

214. Comparing aircraft effectiveness in the monsoon months of June and July with that of February and March, 1945, it appeared that the effectiveness dropped to 70 per cent.

As the average length of trip was less during June and July, however, the cargo tonnage carried per aircraft dropped only to 76.5 per cent. of the fine weather standard.

215. An indication of the monsoon's toll on aircraft and crews may be seen from the study of figures of losses for the month of June, 1945. During this period No. 232 Group lost 12 aircraft due to bad weather; casualties to crews and passengers inclusive of those killed, injured and missing totalling 72. This was a high price paid in men and material for the continued success of air supply in Burma.

216. It is on record that one Dakota aircraft flying over Burma actually found itself turned upside down in a storm, and it was only the skill and presence of mind of the pilot which averted disaster.

217. Yet another example of the hazards which faced transport supply crews in Burma during that monsoon was the experience of a pilot who found himself completely closed in with cumulo nimbus cloud during a return journey from Meiktila to Akyab. After three attempts, a break in the cloud was found which brought the aircraft out on to the coast opposite Ramree Island. The aircraft descended to 300 feet but cumulo nimbus again closed in behind, and the pilot, after making several unsuccessful attempts to climb out of the cloud, was eventually forced down to sea level. For almost an hour the aircraft circled around until the pilot finally succeeded in climbing to 7,000 feet where more cumulo nimbus was encountered and the radio compass was rendered unserviceable. The aircraft then turned on a reciprocal course and found a small gap in the cloud which again closed in. In the face of this predicament, the pilot decided there was no alternative but to descend and to risk a blind forced landing. The pilot succeeded in bringing the aircraft to a standstill in a paddy field without injury to any of the crew.

Stocking Rear Airfields with Supplies.

218. Most of the supplies carried by the R.A.F. Transport Squadrons in Burma after the departure of the American units were for the purpose of stocking rear airfields, where the Army organisations distributed the supply to various Army and R.A.F. units. Civil commitments also continued to be fulfilled in Northern Burma.

219. With the experience gained in June regarding the consumption of petrol required by C-47 aircraft for each trip during average monsoon flying conditions, squadrons located at Ramree, Akyab, and Chittagong were instructed to increase their load from 5,500 lb. to 6,000 lb.

220. In preparation for the final showdown with the trapped Japanese forces in Burma, during July, special instructions for supply dropping in the Toungoo area were issued. Weather, however, was again the big handicap, and as dropping operations were frequently impossible in this area, arrangements had to be made to land loads in Central Burma so as to form a stock-pile near the source of ground operations and later take advantage of periods of fine weather in which to deliver the backlog. This system made it unnecessary for aircraft to carry undropped supplies back to base, with a consequent increase in the number of

hours required to deliver them. In the event of abortive trips producing a back log at Toungoo, aircrews were briefed to proceed to that area on supply dropping operations, after which the aircraft landed at Toungoo or Magwe and carried out second and possibly third trips before returning to base.

221. During the flare up in ground operations in the third week in July, when the break-through from the Pegu Yomas by the trapped Japanese forces began, air supply to the Allied ground forces engaging the Japanese assumed considerable importance until the battle had ended. Rainfall was widespread over the whole area of operations, and difficulties under which aircraft had to operate were acute. With exceedingly bitter fighting taking place, and thousands of Japanese troops pressing forward in their anxiety to escape, the state of the ground situation was ever fluid, and made the accurate dropping of supplies no easy task. Many of the dropping zones used, indeed, were less than 100 yards from local enemy forces and there were occasions when a dropping zone was surrounded by Japanese troops and some of the containers overshot the mark and fell into enemy hands. It speaks well for the aircrews trained in dropping supplies that more containers did not fall into the hands of the Japanese, whose desperate plight during the previous two months was due to lack of air supply and to the fact that the enemy were cut off from their Headquarters and bases in Southern Burma and Siam by our land forces. Even in this last and major battle with the Japanese in Burma it was significant that air supply—of which the enemy had none—was one of the cardinal factors in assuring triumph for the Allied ground forces and disaster for the enemy. Air supply in Burma made history which outdistanced in merit and achievement the more publicised air supply operations of the war in Europe such as that of Arnhem, or the food dropping to the Dutch in Holland. These, without doubt, were important and commendable efforts in themselves, but they bore no comparison to the enormous and sustained efforts of transport aircrews who faced the hazards of monsoon weather.

End of the War Affects Air Supply Operations.

222. With the Japanese surrender in South East Asia in August, air supply operations to the Allied ground forces in Burma took on a new aspect in keeping with the new situation.

223. This did not mean that the commitment of the air supply squadrons would cease, or indeed, that fighting in Burma was entirely over. On the contrary, it was expected that in certain respects air supply commitments would increase. There could be no doubt, however, that the nature and the location of loads which would be carried, would greatly change. Evacuation of prisoners-of-war and internees, the "fly-in" of Allied ground forces to occupy large and vast territories held by the Japanese, were all commitments which faced the transport squadrons in South East Asia on the cessation of hostilities. Materiel of war, on the other hand—so important a cargo throughout the campaign in Burma—ceased to have a first priority. Movement of personnel, carriage of rations and civilian supplies replaced the transport of military supplies.

224. Operations of the transport squadrons during August fell into two distinct categories. The first half of the month, when Japan was still at war, supply operations continued much the same as on previous months. After 15th August, when surrender was announced, the situation became somewhat confused.

225. The supply tasks by aircraft during the first half of August were confined principally to the carrying of ammunition and petrol for the two most active areas of fighting in Burma— the Mawchi Road and the lower Sittang— where the remnants of the Japanese forces who had survived the July "Killing" were still holding out. There were, of course, other numerous and important supply tasks, the biggest of which was the stocking of airfields in Southern and Central Burma in preparation for the sustained effort which would be required once the assault on Malaya, under operation "Zipper", began.

226. One squadron during the first half of August had the sole task of taking food supplies to the civilian population of Northern Burma. This was an important commitment owing to the lack of other means of transport.

Operations to relieve Allied Prisoners of War.

227. With the Japanese surrender in the second half of August, there came orders for the move of six R.A.F. Transport squadrons to the Rangoon area to transport stores, and to evacuate Ps.O.W. from Siam, French Indo-China, Malaya and the Netherlands East Indies. As the result of these squadron moves, and the military situation at the time, the number of normal transport operations fell away very considerably. The majority of the trips, indeed, were concerned with moves by squadrons and the stocking up of the Rangoon airfields with provisions for the liberated territories and the P.O.W. Camps.

228. August 28th—the historic date on which Operation "Mastiff" was launched to bring relief to the thousands of Allied Ps.O.W. in the prison camps throughout the vast territories of South East Asia—saw the transport squadrons, as well as other aircraft of the Command, including those of the R.A.A.F., take part in what was described as "one of the greatest mercy missions of the war."

229. Many of the flights undertaken in these operations were equivalent to a Transatlantic flight, and yet 75 per cent. of the crews succeeded in reaching their targets and dropping their messages as well as parachuting medical supplies, Red Cross parcels and teams of medical and signalling personnel provided mainly by airborne formations. Later, many thousands of Ps.O.W. and internees were evacuated from these territories by air.

230. It is not difficult to visualise the plight in which our Allied Ps.O.W. would certainly have found themselves after the official Japanese surrender, had not all resources, including Air Power, been used, and organised quickly, to bring relief, comfort and sustenance to these unfortunate men, many of them too weak to stand on their own legs. Only Air Power could have penetrated these vast territories throughout South East Asia with the speed required to initiate that essential relief. The pin-pointing of many Japanese P.O.W. camps, in addition to the great distances flown,

by aircraft and the hazards of weather encountered in these tropical regions, speaks magnificently for the navigational and flying skill of our aircrews.

231. The period, May to August, 1945—covering the re-entry of the Allied Forces into Rangoon and later the surrender of Japan—cannot be termed spectacular in air supply operations when reckoned against such efforts during the Allied advance down through Burma earlier in the year, when the mobility of Fourteenth Army was almost entirely provided by the Allied Air Forces whose record supply tonnage averaged 2,900 tons per day in April, 1945.

232. The period, May to August, was not only the monsoon period but the period, with the exception of the July battle in Burma, during which the Allied Forces on ground, sea and in the air were building up their organisation and strength to deliver the next blow which would have fallen upon the Japanese in Malaya in early September. Nevertheless, the R.A.F. Transport supply squadrons met the demands required of them, and the supply effort for that period may be summarised as follows:—

	May	June	July	August	Total
Tactical Trips	7,998	7,211	8,258	3,779	27,246
Personnel Carried	7,795	2,321	3,017	4,651	17,784
Casualties Evacuated	3,899	2,515	2,044	1,514	9,972
Supplies Delivered (Short Tons)	23,172	19,978	22,170	9,418	74,738
Estimated Total (Short Tons)	23,951	20,210	22,472	9,883	76,516

CASUALTY EVACUATION

A Prominent Lesson which Emerged from the Campaign in Burma.

233. The great saving of lives and raising of morale due to air casualty evacuation was one of the main lessons which emerged from the Campaign in Burma.

234. This service was easily one of the best morale builders among Allied front-line troops. It inspired the fighting man's confidence and allayed any fears he may have had about being wounded, with the possibility of falling into the hands of the Japanese as a prisoner.

235. Air casualty evacuation, once it became known as the recognised method for dealing with serious cases by flying them out of the forward areas in Burma, was a triumph both for the Allied medical staffs and the aircrews alike. The Japanese had no air organisation for similar evacuation of their troops, and the low condition in which many enemy prisoners were found as a result of acute sickness in the jungle areas was, in itself, a contributory factor to their defeat.

236. The general policy was for supply aircraft to deliver supplies and take back from forward airfields on their return trips loads of casualties to the base hospitals, and the special centres established at Comilla, but when adverse landing conditions compelled supply by dropping, there were temporary difficulties in clearing casualties from Corps and Army medical centres. Austers and L.5 aircraft (Sentinels) were used in the Theatre with conspicuous success in the forward areas.

237. For the purpose of handling casualties from forward medical units and forward transport landing grounds, R.A.F. Casualty Air Evacuation Units were set up. These units were situated on the transport air strip covering a particular area. Emplaning of the casualties on to the aircraft was effected according to their degree of urgency for base hospital medical treatment. The average strength of a Casualty Air Evacuation Unit was 40 British other ranks, with a varied number of Indian personnel. Approximately 100 wounded could be staged at these C.A.E.U.s for as long as was necessary. As many seriously wounded and sick personnel required medical attention whilst travelling in aircraft to base, an air ambulance orderly pool was established at base. This was composed of specially trained nursing orderlies who flew in all aircraft. It is noteworthy to record that these nursing orderlies flew as much as 200 hours a month. They carried with them complete first-aid equipment, including oxygen-giving apparatus. In the Burma Theatre, due to the mountainous nature of the country, portable oxygen equipment proved to be essential in air casualty evacuation work, and its employment actually saved many lives.

238. The Casualty Air Evacuation Units in the forward areas were also responsible for the off-loading, treatment and conveyance of casualties received direct from the battle line in light aircraft such as the L.5. These aircraft proved invaluable in evacuating casualties from jungle clearances and small strips in the forward areas.

239. Air evacuation of casualties began in Burma in the opening months of 1944, when the Allied ground forces found themselves encircled in the Arakan, and later during the period of the Siege of Imphal. By September of that year, some 48,789 casualties had been evacuated by air, and as the months passed, and the campaign developed in intensity, the casualty evacuation figures steadily increased.

240. By the end of April, 1945—three days before the fall of Rangoon—the total casualties evacuated by British and American aircraft in Burma was 110,761, of which 50,285 were evacuated by R.A.F. aircraft.

241. In the period May to August, 1945, the closing stages of the war against the Japanese, R.A.F. aircraft evacuated a total of 9,972 casualties.

242. That air casualty evacuation proved itself a triumph both from the point of view of morale and the lives saved, is undisputed. Perhaps more convincing is the fact that, throughout the campaign, only one death in the air among ground personnel evacuated was recorded, and only one aircraft, carrying 24 casualties, was lost due to weather.

243. H.Q. A.L.F.S.E.A. stated that air evacuation reduced mortality of wounded by 60 per cent.

American Experience in Casualty Evacuation.

244. Since American aircraft operated as part of the Allied Air Forces in the Theatre until integration in the Command ceased on 1st June, 1945, it is not inappropriate to mention something of the interesting experience of American L.5. aircraft employed in Burma in casualty evacuation and in other secondary important tasks associated with supply to the ground forces.

245. A special research report on evacuation of casualties from the forward areas in Burma which was produced in July, 1945 by Air/12G (Research) Headquarters, Allied Land Forces, South East Asia, described the work of two American squadrons operating L.5. aircraft with Fourteenth Army in the campaign.

The purpose of the report was:—

(a) To consider the best method of using L.5. aircraft for casualty evacuation in the light of the American experience.

(b) To estimate the number of aircraft required to evacuate the casualties from a Corps in action with varying degrees of battle activity.

246. Throughout the period considered in the report—November, 1944 to April, 1945—the squadrons worked with 4 Corps and 33 Corps from a rear strip close to the Casualty Clearing Station. The squadrons of light aircraft were allotted on the basis of one for each Corps of three Divisions. The C.C.S. was sited at the edge of the strip. Forward strips were made by the troops, and the location of the strips was signalled to the squadrons. A reconnaissance plane would fly over the site in the early morning and photograph the strip. If it was considered satisfactory for landing and take-off, the required number of aircraft flew out immediately.

247. During the Meiktila-Rangoon advance of 4 Corps, the number of strips constructed was greater than that during a corresponding period at any other time, yet none of the strips was refused by the squadrons. When the strips could be built more than 500 yards long, it was possible to evacuate two sitting cases in one sortie, but there were few opportunities for this.

248. All the squadron commanders understood their primary role to be casualty evacuation. But important secondary tasks were also performed. Except in the case of the fly-in of important medical supplies, these secondary tasks were never allowed to interfere with the evacuation of casualties.

249. The secondary tasks undertaken were:—

(a) The emergency flying-in of medical supplies, especially whole blood.

(b) Flying-in reinforcements, mail, food, ammunition and items of personal kit. These trips were always part of an evacuation sortie.

(c) Transporting V.I.P.s. within the Corps area.

(d) Spotting for artillery.

(e) Dropping and picking up messages.

(f) Reconnaissance flights.

250. The importance of the evacuation of casualties relative to other duties was, indeed, interesting. The total trips by one squadron over a given period of one month, when activity was intense, was 12,017 of which 9,238 were casualty evacuation flights, or 77 per cent. of the total, as against 2,779 secondary missions.

251. In an analysis of the secondary tasks undertaken by these aircraft, the flying-in of reinforcements proved exceedingly valuable, since these missions could be combined readily with the collection of a casualty, while most of the other missions could not. In various ten-day periods, for example, the total number of casualties evacuated was 7,705 as against 3,345 reinforcements flown in. The percentage of evacuated casualties which were replaced by reinforcements was therefore 43.

Evacuating Casualties from a Corps in Action.

252. For the peak period March, 1945, a squadron of 32 American light aircraft operated under 33 Corps.

253. During this period, all the cases required to be evacuated were taken out by air. No cases were evacuated by road or rail. The aircraft were based at Shwebo during the first half of the month and flew as far as Ondaw, 35 miles away. In the second half of the month, the aircraft were based at Ondaw and flew as far as Wundwin, 65 miles away. The numbers of ground forces evacuated and the hours flown in three ten-day periods were as follows:—

Date	Number Evacuated	Hours Flown
1—11 March	1,793	1,604
11—22 March	1,464	1,431
21—31 March	1,362	1,688
Total	4,619	4,723

Maximum distance between base and forward strip (miles)	65
Minimum distance between base and forward strip (miles)	35
Average per cent. aircraft in commission daily	96·7
Average number of aircraft in commission daily	30·6
Average number of hours flown per plane per day	5·2
Average number of hours flown per plane per month	153
Average number of cases evacuated per plane per day	5
Average number of hours flown per day	157
Average number of cases evacuated per day	154
Maximum number of flying hours a pilot a day	9

254. The above achievement by this squadron was a record for the American squadrons in the Group. The effort was believed to be near the maximum which any squadron could reach in similar circumstances.

255. During the period some of the pilots flew for nine hours a day for five consecutive days, and made up seven sorties in one day on several occasions. This intensification of activity for short periods could not have been achieved without the very high level of maintenance attained, nor could it have been exceeded without putting too great a strain on the pilots or replacing some of the aircraft. Three of the pilots had to be replaced before the end of the operation owing to exhaustion, and 14 aircraft had to be replaced when the squadron came out. The deterioration of the engines, however, cannot be ascribed simply to this operation, as the aircraft had had three months of operations before operating with

33 Corps. The Squadron Commander, it was interesting to note, considered that the factor limiting the monthly carrying capacity of a squadron was the ability of the pilots, rather than that of aircraft, to withstand the strain of intense activity. Few of the pilots in question could have remained efficient if the squadron had attempted to carry on for longer than six weeks at the same level of activity.

Maximum Monthly Carrying Capacity of L.5 Aircraft.

256. While the average daily number of cases evacuated per aircraft was 5, some of the aircraft actually exceeded this number, while some failed to reach it. On the other hand, had all aircraft been used to the same extent as those which flew more than the average for the whole squadron, the average daily number evacuated would have been six, or 180 for the squadron of 30 aircraft. This figure was agreed upon by the Squadron Commander, who estimated that the maximum daily carrying capacity of a single squadron of light aircraft was 180 and the maximum monthly capacity 6,000. This, of course, was based on the maximum distance of 65 miles between the rear and forward strips.

257. The situation was somewhat altered in the instance of 4 Corps' advance down the Meiktila-Rangoon road in April, 1945, when an American light aircraft squadron was evacuating cases from Toungoo to Meiktila for a short period. The distance involved was 330 miles for a whole sortie, and the flight lasting approximately four and a half hours. This meant that it was not possible to evacuate more than two cases per plane per day for more than a total of 60 casualties per day for the whole squadron. It was interesting to note in this connection, however, that 4 Corps' rate of advance in April was approximately 14 miles per day. While the distances flown by light aircraft engaged on casualty evacuation were correspondingly great, the squadron was nevertheless well able to handle all cases, because ground casualties were very light.

258. Altogether the data derived as a result of the operational experience of these light aircraft in Burma suggests that one squadron of 32 L.5 aircraft is sufficient to evacuate all the cases requiring evacuation from the forward areas of a Corps of three Divisions, provided the average daily number of cases does not exceed 180 and the average distance flown is not greater than 60 miles per trip (120 miles per round sortie). One other important proviso, of course, is that we have air superiority and that there is no prolonged heavy fighting with an exceedingly high sickness rate.

GENERAL RECONNAISSANCE.

A Period of Great Versatility for G.R. Aircraft.

259. When the period under review opened, offensive general reconnaissance had become effectively established as the primary operational function of air-sea power in this Theatre. The opening weeks of 1945 had incontestably indicated an entire absence of enemy U-boats throughout the vast expanses of the Indian Ocean, and pointed to the urgent need for alternative employment. Thus evolved the plan for an intensive anti-shipping campaign to disrupt the enemy's sea transport in and around the waters of the Andaman Sea. Four months of vigorous anti-shipping strikes and carefully planned air-sea mining operations revealed that these tactics were greatly harassing the enemy, and an intensification of offensive general reconnaissance was rightly considered a remunerative policy to pursue.

260. Although the primary operational rôle of 222 Group in May 1945 was that of sinking and immobilising the enemy's shipping, it must be borne in mind that there were continued and increasing commitments in the spheres of photographic reconnaissance, meteorological flights and air-sea rescue. I had, in fact, delegated the responsibility for the organisation and control of air-sea rescue operations and units to Air Marshal Commanding 222 Group as from 1st April, 1945, for the whole of South East Asia Command. Moreover, there was always the possibility that the enemy might recommence his U-boat warfare with renewed vigour, and the G.R. forces under my control had always to be prepared for such a contingency.

Developing the Anti-Shipping Campaign.

261. With the re-occupation of Rangoon on May 3rd, 1945, it became possible to establish a new and invaluable base from which to develop the anti-shipping campaign in more easterly waters. Sunderland aircraft of 230 Squadron (relieved in July by a detachment of 209 Squadron, similarly equipped) operating from the depot ship S.S. "Manela" under the operational control of 346 Wing were able to spread their tentacles over the areas of the Tenasserim Coast, Kra Isthmus, Gulf of Siam and South China Seas, adding confusion and perplexity to the enemy with their constant armed reconnaissance and timely attacks wherever suitable targets presented themselves.

262. As a counterpart to this newly established base of Rangoon in the north, the development of Cocos Island in the south constituted an equally important strategic base for similar operations off the west coast of Sumatra, the south coast of Java and the Sunda Straits. No. 321 Squadron, equipped with Liberators (Mark VI), commenced operating a detachment of six aircraft from Cocos Island on July 22nd, 1945.

263. No. 354 Liberator Squadron, which had initiated the offensive anti-shipping strike aspect of the campaign in early February, disbanded on 15th May, 1945. No. 203 Liberator Squadron, however, which had commenced strike operations on 20th March, 1945, continued its programme of incessant and forceful attack over the Andaman Sea, Straits of Malacca, Gulf of Siam, Java Sea, Bangka Strait and off the west coast of Sumatra until the cessation of hostilities. This squadron was based at Kankesanturai (North Ceylon) but frequently operated detachments from Akyab, Ramree and Cocos Island under adverse conditions.

264. The paramount problem of the shipping strike operations was the lack of forward bases. Liberator aircraft had been operating from bases far removed from this scene of operations, and the period of patrol in the operational area was inevitably curtailed, thus

detracting from the efficacy of the sorties. Furthermore, flying-boat facilities at Rangoon were inadequate, and prevented the Sunderlands from being used to the fullest operational capacity. For example, there were no slipway or beaching facilities, so that it was impossible for flying-boats to undertake operations likely to cause severe damage to their hulls. Neither the Sunderland nor the Liberator aircraft is ideal for low-level shipping attacks, but the nature of the operation and existing conditions demanded long-range aircraft and these were the only types available.

265. It is interesting to note that Liberator aircraft of Nos. 203 and 354 Squadrons carried out a series of long-range sea reconnaissance patrols during May 13th-19th which proved invaluable in the location and eventual destruction on May 16th of the Japanese heavy cruiser "HAGURO" in the Straits of Malacca by H.M. Naval forces. (26th Destroyer Flotilla—Captain M. L. Power, C.B.E., D.S.O., in H.M.S. "SAUMAREZ".)

266. Having regard to the many and varied complexities of conducting strike operations within this vast theatre of operations, such as the unfortunate paucity of air bases, the irremediable problem of distance and the unsuitability of aircraft, my G.R. Air Forces achieved results both impressive and commendable. The enemy's shipping sustained considerable blows at a time when every ship in his possession was of vital importance. When the war came to an abrupt conclusion, offensive general reconnaissance was getting into its stride. Had hostilities continued, past experience permits an optimistic speculation in connection with the heavy toll general reconnaissance would have taken of Japanese sea transport, particularly on the shipping routes between Batavia and Singapore.

Air-Sea Mining as Part of the Campaign.

267. Mine-laying operations were planned as an essential part of the anti-shipping campaign, to be executed concurrently with the more directly offensive anti-shipping strikes programme. Initially, it was planned to lay mines during the hours of darkness in the shipping lanes of Northern Sumatra and Northern Malaya, and 160 Squadron (Liberators Mk.V.) underwent an intensive period of training in long range flying and the technique of mine-laying to implement these plans. They commenced these operations on 21st January, 1945 and continued until 24th May—a period of 124 days during which 196 sorties were flown. After operational experience had been gained, the mining commitments were increased to include drops in the areas of Sonchkla, Chumborn, Port Swettenham and Singapore. Mine-laying operations were discontinued after 24th May, 1945, because the stage was then being finally set for Operation "Zipper", and to have continued mine-laying beyond that date might have had serious repercussions when Allied landings took place on the west coast of Malaya.

268. It is difficult, if not impossible, to assess accurately and fully, the damage and inconvenience caused to the enemy by these particular operations. The strategy employed was to mine a number of different and well-separated targets at frequent intervals so as to cause the enemy the greatest possible inconvenience in constantly deploying his inadequate force of mine sweeping craft over a large area. It is reasonable to assume that many thousands of tons of enemy shipping were immobilised at a time when they could ill be spared, and the task of constant mine-sweeping must have been heart-breaking if not overwhelming. Whatever the material achievements of these operations, it must be added that the programme was extremely well-conceived and well executed.

Employment of General Reconnaissance Aircraft on Special Duty Operations.

269. The year of final and complete victory in South East Asia Command was a period of strenuous re-orientation for G.R. Air Forces. With the Indian Ocean no longer a hunting-ground for enemy U-boats, the days of vigilant defensive warfare had passed, and it became essential to re-model the defensive Air Forces into a strong and penetrating arm of offence with which to sever the enemy's sea communications. (The broad strategy of general reconnaissance in the Indian Ocean had always been concerned with the passive protection of shipping rather than the hunting of U-boats —a strategy rendered inevitable by the enormous expanse of water to be reconnoitered and the inadequate number of aircraft and few advance bases at our disposal.)

270. Unfortunately, it was impossible to devote our entire G.R. resources to the execution of this offensive plan, for there were more urgent operational demands to be satisfied, and general reconnaissance aircraft could be quickly and satisfactorily diverted to the rescue. When mine-laying operations ceased, it was envisaged that 160 Squadron, together with Nos. 8 and 356 Squadrons, would reinforce the shipping strike campaign, but the growing requirements of the S.D. organisation absorbed these squadrons to the detriment of offensive general reconnaissance. The effort of G.R. aircraft operating in the S.D. role does not properly belong to this chapter, but rather to that of S.D. operations as a whole. Suffice it is to say here that these squadrons acquitted themselves in a creditable fashion, and manifested once again the comparative ease with which Air Power can be moulded into different forms or styles to meet the changing requirements.

271. Towards the end of the war, No. 222 Group had become responsible for the operational control of some six squadrons engaged on S.D. operations, with the result that the functional and administrative experience gained therefrom provided the Command with a competent and well-versed organisation for the vital and intricate operations immediately following the end of the war. No. 222 Group also played a large and important part in Operations "Birdcage" and "Mastiff", for the requirements of these operations were in many ways similar to those of S.D.

272. The achievements of general reconnaissance aircraft engaged upon the relief and liberation of Allied prisoners-of-war, are recorded in the appropriate chapter. It was a satisfying conclusion to the history of general reconnaissance in the Indian Ocean—a history of dexterous and highly competent adaptation to the many and varied exigencies of an immense and complicated theatre of war.

SPECIAL DUTY OPERATIONS.

An Integral Part in the War Strategy of South East Asia.

273. Operations by S.D. aircraft of my Command contributed very materially to the success of the highly organised guerilla forces of this Theatre which, themselves, were an integral part of the strategy of the Supreme Allied Commander, South East Asia.

274. In the initial stages, S.D. operations were primarily in support of our own forces operating in the enemy-occupied territories, concerning which our Intelligence from ground sources was exceedingly scarce. In the closing stages of the war, however, operations by aircraft in introducing personnel to the Japanese-occupied areas of Burma, Siam, French Indo-China, Malaya, Sumatra and Singapore Island, and supplying them as well as the guerilla formations under their control, grew to proportions which called for the maximum effort of aircraft and crews engaged on this special work. Indeed the true picture was that our Liberator position in the Command was exceedingly tight, since the S.D. effort was carried out largely by this type of aircraft.

275. By May, 1945, guerilla organisations in the Theatre had become firmly established, so much so, that the Burmese Guerillas played a prominent part with our Air and Ground Forces in the killing of ten thousand Japanese troops during an attempted mass escape from the Pegu Yomas in July.

276. A brief account of their activities in co-operation with the Tactical Air Forces is covered in another chapter.

Control of the Guerilla Organisations.

277. The control of the Guerilla Organisations in this Theatre was vested in the Supreme Allied Commander, South East Asia, with a branch, known as "P" Division, which delegated part of its functions to special staff officers at various lower formations.

278. Guerilla operations in South East Asia took on an entirely different character from the work of the underground forces in Europe, where patriots speedily organised themselves as a resistance movement. In South East Asia the sympathies of Asiatics had first to be won over to our cause by special agents and leaders, and parties of guerillas organised among the local inhabitants and often fanatical hill tribesmen. Aircraft made flights of 2,000 and 3,000 miles regularly on these expeditions for on aircraft almost entirely did the build-up of these secret forces depend.

279. Briefly, the Guerilla Organisations operating in the Theatre were as follows:—

(a) *Force* 136. This was a British Organisation mainly responsible for raising, training, arming and controlling guerilla forces and sabotage teams. It also had a tactical intelligence role and operational control of "Z" Force which had a more limited but similar function.

(b) *O.S.S.* The American Officers of Strategic Services had a similar object to that of Force 136, and also collected and distributed strategic intelligence.

(c) *I.S.L.D.* The Inter-Service Liaison Department was a British Organisation and was concerned mainly with the collection and distribution of strategic intelligence from many sources.

280. In addition to the above, there were also miscellaneous organisations which had guerilla functions, and sometimes called upon Special Duty aircraft to assist them.

Allied Air Force Units Involved.

281. Liberators, Dakotas, Catalinas, Lysanders and L.5 (Sentinels) were used for the S.D. operations. The principal units employed were:—

(i) *No. 357 Squadron.* This squadron was the one permanent complete S.D. squadron in this Theatre. It consisted of 10 Liberators, 10 Dakotas and a detached flight of up to 10 Lysanders. The role of the Lysanders was the infiltration and withdrawal of men and mail by landing in enemy territory. The Dakotas were also available for similar landings, as well as for parachute operations.

(ii) *No. 240 Squadron.* This G.R. Catalina squadron included three Catalinas for Special Duty Operations in alighting in enemy waters. These Catalinas were also capable of minor parachute operations.

(iii) *No. 358 Squadron.* This heavy bomber squadron was transferred indefinitely from 231 Group to the S.D. role, and consisted of 16 Liberators which were modified to S.D. standards.

(iv) *10th U.S.A.A.F.* Until the withdrawal by the American Army Air Forces from the Command on 1st June, 1945, a proportion of the effort of the 10th U.S.A.A.F., by arrangement with the O.S.S., was allocated to S.D. operations.

(v) *Tactical Groups.* By local arrangements between the Guerilla Organisations and No. 221 Group, Tactical squadrons sometimes carried out S.D. operations authorised by the Group Headquarters.

(vi) *S.D. Air/Sea Rescue Operations.* Special Duty Air/Sea Rescue operations were carried out from time to time by A.S.R. Catalinas under the control of No. 222 Group. These operations were concerned with installing dumps of foodstuffs and equipment for missing aircrews on coasts in enemy waters, and were arranged by "E" Group.

282. As the S.D. squadrons during the closing stages of the war in South East Asia were operating regularly at an intensive rate of effort on these missions, other units were also brought in to supplement the S.D. work.

Planning of S.D. Air Operations.

283. The training of aircrews and army personnel to the R.A.F. standards took as high priority as the operations themselves. Where practicable, and when the Guerilla Organisations agreed, the training of army personnel and aircrews was combined. This was particularly essential during training for night landing operations on enemy territory, and for ground-to-air special radar and signals equipment.

284. It was estimated that a sustained rate of five successful sorties per aircraft per month could be maintained by an S.D. squadron of twelve aircraft, giving a total of

sixty sorties per month. Generally, planning did not exceed more than fifty sorties per month, in view of the maintenance difficulties, the extremely long sorties which had to be flown, and the fact that the Guerilla Organisations might not have continuous operations in hand. While it was possible to carry out the majority of the operations over Malaya with safety during daytime, or under last light conditions, it was not considered wise to make these flights in daylight in the immediate vicinity of Singapore.

285. The three principal home bases for the S.D. operations were at Jessore in Bengal, Minneriya in Ceylon, and later the Cocos Islands. The operations from the Cocos did not begin until mid-July, when sorties were flown to all parts of Malaya. From Bengal, the S.D. operations were principally over Burma and French Indo-China, but flights were also made deep into Malaya, one aircraft logging twenty hours thirty-nine minutes for one of its sorties.

Operations Increased for Malaya.

286. The strategic plan for the assault on Malaya called for an even greater effort by the S.D. squadrons based in Ceylon. By July, the underground forces had been so organised by our personnel, and supplied with arms and equipment to such proportions, that they constituted a very real threat to isolated garrisons of Japanese troops. The time was considered opportune to foster and galvanise these organisations into a formidable fighting force to harass the enemy at the time of our own landings in Malaya. For this purpose, therefore, it was decided to use heavy bomber aircraft, based on the Cocos Islands, to supplement the S.D. operations into Southern Malaya, and to employ these aircraft on the first ten nights of the July and August moon periods. These operations were controlled by Headquarters, No. 222 Group. Aircraft airborne from the Cocos Islands were routed in daylight through the gap in the Sumatra mountain range between 1° North and 2° North, and carrying a payload of 5,000 lbs. In this way, approximately 75 per cent. of the Malayan dropping zones was covered.

287. In order to carry out very long range S.D. operations within the Command with worthwhile payloads, Liberators at one time were operating with an all-up-weight (a.u.w.) of 66,000 lbs. This had paid a great dividend in establishing links with the underground forces in Malaya.

288. To keep the a.u.w. within the margin of safety, however, and at the same time carry the maximum payloads, it was necessary, on occasion, to cut the amount of extra petrol carried to the irreducible minimum; to strip aircraft of non-essential equipment, and to carry only essential crews.

289. In the weeks immediately preceding the Allied landings on Malaya, a considerable weight of weapons, ammunition and concentrated food was dropped to thousands of organised guerillas, together with trained guerilla leaders.

290. The operational records of the aircraft engaged on S.D. operations in the Command show that aircraft of No. 222 Group alone flew nearly 11,000 hours between May and September, 1945. The Cocos squadrons, although not altogether fully experienced in S.D. work, speedily established an enviable reputation for accurate dropping. When it is realised, too, that the sorties carried out by Catalina aircraft entailed, for the most part, night landings on enemy waters in varying conditions of sea, without benefit of flarepath, some idea is gained of the high skill required from these R.A.F. pilots.

291. The sudden end of the war in South East Asia did not conclude the tasks of the S.D. squadrons, but brought instead a new series of commitments under Operation "Mastiff" for the relief and liberation of Allied prisoners-of-war, an aspect which is dealt with in a later chapter of this despatch.

Outstanding Operations by Lysander Aircraft.

292. Any report or narrative on S.D. operations would be far short of completeness without mention of the magnificent work done by light aircraft, notably Lysanders. The untiring efforts of Lysander pilots, indeed, greatly assisted Force 136 to carry on their activities behind the enemy lines during the drive through Burma, and I feel justified in singling them out for especial mention.

293. Particularly outstanding work was done by the Lysander Flight of 357 Squadron. Not only were personnel infiltrated, but seriously wounded personnel were evacuated from the field. In addition to the urgent operational stores flown in, commitments had included transport of Staff Officers to Party Commanders in the field, and the evacuation of enemy prisoners-of-war and documents.

294. The versatility of the flight had increased with each operation. Sorties often necessitated flying in foul monsoon weather and landing on very small strips. On one occasion a landing was attempted at Ntilawathihta, near the Papun-Momaung Road, on a very short strip and on wet and slippery grass. The aircraft slid into a deep ditch at the end of the strip, but escaped with negligible damage. In attempts to extricate the aircraft, lumber elephants would not go near, but the combined efforts of fifty local inhabitants eventually succeeded in hauling the plane back on to the strip; the pilot then flew back to base.

295. On many occasions Lysander sorties came near to failure owing to the presence of Japanese troops in the area. Force 136 nearly always had to cover the landing area for fear of surprise by Japanese patrols.

296. On another occasion, a pilot was involved in a skirmish between Japanese troops and Force 136 Guerillas at Lipyekhi, when his aircraft failed to start for the return journey to Rangoon. Firing took place across the strip, but the aircraft escaped damage. It was rendered serviceable next day by a rescue sortie, and was able to return to base.

297. Another escapade was accomplished when Squadron Leader Turner, Flight Commander, damaged his Lysander in an attempt to pick up personnel at Ngapyawdaw, near Kinmun. Shortly after he had landed, the neighbourhood was compromised by Japanese forces and repair of the aircraft was impossible. Attempts to rescue Squadron Leader Turner were abortive until ten days later,

when a rescue aircraft made a well-timed evacuation. In the meantime, the Flight Commander stayed with Force 136 Guerillas.

The Advantages of the Lysander Aircraft.

298. The advantages of the Lysander for the unique type of work it was called upon to carry out were as follows :—
  (i) Weight lifting capacity.
  (ii) Automatic flap action, meeting all the conditions of flight, e.g. a sudden loss of lift in a sudden violent turn or in conditions of turbulence over the hills.
  (iii) Capability of cruising at low speed in conditions of bad visibility.
  (iv) High rate of turn, of great value in confined spaces.
  (v) Fixed undercarriage, strong and able to stand the shocks of heavy landings.
  (vi) High engine power and light wing loading, facilitating quick take-off from waterlogged strips, and an immediate high rate of climb.
  (vii) Reasonable flying endurance of aircraft, the pilot never being embarrassed in a difficult operation by shortage of fuel.

299. But even with these advantages, the technique required of the Lysander pilots was one of skill, particularly when landing on very small strips. On such occasions the normal approach speed of 85 m.p.h. had to be reduced to 70 m.p.h., and a precision touchdown at the very beginning of the strip, with throttle promptly closed, had to be accomplished.

300. From May, 1945, to October, 1945, 357 Squadron Lysanders flew no less than 1,310 hours. 405 sorties were attempted and 363 of these were successful. Personnel infiltrated had numbered 214, and evacuations, 330. In addition, some 104,580 lbs. of stores were landed behind the enemy lines.

301. A fitting tribute to the Lysander operations was paid by Headquarters, Group "A" of Force 136 on 23rd June, 1945.

PHOTOGRAPHIC RECONNAISSANCE

A Record of Achievement Built on Perseverance of Crews.

302. Photographic reconnaissance has come out of the South East Asia Theatre with a record of achievement built upon the perseverance of its air crews to master the difficulties of climate and terrain. A flight of 2,600 miles in nine hours five minutes was one of the longest flights ever done in P.R.

303. The radius of P.R. cover in December, 1943, when the Command was formed, was not more than 680 miles, since long range reconnaissance by Mosquitos was only in process of being attempted in the coverage of the Andaman Islands from Comilla and, a little later, of Bangkok in Siam. When the war with Japan ended in August, 1945, the range of P.R. aircraft in South East Asia Command was such that coverage of the Andaman and Nicobar Islands from Ceylon, flights deep into Siam and French Indo China from Rangoon, and a detailed coverage of targets in Sumatra, Southern Malaya, Singapore and Java by aircraft based on the Cocos Islands, had become normal routine.

304. The Mosquito indeed made amends for the structural defect which had curtailed its use in this Command, for it set up two records in 1945. Firstly, a Mosquito XVI broke the long distance record on March 22 for this type of aircraft in any theatre of war, with a flight of 2,493 miles in eight hours forty-five minutes, covering the Bangkok—Singapore railway to a point south of the Malayan frontier. This performance, however, was eclipsed by a Mosquito XXXIV based on the Cocos Islands, which on 20th August, 1945, flew 1,240 miles to Penang Island and then went on to cover Taiping town and airfield at 17,000 feet. On the return home a survey run was made on the K8/12-inch camera. This was the longest P.R. flight to be made in the Command, and covered a total of 2,600 miles in nine hours five minutes.

Photographic Survey of Burma.

305. Possibly the two most outstanding contributions by photographic reconnaissance to the war in South East Asia were its survey photography of Burma at the beginning of 1944, and its detailed coverage of enemy occupied territories after the fall of Rangoon in May, 1945, in preparation for the large scale assault on Malaya.

306. The survey photography of Burma fulfilled a long-felt want by supplying accurate and up-to-date maps of Burma which were practically non-existent up to this time—the Air Force and Army having to use 1914-15 ground surveys which, as photographic reconnaissance proved, showed major errors. The new survey of Burma was one of the best examples of R.A.F. assistance to the Army in this Theatre.

307. Faced with the urgent and extensive programme of photographic reconnaissance in Malaya and Sumatra for Operation "Zipper", a detachment of 684 Squadron (Alipore) commenced operations from the Cocos Islands in July, 1945, with four Mk. XXXIV Mosquitos which had just been released for service use in temperate and tropical climates. The P.R. programme for "Zipper" went steadily forward and, by the end of July, was 60 per cent. completed. A second detachment of 684 Squadron Mosquitos was operating at this time from China Bay, Ceylon, for the coverage of the Andaman and Nicobar Islands.

P.R. organisation after fall of Rangoon.

308. At the time of Rangoon's capture in May, 1945, the Photographic Reconnaissance Force was commanded by Colonel Minton W. Kaye, United States Army Air Force, with Group Captain S. G. Wise, D.F.C., as Assistant Air Commander.

309. The Force controlled two R.A.F. Squadrons, No. 681 (Spitfires) and No. 684 (Mosquitos), while the Americans had a P.38 (F.5) Squadron, a P.40, and a B.24 Mapping Squadron. The American Units, however, had completed their task as a P.R. integrated force in the Command and, after carrying out a few P.R. sorties at the beginning of May, they then retired to prepare for withdrawal to China with the remainder of the American Air Forces in the Theatre. The two R.A.F. squadrons, therefore, were left to operate on their own.

310. It became apparent, after the fall of Rangoon, that Photographic Reconnaissance in the Command would have to be endowed with a mobility which would allow it to move forward with the tide of battle. Accordingly, No. 347 P.R. Wing, which was formed in April, became effective as a formation in May, 1945. The new Wing Headquarters absorbed all of the R.A.F. element of the Photographic Reconnaissance Force and certain sections of the Station Headquarters at Alipore and Bally (India), where the two R.A.F. Squadrons of Spitfires and Mosquitos were based.

311. In May, No. 684 Squadron continued to be based at Alipore, but No. 681 Squadron moved to Mingaladon, Rangoon and flew most of their sorties in support of the Twelfth Army's mopping up operations along the Mawchi Road, the Sittang Bend and the road and river communications between Pegu and Moulmein.

312. On 9th June, 1945, the Wing passed to the Command of Group Captain C. E. St. J. Beamish, D.F.C.

Working against the Monsoon in Operational Areas.

313. Bad weather was the enemy which photographic reconnaissance had to combat almost continuously. Only by dint of sheer perseverance were many of the most important covers accomplished.

314. With the arrival of the Monsoon in May over the operational areas in Southern Burma and Siam, coverage from a photographic point of view became extremely difficult and flying more hazardous.

315. The inter-tropical front appeared at the Isthmus of Kra and moved as far north as Mergui, but generally it kept more to the south. By the end of May, weather deteriorated considerably and the Monsoon entered into its own for the season.

316. While Spitfires, based in Southern Burma, were able to take advantage of local weather conditions for short P.R. sorties in support of the Army, the task was more difficult, long range Mosquitos undertaking many flights of more than 2,000 miles for each sortie. More than one aircraft on occasions returned to base with torn fabric and other evidence of severe climatic conditions.

317. In August, with the weeks drawing near for the assault on Malaya, No. 2 Mosquito Detachment of 684 Squadron (based on the Cocos Islands), succeeded in flying 282 operational hours with only four crews. Some of the beach targets necessary for operation "Zipper" were exceedingly exacting, since photography had to be done at low tide in order to secure a full picture of the state and condition of beaches in preparation for the landings.

318. Intimation of Japan's surrender was the signal for P.R. to work at greater pressure than ever. The "Zipper" programme, which was all but complete, was cancelled, and a new programme substituted entailing cover, three times a fortnight, by P.R. aircraft of all important targets ranging from Penang Island to Sourabaja in Java. It is worth noting that P.R. aircraft, during this period of uncertainty among Japanese units regarding their country's surrender, met with more opposition than at any other time. At Palembang, pilots reported that enemy A.A. fire was intense.

319. Probably the most outstanding P.R. sortie from a general and humane interest at this time was that undertaken by a pilot of 681 Squadron (Spitfires) when covering prisoner-of-war camps in the Kanchana Buri area of Siam, ten days after the declaration of Japan's surrender. Prisoners at one of the camps were crowded together and swarming over the watch towers, waving and cheering to the pilot of the aircraft. Signs were also laid on the ground, including a giant Union Jack to indicate to the pilot that the prisoners also knew of events which had caused excitement in the world outside.

PART III.

THE SURRENDER OF JAPAN.

THEATRE BOUNDARIES AND DEPLOYMENT OF AIR FORCES DECIDED AT MANILA CONFERENCE.

320. August, 1945 saw the war against Japan move with over-whelming speed towards its culmination.

321. Throughout the war, research in Britain, America and Germany had pursued the possibility of harnessing to war the potentialities of atomic energy, and the first atomic bombs were dropped with devastating effect on metropolitan Japan at Hiroshima and Nagasaki on 5th and 9th August, 1945, respectively. Adding further to the plight of Japan was the declaration of war by Russia on 8th August, followed by Soviet Forces crossing the Manchurian and Korean borders.

322. From these momentous events, and faced with certain Allied invasion of the homeland, for which air power had paved the way, Japan could see no escape. The end came in the form of surrender, which was broadcast from Tokio on 10th August, and the acceptance of the Allied terms on 14th August.

323. As the result of the Japanese intimation that they were prepared to discuss and to receive surrender terms, the Supreme Allied Commander, South East Asia, directed that a Mission representing himself and his three Commanders-in-Chief should be despatched to Manila in the Philippines. The primary object of this Mission was to discuss the terms of surrender with General MacArthur and his staff, with a view to co-ordinating measures to be adopted to implement the terms of surrender both in the South West Pacific area and in South East Asia.

324. As my representative on this Mission, I selected Air Commodore W. A. D. Brook, C.B.E., Deputy Senior Air Staff Officer. Other members of the Mission which left Kandy by York on 16th August, refuelling at Calcutta en route, and continuing the flight by night over enemy occupied territory, were:—

Major-General Penney, S.A.C.'s representative. Head of the Mission, and also representing C.-in-C., A.L.F.S.E.A.

Vice-Admiral C. Moody, representing C.-in-C., E.I.F.

Colonel Mitford-Slade, representing J.P.S., S.A.C.S.E.A.

Colonel Bull, representing J.P.L.C. S.A.C.S.E.A.

Lieut.-Colonel Maugham, representing Intelligence Branch, S.A.C.S.E.A.

Lieut.-Commander Galley, R.N., Flag Lieutenant to Admiral Moody.

2nd Officer Price, W.R.N.S., Secretary to the Mission.

325. The Mission arrived at Manila shortly after dawn on 17th August. The return journey, following the same route, was completed on 21st August, crossing occupied territory once again by night.

Political Situation at Time of Surrender.

326. At the time of the S.A.C.S.E.A. Mission's arrival at Manila, the visit of the Japanese Mission to obtain the surrender terms was still awaited. It was thought that some delay might have occurred arising out of the political confusion in Japan and the lack of communication facilities generally as the result of continuous and heavy bombing.

327. The general opinion in the South West Pacific Area appeared to be that the South East Asia Command Theatre was being far too precipitate in implementing the surrender terms which had not yet been agreed by the contracting parties. Furthermore, General MacArthur was adamant that any implementation of the surrender terms could only take place after the surrender terms had been formally agreed and signed by the Japanese Government either at Tokio or on board a ship in adjacent waters. This, it was calculated, would be at least a week after the presentation of the Allied terms to be collected by the Japanese Mission to Manila, to whom certain points would need clarification.

328. The Japanese Mission consisting of some eight Japanese officers arrived at Manila on the evening of August 19th, having flown in two Betty Bombers from Japan to Okinawa where they had transferred to a C.54. The Mission was led by Lt.-Gen. Kawaba Takashiro, Vice Chief of the Imperial General Staff. Altogether, the representatives were a dejected looking gathering of very small men, clad in shabby and ill-fitting uniforms. They were treated with respect and allowed to wear their swords throughout their visit—an uncomfortable privilege, as each member was carrying a sword nearly as tall as himself. The members of the Mission were housed in the same building as the S.A.C.S.E.A. Mission —a partially repaired building in which they were granted the hospitality of the top floor, the least repaired of all. After a brief meal on arrival they were summoned to a conference at G.H.Q. where they were presented with the terms of surrender for explanation and transmission to their Government. On their part, they provided full details of their Order of Battle, strength of garrisons and the necessary information regarding Prisoner-of-War camps in various Theatres.

329. The Japanese Mission returned to Okinawa from Manila at midday on 20th August. No untoward events occurred during their visit to the Philippines, but such was the mixture of feeling within their own country at that time regarding the peace terms that they were shot at by their own fighters when leaving Japan for Okinawa. A similar reception was contemplated on their return to Japan, and, in consequence, they took the precaution of approaching Japanese territory in the dark.

330. There is little doubt in my mind that the Japanese Government, at the time of surrender, was up against some very strong opposition from certain fanatical factions. It was stated that in Singapore, before our occupation in September, a group of young Japanese officers had planned to fly to Tokio and there weed out what they considered to be the " corrupt elements " around the Throne, where defeatist policies, they held, had greatly influenced the Emperor.

331. The conference at Manila revealed an exceedingly interesting feature. Opinion in the South West Pacific Area apparently attributed a far higher value to the enemy's fighting qualities than was attributed to those Japanese whom we fought and defeated in Burma. It appeared that the morale and determination of the enemy forces in the metropolitan area was on a far higher level than that experienced in the outer regions of Japanese conquest, where forces had been virtually isolated for months and, in any case, were not directly involved in the defence of their homeland. For this reason, G.H.Q. Manila expected considerable opposition to their occupying forces in Japan proper, in the form of sabotage and other subversive activities by fanatical elements.

332. At this time, the American airborne division was standing by at Okinawa to fly into Japan. The ultimate figure for the build-up of U.S. Army Forces for occupation was put at some 18 Divisions together with the whole of the 5th Air Force, although it was not thought that this would include V.H.B. aircraft owing to the lack of suitable runways in Japan.

333. I think it is important to note the American attitude at that time towards the participation of Air Forces, other than American, in the initial occupation of Japan. General Kenney, Commanding General, Far Eastern Air Forces, was not disposed to discuss the occupation of Japan by Allied Air Forces, which he apparently regarded as unnecessary representation in a country where airfield facilities were limited. Furthermore, it seemed that any inclusion of British Air Forces in Japan would inevitably raise the question of Russian Air Forces in a similar role, to which the Americans were strongly averse in every way. On the other hand, the Americans favourably accepted the occupation of Hong Kong and elsewhere by our Air Forces, since they did not regard Hong Kong as their own problem. The fact that the British " Tiger Force " project for Okinawa was no longer contemplated, as the result of Japan's sudden surrender, also produced for the Americans a general feeling of relief, mainly on logistical grounds. The British airfield engineers, who were already in transit for " Tiger Force " constructional requirements, were delayed at the island of Quajalin in the Pacific, pending further instructions to proceed, and it was suggested to us that we might like to divert these forces for our own airfield requirements in Malaya and elsewhere.

334. Australia, however, let it be known that they had every intention of being represented in the forces of occupation of Japan. General MacArthur was informed, through General Blamey, that the Commonwealth proposed to provide a representative garrison for Japan, including three tactical squadrons of the Royal

Australian Air Force. It is interesting to note that this was the first official intimation which had been received by Headquarters, South West Pacific Area regarding the representation of Allied Air Forces in Japan.

335. With Japan's surrender, H.Q. South West Pacific Area were not unnaturally anxious that we should accept full responsibility, as soon as possible, within the new Theatre boundaries originally discussed at a meeting between Admiral Mountbatten and General MacArthur, which had taken place at Manila during July.

336. In the division of responsibility for implementing the surrender terms, South East Asia Command was allotted the following:—

(a) Andamans.   Nicobars.
    Burma.   Thailand.
    F.I.C. (South of   Malaya.
      16° N.). Java.
    Sumatra.   Lombok.
    Bali.

Australia accepted responsibility for:—

(b) British New   Borneo.
      Guinea.   Solomons.
    Bismarck Islands Timor.
    Flores.   Ceram.
    Soemba.   Amboina.
    Boeros.   Tanimbar.
    Kai Aroe.

Islands in the Arafura Sea.

337. This division, however, left a gap comprising the Celebes, Halmahora Islands and Dutch New Guinea, for which no forces were available to implement the surrender terms unless the Dutch did so—a commitment which would obviously have introduced a shipping problem to transfer the necessary forces from Europe. The Australians, too, were anxious to hand over Borneo to us as soon as possible.

THE SURRENDER IN SOUTH EAST ASIA.

Ceremonies at Rangoon and Singapore.

338. In accordance with the orders of the Supreme Allied Commander, South East Asia, Japanese envoys, headed by Lieutenant General Takazo Numata, Chief of Staff to Field Marshal Count Terauchi, Japanese Expeditionary Force, Southern Regions, arrived at Rangoon by air on August 26th to be given their instructions for the implementation of the local surrender terms. Thus, after inflicting on the Japanese one of the greatest defeats of the war in the Far East, in a campaign which had lasted for over three years and in which the enemy's losses amounted to 100,000 men, it was at Rangoon that the Japanese Generals arrived to take their orders from the Allied Forces in South East Asia.

339. The meetings in Rangoon with the Japanese plenipotentiaries were, in no sense, negotiations. There was no question of discussion of terms. The Japanese were there to accept Unconditional Surrender. It was intended also that a binding act of surrender should be signed at Rangoon and that the official ceremony of surrender would be carried out at Singapore after the Supreme Allied Commander's instructions had been completed at the Rangoon meetings.

340. The conditions insisted upon by the Supreme Allied Commander, South East Asia, included immediate relief to prisoners-of-war and internees; Allied aircraft to begin day and night reconnaissance flights over South East Asia; Allied vessels to begin mine-sweeping operations in hitherto Japanese-controlled waters, and also for Allied vessels to enter ports in Malaya and elsewhere with full facilities provided.

341. The meetings with the Japanese plenipotentiaries, which were resumed at Rangoon in the opening days of September, brought to light many positive facts concerning the plight of the Japanese Army in Burma from the time of the enemy's disastrous retreat at Imphal in June, 1944. It was apparent from one important statement read by Major General Ichida, at Rangoon on September 11th, that the Japanese in Burma had not reckoned with two important and vital factors which upset their calculations and placed their forces at disastrous disadvantages:—

(a) Allied air supply, which permitted ground forces in Burma to consolidate their positions without being forced to retreat, and thus rendered the enemy's infiltration and encircling tactics abortive.

(b) Allied air superiority, which so disrupted Japanese supply lines, both in Burma and further afield, that starvation and illness overtook thousands of Japanese troops facing Fourteenth Army, and also denied them the essential supplies of fuel, equipment and material with which to fight a superior equipped, and better supplied, Allied Force.

342. With the disruption of the enemy's lines of communication, and the systematic attacks on their rear supply bases, it was not surprising that Major General Ichida should declare:—

"From the time of the Imphal operation, last year, our Army in Burma carried on its operations continuously for a period of a year with its main force, and during that period the army hardly ever received any reinforcements in its manpower—none since December last year—the replenishment of military stores also being very meagre."

343. The situation of the Allied ground forces, ranged against them, presented a happier picture. Thanks mainly to Allied air superiority, and resulting air supply, they had withstood the siege of Imphal, and, on the siege being raised, had taken the offensive down through Burma with the knowledge that fuel, rations, ammunitions and miscellaneous equipment would be air-dropped or air-landed to them, throughout the advance, while casualties inflicted by the enemy would be taken care of and evacuated safely to base.

The Ceremony at Singapore.

344. With the Supreme Allied Commander, and other Commanders-in-Chief, it afforded considerable satisfaction to witness General Itagaki sign, for his defeated compatriots, Admiral Mountbatten's terms for Unconditional Surrender in the South East Asia Theatre at Singapore, on 12th September, 1945.

345. There was not displayed at that ceremony any deliberate outward show of pride in Allied military achievement. It was more, I consider, an atmosphere of confident achievement which reflected the mood of the three

services in South East Asia that no matter how long the struggle against the Japanese might have taken, victory would be with us in the end. In South East Asia we had good reason to remember that unequal contest during the dark days of 1941 and 1942, when the enemy, powerful and well prepared, swept through Malaya, occupied Singapore and later Burma. But their ultimate and decisive defeat—when the tide turned against them, must surely have caused them to remember the sting of our air forces which, in due course, swept clear the skies over Burma, and disorganised the land communications of the Japanese army as the ground troops rolled the enemy back through Burma during the advance from Imphal to Rangoon.

346. The Instrument of Surrender was drawn up in English—the only authentic version. In case of doubt as to the intention of our meaning in that Instrument of Surrender, the decision of the Supreme Allied Commander was unequivocal and final.

347. Under the terms of surrender, all Japanese Army, Navy and Air Forces in South East Asia passed to the control of the Supreme Allied Commander.

348. I was much impressed by one noticeable characteristic on the part of our enemies which was in striking contrast to their previous behaviour in this Theatre—some of it an exhibition of unmitigated barbarism. After the surrender there was a widespread attitude of subservient willingness by the Japanese to obey our orders. In Singapore, as in other parts of the Command, I observed that the Japanese, officers and men alike, conducted themselves with strict discipline in our presence. They were super-punctilious too, when paying respects to members of our forces. While this was no doubt correct, it did appear somewhat unreal.

349. If, at Singapore, the Japanese myth of invincibility still lurked in the midst of the more fanatical Japanese elements, the Supreme Allied Commander must have corrected sharply any such belief which was held, in so far as it concerned the campaign in South East Asia. Admiral Mountbatten made it clear and emphatic to Itagaki during the surrender ceremony that it was not a negotiated surrender, but complete capitulation by the Japanese, after total military defeat. He informed Itagaki that not only did he possess superior naval, military and air forces at Singapore, but, in addition, he had a large fleet anchored off Port Swettenham and Port Dickson where, three days previously, on September 9th, considerable forces had started disembarking at daylight. On the 10th, the strength of that force was 100,000 men ashore. Indeed, at the very time of the Japanese signing the Instrument of Surrender at Singapore, R.A.F. units were firmly established at strategic points throughout the vast territories of this Theatre which, a few weeks beforehand, had been held by the Japanese.

350. It was also emphasised at the Singapore ceremony that the invasion of Malaya would have taken place on September 9th whether the Japanese had resisted or not, and it was stressed for the particular benefit of General Itagaki, therefore, that the Japanese were surrendering to a superior Allied force in Malaya.

PART IV.

THE RE-OCCUPATION OF JAPANESE OCCUPIED TERRITORIES ON SURRENDER.

OPERATIONS "TIDERACE" AND "ZIPPER".

351. South East Asia Command's assault on Malaya, planned for 9th September, 1945, was forestalled by Japanese surrender, thus bringing about a last minute change in plan involving more than 500 aircraft of the Strategic, Tactical and General Reconnaissance units of the R.A.F. which had been assembled in India, Burma, Ceylon and the Cocos Islands for the attack.

352. While Operation "Zipper" went forward on 9th September as arranged, it did so on a much modified scale, having quickly transferred a proportion of its original strength to Operation "Tiderace" and leaving itself more in the nature of a display to show the flag.

353. The sudden capitulation of Japan on August 14th had brought with it the gigantic task of effecting rapid occupation of the principal key points throughout the Japanese occupied territories in South East Asia and further afield.

354. South East Asia, in this respect, bore no comparison to the situation in Europe where, on the eve of Germany's capitulation, the armed might of the Allied forces could roll along the roads of the Reich to Berlin, and the Air Forces sweep over Germany at will from their bases behind the victorious troops. In South East Asia, the Japanese occupied territories were vast. They covered Siam, French Indo-China, the Tenasserim Coast of Southern Burma, Malaya, Singapore Island, Sumatra, Java and Borneo. Even far off Hong Kong became a commitment.

355. Headquarters, Air Command, South East Asia, based at Kandy, Ceylon, was 1,500 miles distant across the Bay of Bengal from its principal air bases in Burma. Yet, such was the flexibility of air power, and despite the many and intricate formalities with which the Command was confronted in implementing the surrender terms on the eve of the planned invasion of Malaya, that air formations occupied bases at Penang on September 5th, Singapore on the 6th, Bangkok on the 5th and Saigon and Hong Kong on September 12th.

356. More vital still was the fact that the air forces of my Command had also launched upon one of the greatest missions of mercy of the war—the relief and liberation of thousands of Allied prisoners-of-war from the misery and privations of their prison camps, and assisting in their transportation westwards.

The Advent of "Tiderace" for Occupation of Singapore.

357. Capitulation by Japan naturally rendered planning and preparations for the assault on Malaya somewhat abortive. But this was only on a limited scale.

358. At the end of July, the mounting curve of Allied air assaults on Japan was such that it did seem reasonable to presume that an early collapse was a distinct possibility. Accordingly, emergency planning was put in preparation for the rapid occupation of Singapore

at an early date should the enemy agree to accept the terms of the Potsdam declaration of July 26th.

359. The wisdom of this planning made itself apparent early in August when the first atomic bomb was dropped on the Japanese homeland and Russia entered the war.

360. It was the possibility of Japanese treachery, however, which decided the course that planning would take, and the initial occupation of Singapore, known as Operation " Tiderace " was, therefore, mounted from resources other than those earmarked for Operation " Zipper ". In this way, it was possible to counter any Japanese opposition to " Tiderace " which may have taken place, by continuing to mount the strong fighting " Zipper " operation as originally planned.

361. Although the first objective in the reoccupation plan was Singapore, a necessary step in order to establish an advanced air and naval base to clear the Straits of Malacca for shipping, it became clear that Bangkok in Siam, and Saigon in French Indo-China, would also have to be occupied soon after the Japanese surrender.

362. Operations known as " Bibber ", which involved the occupation of the Bangkok area, and " Masterdom ", involving the re-entry into French Indo-China to gain control over the forces of Field Marshal Count Terauchi, whose Southern Army Headquarters were at Saigon, had therefore to be worked out in detail. Moreover, it had been indicated by the British Chiefs of Staff that the former British port of Hong Kong must also be occupied at an early date.

363. To meet these exigencies, therefore, it was found necessary to modify to some extent the air effort for Operation " Tiderace " so that the Dakota Squadrons, based in Rangoon, could be utilised for essential trooping and air lift during the occupation of Bangkok and subsequently of Saigon. This was exceedingly important, since a long voyage with troops from existing Allied bases to Siam and French Indo-China would almost certainly have prohibited the speedy occupation of these territories had not the ground forces been lifted by air.

364. That 14,000 Army and Air Force personnel for the garrison at Bangkok and Saigon were carried in by our Air Forces without loss after the Japanese surrender, was evidence of the additional role which the Air Forces of my Command were called upon to play on the cessation of hostilities, at a time when it was imperative to establish ground troops at key points within the scattered enemy-occupied territories in the quickest possible time.

Original " Zipper " Plan Forestalled.

365. The Surrender by Japan cut right across the ambitious air plan for Operation " Zipper " which had been so carefully conceived to support the landings by ground troops on the Southern region of the Malay Peninsula.

366. Landings on the beaches at Ports Swettenham and Dickson on D-Day, September 9th, were to have been made under air cover provided by carrier-borne aircraft of the Royal Navy, whose task would have included attacks on the enemy's lines of communication and troop concentrations until the fly-in of R.A.F. fighters was accomplished. Two aircraft carriers, H.M.S. SMITER and H.M.S. TRUMPETER, carrying short-range Spitfires and Sentinels and Austers for casualty evacuation, were to carry these aircraft to a point off shore for pilots to fly them from off the carriers and land them on the newly-occupied aerodromes.

367. The planned effort of the naval carrier-borne fighters was 190 sorties a day from the moment of their arrival in the areas of the bridgeheads for about a week. This would be further augmented, within six days, by an additional 72 sorties a day from the first land-based squadrons of R.A.F. Spitfires, and six sorties per night from the night fighter Mosquitos. From the outset, therefore, air superiority was assured. The enemy was not expected to produce any serious air threat which could not be dealt with adequately by our fighters.

368. As more than a thousand miles separated the existing R.A.F. bases in Rangoon and the Cocos Islands from the landing beaches, and almost 1,500 miles in respect of other R.A.F. bases in Ceylon and Ramree Island, it was impossible for light bomber, fighter and fighter bomber squadrons to operate in immediate support of the bridgehead ground forces until the position ashore was consolidated, an airfield captured, repairs effected and runways made serviceable.

369. Basing its time-table on the speed of the Army's advance and the rapidity by which constructional engineers could repair damaged runways and taxi-tracks, it was estimated that strips could be brought into operation at the rate of approximately one per week. Once the newly-occupied airfields had been established, the long-range Thunderbolts, Mosquitos and Dakotas, flying a thousand miles from Rangoon, would then make the flight south to Malaya, being guided on the way by three navigational aid ships at specified positions off the Tenasserim Coast and Malayan Peninsula.

370. The first strip —Kelanang—was calculated to be operational by D plus 6; Port Swettenham by D plus 12 and Kuala Lumpur by D plus 20. It was possible that a fourth strip might be established at Batu Pahat, or Malacca, in order to accommodate a light Mosquito bomber and rocket-firing Beaufighter aircraft by D plus 40.

371. The value of the Cocos Islands prior to and during Operation " Zipper " would have been considerable. The Strategic and G.R. squadrons were to have taken part in large-scale pre-D-Day operations directed against radar installations covering the approaches to the assault area, and also to cutting the Bangkok-Singapore railway north of Kuala Lumpur. Other tasks included the neutralising of the Japanese Air Force, estimated at a little more than 170 aircraft in Malaya and Sumatra, also attacking enemy shipping employed in carrying supplies or reinforcements to Malaya to oppose our landing. The aerodromes at Kelanang, Port Swettenham and Kuala Lumpur were not to be bombed, since they were the first objectives on establishing the bridgehead.

372. Five R.A.F. Wings were detailed to operate in the tactical forces contained within Air Vice Marshal Bandon's 224 Group, whose advanced Headquarters were to be established

ashore on D-Day to set up control communications and radar screens, as an early occupation of Kelanang air strip in a serviceable condition would allow Spitfires to be flown in the following day and made ready for action.

373. The R.A.F. Wings made available for the operation were Nos. 901 Wing, to be first located at Kuala Lumpur; 902 Wing at Kelanang; 904 Wing at an air strip to be sited and constructed; 905 Wing at Port Swettenham and 907 Wing at Batu Pahat or an alternative.

374. A prominent role in the "Zipper" operation was also allocated to the R.A.F. Regiment. Five Wings of nearly 2,500 officers and men, made up of nine Field Squadrons and five Light Anti-Aircraft Squadrons were to capture and hold the aerodromes and also to protect radar sites. The majority of the men had been on active service in India and Burma.

Other Operational Aspects of "Zipper".

375. Air operations in "Zipper", once our position ashore had been consolidated and airfields established, would have followed closely to plan thus:—

(*a*) Eight squadrons of Thunderbolts would have supported the drive on Singapore.

(*b*) Fighter Reconnaissance cover would have been provided by Spitfire F/R Mk. XIV's, and, as in Burma, they would have flown protective patrols over the traffic lanes of the supply dropping Dakotas.

(*c*) Two squadrons of Transport Command supply freighters were allocated to the task of carrying supplies from the beach head air strip at Port Swettenham to the forward troops. A start would first be made with a target of 150 tons per day from D plus 23.

(*d*) With the possibility of an airborne assault force deep behind enemy lines after the third or fourth week of the operation, six squadrons of Dakotas would have been flown in from Rangoon and out again immediately afterwards for this purpose.

(*e*) Mosquitos were to be employed as light bombers, night fighters and photographic reconnaissance aircraft.

(*f*) Air evacuation of casualties was to have been the task of Sentinel and Auster aircraft. As in Burma, they were to operate from a main strip flying as required to 400 yard clearings in the flight zone to pick up wounded and to carry them back to the Dakotas. The more seriously wounded were to have been ferried by Dakotas to Rangoon.

(*g*) Three D.D.T. spraying Dakotas operating from Kelanang were to spray mosquito infested zones over a wide area.

(*h*) To answer emergency calls from D plus 4, three Sunderland aircraft were to be available for air-sea rescue while three high-speed launches were also to be deck-carried to the beach head.

(*i*) Rocket firing Beaufighters were to be employed from about D plus 43 in attacks on shipping, enemy rolling stock, targets on Singapore Island and also in assisting in the bombardment plan for the crossing of the Johore Strait for the final assault on Singapore itself.

Modified Operation "Zipper" Goes Forward.

376. In the closing days of August, before even the "Zipper" convoys had left India for Malaya, the emergency operation "Tiderace" was ordered, since it was essential that air units should fly into Penang and Singapore without further delay. This brought No. 185 Wing, controlling Dakotas, Spitfires and Mosquitos from Burma to Penang, and No. 903 Wing from Akyab to Singapore, together with Nos. 152 and 155 Spitfire Squadrons flying Zayatkwin (Rangoon)—Penang—Singapore (Tengah), and 110 Squadron from Hmawbi (Burma)—Penang—Singapore (Seletar). No. 903 Wing elements reached Singapore on 6th September, some three days before the first "Zipper" elements arrived off the west coast of Malaya on September 9th.

377. With "Tiderace" operation completed, and air, ground and sea forces occupying Singapore, the modified "Zipper" operation went forward on September 9th with convoys standing off the beaches at Ports Swettenham and Dickson. The naval air support programme, however, had been called off.

378. The air effort for the original "Zipper" was considerably reduced and of the five R.A.F. Wings scheduled to take part in the operation, the following wings did not enter Malaya and were phased out:—
No. 901 Wing. No. 904 Wing. No. 907 Wing.

This left the Wing Order of Battle for "Zipper" as under:—

No. 902 Wing. Tengah.	No. 905 Wing. Kuala Lumpur.
No. 185 Wing. Penang.	No. 903 Wing. Kallang.

S.S. "Manela" Sunderland H.Q. Ship—Seletar.

379. The following squadrons were also phased out:—

Spitfires	... ...	Squadrons No. 132 and 615
Thunderbolts	... ...	Squadrons No. 530 and 261.
Dakotas	... ...	Squadrons No. 96 and 62.
Beaufighters	... ...	Squadrons No. 22, 217 and 45.
Mosquitos	... ...	Squadrons No. 82 and 211.

leaving the undernoted squadrons of the original plan:—

Spitfires	... ...	Squadrons No. 11, 17 and 681.
Thunderbolts	... ...	Squadrons No. 131, 258, 81 and 60.
Mosquitos	... ...	Squadrons No. 89, 684 and 84.
Austers	... ...	Squadron No. 656.
Sunderland Det.	...	Squadron No. 205.

The "Zipper" Landings which took place.

380. On D-Day, September 9th, the first of the "Zipper" landings under the modified plan took place, with ground forces and R.A.F. parties leaving the anchored convoys and going peacefully ashore in the Port Swettenham and Dickson areas.

381. This was the start of the large scale landing in Malaya—and under very different circumstances from what had been envisaged when the operation was first planned.

382. Included in the convoy was Headquarters ship H.M.S. BULOLO which carried Air Vice-Marshal Bandon and his advance H.Q. 224 Group staff who moved ashore to Kelanang airfield on September 10th; Telok Datok on September 14th; Kuala Lumpur on September 18th and Singapore on September 22nd.

383. The landing at Port Dickson, some fifty miles south of Swettenham, went forward as planned and without untoward incident.

384. On the eve of the 11th September, the D-plus-3 convoy dropped anchor among the great concentration of shipping already lying off Morib Beach. The scene, with every vessel twinkling lights, resembled more a Cowes regatta than one of the largest amphibious operations of the campaign.

385. The landings at Morib cannot be described as attaining the same degree of success as those experienced at Ports Swettenham and Dickson—due principally to the difficulties encountered on the water-covered beaches which, at that part of the coast, are nothing more than mud brought down by the Klang River. Morib is some 20 miles south of Port Swettenham and 30 miles north of Port Dickson. While there was much to commend Port Swettenham and Port Dickson for landings by a fighting force, this unfortunately, could not be said of Morib. A number of M.T. vehicles which were driven off the landing craft by their Army drivers into what was considered axle-deep water, later plunged into slime and mud while negotiating the shore and remained fast. There were several casualties.

386. These are important factors which might well have produced serious consequences had "Zipper" been mounted against opposing forces on dry land at this part of the coast.

SOME ASPECTS OF THE OCCUPATION OF SIAM, F.I.C. AND HONG KONG.

387. On the occupation of Siam, the Don Muang airfield at Bangkok provided two important functions. It enabled released Allied prisoners-of-war to be evacuated by our aircraft to Rangoon and Singapore, while it also formed a valuable staging post to Saigon in French Indo-China as well as a refuelling point for aircraft lifting there.

388. In Bangkok, the Siamese Air Force was found to be extraordinarily co-operative and markedly pro-R.A.F., since many of them had, in fact, been trained in England.

389. An unusual document, giving an outline of the activities and organisation of the Siamese Air Force, and also emphasising its attitude of passive resistance to the Japanese throughout the enemy's occupation of Siam, was handed over by the Siamese Air Force to R.A.F. Intelligence.

390. History must judge this document for itself. Whatever may have been happening politically behind the scenes in the Far East, in these dark days of December, 1941, there seems to be no doubt that units of the Siamese Air Force, on December 8th, took the air to resist the Japanese invader, only to be outnumbered and overwhelmed by units of the more superior Japanese Air Force. While this commendable spirit of resistance by the Siamese Air Force may have been evident, they were to learn sadly, the same day, that the Siamese Government in Bangkok was actually negotiating with the Japanese Ambassador.

391. "From outer appearances we played up to mislead the Japanese", is one comment in the Siamese document when discussing the defence of Siam during the period of Japanese occupation. In their participation in the defence of Don Muang airfield and Bangkok against Allied aircraft, it was maintained by the Siamese Air Force that "we just did it in a formal fashion. The United Nations aircraft would fly one way and our aircraft the other way, or at different heights. If by rare chance we had to meet we carried on just for appearances sake."

392. Such are some of the statements by the Siamese Air Force. But it is on fact, rather than on professions of loyalty, that any final assessment must be made. In this respect, there is one incontrovertible fact concerning Allied prisoners-of-war, which does reveal the silent co-operation rendered by the Siamese Air Force from the time of their first prisoner-of-war—William MacClurry, an American pilot from the American Volunteer Group (Tiger Squadron), who bailed out at Cheing Mai at the onset of the war in the Far East, and whose custody by the Japanese was vigorously contested by the Siamese Air Force, until they finally confined him themselves to ensure his better treatment and safety.

393. It must also be marked to the credit of the Siamese Air Force that they did, to our knowledge, assist in furthering liaison and communication work within Siam, which included the conveyance of passengers in and out of the country; rendering assistance to, and providing safeguard for Allied personnel sent into Siam to gather information, and also indicating for our benefit, precise targets in the hands of the Japanese. Such acts of co-operation were fraught with grave risk, and it is not surprising that the Japanese ultimately adopted an attitude of suspicion.

The occupation of Saigon.

394. The outward welcome accorded to the Allied Forces from both the French and Annamese alike on our entry into French Indo-China was decidely embarrassing. Our Forces obviously found themselves in a divided house.

395. The main R.A.F. party flew into Saigon from Burma on September 12th, and was given a demonstrative reception by the French. At the same time, there were banners throughout Saigon's streets erected by the Annamese which welcomed the Allies but bore caustic anti-French slogans.

396. R.A.F. reconnaissance parties who inspected Japanese Air Force installations at Than Son Nhut and Saigon, found them most disappointing. Comparatively few aircraft were discovered, and none, indeed, were serviceable. It appeared that all serviceable aircraft had either been withdrawn for the defence of Japan or flown to Phu My aerodrome, twenty miles east of Saigon, after the cessation of hostilities. The majority of Japanese Air Force personnel previously at Saigon had also been withdrawn.

397. The Saigon-Than Son Nhut area was the maintenance and repair unit base for the Japanese in French Indo-China, but, since only

two engine test benches were found, the normal capacity for engine repairs must have been very low. No sign of any centralised production line was apparent.

398. Of characteristic orderliness in Japanese storage equipment there was none. All kinds of equipment were found mixed together in each warehouse apparently without rhyme or reason, and there appeared to be little attempt to keep any detailed record of stock and issues. It is surprising how any items were found when required, or further commitments even calculated.

399. Arms discovered tallied with the list provided by the Japanese, but there was nothing to show that this list was, in fact, definite. Judging by the aggressive attitude of the Annamese towards the French at this period, it may well have been that considerable stocks of Japanese arms had not been declared.

The occupation of Hong Kong.

400. On August 29th a strong naval force under Rear Admiral C. H. J. Harcourt, C.B., C.B.E. (Flag in H.M.S. SWIFTSURE) arrived off Hong Kong and landed a force on August 30th, being joined by Rear Admiral C. S. Daniel, C.B., C.B.E., D.S.C. (Flag in H.M.S. ANSON). The formal surrender of the Japanese at Hong Kong took place on September 16th. An air headquarters was established on September 12th.

401. One Spitfire squadron was conveyed in an aircraft carrier and the remainder of the air units, which included a Mosquito L.B. squadron, another Spitfire squadron, a Sunderland squadron, and one Dakota squadron, were flown in to Kaitak Airfield at Kowloon, on the mainland.

402. Air defence of Hong Kong, and the provision of air support for any operations which might be necessary by the ground forces involving security of the base, were the primary duties of the air forces as planned. In addition, however, Hong Kong provided a link in the chain of air communications for, and reinforcement of the British and Dominion Air Forces which would garrison Japan.

403. The "Shield" convoy, which was at sea at the conclusion of the Japanese war and, accordingly, was diverted while proceeding to Okinawa in connection with the Pacific "Tiger Force" operation, arrived in Hong Kong on September 4th with 3,400 officers and men of various R.A.F. units. A large percentage of "Shield" Force was composed of personnel of No. 5,358 Airfield Construction Wing, whose original task had been rendered redundant.

404. The variety of rehabilitation tasks undertaken by R.A.F. personnel on the occupation of Hong Kong and Kowloon on the mainland, and accomplished without any previous experience, showed that the Royal Air Force, apart from its qualities as a fighting service, could be extremely versatile in other spheres. It was gratifying to observe at Hong Kong how aircrew personnel, mainly fighter pilots, could apply themselves to ground duties varying from prison supervision to billeting and requisitioning, whereas those with greater technical knowledge, such as R.A.F. Airfield Construction Personnel, were largely responsible for the initiation and maintenance of the public services; power, light, transport, etc.

405. In the first few days of occupation, some 18,000 Japanese forces, including many senior officers, were rounded up, disarmed, and concentrated in Shamshui Po prison, previously a concentration camp on the mainland.

406. The first commandant of what, under British occupation, became a Japanese concentration camp, was a R.A.F. squadron leader whose previous experience had been limited to operational flying. He proved himself a competent prison governor during his short term of office before handing over his duties to an Army officer.

R.A.F. undertake many public services.

407. The total neglect of civic administration by the Japanese in Hong Kong and Kowloon, except in so far as it affected themselves, was all too apparent. Transport did not exist; electric power was unreliable and the supply severely limited; public health services had been totally ignored, and the streets stank with accumulated rubbish and filth. There was, too, large scale looting by the Chinese who, until checked, literally stripped every house they entered of all furniture, fittings and every piece of wood including floor boards and window and door frames. Wood for fuel purposes, indeed, was at a premium in Hong Kong due to the absence of coal.

408. The problems of occupation which faced our forces on arrival were so numerous and varied that it was difficult to know where to make a start. Yet, at this time, when the R.A.F. personnel were busily engaged in establishing an occupation force, many important public services were undertaken with willingness.

409. To overcome the transport difficulties, every motor car available was requisitioned. This in itself involved considerable labour for R.A.F. personnel in rehabilitating and maintaining decrepit and mechanically unsound vehicles which had been left behind by the Japanese. In particular, restoration of the dock area to a standard capable of unloading the freight ships of "Shield" convoy presented big difficulties. The wharves were broken in many instances and covered with debris and dilapidated equipment. Sunken vessels in the bases were also hazards to navigation.

410. The power station at Kowloon was manned by a R.A.F. supervisory staff. While the plant did not work to full capacity, principally on account of fuel shortage, it was, nevertheless, made to function and supply all the requirements of light and power in Kowloon and the docks area. This work included the reconditioning of furnaces, boilers, and the repair of certain turbine power units.

411. In their search for wood as fuel, an R.A.F. reconnaissance party of ground personnel penetrated into the New Territories which were still occupied by the Japanese. Large stocks of wood were discovered at Taipo and Fanling, twenty and fifteen miles respectively. An incidental on this trip was that a chit was given to the Chinese Communist Army Troops which allowed the party to cross over the border to collect a number of abandoned

railway trucks. A fuel supply for the Kowloon power station was thus assured, but the margin was so close that on one occasion the power house was within 15 minutes of closing down completely.

412. Railway workshops were also under the initial supervision of a R.A.F. staff, which was later augmented by suitable personnel through arrangements with Civil Affairs. Under R.A.F. supervision these workshops completed repair to three locomotives, some twenty goods wagons, and three passenger coaches. As a result, the rolling stock augmented by this output from the railway workshops was sufficient to meet the requirements of the railway within the colony.

413. Even Hong Kong's municipal water supply included an element of R.A.F. supervisory staff, though in this respect the water supply as a whole had suffered little during enemy occupation and therefore met existing requirements.

414. The morale of our Air Forces in the execution of these extraordinarily varied tasks was wonderfully high, and once the initial excitement and novelty associated with their misemployment in the role of shock troops, guards, policemen and municipal authorities had worn off, R.A.F. units took stock of the situation and turned their attention to the tasks of resuming their normal service duties.

THE LIBERATION OF ALLIED PRISONERS OF WAR AND INTERNEES

Operations "Birdcage" and "Mastiff"

415. The relief and liberation of almost 100,000 Allied prisoners-of-war and internees confined in Japanese prison camps throughout the vast territories of South East Asia, is an episode in the Far Eastern War which relied almost entirely upon Air Power for its success in the initial but vital stages of its operation.

416. It would be inaccurate to record that the Air Forces alone were responsible for the ultimate rescue and liberation of these thousands of prisoners, but the Air Forces of this Command carried out vital tasks as follows:—

(a) Spread the news of Japanese surrender in millions of leaflets dropped over the principal towns and known sites of Japanese prison camps scattered throughout South East Asia.

(b) Warned Allied prisoners-of-war and internees of their impending liberation.

(c) Dropped medical supplies, medical teams, administrative personnel and W/T operators to make first contact with prisoners and to signal back vital information regarding numbers imprisoned and supplies required.

(d) Air dropped, or air landed, quantities of food, clothing and other necessities to relieve the privations suffered at prison camps.

(e) Evacuated by air hundreds of prisoners from Malaya, Siam, French Indo-China, Sumatra and Java, including cases of very serious illness.

417. In a message to all formations of Air Command which took part in the inauguration of this task on August 28th, 1945, the operation was described as "the greatest mercy mission of the war".

418. It was a mission of paramount importance to thousands of families in Britain, the Dominions and, indeed, in Holland, who eagerly awaited information about relatives interned and captured during the Japanese conquest of Malaya in 1942.

419. In Singapore alone, about 35,000 prisoners were held in the various Japanese prison camps throughout Singapore Island, the most notorious of which was the Changi Gaol. The inmates of these camps had been subjected to coarse indignities and even torture.

420. The feeling in Britain found expression in a message from the British Foreign Secretary to the Supreme Allied Commander, South East Asia, in which he drew Admiral Mountbatten's attention to the numerous enquiries which the Government had received since the publication of atrocity stories from Singapore and elsewhere, and saying that there was grave concern in respect of Sumatra, since deaths actually reported by the Japanese through the International Red Cross were much higher in proportion to numbers anywhere else in the Far East.

421. It can be seen, therefore, how well suited was Air Power to perform this vitally important task involving great distances across great tracts of land—a task also in which speed was essential for its success.

Operation "Birdcage" launched.

422. As soon as the Japanese surrender had been universally accepted and confirmed, action was taken to issue instructions contained in specially prepared leaflets to:—

(a) Japanese Prison Guards.
(b) Allied Prisoners-of-war.
(c) Local Japanese forces.
(d) The local native population.

423. The operation to implement this action was allotted the code name of "Birdcage," and was launched by the Air Forces of Air Command on August 28th, operating from bases in Ceylon, Cocos Islands, Bengal and Burma.

424. Thereafter, Operation "Mastiff", was planned to ensure that medical aid, comforts, food, clothing, R.A.P.W.I. Control Staffs where necessary, and any other essential preliminary needs were introduced into the camps as early as possible.

425. Operation "Birdcage" was completed by August 31st. In the space of four days, leaflets had been dropped over 236 localities and 90 prisoner-of-war camps throughout Burma, Siam, French Indo-China, Malaya and Sumatra. Where sorties were at first rendered abortive by weather and by difficulty in locating targets or by mechanical trouble, they were persisted with on the following days. Very few priority targets remained uncovered. One group of towns in the hinterland of Malaya was successfully covered only at the third attempt.

426. In addition to Liberator sorties flown from bases in Ceylon, Cocos Islands and Bengal, Thunderbolts operating from Burma dropped one million leaflets on thirteen localities in Southern Burma extending as far south as the Kra Isthmus. No target was left uncovered. One Thunderbolt was lost during these operations—the aircraft crashing in flames at Kraburi.

427. I think it is worthy of note that Operation "Birdcage" was carried out in very indifferent conditions. Even more important still was the fact that an all round trip of many of the sorties was equivalent to a trans-Atlantic flight. Nevertheless, 75 per cent. of the crews reached their targets, which included towns and camps as far east as Hanoi, Tourane and Saigon.

Success of Leaflet Dropping.

428. The news of Japanese surrender contained in the millions of leaflets dropped met with great enthusiasm throughout the scattered territories of South East Asia. They were picked up on the streets of towns and read eagerly by the civilian population. The messages also dropped to the Allied prisoners-of-war stated, "We want to get you back home quickly, safe and sound".

429. Many of the prisoners had been Japanese forced labour for the building of the notorious Bangkok-Moulmein railway—a slave task which will take its place among the list of incredible efforts carried out by captive men.

430. August, 1945, saw the greatest effort in leaflet dropping attempted by aircraft of the Command.

431. Prior to the surrender, and immediately after, some 33,000,000 leaflets were dropped over the enemy-occupied territories in South East Asia. This form of psychological warfare had been stepped up very considerably after the defeat of the Japanese in Burma, and in July the total dropped by aircraft of the Command reached 22,000,000.

432. One particular form of leaflet, dropped over the trapped Japanese forces in the Pegu Yomas of Southern Burma during July, not only called upon the enemy to surrender after telling them of the hopeless position of their homeland, but, on the reverse side offered them a safe conduct through the Allied lines with the added assurance that they would be given food, medical attention and honourable treatment.

Launching of Operation "Mastiff".

433. The saturating of towns and prison camps with leaflets announcing the Japanese surrender was, in itself, a laudable effort, but the main task which awaited the Air Forces was unquestionably that of Operation "Mastiff" in bringing practical relief and comfort to those who needed them most.

434. Hundreds of these prisoners were emaciated, gaunt and pitiful beings—some, indeed, were too weak to stand upon their legs. The majority of prisoners were deficient of proper clothing. There were instances, too, where some were completely naked.

435. The need of medical supplies was perhaps the greatest, for the Japanese had shown little ability or willingness to appreciate the needs of prisoners-of-war in many cases. The immediate requirements in drugs, therefore, could only be taken to sufferers by air, and, as a large percentage of prisoners and internees, particularly in Singapore, were affected by malaria, it was estimated that 1,250,000 tablets of Atabrine, or substitute, were essential for delivery each week.

436. The "Mastiff" operation in the early stages was carried out by ten Liberator squadrons (including one R.A.A.F. squadron) and one Dakota squadron. Three Liberator squadrons operated from bases in Bengal—Jessore, Salbani and Digri—covering targets chiefly in Siam and French Indo-China. From bases in Ceylon another three Liberator squadrons operated over Malaya and Sumatra, while areas in Malaya and Java were supplied by three Liberator squadrons based in the Cocos Islands, though these were chiefly employed on targets in Sumatra.

437. The Dakota squadron operated from Rangoon over Siam and the Tenasserim Coastal Area of Southern Burma. The tasks undertaken by this Dakota squadron must not be confused with the all-out effort made by five Dakota squadrons of No. 232 Group, R.A.F., based on Rangoon, which were employed on the air-lift to Bangkok, where the Don Muang Airfield was quickly in use. The operations of these Dakota squadrons in the air landing of supplies and in the evacuation of prisoners-of-war was one of the outstanding features of the air operations associated with "Mastiff".

438. From 1st to 5th September, approximately 200 Dakota sorties were flown from Rangoon, and some 400 tons of stores were dropped or landed. The same aircraft carried back 4,000 prisoners-of-war and internees. On the following week the Dakotas carried out a further 360 sorties, and dropped or landed 600 tons of stores. On their return trips they carried back some 3,700 prisoners-of-war. It was a tribute to the enthusiasm shown by the Dakota aircrews at this time that 12th Army, by September 10th, was able to report that approximately 9,000 prisoners-of-war had been carried back to Rangoon from Bangkok. Early in the month, practically all the U.S. prisoners-of-war had been evacuated from the Bangkok area, the figure being approximately 162. This evacuation was carried out chiefly by U.S. airlift, which was also responsible for bringing out a number of British and Allied sick.

Use of Thunderbolts and R.A.A.F. Liberators.

439. Though not actually engaged upon Operation "Mastiff", a number of Thunderbolt aircraft flew from their bases in Burma and assisted in the problem of locating camps and determining their circumstances. Many of these Thunderbolt sorties were rendered abortive by weather, but other sorties resulted in the bringing back of valuable information. It was noted, for example, that several of the prison camps on the Burma-Siam railway, in the area stretching N.W. from Kanchanaburi, were deserted and empty, while prisoners-of-war in other scattered camps greeted the appearance of the Thunderbolts with understandable enthusiasm expressed by frantic cheering and waving.

440. The inclusion of a series of sorties by Liberators of the R.A.A.F. which took off from bases in North Western Australia to drop supplies over Magelang Airfield, in Java, also greatly assisted in the success of operations in the opening weeks. These aircraft landed in the Cocos Islands, loaded up with fresh supplies, and repeated the drop on Java en route back to Australia. The R.A.A.F. Liberators completed 21 sorties, all of which were successful. Other sorties of a similar nature were

flown by these aircraft. At this time too, the presence in Singapore of Dakotas belonging to 31 Squadron, which operated over Sumatra, assisted materially in bringing out of Sumatra some of the first prisoners-of-war.

441. For purposes of comparison, the undernoted table shows the air effort over different target areas of South East Asia for the first three weeks during which Operation "Mastiff" was in progress, and which covers the particular period of my Despatch.

Target Area	August—September Week 30th—5th			September Week 6th—12th			September Week 13th—19th		
	Successful	Abortive	Missing	Successful	Abortive	Missing	Successful	Abortive	Missing
Siam	42	8	—	49	—	—	49	3	—
F.I.C.	13	1	1	11	—	—	11	1	2
Malaya	22	2	—	10	2	—	6	—	—
Sumatra	23	2	1	29	1	—	38	4	—
Java	—	—	—	2	—	—	22	1	—
	100	13	2	101	3	—	126	9	2

Working of RAPWI and the S.D. Squadrons.

442. The evacuation of prisoners-of-war and internees required the maximum co-operation between Naval, Land and Air Forces.

443. An Inter-Services Inter-Allied Committee was therefore established at the Headquarters of the Supreme Allied Commander, at Kandy, Ceylon, for planning and co-ordination of control. This Committee acted as the clearing house for information, and declared the decisions of the Supreme Allied Commander on policy, priorities, and allocation of responsibility.

444. The working organisation was known as RAPWI (Release Repatriation of Allied Prisoners-of-war and Internees), which had a Central Control for aid by air at Kandy, with Army and Air Force Officers, and Sub-Controls at Calcutta, Rangoon, Colombo and Cocos. As the necessity for air dropping decreased, these Controls were incorporated in the RAPWI Control Organisations with Naval, Army, Air and Allied representation. Subsequently a Control was opened at Singapore.

445. The RAPWI Controls were responsible for co-ordination of executive action in all matters of supplies for RAPWI, and the evacuation of personnel by aircraft and white and red ensign ships.

446. For the prodigious effort put up by the Cocos based squadrons engaged on operation "Mastiff", Red Cross and other stores for RAPWI were packed at Sigiriya, Ceylon, and handed over to the R.A.F. for delivery to the Cocos Islands. This demanded a very heavy ferrying commitment to the Cocos as two-thirds of the prison camps were supplied by the Cocos based squadrons. Every available Liberator and Sunderland aircraft was used during the inauguration of "Mastiff".

447. This extra effort by the S.D. Liberators based on the Cocos was due to the large loads which had to be carried to the prison camps at Singapore and Southern Sumatra—loads which averaged from 3,500 to 4,000 lbs.

448. No praise could be too high for the air and ground crew personnel of these Cocos based squadrons. Despite the severe shortage of experienced crews and, indeed, aircraft, a daily average of seven sorties, and sometimes nine, was maintained. One squadron flew to widely differing dropping zones throughout Malaya, Sumatra and Java. Ninety-five personnel were dropped on these sorties, of which 65 were doctors or medical orderlies, and all arrived safely despite the short notice at which most of the sorties were laid on. On the first day of the "Mastiff" operations, indeed, one of the aircraft dropped a medical team on Changi Airfield at dawn on August 29th, making a round trip of 3,400 miles.

449. The great distances covered and the adverse weather conditions encountered were difficulties which were not overcome lightly and without danger. A Liberator on a supply dropping mission to the prison camps at Palembang was seen to spin whilst executing a steep turn and all nine crew members were killed.

450. It became obvious that Operation "Mastiff" would continue for some considerable time until the last prisoner of war and internee had been evacuated from all areas by air and sea. As September advanced the numbers brought out mounted steadily. There has been praise on all sides for our squadrons co-operating with the other Services in this rescue of men and women who have endured untold hardships, indignities and, in some cases barbarous cruelties—comments of praise which I have confirmed myself during talks with repatriated prisoners of war flown out of the prison camp areas.

THE JAPANESE PLANNED COUNTER MEASURES TO INVASION OF MALAYA.

451. The the Allies' powerful "Zipper" operation for the landing in Malaya would have succeeded, and that mastery of the air covering the landing would have been secured almost from the start, seems a justifiable claim after careful examination of evidence made available through interrogation of Japanese officers following the surrender in South East Asia

452. It was evident that the Japanese, in their defence of Malaya, were unable to conform to one of the first principles of modern warfare—that air superiority must be gained, and that the battle in the air must first be won, before ground forces can wage their operations with any likelihood of success.

453. The Japanese counter invasion plan was based on the fact that very few operational aircraft were available since it had been

decided to concentrate all forces for the defence of the homeland. The aircraft available, therefore, were mainly trainers which were not easy to send back to Japan. In all, the enemy had, for the defence of Malaya, Sumatra and Java, approximately 800 serviceable aircraft all of which, in the last resort, were to be used as Tokkoki (special attacker suicide aircraft).

454. On D-Day, the enemy planned that there should be no daylight sorties whatever owing to the difficulty in providing sufficient fighter cover to break through the British fighter defences. About 50 to 60 suicide sorties were to be made at twilight with a fighter escort of 30 to 40 aircraft. The suicides were to fly in flights of about 5 aircraft and all attacks were to be concentrated on shipping. Even if balloons were used by the Allied convoys no other method of attack than that of suicide attack was considered feasible. Ground targets were also to be ignored and no fighter defence put up against R.A.F. bomber attacks. Once the Japanese fighters had fulfilled their escort tasks to the suicide aircraft they, in turn, were to be used as suicide aircraft themselves since there were not enough aircraft to use for both purposes.

455. One Japanese source of information, as the result of interrogation, was extremely revealing. This source declared that the whole of the aircraft available to the Japanese for the defence of Malaya against the Allied invasion would, as the result of the mass suicide attack policy, "have been knocked out in about a week".

Direct attack on Mainland not Expected.

456. Following upon the Allied victory in Burma, and the capture of Rangoon in May, the Japanese expected attacks by the Allies on the Andamans, Nicobars, Mergui and Puket in August or September, with the main attack on Malaya coming at the end of October or nearly in November.

457. As soon as the airfields around Rangoon had been made serviceable by the Allies, the Japanese expected there would be a programme of softening-up attacks on Japanese bases by R.A.F. aircraft, with some 200 bomber sorties and 200 escorting fighter sorties daily. The enemy intended to put up little opposition on air attacks against Mergui, the Nicobars or Andamans, while no defensive fighter sorties were to be flown against the R.A.F. softening-up attacks unless Singapore itself were attacked.

458. A direct landing on the mainland of Malaya was not anticipated at the outset. Instead it was expected that the Allies would work gradually south, during which time there would be consolidation and the systematic building up of bases. In this connection, it is interesting to note that the Japanese considered any landing in the Puket area (an operation which we had earlier planned and then abandoned after the fall of Rangoon) would have proved exceedingly dangerous for them, as the short range of the available Japanese fighter aircraft would have made it most difficult to oppose a landing there. The area of Port Swettenham on the Peninsula, it was believed, would not be reached until the end of 1945.

459. As "Zipper" was planned for September, and would undoubtedly have taken place on that date but for the cessation of hostilities, it is evident that the dispositions by the Japanese for counteracting the Allied invasion would have been lamentably behind schedule.

Japanese Build up of Suicide Aircraft.

460. Taking into account the enemy's limited aircraft resources, the Japanese air strategy, on paper, was quite logically prepared.

461. In February, a little more than six months before surrender came, the Japanese Southern Area Army in South East Asia was informed by Tokio that there must be a change in air strategy in the Southern Area. The High Command had visualised that, before long, the Southern Area (French Indo-China, Siam, Malaya, Burma and Netherland East Indies) would be almost entirely cut off from the Empire and would have to develop their own air defence from an already diminishing air force in that area.

462. Training was accordingly speeded up, and all training aircraft and some operational and second line aircraft were ultimately modified to carry bombs.

463. As far back as February, 1945, the Japanese had already had some experience in the use of suicide attacks in the Philippines campaign and had seen how effective these suicide attacks could be against concentrations of shipping and, in particular, against large battleships and carriers.

464. It was the eventual plan of the Japanese, once the Allied invasion of Malaya had started, to use all their aircraft (first line, training and transport) as suicide aircraft against Allied shipping and then continue to fight on the land without an air force.

465. In the Southern Area, all Japanese aircraft were widely dispersed over the vast areas of Malaya, Sumatra and Java, while airfields were, in many instances, poor in condition. To effect this concentration of aircraft in Malaya, Sumatra and Java in preparation for the Allied invasion of Malaya, the Japanese had left Siam and French Indo-China almost bare of aircraft, except for some trainers, and it had not been thought possible to transfer to Malaya.

No Shortage of Suicide Pilots.

466. It seemed that there was no shortage of pilots in the Southern Area to man Japanese suicide aircraft, and that Major-General Kitagawa, G.O.C., 55th Air Training Division could, on his own admission, have called on 2,000 pilots for the 8/900 suicide aircraft at his disposal. On the other hand, few had any operational experience and consisted of training instructors and student pilots with little more than 100 hours flying. It was from these that only the best were selected as suicide pilots. Here, however, an exceedingly interesting and important factor must be noted. This special attack corps of suicide pilots was made up of ardent volunteers. They had determination to proceed to their doom elated in the thought that they were dying for their Emperor.

Major Factors Overlooked by Japanese.

467. The Japanese considered that they would have been able to defeat the Allies' first attempt at landing in Malaya by the use of their suicide aircraft, but considered that when the second attempt at landing was made by the

Allies, they would have no more aircraft left and the second landing would therefore have been easy.

468. I refute the Japanese contention that the first attempt at landing by the Allies would have met with reverse. On impartial examination of the facts made available by the Japanese after surrender, there were several major factors which the Japanese most decidedly overlooked. Briefly these factors were:—

(i) No attacks were to have been made by Japanese suicide aicraft until dusk on D-Day, thus giving our air forces taking part in the large scale invasion of Malaya at least twelve hours to neutralise, as they would have done, Japanese aircraft in the Penang/North Sumatra area.

(ii) R.A.F. Intelligence had estimated that 175 Japanese first line aircraft would be immediately available in Malaya and Sumatra. Of this number, only 20 were thought to be bombers, and 120 fighters—the remainder being reconnaissance and floatplanes.

The general preparation of all the trainer units in these areas for suicide attacks was well known to the R.A.F., and the estimated number available in Malaya and Sumatra was 245 in Malaya and 20 in Sumatra. The estimated number of trainer aircraft in Java was 346.

By early September, the intended move of the Japanese trainer aircraft in Java to airfields in North Sumatra and Central Malaya had only just got under way, so that it seems fairly certain that many of these trainer aircraft would never have been able to leave Java, as the Japanese had quite overlooked the Allied threat by our air forces established in the Cocos Islands which had started operations in August.

(iii) It was unlikely that any reinforcements of aircraft could have been withdrawn from French Indo-China and Siam. In any event, the numbers and types of aircraft available from that source were negligible—a fact borne out on the entry of the R.A.F. into French Indo-China during the course of occupation after the surrender.

(iv) Without exception the Japanese officers interrogated after surrender were well aware of the fact that their communications were so unreliable that no High Command such as 3rd Air Army could have hoped to control operations once "Zipper" had started. Decisions, it should be noted, were to have been left to subordinate commanders and even to unit commanding officers. This undoubtedly would have meant a great deal of wasted effort.

(v) The Japanese had planned to rely on air reconnaissance for advance information on "Zipper" and the location of targets for suicide attacks in the preliminary stages of the invasion. They were so short of aircraft for this essential commitment, however, that it would have been exceedingly difficult for them to spot and hold any of the Allied Forces. Indeed, it is more likely that complete surprise would have been achieved on D-Day by the R.A.F. units taking part in "Zipper" and that large numbers of Japanese aircraft would most certainly have been destroyed on the ground.

(vi) Lastly, the Japanese Air Force had anticipated a breathing space between the air attacks on the Penang area and the attacks on Singapore. It is doubtful, however, if they could have withdrawn and re-deployed many of their aircraft from that area as well as from Sumatra without our knowledge through superior photographic reconnaissance.

MAINTENANCE.

Meeting the needs of overhaul in face of advancing front

469. The Maintenance Organisation in South East Asia was faced with two major issues during the period May to September, 1945, following upon the re-occupation of Rangoon and, later, the sudden termination of hostilities in August.

470. The influencing factors were:—

(a) The need for a re-orientation of the Maintenance Organisation as the result of the battle front having moved further away from the static repair and overhaul bases which had been built up in India.

(b) The termination of Lend/Lease by America to the United Nations following upon the surrender of Japan, this causing acute difficulties in providing replacements and spares for American types of aircraft in operational use within the Command.

471. On the one hand, the re-organisation of maintenance to meet the needs of the advancing front was not an insuperable task and soon righted itself once necessary changes had been effected, but the denial of spares, on the cessation of Lend/Lease, was distinctly serious as there were some 1,600 American aircraft and gliders in India and South East Asia for which spares were absolutely essential.

472. With the arrival in Southern Burma of the victorious Air Forces in May, it was considered that a reversion from the existing centralised system of maintenance in the Theatre should be initiated. The six months rapid advance down through Burma had been a testing time for every branch of maintenance. Burma could not be compared to the great flat desert stretches of the Middle East. Transport of the mobile units negotiated appalling roads after an equally difficult journey from India. At one time, indeed, it was doubtful if transport would last until Rangoon was reached.

473. These difficulties must be emphasised because it was to this mobile ground organisation, embracing Repair and Salvage Units, Air Stores Parks, Motor Transport, Maintenance Units and Motor Transport Light Repair Units, that the Air Forces in Burma were tied and were fully depndent upon for their servicing if not their very existence during operations.

474. The re-organisation of Maintenance which took place after our arrival in Southern Burma can be summarised as follows:—

(a) The Forward Repair Depots in the operational areas were abolished and Salvage units built up.

(b) Group Commanders were invested with the responsibility of repair and overhaul of their squadron's aircraft.

(c) Squadrons were given their full U.E. of aircraft instead of retaining a proportion of them in the Maintenance organisation as hitherto.

(d) Each Repair and Salvage Unit and Air Stores Park worked for a wing and specialised in the types of aircraft operated by the wing.

475. Re-organisation was necessary for yet another important reason. The great distance which, at that time, obtained between operational areas in Burma and bases in India, precluded the return of short range aircraft to Maintenance Units for major inspections and engine changes. Thus, it became necessary to transfer the responsibility for this maintenance work to the squadrons and other flying units. Owing to the different problems, including beaching facilities, involved in carrying out major inspections on flying boats, this maintenance continued to be centralised at Koggala in Ceylon.

476. Hitherto, all repair and salvage units in the Command were controlled by Headquarters, Base Air Forces through Nos. 222, 226 and 230 Groups on a regional basis. In the re-organisation no change in policy, however, was effected in the case of units under 222 Group, Ceylon, and 226 Group, whose area extended throughout India, but excluded Bengal and Assam. The R. & S.U.s. on the other hand, had, of necessity, to be fully mobile and to move with the units they supported.

477. When the re-organisation was put into effect the establishments of flying units were increased by 25 per cent. in order to cover aircraft undergoing major inspections at units. This increase was effected by feeding in additional aircraft from the R. & S.U.s. as and when the squadron or unit became due for a major inspection.

478. The base at Rangoon carried heavy responsibilities—not only for the continuance of operations during the mopping up period in Burma, but in preparing its organisation to meet the coming operations against Malaya.

479. A Forward Equipment Unit and a Forward Repair Unit were maintained in Rangoon to support the Air Forces in Southern Burma and to act as backing, if necessary, for the "Zipper" forces which would deploy through Southern Burma bases. The pressure on maintenance at this crucial period is illustrated by the amount of work tackled. During the months from May to August, the Repair and Salvage Units returned to service 830 aircraft and dismantled a further 420 which had been written off. The heaviest month was May, after the entry into Rangoon, when 300 aircraft were repaired—an indication of the strenuous use to which they had been subjected during the last stage of the lightning advance to Rangoon.

480. It was thought that the Repair and Salvage Unit in Rangoon would build up a fairly extensive repair depot, but with the capitulation of the Japanese in August this was no longer necessary, and personnel were switched to Singapore to re-occupy and build up the original Repair Depot at Seletar on Singapore Island.

Difficulties arising from Lend/Lease termination.

481. President Truman's announcement of the Surrender of Japan brought with it the declaration that Lend/Lease to Allied Governments was at an end except for assistance to forces engaged against Japanese who had not surrendered.

482. The repercussions in Air Command, South East Asia were serious. There was a world-wide shortage of Dakota spares. The U.S.A.A.F., however, as a result of the termination of Lend/Lease had cancelled the production of spares for their earlier Marks I, II and III and there were 200 Dakotas included in this range within South East Asia Command.

483. To ascertain the position as it affected Air Command, investigation revealed that, excluding Dakotas, Expeditors, Thunderbolts and Cornells, there were some 1,600 American aircraft and gliders in India and South East Asia which would gradually become unserviceable through lack of spares.

484. The Command's most urgent attention at the beginning of September, therefore, was directed with the utmost speed to securing alternative arrangements for supply of necessary spares. In some respects, but by no means all, the situation was partially alleviated by the arrangement reached at Washington that the U.S.A.A.F. would meet, on a cash basis, limited demands in respect of Liberator, Dakota and Skymaster aircraft only. No stock demands, however, were permitted. The literal interpretation of this ruling was that a demand could not be raised until an aircraft was actually grounded or until repair was held up. A period of from eight to ten weeks also must elapse before the necessary parts could be obtained from America.

485. What became quite certain was that no demand whatsoever would be met in other types of aircraft, which included the following:—

Thunderbolt.	Cornell.
Sentinel.	Vengeance.
Argus.	Catalina.
Expeditor.	Harvard.

486. It was clear, therefore, that as stocks for any particular item became exhausted, so also would the repair of aircraft, their engines, and associated equipment automatically cease. Cannibalisation, or robbing another aircraft, was of very limited value as the bulk of the spares required were rendered necessary by wear and tear or by climatic deterioration.

487. In a signal to the Air Member for Supply and Organisation, I stated that if we did not get the essential parts, I could foresee us falling down badly on our agreed commitments, and urged that dollars should be made available for purchase of our essential requirements for replacement arising from wear and tear.

488. But the difficulties in England over the termination of Lend/Lease were greater than it was at first realised. There were dollar quotas to be considered, and in this connection it was learned that demands on available dollars were extremely heavy, especially for foodstuffs. The situation in respect of aircraft spares and replacements, therefore, was

not cheerful. As regards a British replacement for the Dakotas, we could no longer demand the highest priority for labour in Britain, now that the war had ended, thus making progress automatically slow in production.

R.A.F. REGIMENT OPERATIONS.
A record of achievements in the South East Asia Command.

489. In the various campaign stages of the war in South East Asia I have been left in no doubt whatsoever about the usefulness, efficiency and fine example of that most junior of all our forces—the R.A.F. Regiment.

490. The R.A.F. Regiment adequately carried out the task of close defence of airfields in Burma and in other operational areas in South-East Asia.

491. I have it on record from one of my Group Commanders who moved with Fourteenth Army all the way through Burma, that he considered it probable that the Group could not have occupied air strips as far forward as they did—with consequently better air support for the Army—had he not been confident that the R.A.F. Regiment could have maintained the necessary security.

492. In South East Asia the R.A.F. Regiment proved itself a force capable of carrying out more than the tasks which its originators claimed the Regiment could accomplish. It was not a force of men dressed up as guards and picqueted around some airfield or supply dump with guns propped in their hands. These men were so trained in the art and strategy of ground defence and of jungle warfare, that they were able to undertake with success counter measures against Japanese infiltration parties who might set themselves up near the perimeter of some airfield and constitute a menace until hunted down and destroyed.

493. When the advance through Burma began in January, 1945, there were ten Field Squadrons, seven A.A. Squadrons and seven Regiment Wing Headquarters working with the Tactical Air Forces. On the capture of Rangoon in May, 1945, these had been increased to fourteen Field Squadrons, nine A.A. Squadrons and eight Wing Headquarters.

494. For the D-Day operations planned for the assault on Malaya, the Regiment was also scheduled to play a prominent part. Five Regimental Wings of nearly 2,500 officers and men, made up of nine Field Squadrons and five A.A. Squadrons were available. One A.A. Squadron had been brought out of the Cocos Islands, where its twenty millimetre Hispano cannons had given protection to the heavy bomber and transport airfield there.

Defence of Airfields and Mopping Up.

495. When it is considered that few Japanese were ever taken prisoner in Burma, electing to face death rather than capture, and that the principal task of the R.A.F. Regiment was to protect our air strips rather than to make enemy captives, the effort of the Regiment between January and May, 1945, in all forms of service was exceedingly high. While operating at seven strips during that period, the A.A. Squadrons succeeded in destroying one enemy aircraft and registering hits on three others out of a total of nine enemy aircraft attacking these particular strips.

496. The most outstanding episode of the R.A.F. Regiment's service in this theatre was the assistance they gave in the defence of Meiktila airfield. It was essential to comb the airfield and its environs each morning for snipers before permitting aircraft to land. Every gully, fox-hole or other feasible hiding place of a sniper had to be examined. The patrols started just after daybreak and took almost two hours to complete. It was thorough and effective, but the only sure method of clearing the area of the enemy, to ensure the safety of our aircraft.

497. In mopping up isolated parties of Japanese in Burmese villages at the time of the advance on Rangoon, certain units of the R.A.F. Regiment gave considerable assistance to Civil Affairs Officers and also helped in the clearing and disposal of mortar bombs, booby-traps, mines and anti-tank traps. Extensive searches, including patrols up rivers, were also carried out by the Regiment in their efforts to arrest wanted and known collaborators and to enforce the surrendering of illegally held arms and ammunition. The river patrols on these occasions were necessary owing to the difficulties of communication and the nature of the country. During March and April, for example, one Field Squadron covered an area of 2,600 square miles, visited or "raided" 250 villages, arrested 100 Japanese collaborators and recovered 26 rifles. Large quantities of ammunition of British and Japanese make were also recovered, together with clothing, equipment, parachutes and rations.

The Occupation of Singapore.

498. In the protection of newly captured airfields and the guarding of vital radar sites once the assault on Malaya had begun, the R.A.F. Regiment would have been indispensable to the Air Force and could have been relied upon to fulfil its task thoroughly and well. Even in the peaceful occupation of Singapore, units of the Regiment, within 24 hours, were maintaining the security of Kallang, Changi, Seletar and Tengah airfields— one of which had three hundred police in peacetime.

499. Up country in Malaya, during the early days of occupation by our forces, a squadron of the R.A.F. Regiment sent out a patrol into one of the thickly wooded areas and succeeded in recovering 600 gallons of petrol from a party of Malays and Chinese.

500. On September 10th, two days before the official surrender ceremony at Singapore, No. 1329 Wing R.A.F. Regiment, with four Field Squadrons, arrived at Penang and took over the entire garrison duties from the Royal Marines. On the day following it was decided that the Regiment should also occupy Port Butterworth and Prai area, Province Wellesley, as part of the Penang commitment.

501. If the R.A.F. Regiment in South East Asia had done nothing more than provide vital protection for our airfields, the record of its achievements would still read with commendable credit. That it was able to perform further additional services and maintain a smartness and discipline which called forth praise from Army and Navy alike, demonstrates the value of the Regiment as an adjunct to the Royal Air Force. In my many

tours and inspections throughout this Theatre I have noted the almost "jealous-like" pride which the Regiment Squadrons have in their own service.

PART V.
ADMINISTRATIVE AND OTHER ASPECTS.

THE REPERCUSSIONS FELT BY AIR COMMAND AFTER DEFEAT OF GERMANY AND JAPAN.

502. The period May to September, 1945, witnessed a series of important changes associated with the administrative development of Air Command, South East Asia, and the recasting of plans already made to meet the changed conditions after the defeat of Germany and, later still, defeat of Japan.

503. The Command felt the full effects of the global shipping and manpower shortages; of pre-election uncertainties in England; of the change in emphasis of attacks on Japan's outlying conquests to the Japanese homeland; of the vastness of the task involved in building up the Southern Burma net of all-weather airfields in preparation for coming operations; of the monsoon; the sharp contraction in air supply resources consequent upon the withdrawal of the American squadrons, and finally, the task of re-occupying liberated territories.

504. Following the reconquest of Burma in May, the future trend of the Command's administrative development was largely influenced by the following factors:—

(i) Disbandment of the integrated Eastern Air Command Headquarters on 1st June, 1945 and the withdrawal of the United States Army Air Forces from the Command.

(ii) Reorganisation of Headquarters, R.A.F., Burma, on the assumption of full operational and administrative control of the Air Forces in Burma.

(iii) Administrative planning in anticipation of the forthcoming operations in South East Asia associated principally with the re-conquest of Malaya and the build-up of the strategic base of Singapore.

(iv) Planning for the reorganisation of the Command, subsequent to the re-occupation of Singapore.

505. It was not unnatural, on the defeat of Germany, that attention should be focussed suddenly upon the impressive array of air power promised for South East Asia in Phase II of the war. Not only was the number of squadrons expected to be increased, but more modern and more powerfully armed aircraft were envisaged. There were expectations too, of plentiful supplies of spares and ancillary equipment calculated to abrogate, for the duration of the Far Eastern war, the parsimony of indigenous industrial resources. South East Asia, it was confidently hoped, would achieve a higher place in the list of priorities as from VE-Day. But this illusion was soon shattered. At the beginning of June it was officially revealed that the Pacific Tiger Force and post-war events in Europe would take priority over South East Asia's demands. The decision was occasioned not so much by the shortage of equipment as by the global deficiencies in shipping and manpower which implied that drastic cuts in the Phase II Target of 116 squadrons would have to be accepted. It became evident, therefore, that the basis for planning was not what the Command was entitled to expect, but what was actually available.

506. In spite of these difficulties—and they had been many in South East Asia—it was necessary to cut the administrative cloth to suit the operational coat. A target of 87 squadrons which, it was reckoned, would have to meet the air effort, both for "Zipper" and "Mailfist" and other commitments, was therefore accepted.

507. Although these factors did not seriously affect Operation "Zipper", the enforced economy would have had some bearing upon the final assault on Singapore itself and upon operations contemplated early in 1946 into Siam, had the war with Japan continued. Other tasks too, included action on the development of the air base in Southern Burma and the Cocos Islands, both closely associated with "Zipper" and the redeployment of the strategic forces, once heavy bomber bases further east and south east became available.

Important Changes After Fall of Rangoon.

508. The ease with which Rangoon fell caused future administrative planning to proceed along more ambitious lines. Before further operations could be undertaken, however, it was necessary to have a reshuffle of offensive and defensive units; introduce a revised maintenance policy and new equipment to meet conditions of the Malay Peninsula; to withdraw many air forces from Burma for rest, refit and concentration for "Zipper".

509. The most important change in Command organisation at this time was the departure of the American Air Forces which were withdrawn from the Theatre as from 1st June, 1945. The disintegration of the British and American Air Forces in Burma involved the disbandment of Headquarters, Eastern Air Command, and the transfer of the Air Staff from that Headquarters to H.Q. R.A.F., Burma, which then became an independent R.A.F. Command under H.Q. Air Command, South East Asia.

510. A series of other changes was brought about as a result of the revised responsibilities of Headquarters, R.A.F. Burma, upon disbandment of Eastern Air Command. Operational control of all R.A.F. formations and units, formerly under Eastern Air Command, was taken over by H.Q. R.A.F., Burma.

511. The title of "Strategic Air Force", which had included British and American squadrons, ceased to be used with effect from 1st June, 1945, and No. 231 Group, R.A.F., continued strategic operations alone. In the same way the disintegration of Combat Cargo Task Force was carried out and, on the departure of the American squadrons, No. 232 Group took over the full operational control of all R.A.F. transport units in the A.L.F.S.E.A. area.

512. Yet another important change at this time was the reorganisation of the R.A.F. Element of H.Q. Photographic Reconnaissance Force as a Wing (No. 347 Wing), after the withdrawal of the American Forces. Included in the wing's establishment was No. 1 Photographic Interpretation Detachment. The object

of the change was to give the former R.A.F. Element of Photographic Reconnaissance Force more mobility as a wing which could be moved forward as required for operational purposes.

513. Throughout the campaign in Burma, Headquarters 230 Group had been charged with the control of all maintenance and storage units in the area of Headquarters, R.A.F., Burma, but the Group itself was under the direct control of the C.M.O., Headquarters, Base Air Forces. This arrangement was unsatisfactory because it meant that the R.A.F. operational commander in Burma did not have complete control of his maintenance organisation. It was therefore decided to disband No. 230 Group and to absorb the Maintenance Staff of the Group into Headquarters, R.A.F., Burma, with effect from 15th May, 1945. The units under No. 230 Group were, at the same time, placed directly under the operational groups they served, and the staffs of these groups were increased to cope with this commitment by the addition of some of the posts thrown up from the disbandment of No. 230 Group.

Withdrawal of 224 Group in Preparation for "Zipper".

514. The main assault on Malaya, scheduled for early September, made necessary the withdrawal of No. 224 Group and units from the Arakan and Burma.

515. This was started early in May. The withdrawal was handled directly between Headquarters, R.A.F., Burma, and Headquarters, Base Air Forces. As from 1st June, 1945, H.Q. 224 Group was placed directly under the control of H.Q. Base Air Forces for the purpose of mounting operation "Zipper", but the A.O.C. 224 Group and his staff retained the right to visit all units during mounting and to advise on all matters concerning the training of units for their various tasks. Headquarters 224 Group undertook the responsibility for force planning.

516. It was decidedly unfortunate, if not serious, that owing to the acute shortage of shipping, the withdrawal of units from Burma did not go off as smoothly as might have been expected. Many of the units, indeed, came out of the Arakan with no equipment or M.T., while the equipment and M.T. of other units which arrived in India lay on the docks awaiting the arrival of the units for many weeks. When units ultimately reached India they were deployed on airfields which had been prepared for them, but owing to the non-arrival of equipment or personnel, the commencement of training was badly delayed.

Re-organisation of Air Command in 1945-46.

517. In view of the extension of the responsibilities of Air Command, South East Asia, towards Singapore and beyond, the future organisation of formations in the Command required consideration.

518. The principal factors which necessitated reorganisation were as follows:—

(a) Mopping up operations of the enemy in Burma would continue for some time, but, so far as the Air Forces were concerned, these could be undertaken by one composite group (No. 221).

(b) Since No. 224 Group had been withdrawn from Burma for participation in Operation "Zipper", the Group would come directly under the operational control of Headquarters, Air Command, during the next stage of the Campaign.

(c) The Heavy Bomber Group (No. 231) was no longer suitably located in Burma. It would be based at the Cocos Islands for "Zipper" support.

(d) Photographic Reconnaissance, Special Duties and Air Supply Operations would no longer be concentrated on Burma, but would be required in widely separated areas. This called for direct control from the Headquarters of the Air Command of the groups engaged in these duties.

(e) The above factors reduced the responsibilities of H.Q. R.A.F. Burma, which had hitherto controlled several functional groups.

(f) The altered military situation had also called for the move of Headquarters, Allied Land Forces to Kandy, while Headquarters, Supreme Allied Command, together with the Headquarters of the three Commanders-in-Chief, would move to Singapore at the earliest practicable date.

(g) The 10th U.S.A.A.F. had been moved to China and Eastern Air Command dissolved. At the same time the R.A.F. Target Force for South East Asia in Phase II was not to be as large as originally planned.

519. These factors, it was considered, required revision of previous operational plans, and would enable a considerable reduction of planned overheads to be effected in Headquarters and Administrative Services.

520. On the fall of Singapore the following moves were scheduled to take place:—

(a) Headquarters, Air Command would move there in company with Headquarters, Supreme Allied Commander, H.Q. Allied Land Forces and part of the E.I.F. H.Q.

(b) Headquarters, No. 222 Group would move from Ceylon to Singapore and undertake responsibilities in that area similar to those undertaken by Mediterranean Allied Coastal Forces or Air Defences, Eastern Mediterranean.

(c) Headquarters, No. 231 Group would move to Singapore and be possibly employed either as a heavy Bomber Group Headquarters, the Headquarters of a Task Force, or be disbanded.

(d) Headquarters, No. 224 Group would also move to Singapore area and remain a composite group, being modelled as necessary to undertake further operations for the reconquest of Sumatra, Java and Borneo.

521. A small Headquarters, R.A.F. Ceylon, was also planned to take over area responsibilities for:—

(a) Ceylon.

(b) Island Flying-boat, Emergency Landing Grounds and Met. Stations to the south.

(c) Cocos for administrative services.

522. Although the future strategy for South East Asia Command was not yet determined, making it impossible to forecast reliably for the future deployment of forces, it was considered that the reorganisation as planned would meet all the probable requirements.

THE MANPOWER SITUATION IN SOUTH EAST ASIA

523. The energetic stepping up of operations in the Pacific directly against Japan, brought about a wide variety of circumstances which combined to deny Air Command, South East Asia that priority in personnel which the Command had expected would be forthcoming.

524. Demands in Europe and the Pacific for shipping; the sudden announcement, preceding the General Election, to reduce the Overseas Tour for Army personnel by approximately 10 per cent; the operation of the Release Scheme, and the priority accorded to the Pacific "Tiger Force", all adversely reacted upon Air Command, South East Asia.

525. In May, 1945, the establishment and strength of the Command for British personnel were as follows:—

	Estab.	Strength	Surplus/Deficiencies	
Ground Officers	8,103	7,573	—	530
Other Ranks ...	105,470	110,459	4,989	—

526. The 6½ per cent. deficiency in ground officers affected principally the branches in Administration, Code and Cypher, Tech. (E) and Catering. On the other hand, the position as regards airmen was that the technical trades carried a surplus of 7,100, whilst the trade of Clerk G.D. was deficient by not less than 36 per cent., equipment assistants by 20 per cent. and cooks by 28 per cent.

527. By September, 1945, the position had so deteriorated that an overall deficiency was shown, although certain trades continued to carry a surplus. The strength of personnel was as follows:—

	Estab.	Strength	Surplus/Deficiencies	
Ground Officers	8,116	7,525	—	591
Other Ranks ...	123,466	114,419	—	9,047

528. The 7 per cent. deficiency in ground officers was spread over a great many branches. Physical Fitness carried a deficiency of 36 per cent. and Code and Cypher a deficiency of 22 per cent.

529. The overall 8 per cent. deficiency in other ranks, however, clouded the very large deficiencies carried in the following trades:—

	Per cent. deficiency.
Clerks G.D.	43
Clerks Acctg.	36
Cooks	32
Driver M.T.	18
Equip. Asst.	36

530. The Command had clearly to take measures to rectify this weakness if it was to function administratively, and compulsory misemployment of surplus tradesmen and aircrew was therefore introduced. It was fortunate that, on the defeat of Japan, an opportunity was offered for a large scale reduction of establishments and disbandments to begin.

531. The Release Scheme, coming so soon after the cessation of the European War, reacted very materially against the Command. It brought further grave losses in the difficult trades at a time when the efficient administration of the Command was essential for the prosecution of the war against Japan.

532. An even greater disadvantage was the fact that it withdrew from the Command the more senior and experienced personnel. Consequently, while the position in a branch or trade as far as actual personnel were concerned, may have appeared satisfactory on paper, it was not always so in actual performance of work, and efficiency thereby suffered.

Reduction in overseas tour for personnel.

533. On 6th June, 1945, the War Office suddenly announced a reduction in the overseas tour of Army personnel. This factor had every promise of producing serious repercussions in South East Asia, in which either coming operations, or morale, or both, might well have been affected. The fulfilment of the War Office announcement was rendered virtually impossible by the lack of homeward personnel shipping and the congestion in transit camps in India.

534. To avoid a parallel situation with regard to the Air Force in this Command, I signalled the Chief of Staff emphasising that any announcement of a reduction in overseas tour for the Air Force would be premature and impracticable at this juncture.

535. At the same time, I strongly recommended that shipping and air transport should be found in order to bring into effect, by 1st December, 1945, a reduction of tour from four to three and a half years, for all single officers and airmen. This reduction was agreed upon in August in principle, but was not fully implemented until December.

536. Between May and September, 1945, some 559 officers and 2,263 airmen left the Command under the Release Scheme. During the same period 2,201 officers and 12,932 airmen were repatriated in addition to those despatched on release.

537. The celebration of V.E.-Day in the Command was a sincere enough occasion for everyone, though it was only natural that it did not hold the same high spirit of enthusiasm for those in the East still fighting the last of the remaining Axis powers. The announcement that the Burma Star had been inaugurated gave general satisfaction to personnel serving in Burma—an award well merited—but personnel in India and Ceylon felt that the burden of their overseas service was not sufficiently recognised by the award of the Defence Medal.

538. The postal voting scheme for the General Election in July, 1945, was put into operation successfully during May and June, and ballot papers for personnel in South East Asia were flown out from England by transport aircraft. The papers were given priority over all other mails handled by R.A.F. Post Staffs. The total number of completed application forms for postal voting received by 25th June at R.A.F. Post Karachi was 33,500. A last minute supply of forms to the Cocos Islands, whose original consignment was mislaid in transit, produced satisfactory results.

539. Altogether, a total of 30,013 ballot papers was finally forwarded by air to the U.K. from the Command.

PART VI.
CONCLUSIONS

Japan's defeat.

540. Japan, in her disastrous war against the Allied Powers, was defeated largely by her own misjudgment—embarking upon a policy of expansion which lengthened too far her lines of communication without providing adequately armed forces for their protection and maintenance.

541. Expansion brought the Japanese, in their initial flush of success, to the very threshold of India at a time when the Allies were least prepared to resist her westward march.

542. Defeat for the Japanese in South East Asia, I consider, had its begnning in the air battles over the Arakan in late 1943 and the opening months of 1944, when Allied air superiority was obtained.

543. It is my opinion that the cardinal weakness in Japan's war of aggression was undoubtedly a badly balanced war machine, which showed too heavy a bias in favour of land forces, and a much too weak air force, also air potential.

544. Without air support, the Japanese Army in South East Asia fought a losing battle after Allied air superiority had been won. The numbers actually killed during their campaign in Burma were enormous, whilst the number that perished in the jungle will never be known. This Japanese Army provided a grim reminder to any Army that embarks upon operations without adequate air support.

Close Support operations.

545. According to the Japanese, it is impossible to state definitely which of our Allied fighters had the greatest effect morally upon their ground forces in South East Asia, as each fighter had its own characteristics. The effect differed according to the nature of the target attacked and the time of the attack, whether by day or by night. On an assessment of the Allied fighter aircraft individually, however, it appears that the enemy considered the Spitfire, the Thunderbolt and the Mustang surpassed all others.

Fighter, and fighter/bomber offensive operations.

546. The effect of the Beaufighter and Mosquito attacks on Japanese shipping in the Gulf of Martaban during the early months of 1945 was such that the enemy stopped movement of shipping by day, and did movements only at night. In this way enemy shipping was conserved.

547. On the other hand, the harassing attacks these aircraft carried out on the enemy's road, rail and river transport areas was exceedingly effective. While it cost them few casualties to men, the air attacks, according to the Japanese, made troop as well as supply movements virtually impossible. Materials and food, they stated, became difficult to move, and this had a bad effect upon the civilian population.

548. Our policy of surprise raids on the enemy's rear airfields was most effective. In this respect the American fighter attacks on these airfields were not only effective, but greatly helped to reduce the operational strength of the Japanese Army Air Force.

Heavy Bomber Operations.

549. The heavy bomber attacks which our aircraft carried out on Rangoon, and on supply dumps in the vicinity, cannot be compared, in effectiveness, to the heavy air attacks made on bridges, railway tracks, marshalling yards and important installations in other enemy occupied areas. The dumps in the Rangoon area which were targets of attack were, according to the enemy, destroyed to some extent, but they did not greatly affect Japanese morale. The bombing of Rangoon itself, however, which was continued for almost a month before the enemy's evacuation, had a marked effect upon their morale. The effect of the bombings on the civilian population appeared to be small because only military targets were bombed.

550. Bombing raids on military installations in the rear areas were admitted by the Japanese to be most effective, and many targets, some highly important to the Japanese war effort, were destroyed. The attacks, it appears, could have been even more effective had our bombers struck at the targets over a wider area, as enemy installations were immediately divided up into sections and scattered once a target area was hit.

Air Mining Operations Affect Supply.

551. I consider it exceedingly gratifying, and indeed, interesting, to have it confirmed by the Japanese themselves that the isolation of large sea transports, as the result of our air mining operations, seriously affected the Japanese supply situation. The mines were laid by our aircraft in the Rangoon River and off the Tenasserim and Malayan coasts. The sowing of these mines, the Japanese stated, was directly responsible for the sinking of important supply ships.

552. Our air mining programme, which began on 21st January, 1945, and was discontinued on 24th May, 1945, since the stage was then being set finally for the assault on Malaya, resulted in a total of 925 mines being dropped in the specified areas. The minelaying operations were 86.9 successful—only 29 mines being dropped foul, and 80 being brought back by aircraft to base.

553. From a tactical point of view, I was interested to learn that. of all the weapons which we used against the Japanese in Burma—rockets, machine-guns, cannon, bombs and Napalm—the machine-guns had the most effect, both morally and physically, upon their ground forces.

554. During the advance of our ground troops, the feints and dummy attacks by our supporting aircraft proved very effective in keeping the Japanese under cover—a highly important factor when troops are storming strongly-held positions.

555. Close support by the Japanese Army Air Force was negligible. Its development was dependent upon adequate air strength, and as the Japanese Army Air Force gradually dwindled away to nothing, close support for their ground forces was therefore impracticable.

556. While the Japanese also used Visual Control Posts to indicate targets to their aircraft, shortage of wireless equipment greatly hindered them in putting through demands for air support. This is in striking contrast to our own use of V.C.P.s, which we exploited to the full with excellent results.

Air supply.

557. Burma proved how an Army could march for a thousand miles through some of the worst country in the world so long as air supply was guaranteed by our retaining air superiority and having adequate air transport.

558. There is no doubt that the Japanese fully appreciated how vitally important Allied air supply was to the success of our operations. They confessed that all means possible were used to interfere with Allied air supply, but, due to the small size of their Air Force, they failed in their efforts.

559. Burma, I consider, has given us the classic example of an Army in the field existing on air supply, and the technique evolved from these air supply operations must surely command serious attention.

Lessons which emerged in South East Asia.

560. The war in South East Asia, has immeasurably enriched our experience in air operations in the East; quickened our perception to the dangers of a purely static defence system for these Empire territories, and shown how essential is air power for future defence.

The need for greater squadron mobility.

561. One of the most noticeable features of our operations in South East Asia was the clumsy and inadequate method which we had been forced to employ to maintain the mobility of our squadrons, their personnel and equipment.

562. This implies no reflection on the ground staff and maintenance organisation, who succeeded in achieving good results with the equipment and facilities available when moving the squadrons forward, month after month, through a country devoid of proper communications and faced with flooding during the monsoon, when roads turned into quagmires.

563. But a squadron working in support of front-line troops must have greater mobility to enable its ground organisation to move to its next base, and not find itself on some narrow inadequate road, choked for miles ahead with slow moving army transport.

564. It is on record that during April, 1945, when over 80 R.A.F. units moved forward in Burma to new bases in keeping with the overall plan of advance, one R.A.F. wing, having insufficient road transport, had to use bullock carts. Against this, there is the more logical instance of another R.A.F. wing which moved from Akyab to Rangoon by air, taking with it all its equipment and personnel and leaving behind only M.T., since it was picking up a new allotment of vehicles at its destination.

565. With so many moves by squadrons in the forward areas—many going ahead with the bare minimum of staff to keep aircraft operational pending the arrival of the remainder of their ground personnel bringing up essential equipment—squadrons often found themselves separated from a proportion of their servicing echelons for several days due to lack of transport. Until the full staff of the echelons arrived, an enormous amount of work was thrown upon ground crew, since aircraft at the time were being pressed into service in support of the advance and had to be loaded with bombs and with ammunition. They also needed daily servicing.

566. This, I consider, is one of the most important lessons which emerged from operations in South East Asia. Experience has shown that Air Power, in the movement of its ground organisations, must have infinitely greater mobility in future, and be air-lifted by its own transports.

K. R. PARK,
Air Chief Marshal,
Allied Air Commander in Chief,
South East Asia.

August, 1946.

LONDON
PRINTED AND PUBLISHED BY HIS MAJESTY'S STATIONERY OFFICE
1951
Price 3s. 0d. net

Numb. 39367

SUPPLEMENT TO
The London Gazette
OF TUESDAY, 23rd OCTOBER, 1951

Published by Authority

Registered as a newspaper

MONDAY, 29 OCTOBER, 1951

THE PART PLAYED BY THE ALLIED AIR FORCES IN THE FINAL DEFEAT OF THE ENEMY IN THE MEDITERRANEAN THEATRE, MARCH TO MAY, 1945.

The following despatch was submitted to the Secretary of State for Air in September, 1946, by Air Chief Marshal Sir GUY GARROD, K.C.B., O.B.E., M.C., D.F.C., Commander-in-Chief, Royal Air Force, Mediterranean and Middle East, and Deputy Air Commander-in-Chief, Mediterranean Allied Air Forces.

INTRODUCTION.

1. This despatch bears witness to the part played by the Air Forces in the final stages of the Mediterranean campaign. Their contribution was one of the deciding factors in the final victory in that Theatre. The despatch covers the period of my appointment as Commander-in-Chief, Royal Air Force, Mediterranean and Middle East, and as Deputy Air Commander-in-Chief, Mediterranean Allied Air Forces, from 16th March, 1945, when I assumed command from Air Marshal Sir John Slessor, until hostilities ceased in the Theatre—on 2nd May, 1945, for the Italian Sector, and 8th May, 1945, for the Balkan Sector.

2. The purpose of a despatch is to give a short and lucid account of the main events during the period of a Commander-in-Chief's appointment. This task may not present any major difficulty in the case of a Command such as Bomber Command, which is purely functional, with singleness of aim and resources. But in the case of a geographical Command such as MEDME, the task is more complicated. Not only did my Command contain within it the three main types of functional command— Strategic, Tactical and Coastal—so that I was responsible for a complete range of operational air activity, but it also presented a large number of problems not directly operational in character, some of them purely air matters, such as questions of Transport Command bases, some of them of a political nature, such as my dealings with the Greek and Jugoslav governments.

3. Then again, MEDME command had an unusual structure, arising out of the development of the war in the Mediterranean, in that it contained as a sub-command the R.A.F. Middle East, whose chief problems in 1945 concerned internal security and training matters. It was desirable therefore that the A.O.C.-in-C. R.A.F. Middle East, though under my command, should exercise a large measure of autonomy.

4. Finally, the operations of the Royal Air Force in MEDME were inextricably bound up with those of the United States Army Air Force. An integration of Command had been achieved which was more complete than that to be found in any other Theatre. So it would be quite impossible to write a despatch dealing only with R.A.F. activities—it would be like trying to build a house with only two walls..

5. Under these circumstances, I have not attempted to deal with every subject which arose during my period of command, but only with outstanding events. I have given only as much detail as was necessary to present a balanced picture of these events. In particular, I have not attempted to cover the problems which arose in the Middle East, nor have I given a complete history of each of the R.A.F. formations under my command—their activities are covered only in so far as they participated in the main events described.

6. The period falls into two main parts. The first is from 16th March to 8th April, the time from my assumption of command to the beginning of the final ground offensive in Italy, and the second is from 9th April to 2nd May, in which the final Italian offensive took place.

7. There was one event, however, which was taking place during the whole of the period, and therefore cannot conveniently be dealt with in the arrangement of parts I have described; I refer to the offensive by Marshal Tito's Fourth Army in Jugoslavia. It began before the Allied offensive in Italy and continued a few days after the German surrender in Italy. Because of this, I have devoted an early part of the despatch entirely to this subject and this has enabled me also to describe, more fully than would otherwise have been possible, the special organisation of command of the Balkan Air Force, and the special problems with which it had to contend.

PART I.
CONDITIONS IN THE MEDITERRANEAN THEATRE ON MARCH 16TH, 1945.

The Ground Situation.

8. The enemy ground forces in the Italian theatre consisted of the German 10th and 14th Armies comprising some twenty-five divisions, which were stretched along a line reaching roughly from Lake Comacchio on the Adriatic Coast through Vergato, South of Bologna, to Pietrasanta on the west coast. This was the line which had been finally stabilised after the Allied Offensive in the summer of 1944 had battered its way from Cassino up the Italian peninsula, and had only just failed to overflow into the Po Valley. The Fifth Army had been unable to reach Bologna before winter conditions had made operations in the mountains impossible, and the Eighth Army, when it reached the Po Valley on the East coast after long and hard fighting, found itself confronted by a series of formidably defended river lines which it was unable to pierce without sustaining very heavy casualties.

9. It did not prove possible to make any further progress during the winter. Both Allied Armies were very tired after a most exhausting campaign, while the enemy had managed to improve his supply position since he had been falling back on his dumps. Moreover, the Allied ground forces were weakened by the withdrawal of divisions to reinforce other theatres, with the consequence that a large number of anti-aircraft gunners had to be trained as infantry, and this required time.

10. It was decided at the beginning of January 1945 that the 15th Army Group would plan for an all-out offensive in the early Spring. The date of the attack would be at a time when good weather could be expected for air and armoured operations and when both armies could deploy their maximum strength against the enemy, having rested those divisions required for the assault and built up adequate reserves of supplies and a great superiority of tanks and guns.

11. To the Allies it was clear that the enemy would at all costs stand and fight where he stood. He was forced to adopt this attitude by the complete superiority of the Allies in the air*. He dared not retreat since air action had deprived him of practically all means of transporting fuel from Germany into Italy, and any considerable withdrawal would have meant the expenditure of almost all of his slender fuel reserves. In any event he could not afford to abandon without a fight territory whose possession would have enabled us to move our bomber bases so much nearer to Germany itself. Furthermore, any large scale movement would have been extremely hazardous, as he would have laid himself open to intensive and continuous air attack both by day and by night.

12. By the beginning of April the Allied armies were ready once again to resume the offensive, rested and re-equipped. The enemy on the other hand, constantly harassed by air attack throughout the Winter and Spring, had had but little rest, and only a trickle of new equipment had come to him, so that he was forced to rely mainly on such of his old material as the Allied Air Forces had left him intact.

13. It was, of course, obvious to the enemy that the Allies intended to launch a major offensive in the near future. The disposition of his forces suggested that he was awake to the possibility of amphibious operations at the head of the Adriatic, combined with a frontal attack. He had split his mobile reserve of two divisions accordingly to deal with either or both eventualities. He also showed his appreciation of the vulnerability of the Argenta-Ferrara axis, and of the area West of Bologna where the Allies were in a favourable position to carry out an outflanking thrust towards Modena.

14. The following table gives some figures to illustrate the comparative strengths of the Allied and German resources employed in the opening phases of the offensive:—

	Infantry	Artillery			Tanks	
		Hvy.	Med.	Fld.	Med.	Light
15TH ARMY GROUP	82,100	134	492	1,424	2,426	612
10TH AND 14TH GERMAN ARMIES ...	74,500	25	250	771	200	—

NOTE.—The above figures do not show the number of men manning the Artillery and the Tanks. Moreover, they do not include men and equipment not actually employed in a fighting rôle in the opening phases of the battle.

The American Fifth and British Eighth Armies comprised seventeen divisions and ten brigades of many nationalities—British, American, New Zealand, South African, Indian, Palestinian, Polish and Brazilian—while four Italian Gruppi also played an important part.

The Air Situation.

15. On March 16th the enemy in the Italian theatre could put into the air at most 130 aircraft. The Allies could put 4,000. Such figures speak for themselves—the enemy was outnumbered in the air by approximately 30 to 1. Air superiority—which is nowadays the essential pre-requisite to victory on the ground—had been attained in North Africa and never again relinquished, for although enemy air

* See paras. 15-17 below.

resistance flickered up in Sicily, the bid to regain superiority failed. The cumulative effect of our air strategy and fighting had been so to reduce his numerical strength and ability to hit back, that during the final Italian offensive enemy air action could be virtually disregarded as an effective factor.

16. Although the enemy's air force in Italy was a negligible quantity, he had in that country a formidable array of 1,000 heavy and 2,200 light flak guns as well as countless small arms in an anti-aircraft role. He was therefore capable of putting up a very strong defence at important targets, and the Tactical Air Force had been compelled to develop a fairly complicated system of anti-flak tactics in order to avoid undue losses.

17. The freedom of the air enjoyed by the Allies in the Italian theatre allowed the greatest flexibility in the use of air effort, resulting in a high degree of efficiency. Moreover, its effect upon the morale of the German troops was most depressing; it kept them constantly reminded of the great advantage in material and weapons enjoyed by the Allies.

The Naval Situation.

18. The Allied Navies in the Mediterranean were as much masters of the seas as the Allied Air Forces were masters of the air. There were no major enemy surface units left in the theatre, while submarines had been driven from it by the thoroughness and efficiency of our combined naval-air operations, and by the overrunning of their bases. The chief threat which remained was offered by small craft and midget submarines.

19. The major task of the Allied Navies was to maintain the assault on the enemy's few remaining coastal sea routes, whose importance increased as the Air Forces' policy of destroying the enemy's land communications achieved substantial successes. This assault was carried out by British and United States Coastal Forces and destroyers, operating from Naval Advanced Bases at Ancona, Leghorn and in the South of France. In addition a mixed force of French, British and United States cruisers and destroyers, under a French Admiral, was operating continuously in support of the seaward flank of the Allied Forces holding the Franco-Italian frontier, giving gun-support from the sea. This force, which was known as " Flank Force," was under constant threat of attack from the enemy's explosive motor boats and midget submarines.

20. The enemy had carried out a programme of intensive mining, both to protect his coastal convoy routes and to hamper naval operations in support of the coming offensive. As these mines could be easily and quickly laid from small craft of various types, and as he had an adequate stock of mines, the result was to produce a minesweeping problem greater than any which had previously confronted the Navy in the Mediterranean. It was estimated that some 7,000 mines had been laid in the Gulf of Genoa, and 12,000 in the Northern Adriatic, where the whole area was particularly suitable for mine laying. The enemy also prepared detailed plans for the denial of harbours by demolitions, blocking and mining, in all of which work he had by this time had a great deal of experience.

The Maintenance Aspect.

21. By dint of the fine efforts of the R.A.F. Maintenance Organisation the degree of aircraft serviceability was high when the land battle started. The policy during the battle was to use our air forces to the maximum extent of which the aircrews and maintenance personnel were capable. It was confidently believed that the enemy could be defeated within 21 days, and the event proved that this estimate and the policy of an all-out effort was sound.

22. The same policy was followed by the Army, which had sufficient ammunition and supplies and reserves for only about 21 days of intense operations.

23. From the foregoing paragraphs it will be seen that we had all the necessary superiority in equipment—especially aircraft and tanks—to launch a successful offensive. Most important was our predominance in the air, which meant that our own army was safe from air attack and at the same time could be led forward and constantly assisted by the Air Force.

PART II.

THE ORDER OF BATTLE.

ORDER OF BATTLE ON MARCH 16TH, 1945.

24. The Mediterranean Allied Air Force was formed on December 10th, 1943. By March, 1945, it had already built up a fine reputation of accomplishment, and I was privileged to be in command during its highest peak of achievement and ultimate victory. The work of this integrated British-American Command has now finished, but let us hope that the lessons and advantages of co-operation which have been learned will be put to even better use in peace.

25. M.A.A.F. consisted of all operational units in the Mediterranean Theatre (which included Turkey, the Balkans, Central and South Western Europe, but excluded the Middle East); the main components were the Royal Air Force (including units of the Dominion Air Forces under its command) and the United States Army Air Forces. Operational control of all these units was exercised by the Air Commander-in-Chief, who was responsible through the Supreme Allied Commander to the Combined Chiefs of Staff. The Air C.-in-C. also held the appointment of Commanding General United States Air Forces, Mediterranean Theatre of Operations.

26. As Deputy Air Commander-in-Chief, M.A.A.F., I exercised such responsibilities in regard to the Allied Air Forces as might be delegated to me by the Air Commander-in-Chief. As Commander-in-Chief Royal Air Force Mediterranean and Middle East, I was responsible for all R.A.F. operations in the MEDME Theatre; responsible to the Air C.-in-C., M.A.A.F., for those in that part of MEDME falling within his province, and to the Chief of the Air Staff for those in the remainder of the theatre. When I took over from Air Marshal Sir John Slessor, K.C.B., D.S.O., M.C., on March 16th to become Deputy C.-in-C., M.A.A.F., and C.-in-C., R.A.F., MEDME,

A 2

Lieutenant-General Eaker had been in Command of M.A.A.F. since January 15th, 1944. He was succeeded by Major-General J. K. Cannon on March 28th, 1945.

27. By the beginning of April practically all the squadrons were based in Italy. An analysis shows that at this time the Air C.-in-C., M.A.A.F., had under his operational command a total of 258 Squadrons consisting of 155 American, 77 Royal Air Force and Dominion Air Force, 13 co-belligerent Italian, 5 French, 2 Jugoslav, 2 Polish, 3 Greek and 1 Brazilian. To man and maintain these squadrons there were 164,000 American personnel and 79,000 British personnel, besides many of our other Allies. I should like to mention here the fine contribution made to the British effort by the South African Air Force which, at this time, maintained a total of 23½ squadrons in the Mediterranean and Middle East Theatre.

HEADQUARTERS, MEDITERRANEAN ALLIED AIR FORCES.

28. The Air Commander-in-Chief's Allied Headquarters was a comparatively small one, consisting of integrated staff sections for planning, operations, intelligence and signals. The keynote of these sections was the inter-leaving of British and American personnel.

THE CHIEF FIGHTING FORMATIONS.

29. The chief fighting formations under the Command of the Air Commander-in-Chief were the Mediterranean Allied Strategic Air Force, the Mediterranean Allied Tactical Air Force, the Mediterranean Allied Coastal Air Force and the Balkan Air Force.

Mediterranean Allied Strategic Air Force.
(*Major-General N. F. Twining, Commanding General.*)

30. M.A.S.A.F. was predominantly an American organisation, and consisted of the United States 15th Air Force, and 205 Group of the Royal Air Force (Commanded by Brigadier J. T. Durrant, C.B., D.F.C., S.A.A.F.). There were 109 U.S.A.A.F. and 8 R.A.F. and Dominion Squadrons.

31. M.A.S.A.F. formed part of the team of Allied Strategic Air Forces in Europe, the other members being the United States Eighth Air Force and the Royal Air Force Bomber Command. The aim of these forces was the progressive destruction and dislocation of the German military, industrial and economic system, and the direct support of land and naval forces. All M.A.S.A.F. squadrons were based in South-East Italy, chiefly on the Foggia Plain.

Mediterranean Allied Tactical Air Force.
(*Major-General J. K. Cannon, Commanding General.*)*

32. M.A.T.A.F. was composed of the United States 12th Air Force and the Royal Air Force Desert Air Force, which were roughly equal in size. The role of M.A.T.A.F. was to provide the air support required for the operations of Allied land forces in the Italian theatre. To perform this task it had 89 Squadrons, consisting of 42 U.S.A.A.F., 44 R.A.F. and Dominion, 1 Brazilian and 2 Polish.

* Major-General Chidlaw from April 5, 1945.

33. There were four main operational formations within the organisation of M.A.T.A.F.— the Desert Air Force, 22nd Tactical Air Command, the 57th Wing (Medium bombers) and the 51st Troop Carrier Wing.

34. *The Desert Air Force,* commanded by Air Vice-Marshal R. M. Foster, C.B., C.B.E., D.F.C., consisted of a total of 43 squadrons, and was employed chiefly in support of the British Eighth Army. It was composed for the most part of Royal Air Force and Dominion squadrons (11 of which were South African Air Force) but it had also under its operational control three squadrons of American long range fighter-bomber aircraft in order to give it a flexibility not obtainable with the British types of aircraft at its disposal.

35. *The 22nd Tactical Air Command,* commanded by Brigadier-General Chidlaw, was employed chiefly in support of the American Fifth Army and consisted mostly of U.S.A.A.F. squadrons. It did, however, have under its operational control two R.A.F. tactical reconnaissance squadrons and four R.A.F. and Dominion short range fighter and fighter-bomber squadrons.

36. *The 57th Wing* was a purely American formation controlling twelve squadrons of B.25 medium bomber aircraft, and was employed anywhere within the Italian theatre as required. This wing played an outstanding part in the strangling of the enemy's communications.

37. *The 51st Troop Carrier Wing* was also a purely American formation, controlling twelve squadrons of C-47 transport aircraft. It performed a wide variety of functions, including airborne assaults if required, supply dropping, and air ambulance work.

38. Headquarters Desert Air Force and Headquarters 22nd Tactical Air Command were always located alongside Headquarters Eighth Army and Fifth Army respectively. Demands for air support were passed by each Army Headquarters to its fellow Air Headquarters.

Mediterranean Allied Coastal Air Force.
(*Air Vice-Marshal J. Whitford, C.B., C.B.E., Air Officer Commanding*)

39. The direction of M.A.C.A.F. was almost entirely an R.A.F. concern by March, 1945, by which date the formation consisted of seven R.A.F. and Dominion squadrons, four Italian squadrons, four French squadrons and two U.S.A.A.F. squadrons. The operational role of M.A.C.A.F. was the air defence of Allied shipping, the attack of enemy shipping, the air defence of the Italian peninsula (with the exception of the forward areas where the responsibility was M.A.T.A.F.'s) and finally the operation of Air Sea Rescue services in the Adriatic and the Western Mediterranean up to the area of responsibility of Air Headquarters, Malta. By the Spring of 1945 M.A.C.A.F.'s operational activities had been greatly reduced, and in fact it had all but finished its work, and had won a hard battle against what had once been great odds.

The Balkan Air Force.
(*Air Vice-Marshal G. H. Mills, C.B., D.F.C., Air Officer Commanding.*)

40. The functions and organisation of the Balkan Air Force are dealt with fully in Part III and here I shall deal only with its purely

Air Force aspects. It consisted of 29 Squadrons, 13 Royal Air Force, 2 U.S.A.A.F., 3 Royal Hellenic Air Force, 2 Jugoslav Air Force and 9 Italian Air Force. These forces were divided between Greece and Italy. B.A.F. also had operational control of part of a No. 216 Group Transport squadron located at Bari, which was used for special duties operations to Jugoslavia.

OTHER FORMATIONS UNDER THE COMMAND OF AIR C.-IN-C. M.A.A.F.

41. In addition to the four main fighting formations, the Air C.-in-C. M.A.A.F., also had under his control Air Headquarters Malta, No. 336 Photo Reconnaissance Wing, and the Mediterranean Air Transport Service.

Air Headquarters, Malta.
(*Air Vice-Marshal K. B. Lloyd, C.B.E., A.F.C., Air Officer Commanding.*)

42. Air Headquarters, Malta, had at one time formed part of M.A.C.A.F. but was placed directly under Headquarters M.A.A.F. in February, 1945. As the battle front moved northwards the importance of Malta as an operational base decreased. It still remained, however, a natural centre for the direction of oversea air operations in the Mediterranean. Since Malta was a permanent R.A.F. base, the A.O.C. Malta had responsibilities in two directions—his responsibility to the Air Ministry for the implementation of R.A.F. long-term policy, and his responsibility to the Air C.-in-C. for such war commitments as he was required to undertake. The latter consisted of the air defence of Malta and North Africa, the conduct of all anti-submarine operations within his operational area under the general co-ordinating direction of A.O.C., M.A.C.A.F., and air sea rescue services within his area. The air defence and anti-submarine requirements had almost completely disappeared, and A.O.C. Malta's chief commitment in this direction was the maintenance of a skeleton organisation which could be rapidly expanded should a new air or submarine threat arise.

43. The A.O.C. Malta had therefore under his command only one air sea rescue squadron in Malta, and one air sea rescue squadron and one French single-engine fighter squadron in North Africa.

No. 336 Wing.

44. This wing, which consisted of one twin-engined and two single-engined squadrons, had previously formed part of the Mediterranean Allied Photographic Reconnaissance Wing. The latter had, however, been dissolved before I assumed command when it became American policy to make each of their air forces as self-contained as possible. No. 336 Wing remained as a completely R.A.F. formation under the operational control of M.A.A.F. It met the photographic reconnaissance requirements of all three services—Navy, Army and Air Force —working on priorities allotted to it by the Mediterranean Photo Reconnaissance Committee, which also co-ordinated the work of the American photo reconnaissance elements of XIIth and XVth Air Forces.

Mediterranean Allied Transport Service.
(*Brigadier-General L. V. Beau, Commanding General.*)

45. M.A.T.S. was an integrated British-American organisation whose principal function was the co-ordination and direction of all air transport activities within the limits of the Command jurisdiction of the Air C.-in-C. M.A.A.F.

46. M.A.T.S. was responsible for co-ordinating those services which the R.A.F. Transport Command Group in MEDME (No. 216 Group), and the U.S.A.A.F. Air Transport Command operated within the Air C.-in-C.'s theatre.

47. In addition M.A.T.S. had under its immediate operational control a pool of American transport aircraft, which varied in strength, but which normally consisted of three squadrons.

R.A.F. FORMATIONS IN MEDME NOT UNDER COMMAND OF AIR C.-IN-C. M.A.A.F.

48. All the formations described above came under the operational control of the Air C.-in-C. and therefore as deputy Air C.-in-C. I had such responsibility with regard to them as was delegated to me by the Air C.-in-C. However, as Commander-in-Chief, R.A.F., MEDME, I was responsible for certain other formations which did not come within the jurisdiction of the Air C.-in-C. These were:— Headquarters R.A.F. Middle East and the Directorate of Maintenance and Supply.

Headquarters, Royal Air Force, Middle East.
(*Air Marshal Sir Charles E. H. Medhurst, K.C.B., O.B.E., M.C., Air Officer Commanding-in-Chief.*)

49. Headquarters R.A.F. Middle East was the basis from which the R.A.F. organisation in the Mediterranean had been created. It now had very few operational commitments and its chief functions were the provision of operational training and maintenance facilities, serving the requirements both of MEDME and Air Command, South East Asia. In March, 1945, it had only four squadrons under its command —one air sea rescue, one general reconnaissance, one photographic reconnaissance and one single-engined fighter.

50. There were located in Aden and East Africa six general reconnaissance squadrons, but these were under the operational control of Air Command South East Asia.

The Directorate of Maintenance and Supply.
(*Air Vice-Marshal C. B. Cooke, C.B.E., Director of Maintenance and Supply.*)

51. The Director of Maintenance and Supply (D.M. & S.) was responsible for all Maintenance and Supply matters within MEDME Command. The maintenance organisation was a functional one, and D.M. & S. was responsible to me for the technical direction of all maintenance units and operational formations. His Headquarters, named Rear Headquarters, MEDME, was at Algiers, and he controlled three maintenance groups—No. 206 in Egypt, No. 214 in Italy, and No. 218 in North Africa. In my headquarters at Caserta, there was a small maintenance policy and planning staff, headed by the Command Maintenance and Supply Officer (C.M.S.O.), who was responsible for advising me on behalf of D.M. & S., and also for informing D.M. & S. of all policy decisions so that plans could be prepared to implement them.

52. A close liaison was maintained with the U.S.A.A.F. supply services, and where convenient, supplies of "common user" items were pooled to achieve maximum efficiency. A particular instance of this was 1,000 lb. bombs, of which there was a shortage in both services.

ORDER OF BATTLE FOR THE FINAL ITALIAN OFFENSIVE.

53. With but a few minor exceptions, the order of battle I have described above remained unchanged for the final Italian offensive, and in particular, no changes were made which would impair the effectiveness of M.A.S.A.F., M.A.T.A.F., or B.A.F. for giving support to the ground forces.

54. One change was the transfer of the two U.S.A.A.F. special duties squadrons from B.A.F. to M.A.T.A.F., in order to increase the effort available for supplying the Italian Partisans in Northern Italy.

55. On 16th March, I was informed by the Chief of the Air Staff that in view of the services overall manpower deficiencies, which had already arisen in the Royal Air Force, and which would increase still further in the next six months unless corrective action were taken, it was essential that there should be a reduction in the number of R.A.F. first line squadrons. The contribution that MEDME would be required to make was:—

(*a*) the rolling up of 6 heavy bomber squadrons of No. 205 Group at the rate of one per month, commencing in April;

(*b*) the rolling up of 3 light bomber squadrons of Desert Air Force immediately;

(*c*) the rolling up of 4 day fighter or fighter-bomber squadrons at the rate of one per month commencing in April;

(*d*) the transfer of 2 South African medium range general reconnaissance squadrons to A.C.S.E.A., when operational, so that two R.A.F. squadrons could be rolled up in that theatre;

56. The Chief of the Air Staff emphasised that he was prepared to consider alternative proposals provided that they produced no less saving in manpower.

57. I discussed this matter with my operational commanders, and decided that in view of the forthcoming offensive in Italy, it was most important that the fighter and fighter-bomber strength of M.A.T.A.F. should not be reduced, and that because of the preliminary success of Marshal Tito's offensive in Jugoslavia, the strength of B.A.F. should also be maintained as far as possible. On 22nd March, therefore, I replied to the Chief of the Air Staff, proposing an alternative programme of reductions, which would provide the same savings in manpower, and yet not affect the air power available for the direct support of the land forces. At the same time I strongly recommended that earnest consideration should be given to the possibility of postponing all reductions for this theatre until after the end of May, when it was expected that the operations then imminent would have passed their critical phase; and if that were not possible, that at least the postponement of the disbandment of 2 heavy bomber squadrons, and one light bomber squadron, which I had included in my programme, should be considered.

58. As a result of these representations, I was informed by the Air Ministry on the 2nd April that I should be required to reduce my strength in April by only 3 squadrons—one Beaufighter anti-shipping squadron, and 2 fighter or fighter-bomber squadrons. More extensive reductions were to follow from June onwards.

59. The three squadrons to be rolled up in April were found from M.A.C.A.F. and B.A.F., the former supplying the Beaufighter anti-shipping squadron and a fighter squadron engaged on the escort of air sea rescue aircraft, and the latter a fighter squadron based in Greece. Thus the striking power available for the direct support of the land forces was not affected.

60. As events turned out, the war in Europe had finished before the time had come to begin the reductions scheduled for June, and an alternative programme was put into effect.

PART III.

THE BALKAN AIR FORCE AND AIR OPERATIONS IN SUPPORT OF THE JUGOSLAV FOURTH ARMY OFFENSIVE.*

THE FORMATION OF BALKAN AIR FORCE AND ITS CO-ORDINATING RESPONSIBILITIES.

61. The situation in the Western Balkans, as the year 1944 progressed, was that considerable German forces were holding the principal towns and the communications between them in the face of numerous but ill-co-ordinated Partisan attacks. The Partisans were provided with Allied arms and equipment and were supported by small Allied raiding forces and by air and naval attacks. This support was, however, less effective than it might have been, because, while there was a measure of intelligence co-ordination which enabled the various air forces concerned to operate fairly successfully, there was during the first half of 1944 no Headquarters which provided operational co-ordination without need for constant reference to Allied Force Headquarters and M.A.A.F.

62. In order to provide such co-ordination, it was decided in May 1944 to apply to trans-Adriatic operations the principle of three co-equal Commanders of whom one was to be charged with the co-ordination of planning and execution of operations. This was not quite parallel to the system in force at A.F.H.Q., where the Supreme Allied Commander was a "commander" and not a "co-ordinator", nor to that in force in the Middle East where the three service commanders were co-equal. So far as the Balkans were concerned, moreover, it was appreciated that operations could not be divorced from politics and were closely inter-related also to "special" activities.

63. It was thus regarded as essential that some machinery of co-ordination should also be provided between the three service Commanders and the Foreign Office and State Department representatives in Bari, and between the three service Commanders and the Special Operations formation concerned with the Western Balkans.

* As the final offensive in Jugoslavia started earlier than that in Italy, it will be convenient to trace it to its completion before dealing with events in the main theatre.

It was also agreed that as the air force would necessarily play the predominant role in trans-Adriatic operations, the co-ordinator should be the Air Force Commander.

64. In a directive dated 7th June 1944 from the Air Commander-in-Chief, M.A.A.F., a new composite group was formed known as Balkan Air Force. The operational units of Balkan Air Force consisted on an average of twenty-two squadrons excluding those employed on special supply operations. They operated fifteen types of aircraft, flown by air-crew of eight different nationalities (British, South African, Italian, Greek, Jugoslav, and for the supply dropping operations, American, Polish and Russian). It will be seen how " international " were the responsibilities of the A.O.C., B.A.F. as an Air Commander.

65. The responsibilities of A.O.C. B.A.F.* as co-ordinator of trans-Adriatic operations were contained in a directive from the Supreme Allied Commander which became effective on the 15th June 1944. In this directive it was laid down that, apart from the air units coming under his direct command, the A.O.C. B.A.F. was also responsible for co-ordinating the planning and execution of trans-Adriatic operations by all the three services. The land forces affected were known as Land Forces Adriatic (L.F.A.), while the naval forces concerned were those under the command of Flag Officer, Taranto and Liaison with the Italians (F.O.T.A.L.I.). Other formations whose activities the A.O.C. B.A.F. was required to co-ordinate were:—

(a) No. 37 Military Mission (known as the Maclean Mission) which was attached to the Headquarters of Marshal Tito in Jugoslavia.

(b) Force 399, which was responsible for Military Missions in Albania and Hungary and, in a liaison capacity, for missions and special operations in Greece.

(c) Headquarters Special Operations (Mediterranean)—abbreviated title S.O.(M).— which was responsible for the co-ordination and general supervision of special operations throughout the Mediterranean.

66. It was, however, implicit in the directive that while the Air Officer Commanding Balkan Air Force was responsible for the co-ordination of trans-Adriatic operations, the Naval and Army Commanders were ultimately responsible to their respective service Commanders-in-Chief for the day-to-day conduct of operations.

67. The Commander-in-Chief, Mediterranean, had always been of the opinion that it was unnecessary to associate the Flag Officer, Taranto and Liaison with the Italians (F.O.T.A.L.I.) so closely with the other two service commanders as to necessitate moving his Headquarters from Taranto to Bari. From the point of view of naval strategy, too, it was desirable that his Headquarters should remain at Taranto. He was accordingly represented at Balkan Air Force Headquarters by a Naval Liaison Officer who filled the position more of an additional Chief of Staff than an actual Liaison Officer.

68. Located in the same building at Bari was the Rear Headquarters of the Maclean Mission. Force 399 was located partly in the R.A.F. building and partly elsewhere in Bari.

* A.V.M. Elliot was succeeded by A.V.M. Mills on 13th February, 1945.

69. There was therefore set up in one building in Bari what amounted to a miniature G.H.Q. Major issues of policy were discussed at periodic conferences between the three commanders at which their political advisers and representatives of 37 Military Mission and Force 399 were present as required. Day-to-day inter-service discussions also took place at a morning War Room Conference and subsequently between operations and intelligence officers of the three services at a conference presided over by the Senior Air Staff Officer, B.A.F.

70. In order to deal with the various political problems which are inevitably produced by war in the Balkans, representatives in Bari of the British Resident Minister, Central Mediterranean, and of the U.S. Political Adviser, A.F.H.Q., were made the Political Advisers of the A.O.C. Balkan Air Force, and he presided over a Policy Committee which, besides the other two service Commanders, included his Political Advisers and the representatives of the Maclean Mission, Force 399 and H.Q., S.O. (M).

71. As part of the machinery of inter-service co-ordination and to effect the necessary liaison between the three services, the offices of the political representatives and the various " special " forces, an Inter-Service Secretariat was added to the staff of A.O.C., B.A.F.

72. Joint Planning and Joint Intelligence Staffs were also set up and the Intelligence Staff was given the task of providing Balkan intelligence on a wide scale to meet not only the requirements of B.A.F. and L.F.A. but for Force 399 and S.O. (M). A small joint Public Relations Office was also set up.

73. There was a Combined Signals organisation and a Chief Signals Officer (Army) B.A.F. was appointed who was responsible to the Air Officer Commanding in his capacity as co-ordinator of Balkan operations. Necessarily he worked in the closest touch with the Chief Signals Officer (Air) who was responsible for B.A.F. Signals.

74. The joint organisation worked well. Inter-service contacts were maintained all day and every day and the close relations which were established with the political and special forces represented in Bari were of the utmost value in handling the various politico-military problems of the Balkan war. So close was this day-to-day contact that in fact it was found possible to discontinue the meetings of the Committee which had been set up to deal with Special Operations matters.

75. Another feature of the joint organisation was that a system of inter-service command responsible to B.A.F., F.O.T.A.L.I. and L.F.A. was established on the island of Vis and subsequently on the mainland at Zadar, which became known as C.O.Z.A. (Combined Operations Zadar).

76. It was made clear in the A.O.C.'s directive that the primary object of trans-Adriatic operations was " to contain and destroy as many enemy forces as possible in the Balkans." From the Allied resources at that time employed against the Germans it was not to be expected there would be much to spare for operations in the Balkans. Moreover, it was the policy of the U.S. Chiefs of Staff that U.S. forces, apart from some special service units, should not be employed in an operational role in the Balkans.

THE IMPLEMENTATION OF THE DIRECTIVE.

Introduction.

77. Before proceeding to deal with Balkan operations, it is most important to note some of the main problems with which the Balkan Air Force was faced, in so far as they were special conditions which had hitherto not been met by previous air forces. On the purely combat side, implementation of the Directive called for two major tasks:—

(a) air support for the Partisans, or, as they were called from the beginning of 1945, the Jugoslav Army of National Liberation (J.A.N.L.),

(b) attacks on the enemy's road, rail and sea communications on which he was so dependent for the maintenance of his position in the Balkans, and where, when he had to move, he offered the best chance of being effectively engaged.

78. The degree and kind of support afforded to those Partisans operating in the liberated sections of Jugoslavia, did not differ from that given to Partisans operating in the zones still under the general control of the Germans. The boundary between the liberated and unliberated zones was at all times extremely uncertain.

Support Operations.

79. Operations in support of the Partisans were, throughout, seriously hampered by the guerilla nature of the forces, inadequate communications between them and Balkan Air Force, and the inability of the Partisan leaders to appreciate what the Air Force could, or could not, do for them. From the first, R.A.F. Liaison Officers with W/T links to B.A.F. were established with the Partisan Corps, but this sketchy W/T communication could not be maintained on a 24-hour basis. These facts, coupled with Partisan reluctance to disclose their plans or to frame time-tables to which it was possible for us to adhere, severely limited the opportunities for really close support. A further drawback was the reluctance of the Partisans to make an attack in daylight and the inability of our aircraft to attack at last light and return the 200 miles or more to their bases in darkness.

80. Added to this was the fact that the Partisans were primarily guerillas, and as such moved rapidly and frequently; some villages changed hands as many as fifty or sixty times, and areas that were Partisan controlled one day, were often over-run by the enemy on the next and vice versa. This made the task of keeping up-to-date situation maps a big one.

81. Operations under this heading, therefore, normally consisted of fighter-bomber, rocket projectile, or bomber attacks on communications leading up to, or strongpoints in, areas where the Partisans were engaging the enemy offensively or defensively on a considerable scale; or on strongpoints or enemy-held villages near which isolated Partisan formations were being hard-pressed. Beaufighters, in particular, became highly effective in specialised attacks of this nature.

82. For the Jugoslav Fourth Army offensive in Croatia in the Spring of 1945, these difficulties were considerably reduced by an increase in the number of Liaison Officers and an improvement in communications; for instance, for long periods there was a direct telephone line from the Jugoslav 4th Army Headquarters to Balkan Air Force Advanced Command Post at Zadar. This allowed much better support to be given to the Partisans, though naturally it never reached the highest standard achieved between modern air forces and armies.

Attacks on Communications.

83. Apart from shipping attacks, operations against communications fell into three main categories:—

(a) attacks on large scale concentrations of Motor vehicles when the enemy moved in force. A typical instance was the German withdrawal from the Sarajevo salient in April, 1945. On these targets all types of aircraft were concentrated, and help was called for from other formations. The brunt of these attacks was, however, normally borne by fighter-bombers.

(b) armed reconnaissance of railways and roads. Railways provided profitable targets throughout. In the first days roads also gave good results, but later, unless large scale movements were afoot, few targets were seen and the main value of the reconnaissance lay in denying the use of the roads to the enemy by day and forcing him to use them by night, when they were always liable to Partisan attacks. These armed reconnaissances were almost entirely the task of Spitfires, Mustangs and P.39s.

(c) attacks on marshalling yards, rail tracks and bridges. These were mainly the task of the light bombers and R.P. Beaufighters, with incidental fighter-bomber attacks usually made when no other targets were offered on the particular stretch of road which was being swept. Apart from the actual casualties or damage inflicted upon personnel and material, these attacks occasioned sufficient damage to installations to prevent the enemy ever really catching up with repairs, and this had a definite effect in slowing up movement by rail.

Attacks on Sea Communications.

84. These were the task of the Rocket Projectile Hurricanes and, occasionally, Beaufighters. All enemy sea traffic up the Adriatic coast and amongst the islands was virtually stopped after the establishment of the advanced bases at Vis and Zadar brought it within effective range of the Hurricanes.

85. In addition to attacks on the actual craft themselves, attacks on enemy small naval craft bases in the Northern Adriatic played a major part in denying their use to the enemy and thus eliminating what was potentially a serious threat. R.P. Hurricanes and Beaufighters proved very effective for this work. Anti-flak support was normally given for these targets by Spitfires or Mustangs. Several attacks of this kind were made in co-operation with light Naval forces. Special mention should also be made of the highly successful attacks carried out by XV Air Force (U.S.A.A.F.) on Pola, Trieste and Fiume.

Bases.

86. Normally all except Special Operations aircraft operated from strips at Canne and Biferno, just south-east of Termoli, which is itself just north of the spur formed by the

Gargano peninsula. Special Operations aircraft operated from Brindisi and Lecce. On occasions, however, particularly when the Germans were withdrawing from Greece, Brindisi was used as an advanced base by all types.

87. In addition to bases in Italy, an advanced base was available on the island of Vis throughout B.A.F.'s period of operations. Owing to the shortness of the landing strip and bad approaches, this was normally only used by fighter-bombers, with a daily average of some 35 sorties. During 1945 it became more and more a special advanced base of the Italian Spitfire and P-39 squadrons. It was not suitable for Macchis.

88. From February onwards, an advanced landing ground was established at Prkos, near Zadar, and gradually developed until, by the end of April, No. 281 Wing, which by then comprised all single-engined squadrons except the Italians, was based there.

Operational Conditions.

89. The lack of adequate air bases on the east side of the Adriatic meant that a very great majority of sorties flown by Balkan Air Force involved a double sea crossing of at least 100 miles in each direction, and often much more, which added considerably to the strain on aircrew, particularly after facing heavy flak.

90. Added to this were the dangers inseparable from operations in mountainous country during the extremely cloudy weather conditions prevalent during the winter. Moreover, when aircraft reached the target area, the rugged mountainous nature of the country often made attacks difficult to carry out, as for instance, when targets were road or rail movement running through ravines, as was frequently the case.

91. These conditions combined with the nature of the work to make operations in the Balkans, particularly by fighter-bombers and Beaufighters, as tough as those normally carried out in other theatres in spite of the almost complete lack of air opposition. On the other side, however, was the compensating advantage that if shot or forced down in the Balkans there was always a good chance of falling into friendly hands and sooner or later getting back to Italy. Towards the end, missing aircrews would very often be back with their units within two or three days.

92. Another result of these conditions was that calls from the Partisans for support were very often impossible to meet. The difficulties were not always appreciated by the Partisans who, except when weather conditions obviously made an attack impossible, were apt to interpret the non-fulfilment of a task as an example of bad faith and non-co-operation.

British Liaison Officers and Target Information.

93. With friendly forces located throughout Jugoslavia and Albania, and with excellent information being passed by the British Liaison Officers attached to all main Partisan Headquarters, a wealth of data on German formations and enemy movement was always available. A vast amount of intelligence of all kinds was received at Headquarters, and collated and evaluated by the intelligence staffs of the three services.

94. In a very great number of cases however when Partisan Headquarters desired air attacks to be made on specific targets they did not pass adequate or detailed information on the target through the British liaison officers, and often requests to attack German garrisons in towns failed to give detailed aiming points. The obtaining of such vital information therefore led to delays before attacks could be carried out.

Target Clearance.

95. One of the major difficulties encountered in operating over Jugoslavia was the fact that targets could not be attacked without prior clearance from Partisan G.H.Q. This authority was delegated, as regards tactical targets, to Partisan subordinate Army H.Q.'s; but as far as major strategical targets were concerned, delays by Partisan G.H.Q. in giving clearance often seriously delayed or hindered attacks of considerable importance. On occasions, clearance was refused and attacks could not be made.

96. One could understand the reluctance of the Jugoslavs to clear targets in their own country for heavy air attack, with the inevitable damage to their towns and civilians, but often this permission was refused or withheld for long periods in spite of the fact that the enemy were obviously attaching great importance to the targets and possibly taking advantage of such "immunity." Thus Ljubljana marshalling yard, which had over 1,000 units of rolling stock in the later stages, was not cleared for attack. It is only fair to state, however, that permission was normally withheld only when targets lay in built-up areas.

97. Balkan Air Force was responsible for approving all targets in the Balkans selected for air attack. This was done by means of daily signals to all other air forces and by holding daily target conferences which were attended by Intelligence and Operations Officers of the XV Air Force, 205 Group and 37 Military Mission. A representative of B.A.F. also attended the daily target conference of M.A.S.A.F. In this way a most satisfactory liaison was kept up. Day attacks of the XV Air Force and 205 Group heavy bombers were closely co-ordinated with sweeps by B.A.F. fighters and those of Desert Air Force.

The Bomb Line.

98. Mention has already been made of the difficulty of maintaining up-to-date information on Partisan positions and intentions. This was increased when the Russians entered Jugoslavia and showed the same reluctance to give information as the Partisans, while their communications with the Mediterranean theatre were even more circuitous and inadequate. These factors led to the establishment of a bomb line which gave a very generous safety margin except when close tactical support had been called for by the Partisans. In the Russian case this was 80 miles ahead of their last known position, unless previous clearance was obtained through Moscow.

99. In spite of these precautions, instances unfortunately occurred of Partisan forces being attacked by Allied aircraft, due in most cases to their having moved without intimation. These, however, never led to serious repercussions.

Operations with Light Naval Forces.

100. The air force role in these operations was to silence the large coastal defence (C.D.) batteries (especially on Cherso, Rab, and Lussin islands) by intensive air attack so that Naval craft could bombard from close range in safety. These batteries consisted of guns up to 150 mm. in calibre, and with all aircraft often operating from the same airfield, Biferno, it was possible to carry out several very effective attacks.

101. Marauders and Baltimores attacked from medium level, while R.P. Beaufighters, with Mustangs as anti-flak escort, came in at low level in a co-ordinated attack. These batteries were also attacked from low level by Mustangs carrying Napalm fire bombs. As a result, at least four major C.D. batteries were silenced, thus permitting the Navy to bombard the anchorages and to operate their M.T.B.'s close inshore to disrupt the enemy's coastal shipping routes.

Co-operation by M.A.T.A.F.

102. When operations in Italy permitted, M.A.T.A.F. allotted a force of eight squadrons for operations over the Balkans, and this was supplemented by additional squadrons when weather conditions were unfavourable in Italy. They were normally given a specific area in which to sweep roads and railways. On occasions, Mustangs were asked to take on particular targets such as bridges, as B.A.F.'s own aircraft of this type could not carry 1,000 lb. bombs.

THE OFFENSIVE BY THE JUGOSLAV FOURTH ARMY.

The ground position at the beginning of the offensive.

103. The withdrawal of the German Army Group "E" from the Aegean, Greece and Albania had begun in late 1944. The movement of the German 21 Mountain Corps from Northern Albania and Montenegro into Croatia was one of the major parts of this withdrawal, and by the end of March, 1945, the Corps had reached Sarajevo and were in the process of withdrawing northwards towards Brod and thence to Zagreb. There had been a general thinning out of the German forces on the west coast, and following the Jugoslav Army's success in pursuing the retreating Germans, it remained to carry out a final offensive to clear the rest of Northern Jugoslavia of the enemy.

Preparations for the Offensive.

104. Consideration had at one time been given to the possibility of launching an ambitious operation from the Zadar area using considerable forces from the 15th Army Group, which would be aimed at Trieste and Ljubljana Gap and which would be made in conjunction with an offensive on the Italian front. However, when at the end of February, 1945, the Supreme Allied Commander had a long-postponed meeting with Marshal Tito no further mention of the proposal for this operation was made. The 15th Army Group had recently lost several divisions to the Western Front and, apart from any strategic considerations, there were no troops to spare for diversions across the Adriatic. Instead, it was agreed that a large scale offensive should be carried out in Dalmatia by units of the Jugoslav Fourth Army under General Drapsin, which was composed of the former 8 Corps and 11 Corps of the Jugoslav Army of National Liberation. The first object of the operations was to clear the enemy from the Gospic and Bihac areas and then to liberate the whole of the northern Dalmatian coast and islands.

105. In his talks with Marshal Tito, the Supreme Allied Commander promised that the maximum air support should be given by B.A.F. for this operation, subject to its other commitments in the Balkans, that Allied naval craft should co-operate as far as possible, and that the maximum quantity of supplies should be sent to the various Jugoslav formations concerned in the operation.

106. The plans for the original ambitious operation from the Zadar area had included the establishment of an air base there. The plan for the setting-up of this air base was called Operation "Accomplish," and was completed by the 7th February after protracted and difficult negotiations with the Jugoslavs. In the meantime, by the end of January, a refuelling and rearming party had been sent to Prkos airfield at Zadar, mainly with the object of providing for Allied aircraft which landed there in distress.

107. When the plan for an offensive by the Jugoslav Fourth Army was decided upon, arrangements were at once made for providing the maximum air support possible. An Air Adviser was attached to General Drapsin's Headquarters, and R.A.F. liaison officers were attached to each of the Partisan Corps concerned in the offensive in order to supplement the work of the ordinary British liaison officers. I did not consider it advisable, however, to build up the Air Forces at Zadar itself as had been envisaged under Operation "Accomplish," even though this would have been very desirable, because of the danger of an attack against the base by German land forces.

108. However, when the offensive started on 19th March, it very soon became evident that it was going very well and that the risk of incursion by German land and sea forces had considerably diminished. Accordingly, on 22nd March I pressed the Supreme Allied Commander to approve a modified form of Operation "Accomplish" named Operation "Bingham," and he agreed that this operation should take place at the earliest possible date. It was therefore started on the 2nd April, and as a result No. 281 Wing, which comprised all the short range single-engined fighter squadrons in B.A.F. except the Italian ones, was fully established at Zadar by the end of April. The effect of this was to enable B.A.F. to give an increased and closer Air Support to Marshal Tito's forces.

109. A naval agreement had been signed in Belgrade in January which permitted the use of Zadar as a base for light naval craft. In the middle of February units of L.F.A., including one squadron of the Long Range Desert Group, and one squadron of the Special Boating Service, were sent to Zadar. The establishment of an air base there resulted in a rather complex problem of inter-service co-ordination, which was solved by the creation of a headquarters to control raiding operations involving all three services, called Combined Operations, Zadar (C.O.Z.A.).

Air Operations in support of the Offensive

110. Active air operations in support of the Fourth Army commenced on the 19th March and continued with unabated vigour until the end of hostilities on the 8th May 1945. At the same time a considerable effort was maintained against the enemy in the Sarajevo area, and against his communications throughout Jugoslavia to prevent reinforcement of his forces in front of the Fourth Army.

111. The detailed description of air operations in support of the Jugoslav Fourth Army offensive follows in the next section of this part. It is never a simple task to give a compact and lucid account of air operations in support of a land battle, because of the constant necessity to relate those operations to events on the ground and to the overall picture of the battle. In this particular case, the task is far more difficult than usual, simply because a clear picture of exactly what was happening on the ground was, more often than not, not available to the air forces. Some of the difficulties of co-operating with the Partisans have been indicated in earlier paragraphs,* and though these were reduced for this particular offensive, the degree of liaison and close co-operation achieved never approached that which existed between the Armies and Air Forces in Italy. Because of this, there could be only a minimum of advance planning, and air operations were therefore, of necessity, much more of an ad hoc nature. This fact is reflected in the account of the air operations which follows. Moreover, political developments following the cessation of hostilities made impossible an accurate assessment of the value of the operations by Balkan Air Force, since the Allies were not allowed to examine targets, to have discussions with the Jugoslavs themselves, or to interrogate their prisoners.

Operations during the Offensive.
The first phase—capture of Bihac

112. On the 19th March, Marauders and Baltimores heralded the opening of the Jugoslav Fourth Army's attack on Bihac with intensive bombing of strongpoints south-west of the town. From then until the 25th, when Bihac was entered, uninterrupted aid was given to the land forces by tactical support and attack on communications in the enemy's rear.

113. Simultaneously, attacks were mounted against Gospic, Senj and Ogulin and throughout the same period practically the whole of the road and rail system of North Jugoslavia was subjected to straffing and bombing. Aircraft of M.A.S.A.F. and M.A.T.A.F. added weight to this concentrated and widespread effort. Mustangs of D.A.F. gave special assistance by highly successful attacks on road and rail bridges.

114. The Fourth Army successfully completed the first phase of its offensive with the capture of Bihac on the 28th March. They claimed to have killed 4,000 enemy and taken 2,000 prisoners.

Second Phase—clearing of Islands and advance to Fiume

115. Determined to hold the Northern Adriatic coast at all costs, the enemy continued his policy of strengthening the coast and inland defences, but the toll taken by B.A.F. and the Royal Navy of his shipping, apart from the threat of invasion, was causing him much embarrassment and he finally evacuated them.

116. No summary of the operations during March would be complete without mention of the outstanding work of the Long Range Desert Group patrols established in Istria, and on the Island of Rab. These patrols were set up in enemy-held territory and were frequently located by them. Nevertheless, they continued to send out most valuable information for the R.A.F.

117. April was the climax of B.A.F.'s effort in support of the Jugoslav Fourth Army, and indeed, to the whole of its operations over Jugoslavia during the past year. Flying well over 3,000 sorties, fighters, fighter-bombers and medium bombers destroyed or damaged during this month approximately 800 M.T., 60 locomotives, and 40 naval craft.

118. On the 4th of April, a co-ordinated attack was put in against the island of Pag, the coastal garrison of Karlobag and the town of Gospic, and by the 6th all three objectives had been cleared of the enemy. In quick succession followed the fall of Rab, Krk, Lussin and Cherso.

119. The task of the ground and naval forces was lightened immeasurably by the air support given by B.A.F., so much so that little or no interference was experienced from the formidable defences during the actual assaults. Along the coastal road, under cover of our fighters, Fourth Army forces also moved up without air or ground opposition, and by the 15th the coastline had been cleared up to and including Kraljevica.

120. In the hinterland, however, the enemy appeared momentarily to have stabilised the situation, but B.A.F. kept up the attacks on communications. In anti-shipping strikes over the Northern Islands R.P. Hurricanes and Spitfires reaped a good harvest, disabling and sinking several vessels.

121. Between the 20th and 27th April, a large number of close support attacks was put in against gun positions when the Fourth Army were held at the outskirts of Fiume, and attacks were maintained on shipping.

Third phase—link-up with 15th Army Group and clearing of Northern Jugoslavia

122. During the final week of April the Jugoslav Fourth Army made a break-through in North Istria to the River Izonzo and near Monfalcone met the advanced spearheads of the British Eighth Army. This left the Germans with a number of isolated and ill-garrisoned strongpoints running from Novo Mesto (on the road from Karlovac to Ljubljana) to Gorizia.

123. The final assault on Fiume was made on April 30th; the drive to Trieste met with comparatively little opposition.

124. Evidence that the enemy realised the hopelessness of his position in the Istrian Peninsula and elsewhere was shown on 1st May—a week before hostilities ceased—when approximately 25 vessels of all types surrendered to

---
* 79—82 and 94.

R.P. Hurricanes in the Gulf of Trieste. Mustangs and Spitfires remained at readiness throughout the week for support of the 4th Jugoslav Army, but few requests were made.

125. By the 6th May the enemy's withdrawal in Slavonia was rapidly reaching its end. Koprivnica (S.E. of Varazdin) and Bjelovar (E. of Zagreb) fell to the 3rd Jugoslav Army, and with the capture of Kocevje (S. of Ljubljana) by VII Corps the German position was further imperilled in the Novo Mesto area. Generalski Stol was taken and Karlovac threatened. The end of the day saw the enemy pocket northwest of Fiume surrender, and the following day B.A.F. flew its last six sorties.

126. Among the enemy formations caught in Jugoslavia were 15 Mountain Corps, 21 Mountain Corps (including 118, 22 Divisions, and 11 G.A.F. Division) and 91 Corps (including 104 Jaeger, 7 S.S. and 41 Divisions). Elements of 7 S.S. Division succeeded in reaching Central Austria.

127. Outside the borders of Jugoslavia, 188 Mountain Corps, 237 Infantry and remnants of 392 Germano-Croat Divisions, cut off northwest of Fiume, surrendered to Jugoslav forces, but were subsequently allowed to make their way north into Austrian territory.

Summary.

128. Altogether, more than 7,000 sorties were flown by Balkan Air Force during the Fourth Army offensive, between March 19th and 3rd May. More than 100 static targets were attacked, including gun positions, strongpoints, headquarters, barracks, troop concentrations, railway stations, dumps and bridges.

129. So concluded air operations in the Balkans. The task of Balkan Air Force was completed and on 8th May instructions were issued by the Supreme Allied Commander that the A.O.C. should cease to exercise co-ordinating functions in respect of trans-Adriatic operations. Until its final disbandment on 15th July, 1945, Headquarters, Balkan Air Force, therefore continued as an ordinary R.A.F. Headquarters with responsibility only for the control of its various Wings and units.

SPECIAL OPERATIONS.

130. Apart from the normal air operations, considerable effort was expended on Special Operations. Large quantities of ammunition, food and clothing were landed and dropped throughout the country for the Jugoslav Army, utilising a highly developed system of landing grounds and dropping points. Very large numbers of wounded Partisans, together with women and children, were evacuated to Italy from the most seriously threatened areas, their presence in Jugoslavia being a serious embarrassment to the Jugoslav Army. By the end of the war in Europe 36 landing strips had been prepared in Jugoslavia.

131. During the period I was in Command, a Special Operation was carried out involving the evacuation of approximately 2,000 refugees from Slovenia. Marshal Tito had requested this especially as they were in danger of being killed by the Germans withdrawing through the area.

132. The extent of these Special Operations can be seen from the fact that from the formation of B.A.F. until May, 1945, 11,632 sorties were flown to Jugoslavia and 16,469 gross tons of stores were dropped or delivered to the country. By means of Pickups (landing operations) approximately 2,500 personnel were sent in and approximately 19,000 brought out.

CONCLUSIONS.

133. I have divided this section into two parts, the first part dealing with conclusions from the operational point of view, and the second part dealing with conclusions concerning the Balkan Air Force as a whole.

Conclusions (Operational).

134. A scientifically accurate assessment of the value of the operations by Balkan Air Force in the Balkans has been impossible, as political developments have almost entirely prevented examination on the spot, discussion with the Jugoslavs themselves, and interrogation of prisoners. Even so, from the meagre evidence available from Liaison Officers, congratulatory messages from Partisan Commanders, and from the fact that they were always keen to call for air support, it is certain that our aircraft gave decisive material, and even more moral, assistance to the Partisans.

135. For the reasons given above, the effectiveness of attacks on communications cannot be assessed with precision. The fighter-bombers did not carry cameras, but there is ample evidence that claims for damage to M.T. were on the conservative side and there can be no doubt that these attacks very seriously hindered the enemy's power of movement. Possibly the claims against railway engines were over-optimistic and many more were damaged than destroyed. There is evidence that in attacks on marshalling yards and railway tracks serious damage was inflicted in one third of the attacks. What effect this had cannot be assessed, but from photographic evidence it is fair to say that the damage inflicted slowed up enemy movements effectively, and caused considerable congestion.

136. At sea there is no doubt that the attacks on shipping, which virtually stopped all traffic by day, seriously hindered the enemy and probably convinced him of the impossibility of holding the Northern Adriatic Islands since the adjacent coastline on the mainland had been liberated by the Partisans. The effect of air attack on the enemy's midget craft bases has already been mentioned.

137. There is evidence from photographs, confirmed in some cases from examination on the spot, that the numerous attacks on the enemy's coast defence guns on the Northern Adriatic Islands, particularly on Rab and Krk, neutralised these defences and prevented their effective use against the Partisan forces which took the islands. It would be too much to claim, however, that these attacks did more than cut down losses, as the Partisans were usually careful not to stage an attack until they had reliable information that the enemy had decided to abandon an island.

138. Finally, the air was kept clear for Special Operations aircraft who were able to take in supplies and evacuate personnel by day without interference. This very greatly increased the material aid given to the Partisans. This was achieved even though the enemy knew what was going on, were often within easy reach of the landing strips, and at times bombed them. Our fighters, however, prevented any effective interference at any time.

139. In addition, the extremely rapid German withdrawal northwards was, to a large extent due to his realising that a properly organised and equipped Jugoslav Army, supported by tanks and aircraft, was facing him. He first felt the weight of this on the Karlobag-Gospic-Bihac line, where combined Air/Ground attacks quickly broke up his forward positions. This fact, together with the overall effect of our aircraft in "keeping the enemy's head down" was a decisive contribution to the rapid Jugoslav advance and the over-running of many of his supply dumps and isolated garrisons.

Conclusions (General).

140. Balkan affairs have always been of a complicated nature and this was especially so during the second World War. At the beginning of 1943 there were a variety of Navy, Army and Air formations engaged in various activities connected with Balkan affairs with influence and controls stretching from London to Caserta, Bari and Cairo.

141. It became increasingly clear that with the growing strength of the Resistance movements in the Balkans, together with the overall effect on the war in Italy, it was most important to co-ordinate these activities in one place and on a proper inter-service integrated basis. The fact that the only feasible way of carrying on the war in the Balkans was by air indicated that an Air Officer should be appointed as the Co-ordinator.

142. The Commanders, Navy, Army and Air, their efforts co-ordinated by the Air Commander, had at their disposal staff sections composed of officers who were specialists in their particular task.

143. Thus, any problems which arose could be dealt with quickly and efficiently by the integrated section, on an inter-service basis, whether it was a question of operations, intelligence, signals, or plans; and a co-ordinated solution could be presented to the Commander. A most important advantage, too, was the way in which each service learned to appreciate the others' points of view. The spirit of co-operation and understanding brought about by the physical proximity of the various services and sections facilitated the solution of the most difficult problems. The actual operational air units of the Balkan Air Force were small in number and of various types, but the results achieved were most satisfactory.

144. As a venture in "Combined Operations" it was an experiment which subsequent events proved to have been an outstanding success and an example which could well be followed in future similar circumstances. For these happy results great credit is due to Air Vice-Marshal W. Elliot who commanded the Balkan Air Force from its formation in June 1944 until February 1945, and to Air Vice-Marshal G. H. Mills who succeeded him in command until the Force was dissolved in July 1945.

PART IV.

AIR ACTIVITIES PRIOR TO THE FINAL OFFENSIVE IN ITALY.

INTRODUCTION.

145. When I assumed command of the Royal Air Force in MEDME in mid-March, 1945, it was obvious that the German War was drawing rapidly to a close. On the Western Front, the enemy had been pushed back to the east bank of the Rhine, and a bridgehead of great strategic importance had been gained at Remagen. By the end of the month, the last great offensive, across the Rhine and into the heart of Germany, had begun, which was to end in the final capitulation on the 8th May of all enemy forces opposed to the Allied Armies in the west.

146. On the Eastern Front, the Russians were engaged in the capture of the East Prussian ports of Danzig, Gdynia and Koenigsberg on their northern flank; they had reached the Oder at Kuestrin, which gave them a good jump-off point for their coming offensive for the capture of Berlin; to the south, they had reached the area of Breslau; and further south still, they were fighting to the west and north-west of Budapest, and were very soon to push on to capture the Bratislava Gap and Vienna.

147. In the Italian theatre, the front was quiet, while the Allied Armies made their preparations for the final offensive which was to start in April and to lead to complete victory. In Jugoslavia, the offensive by Marshal Tito's Fourth Army was just about to start, and was not to stop until it had reached Trieste.

148. This then was the background against which M.A.A.F. was to continue its air warfare in the seven weeks which remained until the war in Europe had ended.

OPERATIONAL DIRECTIVE FOR THE PERIOD 16TH MARCH-8TH APRIL.

Mediterranean Allied Strategic Air Force.

149. During March the overall mission of the Mediterranean Allied Strategic Air Force remained to carry out its portion of the aim of the Allied Strategic Air Forces in Europe, i.e. "the progressive destruction and dislocation of the German military, industrial and economic systems, and the direct support of land and naval forces."

The strategic objectives in order of priority were:—

(a) The reduction of the enemy's sources of fuel, particularly petrol, his most critical military supply.

(b) Destruction of lines of communication in Germany, and of facilities for the production, assembly and repair of armoured fighting vehicles.

(c) Attacks in support of land operations. To meet the needs of an urgent tactical situation, temporary diversions of the effort of the M.A.S.A.F. from its primary function could be ordered by the Supreme Allied Commander. Moreover whenever weather or other conditions prohibited operations under (a) or (b) above, elements of M.A.S.A.F. could be made available to augment the Tactical Air Force effort in Italy or Jugoslavia, or to support Russian operations.

(d) Attacks on important industrial areas, when weather or tactical conditions were unsuitable for operations against any of the objectives given above.

(e) Counter air force attacks. These were adjusted so as to maintain the air superiority which had already been gained. No fixed priority was therefore assigned to such attacks and in practice they were normally limited to attacks on jet-propelled fighter installations.

(f) Attacks against communications outside Germany. Attacks against these targets included the following, the priority of which was determined by reconnaissance and other intelligence and which was specified by special instructions from Headquarters M.A.A.F.

(1) Railway communications between S.E. Germany and the Danubian Plains.

(2) Railway communications between South Germany and Austria, and Italy.

(3) Communications in Jugoslavia.

(4) Communications in Italy.

Mediterranean Allied Tactical Air Force.

150. The general commitments of the Tactical Air Force for March remained basically the same as in the previous two months. Their priority and scope were:—

(a) the disruption of enemy lines of communication;

(b) the destruction of enemy supplies and dumps;

(c) the support of ground operations by air attacks;

(d) reconnaissance duties;

(e) counter air force operations and provision of air protection over the forward areas;

(f) the dropping of supplies to Italian Partisans and other Special Duties operations.

151. The Commanding General, M.A.T.A.F., was responsible for the selection of targets for offensive air operations in Italy, and no targets in Italy were to be attacked by other formations except upon his request or approval. He maintained at H.Q., M.A.S.A.F., and H.Q., M.A.C.A.F., a list of targets from which individual objectives could be selected by them when an opportunity for attack occurred. If M.A.T.A.F. required priority assistance from M.A.S.A.F., a request was made to Headquarters M.A.A.F. for approval.

152. Owing to the negligible effort of the German Air Force, the counter air force operations and air protection for our forward areas were only minor activities. The major objective was to reduce the enemy army's ability to fight by attacks on his lines of communications and supply dumps. Reconnaissance work was a constant need and was handled by the specialised squadrons concerned.

The Balkan Air Force.

153. The function of Balkan Air Force during March was primarily to give all possible air support to Marshal Tito's Jugoslav Army of National Liberation, in both bombing and Special Duties operations. Details of this have been given in Part III, which deals specifically with the subject. In addition, B.A.F. was responsible for the selection of targets for air operations in Jugoslavia, and the communication of this list to M.A.S.A.F., M.A.T.A.F., and M.A.C.A.F. When the other air forces found an opportunity to operate against previously accepted targets in Jugoslavia consistent with their other priorities, they confirmed with B.A.F. that the targets selected were still cleared for attack. If B.A.F. desired either to solicit additional assistance from M.A.S.A.F. or to obtain a higher priority on accepted targets, it forwarded a request to Headquarters M.A.A.F. for decision.

Mediterranean Allied Coastal Air Force.

154. The primary task of the Mediterranean Allied Coastal Air Force continued to be the protection of our own shipping, the attacking of enemy shipping of all types and the provision of air sea rescue facilities. In addition to this, tactical sorties were flown, giving assistance to Balkan Air Force activities in Northern Jugoslavia, and to M.A.T.A.F.'s programme of interdiction in the western part of the Po Valley.

OPERATIONAL EFFORT PRIOR TO THE ITALIAN OFFENSIVE.

155. An analysis of the bombing effort of the Command during March and early April shows that there were four broad objectives.

(a) The completion of the destruction of the enemy's oil resources.

(b) Attacks on communications in South-East Europe in order to aid the Russian drive into Austria and Northern Jugoslavia.

(c) Interdiction of the enemy's communications, leading into, and inside Italy, and the destruction of his supply dumps and installations, in preparation for the army's final offensive.

(d) Support for the offensive of the Fourth Jugoslav Army.

The first three tasks are dealt with in detail below, while the fourth has been dealt with in Part III.

Oil Targets.

156. By the middle of March, 1945, the air campaign against enemy oil targets had achieved almost complete success. Begun nearly a year before, as a co-ordinated offensive with Bomber Command and the VIIIth Air Force operating from the United Kingdom, it had, assisted by the advances of the Russian armies, so nearly completed its task, that there were by March, 1945, only six known active plants within range of M.A.S.A.F. Of these the most important was that at Ruhland, seventy miles south of Berlin and over 700 miles from M.A.S.A.F. bases. In the third week in March, it was attacked three times by M.A.S.A.F. Fortresses with over one thousand tons of bombs, and successfully neutralised. In March also, attacks were made on the already damaged refineries in the Vienna area, and on two small refineries in the Western Hungarian oil region.

157. These raids brought the offensive to a successful conclusion, for on March 26th, the petrol output of refineries still in enemy hands and within range of M.A.S.A.F. was estimated to be, for all practical purposes, nil; and during April, it was judged to be a waste of effort to make any further raids on oil targets from Italian bases.

158. The overall result of the Anglo-American two-way bombing and of Allied ground advances by the end of March, even allowing for some small production from new underground plants, was to reduce the enemy's production of liquid fuels and lubricants to less

than 20 per cent. of the April, 1944, level, and of petrol to about 10 per cent. It can be truly said that the attacks on the enemy's fuel production constituted one of the most successful air offensives ever waged.

Assistance to the Russians.

159. In November, 1944, it became evident that the advance of the Soviet forces through Hungary was destined to be one of the decisive thrusts of the war. It was equally clear that an excellent opportunity was presented to M.A.S.A.F. of using its striking power to aid our Russian Ally, by limiting the supply and reinforcement of the defending Axis troops south of the Tatra mountains. To achieve this aim, the air offensive had to dislocate the enemy's railway systems in Austria, Western Hungary, and Northern Jugoslavia. Although considerable damage had already been inflicted on vulnerable points of these systems, a far more comprehensive programme of air attacks was now necessary, but before this could be implemented, an exact picture had to be drawn up of the whole flow of enemy traffic to the south-eastern front. Before the end of 1944, by means of constant photographic reconnaissance and reports from ground agents and prisoners of war, the necessary information had been obtained and collated.

160. The first requirement of the Russian High Command was the dislocation of the railways from Linz and Vienna to Zagreb and the connecting lines to North-East Italy. This phase lasted approximately from the beginning of 1945 to 23rd February, 1945. Thereafter an additional commitment was the destruction of Western Hungarian marshalling yards and railway targets in Northern Jugoslavia, in order to dislocate the enemy troop movement northwards across the Drava river.

The Main Targets.

161. Before considering the implementation of the plan to aid the Russian armies, it is necessary to give a brief survey of the principal communication targets involved.

162. The key target of the whole railway network was the complex of marshalling yards immediately to the south-east of Vienna. Before the air offensive began in earnest, most of the military supplies and material from the Reich and Czechoslovakia were handled in these yards, which had ample facilities for the purpose. Of slightly lower priority, but equally large and complex, was the railway centre at Linz, further to the west. And between the two were the spacious yards at Amstettin, capable of dealing with all military traffic and unhampered by industrial commitments.

163. Southwards on the line from Vienna to Zagreb were four important railway centres at Wiener Neustadt, Bruck, Graz and Maribor, which had large classification yards with full facilities and repair depots.

164. East of the Vienna-Zagreb route the lines from the Austrian capital to Budapest were serviced by the Bratislava and Ersekujvar centres, north of the Danube, and those at Hegyeshalom and Komarom to the south of the river.

165. Further south, a number of minor lines branched east from Wiener Neustadt and Graz, passing through the centres at Sopron and Szombathely.

166. Complementary to the major targets were minor yards and sidings along the various lines, while rail traffic offered tempting targets to M.A.S.A.F. fighters.

The Air Effort in March.

167. In January and February well over 13,000 tons of bombs were dropped in meeting this commitment, and March saw a further stepping up of the effort. In that month, some 18,000 tons were dropped on Austrian, Bavarian, Hungarian and Jugoslav railway communications in order to aid the Red Army drive into Austria and Jugoslavia.

168. On about one third of the day missions, visual bombing was possible and the accuracy achieved was exceptional. Night bomber raids by No. 205 Group added to the disruption caused by the Fifteenth Air Force attacks.

169. In addition to the continued policing of the Vienna-Graz-Zagreb route, in answer to Russian requests, M.A.S.A.F. now intensified its attacks on the western Hungarian marshalling yards and northern Jugoslav railway targets so as to dislocate the enemy's northward movement across the Drava.

170. In neutralising the Germans' forward marshalling yards in western Hungary nearly 2,500 tons of bombs were dropped at Hegyeshalom, Komarom, Sopron, Szombathely and Ersekujvar (Nove Zamky). A further 132 tons were dropped on the Bratislava yards, just inside Czechoslovakia.

171. Meanwhile, in completing the disruption of the railway communications in Austria, southern Germany and northern Jugoslavia, M.A.S.A.F. dropped some 15,000 tons of bombs.

172. Of the fifteen bombing attacks delivered against the Vienna-Graz-Zagreb line the most important were five directed against Wiener Neustadt which, except for Bruck, was the only remaining railway centre on the line with a large and relatively intact marshalling capacity. The 1,743 tons of bombs dropped on this target left the yards severely damaged and completely blocked. Three heavy attacks were also made on the crowded yards at Amstettin, which had become the main centre for the sorting of traffic after the previous month's crippling attacks on Linz and Vienna, and these likewise resulted in the destruction of installations and the blocking of the yards with the wreckage of rolling stock.

173. Meanwhile, the air offensive was continued against railway targets at Vienna, Linz and Graz at high intensity. Among the many other railway targets attacked the strongest efforts were directed against those at Wels, Villach, Bruck, Steyr, Gmund, St. Veit, Klagenfurt and St. Polten in Austria; at Muldort and Landshut in Bavaria; and Maribor, Zagreb and Dobova in northern Jugoslavia.

174. No. 205 Group again supplemented the havoc wrought by the United States day bombers by effective night attacks.

During the first seventeen days of March, also, M.A.S.A.F. fighters flew 333 effective sorties on straffing missions, which met with excellent results, particularly in the destruction of locomotives.

The air effort in April.

175. In April the need to help the Allies' last assault in northern Italy (considered later) called for a vastly increased M.A.S.A.F. effort in the area and the commitment of disrupting the enemy's communications supporting the south-eastern front was relegated to second place. Nevertheless, the latter targets still felt a very appreciable weight of M.A.S.A.F. bombs.

176. Main targets in the first week of the month were the constantly attacked Maribor railway bridge, the less visited Dravograd railway bridge, also in Jugoslavia, and the Graz, St. Polten and Krems marshalling yards. In particular, the blocking of the two latter yards cut Linz from Vienna at a very critical stage in the battle for the Austrian capital. No. 205 Group meanwhile hit the Nove Zamky marshalling yards by night and the Strategic fighters operating over a wide area destroyed nearly 100 locomotives and numerous units of rolling stock.

177. With Vienna virtually isolated, the Red Army increased the speed of its advance: from 7th to 13th April bitter street fighting occurred in the capital, culminating in its complete occupation.

178. While the heavy bombers were switching their effort to the Italian theatre, the Strategic fighters continued the work, effectively dive-bombing Austrian bridges and straffing rail traffic in southern Germany. Results of the latter activity during the week ending 15th April included 227 locomotives and 354 units of rolling stock destroyed or damaged.

179. Features of the final assaults were the complete destruction of the Rattensburg railway bridge; the Strategic fighters' continued dive-bombing and straffing effort; the night bombing of the Freilassing marshalling yards, and the severe damage inflicted on the Linz marshalling yards, the last major Austrian traffic centre on the Linz—Budejovice—Prague railway, which after the fall of Vienna, became the enemy's last important lateral communication line behind the rapidly closing eastern front, and an objective of American troops advancing from the southern end of the western front.

General results.

180. It has not proved possible to assess in detail the effects of M.A.S.A.F.'s four month's attacks on railway communications to help the Red Army's advance into Austria. The evidence of photographic reconnaissance, ground reports, and aircrew observations, however, examined in the light of experience gained in investigations in France and Roumania, is sufficient to give a general picture of the effect of the offensive.

181. The air attacks were always ahead of the enemy's programme to repair his battered railway centres, and troop and supply movements to the south-eastern front were seriously limited and delayed. Furthermore, the elimination of marshalling facilities in Austria and Western Hungary forced the Germans more and more to adopt the unsatisfactory practice of making up unit trains far in the rear, so that further handling before arrival at the battle area could be avoided. Additional disruption was caused by the destruction of moving trains. A conservative estimate of units of rolling stock destroyed or severely damaged is 18,000 (including more than 1,600 locomotives). Many of the destroyed wagons were laden with supplies, and tank cars were filled with oil products. Further destruction of tanks and ordnance was effected at loading points. The cumulative effect was to cripple completely the enemy's land operations against the Russians in this area.

THE INTERDICTION OF ITALIAN COMMUNICATIONS

182. When it became evident, at the beginning of 1945, that it would be impossible to launch a major offensive until the Spring came, and that until that time, holding operations only were possible on the ground, the Air Force's chief task as far as the Italian theatre was concerned became the reduction of the enemy's fighting capacity on land to the greatest degree possible. To do this, it was necessary, above all, to deny him freedom of movement. Without such freedom, he would be unable to achieve the build-up of supplies and reinforcements required to withstand a major offensive.

183. But, equally important, the enemy would also be unable to adopt the alternative of withdrawing large land forces and using them to reinforce other fronts, where they were urgently required. It would indeed place him on the horns of a dilemma—he would not be able to use his troops effectively where they were, and would not be able to withdraw them for more effective use elsewhere.

184. A third consequence, rather more strategic than tactical, would be to prevent the Germans from exporting foodstuffs, industrial products, and loot generally from Italy, and from importing raw materials and coal for use in the North Italian industrial areas.

185. By far the most important of the enemy's lines of communication into Italy, especially in view of the campaign being waged against his oil resources, were the railways. These, because of the mountainous nature of the terrain on the northern borders of Italy, were limited in number, and so their interdiction did not present a task which was beyond the capacity of the resources at the disposal of the Air C.-in-C.

186. The Commanding General, M.A.T.A.F., was responsible for the execution of the interdiction policy, and from January until the ground offensive began in April, he used by far the greater part of his effort on this task. Supplementary aid was provided by M.A.S.A.F., when weather or other considerations prevented the heavy bombers from being used to attack targets higher in priority in the strategic effort, and also to a limited extent by M.C.A.F.

Interdiction of Railway Communications.

187. There were eight main routes leading into Northern Italy from the rest of Europe. Of these, the two from France were no longer available to the enemy, while in March an economic agreement with the Swiss Government was concluded which vetoed the passage on the two lines through Switzerland of war material between Italy and the Reich.

188. Of the remaining four routes, which were the ones to which the main weight of the interdiction programme was applied, the most important was the Brenner line running south from Innsbruck via Trento to Verona. The remaining three routes ran across Italy's north-eastern frontier. They were: —

(a) the Tarvisio route running from Tarvisio to Udine and on to Treviso;

(b) the Piedicolle route via Jugoslavia, which joined the Tarvisio route at Udine; and

(c) the Postumia route, also via Jugoslavia.

189. Though the four routes mentioned above were the most important from the point of view of the interdiction policy, attention was also given to the moderately dense network of railways serving Northern Italy.

190. The interdiction was carried out in a series of zones. The Brenner route was attacked along its whole length from Innsbruck to Verona, while the three north-eastern frontier lines were attacked in the frontier zone, and also along the Tagliamento, Livenza, Piave, Brenta and Adige River zones, to the south-west across the Venetian Plain. Lastly the routes in the Po Valley were attacked at the crossings of the Po River and its tributaries. The whole system provided a series of good targets in the way of bridges, viaducts, marshalling yards and sidings.

Air Effort in January and February.

191. The interdiction programme began in earnest on 10th January, 1945, and from then until the ground offensive began on 9th April, M.A.T.A.F. devoted some 75 per cent. of its total effort to this task. Previously, M.A.T.A.F. had operated primarily in the Po Valley, but during January and February air operations against the frontier railway zones were given top priority, and action against the more southerly communications leading to the battle area became a secondary consideration.

192. The 57th Wing concentrated mainly on the Brenner Pass route, assisted by the XXIInd Tactical Air Command, while the Desert Air Force attacked the north-eastern frontier routes. In the less important Po Valley, XXIInd T.A.C. operated against communications west of Vicenza, while D.A.F. concentrated on the Imola-Budrio-Medicina-Molinello area east of Bologna. The Strategic Air Force heavy bombers gave assistance with some 5,000 tons of bombs, most of which were dropped on marshalling yards, and of which some 3,000 tons were on the Brenner route.

193. This heavy effort showed immediate results. In January, the Brenner route was definitely blocked to through traffic for fifteen days, and probably for another five; in February, at no time was the route open to continuous through traffic. On the north-eastern frontier routes, through rail traffic was denied the Germans for the whole of January, and although it was possible on a few days during the early part of February, the state of interdiction during the latter half of the month was the most complete achieved up to that time.

194. This success quickly had the effect of obliging the enemy to lean more and more upon the roads for his communications. Thus in January, heavy road movement at night was reported along the Adige Valley and down both sides of Lake Garda, and photographic reconnaissance and ground reports showed that there was little rail activity south of Trento. The transport of supplies and heavy equipment clearly presented a great problem to the enemy, though the movement of troops could still be accomplished, albeit with a great time lag. Petrol was by then a very scarce commodity indeed, and quite insufficient for large scale motor transport movement, quite apart from the continual hazards of Allied air attacks.

Air Effort in March.
The Brenner route.

195. March witnessed a still greater air effort against this vital line, in particular by the medium bombers of the 57th Wing, who dropped some 3,000 tons of bombs on it in the course of 1,600 sorties—some 60 per cent. of their total effort for the month. Bridges and diversions along almost the entire route remained the main objectives, with targets at Ora and San Michele, in the central Brenner zone, receiving the chief attention. Other targets heavily attacked were at Ala, San Ambrogio and San Margherita, on the lower Brenner line, and Campo di Trens on the upper Brenner line.

196. Simultaneously, XXIInd T.A.C. maintained heavy pressure on the central and lower portions of the route by day, while night intruder aircraft did the same by night. In these attacks, not only were the blocks created by the medium bombers further enlarged, but additional bridges were destroyed, tracks cut, and traffic both bombed and straffed.

197. The M.A.S.A.F. bombers again co-operated by dropping some 1,300 tons of bombs on Verona marshalling yards. In addition their disruption of the Austrian railway system was having its effect on communications further south.

198. In spite of the enemy's desperate repair efforts, and of a spell of bad weather from 26th to 29th March, through traffic on the Brenner route was again impossible for the whole of the month. The interdiction, in fact, reached the highest level yet attained. Ten or twelve blocks on the route at one time was a common occurrence and on one occasion there were at least fifteen blocks on the stretch between Bolzano and Verona.

The north-eastern routes.

199. The main burden of the attacks on these lines again fell on the Desert Air Force, which concentrated chiefly on the Tarvisio-Udine line. In addition, the 57th Wing flew 364 sorties against bridges and diversions in the five river zones in the Venetian Plain, while XXIInd T.A.C. fighter-bombers, and the night intruders, attacked targets primarily in the Casarsa area. M.A.S.A.F. aircraft co-operated by dropping 700 tons of bombs, with the Treviso and Padua marshalling yards as the main targets.

200. These attacks caused the three north-eastern frontier routes to be blocked for the whole of the month, and, moreover, little traffic was able to pass over the more southerly stretches of the lines across the Venetian Plain.

The Po Valley and North-West Italy.

201. The switching of the main air effort northwards against the frontier routes implied that more freedom of movement than formerly was permitted the enemy in the Po Valley. During the period of static ground operations, however, this was considered of minor importance. Nevertheless, a considerable M.A.T.A.F. effort was continued against the principal lines of communication immediately behind the battle area, especially when bad weather prevented operations further afield. During the period, sorties were flown against the Po River zone and in the Mincio, Oglia and Adda river zones, branching northwards from the Po River. Particular attention was paid to the disruption of lines leading to Milan, Turin, and Genoa in order to hinder the transportation of looted industrial and agricultural products bound for the Reich. Also in March, the night intruder effort was increased considerably, particularly in the form of a greater number of attacks on damaged bridges and diversions to demoralise the enemy's repair gangs. Generally, both the day and night attacking aircraft in the Po valley were increasingly concerned with destroying rail and road traffic and rolling stock in marshalling yards rather than the wrecking of the railway system itself.

Air Effort in April.

202. In April M.A.T.A.F. maintained the interdiction of communications between Italy and the Reich until the 9th, when its main effort was switched to the close support of the 15th Army Group's offensive. During the first eight days of the month, the various elements of M.A.T.A.F. continued to attack the same targets as during March. In particular, the medium bombers flew nearly 400 sorties against the Brenner Line, their main targets being the bridges. By the 9th of April the route was blocked in eleven places. Desert Air Force meanwhile continued to attack the lower reaches of the north-east frontier routes and the lines across the Venetian plain. On the eve of the Allied offensive, the north-east frontier zone remained well disrupted, and no through traffic was possible across the Venetian plain. The state of interdiction in the Po Valley itself was also very satisfactory. The XXII T.A.C. fighter-bombers paid a considerable amount of attention to the east-west lines north of the Po and their connecting lines, while the medium bombers made fairly constant attacks on bridges.

203. M.A.S.A.F.'s April effort against the enemy's railway communications in northern Italy was further increased. During the four days prior to the opening of the Army's offensive on the 9th April the heavy bombers dropped 2,000 tons of bombs on bridges and marshalling yards on the Brenner Pass route and also attacked bridges, marshalling yards and locomotive depots on lines to the west of the route and a marshalling yard on the Piedicolle route. Even after the offensive started, M.A.S.A.F. continued to bomb the Italian railway system, in addition to providing close support to our advancing troops.

Enemy Repair Organisation.

204. The enemy's chief means of combating the interdiction programme was a large and very efficient repair organisation.

205. He showed extraordinary energy in effecting repairs and much resourcefulness in reducing the vulnerability of targets. Troops which were held up by the breaks were pressed into the repair gangs; bridges were sometimes replaced in 48 hours and craters were filled in in far less time. In spite of frantic efforts at repair work and brilliant organisation, the enemy was never able to counter our air attacks sufficiently to make an appreciable difference to his desperate situation. The whole area was sterilized and the German Army was becoming more and more impotent because of the impossibility of movement—even by night.

206. During the latter part of 1944 the enemy resorted to deception to supplement his repairs and it certainly became a very clever and much used means to increase the flow of traffic. At Calcinato, a span of the bridge was constantly seen to be out during air reconnaissance, but accumulated evidence proved that traffic was passing over at night. In fact, when a night reconnaissance was flown, the missing span was revealed in place. This particular bridge at Calcinato became known as the first " night operational " bridge.

207. As our attacks increased in number, so the number of " night operational " bridges increased also. During April eleven of these bridges were noted; ten of them were attacked and put out of service for varying lengths of time.

208. Another method of deception used by the enemy was to maintain the unserviceability of selected bridges when there was no immediate need for their use. Certain damaged bridges were repaired up to a certain point— left so that they looked quite impassable—yet could be made passable in a few hours.

209. Full maintenance of the interdiction depended on the weather. Good weather made it possible to achieve complete success, but in periods of bad weather prohibiting flying, repairs were rapidly carried out by the enemy and supplies adequate for some days hurriedly passed through. In spite of these weather difficulties, the railways (as has been shown) were blocked almost continuously.

Interdiction of road communications.

210. Road movement was also dealt with in a systematic way. The whole area of enemy occupied Italy was divided up into a number of areas and regularly patrolled by aircraft of Tactical Air Force both by day and by night. In this way, it was possible to keep an accurate check on all enemy road movements and to attack road transport wherever it was found. However, German road movements were strictly limited because of the shortage of oil fuel. Oxen were used to tow lorries, and so valuable had even small quantities of petrol become that members of the German 98th Division were offered a reward of a thousand cigarettes if they returned from a patrol with a tin of captured petrol.

Interdiction of water communications.

211. As a result of the attacks on his other forms of communication the enemy made an increasing use of waterborne traffic. Shipping travelling by night carried supplies from Trieste and the Istrian ports, while barges were used in the waterways of North-East Italy to support

front line troops. Consequently barges were attacked wherever found and lock gates linking rivers with canals were effectively put out of action by bombing. Attacks were also made on shipping and harbour installations at Trieste and other Istrian ports, and on one occasion on shipping in Venice harbour.

Attacks on dumps and installations.

212. As a complement to that part of the interdiction programme which aimed at stopping the flow of supplies into Italy for the enemy ground forces, a campaign was also undertaken against his dumps, supply points and installations, in a further effort to reduce his strength and ability to withstand an Allied offensive. This campaign reached its climax in March when over 2,000 sorties were flown against such targets; 42 ammunition, 19 fuel and 3 other supply dumps were destroyed, while 18 factories were destroyed and 16 damaged.

213. This effort was continued during early April prior to the Army offensive and a new feature was added by attacks against the enemy's methane gas plants. Twenty-five such targets were destroyed or damaged, again restricting the enemy's fuel supplies since this gas could be used as a substitute for petrol.

214. In April M.A.S.A.F. further increased its effort in the campaign against supplies, and in particular dropped 860 tons of bombs on Italian armament works and 768 on stores targets.

The results of the interdiction policy.

215. The claims made by M.A.T.A.F. against enemy communications in the first three months of 1945 are an indication of the success achieved by the interdiction policy. In that period, 242 road and railway bridges were destroyed; 416 damaged; 4,155 road blocks and rail cuts were made; 2,249 M.T. and armoured vehicles were destroyed, 2,255 damaged; 267 locomotives were destroyed, 982 damaged; 10,244 units of rolling stock were destroyed or damaged; 126 vessels and small boats were sunk, 466 damaged.

216. Though I should be the first to admit that bare figures such as these do not necessarily prove that the interdiction policy achieved its aims, the statements of responsible prisoners-of-war show that it did prevent the enemy building up his strength sufficiently to withstand our ground offensive in April, and most seriously impeded his troop movement. For instance, General von Senger, Corps Commander of the German XIV Panzer Corps, stated:—" The effect of Allied air attacks on the frontier routes of Italy made the fuel and ammunition situation very critical." Again, General von Vietinghoff, German Supreme Commander, Italian Theatre, stated:—" Rail traffic was struck in the most protracted fashion by the destruction of bridges. Restoration of bridges required much time; the larger bridge sites were detoured, or the supplies were reloaded. With the increasing intensity of the air attacks, especially on the stretch of the Brenner, the damaged sections were so great and so numerous that this stretch, despite the best of repair organisation and the employment of the most powerful rebuilding effort, became ever worse and was only locally and temporarily usable."

217. The interdiction policy was also largely successful in its other objective—that of preventing any large scale withdrawal from the Italian front. In an attempt to provide reinforcements for the Western front, the enemy did in fact withdraw three divisions by the end of March, but it must have been a heartbreaking affair for him. The distance they had to travel from the front to Austria was about 150 miles and given uninterrupted facilities, this should have taken them about five days. The first, the 356th, Division, took three weeks; the second, the 16th S.S. Division, took a month; while the third, the 715th Division, also took a month. Perhaps the most significant fact was that these divisions left much of their heavy equipment behind them.

218. It can be stated with complete confidence that the success of the interdiction policy was a major factor contributing to the defeat of the enemy in the Italian theatre. Air power had successfully accomplished the task of preparing the way for the Army's offensive.

PART V.

THE FINAL OFFENSIVE IN THE ITALIAN THEATRE.

INTRODUCTION.

219. This Part of my despatch covers the period from April 9th to May 2nd—the twenty-four days in which German power in the Italian theatre was completely destroyed. It falls into three main parts; a section on the planning for the offensive, a section on the use of air power during the battle, and a section on the battle itself.

220. In my description of the battle, I have attempted to relate the air activities to the particular activities on the ground to which they pertained. In some cases, it has been possible to do this by a day to day narrative, taking air and ground activities together. In other cases, a day to day narrative, to be clear, would require to be more detailed than is desirable for the purposes of this despatch, and in such instances, I have taken a complete phase of the ground activities over a period of days and then followed it by a description of the air effort connected with it.

221. Using this treatment, the description of the battle falls into five parts:

(a) The Eighth Army battle from 9th to 14th April, which breached the Senio and Santerno River lines. This is described day by day.

(b) The Fifth Army battle from 14th to 20th April, in which the Fifth Army fought its way to the Po Valley. The initial part of this is treated day by day, and the latter part as a complete phase.

(c) The Eighth Army battle from 15th to 20th April, in which a route was forced through the Argenta Gap. This is treated as a complete phase.

(d) The combined Eighth and Fifth Armies' offensives from 21st to 24th April, in which the enemy tried to escape across the Po. This is treated as a complete phase.

(e) The final stages of the battle, from 25th April to 2nd May, treated as a complete phase.

222. It should, perhaps, be mentioned that plans were made, and all preparatory action taken for an airborne assault at brigade strength in the initial phases of the battle. Since this assault was not carried out, for reasons of an Army nature, I have made no further reference to it.

PLANNING FOR THE BATTLE.

The Army Plan.

223. The task before the 15th Army Group was to destroy some 25 divisions of the enemy before they could retire north-east into the Alps towards Austria, and prolong the struggle from there.

224. The task was a formidable one. On this west flank, the enemy was firmly planted in the rugged mountains. On his east flank he was solidly entrenched behind the Senio, Santerno, Sillaro and Idice rivers, all comparatively wide and steeply banked; an attacker there faced a maze of ditches, dikes and flooded fields.

225. Beyond these rivers there were still others which made good defence lines for the enemy—the Po and the Adige, both of which were already fortified. Beyond these again, were more river lines, and mountains, across the road to Austria.

226. Against these advantages the enemy was short of transport, his communications were under constant air attack, his air power was negligible, he had very little petrol, and he was woefully inferior in tanks and guns. The relentless air attacks to which he had been subjected in recent months had destroyed his mobility and had decisively undermined his whole powers of resistance.

227. It was certain that he would fight desperately to retain the Po Valley. If, therefore, the 15th Army Group could achieve a quick break-through and a rapid exploitation, huge enemy forces might well be destroyed or captured before they could retire across the Po.

228. The possible lines of attack were severely restricted. The 15th Army Group's front now ran from the Comacchio lagoon on the Adriatic to just below Massa on the Ligurian Sea skirting south of Bologna. The Fifth Army held the mountainous zig-zag line from Massa to Monte Grande, ten miles southeast of Bologna; the Eighth Army line ran south-east from Monte Grande, across the Sillaro and Santerno Rivers, and then northeast along the Senio's south bank to the southern shore of Lake Comacchio and the Adriatic.

229. It was decided that the main effort of 15th Army Group should be launched in the Bologna area by the Fifth Army, since once the latter reached the Po valley, the terrain in their front favoured a quick break-through and a rapid advance.

230. This main thrust by the Fifth Army was to be preceded by an Eighth Army attack, with the object of drawing enemy reserves away from the Fifth Army front.

231. The plan therefore fell into three main parts, which were to follow each other without any pause. In the first stage, each Army would break through the heavily defended enemy lines opposing it—the Eighth Army first, breaching Senio and the Santerno lines and attacking towards Bastia and Budrio; the Fifth Army second, breaking out of the mountains and into the Po Valley, with the secondary mission of capturing or isolating Bologna.

232. The second stage provided for a breakthrough by either or both Armies to encircle the enemy forces south of the Po. The Eighth Army was to go through the Argenta Gap to seize the Po crossings at Ferrara and Bondeno, and there make contact with Fifth Army columns exploiting north-east from Route 9 down the corridor north of the Reno. A secondary Fifth Army effort was to be made northward on Ostiglia.

233. In the third stage, operations were to be directed toward crossing the Po and exploiting northward, especially with the object of capturing Verona. If the situation permitted, further exploitation toward and across the Adige River was to follow.

234. As a prelude to this main attack, two important subsidiary operations were to be carried out. The first of these was an attack against Massa, on the extreme left of the battle front, in order to keep the Germans in that area occupied. The second was an amphibious operation to capture the isthmus projecting between Lake Comacchio and the Adriatic, which would give the Eighth Army free access to the Lake, and prepare the way for further amphibious operations which were to aid in opening the road through the Argenta Gap to Ferrara.

The Naval Plan.

235. The Navy plan for the final offensive was drawn up to give the Army as much support as possible. On the Eighth Army front the capture of the Argenta gap would require an assault in tank landing vessels, across the flooded country surrounding the Valle di Comacchio. A Naval party was to be formed to assist the Army in training L.V.T. (landing vessel, tank) squadrons, and to act as navigational leaders in the assault.

236. The coast northwards of Ravenna was generally unsuitable for amphibious landings. The enemy was, however, sensitive in this area, and a concentration of tank landing craft in the Ravenna-Porto Corsini Canal, combined with a dummy assault and shore bombardment by landing craft at Porto Garibaldi, was to be undertaken in order to delay the movement towards the battle area of the coastal defence division stationed there.

237. On the west coast, gun support to the advance of the Fifth Army along the coast was to be given by cruisers and destroyers. The clearing of a gunfire support area between Viareggio and Spezia would entail further minesweeping.

238. A flotilla of assault landing craft manned by Royal Marines was to be carried overland from Ancona on tank transporters, and launched into the Po River to assist in the crossing.

239. Plans were made for the harbours of Genoa, Trieste and Savona to be opened, and also the Port of Venice as a standby, in case there should be difficulty with the Jugoslavs over the use of Trieste.

The Air Force Plan.

240. The Air Force plan was to give maximum assistance to the Armies by close support operations; to prevent the withdrawal of the enemy north of the River Po; and, when the enemy was in sufficient concentration, to ensure his destruction.

241. To achieve these aims, the whole striking power of M.A.T.A.F. and M.A.S.A.F. was to be used, support of the land forces becoming the over-riding priority for both Air Forces as soon as the offensive began.

242. In general the Desert Air Force was to support the Eighth Army and XXII Tactical Air Command the Fifth Army, although one would lend assistance to the other as the ground situation required, and as determined by H.Q. Tactical Air Force. The prior objective of these two forces was to give close support in the immediate battle areas. The 57th Bombardment Wing of medium bombers was to be used on either Army front for close support operations as the situation required.

243. The Strategic Air Force was to be used in close support operations at the beginning of the offensives by each Army. Thereafter, it was to be available to attack communications targets in Italy, nominated by the Commanding General M.A.T.A.F., in order to maintain the interdiction already accomplished while M.A.T.A.F. forces were employed upon immediate battlefield objectives.

244. The opening of the offensive by the Eighth Army was conditional on a preceding air assault by both M.A.S.A.F. and M.A.T.A.F. Entry into the battle of the Fifth Army was to be dependent upon the gains made by the Eighth Army, and was therefore to be made whether or not it was possible to precede it with an air bombardment.

245. Preceding the 8th Army offensive some 800 Fortresses and Liberators were to bomb troop concentrations and gun installation areas 3,000 yards behind the enemy front line on D-day. Roughly 170 medium bombers were also to attack gun areas, after which 700 fighter-bombers were to follow with attacks on headquarters buildings, strong points and targets of moment. Approximately 100 Boston, Baltimore and Mosquito aircraft and the whole of No. 205 Group were to maintain the attacks during the night hours.

246. In addition to the close support operations full tactical and artillery reconnaissances were to be flown and four " Rover "* stations made available.

247. This air programme was planned for four days and thereafter as required. Its execution, together with that for the 5th Army offensive, is described fully in the narrative of the final offensive.

THE BATTLE.

Preliminary Phase.

248. At 0300 hours on 2nd April the preliminary phase of the battle began. Commandos in powered storm boats attacked at its western shore the Spit that divides Lake Comacchio from the Adriatic. After two days fighting, the Spit had been taken, together with nearly 1,000 prisoners, thus eliminating enemy observation of the Eighth Army's right flank. This attack was helped, especially on the 2nd April, by fighter bombers and medium bombers, who bombed gun positions, troops, and other battlefield targets.

249. A further attack was made on the night of the 6th April across the Reno River on the Lake's southern shore and by the 8th, a bridgehead had been secured across the River. These two operations had secured the Eighth Army's right flank for their main attack.

250. On the 5th April, on the extreme left of the battle-front, an operation was undertaken to capture Massa. This was a diversion to keep the Germans busy in the west. Air support for this operation was provided by fighter bombers and medium bombers. The latter also flew missions against coastal guns near La Spezia which threatened to menace the Army advance up the western coast.

THE EIGHTH ARMY OFFENSIVE.

251. The first phase was to break the series of river lines—Senio, Santerno, Reno and Sillaro—in which the enemy was very strongly entrenched. The Air Forces' task was to make these defence lines one by one untenable.

252. The first main assault began on 9th April when M.A.S.A.F. was used to pound the enemy's front line positions. Some 800 Fortresses and Liberators of 15th Air Force attacked troop concentrations between the Rivers Senio and Santerno. Medium bombers supplemented the attack and concentrated on gun positions. These in turn were followed by the full weight of Tactical Air Force fighter-bombers, who bombed, straffed and fired rockets at enemy positions to the West of the Senio River and along the floodbanks of the river itself.

253. At 1920 hours the Eighth Army's V Corps on the right and the II Polish Corps on the left opened the assault on the Senio positions near Lugo. By nightfall a bridgehead had been gained and bridges thrown across the river.

254. The effect of the preliminary air bombardment can be judged from the fact that, in spite of extremely difficult terrain and formidable defences, the army gained its objectives with remarkably light losses. The New Zealand Division, for instance, crossed the Senio without a single casualty, killed or wounded.

Night 9th-10th April—Eighth Army Front.

255. Following up the heavy raids of the afternoon, 72 Liberators of No. 205 Group dropped a further 200 tons of bombs on fortified positions along the Santerno River, to which the enemy had retreated after the heavy air attack in the afternoon and to which he had also brought forward two reserve divisions. This raid was in preparation for the Army attack on the Santerno positions which was to take place the following day. The employment of heavy bombers by night so close to our own positions was a new development, and undoubtedly surprised and dismayed the enemy. The attack was carried out within a period of four minutes and not a single bomb

---

* The "Rover" system was used for bringing aircraft on to targets visible to a controller who was usually in a specially adapted armoured car or jeep—so that close support aircraft could be up to the minute with a rapidly advancing ground force.

fell outside the target areas. A message of thanks from the Army was received, which said " Bombing quite remarkable and accuracy very impressive."

256. In addition to No. 205 Group's attack on the Santerno defences, the night intruders of Desert Air Force—Bostons, Baltimores and Mosquitoes—flew the record number of 169 sorties, attacking gun positions from Castel Bolognese to Massa Lombarda, watching for any movement on the roads in the Po Valley, or on the Po River itself, and bombing strongpoints in the battle area.

Day 10th April—Eighth Army Front.

257. The following morning, again preceded by a heavy air assault by fighter-bombers, the infantry pushed forward to the line of the Lugo Canal, and by mid-day had reached it in strength. New Zealand troops attacked across the Lugo Canal soon after mid-day and by the evening had reached the Santerno River; at the same time Lugo town itself was captured. Further South the Polish Corps also reached the Lugo Canal.

258. In the afternoon the XVth Air Force made an even greater effort in support of the ground forces, despatching 1,261 bombers and fighters to continue the attack on the Santerno defences begun by No. 205 Group the previous night. The object was again to disorganise the enemy and attack troop concentrations, gun positions and defence installations in the area immediately ahead of the Eighth Army.

259. Desert Air Force flew 662 sorties during the day of which 608 were in close support of V Corps and Polcorps. Four squadrons of Marauders of the S.A.A.F. bombed gun areas at Menate, near the South shore of Lake Comacchio.

260. On the Polcorps sector, attacks were made at Solarolo, Gaiano, Bagnara and against gun areas on both sides of the Santerno. The Mordano bridge over the Santerno was bombed by Thunderbolts, scoring four direct hits on the bridge as well as others on the approaches.

Night 10th-11th April—Eighth Army Front.

261. Desert Air Force continued its watch over the battlefield during the night, but after attacks had been made on the primary targets such as headquarters buildings, gun areas, factories and dumps, the ensuing reconnaissance revealed very little movement, and what little there was appeared very scattered.

262. During the early hours of the morning an attack by the army was launched on the extreme right flank from the bridgehead across the Reno gained in the operations preliminary to the main assault and reached a point some five miles south-east of Argenta, to the north of Route 16. The enemy reacted very strongly as this was a dangerous threat to his key towns of Bastia, Argenta and Ferrara, guarding the Argenta gap, and the way to the Po Valley along Route 16.

Day 11th April—8th Army Front.

263. During the day and through the following night the Eighth Army fought for the Santerno crossings and by the morning of the 12th April had considerable forces across the river. During the day 824 sorties were flown by Desert Air Force. The majority of these were close support missions under " Rover " control, against targets in the immediate battle area nominated by the Army. Spitfires and Mustangs were constantly straffing enemy positions. Search by tactical reconnaissance aircraft for enemy movement in and behind the battle area again revealed very little. In fact his powers of movement had been practically destroyed by our previous heavy air attacks in preparation for this battle. Artillery reconnaissance aircraft secured the engagement of hostile batteries throughout the day, and photo reconnaissance aircraft covered the battle area, Ferrara, Rovigo marshalling yards and any port activity in the North. The day's activity was typical of the work carried out by the Air Force during the offensive.

Night 11th/12th April—8th Army Front.

264. Further bombing was carried out by No. 205 Group when 225 tons of bombs were dropped on enemy concentrations, defences and dumps in the Bastia area, some two to three thousand yards in front of our own troops. The success of these attacks especially on the enemy's communications caused him to abandon Highway 16 where it crosses the Reno and divert his withdrawal to a point ten miles north-west of Bastia.

265. Desert Air Force night intruders continued their attacks in the battle area and communications behind it.

Day 12th April—8th Army Front.

266. During the day the bridgeheads already gained across the Santerno were consolidated into one, and a reserve division moved up through its northern part with the object of producing a local pincer movement against Bastia in conjunction with the force attacking north of Route 16.

267. Further south, Polish forces attacked up Route 9, capturing Castel Bolognese and in the late afternoon, Mordano on the west bank of the Santerno.

268. On this day the majority of the 729 sorties flown by D.A.F. helped the New Zealand and Polish Forces to consolidate and enlarge their bridgeheads across the Santerno River. One hundred and six sorties were directed against targets in the immediate battle area. The usual round of attacks on gun positions and on tanks took place with considerable success.

Night 12th/13th April—8th Army Front.

269. During the night No. 205 Group attacked the key communications centre of Argenta on Route 16, which was now being threatened by the Eighth Army's thrust north and south of the road. The destruction was very great; roads were cratered and blocked with rubble thus impeding the enemy's use of this line of communication.

270. Bostons, Baltimores and Mosquitoes continued their vigil throughout the night, patrolling the battle area, the Po River crossings and intruding further North.

Day 13th April—8th Army Front.

271. At dawn on the 13th April yet another amphibious assault was launched behind the enemy's left flank on the north-western shore of Lake Comacchio. To the south of Route 16 an attack was begun on Conselice, and further progress was made north and north-west of Massa Lombarda.

272. The bulk of the 766 sorties in the tactical area on the 13th were devoted to direct support of the amphibious landing on the right flank. One notable incident during the day was when Spitbombers saw a Tiger tank disappear into a house. They bombed the house and produced a large explosion.

273. A Brigade Commander, commenting on an attack on a strong point by fighter-bombers, said, " The resistance was completely broken. My own troops were able to advance 1,000 yards without resistance and 100 prisoners were taken after the bombing attack ".

Night 13th/14th April—8th Army Front.

274. Heavy bombers of No. 205 Group were again airborne to attack the town of Porto Maggiore which was another key point on the route through the Argenta Gap to the Po River, which the retreating Germans would have to use. Desert Air Force's contribution to the night's effort was aimed at harassing enemy movement in and behind the battle area. Motor transport, barges, the Po River crossings, and the road junction at Consandola were the targets. During the night a Mosquito night-fighter destroyed one F.W.190 and damaged another.

Day 14th April—8th Army Front.

275. At dawn the 2nd New Zealand Division attacked over the Sillaro River due east of Massa Lombarda and towards Medicina, and by mid-day had established a firm bridgehead. To the north, Conselice was finally occupied, while to the south, the Polish Corps captured Imola on Route 9, and swept on towards Castel San Pietro.

Summary of the First Phase.

276. Thus by the 14th April the first three of the river lines on which the enemy depended had been breached, and the Eighth Army's advance was gathering momentum. On the right flank the threat to the Argenta gap was growing, and the ground forces would soon be able to break out along Route 16 to the Po River. On the Eighth Army's left flank good progress was being made along Route 9 towards Bologna.

277. The time had therefore come to launch the Fifth Army into the Po Valley to be the left thrust of the pincer movement aimed at encircling the enemy south of the Po. On the morning of the 14th April the Fifth Army joined in the general offensive.

THE FIFTH ARMY OFFENSIVE.

Day 14th April—Fifth Army Front.

278. The attack was opened by the IV Corps at 09.45 hours some 20 miles south-west of Bologna in the mountainous country just west of Highway 64, which follows the upper valley of the Reno River. It was aimed at Mt. Pero, Vergato and Montese. The attack was preceded by a forty-minute " set piece " air attack by fighter-bombers, and during the day XXII T.A.C. flew a total of 514 sorties, of which all but 55 were on army support.

Day 15th April—Fifth Army Front.

279. A tremendous effort was made by the heavy bombers of 15th Air Force in the afternoon. Every available aircraft that could possibly be used—even some which had previously been considered unfit for operations—was pressed into service. A total of 1,790 bombers and fighters were airborne. This force was given two tasks. The first was to attack 21 targets nominated by the Fifth Army, such as command posts, dumps and enemy-occupied areas, in the area south of Bologna; the second was to attack communications and stores targets further north. Some 1,600 tons of bombs were dropped by the first force, and some 800 tons by the second. The effort by the heavy bombers was augmented by that of 258 medium bombers of Tactical Air Force, which attacked enemy reserve areas at Praduro on Route 64, and at Medicina, though the latter was more intimately concerned with Eighth Army operations. Meanwhile, XXII T.A.C., in missions against targets along the front, including ground positions, command posts, occupied buildings and dumps, flew just under 500 sorties.

280. By the evening of the 15th, Vergato and Montese had been captured, and during the night, the Fifth Army II Corps, on the right of the 4th Corps, joined in the attack.

Ground and air effort, 16th to 19th April, Fifth Army front.

281. During these four days, all the Fifth Army forces were engaged in heavy fighting among the mountains which the enemy held so strongly, but gradual progress was made towards Bologna. Immense assistance was given in this task by both Strategic and Tactical Air Force aircraft, and the heights guarding the approaches to Bologna became universally scarred and pitted with bomb craters.

282. The planned assistance of the Strategic Air Force was largely foiled on the 16th by cloud over the Bologna area which prevented positive identification of targets, and only some 200 tons of bombs were dropped. In the meantime, XXII T.A.C. again directed almost its entire effort of some 500 sorties against battlefield targets to the south and south-west of Bologna. On the 17th and 18th weather conditions were more favourable for accurate bombing, and in the course of the two days, XVth Air Force aircraft dropped a total of 2,700 tons of bombs on tactical targets ahead of the advancing Fifth Army troops. The objective, as in the preceding attacks, was the maximum disorganisation of enemy forces, and the destruction of equipment and installations, prior to an attack by Allied ground forces. As in the case of previous attacks, virtually every building in the areas attacked was destroyed or heavily damaged. This effort was supplemented by that of the medium bombers, while XXII T.A.C. continued to devote almost all its attention to close support work.

283. The night of 16th/17th April provided No. 205 Group with another communications target of importance. Casalecchio, which is located three miles south-west of Bologna, offered an excellent opportunity for the interdiction of the flow of German reserves from Bologna which was attempting to stem the Fifth Army advance. The raid was successful, the road bridge in the town being destroyed, and much other damage being caused.

Day 20th April. Fifth Army front.

284. On the morning of the 20th the leading elements of the Fifth Army broke out of the Appenines into the Po Valley, and took up positions astride Highway 9 between Bologna and Modena. Preparations were immediately made for an attack on Bologna, all the high ground before it having by now been cleared.

285. At last the Fifth Army was ready to begin its drive across the Po Valley, first between the Rivers Reno and Panaro, and then across the latter and up to the Po.

THE EIGHTH ARMY OFFENSIVE.

286. I have now reached a suitable stage in the narrative to go back to the activities of the Eighth Army. It will be remembered that I had taken their story to the 14th April, when a bridgehead had been gained over the Sillaro River and a strong threat developed towards the Argenta Gap.

Ground effort 15th to 20th April. Eighth Army front.

287. On the right flank, four days were spent in forcing the Argenta Gap, but on the 16th Bastia succumbed. On the 19th the infantry fanned out into the open country beyond Argenta, though resistance from strong points and defence posts, and at canals, was still met. An armoured brigade previously held in reserve was committed, and began to move through the gap to break the defence wide open.

288. In the centre, on the 17th April, a sweeping advance was made from the bridgehead across the Sillaro, along the Medicina-Budrio railway, until it was halted by yet another defended river position on the Gaiano. By the 20th this river had been crossed and the advance continued to the next river, the Idice. By this time the resistance was faltering, and a bridgehead was quickly gained here.

289. On the southern flank, the Polish Corps pressed on along and north of Route 9, and on the evening of the 17th opened long-range artillery fire on the enemy in Bologna. By the 20th the core of resistance in this sector was broken, and the advance here, together with that in the centre, was menacing the enemy's escape route from Bologna along Route 64 to Ferrara.

Summary of the air effort from 15th to 20th April.

Eighth Army front.

290. During these days the Desert Air Force continued its effort over the entire Eighth Army front at full intensity—a typical effort being that of the 16th when some 800 sorties were flown on Army support targets. A great deal of the D.A.F. air effort was concentrated on assisting our troops through the Argenta Gap. A secondary effort was aimed at assisting the advance in the centre.

291. As the enemy was forced from his front line positions, the distribution of his forces became increasingly disorganised, and it became difficult, therefore, to brief fighter-bomber pilots concerning their targets before take-off. In these conditions, briefing in the air by advanced mobile operations sections—" Rovers "—paid rich dividends. Of D.A.F.'s effort on the 16th April, of 800 sorties on close support targets, **two-thirds** were directed by forward " Rovers ". " Timothies ", a code name for assaults by relays of fighter-bombers against points of resistance in the path of our advancing troops, were flown all day and every day. A feature of the attacks was the increased employment of fuel tank incendiary bombs which created widespread havoc over gun areas and strong-points.

292. There can be no doubt that the assistance given by the Air Force to the Army during this period of reducing the enemy's highly organised defences had a decisive effect. For instance, during the twelve days 9th-20th April, over 3,200 enemy-occupied buildings were destroyed or damaged by M.A.T.A.F. aircraft.

293. The Tactical medium bombers' main effort during this period on the Eighth Army front was directed to helping in the penetration of the Argenta Gap by bombing assembly areas and troop concentrations in that area, as well as those further north around Porto Maggiore.

294. No. 205 Group again gave considerable assistance by attacks on the enemy's lines of retreat. The first was made on the night of 17th/18th April against Porto Maggiore in the Argenta Gap. The attack was extremely successful, and the roads of the town were entirely covered with rubble and craters. The second attack—and this was the last made by the Group in direct support of the Army—was made on the night of 19th/20th April on Malalbergo, on Route 64 between Bologna and Ferrara. The town was at the time being used as a lateral communication route for enemy troops facing the Eighth Army and as a normal rear communication route for those facing the Fifth Army front. The attack was so successful that thereafter it could be said that Malalbergo ceased to exist as a communications centre.

295. The night intruders of Desert Air Force also did extremely valuable work during this period, attacking villages immediately to the rear of the enemy's front line, bombing crossings, barges and pontoons on the Po and Adige Rivers, adding weight to the attacks made by No. 205 Group on key communication centres, and attacking all road movement to the enemy's rear wherever it could be found. A tribute to the work of these aircraft was paid by General Von Senger, commanding the German armoured forces, who stated: " The night bombing was very effective, and caused heavy losses."

296. A special air operation (bearing the code name " Herring ") added materially to the enemy's discomfiture at the beginning of his retreat. This was on the night of 20th/21st of April when a force of over 220 Volunteer Italian Parachutists was dropped just behind the enemy's lines in the Po Valley (mainly north and north-west of Bologna) by 15 C.47's of the 51st Troop Carrier Wing. They achieved considerable success, killing or capturing over 1,000 Germans and carrying out a varied programme of sabotage and demolition.

THE FIFTH AND EIGHTH ARMIES' OFFENSIVE.
21st to 24th of April.

297. In these four days the German Armies in the Po Valley were cut to ribbons. Considering the enemy's small reserve and limited supplies of petrol and ammunition, normal military strategy would have dictated withdrawal across

the Po at an early stage of the battle before disorganisation was too great for a controlled retreat. But the German Commander, von Vietinghoff, did not give the order to pull back until the Eighth Army had broken through the Argenta Gap and was across the Idice River near Budrio, and Fifth Army troops had reached Route 9 west of Bologna. By then, an orderly withdrawal would in any case have been difficult as all reserves had been committed to the battle; and the attempt that was made was completely smashed by the power of the Allied Air Forces.

298. On the 21st April, Bologna was captured, Polish troops of the Eighth Army entering it from the east at the same time as American troops of the Fifth Army entered it from the south-west. The main part of the German garrison had withdrawn during the previous night.

299. On the Eighth Army's right flank, the drive to the Po along Route 16 was completed, leading elements reaching it on the 23rd, and on the 24th Ferrara was captured. The situation was then that some five German divisions were being contained against the Po east of Ferrara, and were fully occupying the Eighth Army troops in that area. But west of Ferrara to Bondeno the way was clear of the enemy, so it was decided to make a crossing there. By the 25th a secure bridgehead had been obtained, and the division making the crossing later revealed that the total forces opposing it consisted of 14 men.

300. In the meantime Eighth Army troops, advancing westwards south of Route 16, and in the central sector, had linked up with the Fifth Army troops advancing north between the Rivers Reno and Penaro. Meetings were made near Bondeno and Finale, and again near Cento.

301. The Fifth Army had reached the Po River at San Benedetto on the evening of the 22nd and a crossing was made at this point on the 23rd. On the 24th, the bridgehead was enlarged and Fifth Army troops began to pour across the River.

302. Meanwhile, another Fifth Army column was racing west along Route 9, capturing Reggio and approaching Parma. On the west coast, La Spezia was occupied on 23rd April without opposition.

303. In this period many thousands of prisoners were taken and the complete disorganisation of the German Armies was achieved.

Summary of the Air Effort from 21st to 24th April

304. Since September, 1944, constant reconnaissance of the Po River had been maintained, and an assessment made of the crossings which would most probably be used by the enemy if and when he tried to retire across the river. When, therefore, aerial reconnaissance carried out on the night of the 20th/21st April revealed that practically the whole stretch of the Po from Ostiglia to Crespini (halfway between Polesella and Berra) was active with pontoon bridges and other crossing activity, plans which had previously been prepared were carried into effect, and the full power of the Tactical Air Force was concentrated on the task of making the German retreat a shambles.

305. Constant attacks by the medium bombers made it impossible for the Germans to use the pontoon bridges and the ferries for heavy armour and motor transport. During the four days, 21st to 24th April, B-25 aircraft of the 57th Bombardment Wing made 38 attacks on active sites flying 605 sorties. At the same time, fighter-bombers of XXII T.A.C. and D.A.F. kept constant patrols above the river, and destroyed all craft which they found trying to cross during the day. In the same four days, some 220 boats and barges were destroyed or damaged.

306. In addition to attacking all attempted traffic across the river, the Tactical Air Force fighter-bombers paid great attention to searching out enemy movement on the roads and destroying the vehicles when they were found, and to cratering roads to impede the retreat. For instance, in the middle of the morning of April 24th, a collection of enemy armour, motor transport and guns was seen between Polesella and Berra—at that time the stipulated bombline. A special bomb-line was immediately laid down, and under " Rover " control, fighter-bombers attacked the target until late in the evening. In all, there were some three hundred vehicles in the area, and by the end of the day the majority of them had been destroyed.

307. It was in this period too, that the night-intruders put out their greatest effort of the offensive, maintaining during the night the interdiction of traffic across the river established by the medium and fighter-bombers during the day. They attacked pontoon bridges, ferries, boats and barges and concentrations of troops and vehicles assembled near the crossing points. For example on the night of 22nd/23rd April, the Bostons, Baltimores and Mosquitoes of D.A.F. flew a record number of sorties—174. Almost every aircraft was flown twice during the night and some crews made three sorties. The results achieved were also a record—55 motor vehicles destroyed, and 105 damaged, together with six barges. In addition, many direct hits were seen on bridges, wharves, ferry points and pontoons.

308. There can be no doubt that the efforts of the Tactical Air Force played a very important part in the crippling losses in armour and equipment which were inflicted on the enemy south of the River. During the four days 21st to 24th April 3735 motor vehicles were destroyed or damaged by Tactical Air Force. At the same time, claims against occupied buildings fell to 414 destroyed or damaged as compared with over 1,300 during the previous four days, which is indicative of the greatly lessened resistance put up against our advancing troops.

309. The air attacks carried out on the crossings during this period undoubtedly caused the enemy to abandon most of his equipment on the south side of the river. In the stretch between Pontelagoscuro (due north of Ferrara) and Polesella, for instance, where 76 Panzer Corps crossed, 900 vehicles, 100 guns of all calibres, and 59 Mk.4 Tanks, were counted left abandoned on the South side of the river, and this Corps was believed to have suffered fewer losses than other German formations. The air attacks against the Po crossings played a major part in rendering the enemy too weak

and disorganised to prevent the Allied ground forces' quick pursuit across the river in strength, and in causing the collapse which followed.

310. Confirmation of this is given by the statement by General von Senger, commanding the German XIV Panzer Corps "It was the bombing of the River Po crossings that finished us. We could have withdrawn successfully with normal rear-guard action despite the heavy pressure, but due to the destruction of the ferries and river crossings we lost all our equipment. North of the River we were no longer an Army".

311. Similarly General von Vietinghoff, German Supreme Commander, said: "The crossings of the Reno and the Po Rivers were decisively influenced by the employment of the Allied Air Forces. The smashing of almost all ferries and bridges made an ordered retreat across the Po no longer possible. The troops amassed at the crossing points and often had to swim to the other bank without heavy weapons".

The Final Stages of the Battle. 25th April to 2nd May.

312. On the 25th, both Eighth and Fifth Armies were largely across the Po. From their bridgeheads, a series of columns were sent racing northwest, north and northeast, and before long had severed the escape route into the foothills of the Alps north of Milan, so that those elements of the German army which had managed to get across the Po to the west of the main Allied crossings, soon found themselves confined in what was, for all practical purposes, a very large prisoner of war camp. In northeast Italy, on the 1st May, New Zealand forces had linked up with the forces of Marshal Tito in the Trieste area.

313. Towards the end of April, with only four German Divisions left which bore any resemblance to intact fighting formations, it was clear that any attempt to hold the Southern Redoubt was hopeless, particularly as Army Group "G" in Southern Germany was also on the point of collapse. One course alone was open to the German Commander—unconditional surrender. The surrender instrument was signed at Field Marshal Alexander's Headquarters at the Royal Palace of Caserta on the 29th April, and the "cease fire" took effect on the 2nd May.

Air Effort in the final stages of the Battle. 25th April to 2nd May.

314. The outstanding air activity in support of the Army's pursuit of the defeated enemy was an operation named "Corncob," which aimed at blocking or delaying his retreat into north-eastern Italy by destroying the road bridges over the Adige and Brenta Rivers.

315. On the 20th April, there were nine road bridges serviceable across the Adige between Verona and the Adriatic coast. On that day, 272 M.A.S.A.F. heavy bombers destroyed three of these at Rovigo, Barbuglio and Lusia. On the 23rd April another attack was delivered by M.A.S.A.F. aircraft which put out of action the bridges at Badia Polesine, Legnago, Bonavigo, Alboredo, and Zevio. The ninth bridge, at Cavarzere, was destroyed on the 24th April by Tactical Air Force medium bombers.

316. With all the road bridges down over the Adige river the retreating Germans sought to use ferry crossings instead. They were prevented from doing this to any large extent by constant patrols of Desert Air Force aircraft from the 24th to the 26th April. On the 26th, Spitbombers found well over one hundred motor vehicles waiting to be ferried across the river and immediately attacked them. The damage inflicted was, however, curtailed by the onset of bad weather.

317. The second phase of Operation "Corncob" was the interdiction of road bridges across the River Brenta, between Bassano and the east coast. Along this stretch of the river there were still ten bridges serviceable for motor vehicle traffic. Bad weather interfered with the execution of the plan, but nevertheless from 23rd to 26th April, seven of the ten targets were cut or blocked by either M.A.S.A.F. heavy bombers or M.A.T.A.F. medium bombers. The targets affected were the three road bridges at Padua, the Chioggia railway bridge (which had been converted for the use of road traffic), the diversion around the previously destroyed bridge at Friola, the bridge at Corte, and a bridge west of Chioggia.

318. During the early days of the retreat, fighter-bombers by day and night intruders by night continued to attack enemy movement wherever it could be found. After the 27th of April, it could be said that the Air Force's task was finished. The Army was moving so fast against little resistance that pre-arranged targets were no longer possible. In fact, the ground forces did not meet any defence which required bombing from the air, and the battle, such as it was, had passed out of the range of the Spitbombers.

319. After the unconditional surrender took effect on the 2nd of May, sweeps were made in the Trieste area on the 3rd of May to impress unruly elements there, and prevent any incident on a large scale arising from the Jugoslav claim to the city.

Interdiction of Railways during the period of the Offensive.

320. Although the blockade of Northern Italy by the disruption of the frontier railway routes continued to be an important item of the air programme throughout April, the satisfactory interdiction prevailing as the result of the previous long offensive made it possible to reduce the M.A.T.A.F. effort against these distant rail targets as soon as the ground conflict re-opened.

321. The most striking feature of the attacks on railways was now the big effort of the M.A.S.A.F. bombers, which operated against targets nominated by M.A.T.A.F., and thus allowed the latter to concentrate primarily on operations directly connected with the battle. Following their big effort of 8th April, 265 U.S. heavies four days later hit rail targets across the Venetian plain and along the Brenner route. Another large scale assault, prior to the enemy's retreat, was made on the 20th by 500 escorted American heavy bombers who attacked the Brenner route bridges and marshalling yards.

322. When it became evident that the enemy was being driven from the Po Valley a policy was formulated of conserving railway facilities in North Italy. Only targets definitely associated with the supply or withdrawal of the

German Armies were attacked, and we had now to consider military needs after the end of the Italian battle, and those of the civil economy. The Strategic day bombers' last big attack on Italian railway targets was made on the 24th April, when a high proportion of 1,200 bombers and fighters bombed or straffed railway communications in North-East Italy and along the Brenner route, while the remainder attacked the continuation of these lines in Austria, Italian road bridges and supply targets. By night, in the meantime, No. 205 Group made two raids on the Verona Parma bridge, at the southern end of the Brenner. The operations of the M.A.S.A.F. day and night bombers against the railway system in Austria, Jugoslavia and Southern Germany, which in many cases directly affected the supply of Italy, are considered in Part IV.

323. From the 9th to 16th April, when the battle raged at full intensity, the Tactical medium bombers were able to devote little attention to their customary railway targets; from the latter date until the 27th (when bad weather grounded the mediums for the rest of the month) the offensive was continued against Brenner line targets and a smaller effort was directed against the north-eastern routes and two bridges in southern Austria and north-west Jugoslavia. The total sorties flown by the Tactical mediums during April against railway communications amounted to 1,374 in the course of which 2,688 tons of bombs were dropped. Seventy-seven per cent. of these sorties were flown against Brenner line targets.

Results of the interdiction policy during April.

324. Definite blocks on the Brenner route varied between five and eighteen throughout the month, so that at no time was continuous through traffic possible.

325. The three north-eastern frontier railway routes remained out by the destruction of bridges for the third month in succession. The important northern line was apparently given priority for repairs, but despite this, was never made fully serviceable. Spasmodic attempts were made to repair the central line for a time, but at last the unequal struggle was given up altogether. This had been the case with the southern lines for a long time.

326. Further south, through traffic was at no time possible across the Venetian Plain. The Brenta zone of interdiction was well maintained; in particular, an attempt to make the Padua north railway bridge serviceable was forestalled by a M.A.S.A.F. attack on the 11th April. More repair activity was apparent in the Piave River zone, but here again, M.A.S.A.F. heavy bombers prevented any return to serviceability of the Nervesa and Ponte di Piave diversions. Less interdiction was maintained at the Livenza River zone, but this was comparatively unimportant owing to the disruption at Nervesa, further west. In the Tagliamento River zone, the Latisana diversion was still incomplete when it fell into Allied hands, and that a Casarsa, kept out of action by M.A.T.A.F. fighter-bombers until the 12th, was knocked out for the last time by M.A.S.A.F. on the 24th.

327. In the north-central zone of the Po valley, through traffic was impossible between Verona and Milan until the 22nd April, but the few bridges which were made serviceable after that date obviously availed the enemy little as the result of the campaign was then a foregone conclusion.

328. All the permanent railway bridges over the Po from Bressana Bottarone to the east coast remained out of action and no attempt was made to repair them.

The part played by M.A.C.A.F. in the final offensive.

329. In my description of the part played by the Air Forces in the final offensive, I have not thus far mentioned the work done by M.A.C.A.F. I should therefore like now to make specific reference to its efforts.

330. In operations connected with the Italian campaign during the month of April, M.A.C.A.F. destroyed 328 motor vehicles and damaged 234 more; destroyed or damaged 30 locomotives and over 230 units of rolling stock; and damaged three bridges. These operations were carried out especially at the western end of the Po Valley, thus enabling M.A.T.A.F. aircraft to be concentrated on the main battle front.

331. In its own particular sphere of activity, M.A.C.A.F. during the month of April damaged one ship over 1,000 tons, sank 12 smaller craft (including a midget submarine), and damaged 32 more. Air-sea rescue operations resulted in the saving of 118 aircrew personnel.

Other Air Force activities during the battle period.

332. With the very small air force at the enemy's disposal, only a very small part of the Allied Air Force's effort was required in counter-air activity. The enemy air effort was limited to occasional unsuccessful attacks on Allied photographic reconnaissance aircraft, and to small-scale ground attack activity by Stukas and Me. 109 fighter bombers in the battle area. This latter effort reached its peak on the night 22nd-23rd April, when ten to fifteen sorties were reported on the Fifth and Eighth Armies' fronts. After that date this harassing activity quickly declined as the Allied ground-forces over-ran the bases at Villafranca (10 miles S.W. of Verona) and Ghedi (10 miles SSE. of Brescia) and later at Thiene (15 miles N. of Vicenza).

333. Both long-range and short-range reconnaissance by the enemy was on a reduced scale during the battle and quite inadequate to give the German commanders any picture of developments on our armies' fronts and in the rear areas.

334. On sixteen of the seventeen nights from 8th to 25th April, Tactical Air Force night-fighters flew reconnaissance flights over the Ghedi, Villafranca, Bergamo (30 miles NE. of Milan) and Thiene airfields, and made attacks when opportune. Day attacks on airfields resulted in a total of 40 enemy aircraft destroyed on the ground and 27 damaged.

335. In April, M.A.T.A.F. supply dropping aircraft working with Italian Partisan Forces flew 711 sorties, of which 485 were effective; of the non-effective sorties, 107 failed because of lack of signals in the dropping areas. Nearly 950 tons of supplies were dropped, of

which by far the greater proportion was in Italy. The dividends paid by the supply dropping became increasingly evident as the Allied armies made their advance. In addition to harassing the enemy's retreating columns, the Italian Partisans in many cases entered towns before the arrival of our troops and succeeded either in occupying them, or in reducing enemy opposition to our attacking forces.

THE EMPLOYMENT OF AIR FORCES DURING THE BATTLE.

336. By way of Summary I should like to draw attention to the salient features of the employment of the Air Forces during the battle. Initially, before the armies could move without sustaining heavy casualties, the way had to be blasted open by the Mediterranean Allied Strategic Air Force and kept open by the Tactical Air Force. Whenever there was a commitment too big for the Tactical Air Force to deal with, the heavy bombers of Strategic Air Force were called upon. On the Tactical side, the development by Desert Air Force of fighter-bomber technique reached perfection. Strong points and defended obstacles a few hundred yards ahead of our ground forces were habitually attacked on call from the ground forces concerned.

337. The air attacks were maintained throughout the night as well as the day and caused heavy enemy losses. Before the battle, all our Boston and Baltimore Squadrons had been trained for effective tactical bombing by night. Joined by a number of Mosquitoes, they were able to maintain at night the interdiction and close support already successfully accomplished by day; they did this with outstanding success and gave the army tremendous help, fully justifying their conversion from day to night bombers.

338. The inclusion, also of No. 205 Group (Night Bombers) in the Strategical Air Force made possible a round-the-clock employment of heavy bombers in a tactical role. The importance of this was not so much in the weight of bombs dropped, but in the fact that we had at our command a heavy night bomber force, so trained that it could paralyse at one blow a vital communications centre or a concentration of enemy troops. The perfection of a technique for close support for twenty-four hours a day helped the ground forces immeasurably in attaining their object of destroying the enemy South of the Po.

339. The scope of the Air Force's effort can best be gauged by an Army Commander's remark:—"I don't suppose there has ever been a campaign where the Army has asked so much of the R.A.F. and where the R.A.F. has given such wholehearted and devastating support, always in the closest proximity to our men." This close support by our aircraft gave our troops great moral as well as material aid. Whenever a difficult position or obstacle was reached by the Army they were able to call on the air forces to attack and remove it. The positions were invariably very close to our own troops and to see them reduce with such effective accuracy and without any air opposition by the enemy kept the morale of our troops at a very high pitch.

340. From the enemy's own description, taken from a captured document, a very clear picture of the intensity and "attention to detail" with which our fighter-bombers pinned down enemy movement can be obtained. The German document covers the few days from the 9th to 13th April:—"Even single despatch riders, isolated telephone line maintenance personnel, messengers and bicyclists were attacked by fighter-bombers. Single tanks were attacked by as many as fifteen fighter-bombers at a time." It was little wonder that the Germans were unable to move.

341. The battle began, as indeed it continued, as an outstanding example of combination and co-operation, not only between the personnel of the British and American nations, for that had already been achieved, but within the Allied Air Forces themselves. Day bombers, night bombers; day fighters, night intruders; all worked with perfect precision and unceasing devotion to duty. Before the last day fighter had landed, Mosquito intruders were airborne and covering the dusk period, closely followed by other Mosquitoes, Bostons, Baltimores and Invaders keeping the battle area, and beyond, constantly covered throughout the night. In the morning the day fighters were airborne before the Mosquitoes flying through the dawn period had landed. This constant vigil was maintained till the German surrender. And reinforcing the constant jabbing by these Tactical Air Force aircraft, would come the sudden massive blows of the heavy bombers, who were employed both day and night closer to our forward troops than ever before in the Mediterranean theatre.

A BRIEF ASSESSMENT OF THE CONTRIBUTION OF AIR POWER TO THE VICTORY IN THE ITALIAN THEATRE.

342. My object in the next few paragraphs is to set down some of the outstanding ways in which air power contributed to the victory in Italy. I do not pretend that it is anything like an exhaustive analysis, since that would require an examination of many factors which are outside the scope of this despatch, and are rather matters for the historian, such as the effect of the Allied strategic bombing of German industry upon the ability of the German Armies in Italy to make war. I have confined myself chiefly to the facts that were apparent in the Italian situation, and the ways in which Italian-based air power was known to have affected that situation.

343. In the first place, the enemy's position on the eve of the battle was undoubtedly critical, and air power was the major factor in causing this situation. Though his ground positions were strong enough, he was desperately short of all those things which are required to wage modern warfare successfully, e.g. fuel, ammunition, transport, aircraft, tanks and guns. And it was the Air Forces which had caused him to lack all these vital things.

344. His shortage of fuel was due directly to the strategic use of air power, assisted by the advance of the Russian Armies. This advance in itself was greatly assisted by that same strategic air power. Whatever may have been the overall supply position of ammunition, tanks and guns for all the German Armies on all the fronts, those in Italy without doubt received such reduced supplies that their position was

critical. As for morale, in the words of the German Supreme Commander: "Allied air power was decisive in that as a result of their complete lack of an air force of their own, and without the promise of the help of a like force, the German troops felt still more the Allied superiority of materials."

345. To add to the cares of the German commanders, because of their limited ability to make air reconnaissance they could have had only a very imperfect knowledge of the detailed preparations that were being made for the offensive, while the Allied commanders, through the unfettered freedom of air reconnaissance enjoyed by M.A.A.F. were completely informed about the enemy's defences and dispositions.

346. The extreme effectiveness of the assistance given by the Air Forces to the ground forces during the battle itself is also beyond doubt. I shall not attempt to evaluate which of the forces made the greater contribution—nothing would be gained by that since they were so essentially a team, working together in perfect harmony, the one taking advantage of the opportunities created by the other; but the following points show the great importance of the part played by air power at this time.

347. The air bombardment of the German fixed defences in the early days of the battle was probably the decisive factor in enabling our ground forces to overcome them rapidly and with a minimum of casualties. German prisoners of war testified that the dropping of fragmentation bombs on such a large scale caused many casualties, and, especially in the region of Ferrara and Lake Comacchio, greatly reduced the resistance of the German troops. Again, communications between higher and lower commanders were completely disrupted; even radio and telephone communications were delayed threefold. The German Supreme Commander's statement testifies to the effect of this. " The smashing of all communications connections was especially disastrous. Thereafter, the orders failed to come through at all, or failed to come through at the right time. In any case, the command was not able to keep itself informed of the situation at the front, so that its own decisions and commands came, for the most part, too late."

348. Even when those decisions were made, and the commands given, air power prevented their being carried out effectively. Movement of local reserves by day was to all intents and purposes prohibited by the inevitably high losses which would have followed, while movement by night, though still possible, was also attended by heavy losses. To quote the German Supreme Commander once again: " Local reserves, which should have moved by day, often arrived with great delay at the ordered position. Even tanks could not move by day because of the employment of fighter-bombers. The effectiveness of fighter-bombers lay in that their presence alone over the battlefield paralysed every movement."

349. Another important point was that because of the complete air superiority enjoyed by the Allies, our Air Observation Post aircraft could operate completely unhindered and therefore with maximum efficiency. The final result was that these aircraft had only to appear within sight of the German artillery to cause the latter to cease fire, and so in this manner, in vital phases of the battle, an essential element of the enemy's defence system was denied him.

350. Orderly retreats could not be conducted by the Germans because of the air attacks on their lines of communication in the battle area. Through the destruction of almost all the crossings of the numerous canals, trans-shipment was made much more difficult, forcing the enemy to leave much heavy equipment behind. In that way, retreat imposed by the ground forces was turned into a rout by the air forces.

351. And at the Po crossings, as I have already shown earlier on in the description of the battle, rout was turned into destruction, again by the use of air power.

352. Such were the effects of air power upon the Germans. There was a reverse effect upon our own troops. Their morale was heightened by the constant presence of friendly aircraft, by the complete absence of enemy aircraft, and by the knowledge that their casualties would always be kept to a minimum because the air forces would be there to lend a hand with the task.

FINAL REMARKS.

353. In concluding this despatch I wish to place on record the remarkable team work of the three Services under the leadership of Field Marshal Alexander, the Supreme Allied Commander. The mutual understanding was complete at every level within the Theatre, between the three Services themselves as between the Allied Forces generally. This atmosphere of the happy family working for a single purpose, with no thought except for the general good, was a decisive factor in the success of the operations.

354. Finally, I wish to pay my tribute to the magnificent spirit shown by the officers and airmen under my command whose achievements I have described. When I assumed command of them they had made a long journey from Egypt to Northern Italy. Many of the Squadrons had been engaged for over four years in continuous and bitter fighting. The airfield strips were far from ideal. The Heavy Bomber Squadrons on the Foggia plain had been living under canvas throughout the winter in camps which were often a sea of mud. The Maintenance and Administrative Units had also been operating under the most severe conditions of weather and accommodation.

355. Yet the spirit of all ranks in every unit remained at the highest level. The one desire of the Squadrons was to get to grips with the enemy, and if he was not to be found in the air they sought him out relentlessly on the ground. The maintenance personnel in Squadrons and in supporting units toiled ceaselessly to keep the aircraft flying at the very high rate of effort that the battle demanded. It was a joy and an inspiration to command such a force, whose mastery over the enemy resulted in so complete a victory.

GUY GARROD,
Air Chief Marshal,
*lately C.-in-C., Royal Air Force,
Mediterranean and Middle East.*
August, 1946.

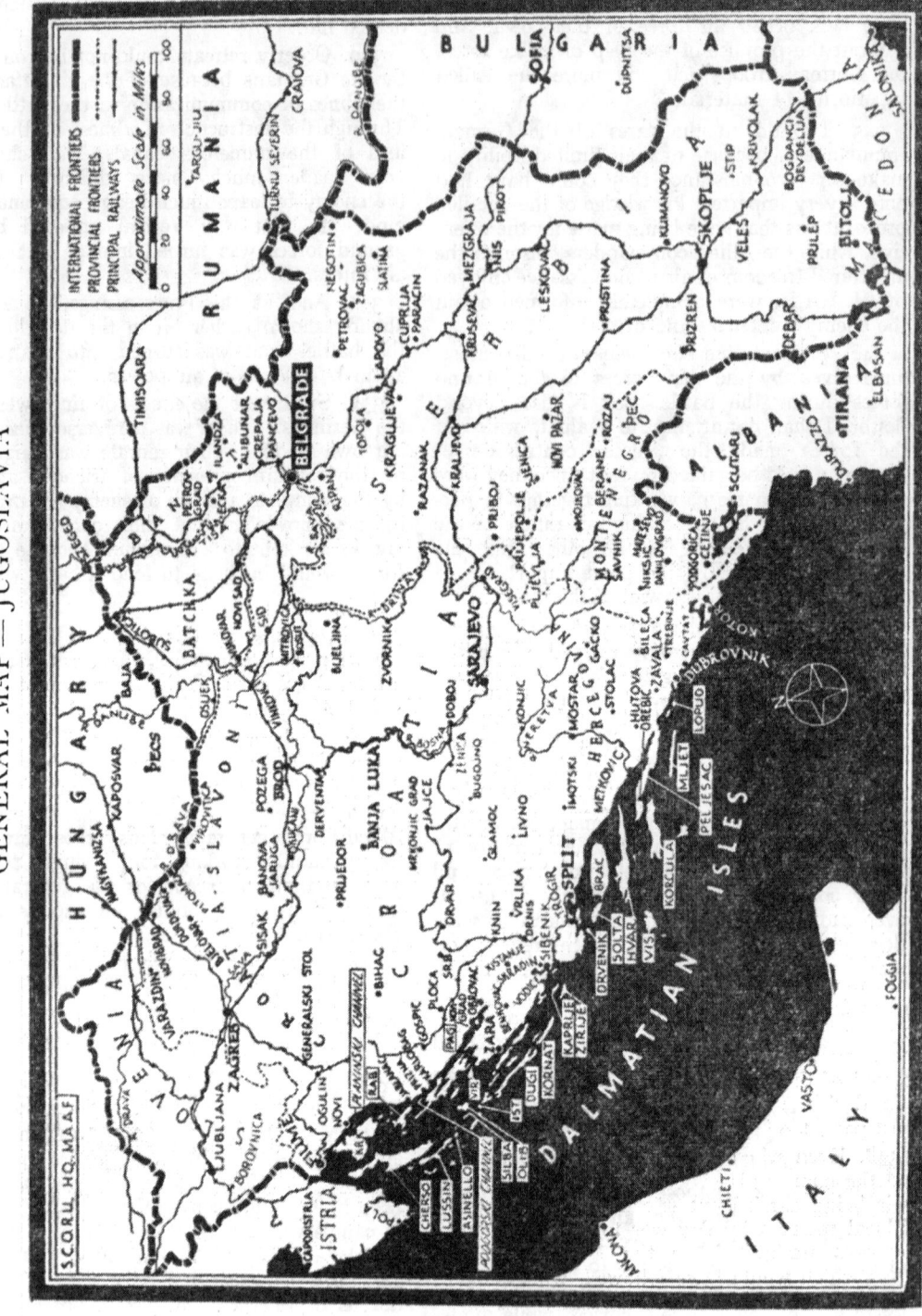

www.ingramcontent.com/pod-product-compliance
Lightning Source LLC
Chambersburg PA
CBHW080811010526
44111CB00015B/2542